South-East Asia
on a shoestring

Hugh Finlay

David Andrew   Paul Hellander
Michael Clark   Clem Lindenmayer
Joe Cummings   Mic Looby
Mason Florence   Nick Ray
Paul Greenway   Chris Rowthorn
Paul Harding   Peter Turner

LONELY PLANET PUBLICATIONS
Melbourne • Oakland • London • Paris

SOUTH-EAST ASIA

Kaohsiung **TAIWAN**

Batan Islands

Luzon Strait

Babuyan Islands

Laoag

PHILIPPINE

Baguio *SEA*

Luzon

Polillo
Islands

Manila

Lucena Catanduanes

Naga

Mindoro *Sibuyan* **PHILIPPINES**

Calamian *Sea*

Group Tablas Masbate Samar

Panay *Visayan*
Sea

Iloilo Tacloban

Bacolod **Cebu** Leyte

Cebu Dinagat

Palawan Bohol Siargao

Negros *Bohol Sea*

Sulu Sea Cagayan de Oro

Mindanao

Zamboanga Davao

Jolo Basilan

Sulu
Archipelago

Tawi-Tawi Talaud

Sulawesi Sea Sangir
Islands

Manado Morotai

Halmahera

Waigeo

Teluk Togian Is Biak

Palu *Tomini* *Maluku Sea* Kota Biak

Bacan Manokwari Yapen Jayapura

Poso *Helmahera* *Cenderawasih*

Sula Islands *Sea* *Bay*

Sulawesi Obi

Banggai Misool

Islands *Seram Sea* Puncak Jaya

Buru Seram 5030m

Pare Kota Ambon **Irian Jaya**

Pare *Teluk* Ambon

Bone **Maluku** Banda

Bone Butung

Ujung (Watapone) (Buton) Kai Aru

Pandang Islands Islands Yos
Sudarso

Selayar *Banda Sea*

Wetar

Flores Sea Leti

Komodo **Nusa Tenggara** Alor Islands Tanimbar

Bima Ruteng Flores Islands Dili Babar Islands

Ende Solor Is Islands

Waingapu Timor *Arafura Sea*

Sumba *Sawu* Kupang

Sea Roti *Timor Sea*

Sawu

120°E Darwin *Gulf of*
Carpentaria

AUSTRALIA *140°E*

PACIFIC OCEAN

PAPUA NEW GUINEA

PALAU

MYANMAR

CHINA

INDIA Myitkyina *25°N*

Imphal *Tropic of Cancer*

MYANMAR
(BURMA)

BANGLA- Kyaingtong
DESH **Mandalay**

Bagan Taunggyi **LAOS**

Inle
Lake Chiang Rai

Sittwe

20°N Pyay **Chiang Mai**

THAILAND

BAY OF Bago

BENGAL Pathein

Yangon
(Rangoon)

Same Scale
as Main Map

Gulf of
Martaban

95°E *100°E*

Ayeyarwady

South-East Asia
10th edition – May 1999
First published – 1975

Published by
Lonely Planet Publications Pty Ltd A.C.N. 005 607 983
192 Burwood Rd, Hawthorn, Victoria 3122, Australia

Lonely Planet Offices
Australia PO Box 617, Hawthorn, Victoria 3122
USA 150 Linden St, Oakland, CA 94607
UK 10a Spring Place, London NW5 3BH
France 1 rue du Dahomey, 75011 Paris

Photographs
All of the images in this guide are available for licensing from
Lonely Planet Images.
email: lpi@lonelyplanet.com.au

Front cover
Illustration of gecko by Mic Looby

ISBN 0 86442 632 1

Printed by The Bookmaker Pty Ltd
Printed in China on acid-free paper from Brazilian plantations

Contents – Text

THE AUTHORS   **10**

THIS BOOK   **15**

FROM TONY WHEELER   **16**

FOREWORD   **20**

INTRODUCTION   **23**

REGIONAL FACTS FOR THE VISITOR   **25**

Highlights 25	Newspapers & Magazines 33	Travel with Children 36
Suggested Itineraries 27	Radio & TV 34	Dangers & Annoyances 36
Planning 27	Photography & Video 34	Activities 37
Visas & Documents 28	Time 34	Courses 38
Embassies & Consulates 30	Electricity 35	Work 38
Customs 30	Weights & Measures 35	Accommodation 39
Money 30	Toilets & Showers 35	Food 39
Post & Communications 32	Women Travellers 35	Drinks 40
Internet Resources 33	Gay & Lesbian Travellers 36	
Books 33	Disabled Travellers 36	

GETTING THERE & AWAY   **41**

Air 41	Land 45	Sea 46

GETTING AROUND SOUTH-EAST ASIA   **47**

Air 47	Bus 52	Bicycle 52
Overlanding in South-East	Train 52	Hitching 53
Asia 48	Car & Motorcycle 52	Boat 53

BRUNEI DARUSSALAM   **54**

Facts about Brunei 54	Customs 57	Drinks 59
Arts 55	Money 58	Getting There & Away 60
Society & Conduct 56	Post & Communications 58	Getting Around 60
Religion 56	Books 58	Bandar Seri Begawan 60
Language 56	Health 59	Around Bandar Seri
Facts for the Visitor 56	Women Travellers 59	Begawan 64
Highlights 56	Business Hours 59	Beaches 64
Planning 56	Public Holidays & Special	Jerudong Playground 64
Tourist Offices 56	Events 59	Kuala Belait 64
Visas & Documents 56	Accommodation 59	Temburong District 64
Embassies 57	Food 59	

CAMBODIA   **66**

Facts about	Planning 71	Books 74
Cambodia 66	Tourist Offices 71	Health 75
Arts 70	Visas & Documents 71	Women Travellers 76
Society & Conduct 70	Embassies & Consulates 72	Gay & Lesbian Travellers 76
Religion 70	Customs 72	Disabled Travellers 76
Language 70	Money 72	Senior Travellers 76
Facts for the Visitor 70	Post & Communications 73	Travel with Children 76
Highlights 70	Internet Resources 74	Useful Organisations 76

2 Contents – Text

Dangers & Annoyances 76
Legal Matters 77
Business Hours 77
Public Holidays & Special
Events 77
Activities 77
Work 77
Accommodation 78
Food 78
Drinks 78
Entertainment 78
Spectator Sports 79
Shopping 79
Getting There & Away 79

Getting Around 81
Phnom Penh 82
Around Phnom Penh 94
Angkor 95
Siem Reap 95
Temples of Angkor 100
South Coast 104
Sihanoukville 104
Kampot 107
Kep 109
Rabbit Island 109
Bokor Hill Station 109
Western Cambodia 110
Battambang 110

Around Battambang 112
Central Cambodia 113
Kompong Chhnang 113
Kompong Cham 114
**North-East
Cambodia** 115
Kratie 115
Stung Treng 115
Ratanakiri 116
Banlung 116
Around Banlung 116
Mondolkiri 117

INDONESIA 118

Facts about Indonesia 118
Society & Conduct 122
Religion 122
Language 123
Facts for the Visitor 123
Highlights 123
Planning 124
Tourist Offices 124
Visas & Documents 125
Embassies & Consulates 126
Customs 126
Money 126
Post & Communications 128
Internet Resources 128
Books 130
Health 130
Women Travellers 131
Gay & Lesbian Travellers 131
Dangers & Annoyances 131
Business Hours 131
Public Holidays & Special
Events 131
Accommodation 132
Food & Drinks 132
Shopping 132
Getting There & Away 133
Getting Around 134
Java 140
Jakarta 144
Pulau Seribu 153
Bogor 153
Bogor to Bandung 156
Bandung 157
Tangkuban Perahu Area 161
Pangandaran 162
Around Pangandaran 165
Wonosobo 165
Dieng Plateau 166

Yogyakarta 167
Around Yogyakarta 175
Solo 177
Around Solo 182
Surabaya 182
Around Surabaya 186
Madura 186
Gunung Bromo 187
Bali 189
Denpasar 195
Kuta 198
Bukit Peninsula 205
Sanur 206
Ubud 207
Around Ubud 213
Pura Besakih 213
Gunung Agung 214
Semarapura (Klungkung) ..214
Nusa Lembongan 214
Padangbai 214
Tenganan 215
Candidasa 215
Amlapura 216
Tirta Gangga 217
North-East Coast 217
Tulamben 218
Singaraja 218
Around Singaraja 218
Lovina 219
Around Lovina 221
South-West Bali 222
West Bali 222
Gunung Batur Area 222
Danau Bratan Area 223
Other Mountain Routes 224
Sumatra 224
Medan 229
Banda Aceh 235

Around Banda Aceh 236
Pulau Weh 236
Bukit Lawang 237
Berastagi 239
Around Berastagi 241
Danau Toba 241
Parapat 241
Pulau Samosir 243
Sibolga 246
Pulau Nias 247
Bukittinggi 249
Around Bukittinggi 254
Danau Maninjau 254
Padang 255
Mentawai Islands 258
Pekanbaru 258
Dumai 259
Batam 259
Pulau Bintan 260
Bandarlampung 261
Kalianda 262
Way Kambas 262
Bakauheni 262
Nusa Tenggara 263
Lombok 263
Mataram 267
Around Mataram 269
Senggigi 270
Lembar 272
Kuta 272
Labuhan Lombok 273
Gunung Rinjani 273
Tetebatu 274
Gili Islands 274
Sumbawa 277
Poto Tano 278
Sumbawa Besar 278
Pulau Moyo 279

Huu 279	Kefamenanu 294	Tentena 315
Bima 279	Atambua 294	Poso 315
Sape 280	Dili 294	Palu 315
Komodo & Rinca 280	Around Dili 295	Donggala 316
Flores 281	**Sumba** 295	Ampana 316
Labuanbajo 282	Waingapu 296	Togian Islands 316
Ruteng 283	Around Waingapu 296	Manado 317
Bajawa 283	Waikabubak 297	Around Manado 318
Riung 284	Around Waikabubak 297	**Maluku (Moluccas)** 319
Ende 284	**Kalimantan** 298	Pulau Ambon 321
Kelimutu 285	Tarakan 298	Around Pulau Ambon 323
Moni 285	Samarinda 300	Banda Islands 324
Maumere 286	Up Sungai Mahakam 300	Pulau Ternate & Tidore 325
Around Maumere 287	Balikpapan 301	**Irian Jaya** 326
Larantuka 288	Banjarmasin 301	Jayapura 328
Solor & Alor Archipelagos ..288	Around Banjarmasin 304	Sentani 330
Timor 289	Pontianak 304	Pulau Biak 331
Kupang 290	**Sulawesi** 306	Around Pulau Biak 332
Around Kupang 293	Ujung Pandang 306	Cenderawasih Bay 333
Roti 293	Tana Toraja 310	Ballem Valley 334
Soe 293	Around Tana Toraja 313	Around the Baliem Valley ..335
Around Soe 293	Pendolo 314	

LAOS 337

Facts about Laos 337	Health 348	Shopping 352
Arts 341	Women Travellers 348	**Getting There & Away** 353
Society & Conduct 341	Gay & Lesbian Travellers 348	**Getting Around** 355
Religion 341	Disabled Travellers 348	**Vientiane** 358
Language 341	Senior Travellers 348	Around Vientiane 370
Facts for the Visitor 341	Travel with Children 348	**Northern Laos** 372
Highlights 341	Dangers & Annoyances 348	Luang Prabang 372
Suggested Itineraries 342	Business Hours 349	Around Luang Prabang 379
Planning 342	Public Holidays & Special	Xieng Khuang Province 380
Tourist Offices ...342	Events 349	Hua Phan Province 381
Visas & Documents 342	Activities 350	Luang Nam Tha
Travel Restrictions 343	Courses 350	Province 382
Embassies & Consulates 344	Work 350	Bokeo Province 384
Customs 344	Accommodation 351	**Southern Laos** 385
Money 344	Food 351	Savannakhet Province 385
Post & Communications 345	Drinks 351	Salavan Province 388
Internet Resources 346	Entertainment 352	Champasak Province 388
Books 346	Spectator Sports 352	

MALAYSIA 394

Facts about Malaysia 394	Customs 401	Travel with Children 404
Arts 397	Money 401	Dangers & Annoyances 405
Society & Conduct 398	Post & Communications 402	Legal Matters 405
Religion 398	Books 403	Business Hours 405
Language 398	Health 404	Public Holidays & Special
Facts for the Visitor 399	Women Travellers 404	Events 405
Highlights 399	Gay & Lesbian	Activities 406
Planning 399	Travellers 404	Courses 406
Visas & Documents 399	Disabled Travellers 404	Accommodation 406
Embassies 400	Senior Travellers 404	Food 407

Drinks 407
Getting There & Away **408**
Getting Around **411**
Peninsular Malaysia –
West Coast **413**
Kuala Lumpur 413
Around Kuala Lumpur 424
Johor Bahru 424
Melaka 425
Port Dickson 430
Seremban 430
Genting Highlands 430
Fraser's Hill 430
Cameron Highlands 430
Ipoh 433
Lumut 434
Pulau Pangkor 434
Kuala Kangsar 435
Taiping 435
Penang 435
Alor Setar 443
Kuala Perlis 443
Langkawi 444
Peninsular Malaysia –
East Coast **445**
Johor Bahru to Mersing 445
Mersing 445
Pulau Tioman 446
Other South-East Coast
Islands 448
Kuantan 449

Around Kuantan 450
Tasik Chini 451
Cherating 451
Rantau Abang 452
Marang 453
Pulau Kapas 453
Kuala Terengganu 453
Around Kuala
Terengganu 455
Merang 455
Pulau Redang 455
Kuala Besut 456
Perhentian Islands 456
Kota Bharu 459
Around Kota Bharu 461
Kota Bharu to Kuala
Lumpur **461**
The Jungle Railway 461
Kuala Lipis 461
Jerantut 462
Taman Negara 463
Sarawak **465**
Kuching 467
Around Kuching 471
Up the Batang Rejang 472
Sibu 472
Kapit 473
Belaga 474
Bintulu 474
Niah National Park &
Niah Caves 474

Lambir Hills National
Park 475
Miri 475
Marudi 476
Gunung Mulu National
Park 476
Kelabit Highlands 477
Limbang 477
Lawas 478
Sabah **478**
Kota Kinabalu 478
Around Kota Kinabalu 482
Rafflesia Forest Reserve 482
Tambunan 483
Beaufort 483
Pulau Labuan 483
Tenom 484
Kota Belud 484
Kudat 484
Mt Kinabalu 484
Ranau 485
Poring Hot Springs 485
Sepilok Orang-utan
Rehabilitation Centre 486
Sandakan 486
Turtle Islands National
Park 487
Batang Kinabatangan 487
Semporna 488
Tawau 488

MYANMAR 489

Facts about Myanmar **492**
Arts 497
Society & Conduct 498
Religion 499
Language 500
Facts for the Visitor **500**
Highlights 500
Planning 500
Tourist Offices 500
Visas & Documents 500
Embassies 502
Customs 502
Money 502
Post & Communications 504
Books 505
Health 506
Dangers & Annoyances 507
Public Holidays & Special
Events 507
Courses 508
Accommodation 508

Food 509
Drinks 509
Shopping 510
Getting There & Away **510**
Getting Around **511**
Yangon (Rangoon) **514**
Around Yangon **523**
Thanlyin (Syriam) &
Kyauktan 523
Twante 524
Bago 524
Pyay (Prome) 526
Letkhokkon Beach 527
Pathein 527
Chaungtha Beach 528
Mandalay Region **529**
Mandalay 529
Around Mandalay 535
Bagan Region **537**
Bagan (Pagan) 537
Around Bagan 541

Meiktila 542
Thazi 542
Shan State **542**
Kalaw & Pindaya 542
Inle Lake 543
Taunggyi 545
Kyaingtong (Kengtung) 546
Hsipaw 546
Lashio 547
Kachin State **548**
Bhamo 548
Myitkyina 549
Putao 549
South-Eastern Myanmar **549**
Kyaiktiyo 549
Mawlamyine (Moulmein) ..550
Around Mawlamyine 551
Pa-An 552
Dawei (Tavoy) 552
Myeik (Mergui) 553
Kawthoung 553

Western Myanmar 553
Sittwe 554

Mrauk U 555
Ngapali Beach 556

Thandwe (Sandoway) 557
Southern Chin State 557

PHILIPPINES   558

Facts about the
Philippines 558
Arts 563
Society & Conduct 564
Religion 565
Language 565
Facts for the Visitor 565
The Best & Worst 565
Suggested Itineraries 565
Planning 566
Tourist Offices 567
Visas & Documents 567
Embassies & Consulates 568
Customs 568
Money 569
Post & Communications 570
Internet Resources 571
Books 571
Health 572
Women Travellers 572
Gay & Lesbian Travellers 572
Disabled Travellers 573
Senior Travellers 573
Travel with Children 573
Dangers & Annoyances 573
Business Hours 573
Public Holidays & Special
Events 573
Activities 574
Work 574
Accommodation 574
Food 574
Drinks 575
Entertainment 575
Spectator Sports 575
Shopping 575
Getting There & Away 575
Getting Around 576
Manila 580
Around Manila 592
Corregidor 592
Olongapo & Subic 594
Angeles 594
Around Angeles 595

Las Piñas 595
Tagaytay (Taal Volcano) 595
Nasugbu & Matabungkay ..596
Batangas 596
Los Baños & Calamba 596
San Pablo & Alaminos 596
Pagsanjan 597
Lucena 597
North Luzon 597
Hundred Islands, Lucap &
Alaminos 597
Lingayen, Dagupan &
San Fabian 598
Agoo & Aringay 598
San Fernando (La Union) ..598
Around San Fernando 599
Baguio 600
Rice Terraces 602
Bontoc 603
Sagada 603
Banaue 604
Batad 604
Vigan 605
Laoag 606
Tuguegarao 606
South Luzon 607
San Miguel Bay 607
Naga 607
Legaspi 608
Around Legaspi 608
Mayon 608
Tabaco 609
Sorsogon 609
Bulusan & Irosin 609
Matnog 609
Islands Around Luzon 610
Batanes 610
Catanduanes 610
Marinduque 610
Mindoro 611
Cebu 614
Cebu City 616
Around Cebu 619
Bohol 621

Tagbilaran 621
Around Tagbilaran 621
Chocolate Hills 621
Talibon 622
Panglao Island 622
Leyte 623
Tacloban 623
Ormoc 623
Samar 624
Calbayog 624
Catbalogan 624
Romblon Islands 624
Romblon 624
Tablas 625
Sibuyan 625
Panay 625
Iloilo City 626
Around Iloilo City 626
Guimaras 626
Kalibo 627
Caticlan 627
Boracay 627
Negros 630
Bacolod 631
Around Bacolod 631
Dumaguete 632
Around Negros 633
Mindanao 633
Surigao & Siargao Island 634
Butuan 634
Cagayan De Oro 635
Dipolog 635
Dapitan 636
Zamboanga 636
Davao 637
Around Davao 640
Camiguin 640
Mambajao 640
Around the Island 640
Palawan 641
Puerto Princesa 641
Around Puerto Princesa 642
South Palawan 643
North Palawan 643

SINGAPORE   645

Facts about
Singapore 645
Society & Conduct 648
Religion 649

Language 649
Facts for the Visitor 649
Highlights 649
Planning 649

Tourist Offices 650
Visas & Documents 650
Embassies 650
Customs 650

6 Contents – Text

Money 651
Post & Communications 652
Books 652
Health 652
Dangers & Annoyances 653
Business Hours 653

Public Holidays & Special
Events 653
Accommodation 653
Food 653
Getting There & Away 654
Getting Around 656

Things to See & Do 657
Places to Stay 668
Places to Eat 671
Entertainment 674
Shopping 675

THAILAND   676

Facts about Thailand 676
Arts 682
Society & Conduct 683
Religion 684
Language 685
Facts for the Visitor 685
Highlights 685
Suggested Itineraries 685
Planning 687
Tourist Offices 688
Visas & Documents 689
Embassies & Consulates 690
Customs 690
Money 691
Post & Communications 692
Internet Resources 692
Books 693
Health 695
Women Travellers 696
Gay & Lesbian Travellers 696
Disabled Travellers 696
Senior Travellers 697
Travel with Children 697
Dangers & Annoyances 697
Business Hours 698
Public Holidays & Special
Events 698
Activities 699
Courses 699
Work 701
Accommodation 701
Food 701
Drinks 702
Entertainment 702
Spectator Sports 703
Shopping 703
Getting There & Away 704
Getting Around 708
Bangkok 712
Around Bangkok 731
Ayuthaya 731
Bang Pa In 735

Lopburi 735
Saraburi 736
Nakhon Pathom 736
Ratchaburi 736
Kanchanaburi 737
Around Kanchanaburi 739
Sangkhlaburi & Three
Pagodas Pass 739
Pattaya 740
Rayong 741
Ko Samet 741
Trat Province 743
Ko Chang National Marine
Park 743
Northern Thailand 744
Chiang Mai 747
Around Chiang Mai 754
Phitsanulok 756
Sukhothai 756
Around Sukhothai 758
Kamphaeng Phet 759
Tak 759
Mae Sot 759
Mae Hong Son 760
Pai 761
Fang & Tha Ton 761
Around Fang & Tha Ton 761
Chiang Rai 762
Chiang Saen 764
Around Chiang Saen 764
Mae Sai-Mae Salong Area   764
Nan 766
North-Eastern Thailand 767
Nakhon Ratchasima
(Khorat) 767
Phimai 769
Prasat Hin Khao Phanom
Rung Historical Park 770
Khon Kaen 770
Udon Thani 771
Nong Khai 772
Around Nong Khai 772

Nong Khai to Loei 772
Loei 773
Lom Sak 773
Beung Kan 773
Nakhon Phanom 773
That Phanom 774
Yasothon 774
Mukdahan 774
Ubon (Ubol) Ratchathani ..774
Surin 775
Southern Thailand 775
Phetburi (Phetchaburi) 776
Around Phetburi 776
Hua Hin 776
Prachuap Khiri Khan 777
Ranong 777
Around Ranong 778
Chaiya 778
Surat Thani 778
Ko Samui 779
Ko Pha-Ngan 783
Ko Tao 785
Nakhon Si Thammarat 786
Phattalung 786
Songkhla 787
Around Songkhla 789
Hat Yai 789
Around Hat Yai 791
Satun 791
Ko Tarutao National Marine
Park 792
Phuket 792
Khao Sok National Park 797
Phang-Nga 797
Krabi 797
Around Krabi 799
Ko Phi Phi 799
Trang 799
Around Trang 800
Sungai Kolok & Ban Taba ..800

VIETNAM   802

Facts about Vietnam 802
Arts 806

Society & Conduct 806
Religion 806

Language 807
Facts for the Visitor 807

Highlights 807
Planning 807
Tourist Offices 807
Visas & Documents 807
Embassies & Consulates 808
Customs 810
Money 810
Post & Communications 810
Internet Resources 811
Books 812
Health 813
Women Travellers 813
Gay & Lesbian Travellers 813
Dangers & Annoyances 813
Legal Matters 814
Business Hours 814
Public Holidays & Special
Events 814
Activities 814
Courses 814
Work 814
Accommodation 815

Food 815
Drinks 815
Entertainment 815
Shopping 816
Getting There & Away 816
Getting Around 817
Hanoi 820
Around Hanoi 830
The North 831
Ninh Binh 831
Around Ninh Binh 831
Cuc Phuong National
Park 832
Haiphong 832
Around Haiphong 832
Halong Bay 833
Cat Ba Island 833
Bai Tu Long Bay 834
Ba Be National Park 835
Hoa Binh 835
Mai Chau 836
Lao Cai 836

Bac Ha 836
Sapa 837
Dien Bien Phu 839
Central Coast 840
Hué 840
DMZ & Vicinity 845
Danang 845
Hoi An (Faifo) 847
Around Hoi An 850
Nha Trang 851
Ca Na 855
Phan Thiet 855
Central Highlands 856
Dalat 856
Buon Ma Thuot, Pleiku &
Kon Tum 860
**Ho Chi Minh City
(Saigon)** 860
Around Saigon 874
Mekong Delta 878
Mytho 878
Other Places 879

APPENDIX 880

**Languages of South-East
Asia** 880
Cambodia (Khmer) 880
Indonesia (Bahasa) 881
Laos 882
Malaysia (Bahasa) 885
Myanmar (Burmese) 886

Philippines (Pilipino) 887
Thailand 888
Vietnam 889
**South-East Asia History
Chart** 890
**Religions of South-East
Asia** 892

Buddhism 892
Hinduism 892
Islam 892
Christianity 893
Other Religions 893
Health 893
Climate Charts 907

GLOSSARY 908

ACKNOWLEDGMENTS 910

INDEX 920

METRIC CONVERSION inside back cover

Contents – Maps

INTRODUCTION

South-East Asia 23

GETTING THERE & AWAY

Asia Air Fares.........................47

BRUNEI DARUSSALAM

Brunei Darussalam 55   Bandar Seri Begawan 62

CAMBODIA

Cambodia 67   Siem Reap 96   Kampot 108
Phnom Penh...................84-5   Temples of Angkor 102-3   Battambang.......................111
Central Phnom Penh 88   Sihanoukville 105

INDONESIA

Indonesia...........................119   Kuta-Legian 200   Gili Air 275
Indonesia Air Fares.............135   Seminyak 203   Gili Meno..........................276
Pelni Shipping Ports 138   Ubud Area 208-9   Gili Trawangan.................277
Java.................................140-1   Central Ubud 210   Kupang 291
Sunda Kelapa & Kota 145   Candidasa 216-7   Central Kupang 292
Central Jakarta...................146   Lovina Beaches 220-1   Kalimantan.......................299
Jalan Jaksa Area 148   Sumatra 226-7   Banjarmasin 302
Bogor................................154   Medan 230-1   Pontianak.........................305
Bandung 158   Berastagi 240   Sulawesi...........................307
Pangandaran 163   Danau Toba 242   Ujung Pandang 309
Yogyakarta........................168   Tuk Tuk Peninsula 244   Tana Toraja 311
Sosrowijayan Area 171   Pulau Nias 248   Maluku 320
Around Yogyakarta 175   Bukittinggi 250   Kota Ambon 322
Solo..................................178   Padang 256   Irian Jaya 327
Surabaya 184   Nusa Tenggara 264-5   Jayapura 329
Bali.................................190-1   Lombok 266   Kota Biak 332
Denpasar 196   Mataram 268
Tuban (South Kuta) 199   Senggigi Beach.................271

LAOS

Laos...................................338   Northern Laos 373   Pakse 389
Laos Air Fares 356   Luang Prabang..................374   Si Phan Don......................393
Vientiane 360-1   Southern Laos 386
Central Vientiane 364   Savannakhet 387

MALAYSIA

Malaysia Air Fares 411   Penang 436   Kota Bharu 458
Peninsular Malaysia 414   Georgetown......................438   East Malaysia 466
Kuala Lumpur.................416-7   Pulau Tioman (Tioman   Kuching 468
Central Kuala Lumpur 420   Island) 447   Kota Kinabalu 480
Melaka City 426   Kuantan...........................450
Cameron Highlands 431   Kuala Terengganu 454

MYANMAR

Myanmar........................490-1   Inner Yangon 518   Bago 525
Myanmar Air Fares.............512   Central Yangon 520   Pathein 528
Yangon 516   Around Yangon 524   Mandalay.........................530

Central Mandalay 532	Bagan Region.....................539	Sittwe 555
Around Mandalay 535	Inle Lake 543	
Around Bagan 538	Nyaungshwe 544	

PHILIPPINES

Philippines 559	Around Manila....................593	Cebu City 618
Philippines Air Fares...........577	Baguio 600	White Beach Boracay..........628
Metro Manila 582-3	Around Puerto Galera &	Davao 638
Intramuros & Rizal Park 584	Sabang...............................612	
Ermita, Malate & Paco 586	Visayas 614-5	

SINGAPORE

Singapore 646-7	City Centre 660-1	Orchard Road 666-7
Central Singapore 658-9	Little India & Arab Street 664	

THAILAND

Thailand 678-9	Central Ayuthaya 732	Nakhon Ratchasima
Thailand Air Fares &	Kanchanaburi.....................738	(Khorat) 768-9
Railways............................709	Ko Samet 742	Ko Samui 780
Greater Bangkok............714-5	Central Chiang Mai 748	Ko Pha-Ngan 784
Central Bangkok.............718-9	Sukhothai Historical	Songkhla 788
Banglamphu......................722	Park...................................757	Hat Yai...............................790
Thanon Khao San	Chiang Rai 763	Phuket Province.................793
Area..................................724	Golden Triangle 765	Phuket Town 794

VIETNAM

Vietnam.............................803	Hoi An (Faifo) 848	Central Saigon 866
Vietnam Air Fares...............818	Nha Trang 852	Pham Ngu Lao Area...........868
Central Hanoi 822-3	Central Nha Trang 854	Dong Khoi Area 870
Old Quarter.......................826	Dalat Area 857	Central Vung Tau...............875
Sapa 838	Central Dalat 858	Vung Tau Peninsula 876
Hué 842-3	Ho Chi Minh City	
Danang 846	(Saigon) 862-3	

MAP LEGEND – SEE BACK PAGE

The Authors

Hugh Finlay

Hugh lives in central Victoria with his partner Linda and daughters Ella and Vera. He joined Lonely Planet in 1985 and has worked on numerous guidebooks, including *Malaysia, Singapore & Brunei*. Hugh coordinated this edition of South-East Asia and travelled to many of the outer islands of Indonesia.

David Andrew

After stints as a public servant, restaurant manager and research assistant, David decided there are few things in life more fun than birdwatching and travelling. He started *Wingspan*, Australia's first magazine for birdwatchers; edited *Wildlife Australia* for a time; started another bird magazine, *Australian Birding*; and then began work at Lonely Planet as an editor. In his spare time he travels around the world looking for rare wildlife and attempting to paint it. David updated the Brunei chapter and the Sabah and Sarawak sections of the Malaysia chapter.

Michael Clark

Michael first visited Myanmar in 1987 while working in Malaysia as a university lecturer. His overseas travels began in the merchant marine, followed by a hitchhiking trip to Greece and then a two year stint in Malawi as a Peace Corps volunteer. Before that, he graduated from the University of California at Los Angeles and later completed graduate work at the University of Hawaii. When not on the road, Michael teaches English to international students at UC Berkeley. He lives in Oakland with his wife Janet and kids Melina and Alexander. He is a coauthor of Lonely Planet's *New York, New Jersey & Pennsylvania* guidebook. Michael updated the Myanmar chapter for this edition.

Joe Cummings

Joe began travelling in South-East Asia shortly after finishing university. Before writing became a full-time job, he was a Peace Corps volunteer in Thailand, a graduate student of Thai language and Asian art history at the University of California at Berkeley, an East-West Center scholar in Hawaii, a university lecturer in Malaysia and a Lao bilingual studies consultant in the USA. Joe is the author of Lonely Planet's *Thailand, Bangkok, Laos* and *Myanmar* guidebooks. As a freelance journalist he has written for many periodicals, including *Asia Magazine,* the *Bangkok Post, Geographical*, the *San Francisco Examiner* and the *Asian Wall Street Journal*. Joe updated the Laos and Thailand chapters.

Mason Florence

Mason gave up a budding career as a rodeo cowboy in 1990, trading in his boots and spurs for a Nikon and a laptop and relocated from Colorado to Japan. Now a Kyoto-based photojournalist, he spends half the year on the road in Asia and free moments in Japan restoring an old thatched-roof farmhouse in rural Shikoku and frequenting Kyoto's finest honky-tonk bars. Mason has worked on Lonely Planet's *Japan, Kyoto, Vietnam* and *Ho Chi Minh City* guidebooks, and his photographs and articles have appeared in publications around the world. He updated the Vietnam chapter for this edition.

Paul Greenway

Gratefully plucked from the blandness and security of the Australian public service, Paul has worked on many Lonely Planet guidebooks, including *Indonesia, Madagascar, Mongolia* and *Iran*. During the rare times that he is not travelling – or writing, reading and dreaming about it – Paul relaxes to tuneless heavy metal music, eats and breathes Australian Rules football and will do anything (like going to Mongolia and Iran) to avoid settling down. Paul updated the Bali and Lombok sections of the Indonesia chapter for this edition.

Paul Harding

Paul started life as a newspaper journalist in Castlemaine, Victoria, before heading blindly into the wide world. Travels around Europe and South-East Asia were punctuated by a spell in London, including a year as editor of a small independent travel magazine. Returning to Australia, Paul joined Lonely Planet as an editor in 1996 and continues to travel whenever possible. This is his first update for Lonely Planet, but his third foray into Indonesia. Paul updated the Java and Sumatra sections of the Indonesia chapter for this book.

Paul Hellander

Paul has never really stopped travelling since he was born in England to a Norwegian father and English mother. He arrived in Australia in 1977, via Greece and 30 other countries. He then taught Modern Greek and trained interpreters and translators for 13 years before throwing it all away for a life as a travel writer. Paul joined Lonely Planet in 1994 and his first assignment in Asia was to update the information on Singapore for the *Singapore city guide, Malaysia, Singapore & Brunei* and *South-East Asia*, and was last heard of heading for Israel. Paul updated the Singapore chapter for this book.

Clem Lindenmayer

Clem's strong interest in languages led him to study – interrupted by repeated bouts of lengthy travel – Asian studies with a major in Mandarin. A keen mountain-goer, Clem researched and authored Lonely Planet's *Trekking in the Patagonian Andes* and *Walking in Switzerland*, and will be a coauthor of Lonely Planet's forthcoming *Hiking in the USA*. He has previously worked on *China, Western Europe* and *Scandinavian Europe* guidebooks. Clem helped update the Malaysia chapter of this book.

Mic Looby

On a flimsy journalism and English literature degree, Australian-born Mic Looby paddled all around South-East Asia before clambering onto a ledge in Hong Kong and impersonating a newspaper editor and cartoonist. Two years later he fled, only to be arrested in Melbourne and put to work as an editorial prisoner in the field of travel guides. Finally, Lonely Planet told him to get lost ... in the Philippines. Now he is only a danger to himself, for whom he works as a writer and illustrator. He can be found at mlooby@hotmail.com.au. Mic updated the Philippines chapter for this edition.

Nick Ray

A Londoner of sorts, Nick studied history and politics at the University of Warwick, a course which gave him a taste for strange happenings in strange places. Dabbling in journalism for a time, he discovered Cambodia a few years ago and just keeps going back. When not writing, he has been known to lead people astray on adventure tours in countries such as Morocco and Vietnam. Nick updated the Cambodia chapter for this edition.

Chris Rowthorn

Chris was born in England and grew up in the USA. After graduation, he dabbled in several fields before moving to Japan on a whim. Upon finding that teaching English was not his dream job, he picked up the pen and started writing, first for the *Japan Times* and then for Lonely Planet. Chris has contributed to Lonely Planet's *Japan* and *Tokyo* guidebooks. He has travelled extensively in South-East Asia, Europe and North America. When he's not travelling, he spends his time doing in-depth research on Kyoto's nightlife. Chris updated parts of the Malaysia chapter for this edition.

Peter Turner
Peter Turner lives in Melbourne and has a long held interest in Indonesia and South-East Asia. Since his first extended trip though Indonesia in 1978, he has returned to Indonesia numerous times, travelling throughout the archipelago. He joined Lonely Planet in 1986 as an editor, and worked in the field on Lonely Planet's *Malaysia, Singapore & Brunei, Singapore city guide, Indonesia, Jakarta, Java* and *Indonesia's Eastern Islands*. He updated the Nusa Tenggara section of the Indonesia chapter for this book.

FROM THE AUTHORS

David Andrew I am indebted to many people for their willing help in updating the Sarawak and Sabah sections of the Malaysia chapter and the Brunei chapter of this book. In particular Mr Sim of Hornbill's Corner Cafe, Kuching, for his fine draught beer and candid views on life in Sarawak; Guy Pilcher-Clayton, Dave Bennet and Dina for helping me investigate the night life of Mire; John and Karen Tarawe for their hospitality in Bario; Ann Otigil of Innoprise Corporation, Sabah; Haji Ahmad Bin Datuk Haji Mohd Kassim of the Australian consulate in KK; and, for allowing me to tap into their 1st class information networks, Hilda Benidip-Chong of Tourism Malaysia and Molly Hj Johar of the Sarawak Tourist Association. Thanks also to all the travellers I met along the way for their comments, complaints and tips. And back in Australia, special thanks are owed to Jim Truscott of SASR for providing maps of the Kelabit Highlands; Doug Laing of the Department of Foreign Affairs and Trade, Canberra; and to my partner Robyn for putting up with me during the long weeks of writing.

Michael Clark Special thanks to Steve Browning, Ko Zaw Tun, Julius and Kirstin, Percy Win Swe, the Three Sisters, Tour Mandalay, the Moustache Brothers and Gigi Porter.

Joe Cummings Joe wishes to thank the following people in Thailand and Laos: Oliver Bandmann, Jennifer Bartlett, Frank Carter, the Chandler girls – Nancy, Nima and Siri – Kaneungnit Chotikakul, Lynne Cummings, Michael Hodgson, Teak House, Santi Inthavong, Steven Martin, the Mutmee Circle, Tara Sauvage and Patrizia Zolese.

Mason Florence Enormous thanks to Sinh and Tram, Nhut, fearless drivers Hien, Linh and Binh, Mark Procter, Linh, Vinh, Thang and the TF Boys, FREC, Fiona Reddaway, Jamie Uhrig, Douglas Thompson, Gino, Virginie Meyniac, Annalisa Koeman of IUCN, Mike Gebbie, Richard Craik, UK Peter, Hans Kemp and Justin Giffin.

Paul Greenway Thanks to the many travellers and people in Bali who helped with information and directions, or, at least, a smile. The tourist offices in Denpasar, Kuta and Mataram were especially helpful. I am also grateful to Anne-Marie van Dam, my

'Dutch connection', who loves Indonesia as much as I do; Graeme Fay, at the Australian consulate in Denpasar; and the unknown people at Bali Online.

Paul Harding Paul would like to thank the staff at various tourist offices in Java and Sumatra; Terry for company in Jakarta; Kylie at home; and Kristin and Sue at Lonely Planet for their assistance and faith.

Paul Hellander During a frenetic and more often than not hot and sticky five weeks of wandering the streets of Singapore, several people come to mind who should be thanked: Elaine Lim of the Singapore Tourism Board and the Sydney office of the STB for a wealth of printed material; Véronique le Petit for her constant stream of tips and advice on eating places and homely hospitality; Matt Donath for information on Singapore Web sites; the efficient and public-spirited people of Singapore for their interest in and assistance with my research while in their country; my wife Stella for her continuing support and willingness to hold the fort; and finally Hup Yick for inspiration. My work is dedicated to Marcus and Byron who may one day make sense of their father's constant wanderings.

Clem Lindenmayer I would like to thank all the staff at tourist offices in the cities I researched for their help.

Mic Looby Thanks to Charlie Wood for not strangling that prize rooster; Kylie Paatsch at Flight Centre; Christophe and Claire for first-aid par excellence; Esther, Ursula and Els for Dutch courage; John Pyle for constructive criticism; Judith and Tani; Bernie and his magic tricycle; Viol Gunn and her gang; Alfred (Fred) Catalonia; Wendy, Chantalle and Karen; Julia & Joel Dorman, Sarah Lowther and Jane Lavin; and, most importantly, the Bear ... for the tailgate.

Nick Ray Nick would like to thank Andrew Dear (UK), Andrew Burke (Oz), Teresa Isabel (US), Nic B (UK), Heath Korvola (US), Miguel (Port), Ross Morgan (UK), Zeman McCreadie (UK) and the Bayon Pearnik team (Cam), Paulin (US) and the UNDP National Parks team, Kay Socha (Cam), Vannat (Cam), and of course all those who fly the flag for Cambodia worldwide and, more importantly, the wonderful Khmer people who deserve better.

Chris Rowthorn I would like to thank Chiori Matsunaga, Ben Soo, Zurina Susan Binti Abdullah, Chan Mun Onn, Helena Thomas, Omar Bentris, Razaleigh Zainal and Chandra Sehgaran.

This Book

FROM THE PUBLISHER

This 10th edition of *South-East Asia on a shoestring* was produced in Lonely Planet's Melbourne office. Editing was coordinated by Linda Suttie, with the able assistance of Russell Kerr, Tony Davidson, Errol Hunt, Mic Looby and Sally O'Brien. Glenn Beanland had overall responsibility for the design and layout of the book, and Simon Bracken designed the cover. The challenging task of overseeing mapping was performed by Mark Germanchis, Chris Thomas and Rachael Scott. Anna Judd, Tim Fitzgerald, Maree Styles, Andrew Smith, Shahara Ahmed, Sarah Sloane and Glenn Beanland all helped out with the maps. Special thanks to Russell Kerr for compiling the index, Isabelle Young for researching the Health section, Tim Uden for assisting with layout, Quentin Frayne for editing the Language section, Chris Thomas and Jamieson Gross for the *South-East Asia on a shoestring* covers graphics and Dan Levin for supplying special fonts.

THANKS

Many thanks to the travellers who used the last edition and wrote to us with helpful hints, advice and interesting anecdotes. Your names appear in the back of this book.

From Tony Wheeler

In early 1974 Tony and Maureen Wheeler set out to travel around South-East Asia to research a new guidebook to the region. Twenty-five years later Tony looks back at that pioneering trip:

The plan was a simple one: we'd ride a motorcycle up to Darwin at the top end of Australia, we'd air-freight it across to Portuguese Timor (East Timor), we'd spend the whole year going everywhere we could in South-East Asia and we'd produce a guidebook from our travels. A quarter of a century later it's intriguing to look back at that trip and note where things have changed and where they've stayed the same.

Of course the very first change was the first country we went to: Portuguese Timor simply does not exist anymore. We flew in to Bacau and spent a couple of weeks bouncing and jolting our way around the country over some of the worst roads we would experience for the whole trip. It was pretty clear the cash-strapped Portuguese were not putting much into their most remote colony and it was hardly surprising when, just over 12 months later, the whole thing fell apart. In Dili we, along with most of the small travelling fraternity passing through at the time, camped out in an open shed on the beach under a wooden sign proclaiming it was the 'Hippy Hilton'. When I went back to Dili a few years ago the shed was still there.

We rode across the border to the Indonesian side of the island, then took a ship across to Flores. The island is still a little bit off the beaten track, but 25 years ago it was way out on a limb. Today Moni, the village at the foot of the amazing Kelimutu volcano, has a dozen or so places to stay but back then we slept on the floor of a villager's hut. At the western end of Flores, we got together with two other Australians and two New Zealanders

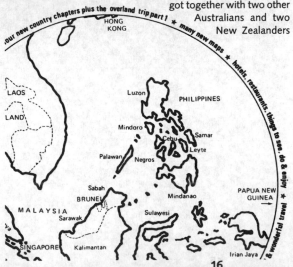

Detail from the cover of the 2nd edition of *South-East Asia on a shoestring.*

Top: 1974 – Maureen at the 'Hippy Hilton', Dili, Portuguese Timor

Middle: 1975 – Maureen putting together the first edition of *South-East Asia on a shoestring*, Palace Hotel, Singapore

Bottom: 1974 – Unloading the motorcycle, Sumbawa, Indonesia

Far left: 1974 – Tony on rocky road in Portuguese Timor towards the Indonesian border

Left: 1974 – A little off-road motorcycle travel, Maumere, Flores, Indonesia

MAUREEN WHEELER

MAUREEN WHEELER

First edition of *South-East Asia on a shoestring*, published in 1975, and (left) editions 2 through 9

and chartered a fishing boat to take us from Labuanbajo to Komodo and on to Sumbawa. Again, visitors were few and far between and facilities distinctly limited; we slept on the veranda of the police station at Labuanbajo.

Sumbawa and Lombok were our next stops but nobody had even dreamed of beach resorts at Senggigi and on the Gili Islands back in 1974. After all Kuta Beach, our first stop in Bali, was still a quiet little beach centre with sand roads winding between a few dozen losmen. We'd paused in Kuta in 1972, on our way to Australia from Europe, and in the intervening two years Legian had just started to develop, but it was an entirely detached village, separated from Kuta by a walk through the country! Back in those days Denpasar was still a quiet alternative to the beach and we stayed for a week or two at the popular Adi Yasa and also tried out the Two Brothers, both long-term survivors although very few travellers stay in Denpasar today.

As for Ubud, well there were a couple of losmen along the main street and we ate dinner each night by the light of oil lamps at Canderi's, for there was no electricity in Ubud. Beyond the football field there were no more buildings: it was just rice paddies all the way to the Monkey Forest. Around the rest of the island there were small local losmen in a number of towns, but Kuta and Sanur were the only beach resorts. Nusa Dua wasn't even a line on a drawing board and local fishing boats were all you found at Candidasa and Lovina Beach.

We continued west, pausing at Mt Bromo, Surabaya and Solo, then making a longer stop at Yogyakarta where the Sosrowijayan backpackers enclave was not very different than it is today. Many of the losmen from 25 years ago are still in existence, although Superman's was still to be invented. Then it was on to Bandung and Bogor before we reached Jakarta. We had unfond memories of our first visit to Jakarta, two years earlier, but this time it wasn't so bad, although the popular Wisma Delima was known simply as 'Jalan Jaksa' because it was the only place to stay on the whole street!

The ferry carried us across to Sumatra but after Palembang the island was very hard going. Sumatran roads in the mid-70s were a real ordeal and we were very glad to take an enforced break at Padang when three days of torrential rain kept us pinned down in our losmen. Bukittinggi was a delight but Lake Toba, just kicking off as a travellers' destination at the time, was heaven on a stick. We had to drag ourselves away to carry on to Medan and Malaysia.

I've been back to Penang many times since and it hardly seems to have changed over the years; again, many of the small Chinese hotels from that visit are still in operation today. We continued down the western side of the Malay peninsula to Singapore and checked into the Palace Hotel – which is now under renovation – and put a box of maps and notebooks into storage while we headed off to north Borneo, deck class on a ship of the Straits Shipping Company. We shared the deck with a De Tomaso Mangusta, on its way to a new home in the sultan of Brunei's garage. He'd only just started collecting cars back then.

Six weeks later we were back in Singapore again, from where

we meandered up the east coast of Malaysia, then back down again to cross to the west and make our way north into Thailand. We stopped at Hat Yai and chartered a fishing boat from Krabi to visit Ko Phi Phi, an island we'd heard might be worth investigating. It was certainly delightful and the villagers were amazed to see their first western visitors, but there was nowhere to stay apart from sleeping on the beach so we continued on to Phuket. Beach resorts were yet to arrive at Phuket as well, although Patong had an open shelter where you could camp for 3 baht a night! It was pouring with rain again so we didn't hang around.

Two years earlier we'd discovered the Malaysia Hotel in Bangkok and between times it had become the city's number one backpacker haven with a noticeboard which was to be a prime research facility for us. Our trusty Yamaha sat in the Malaysia's car park for a week while we did a high speed circuit of Burma and installed Pagan as the high point of the whole year's travel. Just a year later it was badly damaged in a huge earthquake.

Back in Thailand we continued north, stopping at Ayuthaya and Sukhothai on our way to Chiang Mai and the north. In the mid-70s Malaysia was still beset by the tattered remnants of the old Malaysian Communist Party, hiding out in the jungles in the north of the country, and Thailand also suffered from a low level insurrection which was often closer to banditry. Buses were periodically held up in the south, and at Sukhothai visiting the more remote temples was not 100% safe.

By the time we got to Chiang Mai our year, and our money, was starting to run out and we debated whether we should think about including Indochina in our travels. In fact the fall of Saigon was only a few months away and Cambodia looked even more desperate, so our ambitions to visit Angkor Wat would be put on hold for nearly 20 years. But the doors to Laos were still open and leaving our motorcycle behind in Chiang Mai we made a long loop out to the east and crossed the Mekong to Vientiane, where it was clear the Royalists were not going to hold on for much longer. For nearly a year, drinking more than an occasional beer was quite out of our financial range but we joined in to try and demolish the city's supply of French wine. Vientiane's restaurant wine cellars were obviously going to be the first to go when the Pathet Lao took over. Finally we made our way to Luang Prabang, flew to Huay Xai (Ban Houei Sai in our original guidebook) and crossed back into Thailand.

We made our way back through Chiang Rai to Chiang Mai and then, right at the end of the year, we suffered a string of annoying setbacks. First our motorcycle was stolen from outside a Chiang Mai temple. Abandoning it to its fate (it turned up three months later), we travelled by bus and train back through Bangkok and on to Malaysia. There we met my parents in Penang for Christmas and for the first time saw all the colour slides we'd taken all year and sent back to them for developing. The next morning we had a bag stolen and lost the lot! And the portable typewriter we'd bought in Singapore and been carting around on the back of the bike. And all the notes I'd been assiduously typing

Detail of a map of Pagan, Burma, produced for the 5th edition of *South-East Asia on a shoestring.*

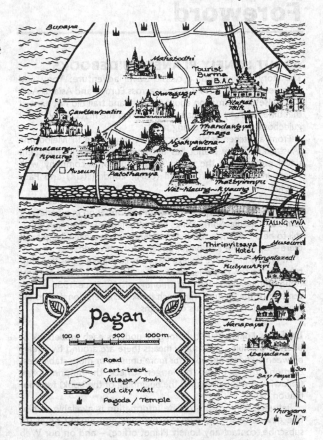

up as we went along. Fortunately I had that primitive predecessor to a backup disk in another bag – carbon copies.

That was the end of the year's travels. In early January 1975 Maureen and I settled down in the Palace Hotel in Singapore and over the next three months wrote, mapped and designed the first edition of this book in the room at the back. A year later our friend and competitor Bill Dalton would write his *Indonesia Handbook* in the same room.

The first edition of *South-East Asia on a shoestring* ran to all of 148 pages and sold for $2.95. The standard price for a losmen at Kuta Beach back in those days was 600 rp, although you only got 400 rp for the US dollar. In Singapore the Palace Hotel cost us S$8 a night, about US$3.50 at the mid-70s rate of exchange. In Bangkok a night at the Malaysia Hotel cost less than 100 baht, US$4 at the time, although we noted that was 'more expensive than other Bangkok cheapies.' In one of Vientiane's French restaurants you could have a five course dinner for US$2.50, although a bottle of French wine would set you back another US$3. ■

Foreword

ABOUT LONELY PLANET GUIDEBOOKS

The story begins with a classic travel adventure: Tony and Maureen Wheeler's 1972 journey across Europe and Asia to Australia. Useful information about the overland trail did not exist at that time, so Tony and Maureen published the first Lonely Planet guidebook to meet a growing need.

From a kitchen table, then from a tiny office in Melbourne (Australia), Lonely Planet has become the largest independent travel publisher in the world, an international company with offices in Melbourne, Oakland (USA), London (UK) and Paris (France).

Today Lonely Planet guidebooks cover the globe. There is an ever-growing list of books and there's information in a variety of forms and media. Some things haven't changed. The main aim is still to help make it possible for adventurous travellers to get out there – to explore and better understand the world.

At Lonely Planet we believe travellers can make a positive contribution to the countries they visit – if they respect their host communities and spend their money wisely. Since 1986 a percentage of the income from each book has been donated to aid projects and human rights campaigns.

Updates Lonely Planet thoroughly updates each guidebook as often as possible. This usually means there are around two years between editions, although for more unusual or more stable destinations the gap can be longer. Check the imprint page (following the colour map at the beginning of the book) for publication dates.

Between editions up-to-date information is available in two free newsletters – the paper *Planet Talk* and email *Comet* (to subscribe, contact any Lonely Planet office) – and on our Web site at www.lonelyplanet.com. The *Upgrades* section of the Web site covers a number of important and volatile destinations and is regularly updated by Lonely Planet authors. *Scoop* covers news and current affairs relevant to travellers. And, lastly, the *Thorn Tree* bulletin board, and *Postcards* section of the site carry unverified, but fascinating, reports from travellers.

Correspondence The process of creating new editions begins with the letters, postcards and emails received from travellers. This correspondence often includes suggestions, criticisms and comments about the current editions. Interesting excerpts are immediately passed on via newsletters and the Web site, and everything goes to our authors to be verified when they're researching on the road. We're keen to get more feedback from organisations or individuals who represent communities visited by travellers.

Lonely Planet gathers information for everyone who's curious about the planet – and especially for those who explore it first-hand. Through guidebooks, phrasebooks, activity guides, maps, literature, newsletters, image library, TV series and web site we act as an information exchange for a worldwide community of travellers.

Research Authors aim to gather sufficient practical information to enable travellers to make informed choices and to make the mechanics of a journey run smoothly. They also research historical and cultural background to help enrich the travel experience and allow travellers to understand and respond appropriately to cultural and environmental issues.

Authors don't stay in every hotel because that would mean spending a couple of months in each medium-sized city and, no, they don't eat at every restaurant because that would mean stretching belts beyond capacity. They do visit hotels and restaurants to check standards and prices, but feedback based on readers' direct experiences can be very helpful.

Many of our authors work undercover, others aren't so secretive. None of them accept freebies in exchange for positive write-ups. And none of our guidebooks contain any advertising.

Production Authors submit their raw manuscripts and maps to offices in Australia, USA, UK or France. Editors and cartographers – all experienced travellers themselves – then begin the process of assembling the pieces. When the book finally hits the shops some things are already out of date, we start getting feedback from readers, and the process begins again.

WARNING & REQUEST

Things change – prices go up, schedules change, good places go bad and bad places go bankrupt – nothing stays the same. So, if you find things better or worse, recently opened or long since closed, please tell us and help make the next edition even more accurate and useful. We genuinely value all the feedback we receive. Julie Young coordinates a well-travelled team that reads and acknowledges every letter, postcard and email and ensures that every morsel of information finds its way to the appropriate authors, editors and cartographers for verification.

Everyone who writes to us will find their name in the next edition of the appropriate guidebook. They will also receive the latest issue of *Planet Talk*, our quarterly printed newsletter, or *Comet*, our monthly email newsletter. Subscriptions to both newsletters are free. The very best contributions will be rewarded with a free guidebook.

Excerpts from your correspondence may appear in new editions of Lonely Planet guidebooks, the Lonely Planet Web site, *Planet Talk* or *Comet*, so please let us know if you *don't* want your letter published or your name acknowledged.

Send all correspondence to the Lonely Planet office closest to you:

Australia: PO Box 617, Hawthorn, Victoria 3122
UK: 10A Spring Place, London NW5 3BH
USA: 150 Linden St, Oakland CA 94607
France: 1 rue du Dahomey, Paris 75011

Or email us at: talk2us@lonelyplanet.com.au

For news, views and updates see our web site: www.lonelyplanet.com

HOW TO USE A LONELY PLANET GUIDEBOOK

The best way to use a Lonely Planet guidebook is any way you choose. At Lonely Planet we believe the most memorable travel experiences are often those that are unexpected, and the finest discoveries are those you make yourself. Guidebooks are not intended to be used as if they provide a detailed set of infallible instructions!

Contents All Lonely Planet guidebooks follow the same format. The Facts about the Country chapters or sections give background information ranging from history to weather. Facts for the Visitor gives practical information on issues like visas and health. Getting There & Away gives a brief starting point for researching travel to and from the destination. Getting Around gives an overview of the transport options when you arrive.

The peculiar demands of each destination determine how subsequent chapters are broken up, but some things remain constant. We always start with background, then proceed to sights, places to stay, places to eat, entertainment, getting there and away, and getting around information – in that order.

Heading Hierarchy Lonely Planet headings are used in a strict hierarchical structure that can be visualised as a set of Russian dolls. Each heading (and its following text) is encompassed by any preceding heading that is higher on the hierarchical ladder.

Entry Points We do not assume guidebooks will be read from beginning to end, but that people will dip into them. The traditional entry points are the list of contents and the index. In addition, however, there is a complete list of maps and an index map illustrating map coverage.

There's also a colour map that shows highlights. These highlights are dealt with in greater detail in the Facts for the Visitor chapter, along with planning questions and suggested itineraries. Each chapter covering a geographical region begins with a locator map and another list of highlights. Once you find something of interest in a list of highlights, turn to the index.

Maps Maps play a crucial role in Lonely Planet guidebooks and include a huge amount of information. A legend is printed on the back page. We seek to have complete consistency between maps and text, and to have every important place in the text captured on a map. Map key numbers usually start in the top left corner.

Although inclusion in a guidebook usually implies a recommendation we cannot list every good place. Exclusion does not necessarily imply criticism. In fact there are a number of reasons why we might exclude a place – sometimes it is simply inappropriate to encourage an influx of travellers.

Introduction

South-East Asia has so many highlights it is difficult to know where to begin. Soaring mountains, deep jungles, ancient temples, hustle-bustle cities, palm-fringed beaches and spellbinding ritual – South-East Asia has it all. Indeed there is nowhere in the world where travellers can whisk through such a diversity of cultures and geography with such ease.

Most travellers arrive at one of the sprawling Asian gateways. Don't be put off by first impressions. True, most Asian capitals are polluted snarls of honking traffic and hastily thrown together shopping malls – at least that's probably the view you'll have coming in to town from the airport. But probe beneath the surface and you'll find fascinating markets, back-street temples, raucous street vendors and, at times, an almost overwhelming air of go-get-it vibrancy. Jakarta is the melting pot of Indonesia; push-and-shove Bangkok is in your face – at turns shocking, at turns seductive – but provides an earthy

contrast to sanitised Singapore, where 'shocking Asia' morphs into 'shopping Asia'.

Mind you, the occasional quiet backwater capital lingers on (though who knows for how much longer?): Vientiane is lazily stirring itself from a long nap. Yangon (Rangoon), the capital of Myanmar (Burma), is a decrepit (some say 'charming') lesson in how not to run your country. Hanoi has unhurried French charm and wide, clean socialist boulevards. Even increasingly visited Phnom Penh is a city rich in colonial history.

But for most visitors Asia's real sights are in the countryside: in the Philippines, Mayon, the 'most perfect' volcano; in Java, the moonscapes of Gunung Bromo; in Malaysian Borneo, Mt Kinabalu; in Sumatra, the unforgettable panorama presented by Danau (Lake) Toba; and in Flores, the bizarre, three-coloured lakes of Kelimutu.

Trying to choose the best beaches is a good way to start an argument. Thailand probably takes the prize with Phuket and the islands of

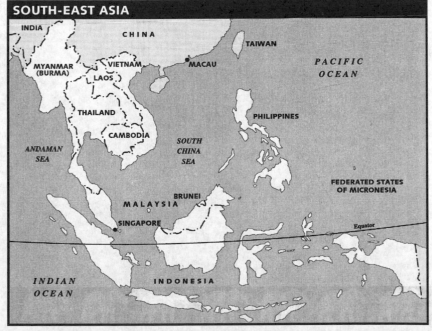

SOUTH-EAST ASIA

Ko Samui, Ko Pha-Ngan, Ko Tao, Ko Phi Phi, Ko Chang ... the list keeps growing. The east coast of Peninsular Malaysia has a few contenders, notably Tioman and the Perhentian islands. The Philippines is no slouch in the sea and sand department – Boracay is the most famed, but there's also Puerto Galera, Malapascua and dozens of other resorts. Indonesia also has its fair share scattered around the archipelago, from Pulau Nias off Sumatra to Bali's Kuta and the Gili Islands off Lombok. Vietnam is the new kid on the block, but beaches like Nha Trang are already well on the way to big resort status. If you want to find that deserted paradise, Indonesia and the Philippines have hundreds of islands to choose from.

And of course there's the history too. Ancient temple complexes such as Cambodia's Angkor, Myanmar's Bagan and Indonesia's Borobudur are awe-inspiring sights that are simply not to be missed. Other temples around the region jostle for your attention, but – without a doubt – the most fabulous is Shwedagon Paya: the gilded, jewel-encrusted pagoda that dominates the city of Yangon.

More? Well there's great food, jungle trekking, giant lizards, superb coral reefs ... in South-East Asia deciding what *not* to do is the problem.

And now is a good time to go. The region has suffered a serious economic downturn, which has seen booming economies brought to a virtual halt and currencies crash. This makes the area less expensive for western travellers but, more importantly, by visiting and spending your foreign currency you will be doing a little bit to reinvigorate the local economy.

Regional Facts for the Visitor

HIGHLIGHTS

South-East Asia is packed with highlights. Listed here are some of the more interesting/fun highlights of a trip through the region.

Beaches

There are excellent beaches in the Philippines, Indonesia and Malaysia; there are even some OK beaches in Vietnam and Cambodia. But it's Thailand that pulls in the crowds.

Thailand Most of Thailand's best beaches are on islands in the south. **Phuket** (largely upmarket these days) and **Ko Samui** were two of the earliest islands to be developed, and consequently they now offer a wide range of accommodation, dining and entertainment options.

Ko Pha-Ngan, not far from Ko Samui, has achieved fame as the venue for massive full-moon parties. **Ko Tao** is a small, remote island, accessible from Ko Pha-Ngan, and is the place to get away from it all.

Ko Phi Phi, on the western side of the isthmus, is arguably overdeveloped but still a popular beach retreat. Other popular islands are **Ko Samet** (with easy access from Bangkok) and **Ko Chang**, which is close to the Cambodian border.

Philippines The Philippines' most celebrated beaches are on **Boracay**, a small island just off the northern tip of Panay.

Malaysia On the east coast of Peninsular Malaysia there's a string of resorts and budget beach havens. The most popular places are **Pulau Tioman**, **Cherating** and the stunning but alcohol-free and slightly boring **Perhentian Islands** – Malaysian beaches are generally more straight-laced than those elsewhere in the region.

Indonesia Bali's famous beaches, such as **Kuta**, are a favourite of package tours, but Indonesia's most stunning beaches are further afield. **Pulau Bunaken** in Sulawesi, **Nias** off the Sumatran coast, or the islands of **Maluku** have some great beaches.

Historical Sights

South-East Asia has two historical sights that vie with each other for top billing: **Bagan**

(Pagan) in Myanmar and **Angkor** in Cambodia. At Bagan there are more than 5000 temples to explore. Angkor doesn't quite rival Bagan in numbers, but there are few sights in the world that measure up to the grandeur of Angkor Wat.

Indonesia's prime historical attractions are in Java. The most famous is **Borobudur**, which predates the temples of Bagan and all but the very earliest Angkor structures (there are probably historical connections between the makers of Borobudur and the early temples of Angkor). Less well known, but also impressive, is the temple complex at **Prambanan**.

Thailand is brimming with wats but it has no world-famous historical attractions. The best places to get a glimpse of Thailand's past are **Ayuthaya**, the capital until 1767, and **Lopburi**, its 10th century capital. **Chiang Mai** is something of a noisy tourist trap these days, but it also has some good historical sights.

Colonial Legacy

There's still a great deal of colonial architecture lingering in the region. The British left their mark in Singapore, parts of Malaysia (mainly on the west coast of the peninsula) and Myanmar; the French in Indochina; the Dutch in Indonesia; and the Spanish in the Philippines.

If it's derelict colonial architecture you're interested in, you'll have to head to Myanmar or Indochina. Much of **Yangon** in Myanmar, however, remains in a photogenic state of disrepair. The most charming of the Indochinese cities is **Hanoi**, with its leafy boulevards and French villas; **Phnom Penh**, too, is not without its charm.

Most travellers tend to forget the Philippines when it comes to colonial architecture, but there are some fine sights here too. In northern Luzon, **Vigan** is probably the best preserved Spanish town in the whole archipelago – a stay here is a wonderful trip back in time. Nearby **Laoag** has some wonderful Spanish churches.

Finally, amid all the new, Singapore, Malaysia and Indonesia have some worthwhile colonial architecture. Singapore's **Colonial District** is an interesting area to explore on foot and contains famous landmarks like the **Raffles Hotel** – renovated but still evocative of the past. In Malaysia, **Kuala Lumpur** and **Melaka** have some good historical buildings. **Jakarta** has some of the oldest colonial architecture in the east.

Places to Hang Out

For many travellers, South-East Asia is as much hanging out, drinking shakes and scoffing banana pancakes as it is travelling. Starting in **Indonesia**, Lombok has the **Gili Islands**, three coral-fringed specks of paradise that are each packed with inexpensive guesthouses (*losmen*). Lombok's next door neighbour is **Bali**, a legendary destination where the crowds can reach legend-making proportions.

Kuta was Bali's original budget beach area, but it has long been appropriated by mid-range and top-end tourism. The rock-bottom places are harder to find, but while you may pay a little more than in some other parts of Indonesia, you get a lot more for your money. Budget travellers with time to kill tend to gravitate to **Lovina** or **Candidasa**, though the beaches themselves are not as good. **Ubud**, the central arts and crafts capital of Bali, is still popular, despite its ever-increasing size.

In Java, sooner or later everyone ends up in **Yogyakarta** (pronounced 'Jogjakarta'). There's plenty to see in and out of town, and there are frequent cultural performances.

In Sumatra, the mountain retreat of **Bukittinggi** is a popular stopover and **Lagundri**, on **Pulau Nias**, is a popular beach hang-out. But the jewel in Sumatra's crown is probably **Danau Toba**, a crater lake with an island almost the size of Singapore. Most budget accommodation (some of the cheapest in Indonesia) is at Tuk Tuk on the island of Samosir.

Very few travellers linger in Singapore, but in **Malaysia** there are some popular places to hang out. On the west coast of Peninsular Malaysia, **Melaka**, a historical town, and **Penang**, with its wonderful old-world Chinatown, are popular spots. On the east coast is **Pulau Tioman**, arguably one of the most beautiful islands in South-East Asia. **Kota Bharu** is a laid-back town up near the Thai border – it is another place where travellers tend to linger, though when compared with other major South-East Asian attractions it's difficult to understand why.

Thailand is packed with popular places to hang out. The most popular of the southern

islands are **Ko Pha-Ngan**, **Ko Tao** and **Ko Samui** – even though Ko Samui is very touristed nowadays. There are also popular island getaways on the east coast – **Ko Samet** and **Ko Chang** both attract large numbers of long-timers. In the north, border areas like **Mae Hong Son** and **Mae Sai** (which lies at the heart of the Golden Triangle) are also favoured.

In **Indochina**, **Luang Prabang** in Laos and **Angkor** in Cambodia have emerged as two places where travellers stop over for more than just a day or two.

Wildlife

South-East Asia's national parks are not all that well developed, and there is nothing like the game parks of Africa. The variety of fauna is astonishing, but not all that easy to see. Nevertheless, tourism geared towards seeing wildlife and national parks is gradually developing, although in many places you're still pretty much on your own. On the whole, national parks are relatively untouristed and, if you have plenty of time and patience, they present good opportunities for exploring the countryside and seeking out wildlife.

Thailand has the most extensive national park network, but accommodation and facilities are limited.

Malaysia has excellent national parks and the best setup in South-East Asia for observing wildlife, but the numbers of big game (elephants, tigers, rhinoceroses etc) are low and the chances of spotting them in the dense jungle are slim. **Taman Negara National Park** has a system of hides to view the animals, while over in Borneo the **Kinabatangan River** and **Danum Valley** in Sabah are rich in wildlife.

Borneo is also home to three of the world's four orang-utan rehabilitation centres (the other is in northern Sumatra), although one, at Semenggok in Sarawak, was due to close in late 1998 and another, Camp Leakey in Kalimantan, is extremely difficult to reach. This leaves the Sepilok Centre in Sabah. It is very well organised and easy to reach, but perhaps a little too touristy. The easiest of all to visit (and therefore the most popular) is the Orang-Utan Rehabilitation Centre at Bukit Lawang in northern Sumatra. It's in a beautiful setting with plenty of budget accommodation.

Indonesia's best and most accessible national parks for wildlife are **Gunung Leuser** and **Kerinci Seblat** in Sumatra, and of course there are those infamous 'dragons' on **Komodo** and nearby **Rinca**.

In the **Philippines, Quezon National Park** in South Luzon and the **Mt Ilig-Mt Baco National Wildlife Sanctuary** in Mindoro are worth a visit. **Mt Kanlaon National Park** on Negros is a major refuge for wildlife in the central Philippines, but visitor facilities are limited.

SUGGESTED ITINERARIES

This section could easily get out of hand – there are just too many possibilities! Unless you have unlimited funds, and years to spend, you can rule out going everywhere. You could spend two months each in the Philippines and Indonesia and only see a tiny fraction of what these two vast archipelagos have to offer. And assuming you are on a six month trip, this only leaves two months for Singapore, Malaysia, Thailand, Myanmar, Vietnam, Laos and Cambodia. Most people end up deciding on a route through the region that takes in some of the highlights, perhaps indulges some special interests and includes some R&R on a beach retreat.

There is one basic itinerary on the South-East Asian trail: the south-to-north route from Indonesia, although you can of course tackle it in the opposite direction. A flight from Australia to Bali or to Timor, for example, allows you to travel through Java, Sumatra, Peninsular Malaysia (and Singapore) and Thailand without once taking a flight.

Once you get to Bangkok, it's decision time, as the possibilities multiply. After visiting northern Thailand, you might fly to Myanmar and then on to Calcutta on the Indian subcontinent; or really take up the overland challenge and travel east through Laos to Vietnam, with a side trip to Cambodia, and on to China (though the China leg of this trip is not covered by this book – look out for Lonely Planet's *China*).

The wild cards on the South-East Asian trail are the numerous islands – the Philippines, Malaysian and Indonesian Borneo, and outlying islands of Indonesia, such as Nusa Tenggara, Sulawesi, Maluku and Irian Jaya. These are all very much detours from the main circuit and thus see much lower volumes of tourist traffic – if you want to get away from banana pancakes and Bob Marley tapes, these places give you the opportunity to do so.

PLANNING

When to Go

Any time for any amount of time might be the answer to this one.

Although there are wet and dry seasons, monsoonal activity is rarely an impediment to travel in South-East Asia. Throughout the region, the rainy season is usually marked by sudden downpours of torrential rain followed just as suddenly by sunshine – bring a raincoat or buy an umbrella and you'll be fine.

As a rule of thumb, from Singapore north (including the Philippines), rainfall peaks between the months of May and September; south and east of Singapore (Indonesia) rainfall is at its heaviest between December and March. Check the climate charts at the back of this book and the Climate sections in the individual country chapters for more details.

Maps

There's very little in the way of decent maps that cover the whole of South-East Asia. Bartholomew's *Asia, South-East World Travel Map* is a fold-out affair with a scale of 1:5,800,000. Very similar is International Travel Maps' *South-East Asia*, at a scale of 1:6,000,000.

Nelles Verlag publishes the *South-East Asia Map*, and Ravenstein has the *South & East Asia Road Map* produced at a scale of 1:9,000,000.

Periplus, a Singaporean publisher, produces a range of excellent South-East Asian regional maps, but as yet there is no map of the entire region. Look out too for Lonely Planet's travel atlases for *Thailand*, *Vietnam* and *Laos*.

What to Bring

As little as possible is the best policy – but not so little that you have to scrounge off other travellers, as some of the 'super lightweight' travellers do, or don't have anything relatively smart to wear when the occasion demands it. It's very easy to find almost anything you need along the way – it's better to start with too little than too much.

Clothes Clothing is definitely cheaper in South-East Asia than in the west, so it makes sense to bring as little as possible and shop for what you need as you travel. Many travellers flying into Bangkok or Bali seem to stock up on a whole wardrobe within days of arriving.

For those who like to be prepared, a check-list of clothing to bring might include:

- underwear and swimming gear
- a pair of long pants and a pair of shorts (not brief)
- a few T-shirts and shirts
- a sweater for cold nights
- a pair of runners or shoes
- sandals or thongs
- a lightweight jacket or raincoat
- a set of 'smart' clothes

Bear in mind that modesty is rated highly in Asian countries, especially for women. Wearing shorts (or skimpier apparel) away from the beach is generally perceived as undignified.

Other Needs There are a host of travel accessories you might bring besides a basic wardrobe. A medical kit is worth considering (see the Health section in the appendix). A good pair of sunglasses with UV protection is essential in the tropical sun, as is high-factor sunscreen, and you might also bring:

- washing gear
- sewing kit
- padlock
- Swiss army knife
- money belt
- extra camera batteries
- water bottle
- torch (flashlight)

A padlock is useful to lock your bag to a train or bus luggage rack, or to secure your hotel room – which often locks with a latch. A folding umbrella will almost certainly come in handy, but these are readily available throughout the region. Soap, toothpaste and so on are always easy to get, but toilet paper and tampons can be difficult to find in remote areas. If you are likely to need condoms, bring these with you as locally produced ones are not always reliable.

Sleeping Bag Should you, shouldn't you? The fact is, in South-East Asia you will get very few opportunities to use a sleeping bag. If you are planning to hike up mountains or do some serious trekking in areas that see few foreigners (there are not many places like this left), it may be worth bringing one; otherwise, you are probably better off saving the space in your pack for something else. Many travellers find that a locally bought sarong serves perfectly as a sheet, as well as functioning as a towel, a beach wrap or a dressing gown.

How to Carry It A backpack is still the best way to carry gear because it's commodious and perfect for walking. On the debit side, a backpack is awkward to load on and off buses and trains; it doesn't offer too much protection for your valuables; the straps tend to get caught on things; and some airlines may refuse to take responsibility if it's damaged or broken into.

Travelpacks – a combination of backpack and shoulder bag – are also popular. The backpack straps zip away inside the pack when not needed so you almost have the best of both worlds. Although not really suitable for long hiking trips, they're much easier to carry than a bag. Access to your gear is also easier – the top zips open so you don't have to take out everything to find something at the bottom – and they are easier to lock than a backpack. Another alternative is a large, soft zip bag with a wide shoulder strap so it can be carried with relative ease. Backpacks and travelpacks can be made reasonably thief-proof with small padlocks. Forget suitcases.

The secret of successful packing is plastic bags, also called 'stuff bags' – they not only separate the items in your pack, they keep them clean and dry.

Airlines do lose bags from time to time, but you've got a much better chance of it not being yours if you tag it with your name and address *inside* the bag, as well as outside. Outside tags can fall off or be removed.

VISAS & DOCUMENTS
Passport
To enter many countries your passport must be valid for at least six months, even if you're only staying for a few days. It is probably best to have at least a year left on your passport if you are heading off on a trip around South-East Asia.

Make sure it has plenty of pages left for those stamp-happy Asian officials to do their bit too. On a long trip, it's surprising how quickly a passport can fill up. A new one is relatively easy to organise in most major South-East Asian cities, but the processing may cause delays to your trip. Some nationalities (Americans for example) can simply have an extra, concertina-style, section added when their passport gets full.

Visas

Visas are stamps in your passport that permit you to enter a country and stay for a specified period of time. Visas are available for most nationalities on arrival in Indonesia, Singapore, Malaysia, Brunei, Thailand, Cambodia and Laos but are still required for Myanmar and Vietnam. It may be that by getting a visa in advance you can get a longer initial period of stay (Laos) or that at the place where you want to enter the country an advance visa is required (some ports in Indonesia), so be sure you are familiar with requirements before just rocking up at a border or port.

As far as possible, get your visas as you go rather than all at once before you leave home: first, they often expire after a certain number of days; second, it is often easier and cheaper to get them in neighbouring countries than it is from far away. Visas for Myanmar, Laos and Vietnam are readily available in Bangkok and Hong Kong.

Visa regulations vary from country to country. In some cases, for example, extensions are near impossible, in others a mere formality. See the Visas sections under the individual countries in this book for further information. And remember the most important rule: treat visits to embassies, consulates and borders as formal occasions and look smart for them.

Photocopies

A sensible security precaution is to keep photocopies of essential documents separate from the documents themselves. You should do this with the data pages of your passport, birth certificate, credit cards, airline tickets and any other important documents you're carrying. Best of all, leave a copy of this information with someone at home too.

While you're compiling that information, add the serial numbers of your travellers cheques and US$50 or more as emergency cash. Keep this emergency material separate from your passport, cheques and other cash.

Onward Tickets

In some countries in South-East Asia (Indonesia, for example) you are required to have an onward ticket out of the country before you can obtain a visa to enter. In practice, however, as long as you look fairly respectable, it's unlikely that your tickets will be checked. The best insurance against being turned away is to buy the cheapest ticket out of the country and cash it in later.

Travel Insurance

A travel insurance policy to cover theft, loss and medical problems is a good idea. Some policies offer lower and higher medical-expense options; the higher ones are chiefly for countries such as the USA, which have extremely high medical costs. There is a wide variety of policies available, so check the small print.

Some policies specifically exclude 'dangerous activities', which can include scuba diving, motorcycling, even trekking. A locally acquired motorcycle licence is not valid under some policies.

You may prefer a policy which pays doctors or hospitals directly rather than you having to pay on the spot and claim later. If you have to claim later, make sure you keep all documentation. Some policies ask you to call back (reverse charges) to a centre in your home country where an immediate assessment of your problem is made.

Check that the policy covers ambulances or an emergency flight home.

Driving Licence & Permits

There are parts of South-East Asia where car and motorbike hire are options for getting around. Malaysia is a good country to drive a car in, and in parts of Thailand and Indonesia motorcycle hire is popular. If you are planning to do any driving, get an international driver's licence before you leave your home country – they are inexpensive and valid for one year.

Hostel Card

Hostelling International (HI) has only a handful of hostels in South-East Asia, and as budget accommodation is usually provided by guesthouses, a hostel card is not essential. A hostel card will get you a small discount in the few hostels available in Thailand, Malaysia, Indonesia, the Philippines and Brunei, but hostels are only slightly cheaper than guesthouse accommodation. Some HI hostels are supposedly only for members, but a student card will often get you in.

Student & Youth Cards

The International Student Identity Card (ISIC), a plastic ID-style card with a photograph, is the official student card to have. The problem in South-East Asia is that there are so many fakes floating around it is next to useless. Discounted international air tickets and so on are available to all and sundry providing you shop at the right agencies. A student card will occasionally get you discounts on domestic flights and entry to attractions. If you are eligible for an authentic student card, by all means get one and bring it with you – just don't expect too much of it.

Seniors' Cards
Generally seniors' cards won't prove to be particularly useful in South-East Asia, but it's worth asking for discounts on domestic flights.

International Health Card
You will need an international health card only if you are arriving in South-East Asia from areas with yellow fever, such as Africa and South America.

EMBASSIES & CONSULATES
It's important to realise what your own embassy – the embassy of the country of which you are a citizen – can and can't do to help you if you get into trouble.

Generally speaking, it won't be much help in emergencies if the trouble you're in is remotely your own fault. Remember that you are bound by the laws of the country you are in. Your embassy will not be sympathetic if you end up in jail after committing a crime locally, even if such actions are legal in your own country.

In genuine emergencies you might get some assistance, but only if other channels have been exhausted. For example, if you need to get home urgently, a free ticket home is exceedingly unlikely – the embassy would expect you to have insurance. If you have all your money and documents stolen, it might assist with getting a new passport, but a loan for onward travel is out of the question.

Some embassies used to keep letters for travellers or have a small reading room with home newspapers, but these days the mail holding service has usually been stopped and even newspapers tend to be out of date.

Most travellers should have no need to contact their embassy while in South-East Asia, although if you are really going off the trail it may be worth letting your embassy know. The important thing to remember here is that if you do tell people that you are going to X for a certain period of time, be sure to let them know when you return. In this way valuable time, effort and money aren't wasted looking for you while you may be relaxing on the beach somewhere in a different country, having already left X, and the country it's in, without informing these same people.

See the individual country chapters for details of the embassies found there.

CUSTOMS
Customs regulations vary little around the region. A dim view is taken of drugs and arms – the death sentence or a lengthy stay in prison are common measures taken to discourage travellers sneaking drugs across borders. Check the Customs sections of the countries in this book for details on duty-free allowances.

MONEY
Exchanging Money
Currency exchange is generally straightforward throughout the region. Myanmar is an exception, enforcing extortionate official exchange rates that bear little relation to the value of the local currency, although it's possible to avoid this nonsense to a large extent. In Vietnam and Cambodia you needn't exchange money at all if you have a supply of US dollars cash.

The currency of choice is US dollars – cash or travellers cheques. No matter how remote, if there's a bank around that accepts foreign currency, you can be sure it will be familiar with US dollars and will usually have current rates.

Other major currencies are easy to change in the main centres; it's when you start getting away from regularly touristed areas that your currency options become more limited. This applies especially to Laos, but is equally true in other places such as the outer islands of Indonesia.

Cash Nothing beats cash for convenience ... or risk. If you lose it, it's gone forever – very few travel insurers will come to your rescue. However, it is a good idea to take some cash with you. Often, it is much easier to change just a few dollars (when leaving a country for example) in cash rather than cheques – and more economical.

Cash is also very handy when banks are closed, or nonexistent. Even in remote villages it seems there's always someone who knows what the greenback is worth, and you can often find someone who will accept US dollars in an emergency.

Travellers Cheques American Express or Thomas Cook travellers cheques are probably the best to carry because they are widely accepted and have 'instant replacement' policies. Amex has offices in most of the major cities.

The main idea behind carrying travellers cheques rather than cash is the protection they offer from theft, although it doesn't do a lot of good if you have to go back home to get the refund. Remember that 'instant replacement' may not be exactly instantaneous, although overall most people seem to be pretty satisfied with the service.

Keeping a record of the cheque numbers and the initial purchase details is vitally important. Without this you may well find that 'instant' is a very long time indeed. If you're going to really out-of-the-way places, it may be worth taking a couple of different brands of travellers cheques since banks may not always accept all varieties. Once again, take only well known brands and stick to major currencies.

Take nearly all the cheques in large denominations, say US$100s. It's only at the very end of a stay that you may want to change a US$20 or US$10 cheque just to get you through the last day or two. A number of institutions charge a per-cheque service fee, so changing US$100 in 20s can end up five times as expensive as a single US$100 cheque.

ATMs & Credit Cards Credit cards have a number of uses and are well worth carrying if you can get one. The most obvious use is to make major purchases, such as airline and boat tickets, car rental and even souvenirs. It is often surprising how many places such as small hotels accept credit cards.

Credit cards also allow you to draw cash over the counter at selected banks and, increasingly, make cash withdrawals at automatic teller machines (ATMs) in the more developed countries of the region. In these countries it is also possible to access overseas savings accounts through ATMs which support Cirrus and Maestro – check with your bank at home before you leave.

Credit cards are a convenient way to carry your money: your money isn't tied up in travellers cheques in a currency that is diving; and the exchange rates are often better than those offered by local banks or moneychangers for cash or travellers cheques. The disadvantages are that interest is charged, unless your account is always in the black, and credit limits can be too limited. There's usually a transaction fee charged by your home bank for cash advances made overseas, and these can be high, so check before you leave.

Not all banks in South-East Asia will give cash advances on a credit card, and it can be difficult outside major cities. Malaysia, Thailand and Indonesia are pretty credit-card friendly, but don't rely on a credit card in Myanmar or Laos.

While credit cards offer a good option for accessing money, it's not a good idea to rely exclusively on cards; carry travellers cheques and/or cash as a backup. Nobody wants to be short of cash only to see 'Funds unavailable – contact your bank' flash up on an ATM when their bank is thousands of miles away.

Visa and MasterCard are equally acceptable, and American Express has a large network of offices.

Finally, always check purchases and receipts when you buy something with a credit card, and against accounts when you get home. Credit card fraud, especially in Bangkok, is not unknown.

International Transfers It is possible to instruct your bank at home to transfer money (assuming you've got it) to a bank overseas where you can collect it. You need to specify the bank and its address. If you're unsure which local bank is best to use, you can ask your bank at home.

A telegraphic transfer is the quickest way to send money – it should reach you in a couple of days. When it gets there, it will most likely be converted into local currency – you can take it as it is or buy travellers cheques. Singapore is easily the best place included in this book to transfer money to. Malaysia and Thailand are not bad either, but even in Indonesia and the Philippines it's fairly straightforward.

Black Market You can travel through much of South-East Asia and never have to use the black market to change money – in most countries there isn't one. Myanmar has a thriving black market, mainly in US dollars.

In Indochina the US dollar is a generally accepted currency – changing it for local currency is something that almost anyone with access to a cash register can do. See the relevant country chapters for more details.

Costs

With the Asian economic crisis of the late 1990s, which has seen local currencies plunge in value against the dollar, travel in South-East Asia is once again a real bargain. This is especially so in Indonesia, where the currency fell to a fraction of its previous value in less than 18 months. The situation in the other countries is not as severe, but all currencies have been affected to some extent.

As always, top-end travellers can spend as much per day in some parts of the region as they would in any other popular tourist destination around the world. Off the beaten track, however, in places like Indonesia, north-east Thailand, Laos, Cambodia and Vietnam, budget travel is still possible. And even in the biggest cities, where accommodation can be expensive and tight, there are always a few rock-bottom options.

Your budget is dependent upon how you live and travel. If you're moving fast and living it up in the big cities, your day-to-day living costs are going to rise. On the other hand, if you stick to the less touristed parts of the region and travel at a relaxed pace, it's still possible to keep costs down to US$10 per day (and less) in most South-East Asia countries.

But remember, keep costs in perspective. When bargaining over a few dong, riel or rupiah, bear in mind that that small amount of money is worth far more to the local person than it is to you if you're from a western country with a strong economy.

Carrying Money

Obviously you don't want to have all your money swiped from your back pocket. Find somewhere safe to store it. The pouches that buckle around the waist are not good places to store large amounts of money, but a money belt or pouch that fits inside your clothes *is*, and some travellers even have pouches sewn inside their clothes. Another option is take a pair of nylon stockings, fold one leg inside the other and tie it around your waist (inside your clothes of course) with your valuables positioned at the small of your back.

It's sensible to keep a small emergency stash – say US$50 – separately from the bulk of your funds.

Tipping & Bargaining

Tipping is not usually expected in South-East Asia. In Singapore a tip may sometimes be expected, and the same is true of heavily touristed parts of Thailand. Elsewhere there should be no need, unless you are staying in an upmarket accommodation where international rules apply.

You may not need to tip, but you will certainly have to bargain. Haggling over prices is the rule outside supermarkets and department stores, where prices are fixed. If you buy anything in a market, at a street stall or even in a souvenir shop, some bargaining is called for. Remember to keep it friendly – if you think you're being ripped off, walk away and shop somewhere else.

POST & COMMUNICATIONS

Post

Postal services are generally reliable across the region. Of course, it's always better to leave important mail and parcels for the big Asian centres like Bangkok, Singapore, Kuala Lumpur and Jakarta.

There's always an element of risk in sending parcels home by sea, though as a rule they eventually reach their destinations. If it's something of value to you, it's worth considering air freight – better still, register the parcel or send it by courier.

Inquire at the post office before you bring in a parcel, because there may be special wrapping requirements or it may have to be inspected (as in Indonesia) before being wrapped.

Poste Restante

Poste restante is widely available throughout the region and is the best way of receiving mail. American Express has client mail services. Some travellers use hotels as poste restante services – sometimes this works, sometimes it doesn't. Very few embassies will hold mail for their people – they'll just forward it to poste restante.

When getting people to write to you, ask them to leave plenty of time for mail to arrive and to print your name very clearly. Underlining the surname also helps.

Warning

Because of the volatility of South-East Asian currencies, the rates of exchange and prices given in this book, accurate at the time of writing, may vary considerably at the time of your visit. Prices given in US dollars are the most stable.

Monks at Doi Suthep wat, Chiang Mai, Thailand

The quiet, patient face of 'Burmese-ness'

Huge guardians of Buddhist compassion at the Bayon in Angkor Thom, Cambodia

Young Vietnamese woman at work

Sunrise over Bagan, Myanmar (Burma)

FRANK CARTER

Hill tribes mingle at Muang Sing's market, Laos

RICHARD I'ANSON

Jeepneys, the jewels of Philippines roads

ANDREW BROWNBILL

Bromo-Tengger-Semeru National Park in East Java, Indonesia

RICHARD I'ANSON

Cameron Highlands tea plantation, Malaysia

SARA-JANE CLELAND

Krabi beach and limestone rocks, Thailand

International Calls

The international phone system varies from country to country across South-East Asia, but it is generally easy to make international calls. Many guesthouses can organise direct-dial or reverse-charge calls.

In Singapore, Malaysia, Indonesia and Cambodia international card phones are also widely available. Check the individual country chapters for more details.

Fax

Fax services are widely available in most countries across the region. Try to avoid the business centres in upmarket hotels – tariffs of 30% and upwards are often levied on faxes and international calls.

Email & Internet Access

Internet users can access email and Internet services in all countries of the region with the exception of Myanmar, although casual use is not readily available in Laos or Cambodia. Services vary from cybercafes in Bali and Singapore to post offices or service providers with public access. The cost is generally low.

INTERNET RESOURCES

The World Wide Web is a rich resource for travellers. You can research your trip, hunt down bargain air fares, book hotels, check on weather conditions or chat with locals and other travellers about the best places to visit (or avoid!).

There's no better place to start your Web explorations than the Lonely Planet Web site (www.lonelyplanet.com). Here you'll find succinct summaries on travelling to most places on earth, postcards from other travellers and the Thorn Tree bulletin board, where you can ask questions before you go or dispense advice when you get back. You can also find travel news and updates to many of our most popular guidebooks, and the sub-WWWay section links you to some of the most useful travel resources elsewhere on the Web.

BOOKS
Lonely Planet

A guidebook which covers an area as vast as South-East Asia can only hope to scratch the surface. For more detailed information on a specific area or country, refer to the large range of travel guides produced by Lonely Planet. These are updated regularly and

provide useful maps and a wealth of information for travellers.

The titles to look for are:

Bali & Lombok
Cambodia
Indonesia
Indonesia's Eastern Islands
Java
Laos
Malaysia, Singapore & Brunei
Myanmar (Burma)
Philippines
Thailand
Thailand's Islands & Beaches
Vietnam

Look also for the following city guides:

Bangkok city guide
Ho Chi Minh City (Saigon) city guide
Hong Kong city guide
Jakarta city guide
Singapore city guide

Phrasebooks

Also of interest to travellers in South-East Asia are Lonely Planet's range of phrasebooks, which includes:

South-East Asia phrasebook
Burmese phrasebook
Hill Tribes phrasebook
Indonesian phrasebook
Lao phrasebook
Malay phrasebook
Pilipino phrasebook
Thai phrasebook
Vietnamese phrasebook

NEWSPAPERS & MAGAZINES

Each of the countries of South-East Asia has its own English language dailies. They vary in quality and are sometimes not available away from the major tourist centres.

International newspapers and magazines are also available in the major regional centres. The newspapers you are most likely to come across are the *International Herald Tribune*, the *Asian Times* and the *Asia Wall Street Journal*, probably in that order. In some places you will come across three or four-day-old British, European and Australian dailies. French dailies are widely available in Indochina.

On the magazine front, *Time* and *Newsweek* are the big ones, but *The Economist* also makes regular appearances on newsstands.

Asiaweek, Far Eastern Economic Review and *Asia Inc* are Hong Kong productions with good coverage of regional news.

RADIO & TV

A short-wave radio is not a bad idea if you like to keep up with world events, as local coverage is often not what it might be.

Satellite TV is extremely popular across the region, and can be seen in restaurants, airport lounges and mid-range to top-end hotels. Popular English-language channels are CNN (American international news service), BBC (British news), HBO (movie channel), Star TV (three channels – sports, popular entertainment and Chinese) and MTV.

PHOTOGRAPHY & VIDEO
Film & Equipment

You'll run through plenty of film in South-East Asia, and in Singapore it's fairly cheap. Film is readily available elsewhere (Malaysia, Thailand and Indonesia, for example), but slide film is often difficult to obtain.

Cameras are also cheap in Singapore, where the choice of camera equipment is staggering. If you have any difficulties these are also the places to have your camera attended to.

Technical Tips

When taking photos in the region compensate for the intensity of the light – for a few hours before and after midday the height of the sun will tend to make pictures very washed out. Try to photograph early or late in the day. There will also be plenty of occasions when you'll want to use a flash, either for indoor shots or in jungle locations where the amount of light that filters through can be surprisingly low.

Video

Properly used, a video camera can give a fascinating record of your holiday. As well as videoing the obvious things – sunsets, spectacular views – remember to record some of the ordinary everyday details of life in the country. Often the most interesting things occur when you're actually intent on filming something else. Remember too that, unlike still photography, video 'flows' – so, for example, you can shoot scenes of countryside rolling past the train window.

Video cameras have amazingly sensitive microphones and you might be surprised by how much sound is picked up. This can also be a problem if there is a lot of ambient noise – filming by the side of a busy road might seem OK when you do it, but viewing it back home might simply give you a deafening cacophony of traffic noise. Two good rules for beginners are: try to film in long takes, and don't move the camera around too much – otherwise, your video could well make your viewers seasick! If your camera has a stabiliser you can take good footage while travelling on various means of transport, even on bumpy roads.

Finally, remember to follow the same rules regarding people's sensitivities as for still photography – having a video camera shoved in their face is probably even more annoying and offensive for locals than a still camera. Always ask permission first.

Photographing People

Always try to make contact with people before you photograph them. Often a smile will do the trick. For portraits, it is best to ask politely. Don't stick cameras in people's faces indiscriminately.

Airport Security

X-ray machines that claim to be film-safe generally are. You are advised to have very sensitive film (1000 ASA and above) checked by hand. Most professionals insist that all their film be checked by hand, and in some cases they will take the extra precaution of using a lead-lined bag.

TIME

Most of South-East Asia is either seven or eight hours ahead of GMT/UTC (Greenwich Mean Time/Universal Time Coordinated).

Malaysia, Brunei, Singapore, Macau and the Philippines are all eight hours ahead of GMT/UTC. Thus, when it's noon in Kuala Lumpur, it's 8 pm the previous day in Los Angeles, 11 pm the previous day in New York, 4 am in London and 2 pm in Sydney.

Thailand, Vietnam, Cambodia and Laos are seven hours ahead of GMT/UTC. When it is noon in Bangkok, it is 9 pm the previous day in Los Angeles, midnight in New York, 5 am in London and 3 pm in Sydney.

Myanmar is six and a half hours ahead of GMT/UTC, half an hour behind Bangkok time. When it is noon in Yangon, it is 9.30 pm the previous day in Los Angeles, 12.30 am in New York, 5.30 am in London and 3.30 pm in Sydney.

There are three time zones in Indonesia: Sumatra, Java and west and central Kalimantan are on West Indonesian Time, which is seven hours ahead of GMT/UTC; Bali, Nusa Tenggara, south and east Kalimantan and Sulawesi are on Central Indonesian Time, which is eight hours ahead of GMT/UTC; and Irian Jaya and Maluku are on East Indonesian Time, which is nine hours ahead of GMT/UTC. Thus when it is noon in Jakarta, it is 9 pm the previous day in Los Angeles, midnight in New York, 5 am in London, 1 pm in Bali and Ujung Pandang, 2 pm in Jayapura and 3 pm in Sydney.

ELECTRICITY

If you want to bring your ghetto blaster, notebook computer or hair drier, try to make sure that it can handle different voltages and cycles, and bring socket adaptors. Better still, make sure that it also runs on batteries.

Reliability of supply is in direct relation to the affluence of the country. Myanmar, the Philippines and Indochina have frequent blackouts and Indonesia is generally reliable but not always, especially in the more remote islands; elsewhere you shouldn't have any problems.

Voltages & Cycles

The going voltage is 220V at 50Hz (cycles), except for the Philippines, which is 220V at 60Hz. Note that 240V appliances will happily run on 220V.

Plugs & Sockets

It's best to be prepared for anything. Malaysia and Singapore use the flat three-pin type as used in the UK. Most other countries use the round two-pin type as found in Europe. Exceptions are the Philippines, which uses the flat, vertical, two-pin plug used in the USA. Outlets in Indochina generally take European plugs, but some outlets take the US flat-pin type. Buy socket adaptors before you leave – they can be difficult to find in Asia.

WEIGHTS & MEASURES

The metric system is used across most of South-East Asia. Refer to the conversion table on the inside back cover of this book if you have problems with metric measurements.

TOILETS & SHOWERS

Across the region, the 'squat toilet' is the norm except in hotels and guesthouses geared toward tourists and international business travellers.

Next to the typical squat toilet is a bucket or cement reservoir filled with water. A plastic bowl usually floats on the water's surface or sits nearby. This water supply has a two-fold function: toilet-goers scoop water from the reservoir with the plastic bowl and use it to clean their nether regions while still squatting over the toilet; and a bowl full of water poured down the toilet takes the place of the automatic flush. More rustic toilets in rural areas may simply consist of a few planks over a hole in the ground.

Even in places where sit-down toilets are installed, the plumbing may not be designed to take toilet paper. In such cases the usual washing bucket will be standing nearby or there will be a waste basket where you're supposed to place used toilet paper.

Public toilets are common in cinemas, department stores, bus and railway stations, larger hotel lobbies and airports. Elsewhere you'll have to make do; while on the road between towns and villages it is acceptable to go discreetly behind a tree or bush.

Bathing

Some hotels and most guesthouses do not have hot water, though places in the larger cities will usually offer hot water of some kind – either by the tap or bucket.

Many rural people bathe in rivers or streams. At basic hotels in towns or cities the bathrooms usually have a large jar or cement trough filled with water for bathing purposes. A plastic or metal bowl is used to sluice water from the jar or trough over the body – don't jump in the trough! Even in homes with showers, heated water is uncommon.

WOMEN TRAVELLERS

South-East Asia is generally a fairly safe region for women to travel in. In some places, the widespread myth of the easy virtue of western women is still taken as fact, but most of urban South-East Asia has become more sophisticated over recent years and this is less a problem than it once was.

Attitudes Towards Women

South-East Asia is not the Middle East. Women play an active role in day-to-day public life. Providing you dress appropriately and interact respectfully with the locals you too will be treated with respect. Bear in mind, however, that solo travel is an alien concept for many South-East Asians, particularly if carried out by a woman. It's always a good idea to have a companion.

While most of Indonesia and Malaysia is Muslim, it is not of the fundamentalist variety – you will not be tackled by religious zealots for baring an ankle. Nevertheless, women travellers can experience some difficulty in Sumatra, along the east coast of Peninsular Malaysia and in the southern Philippines, so extra care should be taken there. Respectful dressing is certainly necessary – beach wear should be reserved for the beach and basically the less skin you expose the better.

Safety Precautions
Attitude can be as important as what you wear. Never respond to come-ons or rude comments. Completely ignoring them is always best. A haughty attitude can work wonders!

A husband (which means any male partner) or children also confer respectability, although the husband doesn't have to be present. Some women travellers wear a wedding ring simply for the impression it makes. The imaginary husband doesn't even have to be left at home – who is to say you're not meeting him that very day?

Some precautions are simply the same for any traveller, male or female, but women should take extra care not to find themselves alone on empty beaches, down dark streets or in other situations where help might not be available.

Be deeply suspicious of any holes in the walls of cheap hotels, especially in showers. In some parts of the region cheap hotels often double as brothels; if you find yourself in one of these, turning the haughty attitude up a notch may help. However, as often as not it's no problem: some people may be there because it's a brothel, but it will be recognised that you're there because it's a cheap hotel. Nevertheless, you should take care, especially at night, and if you're uncomfortable move to another hotel.

Solo women travellers, just like solo males, should be wary when strangers are unexpectedly friendly. See the note about theft in the following Dangers & Annoyances section.

GAY & LESBIAN TRAVELLERS
In general, gay men are more accepted in South-East Asia than gay women. Public dis-

plays of affection, heterosexual or homosexual, are frowned upon across the region. It would pay to be discreet, if not obsessively so, but your private sexual conduct will not attract the attention of authorities in South-East Asia – unless it involves children!

DISABLED TRAVELLERS
Travellers with serious disabilities are unlikely to find South-East Asia very user friendly. Even the more sophisticated cities are very much push-and-shove places. In general, care of the disabled is left to close family members and throughout the region it is unrealistic to expect much in the way of public amenities.

TRAVEL WITH CHILDREN
South-East Asia is a good place to travel with children. They'll be fussed over and looked after wherever you go, and kids are perfect ice-breakers – you'll get to meet far more locals if you have the children along. For more details on how to get the most out of your trip, pick up a copy of Lonely Planet's *Travel with Children*.

DANGERS & ANNOYANCES
Theft
Theft is not the problem that many people imagine it to be in South-East Asia. To be sure, if you wander around with money hanging out of your back pocket or with your bag open, you can expect things to go missing. But with a small amount of common sense and routine caution there's no reason why you should have anything stolen on your travels. The most important things to guard are your passport, certain documents, tickets and money. It's best to always carry these in a moneybelt or a sturdy leather pouch next to your skin.

Theft in South-East Asia is usually carried out by stealth. Be alert to the possible presence of snatch thieves, who will whisk a camera or a bag off your shoulder. Don't store valuables in easily accessible places. Violent theft is very rare but occurs from time to time – usually late at night and after the victim has been drinking. Be careful walking alone late at night and don't fall asleep in taxis. Feel free to relax a little in affluent cities like Singapore and Kuala Lumpur.

Always be diplomatically suspicious of over-friendly locals. Don't accept gifts of food and drinks from someone you don't know. In Thailand, thieves have been known to use drugged food and drinks to knock travellers out and get at their belongings.

Finally, don't let paranoia ruin your trip. With just a few sensible precautions most travellers make their way across the region without incident.

Scams

Most scams assume you're either very gullible or very stupid – if you have your wits about you, there's no reason to become a victim of one.

Two perennial scams are airline-ticket rackets and gemstones (buy here cheap, sell at home for huge profits). It seems obvious, but it's not a good idea to fork out wads of cash for an airline ticket to an 'agency' that operates from a kitchen table – it's always better to spend a little more and buy from an established operator. As for gemstones, if there really were vast amounts of money to be made by selling them back home, there would be queues outside Bangkok jewellery shops.

There are any number of scams, but they all revolve around the unlikely scenario of a local presenting you with an opportunity to save or make lots of money. Gambling rackets, 'losing' travellers cheques, guaranteeing loans – they're all scams on which unfortunate or foolish travellers have lost their shirts.

Drugs

The risks associated with drug use have grown to the point where, in most parts of the region, you won't even see joints being passed around. These days, even a little harmless grass can cause a great deal of trouble. To get mixed up with anything heavier would be to court a long jail sentence or, in some places, the death penalty. There are enough foreign travellers languishing in South-East Asian jails as it is; don't add to their numbers.

The days of paying off a few cops and making a speedy exit from the country have disappeared. Even easy-going Bali now has a jail just down the road from Kuta Beach where a number of travellers are enjoying the tropical climate much longer than they intended. In Indonesia, you can actually end up behind bars because your travel companions had dope and you didn't report them.

Other places can be a whole lot worse. A spell in a Thai prison is nobody's idea of a pleasant way to pass the time, while in Malaysia and Singapore, a prison spell may be supplemented with a beating with the *rotan*. In those countries simple possession can have you dangling from a rope, as two Australians discovered in 1986 in Malaysia. On a per capita basis, the Malaysians execute far more people for drug-related offences (and with far less publicity) than the Americans do for murder.

Don't bother bringing drugs home with you either. Back home in the west you may not get hanged for possession, but with all those South-East Asian visa stamps there's a good chance customs officials will take a good look at your luggage.

ACTIVITIES
Trekking

Trekking in South-East Asia doesn't take on the same proportions as in Nepal, but plenty of good treks are possible, particularly jungle hikes. Most visitors at least hike up a mountain or volcano somewhere in their travels – this inevitably involves a shivering, pre-dawn climb to catch the sunrise.

Trekking in the hill tribe regions of **Thailand** features on many travellers' itineraries. It's not a unique experience, but despite mass tourism many still find it rewarding. Shop around in Chiang Mai for a trek. Most last from three to seven days and may include rafting and elephant rides. Treks can also be organised in Chiang Rai, Mae Hong Son and other northern centres.

One of **Malaysia's** highlights is its national parks, and Taman Negara National Park has some excellent walks. Some good treks can also be organised in East Malaysia, particularly in Sarawak, at Gunung Mulu, and around Bario for the more adventurous. No trip to Sabah is complete without visiting the towering summit of Mt Kinabalu, a relatively easy two day climb.

In **Indonesia**, Sumatra has some good jungle treks, particularly in Gunung Leuser National Park, and it is easy to organise treks in Berastagi or Bukit Lawang. Java has some good walks in the national parks, but is noted more for its volcanic peaks: Gunung Merapi can be a taxing climb, while spectacular Gunung Bromo is more of a stroll. Batur and Agung volcanoes, on Bali, are popular day trips, or try Gunung Rinjani on neighbouring Lombok for an excellent three day hike. Indonesia's outer regions, particularly Irian Jaya and Sulawesi, present plenty of more adventurous jungle trekking opportunities.

In the **Philippines**, the Mayon volcano is a 'must climb', although recent eruptions have made it more difficult. You can arrange walks around Banaue in North Luzon and Quezon National Park.

In **Vietnam**, Tam Dao has some of the best walks.

Surfing

Indonesia is the big surfing destination in Asia, and for years surfers have been carting their boards to isolated outposts of the archipelago in search of long, deserted waves. Ulu Watu in Bali, Grajagan in Java and Nias in Sumatra are famous surfing destinations, but there is surf right along the southern coast of the inner islands – from Sumatra through to Sumbawa, Sumba and across to Irian Jaya.

Diving & Snorkelling

South-East Asia is an underwater paradise that presents countless opportunities for diving and snorkelling. Indonesia, Malaysia and Thailand have the best facilities, and many easily accessible reefs, but the Philippines and even Vietnam also have some diving spots.

Many beach resorts rent out masks, snorkels and fins, and novices will require little outlay. But if you intend to do a lot of snorkelling it is worth bringing your own equipment: rental gear is not always of good quality and it soon becomes more economical to buy rather than rent.

You don't have to hire boats or venture to far-flung islands to find good snorkelling – Lovina Beach (Bali) and the Gili Islands (Lombok) in Indonesia; Tioman and the Perhentian islands on Malaysia's east coast; and Ko Pha-Ngan in Thailand are all very popular beach resorts with easily accessible snorkelling.

Scuba diving is generally cheap in South-East Asia and there are some very good operators around. However, it isn't always the best place to get a diving certificate because fewer operators are qualified to offer diving courses and those that do are not always of the highest standard. It is usually better to get a certificate before arriving, eg diving courses in Cairns, Australia, are often of high quality and just as cheap as those in South-East Asia.

Indonesia offers extensive opportunities for diving: Bali has some excellent dives and, because it is the main tourist area, there are plenty of operators; there are countless small islands and reefs between Labuanbajo, in Flores, and Komodo; Flores, Timor and Maluku all have good diving; and the 'sea gardens' of Sulawesi, particularly around Manado, are legendary.

There is some diving on the west coast of **Malaysia**, but it is better on the east coast, where the islands of Tioman, Kapas, Redang and the Perhentians are just some of the possibilities. Some of the best diving in Malaysia is found in Borneo; Sabah, in particular, has excellent diving and very professional dive outfits. Sipadan Island and its amazing wall is the most famous (and expensive) dive site.

In **Thailand**, Pattaya is crammed with dive shops and is popular because of its easy access and proximity to Bangkok. Phuket is the next most popular and presents the best diving opportunities on plenty of nearby islands, including Ao Phang-Nga and the world-famous Similan and Surin islands, in the Andaman Sea. In the Gulf of Thailand off the east coast, the popular islands of Ko Samui, Ko Pha-Ngan and Ko Tao off Surat Thani all have dive outfits.

Unfortunately, many of the coral reefs in South-East Asia are under threat. Dynamite fishing has been a major culprit: explosives are dropped into the water to stun fish, and then it is an easy matter to scoop up the catch from the surface. In the process the delicate coral is devastated. Other threats to the reefs include silting, caused by deforestation, over-development in the tourist areas and coral harvesting (live coral for board room fish tanks can bring big money). Moves are afoot to establish marine parks throughout the region, but it may be a case of too little too late.

COURSES

There are a variety of courses available throughout the region, from language to meditation, massage, Thai boxing and cooking. In some cases you'll need to apply for a special visa, or there may be other prerequisites. See the individual chapters for details.

WORK

Finding work in Asia was always a bit of a hit or miss affair, but with the current economic downturn in the region it's likely that opportunities will be even more limited.

Jobs are sometimes available teaching English. Wages are generally poor (unless you are properly qualified), but will at least cover your living expenses. Cambodia and

Thailand, and to a lesser extent Laos, all offer possibilities in this area.

Volunteer organisations are another possibility, but obviously this is not paid work, and often you need to arrange this kind of thing before you actually arrive in the country.

The other stand-by of the traveller is buying and selling. Unless you're highly motivated, able to order in bulk and have contacts in retail outlets at home, you are not realistically going to make much money out of this. Buyers who purchase collectables or gems are experts (if they are making any money at it).

ACCOMMODATION

South-East Asia is crammed with hotels, and it is very unusual to have problems finding somewhere to stay. The exception to this rule is at peak tourist periods, such as Christmas, when popular destinations like Bali, and Ko Samui and Phuket in Thailand, get packed out. Indochina's busiest time is around Chinese New Year. Keep away from the big name destinations at busy times of the year.

All the major attractions on the South-East Asian circuit have inexpensive guesthouse (losmen in Indonesia) accommodation, but off the beaten track you may find yourself staying in Chinese hotels where prices verge on mid-range.

If you stick to the travellers' circuit, you should be able to keep accommodation costs down to US$5 to US$10 per day for a double. In expensive destinations, such as Singapore, Brunei and Kuala Lumpur, you will have to pay more or stay in a dorm.

There is often a hotel booking desk at international airports, although they usually do not cover the lower strata of hotels. Some airports (like Bangkok's) are better than others (like Singapore's) for this game. Otherwise, you'll generally find hotels clustered near bus and train stations – always good places to start hunting. Check your room and the bathroom before you agree to take it. If the sheets don't look clean, ask to have them changed right away.

If you think a hotel is too expensive, ask if they have anything cheaper. A very important point to remember in Chinese hotels is that a 'single' room usually has a double bed while a 'double' has two beds. A couple can always request a single room. Many cheaper hotels throughout the region supply only one sheet on the bed; if you want a top sheet (useful for keeping mosquitoes away) you'll have to ask

for one (which may or may not be forthcoming) or supply your own (a sarong is very useful here).

FOOD

In general, food in South-East Asia is healthy. A good rule of thumb is to glance at the restaurant or food stall and the people running it – if it looks clean and they look healthy, then chances are the food will be OK too.

Be wary of salads and other uncooked food – it's no good avoiding the water if you then eat fruit or vegetables that have been washed in that unhealthy water. Cooked food that has been allowed to go cold can also be dangerous.

In general, you should have few problems and, in places like Singapore, you can usually eat from street stalls with impunity. Of course, you'll also find Coke and other hygienically pure western delights. McDonald's is spreading its tentacles through the region too and you'll find branches of it in Indonesia, Malaysia, the Philippines, Singapore and Thailand. KFC has spread its influence even more widely.

Despite the pleasures of the local cuisine, some travellers feel there are benefits to be had by preparing their own food. This requires carrying cooking gear and a gas cooker (replacement cylinders are available in most places in the region), but you can save money this way and also eat well.

Fruit

Fruit can be one of the special taste treats of South-East Asian travel. Apart from all those mundane bananas, pineapples and coconuts, there is a host of fruits that will do wonderful things to your taste buds.

Durian The most infamous fruit of the region, the durian is a large green fruit with a hard spiny exterior. Crack it open to reveal the biggest stink imaginable! Drains blocked up? No, it's just the durian season. If you can hold your nose and eat at the same time, you might learn to love them. The Chinese regard them as an aphrodisiac.

Jeruk *Jeruk* is the all-purpose term for citrus fruit. There are many kinds available, including the huge *jeruk muntis* or *jerunga*, known in the west as a pomelo. It's larger than a grapefruit and has very thick skin, but tastes sweeter – more like an orange.

Mangosteen The small purple-brown mangosteen cracks open to reveal tasty white segments with a very fine flavour. Queen Victoria once offered a reward to anyone able to transport a mangosteen back to England while still edible.

Nangka An enormous yellow-green fruit, the *nangka* can weigh over 20kg. Inside are dozens of individual bright yellow segments. Also called jackfruit, the taste is distinctive and the texture slightly rubbery.

Rambutan A rambutan is a bright red fruit covered in soft, hairy spines; the name means 'hairy'. Break it open to reveal a delicious, white, lychee-like fruit inside.

Salak Found chiefly in Indonesia, the *salak* is immediately recognisable because of its brown 'snakeskin' covering. Peel the skin off to reveal segments that taste like a cross between an apple and a walnut. Bali salaks are much nicer than any others.

Starfruit Called *belimbing* in Indonesia and Malaysia, the name is obvious when you see a slice – it's star shaped. It tastes cool, crisp and watery.

Zurzat Also spelt *sirsak* and known in the west as soursop or custard apple. A warty green skin covers a thirst-quenching interior with a slight lemony taste. They are ripe when they feel squishy.

Other The *sawo* looks like a potato and tastes like a pear. *Jambu* is pear shaped but has a radish-like crispy texture and a pink, shiny colour. *Papaya*, or *paw paw*, has a sweet, yellow pulp.

DRINKS
Nonalcoholic Drinks

It's rarely safe to drink tap water in South-East Asia – Singapore is the exception. It's a good idea to be careful with ice too, at least in budget eateries. Bottled water is widely available and is the only alternative if you don't want to purify your own water. Unfortunately, discarded plastic water bottles are the cause of an increasingly wide environmental problem – and not just in South-East Asia.

One of the great pleasures of dropping into the more touristed parts of South-East Asia (Bali, the southern beach retreats of Thailand etc) is the wide range of shakes and fruit juices. Canned and bottled drinks are also available everywhere – there's no escaping Coke, even if you trek days into the interior of Kalimantan.

Alcoholic Drinks

Beer is available nearly everywhere (Brunei is the odd one out), but prices vary dramatically from place to place. If such things are important to you, Indonesia has the lowest beer prices, and the Philippines and Cambodia follow not far behind. In Thailand and Malaysia beer is more of a luxury item.

Wine drinkers will be disappointed by South-East Asia. Unless you go upmarket you're unlikely to come across it in restaurants, though inexpensive eastern European wines are available in Indochina.

Most countries in the region also have their local firewaters – see the country chapters for more details.

Getting There & Away

Step one is to get to Asia and, in these days of intense competition between the airlines, there are plenty of opportunities to find cheap tickets to a variety of 'gateway' cities. You have virtually no choice apart from flying, though – regular shipping services to South-East Asia are just about nonexistent and China-Vietnam and China-Laos are the only overland options.

AIR
Airlines
The major Asian gateways for cheap flights are Singapore, Denpasar and Bangkok. They are all good places to fly to and good places to fly from. Penang is another good place to shop for tickets. Hong Kong is not the place for cheap tickets that it once was.

The economic crisis has also led to some turbulence within the airline industry across the region. At least two of the major (and cheaper) carriers – Garuda Indonesia and Philippine Airlines – are in serious financial trouble and at the time of writing it's difficult to predict the final outcome. Both airlines have already cut back services, and more seem destined to follow.

Buying Tickets
Cheap tickets are available in two distinct categories – official and unofficial. Official ones are advance purchase tickets, budget fares, Apex, super-Apex or whatever other promotional devices airlines can think of to get 'bums on seats'.

Unofficial tickets are simply discounted tickets which the airlines release through selected travel agents. Don't go looking for discounted tickets straight from the airlines – they are available only through travel agents. Generally, you can find discounted tickets at prices as low as, or lower than, the Apex or budget tickets; there is no advance-purchase requirement nor should there be any cancellation penalty, although individual travel agents may institute their own cancellation charges.

It is necessary to exercise a little caution with discounted tickets. For example, make sure 'OK' on the ticket really means you have a confirmed seat. Phone the airline and reconfirm; it's better to find out immediately if the agent has made a firm booking.

Plane tickets will probably be the most expensive items in your budget, and buying them can be an intimidating business. There is likely to be a multitude of airlines and travel agents hoping to separate you from your money, and it is always worth putting aside a few hours to research the state of the market.

Start early: some of the cheapest tickets have to be bought months in advance and popular flights can sell out quickly. Talk to other recent travellers – they may be able to stop you making some of the same old mistakes. Look at the ads in newspapers and magazines (not forgetting the press of the ethnic group whose country you plan to visit), consult reference books and watch for special offers.

Phone several travel agents for bargains. (Airlines can supply information on routes and timetables, but, except during interairline wars, they do not supply the cheapest tickets.) Find out the fare, the route, the duration of the journey and any restrictions on the ticket. Then sit back and decide which is best for you.

You may discover that those impossibly

Warning

The information in this chapter is particularly vulnerable to change: prices for international travel are volatile, routes are introduced and cancelled, schedules change, special deals come and go, and rules and visa requirements are amended. Airlines and governments seem to take a perverse pleasure in making price structures and regulations as complicated as possible. You should check directly with the airline or a travel agent to make sure you understand how a fare (and ticket you may buy) works. In addition, the travel industry is highly competitive and there are many lurks and perks.

The upshot of this is that you should get opinions, quotes and advice from as many airlines and travel agents as possible before you part with your hard-earned cash. The details given in this chapter should be regarded as pointers and are not a substitute for your own careful, up-to-date research.

Air Travel Glossary

Baggage Allowance This will be written on your ticket and usually includes one 20kg item to go in the hold, plus one item of hand luggage.

Bucket Shops These are unbonded travel agencies specialising in discounted airline tickets.

Bumped Just because you have a confirmed seat doesn't mean you're going to get on the plane (see Overbooking).

Cancellation Penalties If you have to cancel or change a discounted ticket, there are often heavy penalties involved; insurance can sometimes be taken out against these penalties. Some airlines impose penalties on regular tickets as well, particularly against 'no-show' passengers.

Check-In Airlines ask you to check in a certain time ahead of the flight departure (usually one to two hours on international flights). If you fail to check in on time and the flight is overbooked, the airline can cancel your booking and give your seat to somebody else.

Confirmation Having a ticket written out with the flight and date you want doesn't mean you have a seat until the agent has checked with the airline that your status is 'OK' or confirmed. Meanwhile you could just be 'on request'.

Courier Fares Businesses often need to send urgent documents or freight securely and quickly. Courier companies hire people to accompany the package through customs and, in return, offer a discount ticket which is sometimes a phenomenal bargain. In effect, what the companies do is ship their freight as your luggage on regular commercial flights. This is a legitimate operation, but there are two shortcomings – the short turnaround time of the ticket (usually not longer than a month) and the limitation on your luggage allowance. You may have to surrender all your allowance and take only carry-on luggage.

Full Fares Airlines traditionally offer 1st class (coded F), business class (coded J) and economy class (coded Y) tickets. These days there are so many promotional and discounted fares available that few passengers pay full economy fare.

ITX An ITX, or 'independent inclusive tour excursion', is often available on tickets to popular holiday destinations. Officially it's a package deal combined with hotel accommodation, but many agents will sell you one of these for the flight only and give you phoney hotel vouchers in the unlikely event that you're challenged at the airport.

Lost Tickets If you lose your airline ticket an airline will usually treat it like a travellers cheque and, after inquiries, issue you with another one. Legally, however, an airline is entitled to treat it like cash and if you lose it then it's gone forever. Take good care of your tickets.

MCO An MCO, or 'miscellaneous charge order', is a voucher that looks like an airline ticket but carries no destination or date. It can be exchanged through any International Association of Travel Agents (IATA) airline for a ticket on a specific flight. It's a useful alternative to an onward ticket in those countries that demand one, and is more flexible than an ordinary ticket if you're unsure of your route.

No-Shows No-shows are passengers who fail to show up for their flight. Full-fare passengers who fail to turn up are sometimes entitled to travel on a later flight. The rest are penalised (see Cancellation Penalties).

On Request This is an unconfirmed booking for a flight.

cheap flights are 'fully booked, but we have another one that costs a bit more ...' Or the flight is on an airline notorious for its poor safety standards and leaves you in the world's least favourite airport in mid-journey for 14 hours. Or they claim only to have the last two seats available for that country for the whole of July, which they will hold for you for a maximum of two hours. Don't panic – keep ringing around.

Air Travel Glossary

Onward Tickets An entry requirement for many countries is that you have a ticket out of the country. If you're unsure of your next move, the easiest solution is to buy the cheapest onward ticket to a neighbouring country or a ticket from a reliable airline which can later be refunded if you do not use it.

Open Jaw Tickets These are return tickets where you fly out to one place but return from another. If available, this can save you backtracking to your arrival point.

Overbooking Airlines hate to fly empty seats and since every flight has some passengers who fail to show up, airlines often book more passengers than they have seats. Usually excess passengers make up for the no-shows, but occasionally somebody gets bumped. Guess who it is most likely to be? The passengers who check in late.

Point-to-Point Tickets These are discount tickets that can be bought on some routes in return for passengers waiving their rights to a stopover.

Promotional Fares These are officially discounted fares, available from travel agencies or direct from the airline.

Reconfirmation At least 72 hours prior to departure time of an onward or return flight, you must contact the airline and 'reconfirm' that you intend to be on the flight. If you don't do this the airline can delete your name from the passenger list and you could lose your seat.

Restrictions Discounted tickets often have various restrictions on them – such as needing to be paid for in advance and incurring a penalty to be altered. Others are restrictions on the minimum and maximum period you must be away, such as a minimum of 14 days or a maximum of one year.

Round-the-World Tickets RTW tickets give you a limited period (usually a year) in which to circumnavigate the globe. You can go anywhere the carrying airlines go, as long as you don't backtrack. The number of stopovers or total number of separate flights is decided before you set off and they usually cost a bit more than a basic return flight.

Stand-by This is a discounted ticket where you only fly if there is a seat free at the last moment. Stand-by fares are usually available only on domestic routes.

Transferred Tickets Airline tickets cannot be transferred from one person to another. Travellers sometimes try to sell the return half of their ticket, but officials can ask you to prove that you are the person named on the ticket. This is less likely to happen on domestic flights, but on an international flight tickets are compared with passports.

Travel Agencies Travel agencies vary widely and you should choose one that suits your needs. Some simply handle tours, while full-services agencies handle everything from tours and tickets to car rental and hotel bookings. If all you want is a ticket at the lowest possible price, then go to an agency specialising in discounted tickets.

Travel Periods Ticket prices vary with the time of year. There is a low (off-peak) season and a high (peak) season, and often a low-shoulder season and a high-shoulder season as well. Usually the fare depends on your outward flight – if you depart in the high season and return in the low season, you pay the high-season fare.

Use the fares quoted in this book as a guide only. They are approximate and based on the rates advertised by travel agents at the time of writing. Quoted air fares do not necessarily constitute a recommendation for the carrier.

If you are travelling from the UK or USA, you may find that the cheapest flights are being advertised by obscure bucket shops whose names haven't yet reached the telephone directory. Many such firms are honest and solvent, but there are a few rogues who will take your money and disappear, to reopen elsewhere a month or two later under a new name.

If you feel suspicious about a firm, don't give them all the money at once – leave a deposit of 20% or so and pay the balance only when you get the ticket. If they insist on cash in advance, go somewhere else. And once you have the ticket, ring the airline to confirm that you are actually booked on the flight.

You may decide to pay more than the rock-bottom fare by opting for the safety of a better known travel agent. Firms such as STA Travel, which has offices worldwide, Council Travel in the USA and Travel CUTS in Canada are not going to disappear overnight, leaving you clutching a receipt for a nonexistent ticket, and they offer good prices to most destinations.

Once you have your ticket, photocopy it or write its number down, together with the flight number and other details, and keep this information somewhere separate and safe. If the ticket is lost or stolen, this will help you get a replacement.

It's sensible to buy travel insurance as early as possible. If you buy it the week before you fly, you may find, for example, that you're not covered for delays to your flight caused by industrial action.

Round-the-World Tickets

Round-the-World (RTW) tickets are very popular, and airline RTW tickets are often real bargains, working out no more expensive or even cheaper than an ordinary return ticket. Prices start at about £850, A$2000 or US$1400.

The official airline RTW tickets are usually put together by a combination of two airlines and permit you to fly anywhere you want on their route systems, so long as you do not backtrack. Other restrictions are that you (usually) must book the first sector in advance and cancellation penalties then apply. There may be restrictions on how many stops you are permitted. Usually the tickets are valid for a period of between 90 days and a year. An alternative type of RTW ticket is one where a travel agency combines a number of discounted tickets.

RTW tickets usually involve the larger airlines and are therefore limited to the major airports of the region – Singapore, Bangkok, Kuala Lumpur, Hong Kong.

The USA

Intense competition among Asian airlines on the US west coast and Vancouver has resulted in ticket discounting.

The *New York Times*, the *Chicago Tribune*, the *Los Angeles Times* and the *San Francisco Examiner* all produce weekly travel sections in which you'll find any number of travel agents' ads. Student travel specialists Council Travel and STA Travel have offices in major US cities. The magazine *Travel Unlimited* (PO Box 1058, Allston, MA 02134, USA) publishes details of the cheapest air fares and courier possibilities for destinations all over the world from the USA.

From the US west coast, fares to Singapore, Bangkok or Hong Kong cost around US$399/680 one way/return, while Bali flights cost from US$434/787 in the low season (outside summer and Christmas). Flights to Malaysia are about US$434/729. There are plenty of competitive fares offered to Indonesia from the USA.

From Kuala Lumpur you can fly to the US west coast for around RM1350. From Singapore, one way fares to the US west coast start at around S$990.

If you shop around the travel agents in Manila, you should be able get tickets to the US west coast for around US$500. From Bangkok, one way flights to Los Angeles or San Francisco cost from US$400.

Canada

The *Vancouver Sun* and the *Toronto Globe & Mail* carry many travel agents' ads, and Travel CUTS has outlets throughout Canada.

Australia & New Zealand

Since there are far fewer airlines flying to and from Australia and New Zealand than there are to and from Europe and North America, you won't find the same wide range of fares. Nevertheless, bargains can still be found with a little shopping around. STA Travel and Flight Centre offices are major dealers in cheap air fares. Check them for starters or simply scan the ads in newspaper travel sections.

Regular excursion return fares from New Zealand and Australia usually have a low and a high season. The high season normally only applies for a limited time over the December-January school holiday period. There are also 'special fares', usually operated by airlines which are not regulars over that route or which take a more roundabout route.

One way/return fares from Melbourne or Sydney include: Singapore, A$510/780 to A$660/860; Kuala Lumpur, A$580/880 to A$700/1000; Bangkok, A$520/780 to A$750/1100; Hong Kong, A$740/920 to A$950/1200; and Manila, A$630/700 to A$800/1100. Logically it should be cheaper to fly to Denpasar (Bali), but its popularity as a holiday destination means that fares are around A$660/820 to A$740/1000, and the maximum stay is usually only 90 days. Low fares quoted here are for specials available through travel agents and restrictions usually apply; high fares are for more flexible tickets of six to 12 months' duration.

The cheapest flights to Asia are from Darwin and Perth. The Merpati flight from Darwin to Kupang (on the Indonesian island of Timor) costs A$244/396 one way/return ($319/536 in the high season) and is an economical and interesting way out of the country.

From Kupang to Darwin the price is US$180 one way, often slightly cheaper through a travel agent in Kupang. You won't be allowed on the plane without an Australian visa – obtainable in Denpasar or Jakarta, not Kupang.

Other low-season fares from Darwin or Perth include: Denpasar, A$510/730 one way/return; Singapore or Kuala Lumpur, A$560/700; Bangkok, A$580/920; and Manila, A$610/935.

From Auckland, you can get return flights to Denpasar for around NZ$1215 and to Bangkok for around NZ$1225. The Singapore run has the most competition, with flights from NZ$1165 return or NZ$845 one way.

From Penang in Malaysia, you can get one way fares to Sydney from RM930; Perth is about RM890 one way, but you can get return fares for the same amount. From Singapore, fares to Australia include Sydney or Melbourne for S$590 one way, or Perth for S$460. From Bangkok, fares to Sydney/Melbourne are available for around US$400, to Perth US$280.

The UK

Ticket discounting has long been established in the UK and it's wide open – the various agents advertise their fares and there's nothing under the counter about it at all.

Trailfinders, in West London, produces a lavishly illustrated brochure which includes air fare details. STA Travel also has branches in the UK. Look for ads in the Sunday papers and *Exchange & Mart*. Also look out for free magazines which are widely available in London. Start by looking outside the main railway stations.

Most British travel agents are registered with the Association of British Travel Agents (ABTA). If you have paid an ABTA-registered agent for your flight and the agent then goes out of business, ABTA will guarantee a refund or an alternative. Unregistered bucket shops are riskier but also sometimes cheaper.

The Globetrotters Club (BCM Roving, London WC1N 3XX) publishes a newsletter called *Globe* which covers obscure destinations and can help in finding travelling companions.

Rock-bottom fares (low season) from London to South-East Asia for one way/return include Bangkok, £192/355; Singapore, £216/399; Jakarta, £216/414; Denpasar, £332/499; Manila, £270/478; and Hong Kong, £259/515. From London to Malaysia, you're looking at UK£275/475 one way/return. Flights from London to Australia or New Zealand with stopovers in South-East Asia are available from around £350 one way. You can get a London-Australia return ticket with a stopover in Jakarta or Bali, Singapore or Bangkok for around £640.

To fly to London from Kuala Lumpur, fares start at around RM940 with the less popular airlines such as Aeroflot. Fares with better airlines are around RM1300. From Singapore, fares to London or other European destinations cost from S$690 one way with the East European airlines, and from S$830 one way with the better airlines. From Bangkok, fares to London cost about US$450 to US$550.

Europe

On the Continent, Amsterdam and Antwerp are among the best places for buying airline tickets. In Amsterdam, NBBS is a popular travel agent.

LAND
China

The only land borders between South-East Asia and the rest of Asia are the frontier that Myanmar shares with India, and the Chinese border with Myanmar, Laos and Vietnam. For decades they have been closed to foreign tourists, but for a few years now it has been possible to travel overland between China and Vietnam and China and Laos. It is rumoured that the crossing from China to

Myanmar may open up to independent travellers; in the past it has been open only to package tours.

Vietnam

China-Vietnam border crossings are at Hekou-Lao Cai and at Pingxiang-Dong Dang, on the rail line between Beijing and Hanoi. A special visa is required to enter Vietnam from China – it is not difficult to get but costs extra. There are no special requirements for entering China.

Laos

From Mengla district in southern Yunnan Province in China it is legal to enter Laos via Boten in Luang Nam Tha Province if you possess a valid Lao visa.

Myanmar

The crossing from Ruili in Yunnan Province in China to Mu-se in Myanmar is rumoured to open up to independent travellers soon.

SEA

With the exception of the short hop from

Papua New Guinea to Irian Jaya (Indonesia), no ships or ferries connect South-East Asia with destinations outside the region on a regular basis. Proposals to reopen the old Chennai (Madras)-Penang ferry surface from time to time, and rumours about the opening of a Darwin-Kupang ferry service are perpetual, but flying is still the only way to cover these runs.

Some cargo ships from Europe and the US take passengers and stop in South-East Asia, but though this may be a romantic way to see the world, it is much more expensive than flying. The other option is to get hired as crew for private boats to Indonesia, or tag along and pay for your keep. This is certainly possible from Darwin, especially at the time of the Darwin-Ambon yacht race if you are an experienced sailor.

Papua New Guinea

In recent years there has been an irregular ferry service between Jayapura (Irian Jaya) and Vanimo (PNG). At the time of writing it was operational, but make inquiries before making plans to use this service.

Getting Around South-East Asia

AIR

All sorts of ticket bargains around the region are available to you once you arrive in South-East Asia. These intra-Asia fares are widely available, although Bangkok, Singapore, Penang and Hong Kong are the major ticket discounting centres.

A little caution is necessary when looking for tickets in Asia. First of all, shop around – a wise move anywhere, of course. Secondly, don't believe everything you are told – ticket agents in Penang (Malaysia) are very fond of telling people that tickets there are cheaper than in Bangkok or Singapore or wherever. In actual fact, they are often much the same price anywhere; if there is any difference it's likely to be in the favour of the originating city. For example, you're unlikely to find a Bangkok to Kathmandu ticket cheaper in Penang than in Bangkok. Or a Penang to Hong Kong ticket cheaper in Singapore than in Penang.

Most important of all, be very careful that you get what you want before handing over money and that the ticket is precisely what you pay for. Over the years, we have had many letters from people complaining that they were done by various agents.

ASIA AIR FARES

Full one-way economy fares in US$
(discounts available on most flights)

Tokyo
Kathmandu
Calcutta 305
795
Chennai (Madras)
Colombo
Vientiane 330 500 340
Yangon (Rangoon) 121 450
Bangkok 132
390
635
300
Penang 140
Medan 80 110
635
Singapore 375
450
256
Hong Kong
220
480
309
Ho Chi Minh City 290
260
Kota Kinabulu 254 220
350
Manila 241
Cebu
Davao 150
Manado
260
350
580 Ujung Pandang
Jakarta
Denpasar
680
1100
150
249

0   500   1000 km

Favourite tricks include tickets with very limited periods of validity when you have been told they are valid all year round. Or you could find a ticket is marked 'OK', indicating that you have a seat reservation, when no reservation has been made. Also, you could find that an airline will not accept your ticket for a subsequent sector of your travels.

Take care, but don't get too uptight about it – most agents are reliable. People who buy tickets from 'agents' who operate from coffee-bar tables are asking for trouble. And remember to reconfirm. It doesn't hurt to re-confirm the moment you get your ticket, and that is the most certain way of finding out if the 'OK' on your ticket really is OK.

Most airports in South-East Asia charge a departure tax, so make sure you have that final necessary bit of local currency left.

Approximate intra-Asia fares are shown in the chart at the start of this section.

Student Travel

There are student travel offices in most South-East Asian capitals, most of them associated in some way with STA Travel. In Asia, student fares rarely have an edge over simple discount fares (available at all agencies), but at least STA Travel is a reliable operator.

Other services they can provide include local tours and accommodation bookings. Usually the hotels they deal with are somewhat upmarket and even with discounts they're outside the usual budget travellers' range. If you're a real student, they can also provide student cards.

OVERLANDING IN SOUTH-EAST ASIA

With all the water in the way, 'overlanding' through South-East Asia seems a misnomer. However, if by the term overlanding you mean travelling from place to place by local transport with the minimum use of aircraft, then South-East Asia offers enormous scope.

Indonesia & Singapore

If you want to trek right through Indonesia from the Australian end, the logical starting point is Kupang in Timor. There are regular flights from Darwin in Australia's Northern Territory to Kupang. From Kupang, you could work your way through the amazing and varied islands of Nusa Tenggara. Along the way you could climb to see the multi-coloured lakes of Kelimutu in Flores, see the

dragons of Komodo and pause at the wonderful Gili Islands off Lombok.

From Bali, after you've explored that magical island, the next stage is to hop on a bus to Surabaya, usually an overnight trip. On the way to Surabaya, it's worth stopping off to climb the extraordinary Gunung Bromo in Java. From Surabaya, you can continue to Yogyakarta, the cultural heartland of Java and Indonesia.

On from Yogya, you can catch a train or bus to Jakarta, although if you have time, there are interesting stops en route at, for example, the Dieng Plateau, Pangandaran, Bandung and Bogor.

At Jakarta, you may be forced to make a decision. If your visa is running short – and unfortunately present visa limitations make it virtually impossible to explore Indonesia in one bite – you have to leave. If you're in that situation head to Singapore, from where you can then re-enter Indonesia and start again. There's no need to return to Jakarta though.

From Singapore ferries operate to Batam and Bintan islands in the Riau Archipelago, and from there speed boats go to Pekanbaru in Sumatra. If you're not embroiled in visa problems back in Jakarta, you could continue by bus or train, and then by ferry, to Sumatra.

Travel in southern Sumatra involves long bus trips to get to the north, so many people opt instead for the regular ship or flight from Jakarta to Padang. After Padang, the road through Sumatra continues north through delightful Bukittinggi, with perhaps a side trip to Pulau Nias and then a well-earned rest at relaxing Danau (Lake) Toba.

Finally, you exit Sumatra by taking the ferry or flying from Medan to Penang in Malaysia. An alternative to this route would be to go from Singapore up to Penang and enter Sumatra at Medan and then do the trip through Sumatra in reverse, finally exiting to Jakarta or to the Riau Archipelago and/or Singapore.

And of course, there are numerous other Indonesian islands to the north and east, including Kalimantan (the southern half of Borneo), wonderful Sulawesi, Irian Jaya and Maluku. To Sulawesi, Pelni passenger ships go from Java, Lombok, Sumbawa and Flores. It is then possible to travel by Pelni boat or fly from Manado in northern Sulawesi to the Philippines, or you can fly to Singapore or take a boat from Sulawesi to Kalimantan and then cross overland to East Malaysia.

Malaysia & Thailand

Assuming you've followed the traditional path up through Indonesia, you're now in Penang, and after enjoying yourself there you can head south to the hill stations such as the Cameron Highlands, to Pulau Pangkor, to modern Kuala Lumpur, to historic Melaka and, finally, arrive at Singapore. Then you can head up the east coast and sample Malaysia's beaches and offshore islands. Travel in Malaysia is just about the most hassle-free of anywhere in Asia. There are excellent train and bus services, and very economical share-taxis; even the hitching is easy.

The north Borneo states – Malaysia's Sabah and Sarawak, and the independent kingdom of Brunei – are most easily visited from Singapore or Peninsular Malaysia, because connections between north Borneo and Kalimantan are limited. You can fly from Sabah direct to Manila or Hong Kong.

There are a variety of ways of crossing to Thailand from Malaysia, but the usual routes are to take a taxi or train from Penang to Hat Yai if you're on the west coast, or simply to walk across the border from Rantau Panjang to Sungai Kolok on the east coast.

From Hat Yai, the major city in the south of Thailand, you can continue by bus to Phuket, a resort island with superb beaches. Then continue north to Surat Thani and the equally beautiful islands of Ko Samui, Ko Pha-Ngan and Ko Tao. Finally, you reach hyperactive Bangkok and decide where to head next.

For most travellers, that decision will be to continue north to Chiang Mai – the second city of Thailand and another great travellers' centre. On the way, you could pause to explore the ancient cities of Ayuthaya and Sukhothai. From Chiang Mai, you can make treks into the colourful hill tribe areas or you can loop back to Bangkok through the north-east region. Bangkok is more than just the sin city of South-East Asia, it's also a centre for cheap airline tickets, so the next question is where to fly to.

Myanmar (Burma) & West

Since you can now get 28-day visas for Myanmar, it's a bit less of a rush around the attractions of that unusual country. You can visit Myanmar as a foray from Bangkok, or use Myanmar as a stepping stone between South-East Asia and West Asia. If the latter is your intention, then it's time to pack *South-East Asia on a shoestring* away and pick up other Lonely Planet guides on Bangladesh, India, Nepal and beyond.

Vietnam, Laos & Cambodia

This area of South-East Asia, often referred to as Indochina, has opened its doors to foreign travellers, but options for entering the area are still fairly limited. More border crossings should open, but as yet the only regular overland crossings are Thailand-Laos, Thailand-Cambodia, China-Vietnam, China-Laos and Vietnam-Cambodia.

The main option is still to fly. There are a number of flights to and from Ho Chi Minh City or Hanoi. Bangkok is the cheapest and most popular gateway.

The main overland option from Thailand is to enter Laos via the Nong Khai crossing near Vientiane. See the Laos chapter for other border crossings.

There are currently two crossings between Laos and Vietnam: at Lao Bao and Kaew Neua (also called Nam Phao).

No border crossings are permitted between Laos and Cambodia, although it's possible the border between Champasak Province in Laos and Stung Treng Province in Cambodia will open at some stage.

Buses run regularly between Phnom Penh in Cambodia and Vietnam's Ho Chi Minh City. The land border between Cambodia and Thailand at Poipet was opened to foreigners in 1998.

The most cost-effective way to tour Indochina is to take a flight from Bangkok to Phnom Penh or Ho Chi Minh City, then travel through Cambodia and up through Vietnam to the north. Then continue to China or fly from Hanoi to Laos. From Laos you can continue back overland into Thailand.

Hong Kong & East

From Hong Kong, the frenetic city-state and gateway to China, you've got a choice of heading further east or west (in which case you'll need Lonely Planet's *North-East Asia on a shoestring* for China, Japan, Korea and Taiwan), turning south for Vietnam or flying to the Philippines. Travelling across China to the far west then down into Pakistan via the Karakoram Highway from Kashgar, or into Nepal via Lhasa, are adventurous routes.

Philippines

Manila is overwhelmingly the gateway to the Philippines, but there is an interesting short flight or fortnightly Pelni boat connection between Davao in Mindanao and Manado in

Land Border Crossings for South-East Asian Countries

Brunei
From Malaysia

A one week visa is automatic; a two week visa is easy to get.

- The most popular crossing is Kuala Baram (M)/Kuala Belait (B) (road; for Miri in Sarawak to BSB).
- Limbang (M)/Bangar (B) (road).
- Trusan (M)/Labu (B) (road; for Lawas to Bangar).
- Also, sea connections between Brunei and Sarawak and Sabah.

Cambodia
From Thailand

Cambodian visas are not available at the border; get one in Bangkok.

- Aranya Prathet (T)/Poipet (C) (road; to Siem Reap).
- Hat Lek (T)/Koh Kong (C) (boat & road; for Trat to Sihanoukville).

From Vietnam

- Moc Bai (V)/Chiphu (C) (road; for Ho Chi Minh City to Phnom Penh). When leaving Vietnam you must have Moc Bai stamped on your Vietnamese visa.

Indonesia
From Malaysia

- Tedebu (M)/Entikong (I) (road; for Kuching in Sarawak to Pontianak in Kalimantan). Visa-free entry point for Indonesia.
- Also, sea connections between Sabah and Kalimantan; and Peninsular Malaysia and Sumatra.

Laos
From Thailand

Lao visas are available at Nong Khai and Chiang Khong.

- The main crossing is at Nong Khai (T)/Vientiane (L) (Friendship Bridge).
- Chiang Khong (T)/Huay Xai (L) (ferry).
- Chong Mek (T)/Pakse (L) (road & ferry).
- Mukdahan (T)/Savannakhet (L) (ferry).
- Nakhon Phanom (T)/Tha Khaek (L) (ferry).

From Vietnam

Lao visas are not available at the border.

- Lao Bao (V)/Sepon (L) (road; for Danang to Savannakhet). When departing Vietnam via Lao Bao, Vietnamese visa must indicate Lao Bao border crossing.
- Cau Treo (V)/Kaew Neua (L) (road; from Vinh in Vietnam).

From China

- Mohan in the Mengla district in Yunnan Province (C)/Boten in Luang Nam Tha Province (L) (road). Lao consulate in Kunming issues only seven-day transit visas. Lao visas are not available at the border.

Malaysia
From Brunei

- The most popular crossing is Kuala Belait (B)/Kuala Baram (M) (road; for BSB to Miri in Sarawak).
- Bangar (B)/Limbang (M) (road)
- Labu (B)/Trusan (M) (road; for Bangar to Lawas).
- Also, sea connections between Sarawak and Sabah and Brunei.

From Indonesia

- Entikong (I)/Tedebu (M) (road; for Pontianak in Kalimantan to Kuching in Sarawak).
- Also, sea connections between Kalimantan and Sabah; and Sumatra and Peninsular Malaysia.

From Singapore

- Most travellers use the Singapore/Johor Bahru (M) Causeway crossing.
- Tuas (S)/Tanjung Kupang (M) (bridge).
- Also, ferry services to Pengerang, Tanjung Belungkor and Pulau Tioman.

From Thailand

- Most travellers use the Sadao (T)/Bukit Kayu Hitam (M) crossing (road; for Hat Yai to Penang).

Land Border Crossings for South-East Asian Countries

- Thung Mo (T)/Padang Besar (M) (road & rail; the Bangkok-Penang express train crosses the border here).
- Sungai Kolok (T)/Rantau Panjang (M) (road & rail).
- Betong (T)/Keroh (M) (road).
- Ban Taba (T)/Kota Bharu (M) (road).
- You can also get from Satun (T) to Pulau Langkawi (M) by boat.

Myanmar (Burma)
From Thailand

- Mai Sae (T)/Tachilek (M) (road). From Tachilek you can travel overland only as far as Kyaingtong. However, you can fly from Tachilek to other cities in Myanmar.
- Ranong (T)/Kawthoung (M) (boat). You must fly out of Kawthoung to other places in Myanmar.

From China

- The crossing at Ruili (C)/Mu-se (M) may open up to independent travellers soon.

Singapore
See under Malaysia.

Thailand
From Cambodia

- Poipet (C)/Aranya Prathet (T) (road; from Siem Reap).
- Koh Kong (C)/Hat Lek (T) (boat & road; for Sihanoukville to Trat).

From Laos

- The main crossing is at Vientiane (L)/Nong Khai (T) (Friendship Bridge).
- Huay Xai (L)/Chiang Khong (T) (ferry).
- Pakse (L)/Chong Mek (T) (road & ferry).
- Savannakhet (L)/Mukdahan (T) (ferry).
- Tha Khaek (L)/Nakhon Phanom (T) (ferry).

From Malaysia

- Most travellers use the Bukit Kayu Hitam (M)/Sadao (T) (road; for Hat Yai to Penang).
- Padang Besar (M)/Thung Mo (T) (road & rail; the Penang-Bangkok express train crosses the border here).

- Rantau Panjang (M)/Sungai Kolok (T) (road & rail).
- Keroh (M)/Betong (T) (road).
- Kota Bharu (M)/Ban Taba (T) (road).
- You can also get from Pulau Langkawi (M) to Satun (T) by boat.

From Myanmar

- Tachilek (M)/Mai Sae (T)(road).
- Kawthoung(M)/Ranong (T) (boat).

Vietnam
From Cambodia

- Chiphu (C)/Moc Bai (V) (road; for Phnom Penh to Ho Chi Minh City). When entering Vietnam you must have Moc Bai stamped on your Vietnamese visa.

From Laos

- Sepon (L)/Lao Bao (V) (road; for Savannakhet to Danang). When entering Vietnam you must have Lao Bao stamped on your Vietnamese visa.
- Kaew Neua (L)/Cau Treo (V) (road; to Vinh in Vietnam).

From China

- The busier crossing is Pinxiang (C)/Dong Dang (V) (road; crossing point known in Vietnamese as Huu Nghi Quan, or Friendship Gate).
- Hekou (C)/Lao Cai (V) (rail; for train from Kunming to Hanoi).

China
From Laos

- Boten in Luang Nam Tha Province (L)/Mohan in the Mengla district in Yunnan Province (C) (road).

From Myanmar

- The crossing at Ruili in Yunnan Province (C)/Mu-se (M) may open up to independent travellers soon.

From Vietnam

- The main crossing is Dong Dang (V)/Pinxiang (C) (road).
- Lao Cai (V)/Hekou (C) (rail; for train from Hanoi to Kunming).

Sulawesi (Indonesia). It is also possible to fly directly from Singapore to Cebu.

From Manila you can head north to the rice terraces and beaches of north Luzon, and south to the Mayon volcano and other attractions of south Luzon. Or island-hop through the tightly clustered Visayas.

Eventually, you can hop back to Manila and decide where to go next – on to Australia or further afield. A good loop through the region includes travelling from Australia to Indonesia, Singapore, Malaysia, Thailand, Indochina, Philippines and, finally, back to Australia. But, of course, there are lots of other possibilities.

BUS

Bus travel can be absurdly comfortable, certainly by the standards further west in Asia, but there are always opportunities for crowded, bone-shaking rides shared with chickens, goats and all sorts of local produce.

Air-con luxury buses are widespread in Malaysia and Thailand (where they really are gigantic). In Indonesia air-con buses cover the main runs from north Sumatra right though to Flores, and the Philippines also has a number of air-con services. A host of cheaper, regular buses of a variety of standards cover the major and minor routes; minibuses also operate and sometimes provide luxury services.

Regular buses tend to be cheap and frequent, but they are often crowded and leg room is at a premium. They are usually fine for short to medium hops.

TRAIN

The main train services are found in Thailand, Malaysia, Vietnam, Myanmar and on Java, in Indonesia. Buses are generally more convenient, more frequent, and often faster and cheaper, but the trains are still worth considering. Standards can vary enormously. In Thailand and Malaysia trains are very comfortable and a good alternative to the buses. The *International Express* runs between Thailand and Malaysia. Some of the crowded economy trains in Java are best avoided, but other services are excellent and cheap. Myanmar and Vietnam have dilapidated trains, but even they can be better than the dilapidated buses. Cambodia's rail services are very cheap but exceedingly slow and tedious.

Rail passes are offered in some countries, but unless you are travelling quickly and extensively by train, they are often not economic. See the individual country chapters for a full rundown of rail services.

CAR & MOTORCYCLE

Of course, you could hit the road with your own transport, but you really cannot go too far in South-East Asia: it's not like former days, when entire continents could be crossed overland. You could always buy a motorbike in Singapore, but once you've ridden it through Malaysia and Thailand you've come to the end of the road. Land borders to Myanmar are firmly shut, so the idea of crossing Burma and heading across Asia to Europe is just a dream.

Remember too that many places (including Thailand and Indonesia) require a carnet – an expensive customs document which guarantees that you will later remove the vehicle from their country.

If you must have your own wheels, it's better to hire them when necessary. Car hire is becoming much more readily available in the region. Malaysia is like most countries in the west when it comes to car hire, and you can also easily hire cars in Indonesia and Thailand. Motorbikes can be hired in many places in Malaysia and Thailand, and, of course, in Bali and other parts of Indonesia.

BICYCLE

Cycling is a cheap, convenient, healthy, environmentally sound and above all fun way of travelling. You can hire bicycles for day tripping in most tourist centres, including Bali, Penang, Chiang Mai and Bagan (Myanmar), but they don't rent bicycles for long-distance travel. Top quality bicycles and components can be bought in major cities like Singapore, but generally 10-speed bikes and fittings are hard to find – and impossible in places like Vietnam. Bring your own.

Before you leave home, check your bike carefully and fill your repair kit with every imaginable spare. As with cars and motorbikes, you won't necessarily be able to buy that crucial gismo for your machine when it breaks down somewhere in the back of beyond as the sun sets. A basic kit starts with Allen keys, spoke key, tyre levers and a small Swiss army knife.

Bicycles can travel by air. You can take them to pieces and put them in a bike bag or box, but it's much simpler to wheel your bike to the check-in desk, where it should be treated as a piece of baggage. You may have to remove the pedals and turn the handlebars sideways so that it takes up less space in the aircraft's hold; check all this with the airline well in advance, preferably before you pay for your ticket.

Thailand is a good destination for bicycle touring and an increasing number of travellers take their bicycles and continue through to Malaysia and Singapore. Road conditions are good enough for touring bikes in most places, but mountain bikes are recommended for forays off the beaten track, or for travel further afield in South-East Asia. Vietnam is a great place to take a (mountain) bicycle – traffic is relatively light, buses take bikes and the entire coastal route is feasible, give or take a few potholes and hills. Indonesia is a more difficult proposition: distances in Sumatra, congested roads in Java, hills in Bali and poor road conditions in the outer islands all conspire against it – although they don't deter a steady stream of dedicated cyclists.

HITCHING

Hitching is never entirely safe in any country in the world and we don't recommend it. Travellers who decide to hitch should understand that they are taking a small but potentially serious risk. People who do choose to hitch will be safer if they travel in pairs and let someone know where they are planning to go.

Bearing all that in mind, it's handy to know that hitching in Peninsular Malaysia is a breeze, and it's not too bad in Thailand either.

BOAT
Ferry

Because many South-East Asian countries are separated by water, you'll unavoidably have to spend more on transport than you would in other parts of Asia. However, some of these trips can be great experiences. There are not a lot of inter-country shipping services – most are between Indonesia and Malaysia or Singapore – although those that are available are often very interesting. One very handy one is the fortnightly Pelni connection between Manado (Sulawesi, Indonesia) and Davao (Philippines).

Indonesia and the Philippines are paradise if you love sea travel. Both countries have extensive ferry/passenger ship services.

Yacht

With a little effort, it's often possible to get yacht rides from various places in the region. Very often, yacht owners are also travellers and they often need an extra crew member or two. Willingness to give it a try is often more important than experience and all it may cost you is a contribution to the food kitty. Check out anywhere that yachts pass through, or towns with western-style yacht clubs.

Brunei Darussalam

Brunei is a tiny Islamic sultanate lying in the north-eastern corner of Sarawak. Indeed, at just 5765 sq km, Brunei is one of the smallest countries in the world. Its vast oil reserves also make it one of the wealthiest.

Brunei is a very expensive place to visit, and most travellers see it only fleetingly en route between the Malaysian states of Sabah and Sarawak. While the lavish architecture of the capital Bandar Seri Begawan (known as Bandar or BSB) is not without interest, Brunei is like a rule-bound Islamic Singapore, with prohibitions on alcohol, and girls and boys holding hands (among other things). In its defence, however, the locals are among the friendliest people you'll meet anywhere.

Facts about Brunei

HISTORY

In the 15th and 16th centuries Brunei was a considerable local power, its rule extending throughout Borneo and into the Philippines. In 1838 James Brooke, a British adventurer with an inheritance and an armed sloop, arrived to find the Brunei sultanate fending off rebellion from warlike inland tribes. Brooke put down the rebellion and in reward was granted power over part of Sarawak. Appointing himself Raja Brooke, he pacified the 'natives', suppressed head-hunting and eliminated the much feared Borneo pirates.

A series of 'treaties' was forced onto the sultan by Raja Brooke, whittling the country away until finally, in 1890, the country was actually divided in half. Throughout their rule, which lasted until after WWII, the Brooke dynasty of 'white rajas' continued to bring ever-growing tracts of Borneo into their control.

In 1929 oil was discovered. That windfall allowed Brunei to flourish with no income tax, pensions for all, magnificent and pointless architecture and perhaps the highest per capita consumption of cars in South-East Asia.

In early 1984 the sultan, the 29th of his line, led his country somewhat reluctantly into complete independence from Britain. He celebrated by building a US$350 million palace and giving the country its current name, which means 'Abode of Peace'.

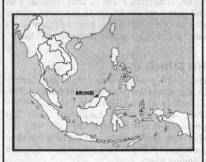

Brunei is the most Islamic country in South-East Asia. In 1991 the sale of alcohol was banned, stricter dress codes have been introduced, and in 1992 Melayu Islam Beraja (MIB), the national ideology stressing Malay culture, Islam and monarchy, became a compulsory subject in schools. Still, there are signs that change is afoot. A government committee recently recommended constitutional changes that would allow for an elected parliament. This a sign, perhaps, that even the sultan is aware that, as an absolute Islamic monarchy, Brunei is out of step with its neighbours.

GEOGRAPHY

Brunei consists of two areas separated by the Limbang District of Sarawak. The western part of Brunei contains the main towns: BSB, the oil town of Seria and the commercial

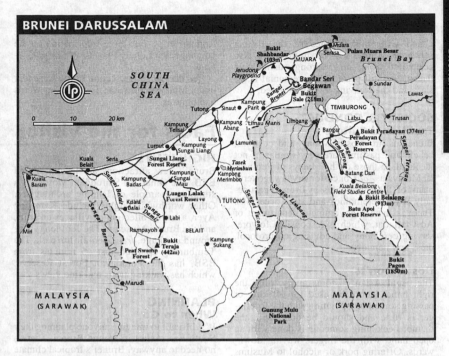

BRUNEI DARUSSALAM

town of Kuala Belait. The eastern part of the country, Temburong District, is much less developed. Brunei is mainly jungle, and approximately 75% of the country is covered by forest.

CLIMATE
Brunei is warm to hot year-round with heavy rainfall that peaks from September to January. See the BSB climate chart in the Appendix.

GOVERNMENT & POLITICS
Brunei is a monarchy, and the sultan appoints ministers to assist him in governing the country. The sultan is both prime minister and defence minister. Two of the sultan's brothers are also ministers – one brother, the finance minister was sacked in late 1998 for mismanaging the vast Brunei Investment Agency. The only democratic elections ever held were in 1962 and resulted in an attempted coup.

ECONOMY
Oil! The country is virtually dependent on the stuff, although some economic diversification

plans are now being instituted for that fearsome day when the pump runs dry. However, the prospect of an oil-less Brunei is still a long way off. Brunei has increased its oil production in the 90s, and new fields have been discovered. Brunei is also one of the world's largest exporters of liquefied natural gas. A small amount of rubber is also exported. Around 80% of the country's food requirements have to be imported.

POPULATION & PEOPLE
The latest estimate of Brunei's population was about 305,100. Malays, including indigenes of various tribes constitute 67% of the population; Chinese make up 15%; and Indians and some 20,000 expatriate workers from Europe and Asia make up the remainder of the population.

ARTS
Traditional arts have all but disappeared in modern Brunei. In its heyday the sultanate was a source of brassware in the form of gongs, cannons and household vessels (such as kettles and betel containers) that were

prized throughout Borneo and beyond. The lost wax technique used to cast bronze declined with the fortunes of the Brunei sultanate. Brunei's silversmiths were also celebrated. *Jong sarat* sarongs, using gold thread, are still prized for ceremonial occasions and the weaving art has survived.

SOCIETY & CONDUCT
Traditional Culture
Bruneians are mostly Malay, and customs, beliefs and pastimes are very similar, if not identical, to those of the Malays of Peninsular Malaysia. *Adat*, or customary law, governs many of the ceremonies in Brunei, particularly royal ceremonies and state occasions. There is even a government department of Adat Istiadat, which is responsible for preserving ceremony and advising on protocol, dress and heraldry.

Dos & Don'ts
The usual Asian customs apply: only the right hand should be used for offering or passing something; pointing with the forefinger is rude and should be done with the thumb; beckoning someone is done with an open hand with the fingers waving downwards. Offering pork or alcohol to Muslims not only may cause offence – it is tempting them to break the law. Eating shellfish and smoking are tolerated but not considered the done thing. Before entering a mosque or a house, remove your shoes.

RELIGION
Brunei is quite a strict Muslim country, and a Ministry of Religious Affairs has been set up to foster and promote Islam. The ministry also has special officers who investigate breaches of Islamic law by Muslims, and apparently government men prowl the streets after dark looking for unmarried couples standing or sitting too close to each other. Getting nailed for this crime, known as *khalwat*, can mean imprisonment and a fine. The constitution does allow other religions to be practised in the country – non-Muslim visitors need not worry about being spat upon and abused as infidels. Bruneians are very friendly and hospitable people, and not all are as zealous as their government.

LANGUAGE
The official language is Malay but English is widely spoken. Jawi, Malay written in Arabic

script, is taught in schools, and most signs in the country are written in both Jawi and the Roman script. For more information on the language, see Lonely Planet's *Malay phrasebook*.

See the Language section in the Appendix under Malaysia for some useful Malay words and phrases.

Facts for the Visitor

HIGHLIGHTS
Brunei's few attractions are in and around BSB. The Omar Ali Saifuddien Mosque is a stunning example of Islamic architecture. Other worthwhile sights include Kampung Ayer, a large collection of villages on stilts, and the Brunei Museum. The Jerudong Playground is a huge, *free* open-air fun park. The Temburong District, just 45 minutes from BSB, has the Peradayan Forest Reserve, which has walking trails and fine views.

PLANNING
When to Go
It's difficult to imagine anyone planning their South-East Asia trip around Brunei. There's no need to anyway. Brunei's tropical climate has year-round hot weather, though you can expect occasional heavy downpours, particularly between September and January. Being part of Borneo, Brunei is outside the hurricane belt.

Maps
Explore Brunei, the free government tourist booklet, has a good map of Bandar Seri Begawan. It's available at some travel agents and at the tourist office at the airport.

What to Bring
Apart from alcohol, you can buy anything you need in Brunei.

TOURIST OFFICES
There's an information counter at the airport, but otherwise you're pretty much on your own. *Explore Brunei*, the free government tourist booklet, contains much useful information for visitors. It is available at major hotels, travel agents and the airport information desk.

VISAS & DOCUMENTS
For visits of up to 14 days, visas are not nec-

essary for citizens of Belgium, Canada, France, Germany, Indonesia, Japan, Luxembourg, the Netherlands, New Zealand, Norway, the Philippines, South Korea, Sweden, Switzerland, Thailand and the Republic of the Maldives. British, Malaysian and Singaporean citizens do not require a visa for visits of 30 days or less. US citizens do not need a visa for visits of up to 90 days.

People of all other nationalities, including British overseas citizens and citizens of British dependent territories, must have a visa to visit Brunei. Brunei embassies overseas have been known to give incorrect advice, so you should double-check if your nationality is not listed above and you are told that you do not require a visa to enter the country.

If entering from Sarawak or Sabah, there's no fuss on arrival and a one week stay is more or less automatic. If you ask, you can usually get two weeks. What you'd do with them is another thing.

Transit passengers are issued a 72 hour visa at Brunei International Airport and if you intend to make a short trip to Brunei, it would be worth taking advantage of this visa. Three days is enough to see most of the sights, but this visa ties you to air travel.

EMBASSIES
Brunei Embassies

Brunei embassies abroad include:

Australia
(☎ 02-6290 1801)
16 Bulwarra Close, O'Malley, ACT 2606
Canada
(☎ 613-234 5656)
No 395 Laurier Ave East, Ottawa, Ontario
K1N 6R4
France
(☎ 01 53 64 67 60)
7 rue de Presparg, 75017 Paris
Germany
(☎ 0228-672044)
No 18 Kaiser Karl Rinc, 53111 Bonn 1
UK
(☎ 020-7581 0521)
20 Belgrave Sq, London SW1X 8PG
USA
(☎ 202-342 0159)
Suite 300, Watergate Bldg, 2600 Virginia Ave
NW, Washington, DC 20037

See the other chapters in this book for Brunei embassies in those countries.

Embassies in Brunei

Countries with diplomatic representation in BSB include:

Australia
(☎ 229435)
4th floor, Teck Guan Plaza, Jalan Sultan
Canada
(☎ 220043)
Suite 51/52, Britannia House, Jalan Cator
France
(☎ 220960)
301-306, Kompleks Jalan Sultan, Jalan Sultan
Germany
(☎ 225547)
6th Floor, Wisma Raya, Jalan Sultan
Indonesia
(☎ 330180)
Lot 4498, Sungai Hanching Baru, Jalan Muara
Malaysia
(☎ 345652)
Simpang 396-39, Kampong Sungai Akar,
Mukim Berakas B, Jalan Kebangsaan
Myanmar
(☎ 450506)
Simpang 212, Lot 2185 Jalan Kampong
Rimba, Gadong
Netherlands
(☎ 372005)
c/o Brunei Shell Petroleum Co, Seria
New Zealand
(☎ 331612)
36A Seri Lambak Complex, Jalan Berakas
Philippines
(☎ 241465)
Badiah Complex, Jalan Tutong
Singapore
(☎ 227583)
5th Floor, RBA Plaza, Jalan Sultan
Thailand
(☎ 448331) 1 Simpang 52-86-16
UK
(☎ 222231) Level 2, Block D, Complex
Yayasan Sultan Haji Hassanal Bolkiah
USA
(☎ 229670) 3rd floor, Teck Guan Plaza,
Jalan Sultan
Vietnam
(☎ 343167)
Lot 13489, Jalan Manggis Dua (off Jalan Muara)

CUSTOMS

Duty-free allowances for persons over 17 years of age are 200 cigarettes or 250g of tobacco, 60ml of perfume and 250ml of toilet water. Non-Muslims may import two bottles of liquor and 12 cans of beer, which must be declared upon arrival.

The importation of drugs carries the death penalty.

MONEY

Currency

The official currency is the Brunei dollar (B$), but Singapore dollars are equally exchanged and can be used (nobody's interested in Malaysian ringgit – there's about a 40% difference between the B$ and the RM). Banks give around 10% less for cash than travellers cheques.

Brunei uses 1c, 5c, 20c and 50c coins, and notes in denominations of B$1, B$5, B$10, B$50, B$100, B$500, B$1000 and B$10,000.

Exchange Rates

Exchange rates are as follows:

country	unit		B dollar
Australia	A$1	=	B$1.04
Canada	C$1	=	B$1.06
euro	€1	=	B$1.98
France	10FF	=	B$3.00
Germany	DM1	=	B$1.00
Japan	¥100	=	B$1.38
New Zealand	NZ$1	=	B$0.89
Singapore	S$1	=	B$1.02
UK	UK£1	=	B$2.80
USA	US$1	=	B$1.65

Costs

If you are on a tight budget, the cost of accommodation in Brunei will probably give you apoplexy. Transport costs within the country are comparable to prices in East Malaysia; food is reasonably priced unless you eat at western restaurants, but since you can't obtain alcohol anywhere you could even save money on dining out.

POST & COMMUNICATIONS

Post

Post offices are open from 7.45 am to 4.30 pm from Monday to Thursday and on Saturday; opening hours on Friday are 8 to 11 am and 2 to 4 pm. All post offices are closed on Sunday. The cost of an air mail postcard to Malaysia and Singapore is 20c; to most other countries in South-East Asia it's 35c; to Europe, Africa, Australia and the Pacific 50c; and to the Americas 60c.

Telephone

Phone cards – Hallo Kad and JTB are the most common – are available from Telecom offices and retail stores in denominations of B$10, B$20, B$50 and B$100. They can be

Telephone Codes

The country code for Brunei is 673. The international dialling code is 01. Following are area codes for some cities. You must dial the zero when calling from within Brunei.

Bandar Seri Begawan	☎ 02
Kuala Belait	☎ 03

used in public booths to make international calls. Most hotels have IDD phones, and faxes can be sent from the Telecom office or from major hotels.

BOOKS

By God's Will – A Portrait of the Sultan of Brunei by Lord Chalfront is a measured look at the sultan and Brunei. *Brunei Darussalam, A Guide* is an excellent glossy publication that will be of use for those planning a long stay in Brunei.

NEWSPAPERS & MAGAZINES

The *Borneo Bulletin*, published in Kuala Belait, is the country's only daily newspaper. Malaysian and Singaporean newspapers are available, as are some foreign magazines, such as *Time*, *Newsweek* and *Asiaweek*.

RADIO & TV

Brunei has two radio channels transmitting on both the medium wave and FM bands. One is a Malay channel, while the other transmits in English, Chinese and Gurkhali. English transmission times are from 6.30 to 8.30 am, 11 am to 2 pm and 8 to 10 pm. London's Capital Radio and Capital Gold can be picked up on the FM band.

TV is broadcast on channel 5 for most of the country, while Belait District receives transmission on channel 8. Malaysian TV can also be received.

Five times a day, during Muslim prayer times, the radio and TV transmit the muezzin's call nationally.

ELECTRICITY

Electricity supplies are dependable and run at 220-240V and 50Hz. Plugs are of the three-square-pin type, as used in Malaysia and Singapore.

WEIGHTS & MEASURES

Like almost everywhere else in the world, Brunei uses the metric system.

LAUNDRY

It would be cheaper to leave your laundry for Sabah or Sarawak. Laundry services are available at Brunei hotels but are expensive.

HEALTH

There is no risk of malaria in Brunei but dengue fever occurs, so it's worth taking measures to avoid mosquito bites. The usual precautions should be taken to avoid heat exhaustion and dehydration. For more general information on these and other health matters, refer to the Health section in the Appendix.

The tap water is safe to drink and malaria has been eliminated. Smoke haze is another matter and at its worst face masks are *de rigueur* in downtown BSB. At times the smoke is dangerous enough to force the closure of schools. Seek information before you arrive, especially if taking young children; it's probably as well to avoid Brunei altogether if the situation is bad.

The Hart Medical Clinic (☎ 225531) at 47 Jalan Sultan is a clinic close to the centre of BSB. The RIPAS hospital just north of Jalan Tutong is a fully equipped, modern hospital.

WOMEN TRAVELLERS

Brunei is a very safe country to travel in. Muslim women are required to cover up from head to toe, with only the face and hands exposed, but because of the large expat population many Bruneians are used to western ways. Bruneian men are generally very polite, and seem less inclined to leer openly than their Malaysian counterparts. Bare shoulders and short dresses are inappropriate.

BUSINESS HOURS

Government offices are open from 7.45 am to 12.15 pm and 1.30 to 4.30 pm, Monday to Thursday and Saturday. Private offices are generally open from 9 am to 5 pm Monday to Friday, and from 9 am to noon on Saturday, while banks are open from 9 am to 3 pm during the week and from 9 to 11 am on Saturday. Shops open around 9 am, and in the big shopping malls stay open until 9 or 9.30 pm. Most shops in the central area are closed by 6 pm.

PUBLIC HOLIDAYS & SPECIAL EVENTS

As in Malaysia, the dates of most religious festivals are not fixed, as they are based on the Islamic calendar. Fixed holidays are:

New Year's Day
  1 January
National Day
  23 February
Anniversary of the Royal Brunei Armed Forces
  31 May
Sultan's Birthday
  15 July
Christmas Day
  25 December

Variable holidays include:

Chinese New Year
  January or February
Isra Dan Mi'Raj
  February
Awal Ramadan (1st day of Ramadan)
  March
Anniversary of the Revelation of the Koran
  April
Hari Raya Aidilfitri (end of Ramadan)
  April
Hari Raya Haji
  June
First Day of Hijrah
  July
Hari Moulud (Prophet's Birthday)
  July or August

ACCOMMODATION

The accommodation situation in Brunei is unlike any other country in South-East Asia. There is just one budget option (in BSB). All other accommodation is expensive mid-range and top-end hotels. Outside BSB the only places to stay are in Kuala Belait.

FOOD

Like Malaysia, Brunei has an interesting mix of Malay and Chinese food. See the Food section of the Malaysia chapter for information on the local cuisine. The expat population has fostered a high standard of more expensive western restaurants.

DRINKS
Nonalcoholic Drinks

Again, see the Drinks section of the Malaysia chapter for more information on local drinks. Brunei is a modern place, and all the international soft-drink labels can be found there.

Alcoholic Drinks
Just kidding. Brunei is strictly BYO.

Getting There & Away

AIR
Airports & Airlines
Brunei has one airport, 8km from the centre of the capital, BSB.

Royal Brunei Airlines has direct flights from BSB to 27 destinations, including regional capitals such as Singapore, Kuala Lumpur, Manila, Taipei and Hong Kong; major centres in Borneo, such as Kuching, Gunung Mulu National Park and Kota Kinabalu; Darwin, Perth and Brisbane in Australia; Bali and Jakarta in Indonesia; and further afield to Abu Dhabi, London and Frankfurt. Malaysia Airlines, Singapore Airlines, and Thai Airways International also cover the routes to their home countries.

Although published rates for flights with Royal Brunei may seem extortionate, good discounts are usually available if you buy your ticket in the country of your departure. Being a Muslim airline, Royal Brunei does not serve alcohol on its flights.

Departure Tax
The departure tax is B$5 to Malaysia and Singapore, and B$12 to all other destinations.

Malaysia & Singapore
To Kuching the economy fare is B$243 (RM309 from Kuching); to Kota Kinabalu, B$81 (RM103 from KK); and to Kuala Lumpur, B$411 (RM544 from KL). Because of the difference in exchange rates, it is around 40% cheaper to fly to Brunei from Malaysia than vice versa.

The standard economy fare to Singapore is B$389 one way (S$389 from Singapore) or 30 day excursion fares are available for B$530 (S$530) return. Discounts are not usually available on these flights.

Around South-East Asia
Published return fares to other Asian destinations include Bali and Jakarta, B$471 (US$450 from Bali); Manila, B$458 (US$468 from Manila); Taipei, B$763; and Hong Kong, B$686. On flights where Royal Brunei has competition, discounting of up to 20% is available if tickets are bought through a travel

agent. To Bangkok the discounted fare is around B$520 and to Manila B$458. From Bangkok to Perth or Darwin some of the cheapest flights go via Brunei.

LAND
The main overland route is via bus from Miri in Sarawak. See the Bandar Seri Begawan (BSB) Getting There & Away section for details. It is difficult but possible to travel overland between Limbang in Sarawak and Bangar in the eastern part of Brunei, and a boat to BSB is the usual method. Overland travel between Lawas (Sarawak) and Bangar is possible but expensive.

SEA
Boats connect Brunei to Lawas and Limbang in Sarawak, and Labuan Island, from where boats go to Sabah. See the BSB Getting There & Away section for details of travel to Limbang. All other services depart from the terminal at Muara, 25km north-east of BSB. To get to the ferry terminal, take an express bus from the Multistorey Carpark in BSB; there are regular departures and the fare is B$2.

For Labuan, there are four or five high-speed ferry services daily (B$15, 1½ hours). There is an express boat daily to Lawas (B$15, two hours).

Getting Around

The cheapest way to get around Brunei is by bus, but buses are reliable only around BSB and between major centres. Buses on the main highway between BSB and Kuala Belait are fairly regular, but you may be in for a long wait on other routes. Hitchhikers are such a novelty that the chances of getting a lift are good.

Bandar Seri Begawan

The capital, Bandar Seri Begawan (usually called BSB or Bandar), is the only town of any size and one of the few places to go in Brunei. It's neat, very clean, modern and just a little boring. Islam and oil money are BSB's defining characteristics. Arabic script graces the street signs, domes and minarets dot the skyline. Most visitors find themselves scratching for something to do after a couple of days.

Orientation

The centre of BSB lies at the confluence of Sungai Brunei (the Brunei River) and Sungai Kedayan and is compact enough to explore in about an hour. It's easy to find all shops, hotels and services.

Information

Tourist Offices Pick up a copy of *Explore Brunei* from the tourist information booth at the airport. Apart from this free booklet, the office is next to useless.

Money The Hongkong Bank in the centre of town is one of the most efficient places to change money.

Post & Communications The post office is on the corner of Jalan Sultan and Jalan Elizabeth Dua. It is open from 7.45 am to 4.30 pm daily except Friday and Sunday. Next door is a JTB (a telecommunications company) office where you can buy phone cards, make local and international calls, and send faxes.

Travel Agencies The Teck Guan Plaza complex has a few travel agencies, including Ken Travel (☎ 223127) on the 1st floor, which acts as an American Express agent. Jasra Harrisons (☎ 243911), on the corner of Jalan McArthur and Jalan Sungai Kianggeh, can organise local tours and trips to Temburong. Half day tours of BSB start at B$45 per person; and a range of expensive trips into the countryside start at B$55 (B$25 for children).

Bookshops For books and magazines try the Best Eastern on the ground floor of the Teck Guan Plaza building, on the corner of Jalan Sultan and Jalan McArthur.

Cultural Centres The British Council is a long way out of town at 45, Simpang 100, Jalan Tungku Link. It is open Monday to Thursday from 8 am to 12.15 pm and 1.45 to 4.30 pm, on Friday and Saturday from 8 am to 12.30 pm.

Things to See

The **Omar Ali Saifuddien Mosque**, named after the 28th sultan of Brunei, was built in 1958 at a cost of about US$5 million. The golden-domed structure stands close to Sungai Brunei in its own artificial lagoon and is one of the tallest buildings in Bandar Seri Begawan. It's also one of the most impressive structures in the east. It's closed to non-Muslims on Thursday, and on Friday it is only open from 4.30 to 5.30 pm. From Saturday to Wednesday you may enter the mosque between the hours of 8 am and noon, 1 and 3 pm and 4.30 and 5.30 pm (ie outside of prayer times).

Kampung Ayer is a collection of 2ᵘ water villages built on stilts on either side of Sungai Brunei and houses a population of around 30,000 people. It's a strange mixture of ancient and modern; old traditions and ways of life are side by side with modern plumbing, electricity and colour TV. A visit to one of the villages is probably the most rewarding experience you'll have in Brunei, though the garbage that floats around them has to be seen to be believed. The villages are at their best at high tide. To get there, take the path from behind the Omar Ali Saifuddien Mosque or take a water taxi (around B$1) across the river.

The **Brunei Museum** is housed in a beautiful building on the banks of Sungai Brunei at Kota Batu, 4.5km from the centre of BSB. Historical treasures and a good ethnography section are the highlights. The adjoining **Malay Technology Museum** is also worth a visit.

The **Jame'Asr Hassanal Bolkiah Mosque** is the latest minaretted and domed addition to the Bruneian skyline. It is the largest mosque in the country, constructed at great expense, and as the local tourist literature trumpets, 'a symbol of Islam's firm hold in the country'. It's a fabulous sight and is in Gadong, a few kilometres north of town.

Another photogenic attraction is the **Istana Nurul Iman**, the magnificent sultan's palace. It looks particularly impressive when illuminated at night. The *istana* is open to the public only at the end of the fasting month of Ramadan and is 4km out of town on the Tutong road.

Places to Stay

Pusat Belia (☎ 229423), the youth centre on Jalan Sungai Kianggeh, is a short walk from the town centre. It is the only budget option. A bed in an air-con four bed dorm costs B$10 per night for one to three nights and B$5 for each subsequent night. The centre has a swimming pool (entry B$1) and a cafe with a very limited menu. Officially you need a youth hostel or student card to stay. Entry without a card is at the discretion of the manager, who may make things difficult and

BANDAR SERI BEGAWAN

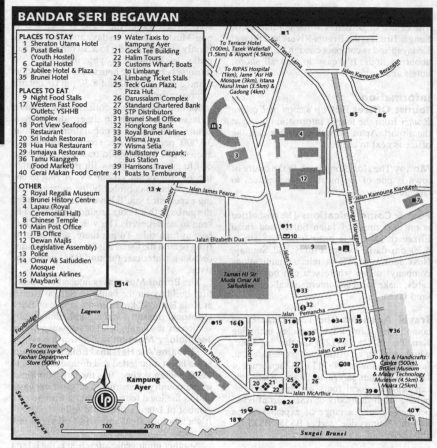

PLACES TO STAY
1 Sheraton Utama Hotel
5 Pusat Belia
   (Youth Hostel)
6 Capital Hostel
7 Jubilee Hotel & Plaza
35 Brunei Hotel

PLACES TO EAT
9 Night Food Stalls
17 Western Fast Food
   Outlets; YSHHB
   Complex
18 Port View Seafood
   Restaurant
20 Sri Indah Restoran
28 Hua Hua Restaurant
29 Ismajaya Restoran
36 Tamu Kianggeh
   (Food Market)
40 Gerai Makan Food Centre

19 Water Taxis to
   Kampung Ayer
21 Gock Tee Building
22 Halim Tours
23 Customs Wharf; Boats
   to Limbang
24 Limbang Ticket Stalls
25 Teck Guan Plaza;
   Pizza Hut
26 Darussalam Complex
27 Standard Chartered Bank
30 STP Distributors
31 Brunei Shell Office
32 Hongkong Bank
33 Royal Brunei Airlines
34 Wisma Jaya
37 Wisma Setia
38 Multistorey Carpark;
   Bus Station
39 Harrisons Travel
41 Boats to Temburong

OTHER
2 Royal Regalia Museum
3 Brunei History Centre
4 Lapau (Royal
   Ceremonial Hall)
8 Chinese Temple
10 Main Post Office
11 JTB Office
12 Dewan Majlis
   (Legislative Assembly)
13 Police
14 Omar Ali Saifuddien
   Mosque
15 Malaysia Airlines
16 Maybank

To Terrace Hotel
(100m), Tasek Waterfall
(1.5km) & Airport (4.5km)

To RIPAS Hospital
(1km), Jame 'Asr HB
Mosque (3km), Istana
Nurul Iman (3.5km) &
Gadong (4km)

Jalan Tasek Lama
Jalan Kampung Berangan
Jalan James Pearce
Jalan Stoney
Jalan Elizabeth Dua
Jalan Sultan
Jalan Kampung Kianggeh
Jalan Sungai Kianggeh
Taman HJ Sir
Muda Omar Ali
Saifuddien
Lagoon
Footbridge
To Crowne
Princess Inn &
Yaohan Department
Store (500m)
Kampung
Ayer
Sungai Kedayan
Jalan Roberts
Jalan Pretty
Jalan Pemancha
Jalan Cator
Jalan McArthur
To Arts & Handicrafts
Centre (500m),
Brunei Museum
& Malay Technology
Museum (4.5km) &
Muara (25km)
Sungai Brunei

0   100   200 m

---

will probably tell you to come back in a few
hours if he doesn't like the look of you. Some
males with long hair have been turned away.
There are no budget alternatives.

The **Capital Hostel** (☎ 223561), off Jalan
Tasek Lama just behind the Pusat Belia, has
faded singles/doubles costing from B$80/95
to B$118/138. The restaurant downstairs
serves reasonably priced meals and western
breakfasts.

The **Crowne Princess Inn** (☎ 241128), Km
2.5 Jalan Tutong, is across Sungai Kedayan
near the Yaohan department store – take the
footbridge behind the Omar Ali Saifuddien
Mosque. It is inconveniently located but
rooms are reasonably priced at B$110, and a
discount can make this very good value by
Brunei standards.

Places to Eat

The **Gerai Makan** food centre on the riverfront just over the canal from the customs
wharf is a good place to eat, although, as is
the case all over BSB, not much happens in
the evenings. For takeaway food, try the
Tamu Kianggeh market or, in the evenings
only, the **food stalls** that spring up behind the
Chinese temple, opposite the post office.
Satay, barbecued fish, chicken wings and
kueh melayu (sweet pancakes filled with
peanuts, raisins and sugar) are all available
here.

The main street, Jalan Sultan, has the
cheapest restaurants in town. **Ismajaya
Restoran** has rice and curry meals for around
B$3, and a few doors down, the **Sin Tai Pong**
has chicken rice for B$2.50. The **Hua Hua**

Restaurant nearby is more expensive – about B$6 to B$8 for most dishes – but the food is very good. The Hua Hua and the Ismajaya stay open until 9 pm. On Jalan McArthur the *Sri Indah Restoran* has decent *roti* and *murtabak*.

Delifrance, in the YSHHB Complex near the Omar Ali Saifuddien Mosque, has good European-style pastries and sandwiches. You'll find a good range of western fast food around the town centre, but it's not particularly cheap. In the YSHHB Complex, there's a *SugarBun*, *Jollibee*, *KFC* and *Pizza Hut*. Another branch of *Pizza Hut* on the corner of Jalan Sultan and Jalan McArthur does take-away slices for B$1.90.

Getting There & Away
Air Airline offices or general sales agents in BSB include:

British Airways
 (☎ 243911)
 Harrisons, corner of Jalan Kianggeh
 and Jalan McArthur
Malaysia Airlines
 (☎ 224141)
 144 Jalan Pemancha
Royal Brunei Airlines
 (☎ 242222)
 RBA Plaza, Jalan Sultan
Singapore Airlines
 (☎ 244901)
 49-50 Jalan Sultan
Thai Airways International
 (☎ 242991)
 51 Jalan Sultan

Bus Brunei's main highway links BSB with Sarawak via Seria and Kuala Belait. Getting to Limbang (Sarawak) by road is difficult but not impossible. It is possible but expensive to travel by road to Lawas in Sabah – it's better to travel to Sabah by boat. The BSB bus station is on Jalan Cator, beneath the Multistorey Carpark (that's the official name).

To get to Miri in Sarawak, take a bus to Seria (B$4), change buses to get to Kuala Belait (B$1), then take a bus to Miri (B$10.20). Immigration and customs formalities are taken care of on both sides of the Brunei-Sarawak border.

Boat With the exception of boats to Limbang in Sarawak, all international boats leave from the terminal at Muara, 25km north-east of BSB (see the earlier Brunei Getting There & Away section for details).

Limbang boats dock at the end of Jalan Roberts in BSB, where immigration formalities are taken care of. There are a number of regular ekspres boats for Limbang (B$10, 30 minutes).

Getting Around
To/From the Airport Purple bus Nos 11, 23, 24, 36, 38 and 57 will get you between the Multistorey Carpark and the airport for B$1. As you leave the terminal, walk diagonally right across the car park to get to the bus stop.

Some major hotels have courtesy phones at the arrivals hall where you can request a free pick up. You could always take the ride, say the rooms don't meet your standard then walk to the youth centre.

If you don't have too much baggage you could take a purple taxi for B$3; it will drop you about 100m from the terminal. A metered taxi will cost you around B$20. The big, modern airport is situated 8km from the city.

Bus The government bus network reaches most sights in and around the city, and out to the international ferry terminal at Muara. The bus station is beneath the Multistorey Carpark on Jalan Cator and route numbers are emblazoned on the front of each bus. A route map is displayed at the terminal and reproduced in colour in tourist leaflets. Apart from the Muara express service (B$2), all fares are B$1.

Taxi City Transport Service (CTS) taxis (better known as purple taxis) can take you anywhere within the city limits for a fixed B$3 (plus B$1 if you book by phone). They are not allowed to drop you at the airport terminal but will take you to within a short walk. Purple taxis operate from 6 am to 10 pm and can be found at the Multistorey Carpark or booked on the CTS hot line (☎ 343434). Outside these hours, you will have to take an expensive metered taxi.

Water Taxi Water taxis, popularly known as flying coffins, are most easily caught near the customs wharf or the Tamu Kianggeh food market. Fares start at 50c and go up to B$2, but you can expect to pay much higher charter rates. To charter a boat for a tour of Kampung Ayer and the river shouldn't cost more than B$20 per hour, or less if you bargain hard.

Around Bandar Seri Begawan

The countryside has a lot of pristine forest, with waterfalls and reserves that make pleasant day trips. There are a few other points of interest – decent beaches, longhouses and some more impressive istanas – but the problem is getting to them. A car is essential to reach most of these places.

BEACHES

Muara Beach, 2km from Muara, is a popular weekend retreat. The white sand is clean, but like many beaches in Borneo it is littered with driftwood and the debris of logging. Other beaches around Muara include Serasa and Meragang.

Purple bus No 33 will take you to Muara or Serasa beaches; the fare is $1. You'll have to get to Meragang under your own steam or hitch a ride; the beach is about 4km west of Muara along the Muara-Tutong Road.

JERUDONG PLAYGROUND

Jerudong Playground is near the coast north of BSB and claimed to be the biggest amusement park in the world (though the Disney Corporation may dispute this). All rides are free and you rarely have to queue for any of them. However, just to remind you that this is Brunei, women with sleeveless tops are not allowed on the rides.

The playground is open Monday to Wednesday from 5 pm to midnight, Thursday and Saturday from 5 pm till 2 am, and Friday, Sunday and public holidays from 2 pm until midnight. There are food and drink stalls at the car park.

Getting There & Away

It's easy to get to Jerudong Playground – just take purple bus No 55 or 57 from the Multistorey Carpark – but the last bus leaves at 5.30 pm and getting back can be a problem. Major hotels have shuttle services with prearranged pick-up times; for B$20 per person it is hardly cheap, but unless you cadge a ride from a friendly local, it's that or take a metered taxi.

KUALA BELAIT

The last town before Malaysia, Kuala Belait is the place to get buses for Miri in Sarawak. It's not completely without interest, but

hardly anyone lingers here. The best place to change money is at the Hongkong Bank opposite the bus station.

Places to Stay

The *Government Rest House* (☎ 334288) charges around B$30 but it's very unlikely you will be allowed to stay. The only alternatives are ridiculously expensive. The cheapest is the *Sentosa Hotel* (☎ 334341) at 92 Jalan McKerron; it charges B$135, although a discount may be available. The *Seaview Hotel* (☎ 332651), Jalan Maulana, is better value than the Sentosa and singles/doubles cost B$100/110 including breakfast, but it is 4km from town on the beach road to Seria.

Getting There & Away

Five buses a day leave for Miri in Sarawak and the fare is B$10.20.

See the BSB Getting There & Away section for details on travel between the capital and Kuala Belait.

TEMBURONG DISTRICT

Temburong District is the eastern slice of Brunei, surrounded by Sarawak. This quiet backwater, rarely visited by travellers, is reached by boat from BSB and can be visited as a day trip. Much of the district is virgin rainforest.

Bangar, a sleepy town on the banks of Sungai Temburong, is the district centre. It has a mosque, but not much else. **Batang Duri** is an Iban (the local Dayak tribe) longhouse on Sungai Temburong, 17km south of Bangar. About 2km before Batang Duri is the **Taman Batang Duri**, a park and small zoo with civets, monkeys, otters and birds.

Kuala Belalong Field Studies Centre is a scientific research centre located in the Batu Apoi Forest Reserve, a large area of primary rainforest that covers most of southern Temburong. It is primarily for scientists and school groups, though interested overseas visitors can arrange to stay through travel agents in BSB – it's not cheap.

The **Peradayan Forest Reserve** protects the peaks of Bukit Patoi and Bukit Peradayan, which can be reached along a walking trail – bring water and food for the walk. The one hour walk through rainforest to Bukit Patoi provides some fine views. It starts at the park entrance, 15km from Bangar. Most walkers descend back along the trail, but it is possible to continue over the other side of the summit and around to Bukit Peradayan. This trail is harder, less distinct and takes two hours.

Getting There & Away

Regular boats to Bangar leave from the wharf near the Gerai Makan food centre in BSB. They cost B$7 and take 45 minutes.

Getting Around

The only way to get around Temburong is by taxi – negotiate the fare. A round-trip ticket to Batang Duri should cost B$20. For the Peradayan Forest Reserve and the walk to Bukit Patoi, taxis also charge B$20 to drop you off and pick you up at an arranged time. Hitching generally involves long waits.

Cambodia

Modern day Cambodia is the successor-state of the mighty Khmer Empire, which during the Angkorian period (9th to 14th centuries) ruled much of what is now Vietnam, Laos and Thailand. The remains of this empire can be seen in the fabled temples of Angkor. These stunning monuments, surrounded by dense jungle, are easily accessible from Phnom Penh.

Cambodia is still recovering from two decades of warfare and violence, including almost four years (1975-79) of rule by the genocidal Khmer Rouge, who killed as many as two million of Cambodia's seven million people and systematically sought to obliterate the country's pre-revolutionary culture. Small Khmer Rouge units remain a problem in northern areas of Cambodia, especially near the Thai border. At the time of writing, travelling around the country is safer than at any time since the 1960s. However, circumstances can change quickly, so always check security conditions before setting off on a road journey.

Facts about Cambodia

HISTORY

From the 1st to the 6th centuries, much of present day Cambodia was part of the kingdom of Funan, whose prosperity was due in large part to its position on the great trade route between China and India.

The Angkorian era, known for its brilliant achievements in architecture and sculpture, began under Jayavarman II around the year 800. During his rule, a new state religion establishing the Khmer ruler as a *devaraja* (god-king) was instituted. Vast irrigation systems facilitated intensive cultivation of the land around Angkor and allowed the Khmers to maintain a densely populated, highly centralised state.

For 90 years, from 1864, the French controlled Cambodia as an adjunct to their colonial interests in Vietnam. Independence was declared in 1953. For 15 years King Norodom Sihanouk (later prince, prime minister and chief-of-state, and now king again) dominated Cambodian politics. But, alienating

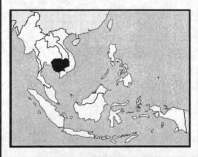

both the left and the right with his erratic and repressive policies, he was overthrown by the army in 1970 and went into exile in Beijing.

From 1969 Cambodia was drawn into the Vietnam conflict. The USA secretly commenced carpet-bombing suspected communist base camps in Cambodia and, shortly after the 1970 coup, American and South Vietnamese troops invaded the country to root out Vietnamese communist forces. They failed. But the invasion did push Cambodia's indigenous rebels, the Khmer Rouge (French for 'Red Khmer'), into the country's interior. Savage fighting soon engulfed the entire country, ending only when Phnom Penh fell to the Khmer Rouge on 17 April 1975, two weeks before the fall of Saigon.

After taking Phnom Penh, the Khmer

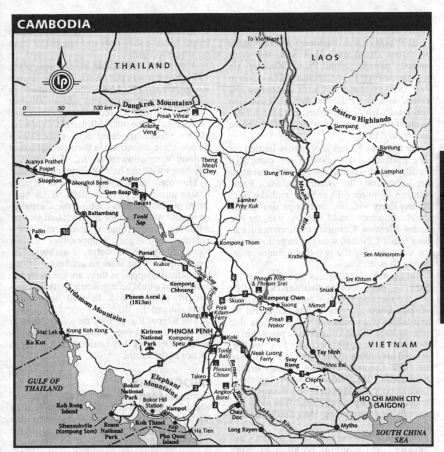

CAMBODIA

Rouge, under leader Pol Pot, implemented one of the most radical, brutal restructurings of a society ever attempted. Its goal was the transformation of Cambodia into a Maoist, peasant-dominated, agrarian cooperative.

During the next four years, hundreds of thousands of Cambodians, including the vast majority of the country's educated people, were relocated into the countryside, tortured to death or executed. Thousands of people were branded as 'parasites' and systematically killed solely because they spoke a foreign language or wore spectacles. Hundreds of thousands more died of mistreatment, malnutrition and disease. At least one million, perhaps even two million, Cambodians died between 1975 and 1979 as a result of the policies of the Khmer Rouge government.

At the end of 1978, Vietnam invaded Cambodia and overthrew the Khmer Rouge, who fled westward to the jungles on both sides of the border with Thailand. They maintained a guerrilla war throughout the 1980s, armed and financed by China and Thailand (and with indirect US support), against the Vietnamese-backed government in Phnom Penh.

In 1991 the warring sides came together in Paris to sign a peace accord which enabled the mid-1993 UN-administered elections in Cambodia. A constitution was drawn up and passed, and Norodom Sihanouk was once again made king. The government was a volatile coalition of the United Front for an Independent, Neutral and Free Cambodia (Funcinpec), led by Prince Norodom Ranariddh, and the Cambodian People's Party

(CPP), led by Hun Sen. Cambodia had two prime ministers.

Real power was wielded by Cambodia's so-called strongman, Hun Sen, the erroneously named Second Prime Minister. He overthrew First Prime Minister Ranariddh in July 1997 on charges of arms smuggling and collusion with the Khmer Rouge. Ranariddh was finally tried and pardoned in March 1998 in order that a free and fair election take place on 26 July 1998.

As many as 39 political parties battled for 122 parliamentary seats in the campaign leading up to election day. Despite threatening a boycott, the National United Front alliance (grouping Funcinpec and the Sam Rainsy Party with two smaller parties) joined the election fray. On 14 August 1998, the National Election Committee announced that Hun Sen's CPP had won the largest share of the vote, but not the two-thirds majority required to rule alone.

International observers had already returned home, declaring themselves satisfied that the election was free and fair. Hundreds of complaints alleging voting fraud and intimidation were rejected, while claims that around 30 political killings took place during the election campaign were said to be exaggerated according to the Cambodia Office of the High Commissioner for Human Rights. Nonetheless, the following month saw thousands of people in Phnom Penh join opposition leaders Sam Rainsy and Prince Norodom Ranariddh in condemning Hun Sen's 'unfair' election win.

Following several months of tortuous negotiations and posturing on all sides, King Sihanouk managed to broker an agreement in November which saw the CPP and Funcinpec form a coalition once more, only this time with Hun Sen firmly in control. Hun Sen is prime minister, while Ranariddh has been made president of the National Assembly, abandoning his alliance with maverick outsider Sam Rainsy.

The Khmer Rouge

The Khmer Rouge was decimated by a series of mass defections which took place from late-1994 onwards. Particularly damaging was the 1996 split which saw forces loyal to former Khmer Rouge foreign minister Ieng Sary in the Pailin area come over to the Royal Cambodian Armed Forces' (RCAF) side. This cut off much-needed revenue generated by gems and logging that the remainder of the

Khmer Rouge needed to wage their war. Furthermore it made the RCAF's task much easier because they only had one major front on which to fight.

A series of remarkable events took place 1997; Pol Pot was put on trial by the Khmer Rouge, General Ta Mok assumed leadership of the fractured movement and an alliance was formed with the remnants of Funcinpec forces loyal to the ousted Ranariddh. By mid-1998 the rebels appeared to be in their death throes. More defections in their stronghold of Anlong Veng allowed the RCAF to capture key bases with the help of former guerrillas.

The man most associated with Khmer Rouge atrocities, Pol Pot, died on 15 April 1998, perhaps forever robbing the Cambodian people of the chance for truth and justice. Although there remains much talk of a posthumous trial and the appearance of other Khmer Rouge leaders before some sort of international tribunal, it seems unlikely anything will actually happen as there are too many big names that would be implicated both in Cambodian politics and beyond in China, Thailand and the USA.

The Khmer Rouge may be weaker than at any time since its overthrow, but lacking conventional territory they could resort to terrorist tactics in the future.

GEOGRAPHY

Cambodia covers an area of 181,035 sq km, which is a little over half the size of Italy or Vietnam. The country is dominated by two topographical features: the Mekong River and the Tonlé Sap (Great Lake). There are three main mountainous regions: in the southwest (the Elephant and Cardamom mountains), along the northern border with Thailand (the Dangkrek Mountains) and in the country's north-eastern corner (the Eastern Highlands).

The Tonlé Sap is linked to the Mekong at Phnom Penh by a 100km-long channel sometimes called the Tonlé Sap River. From mid-May to early October (the rainy season), the level of the Mekong rises, backing up the Tonlé Sap River and causing it to flow northwestward into the Tonlé Sap. During this period, the Tonlé Sap swells from around 3000 sq km to over 7500 sq km. As the water level of the Mekong falls during the dry season, the Tonlé Sap River reverses its flow, and the waters of the lake drain back into the Mekong. This extraordinary process makes the Tonlé Sap one of the world's richest sources of freshwater fish.

CLIMATE

The climate of Cambodia is governed by two monsoons, which set the rhythm of rural life. The cool, dry, north-eastern monsoon, which carries little rain, occurs from around November to April. From May to October, the south-western monsoon brings strong winds, high humidity and heavy rains. But even during the wet season, it rarely rains in the morning – most precipitation falls in the afternoon, and even then, only sporadically.

See the Phnom Penh climate chart in the Appendix.

FLORA

The Cambodian landscape is a blend of cultivated rice paddies, overshadowed by numerous sugar palms, grasslands, lush rainforest cloaking the remoter areas, and, at higher elevations, pine forests. Much of Cambodia remains forested, but hardwoods are being logged at an alarming rate in some provinces, often with the connivance of political and military leaders.

FAUNA

Cambodia is home to a number of large animals, although numbers are extremely vague because of the isolation of their habitat and the impact of hunting. They include bears, elephants, rhinoceroses, leopards, tigers and wild cows and deer. There are several dangerous snake species, including the king cobra, banded krait and the small hanuman.

There are many bird species in the country, including cormorants, cranes, kingfishers and pelicans. Ornithologists might like to visit the **Prek Toal Bird Sanctuary**, on the Prek Toal River at the Battambang end of the Tonlé Sap, which has rare birds such as the lesser and greater adjutants, the milky stork and the spot billed pelican. If you are interested in visiting this abundant sanctuary call the project director (☎ 023-360991).

There are also some large fish in Cambodia's rivers, including the huge Mekong catfish, which reaches up to 5m in length, and the rare Irrawaddy freshwater dolphin, which inhabits areas north of Kratie.

NATIONAL PARKS

Cambodia has four national parks, although facilities at each are pretty nonexistent to date. They are: **Virachey**, in the far northeast, spanning Ratanakiri and Stung Treng Provinces; **Kirirom**, off National Hwy 4 on the road to Sihanoukville; **Ream**, a maritime park just outside Sihanoukville; and **Bokor**, a former French hill station not far from Kampot.

GOVERNMENT & POLITICS

Cambodia is a constitutional monarchy headed by King Norodom Sihanouk. Its government, recently re-formed following an election victory by Hun Sen's CPP in July 1998, is characteristically unstable. Hun Sen's strong-arm tactics have been called into question by opposition forces.

ECONOMY

Cambodia is one of the poorest countries in Asia – about 80% of the population is employed in agriculture. All fuel and most raw materials, capital equipment and consumer goods must be imported. In recent years the country's main export has shifted from rubber to timber, which accounts for around half of Cambodia's export earnings.

Foreign aid accounts for the majority of the government's budget and many aid groups are assisting the Cambodian people.

Other economic mainstays are gems, the transhipment of gold and cigarettes and a huge informal sector, including the lucrative business of heroin trafficking.

POPULATION & PEOPLE

The current population of Cambodia is about 11 million. Infant mortality rates are, with Laos, the highest in the region at 90 per 1000. Women account for around 54% of the population.

Official statistics put 96% of the Cambodian population as ethnic-Khmers (ethnic Cambodians), making the country the most homogeneous in South-East Asia. In actual fact, there are probably much larger numbers of Vietnamese in Cambodia than the government cares to admit and such figures do not take account of generations of intermarriage that has occurred.

The most important minority group in Cambodia is undoubtedly the ethnic-Chinese, who, until 1975, controlled the country's economy and who, with the help of overseas Chinese investment, are once again a powerful economic force within Cambodia. Official estimates put their numbers at around 50,000; unofficially there may be as many as 400,000.

CAMBODIA

Cambodia's Cham Muslims (Khmer Islam) officially number some 200,000, though this is another figure that may be an underestimation – some observers claim half a million. They suffered vicious persecution between 1975 and 1979 and a large part of their community was exterminated.

Cambodia's diverse ethno-linguistic minorities (chunchiets), who live in the country's mountainous regions, number around 60,000 to 70,000.

ARTS
Dance
Cambodia's highly stylised classical dance, adapted from Angkor dances (and similar to Thai dances derived from the same source), is performed to the accompaniment of an orchestra and choral narration. There are sometimes opportunities to see classical Khmer dance in Phnom Penh and in Siem Reap (near Angkor).

Architecture
Khmer architecture reached its zenith during the Angkorian era. Some of the finest examples of architecture from this period are Angkor Wat and the structures of Angkor Thom. Many of the finest works of Khmer sculpture are on display at the National Museum in Phnom Penh.

SOCIETY & CONDUCT
Dos & Don'ts
The Khmers are among the easiest people to get along with in all of South-East Asia. Like the Thais, they greet each other with a bow, the hands meeting in prayer. As is the case elsewhere around South-East Asia you should beckon with the palm facing downwards and should refrain from patting children (or anyone else) on the head.

Proper etiquette in wats (temples) is mostly a matter of common sense. A few tips might include:

- Don't wear shorts or tank tops.
- Take off your hat when entering the grounds of the wat.
- Take off your shoes before going into the vihara (sanctuary).
- If you sit down in front of the dais (the platform on which the Buddhas are placed), sit with your feet to the side rather than in the lotus position.
- Never point your finger – or, nirvana forbid, the soles of your feet! – towards a figure of the Buddha (or towards human beings either).

RELIGION
Hinayana Buddhism is the dominant religion in Cambodia and was the state religion until 1975. It was reinstated as the state religion in the late 1980s. Between 1975 and 1979, the vast majority of Cambodia's Buddhist monks were murdered by the Khmer Rouge, who also destroyed virtually all of the country's 3000 wats. The 1990s have seen the restoration of many of the wats and mosques of Cambodia, and monks with alms bowls are once again a common sight.

See the section on Religions of South-East Asia in the Appendix.

LANGUAGE
Cambodia's official language is Khmer. For most westerners, writing and pronouncing this language proves somewhat confusing and difficult.

For more than a century, the second language of choice among educated Cambodians was French, which is still spoken by many people who grew up before the 1970s. English is now the language of choice among young Khmers, and even in Cambodia's rural areas English schools are packed with eager students.

See the Language section in the Appendix for some useful Khmer words and phrases.

Facts for the Visitor

HIGHLIGHTS
At the time of writing, more of Cambodia was open to the visitor than at any time for three decades. Most travellers restrict their visit to the lively capital of Phnom Penh and the famous temples at Angkor. However, people are increasingly heading to the south coast to relax on the empty beaches at Sihanoukville and looping back to Phnom Penh via Kampot and Kep.

Generally, Cambodia has few of the must-see attractions of some of its neighbours, but the Khmer people and their way of life often attracts visitors to stay much longer than anticipated. Many of the provincial towns offer a combination of colonial architecture, sleepy riverside locations and some extremely friendly local people. Easiest to visit are Kompong Cham and Kompong Chhnang, and perhaps the most rewarding is Battambang.

Before planning any trips upcountry by road, it is essential that you check the latest situation with local people and other backpackers, and, if possible, with nongovernmental organisations (NGOs) in Phnom Penh. Cambodia remains a volatile country where unexpected dangers are often not as far away as they might seem. What is safe one week is not necessarily safe the next. Risks that backfire could have repercussions not just for you individually but also for the whole travel industry in Cambodia.

PLANNING
When to Go
Cambodia can be visited any time of year, though the ideal months are December and January. At this time of year humidity levels are relatively low and there is little likelihood of rain. From early February, temperatures start to rise until the hottest month, April, in which it can reach more than 40°C. In late April or early May the south-west monsoon brings rain and cooler weather.

The wet season, which lasts from May to October, need not be a bad time to visit Cambodia. Angkor is surrounded by lush foliage and the moats are full of water at this time of year.

Maps
Tourist maps of Cambodia and Phnom Penh are available in Phnom Penh and Siem Reap. The Periplus *Cambodia Travel Map* at a scale of 1:1,100,000 is probably the best around and is available in Phnom Penh and Bangkok bookshops.

Nelles' *Vietnam, Laos & Cambodia* map at 1:1,500,000 scale is another good map of the country. Point Maps & Guides produces some nice 3D maps of Phnom Penh and Siem Reap.

What to Bring
The usual rules apply: bring as little as possible. Phnom Penh is well stocked with travel provisions, so if you have forgotten or lost anything it should be possible to replace it there. However, many basics such as toiletries and repellent are cheaper in Thailand or Vietnam.

TOURIST OFFICES
Cambodia only has a handful of tourist offices, and these have little to offer the independent traveller. See the Phnom Penh and the Siem Reap sections for information on

tourist offices there. You may actually find the tourist offices in provincial capitals quite helpful as the staff are often so shocked to see visitors.

Cambodia has no tourist offices abroad and it is most unlikely that Cambodian embassies will be of much assistance in planning a trip.

VISAS & DOCUMENTS
Visas
Most nationalities receive a one month visa on arrival at Phnom Penh's Pochentong airport. The cost is US$20 and one passport-size photo is required. Easily extendable one month business visas are available for US$25.

Coming overland from Thailand, visitors have to obtain a visa in Bangkok as they are not available at Poipet or Koh Kong. Travellers arriving overland from Ho Chi Minh City (Saigon) will have to obtain a visa before they arrive, but these are easy to get in Vietnam. You must have Moc Bai as an exit point on your Vietnamese visa to use this route.

Visa Extensions Visa extensions can be granted in Phnom Penh. It is simply a matter of having the cash at hand, and the more the merrier. One passport-size photograph is required. If you are planning to work in Cambodia get a one month business visa for US$25 as it can be extended indefinitely, whereas a tourist visa can be extended only once for one or three months.

Officially one month costs US$30; three months, US$60; six months, US$100; and one year, US$150. However, this way the police will keep your passport for about 25 days. Strangely enough the office offers an express, next day service at inflated prices: US$45 for one month, US$80 for three months and so on. If you try to get your passport returned early at standard price, you may well find the extension cancelled, in which case you have to pay the US$3 per day overstay charge on departure.

Other Documents
Passport-size photographs are readily obtainable in Phnom Penh. If you are thinking of applying for work with NGOs in Phnom Penh, you should bring copies of your educational certificates and work references with you.

EMBASSIES & CONSULATES
Cambodian Embassies & Consulates
Cambodian embassies and consulates abroad include:

Australia
(☎ 02-6237 1259)
5 Canterbury Court, Deakin, ACT 2600
France
(☎ 01 40 65 04 70)
11 avenue Charles Floquet, 75007 Paris
Germany
Consulate:
(☎ 030-555165)
Arnold Zweing Strasse, 1013189 Berlin
USA
Embassy:
(☎ 202-726 7742)
4500 16th St, Washington, DC 20011
Consulate:
(☎ 718-830 3770)
53-69 Alderton St, Rego Park, New York 11374

See the other chapters in this book for Cambodian embassies in South-East Asia.

Embassies & Consulates in Cambodia
For Laos, one month visas cost US$35 and take one day. This is cheaper than in Vietnam. For Vietnam, one month single entry visas are US$50 and take five working days. There is no surcharge for Moc Bai as a valid entry point. Some of the embassies in Phnom Penh are as follows:

Australia
(☎ 426000) 11 254 St
Canada
c/o Australian Embassy
China
(☎ 427428) 256 Mao Tse Toung Blvd
France
(☎ 430020) 1 Monivong Blvd
Germany
(☎ 426381) 76-78 214 St
Indonesia
(☎ 426148) 179 51 St
Laos
(☎ 426441) 15-17 Mao Tse Toung Blvd
Malaysia
(☎ 426176) 161 51 St
Philippines
(☎ 280048) 33 294 St
Thailand
(☎ 426124) 4 Monivong Blvd
USA
(☎ 426436) 27 240 St

UK
(☎ 427124) 29 75 St
Vietnam
(☎ 725481) 436 Monivong Blvd

CUSTOMS
If Cambodia has customs allowances, it is keeping tight-lipped about them. A 'reasonable amount' of duty-free items are allowed into the country. Travellers arriving by air might bear in mind that alcohol and cigarettes sell at duty-free (and lower) prices on the streets of Phnom Penh – a carton of Marlboro costs just US$8!

Like any other country, Cambodia does not allow travellers to import weapons, explosives or narcotics – there are enough in the country already.

MONEY
Currency
Cambodia's currency is the *riel*, abbreviated here by a lower-case r written after the sum. From around 200r to the US dollar in mid-1989, the riel plummeted in value to stabilise at about 2500r to the dollar. The regional crisis of late-1997 did not initially weaken the currency as much as other countries, but it has dropped to around 3800r to the US dollar.

The riel comes in notes with the following values: 100, 200, 500, 1000, 2000, 5000, 10,000, 20,000, 50,000 and 100,000.

Cambodia's second currency, some would say first, is the US dollar, which is accepted everywhere and by everyone, though your change may arrive in riel.

Exchange Rates
Currency exchange rates are as follows:

country	unit		riel
Australia	A$1	=	2403r
Canada	C$1	=	2469r
euro	€1	=	4592r
France	10FF	=	6950r
Germany	DM1	=	2330r
Japan	¥100	=	3198r
New Zealand	NZ$1	=	2060r
Thailand	100B	=	10011r
UK	UK£1	=	6500r
USA	US$1	=	3820r

Exchanging Money
Cash In the interests of making life as simple as possible, organise a supply of US dollars

before you arrive in Cambodia. If you have cash in another major currency, you will be able to change it without any hassle in Phnom Penh or Siem Reap.

Travellers Cheques Most banks charge a commission of 2% to change travellers cheques. Some of the more upmarket hotels in Phnom Penh and Siem Reap will also cash travellers cheques.

Credit Cards Cash advances on credit cards are available in Phnom Penh, Siem Reap, Sihanoukville and Battambang, but charges are high with most banks advertising a US$10 minimum charge. If you want US$250 or under, go to the Foreign Trade Bank in Phnom Penh as they charge a flat 4%.

Commercial Cambodian Bank (CCB) is the only credit card option beyond the capital.

There are no ATMs in Cambodia.

Costs

Budget travellers will find that accommodation rates are reasonable in Cambodia and rooms can be had for US$5 and below. Travel is not so cheap, but as more road journeys become possible expenses come down. Food and drink prices in Phnom Penh and Siem Reap tend to be inflated by the presence of a large expat population, but in local markets and Khmer restaurants prices are low.

Rock-bottom travellers can probably manage Phnom Penh on around US$10 a day. It is generally possible to eat fairly well for US$2 to US$3, much less if you eat local dishes from street stalls and markets.

Visitors to Angkor will have to factor in the cost of entrance fees, which are US$20 for one day, US$40 for three days and US$60 for one week. An additional expense out at Angkor is the government ruling against travellers visiting the ruins without a guide. A guide with a motorbike will cost a minimum of US$6 per day.

Tipping & Bargaining

Tipping is not expected in Cambodia, but as is the case anywhere if you meet with exceptional service or out-of-the-way kindness a tip is always greatly appreciated. Salaries remain extremely low in Cambodia.

Bargaining is the rule in markets, when hiring vehicles and sometimes even when taking a room. The Khmers are not ruthless hagglers. A smile goes a long way.

POST & COMMUNICATIONS

Post is routed by air through Bangkok, which makes Cambodia's postal services much more reliable than they once were. Telephone connections with the outside world have also improved immensely, though they are not cheap.

Postal Rates

Postal rates are listed in the Phnom Penh main post office. Postcards cost 1400r to 1900r internationally. A 10g air mail letter to anywhere in the world costs 1800r to 2300r, while a 100g letter costs 6760r to anywhere in Asia, 7700r to Australia and Europe, and 9800r to the USA.

Parcel rates are 23,800r for 500g within Asia, 29,000r to Australia and Europe, and 39,500r to the USA. There is a 7000r fee for registered mail, but for larger items it is worth it.

Letters and parcels sent farther afield than Asia can take up to two or three weeks to reach their destination.

Receiving Mail

The Phnom Penh main post office has a poste restante box at the far-left-hand end of the post counter. Basically anybody can pick up your mail, so it is not a good idea to have anything valuable sent here.

Telephone

Many hotels and guesthouses in Phnom Penh will allow you to make local calls free of charge. International calls can be made from

Telephone Codes

The country code for Cambodia is 855. The international dialling code is 00. Following are area codes for some cities. You must dial the zero when calling from within Myanmar. Numbers starting with 012, 015, 017 and 018 are mobile phone numbers.

Battambang	☎ 053
Kampong Cham	☎ 042
Kampot	☎ 033
Mondolkiri	☎ 075
Phnom Penh	☎ 023
Ratanakiri	☎ 075
Siem Reap	☎ 063
Sihanoukville	☎ 034

the public phone-card booths, which are available in Phnom Penh, Siem Reap, Battambang and some provincial towns.

Phone cards are available in denominations of US$2 to US$100. International phone rates are expensive, with most calls working out at a minimum of US$3 a minute. Post offices offer a discount of 20% on Saturday and Sunday. Telephoning from Battambang is cheaper as the Interphone offices route calls via Thailand.

Fax

If possible, save your faxes for somewhere else. They cost at least US$6 a page in Cambodia.

Email & Internet Access

Internet access is available in Phnom Penh – see that section for details. Siem Reap was due to be connected in late 1998, but rates are bound to be exorbitant as it will require a long-distance call to the capital.

Business centres in Phnom Penh and Siem Reap offer monthly email accounts with unlimited use for about US$20 to US$30. This is good value if you are intending to stay in Phnom Penh for a long period.

INTERNET RESOURCES

The Internet Travel Guide (www.datacomm. ch/pmgeiser/cambodia) provides a good introduction to Cambodia for travellers. The Cambodian Information Center (www.cambodia. org) lives up to its name with a comprehensive list of sites relating to Cambodia. Stephen Wallace has some great snaps in his Cambodia portfolio (www.wirephoto.com/swallace/ cambodia/cmbd.html). Beauty and Darkness: Cambodia in Modern History (members.aol. com/cambodia/index.htm) con-centrates on the Khmer Rouge period.

BOOKS

All the books listed are available in Bangkok, the majority can be found cheaply in Cambodia's markets and a few might turn up in Ho Chi Minh City (Saigon).

Lonely Planet

For more information about travelling in Cambodia look for Lonely Planet's *Cambodia*.

Guidebooks

Another interesting guidebook and travel diary is *The Cambodia Less Travelled* by Ray Zepp, which chronicles the author's journeys to remote parts of the country. It is getting hard to find, but be sure to seek out a copy if heading out to the provinces.

Travellers heading for Angkor might want to pick up a copy of *Angkor – An Introduction to the Temples* by Dawn Rooney. Also recommended is the pocket-size *Angkor – Heart of an Empire* by Bruno Dagens.

Travel

The classic travel book is Norman Lewis' *A Dragon Apparent*, available in the Norman Lewis Omnibus, a collection of three books recounting Lewis' travels in Asia. A more recent account of travels in Cambodia is *Gecko Tails* by Carol Livingstone, which deftly covers her time in the country during and after the United Nations Transitional Authority in Cambodia (UNTAC) period.

History & Politics

The best widely available history of Cambodia is David P Chandler's *A History of Cambodia*. It is available in Cambodia and Bangkok.

Those wanting to understand the horrors of the 1970s should look out for Ben Kiernan's *How Pol Pot Came to Power* and *The Pol Pot Regime*; David Chandler's biography of Pol Pot, *Brother Number One*; Nayan Chanda's *Brother Enemy*, an incredible insight into how Cambodia and Vietnam descended into war with a little help from their 'friends'; and *Cambodia Year Zero*, a chillingly accurate second-hand account of events between 1975 and 1977, by François Ponchaud.

Jon Swain's *River of Time* and Tim Page's *Derailed in Uncle Ho's Victory Garden* take the reader back to an old Indochina and the madness of war. Finally, Christopher J Koch's *Highways to a War* is a powerful fictional insight into life as a correspondent during the civil war.

NEWSPAPERS & MAGAZINES

The *Cambodia Daily* is available from Monday to Saturday. It costs just 1000r. The *Cambodge Soir* is a French paper that comes out twice weekly.

The *Phnom Penh Post* is a newspaper published every two weeks that provides a very good overview of events in Cambodia. It also has a lift-out map of Phnom Penh with restaurants and business services, all for 2500r.

For the lighter side of life in Cambodia, the free monthly *Bayon Pearnik* combines humorous stories with human interest features from around the country and is a refreshing counterbalance to the darker subjects dealt with by the mainstream press. The *Bayon Pearnik* team are also known for hosting regular parties so look out for posters in guesthouses.

The *Bangkok Post* and *The Nation* are Thai English-language dailies widely available in Phnom Penh, usually by mid-afternoon on the day of publication. *The Economist, Far Eastern Economic Review, Asia Week, Time, Newsweek* and others are readily obtained at bookshops around Phnom Penh.

RADIO & TV

The BBC has broadcasts in Khmer and English on 100MHz FM in the capital. There are also several nascent tourist stations floating on the airwaves around 98 and 99MHz FM.

Most of the mid-range hotels in Phnom Penh have satellite TV, which means that you should have access to the BBC, CNN, Star TV, Channel V (the regional answer to MTV) and Cartoon Network. Otherwise you are restricted to Channel 2 (which is French).

PHOTOGRAPHY

Film and processing are cheap in Cambodia. A roll of 36 Kodacolor Gold 100 or Fujicolor Superia 200 costs about US$2.50. Konika film is even cheaper. The cheapest places for fast printing are the Konika photolabs, which can be found all over Cambodia. Shops generally charge US$4 for 36 standard prints.

Decent cheap slide film is widely available in Phnom Penh. Fuji's Velvia and Provia ranges are US$6 for 36. Sensia and Kodak's Elite are cheaper at US$5 for 36. The variety is similar in Siem Reap, but elsewhere in the provinces you are unlikely to find anything but print so come prepared.

Black-and-white film is also available in Phnom Penh at about US$2.50. Monivong Blvd is the best place for photo supplies. Many labs offer instant passport photos for US$3 to US$4.

ELECTRICITY
Voltages & Cycles

Electricity in Phnom Penh and most of the rest of Cambodia is 220V, 50Hz. Power is in short supply, however, and power cuts are frequent. Most guesthouses, hotels and restaurants have their own generators.

Plugs & Sockets

Electric power sockets are generally of the round two-pin variety. Three-pin plug adaptors can be bought at the markets in Phnom Penh.

WEIGHTS & MEASURES

Cambodia uses the metric system. For those unaccustomed to this system, there is a metric/imperial conversion chart inside the back cover of this book.

LAUNDRY

Laundry is never a problem in Cambodia. All guesthouses and hotels in the country provide a laundry service and it is either free or very reasonable.

TOILETS

Public toilets are pretty scarce in Cambodia, although there are a few in and around the temples of Angkor. The best bets for relief are hotels and restaurants, which usually have western style facilities. *Never* wander off the sides of rural roads in search of privacy as there is always the very real danger of landmines.

HEALTH

Malaria exists year-round throughout the whole country except Phnom Penh. There have been recent large outbreaks of dengue fever. You should take appropriate precautions against both these serious diseases. Schistosomiasis (bilharzia) occurs in the Mekong Delta, so you should avoid swimming or paddling here. Food and water-borne diseases, including dysentery, hepatitis and liver flukes, occur, so it's worth paying particular attention to basic food and water hygiene.

Note that although liver flukes are usually contracted through the eating of raw fish, you can also get them by swimming in the southern reaches of the Mekong River. For more information on these and other health matters, refer to the Health section in the Appendix.

Medical services are poor for the most part. In the event of a medical emergency, you will probably need to get to Bangkok. At the very least, it will be necessary to get to Phnom Penh.

See the Phnom Penh section for details of medical facilities in the city.

WOMEN TRAVELLERS
Attitudes Towards Women
As far as Cambodia can be described as safe, women will generally find the country to be a hassle-free place in which to travel. Foreign women are unlikely to be particularly targeted by the attentions of local men, but at the same time it pays to be careful.

Khmer women dress fairly conservatively, and it's best to follow suit, particularly when visiting wats. In general, long-sleeved shirts and long trousers or skirts are preferred.

GAY & LESBIAN TRAVELLERS
While Cambodian culture is tolerant of homosexuality, the scene is nothing like that of neighbouring Thailand. Public displays of petting, whether heterosexual or homosexual, are frowned on.

DISABLED TRAVELLERS
Depending on your disability, Cambodia is not going to be an easy country in which to travel. Local labour at least is inexpensive, which means that you can hire a guide for around US$10 a day or less. But on the whole it will probably be difficult: the roads are bad, many hotels are without lifts and touring the country's major attraction, Angkor, would be near impossible. Travellers with major disabilities would be advised to look into taking a tour.

SENIOR TRAVELLERS
Senior travellers will not be eligible for anything in the way of discounts in Cambodia – all foreigners are rich as far as Cambodians are concerned.

TRAVEL WITH CHILDREN
Travellers visiting Cambodia with children can pick up a copy of Lonely Planet's *Travel with Children*. If you are just planning a visit to Angkor and Phnom Penh, there should be no problems. More adventurous travel in Cambodia with children is not recommended.

USEFUL ORGANISATIONS
Cambodia hosts a huge number of NGOs. The best way to find out who exactly is represented in Cambodia is to call in to the Cooperation Committee for Cambodia (CCC) (☎ 426009), at 35 178 St, Phnom Penh. This organisation has a handy list of all NGOs, both Cambodian and international.

DANGERS & ANNOYANCES
Security
Sadly, civil strife drags on in Cambodia. In the last few years several foreign visitors have been killed. The Khmer Rouge may be almost finished, but bandits and even elements of the military and police can be a threat to your safety. However, much of Cambodia is not as dangerous as the international media would have you believe, reporting only the bad news. The *Bangkok Post* is a good source of coverage to catch up on the latest stories before entering the country; better still is the Phnom Penh Post Web site (www.newspapers.com.kh/PhnomPenhPost).

Always make a point of checking on the latest security situation before making a trip that you know not many travellers undertake, particularly if using a motorcycle. Moreover, do not rely only on information provided by local people – they often undertake dangerous trips as a matter of necessity and have no way of assessing the risks for a foreigner. Talk to other travellers and NGOs for a more balanced assessment. Embassies are not a great source of information as they tend to be over-cautious. Road conditions change from week to week so the importance of checking the current situation cannot be overstated.

Mines, Mortars & Bombs
Never, ever touch any rockets, artillery shells, mortars, mines, bombs or other war material you may come across. In Vietnam most of it is at least 20 years old, but in Cambodia it may have landed there or been laid quite recently. Cambodia is one of the most heavily mined countries in the world and although exact numbers are unknown it is estimated that there are between four to six million of these enemies within littering the countryside. In short: *do not* stray from well marked paths under any circumstances, even around the monuments of Angkor. If travelling by taxi or motorbike in remote areas do not step off the road, even for nature's calling.

Mine clearing organisations are working throughout the country to clear these arbitrary killers, but even with their crucial presence, the most common way a landmine is discovered is by a man, woman or child losing a limb.

Snakes
Visitors to Angkor and other overgrown archaeological sites should beware of snakes, including the small but deadly light-green hanuman snake that hunts after rainstorms.

Theft & Street Crime

Given the number of guns about in Cambodia, there is less armed theft than you might suppose. Still, motorcycle theft is a problem in Phnom Penh. There is no need to be overly paranoid, just cautious. Driving your own motorbike late at night is not a good idea and even on *motos* it is better to stay in pairs in the early hours.

Pickpocketing and theft by stealth is more of a problem in Vietnam and Thailand than it is in Cambodia. Again, though, it pays to be careful. Don't make the job of potential thieves any easier by putting your passport and wads of cash in your back pocket.

Begging

Cambodia is an extremely poor country and begging is prevalent in Phnom Penh and Siem Reap. The riverfront area in the capital is a particular magnet, as is the Central Market. Many visitors become numb to the pleas after a couple of weeks, but it is worth remembering that amputee soldiers have lost limbs trying to make Cambodia a safer country and then been kicked out of the army as they are no longer able to fight. In a country with poor employment opportunities, civilian amputees may find it hard to earn money other than by begging.

LEGAL MATTERS

Contrary to popular belief, marijuana is not legal in Cambodia. It's probably only a matter of time before the Cambodian police turn busting foreigners into a lucrative sideline. However, for the time being it remains dirt cheap and readily available all over the country and it is sometimes used as a mild flavouring in Khmer cooking.

Moral grounds alone should be enough to deter foreigners from seeking underage sexual partners in Cambodia. Paedophiles are treated as criminals by the authorities and several have served or are serving jail sentences as a result. Many western countries have also enacted much-needed legislation to make offences committed overseas punishable at home.

BUSINESS HOURS

Government offices, which are open Monday to Saturday, theoretically begin the working day at 7 or 7.30 am, breaking for a siesta from 11 or 11.30 am to 2 or 2.30 pm and ending the day at 5.30 pm. However, it is a safe bet that few people will be around early in the morning or much after 4 pm, and some will not turn up at all as their real income is earned elsewhere.

Banking hours tend to vary according to the bank, but you can reckon on core hours of 8.30 am to 3 pm. The Foreign Trade Bank in Phnom Penh is open from 7.30 am to 3.30 pm Monday to Friday.

PUBLIC HOLIDAYS & SPECIAL EVENTS

The festivals of Cambodia take place according to the lunar calendar, so the dates vary from year to year.

New Year (Chinese)
 The Chinese community in Cambodia celebrates the new year in late January or early to mid-February. For the Vietnamese, this is called Tet.
New Year (Khmer)
 Called Chaul Chnam, this is held in mid-April. It's a three day celebration, with Khmers making new year offerings at wats, cleaning out their homes, and exchanging gifts of new clothes.
International Workers Day
 1 May.
Chat Preah Nengkal
 Held in mid to late May, this is the Royal Ploughing ceremony, a ritual agricultural festival led by the royal family.
P'chum Ben
 Held in late September, this is a kind of All Souls' Day, when respects are paid to the dead through offerings made at wats.
HM the King's Birthday
 30 October to 1 November.
Bon Om Tuk
 Held in early November, this celebrates the reversal of the current of the Tonlé Sap River (see Facts about Cambodia, Geography).
Independence Day
 9 November.

ACTIVITIES

Tourism in Cambodia is still in its infancy and as yet there is little in the way of activities besides sightseeing. Snorkelling and diving are availablie in Sihanoukville. Boat trips on rivers and around coastal areas can usually be arranged with local boat owners keen to make some money. Elephant rides can be organised in Ratanakiri and Mondolkiri.

WORK

Jobs are available in Phnom Penh and elsewhere around Cambodia. The obvious choice is English or French teaching. There is a lot of English teaching available and experience isn't always required. Another option is volunteer work with one of the many NGOs. For information about work opportunities with the NGOs call into the CCC (see Useful Organisations above), which has a noticeboard for positions vacant and may also be able to give advice on where to look.

Other places to look for work include the classifieds sections of the *Phnom Penh Post* and the *Cambodia Daily*. The Foreign Correspondents' Club of Cambodia in Phnom Penh has a noticeboard with job postings.

Do not expect to make a lot of money working in Cambodia unless you secure a staff job with an international organisation. But if you want to learn more about the country and help the locals to get the place up and running again, it may well be a worthwhile experience.

ACCOMMODATION

There is a reasonably wide range of accommodation options in Phnom Penh and Siem Reap. Elsewhere, options are more limited.

Budget hostels exist only in Phnom Penh, Siem Reap and Sihanoukville. Costs hover around US$3 for a bed. In other parts of Cambodia the standard rate for the cheapest hotels is US$5, but facilities are often good, particularly in Battambang.

In Phnom Penh and Siem Reap, which see a steady flow of tourist traffic, hotels start to improve significantly once you start spending more than US$10. For US$15 or less it is usually possible to find an air-con room with satellite TV, fridge and attached bathroom.

FOOD

Cambodian food is closely related to the cuisines of neighbouring Thailand and Laos and, to a lesser extent, Vietnam, but there are some distinct local dishes. The overall consensus is that Khmer cooking is like Thai without the spices.

Phnom Penh is far and away the best place to try inexpensive Khmer cuisine, though Siem Reap also has some good restaurants. One of the easiest and most affordable ways to acquaint yourself with Khmer cooking is to wander into the food stalls found in markets all over the country and simply sample each dish before deciding what to eat. In Phnom Penh you also have the choice of excellent Thai, Vietnamese, Chinese, French and Mediterranean cooking.

Rice is the principal staple in Cambodia and the Battambang region is the country's rice bowl. Most Cambodian dishes are cooked in a wok, known locally as a *chhnang khteak*.

See the Language section at the back of the book for food vocabulary.

DRINKS
Nonalcoholic Drinks

All the famous international brands of soft drinks are available in Cambodia. Locally produced mineral water is available at 500r to 700r per bottle.

Coffee is sold in most restaurants. It is either served black or with generous dollops of condensed milk, which makes it very sweet. Chinese-style tea is popular and in many Khmer and Chinese restaurants a pot of it will automatically appear as soon as you sit down.

You can find excellent fruit smoothies all over the country, known locally as *tikalok*. Just look out for a stall with fruit and a blender and point to the flavours you want. Keep an eye on the preparatory stages or you may end up with heaps of sugar and a frothy egg.

On a hot day you may be tempted by the stuff in Fanta bottles on the side of the road. Think again, as it is actually petrol (gas).

Alcoholic Drinks

The local beer is Angkor, which is produced by an Australian joint venture in Sihanoukville. Other brands include Heineken, Tiger, San Miguel, Carlsberg, VB, Foster's and Grolsch. Beer sells for around US$1 to US$1.50 a can in restaurants.

In Phnom Penh, foreign wines and spirits are sold at reasonable prices. The local spirits are best avoided, though some expats say that Sra Special, a local whisky-like concoction, is not bad. At around 1000r a bottle it's a cheap route to oblivion.

ENTERTAINMENT
Cinemas

Cambodian cinemas are best avoided. Even if you can understand the proceedings, they tend to be scruffy, hot and sometimes dangerously overcrowded. There are a few exceptions in Phnom Penh – see cinemas in that section for details.

Nightclubs

Phnom Penh is the place for disco nightlife. There are several clubs that see a good mix of locals and expats. Nightlife in Phnom Penh tends to begin fairly late – an 11 pm start is usual, after a leisurely meal and some drinks at a bar. Drink prices can be steep, but you can always pop outside and get a swift half from a street seller.

Outside Phnom Penh, nightlife is dominated by Khmer nightclubs. These are basically 'hostess clubs' aimed at men, but it is no problem for foreign women to enter. They have a live band and are a good place to learn a bit about Khmer dancing.

Traditional Dance

Public performances of Khmer traditional dance are few and far between. Phnom Penh and Siem Reap are the places to find them. Check the local English-language newspapers for news of upcoming events.

Pubs & Bars

Again, Phnom Penh is the best place for pubs and bars. Elsewhere around Cambodia, drinking takes place at street stalls, in restaurants and in nightclubs.

SPECTATOR SPORTS

Sports events are held from time to time at the Olympic Stadium in Phnom Penh, particularly weekend football (soccer) matches now the Marlboro League is up and running. Thai boxing is popular in Cambodia. Check the local English-language newspapers for news of events at the stadium. Mild Seven organises monthly dirt bike races in cities around the country.

SHOPPING

The checked cotton scarves everyone wears on their heads, around their necks or, if bathing, around their midriffs are known as *kramas*. Fancier coloured versions are made of silk or a silk-cotton blend. Some of the finest cotton kramas come from the Kompong Cham area.

For information on where in Phnom Penh to find antiques, silver items, jewellery, gems, colourful cloth for sarongs and *hols* (variegated silk shirts), woodcarvings, papier-mâché masks, stone copies of ancient Khmer art, brass figurines and oil paintings, see Shopping in the Phnom Penh section.

Also see the Phnom Penh section for information on buying craft items produced by Cambodian mine victims, and disabled and women's groups. The proceeds go to good causes, and the products are good quality.

Getting There & Away

AIR

Cambodia is connected only by air to most other South-East Asian countries.

When buying tickets in Phnom Penh it is worth shopping around travel agents in the vicinity of the Central Market as they often have discounts on published fares. Prices listed here are those quoted in Phnom Penh.

Departure Tax

There is a hefty departure tax of US$20 on all international flights out of Cambodia.

Thailand

Flights between Phnom Penh and Bangkok are available daily with Thai Airways International, Royal Air Cambodge (RAC) and Bangkok Airways, and, somewhat infrequently, Kampuchea Airlines. Flights are cheaper in Bangkok than Phnom Penh.

Kampuchea Airlines is the cheapest, but it has an erratic reliability record, and their schedule is constantly shrinking. Fares are US$80/99 one way/return. RAC charges US$120/220 one way/return and Thai Airways flights are US$140/280. Bangkok Airways also flies daily to Siem Reap. Phnom Penh flights are US$142/284 one way/return and those from Siem Reap US$155/310.

Hong Kong

Dragonair flies between Hong Kong and Phnom Penh. It costs US$377/722 one way/return. Definitely buy the ticket through a travel agent as they can save considerable money on this absurd price. Kampuchea Airlines has flights for US$250/373 one way/return.

Laos

Flights between Vientiane and Phnom Penh cost US$125/250 one way/return with Lao Aviation. RAC also offers a Vientiane service at the same price. See also the Air entry in the main Getting There & Away section of the Laos chapter.

Singapore

Silk Air and RAC have flights from Singapore to Phnom Penh. RAC tickets cost about US$250/360 one way/return, while Silk Air flights are about US$260/440. Kampuchea Airlines is a cheaper option at US$145/168 one way/return.

Malaysia

Flights between Kuala Lumpur and Phnom Penh are available with Malaysia Airlines and RAC. RAC charges US$190/330 one way/return and with Malaysia Airlines it is US$195/322.

Vietnam

Vietnam Airlines does the short hop from Ho Chi Minh City (Saigon) to Phnom Penh for US$70/120 one way/return; RAC charges US$65/130.

There are no direct flights to Hanoi, but tickets routed via Ho Chi Minh City cost US$175/350 one way/return.

LAND
Border Crossings
Thailand

Poipet The land border between Cambodia and Thailand at Poipet was opened to foreigners in February 1998. A steady number of travellers has come and gone this way since, and the roads from the crossing to either Siem Reap or Battambang were considered safe at the time of writing, but in terrible condition.

To enter here you need to obtain a Cambodian visa from Bangkok. Sometimes the border may be closed for a short time if the Thai authorities wish to return Khmer refugees to Cambodia. Check the current situation before heading to the border. There is no departure tax by land, but guards may ask for a US dollar. From Poipet you can travel by road to Sisophon and on to either Siem Reap or Battambang. For details on roads and prices, see the Siem Reap, Battambang and Sisophon sections.

It is worth noting that the road between Sisophon and Siem Reap can become impassable at times during the wet season.

After crossing the border at Poipet, you must take a tuk-tuk or pick-up (4B) to Aranya Prathet, from where there are two trains a day to and from Bangkok and buses every two hours. See the Thailand chapter for more details.

Coastal Border The coastal border between Krong Koh Kong and Trat Province in Thailand is officially open. Fast boats between Koh Kong and Sihanoukville costing 500B leave Sihanoukville at 10.30 am and 12.30 pm, although the earlier one may not leave unless full. The boat leaves Koh Kong at 8 am. It takes about 3½ hours.

When entering Cambodia, it is best to take a share taxi (100B per vehicle) or moto (50B) from the Thai border post Hat Lek to Koh Kong and pick up the fast boat to Sihanoukville from its point of origin.

When leaving Cambodia, jump off the boat at the commune of Pak Long, just before Koh Kong, and you can take a small speedboat (30 minutes) to Hat Lek for about 100B. Friendly immigration police usually suggest this as passports are also checked at Pak Long. This is faster and easier than continuing right into Koh Kong.

From the Thai side there are regular 20B pick-ups to Klong Yai, from where you can take a 60B per person share taxi to Trat. Bear in mind buses leave regularly until 6 pm and then break until 11 pm. Move fast unless you don't mind hanging around in Trat.

Vietnam

The only fully functioning land crossing between Vietnam and Cambodia is at Moc Bai in Vietnam. The trip by taxi between Phnom Penh and Ho Chi Minh City (Saigon) should only take six to seven hours. Buses run daily except Sunday between Phnom Penh and Ho Chi Minh City (Saigon) via the Moc Bai border checkpoint. The air-con bus costs US$12, the bus without air-con is US$5, but expect to be delayed at the border for a couple of hours while locals are shaken down.

You must have Moc Bai stamped on your Vietnam visa or you will not be allowed to enter the country, even if you plead. See Getting There & Away in the Phnom Penh section for details.

Laos

The land border with Laos is not currently open to westerners as the Lao authorities are paranoid about security in Cambodia. However, if security improves between Kratie and Stung Treng and with Visit Laos Year planned for 1999, it could open during the lifetime of this book. Check the situation in Phnom Penh.

Getting Around

AIR

Domestic Air Services

Royal Air Cambodge has flights to destinations around Cambodia. Angkor is well serviced and it is usually possible to get on a flight at short notice. But demand for flights to other destinations around the country can often exceed supply.

There are several flights a day from Phnom Penh to Siem Reap (Angkor); the cost is US$55/110 one way/return. For Battambang, there are six flights a week, US$45/90 one way/return. Flights to Ratanakiri are scheduled five times a week, US$55/100.

Other destinations are: Koh Kong, three times a week, for US$50/100; Stung Treng, three times a week, US$45/90; and Mondolkiri, twice a week, US$50/100. There are no flights to Sihanoukville, but buses are safe and comfortable.

Domestic Departure Tax

The airport tax for domestic flights is an outrageous US$10 from Phnom Penh and a more acceptable US$4 elsewhere.

BUS

Bus services in Cambodia are improving fast. Three companies offer fast, comfortable air-con services between Phnom Penh and Sihanoukville. There are also a number of routes out of the capital to towns such as Kompong Chhnang, Udong and Takeo on small air-con buses.

TRAIN

Cambodia's rail network is open to foreigners, but it is really not worth considering unless you are a serious trainspotter or a total miser. Trains are tediously slow, uncomfortable and often overcrowded, but they are extremely cheap at 15r per kilometre. Mechanical problems can mean an unscheduled overnight stop somewhere and bridges are not always maintained, as proven by the collapse of the one in Kampot in early 1998. Trains are easy prey for bandits as they can run along next to them.

CAR & MOTORCYCLE

Car hire is not available in Cambodia. However, a number of travel agencies can arrange a car and driver for anything between US$25 and US$50 a day depending on the destination. Share taxis can also be chartered for a negotiable fee.

Motorcycles are available for rent in Phnom Penh and Sihanoukville, but not in Siem Reap as it is forbidden for foreigners to ride motorcycles without a driver. Costs are US$4 per day for 50cc to 100cc motorcycles and US$7 for a 250cc dirt bike. Drive cautiously as medical facilities are less than adequate in Cambodia and drivers are erratic.

A motorbike is great for visiting out-of-town attractions in the Phnom Penh area. It is possible to take motorcycles upcountry for short tours, but it is inadvisable to try to bike to Siem Reap, Battambang and the north-east as road conditions are dire and security more of an issue because of journey times.

Cambodia is more dangerous than Thailand or Vietnam. Here are a few basic tips:

- Check road security extra carefully.
- Travel in numbers for safety.
- When in a group, stay close together in case of any incident.
- Don't scrimp on petrol (gas), as running out could jeopardise your safety if you get stranded overnight.
- Don't try riding like Evil Knevil after smoking marijuana.

BOAT

Passenger boat services ply the Mekong as far north as Stung Treng, but the most popular services with foreigners are those that run on the Tonlé Sap between Phnom Penh and Siem Reap. The new express services do the trip in as little as four hours in the wet season.

There are also fast boats to Kompong Cham and Kratie. Some travellers also use the fast boat between Sihanoukville and Koh Kong (see Getting There & Away under Border Crossings).

TAXI, PICK-UP & MINIBUS

Long-distance pick-ups take on the dreadful roads for long journeys up to Siem Reap and Battambang. You can sit in the cab or, if you are feeling bold, on the back, and they leave when seriously full. It is best to arrange these yourself as it is cheaper than going through a guesthouse. You often have to haggle patiently to ensure you pay a fair price.

Share taxis are widely available for hire in Cambodia and many travellers use them to get to Vietnam. For major destinations you can either hire them individually or pay for a seat and wait for other passengers to turn up.

When using pick-ups or taxis it is an advantage to travel in numbers as you can buy spare seats to make the journey more comfortable.

Minibuses cover similar routes, but tend to be chartered by Khmer families for outings. As a basic rule, pick-ups are best for bad roads, taxis are best for sealed roads and mini-buses are best if you want a little more space.

LOCAL TRANSPORT
Bus
The only real local bus services running in Cambodia are those in Phnom Penh, but most people use motos or cyclos as buses run on limited fixed routes.

Taxi
The taxi situation has been steadily improving in Cambodia over the last few years. Whereas taxi hire was once available only through government ministries, there are now many private operators working throughout Cambodia. Even in Phnom Penh, however, you'll be hard pressed to find a taxi for short hops, unless leaving popular nightspots late at night.

Fares average about US$0.50 per kilometre for local journeys.

Moto (Motorcycle Taxi)
Motos are a quick way of making short hops around towns and cities. Prices range from 500r to US$1, depending on the distance and town. Most journeys are about 1000r, but you should expect to pay an extra 500r or so late at night.

Moto drivers assume you know the cost of a trip and prices are rarely agreed before starting. Be careful not to put your leg near the exhaust pipe after long journeys as you will get a nasty burn which can take some time to heal in the sticky weather.

Moto drivers almost universally wear baseball caps.

Cyclo
As in Vietnam and Laos, the *samlor*, or cyclo, is a cheap way to get around Cambodia's urban areas. In Phnom Penh, cyclo drivers can either be flagged down on main thoroughfares or found hanging out around marketplaces and major hotels. It is a slower,

more relaxing way to see the sights, but for everyday journeys the cyclo is fast being pushed out of business by the moto.

Cyclo fares can vary wildly depending on your negotiating skills, but aim to pay moto prices.

Remorque-Kang & Remorque-Moto
The *remorque-kang* is a trailer pulled by a bicycle. A trailer hitched to a motorbike is called a *remorque-moto*. Both are used to transport people and goods and are commonplace in rural areas. They are not seen so much nowadays in urban Cambodia.

Phnom Penh

Phnom Penh, capital of Cambodia for much of the period since the mid-15th century (when Angkor was abandoned), is situated at the confluence of the Mekong, the Bassac and the Tonlé Sap rivers. Once considered the loveliest of the French-built cities of Indochina, Phnom Penh's charm – although still evident in many parts – is fast succumbing to a construction boom.

Orientation
The Tonlé Sap and Bassac rivers define the eastern extent of town. The centre of town is roughly the area around the Psar Thmei (New Market, more commonly known as the Central Market).

The major thoroughfares in Phnom Penh run north-south. They are Monivong Blvd (the main commercial drag), Norodom Blvd (mainly administrative) and Samdech Sothearos Blvd (in front of the Royal Palace). The main east-west arteries are Pochentong Blvd in the north, Preah Sihanouk Blvd, which runs past the Independence Monument, and Mao Tse Toung Blvd, in the far south of town.

Besides the main boulevards are hundreds of numbered streets. In most cases, odd-numbered streets run more or less north-south (usually parallel to Monivong Blvd), with the numbers rising as you move from east to west. Even-numbered streets run in an east-west direction and their numbers rise as you move from north to south.

Maps One of the best maps is a 3D one produced by Point Maps & Guides, which also produces an annual guide useful for business travellers. Local maps of Phnom Penh, touted around the restaurants by children, are generally poor. The *Phnom Penh Post* and *Bayon Pearnik* include maps with regularly updated listings.

The *Cambodia Travel Map* published by Periplus is available at bookshops and includes a large fold-out map of Phnom Penh at a scale of 1:17,000.

Information

Tourist Offices The head office of Phnom Penh Tourism is across from Wat Ounalom at the intersection of Samdech Sothearos Blvd and Sisowath Quay. The office is officially open from 7 to 11.30 am and from 2 to 5.30 pm. It's a sleepy place with little in the way of useful information.

The Ministry of Tourism (MOT) (☎ 426876) is in a white, two storey building on the western corner of Monivong Blvd and 232 St. Inside, chaos prevails.

Money The best bank for changing money and obtaining credit card advances is the Cambodian Commercial Bank (CCB), on the corner of Pochentong St and Monivong Blvd. It takes most travellers cheques and can also organise credit card advances for MasterCard, JCB and Visa.

There is a minimum charge of US$10 for transactions of under US$500 and 2% thereafter. A limit of US$2000 is imposed on cash advances. The Foreign Trade Bank on Norodom Blvd charges a flat 4%, which is better value on transactions of less than US$250. Most other banks around town charge US$10 plus commission!

Most banks change travellers cheques for 2% and cash for free.

Post The main post office is just east of Wat Phnom on 13 St. It is open from 7 am to 7 pm daily; it offers postal services as well as domestic and international telephone, fax and telegraph links. International calls are 20% cheaper at weekends.

There is a smaller post office – more convenient to some of the guesthouses and hotels – on the corner of Monivong and Preah Sihanouk Blvds.

Telephone The easiest way to dial locally or internationally is from the Camintel and Telstra phone-card booths that are scattered around town. Phone cards are available at numerous outlets; just look for the little signs on shops. Long-distance international calls work

out at a little over US$3 per minute on average. It's cheaper to call from the post office at weekends.

Fax Apart from the main post office, many of the mid-range hotels and all of the top-end hotels around town have fax services. Sending faxes from Phnom Penh is at least US$6 a page, and it generally costs money to receive them too. The Foreign Correspondents' Club on Sisowath Quay has a business centre where faxes can be sent and received.

Email & Internet Access Monthly email accounts can be arranged with business centres for about US$20 to US$30 and include unlimited usage. Note that this is not an Internet-based service so does not allow you to check Hotmail or Yahoo, but it saves you the US$8-US$10 charge per hour for accessing Internet email.

Internet access is available at the Public Internet Centre, 5 53 St, near the Central Market, for US$10 per hour. Page printing is only 200r so you can arrange takeaways. The Foreign Correspondents' Club on Sisowath Quay offers access at a similar price.

Travel Agencies The area near the Central Market on Monivong Blvd has a few budget travel agencies, including Pich Tourist (☎ 246585), which is above Monument Books.

One of the most reliable outfits in town is Diethelm Travel (☎ 219151), at 65 240 St. Diethelm also has offices in Siem Reap, Bangkok, Ho Chi Minh City (Saigon) and Vientiane, making it a good agency to book regional flights and tours.

Another popular agency is East West Travel (☎ 427118), at 182A 208 St. Transpeed Travel (☎ 427366), at 19 106 St in the same building as Thai Airways, is a convenient option for flight bookings.

Bookshops The best range of books in town is found in Monument Books at 155 Monivong Blvd. This place has almost everything ever published on Cambodia and much on other countries in the region, but prices are quite high.

For books and magazines, the bookshops in the Cambodiana and Le Royal hotels are up to date, although more expensive still. All of the above have a good selection of French newspapers and magazines, and all the international English-language weeklies.

CAMBODIA

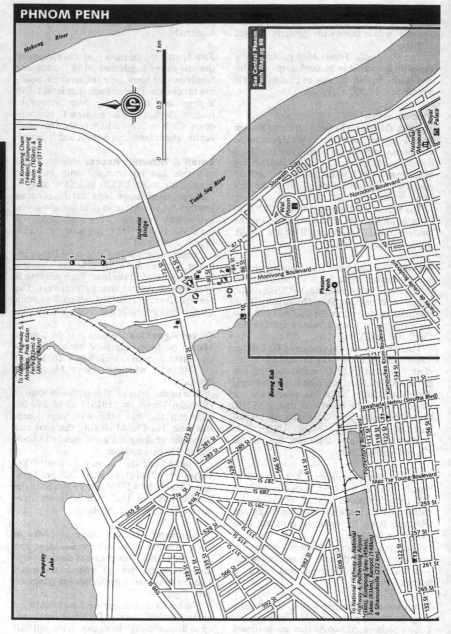

PHNOM PENH

Mekong River

1 km

0.5

See Central Phnom
Penh Map pg 88

To Kompong Cham
(144km), Kompong
Thom (165km) &
Siem Reap (311km)

Tonlé Sap River

Japanese
Bridge

Sisowath Quay

Norodom Boulevard

Wat
Phnom

National
Museum

Royal
Palace

To National Highway 5,
Mosques, Prek Kdam
Ferry (31km) &
Udong (40km)

171 St

70 St

Monivong Boulevard

Phnom
Penh

Charles de Gaulle Boulevard

Boeng Kak
Lake

Kampuchea Krom Boulevard

134 St

211 St

Jawaharlal Nehru (Sivutha Blvd)

156 St

Pochentong Boulevard

112 St

118 St

122 St

Mao Tse Toung Boulevard

253 St

257 St

122 St

261 St

265 St

132 St

273 St

281 St

283 St

285 St

528 St

595 St

614 St

287 St

515 St

514 St

516 St

289 St

291 St

313 St

315 St

317 St

608 St

592 St

253 St

355 St

528 St

337 St

339 St

335 St

996 St

598 St

595 St

Pumpeay
Lake

To National Highway 3, National
Highway 4, Pochentong Airport
(7km), Pochentong (Red River),
Takeo (83km), Kampot (148km)
& Shanoukville (232 km)

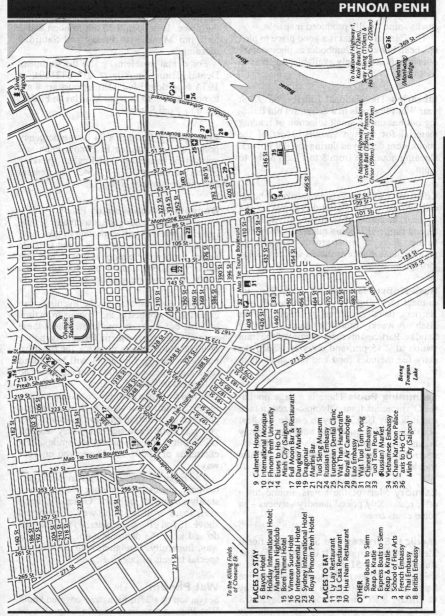

PHNOM PENH

PLACES TO STAY
6 Bayon Hotel
7 Holiday International Hotel;
   Manhattan Nightclub
15 Borei Thmei Hotel
16 Vimean Suor Hotel
20 Intercontinental Hotel
23 Sydney International Hotel
26 Royal Phnom Penh Hotel

PLACES TO EAT
11 Ly Lay Restaurant
13 La Casa Restaurant
30 Hua Nam Restaurant

OTHER
1 Slow Boats to Siem
   Reap & Kratie
2 Express Boats to Siem
   Reap & Kratie
3 School of Fine Arts
4 French Embassy
5 Thai Embassy
8 British Embassy
9 Calmette Hospital
10 International Mosque
12 Phnom Penh University
14 Buses to Ho Chi
   Minh City (Saigon)
17 Full Moon Bar & Restaurant
18 Dangkor Market
19 Dragonair
21 Martini Bar
22 Tuol Sleng Museum
24 Russian Embassy
25 European Dental Clinic
27 Wat Than Handicrafts
28 Royal Air Cambodge
29 Lao Embassy
31 Wat Tuol Tom Pong
32 Chinese Embassy
33 Tuol Tom Pong
   (Russian) Market
34 Vietnamese Embassy
35 Cham Kar Mon Palace
36 Taxis to Ho Chi
   Minh City (Saigon)

The International Stationery & Book Centre is mainly devoted to dictionaries, but it also stocks some locally produced maps.

The Central Market is a good place to pick up cheap books on Cambodia as photocopies of originals are widely available, much as in Vietnam.

Libraries The National Library, on 92 St near Wat Phnom, is in a delightful old building but has only a small selection of reading material for foreign visitors. Most of the books were destroyed during the Pol Pot era. Opening hours are from 8 to 11 am and 2 to 5 pm.

Cultural Centres French speakers should call into the Centre Culturel Français on 184 St (near the corner of Monivong Blvd). It has a good range of reading material. Many embassies have a home-grown selection of periodicals to glance at should you be passing through.

Hash House Harriers A good opportunity to meet local expats is via the Hash House Harriers, usually referred to simply as 'the Hash'. A weekly run/walk takes place every Sunday. Participants meet in front of the train station at 2.45 pm, and entry is US$5; the entry fee includes food and refreshments at the end.

Swimming Pools There is a large pool at the Olympic Stadium, Olympic-sized in fact, and it is only US$2 a day to escape the heat of the city. Women should note that skimpy bikinis are not allowed and some rather attractive frilly numbers are available for hire should this be a problem.

Laundry Most of the hotels around town offer reasonably priced laundry services – in some cases free.

Medical Services The SOS International Medical Centre (mobile ☎ 015-916685), 161 Rue Pasteur at 51 St, is one of the best medical services in Phnom Penh. Office hours are from 8.30 am to 5.30 pm Monday to Friday, 8.30 am to noon Saturday. SOS also has a 24 hour emergency service (mobile ☎ 015-912765) and can organise evacuation to Bangkok.

For specialist advice on tropical diseases you can visit the Tropical & Travellers Medi-

cal Centre (mobile ☎ 015-912000) at 88 108 St, near Wat Phnom. A British doctor runs the place. It is open 8.30 am to noon and 2 to 5 pm Monday to Friday and Saturday morning.

For dental problems, go to the European Dental Clinic (mobile ☎ 015-832159), at 195A Norodom Blvd. Office hours are 8 am to noon and 2.30 to 6 pm Monday to Friday, 8 am to 1 pm Saturday.

Emergency There is a 24 hour emergency police contact number in Phnom Penh and you will be connected to an English-speaking officer: mobile ☎ 018-811542. The general emergency number is ☎ 117.

Dangers & Annoyances Phnom Penh is by no means as dangerous as many people imagine, but it is still important to take care. Armed theft does occur, so it is not sensible to ride a motorcycle alone late at night. Long solitary walks at night are not advisable either, as some neighbourhoods are poorly lit.

Those out clubbing in the evenings can expect to be stopped at checkpoints from time to time, but moto drivers know where these are and tend to avoid them. Ostensibly, police checkpoints are there to check for firearms, but occasionally foreigners will be nabbed for a cigarette or a dollar. You are under no obligation to fork out.

When driving a motorcycle take care not to ignore 'no left turn' signs as there are traffic police at the junction only too willing to help you part with some riel. They may demand US$5, but if you are patient and smile, a few cigarettes or 1000r should see you on your way.

The restaurant areas of Phnom Penh (particularly places with outdoor seating) see a steady stream of beggars. Generally, however, there is little in the way of push and shove. If you give to beggars, do as the locals do and keep the denominations small – this way, hopefully, foreigners will not become special targets of begging.

Wat Phnom

Set on top of a 27m-high, tree-covered knoll, Wat Phnom was once visible from all over the city, and still makes for a good landmark. According to legend, the first pagoda on this site was erected in 1373 to house four Buddha statues deposited here by the waters of the Mekong and discovered by a woman named Penh (thus the name Phnom Penh, the Hill of Penh).

Royal Palace

Phnom Penh's Royal Palace is the official residence of King Norodom Sihanouk, and is seldom open to the public. It is only possible to view the Silver Pagoda and some of the ceremonial buildings nearby. Guides for the Silver Pagoda can walk you around some of the grounds and have a good knowledge of all that has taken place within the walls.

Silver Pagoda

The spectacular Silver Pagoda is so named because the floor is covered with over 5000 silver tiles weighing 1kg each. It is also known as Wat Preah Keo (Pagoda of the Emerald Buddha). The Emerald Buddha, which is presumably made of baccarat crystal, sits on a gilt pedestal high atop the dais. In front of the dais stands a life-size Buddha made of solid gold and decorated with 9584 diamonds, the largest of which weighs 25 carats. There are also many more intricately carved Buddha images on display, some of the finest in the region, and a collection of decorative jewellery worn by royal *apsaras*.

The Silver Pagoda is open to the public daily from 7.30 to 11.30 am and from 2.30 to 5 pm. The entry fee is US$3. There is an additional US$2 charge to bring a still camera into the complex; movie or video cameras cost US$5. Photography is not permitted inside the pagoda itself, so these prices are a little cheeky.

National Museum

The National Museum of Cambodia is housed in a graceful terracotta structure of traditional design (built 1917-20) just north of the Royal Palace. It is open Tuesday to Sunday from 8 to 11.30 am and 2 to 5.30 pm. The entry fee for foreigners is US$2, and English and French-speaking guides are available. Photography is prohibited inside.

The National Museum exhibits numerous masterpieces of Khmer art, artisanship and sculpture dating from the pre-Angkor period of Funan and Chenla (4th to 9th centuries AD), the Indravarman period (9th and 10th centuries), the classical Angkor period (10th to 14th centuries) and the post-Angkor period (after the 14th century).

It is also home to a massive **bat colony** of Cambodian freetails. On a clear evening you can sometimes see thousands of bats streaming out of the roof at sunset.

Tuol Sleng Museum

In 1975 Tuol Svay Prey High School was taken over by Pol Pot's security forces and turned into a prison known as Security Prison 21 (S-21). It soon became the largest such centre of detention and torture in the country. Almost all the people held at S-21 were later taken to the extermination camp at Choeung Ek to be executed. Detainees who died during torture were buried in mass graves in the prison grounds. During the first part of 1977, S-21 claimed an average of 100 victims per day.

S-21 has been turned into the Tuol Sleng Museum, which is a testament to the crimes of the Khmer Rouge. The museum is open daily from 7 to 11.30 am and 2 to 5.30 pm; entry is US$2.

Wat Ounalom

Wat Ounalom, headquarters of the Cambodian Buddhist patriarchate, is on the corner of Samdech Sothearos Blvd and 154 St (across from Phnom Penh Tourism).

Under Pol Pot, the complex, which was founded in 1443 and includes 44 structures, was heavily damaged and its extensive library destroyed. Today the wat is once again returning to prominence as a centre for Buddhist training (for local monks).

Other Wats

Other wats in Phnom Penh worth visiting include: **Wat Lang Ka**, on the southern side of Preah Sihanouk Blvd just west of the Victory Monument; **Wat Koh**, on the eastern side of Monivong Blvd between 174 and 178 Sts; and **Wat Moha Montrei**, east of the Olympic Market on the southern side of Preah Sihanouk Blvd between 163 and 173 Sts.

English St

This is a cluster of private language schools that teach English (and some French). It is situated one block west of the National Museum on 184 St between Norodom Blvd and the back part of the Royal Palace compound. Between 5 and 7 pm, the whole area is filled with students who see learning English as the key to making it in postwar Cambodia. This is a good place to meet local young people.

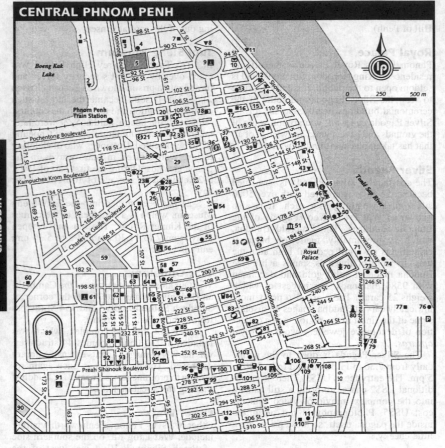

CENTRAL PHNOM PENH

Independence Monument

The Independence Monument, which is at the intersection of Norodom and Sihanouk Blvds, was built in 1958. It is now also a memorial to Cambodia's war dead (or at least those the present government considers worthy of remembering). Do not cross the small barriers as police will give you a hard time.

Colonial buildings

There are quite a number of fine French-era buildings around the city. Some worth photographing include the **National Library**, the **Ministry of Justice** and those in the area around the main post office. The recently restored **Hotel Le Royal** is also worth a visit to get a glimpse of what all these places looked like when first built.

Massage

The Seeing Hands Massage is intended to raise funds to empower disabled Cambodians in the capital. It is administered by well trained blind masseurs and costs US$3 per hour. It is based at the National Centre for Disabled Persons (NCDP) at 3 Norodom Blvd.

Artillery Range

Some travellers decide Cambodia is the place to do the Rambo thing and fire off a few rounds on an AK-47 or aim a rocket launcher at a cardboard cut-out of a tank. It is about US$12 for an AK clip, US$30 for 100 bullets on an M-60 mounted machine-gun and about US$40 for use of a B-40 grenade launcher. The range is just beyond Pochentong airport, so aim low. Go in a group as you can negotiate a discount.

CENTRAL PHNOM PENH

PLACES TO STAY
1 No 9 Guesthouse; Lakeside Guesthouse
3 Tai Seng Hotel
5 Hotel Le Royal
7 Sharaton Hotel; Casa Nightclub
12 Pyco Guesthouse
16 Last Home
17 Cathay Hotel
23 Diamond Hotel; Malaysia Airlines
24 Pailin Hotel; Silk Air
31 Fortune Hotel
40 Dara Reang Sey Hotel
42 Hotel Indochine
60 Sangkor Hotel
62 Lux Orisey Guesthouse
63 Capitol Guesthouse
64 Hong Kong Hotel; Lucky! Lucky! (Motorcycle Rental)
71 Renakse Hotel
77 Sofitel Cambodiana Hotel
88 Narin's Guesthouse
97 Tokyo Hotel
101 Golden Gate Hotel
110 One Way Guesthouse

PLACES TO EAT
2 Café Freedom
8 Il Padrino Restaurant
11 Tonlé Sap Restaurant
14 Saigon House Restaurant
25 Little India Restaurant
32 Mamak's Corner
41 Rendez Vous Restaurant
43 Banana Leaf Restaurant
46 Pon Lok Restaurant
47 Happy Herb's Pizza; The Pink Elephant
50 The Globe Bar & Restaurant
78 Chiang Mai Restaurant
79 EID Restaurant
82 Baggio's Pizza
86 Royal India Restaurant

92 Inexpensive Khmer Restaurant
93 Inexpensive Khmer Restaurant
100 Phnom Kheiv Restaurant
108 Red
109 The Mex

OTHER
4 Seven Seven Supermarket
6 National Library
9 Wat Phnom
10 Main Post Office
13 Thai Airways; Transpeed Travel; Kampuchea Airlines
15 Psar Char (Old Market)
18 NCDP Handicrafts; Seeing Hands Massage
19 Tropical & Travellers Clinic
20 Canadia Bank
21 Cambodian Commercial Bank (CCB)
22 Monument Books; Pich Tourist
26 DH Cambodia Bus Office
27 GST Bus Office
28 Ho Wah Genting Bus Office & City Bus Terminus
29 Psar Thmei (Central Market)
30 Taxis, Pick-ups & Minibuses
33 Public Internet Centre
34 Thai Farmers' Bank
35 Cathouse Tavern
36 Maybank
37 Foreign Trade Bank of Cambodia
38 Bangkok Bank
39 Sharky's (Disco)
44 Wat Ounalom
45 Phnom Penh Tourism
48 Foreign Correspondents' Club of Cambodia (FCC)
49 UNESCO
51 National Museum
52 Banque Indosez

53 Japanese Embassy
54 Heart of Darkness Bar
55 Cooperation Committee for Cambodia (CCC)
56 Wat Koh
57 Centre Culterel Français
58 Ministry of Culture
59 O Russei Market
61 Wat Sampao Meas
65 International Stationery & Book Centre
66 Khemarin Mini Theatre
67 East West Travel
68 Bangkok Airways
69 Immigration (Direction des Etrangers) Bureau
70 Silver Pagoda
72 Ministry of Justice
73 National Assembly Building
74 Chatomuk Theatre
75 Foreign Ministry
76 Naga Floating Casino
80 Cambodia-Vietnam Monument
81 Australian Embassy
83 US Embassy
84 St Tropez Nightclub
85 Diethelm Travel
87 Ministry of Tourism (MOT)
89 Olympic Stadium
90 Olympic Market
91 Wat Moha Montrei
94 Suntan Foodmart
95 Post Office
96 Lucky Supermarket
98 Ettamogah Pub
99 Tom's Irish Pub
102 Cactus Bar
103 Vietnam Airlines
104 Irish Rover Pub
105 Wat Lang Ka
106 Independence Monument
107 Lao Aviation
111 Prayuvong Buddha Factories
112 Khemara Travel

CAMBODIA

Places to Stay

Budget accommodation is spread throughout town.

The longest running, though by no means the best, budget hotel in town is the *Capitol Guesthouse* (☎ 364104), on 182 St not far from O Russei Market. The owners have expanded operations into two adjacent buildings under the names *Happy Guesthouse* and *Capitol II*. Basic singles/doubles (no bath-room, often no window) are US$3/5, while rooms with bathroom cost US$4/6. The Capitol is a good place to arrange transport for sightseeing in the Phnom Penh area as the friendly management are the most experienced in the business. It has an extremely cheap restaurant priced in riels.

Narin's Guesthouse (☎ 213657) is a well established favourite. It's a clean, family-run place that provides excellent meals. The guesthouse is in a residential neighbourhood at 50 125 St, and has overflow annexes in the adjacent two houses offering more than 30 rooms. Rooms with shared bathroom cost US$3/5. There are also some doubles with bathroom for US$7. The family has contacts throughout Cambodia and can help with travel and visa arrangements.

Another popular spot is on the Boeng Kak Lake. *No 9 Guesthouse (mobile ☎ 018-815569)* has a wooden pavilion area with hammocks on the lake itself and a pool table near reception. It's advisable that you check any valuables in with management here as the rooms are not particularly secure. Singles/doubles cost US$2/3.

Next door to No 9 is *Lakeside Guesthouse*, a similar operation and quite often these places are home to long-term residents who can't drag themselves away.

New places near the lake are opening regularly and other choices here include the basic *Sunrise (☎ see No 9)* and the slightly less ramshackle *Cafe Freedom (mobile ☎ 012-807345)*, which even has a small bungalow beside the lake for US$8. Access to this area of town can be a hassle in the wet season, but sunsets over the lake are something not to be missed whether staying up here or not.

Not far from the Capitol on 115 St is the *Lux Orisey Guesthouse,* which has a double bed and bathroom for US$5 and two beds and TV for US$8.

The *Pyco Guesthouse*, formerly Bert's Books, is run by a friendly Khmer doctor, but with little atmosphere for such a good riverside location – a joint venture in waiting. Rooms with fan and bathroom are US$5 or US$10 with air-con.

On the waterfront, at the corner of 144 St, is the *Hotel Indochine (☎ 427292)*, a friendly place with spacious air-con singles/doubles with attached bathroom for US$10/15. The location is excellent and this is the best choice in town for those wanting more than a basic guesthouse offers.

The *Dara Reang Sey Hotel (☎ 428141)* on the corner of 118 and 13 Sts is a great deal with well appointed air-con rooms at US$12/15 a single/double. There are also some fan rooms with bathroom for just US$6. The restaurant has Khmer-priced food and drinks.

The *Cathay Hotel (☎ 427178)* has been around for a while and is popular with resident journalists and photographers. Large air-con rooms with all the trimmings are US$15, making it one of the better deals in town.

Not far from the Cathay, at 2 67 St, is the *Fortune Hotel (☎ 211337)*. It does a steady business with regular visitors to Phnom Penh and seems to have cleaned up its once slightly seedy image. Rooms cost US$15.

The *One Way Guesthouse (☎ 215621)* is a small place at the intersection of 308 St and Norodom Blvd which has four rooms available for US$20 with air-con, TV and bathtub. You may need to book ahead to get in here.

A favourite with long-termers is the *Golden Gate Hotel (☎ 721161)*. There are two buildings; prices on the Preah Sihanouk Blvd side are a little higher. The Golden Gate has a downstairs restaurant, verandas and areas to sit (with magazines provided); the rooms are spotless, with air-con, satellite TV and minibars; and there is a free laundry service. Costs are US$15/20 for a single/double and US$15/30 in the newer building. It is close to the corner of 57 and 278 Sts. If the Golden Gate is full, the *Tokyo Hotel (☎ 722247)* is not far away at 13 278 St. It is good value with rooms at US$15/18.

The *Tai Seng Hotel (☎ 427220)*, at 56 Monivong Blvd, has a good location east of Wat Phnom and is heavily promoted by the tourist office at Pochentong airport. Rooms here start at US$18 and go up to US$25. All rooms have air-con, TV, fridge and hot water and some have good views of Boeng Kak Lake.

Opposite the Royal Palace, hidden among some attractive trees, is a colonial building, the *Renakse Hotel (☎ 722457)*. The rooms have all been modernised and spotless doubles with air-con, TV, minibar and hot-water bath start at US$30 and reach US$40 if you want sofas and a terrace. These rates include breakfast, making this a great treat if, like most, you cannot afford a similar ambience at the Hotel Le Royal.

Places to Eat

Many of the guesthouses have reasonably priced restaurants and some tasty fare, but with so much decent food available in Phnom Penh it is a shame to get into the habit of chowing down on the nearest terrace. They are a good place for trading tales about the latest situation upcountry, but you won't meet many locals dining in guesthouses.

If you want to eat on the Boeng Kak Lake, several of the guesthouses offer reasonably priced food. *Cafe Freedom* has a coffee shop atmosphere and some decent Thai food, although prices are quite high.

Khmer Bargain dining can be found in the markets of Phnom Penh and there is often a good mix of Khmer food as well as a touch of Chinese and Vietnamese. The Central Market dining area offers fish noodle soup and fresh spring rolls for about 2000r and most of the displayed food costs about the same.

Scattered all over town are numerous Khmer restaurants that offer alfresco dining in the evenings. These places often have Angkor Beer signs and are as much about drinking as about eating, but they're lively places for an inexpensive meal. There is a clutter of excellent places on Preah Sihanouk Blvd between 111 and 141 Sts. Most dishes are 4000r to 5000r and popularity seems proportional to the number of beer girls serving there. There are also good places on Monivong Blvd.

For inexpensive Khmer food with a Gallic touch, head down to the *Phnom Khiev Restaurant* on Preah Sihanouk Blvd. The restaurant has a popular garden area out front, and it does good salads and some excellent beef dishes.

There are stacks of glitzy Khmer places just beyond the Japanese Bridge on National Hwy 6. Many are less expensive than they look, some on the right offer dining by the Mekong and all are a good place to find Khmers on a big night out.

Continental The *Foreign Correspondents' Club (FCC)*, on Sisowath Quay, has a restaurant and bar on its 3rd floor with fabulous views of the Tonlé Sap River on one side and the National Museum on the other. The FCC is one of the best places to have that splash-out meal. There are a number of other upmarket European restaurants on the riverfront.

The best pizza in town can be had at *Baggio's Pizza*, on 51 St near the intersection of Preah Sihanouk Blvd. Small pizzas (a meal for one) start at around US$5. *Happy Herb's Pizza*, on Sisowath Quay, is as close as you get to a Phnom Penh institution. If you want your pizza to leave you with a grin for the rest of the day (or evening), tell the waiter you want it 'happy' – those who have nothing pressing on the agenda for a couple of days should request 'very happy'. Even if you are not in the market for being happied, the food here is good.

Indian There are some surprisingly good Indian restaurants in Phnom Penh. The *Banana Leaf* has a riverside location and sells generous portions of quality Indian and Sri Lankan food for US$2 to US$5. *Little India Restaurant*, near the Central Market, has huge vegetarian *thalis* for US$3 including a drink, while those wanting meat will have to pay US$4.

Thai & Vietnamese Just east of the Independence Monument on Samdech Sothearos Blvd is *EID*. It's a small place and very basic, but it has arguably the best Thai food in town. There's a second EID on Sisowath Quay. Most dishes range from US$2 to US$4. *Saigon House* is a good Vietnamese restaurant near the Pyco Guesthouse with prices that won't break the budget.

Other Cuisines Aussie pub grub is available at the *Ettamogah Pub* on Preah Sihanouk Blvd, next door to the Lucky Supermarket. The fish and chips and hamburgers are among the best in town, but they're not cheap.

Mamak's Corner, a Malaysian restaurant opposite the Canadia Bank, is the place for an early morning *roti chanai* and a *kopi susu*. It's possible to eat well here for around US$3.

Mexican fast food is available at *The Mex*, on the corner of Preah Sihanouk and Norodom Blvds. It has both takeaways and inexpensive sit-down meals. You can fill yourself up with a massive burrito for US$2.50.

Self-Catering Baguettes are widely available around town, and usually cost about 500r. The city's markets have heaps of fresh fruit and vegetables at fair prices if you bargain, as well as imported luxuries.

Phnom Penh's supermarkets are remarkably well stocked with goodies. For around US$3 to US$4 you can pick up treats such as salami, Camembert and Brie.

The best of the Phnom Penh supermarkets are the Lucky Supermarket, at 160 Preah Sihanouk Blvd, and the Seven Seven Supermarket, at 13 90 St. Other good supermarkets include the Suntan Foodmart at 477 Monivong Blvd and the Bayon Market at 133 Monivong Blvd.

Entertainment

For entertainment news, check the latest issue of the *Bayon Pearnik*, the *Phnom Penh Post* or the Friday edition of the *Cambodia Daily*.

Traditional dance is infrequently held at the Chatomuk Theatre, just north of the Cambodiana Hotel. Look out for advertisements in the local press.

Bars If you want to save yourself a bit of money, it is worth hitting the early evening happy hours in some of the bars around town as staple drinks are often half-price. One of the most popular evening drinking spots is the *FCC*, on Sisowath Quay. Drinks are a little expensive, but you pay for the ambience as much as anything and it is the best place from which to watch a storm come in over the Tonlé Sap.

There are a few more decent bars on the riverfront including *The Pink Elephant*, which serves Bank's Bitter for US$1.60 a can, and *The Globe Bar & Restaurant,* occupying one of the finest colonial buildings in the city and with a great value happy hour from 5 to 8 pm.

Naga, the floating casino behind the Cambodiana, has surprisingly cheap drinks – the Vegas technique – but you need to take a crowd as it lacks atmosphere. Upstairs, in the world of the high rollers, beer is free.

The *Cathouse Tavern* at the top end of 51 St has an intimate feel and sees its fair share of customers. *Tom's Irish Pub*, on 63 St, just south of Preah Sihanouk Blvd, has a loyal following and cheap drinks for an expat haunt. Farther up Preah Sihanouk Blvd is *Cactus*, a French bar serving meals as well.

The most popular late night haunt in town is *Heart of Darkness*. It's on 51 St, south of the Central Market. The Heart, as locals call it, is generally deserted before 10 pm but often packed after midnight. Most drinks are US$1 to US$2 or not much more, and the music is some of the best in town. There is also a pool table out the back, but get your name up early as it is a popular institution.

Nightclubs If a bar just doesn't satisfy your disco fever, there are a number of good late night spots to strut your stuff, as Phnom Penh is well known for its big nightlife. *Martini Bar* is infamous throughout the city and most moto drivers will try and usher you there later in the evening. It has lost some of its charm recently, as with the clamp-down on city brothels most of the working girls seem to set up shop here at the weekend, but it is still worth one trip just to say you've been.

St Tropez on 214 St is worth a visit, but if you can last until dawn then you'd better head to the capital's number one disco, the *Manhattan Club* at the Holiday Hotel. Drinks at both these establishments are pretty steep, but outside the Manhattan are stalls with cheap beer and tikaloks (fruit smoothies).

The latecomer on the scene is the revitalised *Casa* at the Sharaton Hotel, which has some good drinks promotions and deejays who have found life beyond MTV.

Cinemas The Khemarin Mini Theatre, at 280 Monivong Blvd, shows several western films daily on a reasonably sized screen for US$2. There's a weekly programme available free. The FCC shows films on Sunday and Tuesday evenings for US$2. The Centre Culturel Français shows some good French films every month. You can pick up a free monthly programme from bookshops or the centre itself.

Shopping

The Central Market has four wings filled with shops selling gold and silver jewellery, antique coins, fake name-brand watches and other such items. For souvenir shopping the best place is Tuol Tom Pong Market (Russian Market), in the south of town.

The National Centre for Disabled Persons has a shop called NCDP Handicrafts at 3 Norodom Blvd. Articles on sale include silk and leather bags, slippers, *kramas*, shirts, wallets, purses and notebooks. The standards of artisanship are very high. Prices vary, but some items are reasonable and the proceeds support a number of worthy projects in the capital. Along similar lines is the handicraft shop at Wat Than.

Getting There & Away

Air The Royal Air Cambodge (RAC) booking office (☎ 428891) is at 206 Norodom Blvd.

Opening hours are 8 am to 5.30 pm Monday to Friday and 8 am to noon on Saturday. It is generally possible to get flights at short notice to Siem Reap, but for other destinations try to book in advance. There's another office next door to the CCB bank.

Other airlines around town are:

Air France
  (☎ 426426) Office 11, Sofitel Cambodiana Hotel
Bangkok Airways
  (☎ 426707) 61 214 St
Dragonair
  (☎ 217665) 104 Regency Sq, Intercontinental Hotel, Monireth Blvd
Kampuchea Airlines
  (☎ 426912) 19 106 St
Lao Aviation
  (☎ 426563) 58 Preah Sihanouk Blvd

Malaysia Airlines
(☎ 426588) Diamond Hotel, 182 Monivong Blvd
Silk Air
(☎ 364747) Pailin Hotel, Monivong Blvd
Thai Airways International
(☎ 722335) 19 106 St
Vietnam Airlines
(☎ 364460) 35 Preah Sihanouk Blvd

Bus New bus services are opening regularly as security improves. For Sihanoukville, GST, DH Cambodia and Ho Wah Genting all have large, comfortable air-con buses with kungfu videos and complementary water making the three to four hour run. Tickets cost 12000r. GST departs at 8 am and 1 pm, DH Cambodia at 7.30 am and 1.30 pm and Ho Wah Genting at 7.30 and 9.30 am and 1.30 pm. Buses depart from the ticket offices which are all located near the Central Market.

Buses back to Phnom Penh leave from company offices in the centre of Sihanoukville. See the Sihanoukville map for locations. GST and DH Cambodia operate the same times as from Phnom Penh, but Ho Wah buses depart at 8 am, noon and 2 pm. DH Cambodia offers a return ticket for US$5.

Ho Wah Genting also runs air-con provincial services to towns around Phnom Penh, including Kompong Chhnang via Udong, and Takeo via Tonlé Bati and Phnom Chisor. See the Kompong Chhnang and Around Phnom Penh sections for details.

Ho Chi Minh City (Saigon) There is a daily (except Sunday) bus service to Ho Chi Minh City which leaves at 4.30 am from the Ho Chi Minh bus station on a little dirt road off 182 St just past the Shell garage.

Monday to Wednesday is the clattertrap bus, costing US$5 and Thursday to Saturday is the modern air-con bus for US$12. The office is open from 5 to 10 am. It is often better to use share taxis as the bus gets stuck at the border for ages, making journey times as long as 10 hours.

Train Trains to Kampot leave at 6.20 am every Tuesday, Thursday and Saturday and return the following day. Tickets are about 2500r for the scheduled six hour, 166km trip. At the time of writing, there are no trains to Sihanoukville as the Kampot Bridge is down.

Trains to Battambang depart at 6.30 am every day in both directions. The 274km journey takes about 12 hours and tickets cost just over 4000r.

Car & Motorcycle Car hire is not available, but travel agencies can arrange a car and driver for US$25 and up for excursions. Motorcycles are a liberating way to see places of interest near Phnom Penh. See the following Getting Around section for details.

Taxi & Pick-up Taxis to Sihanoukville leave from the local city bus station area just south of the Central Market. Drivers charge about 10,000r a head and cram six passengers into their vehicles. It's not a pleasant way to travel when compared with the bus services.

Taxis to the Vietnam border take about three hours and cost US$25 to charter or US$5 per person. From Moc Bai it is about US$5 per person to downtown Ho Chi Minh City (Saigon). They leave from near the Olympic Market or from the east side of the Monivong Bridge in the south of town. The Capitol Guesthouse has a US$6 per person service with no more than four to a car.

It is also possible to hire taxis on a per-day basis. Rates start at US$25 for around Phnom Penh and for nearby destinations, and then go up according to distance.

Pick-up trucks tackle some of the country's harsher roads. Siem Reap costs about US$7 if sitting inside and US$3 if sitting in the back. Battambang is US$5 in and US$2 out. There are also services to many other destinations and you can work out how much to pay using Battambang's prices as a benchmark. For more details of other destinations in this chapter see the relevant sections.

Boat The most popular boat services are those to Siem Reap. Express services take just four or five hours to reach Siem Reap. These boats are subject to dangerous overcrowding, and often have nothing in the way of safety gear. It's best to sit on the roof of the express boats, but don't forget some sunscreen. Express boats to Siem Reap cost US$25, but guesthouses can save you a couple of dollars. This is an unofficial foreigner price (locals pay 50,000r), which will hopefully come down as more people opt to take the road. Several companies have daily services at 7 am, arriving at about 11.30 am. Alternatively, you can save some money and see an extra town by taking a cheap bus to Kompong Chhnang and picking up the fast boat there. See the Kompong Chhnang section for details.

There are also daily express boats from Phnom Penh to Kompong Cham (10,000r) and Kratie (30,000r). Boats leave at 7 am and take about three hours to Kompong Cham and six to Kratie. Express services from Phnom Penh to Stung Treng are irregular because of security problems and the river level, but fast boats have been known to do a 10 hour run for 60,000r. For a few months a year, extremely slow boats do the run, but think carefully about how much you'd like being on a cargo boat for two days before taking this trip.

Getting Around
To/From the Airport
Pochentong international airport is 7km west of central Phnom Penh via Pochentong Blvd. Official taxis cost US$7, but you can negotiate a taxi for about US$4 outside. A moto costs about US$1.50 per passenger.

Bus
Phnom Penh has a fledgling bus network, but figuring out where and when the buses go is a matter of fearful difficulty. The city bus terminus is just south of the Central Market, at the north-east end of Charles de Gaulle Blvd. The green and white buses were donated by the Paris metropolitan government. You will need the help of someone who speaks Khmer to figure out where any bus goes. Alternatively you might just hop on one and see where you end up.

Taxi
There are no metered taxis of the sort you see in Vietnam. Vantha Taxi has a couple of old air-con cars, including a groovy 70s Merc, that work out at about US$1 every couple of kilometres and this includes a security guard at night. Ring Vantha Taxi 24 hours on mobile ☎ 018-810267. Unmetered taxis tend to wait outside popular nightspots, but you must agree on a price in advance.

Motorcycle
There are numerous motorbike hire places around town. Bear in mind that motorbike theft is a problem in Phnom Penh, and if yours gets stolen you will be liable. One of the best places for motorbike hire is Lucky! Lucky! on Monivong Blvd next to the Hong Kong Hotel. A 100cc Honda costs US$4 per day or US$25 per week and 250cc dirt bikes cost US$7 per day.

Moto
Motos are easily recognised by the baseball caps favoured by the drivers. In areas frequented by foreigners, moto drivers generally speak English and sometimes a little French. Elsewhere around town it can be difficult to find anyone who understands where you want to go. Most trips are about 1000r and an extra 500r at night, although if you want to get from one end of the city to the other you have to pay more. Prices are rarely negotiated in advance.

Many of the moto drivers who wait outside the Capitol Guesthouse, Narin's Guesthouse and the Hotel Indochine have good English and are able to act as guides. Some at the Capitol Guesthouse have been guiding for about five years.

Cyclo
Cyclos are still common on the streets of Phnom Penh but have lost a lot of business to the moto drivers. Costs are generally 500r for a short trip, 1000r for longer ones.

Bicycle
It is possible to hire bicycles at the Capitol Guesthouse for 4000r a day, but take a look at the chaotic traffic conditions before venturing forth on one.

AROUND PHNOM PENH
Killing Fields of Choeung Ek
Between 1975 and December 1978, about 17,000 men, women and children (including nine westerners), detained and tortured at S-21 prison (now Tuol Sleng Museum), were transported to the extermination camp of Choeung Ek to be executed. Many were bludgeoned to death to avoid wasting precious bullets.

The remains of 8985 people, many of whom were found bound and blindfolded, were exhumed in 1980 from mass graves in this one-time longan orchard. Some 43 of the 129 communal graves here have been left untouched. Fragments of human bone and bits of cloth are scattered around the disinterred pits. Over 8000 skulls, arranged by sex and age, are visible behind the clear glass panels of the Memorial Stupa, which was erected in 1988. Entry is US$2.

Getting There & Away
The Killing Fields of Choeung Ek are 15km south-west of central Phnom Penh. A moto there and back is about US$3. Some guesthouses can arrange a share taxi for US$10 a half day.

Udong
Udong, 40km north of Phnom Penh, is not a major attraction but is a pleasant day trip from Phnom Penh for those with spare time. It served as the capital of Cambodia under several sovereigns between 1618 and 1866.

Phnom Udong, a bit south of the old capital, consists of two hills joined by a ridge. There are good views of the Cambodian countryside and its innumerable sugar palm trees. The larger hill, **Phnom Preah Reach Throap** (Hill of the Royal Fortune), is so named because a 16th century Khmer monarch is said to have hidden the national treasury here during a war with the Thais.

The most impressive structure on Phnom Preah Reach Throap is **Vihear Preah Ath Roes**, or Vihara of the 18 Cubit Buddha. The vihara and the 9m Buddha, dedicated in 1911 by King Sisowath, were blown up by the Khmer Rouge in 1977.

At the north-western extremity of the hill stand three large **stupas**. The first one you come to is the final resting place of King Monivong (ruled 1927-41).

Getting There & Away The cheapest way to get to Udong is by air-con local bus. They leave from Central Market in Phnom Penh and are marked Udong; if you can, get the driver to let you off at the Udong access road, Kompong Chhnang. It is 2500r each way and takes about one hour. Taxis can be rented for US$20 to US$25 a day from guesthouses and hotels if there are enough of you, but this works out more expensive than the bus. A rented motorcycle is a good option as the road is well surfaced.

Tonlé Bati

South of Phnom Penh, the laterite **Ta Prohm Temple** was built by King Jayavarman VII (ruled 1181-1201) on the site of a 6th century Khmer shrine. The main sanctuary consists of five chambers. In each is a statue or linga (or what is left of them after the destruction wrought by the Khmer Rouge). The site is open all day, every day. A Khmer-speaking guide can be hired here for around US$1 a day.

Just north-west of Ta Prohm Temple, a long, narrow peninsula juts into the Bati River. On Sundays, it is packed with picnickers and vendors selling food, drinks and fruit.

Getting There & Away Ta Prohm Temple is 2.5km off National Hwy 2, about 31km south of Phnom Penh. Air-con local buses leave from Central Market and cost 2500r each way for the one hour journey. Motorcycle is a good option as you can combine the trip with a visit to Phnom Chisor.

Phnom Chisor

There is a spectacular view of the surrounding countryside from the top of Phnom Chisor, although it is more striking during the wet season. The main **temple**, which stands at the eastern side of the hilltop, was constructed in the 11th century of laterite and brick. The carved lintels are made of sandstone. On the plain to the east of Phnom Chisor are two other Khmer temples, **Sen Thmol** (at the bottom of Phnom Chisor) and **Sen Ravang** (farther east), and the former sacred pond of **Tonlé Om**.

Getting There & Away Phnom Chisor is around 55km south of Phnom Penh and can easily be combined with a trip to Tonlé Bati. Taxi hire for both destinations should be US$25 for the day.

Angkor

The world-famous temples of Angkor, built between seven and 11 centuries ago when the Khmer civilisation was at the height of its extraordinary creativity, constitute one of humanity's most magnificent architectural achievements. From Angkor, the kings of the Khmer Empire ruled over a vast territory that extended from the tip of what is now southern Vietnam northward to Yunnan in China, and from Vietnam westward to the Bay of Bengal.

The 100 or so temples constitute the sacred skeleton of a much larger and spectacular administrative and religious centre whose houses, public buildings and palaces were constructed out of wood – now long decayed – because the right to dwell in structures of brick or stone was reserved for the gods.

SIEM REAP

The town of Siem Reap is only a few kilometres from the temples of Angkor and serves as a base for visits to the monuments. The name Siem Reap (pronounced see-EM ree-EP) means 'Siamese Defeated'.

Siem Reap is 6.4km south of Angkor Wat and 9.7km south of the Bayon.

Information

Tourist Offices The Angkor office of Cambodia Tourism is in a modern white structure opposite the Hotel Grand d'Angkor. There's a sign saying 'tourist information' but you will be very lucky to find the staff here awake

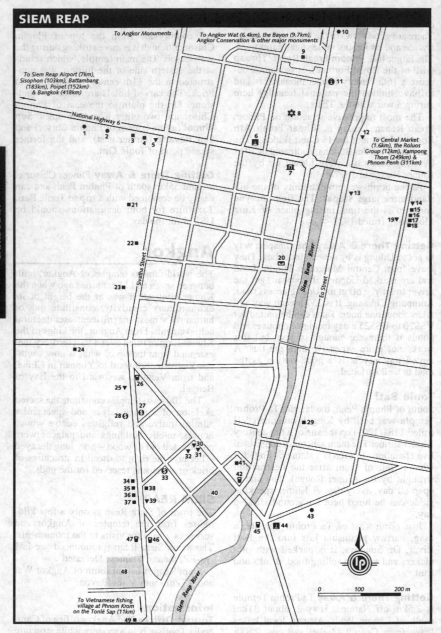

SIEM REAP

To Angkor Monuments

To Angkor Wat (6.4km), the Bayon (9.7km),
Angkor Conservation & other major monuments

To Siem Reap Airport (7km),
Sisophon (103km), Battambang
(183km), Poipet (152km)
& Bangkok (418km)

National Highway 6

To Central Market
(1.6km), the Roluos
Group (12km), Kampong
Thom (249km) &
Phnom Penh (311km)

Sivatha Street

Siem Reap River

Eo Street

Siem Reap River

To Vietnamese fishing
village at Phnom Krom
on the Tonlé Sap (11km)

0   100   200 m

SIEM REAP

PLACES TO STAY			
3	Apsara Angkor Guesthouse	38	Goldan Apsara Hotel
4	Takeo Guesthouse; Chenla Guesthouse	41	Stung Siem Reap Hotel
9	Hotel Grand d'Angkor	49	Popular Guesthouse
15	Garden Guesthouse		PLACES TO EAT
16	Mom's Guesthouse	5	Greenhouse Restaurant
17	Sunrise Guesthouse	12	Arun Restaurant
18	Mahogany Guesthouse	13	Samapheap Restaurant
21	Garden Green Guesthouse	14	Bayon Restaurant
22	Eclipse Guesthouse	19	Chavlit Thai Restaurant
23	Smiley Guesthouse	25	Rasmey Meanchey Restaurant
24	Naga Guesthouse	30	New Delhi Restaurant & Above the Dust Bar
29	Bayon Hotel	31	Little India Restaurant
34	Royal Hotel	32	Chao Saya Restaurant
35	Vimean Thmei Hotel	39	Monorom Restaurant
36	Reaksmey Chanreas Hotel		OTHER
37	Villa Phkay Proeuk	1	Bangkok Airways

OTHER	
2	Royal Air Cambodge
6	Wat
7	Sihanouk's Villa
8	Royal Gardens
10	Minefield Studio
11	Tourism Office
20	Main Post Office
26	Vimean Akas Nightclub
27	Pacific Commercial Bank
28	Cambodian Commercial Bank (CCB)
33	First Overseas Bank
40	Old Market
42	Bar Only One
43	Centre Culturel Français
44	Wat Dam Nak
45	Martini Nightclub
46	Bakheng Nightclub
47	Zanzybar
48	Night Market

unless you come in on a prepaid tour and they're expecting you.

For the most part, budget and mid-range travellers in Angkor get their travel information from other travellers or from their guesthouses.

Fees Visitors have a choice of a one day pass (US$20), a three day pass (US$40) or a one week pass US$60. This gives you access to all the monuments of Angkor.

Passes can be purchased at the entrance booth and upgrading passes from one to three days and three days to a week costs only US$20, so you can decide how much time you need as you go along.

Money There are several banks where you can change money in Siem Reap. The CCB has the usual travellers cheques at 2% commission and credit card cash advances at 2% with a US$10 minimum charge.

Post & Communications The main post office is along the river 400m south of the Hotel Grand d'Angkor.

There are both Camintel and Telstra public phone booths around town. You can buy cards at the main post office; otherwise try one of the hotels or business centres around town.

Dangers Siem Reap itself is perfectly safe to stroll around, even by night. Out at the temples, however, stick to clearly marked trails. There are still mines lurking out there. It is also not recommended that you visit remote sites alone – indeed the local authorities forbid it for your safety. There is the potential of armed robbery or perhaps even kidnapping in remote areas – there is no chance of you taking the wrong road with a moto driver.

Places to Stay

The accommodation boom continues unabated and there are arguably as many hotels and guesthouses as there are temples in the region. Prices are flexible in many places, especially if you are staying for a few days.

The cheapest guesthouse in town is the *Naga Guesthouse*, just off Sivutha St. Rooms cost as little as US$2, and doubles are available for US$3. Low prices ensure its enduring popularity and there is a free pool table in the restaurant area.

Near the Naga there are a couple more good options, including the homely *Smiley Guesthouse* run by the same family as Narin's in Phnom Penh with singles priced at US$3, doubles for US$5 and some with bathroom for US$6.

Farther up Sivutha St is the *Eclipse Guesthouse,* which has big, clean doubles with bathroom at US$6, similar singles at US$5 and rooms with shared facilities for just US$3.

East of the Siem Reap River, just off National Hwy 6, is a cluster of long-running guesthouses which remain popular despite prices edging upwards. *Mom's Guesthouse,* near the Bayon Restaurant, has singles at US$5 and doubles for US$6, or US$8 with bathroom.

Mahogany Guesthouse is a large two storey building with a veranda area for socialising. Singles cost US$5, while doubles with bathroom are US$8 to US$10, depending on the room.

Other guest houses in this area include: *Garden*, which also has singles/doubles at US$5/7 and a couple of rooms with bathrooms for US$8; the friendly and helpful *Sunrise,* with singles/doubles at US$4/6 and some with bathroom at US$8; and *Pailin Guesthouse* with similarly priced rooms. There isn't much to choose between them so go with your instinct on arrival. None of them offer food.

The other budget section of town is the area just west of the Greenhouse Restaurant on National Hwy 6. Pick of the pack is probably the big *Apsara Angkor Guesthouse*. The rooms are spacious and there's a leafy restaurant area in the garden. Singles/doubles cost US$3/5 and food is cheap as the menu is priced in riels.

Takeo Guesthouse is the best value in this part of town at US$2 a person or US$3 with bathroom. Dinner with the family is US$1. Next door is the *Chenla Guesthouse*, a clean family-run place with kitchen facilities. Nice doubles with bathrooms are US$6 in the new building at the back. In the old house it is US$3 for a simple double.

Down near the river on the edge of town is the *Popular Guesthouse,* which has a good selection of rooms including singles/doubles with shared bathroom at US$2/4 and US$5/7 with bathroom inside. They also serve good food.

Moving up in price, the *Golden Apsara Hotel* (☎ 963533) is recommended. It's a hospitable villa with verandas and a pleasant family atmosphere. Fan rooms with attached bathroom start at US$10, while air-con singles/doubles cost US$15/20.

Across the road from the Golden Apsara are several more villa-style hotels. The *Villa Phkay Proeuk* (☎ 380175) has fan singles/doubles for US$5/10 and air-con doubles at US$15. There are a couple of air-con triples, and these are a good deal at US$20. Rooms are large and well equipped, making it the best value place of its kind.

The *Vimean Thmei Hotel* (mobile ☎ 015-636993) and *Reaksmey Chanreas* (☎ 380068) are similar outfits, with fan rooms at US$10

and air-con rooms at US$15. The *Royal Hotel* (mobile ☎ 015-639114) is overpriced at US$20 a room.

One of the best upmarket guesthouses in town is the *Garden Green Guesthouse*, which as the name suggests has a verdant garden in which guests can relax. Rooms go for a bewildering array of prices, ranging from US$8 for fan and bathroom up to US$17 for a fully appointed room in the new building. If this is the sort of money you want to spend this is one of the nicest places to spend it.

If you are willing to fork out even more money, there are many places with rooms in the US$30 to US$50 range. The *Stung Siem Reap Hotel* (☎ 963482) is in a nice old building near the market and has rooms from US$25 to US$35. The riverside *Bayon Hotel* (☎ 963507) has some extremely welcoming staff and rooms run from US$35 to US$50.

Places to Eat

One of the best places in town is the *Bayon Restaurant*, just off National Hwy 6. It has a pleasant garden setting, and food offered on the wide-ranging menu is consistently excellent – try the curry chicken in baby coconut for US$2. It is convenient for those staying in nearby guesthouses, but worth the walk for those on the other side of the river. On the same road is the *Chavlit Thai Restaurant,* which has well prepared Thai food served in a cosy, traditional Thai setting. Most dishes are US$2 to US$3.

The *Rasmey Meanchey Restaurant* looks pretty inconspicuous with its lack of interior design, but do not be deceived by appearances as the food is excellent. There is an English menu, which includes the delicious steamed fish in ginger with black mushroom sauce. Most dishes are between US$1 and US$3.

The *Samapheap Restaurant* is next to the river. It has a Thai atmosphere – complete with twinkling fairy lights at night – and the food is a mixture of Khmer, Thai and generic western. North of Samapheap and also beside the river is the *Arun Restaurant*, an inexpensive Khmer restaurant, with some of the best prices in town.

The *Greenhouse Restaurant* is on the corner of Sivutha St and National Hwy 6. It has a good atmosphere and is the only restaurant in town that sells red and white wine by the glass. It has a large range of Thai, Khmer and western standards on the menu.

There are two Indian restaurants in town, but if they are busy service can be hit or miss. Prices are average at US$2 to US$4 a main course. *Little India* has better food, but *New Delhi* hosts weekend drinking bashes on the roof at the *Above the Dust Bar*. Flyers will forewarn you of a session.

The *Chao Saya Restaurant* has an experienced European chef who can whip up pastas and steaks for US$4 to US$6. Big portions make it worth the extra money and beer gets cheaper if you buy in bulk.

The *old market* has some cheap stalls with signs in English.

Entertainment

Nightlife in Siem Reap has a provincial feel to it despite the number of tourists starting to come through the town.

There are a few expat bars in town, including *Bar Only One* and *Zanzybar*, but slightly inflated prices seem to keep backpackers away.

There are several nightclubs in town. *Vimean Akas* is the most expensive, but possibly the worst. *Martini* has nothing to do with its namesake in Phnom Penh and is worth a visit as there is no dodgy cover band. *Bakheng* is the cheapest with almost guesthouse-priced drinks and the occasional bizarre floor show that includes a ballroom routine and scantily clad dancers with lit candles.

Getting There & Away

Air Daily flights between Phnom Penh and Siem Reap cost US$55 one way, or US$110 return. The Royal Air Cambodge office (☎ 963422) in Siem Reap is on National Hwy 6 out towards the airport. Bangkok Airways (☎ 380191/2) has daily flights to Bangkok for US$155/310 one way/return. The Bangkok Airways office is on the same road and open daily from 8 am to 5 pm.

Boat Ferries from Siem Reap back to Phnom Penh leave from Phnom Krom, 11km south of Siem Reap. A moto out here costs US$1. Most of the guesthouses in town sell ferry tickets and if you buy through them you will likely get a free moto ride.

See the Phnom Penh Getting There & Away section for information about the boats running from Phnom Penh to Siem Reap.

Pick-up As the security situation has improved, travel between Phnom Penh and Siem Reap is becoming increasingly popular among backpackers. Sections of the road are not pretty, but pick-ups complete the journey in about eight hours. It costs about US$7 in the cab, US$3 on the back. Guesthouses can help you arrange this, but you will likely have to pay a bit more for the privilege.

The 152km road to Thailand (Poipet border crossing) is something of a joke as about 50% of the time is spent driving in the paddy fields to avoid potholes and downed bridges. Pick-ups to Poipet take four to five hours and cost about US$5 in the cab and US$2 behind, although be prepared for some negotiating. To Sisophon, where you can change for Battambang, pay about US$3 in the cab and about 5000r on the back for the three to four hour ride.

Getting Around

To/From the Airport Many of the hotels and even some of the guesthouses in Siem Reap have a free airport pick-up service. The 7km ride from the airport on the back of a moto costs US$1. Taxis can be arranged for US$3 to US$5.

Minibus & Taxi Most of the hotels and guesthouses can organise taxi hire to visit Angkor. The going rate is US$20 to US$25. Minibuses are available from Angkor Tourism or from Cambodia Travel & Tours (mobile ☎ 015-918609) located in the south of town. A 12 seat minibus costs around US$40 per day, while a 22 seat minibus is US$80 per day.

Car & Motorcycle Travel agencies can arrange a car and driver for sightseeing. Details are in the Getting Around section earlier in this chapter.

Motorcycles are not available for hire. The government demands that tourists visiting Angkor travel with a 'qualified guide', which in practice means that you are compelled to hire a moto or a car with a driver.

Currently, it is illegal for locals to rent motorbikes to foreigners (unless journalists or NGOs), illegal for them to show visitors back routes into the temple complex and illegal for moto drivers to carry more than one passenger. Don't go trying to persuade residents into bending these rules as they will likely get into a lot more trouble than you, possibly even having their moto confiscated. Also, it is worth remembering that this situation exists in the interests of visitor safety. A few wrong turns could have foreigners in places they shouldn't be, either because of land-mines or isolated cases of robbery.

Moto Motos are available at daily rates of US$6. Some of the drivers have excellent English and can tell you much about the temples as you zip between them. Many people end up going around the temples with the moto driver they take from the ferry to town, particularly if it is a free lift arranged by a guesthouse, but there are many to choose from.

The average cost for a short moto trip within town is 500r.

Bicycle & Cyclo Some of the guesthouses around town hire out bicycles.

You can get around Siem Reap itself in the town's unique and rather uncomfortable cyclos, which are essentially standard bicycles with a two seat trailer in hitch. You can reach anywhere in town for 500r.

TEMPLES OF ANGKOR

Between the 9th and the 13th centuries, a succession of Khmer kings who ruled from Angkor utilised the vast wealth and huge labour force of their empire to carry out a series of monumental construction projects. Intended to glorify both the kings and their capitals, many were built in the vicinity of Siem Reap.

The 'lost city' of Angkor became the centre of intense European popular and scholarly interest after the publication in the 1860s of *Le Tour du Monde*, an account by the French naturalist Henri Mouhot of his voyages. A group of talented and dedicated archaeologists and philologists, mostly French, soon undertook a comprehensive programme of research.

Under the aegis of the Ecole Française d'Extreme Orient, they made an arduous effort – begun in 1908 and interrupted at the beginning of the 1970s by the war – to clear away the jungle vegetation that was breaking apart the monuments and to rebuild the damaged structures, restoring them to something approaching their original grandeur.

The three most magnificent temples at Angkor are the Bayon, which faces east and is best visited in the early morning; Ta Prohm, which has been slowly claimed by the jungle; and Angkor Wat, the only monument here facing westward and at its finest in the late afternoon.

If you've got the time, all these monuments are well worth several visits each. Angkor's major sites can be seen without undue pressure in three full days of touring.

Security has improved considerably recently and it is now possible to visit outlying temples such as the ornately decorated Banteay Srei without paying an exorbitant surcharge for armed protection.

Rumours abound of local scams on the Angkor passes, so if you want to be sure your money is going to the right place, pay for the ticket at the entrance booth. Selling any unused portion of the ticket has been known to work, but it has also failed.

There are a lot of children selling food, drinks and souvenirs in and around the temples. Try and be patient with them: you'll probably find ice-cold water heavenly after you have climbed the steep steps of the temples.

Angkor Thom

The fortified city of Angkor Thom, some 10 sq km in extent, was built by Angkor's greatest builder, Jayavarman VII, who came to power in the 12th century just after the disastrous sacking of the previous Khmer capital, centred on the Baphuon, by the Chams.

The city has five monumental gates, topped by four serene faces of Avalokitesvara, one each in the north, west and south walls and two in the east wall.

The Bayon The most outstanding feature of the Bayon, which was built around 1200 by Jayavarman VII in the exact centre of the city of Angkor Thom, is the eerie and unsettling third level, with its icily smiling, gargantuan faces of Avalokitesvara. There are more than 200 of these staring downwards from 54 towers. Almost as extraordinary are the Bayon's 1200m of bas reliefs, incorporating over 11,000 figures. The famous carvings on the outer wall of the first level depict vivid scenes of life in 12th century Cambodia.

It is best visited for sunrise or sunset as shadows and shafts of light make the faces more enigmatic still. Strangely dull from a distance, once you're inside you'll find it is one of the most stunning of the temples at Angkor.

The Baphuon The Baphuon, a pyramidal representation of Mt Meru, is 200m north-west of the Bayon. It was constructed by

Udayadityavarman II (reigned 1050-66) at the centre of his city, the third built at Angkor. It was in pretty poor shape for many years, but a team of French archaeologists are working to restore its pride.

The decor of the Baphuon, including the door frames, lintels and octagonal columns, is particularly fine. On the western side of the temple, the retaining wall of the second level was fashioned – apparently in the 15th century – into a reclining Buddha 40m in length, but as it was unfinished it is quite difficult to make out.

Terrace of Elephants The 350m-long Terrace of Elephants was used as a giant reviewing stand for public ceremonies and served as a base for the king's grand audience hall. The middle section of the retaining wall is decorated with human-size *garudas* (mythical human-birds) and lions. Towards either end are the two parts of the famous Parade of Elephants.

Terrace of the Leper King The Terrace of the Leper King, just north of the Terrace of Elephants, is a platform 7m in height on top of which stands a nude (though sexless) statue (actually a copy). The figure, possibly of Shiva, is believed by the locals to be of Yasovarman, a Khmer ruler whom legend says died of leprosy.

The front retaining walls are decorated with five or so tiers of meticulously executed carvings of seated apsaras (shapely dancing women).

On the southern side of the Terrace of the Leper King (facing the Terrace of Elephants) is the entry to a long, narrow trench excavated by archaeologists. This passageway follows the front wall of an earlier terrace that was covered up when the present structure was built. The figures look as fresh as if they had been carved yesterday.

At the time of writing, elaborate restoration work was being undertaken.

Angkor Wat

Angkor Wat, with its soaring towers and extraordinary bas reliefs, is considered by many to be one of the most inspired and spectacular monuments ever conceived by the human mind. It was built by Suryavarman II (reigned 1112-52) to honour Vishnu (with whom he, as god-king, was identified) and for use as his funerary temple. The central temple complex consists of three storeys, each of which en-closes a square surrounded by intricately interlinked galleries. Rising 31m above the third level and 55m above the ground is the central tower, which gives the whole ensemble its sublime unity. The temple is surrounded by a vast **moat**, which forms a rectangle 1.5km by 1.3km.

Stretching around the outside of the central temple complex is an 800m-long series of extraordinary bas reliefs. The most famous scene, the **Churning of the Ocean of Milk**, is along the southern section of the east gallery. This brilliantly executed carving depicts 88 *asuras* (devils) on the left and 92 *devas* (gods) with crested helmets on the right, churning up the sea to extract the elixir of immortality.

Phnom Bakheng

This is a popular hilltop location from which to photograph Angkor Wat in the glow of a late afternoon sun and to watch the sunset over the surrounding countryside. It is also home to the first of the **temple mountains**, built by Yasovarman (ruled 889 to 910), in the Angkor area.

Ta Keo

Built by Jayavarman V (ruled 968 to 1001), this massive structure rises more than 50m, but was never decorated with the fine carvings seen at other temples, giving it a rather spartan feel.

Ta Prohm

The 12th century Buddhist temple of Ta Prohm is one of the largest Khmer edifices of the Angkorian period. It has been left just as it looked when the first French explorers set eyes on it more than a century ago. Whereas the other major monuments of Angkor have been preserved and made suitable for scholarly research by a massive programme to clear away the all-devouring jungle, this Buddhist temple has been abandoned to riotous nature.

Inside, it is a maze of narrow corridors and crumbling stonework, areas of which are roped off as the chances of collapse are serious. If you are fit and careful it is worth climbing onto the upper levels to escape any tour groups and find some great photo opportunities of the jungle's ongoing assault.

It is one of the few temples where an inscription provides information on its dependants, which included an incredible 80,000 people to maintain the building.

TEMPLES OF ANGKOR

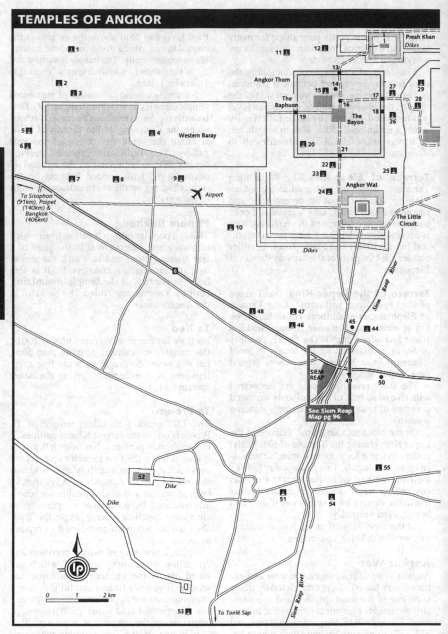

Preah Khan Dikes

Angkor Thom

The Baphuon

The Bayon

Western Baray

To Sisophon
(91km), Poipet
(140km) &
Bangkok
(406km)

✈ Airport

Angkor Wat

The Little Circuit

Dikes

Siem Reap River

SIEM REAP

See Siem Reap Map pg 96

To Tonlé Sap

Dike

Dike

Dike

0   1   2 km

CAMBODIA

TEMPLES OF ANGKOR

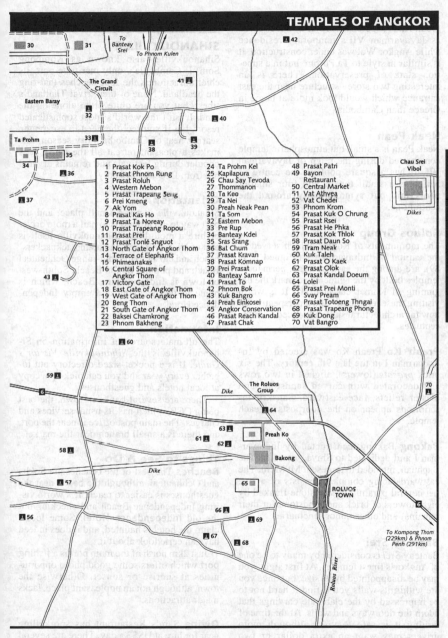

1 Prasat Kok Po
2 Prasat Phnom Rung
3 Prasat Roluh
4 Western Mebon
5 Prasat Trapeang Seng
6 Prei Kmeng
7 Ak Yom
8 Prasat Kas Ho
9 Prasat Ta Noreay
10 Prasat Trapeang Ropou
11 Prasat Prei
12 Prasat Tonlé Snguot
13 North Gate of Angkor Thom
14 Terrace of Elephants
15 Phimeanakas
16 Central Square of
   Angkor Thom
17 Victory Gate
18 East Gate of Angkor Thom
19 West Gate of Angkor Thom
20 Beng Thom
21 South Gate of Angkor Thom
22 Baksei Chamkrong
23 Phnom Bakheng

24 Ta Prohm Kel
25 Kapilapura
26 Chau Say Tevoda
27 Thommanon
28 Ta Keo
29 Ta Nei
30 Preah Neak Pean
31 Ta Som
32 Eastern Mebon
33 Pre Rup
34 Banteay Kdei
35 Sras Srang
36 Bal Chum
37 Prasat Kravan
38 Prasat Komnap
39 Prei Prasat
40 Banteay Samré
41 Prasat To
42 Phnom Bok
43 Kuk Bangro
44 Preah Einkosei
45 Angkor Conservation
46 Prasat Reach Kandal
47 Prasat Chak

48 Prasat Patri
49 Bayon
   Restaurant
50 Central Market
51 Vat Athvea
52 Vat Chedei
53 Phnom Krom
54 Prasat Kuk O Chrung
55 Prasat Rsei
56 Prasat He Phka
57 Prasat Kok Thlok
58 Prasat Daun So
59 Tram Neak
60 Kuk Taleh
61 Prasat O Kaek
62 Prasat Olok
63 Prasat Kandal Doeum
64 Lolei
65 Prasat Prei Monti
66 Svay Pream
67 Prasat Totoeng Thngai
68 Prasat Trapeang Phong
69 Kuk Dong
70 Vat Bangro

Chau Srei
Vibol

Dikes

The Roluos
Group

Dike

Preah Ko

Bakong

Dike

ROLUOS
TOWN

To Kompong Thom
(229km) & Phnom
Penh (291km)

Roluos River

CAMBODIA

Preah Khan

Preah Khan (Sacred Sword) may have served as Jayavarman VII's temporary residence while Angkor Wat was under construction. It is similar in style to Ta Phrom, but in a superior state of preservation. There is an interesting two storey structure near the east entrance which would look more at home in Greece than Cambodia.

Neak Pean

Neak Pean is a small but atmospheric temple constructed during the reign of Jayavarman VII. It has a square pool, in the centre of which is a small tower, and four smaller pools laid out symmetrically around the central one.

Roluos Group

The monuments of Roluos, which served as the capital of Indravarman I (reigned 877-89), are among the earliest large, permanent temples built by the Khmers and mark the beginning of Khmer classical art. It is worth visiting these temples to gain a perspective on how far architectural skills advanced over the centuries.

Preah Ko Preah Ko was erected by Indravarman I in the late 9th century. The six brick *prasats* (towers), aligned in two rows and decorated with carved sandstone and plaster reliefs, face eastward. Sanskrit inscriptions appear on the doorposts of each temple.

Bakong Bakong, constructed by Indravarman I and dedicated to Shiva, was, like The Baphuan, intended to represent Mt Meru. The eastward-facing complex consists of a five tier central pyramid of sandstone flanked by eight towers of brick and sandstone (or their remains) and other minor sanctuaries.

Banteay Srei

Banteay Srei is considered by many to be one of Angkor's finest temples. At first sight, you may be disappointed by its size, but once you are within its walls you'll find it hard not to be impressed by the elaborate carvings that adorn the doorways and walls. At the time of writing it is safe to visit, although moto drivers may want an extra dollar or two towards petrol (gas). Late afternoon is a fine time to visit as the sun's rays enliven the pink sandstone.

South Coast

SIHANOUKVILLE

Sihanoukville (also known as Kompong Som) is Cambodia's only maritime port. Its chief attraction is the four beaches that ring the headland. None of them rival Thailand's finest, but you are quite often alone on the sand. It isn't the world's most sophisticated resort, but if you feel the need to escape the searing heat of Cambodia's dry season, this makes a pleasant retreat all the same. It is popular during festivals and remains dry and hot from December to July.

Orientation

Sihanoukville is not a small place, and the best way to get around is to hail a moto driver or hire a motorbike. Sihanoukville itself is east of Victory Beach, the main backpackers' beach and closer to the mid-range Ochheuteal Beach and popular Sokha Beach. South-west of town is Independence Beach, which is home to the decaying and empty Independence Hotel.

Information

The ultimate source of information on Sihanoukville is the *Sihanoukville Visitor's Guide*. It is a pocket-sized directory put together every year and you can pick up a copy at local hotels and guesthouses.

There are several banks in town, the best being CCB, which has its usual services and charges. The main post office is near the port, and there is a small branch near the market.

Things to See & Do

Beaches The best of the beaches are Sokha and Ochheuteal, although the beach near the guesthouses is easier to reach. It's worth visiting Independence Beach and checking out the old **Independence Hotel**. Some locals claim the hotel is haunted, and it does indeed have an eerie look about it.

Just 2km north of the main port is a **fishing port** which offers some good photo opportunities at sunrise or sunset. Otherwise the town, although not an unpleasant place, lacks major attractions.

Diving Sam's Restaurant has snorkelling gear for hire at US$3 a day. There are several dive operations in town, all offering comparable deals. Condor Dive (mobile ☎ 015-831373) operates out of Pet's Place and offers

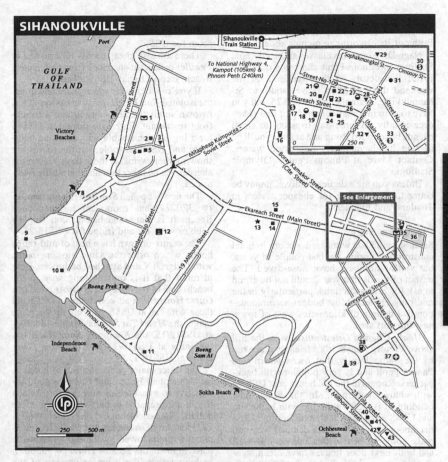

SIHANOUKVILLE

PLACES TO STAY
2 Mealy Chenda Guesthouse
5 Mari Yan Bungalows
6 Bungalow Resort
9 Koh Pos Hotel
10 Independence Hotel
11 Sea Breeze Guesthouse
14 Kampuchea Hotel
15 Guesthouse
20 Angkor Inn Guesthouse
22 Koh Rong Hotel
24 Hotel Tai San
25 Hawaii Hotel
26 Kampong Som Hotel
40 Seaside Hotel
41 Crystal Hotel

PLACES TO EAT
3 Sam's Restaurant
8 Hawaii Seaview
28 Apsara Restaurant
29 Pet's Place; Condor Dive
32 Ly Ay Restaurant
34 Restaurant & Bar
42 Sea Dragon Restaurant
43 Les Feuilles Restaurant

OTHER
1 Main Post Office
4 Independence Square
7 Victory Monument
12 Wat Khrom
13 Police Station
16 Galaxy Nightclub

17 Cambodian Commercial Bank (CCB)
18 Ho Wah Genting Buses
19 Bobo Nightclub
21 GST Buses; Good Luck Motorbike Rentals
23 Angkor Arms
27 DH Cambodia Buses
30 Pacific Commercial Bank
31 SV Rentals
33 First Overseas Bank
35 Post Office
36 Market
37 Hospital
38 Nasa Nightclub
39 Golden Lion Traffic Circle

single tank dives for US$35. Sports Pegasus (mobile ☎ 015-340120) offers similar prices. Both outfits can arrange picnics aboard.

Naga Dive operates classes at the Olympic Stadium in Phnom Penh and has a qualified PADI instructor. At the weekend, at the weekend this operation moves south to Sihanoukville. A single tank is US$25, but you have to chip in for a boat on top of that. They occasionally do three-day trips out to small islands beyond Ko Rong and at least you'll be in safe hands in pretty uncharted waters. Contact Marc at Phnom Penh's Olympic Stadium.

Unless you are a dedicated diver, it may be better to save diving for cheaper waters in Thailand and Indonesia.

Places to Stay

Sihanoukville has witnessed a boom in hotel construction during the last couple of years, but visitor numbers have nose-dived. The upshot of this is that you should not be afraid to ask for rate reductions, particularly in the mid-range hotels. Most budget accommodation is a couple of kilometres west of town, near the port area.

Mealy Chenda Guesthouse is on the hill above Victory Beach. It's a friendly place run by the same family that owns Narin's in Phnom Penh and is very popular with backpackers. Rooms in the old house cost US$3/5 with shared bathroom. In the fancy new building, it is US$7 a double with bathroom and US$8 a triple with shared facilities. The neighbours have obviously decided they can make some money in this business as well and both next door houses have clean, spacious doubles with bathroom for US$8.

Two bungalow resorts operate on the same hill, although unfortunately there are still no beachside huts anywhere. *Bungalow Resort* is the cheaper of the two, with basic huts at US$5 if you haggle. Slightly more upmarket is the *Mari Yan*. Huts with bathrooms are US$8 for one person, US$10 for two and there are rooms in a longhouse for US$6. The setting is pleasant, but restaurant prices seem more geared to expats than backpackers. Both sets of bungalows get pretty hot during the day as they have tin roofs.

Ekareach St (Main St), the road that leads to town from Victory Beach, has recently seen the opening of several family-run guesthouses. The location isn't great, but the prices are some of the lowest in town. The best of the bunch is the nameless *guesthouse* at No

132 which is opposite the Kampuchea Hotel and has spotless rooms with fan and bathroom for US$6.

There are also cheap rooms for rent at *Les Feuilles* restaurant one block from Ochheuteal Beach. Expect to pay US$5 a bed.

If you're looking for some peace and quiet, the isolated *Koh Pos Hotel* is an option. It has its own small stretch of beach and a beachfront restaurant. Rates are posted at US$15 for a big air-con double with attached bathroom and US$20 a triple, but the rooms are showing their wrinkles these days. Given the alternatives on other beaches it is a little overpriced.

The newly opened *Sea Breeze Guesthouse* (☎ 320217) has rooms on Independence Beach. It is clean and has air-con singles/doubles with TV and fridge for US$15/25.

The centre of town has a host of mid-range hotels which offer the same air-con rooms with fridge, TV and attached bathroom. Bear in mind that it is quite a long way to the beach. One of the cheapest is the *Angkor Inn Guest House* with air-con rooms at US$8 and those with fan at US$6. Moving up the price range, the *Hotel Tai San* has singles/doubles at US$12/15, the *Kompong Som Hotel* has the same at US$10/13 and the *Koh Rong Hotel* at US$10/15.

The other major concentration of hotels is on Ochheuteal Beach and this is a good alternative to guesthouses near Victory Beach if you are prepared to part with a few more dollars. The beachfront *Crystal Hotel* (☎ 933-523) has singles/doubles at US$25/35, but is rather overshadowed by the most expensive place in town, the *Seaside Hotel* (☎ 933662), looking rather like a junior version of the Cambodiana in Phnom Penh.

It offers a variety of well appointed rooms for US$25 right up to US$50 for Hun Sen's regular room, suite 214.

Places to Eat

There are a lot of restaurants in the town centre and each of the beaches has one or two, although you are expected to pay higher prices for the pleasures of a sea view. *Mealy Chenda Guesthouse* has an extensive, reasonably priced restaurant with plenty of seafood. It is a good place to watch the sunset, but service can be slow if there's a crowd.

Sam's Restaurant, near Victory Beach, also has a good selection of food for US$1 to US$3. It is a top spot for breakfast as they do a great bacon, cheese and tomato toasted sandwich. It is all too easy to hang around these places if you're staying at this end of town, but it is worth venturing into the centre or to Ochheuteal Beach for an evening out.

The *Apsara Restaurant*, right in the centre of town, has a mixture of Asian cuisine and some western dishes at prices between US$2 to US$4. The *Ly Ay Restaurant* is a cheap noodle shop that stays open late into the night, so it is a good option if you get a munchies attack after the nightclubs close.

Opposite the market is a nameless Angkor Beer emporium that has a couple of menus in English encouraging diners to sample such exotic delights as lizard and deer. 'Fried crap with peper' is one for the brave. *Pet's Place* is the place in town to get western food, but it is also the place to pay western prices. It is a good place to indulge.

Down on Ochheuteal Beach there are a few more restaurants offering the advantage of a sea breeze. *Les Feuilles* has steaks in blue cheese sauce at US$6 and a selection of pastas for about US$4. It also has a pool table. On the seafront is the *Sea Dragon Restaurant*, which has one of the most extensive menus around. It offers just about every combination of food and flavours you can imagine.

Entertainment

Nightlife in Sihanoukville is pretty limited compared with Phnom Penh.

The nameless *beer emporium* is a great place for cheap draught at 1800r a glass. The *Angkor Arms* is on the main drag and aims to offer the atmosphere of a British pub with darts and draught, with slightly higher prices to match.

There are several nightclubs around town, but they are quite expensive for those on a budget and wind down by midnight. Most are of the dark, 'Sha La La La La' variety frequented by Khmers and Chinese and teeming with women who charge for their company. *Galaxy* and *Nasa* are probably the best of this type. The single exception is *Bobo*, which stays open until 2 am, has decent lighting and employs deejays rather than cover bands. It is currently closed for renovations, but should be open by the time you read this.

Getting There & Away

Bus See the Phnom Penh section for details of the three bus companies operating services between Sihanoukville and Phnom Penh.

Train The train service to Sihanoukville is currently out of service as the river bridge in Kampot collapsed in early 1998. Repairs are likely to take some time.

Motorcycle Car hire is not available in Sihanoukville, but taxis can be chartered.

Motorbike rentals can be arranged at Good Luck (you'll need it with some of their bikes) and SV Rentals. It is US$7 a day for 250cc off-roaders, sometimes cheaper if you take them for several days, and they will get you to Kampot without a care for the potholes in about three hours.

The advantage of the motorcycle is it makes a visit to Kep and, particularly, Bokor Hill Station, much easier if security allows. However, it is not a good idea for beginners. National Hwy 4 is a busy road so it is easier to bus down and arrange a motor-cycle in Sihanoukville. However, some travellers do start in the capital – see the Phnom Penh section for details of rentals there.

Taxi Taxis from Phnom Penh to Sihanoukville leave from the area north-west of the Central Market. Prices are negotiable but expect to pay about US$25 a vehicle, 8000r to 10,000r a head in cramped conditions or US$4 each with just three in the back. Most drivers think they are Michael Schumacher so if you don't like blind overtaking you may want to sit in the back with some Valium.

Kampot is 105km from Sihanoukville and the road is excellent while you stay on National Hwy 4, pretty poor for the next 30km and good again for the final stretch. Taxis take about three hours and can be arranged from near the market for about 8,000r a person.

Getting Around

Motorcycle There are two rental shops in town. See Getting There & Away for details.

Moto Apart from hiring your own bike, the only way to get around Sihanoukville is by moto. There are plenty about and in the evenings they tend to wait in droves outside popular nightspots. From the guesthouse area in the west to the market is about 1000r, to Sokha Beach and Ochheuteal Beach more like 2000r, and late at night an extra 500r might be requested.

KAMPOT

The somnolent riverside town of Kampot sees few visitors, but it is a charming place

KAMPOT

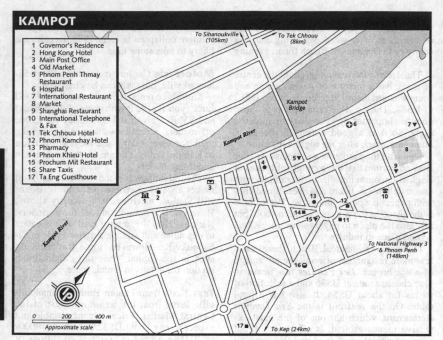

1 Governor's Residence
2 Hong Kong Hotel
3 Main Post Office
4 Old Market
5 Phnom Penh Thmay
   Restaurant
6 Hospital
7 International Restaurant
8 Market
9 Shanghai Restaurant
10 International Telephone
   & Fax
11 Tek Chhouu Hotel
12 Phnom Kamchay Hotel
13 Pharmacy
14 Phnom Khieu Hotel
15 Prochum Mit Restaurant
16 Share Taxis
17 Ta Eng Guesthouse

To Sihanoukville (105km)
To Tek Chhouu (8km)
Kampot Bridge
Kampot River
Kampot River
To National Highway 3 & Phnom Penh (148km)
To Kep (24km)

0   200   400 m
Approximate scale

with some lovely examples of French architecture and a relaxed atmosphere. Security concerns that have kept travellers away in the past are no longer a problem and the town is a good base from which to explore the nearby crumbling beach resort of Kep, and the abandoned hill station of Bokor.

Information

The main post office is on the river to the south of the Kampot Bridge. There are telephone and fax offices around town. There are no banks, so bring a supply of dollars with you.

Tek Chhouu Falls

The Tek Chhouu Falls are 8km out of town. Waterfall enthusiasts should prepare themselves for a disappointment as it is really just a series of small rapids, which don't move very rapidly in the dry season. It is, however, a pleasant bathing spot should you want to cool off, and very popular with locals. There is a proper waterfall 18km farther up a dirt track from Tek Chhouu, but access may be a problem for strangers as the checkpoint en route is policed by Khmer Rouge defectors. Check in town before you head up there.

Places to Stay

There aren't an awful lot of places to choose from in Kampot, and beyond domestic tourists there have been very few people to fill them. The *Ta Eng Guesthouse* is the best value establishment in town. The friendly owner speaks decent English and French and has three double rooms available with net, ceiling fan and shared bathroom for US$5.

Down on a prime riverfront location in the south of town is the *Hong Kong Hotel,* which is a little run-down, but has cheap rooms at US$7 a double with bathroom.

The other hotels in town are clustered around the central roundabout. *Hotel Tek Chhouu* is cheap and run-down, with rooms as low as US$6. The *Phnom Khieu* and *Phnom Kamchay* hotels are more upmarket and offer basically the same deal: rooms are well equipped with air-con, fridge and clean bathrooms and cost US$12/15. The Phnom Khieu is probably slightly the better.

Places to Eat

There are quite a few restaurants in town, although you may have trouble making yourself understood in the hole in the wall places.

The best place in town is the ***Phnom Penh Thmay Restaurant***, one block up from the bridge. It has an extensive menu in English and most dishes cost between US$1 and US$3. Come the evening, the same street plays host to a large number of tikalok (fruit smoothie) sellers.

Prochum Mit Restaurant is right in the centre of town and has good food. If it is riverside dining you are after then you need to visit the *small bamboo stalls* that set up their wares a just west of the bridge after dark.

Nightlife is a bit of a nonstarter, but expats tend to drink at the Phnom Kamchay Hotel.

Getting There & Away

Kampot is 148km from Phnom Penh and, due to the poor condition of National Hwy 3, the journey takes three to four hours, depending on the vehicle and driver. Share taxis cost about US$3 per person and leave from near the Total station in the south-west of town.

Some travellers make their way on 250cc motorbikes from the capital; see the Phnom Penh section for rental details. Then there is the train: check the Phnom Penh section for details, but it is the least sensible option.

The road to Sihanoukville is 105km. Share taxis go from the Total station for 8,000r a person, but minibuses are a better deal at 5000r per person. For road conditions, see the Sihanoukville section.

KEP

The seaside resort of Kep is on a small headland and has a 6km palm-fringed road extending along the coastline. It was founded as a colonial retreat for the French elite in 1908. Cambodian high rollers continued the tradition, flocking here to enjoy gambling and water sports, and like most privileged revolutionaries it is likely the Khmer Rouge had their dachas down here in case things got too hot in the capital. Little remains but skeletons of buildings as locals were forced to loot the villas for materials to sell to the Vietnamese to survive the famine of 1979 and 1980.

There are regular rumours of redevelopment plans, although currently there are only a few new villas in town. The beach itself is rather dirty and often very crowded at the weekend, but there is, nonetheless, a certain atmosphere about the place that brings expats back again and again.

There are two places to stay in town: the ***Phuong Bon Guesthouse*** about 3km on from the mermaid statue, with rooms at US$5 for a double bed and fan and US$7 for two beds and a bathroom; and the decrepit ***Krong Kep Hotel*** with doubles for US$10 to US$15. To be honest, it is a better option to stay in Kampot, which has more hotels and restaurants. Eating in Kep is easy as there are numerous bamboo shacks all along the road offering fresh seafood, although be prepared to agree to a price in advance.

Kep is subject to the south-west monsoon so the best time to visit is from November to June.

Getting There & Away

Kep is 24km from Kampot, 172km from Phnom Penh and 49km from the Vietnamese town of Ha Tien. There is a border crossing 8km north of Ha Tien, but it is not presently open to foreigners. The direct road to Phnom Penh offers some stunning limestone peaks before rejoining National Hwy 3. The journey from the capital takes three to four hours.

RABBIT ISLAND

Just a short boat ride off the coast of Kep is Rabbit Island. It has four **beaches**, all much nicer than those at Kep itself, and it is possible to stay with families on the island as long as you can sort out a price for food and lodging. Malaria is prevalent on most islands off Cambodia's coast so come well armed.

Boats can be arranged at the first cluster of food stalls on the coast road. Expect to pay about US$20 a day for the boat, although the exact price may depend on numbers. You can negotiate your way to the island for somewhat less if you are planning to stay overnight.

BOKOR HILL STATION

The old French hill station of Bokor (elevation 1080m) is known for its cool climate, secluded **waterfalls** and jungle vistas. Currently, Bokor is abandoned and only one villa is under construction, surely for someone who has access to a helicopter. The place really has a ghost town feel and the old **Catholic church** looks like it was locked up only yesterday. The old hotel and casino, the **Bokor Palace**, is straight out of *The Shining*, and if you walk to the edge of what was once a terrace you will be rewarded with a magnificent view over lush jungle stretching almost to the sea.

There are no amenities at present, but this may change if plans to redevelop the place take off.

Warning

Like any rural areas in Cambodia there may be some landmines dotted about here. There was not much fighting in this area, but it is sensible to keep to well marked paths near buildings. Security is on and off so make double sure you check in Kampot before attempting a visit.

Getting There & Away

Bokor Hill Station is 41km from Kampot, 132km from Sihanoukville and 190km from Phnom Penh. The access road is 7km outside Kampot marked by an elaborate interchange system that must have seen its fair share of Renaults and Citroens during the resort's heyday. There is a police post at the bottom of the road, but the police shouldn't stop you unless there is trouble ahead.

The road is in terrible condition for the first 25km and passable only during the dry season on an off-road motorbike or a sturdy 4WD vehicle. It is best visited as a day trip from Kampot. It is possible to get here from Sihanoukville, but it's an arduous trip.

Western Cambodia

BATTAMBANG

Cambodia's second largest city is an elegant riverside town, home of the best-preserved colonial architecture in the country and some of the most hospitable Khmers you can hope to meet. Until recently, security concerns kept Battambang off the map for all but those willing to fly in and out. However, recently improved conditions have opened the city to overland traffic and it makes a great base from which to explore nearby temples and scenic villages.

Orientation

Although it is a major city, Battambang is fairly compact and easily negotiable on foot. The centre of town is the market square and all commercial activity and most of the city's hotels are within a few blocks of streets bordered to the west by the railway line and to the east by the Sangker River.

Information

There are several banks in town. The CCB will do the usual cash advances on credit cards and travellers cheques at 2%.

The main post office is on the riverfront, but for international telephone calls use the Interphone offices located all over town. Calls are routed via Thailand so it is 10B a minute to Bangkok and US$2 a minute for Europe, Australia and the USA.

Things to See & Do

Much of Battambang's charm lies in the network of old French **shophouses** nestled on the riverbank. There are a number of wats around town, including **Wat Phiphitaram**, where a number of the monks speak English and are glad for the chance to practice their conversation. The city has a small **museum** under renovation. Beyond the town are a number of attractions, including hilltop temples, Angkorian-era wats and a large lake (see Around Battambang).

Places to Stay

Battambang's hotels are the best value in the country as many were built to house UNTAC personnel and now have few guests to patronise them. Prices are fairly uniform so you can expect to pay around US$5 for a spacious double with bathroom, TV and fridge, and US$10 for the added luxuries of air-con and hot water. Most hotels have an adult movie channel which kicks in at night and is beyond explicit.

The best choice in town is the *Chhaya Hotel*, right in the centre of town, which has helpful and friendly staff and attentive service, all for US$5. The cheapest rooms are in the nearby *Sekmeas Hotel* at US$4, but they are a little musty.

Other hotels with cheap rooms include *Hotel Asie* and *Phnom Pich Hotel*. The *23 Tola Hotel* was under renovation at the time of writing and will reopen as the *Royal Hotel*. This should prove serious competition to the Chhaya Hotel.

Moving up to the US$10 establishments, the friendliest staff are at the *Golden River Hotel* and the desk manager has excellent English. There is a pool table upstairs.

The top joint in town is the *Teo Hotel* and doubles there go for US$12. The exterior is pretty extravagant, but the rooms are similar to those elsewhere.

If you want to be overlooking the river the only choice is the *Angkor Hotel*, a modern affair incongruously clinging to the end of some fine old buildings.

Other worthwhile options around town include the *Paris Hotel*, *Khemara Hotel* and *International Hotel*, the latter overlooking the bustling market area.

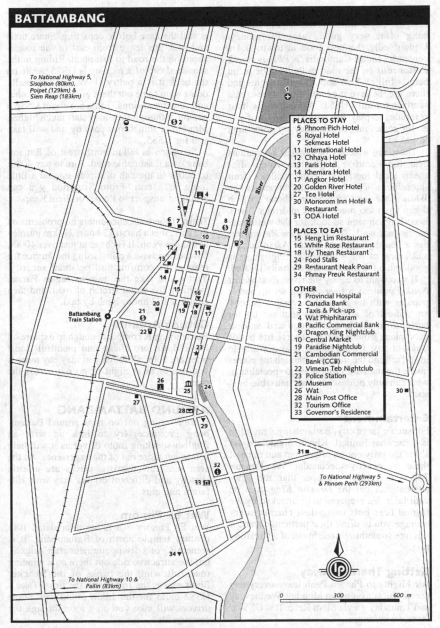

BATTAMBANG

To National Highway 5,
Sisophon (80km),
Poipet (129km) &
Siem Reap (183km)

Sangker River

Battambang
Train Station

To National Highway 5
& Phnom Penh (293km)

To National Highway 10 &
Pailin (83km)

PLACES TO STAY
5 Phnom Pich Hotel
6 Royal Hotel
7 Sekmeas Hotel
11 International Hotel
12 Chhaya Hotel
13 Paris Hotel
14 Khemara Hotel
17 Angkor Hotel
20 Golden River Hotel
27 Teo Hotel
30 Monorom Inn Hotel &
Restaurant
31 ODA Hotel

PLACES TO EAT
15 Heng Lim Restaurant
16 White Rose Restaurant
18 Uy Thean Restaurant
24 Food Stalls
29 Restaurant Neak Poan
34 Phmay Preuk Restaurant

OTHER
1 Provincial Hospital
2 Canadia Bank
3 Taxis & Pick-ups
4 Wat Phiphitaram
8 Pacific Commercial Bank
9 Dragon King Nightclub
10 Central Market
19 Paradise Nightclub
21 Cambodian Commercial
Bank (CCB)
22 Vimean Teb Nightclub
23 Police Station
25 Museum
26 Wat
28 Main Post Office
32 Tourism Office
33 Governor's Residence

0   300   600 m

CAMBODIA

Places to Eat

Like the city's hotels, restaurants in Battambang offer very good value for money. Undoubtedly the best food in town, and a contender for all Cambodia, is *Phmay Pruek Restaurant* on the road to Pailin. The menu here is full of Thai and Khmer delights and there are, believe it or not, Wall's ice-cream sundaes for only US$1. Worth a try is 'four comrades to play fire with shrimp' or if you prefer something super spicy try something 'drunken'.

There are a series of popular restaurants near the Paradise Nightclub which offer cheap local food and divine tikaloks (fruit smoothies). The best of the bunch is the *White Rose* (or Colap So in Khmer), which doesn't put too much sugar in drinks. There is no English sign so look for the white rose on the rear wall. The *Heng Lim Restaurant* has a healthy menu of mixed Asian cuisine and some of the staff speak English. It is good value for money, and centrally located.

If you want to eat by the river, *Restaurant Neak Poan* has a beer garden set up and is popular with locals in the evening. Nearby are a host of street stalls that set up for business in the late afternoon and make a good place from which to observe life in this pleasant city. Cheap dining is also available in and around the market, although the places inside the main building seem to specialise in what can only be described as 'unusable-bits' soup.

Entertainment

For such a large city, Battambang's nightlife is somewhat limited. Khmer nightclubs are about the only option after 9 pm and none of these are exactly spectacular. The *Vimean Teb* is marginally cheaper than the other alternatives, but the *Dragon King* goes on until later. Be prepared to be attacked by the myriad beer girls using their charms to encourage you to drink their particular brand – it is like something straight out of a wrestling ring.

Getting There & Away

Air Flights to Phnom Penh leave every day except Tuesday, and on Monday, Wednesday and Thursday go via Siem Reap. It is US$45/90 one way/return.

Taxi The 293km road to Phnom Penh is a case of the good, the bad and the ugly. It is plain ugly as far as Pursat, bad to Kompong Chhnang and good into Phnom Penh. Security is not currently a problem, but check this is still the case before departing. Share taxis and pick-ups leave from east of the roundabout on the road to Sisophon. Riding in the squashed cab of a pick-up is US$5, while on the back it is a paltry US$2, but you really don't want to be out there given both weather and road conditions. Taxis are about US$6 a person, although they may start much higher. Minibuses sometimes pass by and will take you for US$5.

Sisophon is 80km north-west of Battambang on a reasonable road. Aim to pay 4000r to 5000r in the cab of a pick-up and a little more in a taxi. From Sisophon you can arrange transport to Poipet or Siem Reap.

Train If the train encounters no problems on the way, it is a harsh 12 hour, 274km journey to Phnom Penh. It is cheap at just over 4000r, but locals advise against using the service for reasons of comfort and personal security. You could take the train as far as Pursat, avoiding the worst stretch of road, and then continue to Phnom Penh by taxi.

Getting Around

Battambang is compact enough to explore on foot. Motos are cheap and plentiful. Most rides are 500r, although you may pay more if you use them at night or go out across the river.

AROUND BATTAMBANG

Before setting out on trips around Battambang Province, try to link up with an English-speaking moto driver as it will help you to get more out of the experience. As the area sees few tourists, prices are a little sketchy and different drivers may want different amounts.

Wat Ek Phnom

Wat Ek Phnom is a rather dilapidated 10th century temple north of Battambang. It is something of a disappointment after Angkor, but the attractive ride out there on a winding road following the banks of the **Sangker River** makes the trip worth the time. Take a US$2 moto for the 15km round trip. Some drivers will take you on a loop through the countryside.

Phnom Sampeau

The hilltop temple of Sampeau was formerly the frontline in the government's defence of

Battambang, but with the late-1996 defection of Ieng Sary and his Khmer Rouge units the area is safe to visit. There is a long, hot climb to reach the summit, which is topped by both a small **wat** and a **stupa**.

Nearby are a couple of large field guns, which local children claim are defended with mines. This may not be true, but in the meantime take your photos from the path and do not approach them. Just for this information alone it is worth letting a child tag along with you and giving them something like 1000r at the end.

The children will also guide you to a rather horrific **killing field** located in a cave on another part of the hill. A small staircase leads down to a platform covered in the skulls and bones of victims. Look up to the right and you will see a skylight hole where victims were bludgeoned before being thrown into the pit beneath.

Phnom Sampeau is 26km south-west of Battambang and a moto is US$2 to US$3, including waiting time.

Wat Banan

Wat Banan is like a smaller version of the rather more famous Angkor Wat. Built in the 10th century, it is in a better state than Ek Phnom and its hillside location makes it more striking.

Wat Banan is located 25km south of Battambang and the round trip costs from US$2 to US$3.

Kamping Poy

Kamping Poy is both a lake and the site of one of the Khmer Rouge's grander schemes, a massive hand-built **dam** stretching for about 8km between two hillsides. Some locals claim it was intended as a sort of final solution for enemies of the revolution who were to be invited to witness its inauguration, and drowned as dynamite charges were set to detonate. It was more likely another step on the road to re-creating the complex irrigation network that Cambodia enjoyed under the kings of Angkor. Whatever the truth, as many as 10,000 Cambodians are thought to have perished in its construction. Nearby is a large **lake** which is a popular swimming spot for locals at the weekend.

Kamping Poy is 36km west of Battambang down a small turn-off just after Phnom Sampeau and is best combined with a visit to this wat; a moto for the full day trip is about US$6.

Sisophon

There is nothing of interest in Sisophon, but a number of travellers are finding themselves having to spend the night here coming overland from Thailand. Near the market is the **Phnom Meanchey Hotel** which offers aircon rooms with TV and fridge for US$10. From Sisophon to Poipet is about 5000r in the cab, less on the back, and to Siem Reap it is about 15,000r inside, 6000r outside. Coming from Thailand to Siem Reap, you should spend the night in Sisophon if you arrive much after 2 pm.

Trains run from here to Battambang daily but are absurdly slow when compared to the road. The rail line to Poipet and Thailand is currently in a state of disrepair.

Central Cambodia

KOMPONG CHHNANG

Kompong Chhnang is a tale of two cities: the ugly dockside seen by those travelling to Siem Reap by fast boat, and the old **colonial quarter** with its pleasant parks and handsome buildings. Connecting these very different parts is a long road lined with stilt houses and a maze of narrow walkways.

The town has nothing beyond atmosphere to offer the casual visitor, but for those with limited time who want a feel of provincial Cambodia it makes an economical transit stop between Phnom Penh and Angkor.

Places to Stay & Eat

There are only a couple of hotels in town. The **Rithesen Hotel** is on the Tonlé Sap River and has singles/doubles for US$5/8 or with air-con for US$8/12. It is clean, but it is in the dirtier part of town, where the aromas can get pretty strong, particularly when the river is low.

The **Krong Dei Meas Guesthouse** is in the colonial sector just off the central park and has basic rooms with bathroom for US$5. It sees a number of soldiers staying over on their way back to the capital so can get noisy at night.

There are several small restaurants in both parts of town. The **Mekong Restaurant**, near the Independence Monument, has a small but decent menu including a sound steak and chips, but the prices are high for such a small town. Better value, and arguably with the better food, is a Khmer place with no English name next to the Victory Monument. Most meals cost no more than US$2.

Getting There & Away

Kompong Chhnang is 91km north of Phnom Penh on a good, sealed road. DH Cambodia (7 and 10 am, and 12.30 and 3 pm) and Ho Wah Genting (6.50, 9 and 11.30 am, and 2 and 3.30 pm) run daily buses for 5000r that go past Udong. The fast boats make the trip, but are overpriced compared with the air-con buses. From Kompong Chhnang you can board the fast boat to Siem Reap which comes through just after 8.30 am. Aim to pay about 35,000r.

KOMPONG CHAM

Cambodia's third-largest city is a peaceful provincial capital spread along the banks of the Mekong River. It was an important trading post during the French period and the colonial legacy is evident as you wander through the streets. Even today it remains a crucial travel hub and acts as a gateway to the eastern and northern areas of Cambodia, and this role will only be enhanced with the construction of a Japanese-financed bridge across the Mekong, which is scheduled to begin in late 1998. It could become the Nong Khai of Cambodia one day, but for now it is still a quiet city where you can get away from it all.

Wat Nokor

Just outside town is an 11th century Mahayana Buddhist shrine of sandstone and laterite which today houses Wat Nokor, an active Hinayana wat. It is a kitsch place as it is really a temple within a temple and many of the older building's archways have been incorporated into the new building as shrines for worship. On weekdays, you will find just a few monks in the complex and you can wander slowly among the many alcoves and their hidden shrines, including a large reclining Buddha.

Phnom Pros & Phnom Srei

The names of the two hills translate as Man Hill and Woman Hill respectively. Local legend has it that two teams, one of men and the other of women, toiled by night to be the first to construct a stupa on their summit by daybreak. The women built a big fire, which the men took to be the rising sun and gave up work. The women, having won, no longer had to ask for the man's hand in marriage. Phnom Srei (Woman Hill) has good views of the countryside during the wet season.

Phnom Pros (Man Hill) is an interesting place for a cold drink as the trees are populated by some rather cheeky monkeys.

The hills are a short distance out of town and can be reached by moto for about US$1 round trip depending on waiting time for the moto driver.

Information

There are banks in town that can do travellers cheques and cash, but no credit card advances. Pacific Commercial Bank faces the river and is just around the corner from the market. Canadia Bank is at the river end of Monivong.

Phone calls and faxes can be arranged at offices around town.

Vannat is a good local guide to nearby attractions and if you sip an evening drink by the Mekong, he'll likely find you before long. He speaks English and French.

Places to Stay

There are an incredible number of rooms to rent in this city, as they were originally let to Cambodian soldiers when this was near the frontline in the war against the Khmer Rouge. In most hotels, rates are negotiable.

One street off the market has a whole row of *guesthouses* advertising rooms at 5000r, although most 'guests' here seem to pay by the hour so it could get noisy.

There is another 5000r *guesthouse* establishment on Rue Pasteur just off the river, sporting a Foster's beer sign, and this place presents a cleaner image than its immediate competitors.

If a riverside view is required, the *Chumnor Tonlé* has big doubles with bathroom at US$5 and US$10 with air-con, but the staff speak no English. Farther along the riverfront is the vast *Mekong Hotel*, with corridors you could play frisbee in, which has large, well equipped rooms at US$7 with fan and US$15 with air-con. If business seems to be slow, ask for a discount.

The *Bophear Guesthouse* is a friendly, clean place one block off the river on Rue Pasteur. Doubles with bathroom, fan and complimentary water cost US$5, making this the best of the budget places in town. Other guesthouses between the river and market include *Lucky* and *Monorom* with rooms at US$5.

The newly opened *Mittapheap Hotel* is the most upmarket hotel in town and has large, spotless rooms for US$15.

Places to Eat

The best restaurant in town is the *Kompong Cham Restaurant* on Rue Pasteur, about 1km up from the Mekong River. There are more than 100 dishes on the menu, including Khmer, Thai and Chinese influences. Prices are reasonable and it attracts a number of local expats.

The *Hoa An* was a very good restaurant until it was bulldozed to clear an access road for construction of the proposed bridge. However, the owners have definate plans to build new premises so keep an eye out for its return.

The *Apsara Restaurant* is on the market square, but the consensus is that food and service are not impressive.

There are a lot of unnamed *restaurants* around town selling inexpensive Khmer classics, some stop-and-dip *food stalls* in the market and a number of tikalok (fruit smoothie) *stalls* near the police station.

Entertainment

Leave your platform heels in the capital as the only nightclub in town has closed down at the time of writing. Locals gather on the waterfront outside the Mekong Hotel, where a number of *stalls* sell cheap drinks in the evening.

Getting There & Away

Kompong Cham is 120km north-east of Phnom Penh. The road is being upgraded by the Japanese so is excellent in sections, although the project is not due for completion until mid-1999. At the time of writing buses were not running the route but may be by the time you read this. Shared taxis cost about US$2 a person and go from the Central Market in Phnom Penh, while minibuses are as cheap as 4000r.

National Hwy 7 on to Kratie is in poor condition and swings eastwards almost to Mondolkiri before cutting west again. Pick-ups do the run for about US$3, or less if you ride on the back.

Fast boats heading for Phnom Penh and Kratie leave from an area near the Mekong Hotel. It takes approximately three hours to the capital and is 10,000r. To Kratie it also takes three hours and is 20,000r. There are also slower boats up to Kratie, and, in the wet season, Stung Treng. Travel is slow, departures infrequent and security not always good, but to Kratie is only 8000 to 10,000r, taking six hours.

North-East Cambodia

North-east Cambodia is one of the most inaccessible parts of the country and conditions vary widely between wet and dry seasons. Overland prices tend to be higher than elsewhere in the country and pick-up drivers are not afraid to leave without you if they don't like your price.

KRATIE

This small riverside town, pronounced 'krach-eh', is an overnight stop on the land route to Ratanakiri. It is a well preserved Khmer town as it was spared war time bombing and was 'liberated' by the Khmer Rouge long before other parts of the country. You get some dramatic sunsets over the Mekong and there are some very **old Khmer houses** on the edge of town.

There are a few hotels in town, including the *December 30th Hotel* with large rooms with bathroom at US$4 and the *Heng Heng Hotel* with rooms for US$5.

Getting There & Away

National Hwy 7 puts Kratie 343km north of Phnom Penh and 141km south of Stung Treng. By road from the capital it takes about eight hours and costs about US$5 inside a pick-up.

Quicker and more comfortable are the fast boats that take six hours up, five hours down, and cost 30,000r. Boats leave in both directions at 7 am.

The road north to Stung Treng is one of the least safe in the country as bandit attacks are frequent and some of the potholes would be more at home on a golf course. A number of travellers are now using this route and trucks charge about 25,000r inside and about 15,000r in the back for the six to eight hour journey. Check and double check the security conditions before setting out on this road.

For details of the journey to Kompong Cham, see that section.

STUNG TRENG

About 50km south of Laos, Stung Treng is a real outpost town on the banks of the Tonlé San River, just off the Mekong. Travellers heading between Kratie and Ratanakiri have to stop here for the night, but few hang around. The modern *Sekong Hotel* has fan rooms with bathroom for US$10 and air-con rooms for US$20. The *Amatak Hotel* has prices more in line with provincial Cambodia, with basic rooms for US$5.

Getting There & Away
Flights to and from Stung Treng depart on Monday, Wednesday and Friday and cost US$45/90 one way/return.

The road to Banlung in Ratanakiri is disgraceful and the journey takes about seven to nine hours by pick-up or jeep and costs about 30,000r up front or 20,000r behind, although the driver will start higher.

For details on the journey south, see the Kratie and Phnom Penh sections.

RATANAKIRI
Ratanakiri Province is Cambodia's wild east, home to a variety of shy **hill tribes**, or *chunchiets* (ethno-linguistic minorities), and a diversity of natural attractions including lakes, waterfalls and hidden wildlife. It is best visited in December or January as in the wet season it is difficult to move about and in the height of the dry season the roads are dust tracks that leave you spluttering on the back of a moto and the jungle is fairly subdued.

BANLUNG
Banlung is the provincial capital of Ratanakiri Province and the best base from which to explore the natural attractions of the area. The town itself isn't that interesting, but locals are extremely friendly and help make a visit a lively time. You can also ask around town about arranging an **elephant ride** in one of the surrounding villages.

Information
There are no banks in Banlung, but you can change US dollars into riel at jewellers in town. There is a post office on the road to Bokheo where you can make international calls.

Places to Stay & Eat
One of the nicest places to stay is the *Mountain II Guesthouse* on the road to Voen Sai.

It is an old building with a breezy balcony and double rooms are US$5. Owned by the same woman is the *Mountain Guesthouse*, near the airport, with rooms for the same price. Mrs Kim meets every plane that lands, so she can take you to either establishment.

The *Banlung Guesthouse* is the nearest the airport and small air-con rooms are US$10.

There are two hotels in the centre of town, the *Labansiek Hotel* and the *Ratanakhotel*, both of which have air-con rooms with bathroom for US$10. They are both near the central monument, although the Ratanakhotel has a slightly unfinished feel with wires and poles sticking out everywhere. It also has some fan rooms at US$5, but they can get very hot and you'll probably end up sleeping on the roof if you opt for one of these.

The best place to eat is the *Ratanakiri Restaurant*, also known as the American Restaurant. Various foreign visitors have contributed to the menu during the last few years, which claims to include lobster Thermidor, although given the distance to the coast you may want to leave it alone. Naeh, the owner, is one of the friendliest restaurant owners in Cambodia. You can also get cheap food near the market.

The *Labansiek Hotel*'s restaurant is expensive and the *Angkor Beer Restaurant* is pretty unfriendly.

Out on the road beyond the market are a couple of *nightclubs* that stay open until customers leave.

Getting There & Away
RAC flies to Banlung five times a week and most flights go via Mondolkiri or Stung Treng, regardless of the published schedules. One way/return costs US$55/100.

The road journey from Phnom Penh to Ratanakiri is an arduous three days as you must break it in Kratie and Stung Treng. The road between Banlung and Stung Treng is hopeless; for details of costs and continuing south overland, see the Stung Treng and Kratie sections.

AROUND BANLUNG
Yeak Loam Lake
Yeak Loam Lake is a circular crater lake situated amid lush jungle. It is one of the most peaceful, beautiful locations Cambodia has to offer and the water is extremely clean, with visibility of more than 5m. Entry is 1000r and there is a small centre nearby that has information on chunchiets in the province and on walks around the lake. It is 5km from Banlung, just off the road to Bokheo. Motos are available for about US$1 return.

Waterfalls
There are numerous waterfalls in the province, but many are inaccessible in the wet season and devoid of water in the dry

season. The three most commonly visited are **Chaa Ong**, **Ka Tieng** and **Kinchaan**. It is best to hook up with a local moto driver to visit any of these as they are off the beaten track and can be difficult to find alone. If you are on your own motorcycle and are having trouble finding the way, pick up a villager in the vicinity and they will guide you over the final stretch. The most spectacular of the three waterfalls is Chaa Ong as it is set in a jungle gorge and you are able to clamber behind the waterfall itself.

Other Places

Located on the Tonlé San River, **Voen Sai** is a pleasant little community including Chinese, Lao and Kreung villagers. Across the river is an old **Chinese settlement** dating back to 1700 and farther downstream several Lao and **chunchiet villages**. You can cross the river for 500r or less.

Voen Sai is also the gateway to **Virachey National Park**, the largest such park in Cambodia stretching east to Vietnam, north to Laos and west to Stung Treng. The park has not been fully explored and may be home to a number of larger mammals. Rangers also say there are a number of **waterfalls**, some as high as 100m. Facilities are minimal, but if you contact the ranger post in town you may be able to arrange a walk in the area.

The old provincial capital of **Lumphat** is something of a ghost town these days thanks to American bombing. However, it is an embarkation point for trips on the **Tonlé Srepok**, the river depicted in the film *Apocalypse Now*, in which Martin Sheen crosses the border into

Cambodia searching for the insane Colonel Kurtz, played by Marlon Brando.

The gem mining town of **Bokheo** is pretty dull in itself, but you may want to head out here to take a look at the **mines** themselves, which are 10m-deep circular pits into which the miner descends. You can purchase cheap stones in and around the town. Bokheo is 28km east of Banlung on the road to Vietnam.

MONDOLKIRI

Mondolkiri is another isolated forested province south of Ratanakiri, nestled against Cambodia's eastern border with Vietnam. It offers similar attractions to Ratanakiri Province, but has seen fewer visitors. Sen Monorom is the capital and like Banlung there is a pleasant lake in town. One advantage over Ratanakiri is Sen Monorom's elevated altitude, which ensures cooler temperatures during the dry season. The *Pich Kiri Guesthouse*, signposted at the airport, has rooms from US$5 to US$10 with fan and air-con. Ask around town about **elephant rides** as most of the creatures are found at work in nearby villages.

Getting There & Away

RAC flies to Sen Monorom twice a week for US$50/100 one way return. The road from Phnom Penh is pretty poor after Kompong Cham, although loggers have upgraded it, and it would require an overnight stop in a village along the way. For the time being, flying is the sensible way to go. You can go to Kratie by boat (30,000r) and then go by road from there in one day.

Indonesia

Indonesia is a long chain of tropical islands offering a mixture of cultures, people, scenery, prospects, problems and aspirations unmatched in South-East Asia. For the budget traveller, Indonesia is a kaleidoscope of cheap food, adventurous travel and every sort of attraction – the tropical paradise of Bali, the untouched wilderness of Sumatra, the historical monuments of Yogyakarta, with the overcrowding of Jakarta thrown in to leaven the mix. It's also currently an unbeatable bargain, thanks to the regional economic crisis and the consequent collapse of the rupiah.

Facts about Indonesia

HISTORY

The earliest inhabitants of the Indonesian Archipelago date back to *Pithecanthropus erectus*, or Java Man, one of the earliest human ancestors that migrated via land bridges to Java at least half a million years ago. The people of Indonesia today are of Malay origin, closely related to the peoples of Malaysia and the Philippines, and are descendants of much later migrations from South-East Asia which began around 4000 BC.

Trade brought Hinduism and Buddhism from India as early as the 4th century AD and by the end of the 7th century, small trading posts had grown to become powerful kingdoms in Java and Sumatra. The Buddhist Sriwijaya Empire ruled southern Sumatra and much of the Malay peninsula for six centuries while the Hindu Mataram kingdom presided over Central Java. The two developed side by side as both rivals and partners and Mataram went on to raise inspiring monuments like Borobudur.

Mataram mysteriously declined and power shifted to East Java, where the Majapahit Empire rose to become the last great Hindu kingdom. Founded in the 13th century, it reached its peak under Prime Minister Gajah Mada, ruling Java, Bali and the island of Madura, off Java's north coast, although it also claimed suzerainty over a vast area of the archipelago.

The spread of Islam into the archipelago spelt the end of the Majapahits – satellite

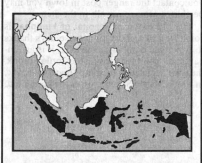

kingdoms took on the new religion and declared themselves independent of the Majapahits. But by the time Islam reached Java, it was less orthodox than in the Middle East and became infused with Javanese mysticism. The Majapahits retreated to Bali in the 15th century to found a flourishing culture while Java split into separate sultanates.

By the 15th century, a strong Muslim empire had developed with its centre at Melaka (Malacca) on the Malay peninsula,

INDONESIA

but in 1511 it fell to the Portuguese and the period of European influence in the archipelago began.

The Portuguese were soon displaced by the Dutch, who began to take over Indonesia in the early 17th century. A British attempt to oust the Dutch in 1619 failed – Melaka fell to the Dutch in 1641 and by 1700 they dominated most of Indonesia by virtue of their supremacy at sea and their control of the trade routes and some important ports. By the middle of the 18th century, all of Java was under their control.

The Napoleonic Wars led to a temporary British take-over between 1811 and 1816 in response to the French occupation of Holland, so Java came under the command of Sir Stamford Raffles. Indonesia was eventually handed back to the Dutch after the cessation of the wars, and an agreement made whereby the English evacuated their settlements in Indonesia in return for the Dutch leaving India and the Malay peninsula.

While the Europeans may have settled their differences, the Indonesians were of a different mind – for five years from 1825 onwards the Dutch had to put down a revolt led by the Javanese Prince Diponegoro. It was not until the early 20th century that the Dutch brought the whole of the archipelago – including Aceh and Bali – under control.

Although Dutch rule softened, dissatisfac-

tion still simmered and, led by Achmad Soekarno, a strong nationalist movement developed despite Dutch attempts to suppress it. The Japanese occupied the archipelago during WWII. After their defeat, Soekarno declared independence on 17 August 1945, but the Dutch returned and tried to take back control of their old territories. For four bitter years up to 1949, the Indonesians fought an intermittent war with the Dutch, who in the end were forced to recognise Indonesia's independence.

Weakened by the prolonged struggle, the transition to independence did not come easily. The first 10 years of independence saw Indonesian politicians preoccupied with their own political games until, in 1957, President Soekarno put an end to the impasse by declaring Guided Democracy with army backing and investing more power in himself.

Soekarno proved to be less adept as a nation builder than as a revolutionary leader. Grandiose building projects, the planned 'socialisation' of the economy and the senseless Confrontation with Malaysia led to internal dissension and a steady deterioration of the national economy.

As events came to a head, there was an attempted coup in 1965 led by an officer of Soekarno's palace guard. The coup was suppressed by the Indonesian army under the leadership of General Soeharto. The reasons for the coup are unclear but it was passed off as an attempt by the Communists to seize power and hundreds of thousands of Communists, suspected Communists and sympathisers were killed or imprisoned. Soeharto eventually pushed Soekarno out of power and took over the presidency.

The invasion of Portuguese Timor, in 1975, stands as much to the world's discredit as Indonesia's, and it was surely no coincidence that then US secretary of state, Henry Kissinger, left Jakarta the day before the invasion. The Dili massacre in 1991 severely tarnished Indonesia's international standing.

Despite graft and corruption being very much a way of life, the economy grew rapidly during the 80s and early 90s with heavy foreign investment and industrialisation, but it all came crashing to a halt in 1997 when the rupiah collapsed as part of a broader Asian economic crisis. Virtually overnight the prospects suddenly became extremely grim, and the International Monetary Fund (IMF) was forced to step in and bail the country out with a $41 billion aid package.

Discontent with the Soeharto regime's culture of corruption, cronyism and nepotism was already well on the rise in the late 90s, but with the country's sudden economic collapse, the discontent rapidly escalated to demonstrations, calls for political reform and for Soeharto to resign and disastrously, in May 1998, violent riots in Jakarta which left over 1000 people dead.

The pressure on Soeharto finally led to his resignation on 21 May 1998. He was succeeded by Vice-President BJ Habibie, a man with strong links to Soeharto and therefore deemed by many as an unacceptable successor. Within days of taking power, however, Habibie's actions showed that his style would be hugely different from his predecessor – a number of political prisoners (some of them East Timorese) were released, the media (both foreign and local) was liberalised, and a law banning discrimination against ethnic Chinese citizens (who were targets during the 1998 riots) was passed. Economic policy also took a new direction, with the acceptance of an independent central bank, transparency in government spending and a tight monetary policy. Habibie stated that general elections would be held in May 1999, and presidential elections on 22 December the same year.

Despite all his manoeuvring, it seems far from certain that Habibie will survive as leader until the elections take place. His most severe handicap is the lack of a power base within the ruling Golkar party. Compounding this is a similar lack of public support. What is even more worrying, perhaps, is the lack of a credible alternative power structure – neither the opposition parties, the Muslims nor the students are as yet sufficiently well organised. Given this lack of either a credible leader or realistic alternative, the country faces an acute power vacuum at a time when it most needs strong leadership to implement the economic and political reforms necessary to ride out the crisis.

GEOGRAPHY
Indonesia has an area of 1.9 million sq km scattered over about 13,700 islands. It is a far less compact mass of islands than the nearby Philippines, the other island nation of the region. Parts of Indonesia are still vast, barely explored regions of dense jungle and many islands have extinct, active or dormant volcanoes.

CLIMATE
Straddling the equator, Indonesia is hot year-round – hot and wet during the wet season, and hot and dry during the dry season. Coastal areas are often pleasantly cool, however, and it can get extremely cold in the mountains.

Generally, the wet season starts later the further south-east you go. In north Sumatra, the rain begins to fall in September, but in Timor it doesn't fall until November. In January and February it can rain often.

In general, the dry season is from May to September. The odd islands out are those of Maluku (the Moluccas), where the wet season is the reverse, running from May to September.

See the regional sections in this chapter and the Jakarta climate chart in the Appendix for more details.

ECOLOGY & ENVIRONMENT
Indonesia's rapid industrial expansion in the past decade and its large and growing population are placing great stresses on the environment. Things are not helped by the fact that the country does not have the resources to give high priority to environmental issues. Nevertheless, there are environmental programs in place in Indonesia, but typically they are poorly funded and enforcement is difficult or ignored.

Despite widespread logging, and development encroaching on the jungle, Indonesia still has large forest reserves, particularly in Sumatra and Kalimantan. The government policy of selective logging and reafforestation is all but ignored and the forests are disappearing at an alarming rate. Forest fires in Kalimantan, lit by loggers and farmers to clear undergrowth, burnt out large areas of Kalimantan in 1997 and again in 1998. The fires were exacerbated by a prolonged drought, and huge palls of smoke covered large parts of the entire region.

Industrial pollution, especially in Java, has come in the wake of industrialisation, and a growing middle class has seen the number of vehicles on the road increase dramatically.

Indonesia is also becoming more urbanised – 30% of the population currently live in cities – and this puts further strain on the environment as rubbish and sewerage inevitably finds its way into the canals and river systems. Most Indonesians are not supplied with safe drinking water, and all water has to be boiled.

FLORA & FAUNA

Indonesia has one of the world's richest natural environments, harbouring an incredible diversity of plant and animal species. The British naturalist Alfred Wallace first classified the Indonesian islands into two zones: a western, Asian ecological zone and an eastern, Australian zone. The 'Wallace Line' dividing these two zones runs between Kalimantan and Sulawesi and south through the straits between Bali and Lombok. Later scientists have further expanded on this classification to show distinct breaks between the ecologies of Sulawesi and Maluku, and further between Maluku and Irian Jaya.

West of the Wallace Line, Sumatra, Java, Kalimantan and Bali were once linked to the Asian mainland, and as a result some large Asian land animals, including elephants, tigers, rhinoceroses and leopards, still survive in some areas, and the dense rainforests and abundant flora of Asia are in evidence. Perhaps the most famous animal is the orang-utan ('forest man' in Indonesian), the long-haired red apes found in Sumatra and Kalimantan.

East of the Wallace Line, Sulawesi, Nusa Tenggara and Maluku have long been isolated from the continental land masses and have developed unique flora and fauna. From Lombok eastwards, the flora and fauna of Nusa Tenggara reflect the more arid conditions of these islands. The large Asian mammals are nonexistent, and mammal species in general are smaller and less diverse. Nusa Tenggara has one astonishing and famous animal, the Komodo dragon, the world's largest lizard, found only on Komodo and a few neighbouring islands.

Irian Jaya and the Aru Islands were once part of the Australian landmass, and the collision of the Australian and Pacific plates resulted in a massive mountain range running along the middle of Irian Jaya, isolating a number of unique environments, although the fauna throughout is closely related to Australia. Irian Jaya has kangaroos, marsupial mice, bandicoots, ring-tailed possums, crocodiles and frilled lizards – all animals found in Australia.

GOVERNMENT & POLITICS

Indonesia is currently in a period of great political uncertainty, and reform of the system which saw Soeharto, his family and those favoured by him amass fortunes seems inevitable.

Under the existing system, executive power rests with the president. Officially, the highest authority lies with the People's Consultative Assembly (MPR), which elects the president every five years. The congress is made up of all members of the elected House of Representatives (which rarely meets), and presidential appointees from various interest groups, most notably the armed forces. Real power lies with the ruling party, Golkar, where the army is a major player, while the real business of government is handled by the president and ministers appointed by and responsible only to the president.

Up until now, democracy has been largely a veneer, although this too is bound to change. The end of the Soeharto era has seen a proliferation in political parties as people start to enjoy the first taste of political reform – 60 new parties were formed within three months of Soeharto's fall. While Soeharto was in power there were only two major political parties allowed in addition to Golkar: the Muslim United Development Party (PPP) and the Indonesian Democratic Party (PDI), led until 1997 by Soekarno's daughter, Megawati Soekarnoputri, who seems likely to play a role in future political developments. Another major player is Amien Rais, leader of the 28-million-strong Muhamadiyah Muslim organisation.

The state philosophy is Pancasila (Five Principles), the sole philosophical base for all political, social and religious organisations.

INDONESIA

The five principles are Faith in God, Humanity, Nationalism, Representative Government and Social Justice. While it the past has been used as an excuse for government authoritarianism, it has also ensured religious and social tolerance in multi-ethnic Indonesia.

ECONOMY

In the 80s and 90s foreign-investment approvals were averaging around US$1 billion per week, the economy was booming, Indonesia was one of the major regional economic players and the outlook seemed extremely bright.

The Asian currency crisis of October 1997 brought all that to a screaming halt, and Indonesia now faces a lengthy period of severe economic hardship. The IMF US$41 billion bail out package for the economy is causing major pain as subsidies are wound back leading to massive jumps in the prices of fuel, transport and basic commodities. Unemployment is tipped to top 20% (up from 5% pre-crisis), inflation romps along (around 70% in mid-98) and the economy was expected to shrink by as much as 20% in 1998. All in all the economic outlook is extremely bleak.

Despite a conspicuously wealthy elite, particularly in the main cities of Java, most Indonesians survive in a rural subsistence economy, and increasing numbers are destined to fall below the poverty line as the economic crisis bites. Corruption and inefficiency are still widespread, and the problems of overpopulation and the accompanying strain on resources all add to a picture of economic hardship for the near future.

POPULATION & PEOPLE

Indonesia is the fourth most populous country in the world. The population is around 200 million and fully 60% are crammed into just 7% of the nation's land area – the island of Java. The people are of the Malay race, although there are many different groupings and a vast number of local dialects. There are distinct cultural differences between islands, and even within islands, making Indonesia the most culturally diverse nation in South-East Asia.

SOCIETY & CONDUCT

Indonesia has a diverse mix of cultures rather than a single one, but the effects of mass education, mass media and a policy of government-orchestrated nationalism have created a very definite Indonesian national culture.

'Keeping face' is important to Indonesians and they are generally extremely courteous – criticisms are not spoken directly and they will usually agree with what you say rather than offend.

Dos & Don'ts

Indonesians will accept any lack of clothing on the part of poor people who cannot afford them; but for westerners, thongs (flip-flops), bathing costumes, shorts or strapless tops are considered impolite except perhaps around places like Kuta on Bali. Elsewhere you have to look vaguely respectable. Women are better off dressing modestly – revealing tops are just asking for trouble. Short pants are marginally acceptable if they are the baggy type which almost reach the knees.

Permission should be requested to enter places of worship, particularly when ceremonies are in progress. Dress decently, and always remove footwear before entering a mosque. It is also customary to take shoes off before entering someone's house.

Asians resent being touched on the head, which is regarded as the seat of the soul and is therefore sacred.

When handing over or receiving things remember to use the right hand – the left hand is used as a substitute for toilet paper. To show great respect to a high-ranking or elderly person, hand something to them using both hands.

Talking to someone with your hands on your hips is impolite and is considered a sign of contempt, anger or aggressiveness. Shaking hands is customary for both men and women on introduction and greeting.

RELIGION

Nominally a Muslim nation, there is actually an amazing diversity of religions and a commendable degree of religious tolerance in Indonesia. From the time of the Dutch, pockets of Christianity have continued to exist on the islands of Timor and Flores, in the Danau Toba region of north Sumatra and the Tana Toraja area of Sulawesi. At one time, Sumatra was predominantly Buddhist and Java was predominantly Hindu – this was before the spread of Islam and its eventual dominance of the region. The last remnants of Hinduism are found on Bali, though much of Muslim Java still follows Hindu tradition and thought.

See the Religions of South-East Asia section in the Appendix for a full discussion of the various religions found in the region.

LANGUAGE

Although there are a vast number of local languages and dialects in the country, Bahasa Indonesia, which is very similar to Malay, is promoted as the one national language.

Like most languages, Indonesian has its simplified colloquial form and its more developed literate language. Indonesian is rated as one of the simplest languages in the world as there are no tenses or genders, and often one word can convey the meaning of a whole sentence. There are often no plurals, or it is only necessary to say the word twice – child is *anak*, and children are *anak anak*. Book is *buku* and books are *buku buku*. With other words, the context makes it clear that it's plural.

Indonesian can also be a delightfully poetic language with words like *matahari*, or 'sun', derived from *mata* (eye) and *hari* (day), so the sun is literally the eye of the day.

Lonely Planet's *Indonesian phrasebook* is a pocket-sized introduction to the language, intended to make getting by in Bahasa Indonesian as easy as possible.

See the Appendix for a list of useful words and phrases.

Facts for the Visitor

HIGHLIGHTS

The most visited islands for overland travellers are Sumatra, Java and Bali, and it is possible to see the main highlights of these three islands in one month, but that doesn't leave much time for relaxation.

Other Indonesian islands are not so accessible, and travel costs are often higher because flying becomes essential unless you have huge amounts of time. Nusa Tenggara and Sulawesi are easier to explore than Maluku, Irian Jaya or Kalimantan, which are still unexplored territory for the vast majority of visitors to Indonesia, though they have plenty to offer.

Java

The cultural city of **Yogyakarta** is the number one travellers' centre and a good base for exploring the awe-inspiring monuments of **Borobudur** and **Prambanan**. Nearby **Solo** is a quieter court city and repository of Javanese culture.

Pangandaran is Java's beach resort, while the **Gunung Bromo** area is one of Indonesia's most spectacular volcanic landscapes.

The big cities of Java tend to be crowded and disorienting, but **Bogor** and **Bandung** have reminders of the Dutch presence. The bustling and increasingly modern capital of **Jakarta** still has the finest remnants of the Dutch era.

Sumatra

Sumatra's main attractions are in the north between Medan and Padang. Spectacular **Danau (Lake) Toba** is on most itineraries, and the **Bukit Lawang orang-utan sanctuary** is easily reached from Medan.

The mountain town of **Bukittinggi** is the cultural heartland of the Minangkabau people and one of the main travellers' centres. **Pulau Nias** also gets a lot of visitors, drawn by both the ancient megalithic cultures and the surf.

Bali

Bali has brilliant green terraced landscapes, fascinating Hindu culture and excellent facilities. Spectacular temples like **Ulu Watu**, **Rambut Siwi** and touristy **Tanah Lot** perch on cliffs over the sea, while hundreds of others come alive during colourful temple festivals.

Kuta is Bali's most famous beach, but other resorts, such as **Lovina, Candidasa** and **Sanur**, also offer sun, sea, surf, snorkelling and/or socialising.

Strange stone figures at **Gunung Kawi** date from the 11th century, while contemporary culture is best experienced at **Ubud**, where modern painting and carving thrive, along with traditional music and dance and the island's finest cuisine. Trekkers are attracted to the smoking caldera of **Gunung Batur**, with 3142m **Gunung Agung** an even bigger challenge.

Nusa Tenggara

Lombok, which is Nusa Tenggara's main destination, gets a lot of the Bali overflow, attracted by fine beaches, islands, towering **Gunung Rinjani** and a more relaxed approach to tourism.

The two most famous attractions of Nusa Tenggara are the fabulous dragons of **Komodo** and the spectacular coloured lakes of **Kelimutu** on **Flores**. Scenic Flores also has traditional cultures to explore around **Bajawa** and some decent beaches at **Labuanbajo** for relaxing.

The island of **Sumba** has fascinating megalithic cultures, and **Timor** is as wild and as traditional as they come.

INDONESIA

Kalimantan

Kalimantan is one of the least visited parts of Indonesia, mostly because its unique cultures, spectacular flora and unusual wildlife, all well away from the ravages of development, are expensive and time-consuming to reach.

Banjarmasin and its river life is the main tourist destination and a good place to start exploring this vast island. The remote Kayan and Kenyah settlements in the **Apokayan** are worth a visit.

Sulawesi

The colourful funerals of **Tana Toraja** are Sulawesi's best known attraction from June to August. The mountains of Tana Toraja are serenely beautiful, as are those of central Sulawesi.

Sulawesi also has some superb beaches and coral reefs. The 'sea gardens' off **Manado**, particularly around **Pulau Bunaken**, offer some of the best snorkelling and diving in Indonesia, while the pristine reefs around the **Togian Islands** are an untouched tropical wonder.

Maluku

The islands of Maluku are known for great beaches, diving and old forts. The main island of **Ambon** makes a good base and has beaches, hiking, diving and a superbly renovated fort. To the north, **Ternate** has stunning volcanic scenery, black-sand beaches and even more forts. The highlight of Maluku, the **Bandas**, has it all: magnificent forts, the awesome **Gunung Api** volcano, and great diving and swimming.

Irian Jaya

The **Baliem Valley**, with its unique culture and trekking among stunning scenery, is the major tourist attraction in remote Irian Jaya. Along the northern coast, **Manokwari** and **Nabire** are pleasant towns with a few islands and lakes to explore.

Biak is a popular stopover with great diving spots, beaches and WWII remnants to explore around the island.

PLANNING
When to Go

Though travel in the wet season is possible in most parts of Indonesia, it can be a definite deterrent to some activities, and travel on mud-clogged roads in less developed areas is difficult. In general, the best time to visit Indonesia is in the dry season between May and September.

See the Climate section earlier for details of regional weather variations.

Maps

Locally produced maps are often surprisingly inaccurate. The Nelles Verlag map series covers Indonesia in a number of separate sheets, and they're usually quite good. Periplus also produces excellent maps of most of the archipelago and includes maps of the major cities. Both series are available in Indonesia and overseas.

TOURIST OFFICES

The National Tourist Organisation of Indonesia produces a *Calendar of Events* for the entire country and a useful *Indonesia Travel Planner* book, which includes some good maps and helpful travel information. They're available from the Directorate General of Tourism in Jakarta and at tourist offices overseas.

Otherwise, Indonesian tourist offices are generally poor, often have limited or no literature or maps, and the staff may not always speak English. The usefulness of individual tourist offices often depends on who works there and who you get to talk to.

Some of the regional tourist offices produce local information, or useful items such as festival calendars. Denpasar on Bali, and Jakarta, Bandung, Yogyakarta and Solo on Java have good tourist offices. Other good regional offices can be found in Bukittinggi and Padang on Sumatra, and Mataram on Lombok. There's also an excellent independent tourist office in Ubud on Bali. Outside of these areas, it often isn't worth the effort.

Tourist Offices Abroad

Indonesian Tourist Promotion Offices (ITPO) abroad can supply brochures and information about Indonesia. Useful publications are the *Travel Planner*, *Tourist Map of Indonesia* and the *Calendar of Events* for the whole country. ITPO offices are listed below. Garuda Airlines offices overseas are also worth trying for information.

Australia
    (☎ 02-9233 3630) Level 10, 5 Elizabeth St, Sydney, NSW 2000
Germany
    (☎ 069-23 3677) Wiessenhuttenstrasse 17 D.6000, Frankfurt am Main 1

Japan
(☎ 03-3585 3588) 2nd Floor, Sankaido Bldg,
1-9-13 Akasaka, Minatoku, Tokyo 107
Singapore
(☎ 534 2837) 10 Collyer Quay, Ocean Bldg,
Singapore 0104
Taiwan
(☎ 02-537 7620) 5th Floor, 66 Sung Chiang
Rd, Taipei
UK
(☎ 020-7493 0030) 3-4 Hanover St, London
W1R 9HH
USA
(☎ 213-387 2078) 3457 Wilshire Blvd, Los
Angeles, CA 90010

VISAS & DOCUMENTS
Passport
Check your passport expiry date. Indonesia
requires that your passport has six months of
life left in it on your date of arrival.

Visas
Visitors from most western countries can
enter Indonesia without a visa, for a stay of
up to 60 days, so long as you enter and exit
through certain recognised airports or seaports. Officially (but not always in practice),
you must have a ticket out of the country
when you arrive. Officially (and almost certainly), you cannot extend your tourist pass
beyond 60 days (business visas can be extended). If you really intend to explore
Indonesia in some depth, then 60 days is inadequate and you will have to exit the
country and re-enter.

Visa Extensions Tourist passes cannot be
extended beyond 60 days. You may get a few
extra days in special circumstances, like
missed flight connections or illness, but don't
count on it. Do *not* simply show up at the
airport with an expired visa or tourist pass
and expect to be able to board your flight.
You may be sent back to the local immigration office to clear up the matter. Overstaying
attracts very steep fines, up to 500,000 rp per
day, or a stint in jail if you can't pay.

If you arrived in Indonesia on a one-month
visitor visa, it is usually extendable only for
two weeks. An extension costs around 50,000
rp, and is obtained through any immigration
office.

Onward Tickets
The onward ticket requirement is randomly
enforced; you may be asked, in which case
evidence of sufficient funds is usually acceptable in lieu – US$1000 seems to be the magic
number (credit cards are often not accepted).
If you don't have it, dress as if you do; otherwise say you are only making a short visit –
a 60 day entry permit is standard regardless
of the length of stay.

If you fly to Kupang (in Timor) from
Darwin, Australia, or take the ferry to Batam
from Singapore, it's unlikely that any great
fuss will be made. Expect to flash your cash
if arriving in Medan (in Sumatra) on the ferry
from Penang (in Malaysia).

On Bali they may still ask to see a ticket but
most Bali visitors are on short-stay package
trips, so you're unlikely to be troubled.

Jakarta can be a hassle. Some visitors have
been forced to buy an onward ticket on the
spot. The main problem is likely to be with
airlines overseas, who may strictly enforce
official requirements and not let you on
flights to Indonesia without an onward ticket.

If you want a simple solution, the Malaysia
Airlines flight between Medan and Penang is
straightforward, reasonably cheap and can be
refunded if you don't use it. The various
flights between Jakarta and Singapore are
also safe and cheap bets. See Getting There
& Away later in this chapter for other short-
hop international flights.

Visa-Free Entry/Exit Points
The visa-free entry system becomes a problem for that tiny minority of travellers who
plan to arrive or depart through an unrecog-
nised 'gateway'. If you fall into that category
you have to get an Indonesian tourist visa
before arriving, and visas are only valid for
one month. Extensions on a one month visa
are usually only for two weeks and cost
around 50,000 rp.

The Indonesian government's list of recognised 'no visa' entry and exit points are the
airports of Ambon, Denpasar, Balikpapan,
Batam, Biak, Jakarta, Kupang, Manado,
Mataram, Medan, Padang, Pekanbaru, Pontianak and Surabaya. Bandung, Banda Aceh
and Solo airports are visa-free only for 30-
day visas rather than the usual 60-day visa.

Also visa-free are the seaports of Ambon,
Batam, Belawan, Bengkulu, Benoa, Dumai,
Jakarta, Padangbai, Semarang, Surabaya,
Tanjung Pinang, Manado and Ujung Pandang.
The only 'no visa' land crossings are at En-
tikong in west Kalimantan, between Pontianak
and Kuching (Malaysia); and Jayapura, from
Vanimo (PNG).

The official list is rarely updated but does

INDONESIA

change, so if you're planning an odd entry or exit find out the latest story. Entering by air on a regular flight is usually not a problem, and the airline will be better informed than an Indonesian embassy.

Entering or leaving Indonesia overland or by unusual sea routes usually requires a visa.

EMBASSIES & CONSULATES
Indonesian Embassies & Consulates

Countries with an Indonesian embassy include:

Australia
(☎ 02-6250 8600)
8 Darwin Ave, Yarralumla, ACT 2600
Consulates in Adelaide, Darwin, Melbourne, Perth and Sydney
Canada
(☎ 613-231 0186)
55 Parkdale Ave, Ottawa, Ontario K1Y 1E5
Consulates in Vancouver and Toronto
France
(☎ 01 45 03 07 60)
47-49 rue Cortambert, 75116 Paris
Consulate in Marseilles
Germany
(☎ 0228-382 990)
2 Bernakasteler Strasse, 53175 Bonn
Consular offices in Berlin, Bremen, Dusseldorf, Hamburg, Hannover, Kiel, Munich and Stuttgart
India
(☎ 011-611 8642)
50-A Chanakyapuri, New Delhi
Japan
(☎ 03-3441 4201)
5-9-2 Higashi Gotanda, Shinagawa-ku, Tokyo
New Zealand
(☎ 04-475 8697)
70 Glen Rd, Kelburn, Wellington
UK
(☎ 020-7499 7661)
38 Grosvenor Square, London W1X 9AD
USA
(☎ 202-775 5200)
2020 Massachusetts Ave NW, Washington, DC 20036
Consulates in Chicago, Honolulu, Houston, Los Angeles, New York and San Francisco

See the other chapters in this book for Indonesian embassies in those countries.

Embassies & Consulates in Indonesia

Countries with diplomatic representation in Jakarta include:

Australia
(☎ 522 7111) Jalan Rasuna Said, Kav 15-16
Brunei
(☎ 571 2180) 8th Floor, Wisma BCA, Jalan Jenderal Sudirman Kav 22-23
Canada
(☎ 525 0709) 5th Floor, Wisma Metropolitan I, Jalan Jenderal Sudirman, Kav 29
France
(☎ 314 2807) Jalan Thamrin 20
Germany
(☎ 390 1750) Jalan Thamrin 1
Japan
(☎ 32 4308) Jalan Thamrin 24
Malaysia
(☎ 522 4947) Jalan Rasuna Said Kav X/6 No 1
Myanmar (Burma)
(☎ 314 0440) Jalan H Augus Salim 109
Netherlands
(☎ 525 1515) Jalan Rasuna Said, Kav S-3, Kuningan
New Zealand
(☎ 570 9460) Jalan Diponegoro 41
Philippines
(☎ 310 0334) Jalan Imam Bonjol 6-8
Singapore
(☎ 520 1489), Jalan Rasuna Said, Block X, Kav 2 No 4
Thailand
(☎ 390 4055) Jalan Imam Bonjol 74
UK
(☎ 390 7484) Jalan Thamrin 75
USA
(☎ 344 2211) Jalan Merdeka Selatan 5
Vietnam
(☎ 310 0357) Jalan Teuku Umar 25

CUSTOMS

Customs allows you to bring in a maximum of 2L of alcoholic beverages and 200 cigarettes or 50 cigars or 100g of tobacco.

Bringing narcotics, arms and ammunition, cordless telephones, pornography, printed matter in Chinese characters and Chinese medicines into the country is prohibited. Officially, cameras, computers, radios and the like should be declared upon arrival, but in effect customs officials rarely worry about how much gear tourists bring into the country – at least if you have a western face. Personal effects are not a problem.

MONEY
Currency

For many years the Indonesian rupiah was a relatively stable currency based primarily on the US$, trading at around 2000 rp to 2400 rp to the dollar. Then in late 1997 the currency crises of Thailand and then Malaysia spilled over into Indonesia. The central bank was unable to defend the rupiah and abandoned the currency to the market. Within weeks the rupiah plunged to over 10,000 rp to the US dollar.

The currency continues to fluctuate wildly based on the latest rumours or IMF pronouncements. Your foreign currency should go a long way, despite rampant inflation.

Exchange Rates

At the time of writing exchange rates were as follows:

country	unit		rupiah
Australia	A$1	=	5498 rp
Canada	C$1	=	5650 rp
euro	€1	=	10,507 rp
France	10FF	=	15,900 rp
Germany	DM1	=	5332 rp
Japan	¥100	=	7316 rp
New Zealand	NZ$1	=	4713 rp
Singapore	S$1	=	5387 rp
UK	UK£1	=	14,873 rp
USA	US$1	=	8740 rp

Exchange rates within the country vary wildly depending on where you go – the more remote the place the worse the rates will be. In 1998, when the official rate for the rupiah was around 10,000 rp for US$1, moneychangers on Bali were offering around 9000 rp, banks slightly less, while in Irian Jaya banks were quoting a shade over 5000 rp! For this reason it makes good sense to get cash advances from a credit card whenever possible, as you will get the daily international market rates rather than whatever rates the local bank happens to be using (see Cash Advances in this section).

US dollars are easily the most widely accepted foreign currency and often have a better exchange rate than other currencies – this is especially so outside of Jakarta, Bali and the major tourist areas. If you're going to be in really remote regions, carry sufficient cash with you as banks may be scarce. Even those you do come across may only accept certain varieties of travellers cheques – stick to the major companies.

There are moneychangers in many locales and they're open longer hours and change money (cash or cheques) much faster than the banks. In places like Bali, they offer extremely competitive rates.

ATMs Automatic Teller Machines (ATMs) have proliferated in Indonesia in the past few years to the extent that you could travel through the main tourist areas of Bali, Java and Sumatra and never have to set foot inside a bank, although it's definitely recommended to carry some cash or travellers cheques as a back-up, particularly if travelling away from the main areas – or you can use a plastic card as your back-up.

Even in major regional cities such as Ujung Pandang, Ambon and even Jayapura, you'll find ATMs that accept Visa, MasterCard or Cirrus cards. The ATMs are accessible 24 hours a day and often in cities they don't even have to be near a bank – you can find clusters of them at the post office, in shopping centres or other strategic locations.

Cash Advances MasterCard (and linked services such as Cirrus and Maestro) is the most widely accepted plastic card. BNI, Bank Internasional Indonesia (BII), Bank Bali and some other major Indonesian banks give cash advances for MasterCard, while the Bank of Central Asia (BCA) and BII accept Visa.

Most cards can be used to debit from your savings account rather than racking up credit, and you receive the best exchange rates of the day. Transaction fees may be charged by your home bank and can be ridiculously high, so it makes sense to withdraw as much cash as possible at a time – check with your bank. Always check the transaction record to ensure the correct amount has been debited (some banks such as BNI even give your home account balance in rupiah – instant millionaire).

Apart from using them for cash advances, credit cards can also be used at big hotels, exclusive restaurants and shops.

Costs

Given the huge financial hole the rupiah is in at the moment, Indonesia is an unbeatable bargain, with costs amazingly low, even by South-East Asian standards. A couple of dollars for a hotel or a decent meal and a drink at a good restaurant is par for the course.

If you follow the well-beaten tourist track through Bali, Java and Sumatra, stay at cheap losmen (hotels), eat local food and take the cheapest transport you could get by on US$5 a day! Travellers' centres like Danau Toba, Yogyakarta and Bali are superb value for accommodation and food.

Elsewhere transport costs rise, budget accommodation can be limited and prices are

INDONESIA

higher because competition is less, but they're still comparatively very cheap. Sulawesi and Nusa Tenggara are cheap enough, but accommodation in Maluku and Irian Jaya can be two to three times higher, and transport costs in Kalimantan are also relatively high.

Despite significant recent increases, fuel is still absurdly cheap in Indonesia (US$0.10 per litre), so surface transport costs are also pleasantly low. Air fares have risen considerably to keep pace with the plummeting rupiah, but, once again, they are still cheap by international standards; Denpasar to Ujung Pandang, for instance, costs around US$50, Jakarta to Ujung Pandang is around US$100.

Tipping & Bargaining

Tipping is not a normal practice in Indonesia but is often expected for special service. Someone who carries your bag, guides you around a tourist attraction etc will naturally expect a tip.

Bargaining is required in markets, for souvenirs and any tourist-oriented goods and for transport where prices are not fixed. It may even be required for everyday items, such as a bottle of water or a packet of cigarettes, especially from street hawkers in tourist areas such as Bali. Hotel prices are usually fixed but asking for a discount might bring a reduction, especially at the upper-end hotels.

Bargaining is a complex social game that Indonesians love to play well, and a necessary survival skill in a poor country. As with any social interaction, it is important to maintain equanimity. Remain good-humoured – shouting or aggressiveness will force the trader to lose face and push prices up. Above all, keep things in perspective: the 1000 rp you may overpay for a *becak* (bicycle rickshaw) ride wouldn't buy a newspaper at home, but it is a meal for a poor becak driver.

POST & COMMUNICATIONS
Post

The postal service in Indonesia is generally good and the poste restante service at Indonesian *kantor pos* (post offices) are reasonably efficient in the main tourist centres. Expected mail always seems to arrive, eventually.

Overseas parcels can be posted, insured and registered *(tercatat)* from a main post office but they'll usually want to have a look at the contents first, so there's not much point in making up a tidy parcel before you get there. If you are going on to Singapore, the postal service is more reliable and cheaper from there.

Telephone

International calls are easy to make from private booths in Telkom offices and privately run *wartel (warung telekomunikasi,* telecommunications stall). Reverse-charge calls can be made from Telkom offices free of charge, though private wartels usually charge for the first minute or don't offer the service at all.

Many Telkom offices also have Home Country Direct Dial Phones (press one button to get through to your home country operator) and they can also be found in terminals at major airports and some big hotels.

International calls can also be made from new public phones, the ones which take the credit-card-like stiff plastic cards with the embedded chip (as against the older ones which take a thin flexible card with a magnetic strip). You can also make Home Country Direct calls from these booths (dial 00181, then the country code and number). These phones so far are found only in the main cities, and only on Bali, Java and Sulawesi. Elsewhere, international calls cannot be made from public phones.

Local directory assistance is 108. The police emergency number is 110.

Email & Internet Access

Depending on where you are, access varies from easy to impossible. On Bali and Java Internet cafes are springing up everywhere. They are open long hours and charge anything from 10,000 rp to 60,000 rp per hour.

In Sumatra and Java (and occasionally elsewhere, such as Ambon) major post offices have public Internet access. While they are only open during normal business hours, they are cheaper at 5000 rp to 12,000 rp per hour.

INTERNET RESOURCES

Indonesia hasn't exactly jumped on the web but a growing number of sites sometimes provide useful information. Web pages on Indonesian ISPs (Internet service providers) can be very slow and tend to be updated irregularly.

Bali is well represented with plenty of commercial sites promoting tourism. For a general introduction try werple.mira.net.au /~wreid/ or www.indo.com.

'Grandaddy of them all' is the Australian National University's links site at coombs. anu. edu.au/WWWVLPages/IndonPages/WWWVL -Indonesia.html. Another good links page comes from the University of Auckland: www.auckland.ac.nz/asi/indo/links.html.

Telephone Codes

The international dialling code from within Indonesia is 001 (through Indosat), or 008 (Satelindo); Home Country Direct is 00181.

The country code for Indonesia is 62. Following are area codes for major cities. Dial the initial zero only when calling from within Indonesia.

Java

Bandung	☎ 022
Bogor	☎ 0251
Cilacap	☎ 0282
Cirebon	☎ 0231
Gunung Bromo Area	☎ 0335
Jakarta	☎ 021
Pangandaran	☎ 0265
Probolinggo	☎ 0335
Solo	☎ 0271
Surabaya	☎ 031
Yogyakarta	☎ 0274
Wonosobo	☎ 0286

Bali

Candidasa	☎ 0363
Danau Bratan Area	☎ 0368
Denpasar (also southern Bali)	☎ 0361
Gunung Batur Area	☎ 0366
Kuta Region	☎ 0361
Lovina Beach	☎ 0362
Nusa Dua	☎ 0361
Padangbai	☎ 0363
Sanur	☎ 0361
Singaraja	☎ 0362
Tirta Gangga	☎ 0363
Ubud	☎ 0361

Sumatra

Banda Aceh	☎ 0651
Bandarlampung	☎ 0721
Batam	☎ 0778
Berastagi	☎ 0628
Bukittinggi	☎ 0752
Bukit Lawang	☎ 061
Dumai	☎ 0765
Gunung Sitoli	☎ 0639
Lagundri	☎ 0630
Maninjau	☎ 0752
Medan	☎ 061
Padang	☎ 0751
Parapat	☎ 0625
Pekanbaru	☎ 0761
Sabang	☎ 0652
Samosir	☎ 0625

Sibolga	☎ 0631
Tanjung Pinang	☎ 0771
Teluk Dalam	☎ 0630

Nusa Tenggara

Ampenan	☎ 0370
Bajawa	☎ 0384
Bima	☎ 0374
Dili	☎ 0390
Ende	☎ 0381
Kupang	☎ 0380
Labuanbajo	☎ 0385
Larantuka	☎ 0383
Mataram	☎ 0370
Maumere	☎ 0382
Ruteng	☎ 0385
Soe	☎ 0368
Sumbawa Besar	☎ 0371
Waikabubak	☎ 0387
Waingapu	☎ 0387

Kalimantan

Balikpapan	☎ 0542
Banjarmasin	☎ 0511
Pontianak	☎ 0561
Samarinda	☎ 0541
Tarakan	☎ 0551

Sulawesi

Bitung	☎ 0438
Dongala	☎ 0457
Gorontalo	☎ 0435
Manado	☎ 0431
Palu	☎ 0451
Pare-Pare	☎ 0421
Poso	☎ 0452
Rantepao	☎ 0423
Tentena	☎ 0458
Ujung Pandang	☎ 0411

Maluku

Ambon	☎ 0911
Bandaneira	☎ 0910
Ternate	☎ 0921

Irian Jaya

Biak	☎ 0961
Fak Fak	☎ 0981
Jayapura	☎ 0967
Manokwari	☎ 0986
Nabire	☎ 0964
Sentani	☎ 0967
Wamena	☎ 0969

Although it can be slow and difficult to access at times, the site at www.batavianet.com/links/ is excellent with literally thousands of Indonesian URLs.

For news on Indonesia, there are a number of options. A daily news service of the Royal Institute of Linguistics and Anthropology (KITLV) in Leiden, The Netherlands is at gopher://oasis.leidenuniv.nl:70/11/.kitlv/daily-report. It has news postings in Indonesian and English with reports that you won't find in the regular press, including plenty of East Timor news.

Tempo magazine is one of Indonesia's most respected publications and its Web site (www.tempo.co.id/har/3Ags-2.html) offers a few daily articles, in Indonesian and English.

For information on nature conservation in Indonesia, try www.bart.nl/~edcolijn/index.html.

BOOKS
Lonely Planet
For more detailed information on Indonesia, look for the Lonely Planet guidebooks to *Indonesia, Bali & Lombok, Java, Indonesia's Eastern Islands* and *Jakarta city guide*. If you're interested in diving Lonely Planet's Pisces series includes the detailed *Diving and Snorkeling Guide to Bali and the Komodo Region*.

Lonely Planet's Journeys book *Islands in the Clouds*, although set mostly in Papua New Guinea, crosses the border to Irian Jaya in Indonesia.

Guidebooks
Periplus produce a number of beautifully illustrated and presented regional guidebooks to Indonesia. Although dated, they are particularly strong on background material; less so with practical information.

Travel
One of the better travelogues is *In Search of Conrad* by Gavin Young, who retraces Joseph Conrad's journeys by boat around Sumatra, Java, Kalimantan, Bali and Sulawesi. Or read Conrad's *Victory*, which is set in Indonesia.

History & Politics
An excellent general history is *A History of Modern Indonesia* by MC Ricklefs. It covers Indonesian history from the rise of Islam, circa 1300, to the early 1990s.

General
Indonesia in Focus, edited by Peter Homan, Reimar Schefol, Vincent Dekker & Nico de Jonge, is a Dutch publication with numerous glossy photos and well-illustrated articles exploring Indonesia's rich ethnic diversity.

Various books explore regional cultures in detail. *The Religion of Java* by Clifford Geertz is not only a classic book on Javanese religion, culture and values, but revolutionised the study of social anthropology. Tim Flannery's *Throwim Way Leg* is mostly about research work undertaken in Papua New Guinea, but offers some interesting insights into life in Irian Jaya.

Two good illustrated books on Indonesian fauna are *The Wildlife of Indonesia* by Kathy MacKinnon and *Wild Indonesia* by Tony & Jane Whitten.

The Malay Archipelago by Alfred Russel Wallace is the 1869 classic of this famous naturalist's wanderings throughout the Indonesian islands.

Art in Indonesia: Continuities and Change by Claire Holt is an excellent introduction to the arts of Indonesia. For an overall guide to Indonesian crafts, *Arts and Crafts of Indonesia* by Anne Richter is detailed and beautifully illustrated.

Pramoedya Ananta Toer is Indonesia's best known novelist and was jailed for criticism of the government. His famous quartet of novels set in the colonial era is *This Earth of Mankind, Child of All Nations, Footsteps* and *House of Glass*. Mochtar Lubis is another well-known Indonesian writer. His novel *Twilight in Djakarta* attacks corruption and the plight of the poor in Jakarta in the 1950s.

HEALTH
Malaria risk exists year-round in Irian Jaya and rural areas of the other islands. There is no risk in the big cities or in the tourist areas of Java and Bali. There have been recent large outbreaks of dengue fever, so you should take measures to avoid mosquito bites. Food and water-borne diseases occur, including dysentery and hepatitis, so it's worth paying attention to basic food and water hygiene. Schistosomiasis (bilharzia) occurs in Sulawesi, and rabies exists in Java, Kalimantan, Sumatra and Sulawesi. For more information on these and other health matters, see the Health section in the Appendix.

Unboiled water should be avoided, but bottled water is available everywhere and many hotels and restaurants provide *air putih*, or boiled water, for guests. Take care with ice. Restaurants often provide hygienic, commercially prepared ice, and even roadside food stalls may buy commercial ice – but then chop up it on the side of the road!

WOMEN TRAVELLERS

Indonesia is a Muslim society and very much male oriented. However, women are not cloistered or forced to wear purdah, and generally enjoy more freedom than in many more orthodox Middle Eastern societies.

Plenty of western women travel in Indonesia either alone or in pairs – most seem to enjoy the country and its people, most seem to get through the place without any problems, or else suffer only a few minor hassles with the men. There are some things you can do to avoid being harassed; dressing modestly helps a lot.

Travelling alone is considered an oddity – women travelling alone, even more of an oddity, and it is certainly tougher going for a woman travelling alone in isolated regions. Nevertheless, for a woman travelling alone or with a female companion, Indonesia can be easier going than some other Asian countries.

GAY & LESBIAN TRAVELLERS

Gay travellers in Indonesia will experience few problems. Physical contact between same-sex couples is quite acceptable, even though a boy and a girl holding hands may be seen as improper. Homosexual behaviour is not illegal, and the age of consent for sexual activity is 16 years. Immigration officials may restrict entry to people who reveal HIV positive status. Gay men in Indonesia are referred to as *homo* or *gay*.

Community attitudes to the wider gay community are surprisingly tolerant in a traditional, conservative family-oriented society.

DANGERS & ANNOYANCES

Violent crime is very rare in Indonesia, but theft can be a problem. If you are mindful of your valuables and take precautions, the chances of being ripped off are small. A money belt worn under your clothes is the safest way to carry your passport, cash and travellers cheques. Pickpockets are common and crowded bus and train stations are favourite haunts, as are major tourist areas.

Don't leave valuables unattended, and in crowded places hold your bag or day pack closely. Keep an eye on your luggage if it is put on the roof of a bus, but back-slashing or theft from bags next to you inside the bus is also a hazard. It is good insurance to have luggage that can be locked. Always lock your hotel room door and windows at night and whenever you go out. Don't leave valuables lying around in dorms or outside your room.

BUSINESS HOURS

Most government offices are open Monday to Friday from 7 am to 3 pm, with an extended lunch break for Friday prayers. Private business offices have staggered hours: Monday to Friday from 8 am to 4 pm or 9 am to 5 pm, with a break in the middle of the day. Some offices are also open on Saturday morning until noon. Banks are usually open Monday to Friday from 8 am to 3 or 4 pm. Some banks in major cities also open Saturday mornings, while others may have limited hours for foreign currency transactions, eg 8 am to 1 pm.

Shops tend to open about 8 am and stay open until around 9 pm. Sunday is a public holiday but some shops and many airline offices open for at least part of the day.

PUBLIC HOLIDAYS & SPECIAL EVENTS

Although some public holidays have a fixed date each year, the dates for many events vary each year depending on Muslim, Buddhist or Hindu calendars.

National public holidays are:

New Year's Day	1 January
Lebaran (Idul Fitri)	January or February
Hindu New Year (Nyepi)	March
Good Friday	April
Idul Adha	April
Ascension Day	April
Muharram (Moslem New Year)	May
Waisak Day	May
Mohammad's Birthday	July
Independence Day	17 August
Ascension of Mohammad	December
Christmas Day	25 December

Independence Day is the biggest event, with parades and celebrations held throughout the country. Lebaran marks the end of Ramadan and is a noisy celebration at the end of a month of gastric austerity. It is the major Muslim celebration of two days duration. Nyepi on Bali marks the Hindu New Year, and though it is preceded by festivals, virtually all of Bali closes.

With such a diversity of people in the archipelago there are many other local holidays, festivals and cultural events. On Sumba, for example, mock battles and jousting matches harking back to the era of internecine warfare are held in February and March. The Balinese have the Galungan Festival, during which time all the gods, including the supreme deity Sanghyang Widi, come down to earth to join in. In Tana Toraja, in southern Sulawesi, the end of the harvest season is the time for funeral ceremonies. In Java, Bersih Desa takes place at the time of the rice harvest – houses and gardens are cleaned, village roads and paths repaired.

ACCOMMODATION

Hotels are common, but names such as *losmen* and *penginapan* are other designations for cheap, rock-bottom hotels. The word *wisma*, akin to guesthouse, is also worth watching out for.

Cheap hotels are usually very basic, rarely containing more than a bed and a small table. In compensation, a simple breakfast is often included and tea or coffee is usually provided gratis a couple of times a day. Traditional washing facilities consist of a *mandi*, a large water tank from which you scoop water with a dipper. Climbing into the tank is very bad form! Toilets may also be the traditional hole-in-the-floor variety but in places like Bali, showers and western sit-up toilets are common. Don't expect hot water in budget places though.

Accommodation prices in Indonesia vary considerably – Yogyakarta and Danau Toba are much cheaper than elsewhere. Bali is slightly more expensive on the whole, but many Balinese hotels have pleasant gardens and huge breakfasts and you get much more for only a little extra. There are some really nice places around and finding rooms for less than US$5 a night is possible.

FOOD & DRINKS

A *rumah makan*, literally 'eating house', is the cheaper equivalent of a *restoran*, but the dividing line is often hazy. Cheapest of all is a *warung*, a makeshift or permanent food stall, but again the food may be the same as in a rumah makan. With any roadside food it pays to be careful about hygiene. The *pasar* (market) is a good food source, especially the *pasar malam* (night market). Mobile pushcarts *(kaki lima)*, originally from Java, are now found all over the country, serving cheap snack foods and meals.

As with food in the rest of Asia, Indonesian food is heavily based on rice. *Nasi goreng* is the national dish: fried rice, with an egg on top in deluxe *(istimewa)* versions. *Nasi campur*, rice with whatever is available, is a warung favourite, often served cold. The two other real Indonesian dishes are *gado gado* and *sate*. Gado gado is a fresh salad with prawn crackers and peanut sauce. It tends to vary a lot, so if your first one isn't so special try again somewhere else. Sate are tiny kebabs served with a spicy peanut dip.

The Dutch feast *rijsttafel*, or rice table, consists of rice served with everything imaginable – for gargantuan appetites only. Some big hotels still do a passable imitation. Indonesians are keen snackers, so you'll get plenty of *pisang goreng* (banana fritters), peanuts in palm sugar or shredded coconut cookies.

Padang food, from the Padang region in Sumatra, is popular throughout Indonesia. In a Padang restaurant, a bowl of rice is plonked in front of you, followed by a whole collection of small bowls of vegetables, meat, fish and eggs. Eat what you want and your bill is added up from the number of empty bowls. In Sumatra, food can be spicy enough to burn your tongue.

Bottled water and soft drinks are available everywhere and many hotels and restaurants provide air putih (boiled water) for guests. The iced juice drinks can be good, but take care that the water/ice has been boiled or is bottled.

Indonesian tea is fine and coffee is also quite good. Local beer is good – Bintang is Heineken-supervised and costs from around US$1 a large bottle. Bali Brem rice wine is really potent, and the more you drink the nicer it tastes. *Es buah*, or *es campur*, is a strange concoction of fruit salad, jelly cubes, syrup, crushed rice and condensed milk. It tastes absolutely *enak* (delicious).

See the Language section in the Appendix for food and drinks vocabulary.

SHOPPING

There are so many regional arts and crafts in Indonesia that they're dealt with under the regional sections. For an overview of the whole gamut of Indonesian crafts, pay a visit to the Sarinah department store or the art market of Pasar Seni at Ancol in Jakarta. They've got items from all over the archipelago. While you may not find all the most interesting products, you'll see enough for a good introduction to what is available.

Getting There & Away

AIR
Airports
Indonesia's two main international gateways are Denpasar on Bali and Jakarta in Java, and most flights from Europe and Asia use one of these two airports.

Direct flights link Jakarta with all the capital cities in South-East Asia, and Bali is also well serviced via Jakarta and with direct flights.

Other Indonesian cities with international flight connections, mostly for flights within South-East Asia include: Medan in Sumatra, Bandung and Surabaya in Java, and Ujung Pandang and Manado in Sulawesi.

The cheapest and most popular flights are those between Indonesia and other cities in the region, outlined below.

Departure Tax
Airport tax for international departures is 50,000 rp from Denpasar and Jakarta; 20,000 rp from other airports.

Singapore
Singapore-Jakarta is one of the most popular flights. Many airlines service the route with fares as low as US$65 one way. To Bali costs around US$150.

Silk Air, the regional offshoot of Singapore Airlines, and Garuda have a number of direct flights to regional Indonesian cities, including Manado and Ujung Pandang (Sulawesi); Solo and Surabaya (Java); Pontianak (Kalimantan); and Palembang, Pekanbaru, Padang and Medan (Sumatra).

Malaysia
Popular connections include Penang-Medan for RM185, or US$60 to US$140 from Medan, depending on discounts. Numerous other flights go to Sumatran destinations from Kuala Lumpur, Penang and other Malaysian cities. One of the more interesting is the Penang-Banda Aceh flight with Pelangi Air.

In Borneo, Malaysia Airlines flies between Pontianak in Kalimantan and Kuching in Sarawak (RM276), and Bouraq and Malaysia

Airlines fly between Tarakan in Kalimantan and Tawau in Sabah.

Malaysia Airlines also connects Kuala Lumpur with Ujung Pandang in Sulawesi.

From Jakarta, the cheapest connections are to Singapore from as little as US$65, though Malaysia Airlines has competitively priced flights to Johor Bahru.

Philippines
Garuda flies four times a week between Manila and Jakarta (US$220), and there are also direct flights between Bali and Manila.

Bouraq Airlines flies weekly between Davao, in the south of Mindanao, and Manado in the north of Sulawesi (US$180; US$150 from Manado).

Papua New Guinea
Sadly there are no longer flight connections between PNG and Irian Jaya.

Australia
Bali is the main gateway with connections to all the main Australian cities. A few direct flights go to Jakarta, but most go via Bali.

From Bali, the cheapest flights are to Darwin or Perth for around A$400. Cheapest of all are the Merpati flights from Darwin to Kupang in Timor for A$244 one way (US$180 from Kupang to Darwin).

LAND
Only two countries – Malaysia and Papua New Guinea – have land borders with Indonesia. Regular buses (10 hours) run daily between the Malaysian city of Kuching in Sarawak and Pontianak in Kalimantan, and this is a visa-free entry point.

A boat operates between Jayapura in Irian Jaya and Vanimo in PNG. See the Jayapura Getting There & Away entry for details.

SEA
Malaysia
Most sea connections are between Malaysia and Sumatra. The most popular ferry service is between Penang (Malaysia) and Medan (Sumatra), but ferries also connect Dumai (Sumatra) with Melaka.

Medan to Penang The high-speed ferries *Selasa Ekspres*, *Perdana Ekspres*, *Langkawi Ekspres* and *Bahagia Ekspres* take about 4½ hours to do the run across the Melaka Strait. Between them, there are departures every day

INDONESIA

from Medan and Penang for RM110/90 in 1st/2nd class (about 260,000 rp 2nd class). The fares from Belawan include port tax and bus transport from Medan. Children pay half fare.

Dumai to Melaka From Melaka, daily high-speed ferries (RM80; 2½ hours) operate to Dumai at 10 am. From Dumai the ferries run daily at 3 pm (100,000 rp).

Sumatra to Johor Bahru Yet another possibility is to take a boat from the Bebas Cukai ferry terminal in Johor Bahru. Boats go direct to Batu Ampar and Tanjung Pinang, both in Sumatra.

Tarakan/Nunukan to Tawau There are also boats connecting Kalimantan with Sabah in Malaysia. For boats from Nunukan to Tawau, go to Pelabuhan Tarakan. There are two speedboats daily (except Sunday) to Tawau, leaving around 1 pm (be at the immigration office by 12 noon). Tickets can be bought in KM Sangalaki Express close to losmen Nunukan (16,000 rp or RM25 from Malaysia). There are many other agencies on the road between the city square and the docks, but they sell tickets for the slower boats. You can also take a speedboat from Tarakan via Nunukan. It leaves at 8.30 am and you go through immigration in Nunukan. In Nunukan you can catch a speedboat to Tawau (four hours, 30,000 rp). Make sure that you have 1500 rp left for the harbour tax which is collected just before you board the boat.

There are also much slower longboats from Nunukan, leaving daily at around 9 am and arriving in Nunukan 12 hours later.

There is an Indonesian immigration office in Nunukan where you must finalise your paperwork. Note that if you got a two month tourist visa on arrival in Indonesia, you will need an exit permit from the immigration office in Jakarta. If you have a one month tourist visa before coming to Indonesia, Nunukan can stamp your passport without an exit permit from Jakarta. Some travellers report an easy exit via this route, but many who don't have an exit permit get turned back.

Papua New Guinea
In recent years there has been an irregular boat between Jayapura (Irian Jaya) and Vanimo (PNG). At the time of writing it was operating once or twice a week, but the situation seems to be quite fluid. Make inquiries before making plans to use this service. See the Jayapura entry for contact details.

Singapore
From Singapore to Batam in Indonesia's Riau Archipelago is less than half an hour by ferry, and from Batam boats go through to Pekanbaru in Sumatra. Ferries also run between Singapore and nearby Pulau Bintan, from where passenger boats go on to Jakarta. See the Sumatra Getting There & Away section for more details.

Getting Around

AIR
Domestic Air Services
Indonesia has a number of airlines flying to some pretty amazing places. The national airline, Garuda Indonesia, operates most of the long-distance international connections and many major domestic routes using jet aircraft.

Merpati is the country's main domestic carrier with an extensive network covering just about everywhere, although the network has been wound back somewhat recently. Merpati provides a reasonable service on the main runs, but in the back blocks flights are subject to frequent and unexplained cancellations.

The other domestic airlines are much smaller, operate limited networks and are under severe strain as a result of the economic crisis. Sempati has stopped flying altogether, and while the others were still flying at the time of writing, their future viability seems far from assured. The main airlines are: Bouraq, which has some useful flights to and within Java, Kalimantan, and Sulawesi; Mandala, which operates 737s between Java, Sulawesi and Maluku; and DAS which flies into interior Kalimantan.

Further down the ladder are the tiny regional airlines which just operate a very limited service using small aircraft on short runs.

The entire domestic airline system has been thrown into chaos following the economic crisis, with carriers unable to meet leasing and maintenance payments, which are usually in US dollars while revenue is in increasingly worthless rupiah. After a period of great uncertainty, fare hikes and general confusion, it was announced that in July 1998 the six domestic airlines (Garuda, Merpati, Bouraq, Mandala and DAS) would pool their services, combine their fleets, share domestic routes

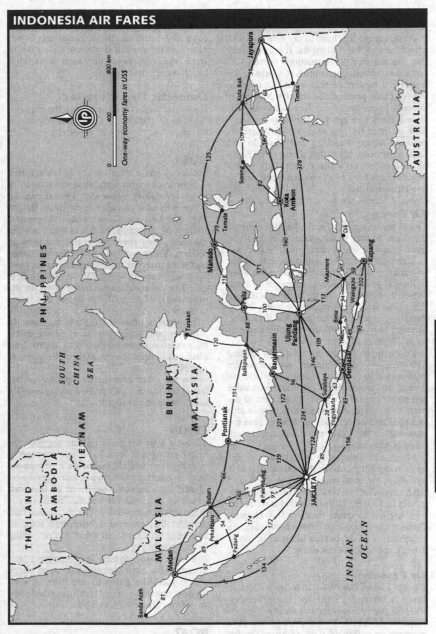

INDONESIA AIR FARES

One-way economy fares in US$

between them and pool the revenue of their operations.

At this stage it is hard to say how this will affect air travel in Indonesia. It seems likely that the number of destinations served will remain relatively unchanged; it would be the frequency of service that would change. In the far flung parts of the country Merpati is the only operator anyway, but in Java and Sulawesi there is a great deal of duplication – four airlines fly less-than-half-full aircraft between Ujung Pandang and Manado and back every day, all within a couple of hours of each other! So a place with daily flights might be cut back to a few each week, and so on. Time will tell.

Air Fares

Ticket prices are fixed and all airlines charge the same or very similar fares – in theory at least. Mandala seems to offer a 25% discount as a matter of course, and discounts of between 18 and 25% are available on the other airlines if you buy the ticket through an agent rather than direct from the airline, although this also varies from place to place – Ujung Pandang is particularly good for discounts. Merpati also offer 25% discount for students up to 26 years of age.

Domestic air tickets attract a 10% tax and 2700 rp insurance. Where and when these are paid seems to vary, but usually the 10% tax is included in the ticket price and insurance and departure tax are paid at the point of departure. Sometimes though insurance is also included and other times neither of these are included in the ticket price. So always ask when buying tickets.

Much like everything else, domestic airlines were hit hard by the *krismon* (*krisis monetere*, or economic crisis) in 1998 and fares skyrocketed. At the time of writing, domestic fares were so volatile that it would be meaningless to quote them in this chapter. Those quoted in the air-fares chart provide a comparative guide, but are likely to be out of date by the time the ink dries.

Air Passes

Garuda issues the Visit Indonesia Decade Pass. It costs US$300 for three sectors, US$500 for five sectors and each additional sector is US$110. You must buy the pass overseas or within 14 days of arrival in Indonesia, and enter the country on Garuda. If arriving on another airline, a surcharge of US$50 applies.

The Garuda pass can be used only on Garuda flights. If your travel is restricted to Java and Sumatra, these passes might not save any money but if you are flying out to Irian Jaya or Sulawesi, they soon start to look much more attractive.

Domestic Departure Tax

Domestic airport tax varies with the airport – 8000 rp to 10,000 rp. This tax is payable at the airport at the time of departure.

BUS

Indonesia has a huge variety of bus services – from trucks with wooden seats in the back to air-con deluxe buses with TV and karaoke – that will take you all the way from Bali to Sumatra. Java and Sumatra have the greatest variety of bus services. Local buses are the cheapest; they leave when full and stop on request. There is a variety of different classes and prices, depending on whether buses have air-con, reclining seats, TV, on-board toilets etc. The deluxe express buses often do the night runs, when traffic is lighter and travel is faster.

Minibuses often do the shorter runs. In Sumatra, and especially Java, deluxe minibuses also operate on the major routes. Bali also has tourist buses plying the popular routes.

On the other islands, the options for bus travel are much more limited and often only local buses are available.

TRAIN

There is a pretty good railway service running the length of Java. In the east, it connects with the ferry to Bali, and in the west with the ferry to Sumatra. Otherwise, there's just a bit of rail into Sumatra but most of that vast island is reserved for buses. Trains vary – there are slow, miserable, cheap ones and fast, comfortable, expensive ones, and some in between. So check out what you're getting before you pay.

Some major towns (eg Surabaya and Jakarta) also have several stations, so check where you'll be going to and from as well. Student discounts are generally available and vary from about 10% to 25%.

BOAT

Indonesia is an island nation, so ships are important. If you're going to really explore you'll have to use them.

Pelni Ships

Pelni is the biggest shipper with services almost everywhere. They have modern, all-air-con passenger ships and operate regular fortnightly or monthly routes around the islands. The ships usually stop for two to four hours in each port, so there's often time for a quick look around.

Pelni has at least 20 vessels running around the islands, and more are being added all the time. More than one ship, and as many as seven, service any one port and there's a lot of overlap on sections of routes, so services on these sections can be quite frequent. Regular ferries are still more convenient for travel between the main islands – you can travel from Sumatra right through to Timor by land/ferry connections – but Pelni ships are often the only alternative to flying for travel to and between Kalimantan, Sulawesi, Maluku and Irian Jaya.

Routes and schedules change every year, and copies of current schedules are as rare as hen's teeth. Pelni offices are generally less than helpful; they *may* have schedules, but it's unlikely. The best bet for schedules and fares are the many travel agents in each port who are Pelni agents, although they can usually only give you details for services to and from that particular port.

Travel on Pelni ships consists of four cabin classes, plus *kelas ekonomi*, which is the modern version of the old deck class. There you are packed in a large room with a space to sleep; but, even in ekonomi, it's air-con and can get pretty cool at night, so bring warm clothes or a sleeping bag. It is possible to book a sleeping place in ekonomi – sometimes – otherwise you have to find your own empty space. Mattresses can be rented for a minimal charge and many boats have a 'tourist deck' upstairs. There are no locker facilities in ekonomi, so keep an eye on your gear.

Class I is luxury-plus with only two beds per cabin and a price approaching air travel. Class II is a notch down in style, with four to a cabin, but still very comfortable. Class III has six beds and Class IV has eight beds to a cabin. Classes I to IV have air-con, TV, hot water and access to a restaurant with good food. The cost of food is included of Class I, II and III tickets, while in ekonomi you queue to collect an unappetising meal on a tray and then sit down wherever you can to eat it. It pays to bring some food with you.

Ekonomi is fine for short trips. Class IV is the best value for longer hauls, but some ships only offer Classes I and II, or III, in addition to ekonomi. Prices quoted in this book are for ekonomi – as a rough approximation Class IV is 40% more than ekonomi, Class III is 60% more, Class II is 120% more and Class I is 200% more.

You can book tickets up to two weeks ahead; it's best to book at least a few days in advance. Pelni is not a tourist operation, so don't expect any special service, although there is usually somebody hidden away in the ticket offices who can help foreigners.

As well as its luxury liners, Pelni has Perintis (Pioneer) ships that visit many of the ports not covered by the passenger liners. They can get you to just about any of the remote outer islands, as well as the major ports. The ships are often beaten up old crates that also carry cargo. They offer deck class only, but you may be able to negotiate a cabin with one of the crew.

Pelni Vessels & Routes The main Pelni ships, and the routes they ply (all fortnightly for the round trip unless otherwise indicated), are listed below. Like most things in Indonesia these details are prone to change without notice so it is advisable to check details locally.

Awu:

Denpasar (B)→Lembar (NT)→Waingapu (NT)→Ende (NT)→Kupang (NT)→Kalabahi (NT)→Dili (NT)→Maumere (NT)→Ujung Pandang (SI)→Nunukan (K)→Tarakan (K), and back via the same ports except Nunukan, reversing Lembar and Denpasar, so it stops at Denpasar before Lembar.

Bukit Siguntang:

Dumai (Sm)→Kijang (Sm)→Jakarta (J)→Surabaya (J)→Ujung Pandang (SI)→Bau Bau (SI)→Ambon (M)→Banda (M)→Tual (M)→Dobo (M) or Kaimana (IJ), and back via the same ports.

Ciremai:

Jakarta (J)→Semarang (J)→Ujung Pandang (SI)→Bau Bau (SI)→Banggai (SI)→Bitung(SI)→Ternate (M)→Sorong (IJ)→Manokwari (IJ)→Biak (IJ)→Jayapura (IJ), and back via the same ports.

Dobonsolo:

Jakarta (J)→Surabaya (J)→Denpasar (B)→Kupang (NT)→Dili (NT)→Ambon (M)→Sorong (IJ)→Manokwari (IJ)→Biak (IJ)→Jayapura (IJ), and back via the same ports.

INDONESIA

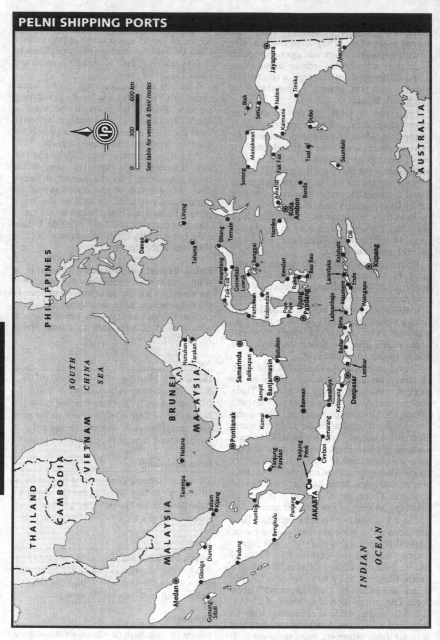

PELNI SHIPPING PORTS

See table for vessels & their routes

0   300   600 km

Kambuna:

Sibolga (Sm)→Pulau Nias (Sm)→Padang (Sm)→
Jakarta (J)→Surabaya (J)→Ujung Pandang (Sl)→
Balikpapan (K)→Pantoloan (Sl)→Toli-Toli (Sl)→
Bitung (Sl), and back via the same ports reversing
Sibolga and Pulau Nias.

Kelimutu:

Shuttles back and forth between Surabaya (J) and
Banjarmasin (K) every two days, substituting
Semarang for Surabaya twice a fortnight.

Kerinci:

Dumai (Sm)→Kijang (Sm)→Jakarta (J)→Surabaya
(J) →Ujung Pandang (Sl) →Balikpapan (K)→
Pantoloan (Sl)→Toli-Toli (Sl)→Tarakan (K)→
Nunukan (K), and back via the same ports except
Tarakan.

Lambelu:

Pulau Nias (Sm)→Sibolga (Sm)→Padang (Sm)→
Jakarta (J)→Surabaya (J)→Ujung Pandang (Sl)→
Bau Bau (Sl)→Ambon (M)→Namlea (M)→Bitung
(Sl)→Ternate (M), and back via the same ports
except Bitung, reversing Pulau Nias and Sibolga.

Lawit:

Cirebon (J)→Pontianak (K)→Tanjung
Pandan→Jakarta (J)→Tanjung Pandan→Pon-
tianak (K)→Semarang (J)→Kumai (K), and back
via the same ports.

Leuser:

Semarang (J)→Sampit (K)→Surabaya (J)→
Batulicin (K)→Pare-Pare (Sl)→Samarinda (K)→
Toli-Toli (Sl)→Tarakan (K)→Nunukan (K), and
back via the same ports except Tarakan, and
substituting Kumai for Sampit

Pangrango:

Ketapang (J)→Semarang (J)→Sampit (K)→
Bawean→Surabaya (J)→Badas (NT)→Labuanbajo
(NT)→Waingapu (NT)→Ende (NT)→Sabu (NT)→
Roti (NT)→Kupang (NT), and back via the same
ports except Roti.

Rinjani:

Surabaya (J)→Ujung Pandang (Sl)→Bau Bau
(Sl)→Ambon (M)→Banda (M)→Tual (M)→Fak
Fak (IJ)→Sorong (IJ)→Manokwari (IJ)→Nabire
(IJ)→Serui (IJ)→Jayapura (IJ), and back via the
same ports.

Tatamailau:

Timika (IJ)→Dobo (M)→Tual (M)→Saumlaki
(M)→Dili ((NT)→Larantuka (NT) →Labuanbajo
(NT)→Bima (NT)→Banyuwangi (J)→Denpasar
(B)→Badas (NT)→Ujung Pandang (Sl)→Bau Bau
(Sl)→Ambon (M)→Amahai (M)→Fak Fak (IJ)→
Kaimana (IJ)→Timika (IJ)→Merauke (IJ); this trip
takes a fortnight. The journey is reversed the
following fortnight, usually missing Timika.

Tidar:

Surabaya (J)→Balikpapan (K)→Surabaya (J)→Pare
Pare (Sl)→Pantoloan (Sl)→Nunukan (K)→Tarakan
(K)→Balikpapan (K)→Pare Pare (Sl)→Surabaya
(J)→Ujung Pandang (Sl)→Balikpapan (K)→
Tarakan (K)→Pantoloan (Sl)→Ujung Pandang
(Sl)→Surabaya (J).

Tilongkabila:

Lirung (Sl)→Tahuna (Sl)→Bitung (Sl)→Gorontalo
(Sl)→Luwuk (Sl)→Kolonedale (Sl)→Kendari (Sl)→
Raha (Sl)→Bau Bau (Sl) →Ujung Pandang (Sl)→
Labuanbajo (NT)→Bima (NT)→Lembar (NT)→
Denpasar (B), and back via the same ports

Umsini:

Jayapura (IJ)→Serui (IJ)→Nabire (IJ)→Manokwari
(IJ)→Sorong (IJ)→Ternate (M)→Bitung (Sl)→
Kwandang (Sl)→Balikpapan (K)→Ujung Pandang
(Sl)→Surabaya (J), and back via the same ports

Note: The port for Jakarta is Tanjung Priok; for Bali
it is Benoa Port; and for Manado (Sulawesi) it is
Bitung. B=Bali, IJ=Irian Jaya, J=Java, K=Kalimantan,
M=Maluku, NT=Nusa Tenggara, Sl=Sulawesi, Sm=
Sumatra. See the Pelni Shipping Ports map for port
locations.

Other Ships

Sumatra, Java, Bali and Nusa Tenggara are
all connected by regular ferries and you can
use them to island-hop all the way from
Sumatra to Timor.

Getting a boat in the outer islands is often
a matter of hanging loose until something
comes by. Check with shipping companies,
the harbour office or anyone else you can
think of.

If you're travelling deck class, unroll your
sleeping bag on the deck and make yourself
comfortable. Travelling deck class during the
wet season can be extremely uncomfortable.
Either get one person in your party to take a
cabin or discuss renting a cabin from one of

the crew (it's a popular way for the crew to make a little extra). Bring some food of your own.

It's also possible to make some more unusual sea trips. Old Makassar schooners still sail the Indonesian waters and it may be possible to travel on them from Sulawesi to other islands, particularly Java and Nusa Tenggara.

LOCAL TRANSPORT

Indonesia has a huge variety of local transport. Public minibuses are everywhere, plying city routes or doing the local runs between towns and villages. The great minibus ancestor is the *bemo*, a three wheeler pick-up with two rows of seats down the sides, and the term bemo is widely used, especially on Bali. Elsewhere minibuses go under a mind-boggling array of names such as *opelet, mikrolet, colt* (since they are often Mitsubishi Colts), and *Kijang*, (Toyota Kijang 4WD look-alike). Minibuses usually run standard routes like buses and depart when full, but can also be chartered like a taxi.

Then there's the *becak*, or bicycle rickshaw – they're the same as in many other Asian countries, but are only found in towns and cities. Increasingly, they are being banned from the central areas of major cities. The *bajaj*, a three wheeler powered by a noisy two-stroke engine, is only found in Jakarta. They're identical to what is known in India as an auto-rickshaw. In quieter towns, you may find *dokar* (called *cidomo* on Bali) and *andong* – a horse or pony cart with two or four wheels respectively.

A handy form of transport in many places is the *ojek*, or motorcycle taxi, as long as you don't mind not having a helmet. You hop on the back, luggage and all, and they go where you want.

On Bali, Yogyakarta and many other centres you can also hire bicycles or motorbikes. Many towns, of course, have taxis (they even use their meters these days in the big cities in Java). You can also hire cheap driveyourself cars on Bali. Then there are all sorts of oddities: you can hire horses in some places.

Java

Indonesia's most populous island presents vivid contrasts of wealth and squalor, majestic open country and crowded filthy cities, quiet

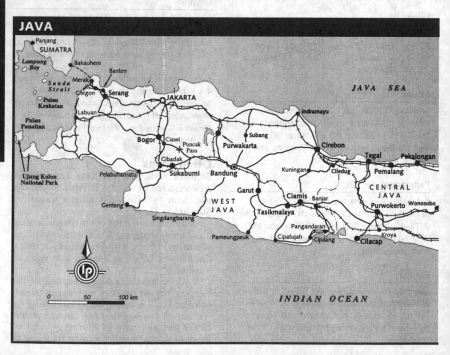

rural scenes and bustling modern traffic. For the traveller, it has everything from live volcanoes to inspiring 1000-year-old monuments.

Java is Indonesia's political stage and the centre for education, history and culture. It was from universities in Bandung, Yogyakarta, Solo, Surabaya and, especially, Jakarta, that students waged a campaign of anti-government demonstrations that eventually led to President Soeharto's resignation in 1998.

Java is a long, narrow island conveniently divided into three sections – West, Central and East Java.

West Java, also known as Sunda, is predominantly Islamic, and it surrounds the capital, Jakarta. The most visited places, other than Jakarta, are Bogor, Bandung and Pangandaran.

Central Java is the centre for much of the island's early culture. Two great Hindu/Buddhist dynasties centred here constructed the immense Borobudur temple and the complex of temples at Prambanan. Later, the rise of Islam carried sultans to power and their palaces, or *kratons*, at Yogyakarta and Solo (Surakarta) can be visited. This is a region for dance drama, or *wayang orang*, *gamelan* orchestras and *wayang kulit*, leather shadow puppet performances.

Finally, there is East Java, the area most likely to be rushed through in the haste to get to Bali. The major city here is the important port of Surabaya. Although East Java's attractions include the ruins at Trowulan and the temples around Malang, the main interest in the region is natural: the settings of the many hill stations and the superb Gunung Bromo volcano.

Most people travelling through Java follow the well-worn route of Jakarta-Bogor-Bandung-Pangandaran-Yogyakarta-Solo-Surabaya-Bali, with short diversions from points along that route. Many only stop at Jakarta and Yogyakarta! There are also a number of interesting towns along the north coast, but they attract few visitors.

History

The history of human habitation in Java extends back over half a million years when 'Java Man' lived along the banks of Sungai Bengawan Solo in Central Java. Waves of migrants followed, coming down through South-East Asia to inhabit the island.

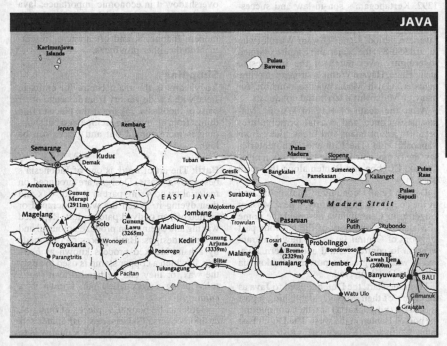

Hinduism and Buddhism first appeared in small coastal trading posts in West Java as early as the 4th century AD. Around the beginning of the 8th century, King Sanjaya founded the first major Hindu kingdom of Mataram, which controlled much of Central Java.

Sanjaya's kingdom was followed by a Buddhist interlude under the Sailendra Dynasty, when work began (probably around 780 AD) on Borobudur. Hinduism continued to exist alongside Buddhism and the massive Hindu Prambanan complex was built and consecrated around 856.

Mataram mysteriously collapsed and its great monuments were abandoned. No great kingdoms were recorded until the rise of civilisation in the Brantas Valley in East Java in the 11th century. King Airlangga was a legendary king who, until his death in 1049, fought to bring much of East Java under his control and extended Javanese influence to Bali.

Early in the 13th century, the kingdom of Singosari, previously a part of the kingdom of one Airlangga's sons, rose to prominence and expanded its power until its last king, Kertanegara, was murdered in a rebellion in 1292. Kertanegara's son-in-law and successor, Wijaya, then established the Majapahit Empire, the greatest empire of the Hindu-Javanese period. Under Hayam Wuruk (who ruled 1350-89) the Majapahit Empire claimed sovereignty over much of the Indonesian archipelago. Hayam Wuruk's strongman prime minister, Gajah Mada, was responsible for many of Majapahit's territorial conquests.

After the death of Hayam Wuruk, Majapahit declined and coastal principalities began to adopt Islam and break away from Majapahit rule. The 15th and 16th centuries saw the rise of new Islamic kingdoms such as Demak, Cirebon and Banten along the north coast.

Demak finally conquered Majapahit, and by the end of the 16th century, a new Muslim kingdom in Central Java assumed the name of Mataram, in memory of the glorious past kingdom of Central Java. The new Mataram went on to control central and eastern Java, and it was the greatest power in Indonesia when the Dutch arrived.

From the start, the Dutch looked to Java as the centre of their colony, establishing a post at Batavia (now Jakarta) and then conquering the port of Banten in the west. The Dutch East India Company (Vereenigde Oost-Indische Compagnie; VOC) successfully repelled Mataram, and began to spread its influence into the interior. The Dutch, while never directly at war, were only too keen to lend their military services to opposing principalities in return for land concessions.

Mataram was racked by internecine war until the Dutch resolved the conflict by splitting it into the principalities of Surakarta (Solo) and Yogyakarta. The Dutch slowly acquired much of Java. In 1799 the Dutch government dissolved the VOC and assumed direct control. The company was bankrupt and the colonial government set about making the colony, particularly Java, pay for itself through plantations. This brought great hardship to the peasantry, which supported Prince Diponegoro's Java War (1825-30). The Dutch held the cities but struggled against Diponegoro's guerilla tactics in the countryside. Diponegoro was treacherously lured into negotiations in Magelang and then exiled to Sulawesi. Thousands were dead and Dutch control over Java was complete.

Java, with its vast human resources and Dutch colonial investment, very much dominated Indonesia. Though the mineral and natural resources of the other islands began to overshadow it in economic importance, Java was the most developed island and sucked in the greatest resources. This is still the case in modern Indonesia, and often causes resentment in the other provinces.

Shopping

Yogyakarta is the main centre for crafts in Java, with a wide variety from Java and other parts of Indonesia. Jakarta is the place to find things from all over the archipelago but shopping is more spread out and prices can be high.

Batik The art of *batik* is one of Indonesia's best known crafts. Designs are produced on material by covering part of it with wax and then dyeing it. When the wax is scraped or melted off, an undyed patch is left. Repeated waxing and dyeing can produce colourful and complex designs. Batik pieces can be made by a hand-blocked process known as *batik cap*, in which a copper stamp is used to apply the wax, or they can be hand drawn *(batik tulis)* using a wax-filled pen known as a *canting*.

Batik can be bought as pieces of material, cushion covers, T-shirts, dresses, dinner sets and paintings. An easy check for quality is to simply turn the item over to ensure the design is of equal colour strength on both sides of the material – that makes it batik and not just printed material. Solo, Yogyakarta and Pekalongan are the major batik centres.

Other Crafts Silverwork can be found in the Kota Gede area, a few kilometres southeast of Yogyakarta. Wayang puppets can be found all over Java. Leather wayang kulit are made in Yogyakarta, while wooden *wayang golek* (three dimensional wooden) puppets are a speciality of West Java. Leatherwork in Yogyakarta is cheap and the quality is usually good. Cane craft can be found in Yogyakarta and other areas but is difficult to transport. Javanese woodcarvers produce some fabulous work, mostly carved furniture at Jepara. Pottery is made everywhere – Kasongan near Yogyakarta and Kelampok near Purwokerto are major centres.

Getting There & Away

Jakarta, Bandung, Surabaya and Solo are visa-free (30 days only), as are the seaports of Benoa Port, Jakarta, Semarang and Surabaya.

You can get to Java by a number of means and from a variety of directions. People usually come to Java from:

Sumatra – either by Pelni ship from Padang, Medan or Batam to Jakarta, or the short trip across the Sunda Strait from Bakauheni to Merak.
Bali – the very short ferry trip from Gilimanuk on Bali to Banyuwangi at the eastern end of Java.
Sulawesi, Kalimantan, Maluku or Irian Jaya – by air or sea.
Singapore – see the Getting There & Away section earlier in this chapter for details.

Air Jakarta is a reasonably good place for shopping around for international airline tickets, although it is not as good as Singapore. Jakarta is the main international and domestic hub, with connections to all of the archipelago. Surabaya is the other main air hub, while Solo receives a few international flights.

Sea Java is a major hub for shipping services from other Indonesian islands. Jakarta and Surabaya are the main ports for Pelni ships. There are also weekly passenger ships between Singapore and Jakarta, and Pasir Gudang (Malaysia) and Surabaya. See the Indonesia Getting There & Away section for details.

Getting Around

Air There's no real need to fly around Java as there's so much road transport available. If you do decide to take to the air, you will get some spectacular views of Java's many mountains and volcanoes. Apart from Jakarta, Java's main airports are Surabaya, Yogyakarta, Solo and Bandung.

Bus Daytime bus travel is often slow and nerve-racking. It is probably just as bad for your nerves at night (if you are awake), but at least travel is much faster. Trains are often better for the long hauls, but bus departures are much more frequent. In some places there are good reasons for taking the bus, such as on the scenic Jakarta to Bandung trip over the Puncak Pass.

There are various fares and bus types. Where the fare isn't ticketed or fixed, it's wise to check the price with other passengers – minibus drivers are the worst culprits for jacking up fares for tourists. Beware of the practice of taking your money and not giving you your change until 'later'.

The cheapest and most frequent buses are the big public buses. There are also *patas* buses, which are air-con services that make fewer stops. Deluxe buses run on important routes, usually at night to avoid traffic. Watch your luggage, especially on the cheaper buses.

Small minibuses, usually called colts or *angkots*, run the shorter routes more frequently.

The easiest and most convenient version of all are the air-con minibuses which operate on the major runs. Called *travel*, they will pick you up at your hotel and drop you off at your designated hotel at the other end. Many hotels can arrange pick-up. They cost quite a bit more than public buses but can often save long trips to and from inconvenient bus stations.

Train Choose your trains for comfort, speed and destination. They range from cheap, slow trains to reasonably cheap fast trains, very expensive expresses and squalid all ekonomi class cattle trains. The schedules change frequently and although departures may be punctual, arrivals will be late for most services and very late for others.

In Jakarta and Surabaya in particular, there are several stations, some of them far more convenient than others. Bear this in mind when choosing your trains. Ekonomi trains are slow, usually run over schedule and can

INDONESIA

be horribly crowded. *Bisnis* trains are a better option and seating is guaranteed.

Student discounts are generally available, but not for the expensive express trains. Try going straight to the stationmaster for speedier ticketing, and to get tickets even when, officially, the train is booked out. Remember that fares for the same journey and in the same class may vary widely from train to train.

Local Transport Around towns in Java, there are buses, taxis, colts, becaks and some very peculiar and purely local ways of getting from A to B.

JAKARTA

Jakarta has undergone a huge transformation in recent years. New freeways, office towers, luxury hotels and shopping malls have replaced much of the squalor and Jakarta has the appearance of a modern Asian boom city – at least in parts. Away from the glossy central business district, it still has its fair share of grime, crime and poverty. This sprawling capital of nine million people is the centre of power and wealth in Indonesia but it is also a vortex that sucks in the poor, often providing little more than the hope of hard work for low pay.

The eyes of the world were on Jakarta when social, economic and political tensions came to a head on Tuesday, 12 May 1998. The shooting of four students by the military during a demonstration at Trisakti University triggered a wave of rioting in which over 1000 died and thousands fled the capital. President Soeharto announced his resignation from the besieged national parliament on 21 May.

When not looking like a war zone, Jakarta has a lot to offer. Apart from a few interesting museums, there is some fine old Dutch architecture and, at the old schooner dock, you can see the most impressive reminder of the age of sailing ships to be found anywhere in the world.

The Dutch took Jakarta and renamed it Batavia back in 1619, when it became the centre of the Dutch empire in Indonesia. The name reverted to Jakarta after the Japanese occupation, and Soekarno declared Indonesia's independence from his Jakarta home in 1945.

Orientation

Jakarta sprawls 25km from the docks to the southern suburbs. Soekarno's towering national monument (Monas) in Merdeka Square

is an excellent central landmark. North of the monument is the older part of Jakarta, including the Chinatown area of Glodok, the old Dutch area of Kota, then the waterfront and the old harbour of Sunda Kelapa. The modern harbour, Tanjung Priok, is several kilometres along the coast to the east. The more modern part of Jakarta is to the south of the monument.

Jalan Thamrin is the main north-south street of the new city and this wide boulevard has Jakarta's big hotels, banks and the Sarinah department store. A couple of blocks east along Jalan Kebon Sirih is Jalan Jaksa, the cheap accommodation centre of Jakarta.

Information

Tourist Offices The very helpful Jakarta tourist information office (☎ 314 2067) is in the Jakarta Theatre building on Jalan Thamrin, opposite the Sarinah department store. It is open Monday to Friday from 8 am to 5 pm, Saturday from 8 am to 1 pm.

The Directorate General of Tourism office at Jalan Merdeka Barat 16-19 has some useful free maps, brochures and publications. There's also a desk at the airport.

Money Jakarta is crawling with banks offering some of the best exchange rates in Indonesia, though it still pays to shop around. Banks offer better rates than moneychangers.

Most banks are open Monday to Friday from 8 am to 4 pm, and Saturday from 8 to 11.30 am. Handy banks to Jalan Jaksa are Bank Duta, Lippobank, and BNI on Jalan Kebon Sirih. In the Plaza Indonesia, the BDNI bank on the 1st level of the Sogo department store is open from 10 am to 9 pm, and offers OK rates. Downstairs, the BII bank also keeps extended hours and has better rates.

Almost all banks give credit card cash advances over the counter. BII bank ATMs allow cash advances on Visa and MasterCard, as does Bank Duta on Jalan Kebon Sirih. Bank Bali, BNI and Lippobank ATMs give cash advances on MasterCard and Cirrus, and the BCA bank ATMs accept Visa.

American Express is represented by Pacto Ltd (☎ 797 5874) at Jalan Taman Kemang II Blok D2/4 in South Jakarta, or at the Borobudur Intercontinental Hotel.

Post & Communications The main post office is behind Jalan Pos Utara, to the north-east of Monas. It is open Monday to Friday from 8 am to 9 pm, Saturday to 7 pm and

Sunday from 9 am to 4 pm. It's a good half-hour walk from the city centre or you can take a No 12 bus from Jalan Thamrin. There's a smaller post office on Jalan Haji Agus Salim, closer to Jalan Jaksa.

The main post office has a well-organised and busy Internet *(Warposnet)* service. Your on-line time is logged and you get a print-out when you're finished. It costs 1500 rp per 10 minutes. At the time of writing another Internet service was just setting up at the wartel on Jalan Kebon Sirih, just around the corner from Jalan Jaksa. Even more convenient is the service at Click! travel agency at Jalan Jaksa 29 (next to the Djody Hostel) but you pay for the privilege – 15,000 rp per half hour.

You can make direct international calls from wartels all over Jakarta. There are a couple of wartels around Jalan Jaksa, including one in the lane near Borneo Hostel. Since the main Telkom office closed down, finding somewhere to make a reverse-charge (collect) call is not so easy. If all else fails, head for the major hotels – the Grand Hyatt business centre will connect you for a 7000 rp fee.

Kota (Old Batavia)

The heart of the old Dutch city is the old town square, Taman Fatahillah, where you'll find Indonesia's best and oldest Dutch architecture. Take a P11 or P10 bus from Jalan Thamrin.

Facing the open cobbled square is the old City Hall, dating from 1710, now the **Jakarta History Museum**, with furniture and paintings from Dutch colonial life. The city hall was also the main prison compound of Batavia – in the basement there are cells and 'water prisons' where often more than 300 people were kept. Admission is 1000 rp. It's open from 9 am to 3 pm Tuesday to Thursday, to 2.30 pm on Friday and 12.30 pm on Saturday. It's closed on Monday.

The old Portuguese cannon **Si Jagur**, or Mr Fertility, opposite the museum, was believed to be a cure for barrenness because of its suggestive clenched fist with protruding thumb. Women offered flowers to the cannon and sat astride it in the hope of bearing children.

Across the square on Jalan Pintu Besar Utara, the **Wayang Museum** has a good display of puppets. Wayang golek or wayang kulit is performed every other Sunday from 10 am to 1.30 pm. Admission and opening hours are the same as the Jakarta History Museum. Guided tours are conducted in English for 10,000 rp.

The **Balai Seni Rupa** (Fine Art Museum),

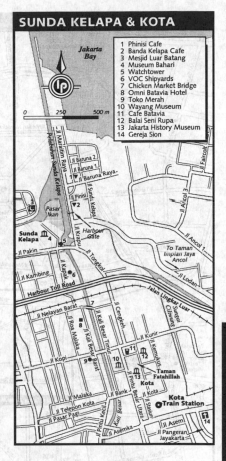

SUNDA KELAPA & KOTA

Jakarta Bay

0   250   500 m

1 Phinisi Cafe
2 Banda Kelapa Cafe
3 Mesjid Luar Batang
4 Museum Bahari
5 Watchtower
6 VOC Shipyards
7 Chicken Market Bridge
8 Omni Batavia Hotel
9 Toko Merah
10 Wayang Museum
11 Cafe Batavia
12 Balai Seni Rupa
13 Jakarta History Museum
14 Gereja Sion

on the east side of the square, has a small gallery of modern Indonesian paintings and a collection of ceramics. It is closed on Monday.

Nearby, at Jalan Pangeran Jayakarta 1, **Gereja Sion** is the oldest remaining church in Jakarta. It was built in 1695 outside the old city walls for the 'black Portuguese' who were brought to Batavia as slaves and given their freedom if they joined the Dutch Reformed Church.

From Taman Fatahillah, you can walk along the grotty Kali Besar canal to the old harbour of Sunda Kelapa. More fine old Dutch architecture lines the canal, including the **Toko Merah**, formerly the home of Governor-General van Imhoff. Further north, the last remaining Dutch drawbridge, the **Chicken Market Bridge**, spans the Kali Besar.

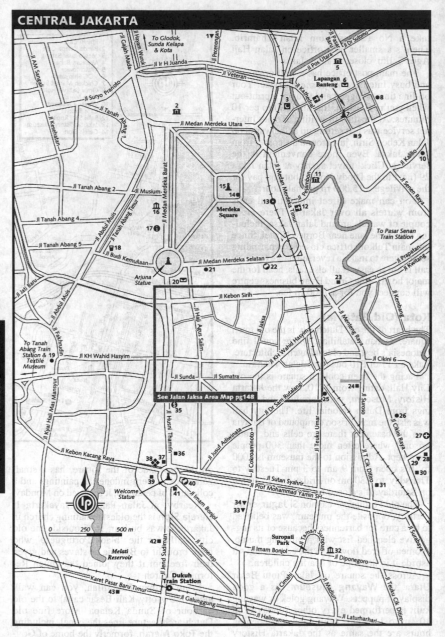

CENTRAL JAKARTA

CENTRAL JAKARTA

PLACES TO STAY					
9	Borobudur Inter-Continental Hotel	29	Oasis Bar & Restaurant	14	Entrance to Monas
23	Hotel Aryaduta	33	Gandy Steakhouse	15	National Monument (Monas)
24	Hotel Menteng I	34	Tamnak Thai Restaurant	16	National Museum
28	Karya II Hotel			17	Directorate General of Tourism Office
30	Hotel Menteng II		OTHER	18	Tanamur Disco
31	Hotel Marcopolo	2	Presidential Palace	19	Pasar Tanah Abang
36	President Hotel	3	Mesjid Istiqlal	20	Post Office Branch
37	Grand Hyatt Jakarta Hotel	4	Catholic Cathedral	21	Garuda Office
39	Hotel Indonesia	5	Gedung Kesenian	22	US Embassy
41	Mandarin Oriental Jakarta Hotel	6	Main Post Office	25	Immigration Office
42	Kartika Plaza Hotel	7	Free Irian Monument	26	Taman Ismael Marzuki (TIM)
43	Shangri-La Hotel	8	Mahkamah Agung & Ministry of Finance Building	27	Hospital
		10	Bharata Theatre	32	Adam Malik Museum
		11	Gedung Pancasila	35	BII Bank
PLACES TO EAT		12	Emanuel Church	38	Plaza Indonesia
1	Seafood Night Market	13	Gambir Train Station	40	British Embassy

To the south of Kota, **Glodok** was the old Chinatown of Batavia. It is a centre of trade and entertainment and was a focus of rioting in May 1998 when Chinese shopkeepers were targeted and shopping centres were burnt down. The lanes off Jalan Pancoran are still crammed with narrow crooked houses, small shops, temples and market stalls.

Sunda Kelapa
This is one of Jakarta's finest sights. The old Dutch port has more colourful sailing ships, the magnificent Buginese Macassar schooners, than you ever thought existed. Sunda Kelapa is a hot but easy walk from Taman Fatahillah or take the unique local transport – a ride on a 'kiddie seat' on the back of a pushbike. Admission to the harbour is 250 rp. The harbour is usually a hive of activity, and old men will take you in row boats around the schooners for about 8000 rp an hour – but an hour is probably too long.

The early morning fish market, **Pasar Ikan**, is close by. In the same area, one of the old Dutch East India Company warehouses has been turned into the **Museum Bahari** (Maritime Museum), open every day except Monday (1000 rp). The old **watchtower** near the bridge has good views of the harbour. Access costs 1000 rp.

Monuments
Inspired tastelessness best describes the plentiful supply of monuments Soekarno left to Jakarta – all in the Russian 'heroes of socialism' style.

Monas (Monumen Nasional), the giant column in Merdeka Square topped with a gold flame, is the most dramatic. It's open every day from 8 am to 5 pm. Admission is 600 rp to the **National History Museum** in the base, or 3100 rp for both the museum and the lift to the top. The museum tells the history of Indonesia's independence struggle in 48 dramatic, overstated dioramas. The lift zips you up for superb (smoggy) views across Jakarta, but the queues are very long on weekends and holidays.

Monas has been dubbed 'Soekarno's last erection' and all the other monuments have also acquired descriptive nicknames. The gentleman at Kebayoran holding the flaming dish is the 'Pizza Man' and the Free Irian Monument at Lapangan Banteng, showing a muscular gent breaking the chains of colonialism, is the 'Howzat Man' (cricket fans will understand).

Indonesian National Museum
Situated on the western side of Merdeka Square, this is one of the most interesting museums in South-East Asia. There are excellent displays of pottery and ancient Hindu statuary, a huge ethnic map of Indonesia and an equally big relief map on which you can pick out all those volcanoes you have climbed. The museum also features some fascinating fossils and examples of costumes and cultural life from all over the archipelago.

It's open daily (except Monday) from 8.30 am to 2.30 pm (Friday to 11.30 am and Saturday to 1.30 pm). Admission is 750 rp, plus

JALAN JAKSA AREA

PLACES TO STAY
6 Hotel Sabang Metropolitan
13 Lia's Hostel
16 Sari Pan Pacific Hotel
30 Bali International Hotel
31 Arcadia Hotel
33 Ibis Tamarind
38 Hotel Indra International
39 Hotel Karya
41 Hotel Tator
42 Djody Hotel
43 Djody Hostel
46 Borneo Hostel
47 Bintang Kejora
50 Nick's Corner Hostel
52 Norbek Hostel
52 Jusran Hostel
59 Wisma Delima
62 Bloem Steen Homestay
63 Kresna Homestay

67 Berlian Hostel
68 Hotel Paragon
69 Cemara Hotel

PLACES TO EAT
5 HP Gardena
7 Bakwan Campur
8 Sakura Anpan Bakery
10 Natrabu
11 Sederhana Padang Restaraunt
12 Sizzler
14 Hoka Hoka Bento
15 Paradiso 2001
22 McDonald's; American Chili's Bar & Grill
26 Sabang Bakery & Cafe
27 Lim Thiam Kie
28 Pho Hoa Bakmie
32 Hazara Indian Restaurant
34 Le Bistro
36 Ayam Goreng Nyonya Suharti

37 Romance Bar & Restaurant
40 Pappa's Kafe
49 Jalan Jaksa International Cafe
56 Ikan Bakar Kebon Sirih Restaurant
58 Sate Khas Senayan
61 Angie's Cafe
64 Margot Cafe; Hotel Le Margot
65 Warung Memori

OTHER
1 BII Bank
2 Bangkok Bank
3 Airlines: Qantas, Thai, Ansett & Continental
4 BDN Building
9 Mosque
17 ATD Plaza
18 Jaya Pub
19 Jaya Building
20 Skyline Building

21 Tourist Office; Jakarta Theatre; Green Pub
23 Hard Rock Cafe
24 Sarinah Department Store
25 Robinson's Department Store
29 Police Station
44 Click! Travel Agency & Internet Cafe
45 Wartel
48 Roberto Kencana Travel
53 Lippobank
54 Wartel & Internet Centre
55 BNI Bank
57 Bank Duta
60 BFC Cafe
66 Wartel
70 Media Taxis

another 1000 rp for your camera. Conducted tours, in a number of languages, are organised by the Indonesian Heritage Society (☎ 36 0551, ext 22).

Taman Mini Indonesia Indah
This 'whole country in one park' is a short bus ride from the Kampung Rambutan bus station south-east of the city centre. Exhibits include 27 traditional houses for the 27 provinces of Indonesia and a lagoon 'map' where you can row around the islands of Indonesia. On Sunday morning there are free cultural performances in most regional houses and a monthly calendar of various events is available at the tourist information office.

Allow 1½ hours to get there and three hours to look around. It's pretty good value. The park is open from 8 am to 5 pm daily (the houses close at 4 pm) and admission is 2000 rp.

Taman Impian Jaya Ancol
Ancol 'Dreamland' is on the water front between Kota and Tanjung Priok harbour. This huge amusement complex has an oceanarium, an amazing swimming pool complex, an Indonesian Disneyland and the excellent Pasar Seni Art Market with its numerous small shops and sidewalk cafes. Admission to Ancol is 2500 rp on weekdays, 3000 rp on weekends – extra for the attractions.

The big drawcard is Dunia Fantasi (Fantasy World), a mini version of Disneyland. It is really quite good if you've got children. Admission (including entry to Ancol) is 21,500 rp on weekdays, 28,000 rp on weekends. Dunia Fantasi is open Monday to Thursday from 11 am to 6 pm, Friday 2 to 9 pm and weekends and holidays from 10 am to 9 pm.

Most visitors find the Pasar Seni of most interest. No extra entry fee applies and it is open from 10 am to 10 pm.

To get there, take a bus to Kota and then bus No 64, 65 or a M15 minibus.

Other Attractions

To the north of Merdeka Square you'll see the gleaming white **Presidential Palace**. To the north-east is the vast **Mesjid Istiqlal**, the largest mosque in South-East Asia.

The **Ragunan Zoo**, in the Pasar Minggu District south of the city, has Komodo dragons, orang-utans and other interesting Indonesian wildlife. The **Jalan Surabaya** market stalls sell antiques, and at Jalan Pramuka there is a **bird market**, featuring tropical birds.

Of Jakarta's many museums one of the most interesting is the **Textile Museum** at Jalan Satsuit Tubun 4, south-west of the National Museum. It has a large collection of fabrics from all over Indonesia plus looms, batik-making tools and so on.

Places to Stay – Budget

Jakarta's cheap accommodation is almost all centred on Jalan Jaksa.

The original guesthouse, *Wisma Delima*, Jalan Jaksa 5, is a bit run down these days but it's still very popular. Dorm beds are 10,000 rp (9000 rp for HI members), or small but tidy singles or doubles are 20,000 rp. Mandis and showers are outside the rooms.

Norbek Hostel (☎ 33 0392) is across Jalan Jaksa at No 14. It's a dark rabbit warren with plywood walls and plenty of rules, but is friendly and well run. Rooms with fan are 20,000 rp. Down a small alleyway nearby, *Jusran Hostel* is a smaller, quiet place. Basic plywood singles/doubles cost 15,000/20,000 rp with fan.

Nick's Corner Hostel (☎ 314 1988) at No 16 is one of the better budget places on Jalan Jaksa. A bed costs 10,000 rp in immaculate, if somewhat cramped, air-con dorms – cool enough to require a blanket. Some of the other rooms are a bit dingy though. Doubles with ceiling fan cost 30,000 rp, and better rooms with bathroom and air-con are 47,000 rp.

Djody Hostel, Jalan Jaksa 27, has small, spartan rooms with shared mandi for 16,500/

24,200 rp. A few doors further up is the related but better *Djody Hotel* (☎ 315 1404) at No 35. Simple rooms without mandi cost 17,600/29,000 rp. Rooms with air-con and bathroom cost 48,000 rp.

Hotel Tator (☎ 32 3940), Jalan Jaksa 37, is a definite step above the others in quality and it's often full. Rooms cost 30,000/45,000 rp with fan, 55,000 rp with air-con and 60,000 rp for hot water as well.

More places can be found in the small streets running off Jalan Jaksa. *Kresna Homestay* (☎ 32 5403), at 175 Gang I, and *Bloem Steen Homestay* next door at No 173, are two smaller places. They're a bit cramped, but reasonable value for Jakarta. The friendly Kresna has rooms for 20,000/25,000 rp without/with mandi; the Bloem Steen has singles/doubles with fan for 20,000/25,000 rp.

On Kebon Sirih Barat 1, running west off Jalan Jaksa, *Borneo Hostel* (☎ 32 0095), at No 35, is popular, well run and friendly and has a lively cafe/bar. Well-kept rooms cost 20,000/30,000 rp without/with mandi. Another reasonable place along this lane is *Bintang Kejora* (☎ 32 3878) at No 52. It has good-sized singles/doubles for 15,000/20,000 rp or 35,000 rp with mandi.

In a very small alley off the southern end of Jalan Jaksa is the quiet *Hostel 36*. It has clean singles/doubles for 20,000/30,000 rp. Getting even deeper into the alleys off Jalan Jaksa, *Lia's Hostel* (☎ 316 2708) is lost in the kampung, but it's a clean, airy place with rooms for 15,000/20,000 rp. The easiest way to get there is to turn left past Bintang Kejora (follow the sign).

Another good choice is *Berlian Hostel* (☎ 314 9317), down a lane on the other side of Jalan Jaksa, where rooms are 20,000 rp a double.

Places to Stay – Mid-Range

Most places in this category add 21% tax and service to the quoted rates. Discounts are readily available at the more expensive hotels.

The prize for the nicest hotel on Jalan Jaksa goes to *Hotel Karya* (☎ 315 0519, fax 314 2781). It's quite reasonably priced at 125,000 rp for well-appointed doubles with air-con, hot water and TV, and 150,000 rp for larger rooms (all including tax, service and breakfast). *Hotel Le Margot* (☎ 391 3830), Jalan Jaksa 15, is a smaller place with plain but comfortable rooms for 115,500 rp (including tax and service).

Jalan KH Wahid Hasyim has a string of

INDONESIA

more upmarket mid-range hotels. *Cemara Hotel* (☎ *314 9985, fax 32 4668*), on the corner of Jalan Cemara, has rooms from 250,000 rp. *Hotel Paragon* (☎ *391 7070, fax 316 0715*), Jalan KH Wahid Hasyim 29, is strangely designed like a multistorey motel but has immaculate rooms from 192,500 rp.

Hotel Sabang Metropolitan (☎ *385 7621, fax 384 3546*) is well-located at Jalan Haji Agus Salim 11. It has a pool, business centre and reasonable rooms with all the facilities from 157,300 rp. There's another enclave of mid-range hotels in Cikini, south-east of Jalan Jaksa.

Places to Eat

Jakarta has the best range of restaurants in Indonesia, with food from all over the archipelago and all over the world.

Many travellers don't get far past Jalan Jaksa though. It has a string of popular places all dishing out the standard travellers' menu. *Romance Bar & Restaurant*, Jalan Jaksa 40, is OK, with air-con, a varied menu and a small bar, while *Margot Cafe*, in front of Hotel Le Margot, is a good restaurant/bar.

At Jalan Kebon Sirih 31A, on the corner of Jalan Jaksa, *Sate Khas Senayan* is an upmarket, air-con sate place. Prices are quite high (sate from 9000 rp) but the food is good and the ice desserts, such as *es kombinasi*, are well worth sampling.

For real Indonesian food at a rock-bottom price, there are lots of *night stalls* along Jalan Kebon Sirih and Jalan KH Wahid Hasyim. Some are of dubious cleanliness, so inspect them first.

The next street west of Jalan Jaksa, Jalan Haji Agus Salim, has a string of cheap to mid-range restaurants. Though it was renamed years ago, everyone still knows it by its former name – Jalan Sabang – and it is famed as the sate capital of Indonesia. Dozens of sate hawkers set up on the street in the evening and the pungent smoke from their charcoal braziers fills the air. Most business is takeaway, but benches are scattered along the street if you want to eat it there.

Restaurants on this stretch include *Natrabu*. For service, decor and price, this is a class above your average *nasi padang* restaurant, but it's a good place to try the spicy Sumatran food. There are cheaper and simpler Padang food places nearby. For standard Chinese fare, the *Lim Thiam Kie* is at No 49, or down an alley a little further north, the *Paradiso 2001* is a tiny Chinese vegetarian restaurant.

Other more expensive restaurants range from *Sizzler*, for chain-food grills, to the *HP Gardena*, serving Chinese steamboat and the *Pho Hoa Bakmie* Vietnamese restaurant.

On the ground floor of the Jakarta Theatre building on Jalan Thamrin, the *Green Pub* is a popular expat hang-out with Mexican food and live music at night. Indonesia's original *McDonald's* is at the front of the Sarinah department store on Jalan Thamrin. *Sarinah* also has a supermarket and an expensive, but good, food-stall area in the basement. For more upmarket western food, the Sarinah building also houses *American Chili's Bar & Grill*, and the *Hard Rock Cafe* here also does good grills.

The Plaza Indonesia further down Jalan Thamrin has plenty of other mall-based eateries, including the *Cira Food Court* on the 3rd level, with a range of excellent Asian and western food stalls.

For a culinary splurge, *Cafe Batavia* on Taman Fatahillah is a wonderfully atmospheric restaurant and bar with pricey but excellent food (see Entertainment). Another well-known place is the classy *Oasis Bar & Restaurant*, among the mid-range hotels of Cikini, where you can get a good traditional rijsttafel.

Entertainment

The Jakarta cultural centre, *Taman Ismael Marzuki*, or TIM, at Jalan Cikini Raya 73, hosts all kinds of top-class cultural performances – western and Indonesian. Events are listed in the TIM monthly program available from the tourist information office.

At 8.15 pm every evening, except Monday and Thursday, wayang orang can be seen at the *Bharata Theatre*, Jalan Kalilio 15, near the Pasar Senen. *Ketoprak* (Javanese folk theatre) performances take place here on Monday and Thursday evenings.

The *Wayang Museum*, on Jalan Pintu Besar Utara in Kota, stages wayang kulit or wayang golek every second Sunday, and *Taman Mini Indonesia Indah* (see the earlier entry for details) has regular cultural performances.

Jakarta has plenty of nightlife. It's the most sophisticated, broad-minded and corrupt city in Indonesia with nightlife to match. Drugs such as Ecstasy can be found in Jakarta's clubs but there are regular crackdowns and penalties for possession can be stiff. Letting your hair down in Jakarta can be a relatively expensive business – discos such as Tanamur charge at least 25,000 rp at the door and around 12,000 rp for a small beer.

On Jalan Thamrin, the Sarinah building houses the ever-popular *Hard Rock Cafe* and, across the road nearby, the *Jaya Pub* is a long-running rock'n'roll place. *Planet Hollywood*, 4km south of the city centre on Jalan Gatot Subroto, is a trendy spot for moneyed Jakartans. *Cafe Batavia*, right in the heart of old Kota on Taman Fatahillah, is a popular upmarket watering hole and a good place to stop for a drink during an afternoon of sightseeing. It's open 24 hours.

Many of the big hotels house smart discos, and the Glodok area, Jakarta's Chinatown, has an interesting collection. The 9th floor disco of *Sydney 2000* has impressive decor and a dazzling laser show.

Jakarta's most infamous disco is *Tanamur* at Jalan Tanah Abang Timur 14. This long-running institution is jammed nightly with gyrating revellers of every race, creed and sexual proclivity, and innumerable ladies of the night.

Many travellers find the bars and cafes on Jalan Jaksa cheap places to hang out in the evening. *BFC Cafe*, right next to Wisma Delima, is a new place with high bar stools, offbeat timber decor and cold draught beer.

Getting There & Away

Jakarta is the main travel hub for Indonesia, with ships and flights to destinations all over the archipelago. Buses depart for destinations throughout Java and for Bali and Sumatra. Trains are a convenient alternative for many destinations on Java.

Air Most flights go from Soekarno-Hatta international airport 35km north-west of the city, although a handful of domestic flights (eg to Bandung and Bandarlampung) use the more central Halim airport in the south-east. Airport tax is 25,000 rp on international flights and 11,000 rp on domestic flights (9000 rp from Halim), payable at check-in.

The domestic airline offices are dotted around the city. The main Garuda office (☎ 380 1901, fax 231 1395) is at Jalan Medan Merdeka Selatan 13. Merpati (☎ 654 8888, fax 654 0620) has an office at Jalan Angkasa Blok B15 in Kemayoran, north-east of the city centre, and another at Gambir station, and Bouraq (☎ 628 8815, fax 600 8729) is at Jalan Angkasa 1-3. Mandala (☎ 424 6100) is at Jalan Garuda 79, one block south of Jalan Angkasa. Travel agents also sell domestic

tickets. Fares were so volatile at the time of writing that any examples would bear little resemblance to reality by the time that you read this.

For international flights, agents on Jalan Jaksa are a good place to start looking. Jakarta is no discount centre, but some reasonably priced tickets can be found. The most popular is the short hop to Singapore, costing as little as US$65 with Pakistan International Airlines or Gulf Air. Other typical one-way fares are: Bangkok US$215, Kuala Lumpur US$85, London US$485, Perth US$288 and Sydney US$355.

Bus Jakarta has four main bus stations, all well out of the centre:

Kalideres, 15km west of the city centre, has frequent buses throughout the day to destinations west of Jakarta such as Merak, Serang and Labuan.

Kampung Rambutan, 18km south of the city, primarily handles buses to destinations south and south-east of Jakarta such as Bogor, Bandung and Tasikmalaya. The trains to Bogor and Bandung are a better alternative.

Pulo Gadung, 12km east of the city centre, has buses to Cirebon, Central and East Java, Sumatra and Bali. Buses to Yogyakarta leave throughout the day from 8 am to 6 pm, with the deluxe night buses leaving around 3 to 6 pm. This is also the main terminal for Sumatran buses, which leave between 10 am and 3 pm. Allow at least an hour to get out to Pulo Gadung by public bus (No 54 from Jalan Thamrin).

Lebak Bulus, 16km south of the city, handles many of the long-distance deluxe buses to Yogyakarta, Surabaya and Bali. Most departures are late afternoon or evening. So many buses leave that you can usually just front up at the terminal and join the chaos, though it pays to book for deluxe buses and during busy holiday periods. Travel agents on Jalan Jaksa sell tickets and usually include transport to the terminal. Their prices are a lot higher but save a lot of hassle.

Minibus Door-to-door travel minibuses are not such a good option in Jakarta because it can take hours to pick up or drop off passengers in the traffic jams. Some travel agents book them, but you may have to go to a depot on the outskirts. Jalan Jaksa travel agents can book direct minibuses to Yogya (45,000 rp).

Train Jakarta has a number of train stations. The most convenient and most important is Gambir, on the eastern side of Merdeka

Square, a 15 minute walk from Jalan Jaksa. Gambir handles mostly express trains to Bogor, Bandung, Yogyakarta, Solo, Semarang and Surabaya. Most trains to Gambir go on to Kota, the station in the old city area to the north. The Pasar Senen station, to the east, has mostly ekonomi trains to eastern destinations. Tanah Abang, to the west, has a couple of slow trains to Merak.

Trains in Java are often subject to delays, but from Jakarta the train stations are much more central than the bus stations and trains don't have to battle the Jakarta traffic jams.

For longer hauls, the express trains are far preferable to the ekonomi trains, and most have cheaper bisnis class in addition to air-con *eksekutif* class. For most express trains, tickets can be bought in advance, either at the station, or some travel agents arrange tickets for a premium.

Gambir station is well set up – as well as cafes, it has a 24 hour Merpati office, wartel and ATMs. From Gambir station you can walk out the front to the main road and hail down a bajaj, which will cost at least 2000 rp to Jalan Jaksa after bargaining, or a metered taxi (around 3000 rp).

Bogor Ekonomi trains to Bogor (900 rp; 1½ hours) leave every 20 minutes or so from Gambir and Kota. Trains can be horribly crowded during rush hour, but otherwise provide a good service. The bisnis trains (2500 rp; one hour) are better, leaving at 7.43 and 11 am, 2.28, 4.48 and 7.03 pm. Air-con services cost 4000 rp.

Bandung The efficient and very comfortable *Parahyangan* service departs to Bandung (15,000/25,000 rp bisnis/eksekutif; three hours) roughly every hour between 5.30 am and 8.30 pm from Gambir station. The more luxurious *Argogede* departs at 10 am and 6 pm, and costs 30,000 rp in eksekutif class.

Cirebon Most trains that run along the north coast, and those to Yogyakarta, go through Cirebon. One of the best services is the *Cirebon Ekspres* departing Gambir station at 7 and 9.45 am, and 4.30 pm (12,000/23,000 rp bisnis/eksekutif; 3½ hours).

Yogyakarta & Solo The *Fajar Utama Yogya* (23,000 rp bisnis; nine hours) departs Gambir at 6.10 am, and the *Senja Utama Yogya* (25,000/55,000 rp bisnis/eksekutif) departs at 7.20 and 8.40 pm. The *Senja Utama Solo* is

the best option to Solo (28,000/57,000 rp bisnis/eksekutif; 10½ hours) and it also stops in Yogyakarta. Expect overruns on the scheduled journey times.

Surabaya Trains to Surabaya either take the short northern route via Semarang or the longer southern route via Yogyakarta. Express trains range from the *Jayabaya Utama* (33,000 rp; 12 hours) to the luxurious *Argobromo* (100,000 rp; nine hours).

Boat See the Indonesia Getting Around section for information on the Pelni shipping services which operate on a regular weekly schedule to ports all over the archipelago. Most ships go through Jakarta, and all arrive at (and depart from) Pelabuhan Satu (Dock No 1) at Tanjung Priok, 13km from the centre of the city. Take the grey Himpunan bus No 81 from Jalan Thamrin, opposite the Sarinah building; allow at least an hour.

The Pelni ticket office (☎ 421 1921) is at Jalan Angkasa 18, north-east of the centre, or you can buy through travel agents, who charge a small premium but are much more convenient.

Direct services from Jakarta include Padang (Sumatra) and Ujung Pandang (Sulawesi) and many more services go via Semarang and Surabaya. Ships also sail from Jakarta to Batam and Tanjung Balai in the Riau Archipelago, from where it is just a short ferry ride to Singapore. As well as the Pelni boats, the MV *Samudera Jaya* leaves Jakarta every Saturday and does the trip to Tanjung Pinang in 18 hours for 95,000 rp. Bookings can be made through travel agents or at PT Admiral Lines, right on Tanjung Priok harbour at 21 Jalan Raya Pelabuhan.

Getting Around
To/From the Airport Soekarno-Hatta is 35km north-west of the city at Cengkareng. Allow an hour to get there, longer during peak hours.

There's a good Damri bus service (4000 rp) every 30 minutes from 3 am to 7 pm between the airport and Gambir train station in central Jakarta.

Alternatively, a metered taxi costs about 40,000 rp, including the airport service charge and the 7500 rp toll road charges, paid on top of the metered fare. Catch cabs from taxi ranks outside the terminal, and avoid offers of 'transport' from unregistered taxis. Some Jalan Jaksa hostels offer minibuses to the airport, but are no bargain if they don't use the toll road.

A taxi from Jalan Jaksa to Halim airport costs 10,000 rp, but twice that in the other direction.

Bus Jakarta has a large network of city buses. Ordinary buses cost 300 rp, express (Patas) buses cost 700 rp and air-con Patas buses cost 1800 rp. Jakarta's crowded buses have their fair share of pickpockets and bag slashers. The more expensive buses are generally safer, as well as being more comfortable.

In addition to the big buses, mikrolets and other minibuses operate in some areas (400 rp). Jakarta still has some Morris bemos, the original three wheelers.

The tourist office has information on buses around Jakarta. Some of the useful services that operate along central Jalan Thamrin include:

No 81 – Blok M to Kota, Ancol and Tanjung Priok
P11, P10 (air-con) – Kampung Rambutan to Kota
P1, B1 – Blok M to Kota
P7A, No 78 – Pulo Gadung to Kalideres via Jalan Juanda

Taxi Jakarta's taxis are modern, well kept, and have air-con and working meters (usually). The first kilometre costs 1500 rp, then 550 rp for each additional kilometre. Taxi drivers expect, if not demand, a tip. It is customary to round the fare up to the nearest 1000 rp for good service. Bluebird Taxis have a good reputation.

Local Transport Bajaj are nothing less than Indian auto-rickshaws – orange three wheelers that carry two passengers (three at a squeeze) and are powered by noisy two-stroke engines. A short ride of a couple of kilometres (such as Gambir to Jalan Jaksa) will cost 2000 rp but bajaj are not allowed along Jalan Thamrin.

PULAU SERIBU
Pulau Seribu, or Thousand Islands, starts a few kilometres out in the Bay of Jakarta. The islands are only a short boat ride from Jakarta's Ancol Marina and have some of the finest white sand beaches in Java. The Jakarta tourist information office has details on the islands.

The closer islands such as **Pulau Bidadari** and **Pulau Ayer** are popular day trip destinations. The further you go from the coast, the clearer the waters become and the more expensive the resorts.

Most resorts have daily boats from Ancol Marina for guests and day-trippers, usually leaving around 8 or 9 am and returning around 3 pm. The resorts provide speedboats, and even the furthest islands take only a little over two hours.

BOGOR
Bogor, 60km south of Jakarta, stands at a height of only 290m but is appreciably cooler than the capital, although visitors in the wet season should bear in mind the town's nickname: the City of Rain. Bogor has probably the highest annual rainfall in Java and has achieved a record 322 thunderstorms in one year.

Bogor is easily visited as a day trip from Jakarta, or you can use it as a base from which to visit Jakarta. It's a pleasant and relaxing enough place, but don't expect a small country town – Bogor's streets bustle with all the fervour of a typical Indonesian city.

Orientation & Information
Bogor's centrepiece is the tranquil Kebun Raya (botanical gardens). The train station is a 10 minute walk to the north-west and the bus station is near the south-east edge.

The tourist office (☎ 33 8053), Jalan Ir II Juanda 10, seems to move every year but is now ensconced next to the town hall (*balai kota*). There's not much information to be gleaned here but it's worth a try. A small branch office is at the entrance to the gardens.

Bank Indonesia International (BII), near the train station on Jalan Dewi Sartika, has an ATM accepting Visa and MasterCard. The BCA bank is at Jalan Ir H Juanda 28, and there's a branch of BNI bank across from the bus station on Jalan Raya Pajajaran.

The post office is on Jalan Ir H Juanda, opposite the BCA bank. It's open Monday to Saturday from 8 am to 5 pm and Sunday to noon. The Internet office inside is open from 8 am to 1 pm and charges 10,000 rp per hour. There's also a 24 hour wartel next door, while the wartel at the entrance to the Kebun Raya has a Home Country Direct phone.

Things to See & Do
The **Kebun Raya** are huge, world class botanical gardens in the centre of Bogor. Stamford Raffles founded the gardens in 1817 during the British period, and they have a huge collection of tropical plants and bizarre trees. A

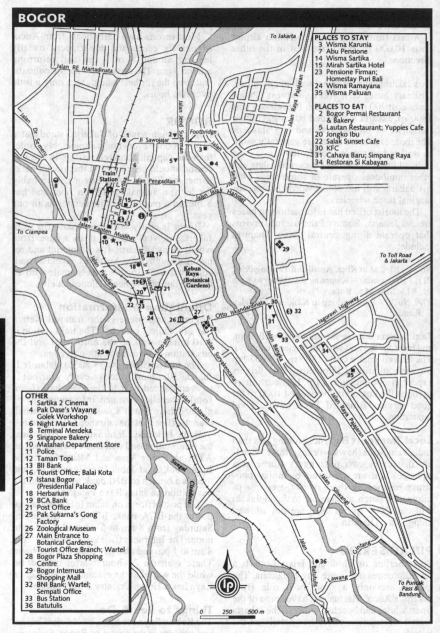

BOGOR

To Jakarta

To Ciampea

To Toll Road
& Jakarta

Footbridge

Jalan RE Martadinata

Jalan Jend Sudirman

Jalan Raya Pajajaran

Jl Sawojajar

Train
Station

Jalan Pengadilan

Jalan Jalak Harupat

Jalan Dewi Sartika

Jalan Kapten Muslihat

Jalan Paledang

Jalan Ir H Juanda

Kebun
Raya
(Botanical
Gardens)

Otto Iskandardinata

Jalan Bangka

Jagorawi Highway

Jalan Empang

Jalan Suryakencana

Jalan Pahlawan

Sungai Cisadane

Jalan Raya Pajajaran

Jalan Siliwangi

Cigintang

Batutulis

To Puncak
Pass &
Bandung

PLACES TO STAY
3 Wisma Karunia
7 Abu Pensione
14 Wisma Sartika
15 Mirah Sartika Hotel
23 Pensione Firman;
   Homestay Puri Bali
24 Wisma Ramayana
35 Wisma Pakuan

PLACES TO EAT
2 Bogor Permai Restaurant
  & Bakery
5 Lautan Restaurant; Yuppies Cafe
20 Jongko Ibu
22 Salak Sunset Cafe
30 KFC
31 Cahaya Baru; Simpang Raya
34 Restoran Si Kabayan

OTHER
1 Sartika 2 Cinema
4 Pak Dase's Wayang
  Golek Workshop
6 Night Market
8 Terminal Merdeka
9 Singapore Bakery
10 Matahari Department Store
11 Police
12 Taman Topi
13 BII Bank
16 Tourist Office; Balai Kota
17 Istana Bogor
   (Presidential Palace)
18 Herbarium
19 BCA Bank
21 Post Office
25 Pak Sukarna's Gong
   Factory
26 Zoological Museum
27 Main Entrance to
   Botanical Gardens;
   Tourist Office Branch; Wartel
28 Bogor Plaza Shopping
   Centre
29 Bogor Internusa
   Shopping Mall
32 BNI Bank; Wartel;
   Sempati Office
33 Bus Station
36 Batutulis

0   250   500 m

monument to Raffles' wife, Olivia, is near the main entrance. The gardens are open from 8 am to 5 pm every day. Admission is 2500 rp, or 1500 rp on crowded Sundays and public holidays.

The **Presidential Palace** (Istana Bogor), built by the Dutch and much favoured by Soekarno (Soeharto ignored it), stands beside the gardens, and deer graze on its lawns. The palace is not normally open to the public, but tours can be arranged through the tourist office.

Near the garden entrance, the **Zoological Museum** has an interesting collection of stuffed animals. Exhibits include a blue whale skeleton, a stuffed Javan rhino and, if you have ever heard about the island of Flores having a rat problem, one glance at the showcase stuffed with the Flores version of Indonesian rats will explain why. The museum is open from 8 am to 4 pm daily (500 rp).

There are a couple of places you can visit to see Javanese artisans at work. Pak Sukarna belts out gongs and other gamelan instruments in his **gong factory** at Jalan Pancasan 7, while Pak Dase makes quality wooden puppets at his **wayang golek workshop** in Lebak Kantion RT 02/VI. Both these places are included in most tours of Bogor organised by guesthouses.

Places to Stay

Bogor has some very good family-run places which make staying here a real pleasure, and a good alternative to Jakarta (though not much cheaper).

Two of the better budget places in town are also conveniently close to the entrance to the gardens. *Pensione Firman* (☎ 32 3246), Jalan Paledang 48, is deservedly a budget favourite and the cheapest around with dorm beds at 10,000 rp and rooms from 20,000 rp with shared bathroom and from 25,000 rp with bath, all including breakfast and free tea and coffee. There's a good view from the upstairs balcony area. *Homestay Puri Bali* (☎ 37 4906), next door at No 50, is also good. It's a quiet place with an attractive garden and semi-Balinese style restaurant. Pleasant, airy rooms cost 25,000 or 30,000 rp for doubles with bath, or 45,000 rp for a huge triple room.

Just around the corner and across from the gardens at Jalan Ir H Juanda 54 is the very colonial *Wisma Ramayana* (☎ 32 0364). Doubles from 26,000 rp without bath are pretty barren, but the larger rooms with bath,

from 36,000 rp to 45,000 rp, have style. Breakfast is included.

Abu Pensione (☎ 32 2893), near the train station at Jalan Mayor Oking 15, is clean, attractive and well set up with travel services. There's a variety of rooms starting with ordinary doubles without bath for 25,000 rp and better doubles with bathroom for 35,000 rp, up to 60,000 rp with air-con and hot water. Breakfast is an extra 5000 rp and there's a 10% tax. On the other side of the train station, *Wisma Sartika* (☎ 32 3747), Jalan Dewi Sartika 4D, is convenient and well run, but the rooms are basic. Doubles cost 30,000/40,000 rp with shower outside/inside, including breakfast and tax.

North of the Kebun Raya, the exceptionally friendly *Wisma Karunia* (☎ 32 3411), Jalan Sempur 35-37, is a little out of the way but quiet and reasonably priced at 15,000 rp for doubles with shared bathroom, and from 30,000 rp to 35,000 rp for rooms with private bathroom. Breakfast is included and the family will prepare you a nice evening meal for 3000 rp.

Mirah Sartika Hotel (☎ 31 2343), Jalan Dewi Sartika 6A, is a central mid-range option. Economy rooms are 55,000 rp and comfortable, well-appointed rooms with air-con and TV are 65,000 rp, including breakfast (but add 15% tax). Further out of town, south of the bus station, *Wisma Pakuan* (☎ 31 9430), Jalan Pakuan 12, is a comfortable guesthouse. Doubles with fan, TV and hot water are 55,000 rp, or 71,500 rp with air-con, all including breakfast and tax. Angkot No 6 will get you there.

Places to Eat

Cheap eats can be found at the *night market* on Jalan Dewi Sartika, and the *Pasar Bogor*, near the Kebun Raya entrance, has good food stalls during the day.

A good restaurant for Sundanese food is the *Jongko Ibu* opposite the post office at Jalan Ir H Juanda 36. Prices are moderate and you can dine buffet-style and try a number of dishes. *Restoran Si Kabayan*, Jalan Bina Marga I No 2, is one of Bogor's most pleasant Sundanese restaurants, with individual bamboo huts arranged around an attractive garden.

The *Salak Sunset Cafe*, near Pensione Firman at Jalan Paledang 38, is a chic but cheap little place with river views.

Cahaya Baru, Jalan Raya Pajajaran 7, is an excellent modern seafood restaurant with a wide variety of dishes for around 12,000 rp to 15,000 rp. The menu also features a few off-beat numbers: fried pigeon in butter sauce and several variations of fried frog. It's wedged in between *KFC* and a *Simpang Raya* Padang restaurant near the bus station.

Getting There & Away

Bus Buses depart frequently throughout the day to Jakarta (1200/3000 rp without/with air-con). Most go to the Kampung Rambutan station – a trip taking only a little over half an hour via the Jagorawi Hwy toll road, but double that time from Kampung Rambutan to central Jakarta. Some services go directly to Jakarta's Pulo Gadung station (1600 rp) and Tanjung Priok harbour (1900 rp) – very useful if you're planning to leave Jakarta immediately from one of these exit points.

There are also regular buses from Bogor to Bandung (3000 rp to 7000 rp; three hours). On weekends, buses are not allowed to go via the scenic Puncak Pass (it gets very crowded) and have to travel via Sukabumi (3300/5500 rp; four hours). Air-con, door-to-door minibuses also go to Bandung for 15,000 rp. These can be booked through most of the guesthouses, or call Erny Travel on ☎ 32 2563.

Train Trains are the best way to reach Jakarta. They leave roughly every 20 minutes until 8.20 pm and take about 1½ hours. The frequent economy trains cost 900 rp to Gambir station or 1000 rp to Kota. Better services are the express trains (2000 rp; four a day), bisnis (2500 rp; three a day) and air-con (3500 rp; three a day).

Getting Around

Bogor's distinctive angkots (300 rp) create lime-green gridlock most of the time, making the going slow, particularly around the train station area. They shuttle around town with regular services between the bus and train station (No 3), and in an anticlockwise loop around the gardens (No 2 from the train station to the entrance to Kebun Raya). Most angkots and colts run to and from Terminal Merdeka.

Becaks are banned from the main road encircling the gardens. There are no metered taxis in Bogor.

BOGOR TO BANDUNG

There are a number of sprawling resort towns and tea plantations on the way up and over the beautiful **Puncak Pass** between Bogor and Bandung – a very scenic bus trip. The area is a popular escape from Jakarta on weekends, when the traffic jams are horrendous. Accommodation tends to be expensive, though budget places can be found in Cisarua on the Bogor side of the pass, or Cibodas and Cipanas on the other side.

The **Gunung Mas Tea Plantation** sprawls just below the summit and is easily reached by angkot (500 rp) from Cisarua. You can wander through the contoured plantation and watch the pickers in action for free, or a tour of the factory costs 1500 rp plus at least 5000 rp for a guide. Don't bother visiting Telaga Warna (coloured lake) at the top of the pass; they charge you twice to get in (200 rp and 1000 rp) and then it's just a murky green pond that supposedly changes colour in the varying light. **Taman Safari Indonesia**, just east of Cisarua, is a drive-in 'safari park'.

At **Cibodas**, just over the Puncak Pass, there is a cooler, high-altitude extension of the Kebun Raya. The gardens are 4km off the main road, 500 rp by angkot from Cipanas. From here, you can climb **Gunung Gede**, a volcano peak offering fine views of the surrounding area. The PHPA (national parks service) office opposite the entrance to the gardens issues permits and has good maps of the route. The walk takes all day, so an early start (usually around 2 am) is essential to reach the summit by dawn.

Places to Stay & Eat

Kopo Hostel (☎ 0251-25 4296) at Jalan Raya Puncak 557 in Cisarua, on the main Bogor-Bandung road, is an excellent base for exploring the Puncak Pass. It has a garden and a small restaurant. Dorm beds are 8000 rp, doubles from 22,000 rp, and the four-bed rooms with bathroom and hot water are good value at 43,000 rp if you're in a group. Hostelling International (HI) members get a small discount and breakfast is included.

In Cibodas village, 500m before the gardens, *Freddy's Homestay* (☎ 0263-51 5473) is a great option. Bright, clean rooms are 20,000 and 25,000 rp, or the dorm is 10,000 rp – all with shared mandi, but breakfast is included. Meals are available and good information is provided. *Pondok Pemuda Cibodas* (☎ 0263-51 2807), near the Cibodas PHPA office, caters mostly to school groups and has large dorms costing 5500 rp per person.

In Cipanas, *Villa Cipanas Indah* (☎ 0263-51 2513), Jalan Tengah 8, has rooms for

30,000 and 40,000 rp with hot water. Good information and guides are on offer.

There are plenty of restaurants along the resort strip. *Rindu Alam Restaurant* is perched up at the top of the pass and its balcony area is a popular place to dine while looking out over the valleys and tea plantations (if they're not shrouded in mist). The food here is excellent and, for such a touristed place, the prices are surprisingly reasonable.

Getting There & Away
You can get up to the towns on the pass by taking a colt or any Bandung bus from Bogor. Plan not to be here on the weekend; if you are and want to travel on to Bandung, you'll have to take a colt to Cianjur (2500 rp), then a bus to Bandung from there. During the week, just flag down any Bandung-bound bus.

BANDUNG
Bandung is Indonesia's third largest city and the capital of West Java, homeland of the Sundanese people. It's a bustling city on the move, a centre for learning and Indonesia's new high-tech industries. Its 750m altitude makes it cool and comfortable, and the leafy northern part of town is home to some of Indonesia's finest Dutch architecture.

The surrounding highlands are dotted with hot springs and volcanoes, the most notable being Tangkuban Perahu.

Orientation & Information
Bandung sprawls over a wide area but the central part of town is along Jalan Asia Afrika and around the *alun alun* (city square). Most of the budget accommodation is conveniently located around Jalan Kebonjati, just south of the train station.

Tourist Offices The very helpful Visitor Information Centre (☎ 420 6644) is at the north-east corner of the alun alun on Jalan Asia Afrika and is open Monday to Saturday from 9 am to 5 pm. This is where you can catch the City Circle Bus (see Organised Tours later in this section). The train station also has a tourist information booth.

Money The Golden Megah Corp moneychanger, which has branches at Jalan Oto Iskandardinata 180 and Jalan Lembong 36, changes cash and travellers cheques at excellent rates and is open Monday to Friday from 8.30 am to 4.30 pm, Saturday to 2 pm. There's a BNI bank with an ATM (MasterCard and Cirrus) just north of the railway line on Jalan Kebonjukut, and a BCA bank with Visa ATM nearby on Jalan Suniaraja.

Post & Communications The main post office is on the corner of Jalan Asia Afrika and Jalan Banceuy and is open every day from 8 am to 7 pm. Their small Wasantaranet Internet service keeps the same hours but is closed Sunday and charges 8000 rp an hour.

There are plenty of wartels in Bandung for international calls and at least two that will connect you for a reverse-charge call. Try Wartel Sandita at Jalan Naripan 39, or Wartel Dewi Sartika at Jalan Dewi Sartika 59.

Museums
Bandung was famous as the venue for the Afro-Asian conference, when Soekarno, Zhou Enlai, Ho Chi Minh, Nasser and other Third World figureheads met in 1955. The **Gedung Merdeka** (Freedom building), on Jalan Asia Afrika, has the full story.

The **Museum Geologi** (Geological Museum) at Jalan Diponegoro 57 has some interesting exhibits including relief maps, volcano models and fossils.

Other museums include the **Museum Mandala Wangsit** (Army Museum) on Jalan Lembong, with its grim and explicit photographs of the Darul Islam rebellion, and the West Java Cultural Museum, south-west of the city centre on Jalan Oto Iskandardinata (Jalan Otista for short). It is closed Monday.

Jeans Street
Bandung is a centre for clothing manufacture and a procession of shops on a 1km-long strip of Jalan Cihampelas in the north of the city compete for business with outrageous shopfronts and decor. Superman, Rambo and Aladdin are all here – it's definitely worth seeing, and the jeans and T-shirts are cheap.

Other Attractions
Bandung is noted for its fine Dutch Art Deco architecture. The **Savoy Homann Hotel** and the **Grand Hotel Preanger**, both on Jalan Asia Afrika, are worth a look. Also take a look at the magnificent **Gedung Sate** (near the Museum Geologi), the regional government building, so-called because it's topped by what looks like a sate stick.

Further north, Bandung's ITB, or **Institute of Technology**, is one of the most important universities in Indonesia and also has some

INDONESIA

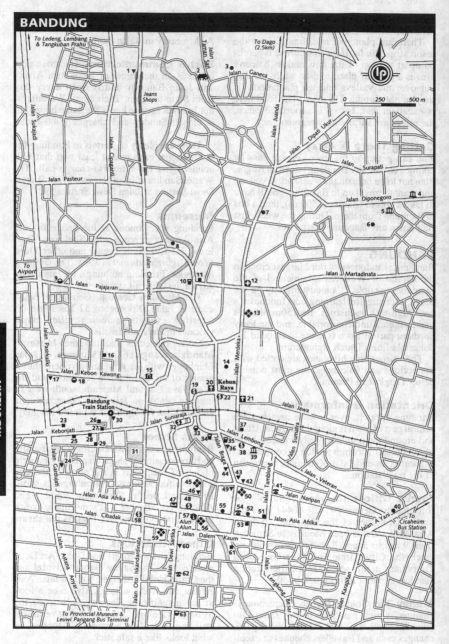

BANDUNG

To Ledeng, Lembang
& Tangkuban Prahu

To Dago
(2.5km)

Jeans
Shops

To
Airport

Jalan Taman Sari

Jalan Ganeca

Jalan Juanda

Jalan Dipati Ukur

Jalan Surapati

Jalan Diponegoro

Jalan Pasteur

Jalan Cipaganti

Jalan Sukajadi

Jalan Champelas

Jalan Martadinata

Jalan Pajajaran

Jalan Pasirkaliki

Jalan Kebon Kawong

Jalan Merdeka

Kebun
Raya

Bandung
Train Station

Jalan Kebonjati

Jalan Suniaraja

Jalan Jawa

Jalan Lembong

Jalan Braga

Jalan Sumatra

Jalan Garduajh

Jalan Tamblong

Jalan Veteran

Jalan Asia Afrika

Jalan Naripan

Jalan A Yani

To
Cicaheum
Bus Station

Jalan Cibadak

Jalan Asia Afrika

Jalan Oto Iskandardinata

Jalan Dewi Sartika

Jalan Dalem Kaum

Jalan Lengkong Besar

Jalan Karapitan

Jalan Astana Anyar

To Provincial Museum &
Leuwi Pangang Bus Terminal

0   250   500 m

BANDUNG

PLACES TO STAY					
11	Bumi Sakinah	49	Braga Restaurant & Pub	32	BCA Bank
16	Hotel Patradissa	60	Warung Nasi Mang Udju	33	4848 Taxis
23	Hotel Patradissa II			34	Braga Disco
25	Hotel Surabaya	**OTHER**		35	North Sea Bar;
26	Sakardana Homestay	2	Zoo		Amsterdam Cafe
27	Losmen Sakardana	3	Bandung Institute of	38	Golden Megah Corp
28	Le Yossie Homestay;		Technology (ITB)		Moneychanger
	STA Agency	4	Museum Geologi (Geological	39	Museum Mandala Wangsit
29	By Moritz		Museum)		(Army Museum)
37	Hotel Panghegar	5	Museum Pos dan Giro	40	Rumentang Siang
51	Grand Hotel Preanger	6	Gedung Sate (Regional	41	Wartel Sandita
53	Savoy Homann Hotel		Government Building)	45	Matahari Department Store
61	Hotel Mawar; Pak Ruhiyat's	7	Galael Supermarket		& Supermarket
	Workshop	8	Flower Market	47	Post Office
		9	Bandung Express Buses	48	Bank Rakyat Indonesia; Polo
PLACES TO EAT		10	Lost World Cafe	50	Sarinah Department Store
1	Boga Boga Cafe	12	Hospital	52	Merpati Office
17	Rumah Makan Mandarin	13	Plaza Bandung Indah	54	Wartel
24	Night Warung	14	City Hall	55	Gedung Merdeka
30	Warung & Restaurants		(Kantor Walikota)		(Freedom Building)
36	Braga Permai	15	Governor's Residence	56	Palaguna Shopping Centre
42	Sindang Reret Restaurant	18	4848 Taxis	57	Visitor Information Centre
43	Canary Bakery	19	BNI Bank	58	Golden Megah Corp
44	London Kafe;	20	Bethel Church		Moneychanger
	French Bakery	21	Catholic Church	59	King's Department Store
46	Night Market Warung	22	BII Bank	62	Wartel Dewi Sartika
		31	Pasar Baru	63	Kebun Kelapa Angkot Station

fine examples of Indo-European architecture. On Jalan Taman Sari, close to the ITB, Bandung's **zoo** has open park space and a wide variety of Indonesian bird life. Admission is 2000 rp.

Down a small alley behind Jalan Pangarang 22, near Hotel Mawar, you can see **wayang golek puppets** being carved at Pak Ruhiyat's workshop at No 78/17B.

On occasional Sunday mornings, traditional **ram-butting fights** are held at Cilimus, near Terminal Ledeng to the north of the city. Check with the Bandung visitor centre to see when they're on.

Organised Tours

The City Circle Tour Bus is an excellent service operating four times a day (9 and 11.20 am, 1.40 and 3.40 pm) from the Visitor Information Centre. The bus has three set routes around town covering the main points of interest, including the Dago teahouse, and you can get on and off where you like. The cost is 10,000 rp including commentary. This is an anomaly among Indonesian buses – it leaves on time, even if it's empty. The tourist office can also arrange interesting walking tours of the colonial city (20,000 rp an hour).

Most of the guesthouses book day tours to Gunung Papandayan (an active volcano south of Bandung), which include a visit to a Hindu temple and various cottage industries. The trip is pretty good value at 45,000 rp.

Places to Stay

Jalan Kebonjati, near the train station and the city centre, is the place to head for budget accommodation. *By Moritz* (☎ 420 7264), Kompleks Luxor Permai 35, Jalan Kebonjati, is a well-managed travellers' guesthouse with a popular restaurant and bar. Dorm beds cost 10,000 rp and spotless singles/doubles with shared bathroom are 15,000/20,000 rp. Breakfast is included.

Le Yossie Homestay (☎ 420 5453), 53 Jalan Kebonjati, is not quite as immaculate but is also good. A dorm bed costs 8000 rp, and singles/doubles are 10,000/15,000 rp. The rooms are light, travel information is available and there is a downstairs cafe with free tea and coffee for guests.

Hidden away down a little alley beside Hotel Melati is the quiet *Losmen Sakardana* (☎ 420 9897) at No 50/7B. Basic rooms are 10,000/15,000 rp. *Sakardana Homestay* (☎ 421 8553), Gang Babakan 55-7/B, further along the same alley, is its more popular copy. It's friendly and has a good upstairs

INDONESIA

restaurant. Tiny singles/doubles are 10,000/15,000 rp.

Jalan Kebonjati also has a few hotels. *Hotel Surabaya* (☎ 43 6791), at No 71, is the most interesting with plenty of colonial ambience. Simple rooms range from 13,000/23,500 rp up to 45,000 rp for attractive rooms with bath in the garden wing.

Hotel Patradissa II (☎ 420 2645), Jalan Pasirkaliki 12, just around the corner from Jalan Kebonjati, has small but spotless rooms with attached bathroom and hot showers for 35,000 rp, including breakfast.

North of the train station, *Hotel Patradissa* (☎ 420 6680), at Jalan H Moch Iskat 8, is larger and also good value. Small singles/doubles with hot showers are 25,000/35,000 rp, larger doubles are 42,000 rp, and air-con rooms are 60,000 rp.

For a home-style retreat, *Bumi Sakinah* (☎ 420 6842), Jalan RE Martadinata 3, is a charming old guesthouse with large rooms from 60,000 rp.

Places to Eat

There's a good *night market* directly across from the Visitor Information Centre. On Jalan Gardujati, opposite Hotel Trio, is a string of lively night-time *warung* and a selection of *Chinese restaurants*. Cheap, if slightly grotty, *warung* can be found directly in front of the train station, facing Jalan Kebonjati.

Jalan Braga, the one-time fancy shopping street of Bandung, has all sorts of interesting places. The centrepiece is the *Braga Permai*, with its open-air cafe, at No 74. It's a more expensive restaurant but cheaper meals are available and the ice cream is superb. Other places on Jalan Braga include the *Canary Bakery* for fast food, the *London Kafe* for pricey European-style coffee, and the *French Bakery* for a snack or light meal, croissants or Danish pastries. The *North Sea Bar* has some excellent, though expensive, steak dishes – the mixed grill at 35,000 rp is a sight to behold.

The *Sindang Reret Restaurant*, Jalan Naripan 9, just around the corner from Jalan Braga, has good Sundanese food, and is noted for its free Saturday-night wayang golek performances.

Just south of the alun alun, at Jalan Dewi Sartika 7A, the *Warung Nasi Mang Udju* has cheap Sundanese food, eaten with the fingers. Not far from the train station on Jalan Kebon Kawong, *Rumah Makan Mandarin*

is a good Chinese restaurant with seafood dishes from around 12,000 rp.

At the top end of Jalan Cihampelas at No 159B, the *Boga Boga Cafe* is a great place to take a break from jeans shopping. It has a range of Indonesian and western dishes, fast food and superb home-made yoghurt drinks.

Entertainment

Bandung is the cultural centre of West Java and a good place to see Sundanese arts. All-night wayang golek puppet performances are held every other Saturday night at *Rumentang Siang*, Jalan Baranangsiang 1, near Pasar Kosambi on Jalan Ahmad Yani. You can also catch a scaled-down version with a meal every Saturday night at the *Sindang Reret Restaurant* (see Places to Eat).

Angklung (shake drum) performances take place at Pak Ujo's *Saung Angklung* (Bamboo Workshop), Jalan Padasuka 118, daily at 3.30 pm (12,500 rp), and you can see the instruments being made. There are a number of other places around the city to see wayang, Sundanese dance, gamelan playing and *pencak silat*, an Indonesian martial art.

Jalan Braga is a good place in the evening for less cultural pursuits. The *North Sea Bar* is a relaxed bar/restaurant popular with expats, while the newer *Amsterdam Cafe*, a few doors down, is quieter but is also a good place for a drink.

There are plenty of expensive discos in Bandung with cover charges of around 25,000 rp. The *Braga Disco*, just off Jalan Braga, is popular, and *Polo* on the 11th floor of the BRI building on Jalan Asia Afrika, is a chic disco with a rave scene.

The *Lost World Cafe* is a trendy new cafe/bar with live music, moderately-priced Indonesian and western food, cocktails from 7000 rp and a cave-like atmosphere. It's north of the centre on Jalan Wastakacana.

Mainstream movie releases (8000 rp) are shown at the modern multi-screen cinema complex on the top floor of *Plaza Bandung Indah* on Jalan Merdeka.

Getting There & Away

Air Merpati flies daily from Bandung to Jakarta and Yogyakarta.

Bus The Leuwi Panjang bus station, 5km south of the city centre on Jalan Soekarno-Hatta, has buses west to places like Bogor (3500 rp to 8000 rp; 3½ hours), Sukabumi (3000 rp; three hours) and Jakarta's Kampung

Rambutan station (5000 rp to 15,000 rp; 4½ hours). Buses to Bogor are not allowed to take the scenic Puncak Pass route on weekends. Door-to-door minibuses also go to Bogor (15,000 rp) via Puncak.

Buses to the east leave from the Cicaheum bus station, on the eastern outskirts of the city. Buses go to Garut (1350 rp; two hours), Banjar (2900 rp; five hours), Cilacap (6000/12,400 rp without/with air-con), Wonosobo (7400/15,200 rp; 10 hours) and Yogyakarta (10,100/28,900 rp; 12 hours). There are frequent departures for Yogyakarta, many of them leaving late in the afternoon for an overnight trip.

There are regular buses to Pangandaran for 4300/8800 rp, or the Budiman express service costs 8500 rp. Sari Harum (☎ 70 8110) has comfortable, air-con minibuses at 7 am and 2 pm (16,500 rp, five hours) – most guesthouses book this service for a little extra. A door-to-door minibus service is also provided by 4848 Taxi (☎ 420 8448, 43 4848) to Pangandaran (9000 rp) from the depot at Jalan Kebon Kawong 49, and Jakarta (20,000 rp air-con) from the depot at Jalan Suniaraja Timur 39.

For luxury night buses to major Javanese cities and Bali, try the STA agency (☎ 43 4356) next door to Le Yossie Homestay on Jalan Kebonjati, or Bandung Express (☎ 43 1333), Jalan Doktor Cipto 5.

Train The Bandung-Jakarta *Parahyangan* is the main service with departures to Jakarta's Gambir station roughly every hour from 4 am to 7 pm (15,000/25,000 rp bisnis/eksekutif). The *Argogede* luxury service departs at 6.30 am and 2.30 pm (30,000 rp; 2½ hours).

Several daily trains also operate between Bandung and Yogyakarta. The journey takes about nine to 10 hours and the fare varies from 9000 rp in ekonomi, and from 20,000 rp in bisnis, to the eksekutif class *Turangga* (50,000 rp). The ekonomi fare to Surabaya starts at 11,000 rp and the express *Mutiara Selatan* is 28,000 rp in bisnis class. Trains also run to Banjar (5000/10,000 rp ekonomi/bisnis) where you can get a bus to Pangandaran.

Getting Around
Bandung's airport is 4km north-west of the city centre, about 4000 rp by metered taxi or 10,000 rp if coming from the airport.

Angkots cost 300 rp to 500 rp around town (400 rp for most destinations). You can get to most places such as Dago, Jalan Cihampelas and Tangkuban Perahu, from the terminal in front of the train station (Stasiun Hall). Abdul Muis at the Kebon Kelapa bus station is another central terminal, with angkots to Cicaheum and Luewi Panjang bus stations. Big Damri city buses Nos 9 and 11 run from west to east down Jalan Asia Afrika to Cicaheum (500 rp).

Metered taxis are common in Bandung, although there are a lot of unmetered ones that require bargaining and are always more expensive. As in other cities, the becaks are being relegated to the backstreets and are no longer seen in great numbers.

TANGKUBAN PERAHU AREA
Tangkuban Perahu (overturned perahu, ie boat) is a huge volcanic crater 30km north of Bandung. Legend tells of a god challenged to build a huge boat during a single night. His opponent, on seeing that he would probably complete this impossible task, brought the sun up early and the boat builder turned his nearly completed boat over in a fit of anger.

Tangkuban Perahu is worth a visit, although the dormant Kawah Ratu (Queen Crater) at the top is hardly spectacular. As cars can drive right to the top, it attracts plenty of tourists and is very commercial – car parks, warung, hawkers, an information centre and an admission fee (2550 rp). You can escape the crowds by walking (anticlockwise) around the main crater and along the ridge between the two craters. To get all the way around takes about an hour and though the track is well marked, parts of it are steep and slippery.

A more interesting sight is **Kawah Domas**, an active volcanic area of steaming vents and bubbling pools about 1km down from the carpark. From here you can follow the trail back to the main road (ask directions) and flag down a colt back to Bandung or on to the hot springs at **Ciater**, a few kilometres beyond the Tangkuban Perahu entrance point. There are more hot springs at **Maribaya**, 5km beyond Lembang, but Ciater is better for a swim and both are commercialised. Guides at Tangkuban Perahu will also offer to lead you to Ciater through the jungle.

You can extend your Tangkuban Perahu trip by walking from the bottom end of the gardens at Maribaya down through a brilliant river gorge (there's a good track) to **Dago**, an exclusive residential suburb of Bandung with a famous teahouse. Allow about two hours for the walk to Dago. It's a good spot to watch the city light up and you can then return on the local angkots, which run to/from the train station in Bandung.

Getting There & Away

Take a Subang-bound colt (3000 rp; 45 minutes) from Bandung's train station, which goes via Lembang to the park entrance, and then a minibus to the top (2500 rp if full). Weekends and mornings are the best time for finding other passengers to share, otherwise you'll have to charter or walk the 4.5km to the top.

PANGANDARAN

The fishing village of Pangandaran lies on a narrow, bulbous peninsula with broad black-sand beaches that sweep back along the mainland. At the end of the peninsula is the Pangandaran National Park.

This is Java's number one beach resort. It is one of the most relaxing and friendly places in Java to hang out, the living is cheap, and apart from the beach, there are walks in the national park and other nearby attractions. The western beach offers good swimming and is lined with colourful stalls, while the eastern beach is where you'll find the fishing boats and the fish market. Further around the coast to the west, the sea is rough and under-tows make swimming dangerous.

Pangandaran is a busy resort on weekends and is positively swarming with local visitors during holiday periods, when prices soar. At other times it is still just an overgrown fishing village and a good place to take a break from travel.

Information

A once-only 2000 rp fee is charged when entering Pangandaran. Entry to the national park is another 1250 rp.

The post office is on Jalan Kidang Panan-jung and the 24 hour Telkom office is further north on the same street. It has Home Country Direct phones. The Bank Rakyat Indonesia, also on Jalan Kidang Pananjung, changes most currencies and major brands of travellers cheques at poor rates, but the moneychangers are worse.

Organised Tours

A host of good-value tours are offered to destinations around Pangandaran. They include the excellent Green Canyon boat trip for 45,000 rp, but the canyon is clogged with an armada of boats on weekends.

The main part of the national park (beyond the recreation area) is closed to the public, but licensed guides can take you in for day trips.

Places to Stay

Almost all of Pangandaran's hotels – even the cheapies – have a two night minimum charge, so it pays to check the place out beforehand. The greatest concentration of hotels is around the northern end of Jalan Pamugaran, facing the west beach, but many of Pangandaran's cheap places can be found around the main street at the southern end of town. There are also some good places along the beach out of town (see Around Pangandaran later).

Rawamangun Hotel, on the corner of Jalan Pasanggrahan and Jalan Kidang Pananjung, is the cheapest around. It's very basic but friendly and only 6000/9000 rp for singles/doubles. *Losmen Mini I*, across the street on Jalan Kidang Pananjung is clean, convenient and popular. Rooms with mandi cost 10,000/15,000 rp, including breakfast.

Further north, near the post office, the new *Pondok Ibu* (☎ 63 9166), Jalan Kidang Pananjung 116, has a nice garden cafe and clean, comfortable rooms for 15,000/20,000 rp including breakfast.

On Jalan Kalen Buhaya *Losmen Mini Dua* (☎ 63 9298) has large doubles with fan and shower for 20,000 rp, including breakfast. At No 20, *Susan's Guesthouse* (☎ 63 9290) is a bigger place with a range of rooms from 20,000 rp to 30,000 rp for large doubles with fan and hot shower. If you want air-con, *Losmen Samudra II* (☎ 63 9394), at No 16, is simple but good value with clean doubles for 35,000 rp.

On the eastern beach, *Panorama Hotel* (☎ 63 9218) is excellent value with pleasant verandah singles/doubles facing the sea for 15,000/20,000 rp with bathroom, including breakfast.

The northern end of town around Jalan Bulak Laut is Pangandaran's Riviera, popular with Europeans and home to a lot of mid-range hotels, but there are some good budget places here as well.

The popular *Holiday Beach Inn* (☎ 63 9285), Jalan Bulak Laut 50, is one of the cheapest. Singles/doubles cost 10,000/20,000 rp with attached mandi, and there's a good restaurant. Next door at No 49, *Mutiara Selatan* (☎ 63 9416) is a bit drab-looking but only 10,000/15,000 rp, including breakfast. Closer to the beach, *Pantai Sari Hotel* (☎ 63 9175)

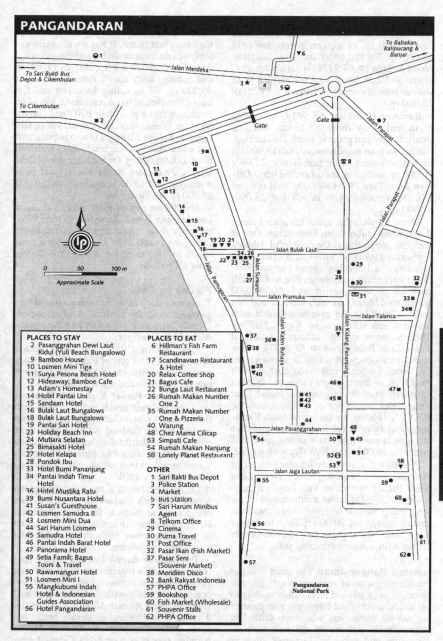

PANGANDARAN

To Babakan,
Kalipucang &
Banjar

To Sari Bukti Bus
Depot & Cikembulan

To Cikembulan

Jalan Merdeka

Gate

Gate

Jalan Parapat

Jalan Parapat

Jalan Bulak Laut

Jalan Sumardi

Jalan Pamugaran

Jalan Pramuka

Jalan Talanca

Jalan Kalen Buhaya

Jalan Kidang Pananjung

Jalan Pasanggrahan

Jalan Jaga Lautan

Pangandaran
National Park

0   50   100 m
Approximate Scale

PLACES TO STAY
2   Pasanggrahan Dewi Laut
    Kidul (Yuli Beach Bungalows)
9   Bamboo House
10 Losmen Mini Tiga
11 Surya Pesona Beach Hotel
12 Hideaway; Bamboe Cafe
13 Adam's Homestay
14 Hotel Pantai Uni
15 Sandaan Hotel
16 Bulak Laut Bungalows
18 Bulak Laut Bungalows
21 Pantai Sari Hotel
23 Holiday Beach Inn
24 Mutiara Selatan
25 Bimasakti Hotel
27 Hotel Kelapa
28 Pondok Ibu
33 Hotel Bumi Pananjung
34 Pantai Indah Timur
    Hotel
36 Hotel Mustika Ratu
39 Bumi Nusantara Hotel
41 Susan's Guesthouse
42 Losmen Samudra II
43 Losmen Mini Dua
44 Sari Harum Losmen
45 Samudra Hotel
46 Pantai Indah Barat Hotel
47 Panorama Hotel
49 Setia Famili; Bagus
    Tours & Travel
50 Rawamangun Hotel
51 Losmen Mini I
55 Mangkubumi Indah
    Hotel & Indonesian
    Guides Association
56 Hotel Pangandaran

PLACES TO EAT
6   Hillman's Fish Farm
    Restaurant
17 Scandinavian Restaurant
    & Hotel
20 Relax Coffee Shop
21 Bagus Cafe
22 Bunga Laut Restaurant
26 Rumah Makan Number
    One 2
35 Rumah Makan Number
    One & Pizzeria
40 Warung
48 Chez Mama Cilicap
53 Simpati Cafe
54 Rumah Makan Nanjung
58 Lonely Planet Restaurant

OTHER
1   Sari Bakti Bus Depot
3   Police Station
4   Market
5   Bus Station
7   Sari Harum Minibus
    Agent
8   Telkom Office
29 Cinema
30 Purna Travel
31 Post Office
32 Pasar Ikan (Fish Market)
37 Pasar Seni
    (Souvenir Market)
38 Meridien Disco
52 Bank Rakyat Indonesia
57 PHPA Office
59 Bookshop
60 Fish Market (Wholesale)
61 Souvenir Stalls
62 PHPA Office

INDONESIA

is very good value and also has a good restaurant. Big, clean doubles with fan and mandi cost 20,000 rp, or air-con rooms are only 25,000 rp. Tucked away on Jalan Sumardi, *Hotel Kelapa* (☎ 63 9329) is set up for travellers and has basic singles/doubles with shower around a central courtyard for 17,500/25,000 rp.

Bamboo House (☎ 63 9419) is further north and away from the beach, but this small, family-run place is worth considering. Rooms without mandi cost 10,000/15,000 rp, or better rooms with mandi are 15,000/20,000 rp including breakfast. Nearby, *Losmen Mini Tiga* (☎ 63 9436) is well run and has clean rooms with mandi for 25,000/30,000 rp.

There are plenty of upmarket places along the northern end of Jalan Pamugaran. One of the most interesting is the delightful *Adam's Homestay* (☎/fax 63 9164) with eclectic architecture, a bookshop, good cappuccinos, direct international phone service and a small pool. Large rooms cost from 54,000/63,000 rp, up to 126,000 rp with air-con and hot water. Check out the excellent double with balcony and sitting room for 90,000 rp. There's more stylish accommodation at *Bulak Laut Bungalows* (☎ 63 9377), where attractive rooms with sitting area and verandah around a leafy courtyard cost 30,000/35,000 rp, or more simple rooms are 20,000/25,000 rp. Further south, another *Bulak Laut Bungalows* (same name, different owners; ☎ 63 9171) is on the corner of Jalan Pamugaran and Jalan Bulak Laut. It has attractive cottages in part stone with sitting room and mandi for 30,000 rp, or 70,000 rp with air-con.

Probably the most idyllic place in all of Pangandaran is *Pasanggrahan Dewi Laut Kidul* (better known as Yuli Beach Bungalows; ☎ 63 9375) at the northern end of the west beach road. Wonderful bungalows with sunken lounge are 80,000 rp (less if staying more than two nights) in a serene jungle setting with a great swimming pool.

Around Pangandaran The quiet beaches outside Pangandaran are increasingly popular places to hang out and relax. They're easy to get to and most of the following guesthouses are run by westerners who have settled in Pangandaran, and are on the ball with information and services. Luxuries such as electricity are not the norm, but that adds to the atmosphere.

Cikembulan, 4km along the beach road to the west, has a small enclave of guesthouses. *Delta Gecko Village* is a popular spot with a high hang-out factor. It has a wide variety of atmospheric bamboo and wood bungalows. A dorm bed costs 10,000 rp, singles 15,000 rp, and doubles with mandi from 20,000 rp to 40,000 rp, all including breakfast and free use of bicycles. It has a restaurant, lots of information and a great fish BBQ and cultural night on Wednesday. Next door, the smaller *Losmen Kelapa Nunggal* is also popular with just a few spotless singles/doubles with bath for 20,000/25,000 rp. On the other side of Delta Gecko, *Francisco Brillo* has a good pizza restaurant and basic bungalows for 20,000/25,000 rp double/triple.

About 4km east of Pangandaran in Babakan, *Laguna Beach Bungalows* (☎ 63 9761) offers stylish mid-range accommodation facing the beach from 22,500 rp for a small single to 45,000 rp for a sea view double. Ring for pick-up.

Places to Eat

There are plenty of decent restaurants in Pangandaran, and the seafood is often superb. Usually, you pick your fish and the price is dependent on weight.

Chez Mama Cilacap, at Jalan Kidang Pananjung 187, is one of Pangandaran's best restaurants with an extensive menu, moderate prices, fresh fish and icy fruit juices.

The *Lonely Planet Restaurant* (no relation), on the east beach near the wholesale fish market, looks no better than your average warung but the seafood is cheap and reportedly some of the freshest around. The basic *Simpati Cafe* also has reasonable prices, serves excellent fruit salads, gado gado and a variety of grilled fish.

On the west beach at the southern end, the no frills *Rumah Makan Nanjung* has good cheap seafood. Next to the Bumi Nusantara Hotel at the southern end of Jalan Pamugaran is a *warung area* with cheap Indonesian dishes and sea breezes.

The *Holiday Beach Inn* has a very good restaurant with a typical travellers' menu and good breakfasts. Across the road, *Bagus Cafe* is a pleasant place with pizzas. Further back from the beach *Rumah Makan Number One 2* has a mixed menu, moderate prices and some style. The original *Rumah Makan Number One* is now on Jalan Kidang Pananjung and is also worth a visit.

In addition to the restaurants, the excellent *Pasar Ikan* (fish market) on the east beach sells fresh fish and a selection of good warung style seafood according to weight.

Hillman's Fish Farm, north of town, is good for a night out. It's a stylish place where you can eat seafood fresh from the ponds surrounding the restaurant.

Getting There & Away

Bus Local buses run from Pangandaran's bus station to Tasikmalaya (5000 rp; three hours), Banjar (3000 rp; 1½ hours) and Kalipucang (1000 rp; 40 minutes).

Budiman express buses run to Bandung 13 times a day (8500 rp; six hours) and there are two buses a day to Bogor (13,000 rp; nine hours). Buses to Jakarta only go as far as Bekasi, 22km east of the city. The Sari Bukti bus depot, 2km west of Pangandaran along Jalan Merdeka, has buses to Jakarta (13,000 rp), Bandung (7500 rp) and Bogor (13,000 rp). Travel agents sell tickets for a premium but include transport to the depot.

The easiest way to reach Jakarta is by the Mitra Marsada Utama bus that picks up in Pangandaran on Wednesday, Friday and Sunday and goes right to Jalan Jaksa for 35,000 rp. Sari Harum has a daily door-to-door minibus to Bandung for 16,500 rp – it saves a trip to or from Bandung's Cicaheum station. Guesthouses and travel agents book these services.

Travel east is usually via the Kalipucang-Cilacap ferry (see the Boat entry following). Otherwise take a bus to Banjar, then another bus to Purwokerto for onward buses to Yogyakarta or Wonosobo. You can take the train from Banjar, but ekonomi services heading east are crowded and slow and it's hard to get a seat.

Boat The most popular way to/from Yogyakarta is via the interesting backwater trip between Kalipucang and Cilacap. This starts with a 17km bus trip east from Pangandaran to Kalipucang. From here the ferry travels across the wide expanse of Segara Anakan and along the waterway sheltered by the island of Nusa Kambangan. It's a fascinating trip, hopping from village to village in a rickety 25m wooden boat, loaded with locals headed to and from market – though popular with tourists it's still very much a local service. It takes four hours to Cilacap and costs 1800 rp. Boats leave Kalipucang at 7 and 8 am and 1 pm. Take an early boat if you want to reach Yogyakarta in one day (it's still possible if you take the 1 pm boat, but it means

a change of bus in Purwokerto and a late arrival). From the Cilacap jetty you can get a becak to the main road, a bemo to the Cilacap bus station, and then a bus to Yogyakarta. From Cilacap, boats depart at 8 am and 1 pm.

The trip is made very easy by the door-to-door travel service between Pangandaran and Yogyakarta that will drop you at the ferry and pick you up on the other side for 17,500 rp, including the ferry ticket. All up the journey takes about eight hours. This trip is also advertised to Wonosobo (for Dieng Plateau), but the minibus drops you at Kebumen and from there it's another two hours by public bus to Wonosobo.

AROUND PANGANDARAN

By hired motorbike you can tour right along the scenic west coast road to **Cipatujah**, 74km south of Tasikmalaya. Of the many beaches, **Batu Karas**, 42km from Pangandaran and 10km off the highway, is the best and has surfing and safe swimming around a sheltered headland. Accommodation, which is favoured by surfers, is available here. Batu Karas can be reached from Pangandaran by bus via Cijulang (2500 rp; one hour).

Near the turn-off to Batu Karas, boats take tours up the emerald-green river to **Green Canyon**, usually organised out of Pangandaran (see Organised Tours earlier).

WONOSOBO

Wonosobo is the main gateway to the Dieng Plateau and has some reasonable budget accommodation, otherwise it's a forgettable place. There is some interesting rice field scenery around Wonosobo – Wisma Duta Homestay can organise day trips.

The tourist office (☎ 21194) at Jalan Kartini 3 is useful (if it's open). The BNI bank on Jalan A Yani changes cash and travellers cheques at passable rates and there's a BCA bank with ATM (Visa) around the corner on Jalan Sumbing.

The Telkom office at the north end of Jalan A Yani is open 24 hours and has Home Country Direct phones.

Places to Stay & Eat

Wisma Duta Homestay (☎ 21674), Jalan Rumah Sakit 3, is the best budget option. Comfortable, bright singles/doubles with mandi cost 10,000/15,000 rp, or better doubles with shower are 30,000 rp, all including breakfast and free tea and coffee.

Also good is the small *Citra Homestay* (☎ 21880) at Jalan Angkatan 45 (down a small alley off Jalan Kawedanan). It has clean rooms with shared bathroom for 15,000/20,000 rp including breakfast.

Wonosobo has plenty of other cheap, uninspiring losmen such as *Losmen Rahayu* on Jalan Resimen for 5000/7000 rp, or the slightly better *Losmen Jawa Tengah*, just off Jalan A Yani, with doubles/triples for 10,000/15,000 rp.

Hotel Nirwana (☎ 21066) at Jalan Resimen 18 No 34 is secure, friendly and probably the best-kept mid-range hotel in Wonosobo. Comfortable rooms cost 50,000 rp with hot shower, or 75,000 rp for large family rooms. Rates are inflated, but a substantial breakfast is included. The slightly threadbare *Hotel Sri Kencono* (☎ 21522), Jalan A Yani 81, is reasonable value. It has huge doubles with hot shower, TV and breakfast for 40,000 rp plus 10% tax.

Food *stalls* and *warung* set up along Jalan Sumbing at night. For restaurant fare, the *Dieng Restaurant*, Jalan Kawedanan 29, has excellent buffet-style food and information on Dieng. The *Asia Restaurant* two doors down has good Chinese food.

Getting There & Away

From Yogyakarta take a bus to Magelang (1500 rp; one hour) and then another to Wonosobo (2000 rp; two hours). Rama Sakti Travel (☎ 21236) and Rahayu Travel (☎ 21217), both on Jalan A Yani, have door-to-door minibuses to/from Yogyakarta for 6500 rp per person. They run six times a day and take three hours.

The bus station is 2km south of the town centre. Regular buses go to Semarang (2500 rp; four hours), Purwokerto (2500 rp; three hours) and Magelang. Buses to Cilacap require a change at Purwokerto. Leave around 6 am to catch the ferry to Kalipucang and on to Pangandaran. You can get to Jakarta's Pulo Gadung terminal in nine hours (10,000/20,000 rp without/with air-con).

Buses to Dieng leave every 10 minutes or so from Terminal Dieng, 500m west of the town centre. They cost 1200 rp to Dieng and 1700 rp on to Batur.

Getting Around

Wonosobo is small and easy to get around on foot. Yellow angkots run around town for 300 rp and to outlying villages. Horse drawn andongs should cost 500 rp for short trips, but most rides will be 1000 rp (eg from the bus station to the town centre) – bargaining is required.

DIENG PLATEAU

This 2000m-high plateau has a few interesting temples, beautiful scenery, good walks and (at night) freezing temperatures. To really appreciate Dieng, it is definitely worth staying here the night rather than day-tripping from Wonosobo.

Dieng is the collapsed remnant of an ancient crater. On the swampy plain in front of Dieng village are five Hindu/Buddhist temples that form the **Arjuna Complex**. These temples are thought to be the oldest in Java, predating Borobudur and Prambanan. Though historically important, they are small, squat and not particularly impressive. Another temple nearby is **Candi Bima**, to the south, and the small site **museum** contains statues and sculpture from the temples.

The plateau's natural attractions and its sense of isolation are the main reasons to visit. From the village, you can do a two-hour loop walk that takes in pretty **Telaga Warna** (Coloured Lake) and **Kawah Sikidang**, a volcanic crater with steaming vents and frantically bubbling mud pools. You can see all the main sights, including the temples, on foot in a morning or afternoon. Other volcanic areas and lakes lie further afield.

The walk to Sembungan, reputed to be the highest village in Java at 2300m, to see the sunrise from the hill 1km from the village is a popular activity. Start at 4 am to reach the top 1½ hours later. Dieng Plateau Homestay and Losmen Bu Djono both offer guides for 5500 rp per person.

It costs 3000 rp to visit the plateau and temples; there's a small ticket office on the right as you enter the village. Further along is a tourist office which has maps of the area, but it's open variable hours.

Places to Stay & Eat

There are only a handful of accommodation choices. The *Dieng Plateau Homestay* and *Losmen Bu Djono* next door are the best options. Bu Djono, with simple doubles for 10,000 rp with shared mandi, is marginally the better of the two. They both have *cafes*, information on Dieng and offer guides.

Other options include the stark *Hotel Asri* with passable singles/doubles for 15,000/20,000 rp, and the absurdly overpriced *Hotel*

Gunung Mas which asks 70,000 rp for the luxury of a hot shower.

Getting There & Away

Frequent buses to Dieng (1200 rp; one hour) leave from Wonosobo throughout the day from about 5.30 am and continue on to Batur.

YOGYAKARTA

The most popular city in Indonesia, Yogyakarta (Yogya) is lively, economical, a shoppers' paradise and, as a centre for Javanese culture, offers plenty of attractions.

Yogyakarta was founded in 1755 when the declining Mataram kingdom fragmented under growing Dutch intervention. Prince Mangkubumi, the brother of the Susuhunan of Surakarta, was granted the territory of Yogyakarta and took the title of 'sultan'. From 1825 to 1830, the great Indonesian hero, Prince Diponegoro, led a bitter revolt against the Dutch in the Yogya area. In this century, Yogya was again a centre of resistance to the Dutch, and after WWII, was the capital of the revolution until independence was eventually won. Today, Yogya is not only the cultural and artistic centre of Java, but a major university town crammed with prestigious institutions.

Although Yogyakarta is spelt with a Y, it's pronounced with a J. Asking for 'Yogya' will get you blank stares – it's pronounced 'Jogja'.

Orientation

Bustling Jalan Malioboro, named after the Duke of Marlborough, is the main street and runs south from the train station, becoming Jalan A Yani at the southern end. Most of the shops are along this street and most of the cheap accommodation places are just off it, in the Sosrowijayan enclave, near the railway line. There's a second enclave, principally of mid-range places, around Jalan Prawirotaman, just south of the Dalem Pujokusuman Theatre.

The Kraton, or Palace, is the centre of the intriguing area of old Yogya, where you will also find the Water Palace and numerous batik galleries.

Information

Tourist Offices The helpful tourist information office (☎ 56 6000), Jalan Malioboro 16, is open Monday to Thursday from 7.30 am to 7.30 pm, Friday and Saturday to 6 pm (with a break from noon to 1 pm). Tugu train station and the airport also have tourist information counters.

Money The BNI bank, Jalan Trikora 1 opposite the post office, is efficient and has good rates for most currencies as well as an ATM accepting MasterCard and Cirrus, or try the BCA bank on Jalan P Mangkubumi. Moneychangers are numerous and keep extended hours but rates are worse than the banks. PT Baruman Abadi, in the Natour Garuda Hotel near Jalan Sosrowijayan, is one moneychanger that gives excellent rates.

American Express is represented by Pacto, also in the Natour Garuda Hotel.

Post & Communications The main post office is on Jalan Senopati at the bottom of Jalan Malioboro and is open Monday to Saturday from 7 am to 9 pm, and from 8 am to 8 pm on Sunday. Their efficient Warposnet (Warung Internet) office is open Monday to Saturday from 8 am to 9 pm and Sunday from 9 am to 8 pm and costs 3000 rp per half hour.

The best place for international calls is the 24 hour wartel behind the main post office at Jalan Trikora 2 (it has a Home Country Direct phone). There's another convenient wartel opposite the train station on Jalan Pasar Kembang and a Home Country Direct phone outside the Bakti Kasih Hotel on Jalan Sosrowijayan.

Numerous private 'Internet cafes' have sprung up in the tourist areas of Yogya – usually just a couple of terminals in an existing shop or business – and more are sure to follow. They're invariably more expensive than the post office but usually more convenient. Right in the heart of the Sosrowijayan area on Gang I is Whizz Kidz Internet (3000 rp for 15 minutes). On Jalan Prawirotaman I, next to the Duta Guest House, Protech 8 charges 7000 rp an hour (minimum 15 minutes) and serves coffee and soft drinks.

Medical Services Ludira Husada Tama Hospital (☎ 51 3651), Jalan Wiratama 4, has a 24 hour clinic.

Dangers & Annoyances Yogya has more than its fair share of thieves – of the break into your room, snatch your bag, steal your bicycle and pick your pocket varieties. The Prambanan and Borobudur buses are reputed to be favourites for pickpockets.

Batik salesmen, posing as guides or simply instant friends, can be a pain, especially around the Taman Sari. Shake them off, or agree on a guide fee (they can be quite helpful), unless you want to endure the inevitable hard sell at a batik gallery.

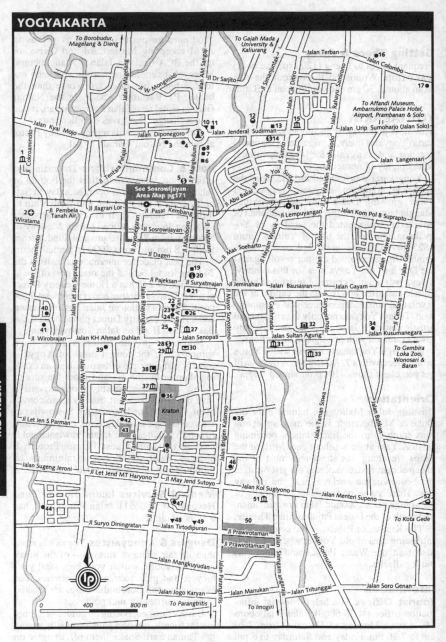

YOGYAKARTA

YOGYAKARTA

PLACES TO STAY		
6	New Batik Palace Hotel	
7	Arjuna Plaza Hotel	
11	Phoenix Heritage Hotel	
13	Java Palace Hotel	
19	Mutiara Hotel	
50	Prawirotaman Accommodation Area; Protech 8	

PLACES TO EAT		
10	Pizza Hut	
22	Cherry Cafe	
23	Griya Dahar Timur	
48	Kedai Kebun	
49	Dutch Cafe	

OTHER		
1	Museum Sasana Wiratama (Monumen Diponegoro)	
2	Ludira Husada Tama Hospital	
3	Merpati Office	

4	Minibus Agents
5	BCA Bank
8	Garuda Office
9	Tugu Monument
12	Terban Colt Terminal & Night Buses
14	BII Bank
15	Army Museum
16	ISI Dance Faculty
17	RRI Auditorium
18	Lempuyangan Train Station
20	Tourist Information Office
21	Terang Bulan Shop
24	Mirota Batik
25	Gedung Negara (Governor's Building)
26	Pasar Beringharjo
27	Benteng Vredeburg
28	BNI Bank
29	Sono-Budoyo Museum
30	Main Post Office; Wartel

31	Museum Biologi
32	Pakualaman Kraton
33	Sasmitaluka Jenderal Sudirman
34	Batik Research Centre
35	Purawisata Theatre
36	Kraton Entrance
37	Museum Kereta Kraton
38	Mesjid Besar
39	Nitour
40	Amri Yahya's Gallery
41	ISI (Fine Arts Faculty)
42	Pasar Ngasem (Bird Market)
43	Taman Sari (Water Palace)
44	Agastya Art Institute
45	Sasono Hinggil
46	Dalem Pujokusuman Theatre
47	Swasthigita Wayang Kulit Workshop
51	Museum Perjuangan
52	Umbulharjo Bus Station

Kraton

In the heart of the old city the huge palace of the sultans of Yogyakarta is effectively the centre of a small walled city within a city. Over 25,000 people live within the greater Kraton compound, which contains its own market, shops, batik and silver cottage industries, schools and mosques. The palace is guarded by elderly gentlemen in traditional costume and a guide shows you around its sumptuous pavilions and halls. The 3000 rp admission (plus 500 rp camera fee) includes the guided tour. The kraton is open from 8.30 am to 2 pm daily, except Friday, when it closes at 1 pm. It is closed on national and kraton holidays.

The inner court has a museum dedicated to Hamengkubuwono IX, the current sultan's father. In the inner pavilion between 9 or 10 am and noon you can see gamelan on Monday and Tuesday, wayang golek on Wednesday, classical dance on Thursday and Sunday, wayang kulit on Saturday and poetry reading on Friday.

Taman Sari & Bird Market

The Taman Sari, or Water Palace, was a complex of canals, pools and palaces built within the Kraton between 1758 and 1765. Damaged first by Diponegoro's Java War and then further by an earthquake, it is today a mass of ruins, crowded with small houses and batik galleries. The main bathing pools have been restored. Admission to the restored area is 1000 rp (plus 500 rp for camera fee), open daily from 9 am to 3 pm.

On the edge of the site is the interesting Pasar Ngasem (bird market). You can enter the northern part of the Taman Sari from here and climb to the top of the outer wall for good views over Yogya.

Museums

Close to the Kraton, on the north-western corner of Kraton Square, the **Sono-Budoyo Museum** has a first-rate collection of Javanese arts, including wayang kulit puppets, *topeng* masks, *kris* and batik, and the outside courtyard is packed with Hindu statuary. It's open from 8 am to 2.30 pm daily except Monday (500 rp).

Between the kraton entrance and the Sono-Budoyo Museum in the palace square, the **Museum Kereta Kraton** holds some opulent chariots of the sultans. It's open from 8 am to 4 pm daily (500 rp).

Yogya has plenty of other museums, usually dedicated to some independence hero or military escapade. Dating from 1765, **Benteng Vredeburg** is the old Dutch fort opposite the post office. Now restored, it houses a museum with dull dioramas showing the history of the independence movement, but the fort architecture is worth a look. Opening hours are Tuesday to Thursday from 8.30 am to 1.30 pm, Friday 8.30 to 11 am, Saturday and Sunday 8.30 am to noon; closed Monday (750 rp).

INDONESIA

Fans of Prince Diponegoro might appreciate the **Museum Sasana Wiratama**, also known as the Monumen Diponegoro. A motley collection of the prince's belongings and other exhibits are kept in this small museum built at the site of his former Yogya residence. It's open daily from 8 am to 1 pm.

Other Attractions
The smaller **Pakualaman Kraton**, on Jalan Sultan Agung, is also open to visitors and has a small museum, a *pendopo* (open-sided pavilion) which can hold a full gamelan orchestra (performances are held every fifth Sunday) and a curious colonial house with fine cast-iron work. The kraton is open Tuesday, Thursday and Sunday from 9.30 am to 1.30 pm.

The main street of **Kota Gede**, 5km southeast of Yogya, is the silverwork centre of Yogya. This is a must for those after silver jewellery or ornaments, and the sacred **grave** of Senopati, the first king of Mataram, can also be seen.

Yogya's **Gembira Loka Zoo** is a spacious but sad affair about 3km east of the centre of town.

Places to Stay
Accommodation in Yogya is remarkably good value and there is a superb choice. There are two particularly popular enclaves – the central Sosrowijayan area for the really cheap places and the Prawirotaman area, a couple of kilometres south of the Kraton, for mainly mid-range hotels.

Sosrowijayan Area South of the railway line between Jalan Pasar Kembang and Jalan Sosrowijayan, the narrow alleyways of Gang Sosrowijayan I and II have most of the cheap accommodation and popular eating places. More good places to stay are in other small gangs in this area. Despite mass tourism, the gangs are quiet and still have a kampung feel to them.

Gang Sosrowijayan I has some very basic places that cost as little as 5000/8000 rp for singles/doubles, but they are dingy and cater mostly to locals. *Losmen Beta* is about the best of these. A bit further along is *Losmen Superman*, behind the restaurant of the same name. Small singles with shared mandi are 8000 rp, but brighter doubles with mandi are 10,000 rp. *New Superman's*, further south, also has good rooms a couple of doors back from the restaurant. Clean singles and doubles with interesting rock garden bathrooms are

10,000 rp. *Rejeki Homestay* is another good choice with singles/doubles with mandi and fan for 10,000/15,000 rp.

There are some good places running off Gang I. *Nuri Losmen* is a new, spotlessly clean place with rooms for 10,000/12,500 rp, and *Losmen Happy II* has decent rooms for 16,500 rp. For a little more outlay, *Hotel Harum* (formerly Losmen Happy) has good, clean singles and doubles with shower for 22,000 rp. On the other side of Gang I, *105 Homestay* is a nice place with colourful decor and singles/doubles for 15,000/20,000 rp with bathroom.

On Gang Sosrowijayan II, *Hotel Bagus* has basic, cheap rooms with shared mandi for 7000/8500 rp, but better places are in the small alleys off Gang II, most of them in a similar rock-bottom price range. *Hotel Selekta* is popular and friendly. It's roomier and lighter than most. Large rooms with mandi cost 15,000 rp, including breakfast, and there are some cheaper rooms. Nearby, *Monica Hotel* (☎ 58 0598), is a small, flash hotel among the cheapies. Very clean rooms around a garden are 25,000 rp including breakfast. Of the other cheap losmen along this alley, the new *Losmen Citra Anda* is secure and has good singles/doubles for 10,000/12,000 rp, *Isty Losmen* is cheap at 6000/7000 rp for rooms without mandi, while *Utar Pension* has comfortable doubles for 12,500 rp.

On the other side of Gang II, *Supriyanto Inn* is a small place with good-value, renovated rooms at 7500 rp a double.

Another new place worth checking out is *Hostel Yogya Backpackers*, down a lane south of Jalan Sosrowijayan. Singles/doubles without mandi are 5000/7500 rp, or 10,000 rp with mandi.

On Jalan Sosrowijayan, between Gang I and Jalan Malioboro, the large *Hotel Indonesia* (☎ 58 7659), Jalan Sosrowijayan 9, is popular but overrated. It has a pleasant open courtyard area but the rooms are pretty dank. They start at 7000 rp; rooms with mandi cost 10,000, 15,000 and 17,500 rp.

Jalan Sosrowijayan also has some good mid-range hotels. *Bladok Losmen & Restaurant* (☎ 56 0452) at No 76 is one of the best with very stylish singles/doubles for 32,000/35,000 rp and 42,000/45,000 rp to 75,000/78,000 rp for air-con and hot water (plus 10% tax). There's a nice pool and a great breakfast buffet. At No 78, the friendly *Hotel Karunia* (☎ 56 5057) is a cheaper alternative with a

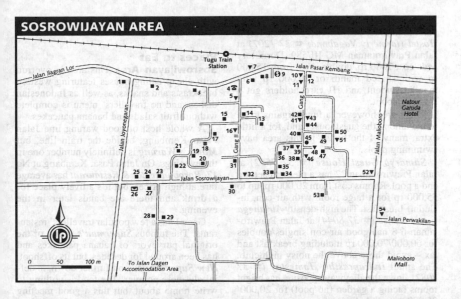

SOSROWIJAYAN AREA

PLACES TO STAY
1 Hotel Kota
2 Berlian Palace
3 Hotel Mendut
6 Batik Palace Hotel
8 Asia-Afrika
12 Kencana Hotel
13 Supriyanto Inn
14 Hotel Bagus
15 Losmen Citra Anda
17 Isty Losmen
18 Utar Pension
19 Losmen Lita
20 Lotus Losmen
21 Hotel Selekta
22 Monica Hotel
23 Bladok Losmen
   & Restaurant
24 Hotel Karunia
25 Yogya Inn
27 Oryza Hotel
28 Ella Homestay
29 Hostel Yogya
   Backpackers
30 Bakti Kasih Hotel
31 Jaya Losmen
33 Dewi Homestay
34 Losmen Rama
35 Hotel Harum
36 Nuri Losmen
37 New Superman's Losmen;
   Losmen Happy II
38 Hotel Jogja
40 Rejeki Homestay
42 Losmen Beta
44 Sari Homestay
47 Lima Losmen
49 Losmen Lucy
50 105 Homestay
53 Hotel Indonesia

PLACES TO EAT
5 Cafe Sosro
7 Mama's Warung
10 Borobudur Bar &
   Restaurant
11 Cheap Warung
16 Anna's
32 Restoran Tanjung
39 New Superman's
   Restaurant
41 N&N
43 Superman's Restaurant
   & Losmen
46 Murni Restaurant
48 Bu Sis
51 Eko Restaurant
52 Prada Cafe
54 Legian Restaurant

OTHER
4 Wartel
9 PT Haji La Tunrung
   Moneychanger
26 Small Post Office
45 Whizz Kidz Internet

good rooftop restaurant. Rooms cost 16,500/
20,000 rp to 40,000 rp.

On Jalan Pasar Kembang, opposite the
train station, *Asia-Afrika* (☎ 56 6219) at No
21 has a pool and an attractive garden cafe.
Prices range from 37,000 rp for fan rooms, to
55,000 and 85,000 rp for air-con rooms with
hot showers. Non-guests can use the pool for

5000 rp. *Hotel Kota* (☎ 51 5844), Jalan
Jlagran Lor 1, is worth a look if you're after
some colonial character, but it's pricey. Tiny
singles are US$8 and US$17 (with air-con)
and better doubles are US$24 and US$32.

There's a less appealing mid-range strip
on Jalan Dagen, one street south of Jalan
Sosrowijayan.

Jalan Prawirotaman The only true budget place in this area is the friendly *Kelana Youth Hostel (formerly Vagabond;* ☎ *37 1207)* at Jalan Prawirotaman MG III/589. Dormitory beds cost 7000 rp, doubles cost from 15,000 rp with shared mandi or 20,000 rp with mandi. Student and HI card holders get a small discount.

There are, however, a few bargains to be found among the guesthouses and, for a little extra, many of the hotels in this area have swimming pools.

Sumaryo Guest House (☎ *37 7552)* at Jalan Prawirotaman 22 has a pleasant setting and a pool. Rooms cost from 20,000 rp, up to 55,000 rp for a huge room with air-con, including breakfast. The high-density *Airlangga Guest House (*☎ *37 8044)* at Jalan Prawirotaman 6-8 has good air-con singles/doubles for 60,000/70,000 rp including breakfast and tax – avoid those above the noisy nightclub. The small *Indraprastha Homestay (*☎ *37 4087),* down the alleyway opposite, has bright rooms facing a garden (no pool) for 20,000/25,000 rp with bathroom.

Further down the street, *Prambanan Guest House (*☎ *37 6167),* at No 14, is a stylish but slightly overpriced place with a pool, attractive garden and very comfortable rooms from US$14/16, to US$30 for large doubles with air-con. It has a Home Country Direct phone and good travel services. The popular and good-value *Rose Guest House (*☎ *37 7991)* at No 22 has a larger than normal pool and a restaurant next to it. A variety of rooms cost from 20,000/25,000 rp with fan to 55,000/60,000 rp with air-con and hot water.

The next street south, Jalan Prawirotaman II, is quieter, cheaper and has some good deals. *Makuta Guest House (*☎*/fax 37 1004)* has spotless rooms with bathroom for 20,000/25,000 rp. Larger rooms with hot water are worth the extra at 25,000/30,000 rp.

Metro (☎ *37 2364),* at Jalan Prawirotaman II 71, is the most popular place and has a garden area. There's a wide range of rooms from 11,000/13,500 rp (shared mandi) to 50,000/60,000 rp with air-con and hot showers, but some are looking shabby. The best value are the mid-priced rooms in the annex across the street, where you'll find the pool. There are plenty of services here, including an Internet cafe (10,000 rp per hour).

Mercury Guesthouse (☎ *37 2320)* at No 595 is a place with a bit of style. It has a pool and an attractive Javanese-style restaurant with low tables and cushions. Comfortable rooms with fan and hot shower are 30,000/45,000 rp but discounts are available.

Places to Eat

Sosrowijayan Area This area is overrun with cheap eating houses featuring western breakfasts and snacks, as well as Indonesian dishes, and no travellers' menu is complete without fruit salads and banana pancakes.

A whole host of good warung line Jalan Pasar Kembang, beside the train line, but *Mama's Warung* is definitely number one in the evenings. On Jalan Pasar Kembang at No 17, *Borobudur Bar & Restaurant* has average fare at high prices, but it's a lively place for a drink and there are bands later in the evening.

Gang I has a few popular travellers' restaurants. The famous *Superman's* is one of the original purveyors of banana pancakes and has been around for decades, but its offshoot, *New Superman's,* a bit further down, is definitely more popular. The food is nothing to write home about, but this a good meeting place. The *Murni Restaurant* has Indian food, while the no-frills *N & N* is popular for its low prices, but for the cheapest eats on Gang I, head to the little cluster of wall-hugging *warung* at the station end.

Gang II also has some good, cheap places, including *Anna's* and *Cafe Sosro.*

Jalan Sosrowijayan has a number of good restaurants. *Bladok Restaurant,* at No 76, is an excellent little place attached to the hotel of the same name. The menu has Indonesian and European specialities. On the corner of Jalan Malioboro, the more expensive *Prada Cafe* has authentic Italian food.

Jalan Malioboro After 10 pm, food stalls replace the souvenir stands on Jalan Malioboro and you can take a seat on the woven mats along the pavement. Most of them serve the speciality of Yogya – *nasi gudeg* (rice with young jackfruit cooked in coconut milk).

On the corner of Jalan Malioboro and Jalan Perwakilan, *Legian Restaurant* is hidden away upstairs. It's very classy but great for a splurge and a worthwhile retreat from the busy streets. They do a good claypot *gudeg ayam* (chicken with jackfruit), but the western dishes are less inspiring.

That big intrusion on Jalan Malioboro – Malioboro Mall – has the usual fast food places. It also has some reasonable cafes inside and the top floor has a so-so food stall area.

Further down, the *Cherry Cafe*, upstairs at

Jalan A Yani 57 next to the Tatiana Batik shop, is a good place to escape the crowds, although the prices here have definitely crept beyond the budget range. The *Griya Dahar Timur*, Jalan A Yani 59, is a cheaper Chinese restaurant with a varied menu.

Jalan Prawirotaman This area has a host of mid-range restaurants of fairly average standard, along with some excellent little cafes. *Tante Lies*, also known as Warung Java Timur, at the Jalan Parangtritis intersection is cheap and has Central and East Javanese dishes. Just around the corner, *Laba Laba Cafe* is a bit more upmarket.

Viu Via, Jalan Prawirotaman 24B, is an excellent Belgian-run travellers' cafe and meeting spot. As well as providing good food that includes a daily changing menu of Indonesian dishes, they organise a variety of activities, from cycling tours to batik and Javanese dance courses. *Hanoman's Forest Restaurant* features Indonesian and western cuisine, but the main attraction is the classical Javanese dance or wayang shows each night.

On Jalan Prawirotaman II, opposite the morning market, the *Amsterdam Cafe* has been recommended for its Dutch food and sates.

Further west, among the batik galleries on Jalan Tirtodipuran, are a couple of interesting cafes serving a mixture of Indonesian and European dishes. The *Dutch Cafe* at No 47A has a selection of imported beer and wine, medium-priced food and good music. *Kedai Kebun* at No 3 is a relaxing garden restaurant with a changing gallery and an appetising menu.

Entertainment
Yogya is an excellent place to see traditional Javanese performing arts. The tourist information office can advise you of what's on. The *Kraton* has daily gamelan, dance or wayang rehearsals. Performances also take place in hotels, restaurants and a variety of performing arts centres.

Wayang kulit can be seen virtually every night of the week. The *Agastya Art Institute* has 3 pm performances every day except Saturday (5000 rp). The *Sono-Budoyo Museum* has performances at 8 pm every evening (5000 rp). Every second Saturday, all-night performances are held at the southern square (Sasono Hinggil) of the Kraton area.

Wayang golek plays are performed at the

Agastya Art Institute on Saturday afternoon and there is a daily Nitour performance, except on Sunday. Wayang orang or *wayang wong* are Javanese dance dramas, and these can also be seen at a variety of venues.

The most famous dance performance is the great Ramayana ballet at Prambanan (see the Around Yogyakarta section). Excellent shortened performances of the Ramayana ballet are held at the *Purawisata Theatre* (☎ 37 4089), Jalan Brigjen Katamso, every night from 8 to 10 pm (50,000 rp for performance only, 80,000 rp for dinner and performance). Guesthouses and travel agents in the accommodation areas book this performance and often provide transport for the same price as buying a ticket at the theatre itself. Another fine troupe performs at *Dalem Pujokusuman* at Jalan Katamso 45 every Monday, Wednesday and Friday from 8 to 10 pm.

Shopping
Yogya is a noted batik centre, but other craft industries in and around Yogya include silver, leather, pottery and wayang puppets. Even if you don't intend to buy, galleries and workshops are open, free of charge, for visitors to observe traditional Javanese crafts in action.

Jalan Malioboro is one great long colourful bazaar of souvenir shops and stalls offering a wide selection of cheap cotton clothes, leatherwork, batik bags, topeng masks and wayang golek puppets. Prices are lowest here, depending on your bargaining skills.

On Jalan A Yani (the continuation of Jalan Malioboro), the Terang Bulan shop at No 108 and Batik Keris at No 71 are fixed-price and have a good range of batik. Mirota Batik at No 9 is a good shop to get an idea of prices for general handicrafts as well as batik. Malioboro's labyrinthine market, Pasar Beringharjo, is always worth a browse, especially for cheap batik and textiles.

Yogya has dozens of batik art galleries. Prices are high at the better known galleries, and ridiculously cheap at the mass production galleries, most of which are found around the Taman Sari. Try to avoid the touts and 'guides' who follow you – you'll end up paying commission on anything you buy and you'll be subjected to unwanted hard-sell tactics. Yogya is crawling with batik sellers and many scams are tried. A time-honoured ploy is the tale about a huge ASEAN exhibition in Singapore which will empty the city of batik and today is your last chance to buy! More common is the 'special exhibition' of Yogya's top students in a gallery just around the corner – for today only ...

Another major area to shop is Jalan Tirtodipuran, the continuation of Jalan Prawirotaman. A string of expensive batik factories, galleries and art shops sell furniture, antiques and curios. Antiques are often instantly aged and prices can be ridiculously high here. Many of the batik workshops here, such as Batik Indah, Jalan Tirtodipuran 6A, give free guided tours of the batik process.

Silverwork can be found all over town, but the best area to shop is in the silver village of Kota Gede. You can get a guided tour of the process at the large factories such as Tom's Silver and MD, with no obligation to buy at their high prices.

Kasongan, the potters' village 7km southwest of Yogya, produces an astonishing array of pottery, mostly large figurines and pots.

Getting There & Away

Air Garuda (☎ 51 4400) and Merpati (☎ 51 4272) both service Yogya. Flights include Jakarta, Denpasar, Surabaya and Bandung.

Bus Yogya's Umbulharjo bus station is 4km south-east of the city centre, but there are plans to move it even further out some time in 2000. Economy/air-con buses include: Solo (1500/2000 rp; two hours), Semarang (3200/6050 rp; 3½ hours), Purwokerto (4900/9850 rp; five hours), Bandung (12,700/29,300 rp; 12 hours), Jakarta (16,200/34,400 rp; 12 hours), Surabaya (8500/18,450 rp; eight hours), Probolinggo (17,000/35,000 rp; nine hours) and Denpasar (43,500 rp with air-con; 16 hours).

For the long hauls, tickets for the big luxury buses can be bought at the bus station, or it's more expensive but less hassle to check fares and departures with the ticket agents along Jalan Mangkubumi, Jalan Sosrowijayan and Jalan Prawirotaman. These agents can also arrange pick-up from your hotel. There are also long-distance night buses from the Terban colt terminal (see below) to Jakarta (35,000 rp), Denpasar (45,000 rp) and other destinations.

From the main bus station, buses also operate regularly to towns in the immediate area: Borobudur (1500 rp; 1½ hours), Parangtritis (1500 rp; one hour) and Kaliurang (1500 rp; one hour). For Prambanan (1000 rp) take the yellow Pemuda bus. For Imogiri (500 rp; 40 minutes) take a colt or the Abadi bus No 5 to

Panggang and tell the conductor to let you off at the *makam* (graves).

From the Terban colt terminal north of the centre on Jalan Simanjuntak, colts go to Kaliurang (1500 rp), Prambanan (1000 rp) and Solo (1000 rp), passing the airport en route.

Minibus Door-to-door minibuses run to all major cities from Yogya. Most will pick up from hotels in Yogya, or there are depots on Jalan Diponegoro. Minibuses go to Solo (6000 rp), Jakarta (40,000 rp), Malang and Surabaya (25,000 rp), Cilacap (10,000 rp), Semarang (7500 rp), Wonosobo (6500 rp), Bandung (30,000 rp) and other destinations. Numerous agents also have direct minibuses to Pangandaran (20,000 rp air-con) and Gunung Bromo (25,000/35,000 rp without/with air-con).

Train Yogya's main Tugu station is conveniently central, although most ekonomi trains run to and from the Lempuyangan station 1km further east.

Good express services to/from Jakarta are the *Fajar Utama Yogya* day trains and *Senja Utama Yogya* night services, which go via Cirebon. Both cost from 25,000 rp in bisnis class to 55,000 rp in air-con eksekutif, and take around 8½ hours. The *Argo Lawu* is a better eksekutif service (80,000 rp) that departs from Yogya at 8.44 am and takes just over six hours. Slower, crowded ekonomi trains depart from Jakarta's Pasar Senen station and stop at Yogya's Lempuyangan station (14,000 rp).

The quickest and most convenient way to get to Solo is on the *Prambanan Ekspres* (2000/5000 rp bisnis/eksekutif; one hour) departing daily at 7.25 and 10.30 am, 1.20 and 4 pm.

There are more than half a dozen trains a day between Yogya and Surabaya, with most of the express services leaving Yogya late at night. The *Sancaka* and *Mutiara Selatan II* (25,000 rp bisnis; five hours) are reasonable services. Ekonomi trains (7000 rp; seven hours) run during the day from Lempuyangan. Other ekonomi train destinations include Probolinggo (10,000 rp), Malang (14,000 rp) and Bandung (9000 rp).

Getting Around

To/From the Airport Taxis from the airport to Yogya, 10km away, cost 10,000 rp. From the main road, only 200m from the terminal, you can get a colt to Yogya's Terban colt terminal or a bus to the Umbulharjo bus station.

Bus *Bis kotas* (city buses) operate on set routes around the city for a flat 350 rp fare. All terminate at the bus station.

Local Transport Bicycles and motorbikes can be hired cheaply but lock them up very securely. There seems to be more becaks in Yogya that the rest of Java combined and the constant hassle can be annoying. Furious bargaining is usually required – the first price is often an outrageous one. Count on 1000 rp for a short trip. Jalan Prawirotaman to Jalan Malioboro or Jalan Sosrowijayan to the kraton should cost no more than 2000 rp. Horse-drawn andongs cost about the same. Metered taxis are readily available at 1300 rp for the first kilometre and 450 rp for subsequent kilometres.

AROUND YOGYAKARTA

Yogya's, indeed Java's, biggest drawcards are the complex of Prambanan and the huge Buddhist centre at Borobudur, but a number of other interesting places can be visited outside the city. There are plenty of organised minibus tours from Yogya that include Prambanan and Borobudur.

Prambanan

The biggest Hindu temple complex in Java, Prambanan is 17km east of Yogya on the Solo road. Though some 50 temple sites have been discovered in and around Prambanan, the main temples are all in the tourist complex fronting the village on the highway.

The largest of these, the **Shiva temple**,

AROUND YOGYAKARTA

soars 47m high and is lavishly carved. The statue of Shiva stands in the central chamber and statues of the goddess Durga, Shiva's elephant-headed son Ganesh and Agastya the teacher stand in the other chapels of the upper part of the temple. The Shiva temple is flanked by the Vishnu and Brahma temples, the latter carrying further scenes from the *Ramayana*. In the small central temple, opposite the Shiva temple, stands a fine statue of the bull Nandi, Shiva's mount.

Built in the 9th century AD, possibly 50 years after Borobudur, the complex at Prambanan was abandoned soon after its completion when the old Mataram kingdom mysteriously declined. Many of the temples had collapsed by the 19th century and not until 1937 was any form of reconstruction attempted. Other temple ruins can be found close to Prambanan and on the road back to Yogya.

There is a 10,000 rp admission charge to the temple complex, including camera fees and a guided tour. The temple enclosure is open daily from 6 am to 6 pm, with last admission at 5.15 pm.

If you are here at the right time, don't miss the great Ramayana ballet. The ballet is performed over four successive nights, twice each month of the dry season, from May to October, leading up to the full moon. Prambanan's Trimurti Theatre has performances throughout the year on Tuesday, Wednesday and Thursday nights from 7.30 pm.

Getting There & Away From Yogya, take the yellow Pemuda bus (1000 rp; 30 minutes) from the main bus station, or a Solo-bound colt from the Terban terminal. A bicycle is an ideal way to explore all the temples in the area via the back roads.

Borobudur

Ranking with Bagan and Angkor Wat as one of the greatest South-East Asian Buddhist monuments, Borobudur is an enormous construction covering a hill 42km from Yogya. With the decline of Buddhism, Borobudur was abandoned and only rediscovered in 1814 when Raffles governed Java.

The temple consists of six square bases topped by three circular ones and it was constructed at roughly the same time as Prambanan in the early part of the 9th century AD.

Over the centuries, the supporting hill became waterlogged and the whole immense stone mass started to subside at a variety of angles. A US$25 million restoration project returned it to its former glory.

Nearly 1500 narrative panels on the terraces illustrate Buddhist teachings and tales, while 432 Buddha images sit in chambers on the terraces. On the upper circular terraces there are latticed stupas which contain 72 more Buddha images.

The **Mendut Temple**, 3km east of Borobudur, has a magnificent statue of Buddha seated with two disciples. He is 3m high and sits with both feet on the ground, rather than in the usual lotus position. It has been suggested that this image was originally intended to top Borobudur but proved impossible to raise to the summit. It's a fine walk to Mendut and the smaller Pawon Temple, otherwise a bus or bemo is 300 rp.

The Borobudur temple site is open from 6 am to 5.15 pm and admission is 10,000 rp, including camera fees and entry to the museum. A guide costs extra.

Places to Stay & Eat The small village of Borobudur has quite a selection of accommodation. The welcoming, well-run *Lotus Guest House* (☎ 0293-88281), on the east side of the temple near the main parking area, has doubles with mandi for 15,000 rp up to 30,000 rp, including breakfast. It has a good cafe, information on things to do in the area and bicycles for rent (2000 rp).

About 1km from the temple, the flash *Pondok Tingal Hostel* (☎ 0293-88245) has bamboo-style rooms from 33,000 rp to 125,000 rp, or a bed in the spotless, often empty dorms costs 7500 rp (add 15% tax to these rates). There's a good restaurant here, a Home Country Direct phone, and occasional free cultural performances.

Opposite the temple complex, *Losmen Borobudur* is a pretty dingy place. Small rooms without/with mandi are 10,000/15,000 rp. Across the road, *Saraswati* (☎ 0293-88283) has clean doubles with mandi and fan for 33,000 rp including breakfast. It also has a nice garden restaurant.

Getting There & Away From Yogya take a direct bus (1500 rp; 1½ hours) via Muntilan. Returning to Yogya you can avoid a trip out to the main Umbulharjo station by getting off at Jombor, north of the city, and catching a No 5 bus to the centre.

Buses also go direct from Borobudur to Magelang (1200 rp), where you can change for Wonosobo.

Kaliurang, Gunung Merapi & Selo

Kaliurang is a pleasant mountain resort on the slopes of Gunung Merapi, 26km north of Yogya. There are great views of the mountains, lovely walks and crisp mountain air.

Gunung Merapi is one of Java's most dangerous volcanoes and has erupted numerous times. Recently, an eruption killed 69 people in November 1994 and since then Merapi continues to rumble and spew lava down its flank. Eruptions in July and October 1998 forced thousands to evacuate their homes. The once popular climb from Kaliurang is now off-limits, but it is possible to climb to a viewpoint below the tree line to see the lava flows – still a spectacular sight. You can only go with a qualified guide – contact the owner of Vogels for information and advice (see Places to Stay). The climb starts at 3 am and costs 10,000 rp (minimum four people) including breakfast.

It is possible, and easier, to climb Merapi from **Selo** on the north side but you cannot see the lava flows.

Places to Stay In Kaliurang, *Vogels Hostel* (☎ 0274-89 5208), Jalan Astamulya 76, has deservedly been the travellers' favourite for years. There's a variety of rooms starting at 4000 rp in the dorm. Doubles range from 10,000 rp, up to good mid-range bungalows at the back with bath for only 22,000 rp. HI card holders get a small discount. It has a good, cheap restaurant and this is the place to arrange treks to Merapi and other good walks.

The nearby *Christian Hostel* is a Vogels offshoot with similar room prices. The rooftop sitting area has views of Merapi and the lava flow. Kaliurang has over 100 other places to stay.

In Selo, *Pak Auto* has simple accommodation for 5000 rp per person and arranges guides.

Getting There & Away Buses and colts run direct from Yogya to Kaliurang (1500 rp). For Selo, take a Magelang bus to Blabak and then a colt or bus. Direct Solo-Magelang buses also pass Selo.

Imogiri & Parangtritis

The royal cemetery of the sultans of Mataram lies 20km south-east from Yogya at **Imogiri**, high on a hillside at the top of 345 steps. Imogiri is a sacred site and many local people visit to pay their respects at the royal graves, especially that of the great Sultan Agung.

All visitors have to sign the Visitors' Book, pay a small donation and hire traditional Javanese dress before they enter the graveyard. The main tombs are only open from 10 am to 1 pm on Monday and from 1.30 to 4 pm on Friday and Sunday, and there is no objection to visitors joining the pilgrims then.

The best known of the beaches south of Yogya, **Parangtritis** is 27km away. It is a scruffy local resort that is packed on weekends and the currents and undertows can be dangerous.

Parangtritis is a centre for the worship of Nyai Loro Kidul, the queen of the South Seas, whose mystical union with the sultans of Yogya and Solo requires regular offerings. Parangtritis attracts all sorts of mystics and meditators.

See the Yogya Getting There & Away section for transport details. Most of Yogya's travel agents offer day trips that include Parangtritis and Imogiri from around 20,000 rp.

SOLO

Only an hour by train from Yogyakarta, Solo (or Surakarta) was for a time the capital of the Mataram kingdom.

Solo competes with its sister city Yogya as a centre of Javanese culture. It has two royal palaces, is a major batik centre and its schools of dance, music and wayang are as highly regarded as Yogya's. This laid-back city offers some fine homestay accommodation, good food and most of Yogya's attractions – without the tourist hordes.

Orientation & Information

Solo's main street is Jalan Slamet Riyadi, running east-west through the centre of the city. The train and bus stations are about 2km north of the centre, while most of the budget accommodation is conveniently clustered around Jalan Yos Sudarso and Jalan A Dahlan. The oldest part of Solo is east of here around the Kraton Surakarta and Pasar Klewer.

The helpful tourist office (☎ 71 1435) is set back from the main road at Jalan Slamet Riyadi 275 and is open from 8 am to 5 pm.

The main post office on Jalan Jenderal Sudirman is open Monday to Friday from 7 am to 8.30 pm and till 1 pm on Saturday. Its Wasantara-net Internet centre is open from 8 am to 3 pm and costs 1600 rp for 15 minutes. There's a wartel next to the Telkom office on Jalan Mayor Kusmanto and a more central one next to Hotel Kota on Jalan Slamet Riyadi.

INDONESIA

SOLO

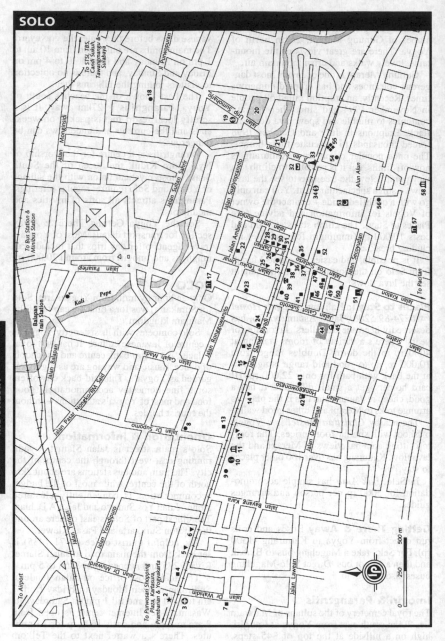

To STSI, TBS,
Candi Sukuh,
Tawangmangu &
Surabaya

Jalan II Purwopuran

18

19   Urip Sumoharjo

20

Jalan Monginsidi

Jalan Sutan Sahrir

Jalan Supriyopranoto

II Jen Sudirman   33
32   54 55
34   Alun Alun
53
56   58
57

To Bus Station &
Minibus Station

Jalan Pasarlegi

Jalan Imam Bonjol

Jalan Ambon
22
Jalan Teuku Umar   26 28 29 25   30 31
27   35   52
25   36   Jalan Yos Sudarso
37
Jalan Secoyudan

17

1   Kali   Pepe   23

Balapan
Train Station

Jalan Balapan

Jalan Rongowarsito   24

Jalan Gajah Mada

15 16   Jalan Slamet Riyadi
14   44   45
40 39   41   46 48   49 50   51
38   47   Jalan Gatot Subroto
Jalan Kraton
To Pacitan
station

Jalan Pasar Nongko

13

Jalan Dr Subomo
8   13   42 43   Jalan Honggowongso
12
9 10 11   Jalan Dr Rajiman

To Airport

Jalan Tunsin

Jalan Yosodipuro

Jalan Dr Muwardi

Jalan Bayang Kara

4
5 6
3   2   Dr Wahidin
7   Jalan Lawean

To Purwosari Shopping
Plaza Kartasura,
Prambanan & Yogyakarta

500 m
250
0

INDONESIA

SOLO

PLACES TO STAY		15	Tio Ciu 99	24	Garuda (Lippobank Building)
4	Solo Inn	25	Jalan Teuku Umar Warung	27	American Donut Bakery
7	Ramayana Guest House	26	Warung Baru	32	Main Post Office
13	Hotel Dana	28	Cafe Gamelan	33	Adpura Kencana Monument
16	Pendhawa Homestay;	30	Monggo Pinarak	34	BCA Bank
	Borobudur Homestay	36	Kusuma Sari	35	Niki Tour
22	Lucie Pension	37	Kusuma Sari Lesahan	39	Wartel
29	Istana Griyer; Steak Warung			40	New Holland Bakery
31	Hotel Keprabon	OTHER		42	Legenda Disco
38	Hotel Kota	1	RRI Radio Station	43	Batik Danarhadi
41	Relax Homestay	2	Police Station	44	Singosaren Plaza
46	Cendana Homestay &	3	Hospital	45	Taxi Stand
	Warung Biru	8	Toko Bedoyo Srimpi	47	Batik Keris
48	Paradise Guest House	9	Sriwedari Amusement Park	50	Akar Sari Health Shop
49	Westerners	10	Tourist Office	51	Vihara Rahayu Chinese
52	Mama Homestay	11	Radya Pustaka Museum		Temple
		17	Kraton Mangkunegaran	53	Mesjid Agung
PLACES TO EAT		18	SMKI School	54	Balai Agung
5	KFC	19	BNI Bank	55	Matahari Department Store
6	Adem Ayam	20	Pasar Gede	56	Pasar Klewer
12	Pujosari	21	Telkom Office; Wartel	57	Kraton Surakarta
14	Cipta Rasa Restaurant	23	Pasar Triwindu	58	Kraton Museum

Kratons

The Susuhunan of Mataram, Pakubuwono II, finally moved from Kartasura into his new palace, the **Kraton Surakarta**, in 1745. A visit to the museum here is particularly interesting, especially with one of the English-speaking guides, and exhibits include three Dutch carriages which have been used for weddings. The oldest, named Kiyai Grudo, was used by the Susuhunan for his stately entry into the new capital.

Admission is 2000 rp, plus 1000 rp for your camera, and it's open every day (except Friday) from 8 am to 2 pm. Dancing practice can be seen on Sunday.

Kraton Mangkunegaran, the minor kraton, was founded in 1757 by a dissident prince, Raden Mas Said. The museum, in the main hall of the palace behind the pavilion, has some unusual exhibits, including an extraordinary gold genital cover. It's also worth having a look in the palace shop at the wayang kulit puppets made by the resident *dalang* (puppet operator).

The palace is open every day from 8.30 am to 2 pm except Sunday, when it closes at 1 pm. Admission is 3500 rp, and guides are available by donation. Dance practice sessions are held at the pavilion on Wednesday from 10 am until noon, and there's gamelan practice on Saturday from 9 to 10 am.

Radya Pustaka Museum

This small museum, next to the tourist office on Jalan Slamet Riyadi, has good exhibits of gamelan instruments and wayang puppets. It's open Tuesday, Thursday and Sunday from 8 am to 1 pm, Friday and Saturday to 11 am (500 rp).

Other Attractions

Solo's markets are always worth a browse, especially **Pasar Klewer**, the multi-storey batik market, and **Pasar Triwindu**, the antique market. **Akar Sari** is an unusual and interesting health shop at Jalan Secoyudan 96 displaying all sorts of bark, roots, seeds and herbs as well as a variety of Chinese and western medicines.

Sriwedari is Solo's amusement park with fair rides, souvenir and sideshow stalls and other somewhat dated diversions.

Solo is a centre for traditional Javanese religion and mysticism and some travellers come here just to meditate. The guesthouses or travel agents can steer you in the direction of the many schools. Batik courses are also popular – the Warung Baru restaurant (see Places to Eat) is a good place to organise a one or two day course for around 20,000 rp including fabric.

Organised Tours

Various travel agents around town run tours to Sangiran and Candi Sukuh and many guesthouses and hotels will book them.

Most of the homestays offer excellent bike tours of Solo's cottage industries. For 11,000 rp,

INDONESIA

a full-day tour takes you through some beautiful countryside to see batik weaving, gamelan making, and tofu, arak and rice-cracker processing.

Places to Stay

Solo has an excellent selection of friendly homestays offering good travel information, tours and a relaxed atmosphere.

Westerners (☎ 63 3106) at Kemlayan Kidul 11, the first alley north of Jalan Secoyudan off Jalan Yos Sudarso, is clean and secure. Solo's original homestay, it is still popular, though it can be cramped. The dormitory costs 6000 rp, small singles cost 6500 rp and good-sized doubles with mandi are 17,500 rp.

In the same alley at No 1/3, *Paradise Guest House* (☎ 54111) is a big place with a *pendopo*-style (traditional palace audience hall) lobby/sitting area and a touch of style. The chalk-white rooms start from 8500 rp for a basic double without fan or mandi. Rooms with private mandi are 25,000 rp to 40,000 rp, up to 50,000 rp with air-con. Add 10% tax to these rates.

A couple of gangs north is *Relax Homestay* (☎ 46417), Gang Empu Sedah 28, one of Solo's better homestays. Rooms around a large courtyard garden cost 9000 rp, or slightly rundown rooms with mandi in the old section are 20,000 and 25,000 rp.

Cendana Homestay (☎ 52821), Gang Empu Panuluh III No 4, has good, clean rooms with mattresses at floor level. Rooms cost 9000 rp for a small double and 13,000/17,000 rp for singles/doubles with bathroom. The very good *Warung Biru restaurant* is attached.

Istana Griyer (☎ 63 4378), Jalan A Dahlan 22, is the newest and tidiest of Solo's homestays. Immaculate rooms of mid-range standard are 20,000/25,000 rp with shared bathroom, 25,000/30,000 rp with private bathroom, up to 45,000 rp with air-con, TV and hot water, all including breakfast. This small place is well set up and central, down a small alley behind the Steak Warung.

Another relatively new place is *Lucie Pension* (☎ 53375), Jalan Ambon 12. There's only a few rooms with mattresses on the floor in this quiet, friendly homestay. The small single is 8000 rp and large, airy doubles with fan are 12,000 rp, including breakfast.

Mama Homestay (☎ 52248), Kauman Gang III, off Jalan Yos Sudarso, has simple singles/doubles for 7000/10,000 rp and 8000/10,000 rp, including breakfast.

Away from the main guesthouse enclave,

but still central, is *Pendhawa Homestay* (☎ 52219) at Jalan Jawa 31A. The rooms are pretty dingy for 10,000 rp, but breakfast is included. *Borobudur Homestay* next door is owned by the same people and has the same room prices.

Solo has dozens of hotels, but they tend to be anonymous places. The long-running *Hotel Kota* (☎ 68 2841), Jalan Slamet Riyadi 125, is a two storey place built around a courtyard. Rooms cost from 15,000 rp to 20,000 rp with mandi, or 35,000 rp to 40,000 rp with air-con. *Ramayana Guest House* (☎ 71 2814), Jalan Dr Wahidin 22, is an attractive house with a garden and stylish dining/lobby area. Huge doubles with bath cost from 25,000 rp to 50,000 rp, plus 15%.

Right in the centre of things, *Hotel Keprabon* (☎ 63 2811) at Jalan A Dahlan 8-12 has reasonably priced rooms from 12,500 rp with mandi to 25,000 rp with hot shower.

Hotel Dana (☎ 71 1976), Jalan Slamet Riyadi 286, is an excellent upper mid-range choice. This old colonial hotel has luxurious, renovated rooms from 102,000 rp (before discount), including breakfast and tax.

Places to Eat

Solo is famous for its all-night warung serving local specialities such as *nasi liwet* (rice with chicken and coconut milk). Another local speciality is *srabi*, small rice puddings served up on a crispy pancake with banana, chocolate or jackfruit on top.

Pujosari is a good selection of warung next to the museum and tourist office in the Sriwedari Park area. The *Lezat*, open 24 hours, and the Chinese *Oriental* are two favourites here.

Jalan Ahmad Dahlan is the centre for budget travellers' eateries. At No 23, the most popular place is the long-running *Warung Baru* for good breakfasts and Indonesian and western fare at very reasonable prices. Across the street, *Steak Warung* is a restaurant and bar – a good place for a late drink. Two doors down is *Monggo Pinarak*, an excellent restaurant specialising in southern Indian food. There's also an Internet cafe here charging 7500 rp per hour. Further north at No 28, the friendly *Cafe Gamelan* is another popular travellers' place. It has a varied menu of Indonesian and western dishes.

For Javanese food, *Adem Ayam*, Jalan Slamet Riyadi 342, is a busy place and does a tasty nasi gudeg. *Kusuma Sari*, on the corner of Jalan Slamet Riyadi and Jalan Yos

Sudarso, has seductive air-con, good hot platter grills and a variety of ice creams at surprisingly reasonable prices. A little further along Jalan Yos Sudarso is the cheaper *Kusuma Sari Lesahan* where you sit on mats at low tables.

Lesahan dining (on mats) is popular on the streets after dark, and numerous sate stalls set up around Jalan Yos Sudarso. The *warung* along Jalan Teuku Umar are also good value.

Entertainment

Solo is an excellent place to see traditional Javanese performing arts. The tourist office has details.

The Sriwedari Theatre at the *Sriwedari Amusement Park*, Jalan Slamet Riyadi, boasts one of the most famous wayang orang troupes in Java, which performs from 8 to 10 pm every night except Sunday (1000 rp).

Radio Republik Indonesia (RRI), Jalan Abdul Rahman Saleh 51, has all-night wayang kulit shows on the third Saturday of every month from 9 pm, and other regular performances.

Both kratons also have traditional Javanese dance practice: Wednesday from 10 am to noon at the *Kraton Mangkunegaran*, and Sunday morning and afternoon performances at the *Kraton Surakarta*.

You can see dance practice between 9 am and 5 pm every day except Friday and Sunday at the *STSI* (Sekolah Tinggi Seni Indonesia), the arts academy in the north-east of the city, and at *SMKI*, the high school for the performing arts on Jalan Kepatihan Wetan.

For a look at contemporary Solonese nightlife, *Legenda*, on Jalan Honggowongso, is the city's most popular disco.

Shopping

Solo is Indonesia's main batik centre and most of the large batik outlets – Batik Keris, Batik Semar and Batik Danarhadi – are based here, with showrooms in the centre of the city. You can see the batik process at the big Batik Keris factory in Lawiyan, west of the city (bicycle tours stop here). Pasar Klewer is the cheapest place to buy batik if you know your stuff.

Pasar Triwindu on Jalan Diponegoro is Solo's famous antique market. Kris and other souvenirs can be purchased from street vendors at the east-side alun alun to the north of the Kraton Surakarta. At the Balai Agung, on the north side of the alun alun, you can see high-quality wayang kulit puppets being made and gamelan sets are for sale.

Getting There & Away

Air Flights are limited from Solo's airport. Garuda has daily flights to Jakarta (358,000 rp), while Silk Air flies directly to Singapore on Tuesday, Thursday and Saturday (US$170).

Bus The well-organised Tirtonadi bus station is just north of the train station, 3km from the centre of town. Frequent buses go to Prambanan (1000 rp; 1½ hours), Yogya (1350/2300 rp without/with air-con; two hours), Semarang (2100/3550 rp; 2½ hours), Bandung (9500/16,100 rp) and Jakarta (13,750/25,350 rp up to 57,000 rp). Going east and south, buses include those to Surabaya (5600/9500 rp; six hours), Malang (5600/12,750 rp; eight hours) and Probolinggo (7500/15,000 rp, eight hours).

Near the main bus station, the Gilingan minibus station has door-to-door minibuses to nearly as many destinations as the buses. They include Yogya (6000 rp), Surabaya (27,000 rp), Malang (28,000 rp) and Probolinggo (40,000 rp). Homestays and travel agents also sell tickets.

Train Solo is on the main Jakarta-Yogya-Surabaya train line. Solo Balapan is the main station, but some local trains depart from Solo Jebres, further east. For Yogya, the efficient *Prambanan Ekspres* (2000 rp bisnis; one hour) departs at 6 and 9 am, noon and 2.40 pm. For Jakarta, good trains include the express *Senja Utama* (28,000/57,000 rp bisnis/eksekutif; 10½ hours) departing at 6 pm, and the *Jayabaya* (28,000 rp bisnis; 9½ hours) at 8.02 pm. Ekonomi trains to Jakarta cost from 11,000 rp, take about 12 hours, and most terminate at the Pasar Senen station.

For Bandung, the *Senja Mataram* (20,000/35,000 rp bisnis/eksekutif; nine hours) departs at 8.15 am, or the *Mutiara Selatan I* (25,000 rp bisnis; eight hours) departs at 9.21 pm.

There are nine trains a day to Surabaya. The *Sri Tanjung* (4500 rp; six hours) is a reasonable and less-crowded ekonomi train departing at 8.28 am, and the *Sancaka* (19,000/30,000 rp bisnis/eksekutif) departs at 4.34 pm. Trains to Malang cost 14,000/30,000 rp ekonomi/bisnis.

Getting Around

A metered taxi to the airport, 10km north-west of the city centre, will cost around 9000 rp, or take a bus to Kartasura and another to the airport. A becak from the train or bus stations into the town centre costs around 2000 rp, a metered taxi around 3500 rp. The orange minibus No 06 costs 300 rp to Jalan Slamet Riyadi.

The city double-decker buses run between Kartasura in the west and Palur in the east, directly along Jalan Slamet Riyadi, and cost a flat fare of 300 rp. The train that shuttles through the middle of Solo along Jalan Slamet Riyadi a couple of times a day carries passengers between Wonogiri and Solo's Purwosari station to the west of the city.

Bicycles can be hired from most of the homestays.

AROUND SOLO
Sangiran
Prehistoric Java Man fossils were discovered at Sangiran, 18km north of Solo, and there is a small museum (1000 rp) with fossil exhibits including some amazing mammoth bones and tusks.

They are still finding things and if you wander up the road past the museum and have a look in some of the exposed banks you may find shells or fossil bones and crabs. To get there take a Purwodadi bus to Kalijambe (500 rp) and it's a 4km walk from there (2500 rp by ojek).

Candi Sukuh & Candi Ceto
Candi Sukuh is a fascinating temple on the slopes of Gunung Lawu (3265m), 36km east of Solo. Dating from the 15th century, it was one of the last Hindu temples to be built on Java and has a curious Inca-like look. Take a bus to Karangpandan (1000 rp), then a Kemuning minibus to the turn-off to Candi Sukuh (750 rp). On market days the bus goes right to the temple; otherwise it's a 2km uphill walk to the site. It is about 1½ hours travelling by bus in total but it's worth it for the superb views and atmosphere. About 10km further up the mountain is Candi Ceto, a simpler temple built in the same style. It can be reached by ojek for about 5000 rp.

SURABAYA
The capital of East Java, Surabaya is a major port and the second largest city in Indonesia. For most visitors it is merely a transit point on the way to or from Bali or Sulawesi. It has an interesting old city, a modern centre full of multi-storey shopping plazas, and heart-stopping traffic – crossing the street is a true test of nerves. If you thrive on big cities, then you'll certainly like teeming Surabaya.

Information
The tourist office (☎ 547 8853) at Jalan Pemuda 118 is open Monday to Saturday from 9 am to 5 pm. Staff can arrange English and German-speaking guides, as well as trips to Madura.

There are plenty of banks including BNI and BII, both with ATMs, on Jalan Pemuda. The main post office is north of the centre on Jalan Kebon Rojo and is open weekdays from 8 am to 8 pm, Saturday till 1 pm. Its Wasantara-net Internet centre is open from 8 am to 3 pm and costs 1500 rp for 15 minutes online. A convenient wartel is in Tunjungan Plaza. International reverse-charge calls can be made from here for a 2500 rp fee.

Things to See
The old part of town to the north is the most interesting. The streets around **Jembatan Merah** have some fine old Dutch architecture, and from here you can wander across to Chinatown. **Pasar Pabean** is a sprawling, dark market, and the interesting 300-year-old **Kong Co Kong Tik Cun Ong** temple has wayang performances on the full moon. **Mesjid Ampel**, in the heart of the Arab Quarter, is the most sacred mosque in Surabaya and pilgrims chant and make rose petal offerings to Sunan Ampel, one of the *wali songo* (nine saints) who brought Islam to Java. The mosque is approached through Jalan Ampel Suci, a narrow, covered bazaar. Plenty of Makassar schooners can be seen at the **Kalimas wharf**.

The Surabaya **zoo** has a large collection of animals and is well maintained, by Indonesian standards. It's open from 7 am to 4 pm (2000 rp). The zoo is 4km south of central Surabaya – take any bus heading down Jalan Panglima Sudirman or bemo M (500 rp). The small **MPU Tantular Museum**, opposite the zoo, has interesting archaeological exhibits. It's open from 7 am to 1 pm daily except Monday (750 rp).

Close to the town centre is the **THR amusement park**, usually dead but worth a visit on Thursday evenings when transvestites perform *dangdut* music (popular Indonesian music with wailing vocals and a strong beat).

Surabaya's newest tourist attraction was in place but not yet open to visitors at the time of writing. The **Monumen Kapal Selam**, across from the tourist office on Jalan Pemuda, is a 1962 Russian submarine. The *Pasopati* once cruised at a depth of 200m, but now it sits alongside the river awaiting a flood of tourists. Expected admission is 5000 rp for a tour of the sub, including a film.

Places to Stay

Bamboe Denn (☎ 534 0333), Jalan Ketabang Kali 6A, a 20-minute walk from Gubeng train station, is a Surabaya institution and has been the number one travellers' centre in Surabaya for over 20 years. It's also the only cheap place in town, with beds in the large dorm for 9000 rp and a few tiny singles/doubles for 9500/17,000 rp.

Across the river from the Bamboe Denn on Jalan Genteng Besar, *Hotel Paviljoen* (☎ 534 3449) is in an old colonial house at No 94. It's central and well-run. Clean doubles with mandi start at 32,000 rp, larger rooms are from 40,000 rp, or 50,000 rp with air-con, including a light breakfast.

Near the Gubeng train station, *Puri Kencana Hotel* (☎ 534 3261), Jalan Kalimantan 9, is a mid-range place but is excellent value in expensive Surabaya. Clean and comfortable rooms with air-con and hot water start at 45,000 rp including breakfast and tax.

Well north of the town centre, near Kota train station, *Hotel Ganefo* (☎ 36 4880), Jalan Kapasan 169-171, is a spacious old hotel with large but very simple rooms. They cost 30,000 rp with shared mandi, 40,000 rp with mandi and fan, or 50,000 rp with air-con and TV. In the same area, *Hotel Irian* (☎ 20953), Jalan Samudra 16, has doubles for 30,000 rp with shared mandi, 40,000 rp with private mandi, and some air-con rooms from 42,000 rp. *Hotel Semut* (☎ 24578), almost across the road, is a much more stylish place, and reasonable value with standard air-con rooms at 46,000 rp plus 21% tax.

Janur Kuning Homestay (☎ 849 4189) would be a good place to stay if it was a little more central. It's about 8km south of Gubeng train station, halfway between the airport and the city centre at Jalan Sidosermo Pdk IV, Kav 139-140. A range of comfortable rooms with spring beds cost from 17,500 rp up to 35,000 rp for air-con and private bathroom. A taxi will get you there for around 5000 rp, or city buses run along nearby Jalan Ahmad Yani.

For something more upmarket, *Cendana Hotel* (☎ 545 5333; fax 531 4367) at Jalan Kombes Pol M Doeryat 6, is good value with well-appointed three-star rooms, including breakfast and dinner, from 110,000 rp.

Places to Eat

For cheap eats, the *Genteng Market* on Jalan Genteng Besar, just across the river from the Bamboe Denn, has good night warung. There's another good selection of warung and lesahan dining to be found on Jalan Embongblimbing, just off Jalan Jend Basuki Rahmat, near the Cendana Hotel. Most other eats in the city centre are expensive and found in the shopping malls.

The ground floor of the Plaza Surabaya on Jalan Pemuda (not to be confused with the Surabaya Mall further north) has a *Food Plaza* with a range of restaurants with Korean, Cantonese and Indonesian food, and western fast food. The best deal is the *Food Bazaar* on the 4th floor.

The Tunjungan Plaza is similarly well stocked with restaurants and fast-food outlets. The 4th level has the *Mon Cheri* ice cream parlour, the Chinese *New Singapore* and the cheaper *Es Teler 77*.

At Jalan Yos Sudarso 15, the *Zangrandi Ice Cream Palace* is an old establishment ice cream parlour with planters chairs and low tables. Jalan Kayun, near the tourist office, has some decent cheap places such as *Depot Jakarta*. Nearby on Jalan Embong Kenongo, *Turin* is a good Chinese restaurant.

For a splurge head to *Cafe Venezia* at Jalan Ambengan 16. Set in a stylish villa with a lovely garden area, Venezia has steak dishes from 15,000 rp, Japanese grills and a variety of desserts.

Entertainment

There are plenty of discos in Surabaya, including *Top Ten* and *Fire* in the Tunjungan Plaza. The big-name hotels are the best places for bars and live bands, although they're not cheap. *Desperado's*, at the Shangri-La Hotel (6km south of the city centre), and the *Tavern*, at the Hyatt Regency, are popular.

Occasional dance and theatre performances are staged at the *Taman Remaja* (Youth Park) on Jalan Kusuma Bangsa.

Getting There & Away

Air Surabaya has a few international departures and is an important hub for domestic flights. There are daily direct flights to Singapore from US$180 and Bangkok from US$229.

Between them, Garuda (☎ 543 5886) and Merpati (☎ 568 8111) have direct flights to Jakarta, Denpasar, Yogyakarta, Ujung Pandang,

INDONESIA

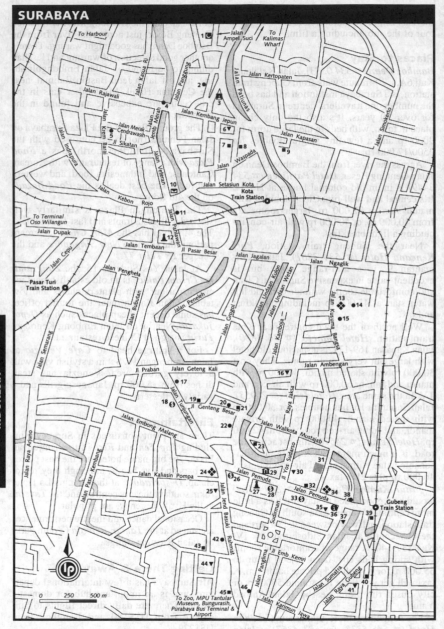

SURABAYA

To Harbour

Jalan Kapasan
Jalan Ampel Suci
To Kalimas Wharf
Jalan Kertopaten
Jalan Patuas
Jalan Kembang Jepun
Jalan Kapasan
Jalan Waspada
Jalan Rajawali
Jalan Kaua Ru
Jalan Patgung
Jalan Merak
Cendrawasih
Jl Sikatan
Jalan Smokerto
Jalan Kremi Barat
Jalan Indapura
Jalan Veteran
Jalan Setasiun Kota
Kota Train Station
Jalan Kebon Rojo
To Terminal Oso Wilangun
Jalan Pahlawan
Jalan Dupak
Jalan Tembaan
Jl Pasar Besar
Jalan Jagalan
Jalan Ngaglik
Jalan Cepu
Jalan Penghela
Pasar Turi Train Station
Jalan Bubutan
Jalan Peneleh
Jalan Undaan Kulon
Jalan Undaan Wetan
Jalan Kusuma Bangsa
Jalan Semarang
Jalan Gogol
Jalan Kamboja
Jalan Ambengan
Jl Praban
Jalan Geteng Kali
Jalan Tunjungan
Jalan Embong Malang
Jalan Kaliasin Pompa
Raya Jaksa
Jalan Walikota Mustajab
Jalan Jend Basuki Rahmat
Jl Yos Sudarso
Jalan Pemuda
Jalan Pemuda
Gubeng Train Station
Jl Emb Kemri
Jalan Pangima
Jalan Sumatra
Jalan Raya Gubeng
Jalan Karimun Jawa
Jalan Raya Arjuno
Jalan Raya Kembang
Jalan Sudirman

0   250   500 m

To Zoo, MPU Tantular Museum, Bungurasih, Purabaya Bus Terminal & Airport

SURABAYA

PLACES TO STAY				
7	Hotel Semut	30	Zangrandi Ice Cream Palace	14 THR Amusement Park
8	Hotel Irian	35	Turin	15 Taman Remaja
9	Hotel Ganefo	37	Depot Jakarta	17 Garuda Office
19	Hotel Paviljoen	41	Kuningan Seafood	18 Bank Bali
21	Weta Hotel	44	Cheap Warung	20 Genteng Market
23	Bamboe Denn			22 Andhika Plaza
32	Garden Palace Hotel	**OTHER**		24 Tunjungan Plaza
39	Sahid Surabaya Hotel	1	Mesjid Ampel	26 Bank Duta
40	Puri Kencana Hotel	2	Pasar Pabean	27 Joko Dolog
43	Cendana Hotel	3	Kong Co Kong Tik	28 BNI Bank
45	Hyatt Regency Surabaya		Cun Ong	29 Governor's Residence
		4	Jembatan Merah	31 World Trade Centre
PLACES TO EAT		5	Gedung PTP XXII	33 BII Bank
6	Kiet Wan Kie	10	Main Post Office	34 Plaza Surabaya
16	Cafe Venezia	11	Pelni Office	36 Tourist Office
25	Galael Supermarket;	12	Tugu Pahlawan	38 Monumen Kapal Selam
	KFC; Swensen's	13	Surabaya Mall	42 Minibus Agents
				46 Bouraq Office

Balikpapan and Bandung, with numerous other connections.

Mandala (☎ 57 8973) offers discounted flights to Jakarta and Ujung Pandang.

Bus Most buses operate from Surabaya's main Purabaya bus station in Bungurasih, 10km south of the city centre. Buses along the north coast and to Semarang depart from the Terminal Oso Wilangun, 10km west of the city.

Normal/air-con buses from Bungurasih include: Malang (2000/4000 rp; two hours), Probolinggo (2200/4500 rp; two hours), Banyuwangi (6500/11,500 rp; six hours), Solo (10,750 rp; 6½ hours) and Yogyakarta (12,750 rp; eight hours). Ekonomi buses also run to Semarang (7500 rp), and to Madura.

Luxury long-haul buses also depart from Bungurasih. Most are night buses leaving in the late afternoon/early evening. Bookings can be made at the terminal, or travel agents in the centre of town sell tickets with a fair mark up. Intercity buses are not allowed to enter the city so you will have to go to Bungurasih to catch your bus. Prices include Jakarta 58,000 rp, Denpasar 32,000 rp and Bandung 48,000 rp.

There are also door-to-door minibus agents along Jalan Jend Basuki Rahmat with buses to Malang (10,000 rp), Yogyakarta (25,000 rp), Solo (23,000 rp) and Banyuwangi (via Probolinggo; 21,500 rp). Try Ranta Tria (☎ 534 5330) at Jalan Basuki Rahmat 38A.

Train Trains from Jakarta taking the quicker northern route via Semarang will arrive at the Pasar Turi station. Trains taking the southern route via Yogyakarta, and trains from Banyuwangi and Malang, arrive at the more central Gubeng station and most carry on to Kota station.

The trip from Jakarta takes nine to 17 hours, although the slower ekonomi trains can take even longer. Fares vary from 13,500 rp in ekonomi class, to 33,000 rp in bisnis and up to 150,000 rp on the luxury *Argobromo* (from Pasar Turi). The cheapest are the ekonomi services like the *Gaya Baru Malam Utara* (13 hours) on the northern route or the *Gaya Baru Malam Selatan* (16 hours) on the southern route. Fares to Bandung range from 15,000 rp in ekonomi to 60,000 rp in eksekutif.

From Gubeng station, trains to/from Solo (four to six hours) and Yogyakarta (five to seven hours) cost from 6000 rp in ekonomi, 19,000 rp in bisnis and 30,000 rp in eksekutif. Trains are faster and cheaper than buses.

There are six ekonomi trains per day to Malang (two hours), continuing to Blitar (from 1900 rp to 3800 rp). There are trains to Banyuwangi (15,000/26,000 rp bisnis/eksekutif; seven hours), with ferry and bus connections to Denpasar, at 8 am and 10 pm, and the ekonomi *Sri Tanjung* departs at 2.10 pm. These go via Probolinggo. If you are arriving at Gubeng, exit through the back of the station where you can catch a metered taxi or walk straight to Jalan Pemuda and into the city.

From Pasar Turi station, trains to Semarang cost 11,000/28,000 rp for bisnis/eksekutif.

INDONESIA

Boat Surabaya is an important port and a major travel hub for ships to the other islands.

Popular Pelni connections are those to Sulawesi, with at least seven Pelni ships doing the Surabaya-Ujung Pandang run (24 hours), and to Kalimantan with ships to Pontianak, Kumai, Banjarmasin, Balikpapan, Batulicin and Sampit. A number of Pelni ships also sail direct between Surabaya and Jakarta (24 hours). See the Indonesia Getting Around section earlier in this chapter for Pelni details. Ekonomi fares include: Ujung Pandang 101,000 rp, Banjarmasin 63,000 rp, Balikpapan 133,000 rp, Jakarta 76,000 rp.

The Pelni ticket office at Jalan Pahlawan 112 is open Monday to Friday from 9 am to 3 pm, and on weekends (if there are ship departures) from 9 am to noon. Ships depart from Tanjung Perak harbour – bus P1 or C will get you there.

Ferries to Kamal on Madura (500 rp; 30 minutes) leave every 40 minutes from Tanjung Perak.

Getting Around

To/From the Airport Taxis from the Juanda airport (15km) operate on a coupon system and cost 12,000 rp to the city centre. The Damri airport bus (2000 rp) drops off in the city centre and at the Purabaya bus station.

Local Transport Surabaya has plenty of air-con metered taxis. Typical fares from central Surabaya include the Pelni office for 4500 rp, the harbour for 8000 rp, Bamboe Denn to Gubeng station for 3000 rp, and the airport for 10,000 rp. Becaks are useful for short distances.

Bemos are labelled A, B, C etc and all charge a standard 500 rp. Bemo M will get you from Jalan Pemuda south to the zoo and N runs between the centre and Pasar Turi train station. Patas (express) buses are labelled P and charge a fixed 500 rp fare. P1 is the most useful service, running from the Purabaya bus station up to Pasar Turi and through the old city to the Kalimas harbour. The buses are crowded and a hassle if you have luggage.

AROUND SURABAYA

Scattered around **Trowulan**, 60km south-west of Surabaya on the Solo road, are the remains of the capital of the ancient Majapahit Empire, the last great Hindu kingdom to rule on Java, driven to Bali by the Muslims in the early 16th century. One kilometre from the main Surabaya-Solo highway, the **Trowulan Museum** houses superb examples of Majapahit sculpture and pottery from throughout East Java. The museum is open from 7 am to 4 pm; closed Monday and public holidays. Reconstructed temples are scattered around the museum, some within walking distance, though you need to hire a becak to see them all.

The hill resort of **Tretes**, 55km south of Surabaya, is a cool break if you have to kill time in Surabaya. Its main claim to fame is as a red-light resort, but it has walks around town and hiking to Gunung Welirang.

On the way to Tretes, **Pandaan**, 40km south of Surabaya, is home to the open-air Candra Wilwatikta Theatre. East Javanese classical dance, a poor cousin of Prambanan's Ramayana ballet, is held here once a month during the dry season from June to October. Seats cost US$3.

MADURA

Only half an hour from Surabaya by ferry, the relatively unspoilt island of Madura has fine beaches and picturesque remote countryside. Coming from Bali, Madura is also accessible by daily ferry from Jangkar, north of Banyuwangi, to Kalianget near the island's eastern tip – you could make a trip through Madura and exit from Kamal to Surabaya.

Madura is a flat, dry and rugged island, and it's a contrast to Java in both landscape and lifestyle. Cattle raising is important, rather than rice growing, and much of Indonesia's salt supply comes from the vast salt tracts around Kalianget.

During the dry season, particularly in August and September, Madura is famed for its colourful **bull races**, the *kerapan sapi*, which climax with the finals held at Pamekasan. The bulls are harnessed in pairs, two teams compete at a time and they're raced along a 120m course in a special stadium. Races don't last long – the bulls can do nine seconds over 100m, faster than the men's world track record. Bull races for tourists are sometimes staged at the Bangkalan Stadium, and race practice is held throughout the year in Bangkalan, Pamekasan and Sumenep, but dates are not fixed. The tourist office in Surabaya can supply details of where and when the bull races will be held.

Near the village of Arosbaya, 28km north of Bangkalan, **Air Mata** is the old royal cemetery of the Cakraningrat family, with beautiful views across the terraced hills.

The south coast road to Pamekasan, 100km east of Kamal where the ferry docks, has fields of immaculately groomed cattle, small fishing villages and a sea of rainbow-coloured *perahus* (outriggers). **Pamekasan**, the capital of Madura, comes alive in the bull racing season, but is quiet the rest of the year. **Camplong**, about 15km west of Pamekasan, has a reasonable beach and calm water.

Sumenep, 53km north-east of Pamekasan, is a more refined, royal town and the most interesting on Madura. You can see Sumenep's 18th century mosque, and the kraton with its water palace and interesting museum. **Asta Tinggi**, the royal cemetery, is only about 3km from the town centre.

Places to Stay

In Pamekasan, *Hotel Ramayana (☎ 0324-22406)*, Jalan Niaga 55, is the best bet. Rooms with shared mandi cost 10,000 rp, bright rooms with mandi are 15,000 rp, and air-con rooms start at 30,000 rp.

In Sumenep, *Hotel Wijaya I (☎ 0328-21433)*, Jalan Trunojoyo 45-47, has good clean rooms from 9000 rp without mandi, 17,000 rp with mandi, and 35,000 rp to 45,000 rp with air-con. The sister *Hotel Wijaya II (☎ 0328-62532)* nearby has the same room prices and is also good.

Bangkalan has a selection of hotels and Camplong has mid-range bungalows on the beach, but there is not a lot of reason to stay at either.

Getting There & Away

It's only half an hour by ferry (500 rp) from Surabaya to Kamal, the harbour town in Madura. From the ferry terminal in Kamal you can take a bus or colt to other main towns, including Bangkalan. Buses also run from Sumenep right through to Surabaya, Malang and Bali.

GUNUNG BROMO

Gunung Bromo is an active volcano lying at the centre of the Tengger Massif, a spectacular volcanic landscape and one of the most impressive sights in Indonesia. The massive Tengger crater stretches 10km across and its steep walls plunge down to a vast, flat sea of lava sand. From the crater floor emerges the smoking peak of Gunung Bromo (2329m), the spiritual centre of the highlands. This desolate landscape has a strange end-of-the-world feeling, particularly at sunrise.

Often the whole area is simply referred to as 'Mt Bromo', but Bromo is only one of three mountains within the caldera of the ancient Tengger volcano; it is flanked by the perfect cone of Batok (2440m) and the larger Kursi (2581m). Further south the whole supernatural moonscape is overseen by Gunung Semeru (3676m), the highest mountain in Java and the most active volcano in these highlands. The whole area has been incorporated into the **Bromo-Tengger-Semeru National Park**.

A visit to this fantastic volcano is easy to fit in between Bali and Surabaya or Yogyakarta. The usual jumping-off point for Bromo is the town of Probolinggo on the main Surabaya to Banyuwangi road. From there, you head to Ngadisari or Cemoro Lawang, high on the Tengger crater.

Get up at 4.30 am or earlier for an easy stroll across to Bromo from Cemoro Lawang. By the time you've crossed the lava plain and started to climb the steps up to Bromo's crater it should be fairly light. Horseback is a popular way of getting to Bromo (6500 rp from Cemoro Lawang), but it's better to ride the return journey when it's light and mostly uphill. The squat, grey cone of Bromo is not in itself one of the great volcanoes of Indonesia – it is the whole landscape that is breathtaking – but from the top you'll get fantastic views down into the smoking crater and of the sun sailing up over the outer crater. In the wet season, the dawn and the clouds often arrive simultaneously, so at that time of year you might just as well stay in bed and stroll across later in the day.

Though Probolinggo is the usual approach, Bromo can also be reached via Tosari from the north-west and Ngadas from the south-west.

Tours come via Tosari because 4WD vehicles can drive all the way to the base of Gunung Bromo. The main traffic from Tosari, however, is minibus tours via a sealed road right to the top of Gunung Penanjakan (2770m) to see the dawn from there. The superb views right across Bromo and the Tengger crater to smoking Gunung Semeru are unsurpassed – this is where those postcards shots are taken. Gunung Penanjakan can also be reached from Cemoro Lawang, and it's well worth the effort. You can walk (one hour) or take a chartered jeep along the road to the 'Penanjakan II' viewpoint, itself a spectacular vantage point, but it's worth walking another hour up the steep trail behind this viewing area to Penanjakan proper.

From Malang, it is possible to travel by mikrolet to Tumpang, and then by another mikrolet to Gubug Klakah, from where you walk 12km to Ngadas. From Ngadas it is 2km to Jemplang at the crater rim, and then three hours on foot (12km) across the floor of the Tengger crater to Gunung Bromo and on to Cemoro Lawang. Alternatively, from Ngadas it is an 8.5km walk to Rano Pani, where Pak Tasrep runs a homestay and can help organise a climb of Gunung Semeru. It is a full day's walk from Rano Pani to Arcopodo, the camp site on the mountain, and you must be equipped for freezing conditions. The rugged ascent is usually done at 2 am the following morning to reach the peak before sunrise.

In January or February, the big annual Kesada festival is held by the local Hindu community when offerings are made to appease Bromo.

Places to Stay & Eat
Cemoro Lawang Situated at the lip of the Tengger crater, Cemoro Lawang is right at the start of the walk to Bromo and therefore is the most popular place to stay.

Cafe Lava Hostel (☎ 54 1009) is the number one travellers' place. Singles/doubles cost 8000/15,000 rp with shared mandi, or 20,000/30,000 rp with private cold-water mandi. Rooms are basic but the hostel is cheap, convivial and has a good restaurant with such alpine touches as hot mulled wine. The fancier co-owned *Lava View Lodge* is along a side road from the bus stop (about 10 minutes walk from Cafe Lava) and right at the edge of the crater with great views. Comfortable rooms with bathroom start at 20,000/30,000 rp, or 30,000/50,000 rp with hot shower, up to 50,000/75,000 rp for the excellent cottages.

Cemara Indah Hotel (☎ 54 1019) is also on the rim of the crater, on the road leading up to the Gunung Penanjakan viewpoint. It offers more great views and has a very good restaurant. Basic rooms are 7000/10,000 rp and comfortable rooms with bathroom and hot water cost 60,000 rp, all including breakfast.

Hotel Bromo Permai I (☎/fax 54 1021), 100m past Cafe Lava, is the classiest hotel in Cemoro Lawang with a good restaurant and bar. Rooms with shared mandi cost from 16,000 rp, and with attached bathroom and hot water from 60,000 rp to 106,000 rp.

Ngadisari Another 3km back towards Probolinggo, Ngadisari has a few decent places to stay. *Yoschi's Guest House* (☎ 54 1018),

just outside Ngadisari village, is an excellent choice. This attractive, friendly inn has doubles from 15,000 rp with shared mandi to 30,000 rp with bathroom, and comfortable family cottages with hot water for 50,000 rp. Hot showers are available for 2500 rp. It has a good restaurant and offers tours and cheap transport to Bromo (1250 rp). A short walk away, *Bromo Home Stay* (☎ 54 1022) has comfortable rooms for 10,000/15,000 rp without/with mandi, or 25,000 rp with hot shower.

Probolinggo On the highway between Surabaya and Banyuwangi, this is the jumping-off point for Gunung Bromo. Most travellers only see the bus or train station before moving on, but the town has plenty of hotels if you get stuck.

Hotel Bromo Permai (☎ 22256), Jalan Panglima Sudirman 237, is the most popular travellers' hotel and has comfortable, clean rooms from 9500 rp with shared mandi and 11,400 rp with shower, to 28,000 rp with air-con. It's on the main road close to the centre of town.

Hotel Ratna (☎ 21597), further west at Jalan Panglima Sudirman 16, is one of the best in town. Good economy rooms cost 10,000 and 12,000 rp, or rooms with bath range from 25,000 rp to 45,000 rp with air-con.

Getting There & Away
Probolinggo's bus station is 5km west of town on the road to Bromo – catch a yellow angkot from the main street or the train station for 300 rp. Regular buses include: Surabaya (2200/4500 rp air-con; two hours), Malang (2300/4500 rp; 2½ hours) and Banyuwangi (7000/9000 rp; five hours). Deluxe buses to Yogya or Denpasar take eight hours and cost around 25,000 rp. There are plenty of 'tourist office' bus agents at the station offering dubious information. For local buses or shorter trips (such as Surabaya and Malang), find the bus and buy your ticket on board rather than from an agent. For the deluxe buses and longer hauls it's better to pay the extra and book a seat with an agent – but shop around. Coming from or heading to Denpasar, it's a lot easier to get a through bus, rather than trying to make the connections at Banyuwangi and Gilimanuk.

Bison minibuses from the terminal go to Cemoro Lawang (2500 rp; two hours) via Ngadisari (2000 rp; 1¾ hours) until around 5 or 6 pm, as late as 9 pm in the main August tourist season. If you're staying at Cemoro Lawang, make sure when you board the minibus that it's going all the way to the top and pay when you get there. You pay the 2100 rp entry fee to the national park at Ngadisari.

Probolinggo's train station is 1.5km north of the centre of town. Ekonomi trains run to Surabaya (6000 rp), Banyuwangi (3500 rp), Malang (3500 rp), Solo (9000 rp) and Yogyakarta (10,000 rp). Bisnis class services include the *Mutiara* to Surabaya and Banyuwangi (7000 rp).

Travel agents in Solo and Yogya sell direct minibus tickets to Bromo (Cemoro Lawang or Ngadisari) for 50,000 rp air-con. Two-day/one-night tours from Solo and Yogya (continuing on to Bali) cost around 100,000 rp, but these use the Bromo Home Stay in Ngadisari and are not particularly good value.

Bali

To westerners, Bali has been both a tropical paradise and an example of the destructive effects of tourism. It has a rich culture, beautiful landscapes and coastline, a small bustling capital, several interesting towns, and hundreds of rural villages, where most Balinese live. The most conspicuous effects of tourism are confined to a few areas, and it's not hard to find fascinating places where tourists are a novelty. Balinese dancing, music, visual arts and architecture are unique and accessible to visitors. Religion is central to Balinese life, and the temples, festivals and offerings are ubiquitous.

History

Bali was populated as early as 3000 BC, but the earliest records are stone inscriptions from around the 9th century AD. By that time rice was grown with a complex irrigation system, and there were the beginnings of a rich culture. Hindu influences from Java grew from the reign of King Airlangga (1019-42) – the rock-cut memorials of Gunung Kawi are a legacy of 11th century links to Java.

The great Majapahit Empire, and its legendary chief minister, Gajah Mada, conquered Bali in 1343. As Islam spread in Java, the Majapahit court progressively moved to Bali, making its final exodus, with priests, artists and intellectuals, in 1478. The priest Nirartha brought many of the complexities of Balinese religion to the island, and established superb sea temples including Rambut Siwi, Tanah Lot and Ulu Watu.

In the 19th century, the Dutch began to form alliances with local princes in north Bali. A dispute over the ransacking of wrecked ships was the pretext for the 1906 Dutch invasion of the south, which climaxed in a suicidal *puputan* (fight to the death) – the Denpasar nobility burnt their own palaces, dressed in their finest jewellery and, waving golden krises, marched straight into the Dutch guns. The rajas of Tabanan, Karangasem, Gianyar and Klungkung soon capitulated too, and Bali became part of the Dutch East Indies. Compliant survivors of the old nobility were used to administer Dutch rule. Balinese culture was actually encouraged by many Dutch officials, international interest was aroused and the first tourists arrived. Dutch rule ended abruptly in 1942, with the Japanese occupation. After WWII, the struggle for national independence was fierce on Bali – 94 resistance fighters under Lt Ngurah Rai were completely wiped out at Marga in 1946, but Dutch losses were even heavier.

Bali languished economically in the early years of independence, and suffered a disastrous eruption of Gunung Agung in 1963. The 1965 coup was followed by the brutal killing of perhaps 50,000 Chinese, suspected Communists and others. Under Soeharto, Bali prospered over a long period of stability and growth, with improving standards of health, education, housing and infrastructure. Much of the improvement has been financed by the phenomenal expansion of tourism, but this has also brought environmental problems, new social tensions and some of the least attractive features of western society.

Climate

Average temperatures are about 30°C year-round, with high humidity. The dry season runs from April to September and the wet season from October to March, though rain storms are possible any time of year. It's cooler and wetter in the mountains, and drier on the east coast, the far west and the Bukit Peninsula.

Flora & Fauna

Picturesque rice fields cover about 20% of the island, with some dense jungle in the interior, scrub and savanna in the drier parts, and barren volcanic regions. The well-watered areas are intensely cultivated, with a huge range of plants, though few are endemic to

INDONESIA

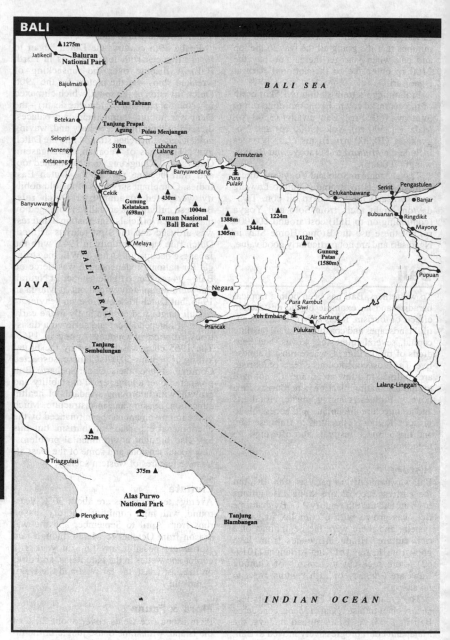

BALI

▲1275m
Jatikecil
**Baluran
National Park**

Bajulmati

BALI SEA

Pulau Tabuan

Betekan

Tanjung Prapat
Agung
Pulau Menjangan

Selogiri

Meneng
310m▲
Labuhan
Lalang
Pemuteran

Ketapang

Gilimanuk
Banyuwedang
*Pura
Pulaki*

Celukanbawang
Seririt
Pengastulen

Cekik

Banyuwangi
**Gunung
Kelatakan
(698m)**
430m▲
▲1004m
**Taman Nasional
Bali Barat**
1388m▲
1224m▲
Banjar

Bubuanan
Ringdikit

Mayong

1305m▲
1344m▲

Melaya
1412m▲

JAVA
**Gunung
Patas
(1580m)**

Pupuan

BALI STRAIT
Negara

*Pura Rambut
Siwi*
Yeh Embang
Air Santang

Prancak
Pulukan

**Tanjung
Sembulungan**

Lalang-Linggah

322m▲

Triaggulasi
375m▲

**Alas Purwo
National Park**

Plengkung
**Tanjung
Blambangan**

INDIAN OCEAN

BALI

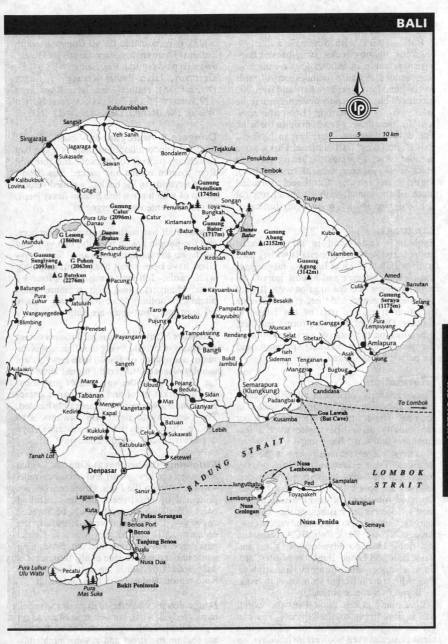

Singaraja
Sangsit
Kubutambahan
Jagaraga
Sukasade
Yeh Sanih
Sawan
Bondalem
Tejakula
Penuktukan
Tembok
Kalibukbuk
Lovina
Gitgit
Gunung Penulisan (1745m)
Songan
Tianyar
Penulisan
Toya Bungkah
Gunung Catur (2096m)
Catur
Kintamani
Batur
Gunung Batur (1717m)
Danau Batur
Gunung Abang (2152m)
Kubu
Pura Ulu Danau
Munduk
G Lesong (1860m)
Danau Bratan
Candikuning
Penelokan
Kedisan
Buahan
Tulamben
Gunung Sangiyang (2093m)
G Pohon (2063m)
Bedugul
Amed
Banutan
Batungsel
G Batukau (2276m)
Pacung
Kayuanbua
Besakih
Gunung Agung (3142m)
Culik
Gunung Seraya (1175m)
Selang
Pura Luhur
Jatuluih
Jati
Pampatan
Kayubihi
Tirta Gangga
Pura Lempuyang
Wangayegede
Taro
Sebatu
Rendang
Muncan
Sibetan
Asak
Amlapura
Blimbing
Penebel
Pujung
Tampaksiring
Selat
Iseh
Ujung
Payangan
Bangli
Sideman
Tenganan
Antasari
Sangeh
Bukit Jambul
Manggis
Bugbug
Marga
Ubud
Pejang Bedulu
Sidan
Semarapura (Klungkung)
Candidasa
Tabanan
Mengwi
Mas
Gianyar
Padangbai
To Lombok
Kediri
Kapal
Kangetan
Batuan
Lebih
Kusamba
Goa Lawah (Bat Cave)
Kukluk
Sempidi
Celuk
Sukawati
Tanah Lot
Batubulan
Ketewel
BADUNG STRAIT
Denpasar
Sanur
Nusa Lembongan
LOMBOK STRAIT
Legian
Junguthatu
Ped
Sampalan
Kuta
Lembongan
Toyapakeh
Karangsail
Pulau Serangan
Nusa Ceningan
Semaya
Benoa Port
Benoa
Nusa Penida
Tanjung Benoa
Bualu
Pura Luhur Ulu Watu
Pecatu
Nusa Dua
Pura Mas Suka
Bukit Peninsula

0   5   10 km

Bali. An enormous variety of flowers grow wild or in gardens.

Bali is thick with domestic animals – chickens, fighting cocks, sway-backed Balinese pigs, cattle, ducks and dogs are the most conspicuous. Wildlife includes small lizards (cecak) and larger geckos, bats and over 300 species of birds. The only endemic bird is the jalak putih or Bali starling (Leucopsar rothschildi), though very few remain in the wild. The only wilderness area, Taman Nasional Bali Barat (West Bali National Park), has a number of wild species, including grey and black monkeys, deer, muncak (mouse deer), squirrels and iguanas. Coral reefs surround much of the island, with colourful tropical fish, dolphins and a few surviving turtles.

Language

English is understood in all the tourist centres, and Bahasa Indonesia is widely used all over Bali. The local Balinese language is completely different and almost impossible for a foreigner to come to grips with. It's not a written language, and there is considerable variation from one part of the island to another. Different linguistic forms are used, depending on the relative social position of the speaker, the person being spoken to, and the person being spoken about.

Information

There are tourist offices in all district capitals, eg Denpasar and Singaraja, as well as in Kuta and Ubud. Staff are often friendly, but can usually offer little more than a few brochures and some basic maps.

Moneychangers are everywhere in the tourist areas. Their exchange rates are usually better than the banks, their service is quicker and they are open a lot longer. Visa, MasterCard and American Express are accepted by most of the bigger businesses that cater to tourists. You can also get cash advances (also through ATMs): Bank Bali, BCA, Danamon and Bank Duta do advances on Visa; and Bank Bali and Lippo Bank do MasterCard. Cash advances attract commissions (about 5%), which are different from bank to bank, so, if you can, check around.

Like many places throughout the world, Bali is now firmly on the Internet. You can get an enormous amount of information about Bali, and even book entire holidays, on the net, and there are Internet centres (with email facilities) at Kuta, Sanur, Ubud and Lovina.

Consulates The Australian consulate, Jalan Mohammed Yamin 4, Renon, Denpasar (☎ 23 5092), is responsible for all Commonwealth citizens. There are honorary consuls for France, Jalan Bypass Ngurah Rai, Sanur (☎ 28 5485); Germany, Jalan Pantai Karang 17, Sanur (☎ 28 8535); Netherlands, Jalan Raya Kuta 599, Kuta (☎ 75 1517); and USA, Jalan Hayam Wuruk 188, Renon, Denpasar (☎ 23 3605).

Dangers & Annoyances Violent crime is relatively uncommon, but there is some bag snatching, picking of pockets and thieving from losmen rooms and parked cars. Don't leave anything in the back of a rented vehicle (most of which are white Suzuki jimny jeeps, obviously rented by foreigners).

Scams Bali has such a relaxed atmosphere, and the people are so friendly, that you may not be on the lookout for scams. Some travellers have been stung badly from gambling with cards, deliberate miscalculations by moneychangers, and high pressure sales pitches for holiday 'timeshare' deals – many are legitimate, but some are dubious.

Hawkers Many visitors regard the persistent attentions of people trying to sell things as the major annoyance on Bali. These hawkers are usually restricted to certain tourist areas like the Kuta region, the environs of just about any upmarket hotel and most tourist attractions, but elsewhere visitors are rarely hassled. The best way to deal with hawkers is to ignore them from the first instance. Eye contact is crucial – don't make any!

Swimming The beaches at Kuta and Legian are subject to heavy surf and strong currents – swim between the flags. Other beaches are protected by coral reefs, but be careful of coral. (Walking on coral should be avoided anyway – it consists of very delicate living organisms.) It can be very sharp and coral cuts can easily become infected. Swimming while under the influence of any intoxicant is dangerous. Lifeguards are only found in the Kuta region, and at Nusa Dua and Sanur.

Drugs You may be offered dope on the street, particularly in Kuta, but you're unlikely to get a good deal. Tablets purported to be Ecstasy are sold on the street and at some nightclubs too, but they could contain just about anything. Bali's famed magic mushrooms (oong) come out during the rainy season.

The government takes the smuggling, use and sale of drugs very, *very* seriously, and entrapment by police and informers is a real possibility. Once you have been caught and put in jail, there is little that your consulate on Bali (if you have one) can do.

Activities

Trekking Bali is too densely populated for remote wilderness treks, but climbing to the top of a volcano is popular. Many people climb Gunung Batur to see the sunrise, and the biggest challenge is Gunung Agung. There are also some limited day treks around Taman Nasional Bali Barat in the far west.

Surfing In recent years, the number of surfers on Bali has increased enormously, and good breaks can get very crowded. Some of the best spots are Kuta Beach, Ulu Watu, Padang Padang, Canggu, Medewi and Nusa Lembongan. A small board is usually adequate for the smaller breaks, but a few extra centimetres on your usual board length won't go astray.

In the Kuta region, you can hire surfboards for about 20,000 rp per day, boogie boards for about 15,000 rp, and even get surfing lessons for about 60,000 rp per day.

Diving With its warm water, extensive coral reefs and abundant marine life, Bali offers some superb diving possibilities. There are a number of dive centres in the tourist centres on Bali which arrange trips all over the island, and offer diving certificate courses. Prices are about US$45 for one dive, plus transport costs. Diving may not be as good during the wet season, as storms tend to reduce visibility.

The best diving spots are at Tulamben, Amed, Pulau Menjangan and around Nusa Lembongan.

For more detailed information, get hold of *Diving & Snorkeling Guide to Bali and The Komodo Region,* one of Lonely Planet's Pisces series.

Snorkelling If you just want to do a little snorkelling, there are pretty good coral reefs off Nusa Dua, Sanur, the Lovina beaches, Padangbai, Amed, Tulamben and various points along the north-west coast. Most areas with coral and tourists will have a place that rents masks, snorkels and fins (about 7000 rp per day), but always check the condition of the equipment.

Rafting Rafting has become very popular, and is best during or just after the wet season. Rafting can usually be done as a day trip from the Kuta region, Sanur, Nusa Dua or Ubud. Operators will pick you up from your hotel, take you to the put-in point, provide all the equipment and guides, give you a buffet lunch and return you to your hotel afterwards. Prices are about US$60.

Shopping

Many people come to Bali to shop, and even if you don't, you will probably end up buying quite a few things. There are a growing number of western-style department stores and shopping centres in Denpasar, Kuta and Nusa Dua, selling a large variety of clothing, shoes, leather goods, music, sports gear and toys – at fixed prices.

All tourist centres have markets and stalls selling souvenirs – at negotiable prices. Ubud, and the road between Denpasar and Ubud, is the best place for traditional art, gold and silver products, handicrafts and clothing. For more traditional items, look for antiques in Semarapura (Klungkung), textiles in Gianyar, paintings in Kamasan, musical instruments in Tenganan, and wood carving at Penarukan.

Getting There & Away

Air Denpasar is a major international gateway. Reconfirm tickets early because flights out of Bali are often full. This can be done over the telephone (staff at all airline offices speak English), or ask your hotel to do it. Almost every international airline has an office at the airport and/or in the Grand Bali Beach Hotel, Sanur.

Air France ☎ 28 8511, ext 1105
Air New Zealand ☎ 75 6170
Ansett Australia ☎ 28 9636
Cathay Pacific Airways ☎ 28 6001
Continental Micronesia ☎ 28 7774
Garuda Indonesia ☎ 22 5245, bookings ☎ 22 7824
Japan Airlines ☎ 28 7577
KLM ☎ 75 6126
Korean Air ☎ 28 9402
Lufthansa Airlines ☎ 28 7069
Malaysia Airlines ☎ 28 5071
Northwest Airlines ☎ 28 7841
Qantas Airways ☎ 28 8331
Singapore Airlines ☎ 28 7940
Thai Airways International ☎ 28 8141

Merpati is the major local carrier. It flies most days from Denpasar to Surabaya; Jakarta; Ujung Pandang; Bima; Kupang; Dili; and

Mataram about ten times a day. However, at the time of writing, fares and schedules were very unstable.

Merpati has an office on Jalan Melati in Denpasar (☎ 26 1238), but you can book at any Garuda office, or travel agency on Bali. Other domestic airlines with some limited flights to/from Denpasar are Bouraq (☎ 24 1397) and Mandala (☎ 22 2751).

All the airlines also have booking offices at the domestic terminal of the airport.

Public Bus The usual route for land travel to Java is on an overnight bus from Denpasar to Surabaya (10-12 hours), though some buses go as far as Yogyakarta (15-16 hours) and Jakarta (26-30 hours). There are also regular buses from Denpasar to Mataram (Lombok), and further east to Sumbawa, but it's generally better to do the latter in individual stages. You can book bus tickets directly at the Ubung terminal in Denpasar, or at travel agencies anywhere on Bali. Prices vary considerably, depending on which company you deal with, and the standard of bus you want. Bus fares include the ferry trip. Some routes avoid Denpasar completely, so you can travel directly between Java and Padangbai or Singaraja.

Shuttle Bus A few tourist shuttle bus companies, such as the Kuta-based Perama service, have buses to Surabaya, Yogyakarta and Jakarta. Before you buy a ticket, however, make sure it is not just a shuttle bus to the Ubung terminal in Denpasar, and then a public bus the rest of the way to Java. Refer to the Lombok entry in the Nusa Tenggara section of this chapter for details about shuttle bus services between Bali and Lombok.

Boat Ferries travel between Gilimanuk in west Bali and Ketapang (Java) every 15 to 30 minutes, 24 hours a day. The actual crossing takes under 30 minutes. The fare is 1000 rp, and there are extra costs for a bicycle (1400 rp), motorbike (2700 rp) and car (10,550 rp).

Ferries also travel between Padangbai in east Bali and Lembar (Lombok) every 60 to 90 minutes, 24 hours a day. The fare is 9000/5500 rp for 1st/2nd class. Bicycles cost 700 rp; motorbikes, 6200 rp; and cars, 35,700 rp. The trip takes at least four hours, sometimes up to seven.

The luxury *Mabua Express* (☎ 37224) provides a fast service (about two hours) between Lembar and Benoa Port (Bali). Tickets cost at least 80,000 rp, depending on demand, and can be booked directly or at any travel agency.

Four Pelni boats, the *Tatamailau*, *Dobonsolo*, *Awu* and *Tilongkabila*, call at Benoa Port about once a fortnight, as part of their regular loop throughout Indonesia. See the Indonesia Getting There & Away section for route details. You can make inquiries and bookings at the Pelni office (☎ 72 1377) at Benoa Port.

Getting Around

To/From the Airport The counters at the international and domestic terminals have pre-paid taxis to Kuta Beach (8000 rp to 10,000 rp); Legian (11,500 rp); Denpasar (15,000 rp); Sanur (17,500 rp); Nusa Dua (17,500 rp); Tanjung Benoa (18,500 rp); and Ubud (47,000 rp). Walk out of the airport car park for a few hundred metres and you'll be on the route of the public bemo to Kuta for about 500 rp.

Public Bus & Bemo Bemos are the main public transport on Bali. They're cheap and fun, but can be inconvenient, particularly to or from southern Bali. Every town has a bemo or bus station, or at least a bemo stop. Denpasar is the hub, and Singaraja, Gilimanuk, Gianyar and Amlapura have major regional terminals. You may have to transit one or more of these terminals to get from one part of Bali to another. On longer routes, larger minibuses and full-size buses operate from the same bemo/bus stations.

It's impossible to be precise about bemo fares, and tourists are regularly overcharged. Watch how much other passengers are paying, and pay while you are on the bemo, so the driver doesn't drive off with your change. You may also be charged extra for a large bag. Bemos rarely leave until they are full, which can take some time.

The Denpasar terminals and some of their major destinations, with current fares, are:

Tegal The terminal for south Bali has blue bemos to Kuta, Legian, Sanur and the airport (about 500 rp); and others to Bualu (for Nusa Dua, 500 rp) and Ulu Watu (1100 rp).

Ubung The terminal for north and west Bali, as well as Java, has bemos and minibuses to: Kediri (850 rp); Negara (2500 rp); Singaraja (3400 rp); Gilimanuk (3900 rp); and Bedugul (2100 rp).

Batubulan The terminal for east and central Bali, 10km north-east of town, has bemos to: Ubud (700 rp); Gianyar (1000 rp); Semarapura (Klungkung) and Bangli (1100 rp); Padangbai (1700 rp);

Candidasa (1900 rp); Nusa Dua (2300 rp) Amlapura (2500 rp); and Kintamani (2500 rp).

Sanglah This terminal has bemos to Suwung and Benoa Port.

Kereneng This is mainly an urban transfer terminal, and has bemos to Sanur.

Wangaya This terminal has bemos to Sangeh, Pelaga and Petang.

Chartered Bemo Many bemos are available for charter – for a trip, by the hour or by the day. The cost depends on time, distance and your bargaining skills; figure on 90,000 rp per day. Petrol may cost extra. For long trips, you will be expected to buy the driver some food and a drink when you stop for a break.

Shuttle Bus Several times a day, tourist shuttle buses travel between the main tourist areas on Bali. They are faster, more convenient and more comfortable than public bemos and buses, but more expensive. They are cheaper than renting or chartering a car or jeep unless you're travelling in a group of three or more. Perama is the most established operator, but there are several others.

As an example, typical fares from Kuta are: Ubud, 7500 rp; Padangbai and Candidasa, 10,000 rp; and Lovina, 12,500 rp, via Bedugul (7500 rp) or Kintamani (10,000 rp). You can buy tickets at any of the shops-cum-travel agencies throughout Bali.

Taxi & Private Car Metered taxis are available in Kuta, Denpasar, Sanur, Ubud and Nusa Dua. The main Denpasar-based companies, Praja Bali Taxis (☎ 70 1111) and Ngurah Rai Taxis (☎ 28 9090), have similar fares, which at the time of research were in a state of flux. The taxis normally crawl along the main roads beeping at tourists. If they use their meters, taxis are still a cheap way of getting around.

You can also rent a private car with a driver, but rates are very negotiable, and you will probably pay more than if you used a metered taxi. These cars are usually not licensed to carrying tourists, so they detour around police stations.

Car Rental The most popular rental vehicle is the four-seater Suzuki jeep known as a jimny. Depending on demand, length of rental and your bargaining ability, these cost from 50,000 rp to 70,000 rp a day, including insurance, but often excluding petrol. A Toyota Kijang, which seats six in reasonable comfort, costs from 85,000 rp per day, plus insurance and petrol.

Get an international driver's licence before you leave home – there are steep fines for unlicensed driving, and insurance may be invalidated. Driving is hazardous, and a car does intrude on the environment and isolates you from it. Parking can be difficult, and costs about 500 rp in a town, or near a tourist attraction. Cops also sometimes find pretexts to extract on-the-spot fines.

Motorcycle Rental Motorbikes cost about 17,500 rp per day, depending on the length of rental, your negotiation skills and the quality of the bike. Prices usually include insurance, and a small amount of petrol. They're more fun, more convenient and less intrusive than cars, but even more dangerous – only for experienced riders. Check the machine first, and ride sensibly.

If your international driver's licence isn't endorsed for motorbikes, you should get a local, three-month licence (valid for Bali, Lombok and Sumbawa). The person renting the bike will help you get this, but the licence costs a ridiculous 150,000 rp. Many riders don't bother, and report that police have no problem if you drive a motorbike with any international driver's licence. Find out the latest situation from other renters. Helmets are compulsory.

Bicycle You can rent bicycles in tourist centres for around 5000 rp per day. They're handy transport in towns, and an ideal way to explore the countryside. Most are multi-gear mountain bikes. If uphill stretches are too arduous, it may be possible to put your bike on the top of a bemo or bus, but drivers will charge extra for the service.

Organised Tours Tours can be a good way to see the sights if time is short, or to visit places like Pura Besakih, where public transport is difficult. Tours cost from 25,000/45,000 rp for half-day/full-day, but prices vary considerably depending on the quality of the tour company and vehicle, and where you buy the ticket. Bookings can be made at your hotel or any shop-cum-travel agency on Bali.

DENPASAR

The capital of Bali, and of its own municipal district, Denpasar (population about 400,000), has good shopping, government offices, universities, temples, mosques and churches. It

INDONESIA

DENPASAR

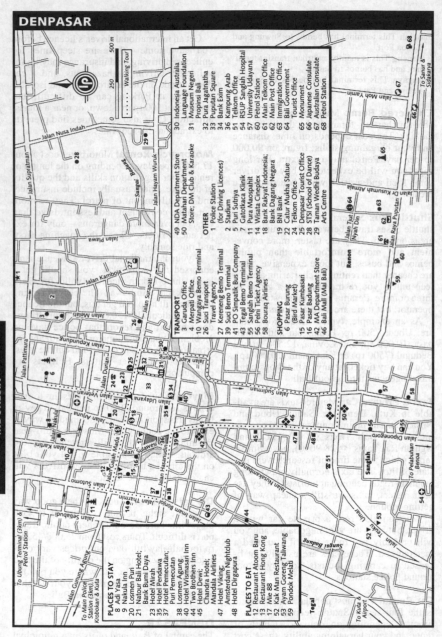

PLACES TO STAY
8 Adi Yasa
9 Nakula Inn
20 Losmen Puri
21 Natour Bali Hotel;
Bank Bumi Daya
23 Hotel Mirah
35 Hotel Pendawa
37 Hotel Pemecutan;
Puri Pemecutan
38 Losmen Agung
40 Hotel Wismasari Inn
44 Two Brothers Inn
45 Hotel Dewi;
Chandra Hotel;
Mandala Airlines
47 Hotel Viking;
Amsterdam Nightclub
48 Hotel Dirgapura

PLACES TO EAT
12 Restaurant Atoom Baru
13 Restaurant Hong Kong
17 Mie 88
52 Kak Man Restaurant
53 Ayam Goreng Taliwang
59 Pondok Melati

TRANSPORT
3 Garuda Office
4 Merpati Office
10 Suci Transport
Travel Agency
26 Wangaya Bemo Terminal
27 Kereneng Bemo Terminal
39 Suci Bemo Terminal
41 PO Simpatik Bus Company
43 Tegal Bemo Terminal
55 Sanglah Bemo Terminal
56 Peini Ticket Agency
58 Bouraq Airlines

SHOPPING
6 Pasar Burung
(Bird Market)
15 Pasar Kumbasari
16 Pasar Badung
42 MA Department Store
46 Bali Mall (Mal Bali)

49 NDA Department Store
50 Matahari Department
Store; DM Club & Karaoke

OTHER
1 Police Station
(for Driving Licences)
2 Stadium
5 Puri Sutriya
7 Gatotkaca Klinik
11 Pura Maospahit
14 Wisata Cineplex
18 Bank Rakyat Indonesia;
Bank Dagang Negara
19 BNI Bank
22 Catur Mukha Statue
24 Telkom Office
25 Denpasar Tourist Office
28 STSI (School of Dance)
29 Taman Wedhi Budaya
Arts Centre
30 Indonesia Australia
Language Foundation
31 Museum Negeri
Propinsi Bali
32 Pura Jagatnatha
33 Puputan Square
34 Bank Exim
36 Kampung Arab
51 Telkom Office
54 RSUP Sanglah Hospital
57 University Udayana
60 Petrol Station
61 Main Telkom Office
62 Main Post Office
63 Immigration Office
64 Bali Government
Tourist Office
65 Monument
66 Japanese Consulate
67 Australian Consulate
68 Petrol Station

has retained some tree-lined streets and pleasant gardens, despite increased traffic, noise and congestion, but there is little reason to linger more than a day.

Orientation

The main street starts as Jalan Gajah Mada in the west, becomes Jalan Surapati in the centre, then Jalan Hayam Wuruk and finally Jalan Raya Sanur in the east. Confusing one-way traffic restrictions and parking problems make it a bad place to drive – take taxis, bemos or walk.

Information

The Denpasar Tourist Office (☎ 23 4569) deals with tourism in the Denpasar municipality, which includes Sanur. They provide free copies of the valuable, annual *Bali Calendar of Events* (relevant for everywhere on Bali), but if you want information about other places on the island, go to the tourist offices in Ubud, Kuta and so on.

All major Indonesian banks have offices in Denpasar. Most have ATMs, and are located around the corner of Jalan Gajah Mada and Jalan Arjuna. The rates offered by moneychangers along the northern end of Jalan Diponegoro are better than the banks in Denpasar, but not as good as the moneychangers in the Kuta region.

The main post office, with the poste restante service, is inconveniently located in Renon. The main Telkom office is also hopelessly inconvenient, but there are wartels all over town.

The city's main hospital, RSUP Sanglah (☎ 22 7911), is open 24 hours, has English-speaking staff, and is regarded by expats as the best on Bali.

Things to See

The **Museum Negeri Propinsi Bali** has some interesting exhibits of traditional tools, crafts, masks and costumes from all over Bali. It's open from 8 am to 3.45 pm on Sunday, Tuesday, Wednesday and Thursday; and closes a little earlier on Friday and Saturday. Tickets cost 750 rp. Opposite the museum, **Puputan Square**, with its heroic Catur Mukha statue, is a meeting place for locals late in the afternoon. It commemorates the suicidal stand against the Dutch. The two most important temples are **Pura Jagatnatha**, the state temple next to the museum, and the 14th century **Pura Maospahit**.

Taman Wedhi Budaya arts centre (☎ 22

2776) has occasional exhibits of paintings, crafts and carvings, and holds traditional dances (6000 rp) every evening. It also hosts the annual Bali Arts Festival in June-July.

Places to Stay

Adi Yasa (☎ 22 2679) is central and friendly, with singles/doubles for 12,500/15,000 rp, rooms for 15,000/20,000 rp are far nicer, but often full. Just to the west, *Nakula Inn* (☎ 22 6446) is better, and worth the extra rupiah. Cool and comfortable rooms cost 25,000/ 30,000 rp.

Handy to the Tegal terminal, *Two Brothers Inn* (☎ 22 2704) has small singles/ doubles, with shared bathroom, for 15,000/ 20,000 rp. The central *Hotel Miruh* (☎ 24 0321) is run by a friendly family, and is good value. Clean rooms, with a portable fan and private bathroom, cost 20,000/40,000 rp. Another good option is the clean, central and surprisingly quiet *Hotel Wismasari Inn* (☎ 33 3437). The better rooms at the back cost 30,000 rp; the cheerless rooms inside are 20,000 rp.

Most mid-range places are along, or near, Jalan Diponegoro. *Hotel Viking* (☎ 22 3992) has very noisy 'economy' rooms for 30,000 rp, and better quieter rooms at the back for 65,000 rp with air-con. *Hotel Dirgapura* (☎ 22 6924) is better value, and more suited to budget travellers, with rooms for 15,000/ 20,000 rp.

Hotel Pemecutan (☎ 42 3491) is an unusual and atmospheric place, with a pretty garden in the middle of a palace. It is good value for 50,000/60,000 rp, with air-con, phone, TV and private bathroom.

Places to Eat

Most places cater for locals, and Indonesian visitors and immigrants, so they offer a good selection of authentic food at reasonable prices. Naturally, the cheapest places are the *warung* at the bemo terminals, and the *food stalls* at the Pasar Kumbasari and Pasar Burung markets.

Restaurant Atoom Baru is a typical Asian (as opposed to western) Chinese restaurant with dishes for 7000 rp to 12,000 rp. Across the road, the classy *Restaurant Hong Kong* boasts an inordinately wide range of Chinese and Indonesian dishes, but prices are high. Far better value can be found at *Mie 88*. Though the menu is not extensive, prices are reasonable (from 4500 rp to 6500 rp). There is not much to choose from in Renon, but

Pondok Melati has good seafood, even if the setting is noisy.

A number of places along Jalan Teuku Umar cater mainly for passing motorists, so if you don't have your own transport, get a bemo. The better places include *Kak Man Restaurant* and *Ayam Goreng Taliwag*. The various shopping centres have upstairs *eateries*, and most have fast food outlets like *McDonald's*, *KFC* or *Pizza Hut*.

Getting There & Away
See the Bali Getting There & Away and Getting Around sections above for details about travel to and from Denpasar.

Getting Around
Regular bemos travel along the main roads, and between the bemo terminals, for about 500 rp. Many taxis prowl the streets of Denpasar looking for fares. If you want to order a taxi, Praja Bali Taxis (☎ 70 1111) and Ngurah Rai Taxis (☎ 28 9090) should use the meter.

KUTA
Kuta is the biggest tourist centre on Bali. It's great for cheap accommodation, food, shopping, surf, sunsets and partying; and there is a Balinese community here, beneath the brash, commercialised surface.

The *kelurahan* (local government area) of Kuta extends for nearly 8km along the beach and foreshore, and incorporates four regions: Tuban, a newly-developed region, south of Kuta, with an excellent beach and upmarket hotels and shops; Kuta, with the greatest choice of hotels, restaurants, shops and the best beach, but the worst traffic and most annoying hawkers; Legian, a slightly quieter version of Kuta, with less of everything, including hotels and hawkers; and Seminyak, which somehow retains a small-town atmosphere, with little traffic and no hawkers – but the beach is scruffy in parts and it is isolated from the 'action' in Kuta.

Information
Tourist Offices The helpful Badung Tourist Office (☎ 75 6176) is responsible for Kuta, Nusa Dua and the Bukit Peninsula (but not for Sanur). The Bali Tourist Office (☎ 75 4090) is responsible for the whole of the island, but is not worth trying to find. Avoid any place which purports to be a 'Tourist Information Centre' – they are just travel agents.

Money The plethora of moneychangers are faster, more efficient and open longer hours than banks. Moneychangers also offer far better exchange rates, which are advertised on billboards outside. But shop around, because the rates do vary enormously.

Most banks along Jalan Legian and around Kuta Square shopping centre provide cash advances. There are ATMs at banks and shops at Kuta Square, and at the airport.

Post & Communications The small main post office has a sort-it-yourself poste restante service. This is the best place to post any large packages back home. Other postal agents, which can send, but not receive, mail, are indicated on the relevant maps. There are wartels about every 100m or so along the main roads.

There are also three Internet centres: Bali@ Cyber Cafe & Restaurant (bi-cafe1@idola. net.id); Legian Cyber Cafe (cyleg1@ idola.net. id); and Kambodja (kambodiana @denpasar. wasantara.net.id).

Medical Services Of the several clinics in the Kuta region, the most accessible is the Legian Medical Clinic (☎ 75 8503). It operates 24 hours a day, offers an ambulance service and dentists, and will call at your hotel.

Activities
There is an incredible range of things to do on Bali – none is typically Balinese or Indonesian, but they're great fun anyway. From the Kuta region you can go surfing or diving, or arrange water sports, rafting, fishing trips or cruises anywhere on Bali, not to mention the crazy adrenaline rides such as bungy, slingshot and so on. The best idea is to pick up some brochures at a travel agency, where you can book everything, and talk to other travellers.

For the kids, visit the pool and slides at Waterbom Park; Timezone video arcades at the two Matahari shopping centres; or try the go-karts at Le Speed Karts.

Places to Stay
Tuban, Kuta, Legian and Seminyak have hundreds of places to stay, so it's impossible to list them all. Listed here are places with some character and tranquillity – at a good price. If the first place you visit is unappealing or overpriced, there will always be several more suitable places nearby.

Most budget places have a private bathroom with a cold water mandi or shower, and

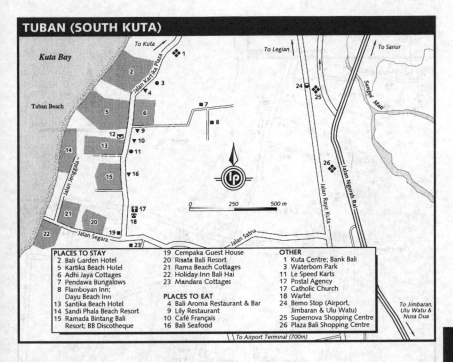

TUBAN (SOUTH KUTA)

PLACES TO STAY
2 Bali Garden Hotel
5 Kartika Beach Hotel
6 Adhi Jaya Cottages
7 Pendawa Bungalows
8 Flamboyan Inn;
   Dayu Beach Inn
13 Santika Beach Hotel
14 Sandi Phala Beach Resort
15 Ramada Bintang Bali
   Resort; BB Discotheque

19 Cempaka Guest House
20 Risata Bali Resort
21 Rama Beach Cottages
22 Holiday Inn Bali Hai
23 Mandara Cottages

PLACES TO EAT
4 Bali Aroma Restaurant & Bar
9 Lily Restaurant
10 Café Français
16 Bali Seafood

OTHER
1 Kuta Centre; Bank Bali
3 Waterbom Park
11 Le Speed Karts
12 Postal Agency
17 Catholic Church
18 Wartel
24 Bemo Stop (Airport,
   Jimbaran & Ulu Watu)
25 Supernova Shopping Centre
26 Plaza Bali Shopping Centre

To Jimbaran,
Ulu Watu &
Nusa Dua

To Airport Terminal (700m)

a fan, and cost from 15,000/20,000 rp for a single/double. If you can live with a fan and cold water, it may be worth paying more (perhaps double), and stay in the cheaper 'standard' or 'economy' rooms at a mid-range place, so you can enjoy the gardens and swimming pool. Beware of throwaway words like 'beach', 'seaview', 'cottage', 'bungalows' and 'inn'. There's a 10% government tax on all accommodation. Cheaper places normally include this in the price, but check first. More expensive places add the tax to your bill, as well as an individual service charge of 5 or 15%.

Most travellers stay for a few days (or much longer), so you should always ask for a discount for a longer stay. In the off-season (November to April), discounts of 50% are not uncommon, so if you normally look for somewhere in the budget range, don't be afraid of checking out somewhere in the mid-range and asking for a substantial discount.

Places to Stay – Budget
South Kuta A number of cheap places are south and/or west of Bemo Corner. Rooms away from the road aren't too noisy.

Bamboo Inn (☎ 75 1935), a traditional little losmen, is quiet and friendly but often full. Simple rooms cost 25,000 rp.

Zet Inn (☎ 75 3135) lacks some character, but is reasonable with singles/doubles for 25,000/35,000 rp, up to 60,000/70,000 rp with air-con.

Central Kuta The quiet alleys and lanes between southern Jalan Legian and the beach is the most popular place to base yourself.

Pleasant singles/doubles at secluded *Bali Sandy Cottages* (☎ 75 3344), in one of the last coconut plantations in Kuta, are good value for 35,000/50,000 rp.

This no-frills *Jus Edith* charges a no-frills 15,000/20,000 rp, but some rooms are better than others.

Kempu Taman Ayu (☎ 75 1855) is a long-running and friendly little place with rooms for 16,000/25,000 rp, though they are not particularly private.

Komala Indah I (☎ 75 1422) is basic, clean and great value considering the location: 15,000 rp for a room with a squat toilet and mandi. *Komala Indah II* (☎ 75 4258) is a little gem. Set in the type of fields and

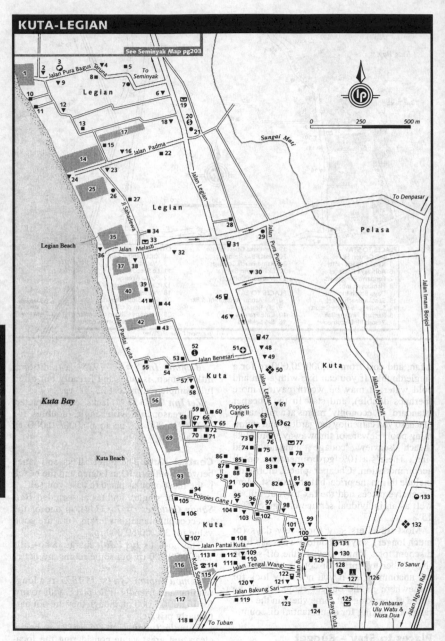

KUTA-LEGIAN

See Seminyak Map pg203

To Seminyak

Legian

Jalan Pura Bagus Taruna

0   250   500 m

Sungai Mati

To Denpasar

Legian

Pelasa

Jalan Legian

Jalan Pura Puseh

Legian Beach

Jalan Melasti

Jalan Sahadeva

Jalan Padma

Kuta

Jalan Benesari

Kuta

Kuta Bay

Poppies Gang II

Kuta Beach

Poppies Gang I

Kuta

Jalan Pantai Kuta

Jalan Bung Sari

To Sanur

Jalan Tengal Wangi

Kuta Square

Jalan Bakung Sari

Jalan Raya Kuta

To Jimbaran
Ulu Watu &
Nusa Dua

Jalan Ngurah Rai

To Tuban

Jalan Imam Bonjol

Jalan Majapahit

PLACES TO STAY
1   Hotel Jayakarta
5   Losmen Made Beach Inn;
     Bamboo Palace
8   Baleka Beach Hotel
10 Puri Tantra Beach
     Bungalows
11 Bali Kelapa Hotel
13 Sinar Indah;
     Bali Sani Hotel
14 Bali Padma Hotel
15 Garden View Cottages;
     Bank Bali
17 Three Brothers Inn
22 Legian Beach Bungalows
25 Bali Mandira
27 Suri Wathi Beach House
28 Surfers Paradise
34 Sorga Beach Inn
35 Legian Beach Hotel
37 Bali Intan Legian
39 Adus Beach Inn
40 Resort Kul Kul
41 Hotel Camplung Mas
     (Ocean Blue)
42 Hotel Kuta Jaya
43 Sayang Beach
     Lodging & Restaurant
44 Hotel Puri Tanahlot
53 Kuta Bungalows
54 Un's Hotel
55 Komala Indah II &
     Restaurant
56 Hotel Istana Rama
59 Suka Beach Inn
60 Bali Dwipa;
     Bali Duta Wisata
68 Bounty Hotel
69 Hotel Sahid Bali
70 Poppies Cottages II
71 Bali Sandy Cottages
72 Hotel Barong
74 Ronta Bungalows
     & Warung
75 Jus Edith
78 Sri Kusuma Hotel
     & Bungalows
80 Penginapan Maha
     Bharata
83 Paradiso Beach Inn
85 Sari Bali Bungalows
86 Sorga Cottages
87 Mimpi Bungalows
88 Suji Bungalow
89 Puri Ayodia Inn
90 Kempu Taman Ayu
91 Rita's House
92 Berlian Inn
93 Hotel Kuta Segara Ceria;
     Kuta Seaview Restaurant
94 Kuta Puri Bungalows;
     Coffee Shop

97   Komala Indah I
102 Poppies Cottages I
104 La Walon Bungalows;
      Masa Inn
105 Sari Yasa Samudra
      Bungalows; Coffee Shop
106 Hotel Aneka Kuta
108 Budi Beach Inn
110 Ida Beach Inn
111 Asana Santhi Homestay
      (Willy I)
112 Kuta Suci Bungalows
113 Yulia Beach Inn
116 Natour Kuta Beach
118 Melasti Bungalows;
      Karthi Inn
119 Hotel Ramayana
124 Bamboo Inn; Zet Inn;
      Jensen's Inn II

PLACES TO EAT
2   Topi Koki Restaurant;
     Bank Bali
4   Rum Jungle Road Bar &
     Restaurant
6   Glory Bar & Restaurant
9   Thai Restaurant,
     Bar & Bakery
12 Poco Loco
16 Joni Sunken Bar &
     Restaurant
18 Warung Kopi
23 Rama Garden Restaurant
24 Surya Cafe & Beach Bar
30 Yanie's
32 Orchid Garden Restaurant
36 Karang Mas Cafe
38 Taman Garden; Legian
     Garden Restaurant;
     Restaurant Puri Bali Indah
46 Aroma's Cafe
48 Mama Luccia Italian
     Restaurant
49 Gemini
57 Brasil Bali Restaurant
61 Mama's German Restaurant;
     Norm's Sports Bar; Lips
64 Batu Bulong
65 Twice Pub
66 Warung 96; Warung Dewi;
     The Corner Restaurant
67 Warung Nanas;
     Warung Ziro
79 Bounty II; Game Fantasia
81 Aquarius Bar & Restaurant
84 Mini Restaurant;
     Expresso Bar & Pizzeria
95 Nusa Indah Bar &
     Restaurant
96 TJ's; Bamboo Corner; Bali Asi
98 Poppies Restaurant
99 Sushi Bar Kunti

101 Made's Warung
103 Fat Yogi's
109 Lenny's Seafood;
      The Bookshop
120 Dayu I
121 Bali Aget
123 Agung Café;
      Agung Supermarket
126 Night Market

BARS & NIGHTCLUBS
31   Peanuts
45   Bounty Restaurant I
47   001 Club
63   SC (Sari Club)
73   Tubes Cafe
76   The Maccaroni Club
107 Hard Rock Cafe &
      Hard Rock Beach Club
122 The Pub
129 Casablanca Bar

OTHER
3   Swiss & Austrian Consular
      Agents; Swiss Restaurant
7   Bali@Cyber Cafe &
      Restaurant
19   Postal Agency
20   ATM Machines
21   The Bookstore
26   Legian Cyber Cafe
29   Bali Bungy
33   Postal Agent; Art Market
50   Matahari Department Store;
      Timezone; McDonald's;
      Cinema
51   Legian Medical Clinic;
      Subway Restaurant
52   Bali Tourist Office
58   Adrenalin Park
62   Bank Panir
77   Postal Agency
82   Perama Office
100 Bemo Corner
114 Kambodja Wartel &
      Internet Centre
115 Kuta Square; Matahari
      Department Store;
      McDonald's; KFC;
      Timezone; Banks
117 Kuta Art Market;
      Artists Cafe
125 Main Post Office
127 Chinese Temple
128 Badung Tourist Office;
      Police Station
130 Public Market
131 BCI Bank
132 Galeal de Wata Shopping
      Centre; KFC
133 Bemos to Nusa Dua;
      Petrol Station

INDONESIA

coconut palms that typified Kuta only thirty years ago, rooms are a bargain at 15,000/20,000 rp.

The friendly and central *Masa Inn* (☎ 75 8507) is very good value, so it's often full. The pool is an attraction, and rooms are cheap for 24,000/27,000 rp.

Down the end of a laneway, the very quiet *Penginapan Maha Bharata* (☎ 75 6754) is recommended. Large, pleasant rooms cost 20,000/25,000 rp.

Puri Ayodia Inn is a small, standard losmen in a quiet, convenient location, and is cheap for 15,000/20,000 rp. Another small losmen, *Rita's House* (☎ 75 1760) is not fancy for 20,000/25,000 rp, but continues to get rave reviews from long-stay travellers.

Ronta Bungalows (☎ 75 4246) provides good, clean accommodation, with a nice garden and central location, so is often full. At 15,000/20,000 rp, it's not hard to understand why.

Another popular place, and better than others in the immediate area is *Suka Beach Inn* (☎ 75 2793). Rooms cost a bargain 15,000/20,000 rp.

Legian Legian is a good alternative to Kuta. The new, family-run *Adus Beach Inn* (☎ 75 5326) is quiet and spotlessly clean; singles/doubles are 25,000/30,000 rp.

Sorga Beach Inn (☎ 75 1609) is good value in a nice area, with rooms for 15,000/20,000 rp. The garden is shady, but the crickets will probably keep you awake at night.

Surfers Paradise (☎ 75 1103) is a quiet 'bed & breakfast' in a pleasant setting, though the rooms for 30,000/35,000 rp could do with some renovation.

The unassuming *Losmen Made Beach Inn* (☎ 75 2127) is excellent value in this neck of the woods, with rooms going for 35,000 rp.

Seminyak For something a little quieter and less-developed, head for Seminyak where you will find the small and friendly *Kesuma Sari Beach Bungalows* (☎ 73 0575) tucked away, with its character-filled rooms for 45,000 rp; the excellent *Mesari Beach Inn* (☎ 75 1401) which has quiet rooms for 20,000/25,000 rp, and charming bungalows for 50,000 rp; and *Puri Mangga Bungalows* (☎ 73 0447), a pleasant place with rooms with hot water and fans, and a manager who is usually willing to negotiate down to 25,000 rp per room.

Places to Stay – Mid-Range

Prices quoted in US dollars are normally negotiable; discounts up to 50% are often possible in the low season. Most rooms have air-con, though not necessarily hot water, and most hotels have swimming pools. The small selection of better places mentioned here are in geographical order; from north to south.

Bali Kelapa Hotel (☎ 75 4167) is one of the best value places in the area. It is friendly and central, and rooms cost 80,000 rp.

The quiet and friendly *Suri Wathi Beach House* (☎ 75 3162) has singles/doubles for US$8/10, or US$12 for a bungalow.

Hotel Puri Tanahlot (☎ 75 2281) has quiet, stylish bungalows, set around a pleasant garden and pool. Rates are negotiable: from US$8/10 to US$25/30.

One of the best in Kuta, *Un's Hotel* (☎ 75 7409) is tucked away, and often neglected. It boasts plenty of foliage with prices from US$17/20 to US$22/30 with air-con. Next is *Sari Bali Bungalows* (☎ 75 3065) where nice bungalows in a spacious garden with a great pool range from 50,000/70,000 rp to 100,000/120,000 rp with air-con. Then there's *Berlian Inn* (☎ 75 1701) which, as the business card says, is 'nice & realy (sic) quiet'. It's also central and realy good value: from US$8/10 to US$22/27.

In an excellent location, *Sari Yasa Samudra Bungalows* (☎ 75 1562) has rooms for US$24/27, and US$42/48 with air-con, fridge and private balcony.

At *Ida Beach Inn* (☎ 75 1205) rooms (US$30/33) are clustered together, but the it's quiet, and has a nice garden – though it's a little hard to find down a laneway.

Yulia Beach Inn (☎ 75 1893) is long-standing place which is still friendly, quiet and central. Basic rooms start at US$7/10, but for a bungalow with hot water, you'll pay US$20/25.

One of several places with good rooms and a quiet location, close to the beach is *Pendawa Bungalows* (☎ 75 2387). It has a spacious garden, and rooms from US$19/23 to US$48/58.

Places to Eat

There are countless places to eat around the Kuta region, from tiny hawker's carts to gourmet hotel restaurants to well-known fast food outlets. The cuisine is international and multicultural – you could stay in Kuta for a month, eat in a different place for every meal and never have to confront so much as a nasi goreng.

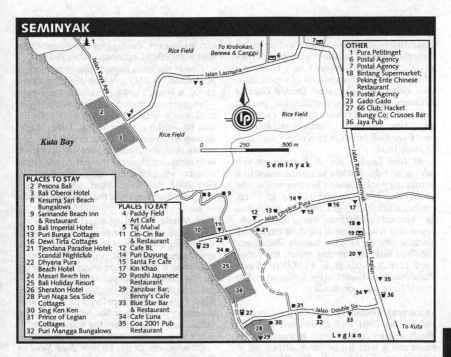

SEMINYAK

Rice Field

To Krokoban,
Berewa & Canggu

Jalan Lasmana

Kuta Bay

Rice Field

Seminyak

0   250   500 m

Legian

To Kuta

OTHER
1 Pura Petitinget
6 Postal Agency
7 Postal Agency
18 Bintang Supermarket;
    Peking Ente Chinese
    Restaurant
19 Postal Agency
23 Gado Gado
27 66 Club; Hacket
    Bungy Co; Crusoes Bar
36 Jaya Pub

PLACES TO STAY
2 Pesona Bali
3 Bali Oberoi Hotel
8 Kesuma Sari Beach
   Bungalows
9 Sarinande Beach Inn
   & Restaurant
10 Bali Imperial Hotel
13 Puri Bunga Cottages
16 Dewi Tirta Cottages
21 Tjendana Paradise Hotel;
   Scandal Nightclub
22 Dhyana Pura
   Beach Hotel
24 Mesari Beach Inn
25 Bali Holiday Resort
26 Sheraton Hotel
28 Puri Naga Sea Side
   Cottages
30 Sing Ken Ken
31 Prince of Legian
   Cottages
32 Puri Mangga Bungalows

PLACES TO EAT
4 Paddy Field
  Art Cafe
5 Taj Mahal
11 Cin-Cin Bar
   & Restaurant
12 Cafe BL
14 Puri Duyung
15 Santa Fe Cafe
17 Kin Khao
20 Ryoshi Japanese
   Restaurant
29 Zanzibar;
   Benny's Cafe
33 Blue Star Bar
   & Restaurant
34 Cafe Luna
35 Goa 2001 Pub
   Restaurant

If you want to eat cheaply, try the places that cater to local workers. There are *food stalls* in the afternoon along Legian Beach, and opposite the Hard Rock Cafe in Kuta. There are also *warung* at the night market near the post office. You can buy food from local supermarkets (the largest are in the two Matahari shopping centres), and from the markets.

Kuta Poppies Gang I, a tiny lane between Jalan Legian and the beach, is named for *Poppies Restaurant*, one of the oldest and most popular in Kuta. The prices are quite high and the food is well prepared and presented, but it seems to survive on reputation alone these days. *TJ's* is a deservedly popular Mexican restaurant, with good ambience, and main courses from 15,000 rp. In the same area, *Made's Warung* is popular, with meals from 10,000 rp to 15,000 rp; and *Nusa Indah Bar & Restaurant* is excellent for seafood at a very reasonable 6000 rp, in a friendly atmosphere.

Bamboo Corner is quaint and a good place to try seafood specials (about 7000 rp). The service is friendly at *Bali Asi*, where lunchtime pizzas only cost 5000 rp.

Poppies Gang II has a lot of cheap eateries, like the popular *Batu Bulong*; *Warung Nanas*, with a very happy hour and specials from 4500 rp to 9000 rp; and *Warung Ziro*, which has daily specials for 6000 rp to 7000 rp. Nearby, *Brasil Bali Restaurant* is one of the best, with a wide range of meals at excellent prices, and permanently cheap drinks.

Other recommended and popular places include *Warung 96*, *Warung Dewi* and *The Corner Restaurant*.

There are almost endless possibilities along Jalan Legian. *Sushi Bar Kunti* has a Japanese set menu for 25,000 rp. *Mini Restaurant*, a huge place despite the name, serves Chinese dishes for 12,000 rp. *Expresso Bar & Pizzeria* has pizzas for 13,250 rp in a pleasant setting. *Gemini* continues to get good reviews for Chinese food, despite its bare appearance. For something completely different, visit the incongruous *Bounty II*, a replica of the famous ship, where you can enjoy a good-value buffet for 30,000 rp. *Aroma's Cafe* is a mid-priced vegetarian restaurant with good food and a delightful garden setting. *Mama Lucia Italian Restaurant* is classy, but expensive at 15,000 rp to 22,000 rp a dish. Several travellers have also recommended *Aquarius Bar & Restaurant*.

INDONESIA

Legian *Warung Kopi* is well regarded for its varied menu of European, Asian and vegetarian dishes, good breakfasts and tempting desserts. *Taman Garden* is very popular for its delicious meals, decent happy hours and effusive staff – it attracts a lot of repeat business. Other good places are *Orchid Garden Restaurant*, which is popular, but pricey; *Legian Garden Restaurant*, with excellent happy hours and cheap breakfasts; and *Restaurant Puri Bali Indah*, which offers excellent Chinese food.

At *Joni Sunken Bar & Restaurant* you can eat and drink while semi-immersed in a swimming pool. It also offers live music, and good-value buffet breakfasts for 8500 rp. Further north, things get more expensive but the standards are higher – this is the fashionable end of town. Some of the most interesting places are the Mexican restaurant, *Poco Loco* and *Topi Koki Restaurant*, which has pretty good French meals from 15,000 rp. *Swiss Restaurant* is adjacent to the Swiss consul so should have some credibility.

Seminyak Restaurants here are good, but not cheap. *Goa 2001 Pub Restaurant* is where trendy expats choose from a multicultural menu and a long list of fancy drinks, all at fancy prices. Further north, *Kin Khao* serves Thai food. Nearby, there are several *warung* serving cheap and tasty Indonesian fare.

Along Jalan Dhyana Pura, *Santa Fe Cafe* is a pretty – and pretty expensive – option for US south-western dishes; and *Puri Duyung* is also classy but pricey. *Cin-Cin Bar & Restaurant* has sensible prices for this part of Seminyak. On the beachfront, you can enjoy the splendid location of *Zanzibar Bar*, which also serves meals; and *Benny's Cafe*, a great place for breakfast, and to watch the sun set at the end of a 'hard day'. For something a little different, share a drink with some mock Easter Island statues at *Crusoes Bar*.

Entertainment

Around 6 pm, the sunset at the beach is the big attraction, perhaps with a drink at one of the beach bars. After a good dinner, many visitors are happy with a video movie, another drink or a stroll in the cool evening air. But a lot of people are here to party, and in the Kuta region that means lots of drinking, loud music and late nights.

Bars, Clubs, Nightclubs & Discos Bars are usually free to enter, and often have special drink promotions and 'happy hours' between about 6 and 9 pm – sometimes longer. For the serious drinker, the biggest concentration of bars is on Jalan Legian and Jalan Padma.

One of the most popular places to party is *Sari Club* (or 'SC'), which features dance music, a young crowd and lots of local guys – but prices are high. Surfers drink beer, play pool, watch surfing videos and work out what will be working tomorrow at *Tubes Cafe*. *Bounty Restaurant I* is built in the shape of a sailing ship, and is easy to spot. It packs them onto the dance floor till the wee hours. Other well-known happening places are *Peanuts*, *Goa 2001 Pub Restaurant*, *66 Club* (pronounced 'double six') or the chic *Gado Gado*.

Live Music To find out what is going on and where, ask around, or read the advertising signs along the streets. One of the newest and most extraordinary places is *The Maccaroni Club*, which features jazz every night, except Sunday, from 10.30 pm, and even invites guests to jam on Friday nights. The new *Hard Rock Cafe* is very popular, with live music and pricey drinks. *Zero Six*, near the beach in Tuban, sometimes offers the unusual combination of rock bands and Balinese dancing.

Other places to try, include *Joni Sunken Bar & Restaurant*, and the Aussie-style 'pubs' along Jalan Melasti. Most upmarket hotels, such as Bali Padma Hotel on Legian Beach, have more laid-back pianists and singers.

Balinese Dance Large hotels and restaurants put on tourist versions of the best known Balinese dances, and these are generally well publicised. At places like Bali Padma in Legian, Ritz-Carlton at Jimbaran on Bukit Peninsula and Kartika Beach Hotel in Tuban they are usually included in a set menu, up to US$25 per head.

Travel agents also arrange evening trips to dances at Bona, Batubulan and Denpasar, usually charging from around 25,000 rp, including transport and ticket. There are also a few dances every evening at nearby Sanur; and a Ramayana ballet at the Taman Festival Bali, near Sanur. Enchanting dances are also held at Ulu Watu – refer to the Bukit Peninsula section following.

Shopping

Parts of the Kuta region are now almost door-to-door shops and over the years these have become steadily more sophisticated, but there are still many simple stalls where T-shirts and beach-wear are the main lines. Often these are crowded together in 'art markets' like the ones at the beach end of Jalan Bakung Sari and on Jalan Melasti. Many shops come and go, so recommending any particular place is not worthwhile.

Don't be pressured into buying things during the first few days of your stay – shop around for quality and price first. Hawkers on the beach and the street ask astronomical prices at first, so you have to haggle like hell. You should also bargain at small stalls and shops. In bigger, more established shops, the 'first price' is more realistic and less negotiable. In shops with marked prices, that's it.

Beware of imitations; you can buy name-brand everything here, but most of it is locally made copies – with local prices and local quality. Much of the leather – belts and bags – at the many shops is actually plastic, but you need to look very hard to pick it.

Getting There & Away
Public Bus Lots of travel agents sell bus tickets to Java, Lombok and Sumbawa, though these are normally the same buses that leave Ubung terminal in Denpasar.

Shuttle Bus Tourist shuttle buses regularly travel between The Kuta region and all tourist centres on Bali, as well as to Lombok. They are convenient, and save you the hassle of catching one or more bemos through Denpasar to your destination. Perama (☎ 75 1551) is the best-known operator, but other shuttle bus companies, such as Simpatik (☎ 75 5814), may have more convenient departure times. You can buy tickets at any of the hundreds of shops-cum-travel agencies.

Bemo Public bemos regularly travel between the Kuta region and Tegal terminal in Denpasar. The fare is about 500 rp, but tourists are often charged a little more. Public bemos may not stop for you along Jalan Legian, so you'll have to go to Jalan Pantai Kuta, east of Bemo Corner – there are no official stops. You may be able to get on a southbound bemo from there to the airport, Jimbaran or Ulu Watu. For all other destinations, you'll have to go to Tegal terminal, and then catch another bemo, probably at another Denpasar terminal.

Getting Around
The Kuta region is *very* spread out. The only local bemo route goes west and north along Jalan Pantai Kuta, east on Jalan Melasti and south on Jalan Legian. The fare is 400 rp, but you will normally be overcharged. Otherwise, it is easy enough to flag down a taxi, but look for one that uses a meter. There are dozens and dozens of places to rent cars and motorbikes, and prices are very competitive. A few places rent bicycles, but the traffic and one-way streets will put off most potential cyclists.

BUKIT PENINSULA
The southern peninsula, often simply known as Bukit (hill), is very dry and quite sparsely populated, but is slated for major tourism development. Just south of the airport, **Jimbaran Bay** is a superb crescent of white sand and blue sea, with a colourful fishing fleet and a few luxury hotels. Beachside *restaurants* do wonderful barbecued seafood every evening for around 15,000 rp. The only place resembling budget accommodation, *Puri Indra Prasta* (☎ 70 1544), is uninspiring, noisy and overpriced, but has a swimming pool. Try to bargain them down from 60,000/ 125,000 rp for a room with a fan/air-con.

A sealed road goes south from Jimbaran to **Pura Luhur Ulu Watu**, where an important temple perches at the tip of the peninsula, and sheer cliffs drop into the sea. Enchanting Kecak dances (7000 rp) are held here at sunset on Wednesday and Saturday. Just before the temple car park, a sign points to **Pantai Suluban**, famous for its great surf.

Nusa Dua
Nusa Dua is Bali's most expensive beach resort – a luxury enclave for tourists who want to experience Bali in very small and sanitised doses, if at all. There's a ritzy shopping centre, and a consistent right-hand surf break on the reef. The nearest thing to budget accommodation is at Tanjung Benoa (see the following entry for details). Infrequent, tourist-riced bemos (2300 rp) go directly to Nusa Dua from Batubulan terminal near Denpasar. It will probably be easier to take a taxi.

Tanjung Benoa
Benoa peninsula is the cheap alternative to Nusa Dua. It is a wonderful, laid-back area for diving and snorkelling, and plenty of dive centres offer expensive parasailing, jet-skiing and water-skiing. You can also hire a speed boat, and cruise on glass-bottom boats. All activities can be booked directly, or through your hotel or any travel agency in south Bali.

Places to Stay & Eat Near the end of the peninsular, there are four good places, all next to each other. *Pondok Agung (☎ 77 1143)* charges US$20 for a room with a fan, hot water and TV, and there's a swimming pool. *Tanjung Mekar (☎ 77 2063)* is a small guesthouse with nice rooms for 30,000 rp. *Rasa Dua (☎ 77 3515)* advertises a few rooms for 35,000 rp. *Pondok Wisata Hasan (☎ 77 2456)* is another friendly, quiet place. Rooms with hot water cost 30,000/60,000 rp with fan/air-con.

There are several nice beachfront restaurants in Benoa village, such as *Mini Restaurant* and *Mina Garden*. For something really classy, *Beluga Marine* has meals for about 15,000 rp, which is not outrageous considering the decor and location. *Cafe Bagus* is away from the beach, but pretty cheap – the 6000 rp buffet breakfast is great value. *Rumah Makan Padma* has sensible prices (about 10,000 rp for seafood), and a menu in German. Cheaper *warung* around the entrances to the resorts cater to local hotel staff, and offer the best value for money.

Getting There & Away Bemos run from Tegal terminal in Denpasar, via Kuta, to the terminal in Bualu village (500 rp), north of Nusa Dua. From there, green bemos go up the Tanjung Benoa road, though not very often. It may be easier to take a taxi.

SANUR

Sanur is an upmarket alternative to Kuta for those coming to Bali for sea, sand and sun, and a down-market alternative to Nusa Dua for those who want a holiday in an air-conditioned hotel with a swimming pool. The beach is wide and white, and sheltered by a reef, but at low tide it's very shallow. Sanur doesn't have the noise, confusion and traffic of Kuta, and you're not constantly badgered to buy things – badgered yes, but not constantly. The nightlife is sedate by comparison, but you can always go over to Kuta for a wild night.

American Express and most airlines are based at the huge Grand Bali Beach Hotel. Nearby is the uninteresting **Museum Le Mayeur**. Most restaurants and hotels are dotted along the main road, Jalan Danau Tamblingan.

Places to Stay

The three cheapest places are huddled together, and behind little art shops along the main road: *Yulia Homestay (☎ 28 8089)*, *Luisa Homestay (☎ 28 9673)* and *Coco Homestay (☎ 28 7391)*. In all three, the atmosphere is friendly, but the rooms for about 25,000 rp each are noisy and not great value. Nearby, the best in this range is *Keke Homestay (☎ 28 7282)*, run by a friendly family. The rooms are quiet, clean and cost 30,000/40,000 rp for singles/doubles.

Just off the main road, *Bali Wirasana (☎ 28 8632)* is also good value for 20,000/40,000 rp, or 60,000 rp with air-con.

All mid-range places have hot water, and air-conditioning, though most have cheaper rooms with fans and cold water. Any place charging US dollars will probably have a swimming pool, but, remember, you will be only a few minutes' walk from a glorious beach.

Opposite the Grand Bali Beach Hotel entrance, *Watering Hole Homestay (☎ 28 8289)* has clean and pleasant rooms for 50,000/80,000 rp with fan/air-con, and 100,000 rp for a large, family-sized room.

At the end of the same road, *Ananda Hotel (☎ 28 8327)* is charming, and has clean and quiet singles/doubles for 40,000/50,000 rp. It is handy if you're catching a boat to Nusa Lembongan.

Along the southern end of the main road, *Penginapan Lestari (☎ 28 8867)* has rooms for 50,000/75,000 rp with fan/air-con; and *Penginapan Jati (☎ 28 9157)* has friendly staff, and good rooms for US$15. Most of the other hotels in Sanur are expensive, and cater almost exclusively to people on packaged tours.

Places to Eat

The cheapest places to grab a meal are the *food stalls* and *warung* at the beach end of Jalan Segara Ayu, or around the Pasar Sindhu night market.

One of the best hotel restaurants is at *Queen Bali Hotel*, on Jalan Pantai Sindhu. Western dishes cost 9500 rp to 12,000 rp, but Chinese and Indonesian meals are a lot less. Opposite, *Kalimantan Bar & Restaurant* (also called the *Borneo*) has main dishes for about 12,000 rp in a tranquil, shady setting.

Just around the corner, *Bali Hai Bar & Restaurant* has meals from 9000 rp to 11,000 rp, and the three-course set menus for about 19,000 rp are very tempting. Nearby, *Puri Mango Guest House* has a restaurant which serves pizzas for 10,000 rp; and good-value three-course menus for about 19,000 rp.

Along the northern end of Jalan Danau Tamblingan, *Warung Wina* (aka *Vienna Cafe*) has good prices, and will appeal to German-speakers; *Kuri Putih* has reasonably priced 'mexi-bali' food for lunch; and *Taman Bayu* has main courses for about 15,000 rp, and Balinese dancing most nights.

Other good places to try include: *Warung Balisun*, popular for sensible prices in a friendly atmosphere; *Warung Agung*; and *Made's Kitchen*, a charming and cheap place for snacks and drinks. Most of the walkway along central Sanur is cluttered with cafes and restaurants, such as *Mango Bar & Restaurant*, *Benno's Corner Cafe* and *Sanur Beach Market Bar & Restaurant*, which is not bad value, and very popular.

Entertainment

Traditional Balinese dancing is held in tourist restaurants and upmarket hotels most nights – check out the advertising outside the premises. Sports fans may want to check out *Bali International Sports Club* on Jalan Kesumasari.

Rumours Nightclub on Jalan Pantai Sindhu probably attracts the biggest dance crowd, mainly tourists plus some local beach boys. The slick *Bali Janger* disco on northern Jalan Danau Tamblingan is also popular with Denpasar yuppies and tourists. For live reggae, try the *Puri Mango Guest House*.

Getting There & Away

There is a bemo stop at the southern end of town, near where Jalan Danau Tamblingan rejoins the Bypass road; and another stop outside the entrance to the Grand Bali Beach. Blue bemos go through the Renon area in Denpasar and across town to Tegal terminal (change here for a Kuta-bound bemo). The green bemos usually go through the eastern outskirts straight to the Kereneng terminal in Denpasar.

Perama, and a few other shuttle bus services, link Sanur with Ubud (5000 rp) and Kuta (5000 rp), as well as other tourist centres on Bali. Book a ticket at any shop-cum-travel agency in the main part of Sanur, or at the Perama office opposite the entrance to the Grand Bali Beach.

UBUD

In the hills north of Denpasar, Ubud is the centre of 'cultural tourism' on Bali. Recently it has developed as fast as the beach resorts, and now has traffic problems in the centre and urban sprawl on the edges. However, it is still a wonderful place to see Balinese arts, handicrafts, dance and music, and it boasts the best restaurants on Bali. Many visitors come for a few days, and end up staying much longer.

Orientation & Information

The once small village of Ubud has expanded to encompass its neighbours – Campuan, Penestanan, Padangtegal, Peliatan and Pengosekan are all part of what we see as Ubud today. The centre of town is the crossroads where the market is located. The friendly tourist office is worth visiting. The post office has a poste restante service, and there are several wartels and Internet centres.

All major banks are represented in central Ubud, and most will change money, and some, such as Bank Bali, give cash advances. However, the dozens of moneychangers along the main streets offer better rates and a quicker service than the banks. The Ubud Clinic (☎ 97 4911; mobile 081 139 6069) is well equipped.

If you are going to spend some time in Ubud, it is worth buying a detailed map at Ary's Bookshop or one of the other bookshops nearby. The best maps for walking around Ubud are Travel Treasure's *Ubud Surroundings* and the *Bali Pathfinder*.

Things to See & Do

The **Museum Puri Lukisan**, in the middle of town, displays fine examples of all schools of Balinese art. The superb **Neka Museum**, in Campuan, has modern Balinese art and fine pieces by western artists who have worked on Bali. Both museums are open daily, and tickets cost 5000 rp. There are also many commercial galleries, but **Neka Gallery** on Jalan Raya and **Agung Rai Gallery** in Peliatan are some of the largest and most important.

The home of the late Gusti Nyoman Lempad, a pioneering Balinese artist, is also a **gallery**, and worth a visit. **Antonio Blanco's home** is also open to visitors (3500 rp). The home of Walter Spies, an influential German artist from the 1930s, is now one of the rooms at Hotel Tjampuhan. The work of Dutch painter Han Snel can be seen in his restaurant.

The **Monkey Forest Sanctuary** in Ubud's south has monkeys which provide entertainment, demand peanuts, and snatch purses, cameras and sunglasses. It is open every day and tickets cost 1100 rp. Other interesting

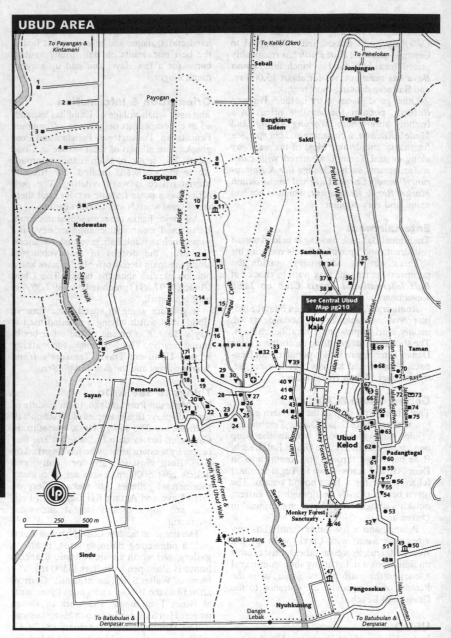

UBUD AREA

To Payangan &
Kintamani

To Keliki (2km)

To Penelokan

Sebali

Junjungan

Payogan

Bangkiang
Sidem

Tegallantang

Sakti

Sanggingan

Kedewatan

Penestanan & Sayan Walk

Campuan Ridge Walk

Sungai Cerik

Sungai Blangsuh

Sungai Ayung

Sungai Wos

Petulu Walk

Sambahan

Ubud
Kaja

See Central Ubud
Map pg210

Jalan Suweta

Jalan Srewedari

Taman

Jalan Sandat

Campuan

Sayan

Penestanan

Monkey Forest &
South West Ubud Walk

Jalan Bisma

Jalan Dewi Sita

Monkey Forest Road

Jalan Hanoman

Raya

Jalan Suqriwa

Jalan Jembawan

Ubud
Kelod

Padangtegal

Sindu

Katik Lantang

Monkey Forest
Sanctuary

Nyuhkuning

Pengosekan

Jalan Hanoman

Dangin
Lebak

To Batubulan &
Denpasar

To Batubulan &
Denpasar

0   250   500 m

INDONESIA

UBUD AREA

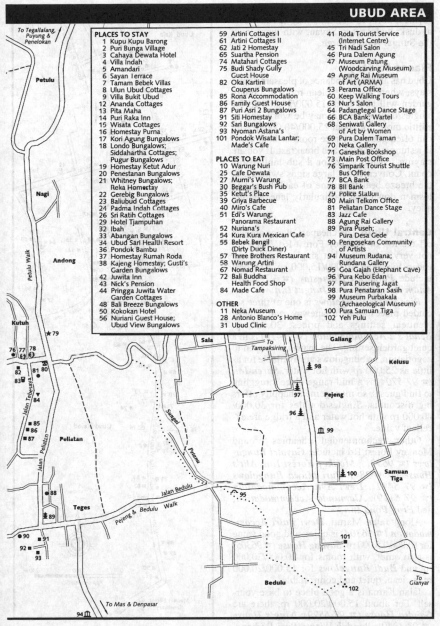

To Tegallalang, Puyung & Penelokan

Petulu

Nagi

Andong

Petulu Walk

Kutuh

★79

Jalan Tebesaya

Peliatan

Jalan Peliatan

Teges

PLACES TO STAY
1 Kupu Kupu Barong
2 Puri Bunga Village
3 Cahaya Dewata Hotel
4 Villa Indah
5 Amandari
6 Sayan Terrace
7 Taman Bebek Villas
8 Ulun Ubud Cottages
9 Villa Bukit Ubud
12 Ananda Cottages
13 Pita Maha
14 Puri Raka Inn
15 Wisata Cottages
16 Homestay Purna
17 Kori Agung Bungalows
18 Londo Bungalows;
   Siddhartha Cottages;
   Pugur Bungalows
19 Homestay Ketut Adur
20 Penestanan Bungalows
21 Whitney Bungalows;
   Reka Homestay
22 Gerebig Bungalows
23 Baliubud Cottages
24 Padma Indah Cottages
26 Sri Ratih Cottages
29 Hotel Tjampuhan
32 Ibah
33 Abangan Bungalows
34 Ubud Sari Health Resort
36 Pondok Bambu
37 Homestay Rumah Roda
38 Kajeng Homestay; Gusti's
   Garden Bungalows
42 Juwita Inn
43 Nick's Pension
44 Pringga Juwita Water
   Garden Cottages
48 Bali Breeze Bungalows
50 Kokokan Hotel
56 Nuriani Guest House;
   Ubud View Bungalows

59 Artini Cottages I
61 Artini Cottages II
62 Jati 2 Homestay
65 Suartha Pension
74 Matahari Cottages
75 Budi Shady Gully
   Guest House
82 Oka Kartini
   Couperus Bungalows
85 Rona Accommodation
86 Family Guest House
87 Puri Asri 2 Bungalows
91 Siti Homestay
92 Sari Bungalows
93 Nyoman Astana's
101 Pondok Wisata Lantar;
   Made's Cafe

PLACES TO EAT
10 Warung Nuri
25 Cafe Dewata
27 Murni's Warung
30 Beggar's Bush Pub
35 Ketut's Place
39 Griya Barbecue
40 Miro's Cafe
51 Edi's Warung;
   Panorama Restaurant
52 Nuriana's
54 Kura Kura Mexican Cafe
55 Bebek Bengil
   (Dirty Duck Diner)
57 Three Brothers Restaurant
58 Warung Artini
67 Nomad Restaurant
72 Bali Buddha
   Health Food Shop
84 Made Cafe

OTHER
11 Neka Museum
28 Antonio Blanco's Home
31 Ubud Clinic

41 Roda Tourist Service
   (Internet Centre)
45 Tri Nadi Salon
46 Pura Dalem Agung
47 Museum Patung
   (Woodcarving Museum)
49 Agung Rai Museum
   of Art (ARMA)
53 Perama Office
60 Keep Walking Tours
63 Nur's Salon
64 Padangtegal Dance Stage
66 BCA Bank; Wartel
68 Seniwati Gallery
   of Art by Women
69 Pura Dalem Taman
70 Neka Gallery
71 Ganesha Bookshop
73 Main Post Office
76 Simparik Tourist Shuttle
   Bus Office
77 BCA Bank
78 BII Bank
79 Police Station
80 Main Telkom Office
81 Peliatan Dance Stage
83 Jazz Cafe
88 Agung Rai Gallery
89 Pura Puseh;
   Pura Desa Gede
90 Pengosekan Community
   of Artists
94 Museum Rudana;
   Rundana Gallery
95 Goa Gajah (Elephant Cave)
96 Pura Kebo Edan
97 Pura Pusering Jagat
98 Pura Penataran Sasih
99 Museum Purbakala
   (Archaeological Museum)
100 Pura Samuan Tiga
102 Yeh Pulu

Sala
To Tampaksiring
Galiang
Kelusu
Pejeng
Samuan Tiga
Jalan Bedulu
Pejeng & Bedulu Walk
Bedulu
To Gianyar
To Mas & Denpasar

Sungai Petanu

INDONESIA

walks are: east to Pejeng, across picturesque ravines; north to Petulu, where herons roost at dusk; and west to Sayan, with views over the Sungai Ayung gorge.

Places to Stay

Ubud has an overabundance of pleasant homestays, where a simple, clean room in a pretty garden will cost from 15,000/20,000 rp for singles/doubles. But it may be worth paying a little more: for about 25,000/40,000 rp, you can often get a very nice room or bungalow, in a stunning garden, and breakfast. If you are staying a while, ask for a substantial discount. Conveniently, large signs swinging in the breeze bear the name of each hotel and losmen down that particularly laneway and alley.

Central Ubud The cheapest places are just off the top of Monkey Forest Rd. They are not very appealing, but singles/doubles are cheap for about 10,000/15,000 rp. The best include *Pandawa Homestay (☎ 97 5698)*, *Anom Bungalows* and *Jungut Inn*.

Rice Paddy Bungalows is one of three secluded places along a laneway, with almost identical settings and prices: 30,000 rp. *Bendi's 2 Accommodation (☎ 96410)* is in a quiet garden setting. The manager is open to negotiation, so bungalows are available for as little as 25,000 rp with hot water. *Saren Inn (☎ 97 5704)* is a mid-range place struggling to find guests, so management happily offers big discounts. Singles/doubles for 30,000/40,000 rp with hot water and a fridge are excellent value.

Other recommended cheapies around Monkey Forest Rd include: *Gayatri Bungalows (☎ 96391)*; *Monkey Forest Inn*; *Alit's House (☎ 96284)*; *Puri Muwa Bungalows (☎ 97 5441)*; *Dewi Ayu Accommodation (☎ 97 6119)*; *Alamanda Accommodation*; and *Frog Pond Inn*.

Along Jalan Maruti, *Dewi Putri Accommodation (☎ 96304)* is quiet, and good value for 10,000/15,000 rp; *Sayong House (☎ 96305)* is also quiet, with rooms for 20,000/30,000 rp; and *Budi Bungalows* for 15,000/20,000 rp is clean, quiet and comfortable.

Jalan Karna is a good place to base yourself. For about 15,000/20,000 rp, there are *Gandra House (☎ 97 6529)*; *Ning's House (☎ 97 3340)*; *Pondok Wisata Puri Widiana*, with a shady garden; and the friendly *Yuni's House (☎ 97 5701)*.

Jalan Goutama is another cheap, quiet and

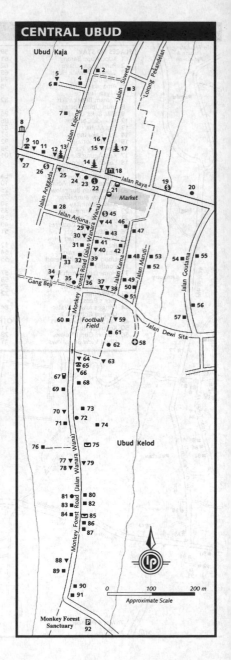

CENTRAL UBUD

CENTRAL UBUD

PLACES TO STAY
1 Artja Inn
2 Arjana Accommodation
3 Suci Inn
4 Shanti Homestay
6 Siti Bungalows
7 Roja's Bungalows
11 Puri Saraswati Bungalows
28 Anom Bungalows; Jungut Inn
31 Alit's House
32 Puri Muwa Bungalows
33 Oka Wati Hotel
39 Gayatri Bungalows
41 Pandawa Homestay &
   Bookshop
42 Gandra House
43 Hibiscus Bungalows
46 Yuni's House
47 Pondok Wisata Puri Widiana
48 Wija's House
49 Ning's House
50 Budi Bungalows
52 Dewi Putri Accommodation
53 Sayong House
54 Darta Homestay
55 Shana Homestay
56 Donald Homestay
57 Agung Cottages
60 Bendi's 2 Accommodation &
   Bendi's Restaurant
61 Wahyu Bungalows
68 Frog Pond Inn;
   Postal Agency; Wartel
69 Ubud Village Hotel
71 Pertiwi Bungalows
73 Puri Garden Bungalows
74 Rice Paddy Bungalows

76 Alamanda Accommodation
80 Ubud Bungalows
82 Saren Inn
83 Dewi Ayu Accommodation
84 Ubud Terrace Bungalows;
   Hotel Argasoka
86 Fibra Inn
87 Ubud Inn
89 Pande Permai Bungalows
90 Monkey Forest Inn
91 Hotel Champlung Sari

PLACES TO EAT
5 Han Snel's Garden Restaurant
10 Mumbul's Cafe
12 Lotus Cafe
15 Bumbu Restaurant
16 Coconut Cafe; Cafe Angkasa
24 Ary's Warung
25 Ryoshi Japanese Restaurant
27 Casa Luna
29 Kul Kul Restaurant
30 Ayu's Kitchen
34 Lillies Garden Restaurant
36 Ibu Rai Bar & Restaurant;
   Cafe Tirta
37 Bamboo Restaurant
38 Tutmak Cafe
40 Gayatri Cafe
44 Canderi's Warung
59 Aries Warung
63 Cafe Bali
64 Noni Orti; Milano Salon
66 Yogyakarta Cafe
70 Cafe Wayan
77 Lotus Lane Restaurant;
   Dian Cafe; Mendra's Cafe

78 Jaya Cafe
79 Monkey Cafe
88 Warung Mama

OTHER
8 Museum Puri Lukisan
9 Wartel
13 Pura Taman Saraswati
14 Pura Desa Ubud
17 Pura Merajan Agung
18 Ubud Palace
19 Bank Danamon
20 Lempad's Home
21 Bemo Stops; Pasar Seni
   (Art Market)
22 Yaysan Bina Wisata
   (Tourist Office)
23 Ary's Bookshop
26 Bank Bali; Toko Tino
   Supermarket;
   Ubud Bookshop
35 Igna Bookshop
45 BNI Bank
51 Cinta Bookshop
58 Puskesmas (Community
   Health Centre)
62 Pondok Pekak Library &
   Resource Center
   (Internet Centre)
65 Wartel
67 Putra Bar
72 Balinet Internet Center
75 Postal Agency
81 Meditation Shop
85 Postal Agency
92 Parking (for Monkey
   Forest Sanctuary)

central area, with plenty of good places to stay. Two of the best are **Shana Homestay**, with large rooms, some with private patios, for 15,000/20,000 rp; and **Darta Homestay**, with a real farmyard atmosphere for 10,000/15,000 rp.

Straddling the budget and mid-range are two recommended places. **Hotel Argasoka** (☎ 96231) has lovely gardens, spacious rooms with hot water, and is excellent value for 50,000/60,000 rp. **Ubud Bungalows** (☎ 97 5537) also has spacious rooms starting at 50,000 rp, and 80,000 rp for a pleasant family room.

Central, pleasant and well-maintained is **Puri Saraswati Bungalows** (☎ 97 5164). Singles/doubles start at US$40/48. The quiet **Oka Wati Hotel** (☎ 96386) has a rice paddy in view, but is a little overpriced with rooms from US$33 to US$55. One gem is **Agung**

Cottages (☎ 97 5414) which is spotlessly clean, and set in a lovely garden. Enormous rooms cost 75,000 rp.

East of Ubud Around Jalan Hanoman, there are a few decent places. **Suartha Pension** (☎ 97 4244) boasts a genuine, traditional family setting, with singles/doubles for 15,000/20,000 rp. **Jati 2 Homestay** (☎ 97 5550) has a small number of delightful rooms for 20,000/25,000 rp, most with wonderful views. **Artini Cottages II** (☎ 97 5689) has a stunning set-up, and a pool. For 100,000/150,000 rp, this is excellent value. **Oka Kartini Couperus Bungalows** (☎ 97 5193) is also central, good value for US$20/25, and has a nice pool.

Also recommended is **Ubud View Bungalows** (☎ 97 4164), which charges 40,000/50,000 rp for down/upstairs rooms with hot water; and **Nuriani Guest House** (☎ 97 5346), which has singles/doubles in another lovely garden for 20,000/35,000 rp.

Jalan Jembawan is a delightful street. *Budi Shady Gully Guest House* (☎ 97 5033) charges 25,000/30,000 rp, with hot water, and is excellent value. *Matahari Cottages* (☎ 97 5459) has bungalows in a picturesque setting for 30,000/35,000 rp.

A little further east, Jalan Tebesaya is reminiscent of a village street. *Puri Asri 2 Bungalows* (☎ 96210) has a lovely garden, and clean rooms for 20,000 rp. *Rona Accommodation* (☎ 97 3229) is a well-established favourite. Good rooms range from 20,000 rp to 40,000 rp with hot water. *Family Guest House* (☎ 97 4054) also has a charming garden, as well as friendly staff. Singles/doubles cost 25,000/35,000 rp.

North of Ubud Places north of Jalan Raya are generally quiet and good value. A long-term favourite is *Suci Inn* (☎ 97 5304), a friendly, relaxed place where singles/doubles are 15,000/20,000 rp. *Pondok Bambu* (☎ 96421) charges 40,000 rp for a large room, with hot water.

Jalan Kajeng is an ideal place to base yourself in northern Ubud. *Shanti Homestay* (☎ 97 5421) is a good option for 20,000/30,000 rp; *Roja's Bungalows* (☎ 97 5107) costs 25,000/30,000 rp, and has a friendly atmosphere; and *Arjana Accommodation* (☎ 97 5583) costs 15,000/20,000 rp. Further up, *Homestay Rumah Roda* (☎ 97 5487) is very friendly and understandably popular, with rooms for 25,000/30,000 rp. *Kajeng Homestay* (☎ 97 5018) has a stunning setting, and rooms for 20,000/30,000 rp.

West of Ubud For some seclusion, within walking distance of central Ubud, many travellers find the places around Campuan and Penestanan very appealing. Among the better in the budget range are the popular *Londo Bungalows* (☎ 62 0361) for 40,000 rp, with hot water; and *Pugur Bungalows* (☎ 97 6672), overpriced but often full anyway, with singles/doubles for 45,000/70,000 rp with hot water. *Homestay Ketut Adur* (☎ 97 5072) is noisy, but reasonable value for 25,000 rp a double. In Campuan, *Homestay Purna* costs 35,000 rp, which is cheap in this area.

Jalan Bisma has a real countryside atmosphere. Of the handful of places along here, *Juwita Inn* (☎ 97 6056) is one of the best. It has bungalows, with hot water, almost lost in a luscious garden, for 35,000/55,000 rp.

Along, or just off, Jalan Bisma, there are a couple of stunning mid-range places, such as *Nick's Pension* (☎ 97 5526). It is popular, and features a pool in a tranquil setting far from any main road. Rooms cost US$20 to US$35, with hot water. *Abangan Bungalows* (☎ 97 5977) has another lovely setting with a pool, and is close to central Ubud. Small rooms cost US$20; larger rooms in the rice-barn style are US$30 to US$35.

Places to Eat

Ubud's numerous restaurants probably offer the best and most interesting food on the island. You can get excellent western and Indonesian meals, and authentic Balinese dishes will often be on the menu as well. There are dozens and dozens of restaurants and warung, but prices are considerably lower in areas where budget travellers normally stay, eg along the roads heading north of Jalan Raya, and along Jalan Sugriwa, Jalan Hanoman and Jalan Jembawan.

Along Jalan Raya, the long-established *Ary's Warung* has moved upmarket, but remains incredibly popular for its setting and diverse menu – meals start from 8500 rp. Across the road, *Lotus Cafe* was for a long time *the* place to eat. A leisurely meal overlooking their lotus pond is still an Ubud institution, but will cost from 15,000 rp a dish. *Casa Luna*, with a superb international menu, is very popular, not least for its freshly baked bread and cakes. Two popular places along Jalan Suweta are *Coconut Cafe* and *Cafe Angkasa*, which may be Ubud's best coffee house.

Most places along Monkey Forest Rd have tourist prices, but a few good cheapies remain. *Canderi's Warung* is run by the endearing Ibu Canderi, and offers huge servings. *Kul Kul Restaurant* and *Cafe Tirta* are popular for cheap western snacks, meals and drinks. *Bendi's Restaurant* has an upstairs area, and is renowned for authentic Balinese meals from 7500 rp. *Gayatri Cafe* is excellent, and offers a range of daily specials for about 7500 rp. *Ibu Rai Bar & Restaurant*, *Noni Orti*, *Lillies Garden Restaurant* and *Cafe Bali* all have elegant settings, and are worth a splurge. *Dian Cafe* has a good range and good prices, as does *Jaya Cafe* and *Yogyakarta Cafe*.

Away from central Ubud, the new *Bali Buddha Health Food Shop* is a popular place to meet other travellers, and relax with something healthy to drink or eat. *Three*

Brothers Restaurant is one of several good-value places along Jalan Hanoman. *Kura Kura Mexican Cafe* has substantial Mexican meals from around 8000 rp. For views, it is hard to beat the charming, but pricey *Murni's Warung* or *Beggar's Bush Pub*.

Entertainment

Entertainment is more cultural, and certainly more sedate, than you would find in southern Bali. You should try to see at least one of the various types of traditional Balinese dances, which are performed for tourists in several places in or near Ubud every night. Tickets range from 10,000 rp to 15,000 rp, and will include transport if the dance is held away from central Ubud. You can buy tickets from any travel agency, most hotels, the tourist office in Ubud, or touts outside Ubud Palace – which is the most accessible dance stage for most visitors.

Beggar's Bush Pub is probably the closest thing to a pub in Ubud. It boasts four levels with wonderful views. Many restaurants, such as *Casa Luna*, *Ubud Restaurant*, *Bamboo Restaurant* and *Yogyakarta Cafe*, show free videos most nights.

Shopping

Ubud has an *enormous* variety of art shops and galleries to explore, or you can use Ubud as a base to investigate the craft and antique shops all the way down to Batubulan – the craft market at Sukawati is a great place to look around. The main galleries in Ubud have excellent selections, and they're very interesting to look through, but prices are typically over US$100. The small shops by the market, and along Monkey Forest Rd and Jalan Hanoman, sell good woodcarvings, paintings and clothing. The two-storey art market (Pasar Seni) also sells a wide range of clothing, sarongs, and souvenirs of variable quality at negotiable prices.

Getting There & Away

Unfortunately, Ubud is on only two bemo routes: small orange bemos stop at Ubud between Gianyar (700 rp) and Pujung, and larger brown ones stop at Ubud between Batubulan terminal (700 rp) near Denpasar and Kintamani, via Payangan. To reach Bedugul, go back to Denpasar; to Lovina, get a connection in Kintamani.

Shuttle buses are particularly useful, and will avoid one or more bemo connections. Perama has daily services directly to Kuta (7500 rp), Sanur (5000 rp), Bedugul (7500 rp), Lovina (12,500 rp) and Kintamani (7500 rp). There are several other local operators, and prices and departure times do vary a little. You can book tickets at any shop-cum-travel agency along the main streets.

Getting Around

Rental prices for cars and motorbikes are quite competitive, and with numerous nearby attractions which are often difficult to reach by public bemo, renting a car or motorbike is an attractive idea. Many places, particularly along Monkey Forest Rd, also rent mountain bikes. However, except for the road between Ubud and Bedulu, the area around Ubud is quite hilly.

AROUND UBUD

About 2km along the main road to Gianyar is the heavily touristy **Gua Gajah**, or elephant cave, discovered in the 1920s and believed to have been a Buddhist hermitage. Nearby is **Yeh Pulu** with its carved bas-relief. A couple of kilometres north is the **Pura Penataran Sasih**, a temple with a huge bronze drum said to be 2000 years old. A legend tells of it falling to earth as the Moon of Pejeng.

Just off the main road north in Tampaksiring, **Gunung Kawi** is a group of large stone memorials cut into cliffs on either side of a picturesque river valley. Believed to date from the 11th century, it's one of the most impressive sights on Bali.

On the main road, a few kilometres north of Tampaksiring, in the shadow of the Soekarno-era presidential palace, is the holy spring and temple of **Tirta Empul**. An inscription dates the spring from 926 AD. There are fine carvings and Garudas on the courtyard buildings. Both sites are open every day. By public transport from Ubud, catch a bemo north to Tampaksiring from the junction in Bedulu, which is south-east of Ubud.

PURA BESAKIH

Nearly 1000m up the side of the mighty Gunung Agung, this is Bali's 'mother temple'. It's big, majestically located and well maintained. There are actually many temples here, but their inner courtyards are all closed to visitors.

If you are travelling independently, try to get there before 9 am, when many tourist buses start to arrive. You have to pay to park, and to enter (1100 rp) – either at the front entrance of the complex, or at a bus lay-off about 1km before the complex. If you don't have a sarong you'll have to rent one for 3000 rp. A few guides will latch on, but you don't need one. There are regular bemos from Semarapura (Klungkung).

GUNUNG AGUNG

Gunung Agung is Bali's highest and most revered mountain, and is not difficult to climb. Start well before dawn, and take a strong torch (flashlight), water, food, and warm and waterproof clothing. It's best to climb during the dry season (April to October), but climbing is not permitted when major religious events are held at Pura Besakih, which includes most of April.

The shortest and most popular route is from Selat or Muncan. This involves the least walking because there are serviceable roads from both towns to the **Pura Pasar Agung** (Agung Market Temple), from where you can climb to the top in as little as two hours. You should report to the police station at Selat before you start from either town, and again when you return. A guide is necessary, and you should pre-arrange one in Selat or Muncan – ask around the markets, or contact the helpful guys at the Selat police station. A guide will charge from 35,000 rp per person, including food – transport is extra.

SEMARAPURA (KLUNGKUNG)

Once the centre of an important Balinese kingdom, Semarapura (also known as Klungkung) is noted for its **palace** and the adjacent **Kertha Gosa**, or Hall of Justice. Disputes that could not be settled locally were brought here, and the accused could study lurid paintings on the roof of wrongdoers suffering in the afterlife. There is also a mildly interesting **museum** inside the complex. Entry to the complex costs 2000 rp.

Loji Ramayana Hotel (☎ 0366-21044), on the road to Candidasa, is a pleasant place to stay and eat, and has good rooms for a negotiable 30,000 rp. Frequent bemos and minibuses stop in Semarapura while travelling between Denpasar's Batubulan terminal and the east coast.

NUSA LEMBONGAN

Of the three islands off the south-east coast known collectively as Nusa Penida, Nusa Lembongan is easily the most developed for tourism. The beach is a lovely arc of white sand with clear blue water, the surfing and snorkelling is excellent, and there are superb views across the water to Gunung Agung on the mainland. Electricity only runs from 5 pm to 7 am. Don't expect to be able to change any money on the island.

Places to Stay & Eat

In Jungutbatu village, *Johnny's Losmen* is very basic, but the singles/doubles for 3000/6000 rp are a bargain. Nearby, the obvious, light-green *Pondok Baruna* has a few spotless rooms and a friendly atmosphere for 20,000/25,000 rp.

Most hotels (which all have restaurants) are along the beach, at the northern end of the island. *Main Ski Inn & Restaurant* is popular with long-stay surfers – bungalows cost from 20,000 rp to 50,000 rp. Their *restaurant* is a little more expensive than others, but it serves good food and has the best view. *Agung's Lembongan Lodge* has cheap double rooms from 20,000 rp, and bungalows for 40,000 rp.

Puri Nusa Bungalows (☎ 0361-29 8613, in Denpasar) is more upmarket, and very popular with surfers and divers. Smart rooms in a two-storey block range from 25,000 rp to 50,000 rp. One place not overrun with surfers and divers is the friendly, family-run *Ketut Bungalows*, with clean and quiet rooms from 25,000 rp to 40,000 rp.

Getting There & Away

Public boats (15,000 rp) leave every day at about 8 am from the beach in front of the Ananda Hotel, in Sanur. Perama has a useful, daily shuttle bus-boat service from Kuta and Ubud (both 25,500 rp). These boats leave from the same spot in Sanur.

PADANGBAI

Located on a perfect little bay, Padangbai is the main port for ferries between Bali and Lombok, and passenger boats to Nusa Penida island. It is also a popular place to break up a journey and relax, and to organise some diving or fishing.

Places to Stay & Eat

The best places are along the beachfront. *Kerti Beach Inn* (☎ 41391) has basic rooms at the front for a bargain 10,000 rp, and double-storey thatched cottages for 20,000 rp. *Padangbai Beach Homestay* (☎ 41517) is the only place with genuine, individual bungalows, even if they could do with some renovation. The price is good – 25,000 rp –

and it is popular. At the end of the bay, *Topi Inn* (☎ *41424*) has small doubles upstairs for 15,000 rp, and some dorm beds for a very reasonable 3000 rp per person.

In the village, *Pantai Ayu Homestay* (☎ *41396*) is very friendly, and singles/doubles cost 15,000/20,000 rp. *Pondok Wisata Dharma* (☎ *41394*) is one of the best, and has rooms for a negotiable 12,000/17,000 rp. The friendly *Bagus Inn* (☎ *41398*) is simple but excellent value for 8000/12,000 rp.

On the main road into Padangbai, *Hotel Madya* (☎ *41393*) is clean and good value for 15,000/20,000 rp, and the rooms are surprisingly quiet.

The seafood is excellent and cheap. Most restaurants are also along the beachfront. *Depot Segara* is the best place for breakfast. *Putri Ayu Cafe* has seafood specials for about 6500 rp, as does *Warung Mangga*. *Ozone Cafe* is an evening gathering place, and the *Pandan Restoran* is also relaxed but a little more expensive than others. The restaurant at the *Topi Inn* is the fanciest place in Padangbai. *Hotel Puri Rai* has the town's one and only (so far) video show.

Getting There & Away

There are two bemo stops. The one used before midday is along the beachfront; in the afternoon, bemos congregate near the wartel along the main road into Padangbai. Regular bemos go to Amlapura, via Candidasa and to Semarapura.

Several buses also travel between Denpasar (Batubulan terminal) and Padangbai every day. Perama shuttle buses stop here on trips between southern Bali and the east coast.

TENGANAN

North-west of Candidasa, about 5km from the main road, is Tenganan, a Bali Aga village with walled homes, a symmetrical layout and unique crafts. The Bali Aga were the original inhabitants of Bali, before the arrival of the Hindu Javanese. It's a charming place, if a bit commercialised, and it has some fascinating festivals. Get a lift up there from the main road by ojek; it's a pleasant walk back down to the main road. A donation is requested as you enter the village.

CANDIDASA

Until the 1970s, Candidasa was just a quiet little fishing village, but now it's shoulder to shoulder tourist development, and many find it overbuilt and unattractive. The main drawback is the lack of beach, which, except for the far eastern stretch, has eroded away. Nevertheless, Candidasa is less hectic than Kuta, it's a good base for exploring east Bali, and budget and mid-range accommodation is surprisingly good value.

Information

Candidasa has a tourist office, but it's rarely open. There are several bookshops, postal agencies and wartels along the main road. The rates offered by the many moneychangers along the main road are not that attractive; Bank Danamon usually has a better rate.

Places to Stay

The popular *Lila Berata Inn* (☎ *41081*) has no-frills singles/doubles going for 8000/10,000 rp. Just east of the lagoon, there are a few good alternatives: *Sindhu Brata Bungalow* (☎ *41825*) has rooms and bungalows for 36,000/45,000 rp; and *Panduwu Bungalows* (☎ *41925*) has a quaint corridor of singles/doubles for 20,000/25,000 rp.

The eastern part of Candidasa is easily the best place to base yourself. *Barong Beach Inn* (☎ *41137*) is quiet and laid-back, and has rooms for 20,000 or 30,000 rp, depending on the views. *Ramayana Beach Inn*, with rooms for a negotiable 15,000/25,000 rp, is very quiet and offers great views from a tiny garden.

Nani Beach Inn Bungalow (☎ *41829*) has quaint, spotless rooms, with something that may be described as a 'beach' in front, for 40,000/50,000 rp.

Hotel Genggong (☎ *41105*) has a real (albeit tiny) beach, and a very pretty garden. Rooms and cottages are great value for 30,000 rp to 40,000 rp.

Standard bungalows around a pleasant garden are 35,000 rp at *Sekar Orchid Beach Bungalows* (☎ *41977*). It's worth splurging on the one and only upstairs room, which offers gorgeous views, sea breezes and hot water for 65,000 rp.

In the mid-range, *Ida Beach Village* (☎ *41096*) has six tastefully-decorated bungalows around a huge garden. At only 35,000 rp to 45,000 rp per bungalow, these are popular, so bookings are essential.

Other decent options include: *Pandan Bungalows* (☎ *41541*) with rooms for 69,000/80,000 rp; and the uninspiring *Resor Prima* (☎ *41373*), which is overbuilt, but the doubles for US$40 have satellite TV and a fridge.

INDONESIA

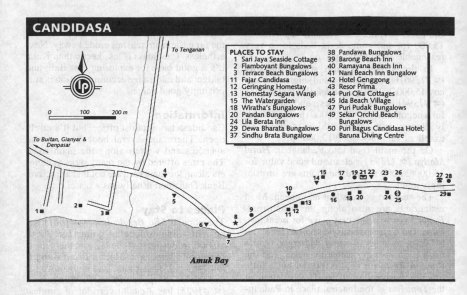

CANDIDASA

To Tenganan

To Buitan, Gianyar &
Denpasar

0 100 200 m

PLACES TO STAY
1 Sari Jaya Seaside Cottage
2 Flamboyant Bungalows
3 Terrace Beach Bungalows
11 Fajar Candidasa
12 Geringsing Homestay
13 Homestay Segara Wangi
15 The Watergarden
18 Wiratha's Bungalows
20 Pandan Bungalows
24 Lila Berata Inn
29 Dewa Bharata Bungalows
37 Sindhu Brata Bungalow

38 Pandawa Bungalows
39 Barong Beach Inn
40 Ramayana Beach Inn
41 Nani Beach Inn Bungalow
42 Hotel Genggong
43 Resor Prima
44 Puri Oka Cottages
45 Ida Beach Village
47 Puri Pudak Bungalows
49 Sekar Orchid Beach
     Bungalows
50 Puri Bagus Candidasa Hotel;
     Baruna Diving Centre

Amuk Bay

Places to Eat

The food in Candidasa is pretty good, particularly the seafood. The cheapest places to eat
are the *food stalls* which spring up every
night, normally near where the main road
almost meets the sea. Most restaurants are
dotted along the main road.

Standard tourist-oriented fare at decent
prices – 4000 rp for Indonesian food; 6000
rp for seafood – can be found at *Rumah
Makan Hawaii*, *Rumah Makan Flamboyant*
and *De Lemod Cafe*. Also worth trying is
Toke Cafe, which offers a good range of
meals with sensible prices. *Warung Srijati*
promises 'the best Balinese food in town',
and for only about 4000 rp a dish, it is worth
a visit.

Further up the price range, *Lotus Seaview*,
part of the Bali-wide chain of upmarket
tourist restaurants, has a wonderful outlook.
TJ's Restaurant is related to the popular TJ's
in Kuta; and *Raja's* is the best for pizzas
(about 12,500 rp).

Entertainment

Traditional Balinese dances (6000 rp) take
place on Tuesday and Friday evening at the
Pandan Harum dance stage in the centre of
Candidasa. Some restaurants, such as *Candi
Agung Warung*, also offer Balinese dances
most nights.

Raja's and *Chez Lilly*, among others, show

video movies most evenings. *Legend Rock
Cafe* offers live music and dancing on some
nights.

Getting There & Away

Candidasa is on the main road between Amlapura and Denpasar, so plenty of bemos and
buses hurtle along, and stop anywhere in
Candidasa. There is no bus or bemo terminal,
so hail down public transport anywhere along
the main road.

Most visitors prefer the more comfortable
and direct shuttle buses, which stop in Candidasa on the daily run between southern Bali
and the east coast. Book a ticket at just about
any hotel, restaurant or shop in Candidasa.

AMLAPURA

Amlapura was called Karangasem until the
1963 eruption of Agung, when the name was
changed to get rid of any nasty associations
which might provoke a recurrence. The old
Puri Agung Karangasem palace was once
the seat of the old Raja of Karangasem. You
can see its faded glory for 2000 rp. The ruins
of the **Taman Ujung** water palace are uninspiring, but nicely located near the coast
about 3km south of Amlapura.

In Amlapura, *Homestay Lahar Mas*
(☎ 0363-21345) has very basic and noisy
singles/doubles for 13,500/15,000 rp. It is

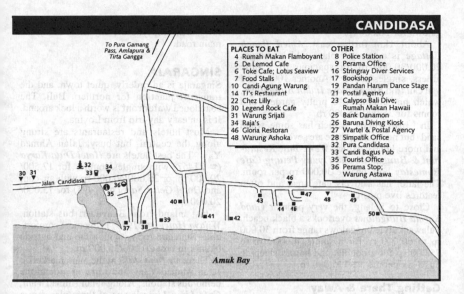

CANDIDASA

PLACES TO EAT
4 Rumah Makan Flamboyant
5 De Lemod Cafe
6 Toke Cafe; Lotus Seaview
7 Food Stalls
10 Candi Agung Warung
14 TI's Restaurant
22 Chez Lilly
30 Legend Rock Cafe
31 Warung Srijati
34 Raja's
46 Gloria Restoran
48 Warung Ashoka

OTHER
8 Police Station
9 Perama Office
16 Stringray Diver Services
17 Bookshop
19 Pandan Harum Dance Stage
21 Postal Agency
23 Calypso Bali Dive;
   Rumah Makan Hawaii
25 Bank Danamon
26 Baruna Diving Kiosk
27 Wartel & Postal Agency
28 Simpatik Office
32 Pura Candidasa
33 Candi Bagus Pub
35 Tourist Office
36 Perama Stop;
   Warung Astawa

To Pura Gamang Pass, Amlapura & Tirta Gangga

Jalan Candidasa

Amuk Bay

best to stay in Tirta Gangga. Amlapura is the major transport terminal for east Bali, and is well-connected to all parts of Bali.

TIRTA GANGGA

The tiny village of Tirta Gangga (Water of the Ganges) is an increasingly popular place to stop off and relax for a day or two. There is a good selection of cheap restaurants and hotels, excellent trekking in the region, and you can admire the delightful **Taman Tirta Gangga** water palace.

Places to Stay & Eat

Opposite the water palace, *Hotel Rijasa* (☎ 21873) has extremely neat and clean single/double bungalows for 15,000/20,000 rp. Within the palace, *Tirta Ayu Homestay* (☎ 22697) has individual bungalows for 30,000/40,000 rp. Nearby, *Dhangin Taman Inn* (☎ 22059) is a relaxed place, though the rooms are fairly ordinary for 10,000/15,000 rp.

Further up the main road, there are a few decent places with excellent views: *Puri Sawah Bungalows* (☎ 21847) has a handful of comfortable and spacious rooms for 65,000 rp; and the *Kusuma Jaya Inn* (☎ 21250) boasts some wonderful views and rooms for a negotiable 15,000/30,000 rp.

All hotels have *restaurants*, and about a dozen *warung* are clustered around the en-

trance to the palace. *Tirtagangga Cafe* serves good pizzas and ice-cold beer.

The restaurants in the *Pura Sawah* and *Tirta Ayu* hotels are worth a splurge for great views and ambience, while *Good Karma* and *Genta Bali* are the trendiest places to hear western music and meet other travellers.

Getting There & Away

Regular bemos and minibuses travelling between Amlapura and Singaraja stop at Tirta Gangga, right outside the water palace or any hotel. Perama shuttle buses travelling between southern Bali and the east coast pass through once or twice a day.

NORTH-EAST COAST

The north-east coast, stretching from Amed south-east to Selang, is starting to attract a number of visitors, who come for secluded seaside accommodation, as well as excellent and accessible diving and snorkelling. The downside is that public transport is infrequent, facilities are limited and the beach is often black and rocky.

Places to Stay & Eat

About 1km east of Amed, *Pondok Kebun Wayan* offers small but charming rooms for 15,000 rp.

In the village of Jemeluk, *Eco-dive* dive

INDONESIA

centre has some simple, but overpriced, bungalows for 28,000 rp.

About 1km further east, *Amed Beach Cottage* is a tranquil place which charges 20,000/30,000 rp for spacious, if a little airless, singles/doubles. Another 100m, and you can find *Kusumajaya Indah Bungalows*, which has character, a pretty garden, and rooms for 35,000/45,000 rp.

In Lipah village, which has some white sand (but not much), there are several warung and more hotels: *Wawa-Wewe Bar, Restaurant & Bungalows* and *Tiyung Petung Cafe Homestay* both charge 30,000 rp per room. The latter has a lovely cafe area, and often features live music.

Close to Selang, the very popular *Good Karma Bungalows* overlooks a black beach. Sulawesi-style bungalows range from 30,000 rp to 60,000 rp for a single, 40,000 rp to 75,000 rp for a double, and homes sleeping up to six people are 115,000 rp.

Getting There & Away
Plenty of minibuses and bemos (and tourist shuttle buses) travelling between Singaraja and Amlapura stop at Culik, sometimes detouring to Amed. Occasionally bemos continue to Bunutan south-east of Amed, but if you don't have your own transport, you will probably need to charter an ojek from Culik.

TULAMBEN
The major attraction here is the submerged wreck of the 1915 US cargo ship, the *Liberty* – probably the most popular dive site on Bali. There's also clear water for swimming and snorkelling, and a few restaurants and hotels. There are dive centres in Tulamben, but most divers come from Lovina.

Overlooking the wreck, *Puri Madha Bungalows* has a few small, clean rooms with sea views for 30,000 rp. About 400m further east, *Bali Coral Bungalows* has a cluster of new and clean bungalows for 40,000 rp. Next door, *Gandu Mayu Bungalows* is better value: 15,000 rp to 25,000 rp per room. Both have excellent restaurants, worth trying if you only come for the day.

Another 500m east, *Paradise Palm Beach Bungalows* costs 35,000 rp a double, and *Matahari Bungalows* is unappealing, but cheap, for 20,000 rp to 25,000 rp. All hotels have restaurants.

Plenty of minibuses and bemos travel between Amlapura and Singaraja, and stop anywhere in Tulamben. The Perama shuttle bus service, based at Gandu Mayu Bungalows, will drop you off anywhere along the main road.

SINGARAJA
Singaraja is an orderly, quiet town, and the transport junction for northern Bali. The abandoned **waterfront** is worth a look around. It is an easy day trip from Lovina.

Most hotels and restaurants are strung along the central, but busy, Jalan Ahmad Yani. The best hotels are *Hotel Duta Karya* (☎ 21467) with singles/doubles for 17,500/ 20,000 rp, or 35,000/40,000 rp with air-con; and *Hotel Gelar Sari* (☎ 21495) for 15,000/ 20,000 rp.

Just inland from Banyuasri bus station, *Wijaya Hotel* (☎ 21915) is the most comfortable. Standard rooms with a fan and outside bathroom cost 20,000/25,000 rp.

There are *food stalls* at the main market on Jalan Ahmad Yani, and *warung* around the bemo/bus stations. Along Jalan Ahmad Yani, *Cafe Lima Lima* is one of three places in a huddle. They all serve cheap, unmemorable Indonesian food and seafood, but no beer.

Getting There & Away
Singaraja has three bus/bemo terminals. From the Sukasada terminal in the south, there's transport to Denpasar (Ubung terminal) via Bedugul. Buses to Gilimanuk and Denpasar (Ubung terminal), and blue bemos to Lovina, leave from Banyuasri terminal in the centre of town. From Penarukan terminal in the east, bemos and minibuses go to Yeh Sanih, and to Denpasar (Batubulan terminal) via Amlapura or Kintamani.

From Singaraja, several companies offer overnight bus services to Surabaya on Java, so you can bypass Denpasar and the rest of southern Bali if you want. Travel agencies along the western end of Jalan Ahmad Yani sell tickets.

AROUND SINGARAJA
Yeh Sanih
Yeh Sanih is a popular spot where freshwater springs are channelled into some clean **swimming pools**. The area is attractively laid out with pleasant gardens. Admission to the complex is 450 rp, and it's open from 8 am to 6 pm every day.

Puri Sanih Bungalows (☎ 23508) has a picturesque *restaurant* inside the complex, overlooking the pools, and two types of bungalows from 20,000 rp to 55,000 rp. Opposite, **Puri Rena Restaurant & Bungalows** (☎ 26589) offers quiet singles/doubles in a pretty garden on a hill for 15,000/25,000 rp. The restaurant is secluded and has great views. There is frequent public transport from Singaraja.

Gitgit

The pretty **waterfalls** in Gitgit are at the end of a well-signed 800m path from the main road – you buy a ticket (1100 rp) about half-way down the path. Opposite the path entrance, *Gitgit Hotel & Restaurant* (☎ 26212) has clean, uninteresting and overpriced rooms from 50,000 rp. The restaurant is also expensive, so eat at one of the *warung* along the path.

Regular buses and minibuses travel from Sukasada terminal in Singaraja to Denpasar (Ubung terminal), via Bedugul, and stop at Gitgit.

LOVINA

To the west of Singaraja is a string of coastal villages which have become a popular budget beach resort, collectively known as Lovina. The beaches are black volcanic sand, and a reef keeps the water calm which is good for snorkelling. Boats take tourists out to see dolphins cavorting in the sea at sunrise. Lovina is the ideal base for day trips along the north coast, and even as far west as Pulau Menjangan.

Information

The tourist office, in the police station, is not worth visiting. The main post office is inconvenient for most visitors, but postal agents and wartels are dotted along the main road. The Spice Dive Center (spicedive@singaraja. wasantara.net.id) runs an Internet service. There are also several other dive centres in Kalibukbuk.

Places to Stay

There are so many places along the Lovina Beach strip that it's impossible to give a complete and up-to-date list of them all. We have mentioned places that are good value, close to the beach and reasonably quiet. Places are listed roughly east to west.

Bungalo Hepi (☎ 41020) has a pool, surrounded by scruffy gardens, and is excellent value: 15,000/30,000 rp for singles/doubles. *Hotel Pantai Bahagia* (☎ 41017) is very cheerful, and has pleasant rooms from 15,000/20,000 rp. *Permai Beach Bungalows*

(☎ 41471) has a nice setting and a pool. The rooms are normally expensive – 50,000/70,000 rp with fan/air-con – but prices are often negotiable, especially if you go diving with them.

Gede Home Stay Bungalows (☎ 41526) is friendly and popular, and has small rooms from 15,000 rp, and better ones with hot water for 30,000 rp. *Mandhara Cottages* (☎ 41476) has a good location and decent rooms for 50,000 rp.

Hotel Yudha (☎ 41183) has a cluster of singles/doubles for 50,000/55,000 rp. Recommended, especially for families, is *Sri Beach Lodging* (☎ 42235). It boasts a great beachfront location, though the rooms, at up to 30,000 rp for a family room, are small.

Jalan Loviana has about a dozen places. The pleasant *Hotel Kalibukbuk* (☎ 41701) has rooms from 35,000 rp with fan, and 50,000 rp with air-con. Back from the beach, *Banyualit Beach Inn* (☎ 41 7889) has a pool, and fan-cooled doubles for 30,000 rp.

Other good budget places nearby are *Yudhistra Cottages* (☎ 41552); the friendly and quiet *Suma Cottages*; *Rays Beach Inn II* (☎ 41088); and *Pondok Wisata Janur* (☎ 41056).

Down Jalan Ketepang, *Rambutan Beach Cottages* (☎ 41388) has a swimming pool set in charming gardens, though there is little that is authentically 'Balinese' about the place. It offers 'budget' rooms for US$10/12; from US$20 with hot water.

The clean and well-run *Rini Hotel* (☎ 41386) is recommended, but prices are likely to have risen following renovations.

The long-standing *Astina Seaside Cottages* (☎ 41187) has some character, and a garden setting. It is good value: from 17,000/20,000 rp with a shared bathroom to 35,000/40,000 rp for a cottage.

Around Jalan Bina Ria, *Nirwana Seaside Cottages* (☎ 41288), on a large slab of privileged beachfront property, has rooms from 45,000/75,000 rp with fans and hot water to 85,000/100,000 rp for an air-conditioned bungalow.

Angsoka Cottages (☎ 41841) has a pool and a range of rooms from 20,000/40,000 rp with fan to 105,000 rp with air-con and hot water.

Palestis Hotel (☎ 41035) has ornate decorations outside, a welcome pool inside, and good-value rooms from 40,000 rp with a fan. Other nearby cheapies are: *Rays Beach Inn I* (☎ 41087); and *Harri's Homestay* (☎ 41152).

INDONESIA

LOVINA BEACHES

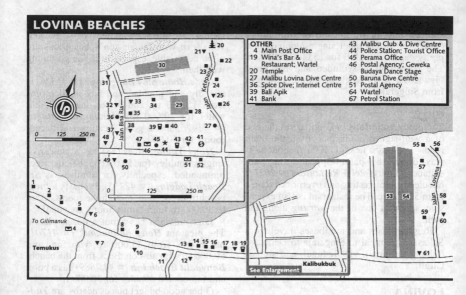

OTHER
4 Main Post Office
19 Wina's Bar & Restaurant; Wartel
20 Temple
27 Malibu Lovina Dive Centre
36 Spice Dive; Internet Centre
39 Bali Apik
41 Bank
43 Malibu Club & Dive Centre
44 Police Station; Tourist Office
45 Perama Office
46 Postal Agency; Geweka Budaya Dance Stage
50 Baruna Dive Centre
51 Postal Agency
64 Wartel
67 Petrol Station

To Gilimanuk

Temukus

Kalibukbuk

See Enlargement

Back on the main road there's a string of other cheapies, such as *Hotel Purnama* (☎ 41043) for 15,000 rp per double; *Mangalla Homestay* for the same price; *Homestay John* (☎ 41260), north of the Mangalla and actually on the beach, for 25,000 rp; *Puri Agung Susila II* (☎ 41080), very cheap at 10,000 rp; *Hotel Mutiara Beach* (☎ 41132), where upstairs doubles cost a reasonable 20,000 rp; and *Parma Hotel* (☎ 41555), with cheap, but noisy, cottages from 20,000/25,000 rp.

Mid-range places nearby include *Bali Lovina Beach Cottages* (☎ 41285), from US$35/42 to US$55/68; and *Aditya Bungalows* (☎ 41059), a big place with a beach frontage, pool, shops and a variety of rooms from US$24 with TV, phone, fridge etc.

Places to Eat

Just about every hotel has a restaurant and bar, where guests and the public are always welcome. Some of the dozens and dozens of places to eat are listed here, but you'll do well to just look around and eat anywhere that takes your fancy. Always keep an eye out for daily specials.

Starting from the Singaraja end, *Harmoni Restaurant* has delicious fresh fish and other seafood dishes, and *Warung Cokot* serves good, cheap Balinese food, such as *babi guling*. *Spunky's Cafe* may have a corny

name, but it's a bright, friendly place, with good food for about 6000 rp. It is one of several newer places along Jalan Loviana.

Surya Restaurant is popular, and has reasonable pizzas (5000 rp) at lunch, and tasty seafood specials. Next door, *Malibu Club* has a bakery, and serves pizzas, but it's overpriced. *Chono Beach Restaurant* is also popular, perhaps more for its happy hour than the food.

On the road to the temple, *Semina Bar & Restoran* has buffets, Balinese dancing and a reasonably-priced à la carte menu in a nice setting. *Warung Warubali* is one the best places to watch the sunset during a happy hour.

On Jalan Bina Ria, the popular *Ruma Ramah Tama* features a more imaginative menu than others, including a wide range of vegetarian dishes. *Kakatua Bar & Restaurant* offers Mexican, Thai and Indian cuisine; and *Warung Kopi Bali* is deservedly very popular, and gets a lot of repeat business. The servings are large, the food is tasty and the prices are reasonable (8000 rp to 12,500 rp). Left at the end of the road, *Sea Breeze Cafe*, right on the beach, has very tasty food and a wonderful outlook.

Entertainment

Some of the hotel restaurants, such as *Rambutan Beach Cottages*, offer traditional dancing with a Balinese buffet meal, or Dutch-style

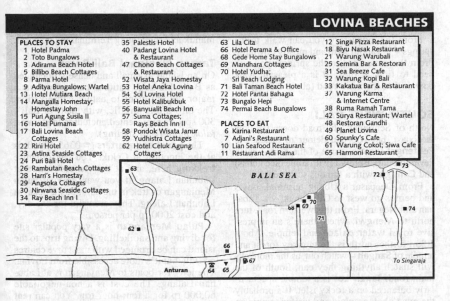

LOVINA BEACHES

PLACES TO STAY
1 Hotel Padma
2 Toto Bungalows
3 Adirama Beach Hotel
5 Billibo Beach Cottages
8 Parma Hotel
9 Aditya Bungalows; Wartel
13 Hotel Mutiara Beach
14 Mangalla Homestay;
   Homestay John
15 Puri Agung Susila II
16 Hotel Purnama
17 Bali Lovina Beach
   Cottages
22 Rini Hotel
23 Astina Seaside Cottages
24 Puri Bali Hotel
26 Rambutan Beach Cottages
28 Harri's Homestay
29 Angsoka Cottages
30 Nirwana Seaside Cottages
34 Ray Beach Inn I

35 Palestis Hotel
40 Padang Lovina Hotel
   & Restaurant
47 Chono Beach Cottages
   & Restaurant
52 Wisata Jaya Homestay
53 Hotel Aneka Lovina
54 Sol Lovina Hotel
55 Hotel Kalibukbuk
56 Banyualit Beach Inn
57 Suma Cottages;
   Rays Beach Inn II
58 Pondok Wisata Janur
59 Yudhistra Cottages
62 Hotel Celuk Agung
   Cottages

63 Lila Cita
66 Hotel Perama & Office
68 Gede Home Stay Bungalows
69 Mandhara Cottages
70 Hotel Yudha;
   Sri Beach Lodging
71 Bali Taman Beach Hotel
72 Hotel Pantai Bahagia
73 Bungalo Hepi
74 Permai Beach Bungalows

PLACES TO EAT
6 Karina Restaurant
7 Adjani's Restaurant
10 Lian Seafood Restaurant
11 Restaurant Adi Rama

12 Singa Pizza Restaurant
18 Biyu Nasak Restaurant
21 Warung Warubali
25 Semina Bar & Restoran
31 Sea Breeze Cafe
32 Warung Kopi Bali
33 Kakatua Bar & Restaurant
37 Warung Karma
   & Internet Centre
38 Ruma Ramah Tama
42 Surya Restaurant; Wartel
48 Restoran Gandhi
49 Planet Lovina
60 Spunky's Cafe
61 Warung Cokot; Siwa Cafe
65 Harmoni Restaurant

BALI SEA

To Singaraja

Anturan

---

rijsttafel. Otherwise, try to find out what is happening at the *Geweka Budaya Dance Stage*.

Lovina's social scene tends to centre on the *Malibu Club*. *Bali Apik*, and several other restaurants and bars nearby have decent happy hours. Especially popular with families are the video nights at *Warung Karma*, *Padang Lovina* and *Bali Apik* restaurants, among others.

Getting There & Away
From southern Bali by public transport you will need a connection in Singaraja (see that section for details). The normal fare on the regular blue bemos from the Banyuasri terminal in Singaraja to Kalibukbuk (or anywhere along the main road) is about 800 rp, but don't expect any change from 1000 rp. At least once a day, Perama shuttle buses link Lovina with tourist centres in southern Bali, via Bedugul, and another via Kintamani.

Getting Around
Lovina is an excellent base from which to explore northern and central Bali. Rental prices for cars and motorbikes are quite reasonable, and can be organised through your hotel, or at most shops-cum-travel agencies. You can easily travel along the Lovina strip by public bemo, or rent a bicycle from several shops in Kalibukbuk for about 6000 rp per day.

AROUND LOVINA
The area immediately west of Lovina has several worthwhile attractions. About 5km west of the middle of the Lovina beach strip, a sign leads to **Air Terjun Singsing** (Daybreak Waterfall). The waterfall is not huge, though the pool underneath is good for a refreshing swim. The falls are more spectacular in the wet season, and may be just a trickle in the dry season.

Banjar
Bali's only **Buddhist monastery**, Brahmavihara Arama, is a handsome structure in a commanding location with views down the valley and across to the sea. The monastery is about 4km up an obvious turn-off from the main road, 8km west of Lovina. If you don't have your own transport, charter an ojek at the turn-off. The road continues past the monastery, winding further up into the hills to Pedawa, a **Bali Aga village**.

Not far from the monastery, the **Air Panas Banjar** (hot springs) are beautifully landscaped with lush tropical plants. You can really indulge yourself here for a few hours, or days. The wonderful *Pondok Wisata Grya Sari* (☎ 92903) is set in the hills, very close to the springs. Pleasant singles/doubles start at US$36/41, and are worth a splurge. The Grya Sari has an expensive restaurant in a lovely setting, otherwise you can eat at the inexpensive *Restoran Komala Tirta*, over-looking the springs.

From the monastery you can walk to the springs – it's about 3km and mostly downhill. From the main road to the springs, you will need to find an ojek. It is a pleasant walk downhill to the main road (about 2.5km).

SOUTH-WEST BALI

North of Seminyak, the road doesn't follow the coast, but you can detour to beaches at **Petitenget** (on the fringe of the Kuta-Legian development), **Berewa** (with some nice hotels) and **Canggu** (with a famous surf break).

From Denpasar's Ubung terminal, buses and bemos go west to Gilimanuk, via Taba-nan and Negara. From this western road, turn north to **Mengwi**, where there's an impressive royal **water palace** and temple. About 10km further north is the monkey forest and temple of **Sangeh** – watch out, as the monkeys will snatch anything they can. South of the main road, **Tanah Lot** is a temple spectacularly balanced on a rocky islet. It's probably the most photographed and visited temple on Bali, particularly at sunset.

The turn-off to the **Medewi** surfing point is well-signed on the main road. *Medewi Beach Cottages (☎ 0365-40029)* dominates the beach, and has singles/doubles from US$17/23 to US$46/52. Nearby, the unsigned *Homestay Gede* has a few, very basic rooms for 10,000 rp. A few hundred metres west of the turn-off, *Tinjaya Bungalows* has pleasant rooms for 25,000 rp to 30,000 rp.

Picturesquely situated on a cliff top over-looking a long, wide stretch of beach, is the superb **Pura Rambut Siwi** temple. It is at the end of a 300m path, south of the main road.

WEST BALI

West Bali is the most neglected part of the island, and most people travelling overland between Bali and Java tend to speed through, which is a shame.

Negara

This major town and transport terminal is quiet, except when the bullock races are held nearby, between July and October each year.

The best hotel is *Hotel Wira Pada (☎ 0365 41161)*. The grounds are spacious, and pleas-ant, quiet singles/doubles cost 20,000/25,000 rp with a fan; 35,000/40,000 rp with air-con. It also serves good food, though it's a little pricey.

Negara is a stop-off for every type of bemo, bus and minibus travelling between Gili-manuk and the Ubung Terminal in Denpasar.

Taman Nasional Bali Barat

On an island as small and densely populated as Bali, this huge national park represents a major commitment to nature conservation. The bird life is prolific, with many of Bali's 300 species represented, including the famous *jalak putih* (Bali starling).

The **park headquarters** (☎ 0365-40060) is at the junction at Cekik. You can organise **trekking** here, and at the visitors' centre at Labuhan Lalang. If you want to visit Pulau Menjangan or trek in the park, buy a ticket at Labuhan Lalang. They are valid for one day, and cost 2000 rp per person.

Pulau Menjangan is a very popular site for diving and snorkelling. Diving trips to the island can be arranged with most dive centres on Bali, but it's more accessible from Lovina. The jetty for boats to Menjangan is at Labuhan Lalang. The cost is a non-negotiable 60,000 rp for a four-hour trip. You can rent snorkelling gear at Lalang (10,000 rp per four hours), snorkellers may be satisfied with the coral close to the shore at Lalang – ask locals about the best sites.

Gilimanuk

Gilimanuk is the terminus for ferries to/from Java. There is a bank, which offers horren-dously low rates, a post office, wartels and an uninformative tourist office underneath the unmissable, hideous stone *thing* stretching across the road.

Penginapan Nusantara II is close to the port, and has airless and overpriced rooms for 25,000 rp. Most other hotels and restaurants stretch along Jalan Raya, the busy main road between Cekik and the port. The best are the new *Sampurna Hotel* which costs 15,000 rp to 25,000 rp for a room with a fan; and *Lestari Homestay*, with a range of rooms from 12,000 rp to 50,000 rp for plush bungalows.

Buses and mini-buses frequently hurtle along the main road between Gilimanuk and the Ubung Terminal in Denpasar, or along the north coast to Singaraja.

GUNUNG BATUR AREA

Danau Batur and the volcanic cones of Gunung Batur are contained in a huge bowl-shaped caldera. One of Bali's natural wonders, Gunung Batur is a great area for trekking, though you can still enjoy the place without exerting yourself. Unfortunately, where visitors are also often hassled by persistent hawkers and would-be guides. Entry to the area costs 1100 rp.

You can also visit the revered **Pura Ulun Danu** temple in Batur village; Bali's highest temple, **Pura Puncak Penulisan** in Penulisan; and the **hot springs** at Toya Bungkah.

Climbing Batur
There are routes up Gunung Batur (1717m) from Toya Bungkah, Songan and Kintamani. Try to reach the top for sunrise, a magnificent sight, and maybe take a longer route down to explore the various volcanic cones. The easiest route is from the north-east, starting near Songan, but it's a hassle to get to the trailhead without your own transport, and parking there is not secure. From Toya Bungkah, start from the ticket office at the entrance to the village, and keep climbing. Allow about two hours to reach the top.

If you have a strong torch (flashlight), a reasonable sense of direction and your own transport to the starting point, you won't need a guide for the usual routes. But a guide is still useful if you can hire one for a decent price. About 15,000 rp per group of up to four people, plus transport, is reasonable, but you will be quoted all sorts of ridiculous prices, often in US dollars. At the top, warung sell welcome drinks and snacks.

Places to Stay & Eat
Penelokan *Lakeview Restaurant & Hotel* (☎ *51464*) charges US$36 for a superior room, and US$48 for 'deluxe', with the best views. The road around the rim is crowded with *restaurants* geared to tour groups. They all have fine views, and prepare buffet-style lunches for 20,000 rp to 25,000 rp, plus 21% tax.

Kedisan & Buahan *Hotel Surya* (☎ *51378*) has clean, comfortable rooms for 20,000 rp; 30,000 rp with hot water. *Hotel Segara* (☎ *51136*) offers 'economy' rooms for the same price, but the better ones for 50,000 rp to 80,000 rp have extra attractions like TV and hot water. Opposite the boat terminal, *Cafe Segara* is good for breakfast and lunch, but closes at 7 pm.

In Buahan, *Hotel Baruna* (☎ *51221*) is friendly and almost guaranteed 'guide-free'. Simple, clean singles/doubles cost 20,000/25,000 rp. There are several other places between Kedisan and Buahan.

Toya Bungkah This scruffy place is the major village by the lake. For singles/doubles at about 15,000/20,000 rp, there's *Hotel Dharma Putra* (☎ *51197*), *Under the Volcano I* (☎ *51666*) and *Nyoman Pangus Bungalows* (☎ *51667*).

Pualam Homestay is cheap, clean and costs a negotiable 10,000/15,000 rp. *Wisma Tirta Yastra* has the best location, but the rooms are very basic for 12,000 rp. *Arlina's Bungalows* (☎ *51165*) is clean, comfortable and friendly, but overpriced at 45,000 rp to 60,000 rp.

Lakeside Cottages (☎ *51249*) is popular with packaged tours. Standard rooms cost US$8/10, and superior rooms with hot water and TV are US$20/25.

Getting There & Away
From Batubulan terminal near Denpasar, bemos regularly travel to Kintamani, via Ubud and Payangan. Buses and minibuses also frequently travel from Singaraja, through Kintamani and Penelokan, and continue to Denpasar. Perama has a shuttle bus service at least once a day from southern Bali, which stops at the Gunung Sari Restaurant near Kintamani, and continues to Lovina.

Getting Around
Plenty of bemos travel between Penulisan and Penelokan. From Penelokan to Toya Bungkah, public transport is infrequent – to Toya Bungkah, Kedisan and along the western side of the inner rim, you may need an ojek. A chartered trip around the lake on a motorised wooden boat is enjoyable – but certainly overpriced (from 40,000 rp per boat). Boats leave from the large terminal in Kedisan, where there is a ticket office, carpark and persistent hawkers.

DANAU BRATAN AREA
Pretty Bratan lake is a quiet, picturesque and less touristy alternative to Gunung Batur. The main village is **Candikuning**, which has a bemo stop and colourful market. Watersports, such as water-skiing and parasailing, and boat rental, are available in the **Taman Rekreasi** (recreation park) at Bedugul, at the southern end of the lake, and from the gardens around the pretty **Pura Ulun Danu Bratan** temple. The cool and attractive **botanical gardens**, near Candikuning and on the slopes of Gunung Pohon, are also worth visiting.

Places to Stay & Eat
Most hotels and restaurants are along the

main road. Opposite the turn-off to Bedugul, *Bukit Strobeli (☎ 21265)* is a huddle of uninspiring, but cheap, rooms for 22,000 rp.

A little closer to the lake, *Hotel Bukit Permai (☎ 21445)* is away from the road and has excellent views. Rooms range from 50,000 rp to 100,000 rp with the best views and TV. In the recreation park, *Bedugul Hotel (☎ 21197)* has motel-style rooms and bungalows, in a good location, but without much charm, for 84,000/108,000 rp for singles/doubles. Discounts of up to 50% are possible.

Just off the road to the botanical gardens, *Penginapan Cempaka (☎ 21042)* has clean, quiet rooms for 25,000 rp to 40,000 rp. In Candikuning, *Sari Artha Inn (☎ 21022)* costs from 15,000 rp to 20,000 rp for simple, and very noisy, rooms; the dearer bungalows at the back are far better.

The best two places are on the western side of the lake. *Ashram Guest House (☎ 21450)* gets mixed reviews, but is often busy in the peak season, so book ahead. It has a range of rooms from 15,000 rp, with shared bathroom, to 70,000 rp. Opposite, *Lila Graha Bungalows (☎ 21446)* is charming and better value, but has limited views. The clean singles/doubles, which have real sheets and a huge bathroom, cost 35,000/40,000 rp.

All hotels have *restaurants*. In Candikuning, *Rumah Makan Ananda* offers the best range and prices for Indonesian food, while near the Ashram, *Bedugul Cafe* has cheap snacks, cold beer and fish meals (6500 rp). Inside the temple gardens, *Restoran Ulun Danu* has a large à la carte menu, and a buffet lunch for 20,000 rp.

Getting There & Away

Plenty of bemos, minibuses and buses travel between Denpasar's Ubung terminal and Sukasada terminal in Singaraja, and stop anywhere along the main road between Bedugul and Pancasari. To Ubud, you will have to change bemos in Denpasar; and to Gunung Batur, get connections in Singaraja – or walk.

Perama, and a few other shuttle bus operators, have daily services linking Candikuning to southern Bali, Ubud and Lovina.

OTHER MOUNTAIN ROUTES

South-west of Danau Bratan is Gunung Batukau, with the remote **Pura Luhur** temple perched on its slopes. The road from there east to Pacung has wonderful panoramas.

Interesting trips by road or on foot can be made to the west around **Danau Buyan** and **Danau Tamblingan**. Further west, **Munduk** is a pretty village. *Puri Lumbung Cottages (☎ 0362-92810)* has well-finished, thatched bungalows for US$60/66 for singles/doubles, and can provide hiking information and guides. The hotel's *Warung Kopi Bali* restaurant has a wonderful outlook and serves an excellent lunch and dinner. The renovated Dutch villas run by *Penginapan Guru Ratna (☎ 0362-92812)* is a charming alternative. Prices range from 40,000 rp per double to US$24 for a mini-home.

Another scenic road winds up from the south, through Blimbing and Pupuan to Seririt. Even less travelled is the route from near Pulukan on the south coast, climbing through spice-growing country and picturesque paddy fields until it joins the road at Pupuan.

Sumatra

Sumatra is Indonesia's island of plenty. It has an extraordinary wealth of natural resources, abundant wildlife, wild jungle scenery, astonishing architecture and a remarkable diversity of cultures.

Most travellers concentrate on the provinces of North and West Sumatra, following a well worn route between Medan and Padang, with a possible diversion to Pulau Nias. Aceh province, occupying the northern tip of Sumatra, is less visited but attractions here include the island of Pulau Weh and the Gunung Leuser National Park. Southern Sumatra (including Jambi and Bengkulu) is the least visited area – places of interest here are few and far between.

Adventure activities such as jungle trekking are popular and widespread in Sumatra, but the vast island is also dotted with wonderful lakes and mountain towns where you can just kick back and relax in between bouts of long-distance travel.

History

Knowledge of Sumatra's pre-Islamic history is sketchy. Mounds of stone tools and shells unearthed north of Medan show that hunter gatherers were living along the Melaka Strait 13,000 years ago, but otherwise there is little evidence of human activity until the appearance about 2000 years ago of a megalithic culture in the mountains of western Sumatra, notably in the Pasemah Highlands near

Lahat. A separate megalithic cult developed at about the same time on the island of Nias.

Sumatra had little contact with the outside world until the emergence of the kingdom of Sriwijaya as a regional power at the end of the 7th century. Presumed to have been based near the modern city of Palembang, Sriwijayan power lay in control of the Melaka Strait, the main trade route between India and China. At its peak in the 11th century, it controlled a huge slab of South-East Asia covering most of Sumatra, the Malay peninsula, southern Thailand and Cambodia. Sriwijayan influence collapsed after it was conquered by the south Indian king Ravendra Choladewa in 1025. For the next 200 years, the void was partly filled by Sriwijaya's main regional rival, the Jambi-based kingdom of Malayu.

After Malayu was defeated by a Javanese expedition in 1278, the focus of power moved north to a cluster of Islamic sultanates on the east coast of the modern province of Aceh. They began life as ports servicing trade through the Melaka Strait. Many of the traders were Muslims from Gujarat (west India), and the animist locals were soon persuaded to adopt the faith of their visitors – giving Islam its first foothold in the Indonesian archipelago.

As well as a religion, these traders also provided the island with its modern name. Until this time, the island was generally referred to as Lesser Java. The name Sumatra is derived from Samudra, meaning 'ocean' in Sanskrit. Samudra was a small port near modern Lhokseumawe that became the most powerful of the sultanates. Marco Polo spent five months in Samudra in 1292, corrupting the name to Sumatra in his report.

After the Portuguese occupied Melaka (on the Malay peninsula) in 1511 and began harassing Samudra and its neighbours, Aceh took over as the main power on Sumatra. Based close to modern Banda Aceh at the strategic northern tip of Sumatra, it carried the fight to the Portuguese and carved out a substantial territory, covering much of northern Sumatra as well as large chunks of the Malay peninsula. Acehnese power peaked with the reign of Sultan Iskandar Muda at the beginning of the 17th century.

When Dutch traders began probing into Sumatra they made little effort to impose themselves militarily until the post-Napoleonic War phase of their empire building. They began their Sumatran campaign with the capture of Palembang in 1825 and worked their way steadily north before running into trouble against Aceh. The Acehnese turned back the first Dutch attack in 1873 but succumbed to a massive assault two years later. They then took to the jungles for a guerrilla struggle that lasted until 1903.

The Dutch were booted out of Aceh in 1942 immediately before the Japanese WWII occupation, and did not attempt to return during their brief effort to reclaim their empire after the war.

Sumatra provided several key figures in the independence struggle, including future vice president Mohammed Hatta and the first prime minister, Sutan Syahrir. It also provided the new nation with its fair share of problems. First up were the staunchly Muslim Acehnese, who rebelled against being lumped together with the Christian Bataks in the newly created province of North Sumatra and declared an independent Islamic republic in 1953. Aceh didn't return to the fold until 1961, when it was given special provincial status.

The Sumatran rebellion of 1958-61 posed a much greater threat. Much debate surrounds the true objectives of the rebels when they declared their rival Revolutionary Government of the Republic of Indonesia (PRRI) in Bukittinggi on 15 February 1958. The main argument with Jakarta concerned the Communist Party's growing influence with President Soekarno. Some have suggested that the rebels had no intention of fighting, and that the Bukittinggi declaration was intended as an ultimatum to Soekarno to back away from the Communists.

The central government showed no interest in negotiations and moved quickly to smash the rebellion, capturing the key cities of Medan and Palembang within a month. By mid-1958 Jakarta had regained control of all the major towns, but the rebels fought on in the mountains of southern Sumatra for another three years, until a general amnesty was granted as part of a peace settlement.

Geography

Stretching nearly 2000km and covering an area of 473,607 sq km, Sumatra is the sixth largest island in the world. It is divided neatly in two by the equator, just north of Bukittinggi.

The main feature is the Bukit Barisan mountains, which run most of the length of the west coast, merging with the highlands around Danau Toba and central Aceh in the

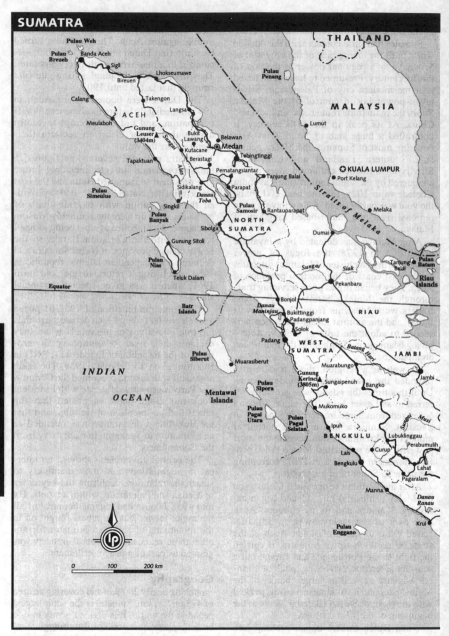

SUMATRA

THAILAND

MALAYSIA

Pulau Weh
Pulau
Breueh
Banda Aceh
Sigli
Bireuen
Lhokseumawe
Calang
Takengon
Langsa
ACEH
Meulaboh
Gunung
Leuser
(3404m)
Bukit
Lawang
Belawan
Kutacane
Medan
Tebingtinggi
Tapaktuan
Berastagi
Pematangsiantar
Tanjung Balai
Sidikalang
Parapat
Danau
Toba
Pulau
Simeulue
Singkil
Pulau
Samosir
Rantauparapat
Pulau
Banyak
Sibolga
NORTH
SUMATRA
Dumai
Gunung Sitoli
Pulau
Nias
Teluk Dalam

Pulau
Penang
Lumut
KUALA LUMPUR
Port Kelang
Melaka
Straits of Melaka
Tanjung
Balai
Pulau
Batam
Riau
Islands

Equator

Batr
Islands
Bonjol
Danau
Maninjau
Bukittinggi
Padangpanjang
Solok
Padang
WEST
SUMATRA
Batang Hari
Muarabungo
Gunung
Kerinci
(3805m)
Sungaipenuh
Bangko
Mukomuko
Ipuh
Lubuklinggau
Perabumulih
BENGKULU
Lais
Curup
Bengkulu
Lahat
Manna
Pagaralam
Danau
Ranau
Krui

Sungai
Siak
Pekanbaru
RIAU
JAMBI
Jambi
Sungai Musi

INDIAN

OCEAN

Pulau
Siberut
Muarasiberut
Mentawai
Islands
Pulau
Sipora
Pulau
Pagai
Utara
Pulau
Pagai
Selatan
Pulau
Enggano

0   100   200 km

north. Many of the peaks are over 3000m (the highest is Gunung Kerinci at 3805m). Spread along the range are almost 100 volcanoes, 15 of them active. The mountains form the island's backbone, dropping steeply to the sea on the west coast but sloping gently to the east. The eastern third of the island is low-lying, giving way to vast areas of swampland and estuarine mangrove forest bordering the shallow Melaka Strait. It's traversed by numerous wide, muddy, meandering rivers, the biggest being the Batang Hari, Siak and Musi.

The string of islands off the west coast, including Nias and the Mentawai Islands, are geologically older than the rest of Sumatra.

Climate

Sitting astride the equator, Sumatra's climate is about as tropical as tropical gets. Daytime temperatures seldom fail to reach 30°C on the coast, but fortunately most of the popular travellers' spots are in the mountains where the weather is appreciably cooler. Places like Berastagi, Bukittinggi and Danau Toba get cool enough at night to warrant a blanket.

The time to visit Sumatra is during the dry season, which runs from May to September. June and July are the best months, and are the most popular with tourists. The timing of the wet season is hard to predict. In the north, the rain starts in October, and December/January are the wettest months; in the south, the rains start in November, peaking in January/February. Bengkulu and West Sumatra are the wettest places, with average rainfall approaching 3500mm.

Flora & Fauna

Large areas of Sumatra's original rainforest have been cleared for plantations, but some impressive tracts of forest remain – particularly around Gunung Leuser National Park in the north and Kerinci Seblat National Park in the central west.

The extraordinary *Rafflesia arnoldii*, the world's largest flower, is found in pockets throughout the Bukit Barisan – most notably near Bukittinggi – between August and November.

Sumatra's forests are home to a range of rare and endangered species, including the two-horned Sumatran rhino, the Sumatran tiger and the honey bear. Gunung Leuser

INDONESIA

National Park is one of the last strongholds of the orang-utan, with more than 5000 living in the wild. The rehabilitation centre at Bukit Lawang is one place where you can be sure of seeing one.

Economy
Sumatra is enormously rich in natural resources and generates the lion's share of Indonesia's export income. The biggest earners are oil and natural gas. The fields around the towns of Jambi, Palembang and Pekanbaru produce three-quarters of Indonesia's oil. Lhokseumawe, on the east coast of Aceh, is the centre of the natural gas industry.

Rubber and palm oil are the next biggest income earners. Timber is another heavily exploited resource, and the forests of the eastern Sumatran lowland are disappearing rapidly into an assortment of pulp mills and plywood factories. Slash and burn agricultural methods were partially responsible for some devastating forest fires in southern Sumatra in 1997. Other crops include tea, coffee, cocoa beans and tobacco. Sumatra was noted as a source of prized black pepper by the Chinese more than 1000 years ago, and pepper remains a major crop in southern Sumatra.

People
Sumatra is the second most populous island in the archipelago with 40 million people. Population density is, however, but a fraction of Bali or Java. Continuing transmigration from these two islands has added to the remarkably diverse ethnic and cultural mix.

Getting There & Away
The international airports at Batam, Medan, Padang and Pekanbaru are visa-free, as are the seaports of Belawan (Medan); Dumai; Bengkulu; Batu Ampar, Nongsa and Sekupang (Pulau Batam); Tanjung Balai (Pulau Karimun); and Tanjung Pinang (Pulau Bintan). Banda Aceh is a visa-free airport, but only for a 30-day visa.

Air A number of Sumatran cities have direct flights to Malaysia and Singapore. Malaysian carrier Pelangi Air offers some good deals for (card-carrying) students, including a 50% stand-by fare on all flights between Indonesia and Malaysia. The discount drops to 25% for a confirmed seat.

Medan Medan is Sumatra's major international airport. Malaysia Airlines does the 40-minute hop to Penang daily for around US$60, and to Kuala Lumpur for US$65. Silk Air flies daily to Singapore (US$140).

Padang Padang is also well served for international flights, and (if it goes ahead) a planned new airport with a capacity for wide-bodied aircraft could make it Sumatra's main international gateway in the future.

Pelangi Air has five flights a week to Kuala Lumpur (US$127) and two to Johor Bahru (US$107). Silk Air has three flights a week to Singapore, and Merpati flies regularly to Pulau Batam with connections to Singapore.

Elsewhere in Sumatra Pelangi has three flights a week from Kuala Lumpur to Pekanbaru (US$110), continuing on to Padang. Pelangi also flies from Pekanbaru to Melaka (US$62) three times a week. Silk Air has direct flights between Pekanbaru and Singapore (US$100).

Pelangi Air flies twice a week from Banda Aceh to Kuala Lumpur (US$138) via Penang (US$110).

Sumatra to Java Garuda and Merpati have direct flights to Jakarta from Medan, Batam and Padang.

Merpati has direct flights to Jakarta from a number of other major Sumatran cities, including Bengkulu, Bandarlampung and Palembang.

Boat The express ferries between Penang in Malaysia and Medan's port of Belawan are the quickest and easiest way to enter Sumatra by water. The route between Singapore and Pekanbaru via Batam is an increasingly popular alternative, as is the crossing from Melaka (Malaysia) to Dumai.

See the Indonesia Getting There & Away section for details of international services.

Singapore to Sumatra via Batam The island of Batam, part of Indonesia's Riau Archipelago, lies just 45 minutes south of Singapore by ferry and is a good stepping stone to the Sumatran mainland.

Ferries shuttle constantly between Singapore's World Trade Centre and Batam's visa-free port of Sekupang from 7 am to 6 pm (S$17). From the domestic ferry terminal there are speedboat connections to mainland towns and to other islands. Pekanbaru is the most popular option. The journey involves a four hour speedboat trip to the mainland bus/ferry terminal of Tanjung Buton, followed by a three hour bus trip, but in practice the trip can take up to nine hours. Fares for the combined ticket start at 35,000 rp. Pekanbaru is about 5½ hours by bus from Bukittinggi.

Jakarta to Sumatra Pelni has ships from Jakarta to a number of Sumatran ports. The weekly Jakarta-Padang-Sibolga-Gunung Sitoli (Pulau Nias) and return route serviced by the *Kambuna* and the *Lambelu* is the one most used by travellers. The boats leave Jakarta for Padang (81,500 rp ekonomi; 30 hours) every Thursday at 10 am, returning from Padang every Sunday at 10 am. The second part of this route continues east from Jakarta through Surabaya, Sulawesi and Ambon.

The *Sinabung* sails from Jakarta to Medan's port of Belawan every four days (118,000 rp ekonomi; 42 hours), stopping at Tanjung Balai in the Riau Archipelago and Muntok on Pulau Bangka. It departs at 4 pm from both Jakarta and Medan.

Merak to Bakauheni Ferries operate 24 hours a day between Merak on Java and Bakauheni at the southern tip of Sumatra. They leave every 36 minutes, so there's never long to wait. The trip across the narrow Sunda Strait takes 1½ hours. You're better off travelling deck class (2000 rp) and enjoying the breeze than sitting in the smoke-filled 1st class lounge. If you travel by bus between Jakarta and destinations in Sumatra, the price of the ferry is included in your ticket – you get off the bus for the ferry journey, but make sure you get back on before the ferry docks, or you might be left behind.

Getting Around

Air An hour on a plane is an attractive alternative to countless hours on a bus, but fares had hiked up at the time of writing and schedules have been cut back, but more changes are likely to have taken place in the meantime. Merpati still has a fairly comprehensive network of services between Sumatra's major cities. SMAC flies some less popular routes, such as Medan to Gunung Sitoli on Pulau Nias.

See the individual destinations for more details.

Bus Bus is the most popular way to get around. If you stick to the Trans-Sumatran Hwy and other major roads, the big air-con buses and tourist coaches make travel a breeze – which is fortunate since you'll spend a lot of time on the road in Sumatra. The best express air-con buses have huge reclining seats, toilets and video. Most of them do night runs to avoid the traffic, so you miss out on the scenery. The non air-con buses are in many cases just older versions of the air-con buses. They can get very crowded but are fine for short trips. Other local buses are sardine cans that pick up everyone and everything possible along the way.

There are numerous bus companies covering the main routes and prices vary greatly, depending on the level of comfort. Tickets can be bought direct from the bus company or from an agent. Agents usually charge about 10% more, but they are generally more convenient. In some towns, they are the only places to buy tickets, but it pays to shop around.

Many travellers take the convenient 'tourist' buses that do the Bukit Lawang-Berastagi-Parapat-Bukittinggi run. Sibolga and Pekanbaru are also covered. They're a good way to meet other travellers, they pick up and drop off at a hotel of your choice and they travel during the day on scenic routes, often making stops at points of interest. On the downside, they can be a bit cramped, and there's usually only one or two departures a day. The cost and journey times are a little more than for air-con buses.

Travel on the backroads is a different story. Progress can still be grindingly slow, uncomfortable and thoroughly exhausting, particularly during the wet season when bridges are washed away and the roads develop huge potholes.

Train Sumatra has a very limited rail network. The only useful service runs from Bandarlampung in the south to Palembang, and then on to Lubuklinggau. There are also passenger trains from Medan to Pematangsiantar, Rantauparapat and Tanjung Balai.

MEDAN

Medan is the capital of the province of North Sumatra and the third largest city in Indonesia with a population of more than two million. It's a sprawling, stifling city and few travellers spend much time here. Most people's abiding memory of Medan is of battered old motorcycle becaks belching fumes into the already heavily polluted air. It's an important entry and exit point, however – Sumatra's

MEDAN

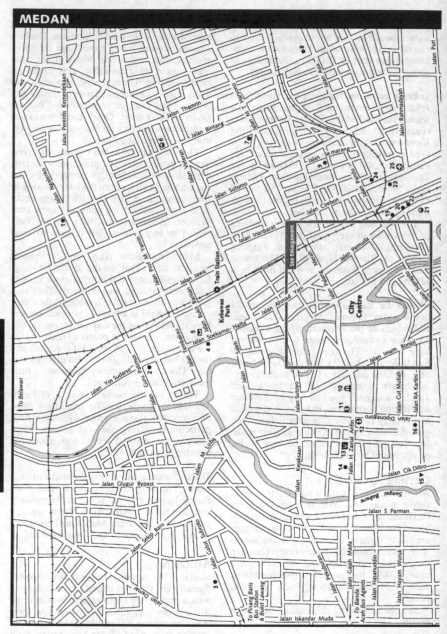

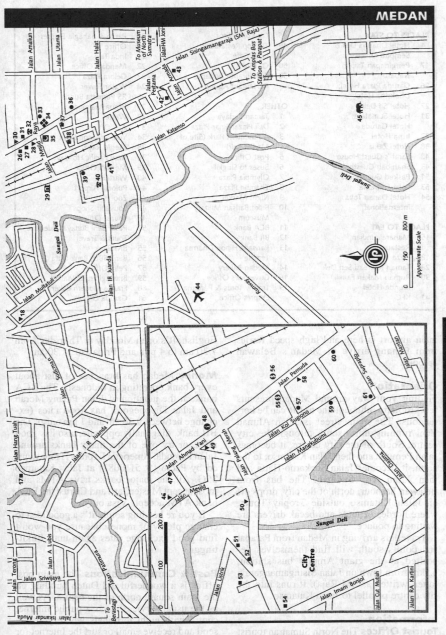

MEDAN

City Centre

Sungai Deli

Sungai Deli

Sungai Deli

INDONESIA

Approximate Scale

To Museum of North Sumatra

To Amplas Bus Station & Parapat

To Berastagi

To Iskandar Muda

MEDAN

PLACES TO STAY			
4	Hotel Dharma Deli & Sempati Office	46	G's Koh I Noor
17	Penginapan Taipan Nabaru	49	Tip Top Restaurant; Lyn's Café
26	Garuda Plaza Hotel; Dhaksina Hotel	50	Oki Suki
27	Hotel Sri Deli	58	Restaurant Cendana; Restaurant Agung
31	Hotel Sumatera; Hotel Garuda		
37	Irma Hotel		**OTHER**
38	Hotel Zakia	1	Taman Budaya
42	Sarah's Guest House	2	Deli Plaza; Sinar Plaza
43	Shahibah Guesthouse	3	Amusement Park (Site of Medan Fair)
51	Pasked Guesthouse	5	Post Office
53	Losmen Irama	6	Buses to Singkil
54	Hotel Danau Toba International	7	Olympia Plaza
		8	Thamrin Plaza
		9	Night Market
PLACES TO EAT		10	Bukit Barisan Military Museum
15	Maharaja Indian Restaurant	11	BCA Bank
18	Pizza Hut	12	BII Bank
28	Taman Rekreasi Seri Deli	13	Parisada Hindu Dharma Temple
30	Rumah Makan Famili; Ibunda Hotel	14	Medan Bakery
41	KFC	16	Governor's Office
		19	Trophy Tours & Perdana Ekspres Office

20	Pacto & Bahagia Ekspres Office
21	Inda Taxi
22	Mandala Office
23	Gelora Plaza
24	Water Tower
25	RS Permata Bunda
29	Istana Maimoon
32	Wartel
33	ALS Office
34	Yuki Simpang Raya
35	Mesjid Raya
36	New Pacific Holiday
39	Merpati Office
40	Wartel
44	Polonia Airport
45	Zoo
47	Souvenir Shops
48	Tourist Office
52	Pasar Seni Budaya; Valentine Tours & Travel
55	BNI Bank
56	Bank SBU; Bank Duta
57	Pelni Office
59	Brastagi Fruits Market
60	France Modern Bakery
61	Garuda Office

main airport is here and high speed ferries from Penang arrive at Medan's Belawan harbour.

Orientation

Finding your way around Medan presents few problems, although the traffic can be horrendous. The main street is Jalan Ahmad Yani running north-south through the city centre. South of the city centre, it becomes Jalan Pemuda and then Jalan Katamso; to the north, it becomes Jalan Soekarno-Hatta and then Jalan Yos Sudarso. The bus from Belawan harbour, north of the city, drops off on Jalan Katamso outside Trophy Tours, where hordes of touts and becak drivers are waiting to pounce.

Travellers arriving in Medan from Parapat and points south will find themselves deposited at the giant Amplas bus station, 6.5km from town on Jalan Sisingamangaraja (often written as SM Raja). It runs into the city centre parallel to Jalan Katamso.

Information

Tourist Offices The North Sumatran tourist office (☎ 53 8101) is in the cream-coloured colonial building at Jalan Ahmad Yani 107. The staff here are friendly and speak good English. It's open Monday to Thursday from 7.30 am to 4 pm, and Friday to 11.30 am.

Money Medan has branches of just about every bank operating in Indonesia. The BCA bank, at the junction of Jalan Palang Merah and Jalan Diponegoro, has good rates (exchange between 9.30 am and 1 pm only). The BII bank, diagonally opposite, also has good rates, or try one of the many banks around Jalan Pemuda. American Express is represented by Pacto (☎ 51 0081) at Jalan Katamso 35G. All the major banks have ATMs and most accept MasterCard and Cirrus; the BCA bank ATM accepts Visa only.

If you're heading south, it's a good idea to change plenty of money because you won't find good exchange rates again until Bukittinggi.

Post & Communications The main post office is a wonderful old Dutch building on the main square north of the centre. As well as the usual services it has a public Internet centre with eight terminals where you can send and receive email or surf the Internet for 6000 rp an hour. It's open Monday to Saturday from 8 am to 6 pm and Sunday to 4 pm.

There are wartels all over town, including

one inside the post office, and there's a Home Country Direct phone at the Tip Top Restaurant on Jalan Ahmad Yani.

Travel Agencies Valentine Tours & Travel (☎ 56 0530) at Jalan Palang Merah 1 is useful for tourist information, tickets to anywhere and organised tours around North Sumatra.

Medical Services A convenient hospital is the RS Permata Bunda (☎ 71 2777) at Jalan SM Raja 7.

Things to See

The city's two finest buildings are within 200m of each other. The **Istana Maimoon** (Maimoon Palace), on Jalan Katamso, was built by the sultan of Deli in 1888, and the family still occupies one wing. Admission is 2000 rp. More impressive is the magnificent black-domed **Mesjid Raya**, nearby at the junction of Jalan Mesjid Raya and Jalan Sisingamangaraja. It was commissioned by the sultan in 1906. Admission is by donation.

The **Museum of North Sumatra** is south of the city on Jalan HM Joni. It has good displays of North Sumatran culture and history, and is open Tuesday to Sunday from 8.30 am to noon and from 1 to 5 pm.

Cultural performances are occasionally staged at **Taman Budaya** on Jalan Perentis Kemerdekaan and, closer to the city centre, at **Pasar Seni Budaya** on Jalan Palang Merah. Ask at the tourist office for details. Don't bother visiting Medan's depressing **Taman Margasawata Zoo**, south of the city on Jalan SM Raja, or the run-down **crocodile farm** at Asam Kumbang.

Places to Stay

Travellers coming from further south in Sumatra will find some of Medan's budget accommodation pretty dire. A good choice is the central *Pasked Guest House* (☎ 56 0530) in the Pasar Seni Budaya Kompleks just off Jalan Palang Merah. It's small but immaculately clean with dorm beds (with fan) for 6000 rp and doubles with fan and private bathroom for 20,000 rp.

Getting out of the city centre (not a bad idea really), some of the best travellers' places are south off Jalan SM Raja. *Hotel Zakia* (☎ 72 2413), right next to the Mesjid Raya on Jalan Sipiso-Piso, is the pick of the bunch. It's friendly and clean with a choice of rooms. Dorm beds are 7000 rp, doubles with fan are 14,500 or 18,000 rp with bathroom. A double

with private mandi in the new section is 23,000 rp. Prices include a breakfast of roti and coffee. Nearby at Jalan Tengah 1B is *Irma Hotel* where basic rooms with fan are 10,000/17,500 rp for a single/double.

Further south on Jalan Armada, *Shahibah Guesthouse* (☎ 71 8528) is popular and well-run. Cot-like dorm beds are 6000 rp and big rooms with fan are 12,000 rp or 20,000 rp with private mandi.

Penginapan Taipan Nabaru (☎ 51 2155) sits on the banks of the Sungai Babura at Jalan Hang Tuah 6. It's a quiet place with dorms for 3000 rp and small doubles with shared bath for 6500 rp, but it's a long way off the beaten track.

If you want air-con, there's a cluster of uninspiring mid-range places on Jalan SM Raja, as well as a few upmarket hotels. *Hotel Sumatera* (☎ 72 1551) at No 21, has standard air-con rooms from 45,000 rp. *Dhaksina Hotel* (☎ 72 0000) at No 20 has rooms ranging from 25,000 rp for a basic twin with fan and mandi to 80,000 rp with air-con and hot shower, but you don't get much for less than 60,000 rp. *Ibunda Hotel* (☎ 74 5555), across the road, has a slightly better standard of rooms from 47,500/62,500 rp for singles/doubles. *Hotel Sri Deli* (☎ 71 3571), at No 30, has larger rooms than the others for 60,000 rp.

Places to Eat

A great place for cheap Chinese food is the *night market* on Jalan Semarang, east of the railway line between Jalan Pandu and Jalan Bandung. By day it's just a grubby side street, but come nightfall it's jam-packed with food stalls.

The *Tip Top Restaurant*, across from the tourist office at Jalan Ahmad Yani 92, is still the most popular place with foreign visitors. It's a pleasant spot, in spite of the continuous traffic jam outside. It serves European and Chinese food as well as Padang food and a range of desserts. The *Taman Rekreasi Seri Deli*, across the road from the Mesjid Raya, is an open-air playground with food stalls.

For Padang food try *Restaurant Cendana* at Jalan Pemuda 20, *Restaurant Agung* nearby at Jalan Pemuda 40, or the *Rumah Makan Famili* at Jalan SM Raja 21B.

Vegetarians looking for something other than gado gado should check out *G's Koh I Noor*, a family-run Indian restaurant at Jalan Mesjid 21. If you're staying out at Penginapan Taipan Nabaru, the *Maharaja Indian*

INDONESIA

Restaurant is nearby on Jalan Cik Ditiro. Mains are around 5000 rp.

Fast food joints are well-represented in Medan: *KFC* is on the corner of Jalan Juanda and Jalan Katamso and at Deli Plaza, and *McDonald's* is in the new Yuki Simpang Raya department store opposite the Mesjid Raya on Jalan SM Raja. The latest in the fast-food scene is the modern Thai steamboat restaurant *Oki Suki* on Jalan Palang Merah, where you choose from a range of uncooked portions then watch them cook in a pot on your table. It's slightly more expensive than Padang food – around 3000 rp a portion.

Brastagi Fruits Market on Jalan Kol Sugiono is an upmarket, air-con shop with a great selection of local and imported tropical fruit. *France Modern Bakery* at Jalan Pemuda 24C is great for cakes and sweet buns.

Getting There & Away

Medan is Sumatra's main international arrival and departure point.

Air There are daily international flights from Medan to Singapore, Kuala Lumpur and Penang. See the Sumatra Getting There & Away section for details.

There are numerous direct flights to Jakarta. Garuda does the trip at least daily, but Mandala has the cheapest fare. Garuda also flies daily to Banda Aceh.

Merpati has daily flights to Batam, four flights a week to Padang and Palembang, and three a week to Pekanbaru and to Pontianak (Kalimantan). SMAC flies from Medan to Gunung Sitoli on Pulau Nias five times a week.

Bus There are two main bus stations. Buses to Parapat, Bukittinggi and other points south leave from the Amplas station, 6.5km south of the city centre along Jalan SM Raja. The best companies for long-distance travel south are ALS and ANS. Their offices are in a separate building behind the station building. They charge similar fares – 4000 rp to Parapat (four hours) and 8000 rp to Sibolga (eight hours); 35,000 rp for air-con services to Bukittinggi, or 45,000 rp for the deluxe buses. You can get all the way to Jakarta in a torturous 48 hours for 120,000 rp (air-con) or 65,000 rp economy. ALS also has a booking office in town at Jalan Amaliun 2, close to the Mesjid Raya. Almost any opelet heading south on Jalan SM Raja will get you to Amplas (500 rp).

Buses to the north leave from Pinang Baris station, 10km west of the city centre on Jalan Gatot Subroto. There are buses to both Bukit Lawang (1500 rp; three hours) and Berastagi (1500 rp; two hours) every half hour between 5.30 am and 6 pm (the last bus to Bukit Lawang leaves at 5.30 pm). There are also frequent buses to Banda Aceh. The journey takes anything up to 13 hours during the day, but the express night buses do the trip in a comfortable (but hair-raising) nine hours. Fares range from 25,000 rp for public buses to 35,000 rp for the latest luxury buses with reclining seats (highly recommended). There are lots of opelets to Pinang Baris along Jalan Gatot Subroto, or take No 64 from Jalan Ahmad Yani. A taxi from the city centre costs about 7000 rp.

Another, more convenient, option for buses to Banda Aceh is the cluster of agents on Jalan Gajah Mada, west of the city centre. Luxury express buses depart from here at 8.30 and 9 pm, arriving in Banda Aceh around 6 am. PMTOH Travel (☎ 55 2546), at No 57, sells tickets for 35,000 rp.

New Pacific Holiday (☎ 72 0652), opposite the junction of Jalan SM Raja and Jalan Sipiso-Piso, has three minibuses a day to Parapat (18,000 rp) and Sibolga (22,000 rp), while Lagundri Tours (☎ 55 3891), west of the city at Jalan Pabrik Tenun 54, runs daily minibuses to Bukit Lawang (18,000 rp), Berastagi (18,000 rp) and Danau Toba (25,000 rp).

Boat The hi-speed ferries to Penang can be booked at the agents on Jalan Katamso. The *Perdana Ekspres* (☎ 54 5803), Jalan Katamso 35C, leaves on Wednesday, Friday and Sunday at 2 pm. Pacto (☎ 51 0081), Jalan Katamso 35G, handles tickets for the *Bahagia Ekspres*, which leaves on Monday and Tuesday at 1 pm, Thursday and Saturday at 10 am. All services cost RM96 (or rupiah equivalent; about US$30), which includes the bus to Medan's port of Belawan.

Pelni boats sail to Jakarta every four days (118,000 rp ekonomi; 42 hours), via Tanjung Balai in the Riau archipelago. The Pelni office (☎ 51 8899) is at Jalan Sugiono 5.

Getting Around

To/From the Airport Airport taxis operate on a coupon system and charge 8000 rp to the city, or 6000 rp to the hotels along Jalan SM Raja.

Local Transport Medan's taxis are less reliable than in some other cities. Even if you can find one with a working meter, it could be 'fixed' or the driver may take you on an unnecessarily circuitous route through grid-lock traffic – agree on a price before getting in or keep an eye on the meter. In theory, flag fall is 1150 rp and fares work out at about 700 rp per kilometre, which is less than you'll pay if you use the becaks that hang out around the travellers' places.

Becak drivers tend to be a bit over-zealous about wanting to take new arrivals to a particular losmen, and there are numerous stories about demands for outrageous amounts of money, almost always as a result of breaking the golden rule of becak travel: agree on the fare beforehand. Most journeys around the city centre should cost no more than 3000 rp. The motorised becaks are slightly cheaper and quicker, but not environmentally friendly.

Opelets are the main form of public transport. They cost 500 rp, although you may be asked to pay double if you have a large backpack. Just stand by the roadside and call out your destination.

BANDA ACEH
Banda Aceh, right at the northern tip of Sumatra, is the capital of Aceh province. Fiercely independent and devoutly Islamic, Aceh was once a powerful state in its own right and later held out against the Dutch longer than almost anywhere else in the archipelago. After independence, the Acehnese took exception to being incorporated into the province of North Sumatra and declared their own Islamic republic (1953-61). Today the Acehnese are kept on side by a deal which gives them autonomy in religious, cultural and educational matters.

Travelling in Aceh during the fasting month of Ramadan (January or February) can be difficult – much of the public transport system shuts down and restaurants are generally closed between sunrise and sunset. It's also wise to dress conservatively here to avoid offence and unwanted attention.

Many travellers simply pass through Banda Aceh in a dash for Pulau Weh, but it's an interesting and relaxed city worth an overnight stop.

Orientation & Information
Banda Aceh is split in two by the Sungai Krueng Aceh. The magnificent Mesjid Raya Baiturrahman (Great Mosque), lies on the southern side. Behind the mosque is the central market and the main opelet terminal.

The tourist office (☎ 23692) is at Jalan Chik Kuta Karang 3, and just around the corner is the post office on Jalan Teukuh Angkasah. There's one Internet terminal here (5000 rp an hour). The Telkom office is nearby on Jalan Nyak Arief.

The best place to change money is the BCA bank at Jalan Panglima Polem 38-40. It also has an ATM which accepts Visa, while the BNI bank on Jalan Kh Dahlan takes MasterCard.

Things to See & Do
With its brilliant white walls and liquorice-black domes, the **Mesjid Raya Baiturrahman** is a truly dazzling sight on a sunny day. The first section of the mosque was built by the Dutch in 1879 as a conciliatory gesture towards the Acehnese after the original had been burnt down. Further domes and minarets have been added at regular intervals. Non-Muslims are not allowed to enter any part of the mosque.

The **Taman Sari Gunongan**, on Jalan Teuku Umar near the clock tower, was built by Sultan Iskandar Muda (ruled 1607-36) as a gift for his wife, a Malayan princess, and was intended as a private playground and bathing place.

The undercover **fish market** on Jalan Sisingamangaraja is one of the most striking and lively in Sumatra, while the **Pasar Aceh** (central market) is also a lively affair and a good place to buy fruit.

Places to Stay
For real Acehnese hospitality, the place to go is *Uncle Homestay* (☎ 26219), Jalan Syiah Kuala 123. There's only a few rooms here and it's out of town, but it's cheap and Abdul and Yulia provide a very homely atmosphere. Singles/doubles are 6000/10,000 rp with fan and mosquito net. There's a lounge with satellite TV and Yulia prepares excellent Acehnese food for dinner. A becak from the central market costs around 2000 rp.

Some of Banda Aceh's cheap losmen are not interested in foreign guests, but you'll be welcomed at *Losmen Raya* (☎ 21427), an old Dutch building 500m from the Mesjid Raya at Jalan Ujong Rimba 30. It has doubles with fan for 15,000 rp and with private bathroom for 20,000 rp, including breakfast.

There are some very reasonably priced mid-range hotels along Jalan Ahmad Yani. *Hotel Medan* (☎ 21501) at No 15 is a good choice. Doubles start from 25,000 rp with fan and 35,000 rp with air-con, but 45,000 rp will get you a very nice air-con room with bath and TV.

Places to Eat

The table-filled square at the junction of Jalan Ahmad Yani and Jalan Khairil Anwar is the setting for Banda Aceh's lively night food market, known as the *Rek*. Since this is where most locals eat out in the evening, many of the central restaurants only open in the morning and afternoon. *Restoran New Tropicana*, Jalan Ahmad Yani 90-92, does upmarket Chinese and seafood. *Rumah Makan Aceh Spesifik*, behind the mosque at Jalan Cut Ali 20-22, is good for Acehnese food. They use the traditional Acehnese method of tenderising meat – by adding a little *ganja* (marijuana) to the cooking pot.

If you're staying south of the river, the place to go is the *Taman Sari Rindang*, opposite Hotel Kuala Tripa on Jalan Ujong Rimba. It's a cafe-style place that's very popular with Banda Aceh's young crowd in the evenings.

Getting There & Away

Air Pelangi Air has two flights a week from Banda Aceh to Penang (US$110) and Kuala Lumpur (US$138). Pelangi's office (☎ 22766) is at Jalan Sri Ratu Safiatuddin 32.

Garuda has a daily flight from Banda Aceh to Medan. The Garuda office is at Hotel Sultan on Jalan Panglima Polem (☎ 22469).

Bus The main bus station is the Terminal Bus Seutui at the southern approach to town on Jalan Teuku Umar. The express services to Medan run at night, take about nine hours and cost from 35,000 rp. Kurnia and PMTOH are both good. The PMTOH office in town is at Jalan Cut Ali 58 (behind the mosque). There are also ekonomi/patas buses (19,000/25,000 rp) to Medan during the day.

Heading down the west coast, PMTOH and Aceh Barat run buses from Banda Aceh to Calang (7000 rp; four hours), Meulaboh (8500 rp; five hours) and Tapaktuan (17,000 rp; 11 hours).

Getting Around

Airport taxis charge a standard 20,000 rp for the 18km ride into town, and 40,000 rp to Krueng Raya (for Pulau Weh).

Opelets (known locally as *labi-labi*) are the main form of transport around town and cost 500 rp. There are also motorised becaks,

which require the usual hard bargaining before you set off. The main opelet terminal is just south of the river near the Pasar Aceh. Minibuses regularly make the trip from here out to Krueng Raya (2000 rp).

AROUND BANDA ACEH
Lhok Nga

Lhok Nga, 17km west of Banda Aceh, is a popular weekend picnic spot and the beaches nearby are good for surfing.

Lampu'uk has a beautiful white-sand Indian ocean beach and some cheap homestay accommodation. *Aceh Bungalows* is a good choice, with rooms for 6000 rp with fan. It also has a small restaurant serving seafood. You can get there by labi labi from Banda Aceh for 1000 rp.

PULAU WEH

This beautiful little island just north of Banda Aceh is the main reason most travellers come to Aceh. Pulau Weh's beaches aren't that spectacular, but it has excellent snorkelling, a rugged, jungle-covered interior and a very laid-back and untouristed atmosphere.

Constant rain is likely from November until early January, and July is supposedly the driest month. Whale sharks can be seen in Sabang harbour and other parts of Pulau Weh, usually in January and February, depending on plankton growth.

Malaria has been reported on the island.

Orientation & Information

Most of the island's population is in the main town and port of Sabang (the whole island is often referred to as Sabang). For most visitors, Sabang is a place to pass through on the way to the beaches at Iboih and Gapang, but this is where you'll find all the information services and there's some cheap losmen and restaurants.

The Stingray Dive Centre (☎ 21265), on the corner of Jalan Teuku Umar and Jalan Perdagangan, books tours and acts as a tourist office. It's open from 8 am to noon and 6 to 9 pm. The post office is on Jalan Perdagangan and the 24-hour Telkom office is next door. The Bank Rakyat Indonesia at Jalan Perdagangan 128 changes only US dollar travellers cheques at poor rates – it's better to change money in Banda Aceh.

Things to See & Do

The most popular beach is at **Iboih**, where

there's a once-only 1000 rp fee to enter the beach reserve at the end of the village. Opposite Iboih, 100m offshore (15,000 rp return by charter boat), is **Pulau Rubiah**, a densely forested island surrounded by spectacular coral reefs known as the **Sea Garden**. This is the most popular snorkelling and diving spot on the island. You can swim across to Pulau Rubiah from Iboih beach, although the current can be quite strong. The Stingray Dive Centre has an office at Iboih beach (Rubiah Tirta Divers). It organises diving trips to a range of locations, hires out equipment and has PADI dive courses from US$220. Most of the accommodation places also hire out snorkelling gear for around 5000 rp.

Gapang Beach, around the headland from Iboih, is good for swimming and there are fewer tourists. Turtles are often spotted here. There are also a few decent beaches around Sabang: **Pantai Kasih** (Love Beach), about a 30 minute walk from town, is a palm-fringed crescent of white sand and a good spot for swimming.

Places to Stay & Eat

Sabang has a couple of reasonable places to stay. Both *Losmen Irma* (☎ *21148*), at Jalan Teuku Umar 3, and *Losmen Pulau Jaya* (☎ *21344*), at No 17-25, cater for travellers. The Pulau Jaya is marginally the better of the two with basic singles/doubles for 5000/9000 rp, better doubles with bathroom for 25,000 rp, or air-con rooms for 30,000 rp.

About 1.5km from town at Jalan Hasanuddin 10, *Pantai Kasih Guesthouse* (☎ *21066*) is a new and attractive family-run place. Immaculate doubles start at 20,000 rp and large, comfy rooms with fan and mandi are 30,000 rp. There's also a pleasant lounge and dining area with TV.

Harry's Cafe, downstairs from Losmen Irma, has a range of pancakes, fruit juices, cold beer and other standard fare. *Dynasty*, Jalan Perdagangan 54, is the top restaurant in town and specialises in Chinese food. *Murah Raya*, next door, has cheap Padang food.

Accommodation at Iboih is in the form of numerous groups of palm-thatch bungalows. From around 7000 rp you get a sturdy bungalow with verandah, mattress and mosquito net. Names to look out for include *Arina*, *Mama's*, *Fatimah*, *Dolphin* and, at the very end of the path, *O'Ong* is more secluded and has a nicer standard of bungalows. Each of these has its own restaurant but there's no obligation to eat where you stay. There are

very few mandis at Iboih – the water supply for bathing is an open well smack in the middle of the reserve. Gapang has similar, though fewer, bungalows.

Another accommodation choice is *Manta Ray Bungalows* at Wind Long Beach on the western side of the island. There are five bungalows (6000 rp) and a small restaurant at this isolated spot. Book at Losmen Irma in Sabang.

Getting There & Away

Ferries to Pulau Weh leave from Krueng Raya, 33km east of Banda Aceh. There are regular bemos from the central market in Banda Aceh (2000 rp; 45 minutes). The *Pulau Rubiah* and *Dingkis* leave Krueng Raya at 9.30 am and 2.30 pm daily, returning at 7.30 am and 3 pm. The voyage takes 2½ hours and costs 4300 rp deck class. There may only be one service a day in the low season.

Getting Around

The ferries to Pulau Weh arrive at the port of Balohan, from where there are bemos for the 15 minute ride to Sabang (2000 rp per person). If you want to go straight to Iboih or Gapang, tell the driver and negotiate a fare depending on the number of passengers – it should be no more than 6000 rp. There are pick-up trucks from Sabang to Gapang and Iboih every day at 10 am, 1 pm and 6 pm, returning at 6 am, noon and 4 pm. They cost 2500 rp and leave from outside the Stingray Dive Centre in Sabang.

The island has a good road network and motorcycles are the ideal way to get around if you want to do some exploring. They can be rented from Harry's Cafe in Sabang for 35,000 rp a day, and from Iboih village for a bit less.

BUKIT LAWANG

Bukit Lawang, 80km north-west of Medan, is on the eastern edge of the huge 9000 sq km Gunung Leuser National Park, separated by the clear, fast-flowing Sungai Bohorok. This is the site of the Bohorok Orang-Utan Rehabilitation Centre, which has turned the once-remote village into one of the most popular tourist attractions in Sumatra. Many travellers spend a few days here, tubing on the river, trekking and enjoying the laid-back lifestyle.

Bukit Lawang gets very crowded with locals from Medan on the weekends – visit during the week for a more pleasant experience.

Orientation & Information

The bus stops where the road ends: a small square near the river surrounded by shops and a few offices, including a small tourist information office. The staff are helpful and speak English, and this is a good place to come for some general information and advice before choosing a guide for a trek in the national park.

Change money before you arrive. There are no banks in Bukit Lawang and the rates at the local moneychangers are appalling. There is no post office, but you can buy stamps at the shops and there are post boxes. There is a small Telkom office by the river, open 24 hours.

Things to See & Do

Bohorok Orang-utan Rehabilitation Centre

The orang-utans can be seen every day at a jungle feeding platform in the national park. While the idea of joining a group of camera-toting tourists might seem a little unnatural and staged, seeing these magnificent creatures come swinging through the jungle towards you – usually with a baby on board – is definitely a rewarding experience.

Before you set off, get a permit from the national parks office in Bukit Lawang – open from 7 am to 3 pm every day. The permit is valid for one day and costs 4000 rp plus 500 rp insurance. There is no limit on the number of permits issued, which is a good reason to avoid going on the weekend. The feeding site is 30 minutes walk from the office in town, including a free crossing of Sungai Bohorok in a dugout canoe. The path into the national park from the river crossing is pretty steep and can get very muddy.

Feeding hour starts at 8 am and 3 pm. These are the only times visitors are allowed to enter the national park other than with a guide or an organised trek.

The **Bukit Lawang Visitor Centre**, opposite the bus stop, has good displays of the park's flora and fauna and a section to explain the orang-utan rehabilitation program. It's open from 8 am to 3 pm. A 50-minute video explaining the program is shown at the centre on Monday, Wednesday and Friday at 8 pm. It's free, but a donation is requested.

Trekking A lot of people use Bukit Lawang as a base for trekking. At last count there were around 65 licensed guides in Bukit Lawang and quite a few unlicensed opportunists – they can be quite persistent in getting you to join a trek. Most of the losmen advertise their own jungle treks, as does the national parks office and the tourist office. Prices are 'fixed' at a relatively steep US$15 for a one-day trek, US$35 for two days and US$65 for three days, but you can certainly bargain for a discount.

Most people enjoy their trek but there have been a few complaints about guides lacking knowledge or even damaging the environment. The best advice is to talk to the rangers at the parks office first, check that your guide is licensed and make sure that the guide you pay for is the one who will accompany you on the trek – last minute guide-swapping has been known to happen.

Other Activities Many of the losmen rent out inflated truck inner tubes (2000 rp) which can be used to ride the rapids of Sungai Bohorok, a pastime known as **tubing**. The river can be dangerous after heavy rain and no safety equipment is available – ask locals for advice on conditions. It's possible to float all the way down the river to the main road (about two hours) where you can catch a minibus back to Bukit Lawang, but the best rapids are upstream around the village anyway.

The Back to Nature Guesthouse offers **whitewater rafting** for US$20 per day.

Places to Stay & Eat

Bukit Lawang has a string of good, cheap losmen spread out along the river and most have associated restaurants. Accommodation is concentrated in two main areas: along the riverbank opposite the town and upstream along the path to the orang-utan feeding site. If you arrive late in Bukit Lawang, staying downstream will save you a pretty strenuous walk in the dark.

The best budget accommodation is upstream near the canoe crossing, about 15 minutes walk from town. *Jungle Inn*, with its creative timberwork and relaxed style, is popular. It has very basic doubles for 5000 rp as well as interesting rooms with balconies and mandi for 15,000 rp.

Losmen Bohorok River has rooms on the riverbank for 10,000 rp, while *Back to Nature Guesthouse* charges 5000 rp for reasonable doubles. Their new rooms right on the riverbank should be finished by now.

If you crave some solitude, *Ariko Inn* is another 1km along the path from the river crossing – at least a 30 minute walk from the bus stop. It has rooms for 5000 rp. About halfway between the village and the river crossing, the **Eden Inn** has cheap rooms for 3000 rp or 5000 rp with mandi, and **Queen Resort** (☎ 57 9159) has a friendly atmosphere and doubles for 7500 rp.

The downstream accommodation is dominated by two large bungalow complexes offering a range of rooms: **Wisma Leuser Sibayak** (☎ 55 0576) has some decrepit cheapies for 3000 rp, comfortable modern rooms by the river for 15,000 rp and 20,000 rp, and a few new rooms with TV and fridge for 35,000 rp; the flashier **Wisma Bukit Lawang Cottages** (☎ 54 5061) charges 7500 rp for basic doubles but has some excellent rooms for 25,000 rp – well worth the money. Ask to see the rooms with a fernery in the mandi. Both these places also have good restaurants.

Besides the losmen restaurants, there are a few popular places along the path towards the rehabilitation centre. **Bamboo Pizza** isn't cheap but its 'Italian-style' pizzas (around 17,500 rp) are good. **La Bento** is a good cafe/bar.

Entertainment
The **Acoustic Cave** is an atmospheric live music venue with bands playing on Sunday, Tuesday and Friday nights. To find the cave entrance, follow the path running past the bridge to Wisma Leuser Sibayak and it's on the left.

Getting There & Away
There are direct buses to Medan's Pinang Baris bus station at least every half hour between 6.30 am and 4 pm (1500 rp; three hours). The public minibuses do the trip in two hours and cost 2500 rp.

As elsewhere, the door to door minibuses are heavily promoted. They leave early in the morning for Medan (20,000 rp), Berastagi (25,000 rp; 4½ hours via Medan) and Danau Toba (35,000 rp; 7½ hours). You can also get a minibus to Banda Aceh via the west coast road.

BERASTAGI
Berastagi is a pleasant hill town in the Karo Highlands, 70km from Medan. At an altitude of 1300m, the climate is refreshingly cool and the setting is dominated by two volcanoes: Gunung Sinabung to the west and the smoking Gunung Sibayak to the north.

The town itself is pretty dull, but it's well set up for travellers. Most people use Berastagi as a base for trekking and other adventure activities.

Orientation & Information
Berastagi is essentially a one street town spread along the broad Jalan Veteran. The tourist office, by the memorial in the centre of town, is friendly and well set up, but the best source of travellers' information is the notice boards at Wisma Sibayak. The post office is opposite the tourist office. Next door is the 24-hour Telkom office.

The best exchange rates are at the Bank PDSU at Jalan Veteran 135. There are several after-hours moneychangers but the rates are not very good.

Things to See & Do
Many people come to Berastagi to climb 2094m **Gunung Sibayak**. You need good walking boots because the path down is steep in places and slippery year-round. The guest books at Wisma Sibayak have more information about this climb, including numerous warnings about the dangers of sudden weather changes. Several people have died or gone missing while climbing Sibayak over the years and travellers are strongly advised not to attempt it alone. However, these days it really is an easy climb and doesn't require a guide.

On the main trail, which begins just beyond the village of Jaranguda, a 7km dirt road leads almost to the top of the mountain, then a concrete path leads up to the crater rim. Finding the alternative path down is a bit trickier, but once you locate the steps on the other side of the ridge it's a steep but straightforward walk down to the village of Semangat Gunung where you can relax in the hot spring bath (500 rp) before catching a local bus back to Berastagi (800 rp) – you can do the whole thing in four or five hours.

To reach the start of the main trail, you can either walk from Berastagi or catch an opelet (300 rp). There's also a more difficult walk up through the jungle on the east side of Sibayak, for which you'll probably need a guide.

Gunung Sinabung (2450m) is a much more demanding climb taking around 10 hours up and back, and is best tackled with a guide.

The town has plenty of guides offering treks along the well-trodden trails through **Gunung Leuser National Park**, particularly to Bukit Lawang or Kutacane.

You can play a round of **golf** on the nine-hole par three course at Hotel Bukit Kubu (☎ 91533).

BERASTAGI

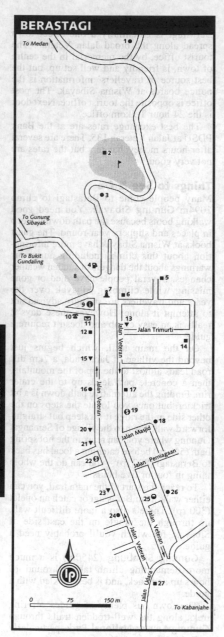

To Medan

To Gunung
Sibayak

To Bukit
Gundaling

Jalan Trimurti

Jalan Veteran

Jalan Veteran

Jalan Masjid

Jalan Perniagaan

Jalan Veteran

Jalan Veteran

Jalan Udara

To Kabanjahe

0   75   150 m

BERASTAGI

PLACES TO STAY

2	Hotel Bukit Kubu
5	Ginsata Guest House
6	Ginsata Hotel & Restaurant
12	Torong Inn; Rumah Makan Garuda
14	Hotel Merpati
17	Losmen Sibayak Guesthouse
27	Wisma Sibayak

PLACES TO EAT

13	Raymond Steakhouse & Coffee Shop
15	Asia Restaurant
20	Europah Restaurant
21	Villa Flores Restaurant
23	Simpana Restaurant

OTHER

1	Peceren Traditional Longhouse
3	Power Station
4	Petrol Station
7	Memorial
8	Fruit Market
9	Tourist Office
10	Telkom Office
11	Post Office
16	Public Health Centre
18	Ria Cinema
19	Bank PDSU
22	Bank Rakyat Indonesia
24	Mini Market
25	Bus & Opelet Station
26	Central Market

Places to Stay

Wisma Sibayak (☎ 91683), at the bottom end of the main street on Jalan Udara, is a very well-run travellers' place. It has dorm beds for 4000 rp and small singles/doubles for 6000/10,000 rp as well as larger triple rooms for 15,000 rp. It's usually packed with travellers and the guest books are full of useful and amusing information and anecdotes. There are no rooms with private mandis, but you can have a hot shower (or at least a hot mandi) for 1500 rp.

The Sibayak's back-up place, *Losmen Sibayak Guesthouse* (☎ 91122) in the middle of town at Jalan Veteran 119, actually has much nicer rooms in the upstairs section for 10,000 rp a double and hot showers for 1500 rp. It also has a pizza restaurant.

There are several reasonable places at the top end of town. *Ginsata Hotel* (☎ 91441), Jalan Veteran 27, has clean doubles with bathroom for 20,000 rp. You can use the hot shower for 1000 rp. In a little side street around the corner is the nicer and more intimate *Ginsata Guest House*, a pleasant old timber building with bright singles/doubles from 8000/10,000 rp.

Across the main road at Jalan Veteran 8, *Torong Inn* (☎ *91966*) is above the Rumah Makan Garuda and has tidy doubles for 10,000 rp. Tucked away on Jalan Trimurti are a few more cheap losmen, including *Hotel Merpati* (☎ *91157*) which is set up for travellers and has small singles/doubles going for 4000/7000 rp or doubles with bathroom for 10,000 rp.

Places to Eat
Most of the budget hotels also operate good restaurants.

Villa Flores at Jalan Veteran 72 is run by an Indonesian woman and her English husband, and specialises in 'Mediterranean cuisine'. It has an interesting menu, including seafood paella, chicken korma and a range of pasta dishes. The food is good and reasonably priced.

Raymond Steakhouse & Coffee Shop is another good place with a range of western food, vegetarian dishes and a family-style Indonesian banquet (9000 rp, minimum of four people). The *Europah Restaurant*, at Jalan Veteran 48G, does good cheap Chinese food.

Being a predominantly Christian area, the local dish is pork – you can sample the *babi pangang* (2500 rp) at *Simpana* on Jalan Veteran.

The colourful *fruit market* is near the memorial, although these days souvenir stalls seem to take up much of the space. Passionfruit is a local speciality – the purple-skinned *marquisa asam manis* make delicious drinks.

Getting There & Away
There are frequent buses to Medan (1200 rp; two hours) from Berastagi's bus station on Jalan Veteran.

Getting to Parapat by public bus is a hassle. It involves changes at Kabanjahe and Pematangsiantar, costs 4300 rp and can take more than six hours. Another option for getting to Danau Toba is to take a minibus from the southern end of Jalan Veteran direct to Pangururan (6000 rp) on the west side of Pulau Samosir. The easy way, however, is to catch one of the tourist minibuses making the Bukit Lawang-Parapat run. Buses depart for Bukit Lawang at 1.30 pm and Parapat at 1 pm (25,000 rp). The four-hour trip on the back road to Parapat is a bumpy old ride, but there are some spectacular views of Danau Toba along the way.

Getting Around
Local transport comes in the form of the horse-drawn *sado*. Rides around town cost from 1500 rp.

Opelets leave from the bus station on Jalan Veteran. They run every few minutes between Berastagi and Kabanjahe (300 rp), the major population and transport centre of the highlands. Opelets heading past the fruit market will get you to Jaranguda (300 rp) for Gunung Sibayak.

AROUND BERASTAGI
There are some fine examples of traditional Karo Batak architecture in the villages around Berastagi. The best known is Lingga, 4km from Kabanjahe, but it's on every tour group itinerary. You're better off heading to Dokan, about 15km south of Kabanjahe, or Cingkes, about 35km south-east. All these places can be reached by opelet from Kabanjahe.

DANAU TOBA
Danau Toba is one of Sumatra's most spectacular sights. It occupies the caldera of a giant volcano that collapsed on itself after a massive eruption about 100,000 years ago. The flooding of the subsequent crater produced the largest lake in South-East Asia, covering an area of 1707 sq km. The waters are 450m deep in places. Out of the middle of this huge expanse of blue rises Pulau Samosir, a wedge-shaped island almost as big as Singapore. The lake is surrounded by steep mountains, ridges and sandy, pine-sheltered beaches. At an altitude of about 800m, the air is pleasantly cool – an attraction in itself after the steamy heat of Medan, 176km to the north.

Danau Toba is the home of the outgoing Toba Batak people. *Horas* is the traditional Batak greeting and it's delivered with great gusto. Most Toba Batak are Protestant Christians and gospel singing can be heard around Samosir on Sunday mornings.

PARAPAT
Parapat is the region's major town and the departure point for ferries to Pulau Samosir. There's no reason to stay in Parapat unless you arrive too late for the ferries, or have to catch an early morning bus. It is, however, a good place to buy Batak handicrafts, and the lively lakeside market on Saturday is worth a visit. Smaller market days are held on Tuesday and Thursday.

INDONESIA

DANAU TOBA

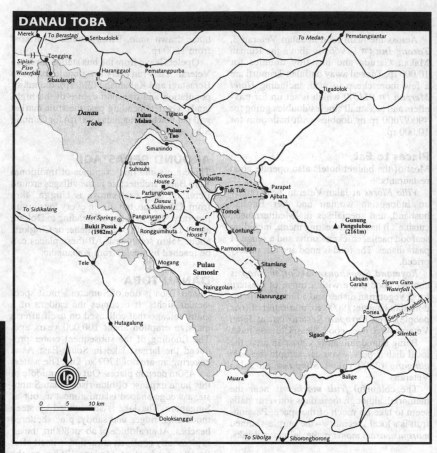

Merek • To Berastagi • Seribudolok

To Medan • Pematangsiantar

Tongging

Sipiso-
Piso
Waterfall

Sibaulangit

Haranggaol • Pematangpurba

Tigadolok

*Danau
Toba*

Pulau
Malau • Tigaras

Pulau
Tao

Simanindo

Lumban
Suhisuhi

Forest
House 2

To Sidikalang

Partungkoan

*Danau
Sidihoni*

Hot Springs

Bukit Pusuk
(1982m)

Pangururan

Ambarita

Tuk Tuk • Parapat

Ajibata

Tomok

Lontung

Ronggurnihuta

Forest
House 1

Parmonangan

Gunung
▲ Pangulubao
(2161m)

Tele • Mogang

Pulau
Samosir

Sitamlang

Nainggolan

Nanrunggu

Labuan
Garaha

Sigura Gura
Waterfall

Hutagalung

Porsea

Sungai Asahan

Sigaol • Silimbat

Muara

Balige

0 5 10 km

Doloksanggul

To Sibolga / Siborongborong

Orientation & Information

The Trans-Sumatran Hwy is known as Jalan Sisingamangaraja through town. The town centre is down by the lakeside marketplace, known as Tiga Raja, about 1.5km away. The two are linked by Jalan Pulau Samosir, which becomes Jalan Haranggaol for the final stretch down to the lake. There is a small tourist office on Jalan Pulau Samosir near the highway.

You can change money at the BNI bank on the highway and it has an ATM which accepts MasterCard and Cirrus. Rates are generally poor for currencies other than US dollars. The post office is on Jalan Sisingamangaraja near the intersection with Jalan Samosir and there are wartels for international calls on the highway and on Jalan Haranggaol by the lake.

Places to Stay & Eat

If you get stuck, there are a few budget places near the ferry dock. *Charlie Bar & Restaurant* (☎ 41277) has a guesthouse upstairs, overlooking the market. Clean singles/doubles are 10,000/15,000 rp. The restaurant downstairs is well set up and offers a range of Indonesian and European food.

Trogadero Guesthouse (☎ 41148), Jalan Haranggaol 112, is a step up in quality with small but clean bungalows for 20,000 rp and a nice lakeside setting. It also has a good restaurant.

If you can't make it any further than the bus station, *Andilo Nancy* (☎ 41548) has accommodation at the back of its office at the station. Simple double rooms without mandi are 7500 rp.

Parapat is dotted with restaurants and the highway strip is well equipped to feed the passing traveller. There are several Padang food places and a number of Chinese restaurants on Jalan Sisingamangaraja, the best of which is the *Singgalang* at No 109, below the hotel of the same name.

Getting There & Away
The bus station is on the highway, about 2km east of town. Buses run to Medan (6000 rp; four to five hours) every hour from 9 am to 2 pm, with less frequent services in the afternoon. Other destinations include Sibolga (12,000 rp; six hours) and Pekanbaru (32,000 rp; 18 hours). For Bukittinggi, most normal buses leave in the morning (29,000 rp; up to 20 hours); express air-con buses bypass Sibolga and travel overnight (37,000 rp; 14 hours); while super deluxe buses leave at 2 and 4 pm (60,000 rp). The same buses continue on to Padang (32,000/40,000/65,000 rp).

Many travellers use the door-to-door tourist minibuses. There are daily buses north to Berastagi (30,000 rp), Medan (25,000 rp) and Bukit Lawang (35,000 rp), and south to Bukittinggi (50,000 rp) and Sibolga (28,000 rp). Tickets for these services are advertised everywhere in Parapat and on Samosir.

Getting to Berastagi by public bus is a hassle. See that section earlier.

Getting Around
Opelets run a constant loop between the ferry dock and the bus station, via Jalan Sisingamangaraja (250 rp).

PULAU SAMOSIR
Samosir has long been Sumatra's premier attraction. It's a good place to unwind after the rigours of Trans-Sumatran Hwy travel, and you couldn't ask for a more spectacular setting.

Most travellers stay in Tuk Tuk, where there is nothing much to do but relax. Those with a serious interest in Toba Batak culture will gain more satisfaction from scrambling over the mountain ridge, or heading around the coast, to the villages on the west side of the island. Visitors to the west will find that Samosir technically isn't an island – it's linked to the mainland by a narrow isthmus at the town of Pangururan.

Information
Change money before you get to Samosir. The rates offered by the island's hotels and moneychangers make the banks in Parapat look generous.

Theft has reputedly been a problem around Tuk Tuk – don't leave valuables in your room and use hotel safety boxes where available.

There's a post office at Ambarita and many of the shops around Tuk Tuk sell stamps. Anju Cottages in Tuk Tuk has a telephone office for international calls and there's a small Telkom office further around the peninsula near Hotel Silintong I. The health centre in Tuk Tuk is equipped to deal with minor ailments and the doctor is on call 24 hours a day.

Tomok
Tomok, 5km south of Tuk Tuk, is the main village on the east coast of Samosir and the souvenir stall capital of the island. Tucked away among the stalls inland from the road is the **Tomb of King Sidabatu**, one of the last animist kings before the arrival of Christianity. It's possible to trek from Tomok to Pangururan on the other side of the island.

Tuk Tuk
This once small village has expanded into a string of hotels and restaurants stretching right around the peninsula. The living is easy and very cheap, and Tuk Tuk is a pleasant base from which to visit the rest of the island. It can be very busy here in the peak months of July and August and during Indonesian holiday periods, but at other times it can be eerily quiet.

Ambarita
A couple of kilometres north of the Tuk Tuk Peninsula, Ambarita is an interesting little village with more souvenir stalls and a small harbour. A group of **stone chairs** outside some traditional Batak houses is where important matters and disputes were once settled. Guides will spin you a yarn about how serious wrongdoers were led to a further group of stone furnishings in an adjoining courtyard, decapitated and then eaten by the cannibalistic villagers. Admission is 1000 rp and the guide is extra.

Simanindo & Pangururan
The fine old **king's house** at Simanindo has been restored and turned into a museum. The adjoining replica of a traditional village compound stages **Batak dance** at 10.30 and 11.45 am every day (11.45 am only on Sunday). Entry is 3000 rp or 1000 rp for the museum only.

TUK TUK PENINSULA

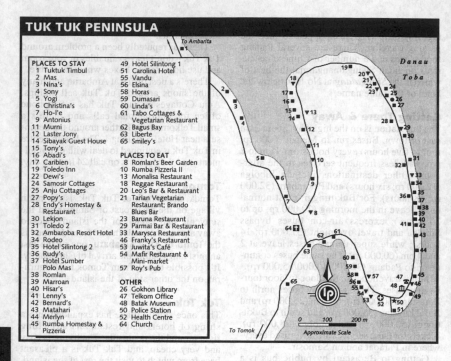

PLACES TO STAY
1 Tuktuk Timbul
2 Mas
3 Nina's
4 Sony
5 Yogi
6 Christina's
7 Ho-l'e
9 Antonius
11 Murni
12 Laster Jony
14 Sibayak Guest House
15 Tony's
16 Abadi's
17 Caribien
19 Toledo Inn
22 Dewi's
24 Samosir Cottages
25 Anju Cottages
27 Popy's
28 Endy's Guesthouse & Restaurant
30 Lekjon
31 Toledo 2
32 Ambaroba Resort Hotel
34 Rodeo
35 Hotel Silintong 2
36 Rudy's
37 Hotel Sumber Polo Mas
38 Romlan
39 Marroan
40 Hisar's
41 Lenny's
42 Bernard's
43 Matahari
44 Merlyn
45 Rumba Homestay & Pizzeria

49 Hotel Silintong 1
51 Carolina Hotel
55 Vandu
56 Elsina
58 Horas
59 Dumasari
60 Linda's
61 Tabo Cottages & Vegetarian Restaurant
62 Bagus Bay
63 Liberte
65 Smiley's

PLACES TO EAT
8 Romlan's Beer Garden
10 Rumba Pizzeria II
13 Monalisa Restaurant
18 Reggae Restaurant
20 Leo's Bar & Restaurant
21 Tarian Vegetarian Restaurant; Brando Blues Bar
23 Baruna Restaurant
29 Parmai Bar & Restaurant
33 Marysca Restaurant
46 Franky's Restaurant
53 Juwita's Café
54 Mafir Restaurant & Mini-market
57 Roy's Pub

OTHER
26 Gokhon Library
47 Telkom Office
48 Batak Museum
50 Police Station
52 Health Centre
64 Church

Pangururan is the biggest town on the island, but it has nothing of interest. There are **hot springs** on the mainland 5km away. You can see the source of the springs, then soak in a concrete bathing pool.

Trekking

There are a couple of interesting treks across the island. Both are well trodden and have a range of accommodation options, so you can proceed at your own pace. Gokhon Library, in Tuk Tuk, has information about the treks.

The shorter trek from Ambarita to Pangururan starts opposite the bank in Ambarita. Keep walking straight at the escarpment and take the path to the right of the graveyard. The climb to the top is hard and steep, taking about 2½ hours. The path then leads to the village of Partungkoan (also called Dolok), where you can stay at *Jenny's Guesthouse* or at *John's Losmen*. From Partungkoan, it takes about five hours to walk to Pangururan via Danau Sidihoni. You can, of course, avoid the initial steep climb by doing the trek in reverse.

A longer version of the trek starts from Tomok. It's 13km from Tomok to Pasang-

grahan (Forest House 1), where you can stay if you wish. From here, you can walk along the escarpment to Partungkoan.

Places to Stay & Eat

Samosir has some of the best-value accommodation in Indonesia. Losmen have moved steadily upmarket over the years, and most places offer a range of rooms, often with hot showers.

Competition is fierce, particularly on Tuk Tuk, so discounts are often available and you'll most likely be approached by touts on the ferry from Parapat.

Every losmen or hotel comes with a restaurant, but there are few surprises around – and very little difference in prices. The restaurants are good earners, and some places get pretty cranky if you don't eat where you stay. There are stories of travellers actually being kicked out for eating elsewhere.

Tuk Tuk This is where the vast majority of people stay. The shoreline is packed solid with hotels and losmen of every shape and size, many adorned with traditional horned-shaped roofs. There is such a choice of places that the best advice is to wander around until you find something that suits – the following is just a small selection.

Starting in the south, the first stop for the ferries is near **Bagus Bay** (☎ 41481), one of the most enduringly popular places in Tuk Tuk. It has large part-stone doubles for 6000 rp, dorms for 3000 rp, and timber Batak-style houses for 10,000 rp, as well as a good restaurant which has a free display of traditional dance every Wednesday and Saturday.

On either side of Bagus Bay are two places that aren't the cheapest in Tuk Tuk, but definitely have style. **Liberte** (☎ 41035) has charming timber Batak-style rooms for 20,000 rp and 30,000 rp, all with attached bathroom and hot water. On the east side, **Tabo Cottages** (☎ 41614) has a few well-appointed bungalows from 15,000 rp to 30,000 rp and an excellent new Batak-style cottage with bath and hot water for 50,000 rp. The vegetarian restaurant and German-style bakery here have long been popular.

Up the hill is **Linda's**, a popular budget place with singles/doubles by the lake for 5000/6000 rp, or 10,000 rp with hot water. Two small places with good views and swimming areas are **Elsina**, which has doubles with cold/hot water for 8000/10,000 rp; and **Vandu** with doubles at 4000 rp or 7000 rp.

Second stop for the ferries is the stylish and long-running **Carolina Hotel** (☎ 41520). Its older bungalows start from 17,500 rp, and there's a range of modern doubles from 35,000 rp to 50,000 rp. Further along is **Rumba Homestay & Pizzeria** with clean doubles for 4000 rp. **Matahari** has shabby rooms for 5000 rp but a good location, while **Bernard's** has huge doubles with a lake view for 20,000 rp and a good restaurant.

Romlan (☎ 41557) is a lovely secluded place set on its own small headland with a private jetty. It has basic rooms for 5000 rp and better doubles in Batak-style houses for 12,000 rp. Cheap places further along include **Endy's Homestay & Restaurant**, which has original Batak houses for 5000 rp and a bakery, and **Popy's** with Batak houses for 6000 rp.

A couple of good mid-range places are **Samosir Cottages** (☎ 41050) and **Anju Cottages** (☎ 41348). Both have rooms for 10,000 rp, and larger modern rooms with hot water from 15,000 rp. Samosir Cottages has a range of better rooms for 25,000 rp and 30,000 rp, as well as offering Batak dancing in its restaurant every Saturday night. Nearby are the popular **Brando Blues Bar** and **Leo's Bar & Restaurant**, which shows free videos every night.

The north-west coast of the peninsula beyond the Toledo Inn is occupied by a string of budget places with good lake views. **Tony's** (☎ 41209) has quiet rooms right by the lake from 5000/7500 rp, and comfortable doubles with hot water for 10,000 rp. The restaurant at the **Sibayak Guest House** next door is quite good. **Abadi's** (☎ 41517) is popular with simple concrete-box rooms from 5000 rp up to 20,000 rp for a large double with hot water.

There are half a dozen more places dotted along the road to Ambarita. **Tuktuk Timbul** (☎ 41374) is friendly and occupies a secluded spot down by the lake. There's a range of rooms from 6000 rp for a Batak-style house to 20,000 rp for a double with hot water.

Ambarita Many people opt to get away from the souvenir shops and bright lights of Tuk Tuk, and there are some very good, quiet guesthouses on the lakeside, north of Ambarita. **Barbara's** (☎ 41230) has a friendly family atmosphere and a good, sandy swimming beach. There's a dormitory for 5000 rp or modern doubles for 15,000 rp and 20,000 rp. The owners will pick you up from Ambarita harbour. Right next door is the **Thyesza Guest House** (☎ 41443), with a similar setup and amiable hosts. Comfortable doubles are 15,000 rp, or 25,000 rp with hot shower and spring mattress.

King's I and **King's II** (☎ 41421) offer some of the cheapest accommodation on Samosir. King's I has a Batak house for 3000 rp and other rooms for 5000/7500 rp, while King's II has modern doubles with hot shower for 10,000 rp. On the main road near King's II, the **No Name Pizzeria** has tasty pizzas for around 15,000 rp.

Way out towards Simanindo, about 6km beyond Ambarita (300 rp on a Simanindo-bound bus), **Le Shangri-La** is quiet with bungalows fronting a sandy beach for 12,000 rp a double.

Pangururan Travellers coming to Danau Toba from the west side might find themselves stuck in Pangururan for a night. **Hotel Wisata Pangururan** (☎ 0626-20050) is the best choice for budget accommodation, with clean but spartan economy rooms going for 6000 rp per person, and better doubles from 20,000 rp.

Getting There & Away

Bus See the Parapat section for information on bus travel to and from Danau Toba. There are daily buses from Pangururan to Berastagi (6000 rp; four hours) and Sidikalang (4000 rp; two hours).

Boat Regular ferries cruise between Parapat and Samosir throughout the day. Ferries between Parapat and Tuk Tuk (1000 rp) operate roughly every hour. The last ferry to Samosir leaves at about 6 pm (or 7.30 pm if there's demand), and the last one back is at about 4.30 pm. Some ferries serve only a certain part of Tuk Tuk, so check at Parapat and you will be pointed to the appropriate boat. Tell them where you want to get off on Samosir when you pay your fare, or sing out when your hotel comes around – you'll be dropped off at the doorstep or nearby. When leaving for Parapat, just stand out on your hotel jetty and wave a ferry down – the first one leaves at around 7 am, in time for the tourist minibuses to Bukittinggi.

Some ferries to Tuk Tuk continue to Ambarita, but four or five boats a day go direct from Parapat. There are also hourly ferries to Tomok from Ajibata, just south of Parapat, for 500 rp.

Every Monday at 7.30 am there's a ferry from Ambarita to Haranggaol (3000 rp; 2½ hours). There are buses from Haranggaol to Kabanjahe (for Berastagi).

Getting Around

There are regular minibuses between Tomok and Ambarita (500 rp), continuing to Simanindo (1000 rp) and Pangururan (2000 rp). Services dry up after 3 pm and the main road bypasses Tuk Tuk.

Motorbikes and bicycles are a great way to see more of the island – the main road is gradually being improved, but it's still very rough in places. Motorbikes can be rented everywhere in Tuk Tuk for about 25,000 rp a day. They come with a free tank of petrol, but no insurance – so take care and check the bike over for any damage before you take it. It takes a full day (about nine hours) to get right around the island, so start early. A decent mountain bike costs around 10,000 rp a day.

SIBOLGA

Sibolga is the departure point for boats to Pulau Nias, so a lot of travellers pass through here. Otherwise it's a pretty unappealing place, although there are some reasonable beaches nearby. Sibolga has a reputation for scams and rip-offs associated with getting to Nias – ignore offers of tickets from people who approach you at the harbour.

Orientation & Information

The town centre is located midway between two harbours. Boats to Nias leave from the Sambas harbour at the end of Jalan Horas.

The ticket office for the boat to Teluk Dalam is PT Simeulue on Jalan Pelabuhan, and tickets for boats to Gunung Sitoli can be purchased at the harbour. If you arrive by tourist minibus, the driver should be able to take you to the appropriate ticket office, then to the boat. Lagundri Tours & Travel (☎ 21149) is conveniently situated opposite the harbour. You can change money at the BNI bank at the beach end of Jalan Katamso.

Places to Stay & Eat

A late arrival in Sibolga will mean spending the night here. The most convenient budget hotels are along Jalan Horas near the port. *Losmen Bunda Kandung* (☎ 21149) at No 152 has basic rooms for 8000 rp and *Hotel Sambas Baru* (☎ 22857) at No 100 has better doubles for 15,000 rp.

Better still is *Hotel Pasar Baru* (☎ 22167), a clean place on the corner of Jalan Imam Bonjol and Jalan Raja Junjungan. It charges 10,000 rp per person for rooms with fan, and 40,000 rp for air-con doubles with TV. It has shared bathrooms only and the rooms facing the street are pretty noisy. There's Chinese food in the busy restaurant downstairs.

As the name suggests, the *Ikan Bakar Siang Malam*, near the BNI bank at Jalan Katamso 45, serves delicious grilled fish for lunch and dinner. Reckon on about 7000 rp per head, including rice and vegetables.

Getting There & Away

Bus Sibolga is a bit of a backwater as far as bus services are concerned. The express buses that travel the Trans-Sumatran Hwy bypass Sibolga by taking a shortcut inland between the towns of Tarutung and Padangsidempuan. There are still plenty of buses, but the going is painfully slow. Typical fares and journey times on public buses from Sibolga are: Medan (11,000 rp; nine hours); Parapat (7000 rp; six hours); and Bukittinggi (15,000 rp; 11 to 15 hours). There's also an express public bus to Bukittinggi that takes only nine hours and costs 20,000 rp.

There are plenty of door-to-door tourist

minibus companies operating out of Sibolga and they make an attractive alternative to the public buses. Lagundri and CV Citra Nasional are down by the harbour on Jalan Horas. Services include Medan (25,000 rp; seven hours), Parapat (20,000 rp; five hours) and Bukittinggi (30,000 rp; eight hours).

Boat Ferries to Nias leave from the harbour at the end of Jalan Horas. There are boats to Gunung Sitoli at 8.30 pm every night except Sunday. Only one ferry sails between Sibolga and Teluk Dalam, leaving Sibolga at 8.30 pm on Tuesday, Thursday and Saturday and returning at 8 pm on Monday, Wednesday and Friday. The journey takes about 12 hours. The fares are 11,750/18,600 rp for deck/cabin class to Gunung Sitoli, and 15,000/20,000 rp to Teluk Dalam. Choose cabin class if you want to get any sleep.

Getting to Nias has been made considerably quicker and easier with the introduction of the 'Jambo Jet', an ageing high-speed ferry which does the journey to Gunung Sitoli every day at 9.30 am. The fare is 26,200/31,200 rp in economy/VIP class for the 3½ hour trip.

The Pelni boats *Kambuna* and *Lambelu* travel from Gunung Sitoli to Sibolga every Saturday, and continue on to Padang and Jakarta.

Getting Around

There are plenty of stories about becak drivers demanding outrageous sums of money, surfers weighed down with bags and boards are the favourite targets, but the story here is no different from elsewhere in Indonesia. It is essential to agree on the fare and destination before you start – bargain hard. The bus station and the harbour are prime spots for being hassled. Becaks should cost about 1500 rp for most distances in town – expect to pay a bit more if you've got a lot of luggage.

PULAU NIAS

Nias is an island almost the size of Bali 125km off the west coast of Sumatra. Magnificent beaches and a legendary surfing break combine with an ancient megalithic culture and unique customs to make it one of Sumatra's most exotic destinations.

Nias is no longer off the beaten track – Lagundri Bay is now part of the world professional surfing circuit – but outside the peak months of June and July it's still relatively deserted. Simple bungalows around the

idyllic crescent-shaped beach are cheap and it's easy to spend long, restful days here.

Chloroquine-resistant malaria has been reported on Nias so take appropriate precautions.

Orientation & Information

Gunung Sitoli, in the north, is the island's biggest town. The only airport is nearby. There is a small tourist information office (☎ 21545) at Jalan Soekarno 6, behind the parade ground. The post office, Telkom office and BPDSU bank are nearby on Jalan Hatta.

Most of the interesting places are in the south and that's where most travellers head. Teluk Dalam is the port and main town of the south, but there is no reason to linger any longer than it takes to organise transport to Lagundri Bay, 13km away. The BPDSU bank in Teluk Dalam offers respectable rates for US dollars (cash and travellers cheques), and exchanges other major currencies. The post office and 24-hour Telkom office are on Jalan Imam Bonjol near the harbour.

Things to See & Do

The perfect horseshoe bay at **Lagundri** is the reason most people come to Nias. The surf break is at the mouth of the bay off **Sorake Beach**. It hosts a leg of the World Qualifying Series in June/July, when some of the best young talent in the southern hemisphere is on display. The surf is at its best from June to October, and the rest of the year the waves are perfect for beginners. Locals at the losmen around Sorake Beach are more than happy to give lessons – a few days and you'll be on your feet is the promise. There is good swimming at the back of the bay on **Lagundri Beach**.

Lagundri is also a good base for visits to the traditional villages of the south. **Bawomataluo**, perched on a hill about 400m above sea level, is the most famous and accessible of them. The houses are arranged along two main stone-paved avenues which meet opposite the impressive chief's house, thought to be the oldest and largest on Nias. Outside the houses are *daro daro*, stone seats for the spirits of the dead. The village is the setting for the **lompat batu** (stone jumping) featured on Indonesia's 1000 rp note. Local boys will offer to give you a demonstration for a price. Bawomataluo can be reached by public bus from Teluk Dalam (1500 rp). From Bawomataluo you can see the rooftops of the village of Orihili through a clearing in the trees – a stone staircase and trail leads downhill to the village.

PULAU NIAS

The small villages of **Botohili** and **Hilimaeta** are both within easy walking distance of Lagundri.

Local legend has it that all Niassans are descended from six gods who came to earth around **Gomo** in the central southern highlands. Menhirs (standing stones) and stone carvings show that Gomo was an important site in megalithic times. The most spectacular examples are at **Tundrumbaho**, 5km from Gomo. It's possible to get to Gomo by local bus, although the roads are pretty bad.

There are easier places to visit, including the much photographed cluster of statues at **Olayama**, 50km from Gunung Sitoli on the way to Teluk Dalam. The statues are found just 300m from the road and are clearly signposted.

Places to Stay & Eat
Gunung Sitoli Most travellers head for the peaceful *Wisma Soliga* (☎ 21815) at Jalan Diponegoro 432, 4km south of town. It's clean, spacious and has a good restaurant specialising in seafood. The cheap rooms for 15,000 rp are pretty basic, but there are better doubles with mandi for 20,000 rp and air-con doubles for 40,000 rp. The manager can organise tickets and transport.

The hotels in town are more convenient but nothing special. *Hotel Gomo* (☎ 21926) on Jalan Gomo, near the parade ground, features a corrugated-iron model of a northern Niassan house on the roof, and has doubles with mandi and fan for 15,000 rp and air-con doubles for 40,000 rp.

There are lots of small restaurants along

the main streets. The *Bintang Terang* turns out a decent serve of fried noodles, while the *Nasional* is the pick of the nasi padang places. Both are on Jalan Sirao.

Lagundri The bay is ringed by dozens of places to stay. Some losmen offer ridiculously cheap lodging (2000 rp a night) just to get customers for their restaurants and owners get very upset if people eat elsewhere. If you want to eat around, it's worth paying a bit more to be a free agent. It's also worth paying a bit more for the extra security – petty theft is a growing problem.

At the end of the Sorake Beach road is the sprawling *Sorake Beach Resort* (☎ 21195), where stylish bungalows start at 187,000 rp (discounts are available). Virtually next door you can have a basic palm-thatch bungalow facing the surf break for 2000 rp to 5000 rp at one of the string of cheap losmen. *Daniel*, *Sun Beach* and *Syparty* are all good and very similar. *Oikhoda* and *Marlynto* are two popular choices further along.

Dolin Guesthouse is a more upmarket place, right next to the judging tower. It has good facilities, a bar, restaurant and clean bungalows from 10,000 rp. There are more places further around the headland, but the beach frontage is not as good.

Non-surfers often prefer to stay near the swimming beach, where the cheapies include *Risky*, with bungalows for 5000 rp, *Dedy Inn* (10,000 rp) and *Erni* (5000 rp). On the western edge of Lagundri Beach, *Harus Damai* (☎ 21227) is a good mid-range choice. It has cheap bungalows for 10,000 rp and secure rooms with shower and fan in its 'hotel' section for 50,000 rp. An added security bonus is that it's opposite the police station.

Teluk Dalam Head straight to Lagundri. No-one in their right mind would consider paying 17,500 rp to stay at the grotty *Wisma Jamburae* on the waterfront.

Getting There & Away
Air SMAC has five flights a week to Medan from Binaka airport, 17km south of Gunung Sitoli, as well as a three flights a week to Padang (via Pulau Batu). People staying in Lagundri can confirm flight bookings at Sorake Beach Resort.

Boat From Gunung Sitoli there are ferries to Sibolga every night except Sunday, departing at 8 pm (11,750/18,600 rp). The high-speed 'Jambo Jet' sails everyday at 3 pm (26,200/ 32,200 rp economy/VIP). There are ticket offices for both services near the parade ground on Jalan Gomo.

From Teluk Dalam, the ferry sails at 8 pm on Monday, Wednesday and Friday only (15,000/20,000 rp), and tickets can be booked at PT Simeuleu (☎ 21058), Jalan Ahmad Yani 41.

Getting Around
To/From the Airport SMAC operates a minibus between Binaka airport and Gunung Sitoli.

Gunung Sitoli to Teluk Dalam There are regular buses between Gunung Sitoli and Teluk Dalam. The fare is 7500 rp and the journey takes about four hours. The most common route is along the sometimes-spectacular east coast road via Tetehosi and Lahusa. Buses run until about 4 pm from Gunung Sitoli but most services are in the morning. There are also public minibuses for 10,000 rp.

Teluk Dalam to Lagundri Lagundri is about 13km from Teluk Dalam; 1500 rp by truck or bemo or 3000 rp by motorbike. If you don't specify a particular losmen when taking a motorbike from the harbour, the driver will probably whisk you to a losmen of his choice.

BUKITTINGGI
This cool, easy-going mountain town is one of the most popular travellers' centres in Sumatra. Most travellers having endured long bus journeys from Jakarta, Parapat or Sibolga to get here, will appreciate that it's a great place to relax for a while, but there are plenty of activities and sights in the region to keep you occupied. At 930m above sea level, it can get quite cool at night. Surrounding the town are three majestic mountains – Merapi, Singgalang and the more distant Sago.

Bukittinggi was a Dutch stronghold during the Padri Wars (1821-37), and it was here that the Sumatran rebels declared their rival government in 1958. Today it is a centre for Minangkabau culture, as well as being a busy market town with a small university. The town is sometimes referred to as Kota Jam Gadang (Big Clock Town), after its best known landmark, the Minangkabau-style clock tower that overlooks the large market square.

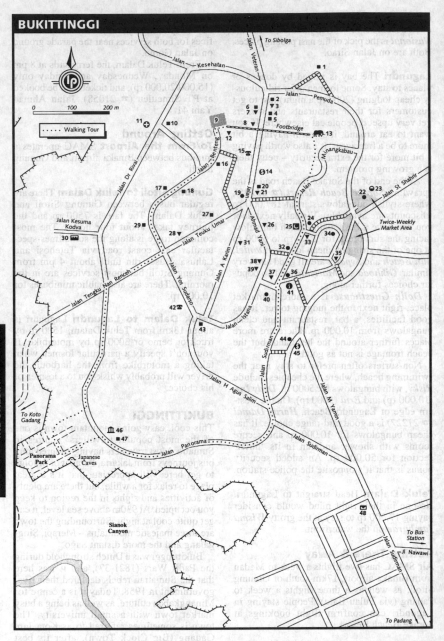

BUKITTINGGI

BUKITTINGGI

PLACES TO STAY		7	Travellers' Tavern	14	Bank Rakyat Indonesia
1	Hotel Tan Dirih	8	The Coffee Shop;	15	Wartel
2	Raja Wali		Stylist Bookshop	19	Toko Buku Setia
4	Bamboo Homestay	12	Benteng Indah Family	22	Pasar Bawah
5	Singgalang Hotel		Restaurant	23	Opelet Station
6	Hotel Murni; Hotel Nirwana	21	Jazz & Blues Cafe	24	Gloria Cinema
10	Merdeka Homestay	26	Mona Lisa	25	Mosque
16	Benteng Hotel	28	Canyon Coffee Shop	30	Swimming Pool
17	Hotel Pemandangan	31	ASEAN Restaurant	32	Toko Eka
18	D'enam Hotel	33	Simpang Raya	34	Pasar Wisata
20	Hotel Dahlia	35	Uni Lis; Post Office Branch	36	Pasar Atas
27	Hotel Kartini	37	Simpang Raya	40	Clock Tower
29	Wisma Bukittinggi	38	Selecta	41	Tourist Office
43	Novotel Bukittinggi	39	KFC	42	Wartel
47	Minang Hotel			44	Medan Nan Balituduang
		OTHER			(Dance Performances)
PLACES TO EAT		9	Fort de Kock	45	BNI Bank
3	Three Tables Coffee Shop;	11	RS Sayang Baya	46	Military Museum
	Rendezvous Coffee Shop	13	Zoo & Museum	48	Main Post Office

Orientation

Bukittinggi is quite spread out, but the town centre is conveniently compact. Most of the cheap hotels, restaurants and travel agencies are at the northern (bottom) end of the main street, Jalan Ahmad Yani. The clock tower and markets are at the top end. Jalan Sudirman runs south from the clock tower to the post office and bus station.

Information

Tourist Offices The tourist office (☎ 22403) is beside the market car park. The staff are friendly and helpful – various brochures, bus information and details of events in the region are available. It's open Monday to Thursday from 8 am to 2 pm, Friday to 11 am and Saturday to 12.30 pm. There's another tourist office next door to the Minangkabau dance centre at Jalan Lenggogeni 1.

Money The BNI bank, at the junction of Jalan Lenggogeni and Jalan M Yamin, is the best place to go. It has an ATM accepting MasterCard and Cirrus. You can also change money at the branch of the Bank Rakyat Indonesia on Jalan Ahmad Yani. After hours, you can change cash and travellers cheques at the various travel agencies around Jalan Ahmad Yani at surprisingly reasonable rates.

Post & Communications The main post office is inconveniently located south of town on Jalan Sudirman. It's open every day from 7.30 am to 4.30 pm (till noon on Sunday). At the time of writing it was about to come on-

line with an Internet service. There's a small post office branch behind Pasar Atas in the market area.

The Novotel also has a public Internet service and is about the only place you can make a reverse-charge (collect) call in Bukittinggi (7500 rp connection fee). There's a wartel on Jalan Ahmad Yani where you can make direct international calls.

Bookshops Bukittinggi is a good place to buy, sell or swap reading matter – there are three or four good second-hand bookshops on Jalan Ahmad Yani alone. Some also have good maps for sale.

Medical Services The Rumah Sakit Sayang Baya on Jalan Dr Rivai has a 24-hour 'special tourist health service'.

Markets

Bukittinggi's large and colourful **market** is crammed with stalls of fruit and vegetables, clothing and handicrafts. Market days are Wednesday and Saturday, when stall-holders spread out down the hillside towards the opelet terminal. The market area is on two levels, connected by steps and labyrinthine streets.

The permanent **Pasar Atas** (upper market) in the square opposite the clock tower was gutted by fire in August 1997, forcing the vendors to set up temporary stalls in the open square. It was in the process of being rebuilt in 1998, but rumour has it that a more modern shopping complex is planned.

INDONESIA

Walking Tour

You can do an interesting loop of Bukitting-gi's main sights in half a day, or as little as two hours, depending on how long you want to linger.

Starting at the **clock tower** (Jam Gadang), walk south down Jalan Sudirman. To the left (if it's not shrouded in mist) looms the impressive Gunung Merapi. Cross Jalan Agus Salim and turn right into Jalan Panorama where you'll pass an interesting mix of colonial and Minangkabau-style buildings. The Tri Daya Eka Dharama **Military Museum** is easily recognisable by the American Harvard B419 plane mounted on the front lawn. Inside is a collection of faded photographs, weapons and memorabilia from the War of Independence. Admission is by donation.

A little further along on the other side of Jalan Panorama is an entrance to **Panorama Park** (500 rp). There are paths leading to several lookout points with views out over the 120m-deep Sianok Canyon and to Gunung Singgalang. Near the entrance, steps lead down to the **Japanese Caves** (Lobang Jepang) (500 rp), a grid-like set of tunnels constructed by the Japanese using Indonesian slave labour during WWII.

You can exit the park further along and continue on Jalan Panorama to the junction with Jalan Tengku Nan Renceh. If you continue straight for another 150m and turn left on Jalan Kesuma Kodva, you can take a dip in the huge local **swimming pool** (1000 rp). Otherwise, turn right and walk up the hill. Just over the crest is the Canyon Coffee Shop, a good place for a rest and a drink, or turn left along Jalan Yos Sudarso and onto Jalan Benteng (past the Benteng Hotel) to the Budaya Kinantan Park (1100 rp). Here you'll find what's left of **Fort de Kock**, built by the Dutch during the Padri Wars.

Crossing the footbridge over Jalan Ahmad Yani to **Taman Bundo Kandung**, there's a good view of Bukittinggi's rusting rooftops and Gunung Singgalang to the south. On the other side is the **Puti Bungsu Zoo**, a motley collection of animals housed in small, bare cages of concrete and rusty iron. It's very popular with local tourists on weekends. The nearby **museum** (500 rp) is a fine example of Minangkabau architecture with its two rice barns at the front. It has a good collection of Minangkabau historical and cultural exhibits. Leaving the zoo you can wander down to the mosque and market area, back to where you started.

Organised Tours

Almost every hotel, coffee shop and travel agency offers tours of the district. They range from trips to the bullfighting (Tuesday and Saturday) and full-day tours of the area's attractions (around 22,500 rp) to activity tours like mountain climbing and pig hunting.

Bukittinggi is the best place to sign up for a trip to the Mentawai Islands (Siberut). There are plenty of guides offering treks at a fixed price of US$150 for 10 days or US$120 for six days. You can also arrange a guide for the climb up Gunung Merapi (US$15), or for a trek to Danau Maninjau (US$20 per day).

Places to Stay – Budget

Bukittinggi's budget hotels are a mixed bunch, but they're cheap enough. Most are close together at the bottom of Jalan Ahmad Yani. The friendly *Bamboo Homestay* (☎ 23388) has dorm beds for 4000 rp and doubles with shared mandi for 8000 rp and 10,000 rp. *Singgalang Hotel* (☎ 21576) at No 130 looks unremarkable but it's a popular place with a central courtyard and doubles for 10,000 rp or 20,000 rp with mandi.

The decrepit-looking *Raja Wali* (☎ 31905) gets plenty of travellers, probably because one of the tourist minibus companies makes its first stop here. It has dorm beds for 4000 rp and singles/doubles with mandi for 8000/9000 rp.

There are several good budget places on the much quieter road to Fort de Kock. The best of them is the friendly and well set up *D'enam Hotel* (☎ 32240) at Jalan Yos Sudarso 4. It has dorm beds for 4000 rp and clean singles/doubles for 8000/10,000 rp or 10,000/15,000 rp with shower.

Hotel Pemandangan (Mountain View Guesthouse; ☎ 21621) across the road has small but bright singles/doubles for 10,000/15,000 rp and a good view of Sianok Canyon and Gunung Singgalang out the back.

The nearby *Wisma Bukittinggi* (☎ 34008) has a wide choice of rooms, from small singles for 12,000 rp to large doubles with shower for 25,000 rp.

Merdeka Homestay (☎ 23937), on the corner of Jalan Dr Rivai and Jalan Yos Sudarso, is a solid old Dutch house with large doubles for 20,000 rp or 25,000 rp with shower.

Places to Stay – Mid-Range

Hotel Dahlia (☎ 22185) at Jalan Ahmad Yani 104-106 has spotless doubles from 20,000 rp or 40,000 rp with hot shower.

There's a much better standard of rooms at the revamped *Hotel Tan Dirih* (☎ 23207), a quiet place down the steps on Jalan Pemuda. Singles/doubles are 30,000/40,000 rp but all rooms have hot showers and it's a bright, relaxing place with a comfortable lounge area.

Hotel Kartini (☎ 22885) at Jalan Teuku Umar 21 is good value; clean and comfortable rooms with hot shower and TV are 30,000/35,000 rp including a big breakfast.

Minang Hotel (☎ 21120), next to the Military Museum at Jalan Panorama 20, has a certain threadbare charm and views over Sianok Canyon. Downstairs rooms are 55,000 rp and upstairs doubles with hot water and balcony are 65,000 and 75,000 rp.

Places to Eat

The coffee shops and restaurants along Jalan Ahmad Yani are designed with travellers in mind and feature everything from omelettes and pancakes to cold beer and toasted sandwiches, and a few Indonesian dishes.

The most popular places to hang out are the *Travellers' Tavern* and the *Rendezvous Coffee Shop* at the bottom end of the street. Both are also good places to pick up information – plenty of guides stop by to offer their services. The *Three Tables Coffee Shop* serves good food. There are several good cafes along Jalan Teuku Umar; the quiet *Canyon Coffee Shop* is a perennial favourite.

Good places to eat cheap Chinese food are the *Selecta* at Jalan Ahmad Yani 3, and the long-running *Mona Lisa*, down the street at No 58. Up near Fort de Kock, the *Benteng Indah Family Restaurant* is another good place.

Naturally enough, Padang food is plentiful. The best places are around the market. *Simpang Raya* has two branches, including one opposite the clock tower. *Nasi kapau* (rice with a selection of meats and vegetables) is a local variation on this spicy Minangkabau speciality – *Uni Lis*, next to the small post office in the market, is the best place to sample it, but you can also try the numerous night-time food stalls.

A number of places, including the western-oriented coffee houses, serve the local speciality, *dadiah campur*, a tasty mixture of oats, coconut, fruit, molasses and buffalo yoghurt.

Entertainment

There are performances of Minangkabau dance/theatre every night at the *Medan Nan Balituduang*, in a hall on the road linking Jalan Sudirman and Jalan M Yamin. The shows start at 8 pm and cost 12,500 rp.

Getting There & Away

The Aur Kuning bus station is about 2km south of the town centre, but easily reached by opelet (300 rp). There are heaps of local buses to Padang (2500 rp; two hours) and Danau Maninjau (1500 rp; 1½ hours), as well as frequent services east to Pekanbaru (5500 rp; six hours) and Dumai (10,000 rp; 10 hours).

All buses travelling the Trans-Sumatran Hwy stop at Bukittinggi. Heading south, you can catch a bus right through to Jakarta from 34,000 rp, up to 100,000 rp for the best air-con services.

The road north to Sibolga and Parapat is twisting and narrow for much of the way. Regular buses take at least 11 hours to Sibolga (15,000 rp), 18 hours to Parapat (21,000 rp) and 22 hours through to Medan (24,000 rp). The express air-con buses cut hours off the journey to Parapat by bypassing Sibolga. They cost about 10,000 rp more, or you can pay a bit extra for the luxury night buses (45,000 rp). Ticket prices vary quite a lot between travel agencies, or you can buy tickets from the agents at the bus station.

Tourist minibuses leave for Parapat every morning and cost from 27,000 rp to 47,000 rp. The latter price includes a night's accommodation at the company's office in Parapat, since you arrive after the last ferry across to Tuk Tuk. Tickets can be booked at a number of places in town. The buses stop just outside Bonjol at the equator, site of a tacky monument and vendors selling 'I Crossed The Equator' T-shirts and other souvenirs. Minibuses to Sibolga cost 25,000 rp or 35,000 rp with air-con and take at least eight hours.

If you're arriving in Bukittinggi from the north (Parapat) or east (Pekanbaru), get off the bus near the town centre to save the hassle of an opelet ride back from the bus station.

Most travel agents sell combined bus and boat tickets to Batam (via Pekanbaru) and Melaka (via Dumai). Again prices vary, but expect to pay from 56,000 rp to Batam and 125,000 rp to Melaka.

Getting Around

Opelets around Bukittinggi cost 300 rp. A *bendi* (horsecart) costs from 2000 rp depending on the distance. Motorbikes are a good way to explore the district and can be hired from travel agents or coffee shops for around 25,000 rp a day (no insurance).

INDONESIA

AROUND BUKITTINGGI

The village of **Koto Gadang**, known for its silverwork, is an hour's walk south-east of Bukittinggi through the Sianok Canyon. Turn left at the bottom of the road just before the canyon and keep going – *don't* cross the bridge.

The bustling small town of **Batu Sangkar**, 41km south-east of Bukittinggi, lies at the heart of traditional Minangkabau country. The massive **Rumah Gadang Payarugung** at the small village of Silinduang Bulan, 5km north of Batu Sangkar, is a smaller replica of the original palace of the area's rulers.

There is a **rafflesia sanctuary** about 16km north of Bukittinggi near the village of Palupuh. A sign in the village indicates the path to the sanctuary. The rafflesia normally blooms between August and November, but the tourist office in Bukittinggi can tell you if there are blooms around.

DANAU MANINJAU

Maninjau, 38km west of Bukittinggi, is another of Sumatra's beautiful mountain crater lakes. The final descent to the lake on the road from Bukittinggi is unforgettable. The road twists and turns through 44 numbered hairpin bends in quick succession, offering stunning views over the shimmering blue lake and surrounding hills. Compared with Toba, the lake is quite small – 17km long, 8km wide and 480m deep in places – giving the true feeling of being enveloped in a crater. Maninjau is well set up for travellers but remains relatively unspoiled and peaceful.

Orientation & Information

The main village is also called Maninjau. The bus stop is at the crossroads where the Bukittinggi road meets the main street, and the post office and telephone office are nearby. The Bank Rakyat Indonesia doesn't change money – either bring enough with you from Bukittinggi, or you can change cash and travellers cheques at PT Maninjau Wisata travel agent next door to Bagoes Cafe. This is also a good place for information on the area.

Things to See & Do

Hanging out by the lake is the reason most people come to Maninjau. The waters are considerably warmer – and cleaner – than at Danau Toba, so it's a good place for swimming. Some of the guesthouses hire or lend dugout canoes or inflated truck inner tubes.

When relaxation becomes too much, many

visitors tackle the road that circles the lake. It's about six hours by bicycle or 2½ hours by motorbike – you can rent them from various guesthouses and travel agencies. The road is fairly flat, but the southern half of the 70km is on a very rocky unsealed road.

There's a strenuous three-hour hike from the lake to **Sakura Hill** and **Lawang Top**, which offer excellent views of the lake and the surrounding area, but it makes far more sense to do this hike in reverse, catching a Bukittinggi-bound bus as far as **Matur** and walking (or taking an opelet) to Lawang Top. From there it's easy to find the path down to the lake. About halfway down is the Anas Homestay, where you can stop for a drink or stay the night for 8000 rp.

Khethek Cafe, a short walk north of Maninjau village, offers two to three-day **batik courses** for 60,000 rp.

Places to Stay & Eat

There are plenty of guesthouses strung out along the road north of Maninjau village as well as a couple of upmarket hotels. Most guesthouses operate their own restaurants.

To really appreciate the tranquillity of Maninjau, the best places to stay are the 'beach' bungalows beyond Bayur village, about 3km north of Maninjau. The pick of these is *Rizal Beach Homestay* (☎ *61404*) which has sturdy bungalows for 12,000 rp, a sandy beach, and a well-designed timber restaurant overlooking the lake. Back along the lakeshore towards Bayur are several more places. *Bayur Permai* has dark but secure singles/doubles for 6000/10,000 rp and *Batu C Beach* is a bigger place with dorm beds for 5000 rp and singles/doubles for 7900/11,900 rp.

In Maninjau village itself, *Pillie Homestay* (☎ *61048*), 200m from the bus stop, charges 5000/10,000 rp for basic rooms. Heading north, *Riak Danau*, *Febby's* and the *Beach Guesthouse* are three places right by the lake with not much to distinguish between them. Rooms range from 5000/8000 rp to 15,000 rp with mandi. Further along, *Happy Homestay* has clean doubles for 8000 rp and 10,000 rp, and the similarly priced *Ananda Cafe & Guesthouse* (☎ *61421*) is another good choice.

For something with a bit more style, *Hotel Tandirih* (☎ *61253*) has comfortable modern rooms with hot water and TV for 55,000 rp.

There are plenty of good cafes among the guesthouses. In Maninjau village, *Srikandi Cafe* does good local fish. About 400m north of the village, *JJ's Coffee Shop* is a convivial meeting place with a good menu and cold beer. Further along, *Maransy* is a very good restaurant overlooking the lake.

The tiny lake mussels sold by vendors opposite the bus stop in Maninjau are called *pense* and the locals eat them like peanuts. Some restaurants will prepare a delicious dish of pense or *rinuak* (lake shrimps).

Entertainment
The *Maninjau View Coffee House*, 500m north of the village, has regular cultural shows in the evenings, and the restaurant at the *Alam Maninjau Guest House*, further back on the hill, has displays of Minangkabau dance on Friday nights.

Getting There & Away
There are buses between Maninjau and Bukittinggi every hour (1500 rp; 1½ hours). Direct buses go to Padang (5000 rp; 2½ hours) via the coast road at 12.30 and 6.30 pm. Otherwise, take one of the regular buses to Lubuk Basing (1500 rp) then a bus to Padang (2500 rp). If you're staying out at Bayur you can wave buses down at the roadside.

Getting Around
Several places rent out mountain bikes for about 5000 rp a day, and motorbikes for 25,000 rp. Opelets cruise between Maninjau and the villages around to the north, including Bayur (300 rp).

PADANG
Few people linger in Padang, a bustling, steamy coastal city of 700,000, but it's a popular entry and exit point and is worth a look.

Padang is the capital of West Sumatra province, home of the Minangkabau people. No ethnic group in Sumatra maintains its cultural traditions more proudly than the Minangkabau. They are staunch Muslims, yet their society remains matrilineal – the eldest female is the head of the family and property is inherited through the female line. The most obvious sign that you are in Minangkabau country is the spectacular peaked roofs of the houses, shaped like buffalo horns.

Orientation & Information
The city centre is quite compact and easy to negotiate. The main street, Jalan M Yamin, runs inland from the coast road to the junction with Jalan Azizcham. Several hotels and the bus station are on Jalan Pemuda, which runs

north-south through the west side of town, while the opelet terminal and central market are on the northern side of Jalan M Yamin.

Tourist Offices There are two useful tourist offices: the West Sumatran tourist office (☎ 34232) at Jalan Sudirman 43, and the regional office (☎ 55711) further north at Jalan Khatib Sulaiman 22 (take an opelet along Jalan Sudirman). Both are open Monday to Thursday from 8 am to 2 pm, Friday to 11 am and Saturday to 12.30 pm.

There's also the Padang city tourist office (☎ 34186) at Jalan Samudera 1.

Money All the major Indonesian banks can be found around the city centre. The BCA bank on Jalan Agus Salim has a Visa ATM, and BNI is south of Jalan M Yani, just off Jalan Hiligoo. Gramedia Bookshop on Jalan Veteran is a useful place – outside are ATMs accepting all major cards. American Express is represented by Pacto (☎ 37678) on Jalan Tan Malaka. There's a 24-hour money-changing service with reasonable rates at the Dipo International Hotel on Jalan Diponegoro.

Post & Communications The main post office is at Jalan Azizcham 7. It has a single public Internet terminal (10,000 rp per hour). The Dipo International Hotel has an Internet cafe with two terminals which you can use for a steep 20,000 rp an hour.

There are plenty of wartels around town, including a central one on Jalan Imam Bonjol.

Things to See & Do
The **Adityawarman Museum**, 500m from the bus station on Jalan Diponegoro, is built in the Minangkabau tradition with two rice barns out the front. It has a small but excellent collection of antiques and other objects from all over West Sumatra. The museum is open daily (except Monday) from 8 am to 6 pm (500 rp). The nearby **Taman Budaya** cultural centre has free performances of traditional dance every Sunday at 10 am. There are free tours of the centre at other times.

Part of the old **railway line** from Padang to Bukittinggi has been re-opened for tourist trains. Every Sunday, there is a train from Padang up the coast to Pariaman at 8.30 am, returning at 2.30 pm, and another train to the Anai Valley, near Padangpanjang, at 8.45 am, returning at 4 pm. Both charge 5000 rp return. The train station (☎ 32200) is east of the city at Jalan Stasiun 1.

PADANG

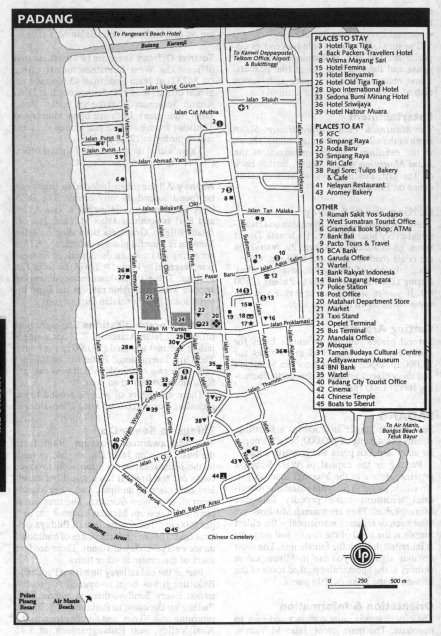

To Pangeran's Beach Hotel

Batang Kuranji

To Kanwil Depparpostel,
Telkom Office, Airport
& Bukittinggi

Jalan Ujung Gurun

Jalan Situjuh

Jalan Cut Muthia

Jalan Veteran

Jalan Purus II

Jalan Purus I

Jalan Ahmad Yani

Jalan Perintis Kemerdekaan

Jalan Belakang Olo

Jalan Tan Malaka

Jalan Sudirman

Jalan Bandung Olo

Jalan Pasar Raya

Pasar Baru

Jalan Agus Salim

Jalan Pemuda

Jalan Proklamasi

Jalan M Yamin

Jalan Diponegoro

Jalan Samudera

Jalan Hiligoo

Jalan Imam Bonjol

Jalan Azizchan

Jalan Alanglawas

Jalan Thamrin

Jalan Mayang Wiruk

Gereja

Jalan Pondok

Jalan Gereja

Jalan Nias

To Air Manis,
Bungus Beach &
Teluk Bayur

Jalan H O S Cokroaminoto

Jalan Niaga

Jalan Nipah Berok

Jalan Batang Arau

Batang Arau

Chinese Cemetery

Pulau
Pisang
Besar

Air Manis
Beach

0   250   500 m

PLACES TO STAY
3 Hotel Tiga Tiga
4 Back Packers Travellers Hotel
8 Wisma Mayang Sari
15 Hotel Femina
19 Hotel Benyamin
26 Hotel Old Tiga Tiga
28 Dipo International Hotel
33 Sedona Bumi Minang Hotel
36 Hotel Sriwijaya
39 Hotel Natour Muara

PLACES TO EAT
5 KFC
16 Simpang Raya
22 Roda Baru
30 Simpang Raya
37 Riri Cafe
38 Pagi Sore; Tulips Bakery
    & Cafe
41 Nelayan Restaurant
43 Aromey Bakery

OTHER
1 Rumah Sakit Yos Sudarso
2 West Sumatran Tourist Office
6 Gramedia Book Shop; ATMs
7 Bank Bali
9 Pacto Tours & Travel
10 BCA Bank
11 Garuda Office
12 Wartel
13 Bank Rakyat Indonesia
14 Bank Dagang Negara
17 Police Station
18 Post Office
20 Matahari Department Store
21 Market
23 Taxi Stand
24 Opelet Terminal
25 Bus Terminal
27 Mandala Office
29 Mosque
31 Taman Budaya Cultural Centre
32 Adityawarman Museum
34 BNI Bank
35 Wartel
40 Padang City Tourist Office
42 Cinema
44 Chinese Temple
45 Boats to Siberut

Places to Stay

There are a few reasonable budget hotels. A good place close to the city centre is the motel-style *Hotel Benyamin* (☎ 22324) at Jalan Azizcham 15, down the lane next to Hotel Femina. The airy rooms on the top floors are better than the rather dingy rooms on the ground floor. Singles/doubles cost from 17,500/25,000 rp and all rooms have fans – a good investment in steamy Padang. *Hotel Sriwijaya* (☎ 23577), at Jalan Alanglawas, has basic clean singles/doubles from 15,000/20,000 rp. There are better air-con rooms for 30,000/35,000 rp.

The *Backpackers Travellers Hotel* (☎ 35751), also known as Hotel Wisma Ransel, sounds promising, but it's a bit sterile and not particularly cheap. It's as clean as a hospital though, and there's a range of rooms. A spotless dorm with fan is 15,000 rp, a small single costs 24,000 rp or an air-con double with TV is 48,000 rp. The hotel is 2km north of the bus station at Jalan Purus II, but there's free transport from the co-owned *Dipo International Hotel* (☎ 34261), Jalan Diponegoro 25.

There are a couple of reasonable budget options just around the corner on Jalan Veteran, including *Hotel Tiga Tiga* (☎ 22123) at (not surprisingly) No 33 with large singles/doubles for 22,000/27,500 rp with fan, mandi and breakfast. Convenient to the bus station, *Hotel Old Tiga Tiga* certainly is old, but it has cheap rooms for 10,000/15,000 rp and reasonable air-con rooms with mandi for 25,000/33,000 rp.

There are several old Dutch houses that have been converted into hotels. The best of them is the friendly guesthouse-style *Wisma Mayang Sari* (☎ 22647), Jalan Sudirman 19. It has clean rooms with air-con, hot water and TV for 40,000/45,000 rp.

Places to Eat

The city is famous as the home of Padang food (nasi padang), the spicy Minangkabau cooking found throughout Indonesia.

Padang food would have to qualify as the world's fastest fast food. There are no menus. You simply sit down and almost immediately the waiter will set down at least half a dozen bowls of various curries and a bowl of plain rice. You pay only for what you eat, and you can test the sauces for free. *Rendang* (beef slowly simmered in coconut milk) is the most famous Padang dish.

Padang food specialists include *Roda Baru*, upstairs in the market at Jalan Pasar Raya 6 and *Simpang Raya*, with branches opposite the post office at Jalan Azizcham 24 and at Jalan Bundo Kandung 3.

Jalan Pondok, which runs through the city's Chinese quarter, is a good place for Chinese food. The *Riri Cafe*, at No 86, is a pleasant little place that opens in the evenings. Further down on the other side of the road, *Tulips Bakery & Cafe* has good sweets and sit-down meals, and *Pagi Sore* is another good nasi padang restaurant.

If you feel like a treat, check out the seafood at the popular *Nelayan Restaurant*, Jalan Cokroaminoto 44. Allow at least 30,000 rp per head for a filling meal.

Getting There & Away

Air Most flights in and out of Padang are domestic, but a new international airport is being planned to replace Padang's Tabing airport and make this a major Sumatran gateway.

Garuda has daily flights to Jakarta and one to Medan. Merpati has regular flights to Jakarta, Medan and Pulau Batam. Mandala has cheaper daily flights to Jakarta (20% discount on published fare), while SMAC flies to Gunung Sitoli on Pulau Nias every Wednesday.

Pelangi Air services Malaysia with five flights a week to Kuala Lumpur (US$142) and two to Johor Bahru (US$107).

Merpati (☎ 32010) and Pelangi Air (☎ 38103) are based at Hotel Natour Muara, Jalan Gereja 34. Mandala (☎ 32773) is at Jalan Pemuda 29A. Garuda (☎ 30173) is at Jalan Sudirman 2 and Silk Air (☎ 38120) has an office at the Sedona Bumi Minang Hotel.

Bus Padang's bus station is conveniently central. Every north-south bus comes through here so there are loads of options, including frequent buses to Bukittinggi (2500 rp; two hours). You can get all the way to Jakarta in 30 hours for 54,000 rp, or 85,000 rp air-con. (There are local buses that do the trip for 35,000 rp in a grinding 48 hours). Fares to Parapat (for Danau Toba) and Medan are the same, ranging from 30,000 rp to 65,000 rp for the best services. Other destinations include Pekanbaru (10,500/13,500 rp), Bengkulu (17,500 rp) and Jambi (20,000 rp).

Boat Between them the Pelni ships *Kambuna* and *Lambelu* call at Padang's port of Teluk Bayur every Friday at 6 pm en route to Gunung Sitoli (36,000 rp deck class; 11 hours) and Sibolga (48,000 rp). They stop again every Sunday at 10 am on the way south to Jakarta (81,500 rp; 30 hours), Surabaya and Balikpapan. The Pelni office (☎ 61674) is at Teluk Bayur, but you can buy tickets from most travel agents in town.

See the Mentawai Islands section later for details of boats to Pulau Siberut.

Getting Around
To/From the Airport Padang's Tabing airport is 9km north of the centre. Airport taxis charge a standard 10,000 rp into town. The budget alternative is to walk from the airport terminal to the main road and catch any opelet heading south (350 rp). Going to the airport, city bus (bis kota) 14A is the best one to get.

Local Transport There are numerous opelets and mikrolets around town, operating out of the Pasar Raya terminal off Jalan M Yamin. The standard fare is 350 rp. Horse-drawn bendi are also common in the town centre.

MENTAWAI ISLANDS
The Mentawais are a remote chain of islands about 100km west of Padang. The largest island, Siberut, is home to most of the population of 30,000. The other islands – Sipora, Pagai Utara and Pagai Selatan – are sparsely populated and seldom visited.

After being left quietly on their own for thousands of years, change is coming at an alarming rate for the Mentawains. Trekking has become big business on Siberut, with a steady stream of travellers heading out into the jungles to catch a glimpse of a primitive culture that is fast disappearing. The villagers, their bodies covered with ritual tattoos and wearing little but loin cloths and decorative bands, are a photogenic lot who have found tour groups to be a good source of income. Tourism is, however, but a minor development alongside logging, transmigration, and government attempts to 'civilise' the islanders.

The islands have some unusual endemic wildlife, including the *siamang kerdil* (dwarf black gibbon). Chloroquine-resistant malaria is a problem.

Organised Tours
Most travellers take the easy option of joining an organised tour. It is also the cheap option in view of the costs involved in chartering

boats and guides on your own. The best place to shop for tours is Bukittinggi, where they are promoted in every coffee shop, losmen and travel agency. Prices are fixed at US$150 for a 10 day tour and US$120 for six days, but the latter is not good value given that it involves nearly three days in transit. Trips can also be organised in Padang – check with the tourist office.

You can expect heavy rain at any time of the year and the treks usually include plenty of mud slogging, river crossings and battles with indigenous insects, so it's definitely not a casual hiking experience. Tours are often cancelled in June and July when the seas are too rough for safe sailing.

Getting There & Away
There are boats to the Mentawai Islands from Padang's Batang Arau harbour four times a week. PT Rusco Lines (☎ 21941), Jalan Batang Arau 31, has boats from Padang to Muarasiberut on Monday and Wednesday, returning on Tuesday and Thursday. The fares are 19,000/25,000 rp for deck/cabin class. The office is to the right through the alleyway opposite the port gates. Boats leave at 7 pm, and the journey takes about 10 to 12 hours.

PT Mentawai Indah (☎ 28200), Jalan Batang Arau 80, has boats to Sikakap (Pulau Pagai Utara) on Monday and Thursday for 20,000/30,000 rp.

PEKANBARU
Before American engineers struck oil in the area shortly before WWII, Pekanbaru was little more than a sleepy river port on the Sungai Siak. Today, it is Indonesia's oil capital, a bustling modern city of more than 500,000 people. There's little reason for travellers to stop here, and people either pass straight through or just stay overnight on the trip between Singapore and Bukittinggi.

Orientation & Information
The main street of Pekanbaru is Jalan Sudirman and most banks, hotels and offices can be found here or close by. Speedboats leave from the wharf at the end of Jalan Sudirman, while the bus station is at the other end of town on Jalan Nangka, off Jalan Sudirman.

The tourist office (☎ 31562) is a long way from the city centre at Jalan Merbabu 16. The BCA bank, at Jalan Sudirman 448, is the best place to change money.

Places to Stay & Eat

Most people head straight to *Poppie's Home-stay* (☎ 33863), a few minutes walk from the bus station on Jalan Cempedak II. There are doubles with mandi for 15,000 rp, small singles for 5000 rp, and a restaurant serving basic meals. The owner speaks good English and can arrange boat tickets to Batam.

The alternative is *Tommy's Place*, 400m from the bus station on Gang Nantongga, next to Jalan Nangka 53. Tommy charges 5000 rp per person and can also arrange tickets for the Batam boats.

There are innumerable cheap places to eat along Jalan Sudirman, particularly in the evening around the market at the junction with Jalan Imam Bonjol. The *New Holland Bakery*, at Jalan Sudirman 153, has a fine selection of cakes and pastries as well as hamburgers and ice cream. It also does fresh fruit juices.

Getting There & Away

Air Simpang Tiga is a busy visa-free entry point. Pelangi Air flies to Kuala Lumpur three times a week for US$110, and to Melaka for US$62. Silk Air flies to Singapore for US$100.

Merpati has direct flights to Jakarta as well as to Medan and Batam.

Bus Bukittinggi is the main destination and there are frequent departures from the bus station on Jalan Nangka. The 222km trip takes five to six hours and tickets cost from 5500/7500 rp without/with air-con.

Boat Agencies all around town sell tickets for the boats to Batam. It's possible to go all the way by boat, leaving from the port at the end of Jalan Sudirman, but most tickets involve a combination of bus to the harbour (3½ hours) and ferry to Batam (35,000 rp; four hours). Total time is around eight hours, reaching Batam in time to catch a ferry to Singapore.

Getting Around

Airport cabs charge 10,000 rp for the 12km trip into town. It's a 1km walk to the main road if you want to catch an opelet (300 rp) into town.

DUMAI

Most of Pekanbaru's oil exits through the port of Dumai, 199km to the north. There's no reason to visit Dumai, but it is an increasingly popular visa-free entry point with ferry links to the Malaysian port of Melaka.

From Melaka, daily high-speed ferries (RM80; 2½ hours) operate to Dumai at 10 am. From Dumai the ferries run daily, except Sunday, at 3 pm (100,000 rp). There are frequent buses from Dumai to Pekanbaru and Bukittinggi.

The Pelni ships *Kerinci* and *Bukit Siguntang* sail from Dumai every Sunday at 4 pm to Jakarta, via Pulau Bintan (97,000 rp; 48 hours).

BATAM

Nowhere in Indonesia is the pace of development more rapid than on Pulau Batam in the Riau Archipelago. For the most part there's a distinct frontier town atmosphere to the place, with high prices, ugly construction sites and no reason to pause any longer than it takes to catch a boat out.

Orientation & Information

Most travellers arrive on Batam by boat from Singapore to the port of Sekupang. It's a minute's walk to the domestic ferry terminal, from where there are speedboats to numerous other Sumatran destinations. Ferries to Pulau Bintan leave from Telaga Panggur in the south-east.

The Batam Tourist Promotion Board (☎ 32 2852) has a small office outside the international terminal at Sekupang. The best exchange rates are in Nagoya, where all the major banks are based. Singapore dollars are as acceptable as Indonesian rupiah.

Places to Stay & Eat

Budget accommodation on Batam is some of the worst in Indonesia and starts at around 25,000 rp. There is a line of utterly rock-bottom places about 1km out of town at Blok C, Jalan Teuku Umar. The *Minang Jaya* is the best of a bad bunch with bare, partitioned rooms.

Restaurants on Batam are expensive, much like everything else, but there are some good seafood places. The best eating in Nagoya is found at the night food stalls along Jalan Raja Ali Haji or at the big and raucous *Pujasera Nagoya* food centre.

Getting There & Away

Air Garuda has daily direct flights from Hang Nadim airport to Jakarta. Merpati has flights to Medan and Padang.

Boat Ferries shuttle constantly between Singapore's World Trade Centre and Sekupang. The trip takes 40 minutes and costs S$17/30 one way/return. There are less frequent services from the World Trade Centre to Batu Ampar and Nongsa.

Speedboats to Tanjung Pinang on neighbouring Pulau Bintan leave from Telaga Panggur, 30km south-east of Nagoya. There's a steady flow of departures from 8 am to 5.15 pm (11,000 rp; 45 minutes).

The main reason travellers come to Batam is to catch an onward boat to Pekanbaru on the Sumatran mainland. Boats leave from the domestic wharf at Sekupang, 100m south of the international terminal. The journey involves a four hour boat trip to Tanjung Buton on the Sumatran mainland, followed by a three hour bus ride. The combined ticket costs about 35,000 rp. There are no services to Pekanbaru after 10 am, so you'll need to make an early start if you're coming from Singapore.

Other destinations from Sekupang include: Pulau Karimun (16,500 rp); Pulau Kundur (17,000 rp); Dumai (35,000 rp); and Kuala Tungkal on the Jambi coast (60,000 rp).

Getting Around
There is a token bus service between Nagoya and Sekupang for 600 rp, but most people use the share taxis that cruise the island: just stand by the roadside and call out your destination to passing cabs. Sample fares from Sekupang include 3000 rp to Nagoya and 10,000 rp to Telaga Panggur.

PULAU BINTAN
Bintan is twice as large as Batam and many times more interesting. The main attractions are the old town of Tanjung Pinang (a visa-free entry/exit point), nearby Penyenget Island and the relatively untouched beaches of the east coast.

Tanjung Pinang
After development-mad Batam, Tanjung Pinang comes as a very pleasant surprise. It may be the largest town in the Riau Archipelago – being the modern administrative centre – but it retains much of its old-time charm.

Information Bong's Homestay (see Places to Stay) is the best source of information. Change money at the BCA bank on Jalan Temiang.

The post office is near the harbour on the main street, Jalan Merdeka. International phone calls can be made from the wartel office on Jalan Hangtuah.

Things to See The old stilted part of town around Jalan Plantar II is well worth a wander. To get there, turn left at the colourful fruit market at the northern end of Jalan Merdeka.

Senggarang is a fascinating village just across the harbour from Tanjung Pinang. The star attraction is an old Chinese temple held together by the roots of a huge banyan tree that has grown up through it. Boats to Senggarang leave from the end of Jalan Plantar II.

You can charter a sampan to take you up the Sungai Ular (Snake River) through the mangroves to see another Chinese temple which has gory murals of the trials and tortures of hell.

Places to Stay & Eat Don't believe a word you're told by the hotel touts at the ferry dock, who will try to persuade you that popular travellers' places don't exist. Lorong Bintan II, a small alley between Jalan Bintan and Jalan Yusuf Khahar in the centre of town, is the place to look. The popular *Bong's Homestay* at No 20 has dorm beds for 10,000 rp and doubles for 15,000 rp, including breakfast. *Johnny's Homestay*, next door at No 22, takes the overflow.

During the day, there are several pleasant *coffee shops* with outdoor eating areas in front of the basketball stadium on Jalan Teuku Umar.

Pulau Penyenget
This tiny island, a short hop across the harbour from Tanjung Pinang, was once the capital of the Riau rajas. The place is littered with reminders of its past and there are ruins and graveyards wherever you walk. There are frequent boats to the island from Bintan's main pier for 1000 rp per person.

Beaches
The best beaches are along the east coast, where there is also good snorkelling outside the November to March monsoon period. There are buses to Pantai Trikora for 2500 rp from the bus station in Tanjung Pinang.

Yasin's Guesthouse (☎ 26770), at the 36km marker near the village of Teluk Bakau, is a laid-back place with half a dozen simple palm huts right on the beach at 25,000 rp per person per day, including three meals.

Getting There & Away
Air Sempati used to connect with Jakarta and Pekanbaru, but like everywhere in Indonesia, domestic air services were in a state of flux

at the time of writing, and these services may or may not have resumed.

Boat Although most of the boats to mainland Riau operate from neighbouring Batam, Tanjung Pinang retains its traditional role as the hub of Riau's inter-island shipping. Most services leave from the main pier at the southern end of Jalan Merdeka, but check when you buy your ticket.

Four boats a day sail direct to Singapore's Tanah Merah ferry terminal for S$39 (1½ hours).

There are regular speedboats to Telaga Panggur on Batam (11,000 rp; 45 minutes), as well as three boats a day direct to Sekupang (13,000 rp; 1½ hours).

There are boats to Tanjung Balai on Pulau Karimun (22,000 rp; 2½ hours), and Dabo on Pulau Singkep (25,000 rp; four hours), as well as a daily express service to Pekanbaru which involves changing boats on Batam. There are also occasional slow boats up the Sungai Siak to Pekanbaru.

For Jakarta, Pelni ships call at the port of Kijang, in the south-eastern corner of the island. The best services are the *Kerinci* and *Bukit Siguntang* which sail between Dumai and Jakarta, stopping at Kijang every Monday (10 am departure) and Saturday (6 pm departure). The journey takes 28 hours and costs around 90,000 rp deck class. The Pelni office (☎ 21513) in Tanjung Pinang is at Jalan Ketapang 8.

Alternatively, the MV *Samudera Jaya* leaves Tanjung Pinang for Jakarta every Thursday (95,000 rp; 18 hours).

Getting Around

Taxis from the airport to Tanjung Pinang cost 15,000 rp. Buses and share taxis to other parts of Bintan leave from the bus and taxi station on Jalan Teuku Umar.

BANDARLAMPUNG

There's not much reason to get off the bus at Bandarlampung, except to use it as a base for visits to Krakatau or Way Kambas National Park.

The capital of Lampung province is Sumatra's fourth largest city, formed by a merger of the old towns of Telukbetung (coastal) and Tanjungkarang (inland). When Krakatau erupted in 1883, almost half of its 36,000 tsunami victims were claimed by the 30m-high wave that funnelled up the Bay of Lampung and devastated Telukbetung.

Orientation & Information

It's difficult to find a convenient centre for Bandarlampung – the bus station, hotel district, provincial tourist office and post office are at far flung corners of the sprawling city. Jalan Raden Intan is the main street running north-south from Tanjungkarang, becoming Jalan Diponegoro then Jalan Patimura as it reaches Telukbetung in the south.

The tourist office (☎ 25 1900) is inconveniently located above the main post office at Jalan Kh Dahlan 21, halfway between Tanjungkarang and Telukbetung. The staff are friendly and speak English. Equally helpful is the Lampung Provincial Tourist Association (☎ 48 2565) at Jalan WR Supratman 39. This is a good place to organise trips to Way Kambas and Krakatau.

Major banks can be found in Tanjungkarang near the train station. BNI has a branch at the roundabout on Jalan Teuku Umar. It has an ATM accepting MasterCard and Cirrus. There's a BCA bank, with a Visa ATM, at Jalan Raden Intan 98, opposite Hotel Arinas.

The post office has three Internet terminals, charging 6000 rp an hour. There's a wartel for international calls next to the Telkom office on Jalan Kartini.

Things to See & Do

There's not a lot to see in Bandarlampung. The **Krakatau Monument** is a steel maritime buoy that was washed out of the Bay of Lampung by the post-Krakatau tidal wave and turned into a monument where it came to rest on a hillside overlooking Telukbetung. It's not much to look at but it is a sobering thought that everything below this point was wiped out by the wall of water.

Diving in the Bay of Lampung is the latest activity being promoted in the hope of luring visitors. The Lampung Dive and Fishing Centre (☎ 48 1481) can arrange dives to Pulau Tegal (from US$88) and Pulau Pagaran (from US$172) – the tourist office has details.

Places to Stay

The best budget option in Bandarlampung is *Hotel Lusy* (☎ 48 5695), Jalan Diponegoro 186. It's a long way from the bus station, but only a 15 minute walk from the provincial tourist office and the Krakatau monument. Clean rooms start at 15,000 rp for a double with fan, up to 30,000 rp with air-con and TV.

Things are pretty grim up at Tanjungkarang. *Hotel Ria* (☎ 25 3974), opposite the roundabout on Jalan Teuku Umar has basic economy rooms from 12,500 rp, doubles with fan for 31,500 rp or 45,500 rp with air-con. *Hotel Gading (☎ 25 5512)*, nearby at Jalan Kartini 72, is another option, with rooms starting at 20,000 rp.

There are some pretty good mid-range hotels clustered together on Jalan Raden Intan. *Hotel Purnama (☎ 25 1447; fax 25 3672)* at No 77-79 is the cheapest with rooms starting at 23,500 rp for a double with fan and 29,500 rp for a basic double with air-con and TV. Add 15% for tax and service.

Places to Eat

The best cheap food in Bandarlampung is at the *Pasar Mambo* night markets in Telukbetung, at the junction of Jalan Supratman and Jalan Malahayati. There are smaller night markets in Tanjungkarang on Jalan Kartini and next to the cinema complex on Jalan Imam Bonjol. The *Sari Bundo* and the *Bedagang I* are a couple of good Padang restaurants on Jalan Imam Bonjol.

The *Golden Dragon Restaurant & Bar* at Jalan Yos Sudarso 272 is a good place for Chinese and seafood.

Getting There & Away

Air Merpati has daily flights to Jakarta (205,100 rp). The Merpati office is at Jalan Kartini 90 (☎ 26 3419).

Bus Rajabasa bus station is one of the busiest in Sumatra, with a constant flow of departures, 24 hours a day, both south to Jakarta and north to all parts of Sumatra. Most people heading north go to Bukittinggi, a long haul that costs from 37,500 rp ekonomi (up to 28 hours) to 81,000 rp air-con (22 hours). The trip to Jakarta takes eight hours and tickets range from 17,500 rp to 27,500 rp air-con, which includes the ferry between Bakauheni and Merak.

Train Three trains a day run between Bandarlampung and Palembang, leaving at 8.30 and 10.30 am, and 9 pm in both directions. The 8.30 am and 9 pm trains have bisnis (20,000 rp) and eksekutif (30,000 rp) class only and take 6½ hours, while the 10.30 am 'market' trains have ekonomi class only (6000 rp) and take an hour longer.

Taxi Share taxis offer a door-to-door service between Bandarlampung and Bakauheni (6000 rp) and Jakarta (45,000 rp). They can save a lot of hassle getting to and from bus stations at both ends. For Bakauheni, try Taxi 4545 (☎ 52264); for Jakarta try Taxi 333 (☎ 48 5579).

Getting Around

Taxis charge a fixed 21,000 rp for the 22km ride from the airport to town. It will cost half that if you can find a metered taxi from town to the airport. The minimum charge for a taxi around town is 3000 rp. There are frequent opelets between Tanjungkarang train station and Rajabasa bus station, and between Tanjungkarang and Telukbetung (300 rp).

KALIANDA

The small coastal port of Kalianda is the best place to arrange boat trips out to **Krakatau**. *Hotel Beringin (☎ 0727 2008)* has good doubles with mandi for 15,000 rp and can organise boats for around 50,000 rp per person. The tourist office in Bandarlampung can also arrange boat charters for around 250,000 rp. The seaworthiness of some of the boats is questionable – check for life-jackets and a two-way radio.

Getting There & Away

There are opelets to Kalianda from Bakauheni (2000 rp) and buses from Bandarlampung (2000 rp).

WAY KAMBAS

Local tourist authorities are keen to promote the attractions of **Way Kambas National Park**, but the soccer-playing elephants of the **elephant training centre** appeal more to domestic tourists than to foreign visitors. The park has other less captive attractions in its 1300 sq km – wildlife includes rare Sumatran tigers and rhinos, and 250 species of birds.

There is a small *guesthouse* at Way Kambas with basic rooms for 30,000 rp a double and there are *food stalls* during the day but nowhere else to eat. Entry to the national park is 1500 rp. The tourist office in Bandarlampung can organise trips to Way Kambas.

Getting There & Away

From Bandarlampung's Rajabasa bus station take a Labuhanmaringgai bus (3000 rp; two hours) and get off at the entrance to Way Kambas. From here you can take an ojek (7500 rp) into the park. Aim to arrive before 5 pm.

BAKAUHENI

Bakauheni is the departure point for ferries to

Java – see the Getting There & Away section earlier in this chapter for details.

There are frequent buses from right outside Bakauheni's terminal building for the 90km trip to Bandarlampung (2000/4000 rp air-con). If you're planning to stay in Bandarlampung, it's worth paying 6000 rp for a seat in a share taxi which will take you to the hotel of your choice.

Nusa Tenggara

Nusa Tenggara is the string of islands that starts to the east of Bali and ends with Timor. Some of the most spectacular attractions of Indonesia can be found in Nusa Tenggara – Gunung Rinjani on Lombok, the dragons of Komodo, the immense stone tombs of Sumba and the coloured volcanic lakes of Kelimutu on Flores.

Although a steady stream of travellers passes through, until recently the lack of transport confined most of them to a limited route. There are now more opportunities for off-the-beaten-track explorations, and the lack of tourists in these places will mean that your reception will be more natural. It does create one problem, though: you will sometimes be the centre of attention, attracting an entourage of children in a small village, all programmed to yell 'hello mister' until either they or you collapse from exhaustion.

You need at least a month to get a reasonable look around the whole chain.

Getting There & Away

Denpasar on Bali is the usual jumping-off point for the islands of Nusa Tenggara – you can go by ferry, hydrofoil or plane across to Lombok, or fly to one of the other islands. Flights from Nusa Tenggara terminate on Bali or Surabaya (Java), with same-day connections on to other parts of Indonesia.

Merpati flies twice a week between Kupang in Timor and Darwin in Australia's Northern Territory. This is an excellent way to travel to Indonesia from Australia. You can then island-hop through Nusa Tenggara to Bali without having to backtrack, as you would on a return trip into the islands from Bali.

Getting Around

Air Flights in Nusa Tenggara are handled by Merpati, although Merpati's theme song – 'It's Merpati and I'll Fly If I Want To' – comes true in Nusa Tenggara. Short flights are subect to cancellation, and bookings are not always

reliable. Mataram, Kupang and Maumere are the main air hubs and the most reliable places to get a flight.

Bus On the islands travel is by bus. Air-con express coaches run right across Lombok and Sumbawa, but elsewhere small buses with limited legroom are crammed with passengers and all manner of produce. They constantly stop to drop off and pick up passengers, and if buses are not full, they will endlessly loop around town searching for passengers until they are full. The main highways are now paved, but narrow and usually winding. Don't underestimate journey times – a trip of only 100km may take three hours or more – and don't overestimate your endurance abilities.

Most buses leave early in the morning, so be prepared for early starts.

Car & Motorcycle A motorbike is an ideal way to explore Nusa Tenggara, but outside Lombok, hiring a motorbike is not always easy, so you really need to bring your own.

Cars with driver can be hired, but outside Lombok, asking rates are very high, count on US$40 a day or more.

Boat Regular vehicle/passenger ferries connect all the main islands, thus making a loop through the islands from Bali and back fairly easy. From Bali through to Flores, schedules don't vary much, but further east the crackpot company in Kupang that runs the ferries is forever fiddling with the schedules, though routes are fairly constant. You'll have to find out the latest schedules on arrival.

Pelni also has regular connections, but routes are also subject to change.

Lombok

Lombok has one main urban area, tranquil countryside, uncrowded beaches and a truly spectacular volcano. Senggigi is an established resort, and basic facilities exist in a few other places, but otherwise there's little tourist development, especially compared to Bali. Most people on Lombok are Muslim, but 10% are Balinese Hindus, and a few follow the indigenous Wektu Telu religion.

Balinese princes ruled Lombok from the mid-18th century until the 1890s, when the Dutch sided with the Sasaks and defeated the Balinese in bloody battles. Economic, historical and religious rivalries still exist between Bali and Lombok.

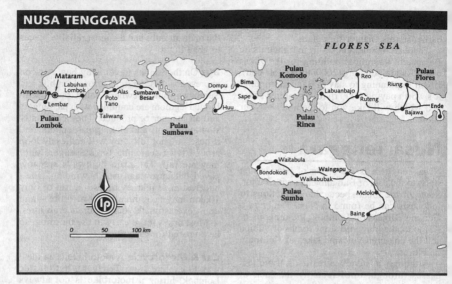

NUSA TENGGARA

FLORES SEA

0   50   100 km

Activities

Gunung Rinjani and its surroundings is a superb area for **trekking**. If you just want to explore the countryside on foot, visit a number of villages in central Lombok, between the main east-west road and the southern slopes of Rinjani.

There is good **snorkelling** and **scuba diving** off the Gili Islands. A few dive centres are located on these islands and along the Senggigi tourist strip, some better than others. The dearth of tourists on Lombok means that substantial discounts are possible, so diving is usually far cheaper than on Bali.

The south and east coasts of Lombok get the same swells that generate the big breaks on Bali's Bukit Peninsula. Lombok's Kuta Beach is the most accessible **surfing** spot, others are often hard to reach by road or boat. The easiest way is on a surf tour on a chartered yacht, usually from Bali. These cost about US$200 per person for a seven-day, all-inclusive trip around Nusa Lembongan (off the south-east coast of Bali), Lombok and Sumbawa. You can book these at surf shops around Bali's Kuta Beach.

Getting There & Away

Air Merpati is the only domestic airline serving Lombok. It has about ten flights a day to Denpasar, as well as daily flights to Bima, Sumbawa Besar and Surabaya, from where there are many onward connections.

Silk Air has direct flights to/from Singapore five times a week for US$220/321 (one-way/return).

Airline Offices The main Merpati office (☎ 36745) is on Jalan Selaparang, in Cakranegara; and there is also a Merpati agency (☎ 33844), opposite the Perama office, on Jalan Pejanggik. The Garuda office (☎ 32305) is in Hotel Lombok Raya. The Bouraq office (☎ 27333) in Hotel Selaparang takes bookings for Bouraq flights elsewhere in Indonesia even though there are no Bouraq flights to/from Lombok. Silk Air has an office in Senggigi (☎ 93877).

Bus Every day, buses from the terminal in Sweta (Mataram) go to most cities in Sumbawa, such as Sumbawa Besar (8950/15,000 rp for economy/air-con class; five hours) and Bima (16,100/27,500 rp; 12 hours); as well as to Denpasar (about 20,000 rp) and Surabaya, Java (about 40,000 rp). All prices include ferry fares. You can buy tickets from travel agents, but they're cheaper at the terminal.

Shuttle Bus The Bali-based operator, Perama, has shuttle bus services between Senggigi, the Gili Islands and Kuta (Lombok), and most tourist centres on Bali, as well as connections from Bali to Java and from Lombok to Sumbawa. A few other companies have similar services at similar prices.

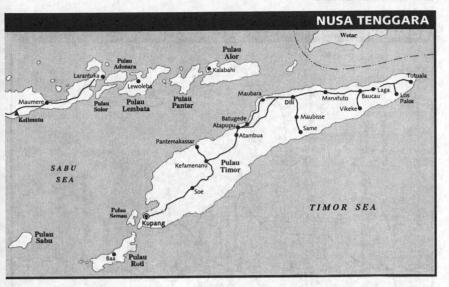

NUSA TENGGARA

Shuttle buses are more expensive than public transport, but they save you considerable hassle changing bemos. Fares include transport on any ferry or boat.

Boat Ferries to Bali leave from Lembar every 60 to 90 minutes, 24 hours a day. The cost for 2nd/1st class is 5500/9000 rp. Bicycles cost an extra 700 rp; motorbikes, 6200 rp; cars, 35,700 rp.

Ferries also leave Labuhan Lombok (also known as Labuhan Kayangan), in eastern Lombok, for Poto Tano (Sumbawa) every 45 to 60 minutes, 24 hours a day. The cost for 2nd/1st class is 2350/3650 rp. Motorbikes cost an extra 6050 rp; and cars, 36,900 rp.

Two Pelni boats, the *Awu* and the *Tilongkabila*, stop at Lembar every week or so during their loop around Indonesia. The Pelni office (☎ 37212) is in Ampenan.

The luxury jet-powered *Mabua Express* (☎ 25895) provides a fast boat service between the Pelni port at Lembar and Benoa Port (Bali). Tickets currently cost 80,000 rp, and you can book at any travel agency on Bali and Lombok.

Getting Around
To/From the Airport Taxis from the airport cost 12,000 rp to anywhere in Mataram, 13,000 rp to Senggigi, and 26,000 rp to Bang-sal (for the Gili Islands). Frequent No 7 bemos travel between the airport, and the Ampenan terminal.

Bemo & Bus The main bus and bemo terminal on Lombok is at Sweta, and others include Praya and Bayan. Away from the main roads, you often need to take a *cidomo* (horse cart), an ojek, charter a bemo or walk.

Car & Motorcycle Cars and motorbikes can only be rented in Senggigi, and at agencies along Jalan Pejanggik in Mataram, and around central Ampenan. Prices and rental conditions are very similar to Bali – refer to that section for details.

Taking Cars & Motorcycles from Bali Reputable rental agencies on Bali should allow you to take a car or motorbike to Lombok for a week or so. Cars on Bali are not normally registered for Lombok, so the rental agency must arrange a special permit (25,000 rp) from the police on Bali. It may be quicker and easier, though not necessarily cheaper, to go to Lombok under your own steam, and rent a car there. No special permit is needed to take a rented motorbike from Bali to Lombok.

Chartering Only some vehicles are registered to take passengers all over Lombok. After some tough bargaining, a chartered bemo or private vehicle will cost about 80,000 rp a day; more for a long trip.

Shuttle Buses Perama is the major shuttle

INDONESIA

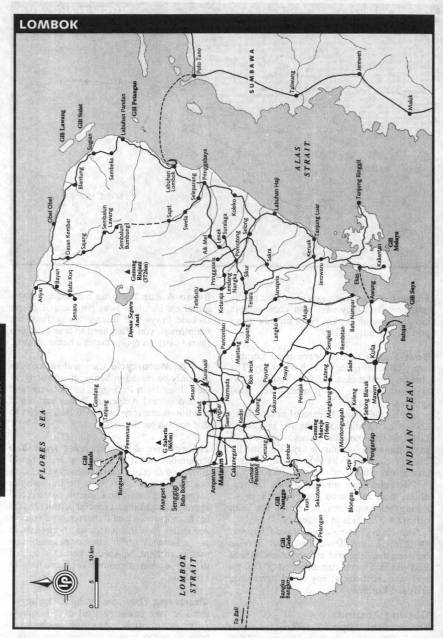

LOMBOK

bus operator, but Lombok Mandiri also has a limited service around Lombok. Perama shuttle buses (and shuttle boats) connect Mataram with Senggigi, Bangsal, the Gili Islands, Teteatu and Kuta (Lombok). But you cannot travel from Kuta (Lombok) to Bangsal, for example, without changing buses first in Mataram – although you can normally get a connection on the same day. You can buy tickets at shops and agencies in the tourist centres.

Cycling Travelling around on a mountain bike would be great as the roads are often reasonably flat, and the traffic is far more bearable than on Bali. Bicycles are available for rent in the tourist centres of Lombok, but for long distances, bring your own.

Organised Tours Organised tours provide a quick introduction to the highlights of the island, and you can always revisit your favourite places independently later. Standard tours include a half-day trip around Mataram, and full-day tours to Kuta and the south coast, to the central craft villages, or to the Gili Islands and the north coast. Prices start at about 25,000 rp per person for a half-day. You can arrange a tour with any travel agency in Senggigi or Mataram, or on Bali.

Boat trips from Lombok to islands further east are widely promoted, especially in Senggigi. The main destination is usually Komodo Island, near Flores, to see the giant Komodo 'dragons' (lizards), with stops at other islands for snorkelling, trekking and beach parties. Some of these trips are pretty rough, with minimal safety provisions. Perama is usually pretty reliable, and offers a variety of trips for 450,000/775,000 rp for four/seven days.

MATARAM

Lombok's main urban area consists of four towns which have merged into one – Ampenan, Mataram, Cakranegara and Sweta. Ampenan, once the main port of Lombok, has some tourist facilities and interesting old buildings and streets. Mataram is the administrative capital of Nusa Tenggara Barat (West Nusa Tenggara), which covers all of Lombok and Sumbawa. Cakranegara (Cakra) has many commercial buildings, and the best range of accommodation and restaurants. Sweta is the main transport terminal of Lombok, and boasts the largest market.

Orientation

Ampenan-Mataram-Cakra-Sweta is spread over 10km. The main road is variously called Jalan Yos Sudarso, Jalan Langko, Jalan Pejanggik and Jalan Selaparang. It's a one-way road, running west to east, for most of its length. A parallel road, Jalan Panca Usaha-Pancawarga-Pendidikan, brings traffic back towards the coast.

Information

Tourist Offices The office (☎ 21658) responsible for West Nusa Tenggara, on Jalan Suprato, is only worth visiting if you need information about Sumbawa. The office (☎ 31730) for West Lombok, ie Mataram and Senggigi, on Jalan Langko, also serves as an unofficial tourist office for all of Lombok. Staff are helpful, and you can get information about airline and Pelni schedules, and book an organised tour.

Money A number of banks along Jalan Selaparang in Cakra will change money. The moneychangers in central Ampenan, Mataram's Cilinaya shopping centre and nearby Senggigi have better rates. You can also change money at the airport.

Post & Communications Mataram's main post office on Jalan Sriwijaya is very inconvenient, but has the only poste restante service on Lombok. A more convenient post office is located opposite the tourist office. The Telkom office in Ampenan has telegram and fax services, and there are several other wartels around town.

Emergency The best hospital on Lombok is the RSU Mataram (☎ 21354). The main police station (☎ 110), where you may have to go for a local motorbike licence (if you haven't got one from Bali), is opposite the tourist office.

Things to See

The **Museum Negeri Nusa Tenggara Barat** has some interesting exhibits about the geology, history and culture of Lombok and Sumbawa, especially about the textiles. It is open from Tuesday to Sunday, 8 am to 2 pm; to 11 am on Friday; and is closed on Monday. The 'special' admission price for tourists is 2500 rp.

The **Mayura Water Palace**, in Cakra, was built in 1744 and was part of the royal court of the former Balinese kingdom on Lombok. Across the road, **Pura Meru** is the largest Balinese temple on Lombok. Both are worth a quick look around.

INDONESIA

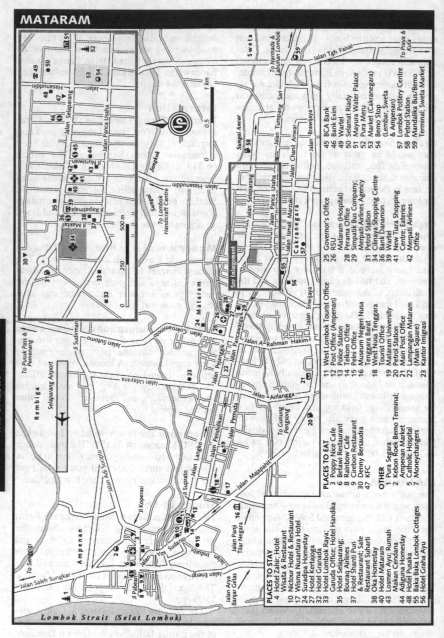

MATARAM

1 km

0.5

0

500 m

250

0

See Enlargement

Cakranegara

Mataram

Sungai Jangkok

Sungai Ancar

To Narmada &
Labuhan Lombok

To Praya &
Kuta

To Lombok Handicraft Centre

To Pusuk Pass &
Pemenang

Selaparang Airport

To Senggigi

Rembiga

Ampenan

To Gunung Pengsong

Lombok Strait (Selat Lombok)

PLACES TO STAY
4   Hotel Zahir; Hotel
     Wisata & Restaurant
10   Nictour Hotel & Restaurant
17   Wisma Nusantara Hotel
24   Suradita Homestay
27   Hotel Kertajoga
32   Hotel Granada
33   Hotel Lombok Raya;
     Garuda Office; Hotel Handika
35   Hotel Selaparang;
     Hotel Shanti Puri
37   Hotel Shanti Puri
     & Restaurant; Sate
     Restaurant Suharti
38   Oka Homestay
40   Hotel Makan
43   Losmen Ayu; Rumah
     Makan Cendana
44   Adiguna Homestay
48   Hotel Pusaka
55   Baka Baka Lombok Cottages
56   Hotel Graha Ayu

PLACES TO EAT
3   Poppy Nice Cafe
6   Betawi Restaurant
8   Rainbow Cafe
9   Cirebon Restaurant
30   Denny Bersaudra
47   KFC

OTHER
1   Pura Segara
2   Kebon Roek Bemo Terminal;
     Ampenan Market
5   Catholic Hospital
7   Moneychangers

11   West Lombok Tourist Office
12   Post Office (Ampenan)
13   Police Station
14   Telkom Office
15   Pelni Office
16   Museum Negeri Nusa
     Tenggara Barat
18   West Nusa Tenggara
     Tourist Office
19   Mataram University
20   Petrol Station
21   Main Post Office
22   Lampangan Mataram
     (Main Square)
23   Kantor Imigrasi
25   Governor's Office
26   RSU
     Mataram (Hospital)
28   Perama Office
29   Simpatik Bus Company;
     Merpati Airlines Agency
31   Petrol Station
34   Cilinaya Shopping Centre
36   Bank Danamon
39   Wartel
41   New Tiara Shopping
     Centre; Eateries
42   Merpati Airlines
     Office
45   BCA Bank
46   Bank Exim
49   Wartel
50   Selamat Riady
51   Mayura Water Palace
52   Pura Meru
53   Market (Cakranegara)
54   Bemo Stop
     (Lembar, Sweta
     & Ampenan)
57   Lombok Pottery Centre
58   Petrol Station
59   Mandalika Bus/Bemo
     Terminal; Sweta Market

Jalan Tgh Faisal

Jalan Tumpang Sari

Jalan Chanil Anwar

Jalan Brawijaya

Jalan Ismail Marzuki

Jalan Panca Usaha

Jalan Selaparang

Jalan Hasanuddin

Jalan Siliwangi

Jalan A. Rahman Hakim

Jalan Pancawarga

Jalan Pejanggik

Jalan Cokroaminoto

Jalan Sutomo

Jalan Sudirman

Jalan Udayana

Jalan Airlangga

Jalan Majapahit

Jalan Pendidikan

Jalan Pemuda

Jalan Langko

Jalan Supato

Jl Koperasi

Jalan Abi Sucipto

Jalan Yos Sudarso

Jl Pabean

Jl Industri

Jalan Panji
Tilar Negara

Jalan Aya
Banjur Gelas

Jalan Energi

Jalan Saleh Sungkar

Jalan Nursiwan

Jalan Regepmaya

Jl Maktal

Jalan Panca Usaha

Sweta

Places to Stay

The most popular and best value places are in Ampenan and Cakranegara – Cakra is the more central and pleasant option.

In Ampenan, *Hotel Zahir* (☎ 34248) is a basic but clean place with singles/doubles for 8000/10,000 rp. *Hotel Wisata* (☎ 26971) has a choice of clean singles/doubles from 12,500/15,000 rp to 35,000/40,000 rp with air-con.

The cheapest place in Mataram is *Suradipa Homestay* (☎ 24576), on Gang Macan VII. At 7500/10,000 rp for rooms with a fan and private bathroom it's very good value. *Hotel Kertajoga* (☎ 21775) is noisy but central, and has fan-cooled rooms for 19,500/23,000 rp, and air-con rooms for 27,500/33,000 rp. *Wisma Nusantara Hotel* (☎ 23492) has a large number of clean, though noisy, rooms. They cost US$11 each, but the manager is open to serious negotiation.

In Cakra, the Balinese-style, family-run *Oka Homestay* (☎ 22406) has a quiet garden and is often full. Singles/doubles cost 12,500/15,000 rp. *Adiguna Homestay* (☎ 25946) is another good budget place with rooms from 12,500/15,000 rp. The popular and friendly *Losmen Ayu* (☎ 21761) is well set up for budget travellers. It offers comfortable rooms at 12,500/15,000 rp, and a range of better rooms over the road for 20,000/25,000 rp.

Good mid-range options are: *Hotel Granada* (☎ 36015) for 70,950/76,450 rp; *Baka Baka Lombok Cottages* (☎ 25378), which has a range of large, quaint cottages for 57,500 rp, with hot water; *Hotel Pusaka* (☎ 33119), which has air-con rooms with TV from 47,500/55,000 rp; and *Nictour Hotel* (☎ 23780), which has quiet, comfortable rooms from a negotiable 90,000/110,000 rp.

Places to Eat

Ampenan has several Indonesian and Chinese restaurants, including the popular *Cirebon Restaurant*. The menu is fairly standard, but most dishes are good value from around 5500 rp. *Poppy Nice Cafe* is as appealing as its name suggests, and has a good range of well-prepared dishes and hospitable staff. One new, excellent spot is *Betawi Restaurant*, where you can enjoy Indonesian and western dishes (for about 7500 rp) in a pleasant upstairs and outdoor setting.

In Mataram, *Denny Bersaudra* is a good place to try authentic Sasak-style food for about 6000 rp a dish. In Cakra, *Sate Restaurant Suharti* is worth visiting for a wide selection of tasty sates for 3500 rp to 5000 rp per plateful. *Rumah Makan Cendana*, handy to the Ayu and Adiguna losmen, has a good range of meals from 3500 rp. Around the junction of Jalan Selaparang and Jalan Hasanuddin there are a number of cheap but unexciting Javanese-style *rumah makans*; none are worth recommending. Most visitors, and affluent locals, end up at the conspicuous *KFC*, the only fast food restaurant on the island.

Shopping

You can shop around at some interesting craft and 'antique' shops along the road between Ampenan and Senggigi, or at the Lombok Handicraft Centre at Sayang Sayang. The Lombok Pottery Centre sells good earthenware, and the Sweta Market has very authentic products.

Getting There & Away

See the Lombok Getting There & Away section for details of air, land and sea transport to Lombok, via Mataram. From Sweta terminal, bemos go to Lembar (700 rp); Praya (700 rp); Labuhan Lombok (2050 rp); Pemenang, for the Gili Islands (700 rp); and Bayan (2100 rp). The terminal in Ampenan has bemos to Senggigi (500 rp). The office of the Perama shuttle bus company (☎ 35936) is at Jalan Pejanggik 66.

Getting Around

Ampenan-Mataram-Cakra-Sweta is very spread out, so don't plan to walk from place to place. Every few seconds, impressive, new yellow bemos shuttle back and forth along the main roads between the Ampenan and Sweta terminals for about 500 rp.

AROUND MATARAM

The region east of Mataram is reminiscent of the best landscapes and scenery that Bali has to offer. **Taman Narmada** is a landscaped hill and lake, laid out as a stylised, miniature replica of Gunung Rinjani and its lake. It's a nice place to spend a few hours, but it's crowded on weekends. It is open from 7 am to 6 pm everyday, and costs 500 rp, plus another 500 rp to swim in the pool. There are frequent bemos from Sweta; the entrance to the gardens is opposite the market in Narmada village.

A few kilometres north-west of Narmada is **Puri Lingsar**, a large temple complex catering for the Bali-Hindu, Islam and Wektu Telu religions. Buy hard-boiled eggs to feed to the holy eels in the temple. *Puri Lingsar Homestay*, about 500m from the temple, on the road towards Suranadi, has pleasant singles/doubles for 15,000/20,000 rp. From Narmada, there are bemos to Lingsar. Look for the 300m path to the temple complex from the main road.

East of Lingsar, **Suranadi** has one of the holiest temples on Lombok, and an uninteresting **forest sanctuary** with an elephant. *Suranadi Hotel* (☎ 33686) has rooms for US$30, and overpriced cottages for US$60. If you can negotiate a better price, this would be a lovely place to stay. The public can stop for a swim in the refreshingly cool pool at the hotel (1500 rp). *Pondok Surya* is a friendly alternative, for 20,000 rp per person, with three meals. Look for the sign at the market in the village.

SENGGIGI

On a series of sweeping bays, Senggigi is the most developed tourist area on Lombok. It has fine beaches, though they slope very steeply into the water, and there's some decent snorkelling. The sunsets over the Selat Lombok strait are superb, and you can enjoy them from the beach, or from one of the beachfront restaurants. Senggigi has experienced a lot of development in the last few years, although with the current downturn in tourism the place is looking forlorn – but this means good discounts for rooms, diving and car rentals.

Orientation & Information

The area known as Senggigi is spread out along nearly 10km of coastal road, but most hotels, restaurants, shops and other facilities are on the main road about 6km north of Ampenan.

You can change money at the few money-changers along the main road, though rates are about 10% lower than in tourist centres on Bali. The Telkom wartel is a little inconvenient, but there are other wartels along the main road. Two Internet centres are Bulan Cybercafe (bulan@mataram.wasantara.net.id) and Planet (planet@mataram.wasantara.net.id). The medical clinic in Hotel Senggigi Aerowisata can be used by guests and the public.

Pura Batu Bolong

Perched on a rocky point south of Senggigi, this Balinese temple is oriented towards Gunung Agung, Bali's holiest mountain.

Legend has it that beautiful virgins were once thrown into the sea from the top of the rock. There are fantastic views of Senggigi and it's a serene place to watch a sunset. During the day, you will be urged to 'donate' 5000 rp for a sash before you enter the temple; 1000 rp is enough.

Diving & Snorkelling

Dive trips from Senggigi mainly go to sites around the Gili Islands, so you may prefer to base yourself there, unless you prefer Senggigi's swankier hotels. The two reliable dive centres are Albatross (☎ 93399) and Blue Coral (☎ 93441), both on the main road.

Around Senggigi, there is good snorkelling off the point and in the sheltered bay around the headland. For some local snorkelling, or if you are going to the Gilis for the day, you can rent snorkelling gear (7500 rp) from places on the beach near Hotel Senggigi Aerowisata. One excellent place for snorkelling is the beach at Windy Cottages, a few kilometres north of Senggigi, and the reef about 50 to 70m off-shore.

Places to Stay – Budget

In Senggigi, *Sonya Homestay* (☎ 63447) is a popular, basic losmen with small rooms for only 15,000 rp. *Pondok Shinta Cottages* is a last resort: very ordinary singles/doubles, with no fan, and next to the main road, cost 8000/10,000 rp.

Lina Cottages (☎ 93237) is central, friendly and good value at 40,000/50,000 rp. *Melati Dua Cottages* (☎ 93288) has quaint, individual cottages for 30,000 rp to 60,000 rp. *Pondok Wisata Rinjani* (☎ 93274) has single/double cottages in a pretty garden for 15,000/20,000 rp, but the place is looking neglected these days. *Hotel Elen* (☎ 93014), easy to miss behind the Hero Photo store, has clean, modern rooms with a ceiling fan, and some style, for 17,500/25,000 rp.

North of Senggigi, *Bale Kampung* has rooms for 16,500/21,000 rp; and quaint, though tiny, bungalows for 14,300/17,600 rp. It also offers cheap food, and good information about local attractions. Further north, in Mangset village, *Pondok Damai* (☎ 93019) is a quiet seaside retreat, with a charming collection of comfortable cottages for 40,000/55,000 rp.

South of Senggigi, *Pondok Wisata Siti Hawa* (☎ 93414) is a family-run homestay fronting a fantastic beach. The handful of bamboo cottages cost 10,000/13,0000 rp. It

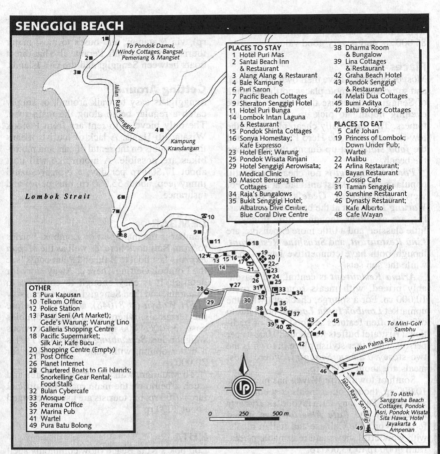

SENGGIGI BEACH

To Pondok Damai,
Windy Cottages, Bangsal,
Pemenang & Mangset

Jalan Raya Senggigi

Kampung
Krandangan

Lombok Strait

PLACES TO STAY
1 Hotel Puri Mas
2 Santai Beach Inn
 & Restaurant
3 Alang Alang & Restaurant
4 Bale Kampung
6 Puri Saron
7 Pacific Beach Cottages
9 Sheraton Senggigi Hotel
11 Hotel Puri Bunga
14 Lombok Intan Laguna
 & Restaurant
15 Pondok Shinta Cottages
16 Sonya Homestay;
 Kafe Expresso
23 Hotel Elen; Warung
25 Pondok Wisata Rinjani
29 Hotel Senggigi Aerowisata;
 Medical Clinic
30 Mascot Berugaq Elen
 Cottages
34 Raja's Bungalows
35 Bukit Senggigi Hotel;
 Albatross Dive Centre,
 Blue Coral Dive Centre

38 Dharma Room
 & Bungalow
39 Lina Cottages
 & Restaurant
42 Graha Beach Hotel
43 Pondok Senggigi
 & Restaurant
44 Melati Dua Cottages
45 Bumi Aditya
47 Batu Bolong Cottages

PLACES TO EAT
5 Cafe Johan
19 Princess of Lombok;
 Down Under Pub;
 Wartel
22 Malibu
24 Arlina Restaurant;
 Bayan Restaurant
27 Gossip Cafe
31 Taman Senggigi
40 Sunshine Restaurant
46 Dynasty Restaurant;
 Kafe Alberto
48 Cafe Wayan

OTHER
8 Pura Kapusan
10 Telkom Office
12 Police Station
13 Pasar Seni (Art Market);
 Gede's Warung; Warung Lino
17 Galleria Shopping Centre
18 Pacific Supermarket;
 Silk Air; Kafe Bucu
20 Shopping Centre (Empty)
21 Post Office
26 Planet Internet
28 Chartered Boats to Gili Islands;
 Snorkelling Gear Rental;
 Food Stalls
32 Bulan Cybercafe
33 Mosque
36 Perama Office
37 Marina Pub
41 Wartel
49 Pura Batu Bolong

To Mini-Golf
Sambhu

Jalan Palma Raja

To Atithi
Sanggraha Beach
Cottages, Pondok
Asri, Pondok Wisata
Sita Hawa, Hotel
Jayakarta &
Ampenan

Jalan Raya Senggigi

0   250   500 m

INDONESIA

caters for budget travellers, and you can rent motorbikes, bicycles and boats. *Atithi Sanggraha Beach Cottages* (☎ 93070) lacks character, but the bungalows are clean, quiet and dotted around a small garden, and cost 20,000/25,000 rp. Not as good, but still cheap, *Pondok Asri* (☎ 93075) has rooms, which are a little noisy, for 15,000 rp to 25,000 rp.

Places to Stay – Mid-Range
Pondok Senggigi (☎ 93273) has rooms facing a pleasant garden, and there's a fine swimming pool. Singles/doubles start from US$9/12, though most rooms with fans cost at least twice that. *Dharma Room & Bungalow* (☎ 93050) has a lovely garden, down to the beach, and charges 45,000 rp for rooms

with a fan, and 130,000 rp for bungalows with air-con and hot water.

Other good options in town are *Graha Beach Hotel* (☎ 93101), which has a good central beachside location, but small rooms from US$45; and *Mascot Berugaq Elen Cottages* (☎ 93365), which offers pleasant Sasak-style and 'seaview' bungalows for US$42 and US$49, with a quiet garden down to the beach.

Elsewhere, *Santai Beach Inn* (☎ 93038) has a homely atmosphere and a lush garden. Economy single/double bungalows, without a fan, cost 26,000/33,000 rp; with a fan, 40,000/52,000 rp. The spacious and charming *Windy Cottages* (☎ 93191) charges 60,000 rp for standard rooms, and 75,000 rp to 90,000 rp for larger bungalows with hot water. *Batu*

Bolong Cottages (☎ 93065) has spacious, well-finished bungalows from 35,000 rp to 86,000 rp, and is very good value.

Places to Eat

Most of the hotels have their own restaurants, and some more remote places north and south of Senggigi will cruise the main road in the evening hoping to pick up (for free) customers. The only really cheap places are the few *warung*, near the Hero Photo store, and the *food stalls*, set up during the day along the beach.

Pondok Senggigi is not cheap, but is still popular from breakfast until late at night. For views and breezes, *Gede's Warung* and *Warung Lino*, lost at the back of the art market, are excellent, though a little pricey. A little classier, and a little more expensive, are *Lina Restaurant*, and *Sunshine Restaurant*, though both have competitive happy hours while the sun sets.

Arlina Restaurant is central, and reasonably priced, with meals from 6000 rp to 10,000 rp. For a splurge, check out what the upmarket *Lombok Intan Laguna* hotel has to offer: it often features seafood, sate or traditional rijsttafel buffets for about 30,000 rp per person. The other stylish place in town is the two-storey *Taman Senggigi*, where most meals are about 20,000 rp.

South of town, *Cafe Wayan* has pizzas for 10,000 rp, though other meals cost considerably more. Two long-term favourites, *Dynasty Restaurant* and *Kafe Alberto*, have joined forces to provide Chinese and Italian meals, with wonderful views and reasonable prices: from 9000 rp to 13,000 rp.

Entertainment

Senggigi has the only nightlife on Lombok. *Pondok Senggigi*, *Kafe Bucu*, *Bayan Restaurant* and *Marina Pub* often have live music. *Lombok Intan Laguna* offers happy hours, live traditional music and discos later in the evening. Ring *Dynasty Restaurant/Kafe Alberto* (☎ 93313) to find out what night it features traditional dancing (currently, Thursday). A couple of the pubs can be quite sociable – *Down Under Pub* at the Princess of Lombok restaurant has good music and pool tables.

Getting There & Away

Public bemos from Ampenan terminal (500 rp) run very regularly. Perama (☎ 93007) has good connections to other tourist centres on Lombok, including Bangsal (5000 rp), Tetebatu (7500 rp) and Kuta (Lombok; 10,000 rp), via Mataram; and buses to most major tourist centres on Bali. Perama also has direct boats between Senggigi and the Gili Islands.

Getting Around

Senggigi is easy to walk around, or simply catch a regular bemo along the main road. The only bicycles to rent are from Pondok Wisata Siti Hawa. A lack of tourists means that discounts on the rental of cars and motorbikes are possible. A motorbike will cost about 17,500 rp per day; a typical Suzuki jimny jeep, about 55,000 rp, plus petrol and insurance.

LEMBAR

Lembar is the main port on Lombok. Ferries to/from Bali dock here, as well as the *Mabua Express* fast boat to Bali, and Pelni boats (see the Lombok Getting There & Away entry for details). It is easy enough to carry on to Mataram, and then Senggigi, but you can stay at *Sri Wahyu* (☎ 81048), about 1km before the terminals, where good singles/doubles cost 13,200/14,800 rp. Opposite the obvious weighbridge, *Serumbung Indah* (☎ 81153) is a better option, with good rooms going for 20,000 rp.

To Mataram, walk out of the port area and catch a bemo on the main road. The official fare is 700 rp, but tourists are usually charged about 2000 rp.

KUTA

Lombok's Kuta Beach (now commonly spelt Kute) is a magnificent stretch of white sand and turquoise sea with rugged hills rising around it, though the vegetation is very sparse and dry. The area is still undeveloped, and has far, *far* fewer tourists and tourist facilities than the (in)famous Kuta Beach on Bali. It really only comes alive during the annual *nyale* fishing festival (in February or March).

You can change money at Anda Cottages or Wisma Segara Anak (which is also a postal agent). There are phones in the hotels, but no wartel.

Surfing

Plenty of good waves break on the reefs around here – many are supposedly 'secret'. There are lefts and rights in the bay in front of Kuta, and more on reefs east of Tanjung

Aan. About 7km east of Kuta, there are several potential breaks on the reefs at the entrance of Teluk Gerupak bay. For tips, repairs and rental of surfboards (15,000 rp per day) and boogie boards (10,000 rp), visit the 'office' (well, shack) of Ocean Blue along the beachfront.

Places to Stay
Most of Kuta's accommodation is along the beachfront road, east of the village. *Anda Cottages* (☎ 54836) was the first, and is still good value for 12,500/15,000 rp for singles/doubles around a spacious garden. The more modern rooms for 25,000/35,000 rp are large and clean.

Wisma Segara Anak (☎ 54834) is well set up, and offers rooms for 10,000/15,0000 rp.

Rinjani Agung Beach Bungalows (☎ 54849) has rooms for 15,000 rp and bungalows for 20,000 rp; and the ones with air-con are good value for 30,000 rp.

Cockatoo Cottages (☎ 54830) is a little more secluded and good value with simple single/double bungalows for 7000/10,000 rp.

The two mid-range places are a little walk from the beach. *Kuta Indah Hotel* (☎ 53781) charges US$21/26 to US$42/49 for decent rooms around a grassy area. The shady and popular *Matahari Inn* (☎ 54832) has economy rooms for 25,000/30,000 rp, which are often full; and the rooms with air-con and hot water are excellent value for 60,000 rp to 110,000 rp.

Places to Eat
There are several cheap *warung* along the beachfront road.

Each hotel has a restaurant: *Cockatoo Cottages* is probably the best value, with western meals for about 8000 rp; *Wisma Segara Anuk* is large, breezy and has the only happy hour in town, though the meals are a little overpriced; and *Matahari Inn* offers decent pizzas from 10,000 rp.

The independent *Bamboo Restaurant*, along the beachfront but close to the village, is good, though some items may be unavailable.

Getting There & Away
Direct public transport from Sweta terminal to Kuta is not regular, so you may have to get a connection in Praya – and even another connection at Sengkol. Perama (☎ 54846), based at Wisma Segara Anak, has one shuttle bus a day to Mataram (10,000 rp).

LABUHAN LOMBOK
Labuhan Lombok, also known as Labuhan Kayangan, is the main port for ferries and boats to Sumbawa (see the Lombok Getting There & Away entry for details). The village is a scruffy place, and there is no need to stay if you're just passing through on your way to/from Sumbawa. If you have to stay here, *Losmen Munawar*, on the road to the port, has very noisy and uninspiring singles/doubles for 5000/10,000 rp; and the nearby *Hotel Melati Lima Tiga* has better rooms for 12,500/18,000 rp.

Frequent buses and bemos travel between Labuhan Lombok and Sweta (2050 rp), via Kopang, and take about two hours, and to Bayan on the north coast. Public transport to Labuhan Lombok is often marked Kayangan or Tanjung Kayangan.

GUNUNG RINJANI
Gunung Rinjani is the highest mountain on Lombok. It has a huge half-moon shaped crater with a large green lake, hot springs and a number of smaller volcanic cones. The view from the rim is stunning – it takes in the amazing crater, the whole north coast of Lombok, and Gunung Agung on Bali. Rinjani is sacred to both Sasaks and Balinese, and many make pilgrimages here. In the wet season, the paths are slippery and dangerous.

Climbing Gunung Rinjani
The most common trek is to climb from Senaru to Pos III (2300m) on the first day, which takes about five hours of steep walking. Most people camp there and climb to the rim (2600m) for sunrise the next morning – this climb takes about two hours. From there you descend into the crater and walk around to the hot springs (2010m), which takes about two hours on a very exposed track. The hot springs are a good place to relax and camp for the second night, before returning all the way to Senaru the next day. The whole trip takes three full days – and probably another day to recover.

To walk to the summit of Rinjani takes at least four days. Two hours walk east from the hot springs, a track branches off to the summit. From this junction (Pelawangan II, at about 2900m), it's a difficult three or four hour climb over loose ground to the top (3726m).

Guides, Porters & Equipment
You can trek from Senaru to the hot springs and back without a guide – the trail is pretty

well defined. To anywhere further, or if you start from Sembalun Lawang or Sapit, you will need a guide. Guides and porters are available in Sapit, Sembalun Lawang and Senaru, and cost about 30,000 rp per day for a guide, and 20,000 rp for a porter. A number of agencies in Mataram and Senggigi organise all-inclusive treks. They are extremely expensive (up to US$100 per person per night), but they do save time and hassle of organising things yourself.

The best places to rent a tent, sleeping bag and stove are the losmen in Senaru mentioned in the following Places to Stay & Eat entry. You'll also need to bring solid footwear, several layers of warm clothing and wet weather gear. It is best to buy food in Mataram or Senggigi, where it's cheaper and there's more choice, but there are some basic shops in Senaru. Also take plenty of water, and a strong torch (flashlight).

Places to Stay & Eat
It's best to stay in Sapit or Senaru. Both villages are worth visiting anyway for views and cool serenity, even if you are not climbing Rinjani. All hotels have restaurants.

In Sapit, *Hati Suci Homestay* (☎ 36545) has pleasant bungalows in a splendid location from 20,000/35,000 rp for singles/doubles. From Pringgabaya on the main road between Labuhan Lombok and Sweta, get a bemo to Sapit. With your own transport, you can use the road north through Sembalun Lawang – as long as the rains hold.

In Senaru, there are several decent places with similar standards and price (about 15,000 rp a double): *Segara Anak Homestay*; *Pondok Guru Bakti*; *Pondok Indah*; *Pondok Wisata Puri Jaya Wijaya*; and *Homestay Bale Bayan*. The rooms at *Pondok Senaru* (☎ 22868) are large, quaint and offer views, but are overpriced at 50,000 rp. From Bayan, there are regular bemos to Senaru until about 4 pm.

TETEBATU
On the southern slopes of Gunung Rinjani, Tetebatu is a lovely, cool mountain retreat, similar to Senaru, though Tetebatu is not a base for treks up the volcano. A shady, 4km path from the main road in the village leads to a **Monkey Forest**. There are two waterfalls, **Air Terjun Jukut** and **Air Terjun Joben**, nearby, accessible by private transport, or on foot with a guide from your hotel.

Almost identical in standard and price (about 15,000/20,000 rp for singles/doubles)

are three places next to each other: *Pondok Wisata Mekar Sari*; *Wisma Diwi Enjeni*; and *Pondok Tetebatu*.

The main, northern road ends at the charming colonial *Soedjono Hotel*, with great views, and a range of rooms from 16,500/22,000 rp.

Along the road heading east from the village, there are several nicer, and slightly more expensive, places: *Cendrawasih Cottages*, *Pondok Wisata Lentera Indah* and the delightful *Losmen Hakiki*.

Every hotel has a *restaurant* serving the usual western-oriented dishes. For some cheap Sasak food, try the friendly *Harmony Warung* or *Shashak Restaurant*.

From the junction at Pomotong, the bemos to Tetebatu, via Kotaraja, are infrequent and the *cidomos* (horse drawn carts) are slow, so take a quick, direct and common ojek.

GILI ISLANDS
Off the north-west coast of Lombok are three small coral-fringed islands – Gili Air, Gili Meno and Gili Trawangan – known as the Gili Islands by the thousands of visitors who come here for the very simple pleasures of sun, snorkelling and socialising. Gili Air is the closest to the mainland, with homestays dotted among the palm trees – it's the prettiest and the most suitable for families. Gili Meno, the middle island, has the smallest population and the fewest tourists – it's the place to play Robinson Crusoe. Trawangan is the largest island, with the most visitors, the most facilities and a reputation as the party island. And there are no vehicles or hawkers on any of the islands!

Orientation & Information
A few shops and hotels on the three islands will change money, but it's best to stock up on rupiah before you come. The Blue Marlin Dive Centre on Trawangan may give cash advances on Visa or MasterCard, with a 3% commission, and has an expensive fax service. All islands have a wartel. On Gili Air, electricity starts at 6 pm every night, though many places have generators; and on Meno, there is no electricity at all (and few generators) in the more remote and cheaper hotels.

Diving & Snorkelling
The coral around the islands is great for snorkelling. Ask locally to find the best spots, many of which you can reach from the shore. For scuba divers, the visibility is fair to good (best in the dry season), and there is some

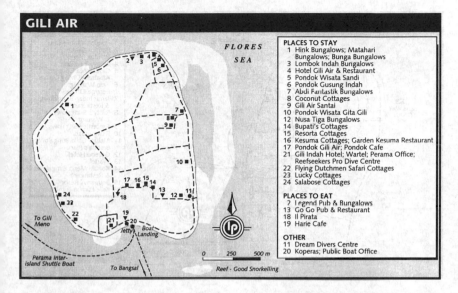

GILI AIR

FLORES
SEA

PLACES TO STAY
1 Hink Bungalows; Matahari
   Bungalows; Bunga Bungalows
3 Lombok Indah Bungalows
4 Hotel Gili Air & Restaurant
5 Pondok Wisata Sandi
6 Pondok Gusung Indah
7 Abdi Fantastik Bungalows
8 Coconut Cottages
9 Gili Air Santai
10 Pondok Wisata Gita Gili
12 Nusa Tiga Bungalows
14 Bupati's Cottages
15 Resorta Cottages
16 Kesuma Cottages; Garden Kesuma Restaurant
17 Pondok Gili Air; Pondok Cafe
21 Gili Indah Hotel; Wartel; Perama Office;
    Reefseekers Pro Dive Centre
22 Flying Dutchmen Safari Cottages
23 Lucky Cottages
24 Salabose Cottages

PLACES TO EAT
2 Legend Pub & Bungalows
13 Go Go Pub & Restaurant
18 Il Pirata
19 Harie Cafe

OTHER
11 Dream Divers Centre
20 Koperas; Public Boat Office

To Gili
Meno

Jetty Boat
Landing

Perama Inter-
island Shuttle Boat

To Bangsal

0   250   500 m

Reef - Good Snorkelling

very good coral reef accessible by boat.
There are quality dive centres on Trawangan
and Air, which also offer diving courses. Discounts of up to 50% are possible, so it is
worth checking around.

Places to Stay & Eat

In the busier season (July, August and around
Christmas) hotels may ask a lot more –
perhaps double the prices listed below.

Gili Air *Lombok Indah Bungalows* has
typical Gili-style bungalows for 15,000 rp.
Legend Pub & Bungalows is also good value
with singles/doubles for 12,000/15,000 rp –
though they may not be too quiet if the 'pub'
there gets rowdy. On the east coast, *Coconut
Cottages* (☎ 35365) has a set of cottages in a
pretty garden for 25,000 rp to 50,000 rp.
Nearby, *Gili Air Santai* (☎ 64 1022) is a little
classier than most places, but still good value
with bungalows ranging from 20,000 rp to
40,000 rp.

On the south-west coast, *Lucky Cottages*,
Flying Dutchman Safari Cottages and *Salabose Cottages* are close to the centre of the
'action', but still secluded. Basic but clean
single/double bungalows cost around 12,500/
15,000 rp. On the far north-west coast, three
cheapies in a row are totally secluded from
the rest of the island (but not from each
other): *Hink Bungalows*, *Matahari Bungalows* and *Bunga Bungalows*.

More central, *Resorta Cottages* is the
cheapest place on the island, with no-frills
bungalows for 7000/10,000 rp. *Bupati's Cottages* is a good, quiet option for 15,000 rp;
and *Nusa Tiga Bungalows* is quiet, spacious
and good value for 12,000/15,000 rp.

Most hotels have decent *restaurants*, serving cheap Indonesian, Chinese and western
food. For something really different, visit *Il
Pirata* – it serves ordinary pasta dishes (from
10,000 rp) on something that looks like a
pirate ship (well, after a few Bintangs, it does).
Garden Kesuma Restaurant has a lovely atmosphere, and good prices; and *Pondok Cafe*
is popular with long-stayers, and a good place
to meet other travellers.

Gili Meno *Pondok Meno* is a quiet, relaxed
place where bungalows cost 15,000 rp.
Pondok Santai is very similar, while *Pondok
Karang Baru* looks newer and sturdier and is
worth paying a little extra: 20,000/25,000 rp
for singles/doubles. *Zoraya Pavilion* (☎ 0370-
27213, in Mataram) has a variety of rooms, at
negotiable prices, from 25,000 rp in a large,
shady area.

In the village, there are a bunch of unexciting places for about 15,000/20,000 rp, though
they are convenient: *Fantastic Bungalows*,
Rawa Indah and *Malia's Child Bungalows*.
Rusty's Bungalows is the best of a bad lot.

If you want reliable electricity, you should
try and stay at a mid-range place. *Janur*

INDONESIA

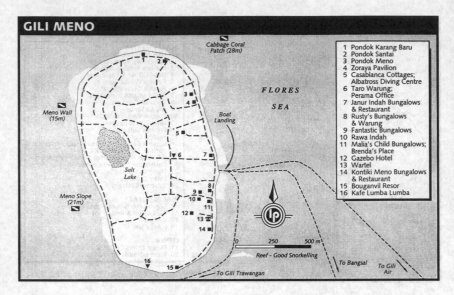

GILI MENO

Cabbage Coral Patch (28m)

Meno Wall (15m)

FLORES SEA

Boat Landing

Salt Lake

Meno Slope (21m)

Reef - Good Snorkelling

To Gili Trawangan

To Bangsal

To Gili Air

1 Pondok Karang Baru
2 Pondok Santai
3 Pondok Meno
4 Zoraya Pavilion
5 Casablanca Cottages;
  Albatross Diving Centre
6 Taro Warung;
  Perama Office
7 Janur Indah Bungalows
  & Restaurant
8 Rusty's Bungalows
  & Warung
9 Fantastic Bungalows
10 Rawa Indah
11 Malia's Child Bungalows;
  Brenda's Place
12 Gazebo Hotel
13 Wartel
14 Kontiki Meno Bungalows
  & Restaurant
15 Bouganvil Resor
16 Kafe Lumba Lumba

Indah Bungalows (☎ 33284) is clean, and has bungalows with a ceiling fan for 50,000 rp. *Casablanca Cottages* (☎ 33847) is back from the beach, but is well set up with a garden and small swimming pool. Single/double cottages cost from US$11/14. The spacious *Gazebo Hotel* (☎ 35795) has tastefully decorated Bali-style bungalows for US$45/55.

The best places to eat are the beachfront *warung* – but don't expect any snappy service on this island. *Janur Indah Bungalows* has reasonable prices (4000 rp to 7000 rp for most dishes). *Brenda's Place* has a wide range of western and Indonesian meals, and a breezy view upstairs. *Rusty's Warung* is deservedly popular for good food and prices – 3000 rp to 7000 rp.

Gili Trawangan The cheapest places are the homestays a few hundred metres from the beach, such as *Alex Homestay* or *Losmen Eky* with singles/doubles for 8000/10,000 rp. Most people will want something nicer and more central. The best among the many cheapies along the main strip are probably: *Halim's*, which is basic but cheap for 10,000/15,000 rp; *Mawar Bungalows* and *Pasir Putih*, both reasonable for about 20,000/25,000 rp; and *Danau Hijau Cottages* for 20,000 rp to 30,000 rp. *Sagitarius Bungalows* is also good value. It has rooms for 15,000 rp, and bungalows for 25,000 rp, set in a nice garden.

The newer, characterless rows of concrete 'bungalows' along the main strip cost from 25,000 rp to 40,000 rp. *Pondok Wisata Kreatif* (☎ 34893) and *Trawangan Cottages* (☎ 23582) are both overpriced with rooms for 35,000/40,000 rp, but they're still popular. Quiet, friendly and good value are *Pondok Kayangan* (☎ 37932), *Melati Cottages* and *Damai Indah*.

Most of the hotels have *restaurants* that offer a selection of inexpensive western and Asian dishes – the fresh seafood can be excellent. *Trawangan Cottages* does passable pizzas for 10,000 rp. *Borobodur Restaurant* has excellent tuna steak for 7500 rp, among other dishes, and cold beer for 8000 rp. Every evening, a couple of places, such as *Halim's*, place the day's catch of fresh fish on a table along the side of the street – just choose, agree on a price and enjoy. Most divers swap stories at the restaurant at the *Blue Marlin Dive Centre*. It is also worth a short walk north to the modestly named *Excellent Restaurant*.

Getting There & Away
Public Bemo & Boat Take a public bemo to Pemenang or anything heading towards Bayan from the west. From Pemenang, it's about 1km off the main road to the harbour at Bangsal by cidomo.

Koperasi Angkutan Laut (Sea Transport Co-operative) is the boat owners' cartel which

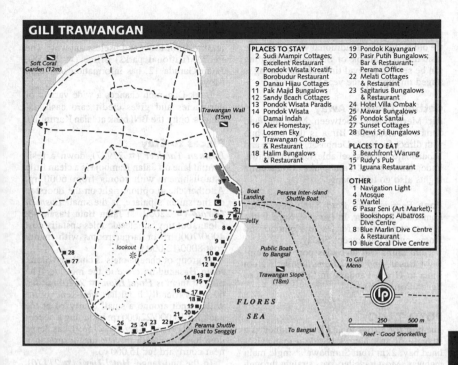

GILI TRAWANGAN

PLACES TO STAY
2   Sudi Mampir Cottages;
     Excellent Restaurant
7   Pondok Wisata Kreatif;
     Borobudur Restaurant
9   Danau Hijau Cottages
11 Pak Majid Bungalows
12 Sandy Beach Cottages
13 Pondok Wisata Paradis
14 Pondok Wisata
     Damai Indah
16 Alex Homestay;
     Losmen Eky
17 Trawangan Cottages
     & Restaurant
18 Halim Bungalows
     & Restaurant

19 Pondok Kayangan
20 Pasir Putih Bungalows;
     Bar & Restaurant;
     Perama Office
22 Melati Cottages
     & Restaurant
23 Sagitarius Bungalows
     & Restaurant
24 Hotel Villa Ombak
25 Mawar Bungalows
26 Pondok Santai
27 Sunset Cottages
28 Dewi Sri Bungalows

PLACES TO EAT
3   Beachfront Warung
15 Rudy's Pub
21 Iguana Restaurant

OTHER
1   Navigation Light
4   Mosque
5   Wartel
6   Pasar Seni (Art Market);
     Bookshops; Albatross
     Dive Centre
8   Blue Marlin Dive Centre
     & Restaurant
10 Blue Coral Dive Centre

Soft Coral Garden (12m)

Trawangan Wall (15m)

Boat Landing

Perama Inter-island Shuttle Boat

Jetty

lookout

Public Boats to Bangsal

Trawangan Slope (18m)

To Gili Meno

FLORES SEA

To Bangsal

Perama Shuttle Boat to Senggigi

0   250   500 m

Reef - Good Snorkelling

---

monopolises public transport to the islands. Its offices at Bangsal, and at the 'ports' on the three islands, sell tickets to Gili Air, Gili Meno and Gili Trawangan. It's a matter of sitting and waiting until there's a full boat load, about 15 people. Public boats leave from Bangsal, and from the islands, at about 8 am – check the departure time the day before.

Shuttle Bus & Boat Perama operates the main shuttle service from Senggigi, and has bus connections from other tourist centres on Lombok and Bali. The Sunshine Restaurant in Senggigi also has a shuttle boat from Senggigi for the same price and at the same time. Shuttle boats leave Senggigi at 9 am, and return from the islands at about 3 pm, so you can day-trip to one or more islands from Senggigi. The one-way fare to Gili Trawangan is 10,000 rp per person; to Gili Meno, 12,500 rp; and to Gili Air, 15,000 rp. You can buy tickets at the Perama office on each island, or from any shop-cum-travel agency.

Chartering a Boat If you are too late for the public or shuttle boats, you can always charter a boat. It is not that expensive if you

deal with the Koperasi, though Perama do charge more. From Bangsal to Gili Air, a boat costs 15,000/25,000 rp one-way/return; to Gili Meno, 18,000/35,000 rp; and to Gili Trawangan, 21,000/40,000 rp.

Island-Hopping Perama runs a shuttle boat service between the three islands every morning and afternoon. This means you can stay on one island, and visit another, although the schedule won't allow you to visit the other two islands and return to your island on the same day. The fare is between 3000 and 4000 rp per person. You can buy tickets at any travel agency on the islands, or at the Perama offices.

Sumbawa

Together with Lombok, Sumbawa forms Nusa Tenggara Barat province. The island was once composed of two main kingdoms, the Sumbawans in west Sumbawa and the Bimans in east Sumbawa. Both were sultanates that extended their influence beyond Sumbawa in the 17th century and today, Sumbawa is strongly Islamic.

Sumbawa is not packed with attractions, but Sumbawa Besar and Bima have traces of the old sultanates. Traditional villages can be visited and Lombok or Sumbawan fighting can be seen at festival times. Horse racing is staged throughout the year.

Getting There & Away

Air Merpati flies between Mataram and Sumbawa Besar but Bima is the main hub with direct flights to Denpasar, Mataram and Labuanbajo and (less reliable) hops to Bajawa, Ende, Ruteng and Tambolaka. Connecting flights also go to Kupang.

Boat Ferries from Poto Tano depart for Lombok every hour. In the east, Sape is the departure point for ferries to Komodo and Flores, every day except Friday.

Pelni ships call at Badas port near Sumbawa Besar, and the *Tatamailau* sails from Bima to Ujung Pandang in Sulawesi and to Benoa Port (Bali).

POTO TANO

The port for ferries to and from Lombok is a straggle of stilt houses beside a mangrove-lined bay, 2km from Sumbawa's single main highway. Most travellers pass straight through to Sumbawa Besar, but you can also head south to the town and **Taliwang** and then on to the fine surf beach at **Maluk**, which has a few losmen.

Getting There & Away

Ferries run regularly between Lombok and Poto Tano (see the Lombok Getting There & Away entry for details). The through buses from Mataram to Sumbawa Besar or Bima include the ferry fare.

Buses also meet the ferry and go to Taliwang (1500 rp; one hour), Sumbawa Besar (3000 rp; two hours) and Bima (8500 rp; nine hours).

SUMBAWA BESAR

Sumbawa Besar is the chief town on the western half of the island, a laid-back, friendly place where horse-drawn cidomos still outnumber bemos and the mosques pack them in on a Friday. Though once a centre for the 'hello mister' cult, the town is now used to a steady stream of tourists.

The chief attraction is the **Dalam Loka**, the wooden, barn-like Sultan's Palace.

Information

The tourist office (☎ 23714), Jalan Bungur 1, is 3km from town and useless anyway. The PHPA (national parks) office (☎ 21358), Jalan Garuda 12, has information on Pulau Moyo.

Bank Danamon changes a wide variety of currencies and gives credit card cash advances, or try the BNI bank at Jalan Kartini 10.

Places to Stay

Losmen Taqdeer (☎ 21987), down a residential lane off Jalan Kamboja is a clean little establishment with rooms from 6000 rp. Another cheap option, right on the doorstep of the sultan's palace, is the small *Losmen Garoto* (☎ 22062) at Jalan Batu Pasak 48. Clean, but tiny, singles/doubles upstairs cost 4000/7000 rp or larger rooms with mandi cost 8000/12,000 rp.

A group of cheap hotels is clustered along Jalan Hasanuddin close to the mosque. The pick of them is *Hotel Dian* (☎ 21708) at No 69. This friendly hotel has well-kept rooms with mandi around a small courtyard at the back for 15,000/22,000 rp, including a decent breakfast. *Hotel Suci* (☎ 21589) has large double rooms with private mandi around a neat courtyard for 15,000 rp.

In the mid-range, *Hotel Dewi* (☎ 21170), Jalan Hasanuddin 60, is bright, spotless and good value with singles/doubles at 12,500/16,500 rp, or 27,500/33,000 rp with air-con up to 55,000 rp for deluxe rooms. *Hotel Tambora* (☎ 21555), on Jalan Kebayan, is arguably the best hotel in town but overpriced. Rooms are 12,600/21,000 rp to 93,000/120,000 rp. Both have restaurants.

Places to Eat

Warung set up in front of the stadium on Jalan Yos Sudarso in the evenings and sell *soto ayam* (chicken soup), sate, *bakso* (meat balls) and other cheap Madurese fare. The *Rukun Jaya*, on Jalan Hasanuddin close to many of the hotels, is a small restaurant with cheap food. *Rumah Makan Mushin*, Jalan Wahidin 31, is a spotless little cafe with simple but very tasty Lombok/Taliwang dishes.

Sumbawa Besar has two very good Chinese restaurants: the *Aneka Rasa Jaya* at Jalan Hasanuddin 14, the *Puspa Warna* at Jalan Cendrawasih 1 and the new *Srikanti* on Jalan Diponegoro.

Getting There & Away

Air Merpati (☎ 21416), Jalan Kebayan 2A,

flies to Mataram and on to Denpasar and Surabaya.

Bus Sumbawa Besar's main long-distance bus station is the Karang Dima terminal, 5.5km north-west of town on the highway, although some morning buses to Bima leave from the Brang Bara station on Jalan Kaharuddin. Fares and approximate journey times from Sumbawa Besar for local buses include: Sape (8500 rp; 7½ hours); Bima (7200 rp; seven hours); Dompu (5500 rp; 4½ hours); Taliwang (3200 rp; three hours); and Poto Tano (3000 rp; two hours). Deluxe, air-con buses are much more comfortable and run through to Bima and Lombok. Hotels can book them the day before.

Boat Pelni's *Pangrango* and *Tatamailau* stop at the small port of Badas, 7km west of Sumbawa Besar, on their respective loops through the eastern islands. The Pelni office is at Labuhan Sumbawa, 3km west of town on the Poto Tano road. (See the Getting Around section of this chapter for details of Pelni schedules.)

PULAU MOYO

Two-thirds of Pulau Moyo, 3km off Sumbawa's north coast, is a reserve noted for its excellent snorkelling and abundant fish. Boat tours between Lombok and Flores stop on the north side of the island, or boats can be chartered to Tanjung Pasir from Air Bari, half an hour north of Sumbawa Besar. The PHPA is helpful in arranging a visits.

HUU

Sumbawa's south coast has some beautiful beaches and good surf. Huu, south of Dompu, is Sumbawa's surfing Mecca. Huu has about a dozen places to stay, from budget to mid-range. *Intan Lestari* is one of the cheapest with bungalows priced from 15,000 rp per person, or the *Mona Lisa* is well-equipped and costs from 15,000/20,000 rp for singles/doubles.

Getting to Huu by public transport is a real hassle. From Dompu's Ginte bus station take a bemo to the hospital, then a cidomo to the Lepardi bus station, then an infrequent bus to Rasabau (750 rp; 1½ hours) and finally a crowded bemo to the beach. Most visitors come here by chartered taxi from Dompu (around 35,000 rp) or Bima airport (around 70,000 rp).

BIMA

This is Sumbawa's main port and the major centre on the eastern end of the island. It's really just a stop on the way through Sumbawa, and there's nothing much to see or do. The only notable attraction of Bima is the large former **sultan's palace**, now a museum, open 8 am to 6 pm daily. The collection is interesting but costs a hefty 5000 rp for tourists. The Jalan Flores **night market** is worth a wander.

Information

The tourist information office (☎ 44331) is near the Telkom office on Jalan Soekarno-Hatta about 2km east of the town centre.

The Bank Rakyat Indonesia on Jalan Sumbawa changes foreign currency and travellers cheques, as does the BNI bank on Jalan Sultan Hasanuddin.

Places to Stay & Eat

Bima is compact and most hotels are in the middle of town, a 10 minute walk from the central bus station. The government-run *Wisma Komodo* (☎ 42070) on Jalan Sultan Ibrahim is a good budget option. Worn double rooms cost 10,000 rp or 15,000 rp with mandi.

The long-popular *Hotel Lila Graha* (☎ 42740), Jalan Lombok 20, has an excellent restaurant, but prices here keep rising, while standards drop. Dingy singles/doubles cost 9000/12,500 rp, or better rooms with mandi start at an expensive 15,000/17,500 rp. Add 10% tax to all rates, but breakfast is included.

Next door, the seedy *Losmen Pelangi* (☎ 42878) has boxy doubles for 10,000 rp, or 15,000 rp with mandi. The cheapest in town is the crumbling *Losmen Kartini* (☎ 42072), Jalan Pasar 11, costing only 4000 rp per person, but it is not recommended for solo female travellers.

The town's best hotel is the new *Hotel La'mbitu* (☎ 42222), Jalan Sumbawa 4. Rooms with fan and hot water cost 27,500 rp; air-con rooms are 44,000 rp or 55,000 rp with fridge.

Apart from the restaurant at Hotel Lila Graha, the nearby *Rumah Makan Sembilan Sembilan* specialises in fried chicken and has other good Chinese and Indonesian dishes. The *night market* has stalls selling interesting snacks and on the same street is the *Rumah Makan Mawar*, a very popular local haunt.

Getting There & Away

Air The Merpati office (☎ 42697) is at Jalan Soekarno-Hatta No 60, east of the town centre. Small planes fly between Bima and Denpasar, Mataram, Labuanbajo, Ruteng, Ende and Tambolaka. Over-booking and cancellations are common.

Bus Buses to destinations west of Bima depart from Bima's central bus station, just 10 minutes walk from the centre of town. Day buses to Sumbawa Besar cost 7200 rp. Numerous express night-bus agents near the bus station sell tickets for air-con buses to Sumbawa Besar (10,000 rp; six hours) and Mataram (22,000 rp; 11 hours). Buses to Mataram leave around 7 am and 7 pm.

Buses to Sape (2000 rp; two hours) depart from Kumbe in Raba, a 20 minute bemo ride east of Bima, but they can't be relied upon to meet the early-morning ferry to Flores and Komodo. The big buses coming through Bima from Surabaya at 4.30 am go through to Sape for 2500 rp. A chartered bemo to Sape costs around 35,000 rp.

Boat The Pelni office, Jalan Pelabuhan 103, is located at Bima's port. The *Tatamailau* and *Tilongkabila* calls at Bima, sailing to and from Ujung Pandang in Sulawesi and Labuanbajo.

Getting Around

Bima has plenty of bemos (300 rp) and dokars for short trips. Bima's airport is 16km out of town; bemos are cheap but infrequent while taxis cost 12,500 rp.

SAPE

Sape is a pleasant enough little town but the only reason to visit is to catch the ferry to Komodo and Flores from Pelabuhan Sape, 3km from Sape.

The PHPA office for Komodo information is 2km from the town towards Pelabuhan Sape.

Places to Stay

Losmen Mutiara, nestled just outside the entrance to the port, is the most convenient. Singles/doubles with shared mandi cost 7500/10,000 rp. In town, *Losmen Friendship* lives up to its name. Clean doubles with shared mandi cost 10,000 rp with private mandi. Two cheaper, more basic places are *Losmen Ratna Sari* and *Losmen Give* with rooms from 7000 rp.

Getting There & Away

Bus Buses go to Sape (2000 rp; two hours) from the Kumbe terminal in Bima-Raba. Buses to Bima meet the ferry from Komodo and Labuanbajo, and air-con express buses run all the way to Mataram or even through to Surabaya.

Boat The car/passenger ferries to Labuanbajo (11,500 rp; eight to 10 hours) on Flores, stopping at Komodo (10,000 rp; five to seven hours) on the way, leave Pelabuhan Sape at 8 am every day except Friday. Cancellations are not unheard of, but this is usually a reliable connection.

Komodo & Rinca

Komodo is a hilly, dry, desolate island sandwiched between Flores and Sumbawa. Its big attraction is lizards – 4m, 130kg lizards, appropriately known as Komodo dragons (*ora*). The best time to see dragons is from June to September, in the dry season, when they come to the watering holes.

The only village on the island is **Kampung Komodo**, a fishing village on the east coast of the island and worth a look. Also on the coast, a half-hour walk from the village, is **Loh Liang**, the park HQ. Some people prefer to visit nearby Rinca island because it is closer to the Flores coast and less touristed. Dragon-spotting is less organised and the chances of seeing them less certain. The PHPA also has a tourist camp on Rinca at **Loh Buaya**.

Permits for Komodo are issued at the PHPA camp at Loh Liang, or on Rinca at Loh Buaya. Permits cost 20,000 rp per person.

Dragon-Spotting

Banu Nggulung, the most accessible place to see dragons, has been set up like a little theatre. The PHPA guides will take you to this dried up river bed about a half-hour walk from Loh Liang. The dragons used to flock here for a free feed of goat provided by tourist groups, but this gruesome ritual has been discontinued. Spotting dragons is no longer guaranteed, but a few of these fabulous beasties are usually in attendance.

A guide costs 3000 rp, or 1000 rp per person for groups of more than three. The PHPA prefers to organise fixed times and take large groups, though smaller groups are less like a zoo.

Around Komodo

While most visitors only stay overnight to see the dragons at Banu Nggulung, Komodo has plenty of other activities.

Gunung Ara can be climbed (3½ hours return) for expansive views across the island. A guide costs 25,000 rp for up to five people. Longer walks are to Poreng Valley and Loh Sabita. The half-hour walk along the beach to Kampung Komodo can be done without a guide.

Wild pigs and deer are commonly seen, and the Komodo dragons occasionally wander into the PHPA camp, but they avoid the kampung because there are too many people. Snakes inhabit the island and signs are posted as a warning.

Good snorkelling can be found at **Pantai Merah** (Red Beach) and the small island of **Pulau Lasa** near Kampung Komodo. The PHPA rents snorkels and masks, and even operates a glass-bottomed boat for US$8 per person.

Places to Stay & Eat

The *PHPA camp* at Loh Liang is a collection of large, spacious, clean wooden cabins on stilts. Each cabin has four or five rooms and singles/doubles cost 10,000/15,000 rp A few more luxurious rooms cost 25,000/35,000 rp. During the peak tourist season around July/August the rooms may be full but the PHPA will rustle up mattresses to sleep on. Accommodation on Rinca is similar and costs 10,000/15,000 rp.

The camp restaurant is limited to below-average *mie goreng* and nasi goreng, plus expensive beverages. Bring some supplies or stock up in Kampung Komodo.

Getting There & Away

The ferries between Labuanbajo in Flores and Pelabuhan Sape on Sumbawa stop at Komodo. The ferries cannot dock at Loh Liang and stop about 1km out to sea, from where small boats transfer you to Komodo for 1500 rp.

Boat tours can be arranged to Komodo and Rinca from Labuanbajo.

Flores

One of the most beautiful islands in Indonesia, Flores is an astounding string of active and extinct volcanoes. The name is Portuguese for 'Flowers'; the Portuguese were the first Europeans to settle the island, on the eastern tip. Flores is 95% Catholic, the church dominates every tiny village and only in the ports will you find any number of Muslims.

The main attraction is the coloured volcanic lakes of Kelimutu near Moni. Labuanbajo is a popular place to kick back for a few days and has decent beaches. Bajawa has become something of a travellers' centre and is the place to visit nearby traditional villages.

Getting There & Away

Air Maumere is the best place for getting to or from Flores by air. Book well in advance for flights from other towns in Flores and always reconfirm. Ende, Labuanbajo and Bajawa only accommodate small aircraft, so seating is limited.

Merpati connects Maumere with Bima in Sumbawa, and with Kupang in Timor. It also connects Bajawa, Labuanbajo and Ruteng with Bima, and Ende with Kupang.

Boat Regular ferries connect Labuanbajo in western Flores with Komodo and Sumbawa. From Larantuka in eastern Flores ferries go to Kupang and the eastern islands of the Solor and Alor archipelagos. From Ende regular boats go to Waingapu in Sumba and to Kupang.

In addition to the ferries, Pelni passenger boats provide a variety of useful links including: Labuanbajo-Waingapu, Ende-Waingapu, Ende-Kupang, Maumere-Ujung Pandang (Sulawesi), Maumere-Dili, Larantuka-Dili, Larantuka-Kupang and Larantuka-Ujung Pandang.

Getting Around

Air Merpati has flights from Labuanbajo to Ende and Ruteng, and between Bajawa and Ende.

Bus The Trans-Flores Hwy loops and tumbles nearly 700 scenic kilometres from Labuanbajo to Larantuka. The highway connects all the major centres and the road is surfaced virtually all the way. Travel is now much easier and more reliable, but still exhausting. Travel in the wet season can be problematic, especially off the highway when vehicles on the unsealed roads get bogged; a trip that might take hours in the dry season can take days.

Public buses run regularly between all the major towns. They are cheap, leave when full (sometimes very full) and stop at all stations. Tickets can usually be bought the day before departure from agents or from the drivers. The big air-con luxury buses you'll find on

Sumbawa or Java don't exist on Flores. The highway is too narrow and winding to accommodate big buses, and the road would quickly turn any 'delux' bus into 'ekonomi'. Open-sided trucks with wooden seats also cover the local runs.

LABUANBAJO
This fishing village at the extreme western end of Flores is a gateway to Komodo and a pleasant enough spot to while away a few days. It's on a pretty harbour sheltered by several small islands. Reasonable beaches, such as Waecicu, are just outside town but the islands have the best beaches and good snorkelling and diving.

Information
The Bank Rakyat Indonesia gives low rates for US dollars, even worse for other currencies. The PHPA office is a five minute walk along the airport road from Hotel Wisata. The Telkom office is just beyond it, and the tourist office (☎ 41170) is nearby.

Organised Tours
Boat tours to Komodo, Rinca and other islands are easily arranged. Boats can be chartered at reasonable rates or the Waecicu Beach/Sinbad shuttle office on the main street in Labuanbajo has daily boats to Bidadari (5000 rp) and Sabola (7500 rp) islands for snorkelling, and to Rinca for 20,000 rp per person. Charter boats to Komodo start at around 75,000 rp for up to six people, which will give you about three hours on the island. Boats to Rinca start at around 60,000 rp. Overnight tours to Komodo and/or Rinca are also widely offered.

Popular boat tours run to Lombok via Komodo, Rinca and then along the north coast of Sumbawa, stopping at Pulau Moyo before continuing on to Lombok. Fares are typically around US$95 for a five or six day trip, though the last day may be at uninteresting Labuhan Lombok. Shop around and find out exactly what is included – entrance fees, equipment, bus transfers to Mataram, what sort of food is served, sleeping arrangements (always on the boat but check the cabin) etc. The Mega Buana Bahari travel agent also tours along the north coast of Flores to Riung.

Places to Stay
Competition is cut throat and rates are very variable. The *Mutiara Beach Hotel* (☎ 41039) has harbour views and very basic singles/

doubles cost 5000/8000 rp, or dark rooms with mandi cost 6000/12,000 rp. The well-appointed *Bajo Beach Hotel* (☎ 41009) across the road is more upmarket. Rooms start at 4000/7000 rp, or those with mandi, from 7000/10,000 rp to 12,500/17,500 rp, are much better.

The popular *Gardena Hotel* has a hilltop position above the main road. Simple bungalows around a garden cost 7000/10,000 rp or 9000/14,000 rp with shower and mosquito nets.

The *Mitra Hotel* (☎ 41003) is a switched-on place offering a variety of services, including tours. Simple but clean rooms cost 6000/8000 rp or 10,000/12,500 rp with mandi.

The well-run *Hotel Wisata* (☎ 41020) competes with the Bajo Beach as the best hotel in the town. Rooms cost 10,000/12,500 rp to 15,000/20,000 rp.

Labuanbajo also has a number of small homestays. The best is *Chez Felix*, run by a friendly family that speaks good English, with rooms from 6000/8000 rp. Nearby is the quiet and similarly priced *Sony Homestay*.

A number of beach hotels are outside the town. Most are reached by boat – free for guests. The *Waecicu Beach Hotel*, a 20 minute boat ride north of Labuanbajo, has long been a popular budget option because of its price – 11,000 rp per person for a basic bamboo bungalow or 13,500 rp with attached mandi, including three meals.

Other expensive options include the *Puri Bagus Komodo* (☎ 41030), a half-hour boat ride away, and the *New Bajo Beach Hotel* (☎ 41047), 2.5km by road south of town.

Two islands have simple bungalows for around 15,000 rp: *Kanawa Island Bungalows* on Pulau Kanawa, and the *Pungu Hotel* (☎ 41083) on Pulau Pungu.

Places to Eat
Labuanbajo has a few good restaurants specialising in seafood at reasonable prices. Pick of the crop is the *Borobudur*, more expensive than most but worth it. It has excellent fish, prawns, a few Thai dishes, steaks and even schnitzel.

The *Dewata* and the *Sunset* restaurants are also good. The *Bajo Beach*, *Gardena* and *Wisata* hotels all have good restaurants.

Getting There & Away
Air Merpati has direct flights between Labuanbajo and Bima with connections to

Mataram and Denpasar. To the east unreliable flights go to Ende and Ruteng.

The Merpati office is 1.5km from town and 1km before the airport. Hotels can arrange a taxi (5000 rp) to meet flights.

Bus Buses to Ruteng (5000 rp; four hours) leave at 7, 9 and 10 am, noon and around 4 pm when the ferry arrives from Sape and Komodo. Buses to Bajawa (10,000 rp; 10 hours) leave at 7 am and 4 pm. The Damri bus to Ende (15,000 rp; 14 hours) meets the ferry, if you are desperate to get to Kelimutu in a hurry and are well stocked with pain killers.

Boat The ferry from Labuanbajo to Komodo (4000 rp; three hours) and Sape (11,500 rp; five to seven hours) leaves at 8 am every day except Friday.

The Pelni passenger ships *Tilongkabila* and *Tatamailau* stop at Labuanbajo and run direct to/from Bima. Pelni schedules are in the Getting Around section of this chapter.

RUTENG

Ruteng, home to the Manggarai people, is basically just another stop on the way through Flores. A number of points of interest lie around town. **Compang Ruteng**, 3km southwest, is a semi-traditional village and **Golo Curu** is a mountain 3km north of Ruteng with panoramic views of the hills and the town. **Gunung Ranaka** is an active volcano just outside town and **Danau Ranamese** is a small lake and local picnic spot 22km east of Ruteng.

Information

Change money at the BNI bank on Jalan Kartini or the Bank Rakyat Indonesia on Jalan Yos Sudarso. The post office is at Jalan Baruk 6.

Places to Stay & Eat

Rima Hotel (☎ 22196), Jalan A Yani 14, is on the ball with information and arranges bus tickets and tours to surrounding attractions. Economy singles/doubles with shared mandi cost 10,000/15,000 rp, or a few lighter and more spacious rooms cost 15,000/25,000 rp and 25,000/35,000 rp.

Hotel Sindha (☎ 21197) on Jalan Yos Sudarso is central and a good option. Rooms with outside mandi for 7000/10,000 rp are bright, roomy and better value than those with mandi for 15,000/18,000 rp. More luxurious rooms cost 20,000/24,000 rp to 45,000 rp.

Wisma Agung II (☎ 21835), behind Toko Agung on Jalan Motang Rua, is basic but

clean and right in the town centre. Economy rooms cost 7500/10,000 rp, or rooms with mandi are 12,500/15,000 rp. *Wisma Agung I* (☎ 21080), Jalan Waeces 10, is the best hotel in town but it's a 15 minute walk from the centre. Pleasant economy rooms are 7000/10,000 rp or renovated rooms with bathroom are 15,000/20,000 rp to 25,000/30,000 rp.

Ruteng has some good Chinese restaurants, including the *Rumah Makan Dunia Baru* on Jalan Yos Sudarso and the *Restaurant Merlin* on Jalan Kartini. On Jalan Motang Rua, the cosy and friendly *Bamboo Den* next to Hotel Karya has fried chicken, sate and other dishes.

Getting There & Away

Air Merpati (☎ 21197) is out in the rice paddies, a 10 minute walk north from the centre of town. It has direct flights to Labuanbajo, Bima and Kupang with onward connections from those centres.

Bus Most buses to Labuanbajo (5000 rp; four hours), Bajawa (5000 rp; five hours) and Ende (10,000 rp; nine hours) leave around 8 am and noon. The Surya Agung bus at 6.30 am goes right through to Maumere (17,000 rp), via Ende and Moni (14,000 rp).

BAJAWA

Bajawa, a little town nestled in the hills, is the centre for the Ngada people of the Bajawa Plateau area. Coming in on the road from Ruteng, you'll see the great volcanic **Gunung Inerie** – a spectacular sight in the setting sun and it can be climbed.

Bajawa is a pleasant enough place for a short stop, but the main attraction is the surrounding traditional villages. The area has many traditional houses and *ngadhu*, basically a carved pole supporting a conical thatched roof, rather like a large umbrella. Ngadhu are a male symbol used in ancestor worship, and to guard against sickness and preserve fertility – both human and agricultural. The female counterpart of this all-round 'tree of life' is the *bhaga*, a structure that looks something like a miniature thatched-roof house.

Bena, 19km south of Bajawa, is one of the most traditional and spectacular villages and also the most visited. Of the many other villages worth visiting, **Bela**, **Nage** and **Wogo** are the most interesting. Guides hang out at the hotels and arrange good trips for 20,000 rp per person and will include a visit to the hot springs.

Places to Stay & Eat

Hotel Korina (☎ *21162)* at Jalan Ahmad Yani 81 is one of the better places, with friendly and efficient staff. Singles/doubles with outside mandi cost 8000/12,000 rp, or new rooms at the back with shower cost 15,000/20,000 rp. Nearby, *Homestay Sunflower* (☎ *21236)*, on a small path off Jalan Ahmad Yani, has long been popular but is a little run down. Small, dark rooms cost 7000/9000 rp or 8000/10,000 rp with mandi. New rooms off to the side on the hill are much better and cost 15,000 rp.

The small *Hotel Ariesta* (☎ *21292)* on Jalan Diponegoro is bright, clean and a good choice. Rooms cost 15,000/20,000 rp with mandi or 10,000/15,000 rp with outside mandi.

The family-run *Elizabeth Hotel* (☎ *21223)* on Jalan Inerie is a fair hike north from the centre of town, but worth the effort. Spotless, bright rooms cost from 7000/10,000 rp to 15,000/20,000 rp with shower. Nearby, the *Stela Sasandy* (☎ *21198)* just off Jalan Soekarno-Hatta is similarly priced but not quite as good.

A group of hotels can be found close to the centre of town, just west of the market. *Hotel Anggrek* (☎ *21172)* on Jalan Letjend Haryono has clean rooms with mandi for 10,000/15,000 rp and a good restaurant. The largest hotel is *Hotel Kembang* (☎ *21072)* on Jalan Marta Dinata with well-appointed double rooms with bath 25,000 rp.

Bajawa has plenty of other less-inspiring hotels.

The popular *Restoran Carmellya* is a cosy travellers' restaurant on Jalan Ahmad Yani, across from Hotel Korina. Their hot competition is the new *Borobudur* further along the street. *Rumah Makan Kasih Bahagia*, near the market on Jalan Ahmad Yani, has cold beer and inexpensive Chinese food. It is better than the similar *Rumah Makan Wisata*.

Getting There & Away

Air Merpati flies from Bajawa to Bima and Ende, with onward connections. The Merpati office (☎ 21051) is opposite the Bajawa Market.

Bus The long-distance bus station is 3km south of town near the highway, but most hotels arrange bus tickets and pick-ups. Buses to Labuanbajo (10,000 rp; 10 hours) leave around 7 am. More frequent buses go to Ruteng (5000 rp; five hours). Buses to Ende (5000 rp; five hours) leave at 7 and 11 am.

Surya Agung and Sayang Indah buses go to Maumere (12,000 rp) via Moni (10,000 rp) at 7 am.

For surrounding villages, small buses and trucks leave from the market.

RIUNG

Riung, on the coast north of Bajawa, is just a mangrove village but the offshore islands of the **Pulau Tujuh Belas** (Seventeen Islands) marine park have beautiful beaches and good snorkelling. Cheap boat trips are easily arranged in Riung. Riung is also home to Komodo dragons, though they are smaller and more brightly coloured.

Riung has a number of basic homestays, including the *Nur Iklas*, *Liberti*, *Madona* and *Tamri Beach*, all costing around 10,000 rp per person including all meals. The church-run *Pondok SVD* has the best rooms but it's expensive at 25,000 rp per person.

Daily buses run between Riung and Bajawa (3500 rp; 2½ hours). Buses to Ende (4500 rp; 4½ hours) go every day except Sunday and Monday, when you'll have to take a bus to Mbay (1500 rp; 1½ hours) and then a bus to Ende.

ENDE

Dominated by the volcanic cones of Gunung Meja and Gunung Iya, Ende is the biggest city on Flores and was once the main Dutch colony where Soekarno was exiled in the 1930s. You can visit the house he lived in, and the regional museum, but otherwise Ende is primarily a stopover to catch buses or the boat to Sumba. Ende also has a good **ikat weaving market** in the main street near the waterfront and trips to nearby villages are worthwhile if you are stuck for something to do.

Information

The Bank Rakyat Indonesia in Hotel Dwi Putri on Jalan KH Dewantara and the BNI bank on Jalan Gatot Subroto near the airport both handle foreign exchange.

Places to Stay & Eat

Near the airport, *Hotel Ikhlas* (☎ *21695)* on Jalan Jenderal Ahmad Yani is in a 'klas' of its own – friendly and on the ball with travel information. Clean, basic singles/doubles cost 3500/6000 rp with shared mandi. Rooms with mandi and fan are 7000/10,000 rp to 10,000/15,000 rp. Good, cheap western and Indonesian food is available. Next door, the spacious and airy *Hotel Safari* (☎ *21499)* has friendly staff and a restaurant. Rooms cost 10,000/15,000 rp with mandi, up to 35,000/40,000 rp with air-con.

The small *Hotel Amica* (☎ *21683)*, Jalan Garuda 39, is a good budget hotel. Rooms go for 10,000/15,000 rp, all with attached bath. The young manager speaks excellent English and can fill you in on excursions around Ende.

Hotel Flores (☎ *21075)* at Jalan Sudirman 28 has a small restaurant and a range of good rooms, from 10,000/15,000 rp with mandi to 55,000 rp with air-con. The large and spotless *Hotel Dwi Putri* (☎ *21685)* on Jalan KH Dewantara is the best in town. Rooms cost 20,000/25,000 rp to 40,000/50,000 rp. The quiet *Hotel Wisata* (☎ *21368)*, on Jalan Kelimutu, is another more upmarket hotel and reasonably priced with large rooms for 15,000/20,000 rp with mandi, and more expensive air-con rooms.

Good restaurants opposite the market on Jalan Pasar include the *Bundo Kandung* for Padang food and the *Istana Bambu*, next door, one of Ende's best restaurants with a long menu of Indonesian, Chinese and seafood dishes. The *Rumah Makan Tanur Merah*, on Jalan Kelimutu near the Telkom office, is an unpretentious but very clean place that does great nasi sate (soup, rice and sate) and other Madurese dishes.

Getting There & Away
Air Merpati (☎ 21355) is on Jalan Nangka, a 15 minute walk from the airstrip. From Ende direct flights go to Bajawa, Bima, Kupang and Labuanbajo.

Bus Buses to the east leave from Terminal Wolowana, 4km east of town. Buses to Moni (2500 rp; two hours) depart between 8 am and noon, or take a Wolowaru bus. Buses to Maumere (6000 rp; five hours) leave between 8 am and 5 pm. Maumere buses will drop you in Moni but charge for the full fare to Maumere.

Buses to the west leave from Terminal Ndao, 2km north of town on the beach road. Buses include: Bajawa (5000 rp; five hours), Ruteng (10,000 rp; nine hours), Labuanbajo (15,000 rp; 14 hours) and Riung (4500 rp; 4½ hours).

Boat Ships dock at Pelabuhan Ipi, the main port, 2.5km south-east of town. The ferry to Waingapu (12,000 rp; 10 hours) leaves Ende on Tuesday at 7 pm. The ferry from Kupang to Ende (17,000 rp; 16 hours) departs on Friday at 7 pm, and returns the following day at 5 pm.

Pelni's *Pangrango* sails from Ende to Waingapu (eight hours) every two weeks and to Sabu on alternate weeks. The *Awu* also sails between Waingapu and Ende and then on to Kupang (11 hours) every fortnight. The Pelni office (☎ 21043) is on the corner of Jalan Pabean and Jalan Kemakmuran.

Getting Around
Bemo fares around town are a flat 400 rp, including the airport, bus stations and Pelabuhan Ipi.

KELIMUTU
This extinct volcano is the most fantastic sight on Flores and one of Nusa Tenggara's main attractions. The crater has three lakes – the largest is light turquoise, the one next to it olive green, and the third one black. Chemicals in the soil account for this weird colour scheme and it changes with time (the green lake was previously a deep maroon/brown) and during the rainy season colours may be a murkier brown.

The best time to see Kelimutu is in the early morning before the clouds roll in, you need strong sunlight to bring out the colours of the lakes.

Getting There & Away
Most visitors base themselves in Moni, the village at the foot of the volcano, and make their way up to the top at 4 am by truck or minibus arranged by the hotels for 3000 rp per person. A few hardy souls walk the 13km to the top in three to four hours. The truck goes down the mountain at 7 am, but many walk back in about two hours.

The park entry post, halfway up the road, charges 1500 rp entry fee. Coming down, there's a shortcut from just beside the entry post which comes out by the hot springs and waterfall. It's fine going down but would be difficult to find, in the dark, on your way up.

MONI
Moni (Mone) is a small village on the Ende to Maumere road at the base of Kelimutu. It is cooler than the lowlands, scenic and a good place for walks. About 2km before Moni, on the Ende side, is the turn-off to the top of Kelimutu.

Moni's Monday **market** is a major local event and attracts a large and colourful crowd. Traditional dance performances are held every evening at the rumah adat near the market and cost 3000 rp.

A good day trip can be made south to **Wolowaru** and traditional villages such as **Ranggase**, **Jopu**, **Wolonjita** and **Nggela**. The villages are an interesting and pleasant three to four-hour walk one way from Wolowaru, so long as you avoid the heat of the day. Ranggase has the most interesting traditional houses, while Nggela is a noted weaving village, though intricately woven sarongs and shawls can be found in other villages. Regular buses run to Wolowaru, 13km from Moni, and one bus runs from Moni to Nggela around 8 am.

Places to Stay & Eat

Moni is a popular stop for a few days and has a collection of basic, cheap homestays clustered together along the road through town. The going rate is 5500 rp per person, or 8250 rp in a room with attached mandi, including breakfast, but competition is cutthroat in quiet periods when prices tumble.

Along the main road opposite the market, *Homestay Daniel* is clean and tidy. *Homestay Amina Moe* is the most aggressive discounter, and also has a few rooms with mandi. Next along, *Homestay Sao Lelegana* is a notch up in standards and has larger rooms with basin and attached mandi. *Homestay Friendly* is another more substantial place with a good aspect and better than average rooms, with and without mandi.

More homestays are clustered about five minutes walk along the road to Ende. They tend to be quieter and less cramped. They include the *Sylvester*, *Lovely Rose*, *Nusa Bunga*, *Regal Jaya*, *Lestari*, and *Hidayai*. *Watugana Bungalow* is one of the best options. New rooms and simple bungalows cost 8000, 10,000 or 12,500 rp a double – breakfast is included, and the higher the price the more substantial the breakfast.

Most of the homestays provide simple buffet meals. Cheap restaurants include the *Moni Indah*, *Sarty* and *Rona* opposite the market. The *Chenty*, above the main road, between the two clusters of homestays has the best aspect but the food is average.

Getting There & Away

Moni is 52km north-east of Ende and 96km west of Maumere. For Ende (2500 rp; two

hours), buses start at around 5.30 am. Other buses come through from Maumere or Wolowaru to Ende until about noon. Late buses come through at around 9 pm. Many buses and trucks leave on Monday market day. Through buses from Maumere go all the way to Bajawa for 10,000 rp.

For Maumere (6000 rp; four hours) the first buses from Ende start coming though at around 9 or 10 am and then later in the evening around 7 pm.

As most of the buses stop in Moni midroute they can be crowded and it's first-come, first-served for a seat.

MAUMERE

Maumere is a medium-size port on the northeast coast and a stopover on the route between Ende and Larantuka. This is still an important mission centre and the Maumere area also has strong ikat-weaving traditions. In December 1992, Maumere was devastated by the earthquakes that hit Flores and the ensuing 20m-high tsunami killed thousands. Most of Maumere has been rebuilt.

Maumere itself has no attractions but some low-key beach resorts are nearby. On Jalan Pasar Baru Timur, the Harapan Jaya Art shop has an excellent selection of ikat cloth.

Information

The tourist office (☎ 21652) is on Jalan Wairklau. The BNI bank on Jalan Soekarno-Hatta is the best place to change money, and the Bank Rakyat Indonesia also handles foreign exchange.

The post office is next to the soccer field on Jalan Pos, and the Telkom office is further south from the town centre on Jalan Soekarno-Hatta.

Places to Stay

Pick of the cheap hotels is the friendly and quiet *Gardena Hotel* (☎ 21489), Jalan Patirangga 28, close to the town centre. This is a good place to contact guides. Well-kept, if bare, singles/doubles cost 10,000/15,000 rp with mandi and fan or 20,000/30,000 rp with air-con.

Hotel Senja Wair Bubak (☎ 21498) on Jalan Komodor Yos Sudarso, near the waterfront, gets a steady stream of travellers but the rooms need a good clean. Rooms cost 6600/11,000 rp or better rooms with mandi start at 11,000/16,000 rp.

Nearby, the small and friendly *Hotel Jaya* (☎ 21292), Jalan Hasanuddin 26, is a good deal, rooms with fan and mandi are 10,000/15,000 rp.

Hotel Beng Goan I (☎ *21041*) on Jalan Moa Toda is a popular local hotel and very central. Rooms range from 6000/10,000 rp to 35,000/50,000 rp with air-con.

Close to the Ende (west) bus station, the well-run *Hotel Wini Rai* (☎ *21388*), Jalan Gajah Mada 50, has a wide variety of rooms from 7500/12,500 rp to 42,500/47,500 rp with air-con. The new *Hotel Wini Rai II* (☎ *21362*) on Jalan Dr Soetomo is right in the centre of town and good for information. Spotless, if dark, rooms cost 7500/12,500 rp with shared mandi or much better rooms are 20,000/25,000 rp with mandi or 32,500/37,500 rp with air-con.

Places to Eat
The best place to hunt out a restaurant is Jalan Pasar Baru Barat, the main street running down to the waterfront. The *Sarina Restaurant* has Chinese food and does good squid. The *Stevani Pub & Restaurant* has small huts dotted around in a garden setting. It's a pleasant place to sit with a drink, and western and Indonesian dishes are served. The nearby *Depot Kanaan* on Jalan Pasar Baru Timur is a spotless little restaurant serving mouthwatering, and cheap, chicken curry and other excellent dishes.

The *Bamboo Den* near Hotel Wini Rai has cheap Indonesian food, good fish and cold beer.

Getting There & Away
Air Maumere's airport handles bigger aircraft and is the best place on Flores for flights to and from other islands. Merpati (☎ 21342), at Jalan Don Thomas 18, flies to Kupang and Bali.

Bus Buses and bemos east to Larantuka (7000 rp; four hours), Geliting, Waiara, Ipir and Wodong leave from the Lokaria (or Wai Oti) terminal, about 3km east of town. Buses west to Ende (6000 rp; five hours) via Moni (5000 or 6000 rp; 3½ hours), Sikka and Ladalero leave from the Ende (or Barat) terminal, 1.5km south-west of town.

Buses often endlessly do the rounds of the town searching for passengers. Hotels can arrange pick-up.

Boat Pelni's *Awu* sails fortnightly between Maumere and Ujung Pandang on Sulawesi (23 hours) and Dili on Timor (18 hours). The Pelni office is on Jalan Slamet Riyadi, or CV Arwana is a Pelni agent on Jalan Dr Soetomo.

Getting Around
The airport is 3km from the town centre, off the Maumere to Larantuka road – 6000 rp by taxi or chartered bemo. Bemos around town and to the bus stations cost 400 rp.

AROUND MAUMERE
Villages and points of cultural interest around town include the weaving village of **Sikka**, 27km south of Maumere, and an interesting museum at the Catholic seminary in **Ladalero**, 19km from Maumere on the Ende road. However, the main attractions are the beaches.

Waiara
Just off the Larantuka road, 13km east of Maumere, Waiara has scuba diving despite reef damage due to the 1992 earthquake. Waiara has two mid-range dive resorts. The *Flores Sao Resort* (☎ *21555*) caters mostly to tour groups and singles/doubles cost US$25/30 to US$65/70. The cheaper *Sea World Club* (☎ *21570*) has simple cabin rooms at US$10/15 up to US$30/35 for very comfortable air-con rooms. Both also offer dive packages.

Wodong/Wairterang
The beach of Wairterang, 28km east of Maumere just outside Wodong village, is developing into quite a scene. The beach is not stunning, but pleasant, and cheap boat tours are offered to offshore islands where the best beaches, diving and snorkelling are found.

Flores Froggies is the original homestay but now looking a little rundown. Simple bungalows are 6000/8000 rp for singles/doubles and some have private mandi for 8000/10,000 rp. *Wairterang Beach Cottage* is a well-kept place with a small bungalows for 5000/10,000 rp. *Pondok Praja* has the largest and best bungalows for 17,500 rp and 25,000 rp.

Pick of the crop, *Ankermi* has attractive grounds and lots of information on nearby attractions. Bungalows cost 7000/10,000 rp or 12,000/17,500 rp with mandi or the dorm bungalow with two mattresses per room costs 5000 rp per person.

Another good option is *Wodong Beach Homestay*, off by itself further around the headland. Under Belgian management, it houses the funky little Coral Bar and runs good trips to the islands. Tiny bungalows are

6000 rp, larger ones 10,000 rp or 15,000 rp with mandi.

All homestays have their own restaurants.

LARANTUKA

This little port nestles at the base of a high hill at the eastern end of Flores. From here, you can see the islands of Solor and Adonara across the narrow strait. It is primarily a place to catch ferries.

The BNI bank and Bank Rakyat Indonesia both change money.

Places to Stay & Eat

The family-run *Hotel Rulies* (☎ 21198) at Jalan Yos Sudarso 44 has the best setup. Clean singles/doubles with shared bath cost 10,000/16,000 rp and food is available. Next door, *Hotel Tresna* (☎ 21072) is slightly fancier but poorly run. Rooms cost 8500/14,000 rp or 15,000/25,000 rp with mandi.

Hotel Kurnia Sederhana (☎ 21066), in the middle of town on Jalan Niaga, looks very unpromising from the outside but rooms at the back for 10,000/15,000 rp are relatively new and well-kept, if a little noisy.

Other hotels are good and reasonably priced but inconveniently located. *Hotel Syalom* (☎ 21464), Jalan WJ Lalamentik 35, is a long grunt uphill from the centre, or *Hotel Fortuna I* (☎ 21140) is 2km north-east of town at Jalan Diponegoro 171, near the Telkom office.

Eating possibilities are limited, but a few warung set up in the evening along Jalan Niaga. *Rumah Makan Nirwana* on Jalan Niaga is a decent Chinese restaurant and the best in town. Nearby, the small *Virgo Cafe*, in the hairdressers of the same name, has fish & chips in addition to the usual nasi and mie meals.

Getting There & Away

Air The Merpati agent's house is at Jalan Diponegoro 64 but flights to Kupang and Lewoleba are almost always cancelled.

Bus Regular buses run between Maumere and Larantuka (7000 rp; four hours). The main bus station is 5km west of the town (400 rp by bemo), but you can pick buses up in the centre. Coming into town, buses can drop you at or near your hotel, depending on the one-way street system.

Boat Ferries to Kupang (14,000 rp; 14 hours) depart Monday and Friday at noon from Waibulan, 4km south-west of Larantuka (400 rp by bemo). Ferries can be crowded, so board early to get a seat. Take some food and water.

The car-and-passenger ferry to Adonara, Lembata and Alor also leaves from Waibulan on Tuesday, Thursday and Sunday at 7 am. More convenient, smaller boats to Adonara, Solor and Lembata leave from the pier in the centre of town. They run twice a day to Lewoleba (4000 rp; four hours) on Lembata at around 8 am, noon and 1.30 pm, stopping at Waiwerang (Adonara) on the way. A boat goes once a week to Lamalera (5000 rp; seven hours) on Lembata on Friday at 9 am.

Pelni's *Tatamailau* calls at Larantuka on its way between Labuanbajo and Dili. The *Sirimau* runs from Larantuka to Kupang and Ujung Pandang in Sulawesi.

SOLOR & ALOR ARCHIPELAGOS

This chain of volcanic, mountainous islands separated by swift, narrow straits lie off the eastern end of Flores and are reached by ferry from Larantuka. The Solor Archipelago consists of the islands of Adonara, Solor and Lembata, the main island of interest where the traditional whaling village of Lamalera can be visited.

Lying between Lembata and Timor are the islands of Pantar and Alor, the main islands of the Alor Archipelago.

It is quite a spectacular ferry ride from Larantuka through the islands past smoking volcanoes, but few travellers make it to this isolated region. It is possible to travel by ferry right through to Atapupu on Timor but allow plenty of time.

Lembata

Lembata Island in the Solor Archipelago is dry, and the sleepy main town of Lewoleba is dominated by the ominous smoking of Ili Api volcano. Traditional villages ring Ili Api and fine ikat comes from the area.

Lewoleba has three hotels but no banks to exchange money. The best hotels here are the switched-on *Lile Ile* homestay halfway between the ferry wharf and the town, and the good *Hotel Rejeki* right in the middle of town, opposite the market. Both hotels serve meals.

On the south coast, **Lamalera** is a whaling village where the villagers still hunt whales using small row-boat's and hand-thrown harpoons. During the whaling season, from May to October, you may see the catch being brought back to the village and hacked up. The village receives a steady trickle of tourists, and you can even go out on a hunt in one of the boats for 15,000 rp. Lamalera has a number of *homestays* costing 10,000 rp per person, including meals. Lamalera is difficult to reach. One boat goes from Lewoleba to Lamalera on Monday nights or from Larantuka a boat leaves on Friday. Otherwise take a truck from Lewoleba to Puor, from where it's a three hour walk, mostly downhill. Bring plenty of water.

Getting There & Away Regular passenger ferries run between Larantuka and Lewoleba.

Ferries to Kalabahi (Alor) depart Lewoleba on Tuesday, Thursday and Sunday at 11 am. They stop for the night in eastern Lembata at Balauring (4500 rp; four hours), which has a losmen or you can sleep on the deck of the boat. At 7 am the next morning the ferry continues on to Kalabahi (9000 rp; nine hours) via Baranusa on Pantar. Bring food and water.

Getting Around The main road across the island is sealed and regular mikrolets, buses and trucks run to destinations around Lewoleba including Waipukang, Loang and Puor (for Lamalera).

Alor

Famed for its highly prized *moko*, bronze drums found mysteriously buried all over the island, Alor is a rugged, scenic island. The island has excellent diving, best arranged in Kupang. Kalabahi is the chief town, and the place for ferry connections. Money can be changed at the BNI bank and the Bank Rakyat Indonesia. The central *Hotel Adi Dharma* or *Hotel Pelangi Indah*, out near the bus station, are the best hotel options.

Getting There & Away Merpati has regular flights between Kupang and Kalabahi.

The ferry to Kupang (16,500 rp; about 16 hours) leaves on Tuesday and Friday at 2 pm. On Sunday at 10 pm a ferry runs to Atapupu (8000 rp; eight hours) on Timor.

Ferries to Lewoleba and Larantuka via Solor leave Sunday, Tuesday and Thursday at 7 am. They stop overnight at Balauring on Lembata.

The Pelni ship *Awu* calls in at Kalabahi on its route between Dili and Kupang.

Timor

Kupang, the 'big city' of Nusa Tenggara, gets a steady stream of travellers passing through on the way to Australia. Outside of Kupang, Timor is one of the most traditional regions of Indonesia, but sees few tourists. Dominated by the scenic central mountains, this large, rugged and dry island is home to a wide variety of cultures. Despite the dominance of Christianity, animism is very much in evidence, and large parts of the island have had minimal contact with Indonesian national culture.

Timor is divided into West Timor and East Timor. Almost all visitors go only to West Timor, because of East Timor's reputation as one of the world's hot spots. However, East Timor is not a war zone, and it is safe and easy to travel to Dili, the capital. You can go right through to Tutuala, East Timor's most easterly point.

History

The Portuguese were the first Europeans to land in Timor, in the early 16th century. The Dutch occupied Kupang in the middle of the 17th century and after a lengthy conflict, the Portuguese finally withdrew to the eastern half of the island in the middle of the 18th century. When Indonesia became independent in 1949, the Dutch half of Timor became part of the new republic but the Portuguese retained the eastern half.

On 25 April 1974, there was a military coup in Portugal and the new government set about discarding the Portuguese colonial empire. Within a few weeks of the coup, three major political parties had been formed in East Timor. After the UDT attempted to seize power in August 1975, a brief civil war between the rival parties, Fretilin and UDT, saw Fretilin come out on top.

However, Indonesia opposed the formation of an independent East Timor and leftist Fretilin raised the spectre of Communism in Indonesian eyes. On 7 December 1975, Indonesia launched a full-scale invasion of the former colony, just one day after US Secretary of State Henry Kissinger had cleared out of Indonesia after a brief visit – presumably having put the US seal of approval on the invasion.

By all accounts, the Indonesian invasion was brutal. Fretilin fought a guerrilla war with marked success in the first two or three years but after that began to weaken considerably. The cost to the Timorese people was horrific, many dying through starvation or disease due to the disruption of food and medical supplies. By 1989, Indonesia had things firmly under control and opened East Timor to tourism, but on 12 November 1991 army troops opened fire on protesters at the Dili cemetery, once again alerting the world to East Timor's plight.

Shortly after taking office in May 1998 President Habibie released a number of East Timorese political prisoners and made some placatory noises about limited autonomy for East Timor. As with so much about Indonesia at the moment, it remains to be seen what will eventuate.

Today, the army well and truly controls East Timor, but isolated resistance continues. While East Timor is normally quiet and travel quite easy, it pays to know the latest situation before venturing outside Dili.

Getting There & Away

Air Merpati flies to Kupang from other parts of Nusa Tenggara and Indonesia. A good way to explore Nusa Tenggara is to fly directly from Bali to Kupang and then island-hop back.

Merpati has a twice weekly service between Darwin in Australia and Kupang. See the Indonesia Getting There & Away section for more details. This is a terrific way of getting to Indonesia; the flight is popular but usually not heavily booked. Kupang is on the no-visa-required entry list.

Boat The Perum ASDP ferry company, based in Kupang, has regular car-and-passenger ferries throughout East Nusa Tenggara. Ferries run from Kupang to Larantuka (Flores), Kalabahi (Alor), Roti, and Waingapu (Sumba) via Sabu. From Atapupu, near Atambua in West Timor, a ferry runs once a week to/from Kalabahi. The routes are fairly constant but schedules are constantly changing – check on arrival in Kupang.

Pelni passenger ships run direct from Kupang to Benoa (Bali), Dobonsolo, Ende, Kalabahi, Larantuka and Sabu with onward sailings to other ports in Nusa Tenggara and Indonesia. Pelni ships connect Dili with Kupang, Ambon and Larantuka.

Getting Around

The good main highway is surfaced all the way from Kupang to Dili, though the buses are of the cramped and crowded version found throughout Nusa Tenggara. Away from the highway, roads are improving but can be impassable in the wet.

KUPANG

Kupang is the biggest city on the island and capital of the province of Nusa Tenggara Timur. It's a small city, but compared with the sedate little towns on Flores and Sumba, Kupang is a booming metropolis. It's not a bad place to hang around – Captain Bligh did, after his *Bounty* misadventures.

Kupang's **Museum NTT**, open 8 am to 3 pm daily, is worth a look.

Information

Tourist Offices The Kupang tourist office (☎ 21540), Jalan El Tari 338, is out in the sticks near the bus station.

Money Kupang is the best place to change money in Nusa Tenggara outside Mataram on Lombok. The Bank Dagang Negara, Jalan Urip Sumohardjo 16, is central and most other banks usually have good rates. If you want a cash advance on Visa or MasterCard, get it here. The currency exchange office at Kupang airport is open when flights arrive from Darwin.

Post & Communications Poste restante mail goes to the main post office, Kantor Pos Besar, at Jalan Palapa 1. A branch post office is at Jalan Soekarno 29. The Telkom office is at Jalan Urip Sumohardjo 11.

Diving

Graeme and Donovan Whitford (☎ 21154), two Australian dive masters based in Kupang, arrange dives to Alor and sites around Timor.

Organised Tours

Many fascinating traditional villages can be visited on Timor, but Indonesian, let alone English, is often not spoken so a local guide is necessary. Guides will find you, and start at around 20,000 rp per day. Big tour companies include Pitoby Tours (☎ 32700), Jalan Jenderal Sudirman 118.

Places to Stay

Accommodation in Kupang is spread out, but the efficient bemo system makes everywhere easily accessible.

Two popular budget options, despite their distance from town (take bemo No 3), are in a quiet area on Jalan Kencil. *Eden Homestay* (☎ 21931) at No 6 is opposite a shady freshwater pool, the local swimming spot. Bungalows are very basic but very cheap at 4000 rp per person. This friendly place offers

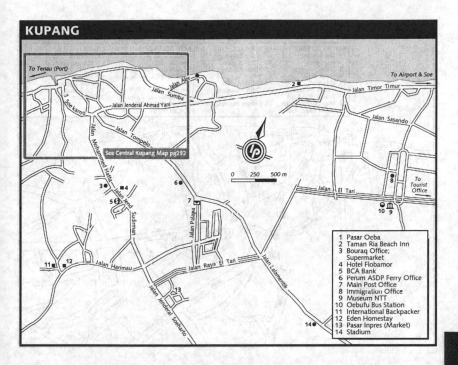

KUPANG

To Tenau (Port)

Jalan Alor

Jalan Sumba

Jalan Jenderal Ahmad Yani

To Airport & Soe

Jalan Timor Timur

Jalan Sasando

Jalan Tompelo

See Central Kupang Map pg292

0   250   500 m

Jalan El Tari

To Tourist Office

Jalan Mohammed Hatta

Jalan Jend Sudirman

Jalan Palapa

Jalan alamentik

Jalan Raya El Tari

Jalan Harimau

Jalan Jenderal Soeharto

1 Pasar Oeba
2 Taman Ria Beach Inn
3 Bouraq Office;
   Supermarket
4 Hotel Flobamor
5 BCA Bank
6 Perum ASDP Ferry Office
7 Main Post Office
8 Immigration Office
9 Museum NTT
10 Oebufu Bus Station
11 International Backpacker
12 Eden Homestay
13 Pasar Inpres (Market)
14 Stadium

meals and cheap tours. *International Backpacker* at Jalan Kencil 37B is one street away. Dormitories and small rooms are more substantial and also cost 4000 rp person. This is another friendly place that also has meals and tours.

Closer to town at Jalan Sumatera 8, *L'Avalon* (☎ 32278) is another popular backpackers. It's a laid-back place, good for information on touring Timor. Well-kept four and six-bed dorms cost 4000 rp per person or the double room costs 10,000 rp.

Nearby, *Cassandra Backpackers* (☎ 22392), Jalan Sumatra 13, is a new and very friendly homestay. Rooms are simple but spotless and cost 4000 rp in three-bed dorms or singles/doubles are 5000/10,000 rp. Good information and services are offered.

Homestay Puteri Australia (☎ 25532), down a small street opposite the Taman Ria Beach Inn, is a small, comfortable homestay run by an Australian woman and her Sumbanese husband. A share room costs 5000 rp and a double with shared mandi is 12,000 rp.

Kupang has dozens of other hotels, most offering rooms in various price ranges. One of the best is *Hotel Susi* (☎ 22172), by the

waterfront at Jalan Sumatera 37. Singles/doubles at the back cost 10,000 rp or 15,000/20,000 rp with fan and mandi. Fancier upstairs rooms, some with great views, cost 18,000/22,000 rp to 25,000/35,000 rp. Nearby, the *Timor Beach Hotel* (☎ 31651) has a restaurant with panoramic sea views. Rooms situated around an elongated courtyard are a little dark, but good value at 12,500/17,000 rp with fan and bath. Air-con rooms go for 24,500/30,000 rp.

Taman Ria Beach Inn (☎ 31320), Jalan Timor Timur 69, is on the beachfront about 3km from the bus station (catch a No 10 bemo). The beach is pleasant enough and the restaurant is good. Worn rooms with mandi and fan are 17,500/25,000 rp and they also rent on a dorm basis at 7500 rp.

Places to Eat

Visiting Darwinites like to hang out at *Teddy's Bar*, Jalan Ikan Tongkol 1-3, for meat pie & chips. The sea views and cold beer compensate for the expensive food. The *Restaurant Karang Mas*, Jalan Siliwangi 88, hangs over the water and is a favourite spot to take in the sunset over a beer. It has seen better days but

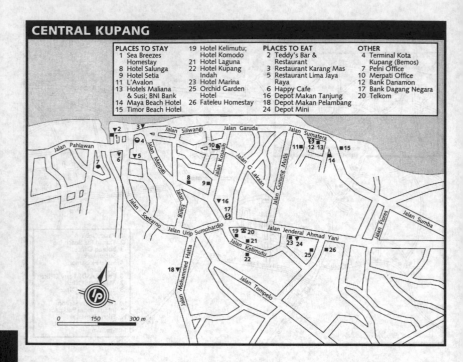

CENTRAL KUPANG

PLACES TO STAY
1 Sea Breezes Homestay
8 Hotel Salunga
9 Hotel Setia
11 L'Avalon
13 Hotels Maliana & Susi; BNI Bank
14 Maya Beach Hotel
15 Timor Beach Hotel
19 Hotel Kelimutu; Hotel Komodo
21 Hotel Laguna
22 Hotel Kupang Indah
23 Hotel Marina
25 Orchid Garden Hotel
26 Fateleu Homestay

PLACES TO EAT
2 Teddy's Bar & Restaurant
3 Restaurant Karang Mas
5 Restaurant Lima Jaya Raya
6 Happy Cafe
16 Depot Makan Tanjung
18 Depot Makan Pelambang
24 Depot Mini

OTHER
4 Terminal Kota Kupang (Bemos)
7 Pelni Office
10 Merpati Office
12 Bank Danamon
17 Bank Dagang Negara
20 Telkom

the food is OK and the beer is cheaper than in the similar *Pantai Laut Restaurant* nearby.

The *Depot Mini* on Jalan Jenderal Ahmad Yani is a spotless restaurant with good, cheap Chinese food. Kupang has many other restaurants – eat up while you can.

Getting There & Away

Air Merpati (☎ 33833) at Jalan Kosasih 2 has direct flights to Denpasar, Dili, Waingapu, Maumere, Kalabahi, Ruteng, Ende and Roti, as well as flights to Darwin (Australia) on Wednesday and Saturday.

Bus Long-distance buses depart from the Oebufu bus station, out near the museum – take a No 10 bemo. Departures include: Soe (4250 rp; three hours), Niki Niki (5250 rp; 3½ hours), Kefamenanu (7500 rp; 5½ hours), Atambua (10,500 rp; eight hours) and Dili (15,500 rp; 12 hours). Bemos to villages around Kupang go from the central terminal, Kota Kupang.

Boat Pelni passenger ships leave from Tenau, 10km west of Kupang (400 rp by

bemo No 12). Ferries leave from Bolok, 13km west of Kupang (600 rp by bemo No 13).

Pelni (☎ 22646), Jalan Pahlawan 3, has connections from Kupang direct to Ende, Dili, Larantuka and Roti, and ships continue on to many other ports including Ujung Pandang (Sulawesi) and Ambon (Maluku).

Perum ASDP has ferries from Bolok harbour to: Larantuka (14,000 rp; 14 hours) on Thursday and Sunday; Kalabahi (16,500 rp; 16 hours) on Thursday and Saturday; and Ende (17,000 rp; 16 hours) on Monday. The Ende ferry continues on to Waingapu (Sumba) and another ferry leaves Kupang on Wednesday for Sabu (14,000 rp; nine hours) and on to Waingapu. Ferries to Roti (5700 rp; four hours) go every day except Friday at 8 am.

Getting Around

To/From the Airport Kupang's El Tari airport is 15km east of the centre. Taxis cost a fixed 12,500 rp. By public transport, turn left out of the terminal and walk a full kilometre to the junction with the main highway, from where bemos to town cost 500 rp. Going to the airport take bemo No 14 or 15 to the junction and then walk.

Bemo Kupang's bemo terminal is at the waterfront, on the corner of Jalan Soekarno and Jalan Siliwangi. Around town, bemos cost a standard 400 rp and are fast, efficient, brightly painted and incredibly noisy – drivers like the bass turned up high and a multispeaker stereo system is de rigueur.

AROUND KUPANG

The beaches around town are not very appealing but **Pantai Lasiana**, 10km east of town, is a half-decent stretch of sand and popular on weekends. **Tablolong**, 27km southwest of Kupang, has a better beach. The small islands of **Pulau Semau** and **Pulau Kera** just off the coast are more interesting, and the backpackers' places run day tours.

The small village of **Baun**, 30km south of Kupang in the hilly Amarasi District, is an ikat-weaving centre, with a few Dutch buildings. You can visit the *rumah raja*, the last raja's house, now occupied by his widow.

Camplong, 46km from Kupang on the Soe road, is a cool, quiet hill town. One kilometre east of town, the Taman Wisata Camplong is a forest reserve that has some caves and a spring-fed swimming pool. The church-run *Wisma Oe Mat Honis* (☎ 50006), at the reserve, has excellent rooms for 7500 rp per person, and 15,000 rp extra for all meals.

ROTI

Roti (also spelled Rote) is the southernmost island in Indonesia, with long ties to Timor. Roti is only four hours by ferry from Kupang and receives a steady trickle of visitors, mostly surfers in search of the excellent break at Nemberala on the west coast. The beach is superb and Nemberala has three cheap losmen costing 10,000 rp to 15,000 rp with meals, or the *Nemberala Beach Resort* is more upmarket. You can also stay in the main town of Baa.

Getting There & Away

Merpati flies Kupang-Roti-Sabu-Roti-Kupang on Friday (maybe).

See the Kupang Getting There & Away section for details on ferries to Roti. Ferries dock at Pantai Baru, from where waiting buses will take you to Baa (2000 rp; 1½ hours), or Nemberala (5000 rp; 3½ hours).

SOE

Soe is a dull sprawl of a town, but is the best base for exploring the scenic hill region of Timor. The surrounding area is very traditional, and thatched, beehive-shaped houses of the Dawan people are dotted everywhere.

The tourist information centre (☎ 21149) on the main street, Jalan Diponegoro, has good information on the surrounding area and can arrange guides. Change money at the BNI bank opposite.

Places to Stay

The travellers' favourite place is *Hotel Anda* (☎ 21323), Jalan Kartini 5. This would have to be the most eccentric losmen in Indonesia, starting with the gaudy statuary and dazzling paint job at the front, and at the back is a huge, home-made replica of a warship. Basic rooms cost around 6500 rp per person, but those in the ship are cute. Pak Yohannes is a wonderful host, speaks English, Dutch and German, and is a wealth of knowledge on the area.

If this is full, *Hotel Cahaya* (☎ 21087), next door, has clean singles/doubles with mandi for 7500/15,000 rp.

Soe has a few mid-range hotels. *Hotel Bahagia 1* (☎ 21015), Jalan Diponegoro 72, is the best and has rooms with outside mandi for 20,000 rp, or with mandi for 22,000/25,000 rp.

Getting There & Away

The Haumeni bus station is 4km west of town (400 rp by bemo). Regular buses run from Soe to Kupang (4250 rp; three hours), Kefamenanu (3000 rp; 2½ hours) and Oinlasi (2500 rp; 1½ hours), while bemos cover Niki Niki (1000 rp) and Kapan (800 rp).

AROUND SOE

On market days in the towns, villagers come from miles around, many in traditional dress. As well as everyday goods, ikat weaving and crafts can be found. The Tuesday market at **Oinlasi**, 51km from Soe, is one of the largest, or the Wednesday market at **Niki Niki**, 34km east of Soe, is just as lively and easier to reach.

The main attraction around Soe is **Boti**, a traditional village presided over by a self-styled *raja* (king). Christianity never penetrated here, and the raja maintains strict adherence to *adat* (tradition). The village is used to tourists, and even gets the occasional tour bus. Buses run to Oinlasi, from where it is 12km on foot along a bad road to Boti. It is best to take a guide who speaks the local dialect. You can stay overnight for a donation.

North of Soe are the **Oehala Waterfall**, the

INDONESIA

cool hill town of **Kapan**, and **Fatumenasi**, surrounded by highland forest and traditional villages.

KEFAMENANU

Kefamenanu, 217km from Kupang, is cool and quiet with a few colonial buildings. On the outskirts of town, 1.5km south of the bus station, **Maslete** is an interesting traditional village. **Temkessi**, 50km north-east of Kefa, is a more spectacular traditional village but very isolated. An interesting side trip can also be made to **Oecussi**, the small, former Portuguese enclave on the coast. The main town, Pantemakassar, has one *losmen* and daily buses run from Kefa.

Hotel Soko Windu on Jalan Kartini is the best budget option with rooms for 7500 rp per person. For something better, *Hotel Ariesta* on Jalan Basuki Rachmat has rooms from 16,500 rp to 55,000 rp.

ATAMBUA

Atambua is the major town and resting place on the overland Dili-Kupang route. **Atapupu**, 25km away, is a port with a ferry to Kalabahi (Alor) on Mondays. The area around Atambua is home to the matrilineal Tetum (or Belu) people. **Betun**, 60km south of Atambua, has losmens and can be used as a base for visiting traditional villages.

In Atambua, the central *Hotel Kalpataru* (☎ 21351), Jalan Gatot Subroto 3, is an oasis of hospitality. Simple but very clean and well kept rooms with outside mandi cost 8500 rp per person. If full, *Hotel Liurai* next door is a good hotel, or Atambua has plenty of others.

DILI

The capital of East Timor is a pleasant, lazy city – the most attractive in Nusa Tenggara. It has a number of reminders of Portugal, such as the villas on the beach road and the **Mercado Municipal**, the old Portuguese market. Near the waterfront is the **Integration Monument**, which has a Timorese rapturously breaking his chains of colonial bondage.

This strongly Catholic city has plenty of churches, and at the eastern end of the bay at **Cape Fatucama**, a massive, new statue of Christ occupies the hilltop headland. It is styled after Rio de Janiero's Christ the Redeemer and there are magnificent views from the hilltop. Some decent beaches, such as Areia Branca (White Sands) are nearby.

Information

The tourist office (☎ 21350), west of the Mercado Municipal on Jalan Kaikoli, is helpful and has maps and brochures. A number of banks change money.

Places to Stay

Head for the very friendly *Villa Harmonia* (☎ 23595), 3km east of town on the road to the Becora bus station (take mikrolet I or bus D). The manager speaks excellent English and this is the best place for travel information. Singles/doubles with outside mandi cost 14,000/18,000 rp. Food and drinks are available.

The other vaguely cheap options are usually 'full' and won't take foreigners. *Wisma Taufiq* and *Basmery Indah* fall into this category.

Everyone will direct you *Hotel Tourismo* (☎ 22029) on the waterfront, on Jalan Avenida Marechal Carmona. It has a delightful garden eating area and a hint of colonial charm. Good mid-range rooms cost 30,000/38,000 rp or 42,000/50,000 rp with a sea view; aircon bumps the price up to 53,000/64,000 rp.

Nearby, *Hotel Dili* (☎ 21871), Jalan Avenida Sada Bandeira 25, is deserted most of the time, but the large rooms for 30,000 and 35,000 rp are clean and have their own sitting areas. *Hotel Lifau* (☎ 24880), Jalan Belarmino Lobo 10, is nothing special but at least it takes foreigners and large rooms with outside mandi cost 30,000 rp.

Dili has a few other expensive, dull hotels.

Places to Eat

Dili has a good range of restaurants, and Portuguese food is a real treat.

For cheap eats, the *Rumah Makan Mona Lisa* on Jalan Alberqueque has Javanese food, and *Depot Seroja* on Jalan Avenida Aldeia has nasi/mie dishes.

Dili's best Portuguese restaurant is the moderately priced *Massau* on the eastern edge of town, a fair hike from the centre – take a taxi. The excellent food is best appreciated with a bottle of Portuguese wine from one of Dili's Chinese shops.

Hotel Tourismo has one of the best restaurants in town, serving Chinese, Indonesian and Portuguese dishes in a lovely garden setting.

Getting There & Away

Air Merpati (☎ 21088) in the New Resende Inn has daily flights to Bali and to Kupang three times a week.

Bus Coming into East Timor on the bus from West Timor, Indonesians are required to show their identity cards at police checkpoints along the way, but they don't seem to bother with foreigners. There is usually one army checkpoint before Dili where the bus jockey will take your passport to be inspected.

Terminal Tasitolo, 7km west of town past the airport, has buses to the west, such as Atambua (5000 rp; 3½ hours) and Kupang (15,500 rp; 12 hours). Tickets can be bought in advance from agents opposite the Mercado Municipal.

Buses east to Baucau (4000 rp; three hours), Los Palos (7000 rp; seven hours) and Vikeke (7000 rp; seven hours) leave from Terminal Becora, 4km east of town. Buses and bemos to Maubisse (3000 rp; three hours) leave from the Balide Terminal, 1km south of town. Most buses leave before 8 am.

Boat The Pelni office (☎ 21415) at Jalan Sebastian de Costa 1 is on the road to the airport near the town centre. Pelni ships connect Dili with Kupang, Kalabahi, Maumere, Ujung Pandang and Ambon.

Getting Around
Dili's Comoro airport is 5km west of the town; the standard taxi fare is 7500 rp. Buses A or B stop on the main road outside the airport and they also go to Terminal Tasitolo. From Terminal Tasitolo, mikrolet No I and bus D run to the Villa Harmonia and Terminal Becora, through the centre of town.

Dili's beat up taxis cost a flat 1500 rp around town.

AROUND DILI
Dili gets a steady trickle of visitors, but outside of Dili a foreigner is a rare sight. Though East Timor is open to tourists, facilities are limited and you will usually have to register with the police on arrival and exit when staying in the towns. The army also sets up checkpoints where you have to show your passport. Be wary of discussing politics.

The old hill towns make a delightful break from the heat of the coast. **Maubisse**, 70km south of Dili, sits high in rugged mountains, surrounded by spectacular scenery. Rooms in the *government guesthouse*, the former Portuguese governor's residence, cost 20,000 rp and 30,000 rp.

Baucau, the second largest town in East Timor, is a charmingly colonial town with many old Portuguese buildings in the Kota

Lama (Old Town). In pre-invasion times, Baucau was the site of the international airport (now a military airbase). **Osolata Beach**, 5km sharply downhill from the town, is breathtakingly beautiful. Stay at the friendly *Hotel Los Amigos* in Kota Baru, opposite the Kantor Bupati on Jalan Kota Baru, or *Hotel Antika*, above the Padang restaurant of the same name on Jalan Kota Lama. The Portuguese-built *Hotel Baucau* costs 20,000 rp per person. It may have been special once, but now nothing seems to work.

From Baucau you can continue on to **Los Palos**, the main plateau town of the Lautem regency. The traditional, high-pitched Fataluku houses in the area are a symbol for all East Timor and grace every tourist brochure. *Losmen Verrisimo*, Jalan Sentral 3, has a few rooms at the back for 8000 rp per person, or the government-run *Wisma Wisata* costs 20,000 rp for rooms with mandi.

From Los Palos, early morning buses go along a bad road to **Tutuala** (2500 rp; two hours), on the eastern tip of the island. The government resthouse is perched on cliffs high above the sea and has breathtaking views along the coast.

Sumba

This dry island, one of the most interesting in the Nusa Tenggara group, is noted for its large, decorated stone tombs and traditional houses. Composed of various linguistic groups, the small warring tribes that inhabited Sumba produced Indonesia's finest horses, used in warfare, and honoured their kings with huge burial stones. Great slabs of rock, weighing up to 70 tonnes, were transported across the countryside by a procession of people and buffalo. These tombs and stone carvings grace many villages.

Though Christianity has made inroads, Sumba's isolation has helped preserve one of the country's most bizarre animist cultures. Sumba is also famous for its ikat blankets with their interesting motifs, including skulls hanging from trees, horse riders, crocodiles, dragons, lions, chickens, monkeys and deer. For ikat, head to East Sumba and the villages around Waingapu, but the most traditional villages are in West Sumba around Waikabubak.

Getting There & Away
Air Merpati operates twice-weekly from Waingapu to Kupang and Denpasar, and between Tambolaka and Bima. Planes are

small, seats limited and flights are subject to cancellation. Book as far ahead as possible.

Boat Waingapu is well-serviced by ferries from Ende on Flores – the main departure point for Sumba. Ferries also run to/from Kupang via Sabu or Ende.

Pelni has useful services between Ende and Waingapu, and Labuanbajo and Waingapu, and long-distance hops from Lombok and to Denpasar.

WAINGAPU

Waingapu is just the main town on Sumba, but can be used as a base for day-tripping to interesting villages.

Orientation & Information

Waingapu has two centres: the older, northern one focuses on the harbour; the southern one is around the main market and bus station, about 1km inland. The BNI bank is on Jalan Ampera near the market, and the Bank Rakyat Indonesia is on Jalan Ahmad Yani.

Places to Stay & Eat

Hotel Permata Sari, otherwise known as Ali's, is near the harbour and handy if arriving by ferry. Ali speaks excellent English and is a mine of information on things to do in Sumba. Well-kept rooms are 5000 rp per person.

Hotel Lima Saudara (☎ 61083) at Jalan Wanggameti 2 is the nearest cheap hotel, with singles/doubles for 9000/17,500 rp, but it's a dive.

Better hotels are in the new part of town near the bus station. The next best budget choice after Ali's is the quiet and friendly *Hotel Kaliuda (☎ 61264)*, Jalan WJ Lalaimentik 3. Rooms with shared mandi cost 12,100 rp and rooms with mandi at back facing the garden are 16,500 rp.

Hotel Elvin (☎ 62097) at Jalan Ahmad Yani 73 is well run, with a good restaurant and large rooms. Renovated singles/doubles with bathroom and air-con cost 15,000/20,000 rp and 25,000/35,000 rp.

In the mid-range, *Hotel Sandle Wood (☎ 61887)*, Jalan Panjaitan 23, has a wide variety of rooms from 11,000/16,500 rp to 27,500/38,500 rp around an attractive garden. *Hotel Merlin (☎ 61300)* on Jalan Panjaitan has better service and is the top hotel in town. Rooms cost 16,500/22,000 rp to 44,000/55,000 rp and the 4th floor restaurant has great views.

The Merlin and Elvin hotels have good *restaurants*, otherwise Waingapu is not over endowed with good eateries. The *Rumah Makan Mini Indah*, Jalan Ahmad Yani 27, is a simple place but has very tasty food. The *Rumah Makan Nazareth* opposite Hotel Kaliuda is the pick of the town's restaurants and serves good Chinese and Indonesian food.

Getting There & Away

Air Merpati (☎ 61329) on Jalan Soekarno has twice weekly flights to Kupang and Denpasar.

Bus Buses to Waikabubak (5000 rp; five hours) depart around 8 am, noon and 3 pm. Bookings can be made at the hotels or the agents opposite the bus station. Buses also head south-east to Melolo, Rende and Baing.

Boat Ferries depart Ende on Tuesday for Waingapu (12,000 rp; 10 hours). From Waingapu, a ferry goes to Sabu (13,500 rp; nine hours) on Monday and continues on to Kupang on Tuesday and one goes to Ende on Wednesday and Saturday.

Pelni ships leave from the Dermaga dock to the west of town (400 rp by bemo). The *Pangrango* calls at Waingapu every two weeks on its way to/from Ende or Labuanbajo. The *Awu* runs from Benoa Port (Bali) via Lembar (Lombok) to Waingapu and on to Ende and Kupang (and vice versa).

Getting Around

Bemos from the town centre to the airport, 6km out, cost 400 rp while a taxi costs 3000 rp. There are regular bemos to villages around Waingapu.

AROUND WAINGAPU

A number of the traditional villages in the south-east can be visited from Waingapu. The stone ancestor tombs are impressive and the area produces some of Sumba's best ikat. The villagers are quite used to tourists. Almost every village has a visitors' book, and a donation of 1000 rp or so is expected. Ikat for sale will appear.

Just 3km south of central Waingapu, a few hundred metres west of the main road to the airport, **Prailiu** is the central village of the old Lewa Kambero kingdom and a busy ikat-weaving centre.

Melolo, a nothing village on the main road 62km south-east of Waingapu, is easily reached by bus and *Losmen Hermindo* has rooms for 5000 rp per person if you want to do more than day-trip from Waingapu. From Melolo infrequent bemos run to nearby traditional villages.

About 7km from Melolo, **Praiyawang** has a massive raja's tomb, good ikat and many traditional houses. **Umabara & Pau**, 4km from Melolo, have several traditional Sumba houses and tombs, and are also noted weaving centres. These villages are a 20 minute walk from the main road – the turn-off is 2km north-east of Melolo.

Some 70km from Waingapu, **Kaliuda** has some of Sumba's best ikat. To get there, take a bus heading to Baing from Waingapu or Melolo and get off at Ngalu – Kaliuda is about a 3km walk from there.

There's good surf between May and August at **Kalala**, about 2km from Baing, off the main road from Melolo. An Australian has set up *bungalow accommodation* along the wide, white-sand beach, costing 35,000 rp per person including meals. Buses from Melolo run to Baing.

Perhaps Sumba's most beautiful beach is at **Tarimbang**, on the coast south of Lewa. Most visitors are surfers, attracted by the break out on the reef, but there are two homestays – the *Bogenvil* is the best and costs 12,500 rp per person including meals. Two buses per day run to Tarimbang from Waingapu.

WAIKABUBAK
Waikabubak is a neat little town with many traditional houses and old graves carved with buffalo-horn motifs. Interesting traditional villages such as **Kampung Tarung**, up a path next to Tarung Wisata Hotel, are right within the town. One of the spectacular attractions of West Sumba is the *Pasola*, or mock battle ritual, held near Waikabubak each year. It's a kind of jousting match on horseback. The Pasola Festival is held at the Lamboya and Kodi districts in February, and at Wanokaka and Gaura in March.

The BNI bank on Jalan A Yani changes most major currencies at good rates. The tourist office is on Jalan Teratai on the eastern outskirts of town.

Places to Stay
The friendly and spacious *Hotel Aloha* (☎ 21245), Jalan Sudirman 26, is a popular budget choice. Clean singles/doubles with shared bath cost 7500/11,000 rp or 10,000/15,000 rp and 15,000/20,000 rp with private bath.

Another good backpackers' hotel, on the ball with travel information and with a restaurant, is *Tarung Wisata Hotel* (☎ 21332), Jalan Pisang 26. It is near the bus station and rooms cost from 5000/9000 rp to 12,500/20,000 rp. It has a great rooftop sitting area looking up at Kampung Tarung.

The small *Gloria Hotel* (☎ 21024), Jalan Gajah Mada 14, is also good value and has rooms for 7000/9000 rp or 12,000/15,500 rp with mandi. It has a good restaurant serving Chinese food.

Just around the corner from the Gloria at Jalan Pemuda 4, *Hotel Manandang* (☎ 21197) is the best in town with rooms around a pleasant garden and a good restaurant. Large, spotless rooms with washbasin and comfy beds are good value at 11,000/16,000 rp. Rooms with private bath range from 20,000/25,000 rp to 40,000/45,000 rp. Prices exclude 10% tax.

Getting There & Away
The Merpati agent (☎ 21051) is at Jalan Ahmad Yani 11. The airport is at Tambolaka, 42km north – Merpati usually has a minibus. There are twice weekly flights between Bima and Tambolaka, but it is not always easy to get a seat.

The bus station is central. Buses run to Waingapu (5500 rp; five hours), Anakalang (1500 rp; 40 minutes), Wanokala (1000 rp), Lamboya (1500 rp), Waitabula (2000 rp; one hour) and Waikelo.

Getting Around
The bigger hotels, such as Hotel Manandang, rent cars. The friendly Warung Sumba Indah (☎ 21633), Jalan Patimura 7, has a variety of motorcycles for rent for 20,000 rp and 25,000 rp – an excellent way to tour West Sumba.

AROUND WAIKABUBAK
At **Anakalang**, 22km east of Waikabubak, some large tombs are right beside the highway, though the more interesting villages are south of town past the market. **Kabonduk** has some fine tombs, and then it is a pleasant 15 minute walk across the fields and up the hill to **Matakakeri** and the original ancestral village for the area, **Lai Tarung**, which has impressive tombs and great views. Lai Tarung is the site of the Purung Takadonga Ratu – a festival honouring the ancestors, held every year around June.

Directly south of Waikabubak is the Wanokaka District, a centre for the Pasola festival in March. **Waigali** and **Praigoli** are interesting traditional villages. The south coast has some fine beaches, particularly **Pantai Rua, Nghiwatu** and **Pantai Morosi**. Pantai Rua and Watukarere (near Nghiwatu) has basic *homestays*.

On the west coast, the coastal village of **Pero** has accommodation at *Homestay Stori* for 13,000 rp per person. It is a popular base for visiting the very traditional nearby villages. Not all are friendly – steer clear of Tosi village. From Kodi a direct bus leaves for Waikabubak (3000 rp; four hours) at around 6 am, returning to Kodi around noon, otherwise take a bus to Waitabula and another to Pero.

Kalimantan

Kalimantan, the southern two-thirds of the island of Borneo, is a vast, jungle-covered wilderness – or at least it was: the loggers and miners are making serious inroads into the region. There are few roads apart from the area around Pontianak and the region from Samarinda to Banjarmasin. The boats and ferries on the numerous rivers and waterways are the chief form of long-distance transport, although there is also a range of flight connections.

Some of the coastal cities have their own remarkable attractions – the canals of Banjarmasin and the fiery orange sunsets over Pontianak, for example. On the whole, however, the native Dayak tribes of the inland areas are the main reason for coming to Kalimantan. Access to such tribes can be time consuming and often expensive.

Forest fires in east Kalimantan in 1997 caused a pall of smoke to cover large areas of Indonesia and Malaysia. Each year fires are lit by farmers and large companies as a way of clearing land, but due to a drought the fires in 1997 (and to a smaller extent 1998) spread rapidly and were impossible to control.

Getting There & Away

Air Bouraq, Merpati and Garuda all fly into Kalimantan. Flights are reasonably frequent into Pontianak, Banjarmasin and Balikpapan.

Boat There are shipping connections to Java and to Sulawesi, both with Pelni and other shipping companies. Many Pelni's ships stop at Kalimantan somewhere along their routes. There are also regular ships from the ports on the east coast of Kalimantan to Pare-Pare and Palu in Sulawesi. See the introductory Indonesia Getting Around section for details of Pelni ships and the routes they take.

For details of boats between Kalimantan and Sabah in Malaysia, see the Indonesia Getting There & Away section.

East Malaysia Despite the long land border with the East Malaysian states of Sabah and Sarawak, options for crossing between the two countries are limited. The only real options are by air or land between Kuching in Sarawak and Pontianak, and by air or sea between Tawau in Sabah and Tarakan.

Malaysia Airlines has flights twice a week between Pontianak and Kuching, or a daily express bus does the trip in about 10 hours. See the Pontianak section for details. Both the land crossing at Entikong and Pontianak airport are visa-free ports.

Malaysia Airlines flies from Tarakan to Tawau, or boats run between Tarakan and Nunukan, and from Nunukan regular boats go to/from Tawau. Tarakan is not a visa-free entry/exit point and an Indonesian visa is required for arrival by air or sea. See the Tarakan section for details of this route.

Indonesian visas can be easily obtained at the consulates in Kuching, Kota Kinabalu or Tawau. Most nationalities do not require a visa to enter Malaysia.

Getting Around

There are roads in the area around Pontianak and in the region from Banjarmasin to Balikpapan and Samarinda, but boat is the main form of transport. Going upriver by boat into some of the Dayak regions is fairly easy from Samarinda or Pontianak. Small boats, ferries and speedboats use the rivers between some of the major towns and cities – there are daily ferries and speedboats between Banjarmasin and Palangkaraya, and longboats between Tarakan and Tanjung Redeb, and Tarakan and Nunukan.

There are flights into the interior with the regular airline companies. Merpati carries the bulk of the traffic, but there are a couple of smaller carriers as well.

TARAKAN

Tarakan, close to the Sabah border, is just a stepping stone to other places. It was the site of bloody fighting between Australians and Japanese at the end of WWII. Unless you have a deep interest in Japanese blockhouses, the only reason to come here is to cross to Tawau in Malaysia.

KALIMANTAN

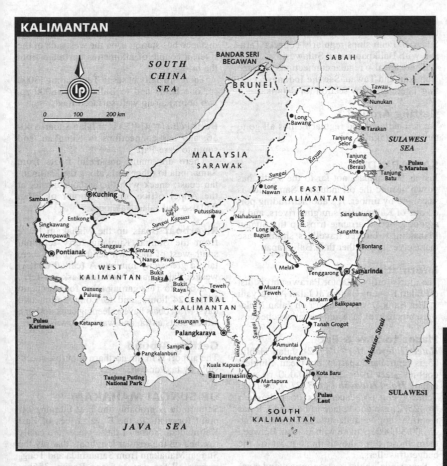

SOUTH CHINA SEA

BANDAR SERI BEGAWAN

SABAH

BRUNEI

Tawau

Nunukan

0   100   200 km

Long Bawang

Tarakan

SULAWESI SEA

MALAYSIA SARAWAK

Tanjung Selor

Kayan

Tanjung Redeb (Berau)

Tanjung Batu

Pulau Maratua

Kuching

Sambas

Entikong

Putussibau

Nahabuan

Long Nawan

Sungai

EAST KALIMANTAN

Sangkulirang

Singkawang

Mempawah

Sungai Kapuas

Long Bagun

Sungai Belayan

Sangatta

Pontianak

Sanggau

Sintang

Nanga Pinoh

Bukit Baka

Melak

Sungai Mahakam

Bontang

WEST KALIMANTAN

Gunung Palung

Bukit Raya

Teweh

Tenggarong

Samarinda

Muara Teweh

Panajam

Balikpapan

Pulau Karimata

Ketapang

Kasungan

Palangkaraya

Sungai Kahayan

Sungai Barito

Tanah Grogot

Makassar Strait

CENTRAL KALIMANTAN

Sampit

Pangkalanbun

Kuala Kapuas

Amuntai

Kandangan

Kota Baru

Tanjung Puting National Park

Banjarmasin

Martapura

Pulau Laut

SULAWESI

SOUTH KALIMANTAN

JAVA SEA

Information

The Bank Dagang Negara on Jalan Yos Sudarso will change some standard travellers cheques and major currencies.

Places to Stay & Eat

Hotel Taufiq (☎ 21347), Jalan Yos Sudarso 26, is a huge rambling place near the main mosque. Its basic but affordable singles/doubles are 12,000/22,000 rp, more with mandi or air-con.

There's a line of cheap and mid-range hotels along Jalan Sudirman including *Losmen Jakarta* (☎ 21704) at No 112, the friendliest of the cheap places, with rates from around 10,000 rp. Nearby, *Losmen Herlina* is basic but habitable.

The lane off Jalan Yos Sudarso near Jalan Sudirman has a wide choice of warung after dark. *Turi*, on the corner of Sudirman and Sudarso, is the popular choice for *ikan bakar* (barbecued fish), a Tarakan favourite.

Rumah Makan Cahaya located on Jalan Sudirman, opposite Losmen Jakarta, is pretty good.

Getting There & Away

Air Merpati (☎ 21911), at Jalan Yos Sudarso 48, flies to Tarakan from Balikpapan or Samarinda.

DAS (☎ 51612), at Jalan Sudirman 9, has useful flights inland, as does MAF (☎ 51011), the missionary airline in the tax building at Jalan Sudirman 133.

Boat The Pelni office is at the main port – take a colt almost to the end of Jalan Yos Sudarso. Pelni ships regularly connect Tarakan with Balikpapan and Sulawesi.

There are also regular connections between Nunukan and Tawau. See the Indonesia Getting There & Away section for details.

Getting Around
Taxis, chartered and regular bemos all go to the airport (5km).

SAMARINDA
Just as Balikpapan, not far to the south, has grown around the oil industry, Samarinda is sustained by timber. It's another trading port on one of Kalimantan's mighty rivers, and is a good place to arrange trips up the Sungai Mahakam – budget travellers should base themselves here rather than Balikpapan.

Information
The tourist office (Kantor Parawisata) is just off Jalan Kesuma Bangsa at Jalan AI Suryani 1. The Bank Dagang Negara on Jalan Mulawarman changes cash and travellers cheques.

Places to Stay & Eat
Hotel Hidayah II (☎ 41712), Jalan Hahlid 25, is central and spartan, but clean. Singles/doubles start from 25,000/30,000 rp with mandi. *Hotel Hidayah I* (☎ 31210), on Jalan Temenggung, is cheaper. Next door, the *Aida* (☎ 42572) is a good place to be based. It has a coffee shop veranda area and rooms from 25,000/30,000 rp, more with air-con. Between them these three hotels host most of the budget travellers.

Samarinda's chief gastronomic wonder are the *udang galah* (giant river prawns) found in the local warung. The Citra Niaga *hawker centre* off Jalan Niaga, a block or two east of the mosque, is a pleasant pedestrian precinct with an excellent range of food.

At the *Mesra Indah shopping centre*, close to Hotel Hidayah II on Jalan Hahlid, are two decent *food centres* and, upstairs overlooking the street, an *ice cream parlour*.

Getting There & Away
Air DAS (☎ 35250), Jalan Gatot Subroto 92, has heavily subsidised and heavily booked flights to the interior – you will need to book at least a month in advance.

Merpati (☎ 43385), Garuda and Bouraq are all at Jalan Sudirman 20. Merpati and Bouraq have flights to Tarakan and Balikpapan.

Bus From Samarinda you can head west to Tenggarong or south to Balikpapan. The long-distance bus station is on the west side of the river, a couple of kilometres upstream from the bridge.

There are daily buses to Tenggarong (3000 rp; one hour) and to Balikpapan (8000 rp, two hours) along well-surfaced roads.

Boat Pelni (☎ 41402) is at Jalan Sudarso 40-56, and has connections to Nunukan, and south to Pare-Pare.

There are many non-Pelni boats from Samarinda to other ports along the Kalimantan coast; check with the harbour master at the Adpel office, on the corner of Jalan Sudarso and Jalan Nakhoda.

Riverboat Boats up the Mahakam leave from the Sungai Kunjang ferry terminal south-west of the town centre. To get there take a green city minibus A (called taxi A) west on Jalan Gajah Mada, and ask for 'feri'.

A boat to Tenggarong takes four hours, to Melak 24 hours, and to Long Bagun two days. Most boats have a sleeping deck upstairs, which costs extra, and warung downstairs.

Getting Around
The airport is in the northern suburbs, accessible by taxi or colt.

UP SUNGAI MAHAKAM
Samarinda is probably the best jumping-off point for visits to the Dayak tribes of East Kalimantan. Some of these places are easily reached on the regular longboats that ply the Sungai Mahakam from Samarinda and Tenggarong all the way to Long Bagun, 396km upriver. Many of the towns and villages have a budget hotel or two, or a longhouse where travellers can stay.

Most people head upriver to **Tanjung Isuy** on the shores of Danau Jempang. Activity focuses on the touristy Taman Jamrot Lamin, a longhouse cum craft centre and tourist hostel. Group tourists flock here for performances of Kenyah, Kayan and Banuaq dancing. Accommodation is provided by the *Taman Jamrot Lamin*, on Jalan Indonesia Australia.

Nearby **Mancong** has another slightly touristy longhouse, where it is possible to stay. To get to Danau Jempang, take a longboat from Samarinda to Muara Muntai (13 hours) first, and spend the night there, before getting a boat to Tanjung Isuy (four hours). **Melak**, 325km from Samarinda, is famous for its 5000 acre Kersid Luwai Orchid Reserve, 16km from Melak by jeep or ojek charter. The *Rahmat Abadi* is the best place to stay.

Long Iram, 409km and 33 hours from Samarinda, is the end of the line if the river is low. Long Iram has become a sort of backwater boom town as a result of gold mining, and accommodation is more expensive.

Further upriver are more longhouses between **Datah Bilang** and **Muara Merak**, including the Bahau, Kenyah and Punan settlements. The end of the line for regular longboat services is **Long Bagun**, or **Long Apari** if the conditions are right. The journey from Samarinda can take three days.

If you want to start your trip from the top, DAS flies to **Data Dawai**, an airstrip near Long Apari, four times a week, although you will need to book weeks, perhaps months in advance.

BALIKPAPAN

Best avoided by budget travellers, Balikpapan is an air-conditioned boom town that has got rich on oil money. It's far from an unpleasant place, sporting some of the best food and undoubtedly the liveliest nightlife in Kalimantan; yet it's simply not cheap and offers very little to see.

Information

The BNI bank on Jalan Pengeran Antasari and its branch at the airport will change major travellers cheques and cash currencies.

Places to Stay

Accommodation is expensive – if possible take a bus (two hours) to Samarinda, where you will find much better value for money.

Hotel Aida (☎ 21006), inconveniently located out of town on Jalan Yani, has airless singles/doubles from 16,000/25,000 rp. Close by, *Hotel Murni* has rooms from 24,000 rp.

One other option is the very central *Hotel Gajah Mada* (☎ 34634), Jalan Sudirman 14, where economy rooms are 30,000/3500 rp, and standard (air-con) doubles are from 78,000 rp; all with private mandi.

Elsewhere around town, room rates are upwards of 90,000 rp.

Places to Eat

Balikpapan has some excellent restaurants. For Padang seafood, try the *Restaurant Masakan Padang Simpang Raya* next to Hotel Murni. The *Restaurant Salero* for *padang/minang* food at Jalan Ahmad Yani 12B is

similarly priced, as is the *Restaurant Sinar Minang* on Jalan Sudirman.

For a splurge, *Bondy's*, on Jalan Ahmad Yani, offers seafood and hearty serves of western fare in an open courtyard.

Getting There & Away

Air Garuda (☎ 22300) is Jalan Ahmad Yani 14; Merpati (☎ 22876) is at Jalan Ahmad Yani 29; and Bouraq (☎ 23117) has an office next to Hotel Budiman.

Handy connections include the daily flights to Palu (the *only* flight linking Kalimantan and Sulawesi) and Banjarmasin, both serviced only by Bouraq. Balikpapan is a visa-free entry/exit point.

Bus Buses to Samarinda (8000 rp; two hours) depart from a bus stand in the far north of the city accessible by a No 2 or 3 bemo.

Buses to Banjarmasin (25,000 rp; 12 hours) depart from the bus station on the opposite side of the harbour to the city. Take a colt from the Rapak bus station to the pier on Jalan Mangunsidi. Charter a speedboat to take you to the other side (2000 rp per person, 10,000 rp charter, 10 minutes).

Boat The Pelni office (☎ 21402) is at Jalan Yos Sudarso 76. The Pelni liners *Kambuna*, *Umsini* and *Tidar* call in fortnightly, connecting Balikpapan to Tarakan, Pare Pare, Pantoloan, Bitung, Ujung Pandang, Surabaya and beyond.

For regular ships to Surabaya and Ujung Pandang try PT Elang Raya Abadi or PT Ling Jaya Shipping (☎ 21577) at Jalan Yos Sudarso 40.

Getting Around

A taxi from Seppingan airport is 20,000 rp.

Bemos do circular routes around the main streets from the Rapak terminal at the end of Jalan Panjaitan, and there are plenty of ojeks.

BANJARMASIN

At first glance it might not look like much, but get out on the canals of Banjarmasin and it quickly becomes one of most stunning cities in Indonesia. With its maze of waterways and other nearby attractions, Banjarmasin is the only city in Kalimantan worth lingering in.

Information

The best place for travel information is the Borneo Homestay (see Places to Stay). The

BANJARMASIN

PLACES TO STAY
2 Wisma Batung Batulis
4 Hotel Rakmat &
  Warung
5 Kuripan
7 Metro
8 Wisma Banjar
13 Borneo Homestay
14 Diamond Homestay
18 Barito Palace
19 Hotel Mentari
20 Kalimantan (Besar)
22 Hotel Sabrina
32 Perdana Hotel
36 Mestika
37 Beauty
38 Hotel Kalimantan
  (Kecil)

PLACES TO EAT
3 Simpang Tiga
28 Depot Taman Sari
30 Tea Stalls
34 Lezat Baru Restaurant
35 Kaganangan

OTHER
1 South Kalimantan
  Tourist Office
6 Hospital
9 Mesjid Raya
  Sabilal Muhtadin
10 Speedboats to
  Palangkaraya
11 Telkom
12 Bank Dagang Negara
15 Garuda/Merpati Office

16 Adi Angkasa Travel
17 BCA Bank
21 DAS
23 Souvenir Shops
24 City Bemos
25 Market
26 Mitra Plaza Shopping
  Centre
27 Taxi Kota Terminal &
  Belauran (Night Market)
29 Utarid Bakery
31 Bank Rakyat Indonesia
33 Post Office
39 Pelni Office
40 City Tourist Office
41 City Hall
42 BNI Bank
43 Banjarmasin Theatre

0   100   200 m

Approximate Scale

To Pasar
Kuin

Jalan Veteran

Jalan Sudirman

Jalan Tendean

Jalan Ahmad Yani

To Bourag
Office, Syamsudin
Noor Airport &
Km 6 Bus Station

Jalan Suprapto

Jalan Sutoyo Siswomiharjo

To Port, Banjar Raya
Pier, Pulau Kaget &
Pulau Kembang

Jalan Pos

Jalan Pos

Jalan Mangkurat

Jalan Lambung

Jalan Bank Rakyat

Jalan Haryono

Jalan Sudimampir

Jalan Ujung Munung

Jalan Hasanuddin

Jalan Pangeran Samudera

Jalan Pangeran Antasari

Jalan Katamso

Jalan Niaga Utara

Jalan Pasar Baru

Jalan Simpang Telawang

Sungai Martapura

South Kalimantan tourist office at Jalan Panjaitan 3, near the mosque, can also be very helpful and arranges guides for trekking in the province.

The Bank Dagang Negara, next to the Telkom office on Jalan Lambung Mangkurat, has the best rates for travellers cheques.

Mesjid Raya Sabilal Muhtadin
In the middle of Banjarmasin is this giant mosque, with its copper-coloured flying saucer-shaped dome and minarets with lids and spires.

Boat Trips
Banjarmasin's two premier attractions are its canals and its floating market. It's possible to tour the waterways of Banjarmasin in a motorised canoe *(klotok)* for around 10,000 rp per hour. Ask around the wharf near the junction of Jalan Lambung Mangkurat and Jalan Pasar Baru. Borneo Homestay runs inexpensive tours of the floating market and canals.

It's worth taking a boat to the river islands of **Pulau Kaget** and **Pulau Kembang**. It takes four to five hours to visit Pulau Kaget, 12km from town, where you can see the famous proboscis, or long-nosed, monkeys. Hire a speedboat from the pier at the end of Jalan Pos.

Places to Stay
Borneo Homestay (☎ 57545), in an alley just off Jalan Pos, is a good information centre. There is a bar and rooftop lounging area overlooking the river. Single rooms without fan cost 15,000 rp, with fan and mandi 35,000 rp.

Diamond Homestay (☎ 50055), on the next alley, is another friendly budget option. Ring the bell above the door at the homestay on Jalan Simpang Hasanuddin or knock on the blue shutters at No 58. This pleasant place charges 15,000/20,000 rp for singles/doubles without fan or mandi.

Just over the iron bridge, *Hotel Rakmat* (☎ 54429) at Jalan Ahmad Yani 9 is sizeable, with a friendly manager. Rooms cost from 15,000/20,000 rp with shared mandi and no fan.

Wisma Banjar (☎ 53561), 100m from the mosque, on Jalan Suprapto 5, is popular. Rooms range from 15,000 rp, to 35,000 rp with air-con.

For something a little more mid-range, the comfortable *Hotel Sabrina* (☎ 54442), Jalan Bank Rakyat 21, has singles/doubles for 30,000/40,000 rp with fan, more with air-con and TV.

Places to Eat
Banjarmasin's excellent array of *kueh* (cake) includes deep-fried breads from the canoe warung at the floating markets. Other breakfast fare includes *nasi kuning* (a local rice and chicken dish) from the **Warung Makan Rakmat** next door to Hotel Rakmat on Jalan Ahmad Yani.

A local speciality is *ayam panggang* (chicken roasted and served in sweet soy), but fish and freshwater cray hold pride of place in Banjar cuisine. There is a string of eateries along Jalan Pangeran Samudera; try the *Kaganangan* at No 30 for local dishes.

If you're on a tight budget or want a taste of street culture, eat at the *tea stalls* along Jalan Niaga Utara between Jalan Katamso and Jalan Pangeran Samudera near Pasar Baru.

Getting There & Away
Air Garuda/Merpati (☎ 54290) are at Jalan Hasanuddin 31; Bouraq (☎ 52445) is inconveniently situated at an office 4km from the centre on Jalan Ahmad Yani 343. DAS (☎ 52902), Jalan Hasanuddin 6, Blok 4, is across the road from Garuda/Merpati.

Bouraq has daily flights to Balikpapan.

Adi Angkasa Travel at Jalan Hasanuddin 27 is a good place to buy air tickets and offers some discounts.

Bus Buses and colts depart frequently from the Km 6 terminal in the south-east for Martapura and Banjarbaru. Night buses to Balikpapan (from 25,000 rp) leave daily between 4 and 4.30 pm and arrive in Panajam, across the river from Balikpapan, about 12 hours later.

Boat Ships dock at Trisakti harbour. To get there take a bemo from the taxi kota terminal on Jalan Pangeran Antasari. The harbour master's office (☎ 54775) is on Jalan Barito Hilir at Trisakti. Opposite is a line of shops with several agencies for boat tickets to Surabaya, but Pelni fares are cheapest from the Pelni counter inside. It's also possible to book tickets at Borneo Homestay.

The Pelni *Kelimutu* shuttles back and forth between Banjarmasin and Surabaya every two days (substituting Semarang for Surabaya twice a fortnight).

Heading inland, speedboats to Palangkaraya (35,000 rp) leave from a dock at the mosque end of Jalan Pos. River ferries *(bis air)* to Palangkaraya depart from the Banjar Raya pier on Sungai Barito, and cost 10,000 rp.

INDONESIA

Getting Around

To/From the Airport The airport is 26km out of town on the road to Banjarbaru. Take a bemo from Jalan Pasar Baru to the Km 6 terminal, and then catch a Martapura-bound colt. Get off at the branch road leading to the airport and start walking (1.5km). Alternatively, a taxi all the way to the airport will cost you around 20,000 rp.

Local Transport Bemos congregate at the junction of Jalan Samudera and Jalan Pasar Baru.

AROUND BANJARMASIN

Banjarbaru

This town, on the road from Banjarmasin to Martapura, has an interesting **museum** (open daily except Monday) with a collection of Banjar and Dayak artefacts along with statues excavated from ancient Hindu temples in Kalimantan. From Banjarmasin take a colt to Martapura and ask to be dropped off at Banjarbaru.

Cempaka

The diamond fields of Cempaka, 43km south of Banjarmasin, are a fascinating excursion. The miners labour in muddy holes – often up to their necks in water – sifting for gold, diamonds and agates. Note that the mines are closed on Fridays.

Take a Banjarmasin-Martapura bemo, and ask to get off at the huge roundabout just past Banjarbaru. From here take a green taxi to 'Alur', and walk the last 500m from the main road to the diamond digs. Borneo Homestay, in Banjarmasin, offers economical tours to Cempaka.

Martapura

The large market at Martapura is at its busiest on Fridays. It is a photographer's paradise – colourfully dressed Banjar women haggle over a cornucopia of exotic snacks and fruit, among other things.

A section of the market sells uncut gems, silver jewellery and trading beads. The diamond-polishing factory and shop are also worth a look.

Frequent colts leave from the Km 6 terminal in Banjarmasin.

PONTIANAK

Pontianak is a sprawling equatorial city that sits astride the confluence of two rivers; Sungai Landak and Sungai Kapuas Kecil. Like Banjarmasin, it really needs to be seen from its canals to be appreciated. Even so, most travellers get out as quickly as possible.

Information

The Kalimantan Barat tourist office is way out at Jalan Ahmad Sood 25 (☎ 36172); don't bother. Staff at the big hotels and private travel agencies often offer better advice. Most of the banks are along Jalan Rahadi Usman.

Mesjid Abdurrakhman

This 18th century royal mosque was built by Syarif Adbul Rahman, sultan of Pontianak from 1771 to 1808. Built in the Malay style, it's an impressive structure with a high, square-tiered roof. It's a short canoe trip across the Sungai Kapuas Kecil from the pinisi (fishing boat) harbour.

Behind the royal mosque is the sultan's former palace, **Istana Kadriyah**. Now a museum, it displays a collection of the royal family's personal effects.

Museum Negeri Pontianak

Near Tanjungpura University, this national museum contains a very good collection of *tempayan*, or South-East Asian water containers. There are also Dayak exhibits that illustrate the tribal cultures of west Kalimantan.

Equator Monument

If you're really stuck for something to do, this monument is to the north of the city centre across the river. Equator monument models are wonderfully kitsch souvenirs.

Places to Stay

Don't expect any bargains in Pontianak. The best budget beds are found at *Wisma Patria* (☎ 36063) at Jalan Merdeka Timur 497. Clean singles or doubles cost from 22,000 rp with fan and mandi, more with air-con.

Another reasonably good budget option is *Berlian Hotel* (☎ 32092), which has fan-cooled doubles with shared bathroom for 25,000 rp.

The modern *Hotel Central* (☎ 37444), Jalan Merdeka Timur 232, is friendly but noisy, and has rooms with air-con, TV and hot water mandi from 45,000 rp.

Orien Hotel (☎ 32650) is in the south of town on Jalan Tanjungpura. It's a good mid-range place; rooms with fan, video and bath are from 45,000.

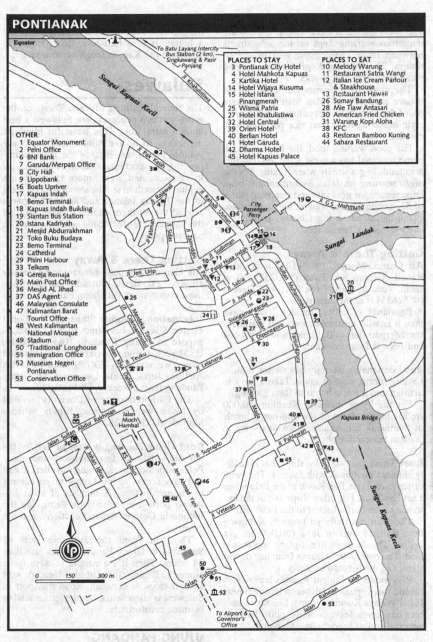

PONTIANAK

Equator

To Batu Layang Intercity
Bus Station (2 km),
Singkawang & Pasir
Panjang

PLACES TO STAY
3 Pontianak City Hotel
4 Hotel Mahkota Kapuas
5 Kartika Hotel
14 Hotel Wijaya Kusuma
15 Hotel Istana
   Pinangmerah
25 Wisma Patria
27 Hotel Khatulistiwa
32 Hotel Central
39 Orien Hotel
40 Berlian Hotel
41 Hotel Garuda
42 Dharma Hotel
45 Hotel Kapuas Palace

PLACES TO EAT
10 Melody Warung
11 Restaurant Satria Wangi
12 Italian Ice Cream Parlour
   & Steakhouse
13 Restaurant Hawaii
26 Somay Bandung
28 Mie Tiaw Antasari
30 American Fried Chicken
31 Warung Kopi Aloha
38 KFC
43 Restoran Bamboo Kuning
44 Sahara Restaurant

OTHER
1 Equator Monument
2 Pelni Office
6 BNI Bank
7 Garuda/Merpati Office
8 City Hall
9 Lippobank
16 Boats Upriver
17 Kapuas Indah
   Bemo Terminal
18 Kapuas Indah Building
19 Siantan Bus Station
20 Istana Kadriyah
21 Mesjid Abdurrakhman
22 Toko Buku Budaya
23 Bemo Terminal
29 Cathedral
29 Pisini Harbour
33 Telkom
34 Gereja Remaja
35 Main Post Office
36 Mesjid AL Jihad
46 DAS Agent
47 Malaysian Consulate
47 Kalimantan Barat
   Tourist Office
48 West Kalimantan
   National Mosque
49 Stadium
50 'Traditional' Longhouse
51 Immigration Office
52 Museum Negeri
   Pontianak
53 Conservation Office

Sungai Kapuas Kecil
Sungai Landak
Sungai Kapuas Kecil
Kapuas Bridge

To Airport &
Governor's
Office

0   150   300 m

INDONESIA

Places to Eat

The local coffee is excellent, and there are numerous *warung kopi* on the side streets between Jalan Tanjungpura and Jalan Pattimura. The *Warung Kopi Aloha* is a good place for coffee and snacks.

The clean little *Somay Bandung*, in the theatre complex on Jalan Sisingamangaraja near Jalan Pattimura, serves delicious Chinese-style *bubur ayam* (sweet rice porridge with chicken).

For good warung food, the Kapuas Indah bemo terminal has a good selection, but this area tends to get smelly when it rains. Try the *night warung* on Jalan Sudirman and Jalan Diponegoro for goat sate and steaming plates of rice noodles, crab, prawns, fish, vegetables.

Pontianak has a big Chinese population and excellent Chinese food.

Getting There & Away

Air Garuda/Merpati (☎ 34142) is at Jalan Rahadi Usman 8A; DAS (☎ 32313) is at Jalan Veteran Baru Blok B/1; and Deraya (☎ 32835) is at the airport.

Pontianak is better connected with Java than it is with destinations around Kalimantan; Merpati flies to Balikpapan twice a week and Jakarta four times a day.

Bus Pontianak's intercity bus station is Batu Layang, north-west of town. Take a ferry to Siantan and a white bemo to Batu Layang.

For the longer hauls to Kuching (50,000 rp; 8½ hours), most of the mid-range hotels in Pontianak can arrange bookings – try to book at least a day ahead.

Boat There are two Pelni ships that regularly connect Pontianak with Jakarta. The Pelni office is on Jalan Pak Kasih at the Pelabuhan Laut Dwikora. For other ships ask at the entrance to the port adjacent to the Pelni office.

There are six daily jet boats to Ketapang near Banyuwangi in Java (50,000 rp; six hours). This is more like a plane trip than a boat. The coastal boat leaves from just downstream of the Siantan car ferry.

Riverboats up Sungai Kapuas leave from behind the Kapuas Indah bemo terminal near Hotel Wijaya Kusuma. Some, like the houseboat bandungs, leave from the pinisi harbour near the end of Jalan Sultan Muhammed.

Getting Around

To/From the Airport Airport taxis into town cost 25,000 rp. Alternatively, walk down the road in front of the terminal building to the main road to Pontianak and from there get a bemo. It is a half-hour drive from the airport to the Kapuas Indah bemo terminal.

Sulawesi

The funeral festivals of Tana Toraja on the south-western peninsula are Sulawesi's best known attraction. This beautiful highland region and its festive culture is all that many visitors get to see. But, as the island's improving transport infrastructure opens access to once-isolated areas, more travellers are venturing north to see the stunning coral reefs of the Togian Islands and the marine parks around the northern capital of Manado, and the unique wildlife of Sulawesi's network of national parks.

Getting There & Away

Air Garuda, Merpati, Bouraq and Mandala all service domestic routes to Sulawesi, with most connections via Ujung Pandang.

International Flights Singapore's regional carrier, Silk Air, has direct flights from Singapore to Ujung Pandang (twice weekly, US$250/361 one way/return) and Manado (twice weekly, US$420/799), and Malaysia Airlines links Kuala Lumpur with Ujung Pandang (twice weekly, US$180/320).

The Philippines city of Davao is serviced by twice weekly Bouraq flights to/from Manado (US$156/262).

Boat Ujung Pandang is a major hub for Indonesia's national ferry network and many Pelni ships stop there, giving travellers cheap and easy access to most other major centres in the archipelago. A number of other Sulawesi ports are serviced by Pelni. See the Indonesia Getting Around section for route details.

The trip from the Javanese port of Surabaya to Ujung Pandang takes less than 24 hours. Then it's a couple of days more around to Bitung (the port for Manado), with several stops in between. Road transport in Sulawesi is often faster, but the ferries tend to be more comfortable.

UJUNG PANDANG

Ujung Pandang is Sulawesi's largest and liveliest city. The Muslim Bugis are the dominant group in Ujung Pandang and the city is

SULAWESI

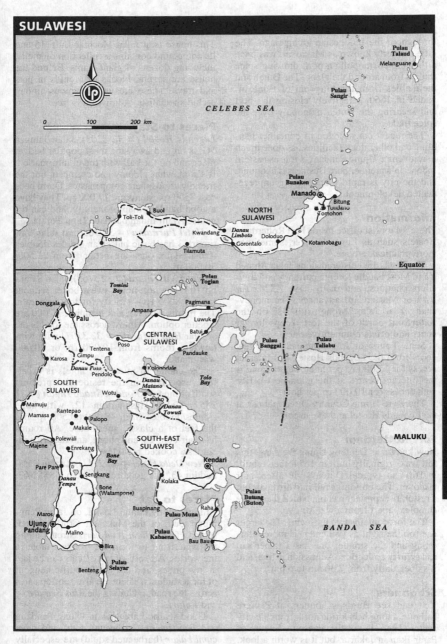

CELEBES SEA

0   100   200 km

Pulau
Talaud
Melanguane

Pulau
Sangir

Pulau
Bunaken
Manado
Bitung
Tondano
Tomohon

NORTH
SULAWESI

Buol
Toli-Toli
Kwandang
Danau
Limboto
Doloduo
Gorontalo
Kotamobagu
Tomini
Tilamuta

Equator

Tomini
Bay

Pulau
Togian

Donggala
Palu
Ampana
Pagimana
Luwuk
Batui

CENTRAL
SULAWESI
Poso
Pandauke

Pulau
Banggai
Pulau
Taliabu

Karosa
Tentena
Gimpu
Kolonodale

Danau Poso
Pendolo
Danau
Matano
Tolo
Bay

SOUTH
SULAWESI
Wotu
Saroako
Danau
Towuti

Mamuju
Mamasa
Rantepao
Palopo
Makale

MALUKU

Majene
Polewali
Enrekang
SOUTH-EAST
SULAWESI

Pare Pare
Danau
Tempe
Sengkang
Kendari

Bone
(Watampone)
Kolaka

Pulau
Butung
(Buton)

Maros
Buapinang
Pulau Muna
Raha

Ujung
Pandang
Malino

BANDA   SEA

Pulau
Kabaena
Bau Bau

Bira
Pulau
Selayar

Benteng

INDONESIA

best known as the home of their magnificent schooners which still trade extensively throughout the Indonesian archipelago. The city, formerly known as Makassar, was once a thriving cosmopolitan port, drawing spice traders from around the globe. The Dutch and their allies from the kingdom of Bone invaded in 1660, effectively closing the port and securing the Dutch monopoly over the spice trade.

The recent construction of container handling and other dock facilities has done much to rejuvenate Ujung Pandang's role as eastern Indonesia's premier port. Business is booming, and the city is rapidly undergoing unprecedented development.

Information
There's a tourist office inside Fort Rotterdam. Hostels such as Legends offer, sometimes more practical, advice.

The banks are clustered along Jalan Ahmad Yani. Most handle foreign currency and travellers cheques, and many have ATMs for Visa or MasterCard advances. The moneychanger at Jalan Monginsidi 42, on the waterfront north of the fort, keeps longer hours and offers competitive rates.

Sena Tours, at Jalan Jampea 1A a few doors from the Legends Hostel, has Internet access for 15,000 rp per hour, better value is the Internet centre at the main post office with access for 10,000 rp per hour.

There are Home Country Direct phones at the Legends Hostel and the airport.

Fort Rotterdam
Now known as Benteng Ujung Pandang, this fort was originally built in 1634, then rebuilt in 1667 in typical Dutch style after their takeover. The buildings fell into disrepair but a restoration project has renovated the whole complex, apart from a wall or two.

The fort contains two museums. The larger one (on the right as you enter) is more interesting and the smaller one has a rather sad and scruffy collection. Admission is free, and it's open daily from 7.30 am to 6 pm.

Schooners
You can see Bugis schooners at Paotere harbour, a long becak ride north from the city centre. There is not the awesome line-up of Pasar Ikan in Jakarta, but it is worth a look. Elsewhere along the waterfront, you may see *balolang*, large outriggers with sails, or *lepa-lepa*, smaller outrigger canoes.

Clara Bundt Orchid Garden & Shell Collection
This house is at Jalan Mochtar Lufti 15 and its compound contains a collection of shells, including dozens of giant clams. Behind the house are several blocks of orchids in pots and trays. These are world famous among orchid specialists. Admission is free.

Places to Stay
Legends Hostel (☎ 32 8203), Jalan Jampea 5G, is far and away the most popular budget place and on the ball with travel information. It's somewhat gloomy and cramped, but the friendly atmosphere compensates. Dorm beds cost 7500 rp, rooms are 17,000 rp. They have a good handout map of the city, and can organise Alam Indah buses to Tana Toraja.

Hotel Purnama (☎ 32 3830) at Jalan Pattimura 3 has basic but clean singles/doubles (the upstairs ones are better) from 21,500/ 30,000 rp.

Hotel Nusantara (☎ 32 3163), Jalan Sarappo 103, has hot, noisy sweat boxes without fan for 8000 rp – strictly for the desperate. The rooms with fan and mandi at 15,000 are a better option. Almost across the road is the similar *Hotel Murah* (☎ 32 3101) with windowless rooms from 10,000 rp, or 20,000 with mandi.

The choice of mid-range hotels is excellent, especially in the residential precinct south of the fort. *Pondok Suada Indah* (☎ 31 2857), Jalan Hasanuddin 12, with huge singles/doubles from 48,400/60,500 rp, has the feel of a classic guesthouse. All rooms have air-con, TV and phone, and the price includes a cooked breakfast.

New Delta Hotel (☎ 31 2711), at Jalan Hasanuddin 43, has good rooms from US$51/63.

Places to Eat
At night along Pantai Losari, on Jalan Penghibur south of the Makassar Golden Hotel, scores of *kaki lima food carts* stretch along the waterfront to form the 'longest table in the world'. All sorts of tasty treats can be had at low prices, and it's the favourite hangout of local students. There are also rooftop cafes across the road, including the *Kios Semarang* and *Fajar*.

Good seafood abounds in Ujung Pandang and *ikan bakar* (barbecued fish) and *cumi cumi bakar* (barbecued squid) are especially popular.

Jalan Sulawesi is a good hunting ground for restaurants – notable places include the

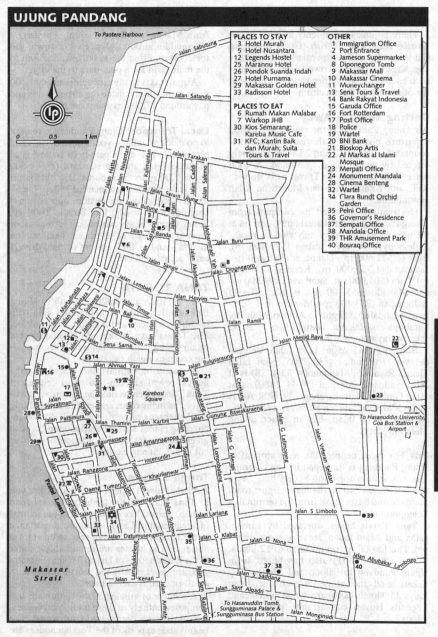

UJUNG PANDANG

To Paotere Harbour →

PLACES TO STAY
3 Hotel Murah
5 Hotel Nusantara
12 Legends Hostel
25 Marannu Hotel
26 Pondok Suanda Indah
27 Hotel Purnama
29 Makassar Golden Hotel
33 Radisson Hotel

PLACES TO EAT
6 Rumah Makan Malabar
7 Warkop JHB
30 Kios Semarang;
    Kareba Music Cafe
31 KFC; Kantin Baik
    dan Murah; Suita
    Tours & Travel

OTHER
1 Immigration Office
2 Port Entrance
4 Jameson Supermarket
8 Diponegoro Tomb
9 Makassar Mall
10 Makassar Cinema
11 Moneychanger
13 Sena Tours & Travel
14 Bank Rakyat Indonesia
15 Garuda Office
16 Fort Rotterdam
17 Post Office
18 Police
19 Wartel
20 BNI Bank
21 Bioskop Artis
22 Al Markas al Islami
    Mosque
23 Merpati Office
24 Monument Mandala
28 Cinema Benteng
32 Wartel
34 Clara Bundt Orchid
    Garden
35 Pelni Office
36 Governor's Residence
37 Sempati Office
38 Mandala Office
39 THR Amusement Park
40 Bouraq Office

Jalan Sabutung
Jalan Satando
Jalan Hatta
Jalan Tarakan
Jalan Nusantara
Jalan Kalimantan
Jalan Caddi
Jalan Saleno
Jalan Serui Ujung
Jalan Butung
Jalan Banda
Jalan Sappo
Jalan Buru
Jalan Mohamm'adi Yeh
Jalan Sangir
Jalan Akademi
Jalan Lembeh
Jalan Diponegoro
Jalan Hasyim
Jalan Mataniata
Jalan Nusantara
Jalan Sulawesi
Jalan Timor
Jalan Bali
Jalan Irian
Jalan Cokroaminoto
Jalan Ramli
Jalan Jampea
Jalan Sumbah
Jalan Serui Sama
Jalan Mesjid Raya
Jalan Bulusaraung
Jalan Ahmad Yani
Jalan Balaikota
Jalan Kajolalido
Jalan Lompob'atang
Jalan Cerekang
Jalan Ujung Pandang
Jalan Slamet
Karebosi Square
Jalan Supratman
Jalan Pattimura
Jalan Thamrin
Jalan Kartini
Jalan Gunung Bawakaraeng
Jalan Baumassepe
Jalan Amannagappa
Jalan Ranggong
Jalan Tompamasa
Jalan Hasanudin
Jalan Daeng Tumpu
Khairilanwar
Jalan Mochtar Lutfi
Jalan Sawerigading
Jalan Datumusengemi
Jalan Lariang
Jalan G Klabat
Jalan G Nona
Jalan G Merapi
Jalan Lompobatang
Incenurdin
Jalan Sudirman
Jalan Salomo
Jalan G Latimojong
Jalan Veteran Selatan
Jalan S Limboto
Jalan S Saddang
Jalan Kenari
Jalan Sam Ratulangi
Jalan Sarif Alqadri
Jalan Monginsidi
Jalan Abubakar Lambogo
Jalan Arifrate
Lamadukkeleng
Makassar Strait
Pasteur Lewari
To Hasanuddin University,
Goa Bus Station &
Airport
To Hasanuddin Tomb,
Sungguminasa Palace &
Sungguminasa Bus Station

0   0.5   1 km

INDONESIA

Rumah Makan Malabar at No 264, famous for its *murtabak* and curries.

There is junk food aplenty at **KFC** or the **Kantin Baik dan Murah** (Good & Cheap Canteen) above the supermarket diagonally opposite the Marannu Tower Hotel. Big hotels such as the Radisson offer western cuisine at the other end of the spectrum.

Getting There & Away

Air Ujung Pandang is the major arrival and departure point for Sulawesi. Airline discounts of between 17 and 25% are routinely offered by agents, so shop around. A good place is Suita Tours & Travel next door to KFC and Kantin Baik dan Murah on Jalan Hasanuddin.

Destinations serviced by Merpati from Ujung Pandang (with official fares, current at the time of writing; they may well be meaningless by now) are: Ambon (573,400 rp), Biak (1,532,600 rp), Denpasar (555,800 rp), Jayapura (1,350,000 rp), Kendari (318,200 rp), Palu (503,000 rp), Surabaya (899,300 rp) and Manado (853,900 rp). Bouraq flies to Balikpapan (923,400 rp), Manado and Surabaya. Mandala has flights to Ambon, Manado, Surabaya and Jakarta. Garuda flies to Biak, Jakarta, Jayapura and Manado.

Bouraq (☎ 45 2506) is at Jalan Veteran Selatan 1; Garuda (☎ 32 2705) is at Jalan Slamet Riyadi 6; Mandala (☎ 32 4288) is at Jalan Saddang; Merpati (☎ 44 2480) is at Jalan Gunung Bawakaraeng 109; Silk Air is in the Makassar Golden Hotel; and Malaysia Airlines (☎ 33 0888) has an office at the Marannu Hotel.

Bus For most people, the next stop after Ujung Pandang is Rantepao in Tana Toraja. The bus station for north-bound buses is a few kilometres east on the main airport road. South-bound buses leave from the terminal at Sungguminasa.

Tana Toraja buses, operated by Liman, Litha and Alam Indah, leave at 8 am and 8 pm. The 15,000 rp trip takes 10 to 12 hours. Liman (☎ 31 5851) also has buses from Ujung Pandang to Palopo and Malili. Buy tickets in advance at the Liman office, Jalan Laiya 25. Hotels can also arrange tickets, and Legends Hostel can arrange pick-up for guests.

Boat Pelni (☎ 33 1401), Jalan Sudirman 38, has a number of vessels making regular stops here.

Getting Around

To/From the Airport *Pete-petes* (bemos) from Makassar Mall to Ujung Pandang's Hasanuddin airport, 22km east of town, run for 2000 rp. From the airport, walk 500m to the main road for a pete-pete to the city.

Airport taxis to the city centre cost 24,500 rp, or walk 100m outside the airport gates and pay around 17,000 rp using the meter.

Local Transport Ujung Pandang is too hot to do much walking – you'll need becaks and pete-petes. The main pete-pete station is at Makassar Mall and the standard fare is 600 rp, or 1000 rp to the suburbs. Big old Damri buses take you any distance for 350 rp. Becak drivers kerb-crawl for custom and are hard bargainers – the shortest fare is 1000 rp. Some enterprising drivers offer menus of tours around town at set prices. Taxis run on meters – and as they are out of date drivers carry adjustment cards.

TANA TORAJA

Tana Toraja is about 320km north of Ujung Pandang. It's a high, mountainous area with beautiful scenery and a fascinating culture. The Toraja have embraced Christianity, but retain strong pre-Christian traditions, including complex death rituals.

Makale (the capital) and Rantepao (the largest town) are the two main centres of Tana Toraja. Bemos link the surrounding villages, but many roads are terrible and walking is a better way of getting around. All the interesting places are scattered around the lush green country surrounding Rantepao – you've got to get out and explore.

Toraja Culture

Architecture The first thing that strikes you in Tana Toraja is the traditional *tongkonan* houses, shaped like buffalo horns (an animal of great mythical and economic importance to the Toraja) with the roof rearing up at front and rear. The houses are remarkably similar to the Batak houses of Danau Toba in Sumatra and are always aligned north-south with small rice barns facing them.

A number of villages in the region are still composed entirely of these traditional houses, but most have corrugated-iron roofs. The beams and supports of the Torajan houses are cut so that they all slot together neatly and the whole house is painted and carved with chicken and buffalo motifs – buffalo skulls

TANA TORAJA

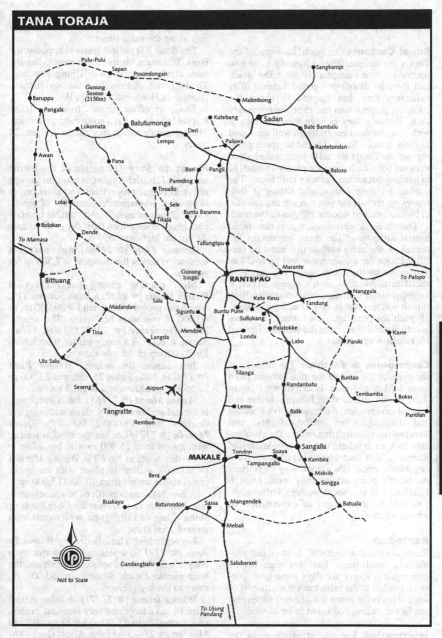

often decorate the front, symbolising the wealth and prestige of the owners.

Burial Customs The burial customs of the Toraja are unique. They generally have two funerals – one immediately after the death and then an elaborate second funeral after sufficient time has elapsed to make the complex preparations and raise the necessary cash. Because they believe you can take it with you, the dead generally go well equipped to their graves. Since this led to grave plundering, the Toraja started to secrete their dead in caves (of which there are plenty around) or in hacked-out niches in rocky cliff faces. The coffins go deep inside, and sitting in balconies on rock-faces you can see the *tau tau*, or life-size carved wooden effigies of the dead.

The funeral ceremonies are the main tourist attraction. The more important the deceased, the more buffalo that must be sacrificed: one for a commoner and up to 24 as you move up the social scale. Pigs are also sacrificed. Animals aren't cheap either: a medium-sized buffalo costs several million rupiah – size, fatness, colour and good horns all push the price up. At a funeral, dress respectfully and don't sit in the areas designated for families and guests.

Ceremonies & Festivals The middle of the year, at the end of the rice harvest from around May onwards, is ceremony time in Tana Toraja; included are funerals, house and harvest ceremonies. All may involve feasting and dancing, often buffalo fights, and Torajan *sisemba* fighting, where the combatants kick each other. Various people around Rantepao will take you to ceremonies for a negotiable price. It's a good way of finding out what's going on – if they speak enough English or if you speak enough Indonesian, you will be able to get an explanation of what's happening.

Rantepao

Rantepao has few sights of its own, but provides a comfortable base for trips to the countryside. Every six days there is a livestock market at the main market north-east of town. This is the prime social event for everyone in the valley, and is not to be missed.

Information The tourist office is in the central square. The staff are sometimes helpful and have the dates of forthcoming ceremonies. There is also a helpful tourist service just south of the hospital on the main street and several other private travel agencies along the main street.

The Bank Rakyat Indonesia is opposite the Bank Danamon on the main street, but the rates aren't as good as in Ujung Pandang. The best rates are from the authorised moneychanger in Hotel Indra Toraja II.

The post office, across from the Bank Rakyat Indonesia, has a poste restante service. The telephone office next door is open 24 hours.

Places to Stay The height of the tourist season is July and August, when tour groups arrive in plague proportions and hotel prices skyrocket. Rantepao has dozens of good-value, clean and usually comfortable hotels – plus many homes open their doors to visitors during the high season.

Losmen Flora (☎ 21586), right next to a mosque, is one of the cheapest at 7,500 rp for singles.

Most popular among backpackers is *Wisma Malita* (☎ 21011), Jalan Suloara 110, which has rooms with mandi for 20,000 rp, or 40,000 if you want hot water. The nearby *Mace Homestay* (☎ 21852), Jalan Tenko Saturu 4, is set in a pretty garden with rooms for 20,000 rp in the low season.

Just across the bridge, *Wisma Rosa* (☎ 21075), Jalan Sadan 28, charges 20,000 rp including breakfast, and is good value.

Wisma Maria (☎ 21165), Jalan Ratulangi, is central and reasonably clean with singles/doubles from 15,000/25,000 rp. *Wisma Monika* (☎ 21216), across the road, is similar with rooms from 25,000 rp with breakfast.

Further south at No 62 is *Wisma Martini* (☎ 21240), a friendly place with basic but comfortable rooms from 10,000/15,000 rp.

A few kilometres north of town, restaurateur Pak Bitty runs *Homestay Chez Dodeng* at the village of Tallunglipu, with rooms from around 15,000 rp.

For something a little better, try *Wisma Te Bass* (☎ 21415), a pleasant place run by a couple – the husband speaks English and the wife speaks Dutch. Rooms are 30,000 rp, more in the high season.

Wisma Irama (☎ 21371) at Jalan Abdul Gani 16 has a large and very pleasant garden, and rooms from 25,000/35,000 rp. *Wisma Monton* (☎ 21675) at Jalan Abdul Gani 14A, in an alley behind the Irama, starts at 60,000 rp.

Less conveniently located but recommended are *Pison Hotel* (☎ 21344), Jalan Pong Tiku

8, with rooms from 27,500/49,500 rp, and the similar *Pia's Poppies* (☎ *21121*) across the lane at No 27A.

Places to Eat Many of the eateries around Rantepao serve Torajan food. A local speciality is *pa'piong*, a mix of meat (usually pork or chicken) and leaf vegetables smoked over a low flame for hours. Order a couple of hours in advance and enjoy it with black rice.

Small, unmarked *warung* along Jalan Andi Mapanyuki and Jalan Suloara offer first-class barbecued fish for considerably less than the restaurants.

Restaurant Mambu, Jalan Ratulangi, serves Indonesian and Torajan food but is also great for western breakfasts. The nearby *Hotel Indra I* has an upmarket Indonesian and Torajan restaurant.

The classy restaurants at the *Pia's Poppies* and *Pison* hotels serve Torajan food. The former also dishes up continental breakfasts, yoghurt, juices and other goodies.

Rumah Makan Rima I, Jalan Mapanyuki, has generous serves of Indonesian food and the best banana pancakes. Pak Bitty's *Chez Dodeng*, Jalan Emi Saelan, is a Rantepao landmark with basic warung fare.

The *River Cafe* a few kilometres north of town has huge serves of Indonesian and other fare, including Mexican. The breezy dining deck overlooks small rapids and a river flat where men spend hours washing and grooming their buffalo. There are crafts and antiques in the gallery next door.

There are many *balok* (palm wine) bars around town, which welcome foreigners, but not in big numbers, so it may be better to go with a local.

Getting There & Away In Rantepao the bus company offices are clustered in the centre of town. The main companies on the Rantepao-Ujung Pandang route are Litha, Liman and Alam Indah. Departures are typically at 8 am, and around 8 pm. The trip to Ujung Pandang (320km) costs 15,000 rp (20,000 rp for the Liman executive bus with air-con and legroom). Pare-Pare to Rantepao takes four to five hours and costs 10,000 rp.

Litha, Alam Indah, Damri and other buses heading north to Tentena, Poso and Palu tend to leave Rantepao mid-morning. Fares to Pendolo (10 hours), Tentena (12 hours) and Poso (13 hours) are all around 30,000 rp. For the long-haulers, the trip to Palu takes 20 hours (40,000 rp).

Bemos run down to the coastal city of Palopo (9000 rp; two hours).

Getting Around Central Rantepao is small and easy to walk around, although there are plenty of becaks.

Kijangs (Toyota van taxis) opposite the post office run almost continuously from Rantepao south to Makale (1000 rp) and you can get off at the signs for Londa, Tilanga or Lemo and walk. From Jalan Diponegoro there are frequent bemos east towards Palopo for the sights in that direction, and bemos north to Lempo (near Batutumonga) start from Jalan Monginsidi. Others leave from Jalan Tappang and the bridge. Almost all services stop around 6 pm.

Motorbikes can be rented from the main street tour agencies for 20,000 rp to 35,000 rp per day. It can be cheaper for a group to charter a bemo or Kijang. If trekking, take a water bottle, something to eat, a torch in case you end up walking at night, and an umbrella or raincoat.

AROUND TANA TORAJA

The following places (the distance in kilometres from Rantepao is shown) are all within fairly easy reach on day trips. If you make longer trips and stay overnight in private homes along the way, pay your way with money or gifts. Guides aren't necessary – the Torajans are friendly and used to tourists, and it's great to escape on your own into the beautiful countryside around Rantepao.

South of Rantepao

Karasbik (1km) Karasbik is on the outskirts of Rantepao, just off the road leading to Makale. The traditional-style houses here are arranged in a square. Apparently the complex was erected some years ago for a single funeral.

Singki (1km) You can climb this small hill just outside Rantepao for a panoramic view over the surrounding area.

Kete Kesu (6km) Just off the main road, south-east of Rantepao, this traditional village is famed for its woodcarving. On the cliff face behind the village are some cave graves and some very old hanging graves – the rotting coffins are suspended from an overhang.

Sullukang (7km) Off to the side of the main road in this village there's a derelict shack on a rocky outcrop which contains several derelict tau tau, almost buried under the foliage. There's also *rante* here – large stone slabs planted in the ground – one of them about 4m high.

Londa (6km) About 2km off the Rantepao to Makale road, this is an extensive burial cave and one of the most interesting in the area. There are a number of coffins containing bones and skulls. Kids hang around outside renting their oil lamps for 4500 rp (you could try bargaining but they're not very amenable to it) to guide you around. Unless you've got a strong torch, you really do need a guide with a lamp.

Tilanga (9km) There are several cold and hot springs in the Toraja area, and this natural cold water pool is very pretty. It's an attractive walk along the muddy trails and through the rice paddies from Tilanga to Lemo – you'll need to ask directions along the way.

Lemo (11km) This is among the largest burial areas in Tana Toraja. The sheer rockface has a whole series of balconies carved out for tau tau. The biggest balcony has a dozen figures – like spectators at a sports event. One tall tau tau stands on a slightly depressed section of floor so he can fit in. There would be even more if they weren't in such demand by unscrupulous antique dealers.

It's a good idea to go early in the morning so you get the sun on the rows of figures – by 9 am their heads are in the shadows. A bemo from Rantepao will drop you off at the road leading up to Lemo, from where it's a 15 minute walk.

Siguntu (7km) Siguntu, a traditional village situated on a slight rise off to the west of the main road, is a pleasant walk from Rantepao. The walk from Rantepao via Singki and Siguntu to the main road at Alang Alang near the Londa burial site is pleasant.

East of Rantepao
Marante (6km) This very fine traditional village is right by the road east to Palopo.

Nanggala (16km) In the same direction (and rather further off the Palopo road) is this traditional village with a particularly grandiose traditional house with a whole fleet – 14 in all – of rice barns. Bemos from Rantepao take you straight there, or they might just drop you off on the main road, from where it's a 1.5km walk.

North & North-West of Rantepao
Palawa (9km) This traditional village a kilometre or two north of Pangli has tongkonan houses and rice barns.

Sadan (13km) Sadan is a weaving centre further to the north. Bemos go there from Rantepao along a road which can be rough at times. The women here have established a tourist market where they sell their weaving.

Batutumonga (23km) From Batutumonga you can see a large part of Tana Toraja. The views are even more stunning from the summit of **Gunung Sesean**, a 2150m peak towering above the village. Most bemos stop at Lempo, which is an easy walk from Batutumonga.

Guesthouses here include *Mama Siska's* at around 25,000 rp per head including meals; *Landorondin Homestay* and its amazing views for 20,000 rp; and *Betania Homestay* for 25,000 rp including meals.

The return to Rantepao is an interesting and easy hike down the slopes to **Pana**, with its ancient hanging graves among bamboo and a few baby graves in nearby trees, through a number of tiny villages. The path ends at **Tikala**, from where there are regular bemos to Rantepao.

Lokomata (26km) There are more cave graves and more beautiful scenery at Lokomata, just a few kilometres past Batutumonga.

Other Villages
At **Pangli (7km)** are house graves; **Bori** (8km) is a funeral ceremony site; and **Pangala** (35km) is a traditional village. One of the most popular **treks** is from Bittuang (58km) to Mamasa in the west.

PENDOLO
A road bears eastwards from Rantepao to Soroako on the shores of Danau Matano in Central Sulawesi. Midway along this road is the village of Wotu, where the Trans-Sulawesi Hwy veers north to the small village of Pendolo on the southern bank of beautiful **Danau Poso**.

The lake and its lovely beaches are the main attractions. You can swim, take boat rides or go for walks. There are daily ferries across the lake to Tentena on the northern side.

Places to Stay & Eat
Homestay Masamba and *Losmen Victory* both overlook the beach adjacent to the jetty

and have small rooms from about 20,000 rp. *Homestay Petezza*, Jalan Pelabuhan 216, a couple of doors up from the Victory, is also good value.

Mulia Hotel, next to the boat jetty, has comfortable rooms from 69,000 rp. The helpful folk at *Pendolo Cottages*, near the Mulia, have rooms from 17,500 rp including breakfast.

TENTENA
This lakeside village lacks Pendolo's fine beaches but has plenty of other attractions including the nearby **Salopa Waterfalls**, set amid unspoilt forest west of Tentena. Take a bemo to Tonusu, then walk the last 3km.

Tentena is host to the undisputed highlight of Central Sulawesi's social calendar, the annual **Lake Poso Festival** in late August, a colourful celebration of culture, with dancing, song, traditional sports and other activities.

Places to Stay
Hotel Victori (☎ 21392) on Jalan Diponegoro 18 has rooms from 22,500 rp. *Hotel Pamona Indah* (☎ 21245), adjacent to the lakeside jetty, is cheaper at around 17,500 rp, and across the bridge *Pondok Wisata Ue'Data* (☎ 21222) is a delightful place with a cafe, and rooms from 15,000 rp.

Getting There & Away
Buses make the run to Poso (2500 rp) in about two hours. Buses to Kolonodale (152km; 15,000 rp) originate in Poso, but you can hail them down from outside the bus station.

POSO
Although it's Central Sulawesi's second largest city, Poso's main attractions are its banks which change foreign currency. There are a number of beaches out of town, all accessible by bemo: **Pantai Madale**, a snorkelling spot, 5km east; the white-sand **Pantai Matako**, 25km east; and **Pantai Toini**, 7km west.

The ebony carving is first-class – check it out at **Lembomawo**, across a footbridge 4km south of Poso.

Information
There is a tourist information office (☎ 21211) at Jalan Sudirman, behind the telephone exchange.

Note that Poso is the last chance for Togian

or Tentena-bound travellers to change travellers cheques. The BNI bank is on Jalan Yos Sudarso.

Places to Stay & Eat
Losmen Lalang Jaya near the dock on Jalan Yos Sudarso is reasonably priced and has unbeatable views of the harbour.

There are a number of other cheap hotels, such as *Hotel Kalimantan* (☎ 21420), Jalan Haji Agus Salim 14; *Hotel Alamanda* (☎ 21333), Jalan Bali 1; and *Losmen Alugoro* (☎ 21336), Jalan Sumatera 20.

Restaurant Depot Anugrah has good cheap Chinese-Indonesian food near the bus offices along Jalan Sumatera.

Getting There & Away
Bus & Bemo There are regular buses from Poso to Tentena (2500 rp). For buses to Palu (10,000 rp; six hours) try Jawa Indah or the other bus offices along Jalan Sumatera. There are daily buses to Kolonodale (15,000 rp) and Ampana (8000 rp).

Boat Check at the port for the current details of boats going to the Togian Islands via Ampana.

PALU
Set in a rain shadow for most of the year, Palu is one of the driest places in Indonesia with less than 600mm of rain a year. Despite perfect swimming weather, the beaches are lousy. Head to Donggala instead (see the following entry).

Information
The regional tourist office (☎ 21795), on Jalan Raja Moili, has maps of the city and hiking suggestions.

Places to Stay & Eat
The central *Purnama Raya Hotel* (☎ 23646), Jalan Wahidin 4, is reasonable value with rooms from 15,000 rp. There is also *Hotel Karsam* (☎ 21776), Jalan Suharso 15, with singles/doubles for 15,000/25,000 rp, and the similarly priced *Taurus Hotel* (☎ 21567) at Jalan Hasanuddin 8.

Jalan Hasanuddin II is a busy alley with many places to eat, including the *Restaurant New Oriental*. On Jalan Wahidin, the *Ramayana* serves all sorts of dishes from the huge woks out front.

Getting There & Away
Air Merpati (π 21171), Jalan Monginsidi 71, has flights to Luwuk (twice a week), Manado (twice a week) and Ujung Pandang (three times a week).

Bouraq (π 21195), Jalan Juanda 87, has flights to Balikpapan (most days) and Ujung Pandang (four times a week).

Bus Buses to Poso, Palopo, Rantepao, Gorontalo and Manado all leave from Terminal Masonda. Palu to Gorontalo takes a day and costs 35,000 rp. Jawa Indah buses to Poso (15,000 rp; six hours) depart from the company's Jalan Hasanuddin office.

Boat Pelni and other large vessels dock at Pantoloan, north-east of Palu. Smaller ships dock at Donggala north-west of Palu, or at Wani, 2km past Pantoloan.

Pelni (π 21696) has an office at Jalan Kartini 96, and another at Pantoloan opposite the road to the wharf. Four modern Pelni boats call at Pantoloan, with connections to Kalimantan and other parts of Sulawesi.

Getting Around
Palu's airport is 7km east of town; take a bemo (3000 rp) or taxi (10,000 rp).

Terminal Manonda has Kijangs to Donggala for 2500 rp, or around 15,000 rp to charter all the way to the beach at Tanjung Karang.

DONGGALA
Donggala's main attractions are the coral reefs at **Tanjung Karang**, north of town. The reef off the Prince John Dive Resort is a delight for snorkellers and beginner divers.

Towale, 12km south-west of Donggala, is another excellent swimming and snorkelling spot.

Places to Stay
Prince John Dive Resort (π 71710) offers simple, clean accommodation from 35,000 rp a head, including meals.

Natural Cottages (π 0451-25020) is an excellent spot on the tip of the peninsula, just past the dive resort. Its cottages cost 35,000 rp, including meals.

Getting There & Away
From Palu you can catch a *taksi Donggala* for 2500 rp. It's another 30 minutes on foot to the beach. Alternatively, you could charter one to Tanjung Karang beach for around 15,000 rp.

AMPANA
Ampana is the stepping-off point for ferries and chartered boats to the Togian Islands. If you need to stay overnight, try *Losmen Irama*, Jalan Kartini 11, about 200m west of the market, from 10,000/14,000 rp for singles/doubles. There's also *Marina Cottage* at Labuhan, 10 minutes east by bendi, and *Penginapan Mekar*, Jalan Kartini 5.

Getting There & Away
Bus Ampana is on the main road from Poso (18,000 rp; five hours). To get to Luwuk (eight hours) get a bemo connection in Bunta.

Boat The ferry from Poso chugs off to Gorontalo via the Togian ports of Wakai, Katupat and Dolong.

There are smaller public boats from Ampana to Bomba (4000 rp; three hours) or to Wakai (3000 rp) every day.

TOGIAN ISLANDS
This remarkably diverse archipelago of coral and volcanic isles is the only place in Indonesia where you can find all three major reef environments – atoll, barrier and fringing reefs – in one location. There are few beaches, but the reefs more than compensate.

Getting Around
Transport within the Togians is a chronic problem. Regardless of where you stay, you need boats to get around, and to reach swimming and snorkelling spots. A convenient (but not cheap) solution is to try to charter a boat from Ampana for a few days. A cheaper and more flexible option is to base yourself on an island and do short snorkelling and whale-watching excursions from there.

The cheapest way between islands is to look out for cargo boats. A boat going from Wakai to Dolong can drop passengers at Katupat or Pulau Malenge for around 5000 rp. Otherwise you might need to spend upwards of 50,000 rp on a charter.

Bomba
This tiny outpost at the south-eastern end of Pulau Batu Daka has nearby reefs and a couple of places to stay. *Losmen Toya Lisa* homestay accommodation in the village costs 20,000 rp including meals. *Homestay Tandongi Reef*, a pleasant place on stilts adjacent to a speck of rock a few hundred metres offshore, costs 30,000 rp a day. *Sisilea Bungalows* is a good newer place for 20,000 rp.

Pulau Kadidiri

This gorgeous beach has three sets of bungalows: *Wakai Cottages* cost 20,000/25,000; *Kadidiri Paradise Bungalows* cost 30,000 rp; and *Pondok Lestari* is 20,000 rp. Diving, trekking and other activities are available at Kadidiri. You can arrange a public or chartered boat from Wakai.

Katupat

A relaxed village on Togian Island, Katupat is also the closest port to the atoll reefs. Stay at *Losmen Melati* at Katupat's main jetty for 40,000 rp or *Losmen Bolilanga Indah* adjacent to the jetty for less.

Malenge

Pulau Malenge is a nature reserve, also close to the atoll reefs. *Malenge Indah Losmen* near the pier charges 25,000 rp a night, including meals. Day trips to the atoll lagoons cost around 30,000 rp, but you will need your own snorkelling gear.

Wakai

Wakai has a port, hotels and some well-stocked general stores, but no beaches. The friendly *Wakai Cottages* costs 25,000/50,000 rp for singles/doubles including three excellent meals. The *Togian Islands Hotel* is an airy weatherboard hotel built over the water near Wakai jetty. Prices start from 25,000.

MANADO

The Minahasan city of Manado is the capital of North Sulawesi, a strongly Christian region with close historical ties to the Netherlands.

Manado is a clean, modern city with little to recommend it, but it does provide a good base from which to explore the region's interesting hinterland, and it is only an hour by motorboat to the brilliant coral reefs off Pulau Bunaken.

Orientation

Mikrolets from every direction loop around Pasar 45, a block of shops, fruit stands and department stores in the heart of town. The market backs on to Jalan Sam Ratulangi, the main road running south, where you will find upmarket restaurants, hotels and supermarkets. Pasar Jengki fish market, north of the centre, is the main launching place for boats to Pulau Bunaken.

Information

Mikrolets marked '17 Aug Wanea' from Pasar 45 will get you to the North Sulawesi tourism office (☎ 86 4299) on Jalan 17 Agustus.

The immigration office (☎ 86 3491) is near the tourist office on Jalan 17 Agustus, and the Philippines has a consulate general (☎ 86 2181) at Jalan Lumimuut 8. There is an Internet centre in the main post office.

Special Events

Festivals include the Tai Pei Kong festival at Ban Hiah Kong temple in February; the Pengucapan Syukur (Minahasan Thanksgiving Day) in June/August; the Bunaken Festival in July; the Anniversary of Manado on 14 July; traditional horse races in the second week of August; and the anniversary of North Sulawesi province on 23 September.

Places to Stay

If arriving by air, expect to be mobbed at the airport by touts for the various hotels (mostly mid-range and better). Don't dismiss them out of hand – business is bad and they offer some remarkably good deals if you can afford a little above rock bottom.

The *Smiling Hostel* (☎ 86 8463), Jalan Rumambi 7, is cheerful and central. There is a small rooftop cafe and advice aplenty from the staff, other travellers and books of tips. Dorm beds cost 7500 rp, and basic singles/doubles start at 11,000/17,000 rp, or doubles with mandi are 22,500 rp.

Manado Bersehati Hotel (☎ 85 5022), Jalan Sudirman 1, is a good choice. It's a Minahasan-style house set off the main road with basic singles/doubles from 12,500/21,000 rp, with mandi for 21,000/27,500 rp and with air-con and TV for 42,500 rp. All prices include breakfast.

An old favourite with travellers (although it's hard to see why) is the charmless *Crown Losmen* (☎ 66277), Jalan Hasanuddin 28, with rooms from 7000/12,000 rp (no fan), 16,500 rp with mandi and 23,500 with aircon. *Jakarta Jaya Hotel* (☎ 86 4330), across the road, has better singles/doubles at 12,500/20,000 rp with fan and bath.

Rex Hotel (☎ 85 1136), Jalan Sugiono 3, is OK if you can afford the air-con rooms at 35,000 rp with mandi; the cheaper rooms have no fan, essential in this climate.

The comfortable *Manado Homestay* (☎ 86 0298), Wanea Lingkungan III, Komplex Diklat Rike, is less conveniently located, but compensates with a homely and welcoming

INDONESIA

atmosphere, and rooms with fan and mandi from 20,000 rp per night. To get there, take a 'Teling' mikrolet from Pasar 45 and ask to get off at Komplex Diklat.

Places to Eat

Manado is a Mecca for adventurous diners. Regional delights include spicy *kawaok* (fried 'forest rat'), tough, gamy *rintek wuuk* (spicy dog meat), *lawang pangang* (stewed bat), the tender and tasty freshwater *ikan mas* (gold fish) and *tinutuan* (vegetable porridge).

Tinoor Jaya, south of the Matahari store on Jalan Sam Ratulangi, is one of the few restaurants in Manado serving regional cuisine.

For basic Indonesian food, there's a whole string of *warung* along Jalan Sam Ratulangi opposite Pasar 45. This area is really bustling at night.

The *Satay House* on Jalan Sudirman has great prawns for 15,000 and, yes, *satay* (sate). Next door is the *Rumah Makan Ria Rio*, although the TV is probably more interesting than the food – the staff certainly think so.

To eat well out of town, stop at the row of restaurants in the Lokon foothills, just before Tomohon, south of Manado. The food at *Tinoor Indah* and the *Pemandangan* is excellent, as are the views over Manado. The drinks of choice are *saguer*, a very quaffable fermented sago wine, and Cap Tikus (literally 'rat brand'), the generic name for distilled saguer.

Getting There & Away

Air Like Ujung Pandang, travel agents can offer discounts of up to 25% on scheduled domestic flights. Try Limbunan (☎ 85 2009), Jalan Sam Ratulangi 159.

Garuda (☎ 85 2154) is at Jalan Diponegoro 15, Merpati (☎ 85 3213) is near Paal 2 terminal, Bouraq (☎ 84 1470) is at Jalan Serapung 27B, Mandala (☎ 85 1743) is at the southern end of Jalan Sam Ratulangi and Silk Air (☎ 86 3744) is at Jalan Sarapung 5.

Useful connections include Bouraq's flights to/from Davao in the Philippines (weekly, US$180/150); Silk Air's direct flights to Singapore (see the Sulawesi Getting There & Away entry for details); flights to Gorontalo (three times a week), Palu (three a week), and Ternate (almost daily) by Bouraq, and daily flights to Ujung Pandang by Bouraq, Mandala, Garuda and Merpati.

Bus Bus fares to Gorontalo (10 hours) range from 20,000 rp to 35,000 rp – the mid-range older air-con buses are the best. Buses go around the gulf to Palu for 50,000 rp, and all the way to Ujung Pandang – if you can tolerate the three day haul. Allow for delays during wet weather. These and the Kotamobagu-bound buses (7,000 rp) all leave from the Malalayang bus station south of Manado.

Boat Pelni (☎ 86 2844), at Jalan Sam Ratulangi 7, has several large boats calling at the deep-water port of Bitung, near Manado. The *Tilongkabila* visits Gorontalo (40,000 rp) and goes all the way to Benoa (Bali, 296,000 rp). The *Kambuna* sails west to Toli Toli (74,000 rp ekonomi) and Balikpapan (141,000 rp), then across to Ujung Pandang (198,000 rp). Some approximate ekonomi fares on the *Ciremai* are Ternate 58,000 rp, Jayapura 250,000 rp and Ujung Pandang 234,000 rp.

Smaller ferries operate out of Manado. They tend to call at ports along the coast, go north to Tahuna (Pulau Sangihe) and Lirung (Talaud Islands) or over to Ternate and Ambon.

Getting Around

To/From the Airport Mikrolets from Sam Ratulangi airport go to Paal 2 terminal, where you change to another to Pasar 45 or elsewhere in the city. Taxis from the airport to the city (13km) cost 13,000 rp, if they use the meter.

Local Transport Transport around town is by mikrolet. Destinations are shown on a card in the front windscreen. There are various bus stations around town for destinations outside Manado – get to any of them from Pasar 45.

AROUND MANADO
Pulau Bunaken

Bunaken offers you the chance to float over some spectacular and accessible coral drop-offs, caves and valleys. You can buy snorkelling gear from the Matahari department store in Manado, or hire well-worn masks and snorkels from places along the beaches on Bunaken. Boats to Bunaken (5000 rp) depart from near Manado's fish market.

The going rate for dive excursions around Bunaken and nearby islands is around US$50 for two dives in the low season, and US$65 in the June/July high season. This is an option for experienced divers. Nusantara Diving Centre (☎ 86 3988), on Molas Beach, Manado, its neighbour Baracuda Diving Resort (☎ 86

2033), and Murex (☎ 86 6280), Jalan Sudirman 28, Manado, all cater for beginners and advanced divers.

There are also a number of Bunaken-based operators. Expat-run Froggies (contact through Smiling Hostel) gets good reports. (Check them out at on the Net at www.divefroggies.com/index.html.)

Places to Stay & Eat There are a number of places to stay on Liang Beach to the west, and on Pangalisang Beach near Bunaken village. Liang is the better of the two. All prices here include meals.

Pantai Liang The popularity of the coral drop-off 100m offshore created a building boom along this beach. None are designed to last.

Papa Boa Bungalow and his neighbours at the far end of the beach charge from 20,000 rp per person. *Bastiong Cottages* is the classiest option – by Bunaken standards – at around 60,000 rp per head. Try to negotiate prices.

Ibu Konda's and *Santika* are also worth a try, both charging 20,000 rp. *Tanta Nona Cottages* gets rave reviews for 30,000 rp.

Pantai Pangalisang Daniel's Homestay is the biggest, most popular place with beds from 30,000 rp, including meals. *Lorenzo Cottage* (☎ 86 7276), next door, is smaller, with cottages for 35,000 rp, or for the same price *Tuwo Kona Cottages* is charming and clean.

Bunaken Seabreeze Bungalows (☎ 85 9379) has bungalows from 25,000 rp and a diving operation.

Getting There & Away Boats leave the fishing harbour in Manado daily except Sunday at around 3 pm, take around an hour and cost 5000 rp. The return from Bunaken is in the morning. A charter costs about 25,000 rp one way.

Tomohon

Minahasa's extraordinary cuisine is served in a string of restaurants on a cliff overlooking Manado, just a few kilometres before Tomohon (see Places to Eat under Manado earlier).

Tomohon has a **vulcanology centre** which monitors and advises on the safety of active volcanoes in the area.

Between Tomohon and Lahendong, there's the extensive **Lahendong hot springs**.

Places to Stay *Happy Flower Homestay* (☎ 35 2787) at the foot of Gunung Lokon is justifiably applauded by all who stay. This simple but delightful refuge costs 10,000/15,000 rp for singles/doubles, or from 27,500 rp for 'deluxe' doubles, including breakfast. From Manado, take a Tomohon-bound bus and get out at Gereja Pniel a few kilometres before Tomohon. Take the path opposite the church, walk 300m, cross a stream and look for the homestay tucked away in trees to the right of the path.

Bitung

Bitung is the chief port of Minahasa and lies to the east of Manado. Despite its spectacular setting, the town is not very attractive. The Pelni office (☎ 21167) is in the harbour compound.

Places to Stay & Eat The *Samudra Jaya* (☎ 21167), Jalan Sam Ratulangi 2, is cheap and central, with rooms from 20,000 rp including breakfast. *Penginapan Sansarino* near the main market is cheaper.

A few kilometres north of Bitung is *Kunkungan Bay Resort*, a swank dive resort amid coconut plantations on a secluded bay. There are helpful staff and excellent diving. Packages, including accommodation and meals, cost around US$170 per day.

Getting There & Away Bitung is 50km from Manado. Mikrolets depart regularly from Manado's Paal 2 terminal. The mikrolet drops you off at the Mapalus terminal just outside Bitung, where you catch another mikrolet for the short trip into town.

See the Manado Getting There & Away section for details of Pelni services from Bitung.

Maluku (Moluccas)

The islands of Maluku are the fabled spice islands to the west of Irian Jaya. Spices, once unique to the islands previously known as the Moluccas, attracted European traders and colonialists hundreds of years ago. Maluku has over 1000 islands, most of which are uninhabited. Visitors to Maluku usually go to Ambon, the provincial capital, the delightful Banda Islands, or Ternate and Tidore, two adjacent islands off western Halmahera. More remote islands are difficult to get to, but are often worth the effort.

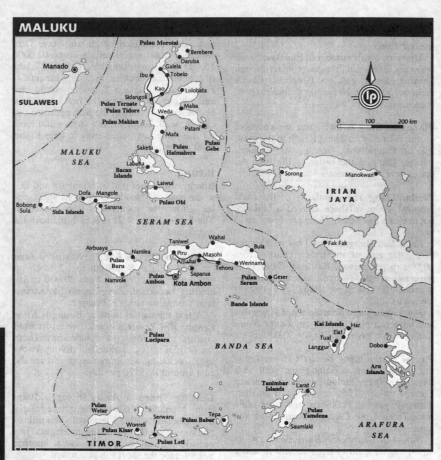

Climate

Timing a visit to Maluku is a bit different from the rest of Indonesia. The dry season is from October to April, and the wet season from May to September, although there are slight variations among the islands. Try to avoid the wet season, but also be prepared for some rain at any time of the year.

Flora & Fauna

The Taman Nasional Manusela on Pulau Seram has unique species of parrots, including the brightly coloured *nuri* (often kept as pets), and cockatoos. Another national reserve on the Aru Islands has the flightless cassowary, and the shy bird of paradise, or *cenderawasih*. In remote parts of Pulau Seram and Pulau Halmahera, you may see a

long-nosed bandicoot, a Timor deer or a miniature version of a kangaroo. Pulau Bacan is famous for its tail-less monkeys.

Some of the vast forests are home to unique species of butterflies, and huge orchids. The nutmeg – that little tree that has caused so much strife in the past – is still cultivated in parts of Ambon and Saparua islands, and the Bandas.

Activities

The **diving** is spectacular, particularly around the Banda Islands, Pulau Ambon and the neighbouring islands of Seram, Saparua and Nusa Laut. The interior of most islands is mountainous, offering unlimited **trekking** opportunities, particularly on Halmahera and Seram islands; and there are volcanoes to climb in the Bandas and on Pulau Ternate. For some of the prettiest **beaches** in Indonesia head to the southern Kai Islands.

Getting There & Away

Air The capital of the province – Kota Ambon on Pulau Ambon – is connected by air to Ujung Pandang (Sulawesi) and Irian Jaya by Merpati, and also to Ujung Pandang by Mandala.

Boat Pelni liners (and many other boats) link Maluku with the rest of Indonesia. Every two weeks the *Lambelu* links Ambon with Bau Bau (south Sulawesi), and goes on to Ujung Pandang and Java; the *Dobonsolo* connects Ambon with Sorong (Irian Jaya), Dili (East Timor) and Java; the *Rinjani* has a great route from Ambon to the Bandas, Tual (Kai Islands) and Fak Fak (Irian Jaya) and back, and then on to Bau Bau and Java; the *Tatamailau* links southern Maluku with Nusa Tenggara and Irian Jaya on a monthly basis; and the *Bukit Siguntang* goes from Ambon to the Bandas and Kai Islands and back, then on to Ujung Pandang and Java.

Getting Around

Air Merpati is the main carrier around Maluku, with flights from the two transport hubs: Kota Ambon and Kota Ternate. To more remote destinations in Maluku, cancellations and delays are common. See individual sections for more details.

Boat Pelni doesn't service islands within Maluku particularly well. See the routes listed earlier under Getting There & Away. Perintis ships, such as the KM *Nagura*, and other more basic vessels, cover the more remote islands.

PULAU AMBON

Pulau Ambon is the main island of Maluku and has some good beaches, diving and a superb fort. The city of Kota Ambon is the administrative capital of Maluku and the main transport hub.

Kota Ambon

Once a pleasant colonial city before it was extensively bombed in WWII, Kota Ambon has an unhurried and easygoing pace, and is pleasantly uncrowded. While the city has little to offer, it's a good base from which to explore a few old forts, picturesque beaches and hiking trails around the island.

Orientation & Information The main shopping streets run parallel to the waterfront, while most of the offices, hotels and restaurants are along, or near, Jalan Sultan Hairun, Jalan Raya Pattimura and Jalan AM Sangaji.

The helpful tourist office (☎ 52471), is at the end of Jalan Pengeringan, which runs towards the coast from Hotel Abdulalie. The post office, which also has public Internet access (15000 rp per hour), is on Jalan Raya Pattimura.

Ambon is the only place (other than Ternate) in Maluku to change money. The best banks are Bank Exim, on Jalan Raya Pattimura, and the BCA bank, on Jalan Sultan Hairun – both are open weekday mornings and have ATMs.

Commonwealth War Cemetery Kota Ambon was the centre of fierce fighting and bombing during WWII. The superb Australian-maintained cemetery for allied servicemen is worth a visit if only for its peaceful garden setting. Take the Tantui bemo (350 rp) from the Mardika bemo terminal.

Siwalima Museum This museum (open every morning, except Monday) has a fine collection of Malukan, Indonesian and colonial artefacts. Take the Amahusu or Taman Makmur bemo (450 rp); the museum is a steep 10 minute walk from the main road.

Other Attractions In the centre of the city, the **Pattimura Monument** was built for the local resistance hero, Thomas Matulessy. Nearby, the few remains of the Dutch **Benteng Victoria** fort are now part of the army barracks. In the suburb of Karang Panjang, another huge **memorial** to another resistance fighter, Martha Christina Tiahahu, offers great views of the city.

Places to Stay Budget hotels, all next to each other, can be found on central Jalan Wim Reawaru. The popular *Penginapan Beta* (☎ 53463) is the best value in Kota Ambon – clean, quiet singles/doubles with mandi cost 15,000/22,000 rp.

Next door, *Hotel Rezfanny* (☎ 42300) has rooms without mandi for 20,000/22,000 rp, or with mandi for 27,500 rp.

Next door again is the modern *Hotel Hero* (☎ 42978), where all rooms are air-con and have mandi, hot water and TV from 49,500 rp for a double rising to 88,000 rp.

KOTA AMBON

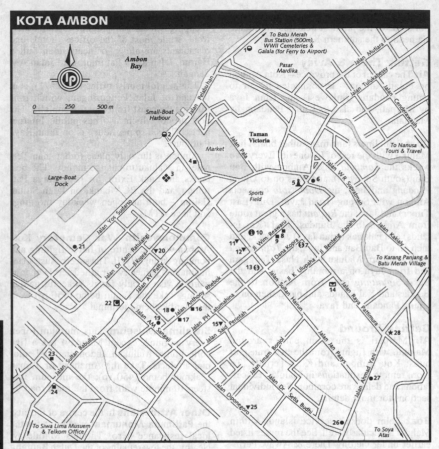

Hotel Elenoor (☎ 52834), Jalan Anthony Rhebok 30, has singles/doubles for 38,000/51,000 rp, with mandi and fan, 51,000/63,000 rp with air-con. Almost next door, *Hotel Gamalama* (☎ 53724) is cheap at 19,250/27,500 rp, with mandi. Get there early; it's often full.

The central *Hotel Sumber Asia* (☎ 56587), near the noisy market, has a good range of rooms starting at 28,000 rp.

In the 'Muslim sector', a little south-west of the main mosque, several good places, such as the quiet *Wisma Jaya* (☎ 41545) and *Hotel Abdulalie* (☎ 52057), have rooms from 14,500/20,400 rp.

See the Around Pulau Ambon section for some good alternatives around the island.

Places to Eat During the evening, the pavement of Jalan AM Sangaji is lined with women selling huge plates of cheap nasi campur. Tiny *warung* congregate around the bemo terminal, port and near Hotel Sumber Asia.

For just a coffee and sweet snack, try one of the popular *rumah kopi*, such as *Sariwangi*, along Jalan Diponegoro.

Halim's Restaurant on Jalan Sultan Hairun is popular with expats. Good Chinese food costs around 10,000 rp to 15,000 rp a dish, and the beer is ice-cold. Almost next door, the *Restaurant Sakura* is also good and somewhat cheaper, although it lacks atmosphere.

Rumah Makan Dedes on Jalan Diponegoro is a great ikan bakar specialist. You select your fish or squid from the fridge, it is

KOTA AMBON

PLACES TO STAY				
4	Hotel Sumber Asia	12	Halim's Restaurant	6	Pelni Office
8	Hotel Rezfanny;	15	Rumah Makan Roda	7	Bank Exim
	Penginapan Beta		Baru	10	Tourist Office
9	Hotel Hero	20	Andre's	13	BCA Bank
16	Hotel Elenoor	25	Rumah Makan Dedes	14	Post Office
17	Hotel Gamalama			18	Pelni Agent
23	Wisma Jaya	OTHER		19	Kedai Kopi Sariwangi
24	Hotel Abdulalie	1	Mardika Bemo Terminal	21	Port Entrance
		2	Speedboats to	22	Al-Fatah Mosque
PLACES TO EAT			Waimana	26	Merpati Office
11	Restaurant Sakura	3	Ambon Plaza	27	Mandala Office
		5	Pattimura Memorial	28	Police Station

then grilled and served with rice and trimmings – excellent! A decent sized fish for one person costs around 10,000 rp.

The **Rumah Makan Roda Baru** serves a wide variety of Sulawesi food, and you get served six or so dishes and just pay for what you eat – around 8,000 rp for a good meal.

The Ambon Plaza has a **KFC** and the **eatery,** on the 3rd floor of the Matahari department store, serves Asian meals.

Andre's on Jalan Kopra has donuts, ice creams and pizza slices (closed Sunday).

Getting There & Away Ambon is a visa-free entry/exit point.

Air Merpati (☎ 52480), Jalan Ahmad Yani 19, flies a number of routes around Maluku, including to Bandaneira (thrice weekly) in the Banda Islands, Ternate (most days) and Langgur (thrice weekly) in the Kai Islands; to the Irian Jayan hubs of Biak (four times weekly) and Sorong (weekly); and flights to Ujung Pandang (four times weekly), with connections to other places such as Kupang, Jakarta and Denpasar.

Mandala (☎ 45997), Jalan Ahmad Yani, flies daily to Ujung Pandang and on to Jakarta every day. The fare is the same as Merpati's, although they seem to offer a 25% 'seasonal' discount as a matter of course.

Boat See the Maluku Getting There & Away and Getting Around sections for details on boats to/from Ambon. The gleaming Pelni office (☎ 48219), opposite the Pattimura Memorial, only sells ekonomi tickets. For all other tickets go to a Pelni agent – there are plenty around, including one opposite Hotel Gamalama on Jalan Anthony Rhebok.

Smaller boats to just about every island around Maluku leave from the small-boat harbour at the end of Jalan Pala. A board outside the harbour shows what's going where and when.

Getting Around Pattimura airport is 36km from the city, on the other side of Ambon Bay. A taxi officially costs 25,000 rp; less if you bargain with the driver in the car park. The cheapest and shortest way is by bemo from outside the airport to Waiame, just south of Poka and half-way up the bay, and then by regular shared speedboat (1000 rp) across to the small-boat harbour at Galala, then another bemo into the city. Allow an hour for all forms of transport.

Local Transport Bemos for Kota Ambon and places near the city leave from the chaotic Mardika terminal, along the waterfront. Buses to places further away on Pulau Ambon, and to Pulau Seram, leave from the Batu Merah terminal, a little further northeast of Mardika.

The city is small enough to walk around, or a becak costs about 1500 rp. (Becaks can only stop around Wisata Hotel, and don't go all the way to the bemo or bus stations.) Local bemos stop at designated places around the city.

Taxis don't cruise for fares; they hang out in the centre on the corner of Jalan Said Perintah, opposite the Rumah Makan Roda Baru.

AROUND PULAU AMBON
Diving

Pulau Ambon, like many nearby islands, offers exciting diving opportunities virtually all year round (roughest between April and June). One or two travel agencies in Kota Am-bon offer some diving hire and trips, but the best place is the Ambon Dive Centre (☎ 55685), opposite the entrance to the Namalatu beach.

INDONESIA

Hila

Hila's strategic position on the north coast has resulted in a long and fascinating pre-colonial and colonial history. Originally built by the Portuguese in 1512, then taken over by the Dutch East India Company (VOC) in the early 17th century, the magnificently restored **Benteng Amsterdam** fort in Hila is the best of its kind in Maluku. A few minutes walk away are the **Wapauwe mosque** (built in 1414), and the quaint **Immanuel Church** (built in 1580, but extensively restored since). Direct buses (2500 rp; one hour – more regular early in the morning) leave from the Batu Merah terminal.

Beaches

A lovely beach not far from the city is **Natsepa**. There are a few restaurants and places to stay; the best, *Bungalow Vaneysa (☎ 61451)*, is right on the beach. Take the Passo or Suli bemo (2000 rp).

In the north-east, **Liang** and nearby **Hunimua** have many secluded beaches but nowhere to stay. **Amahusu** isn't really a beach but is famous as the finishing point for the annual Darwin to Ambon Yacht Race.

The best beaches are south of the city, at **Namalatu**, and nearby at **Latuhalat**. Both are easily accessible from Kota Ambon by direct bemo (1200 rp) and have great snorkelling. At Latuhalat, there are two resorts – *Santai Beach Resort* and *Lelisa Beach Resort* – with nice bungalows from 80,000 rp, and the popular *Homestay Europa*, with homey singles/doubles for 35,000/40,000 rp.

BANDA ISLANDS

The Bandas are an irresistible cluster of islands south-east of Ambon. Various European colonial powers fought for centuries over Banda's spices, and have left a number of forts and colonial houses. With some stunning island and volcanic scenery, and diving, the Bandas are an increasingly popular place to spend some time. Bandaneira, the main village in the Bandas, is situated on the most populous island, Pulau Neira.

Bandaneira

The Bandas are still not geared towards mass tourism. The Bandas offer some extraordinary scuba and skin diving. You can hire snorkelling equipment, boats and guides from local hotels, which are also the best source of diving info.

Information Bandaneira has no bank, so stock up in Ambon. The tourist information counter at the airport is often closed. The post office, near Benteng Nassau, is quaint but often closed, while the incongruously large Telkom office, a becak ride away from hotels, never closes.

Museums & Houses Bandaneira has a number of delightfully restored colonial buildings worth seeing. The **Rumah Budaya Museum** has a small collection of cannons, old coins, modern paintings and Portuguese helmets.

Two homes once occupied by independence heroes, Mohammed Hatta and Sutan Syahrir, have been well restored, and include a lot of memorabilia about their lives. Also worth a look is the Dutch VOC **Governor's Palace**, on the waterfront, and the **Dutch Church** (built in 1680).

Forts Built by the VOC in 1611, the imposing **Benteng Belgica** stands above Bandaneira and offers staggering views of Gunung Api. Below, **Benteng Nassau**, built by the Dutch in 1609 (on the stone foundations laid, but later abandoned, by the Portuguese in 1529) is in need of restoration.

Places to Stay & Eat The best places to stay are the homestays in Bandaneira, which charge from 25,000 rp per person, including three good meals. The best are *Pondok Wisata Rosmina (☎ 21145)* on Jalan Kujali; the *Matahari*, just off Jalan Pelabuhan; and *Likes*, further up the street, both the latter have magnificent sea views.

Good value and slightly more expensive are *Flamboyan Guest House (☎ 21233)* and *Brantz Guest House (☎ 21068)*, both on Jalan Syahrir, and *Delfika I Guest House (☎ 21027)* on Jalan Gereja Tua.

Getting There & Away Three times a week Merpati flies to Ambon; twice via Amahai on Pulau Seram. Flights can be cancelled and are often overbooked. The Merpati office (☎ 21041) is on Jalan Pelabuhan.

Every two weeks the Pelni liner *Rinjani* does a handy trip during the day between Ambon and Bandaneira, and then on to south-east Maluku and Irian Jaya, and back again. Other smaller, less comfortable boats, such as the Perintis ship KM *Iweri*, infrequently link Bandaneira with Ambon, and with the Irian Jayan coast.

Getting Around Bandaneira and Pulau Neira are easy to walk around, although there are a handful of becaks. From the airport, take a free hotel bemo, a public bemo, or even walk for about 15 minutes to your hotel. All sorts of longboats, speedboats and canoes can be rented from the fish market area.

PULAU TERNATE & TIDORE

These islands were one of the first places where the Portuguese (in 1511) and, later, the Dutch established themselves in Maluku. Once bitter rivals, the two islands are littered with the ruins of old European forts, great beaches and beautiful scenery. With air and boat connections to Manado, in northern Sulawesi, Ternate is an ideal place to stop over for a few days.

Kota Ternate

Orientation & Information A lot of places in Kota Ternate are on, or just parallel to, the main street, Jalan Pahlawan Revolusi, which stretches from the Ternate port in the south to the bemo terminal and market.

The tourist office (☎ 22044) is in the governor's office, on Jalan Pahlawan Revolusi. Also on this street are Bank Exim and Bank Danamon for changing money, the post office and, next door, the Telkom office.

Kedaton Sultan Built around 1250, the Sultan's Palace lies just back from Jalan Sultan Baballuh, the road leading to the airport. It's now a **museum** containing an absorbing collection of Portuguese cannons, Dutch helmets and armour, and memorabilia of the past sultans. The best time to find it open is weekday mornings.

Benteng Oranye Opposite the bemo terminal, this fort was built by the Dutch in 1607 on top of an undated Malay fortress. It hasn't been restored, but a walk around gives you a good idea of its former opulence.

Places to Stay The cheapest places are around the entrance to the Ternate port but they're often dreadful. Perhaps the best of this lot are the penginapans *Permata* and *Keluarga* (☎ 22250).

Along Jalan Ake Manako, the family-run but noisy *Wisma Sejahtera* (☎ 21139) is OK at 20,000/25,000 rp for singles/doubles with mandi. On the same street, *Wisma Nusantara* (☎ 21086) is similarly priced.

On Jalan Bosoiri, the central *Hotel Indah* (☎ 21334) is not good value but is clean, with rooms from 27,500/38,500 rp. *Hotel El Shinta* (☎ 21050), on Jalan Pahlawan Revolusi, has a range of rooms starting at 30,250/ 41,250 rp.

Places to Eat Several cheap *Padang restaurants* huddle around the Ternate port.

On Jalan Pahlawan Revolusi, the *Gamalama Restaurant* is good and cheap. On the same street, the *Restoran Garuda* is popular, with a good selection from 6000 rp a plate, but beware of the booming karaoke.

Worth a 10 minute walk north of the terminal, *Bambu Kuring* has an attractive setting and very good, reasonably priced meals.

Getting There & Away Ternate is the hub for northern Maluku. Merpati flies almost daily to Ambon (426,000 rp) and Manado (352,300 rp). The Merpati office (☎ 21651) is on Jalan Bosoiri 81.

Boat Every two weeks, the Pelni liners *Ciremai* and *Umsini* link Ternate with Bitung (northern Sulawesi) and with Sorong (Irian Jaya), and the *Lambelu* comes from Bitung and goes to Ambon (but not vice versa). Perintis and other regular boats go to Pulau Halmahera, Pulau Bacan, Ambon and Sulawesi – information is posted around the various ports.

The ports can be a little confusing. Two ports, only a few hundred metres apart at Bastiong, a few kilometres south of Kota Ternate, have ferries and speedboats to Tidore, Halmahera and the Bacan Islands. Another larger port in Kota Ternate itself caters for Pelni liners, and larger boats to Sulawesi and Ambon.

Getting Around The airport is close to Kota Ternate. You can get a taxi for 10,000 rp, or walk down to the main road from the terminal and catch a bemo for a few hundred rp. The city is small enough to walk around.

Around Pulau Ternate

There are plenty of places to visit around the island during day trips from the city on public transport, or by chartering a bemo for about 15,000 rp per hour.

Forts Built in 1512 by the Portuguese, and restored by the Dutch in 1610, **Benteng Tolukko** is one of the better forts on the island. Near Bastiong, the 1540 Portuguese **Benteng Kalamata** has recently been restored, and consequently has lost a lot of its charm. Still, the setting is pretty, and it's worth a look.

Lakes & Beaches Not far from Takome in the west is **Danau Tolire Besar** (not the scruffy, nearby Danau Tolire Kecil), a stunning, deep volcanic lake (1000 rp by bemo). A trail from the main road leads to the lake, which is believed to have crocodiles, and even the wreckage of a WWII plane.

The beaches are mostly black (volcanic) sand. The best are at **Sulamadaha** (where there is one losmen), picturesque **Pulau Maitara** (a very short boat trip from Rum, on Pulau Tidore) and **Afetaduma**.

Gunung Api Gamalama Completely dominating the island, Gamalama volcano has erupted fiercely many times over the centuries, most recently in late 1994. With a guide (ask at the tourist office or Hotel Merdeka) and some effort, you can trek to the top in a few hours.

Pulau Tidore

Pulau Tidore, the centre of the Central Halmahera District, is less appealing than Pulau Ternate and doesn't have the facilities of its more developed neighbour, but is worth a day trip from Kota Ternate.

In and around **Soa Siu**, the capital of Tidore, there are some **hot springs**, **nice beaches**, an interesting **market** and **Gunung Kiematubu**, which can be climbed or explored. Between Rum and Soa Siu are the compelling but decrepit **Benteng Tohula**, and the engaging (but often closed) **Sultan's Memorial Museum**. Soa Siu has a couple of losmen, but there is no need to stay there.

Speedboats (1250 rp) go every few minutes, and other boats less often, between Bastiong and Rum in northern Tidore.

Irian Jaya

Irian Jaya, the Indonesian side of the island of New Guinea, was only acquired from the Dutch in 1963. Since it had no racial or historical connection with the other Indonesian islands, some interesting arm-bending had to be conducted to get the Dutch to hand it over. Indonesian mining and transmigration have not gone unopposed by some Irianese, particularly the independence movement known as the Free Papua Organisation (OPM), which still engages in some rebellious activities against the Indonesian government.

Irian Jaya is over 400,000 sq km of mostly impenetrable forest and mountains (some permanently snow-capped) with up to 250 designated cultural sub-groups speaking around 500 different languages. It is one of the few areas in the Asia-Pacific region where traditional cultures still survive (but only just). Almost all visitors head to the Baliem Valley – the only part of the interior generally accessible to tourism – via Biak and/or Jayapura, but Irian Jaya has a lot more to offer the traveller with time to spare.

Climate

Generally, the driest – and best – time to visit is from May to October, although it can rain anywhere, anytime. Strong winds and rain are usual along the north coast from November to March. Along some of the south coast, however, it can be wild and woolly from April to October, but this is the dry season in Merauke. The best time for the Baliem Valley is March to August, when the days are drier and cooler, but the nights are usually cold all year around.

Flora & Fauna

Around 75% of Irian Jaya is dense forest in which a unique range of flora and fauna flourishes. Species of the *cenderawasih*, or bird of paradise, still inhabit the remote areas of the Bird's Head Peninsula and Pulau Yapen, and around the southern coastal regions there are large cassowaries and storks. Bandicoots and possums live in many forest regions, and around Merauke wallabies are not uncommon.

The forests have nearly 3000 types of orchids, but be careful because there are also plenty of poisonous snakes and 800 species of spiders. Mangroves and the vital sago palm cover a lot of the coast while eucalypts abound in the south-east. With some effort, you can visit national parks in northern Pulau Biak, between Agats and Nabire, and near Merauke.

Permits

It's possible to visit Jayapura, Sentani, Sorong and possibly Biak without a *surat jalan*, or travel permit, but for other areas, such as Merauke, Agats and the Asmat region, Manokwari and Nabire, as well as Wamena and the Baliem Valley, you will need one.

A surat jalan can easily be obtained at major police stations; it's particularly straightforward in Jayapura, Sentani and Biak. You need two photographs (black & white will

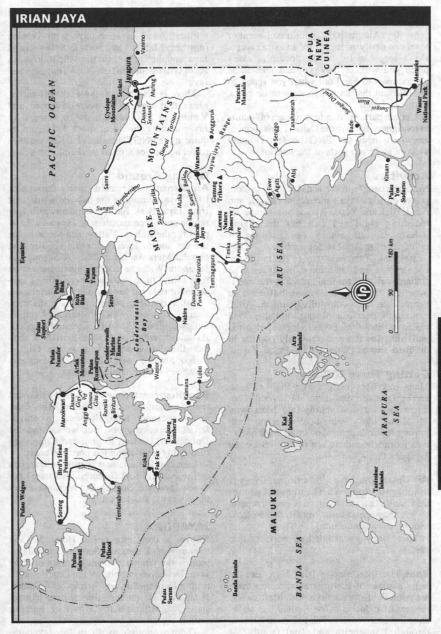

IRIAN JAYA

INDONESIA

do); there is often an 'administration fee' of about 5000 rp; and it should be issued on the same day. Alternatively, your travel agent or hotel can easily arrange it for an extra charge. Don't forget to list on the document every place you will, or may, go, and take some photocopies to hand out when you report to the relevant district police stations or check into your hotel.

Certain parts of Irian Jaya remain off-limits to foreigners, namely the Danau Paniai region, anywhere near the PNG border, Gunung Trikora and most parts of the interior.

Activities

Not surprisingly, most activities for visitors centre on Irian Jaya's mountains, people and coast. Biak and Yapen islands boast some astonishing coral and fish but the diving industry is in its infancy. The best time for diving is from April to September.

Trekking is the best way to really see the countryside and traditional lifestyles. The Baliem Valley is the main place in the interior where trekking is allowed, but it's also permissible, and worthwhile, around the Arfak mountains near Manokwari, and the flood plains north of Merauke. Organised bird-watching tours are increasingly popular in the Bird's Head Peninsula and Pulau Yapen.

Getting There & Away

Many travellers just get on a flight to Biak and/or Jayapura, but there are several more interesting ways of getting into Irian Jaya. These include a Pelni boat or plane from Sorong to the delightful colonial town of Fak Fak, from where there is a flight to Biak and Jayapura through Nabire.

Air Unless you have a lot of time, flying is the only way to travel. The transport centres for Irian Jaya are Sorong, Biak and Jayapura, so you may spend some time in these places waiting for a connection.

There are no scheduled air services into PNG.

Boat The sheer size of Irian Jaya, and the large number of transmigrants, means there are good Pelni connections with Maluku and the rest of Indonesia. The *Rinjani* has an interesting connection to Fak Fak from Ambon, through Bandaneira and Tual (south-east Maluku), and also goes to Surabaya (Java) and Ujung Pandang (Sulawesi); the *Tatamailau* covers the southern coast of Irian Jaya,

and connects it with south-east Maluku and Nusa Tenggara; the *Ciremai* connects the northern coast of Irian Jaya with Ternate (northern Maluku) and ports in Sulawesi and Java; and the *Dobonsolo* links the Irian Jayan north coast with Ambon, Nusa Tenggara and Java.

There is also a boat, the *MV Narimo Express* that travels between Jayapura and Vanimo in PNG once or twice a week. In Jayapura ring the agent on ☎ 31449, or inquire at the PNG Consulate, PT Kuwera Jaya travel agency or around the Pelni ports.

Getting Around

Air Merpati is the main carrier throughout Irian Jaya. Sorong is the hub for north-west Irian Jaya; Biak for the Cenderawasih Bay region and for connections to Jayapura; Jayapura for the Baliem Valley; and Merauke for the far south. Except for the regular and popular Merauke-Jayapura-Biak-Sorong and Jayapura-Wamena routes, most planes are tiny Twin-Otters, which are sometimes cancelled or delayed for any number of reasons.

Other possible alternatives are the missionary services, MAF (Mission Aviation Fellowship) and AMA (Associated Missions Aviation), which will take tourists if they have the room and have some notice. Trigana Cargo Service will also take passengers between Jayapura and Wamena.

Boat Both coasts are well covered by several regular, comfortable Pelni liners. The *Tatamailau* meanders along the southern coast as far as Merauke every four weeks; and the *Dobonsolo, Umsini, Rinjani* and *Cirimai* do fortnightly trips along the northern coast.

Less comfortable and regular boats, such as the Perintis KM *Ilosangi*, also travel between Jayapura, Sorong and Merauke every three weeks, and back again.

JAYAPURA

Known in the Dutch era as Hollandia, and later as Kota Bahru and Soekarnopura, Jayapura is the capital and major town of Irian Jaya. Deliberately built by the Dutch next to the border of the former German New Guinea, Jayapura is an uninteresting modern Indonesian city, although it has a nice harbour setting.

There's enough to do in the Jayapura-Sentani area to make it worth a stay of a few days on your way to or from the Baliem Valley.

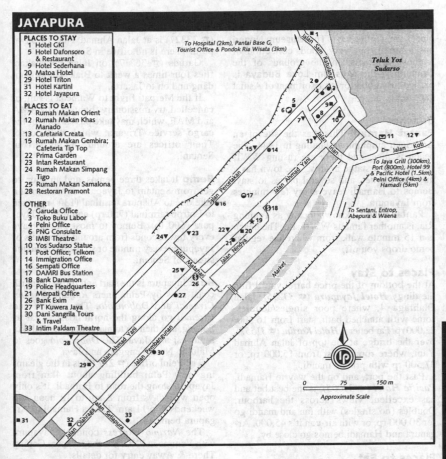

JAYAPURA

PLACES TO STAY
1 Hotel GKI
5 Hotel Dafonsoro & Restaurant
9 Hotel Sederhana
20 Matoa Hotel
29 Hotel Triton
31 Hotel Kartini
32 Hotel Jayapura

PLACES TO EAT
7 Rumah Makan Orient
12 Rumah Makan Khas Manado
13 Cafetaria Creata
15 Rumah Makan Gembira; Cafeteria Tip Top
22 Prima Garden
23 Intan Restaurant
24 Rumah Makan Simpang Tigo
25 Rumah Makan Samalona
28 Restoran Pramont

OTHER
2 Garuda Office
3 Toko Buku Labor
4 Pelni Office
6 PNG Consulate
8 IMBI Theatre
10 Yos Sudarso Statue
11 Post Office; Telkom
14 Immigration Office
16 Sempati Office
17 DAMRI Bus Station
18 Bank Danamon
19 Police Headquarters
26 Merpati Office
26 Bank Exim
27 PT Kuwera Jaya
30 Dani Sangrila Tours & Travel
33 Intim Paldam Theatre

To Hospital (2km), Pantai Base G,
Tourist Office & Pondok Ria Wisata (3km)

Teluk Yos Sudarso

Jalan Sam Ratulang

Jalan Irian

Jalan Koti

Jalan Ahmad Yani

Jalan Percetakan

Jalan Nindya

Jalan Matahari

Market

Jalan Pembangunan

Jalan Ahmad Yani

Jalan Olahraga

Jalan Setiapura

To Jaya Grill (300km),
Port (800m), Hotel 99
& Pacific Hotel (1.5km),
Pelni Office (4km) &
Hamadi (5km)

To Sentani, Entrop,
Abepura & Waena

0   75   150 m

Approximate Scale

INDONESIA

Orientation

Just about everything you will need in Jayapura is confined to Jalan Ahmad Yani, and, parallel to it, Jalan Percetakan.

Information

The tourist office (☎ 33381, ext 2441), open weekdays from 7 am to 3 pm, is a bemo ride north from Jayapura, in the governor's office on Jalan Soa Siu Dok II, but don't waste your time. The best bank to change money is Bank BII on Jalan Percetakan.

The post office, which has an Internet centre, and adjacent Telkom office are along the waterfront. The police station for Baliem Valley permits is on Jalan Ahmad Yani.

Several good travel agencies can arrange local diving and sightseeing trips, as well as tours to the Baliem Valley and Asmat region:

Dani Sangrila Tours & Travel
   (☎ 31060) Jalan Pembangunan 19, Jayapura
PT Kuwera Jaya
   (☎ 31583) Jalan Ahmad Yani 39, Jayapura –
   especially good for diving

PNG Consulate The PNG consulate (☎ 31-250), open weekdays from 8 am to 4 pm, is at Jalan Percetakan 28. All foreigners need a visa to enter PNG, and these are only issued if you have a confirmed air or sea ticket out of PNG. A two-month visa takes a day to issue, and you will need one photo and 20,000 rp.

Museums

Along the Sentani-Abepura bemo route, two places are worth a look. The **Museum Negeri** has a small, but very good, collection of Irianese artefacts. In the grounds of the University, the **Museum Loka Budaya** is particularly good for its assortment of Asmat carvings.

Beaches

Pantai Hamadi This was the site of an American amphibious landing in 1944. The beach is nice, and there are rusting WWII wrecks and a statue nearby. The town has a bustling market, and several places to stay. Bemos to Hamadi leave every few minutes from Jayapura.

Pantai Base G, known locally as Tanjung Ria, is another famous WWII site. The beach is a 15 minute walk from where the regular bemo drops you off.

Places to Stay

At the bottom of the price barrel you'll find the dingy *Hotel Jayapura* (☎ *33216*), Jalan Olahraga 4, where poor singles/doubles, some with attached bath, start from 16,500/22,000 rp. Far better is *Hotel Kartini* (☎ *31557*), over the bridge at the top of Jalan Ahmad Yani, where rooms cost from 15,000 rp, or 37,500 rp with private mandi.

Past the port, and on the way to Hamadi, *Pacific Hotel* (☎ *34005*), is the best bet and has excellent views across the harbour. Doubles (no singles) with fan and mandi go for 30,000 rp, or with air-con it's 45,000. Argapura and Hamadi bemos go close by.

Places to Eat

Night warung can be found along Jalan Ahmad Yani and around the waterfront.

Along Jalan Percetakan, *Rumah Makan Gembira* and *Rumah Makan Simpang Tigo* are simple and good, as is the restaurant in *Hotel Dafonsoro*. *Cafeteria Tip Top* next to the Gembira is a popular place for a light meal and a cool drink.

For the same views as the expensive *Jaya Grill*, *Rumah Makan Khas Manado*, on the way to the port, is recommended – watch your head!

Opposite the Merpati office, the *Prima Garden* is good for Irianese coffee and cakes.

Getting There & Away

Air Merpati flies several times a week to Biak, and Ambon; regularly to Nabire; at least twice a day to Wamena; as well as to Ujung Pandang and Denpasar. Merpati (☎ 33327) is at Jalan Ahmad Yani 15, Jayapura. There is no office in Sentani.

Garuda (☎ 36217), on Jalan Percetakan, flies four times a week to Biak, Ujung Pandang and on to Jakarta.

If the Merpati flight to Wamena is full, or cancelled, try missionary flights run by AMA and MAF, which may take passengers, or the cargo service Trigana, which will do so. Their offices are around the airport in Sentani.

Bemo It takes three bemos, and an hour, to get from Sentani to Jayapura. From Sentani, take one to Abepura terminal (1300 rp), then to Entrop terminal (750 rp) and then to Jayapura (600 rp). Bemos to most places leave every few seconds from around the streets of Jayapura; every minute or so from around the streets of Sentani.

Boat Jayapura is the start and finish for north coast runs by Pelni liners *Rinjani*, *Umsini*, *Ciremai* and *Dobonsolo*. The *Rinjani* and *Ciremai* go along the north coast as far as Sorong, and then on to major ports in Maluku, Sulawesi and Java. The *Dobonsolo* goes to Maluku, Nusa Tenggara and Java.

The Pelni office (☎ 21270) is in the gleaming new Pelni building about 4km from Jayapura along the road to Hamadi. It's only open weekdays from 8 am to 12 noon and weekends 8 to 11 am. Take a Hamadi or Argapura bemo.

The *Narimo Express* connects Jayapura with Vanimo in PNG. See the Jayapura Getting There & Away entry for details.

Getting Around

Jayapura airport is at Sentani, 36km from Jayapura. It's 45,000 rp by taxi from the airport to Jayapura, or you can do it by bemo for 2650 rp.

SENTANI

Sentani, next to Jayapura's airport (36km from Jayapura), and near the shores of the magnificent Danau Sentani, is quieter, cooler (marginally) and more convenient than Jayapura. Sentani has just about all the facilities you may need, so many people prefer to stay here.

The small town is compact, with most facilities on Jalan Kemiri Sentani Kota, the main road to Jayapura.

Information
The post office is on the main road; Telkom just behind it. The Bank Exim on the main road changes money.

Danau Sentani
This magnificent lake is worth a visit to Sentani in itself. You may well see the 9630 hectare lake and its 19 islands as you fly in, and while travelling along the Sentani-Jayapura road.

Renting a boat around the lake can be difficult – try at Yahim or Yabaso harbours or, easier but dearer, at the Yougwa Restaurant (see Places to Eat).

For **breathtaking views**, take a bemo up Gunung Ifar to the **Tugu MacArthur** statue. Alternatively, walk along Jalan Yos Sudarso past Hotel Mansapur Rani for an easy hour to the lake's shore.

If you want to stay out here, *Pondok Wisata Yougwa* (☎ 71570) has delightful rooms overlooking the lake for 85,000 rp.

Depapre
Good **beaches** and **diving** around Depapre are also accessible by bemo from Sentani, which is about 20km to the south-east.

Places to Stay
The popular *Hotel Ratna I* (☎ 91435), just off the main road, is the best value with air-con (only) singles/doubles with mandi for 33,000/44,000 rp including breakfast, free tea or coffee and a lift to the airport on departure (although it's only a few minutes walk).

Close by is the friendly *Hotel Minang Jaya* (☎ 91067), which is poor value by comparison. Small rooms with fan and common bath cost 30,000/35,000 rp, slightly more with mandi, and 50,000/55,000 rp with air-con. A miserly breakfast is included.

Hotel Semeru (☎ 91447), closer to the airport entrance, is OK at 32,500 rp per room with fan, or 42,500 rp with air-con.

In the mid-range, there's the new *Hotel Ratna II* (☎ 92277), also close to the airport, with pleasant air-con rooms at 60,000 rp.

Places to Eat
There are plenty of *rumah makan* along the main street, and night time *warung* can be found at the intersection of the airport and main roads.

Restoran Mickey is about the only eatery in town that offers an alternative to local food, and so is popular with travellers and the numerous expats (mostly missionaries) who live in Sentani. Main dishes cost from 5000 rp, or you could go the whole hog and have Ayam Kentucky Mickey (9000 rp) or 'baked deer on stick'.

The *Yougwa Restaurant*, on the Sentani-Abepura road, is definitely worth a visit for the views of Danau Sentani and the good, reasonably priced food.

PULAU BIAK
Biak, an important part of the battle for the Pacific in WWII, has numerous remnants of those horrific days, and is also a major Indonesian naval base. The island is small and has several attractions, although transport is limited in the north. The only major town, Kota Biak, and particularly the seaside villages of Bosnik and Korim, were heavily damaged by an earthquake and subsequent tsunami in early 1996.

Kota Biak
Orientation & Information Kota Biak is a fairly compact town. A lot of what you need is along Jalan Ahmad Yani, Jalan Sudirman and Jalan Imam Bonjol, all of which meet at the Bank Exim building. This bank, and the nearby Bank Bumi Daya, will change money.

The 24 hour Telkom office, the main post office, and the tourist office (☎ 21663; open weekdays from 7.30 am to 3 pm) are a bemo ride away along the road to the airport. The police station on Jalan Diponegoro is an easy place to get permits for the region and for the Baliem Valley.

Museum Cenderawasih On Jalan Sisingamangaraja, 10 minutes walk east of Hotel Maju, this museum has a mildly interesting stockpile of regional Indonesian artefacts and some WWII memorabilia. Ask someone around the back of the museum to open up for you.

Places to Stay The cheapest are *Hotel Solo* (☎ 21397) on Jalan Monginsidi, where dingy rooms with paper-thin walls cost from 15,000 rp and newer better ones start at 30,000 rp; and the rambling and inconvenient *Hotel Sinar Kayu* (☎ 22137), on Jalan Sisingamangaraja, for 15,600/31,200 rp for singles/doubles.

Hotel Maju (☎ 21841), on Jalan Imam Bonjol, is better value, with singles/doubles from 24,200/35,100 rp with mandi – ask for quieter rooms at the back.

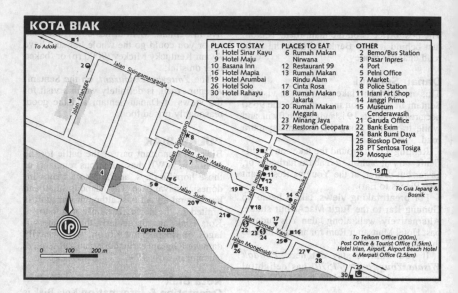

KOTA BIAK

To Adoki

Jalan Sisingamangaraja

Jalan Erlangga

Jalan Diponegoro

Jalan Selat Makassar

Jalan Sudirman

Jalan Imam Bonjol

Jalan Pramuka

Jalan Ahmad Yani

Jalan Monginsidi

Yapen Strait

0   100   200 m

To Gua Jepang & Bonsik

To Telkom Office (200m),
Post Office & Tourist Office (1.5km),
Hotel Irian, Airport, Airport Beach Hotel
& Merpati Office (2.5km)

PLACES TO STAY	PLACES TO EAT	OTHER
1 Hotel Sinar Kayu	6 Rumah Makan	2 Bemo/Bus Station
9 Hotel Maju	Nirwana	3 Pasar Inpres
10 Basana Inn	12 Restaurant 99	4 Port
16 Hotel Mapia	13 Rumah Makan	5 Pelni Office
19 Hotel Arumbai	Rindu Alam	7 Market
26 Hotel Solo	17 Cinta Rosa	8 Police Station
30 Hotel Rahayu	18 Rumah Makan	11 Iriani Art Shop
	Jakarta	14 Janggi Prima
	20 Rumah Makan	15 Museum
	Megaria	Cenderawasih
	23 Minang Jaya	21 Garuda Office
	27 Restoran Cleopatra	22 Bank Exim
		24 Bank Bumi Daya
		25 Bioskop Dewi
		28 PT Sentosa Tosiga
		29 Mosque

More expensive is *Basana Inn* (☎ *22281*), virtually opposite the Maju. It's about the best at 47,000/57,000 rp with welcome air-con and hot water.

Either side of the airport are two places that are good value. To the west, the huge *Hotel Irian* (☎ *21939*) has an agreeable lawn area to sit and admire the sea views and rooms from 38,720/55,660 rp; and to the east, the newer *Hotel Marasi* (☎ *21496*) is clean, quiet and has good service for 46,400/71,600 rp with meals.

Places to Eat Kota Biak isn't blessed with the greatest range of places to eat. *Warung* congregate around the markets and near the bemo/bus station.

On Jalan Imam Bonjol, the *Rumah Makan Jakarta* and *Restaurant 99* are worth a try.

Better are the *Cinta Rosa*, near Hotel Mapia, and, over the road, the *Restoran Cleopatra*. Opposite the Pelni office, on Jalan Sudirman, the *Nirwana* serves wonderful cold fruit drinks and cakes.

Getting There & Away Biak is one of Irian Jaya's transport hubs, so many flights go through here. Merpati flies several times a week to Jayapura; almost daily to Manok-wari; three times a week to Nabire, Ambon and Ujung Pandang; daily to nearby Serui on Pulau Yapen and tiny Pulau Numfor. The

Merpati office (☎ 21386) is opposite the airport.

Garuda (☎ 21416), Jalan Sudirman 3, flies four times a week to Jayapura, Ujung Pandang and Jakarta.

Boat Pelni liners *Ciremai* and *Dobonsolo* stop in Biak and then go on to major ports in Java, Maluku, Nusa Tenggara and Sulawesi every two weeks. Other Perintis boats also regularly stop in Biak. The Pelni office (☎ 21065) is at Jalan Sudirman 37.

Getting Around The Frans Kaisiepo airport is a short bemo ride from town; there is no need to take a taxi. Much of Kota Biak can be covered on foot but the post office, tourist office, main market and bemo/bus station are short bemo rides from most hotels.

AROUND PULAU BIAK

While Kota Biak isn't that exciting, the island does have several interesting places to justify a stopover. All of these can be visited in day trips from the city. Bemos and buses leave regularly from the terminal next to the main market. Chartered bemos around the island will cost a negotiable 25,000 rp per hour.

Gua Jepang

Actually a tunnel, the 'Japanese Cave' pro-vides a chilling impression of a WWII battle where up to 5000 Japanese were killed by US bombs and fires. A museum next door has a fascinating array of WWII memorabilia. The easiest way to the cave is to take a bemo heading towards Bosnik, get off near Dennis Orchard Park (which is nothing to write home about) and walk a few hundred metres up the hill.

Taman Burung dan Anggrek
On the way to Bosnik, the Bird & Orchid Park is worth a quick stop. It's about as close as you will probably get to a bird of paradise.

Wardo
The tiny village of Wardo, set in a pretty bay in the west, is definitely worth a visit. You can hire a boat and guide for an alluring ride along an overgrown jungle river to the **Wapsdori waterfalls**. Climb up a shaky ladder for a dip at the top. Bemos take an hour and cost 3000 rp.

Beaches
The island is littered with pretty beaches and beachside villages, although some were devastated by the 1996 tidal wave. **Bosnik**, another famous WWII site, with boats to the nearby **Padaido Islands**, has a small market and a lovely beach. It's an easy 30 minutes by regular bemo (1200 rp).

Korim (1700 rp; 1½ hours) is further away, and not as nice as Bosnik, but the trip there is interesting.

Diving
Although Pulau Biak and the nearby Padaido Islands boast some of the best scuba diving in Indonesia, the local diving industry is frustratingly undeveloped and unorganised. You *may* be able to rent a boat and guide, but there is no reliable equipment for hire, or instructors. Bring your own gear, and ask around at the travel agencies Janggi Prima (☎ 22973), Jalan Pramuka 5, Hotel Biak Beach, at Bosnik, or the tourist office. The best time to dive is between April and September.

CENDERAWASIH BAY
Stretching from Manokwari to the far east of Pulau Yapen, and incorporating the Taman Laut Cenderawasih, the Cenderawasih Bay region is easily the most underrated and under-visited part of Irian Jaya. With outstanding diving and trekking, wildlife, deserted beaches, isolated islands, traditional cultures

and easy-going towns, the region's potential is, however, still hindered by limited transport and government prohibitions.

Manokwari
The first place in Irian Jaya to be inhabited by missionaries (in 1855), Manokwari is easy to get around and well connected, and nearby there's **trekking** in the Arfak Mountains, the Anggi Lakes and islands such as Pulau Rumberpon.

In Manokwari itself, an easy 5km walk takes you through the lush **Taman Gunung Meja** park, which has plenty of butterflies and a Japanese WWII memorial. A good beach, **Pasir Sen Babai**, is easy to get to, and a canoe trip to **Pulau Mansinam** is a real must.

A good of range of cheap accommodation includes *Hotel Pusaka Sederhana* (☎ 21263), on Jalan Bandung; *Hotel Apose* (☎ 21369), opposite the Merpati office; and *Hotel Arfak* (☎ 21293), Jalan Brawijaya, for city views and decaying charm.

Merpati flies regularly to Biak. The Merpati office (☎ 21133) is on Jalan Kota Baru. All four of the Pelni liners servicing the north coast stop in Manokwari.

Anggi Lakes
Set 2030m high in the Arfak Mountains, the twin lakes of Danau Gigi and Danau Gita offer exquisite scenery and wildlife, and excellent walking and swimming. From Manokwari, Merpati is scheduled to fly to Anggi twice a week, but this is unreliable. Alternatively, catch a regular bus to Ransiki (1200 rp; three hours) and ask at the district office for a guide to the lakes. From Ransiki the trek takes two or three days. You will need to bring all your own gear, and remember that it is always cold at night. At Anggi, you can stay at the home of the village head.

Nabire
Nabire is a worthy stopover on the way to Biak, Jayapura or Wamena. It's a particularly pleasant town, with wide streets, and nearby beaches and islands to explore. And for some reason no one (yet) has learnt how to say 'hello mister'!

The best places to stay are *Hotel Nusantara* (☎ 21180) – which also houses the Merpati office (☎ 21591) – on Jalan Pemuda, for around 30,000 rp; and *Hotel Anggrek* (☎ 21066), on Jalan Pepera. Try the *warung* on the waterfront for huge baked fish.

INDONESIA

Merpati flies daily to Biak, and to Jayapura almost every day.

The Danau Paniai region, which has as much potential as the Baliem Valley for experiencing unique scenery and culture, is still off limits to travellers, but this may change. If regulations allow, you can take a Merpati flight to Enarotali.

BALIEM VALLEY

Easily the most popular destination in Irian Jaya, and the most accessible place in the interior, is the Baliem Valley, where the Dani people were only 'discovered' in 1938. While the Danis have adopted many modern conveniences, and the main town, Wamena, has some up-to-date facilities, the valley is one of the truly fascinating traditional areas still left in the world.

Even in Wamena, a surprising number of Dani men still wear penis gourds and nothing else. You'll regularly see Dani women, dressed only in a grass skirt, carrying string bags from their heads, heavily loaded with vegetables, and even babies and valuable pigs.

The Danis maintain their polygamous marriage system – a man may have as many wives as he can afford. Brides have to be paid for in pigs, the man must give five or six pigs to the family of the wife. Grass skirts usually indicate that a woman is unmarried, although in some parts of the valley married women also wear them. One of the more unusual, but increasingly outdated, customs is for women to amputate part of their fingers when a close relative dies.

For several days every August, Wamena and nearby villages host a spectacular tourist festival with pig feasts, mock wars and traditional dancing.

Wamena

The main town in the Baliem Valley, Wamena is a neat, spread-out place. Although there's not much in the town itself, it's a good base from which to explore nearby villages and the countryside. Wamena is expensive compared with the rest of Indonesia but this is understandable as *everything* has to be flown in from Jayapura.

Orientation & Information While the focal point of town is the scruffy Pasar Nayak Market, a lot of what you will need is on, or near, Jalan Trikora. Bank Exim, and the incongruous Bank Rakyat Indonesia, both on Jalan Trikora, change money, but the rates

are dreadful. The post office is on Jalan Timor, and the 24 hour Telkom office on Jalan Thamrin.

The tourist office (☎ 31365) is on Jalan Yos Sudarso about 1km west of town, and is worth a visit.

Surat Jalan You *must* have a surat jalan, or travel permit, if you want to stay in Wamena and the Baliem Valley. You can't get one in Wamena but they're easy to obtain in Biak and Jayapura. On the surat jalan, list every place you wish to visit, and take a few photocopies to give to regional police stations.

Your surat jalan may be checked by the tourist officer on arrival at Wamena airport, and you then have to report to the police station on Jalan Safri Darwin to have the permit stamped, unless your travel agency, guide or hotel can do it for you. It's all very straightforward but at both places you need to have a photocopy to hand over. You must also report to the local police if you stay outside of Wamena, eg at sub-district centres such as Jiwika and Kurima, but this is usually unnecessary if you're trekking to remote areas. Some more isolated places in the valley may be off limits; the police station in Wamena will fill you in on the current situation.

Travel Agencies Several good – and some not so good – travel agencies catering for trekking tours of the Baliem Valley have sprung up in Wamena, and in Jayapura (see that section for details). In Wamena, the most reliable agencies are the expensive Best Tours & Travel (☎ 32101), Jalan Trikora, opposite Hotel Trendy; and, one of the first and best, Chandra Nusantara Tours & Travel (☎ 31293), Jalan Trikora 17.

Places to Stay Hotel Sri Kandy (☎ 31367), Jalan Irian 16, is quiet, friendly and probably the best value in town. Singles/doubles with attached mandi cost 40,000/55,000 rp including a small breakfast.

Hotel Trendy (☎ 31092), at the north end of Jalan Trikora, has a terrible name but good rooms for the same price, although they can be a bit gloomy.

Nayak Hotel (☎ 31067), directly opposite the airport, has large rooms with mandi from 44,000/66,000 rp, and is a good option.

Hotel Anggrek (☎ 31242), on Jalan Ambon, is clean and comfortable, although overpriced these days at 60,000 rp.

There is very little value in the middle-to-top

range; air-con isn't really needed, and most places don't even offer hot water. The best in this range is *Hotel Baliem Pilama* (☎ *31043*) at Jalan Trikora 177, with singles/doubles around a pleasant courtyard for 58,600/81,000 rp, or 103,000/110,000 rp with hot water, 'bath tube and parabola' (satellite TV).

Baliem Cottages (☎ *31370*), on Jalan Thamrin, has large, quiet and modern 'Dani huts' from 55,000 rp.

See Around the Baliem Valley for cheap alternatives – mostly Dani-style huts – in villages near Wamena.

Places to Eat There's a number of Padang-style places on Jalan Sulawesi behind the market, but they're pretty basic.

The *Rumah Makan Mas Budi* on Jalan Pathinusara is the best place for food; and *Kantin Bu Lies*, next to the airport, is good for simple Indonesian food.

A popular place is the *Cafetaria Nada* on Jalan Thamrin near the Telkom office. They serve a good range of fish and chicken dishes for around 10,000 rp, and novel hot peanut butter bread rolls.

Wamena is officially a 'dry area', so no alcohol is available.

Shopping Souvenir shops selling locally made items of varying quality have sprung up around the market and along Jalan Trikora. Alternatively, you can buy things in the villages or from the increasing number of sellers roaming the streets of Wamena. Naturally, bargaining is the order of the day, and in the villages bartering is also acceptable.

Readily available souvenirs include *noken* (string bags) from 8000 rp to 15,000 rp; intricate hand-woven bracelets; *jogal* or *thali* (grass skirts); *mikak* (necklaces of cowrie shells); the inevitable *horim* (penis gourd) from 2000 rp to 20,000 rp, depending on size and materials; black stone axes for around 15,000 rp (far more for the better ones); and carved bows, arrows and spears from around 10,000 rp.

Getting There & Away Merpati flies at least once a day between Jayapura and Wamena. Flights can be in heavy demand, so book early and reconfirm regularly. Flights are totally dependent on the weather and are often cancelled if the conditions are unfavourable. Don't count on getting back to Jayapura to make a same-day onward connection. The Merpati office (☎ 31488) is at Jalan Trikora 41.

If the Merpati flights are full or cancelled, try Trigana Cargo Service (☎ 31611). They are more expensive (but usually more reliable) than Merpati from Wamena to Jayapura, when the planes are empty, and even more so for the other way. Their office is at the airport.

Getting Around Wamena is easy enough to walk around. There's no shortage of becaks for a very negotiable 500 rp to 1500 rp, although they disappear at night and often, it seems, when it rains!

AROUND THE BALIEM VALLEY

Trekking is certainly the best way to see particular scenery, special ceremonies and more remote cultures. But if you do not have the time, money or inclination to trek, don't be put off coming to the Baliem Valley. With the increasing number of places to stay in the valley, and more transport along new and improving roads, many visitors will be able to see all the traditional people and customs, mummies, markets, scenery and wild pigs they want during day trips from Wamena, Jiwika and Kurima.

Trekking

This is great hiking country but travel light; trails are muddy and slippery. You often have to clamber over stone fences, ford streams and cross trenches and creeks on bridges made of rough wooden planks or a slippery log. Rivers are crossed by dugout canoes or rafts made of three logs loosely lashed together and pushed along with a pole.

It's normally cold at night, and it often rains, so bring warm clothes, an umbrella or jacket, and, if you're camping, a waterproof tent. You can buy food, water and a lot of cooking equipment in Wamena, although it is comparatively expensive. Bring everything else with you.

Staying in village huts, or the homes of teachers or leading local families, should cost from 10,000 rp to 20,000 rp per person per night, or your guide may be able to build makeshift wooden shelters. There are simple Dani-style huts and losmen in a few villages between Akima and Jiwika, as well as in Manda, Kurima and near Wosilimo.

Guides

In Wamena would-be guides will latch onto you as soon as you arrive and, if you show any interest, they can be persistent.

Before committing yourself to a guide, decide if you really want to go trekking (as opposed to day-tripping from Wamena and other villages), ask other travellers and think about where you want to go and for how long.

Prices depend on where you go, for how long, how many in the group and your bargaining power. As a general rule, a good licensed guide will cost from about 30,000 rp to 50,000 rp per day and a porter around 15,000 rp. An all-inclusive price of around 100,000 rp per person per day covers guide, porters, food and accommodation.

Alternatively, the tourist office can arrange 'licensed' guides and porters for you, but this may work out more expensive. There are no proper maps of the Baliem Valley; some hotels sell a passable map, but don't rely on it for trekking.

Baliem Valley – Central & South

Virtually a 'suburb' of Wamena, **Wesaput** is an easy stroll across the runway. The only museum in the valley, the **Palimo Adat Museum**, with its limited collection of local artefacts, is at the end of the trail. On the way, *Wio Silimo Tradisional Hotel* is one of the best Dani-style places around. It costs 20,000 rp per room.

Behind the museum, a long swinging bridge leads to **Pugima**, a flat one hour walk away. Pugima isn't that exciting, but the trail goes past some charming Dani villages and scenery. At the end of Jalan Yos Sudarso, **Sinatma** has charming walks around Sungai Wamena, a market and a swinging bridge.

The road south passes through the village of **Hitigima**. An hour or so on foot from Hitigima (you will need to ask directions or take a guide) are some salt water wells. The road south stops a few kilometres short of **Kurima**, a good base in the south – *Kuak Cottages* losmen is basic but charming. From Kurima, there's more great trekking to places like **Hitugi**, a few hours away. A popular two or three day trek is Wamena-Kurima-Hitugi-Pugima-Wamena.

Baliem Valley – East

Near Pikhe, the northern road crosses mighty Sungai Baliem and passes **Akima**, which is only notable for its mummy. Between Akima and Jiwika, an interesting, flat three to four hour walk, there are several Dani-style huts with Dani-style mandis and breakfast. The better ones are: *Pondok Wisata Dani Home-stay*, just south of Jiwika; *Wiyuk Huts* in Jiwika; and the very pleasant *Pondok Wisata Suroba Indah* in Suroba. **Suroba**, a serene village set 20 minutes off the main road, is worth a stop to admire the countryside and the intricate hanging bridges.

Jiwika (2000 rp by frequent bemo) is a good base. The comfortable *Losmen La'uk* has simple rooms without mandi for 11,000 rp; the same sort of rooms with mandi are less value at 20,000/35,000 rp for singles/doubles. An hour's scramble above the village are some salt wells, and there's a mummy nearby.

North of Jiwika, the **Gua Kotilola** caves are worth a look; ask to be dropped off because there is no sign. In **Wosilimo**, the **Gua Wikuda** caves are more interesting. An hour's walk west of Wosilimo, **Danau Anegerak** has fish and some huts to stay in. From Wosilimo, a hiking trail continues to, and beyond, Pass Valley. Also popular is the one to two day trek from Wosilimo to Pyramid via Meagaima and Pummo.

Public transport continues north to **Manda**, where there are authentic (ie muddy) Dani-style huts and more pretty countryside. From Manda, treks start to the Wolo Valley.

Baliem Valley – West

There isn't a great deal on this side of the valley for trekking, but it's worth a bemo trip anyway as far as **Pyramid**, a graceful missionary village with churches, a theological college, an airstrip and a bustling weekly market. You may be able to stay at **Kimbim**, the nearby sub-district centre. Kimbim is a reasonable place, with some shops and the local police station.

From Pyramid, popular treks go to **Kelila** in the north and to **Pietriver** in the west. If trekking, take the trail from Kimbim to Pummo and along Sungai Baliem to Wamena through Muai, rather than the dull, direct Pyramid-Wamena road.

Danau Habbema, formerly a popular two day trek west from Wamena, is off-limits to foreigners until further notice.

Getting Around

Hopelessly overcrowded bemos go as far south as Kurima; as far north, on the western side of the valley, as Pyramid; and as far north on the eastern side as Manda. To go anywhere else, or to avoid these sardine cans on wheels, you can hire bemos from the terminal from a very negotiable 15,000 rp per hour.

Laos

Laos has been known from antiquity as Lan Xang, or Land of a Million Elephants, and by Vietnam War-era journalists as the Land of a Million Irrelevants. It is one of the least developed and most enigmatic countries in Asia.

Facts about Laos

HISTORY

The country has long been occupied by migrating Thai-Kadais (an ethnolinguistic family that includes Shan, Siamese, Lao and many smaller tribes) and by Hmong-Mien and Mon-Khmer tribal groups practising slash-and-burn cultivation (as they do to this day). The first Lao *meuang* (districts or principalities), however, were consolidated in the 13th century following the invasion of south-western China by Kublai Khan's Mongol hordes.

In the mid-14th century a Khmer-sponsored Lao warlord, Fa Ngum, formed his own kingdom, Lan Xang, around the town of Muang Sawa (now Luang Prabang). In the 17th century Lan Xang split into three warring kingdoms centred on Luang Prabang, Wieng Chan (Vientiane) and Champasak.

By the end of the 18th century most of Laos came under Thai suzerainty but the Vietnamese also demanded tribute. Unable or unwilling to serve two masters, the country went to war with Siam in the 1820s, after which all three kingdoms fell under Thai control. By 1893 colonial French and the Siamese treaties had put Lao territories under the protection of the French.

During WWII, the Japanese occupied Indochina and a Lao resistance group, Lao Issara, formed to prevent a return to French rule at war's end. The Franco-Laotian Treaty of 1953 granted full independence to Laos, but conflict persisted between royalist, neutralist and communist factions. The US bombing of the Ho Chi Minh Trail in eastern Laos commenced in 1964 and greatly escalated the conflict between the royalist Vientiane government and the communist Pathet Lao.

By the 1973 ceasefire, most of the eastern provinces' population had been displaced, and Laos had the dubious distinction of being the most bombed country in the history of warfare.

In December 1975, shortly after the fall of Saigon, the Pathet Lao entered Vientiane and created the Lao People's Democratic Republic.

After 1975 around 300,000 Lao citizens – about 10% of the population – officially resettled abroad. Countless others simply blended into largely Lao-speaking northeastern Thailand.

Although the regime has close political ties with Vietnam, Laos has largely managed to retain a separate identity. Buddhism is deeply ingrained in Laos, and the regime is at pains

LAOS

LAOS

Mekong River

CHINA

VIETNAM

CHINA

MYANMAR
(BURMA)

HANOI

Mengla
Phongsali

Muang
Sing

Boten

Dien Bien Phu

Son La

Xieng Kok

Luang
Nam Tha

Huay Xai

Muang Xai
(Udomxai)

Nong
Khiaw

Sop Hao

Chiang
Khong

Pakbeng

Pak
Mong

Sam Neua

Vieng Xai

Pak Ou

Hua Muang

Luang
Prabang

Nam Seuang

Nam Khan

Sainyabuli

Xieng
Ngeun

Muang Kham

Nong Haet

Kasi

Phonsavan

Muang
Khun

VIETNAM

Vang
Vieng

Nam Ngum

Phu Bia
(2819m)

*Gulf of
Tonkin*

Nam San

Phon Hong

Ang Nam
Ngum

Paksan

Cau Treo

Vinh

SOUTH
CHINA
SEA

Pak Lai

Beung
Kan

Kaew
Neua

Kham
Keut

Kaen
Thao

Chiang
Khan

VIENTIANE

Nong Khai

Mekong River

Nakhon
Phanom

Tha Khaek

VIETNAM

Dong Hoi

Udon Thani

Mukdahan

Savannakhet

Sepon

Lao Bao

Dong Ha

Hué

THAILAND

Se Pon

Se Don

Salavan

Ubon
Ratchathani

Pakse

Se Kong

Sekong
(Lamam)

Se Kaman

Nakhon
Ratchasima

Chong Mek

Champasak

Attapeu
(Samakhi Xai)

Si Phan
Don

Siempang

BANGKOK

Tha Boei

CAMBODIA

*Gulf of
Thailand*

0   50   100 km

LP

to explain that Buddhism and communism are not incompatible. Since 1989 there has been a dramatic relaxation of controls on business and an economic revival.

The country became a full member of the economically oriented Association of South-East Asian Nations (ASEAN) in 1997.

GEOGRAPHY
Laos covers 235,000 sq km and is bordered by Thailand, Cambodia, Vietnam, China and Myanmar (Burma). Over 70% of the country is mountains and plateaus, and two-thirds is forested.

Most of the population is settled along river valleys. The largest river, the Mekong, or Nam Khong, runs the entire length of the country. It provides fertile floodplains for agriculture and is an important transportation artery.

CLIMATE
The annual monsoon cycle gives Laos two distinct seasons: May to October is wet and November to April is dry.

Southern Laos gets the most rain overall; the peaks of the Annamite Chain receive the heaviest rainfall, over 3000mm annually.

The provinces of Luang Prabang, Sainyabuli and Xieng Khuang usually receive only 1000 to 1500mm a year. Vientiane and Savannakhet get about 1500 to 2000mm, as do Phongsali, Luang Nam Tha and Bokeo.

In the Mekong River valley (from Bokeo Province to Champasak Province) the highest temperatures (up to 38°C) occur in March/April and the lowest are in December/January (as low as 15°C).

In the mountains of Xieng Khuang December/January nights can easily fall to 0°C. In mountainous provinces of lesser elevation, temperatures may be a few degrees higher. During most of the rainy season, daytime averages are about 29°C in the lowlands and around 25°C in mountain valleys.

See the Vientiane climate chart in the Appendix.

ECOLOGY & ENVIRONMENT
Although the Ho Chi Minh Trail area suffered herbicides and defoliants – not to mention bombs – during the Vietnam War, Laos as a whole has one of the most pristine (yet unstudied) ecologies in mainland South-East Asia.

Seventeen national biodiversity conservation areas (NBCAs), covering just over 10% of Laos, legally protect habitats. Most of them are in southern Laos, which retains more natural forest cover than the north. The largest of the NBCAs, Nakai-Nam Theun, covers 3710 sq km and is home to the newly discovered Vu Quang ox.

Corruption erodes real environmental protection – illegal timber felling and the smuggling of exotic wildlife species would decrease sharply if all officials were held accountable for their civil duties. However, most Lao still live at or just above a subsistence level, consuming much less of their own natural resources than the people of any 'developed' country.

FLORA & FAUNA
Natural, unmanaged vegetation covers an estimated 85% of Laos. About half the country bears natural forest cover – remarkably, about half of this remains primary forest.

Although the official export of timber is tightly controlled, no one really knows how much teak and other hardwoods are smuggled out of the country into China, Vietnam and Thailand.

In addition to teak and Asian rosewood, the country's flora includes a toothsome array of fruit trees and many bamboo and flowering species, including orchids. In the high plateaus of the Annamite Chain, extensive grasslands, or savanna, are common.

Around 45% of the animal species native to Thailand is shared by Laos, often in greater numbers because there is higher forest cover and fewer hunters.

Notable mammals found in Laos include the concolour gibbon, snub-nosed langur, lesser panda, raccoon dog, pygmy slow loris, giant muntjac, Lao marmoset rat and Owston's civet. Other species common to mainland South-East Asia are a number of macaques (pig-tailed, stump-tailed, Assamese and rhesus), Phayre's leaf monkey, François' leaf monkey, Douc langur, Malayan and Chinese pangolin, Siamese hare, six species of flying squirrel, 10 species of nonflying squirrel, 10 species of civet, marbled cat, Javan and crab-eating mongoose, spotted linsang, leopard cat, Asian golden cat, bamboo rat, yellow-throated marten, lesser mouse deer, serow (a goat-antelope sometimes called Asian mountain goat), goral (another goat-antelope) and 69 species of bats.

Around 200 to 500 wild Asiatic elephants roam areas of open-canopy forest throughout

LAOS

the country, especially in Sainyabuli Province north-west of Vientiane and along the Nakai Plateau. About 1200 captive or domesticated elephants – used for logging and agriculture – can be found scattered around the country.

More rare are the endangered Asiatic jackal, Asiatic black bear, Malayan sun bear, Malayan tapir, barking deer, sambar (a type of deer), gaur and banteng (both are types of wild cattle), leopard, tiger, clouded leopard and Irrawaddy dolphin.

The spindlehorn *(Pseudoryx nghethingensis)* – also known as the *saola* in Vietnam, *nyang* in Laos – is a previously unknown horned animal found in the Annamite Chain along the Lao-Vietnamese border.

A few Javan one-horned and/or Sumatran two-horned rhinos, probably extinct in neighbouring Thailand, are thought to survive in the Bolaven Plateau area of southern Laos. Sightings of kouprey, a wild cattle extinct elsewhere in South-East Asia, have been reported in Attapeu and Champasak provinces as recently as 1993.

The pristine forests and mountains of Laos also harbour a rich selection of resident and migrating bird species. Surveys conducted in 1992-93 recorded 437 species, including 28 globally threatened and near-threatened species. Notable are the Siamese fireback, green peafowl, red-collared woodpecker, brown hornbill, tawny fish-owl, sarus crane, giant ibis and Asian golden weaver.

Endangered Species

Despite widespread hunting (the source of most meat in the Lao diet) for consumption or cross-border trade, habitat loss remains the main threat to species survival in Laos.

Presently the most seriously endangered creature is the Irrawaddy dolphin in the southern Mekong region. Experts say the remaining hundred or so will disappear within 10 years unless gill-net fishing on the Cambodian side of the border is halted or controlled.

The spindlehorn and other recently discovered and extremely rare animals in the Nakai Plateau area are also endangered, but just how much is not known since the population hasn't yet been properly surveyed.

GOVERNMENT & POLITICS

Since 1975 the official name of the country has been the Lao People's Democratic Republic (Sathalanalat Pasathipatai Pasason Lao), or LPDR. Informally, it is acceptable to call the country Laos, which in Lao is Pathet Lao – *pathet* means land or country.

The ruling Lao People's Revolutionary Party (LPRP) is modelled on the Vietnamese Communist Party. In practice, government organs are dominated by the prime minister of the Council of Government (currently Khamtay Siphandone).

Interestingly, the country's 1990 constitution contains no reference to socialism with regard to the economy; it formalises private trade and fosters foreign investment.

Laos is divided into 16 provinces *(khwaeng)* plus the prefecture of Vientiane. Below the province is the meuang, or district, comprising two or more *tatseng* (subdistricts or cantons), which are then divided into *baan* (villages).

ECONOMY

Although rich in minerals, Laos has not yet exploited these resources. Major exports include hydroelectricity and forestry products. Most goods come via Thailand and Vietnam.

Agriculture, fishing and forestry is carried out by 80% of the population. There is very little manufacturing, and foreign aid makes up a large portion of the annual national budget. Much of the domestic trade occurs on the openly tolerated free market. Markets throughout Laos trade freely in untaxed goods smuggled in from Thailand (and elsewhere) and the changing of currency (mostly US dollars and Thai baht) at free market rates is quite open. Laos is still one of the poorest countries in the world, with an annual per capita income of about US$370.

Although the economic turmoil that struck the rest of South-East Asia in 1997-98 also affected the Lao economy, Gross National Product (GNP) growth in the first half of 1998 was estimated to be a relatively strong 6.9% per annum. However, continued devaluations of the national currency, the kip, threaten to undercut real growth.

POPULATION & PEOPLE

The population of Laos is 4.7 million and about half are lowland Lao, most of whom inhabit the Mekong River valley. The rest are tribal Thai (who live in upland river valleys), Lao Theung (lower mountain dwellers mostly of proto-Malay or Mon-Khmer descent) and

Lao Sung (Hmong or Mien hill tribes who live at higher altitudes).

The nation's population density is one of the lowest in Asia, around 20 people per sq km – in other words Laos is roughly the same size as Great Britain with only 8% of Britain's population.

ARTS

Lao art and architecture can be unique and expressive, although limited in range. Most is religious in nature. This includes the pervasive image of Buddha and the *wat*, or temple/monastery. Distinctively Lao is the Calling for Rain Buddha, a standing image with a rocket-like shape. Wats in Luang Prabang feature *sīm*, or chapels, with steep, low roofs. The typical Lao *thâat*, or stupa, is a four-sided, curvilinear, spire-like structure.

Upland folk crafts include gold and silversmithing among the Hmong and Mien tribes, and tribal Thai weaving (especially among the Thai Dam and Thai Lú). Classical music and dance have been all but lost in Laos.

Traditional folk music (usually featuring the *khaen*, or Lao pan-pipe) is still quite popular, however, and inspires much modern Lao pop.

SOCIETY & CONDUCT
Traditional Culture

Traditional culture in Laos has been much influenced by various strains of Khmer, Vietnamese and Thai cultures. As the lowland Lao and the various Thai tribes are all descended from a common ancestry, the similarities between Lao and Thai culture are strong.

Dos & Don'ts

Touching another person's head is taboo and so is the pointing of one's feet at another person or at a Buddha image. Strong displays of emotion are highly discouraged.

The traditional greeting gesture is the *nop* or *wài*, a prayer-like placing together of the palms in front of the face or chest. The handshake is becoming more commonplace, for both men and women.

For all temple visits, dress neatly and take your shoes off when entering religious buildings. Shorts or sleeveless shirts are considered improper dress for both men and women visiting temples.

Shoes are not worn inside homes, nor in some guesthouses and shops.

RELIGION

Most lowland Lao are Theravada Buddhists. Many Lao males choose to ordain as monks temporarily, typically spending anywhere from a week to three months at a wat. After 1975 Buddhism was suppressed but by 1992 it was back in full swing, with a few alterations. Monks are forbidden to promote *phīi* (spirit) worship, which has been officially banned in Laos along with *sāiyasaat* (folk magic).

Despite the ban, phīi worship remains the dominant non-Buddhist belief system. Even in Vientiane, Lao citizens openly perform the ceremony called *sukhwān* or *basi*, in which the 32 *khwān* (guardian spirits of the body) are bound to the guest of honour by white strings tied around the wrists.

Outside the Mekong River valley, the phīi cult is particularly strong among tribal Thai, especially the Black Thai (Thai Dam). Priests *(māw)* who are trained in the propitiation and exorcism of spirits preside at important Black Thai festivals and other ceremonies.

The Khamu and Hmong-Mien tribes also practise animism; the latter group adds ancestral worship. Some Hmong also follow a Christian version of the 'cargo cult' which believes Jesus Christ will arrive in a jeep, dressed in combat fatigues. The Akha, Lisu and other Tibeto-Burman groups mix animism and ancestor cults, except for the Lahu, who worship a supreme deity called Geusha.

LANGUAGE

The official language of Laos is Lao as spoken and written in Vientiane. It has successfully become the lingua franca between all Lao and non-Lao ethnic groups. If you'd like to learn more about the language, get Lonely Planet's *Lao phrasebook*.

See the Language section in the Appendix for some useful Lao words and phrases.

Facts for the Visitor

HIGHLIGHTS

Most visitors begin their journey in Vientiane. Depending on how much time you have available, you might want to save your capital explorations until after you've seen other parts of the country.

Historic Architecture

The former royal kingdoms of **Luang Prabang, Vientiane** and **Champasak** offer the most, be it Buddhist temples or French colonial structures.

Mysterious **Wat Phu**, where human sacrifices may once have taken place, is an intriguing Angkor-period Khmer site in Champasak Province.

Culture

The best mainstream culture sites are on or near the Mekong River, traditional centres for the lowland Lao. **Champasak** and **Si Phan Don** in particular hold fast to older Lao customs. **Vientiane** and **Savannakhet** straddle the traditional and the modern, though Savan shows far less foreign influence than Vientiane.

Hmong-Mien and Thai tribal cultures can be explored in the far northern provinces of **Luang Nam Tha, Bokeo, Udomxai, Phongsali** and **Hua Phan**.

Natural Environment

Laos boasts one of the least disturbed ecosystems in Asia, but access to creatures in the wild is correspondingly limited. Nongovernmental organisations (NGOs) such as the Wildlife Conservation Society may be able to offer some guidance to those with sincere interests. Tour agencies in Vientiane may also be able to help. Camping gear is a must, as virtually none is available in Laos.

Probably the two most rewarding areas for wilderness travel are the **Nakai-Nam Theun NBCA** on the Lao-Vietnamese border and the **Khammuan Limestone NBCA** east of Tha Khaek, both in Khammuan Province.

The area around **Si Phan Don** – a complex of river islands at the Mekong River's widest point – is of major interest for its riparian habitats and waterfalls. Its southernmost reach is also a fragile home to the rare Irrawaddy dolphin.

SUGGESTED ITINERARIES

In a week you can easily take in all the major sights in Vientiane and Luang Prabang, provided you fly between these two cities. A popular alternative is to enter the country at Huay Xai in Bokeo Province, opposite Chiang Khong (Thailand) and then to make the river run from Huay Xai to Luang Prabang, continuing south to Vientiane by plane or road. This saves having to backtrack from Luang Prabang to Vientiane. Or enter at Huay Xai, continue by road to Luang Nam Tha and Udomxai, then south by road or river to Luang Prabang and on to Vientiane.

With two weeks you can add side trips north of Vientiane to Vang Vieng and northeast to Xieng Khuang Province. If you want to see a bit of the south, visit the area between Pakse and the Cambodian border, taking in Champasak, Wat Phu and the Si Phan Don area. If Vietnam is next on your schedule, consider entering it by land via Savannakhet and Lao Bao.

PLANNING
When to Go

The best overall time for visiting most of Laos is between the months of November and February, when it rains least and is not too hot. If you plan on focusing on the mountainous northern provinces, the early rainy season – say May to July – is not bad either, as temperatures are moderate at higher elevations.

Extensive road travel in remote areas like Attapeu, Phongsali and Sainyabuli may be impossible during the main rainy season (July to October), when roads are often unusable for weeks, even months.

Maps

Lonely Planet has a full-colour *Laos travel atlas*, containing the most up-to-date road and place-naming scheme for Laos so far published anywhere.

The National Geographic Service in Vientiane has produced a series of adequate maps of Laos and certain provincial capitals.

TOURIST OFFICES

The government-sponsored National Tourism Authority of Laos (NTAL) is all but useless for accurate, up-to-date information. Its private competitors (see Organised Tours later in this chapter) do a somewhat better job.

NTAL does not supply information by mail and does not maintain any overseas offices. The head NTAL office (☎/fax 21 2013) is situated on Thanon Lan Xang opposite the Centre du Langue Française in Vientiane.

VISAS & DOCUMENTS
Visas

Travellers arriving at Vientiane's Wattay airport and via the Thai-Lao Friendship bridge at Nong Khai can be issued an on-the-spot 15 day tourist visa. To receive this visa on arrival you must present the following:

- US$50 cash (travellers cheques and other currencies, including kip, are not accepted)
- The name of a hotel you will be staying at in Vientiane (pick any one from this guidebook and fill in the blank)
- The name of a contact in Vientiane (most people leave this blank with no problem but if you do know someone in Vientiane by all means write the name in).

For the Wattay airport arrival you're also supposed to possess a valid round-trip air ticket, but we've never seen or heard of this being checked.

It's important to stress that you must have US$50 cash in hand when you arrive at Wattay or at the bridge. Moneychangers at either place are unlikely to be able to give you dollars.

Tourist visas are also issued through travel agencies and Lao consulates abroad. Some places offer the option of a longer 30 day tourist visa. The Lao embassy in Bangkok can usually issue this 30 day visa in 24 hours. The cost is 750B for the visa plus a 300B 'fax fee'. If you only want a 15 day visa, the cost is 250B plus the same fax fee. Some travellers have reported being able to get the shorter visa on the same day of application.

The Lao consulate in Khon Kaen (Thailand) issues 30-day visas for Laos in one to three days for 700B to 1100B depending on your nationality.

The (varying) rate in Vietnam and Cambodia at the time of writing was around US$35 for a 30 day visa. In Yangon the price seemed to vary according to how much the embassy felt like charging that day, usually between US$38 and US$50.

In Thailand you can easily arrange Lao visas through travel agencies in Bangkok, Chiang Mai, Nong Khai, Ubon Ratchathani and Udon Thani. Costs range from 1500B to 2000B depending on the agency and on the speed of visa delivery (24 hours to five working days). In Chiang Khong, Thailand – opposite Huay Xai – all agencies charge US$60 or the baht equivalent for a mere 15 day visa.

Transit Visas The transit visa is the easiest visa to get but is the most restricted. The maximum length of stay on this visa is 10 days (some embassies and consulates offer only five to seven days) and no extension is allowed. No travel is permitted outside the town of Vientiane, and the fee is usually US$25 to US$30.

Visa Extensions Visa extension rules are variable in Laos – of late they are very easy to obtain in Vientiane for US$3 per day. Legally, only the immigration office in Vientiane is authorised to extend your visa, but we have heard of travellers getting the occasional extension in remote provinces such as Phongsali or Sainyabuli – usually for a lot less than US$3 a day. Most immigration offices, however, will simply say you must go to Vientiane.

Overstaying Your Visa If you overstay your visa, you will have to pay a fine at the immigration checkpoint upon departure from Laos. The standard fine is US$5 for each day you've stayed beyond the visa's expiry date.

TRAVEL RESTRICTIONS
In March 1994 travel permits were abolished; foreigners (and Laos) are now theoretically free to travel throughout most of the country. In some 'remote' provinces like Sekong, Attapeu and Hua Phan, travellers may come across officials who bar entry. We don't advise arguing with people who have the power to incarcerate you indefinitely without trial.

Checkpoints
Each time you enter and leave a province – whether by land, air or water – you must stop at a customs or police office and get *jâeng khào* and *jâeng àwk* ('inform enter' and 'inform leave') rubber stamps on your departure card or on a slip of blank paper provided by the checkpoint officials, usually at 100 to 200 kip per chop.

Every airport in the country has a desk or booth where officials check passengers in and out of the province, so if you're flying it's easy to comply with regulations. For road and river travel there are very few controls in most places and local officials don't seem to care whether you're stamped in or not. In fact, it can be very difficult to locate anyone who will give you the necessary chops. A major exception is Luang Prabang province, where stamps are the rule – unstamped visitors may be fined 3000 kip.

Failing to get stamped in or out seems to be a fairly minor offence in most places – the main risk is being sent back to a place you've already been. But as with visa extensions, interprovincial stamps is a very fluid area; it's well worth keeping on top of the general trends.

EMBASSIES & CONSULATES
Lao Embassies & Consulates
Diplomatic representation abroad includes:

Australia
  Embassy:
  (☎ 02-6286 4595)
  1 Dalman Crescent, O'Malley, ACT 2606
China
  Embassy:
  (☎ 010-532 1224)
  11 E 4th St, Sanlitun, Chaoyang, Beijing
  Consulate:
  (☎ 0871-317 6623)
  Room 3226, Camelia Hotel, 154 East Dong
  Feng Rd, 650041 Kunming
France
  Embassy:
  (☎ 01 45 53 02 98)
  74 avenue Raymond Poincare, 75116 Paris
Germany
  Embassy:
  (☎ 0228-23925)
  Amlessing 6, 53639 Koenigswinter 1, Bonn
Japan
  Embassy:
  (☎ 03-5411 2291)
  3-21, 3-Chome, Nishi Azabu, Minato-ku,
  Tokyo
USA
  Embassy:
  (☎ 202-332 6416)
  2222 S St NW, Washington, DC 20008

See the other chapters in this book for Lao
embassies in those countries

Embassies & Consulates in Laos
Countries with representation in Vientiane
include:

Australia
  (☎ 41 3610) Thanon Phonxay
Cambodia
  (☎ 31 4952) Thanon Tha Deua, Ban That Khao
China
  (☎ 31 5103) Thanon Wat Nak Nyai
France
  (☎ 21 5258) Thanon Setthathirat
Germany
  (☎ 31 2111) Thanon Sok Pa Luang 26
Indonesia
  (☎ 41 3910) Thanon Phon Kheng
Japan
  (☎ 41 4400) Thanon Sisangvon
Malaysia
  (☎ 41 4205) Thanon That Luang
Myanmar
  (☎ 31 4910) Thanon Sok Pa Luang

Philippines
  (☎ 31 5179) Thanon Salakokthan
Singapore
  (☎ 21 3570) Novotel, Room 227, Thanon
  Luang Prabang
Thailand
  Visa section:
  (☎ 21 4582) Regent Centre, Thanon Luang
  Prabang (temporary address)
  Consulate in Savannakhet (see that section)
USA
  (☎ 21 2581) Thanon That Dam (Bartholomie)
Vietnam
  (☎ 41 3400) Thanon That Luang
  Consulates in Savannakhet and Pakse
  (see those sections)

CUSTOMS
Customs inspections at ports of entry are very
lax as long as you're not bringing in more
than a moderate amount of luggage. You're
not supposed to enter the country with more
than 500 cigarettes or 1L of distilled spirits.
All the usual prohibitions on drugs, weapons
and pornography apply; otherwise, you can
bring in just about anything you want, including unlimited amounts of Lao and
foreign currency.

MONEY
Currency
The currency is the kip. Although only kip is
legally negotiable in everyday transactions,
in reality three currencies are used for commerce: kip, Thai baht and US dollars.

Notes come in denominations of 1, 5, 10,
20, 50, 100, 500 and 1000 kip. Notes smaller
than 50 kip are almost never seen, however,
and kip coins *(aat)* are being withdrawn from
circulation.

Exchange Rates
Exchange rates are as follows:

country	unit		kip
Australia	A$1	=	2605 kip
Canada	C$1	=	2723 kip
euro	€1	=	5048 kip
France	10FF	=	7660 kip
Germany	DM1	=	2558 kip
Japan	¥100	=	3543 kip
New Zealand	NZ$1	=	2201 kip
Thailand	10B	=	1120 kip
UK	UK£1	=	7087 kip
USA	US$1	=	4205 kip

Exchanging Money

With some exceptions the best exchange rates are available at banks rather than licensed moneychangers. At banks, travellers cheques receive a slightly better exchange rate than cash. Banks in Vientiane can change UK pounds, German marks, Canadian, US and Australian dollars, French francs, Thai baht and Japanese yen only. Outside Vientiane most provincial banks will accept only US dollars or Thai baht.

The best overall exchange rate is generally offered by the Banque pour le Commerce Extérieur Lao (BCEL; Lao Foreign Trade Bank in English). The only advantage of licensed moneychangers is longer opening hours.

Outside Vientiane and Luang Prabang it can be difficult to change travellers cheques; even at Wattay airport the moneychanger is sometimes short of kip (be sure to ask whether they can cover your cheques before signing). Hence visitors are advised to carry plenty of cash outside Vientiane. If you plan to carry Thai baht and US dollars for large purchases (as is the custom), be sure to arrange your cash stash in these currencies before you leave the capital. Even in Luang Prabang it is impossible to get anything but kip at the bank.

Cash

The baht still finds favour for its availability and portability – in a country where the largest note amounts to only a few cents, you can save luggage space by carrying most of your cash in baht for larger purchases, along with smaller amounts of kip and US dollars.

Credit Cards

Many hotels, upmarket restaurants and gift shops in Vientiane accept Visa and Master-Card credit cards. A few also accept American Express; the national representative for Amex is Diethelm Travel Laos.

BCEL on Thanon Pangkham offers cash advances/withdrawals on Visa credit/debit cards for a 2.5% transaction fee if you take kip or 3.5% for US dollars. Thai banks in Vientiane charge more.

Outside of Vientiane credit cards are virtually useless.

Parallel Market

Higher rates than those offered by licensed banks are usually available from retail shops and nonlicensed, freelance moneychangers in Vientiane. Typically these rates run about 25 to 50 kip more per dollar – with no commission – for crisp US$100 or B1000 notes.

Although the changing is sometimes furtive, we've never heard of a foreigner being prosecuted for changing on the black market, so the risk seems very low. Occasional crackdowns on these moneychangers so far haven't lasted more than a few days or a week.

Costs

In Vientiane or Luang Prabang you can squeeze by for about US$10 a day if you stay in the cheaper guesthouses and eat local food; in remote areas you can whittle this figure down to around US$6 to US$8 a day.

Budgets for those who need air-con, hot water and *falang* (western) food leap to around US$25 per day minimum if you economise.

Tipping & Bargaining

Tipping is not customary in Laos except in upmarket Vientiane restaurants where 10% of the bill is appreciated – but only if a service charge hasn't already been added to the bill.

Anything bought in a market should be bargained for; in some shops prices are fixed while in others bargaining is expected (the only way to find out is to try). In general the Lao are gentle and very scrupulous in their bargaining practices. A fair price is usually arrived at quickly with little attempt to gouge the buyer (some tour operators are an exception to this rule).

Remember there's a fine line between bargaining and niggling – getting steamed over 100 kip makes both seller and buyer lose face.

POST & COMMUNICATIONS

Post

Outgoing mail from Vientiane is fairly dependable and inexpensive but incoming mail is unreliable. Forget about mailing things from upcountry Laos.

Telephone

Telephone service in Laos, both domestic and international, is on-again, off-again at best. International calls can be made only from Vientiane and Luang Prabang. IDD is available at selected locations in Vientiane, including the Public Call Office on Thanon Setthathirat

Telephone Codes

The country code for Laos is 856. The international dialling code is 00. Following are selected area codes. You must dial the zero when calling from within Laos.

Luang Prabang	☎ 071
Pakse	☎ 031
Phonsavan	☎ 061
Salavan	☎ 031
Savannakhet	☎ 041
Si Phan Don	☎ 031
Vientiane	☎ 021

in Vientiane, which is open daily 7.30 am to 10 pm. Operators cannot place collect calls or reverse-charge calls. All calls are operator-assisted.

Fax

At the Public Call Office in Vientiane fax services are available daily from 7.30 am to 9.30 pm. You can also send faxes from the main post office.

In provincial capitals fax services are handled at the main post office or at the separate telephone office, where such exists.

Email & Internet Access

In 1998 the government stated that it was only legal to access the Internet through a yet-to-be-established (and probably restrictive) government Internet service provider called PAN-Laos. For more information, log onto www.panasia.org.sg/netlaos.

Of course this hasn't stopped private computer owners from accessing the Net via long-distance calls to Thailand. From a private IDD phone in Laos, calls to Bangkok from Vientiane aren't terribly expensive. For information on LoxInfo, the Thailand service provider, log onto www.loxinfo.co.th. Temporary accounts may be purchased.

INTERNET RESOURCES

The Lao embassy in Washington, DC, maintains a well structured Web site (www.laoembassy.com) which includes up-to-date information on visa regulations and application processes.

The US Library of Congress Web site carries the lengthy *Laos – A Country Study* (lcweb2.loc.gov/frd/cs/latoc.html).

BOOKS

Lonely Planet

Lonely Planet was the first to publish a guidebook on post-1975 Laos in English and the *Laos* guide has recently been updated and reissued in its 3rd edition. LP also publishes the *Lao travel atlas* and *Lao phrasebook*.

Travel

Several classic travel narratives by 19th century French visitors have been translated into English and reprinted, including Henri Mouhot's famous *Travels in Siam, Cambodia, and Laos.*

In 1952 Norman Lewis narrated his trip through French Indochina in *A Dragon Apparent – Travels in Cambodia, Laos and Vietnam*, which contains the quotable passage on Laos: 'Europeans who come here to live, soon acquire a certain recognisable manner. They develop quiet voices, and gentle, rapt expressions.'

Christopher Kremmer's *Stalking the Elephant Kings – In Search of Laos* evokes travel in modern Laos very skilfully while exploring the unsolved mystery of what happened to the country's royal family following the 1975 communist revolution.

Art & Culture

Lao Textiles & Traditions by Mary F Connors is the best overall introduction to the subject. Patricia Cheesman's *Lao Textiles – Ancient Symbols, Living Art* offers a thorough and well illustrated explanation of weaving styles and techniques – old and new – in Laos.

Laurent Chazee's *Atlas des ethnies et des sous-ethnies du Laos* (1995) is sold in Bangkok and Vientiane. This well researched, colour-illustrated book comes with a map tucked into a pocket in the back cover which diagrams the locations of 119 ethnic groups in Laos.

History & Politics

Historical Dictionary of Laos by Martin Stuart-Fox and Mary Kooyman contains a detailed chronology of Laos dating from 500,000 BC to 1991, with lots of trivia you won't find anywhere else.

Stuart-Fox's *Buddhist Kingdom, Marxist State – The Making of Modern Laos* and *A History of Laos* draw post-1975 Lao politics into sharper focus.

The Ravens – Pilots of the Secret War of Laos by Christopher Robbins is an impressive piece of research on the US-directed secret war.

General

Laos – A Country Study is probably the most comprehensive English-language book about Lao society, politics, history and economics. It's also remarkably objective considering it was commissioned by the US Army.

NEWSPAPERS & MAGAZINES

The *Vientiane Times* is a weekly English-language newspaper produced by the Ministry of Information & Culture. It's business oriented, with occasional articles on Lao culture and a short but useful list of ongoing cultural events and social activities in the capital.

The Lao government controls all distribution of the *Bangkok Post* and it is legally available only by subscription. The *Post* can be perused in some hotel lobbies and cafes but otherwise it is rarely seen except in government offices! Raintrees in Vientiane carries *Time, Newsweek, Asiaweek, Far Eastern Economic Review* and a few other news periodicals.

RADIO & TV

Laos has one radio station, Lao National Radio. English-language news is broadcast twice daily on LNR but most expats prefer the English-language news available from the usual short-wave radio programming.

Lao National Television sponsors two TV channels which can only be received in the Mekong River valley and broadcast only from 7 to 11 pm. Typical fare includes Lao-dubbed episodes of *Alf* and *Roadrunner* cartoons. Most Lao watch Thai television, which can be received anywhere in the Mekong River valley. Thailand's channels 5 and 9 telecast a variety of English-language programs.

Satellite TV setups can pick up transmissions from many Asian services.

VIDEO SYSTEMS

The predominant video format in Laos is PAL, a system compatible with that used in most of Europe (France's SECAM format is a notable exception) as well as in Australia. A 'multisystem' VCR has the capacity to play both NTSC and PAL, but not SECAM.

PHOTOGRAPHY & VIDEO
Film

Colour print film is readily available in larger towns like Vientiane, Savannakhet and Luang Prabang. Kodak Ektachrome and Fuji Sensia slide film is available at reasonable prices at a few photo shops in Vientiane. Outside Vientiane, slide film of any kind is rare. Print film generally costs around 3000 to 4500 kip per roll, slide films 9000 to 10,000 kip. For black and white film or other types of slide film bring your own supply.

Restrictions

Lao officials are sensitive about photography of airports and military installations; when in doubt refrain.

Photographing People

In rural areas people are often not used to having their photos taken, so be sure to smile and ask permission before snapping away. In tribal areas *always* ask permission before photographing people or religious totems; photography of people is taboo among several of the tribes. Use discretion when photographing villagers anywhere in Laos, as a camera can be a very intimidating instrument.

Airport Security

So far only Vientiane and Luang Prabang airports use X-ray machines to view luggage, so employ the usual protective procedures (lead-lined bags, hand inspection) if you're flying in or out of either of these cities and are concerned about X-ray damage to film.

ELECTRICITY

Laos uses 220V AC circuitry; power outlets most commonly feature two-prong round or flat sockets. Bring adaptors and transformers as needed. Adaptors for common European plugs are available at shops in Vientiane.

Blackouts are common during the rainy season, so it's a good idea to bring a torch (flashlight).

WEIGHTS & MEASURES

The international metric system is the official system for weights and measures in Laos. In rural areas distances are occasionally quoted in *meun* (12km). Gold and silver are sometimes weighed in *bàat*; one *bàat* is 15g.

LAUNDRY

Most guesthouses and hotels offer laundry services which usually vary in price according to the cost of their rooms. The cheapest places to have laundry done are small laundry shops, found only in Vientiane, Luang Prabang, Huay Xai, Savannakhet, and Pakse.

HEALTH

Malaria exists throughout the year in the whole country, excluding Vientiane. There have been recent large outbreaks of dengue fever. It's very important to take appropriate precautions against both these very serious diseases. Food and water-borne diseases, including dysentery, hepatitis and liver flukes, occur, so it's worth paying attention to basic food and water hygiene. The main risk for liver flukes comes from eating raw or undercooked fish; in particular, avoid eating *pąa dąek*, fermented fish used as an accompaniment to rice. They can also be acquired by swimming in the Mekong Delta. Rabies exists in Laos.

For more information on these and other health matters, see the Health section in the Appendix.

WOMEN TRAVELLERS

Attitudes Towards Women

As in Thailand, Lao women have substantial gender parity in work, inheritance, land ownership and so on, often more so than in many western countries. However, women's cultural standing in Laos is not quite as equal. See the Thailand chapter for further comments on women's status in Theravada Buddhism.

Compared with Thailand, prostitution is much less common in Laos, where it is a very serious criminal offence. Hence, Lao women don't worry about being perceived as prostitutes if they associate with foreign males. Lao women also drink beer and *lào-láo* (rice liquor) in public, which 'proper' Thai females rarely do.

What *is* often perceived as improper or disrespectful behaviour by foreign females is the wearing of clothes that bare the thighs, shoulders or any part of the breasts. Long trousers and walking shorts (for men too), as well as skirts, are acceptable attire; tank tops, sleeveless blouses and short skirts or shorts are not.

Safety Precautions

Everyday incidents of sexual harassment are much less common in Laos than in virtually any other Asian country. Nevertheless women should exercise the usual cautions when travelling alone in remote areas of the country or when out late at night. Lao women almost never travel alone, so a foreign female without company is perceived by most Lao – male and female – as a bit strange.

GAY & LESBIAN TRAVELLERS

Lao culture is very tolerant of homosexuality, although there is not as prominent a gay/lesbian scene as in neighbouring Thailand. Public displays of affection – whether heterosexual or homosexual – are frowned upon.

DISABLED TRAVELLERS

With its lack of paved roads or footpaths (sidewalks) – even when present the latter are often uneven – Laos presents many physical obstacles for the mobility-impaired. Public buildings and hotels rarely feature ramps or other access points for wheelchairs. Public transport is particularly crowded and difficult, even for the fully ambulatory.

SENIOR TRAVELLERS

Seniors' discounts aren't generally available in Laos, but the Lao more than make up for this by the respect they typically show for the elderly.

Cross-generational entertainment is more common in Laos than in China, Vietnam or Thailand. Nightclubs welcome all ages, and at rural temple fairs and other wat-centred events, young and old dance and eat together.

TRAVEL WITH CHILDREN

The Lao love children, and will often shower attention on your offspring, who will find ready playmates and temporary nanny service at practically every stop.

Special nappy-changing facilities, high chairs, car safety seats and the like are virtually nonexistent. For the most part parents needn't worry too much about health concerns. All the usual health precautions apply; children should especially be warned not to play with animals since rabies is very common in Laos.

DANGERS & ANNOYANCES

Road Travel

Road conditions and vehicle maintenance outside the Mekong River valley are quite substandard; it might take days to reach a hospital in the event of an accident. The risk of breakdowns and accidents is moderate to high, though increasing traffic means better odds of quicker assistance.

Trouble Spots

With a couple of exceptions most areas of the country are militarily secure. The once troubled section of Route 13 between Vientiane and Luang Prabang is considered as safe as any road in Laos, but it might be a good idea to ask around in Luang Prabang or Vientiane before setting merrily off down the road.

Ambushes, sometimes fatal, are still frequent on the western portion of Route 7 in Xieng Khuang Province, between the road's westernmost terminus at Route 13 and its crossing over the Nam Ngum river near Muang Sui (east of Phonsavan). At the moment military checkpoints along this section of Route 7 turn back anyone travelling without military escort. Until the area is declared safe, you travel this road AYOR (at your own risk); we recommend flying to Phonsavan or going by road from Nong Khiaw farther north instead. Ask around in Vientiane or Luang Prabang to get the latest story.

South of the aforementioned road is Saisombun Special Zone, a militarised administrative district carved out of eastern Vientiane, south-western Xieng Khuang and north-western Bolikhamsai provinces which is definitely *not* safe as of this writing.

Route 6 north from Paksan through Saisombun Special Zone to just south of Muang Khun (Xieng Khuang Province) continues to be plagued with security problems. North of Muang Khun, all the way to Sam Neua in Hua Phan Province, this road is relatively safe.

Unexploded Ordnance (UXO)
In the eastern portions of the country towards the Vietnamese border – particularly in the provinces of Hua Phan, Xieng Khuang, Sekong and Attapeu – there are large areas contaminated by unexploded ordnance left behind by nearly 100 years of warfare. US-made cluster bombs (known as *bombi* to the Lao) pose by far the greatest potential danger to people living or travelling through these areas and account for most of the estimated 130 casualties per year.

Statistically speaking, the UXO risk for the average foreign visitor is quite low, but travellers should exercise caution when considering off-road wilderness travel in the aforementioned provinces. Stick to well trodden footpaths. *Never* touch an object on the ground that may be UXO, no matter how old, crusty and defunct it may appear.

Theft
On the whole, the Lao are trustworthy people and theft is not much of a problem. Still, it's best if you keep your hotel room locked when you're out and while sleeping at night. If you ride a crowded bus, watch your luggage and don't keep money in your trouser pockets.

Pickpockets are very rare in Laos – most Lao citizens openly carry kip notes in their shirt pockets, or, for larger sums, in an obvious hand pouch or brief.

There's one caveat, however. In Vientiane we've heard of motorcycle duos who sometimes swoop down on pedestrians or bicycle riders, snatching purses, shoulder bags or day packs. So far these incidents have been restricted to night time, usually around 11 pm or later, and typically along dark, secluded sections of road. When walking at night in Vientiane, keep to well lit streets and take a little extra caution with your money and valuables.

BUSINESS HOURS
Government offices are generally open from 8 to 11 am and 2 to 5 pm. Shops and private businesses open and close a bit later, and either stay open during lunch or close for just an hour.

PUBLIC HOLIDAYS & SPECIAL EVENTS
The Lao Buddhist Era (BE) calendar figures year one as 638 BC (not 543 BC as in Thailand), eg 2000 AD is 2638 BE according to the Lao Buddhist calendar.

Festivals in Laos are mostly linked to agricultural seasons or historic Buddhist holidays. The general word for festival in Lao is *bun* (or *boun*).

February
Magha Puja (or Makkha Bu-saa, Full Moon)
This is held on the full moon of the third lunar month. It commemorates a speech given by Buddha to 1250 enlightened monks who came to hear him without prior summons. Chanting and offerings mark the festival, culminating in the candlelit circumambulation of wats throughout the country.
Vietnamese Tet & Chinese New Year
This is celebrated in Vientiane, Pakse and Savannakhet, with parties, deafening nonstop fireworks and visits to Vietnamese and Chinese temples. Chinese and Vietnamese-run businesses usually close for three days.

April
Pii Mai
The 15th, 16th and 17th are official public holidays. The Lunar New Year begins in mid-April

and practically the entire country comes to a halt and celebrates. Houses are cleaned, people put on new clothes and Buddha images are washed with lustral water. Later the citizens take to the streets and dowse one another with water.

May
International Labour Day
1 May is a public holiday.

Visakha Puja (or Visakha Bu-saa, Full Moon)
This falls on the 15th day of the 6th lunar month (usually in May), which is considered the day of the Buddha's birth, enlightenment and *parinibbana*, or passing away. Activities are centred on the wat.

Bun Bang Fai (Rocket Festival)
This is a pre-Buddhist rain ceremony that is now celebrated alongside Visakha Puja in Laos and north-eastern Thailand. This can be one of the wildest festivals in the country, with plenty of music and dance.

July
Khao Phansaa (or Khao Watsa, Full Moon)
This occurs in late July and is the beginning of the traditional three month 'rains retreat', during which Buddhist monks are expected to station themselves in a single monastery.

October/November
Awk Phansaa (or Awk Watsa, Full Moon)
This celebrates the end of the three-month rains retreat.

Bun Nam (Water Festival)
Held in association with Awk Phansaa. Boat races are commonly held in towns located on rivers, such as Vientiane, Luang Prabang and Savannakhet.

November
That Luang Festival (or Bun That Luang, Full Moon)
This takes place at Pha That Luang in Vientiane in early November. Hundreds of monks assemble to receive alms and floral votives early in the morning on the first day of the festival. There is a colourful procession between Pha That Luang and Wat Si Muang.

December
Lao National Day
Held on 2 December. This public holiday celebrates the 1975 victory of the proletariat over the monarchy with parades, speeches etc.

ACTIVITIES
Cycling
The overall lack of vehicular traffic makes cycling an attractive proposition in Laos, although this advantage is somewhat offset by the general absence of roads in the first place. For any serious out-of-town cycling you're better off bringing your own bike, one that's geared to very rough road conditions.

For routes to avoid, see Dangers & Annoyances earlier in this chapter.

Hiking & Trekking
Laos' mountainous, well forested geography makes it a potentially ideal destination for hikers. All 13 provinces have plenty of hiking possibilities, although the authorities view overnight trips that involve camping or staying in villages with suspicion. So far not a single travel agency in Laos has been granted permission to lead overnight treks in any of the tribal areas.

Warning: Be very aware of UXOs. See the earlier Dangers & Annoyances section.

Provinces with the highest potential for relatively safe wilderness walking include Bokeo, Champasak, Khammuan, Luang Nam Tha, Luang Prabang and Vientiane. In particular the 17 NBCAs should be rewarding territory (see the earlier Ecology & Environment section).

COURSES
Language
Short-term courses in spoken and written Lao are available at the following study centres in Vientiane:

Centre de Langue Française
(π 21 5764) Thanon Lane Xang
Lao-American Language Center
(π 41 4321) 22 Phon Kheng, Ban Phon Sa-at
Saysettha Language Centre
(π 41 4480) Thanon Nong Bon, Ban Phonxai
Vientiane University College
(π 41 4873) Thanon That Luang, opposite the Ministry of Foreign Affairs

Meditation
If you can speak Lao or Thai, or can arrange an interpreter, you may be able to study *vipassana* (insight meditation) with Ajaan Sali Kantasilo, the Thai-born abbot of Wat Sok Pa Luang in south-east Vientiane.

WORK
With Laos' expanding economy and the quickening influx of aid organisations and foreign companies, the number of jobs available to foreigners increases slightly each year. Nearly all work will be found in the nation's capital.

Possibilities include teaching English privately or at a language centre in Vientiane (pay is currently around US$8 an hour).

If you have a technical background or international volunteer experience, you might find work with a UN-related program or NGO.

Once you have a sponsoring employer, a visa valid for working and residing in Laos is relatively easy to get.

ACCOMMODATION

Tourist hotels are typically priced in US dollars, while guesthouses and less expensive business hotels (common in Huay Xai, Luang Prabang, Savannakhet and Pakse) are priced in kip or, less frequently, Thai baht.

It is almost always cheaper to pay in the requested currency rather than let the hotel or guesthouse convert the price into another currency. If the price is quoted in kip, you'll do best to pay in kip; if priced in dollars, pay in dollars. Room rates in this chapter are given in the currency quoted by the particular establishment.

Outside the Mekong River valley, most provincial capitals have only two or three basic hotels or guesthouses, although the number and quality of places to stay seems to be increasing every year. Vientiane has a few guesthouses now with rooms costing as little as US$5 or US$6 a night with shared toilet and bathing facilities. In more far flung areas rustic guesthouses with shared facilities cost only 1500 to 3000 kip (about US$0.50 to US$1) per night per person. Though oriented towards local guests, these guesthouses generally welcome foreigners.

Small business hotels in Luang Prabang, Muang Xai, Savannakhet and Pakse cost around US$5 to US$8 per night for simple double rooms. Hotel rooms in Vientiane, Luang Prabang, Savannakhet and Pakse offer private bathrooms and fans as standard features for around US$10 to US$15. Higher cost rooms have air-con, and sometimes hot water, for US$15 to US$25.

Large tourist hotels are beginning to multiply in the larger cities; rooms are typically US$25 to US$60.

FOOD

Lao cuisine is very similar to Thai in many ways. Like Thai food, almost all dishes are cooked with fresh ingredients, including vegetables (*phák*), fish (*pqa*), chicken (*kai*), duck (*pét*), pork (*mūu*), beef (*sìn ngúa*) or water

buffalo (*sìn khwái*). In rural areas wild rather than domestic animals – especially deer, wild pig, squirrels, civets, monitor lizards, junglefowls/pheasants, dhole (wild dog), rats and birds – provide most of the meat in local diets.

Food is salted with *nâam pqa*, a thin sauce of fermented anchovies (usually imported from Thailand), and *pqa dqek*, a coarser Lao preparation which has fermented freshwater fish, rice husks and rice 'dust' as its main ingredients. Common seasonings include the galingale root (*khaa*), ground peanuts (more often a condiment), hot chillies (*màak phét*), tamarind juice (*nâam màak khãam*), ginger (*khíng*) and coconut milk (*nâam màak phâo*). Chillies are sometimes served on the side in hot pepper sauces called *jaew*. *Phõng súu lot* – ajinomoto or MSG – is also a common seasoning, and in Laos you may even see it served as a table condiment in noodle restaurants. In Luang Prabang, dried water-buffalo skin (*nãng khwái hàeng*) is a popular ingredient in local dishes.

All meals are eaten with rice or noodles. Glutinous rice (*khào nío*) is the preferred variety, although ordinary white rice (*khào jâo*) is also common. Sticky rice is eaten with the hands – the general practice is to grab a small fistful from the woven container that sits on the table, then roll it into a ball and dip it into the various dishes. Khào jâo is eaten with a fork and spoon. Noodles may be eaten with fork and spoon or chopsticks. The most common noodles in Laos are *fõe* (flat rice noodles) and *khào pûn* (thin white wheat noodles).

The closest thing to a national dish is *làap*, a spicy beef, duck, fish or chicken salad made with fresh lime juice, mint leaves, onions and lots of chillies. It can be hot or mild depending on the cook.

In Vientiane, Luang Prabang and Savannakhet, French bread is a popular breakfast food. Sometimes it's eaten plain with *kqa-fáe nóm hâwn* (hot coffee with milk), sometimes it's eaten with eggs (*khai*) or in a baguette sandwich that contains Lao-style paté and vegetables. When they're fresh, Lao baguettes are superb. Croissants and other pastries are also available in the bakeries of Vientiane.

DRINKS
Nonalcoholic

Water Water purified for drinking purposes is simply called *nâam deum* (drinking water), whether boiled or filtered. *All* water offered to customers in restaurants or hotels will be purified, so one needn't fret about the safety of taking a sip.

Coffee & Tea Lao-grown coffee is one of the world's best. The usual brewed coffee is served mixed with sugar and sweetened condensed milk – if you don't want either, specify *kạa-fáe dām* (black coffee) followed with *baw sai nâam-tāan* (without sugar).

Chinese-style (green or semi-cured) tea is the usual ingredient in *nâam sáa*, the weak, often lukewarm, tea traditionally served free in restaurants.

Black tea is usually found in the same places real coffee is. An order of *sáa hâwn* (hot tea) almost always results in a cup (or glass) of black tea with sugar and condensed milk. Specify beforehand if you want black tea without milk and/or sugar.

Alcoholic

Beer Lao Brewery Co produces the very drinkable Bia Lao, or 'Beer Lao' (sometimes spelt 'Beerlao'). A draught version *(bīa sòt,* or 'fresh beer') is available only in beer bars in Vientiane and like all Beerlao contains 5% alcohol. Imported Heineken and Tiger beer from Singapore are also available in cans.

Distilled Spirits Rice whisky, or *lào-láo* (Lao liquor), is a popular drink among lowland Lao. Strictly speaking, lào-láo is not legal but no one seems to care. The government distils its own brand, Sticky Rice, which is of course legal and costs around 2000 kip for a bottle. Lào-láo is usually drunk neat, with a plain water chaser.

In a Lao home the pouring and drinking of lào-láo takes on ritual characteristics – it is first offered to the house spirits, and guests must take at least one offered drink or risk offending the house spirits.

In rural provinces, a weaker version of lào-láo known as *lào hái* (jar liquor) is fermented by households or villages. Lào hái is usually drunk from a communal jar using long reed straws. It's not always safe to drink, however, since unboiled water is often added to it during and after fermentation.

ENTERTAINMENT
Music & Dancing

For most nonurban Laos local entertainment involves sitting around with friends over a few jiggers of lào-láo, telling jokes or re-counting the events of the day and singing *phéng phêun múang* (local Lao folk songs).

Almost every provincial capital has a couple of live-music dance halls – called 'discos' by the Lao. There's always food and drink, though most people stick to drinking. The music is mostly Lao, while dance styles range from the traditional *lám wóng* to US country-style line dancing.

Cinema & Video

The arrival of video (along with pirated Thai, Chinese and western videos) has completely killed off local cinema outside the capital.

SPECTATOR SPORTS

Football (soccer) and other stadium sports can occasionally be seen at the National Stadium in Vientiane. Admission is inexpensive. Elsewhere interprovincial games take place on fields or stadiums built in each provincial capital.

Boxing

Though very popular, kickboxing *(múay thai)* is not nearly as developed a sport in Laos as it is in Thailand, and is mostly confined to Thai TV and amateur fights at upcountry festivals.

International boxing *(múay sāakōn)* is officially encouraged in Laos. A local festival program might include three matches in the international style and five in the Lao-Thai style.

Kataw

Kátâw, a game in which a woven rattan – or sometimes plastic – ball about 12cm in diameter is kicked around, is almost as popular in Laos as it is in Malaysia and Thailand (where it's called *takraw*). See the Spectator Sports section in the Thailand chapter for details.

SHOPPING
Handicrafts

Laos' ethnic diversity fosters various silverworks, woodcarving, tribal crafts, ceramics, rattan furniture, textiles and handmade *saa* (mulberry bark) paper, nearly all of which can be bought in Vientiane.

North-eastern Laos is famous for Sam Neua-style textiles, which feature rich brocade and dazzling colours. Original silk designs based on these styles are also produced at weaving centres in Vientiane. Simple Lao-style cotton fabrics are abundant near Pakse and Don Khong, while Sekong and Attapeu feature unique Mon-Khmer weaving.

Hill-tribe crafts and jewellery are most abundantly available in Vientiane, though some very interesting work can also be found in Luang Prabang, Luang Nam Tha, Phongsali, Hua Phan, Bokeo, Salavan, Sekong and Attapeu.

Many of the handicrafts and arts available in Laos are easily obtainable in Thailand. Hill tribe crafts can be less expensive in Laos, but only if you bargain. Most shops now have fixed prices but you can still bargain for fabrics, carvings, antiques and jewellery.

Getting There & Away

AIR
Airports
At the moment Vientiane is the only legal port of disembarkation in Laos for foreign air passengers. However, the Lao government has designated the newly expanded Luang Prabang airport as 'international', and in 1998 Lao Aviation announced plans to begin Chiang Mai to Luang Prabang service.

Airlines
Note: at the time of writing, Thai Airways International (THAI) was the *only* airline with international flights in and out of Vientiane. All other regional carriers, including Lao Aviation, had pulled the plug on this route, mainly because of the current regional financial crisis. Information on non-THAI flights to/from Laos has been left in this book, however, as these flights may well resume soon.

Departure Tax
There is a US$5 departure tax, which can be paid in kip, baht or dollars only. Lao domestic departure tax is 300 kip.

Cambodia
Flights between Vientiane and Phnom Penh cost US$133/250 one way/return with Lao Aviation. Royal Air Cambodge (RAC) planned to introduce services from summer 1998.

China
Lao Aviation flies between Kunming and Vientiane every Sunday, while China Yunnan

Airlines (CYA) does the job every Wednesday, Thursday and Friday. Both airlines usually charge US$155 but special fares as low as US$100 are occasionally available. Lao Aviation and CYA can issue tickets for either airline on this route.

Thailand
Bangkok Bangkok to Vientiane flights operate daily, alternating between Lao Aviation and Thai Airways International airlines. In each case the fare is US$100, though specials as low as US$75 are occasionally available.

Some people save money by flying from Bangkok to Udon Thani in Thailand first, then carrying on by road to Nong Khai and over the Friendship Bridge to Vientiane. Udon Thani is 55km south of Nong Khai and a Bangkok-Udon air ticket aboard THAI costs US$52. THAI operates an express van direct from Udon airport to Nong Khai for 100B per person (around 35 minutes); a local bus is 20B (a bit over one hour).

Chiang Mai Lao Aviation flies to and from Chiang Mai every Thursday and Sunday. The one hour flight costs US$70. Flights between Chiang Mai and Luang Prabang may commence if and when Lao Aviation solves its aircraft shortage.

Singapore
Silk Air flies between Singapore and Vientiane twice weekly for US$355.

Vietnam
Direct flights between Hanoi and Vientiane leave four times weekly aboard Vietnam Airlines, twice weekly with Lao Aviation (US$90).

Lao Aviation flies between Ho Chi Minh City and Vientiane every Friday for US$170. Vietnam Airlines also has four Vientiane flights weekly to/from Ho Chi Minh City via Hanoi for the same fare. Either airline can issue tickets for the other.

LAND
Laos shares land borders with Thailand, Myanmar, Cambodia, China and Vietnam, all of which permit overland crossings for locals, but not necessarily for foreigners. Regulations change from month to month – check with a Lao embassy or consulate for the latest.

China

From Mengla district in southern Yunnan Province in China it is legal to enter Laos via Boten in Luang Nam Tha Province if you possess a valid Lao visa.

The Lao Consulate in Kunming (China) issues only seven-day transit visas. These cost US$25 to US$28 and take three to five days to process. You must bring *four* photos and already have a visa from a third country (such as Thailand) stamped in your passport. Most travellers from Kunming go via Jinghong to Mengla and then to the border at Mohan. As the bus journey from Jinghong takes the better part of the day, you will probably have to overnight at Mengla.

Myanmar & Cambodia

Laos also shares its land borders with Myanmar and Cambodia but, at present, no overland crossing points are usually open for foreigners.

Rumours persist that foreigners will soon be allowed to cross the border between Champasak Province in Laos and Stung Treng Province in Cambodia. Apparently some foreigners have actually managed to accomplish this crossing – most likely with the palms-up cooperation of the local border police – but Lao officials in Vientiane say it's not yet open for everyday travel.

We've had similar reports – balanced by denials from the Lao government – regarding entry from Myanmar at the Lao town of Xieng Kok, on the Mekong River in Luang Nam Tha Province.

Thailand

Nong Khai The Thai-Lao Friendship Bridge spans the Mekong River between Nong Khai Province on the Thai side and Vientiane Prefecture on the Lao side, and is the main land crossing into Laos at the moment. Shuttle buses ferry passengers back and forth across the bridge from designated terminals nearby for 10B per person; there are departures every 20 minutes from 8 am to 5.30 pm. You must arrange your own transport to the bridge bus terminal from Nong Khai.

The bus stops at Thai immigration control on the bridge, where you pay 10B to have your passport stamped with an exit visa. Passengers then reboard the bus and after crossing the bridge stop at Lao immigration and customs, where you pay a fee of 20B to have your passport stamped (40B between noon and 2 pm and on weekends).

From the bridge standard fare is 2000 kip by jumbo (motorcycle taxi), 600 kip by shared jumbo or 200B by car taxi to Vientiane, about 20km away. You can also catch a No 14 bus into town for 400 kip; around 15 buses a day (6.30 am to 5 pm) pass the bridge area on their way from Tha Deua (the old ferry pier) to Vientiane's Talaat Sao (Morning Market).

Chong Mek There's also a land crossing from Chong Mek in Thailand's Ubon Ratchathani Province to Champasak. Specially endorsed visas are no longer necessary for this crossing – any visa will do.

To get to Chong Mek from Ubon, take a bus first to Phibun Mangsahan (15B), then switch to a Phibun-Chong Mek *songthaew* (18B). At Chong Mek you simply walk across the border (Lao immigration and customs are open 8 am to noon and 1 to 4.30 pm) and proceed from Ban Mai Sing Amphon – the village on the Lao side of the border – to Pakse. It is about an hour from the border via bus/taxi and ferry. See under Pakse in the Champasak Province section for further details.

Chiang Khong In 1996 a Thai company announced plans to construct a second bridge over the Mekong between Chiang Khong and Huay Xai but so far nothing has materialised. When (and if) constructed, this bridge is supposed to connect with the 250km road running north-east to the Chinese border via Bokeo and Luang Nam Tha provinces. In the meanwhile the ferry across the Mekong still operates.

Vietnam

Lao Bao Border officials at the border post opposite Lao Bao, a small town on the Vietnam side of the Lao-Vietnamese border near Sepon, will permit visitors holding valid Laos visas to enter the country overland from Vietnam. Lao Bao lies 80km west of Dong Ha and 3km east of the border. There is an international bus running between Danang (Vietnam) and Savannakhet. In Vietnam, you can catch this bus in Danang, Dong Ha or Lao Bao. In Laos, the only place you are likely to board is Savannakhet. This bus is supposed to make its runs on Sunday, Tuesday and Thursday, but this schedule is hardly engraved in stone and will probably increase in frequency as Lao-Vietnamese commerce continues to grow.

Dong Ha to Savannakhet on this bus costs US$15 for foreigners. From the Vietnamese side, departure from Danang is at 4 am, from Dong Ha at 10 am and from Lao Bao at 2 pm. Arrival in Savannakhet is at 7 pm. Border guards (both Lao and Vietnamese) have been known to ask for bribes.

There are also cheaper local buses which just go to the border from either side. These are more of a hassle – it's a 1km walk between the Vietnamese and Lao border checkpoints, and the bus from Dong Ha terminates at Lao Bao, 3km from the actual border checkpoint (though you can cover this 3km by motorbike taxi). Buses from Dong Ha to Lao Bao cost US$1/4 ('standard'/'deluxe' bus). They normally depart twice daily (early morning and noon), but this is approximate since the buses won't leave until completely full.

There is a restaurant on the Lao side of the border, 500m back from the border post. You might be able to sleep in the restaurant if you ask nicely, but there are no hotels here. To say that the facilities around the border are primitive is an understatement.

From the Lao side there's only one local bus a day to Savannakhet. It leaves around 1 pm (but this could change) and takes six hours. If you miss the bus your best bet is to arrange transport to Sepon and spend the night there.

Visas for Laos can be obtained in Saigon, Hanoi or Danang. If you are departing or entering Vietnam via this route, your Vietnamese visa must indicate the Lao Bao border crossing. If you have a Vietnamese re-entry visa, it can be amended at the Vietnamese consulate in Savannakhet.

Kaew Neua The crossing at Kaew Neua (also called Nam Phao) between Bolikhamsai Province and Cau Treo in Vietnam connects with the Vietnamese town of Vinh, 2½ hours by bus from the border. Recent reports say it can be difficult to find a bus from Vinh to the border but this will undoubtedly change as the crossing becomes more established.

From Kaew Neua it's a 40km jumbo ride along Route 8 to Kham Keut. From the latter there are frequent buses to Paksan and to Tha Khaek, both of which are on Route 13, with connections north to Vientiane or south to Savannakhet.

Other Crossings Another crossing at Sop Hun in Phongsali Province to/from Tay Trang (32km west of Dien Bien Phu) is currently open only to Lao and Vietnamese citizens. Stay tuned.

RIVER
Thailand
Since the opening of the Friendship Bridge, the Tha Deua ferry in Nong Khai has been closed to non-Thai, non-Lao citizens. However, it is still legal for non-Thai foreigners to cross the Mekong River by ferry from Thailand into Laos at the following points: Nakhon Phanom (opposite Tha Khaek), Chiang Khong (opposite Huay Xai) and Mukdahan (opposite Savannakhet).

Getting Around

AIR
Domestic Air Services
Lao Aviation handles all domestic flights in Laos with Vientiane as the main hub.

Lao Aviation accepts only US dollars cash for domestic tickets. You can, however, purchase tickets with credit cards through a travel agent. In Vientiane Diethelm Travel Laos and Lao Air Booking are just a block or so away from Lao Aviation on Thanon Setthathirat.

Booking seats can be difficult on domestic flights as demand exceeds supply and scheduling is erratic – flights are sometimes finally set only a day or two in advance.

Wattay international airport reportedly will be expanded with Singaporean assistance. There has also been talk of allowing a Thai company – possibly Bangkok Airways – to supplement domestic flight schedules in Laos.

Safety records for Lao Aviation aren't made public. In most cases pilots must rely on visual flying techniques. When heavy cloud cover is present pilots are forced to circle the area searching for a hole through which to descend; if none is found within the time allotted by fuel capacity, the pilots either return to the original departure point or land at another airport in the same region. After a short wait and refuelling on the ground, they give it another go!

In 1998 the US State Dept and several other foreign consular agencies advised their citizens to avoid using Lao Aviation as the current aircraft shortage and overall lack of equipment maintenance were deemed unacceptably risky.

Domestic Departure Tax
The departure tax for domestic flights is 300 kip. Passengers must also pay immigration officers at each domestic airport 100 kip for

LAOS

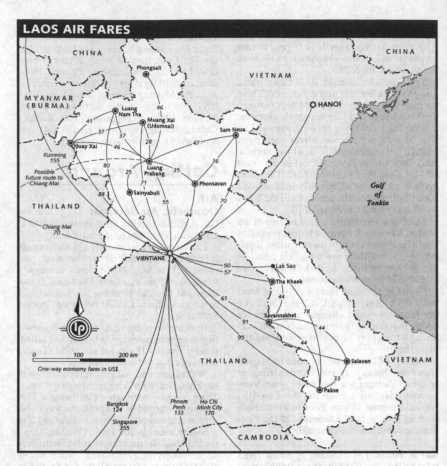

LAOS AIR FARES

One-way economy fares in US$

the privilege of checking in or out of the province each time they arrive or depart by air.

BUS

The road system in Laos remains very undeveloped. Of 22,321km of classified roads (8350km more than the previous year), most aren't pretty. About 16% are tarred; 38% are graded and sometimes covered with gravel; the rest are ungraded dirt tracks.

The roads around Vientiane Prefecture, as far out as Vang Vieng, are surfaced and adequate for just about any type of vehicle. Route 13 north to Luang Prabang and south to Savannakhet has also been paved. Bridge construction over rivers has yet to catch up with road construction, so these routes aren't quite as fast as one might think.

Regular buses ply Route 13 between Vientiane and Pakse an average of two or three times daily. Other routes in the south, such as Pakse to Sekong, typically use large flat-bed trucks mounted with a heavy wooden carriage containing seats in bus-like rows.

In the north, trucks are often converted into passenger carriers by adding two long benches in the back. These passenger trucks are called *thàek-sii* (taxi) or in some areas *sǎwng-thǎew*, which means 'two rows' in reference to the two facing benches in the back.

CAR & MOTORCYCLE

Japanese pick-ups can be chartered between towns or provinces. Because Lao roadways generate a high degree of vehicle wear and tear, hire charges run as high as US$100 a day. Visitors with valid International Driving Permits are permitted to drive in Laos, though a vehicle and driver can be hired for the same price as a rental car in most towns.

Small 100cc motorcycles can be hired at some motorcycle dealers in Vientiane, as well as in Luang Prabang and Savannakhet. The going rate is US$10 to US$12 a day.

Siam Bike Travel (fax 053-21 9211, email davidfl@cm.ksc.co.th) in Chiang Mai, Thailand, arranges two-week, 1500km overland motorbike trips through Laos from Thailand to China and back.

Road Rules

Watch carefully for vehicles making left turns from a side road – Lao drivers typically turn into the left lane before moving over to the right. Motorists also usually merge with oncoming traffic without bothering to look to the rear, reasoning that anything threatening will sound a horn.

Like many places in Asia, every two lane road has an invisible third lane in the middle that all drivers feel free to use at any time. Passing on hills and blind curves is common.

BICYCLE

In Vientiane, Savannakhet, Luang Prabang, Muang Sing and Don Khong it is possible to rent bicycles, although they are usually in rather poor condition. Bicycle rentals elsewhere are as yet unknown.

If you manage to bring your own bicycle into the country, cycling would be an excellent way to see the Mekong River valley area from south Vientiane, which is mostly flat. For the rest of the country you'd need a sturdy mountain bike. You should be able to register it with Lao customs upon entry.

HITCHING

Hitching rides on cargo trucks presents another option. Smaller vehicles will sometimes stop as well. Licence tags will tell you whether vehicles are likely to take on passengers – black tags with yellow letters mean the vehicle is licensed to carry paying passengers; red on yellow means it's privately owned; red is military (not likely to pick up passengers); white on blue is civil service, UN or NGO; and blue-on-white tags belong to embassies or international organisations (who will sometimes pick up foreign passengers). White tags with red lettering mean the vehicle has right-hand drive.

BOAT

Rivers were until recently the true highways and byways of Laos, the main thoroughfares being the Mekong, Nam Ou, Nam Khan, Nam Tha, Nam Ngum and Se Don. The Mekong River is the longest and most important water route and is navigable year-round between Huay Xai in the north and Vientiane. With the increase in road travel, however, passenger services along all rivers are declining year by year.

River Ferry

Large diesel river ferries designed for cargo transport are still used year-round between Huay Xai and Vientiane, but the boats see few passengers south of Luang Prabang now that the Luang Prabang-Vientiane road is sealed. Hence Huay Xai to Luang Prabang is now the main long-distance river trip. The stretch from Vientiane to Pakse sees cargo traffic only.

South of Pakse smaller passenger ferries still ply routes to Champasak and Don Khong, though we are probably seeing the final days of this traffic. At the moment, however, boat transport is still preferable to road transport along these latter routes.

River ferry facilities are quite basic and passengers sit, eat and sleep on the wooden decks. The toilet is an enclosed hole in the deck.

Note that women customarily ride inside the ferries – the outside, front and top decks are considered 'improper' places to sit.

River Taxi

For shorter river trips, such as Luang Prabang to the Pak Ou Caves, it's usually best to hire a river taxi since the large river ferries ply their routes only a couple of times a week. The long-tail boats (héua hãng nyáo) with engines gimbal-mounted on the stern are the most typical, though for a really short trip (eg crossing a river) a rowboat (héua phai) can be hired. The héua hãng nyáo are around 6000 kip an hour for a boat with an eight to 10 person capacity. Larger boats that carry up to 20 passengers are sometimes available for around 8000 kip per hour.

Along the upper Mekong River between Luang Prabang and Huay Xai, Thai-built héua wái (speedboats) – shallow, 5m-long skiffs with 40HP Toyota outboard engines – are common. These are able to cover a distance in six hours that might take a river ferry two days or more. They're not cheap – charters cost about US$20 per hour – but some ply regular routes, so the cost can be shared among several passengers.

LOCAL TRANSPORT

Taxi

Three-wheeled motorcycle taxis are common in the larger towns as well as in some smaller ones. This type of vehicle can be called taxi *(thàek-sii)* or samlor *(sāam-lâw)*, meaning 'three wheels'. The larger ones made in Thailand are called jumbos *(jamboh)* and can hold four to six passengers. Fares are about 500 kip per kilometre per vehicle, but you must bargain to get it. Jumbos aren't usually hired for distances greater than 20km.

Each of the four largest towns – Vientiane, Luang Prabang, Pakse and Savannakhet – has a handful of car taxis, which you'll find only at the airports (at arrival times) and in front of the larger hotels. These taxis can be hired by the trip (pay no more than US$0.50 per kilometre), by the hour or by the day (US$20 to US$40 per day).

Pedicab

The bicycle samlor, once the mainstay of local transport for hire throughout urban Laos, has nearly become extinct. Bicycle samlor fares are about the same as for motorcycle taxis but are generally used only for distances less than 2km. Bargaining is sometimes necessary to get the correct fare, though pedicab drivers seem to be more honest than the motorcycle taxi drivers.

ORGANISED TOURS

Around 16 agencies operate in Vientiane, some of which maintain branches in other cities, such as Luang Prabang, Pakse and Phonsavan. Some agencies advertise tours they can't deliver, while better agencies can go almost anywhere and can create custom itineraries.

For the most part, each agency has a standard set of packages at standard prices. However, per-person rates drop – typically by around US$50 to US$100 per person – for each person added to the group. Costs for one person travelling solo can be US$200 or more per day, while four to six persons travelling together can arrange packages for under US$50 per person per day.

In general, tours arranged by the Vientiane agencies are not bad value as far as package tours go. At each destination, the agencies

arrange all accommodation (double occupancy) and a tour guide. Prices for packages without meals are much lower, and eating out on your own is often more fun than eating pre-arranged hotel meals anyway.

Vientiane Tour Operators

The following are some reputable tour operators in Vientiane:

Diethelm Travel Laos
(☎ 21 5920, fax 21 7151)
Namphu Square, Thanon Setthathirat, PO Box 2657
Inter-Lao Tourisme
(☎ 21 4832, fax 21 6306)
Corner of Thanon Pangkham and Thanon Setthathirat, PO Box 2912
Lane Xang Travel
(☎ 21 2469, fax 21 5804)
Thanon Pangkham, PO Box 4452
Lao Travel Service
(☎ 21 6603, fax 21 6150)
8/3 Thanon Lan Xang, PO Box 2553
SODETOUR (Societé de Development Touristique)
(☎ 21 6314, fax 21 6313)
16 Thanon Fa Ngum, PO Box 70
That Luang Tour
(☎ 21 5809, fax 21 5346)
28 Thanon Kamkhong, PO Box 3619

That Luang and Lane Xang seem to try harder to keep their prices down.

Vientiane

Originally one of the early Lao river-valley fiefdoms (meuang), Vientiane has been controlled by the Burmese, Siamese, Vietnamese and Khmer, and made a capital city by the French, a status it retains in the postcolonial era.

It's one of the three classic Indochinese cities (along with Ho Chi Minh City and Phnom Penh) that conjure up images of exotic Eurasian settings and has remained amazingly laid-back. Vientiane is pronounced 'Wieng Chan'.

Orientation

The city curves along a bend in the Mekong River with the central business district at the middle of the bend. Most of the government offices, hotels, restaurants and historic temples are in this district near the river.

Street signs are mostly written in Lao script only. French designations for street names vary (eg route, rue and avenue) but the Lao script always reads *thanŏn*.

The main streets in the central district are Thanon Samsenthai, which is the main shopping area, Thanon Setthathirat, where several of the most famous temples are located, and Thanon Fa Ngum, which runs along the river. Branching off northward is Thanon Lan Xang, Vientiane's widest street.

To the south-east is the mostly local residential district of Sisattanak and to the west is the similarly residential Sikhottabong.

Maps The *Vientiane Tourist Map*, published by NTAL, is a fairly usable street map. It's available at the National Geographic Service, Raintrees, Phimphone Minimart and several retail shops in the city.

Information

Tourist Offices For information on NTAL, see the earlier Tourist Offices entry under Facts for the Visitor in this chapter.

Money BCEL at Thanon Pangkham and Thanon Fa Ngum, near Lao Aviation and the Lane Xang Hotel, has the best foreign exchange rate of any bank in Vientiane. It's open from 8.30 am to 4.30 pm Monday to Friday, and until 11 am Saturday. Other banks well equipped to handle foreign exchange include Bangkok Bank, Joint Development Bank, Siam Commercial Bank and Thai Military Bank.

Licensed moneychanging booths can also be found in Talaat Sao and in a few other locations around town. You can also change on the 'parallel market' at various shops in town or from the unofficial moneychangers hanging out on Thanon Lan Xang near Talaat Sao. The latter usually offer the best rates in Vientiane but it helps to be on your toes as far as knowing what the going rates are; count your money carefully.

Post The Post, Telephone and Telegraph (PTT) office is on the corner of Thanon Lan Xang and Thanon Khu Vieng, across from Talaat Sao. Business hours are from 8 am to 5 pm Monday to Saturday and until noon on Sunday.

Telephone The Post, Telephone & Telegraph (PTT) office is only for calls within Laos. See Post & Communications in the Facts for the Visitor section for details on overseas calls and faxes.

Emergency The following emergency phone numbers are supposed to bring help immediately:

Fire	☎ 190
Police	☎ 191
Ambulance	☎ 195 or 41 3360

You could also try contacting the police kiosk on Thanon Setthathirat.

Bookshops Raintrees, at 52 Thanon Nokeo Khumman, stocks new and used paperbacks, guidebooks, magazines and other periodicals in English, along with smaller inventories of French and German material. Raintrees also has three smaller branches at: 54/1 Thanon Pangkham (next to the THAI office), in the Lao Hotel Plaza on Thanon Samsenthai and in the Novotel Belvedere on Thanon Luang Prabang.

Laundry Most hotels and guesthouses offer laundry services (a few even include it with room charges). Several laundry and dry cleaning shops can be found in Vientiane's Chinatown area, especially along Thanon Heng Boun and Thanon Samsenthai just east of Thanon Chao Anou.

Medical Services Medical facilities in Vientiane are quite limited. The two state hospitals, Setthathirat and Mahasot, operate on levels of skill and hygiene well below that available in neighbouring Thailand. Mahasot Hospital operates a Diplomatic Clinic 'especially for foreigners' that is open 24 hours. In reality, few foreigners use this clinic.

The 150 bed Hôpital de l'amitié (☎/fax 41 3306) is a centre for trauma and orthopaedics operated by the Association Médicale Franco Asiatique (AMFA) and is on the site of the old Soviet Hospital, north of the city on the road to Tha Ngon.

For medical emergencies that can't wait till Bangkok and can't be treated at one of the local or embassy clinics, you can arrange to have ambulances summoned from nearby Udon Thani or Khon Kaen in Thailand.

Traditional Medicine A state-sponsored, traditional Lao medical clinic (Hong Maw Pin Pua Duay Yaa Pheun Meuang, or Hôpital de Medicine Traditionnelle, ☎ 31 3584) is in the Ban Wat Naak neighbourhood of Sisattanak District. The clinic offers herbal saunas (600 kip per visit) and traditional massage

LAOS

VIENTIANE

To Ban Nong
Bua Thong

●25

Muang
Chanthabuli

●24

**Muang
Sikhottabong**

✈1

To Ban Thalat, Phan Hong
& Kao Liaw Pier

●3

23

📷2

20
19   22
21
●18

17

Thanon Luang Prabang

4■

10 ▼ 11 12
13 ☕ 14

5▼ 6♥ 9■ 8♥
7   15

Thanon Sihom

Thanon Khun Bulom
Thanon Samsenthai
Thanon Setthathirat
Thanon Fa Ngum

Thanon Lan Xang
Thanon Mahasot

26

27

See Central Vientiane Map pg364

57   56 55
59
58

Don Chan
(size varies with
river height)

Mekong River

THAILAND

73

74

75
76
77

78

PLACES TO STAY
4   Auberge de Temple
9   River View Hotel
11 Senesouk Guest House
12 Novotel Belvedere; Raintrees
15 Mekong Hotel
16 New Apollo Hotel
17 Phay Nam Guest House
26 Hotel Royal Dokmaideng;
    Silk Air
29 Le Parasol Blanc Hotel
40 Phonexay Hotel
41 Koto Guest House
47 Villa That Luang
51 Soradith Guest House
54 Heuan Lao Guest House
58 Villa Manoly
62 Chaemchanh
    Guest House
63 Wonderland
    Guest House
65 Vansana Hotel
74 Thieng Thong
    Guest House
77 Muang Lao-China Hotel

PLACES TO EAT
10 Sakura Japanese
    Restaurant
32 Lao Residence
39 Nazim Restaurant
61 Nang Bunmala

EMBASSIES
14 Thai Visa Section
    (Regent Centre)
31 Thai Embassy
33 Vietnamese Embassy
35 Indonesian Embassy
36 Indian Embassy
38 Australian Embassy
66 German Embassy
70 Myanmar Embassy
71 Swedish Embassy

OTHER
1   Wattay International Airport
2   Wat Tai
3   Lao Cotton Factory &
    Showroom
5   Sala Khounta
6   Huamuang Draft Beer
7   Sala Snake
8   Bar Brasserie Anousone
13 Three Elephants Statue
18 Buses to Luang Prabang
19 Talaat Khua Luang
20 Buses to the North
21 Senesabay Bus Co
22 Vientiane Theatre
    (Odeon Rama)
23 Talaat Thong Khan Kham
24 Hôpital de l'Amitié
25 National Circus
    (Hong Kanyasin)

27 Ministry of Interior
28 Patuxai
30 National Geographic Service
34 Ministry of Foreign Affairs
37 Food & Agriculture
    Organisation (FAO)
42 Wat Phonxai
43 United Nations Development
    Programme (UNDP)
44 Unknown Soldiers Memorial
45 Setthathirat Hospital
46 National Assembly
48 Pha That Luang
    (Great Sacred Stupa)
49 Talaat That Luang
50 Wat Ban Fai
52 Talaat Dong Palan
53 Wat Dong Palan
55 Simuang Minimart
56 V&T Computer
57 Wat Phia Wat
59 Wat Si Muang
60 Hospital 109
64 Water Tower
67 Wat Sok Pa Luang
68 Sokpaluang Swimming Pool
69 Hôpital de Medicine
    Traditionnelle
72 Wat Si Amphon
73 China Yunnan Airlines
75 Australian Club (AERC)
76 UNICEF
78 Wat Ammon

LAOS

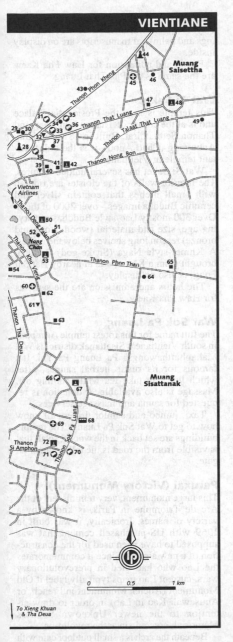

VIENTIANE

Muang
Saisettha

Thanon Phon Kheng

Muang
Sisattanak

Thanon That Luang

Thanon Talaat That Luang

Thanon Nong Bon

Vietnam
Airlines

Thanon Dong Palan

Nong
Chan

Thanon Khu Vieng

Thanon Phon Than

Thanon Tha Deua

Thanon Sok Pa Luang

Thanon
Si Amphon

Thanon Sok Pa Luang

0   0.5   1 km

To Xieng Khuan
& Tha Deua

(600 kip for 15 minutes or 2500 kip for an hour) as well as acupuncture. Other than 'Ban Wat Naak' the clinic has no street address – see the Vientiane map for location. If coming by jumbo, ask the driver to take you to Wat Si Amphon – it's a short walk from the latter (look for small red signs that read 'Hôpital de Medicine Traditionnelle').

Dangers & Annoyances See Theft under Dangers & Annoyances in the Facts for the Visitor section.

Walking Tour
This walk takes you through the central area and past some of the lesser known wats in a leisurely two to 2½ hours. Start at the **fountain** on Thanon Pangkham and walk west on Thanon Setthathirat approximately 250m to **Wat Mixai** on your left. The sīm is built in the Bangkok style, with a veranda that goes all the way around. The heavy gates are flanked by two *nyak*, or guardian giants.

Another 80m west and on the right-hand side of the street is **Wat Hai Sok**, with its impressive tiered roof. Opposite, and just a bit farther on, is **Wat Ong Teu**, and past Thanon Chao Anou on the next block west and on the left again is **Wat In Paeng**. The sīm of this latter wat is nicely decorated with stucco reliefs. Over the front veranda gable is an impressive wood and mosaic facade.

In the reverse direction, go back to Thanon Chao Anou, turn right (south) and walk until you meet Thanon Fa Ngum along the Mekong River. Just around the corner to the left is **Wat Chan**, a typically Lao temple with skilfully carved wooden panels on the rebuilt sīm. Inside is a large bronze seated Buddha from the original temple on this site. In the courtyard are the remains of a stupa with a Buddha image in the Calling for Rain pose.

Continue east on Thanon Fa Ngum until you pass the Lane Xang Hotel on your left. Beyond the hotel a bit, turn left on Thanon Chantha Khumman and walk straight (northeast) about half a kilometre (passing the Hotel Ekalath Metropole on your left) and you'll run into **That Dam**, the Black Stupa. Local mythology says the stupa is the abode of a dormant seven-headed dragon that came to life during the 1828 Siamese-Lao War and protected local citizens.

Pha That Luang

The Great Sacred Stupa is the most important national monument in Laos, a symbol of both the Buddhist religion and Lao sovereignty. Construction began in 1566 and over time four wats were built around the stupa. Only two remain, Wat That Luang Tai to the south and Wat That Luang Neua to the north. The latter is the monastic residence of the Supreme Patriarch (Pha Sangkharat) of Lao Buddhism. In front of the compound entrance is a statue of King Setthathirat.

A high-walled cloister with tiny windows surrounds the 45m stupa. The base of the stupa is designed to be mounted by the faithful, with walkways around each level and connecting stairways.

Each level of the monument has different architectural features in which aspects of Buddhist doctrine are encoded. The tall central stupa is reminiscent of India's first Buddhist stupa at Sanchi.

The cloister measures 85m on each side and contains various Buddha images. A display of classic Lao sculpture and Khmer figures is on either side of the front entrance (inside). Worshippers stick balls of rice to the walls to pay respect to the spirit of King Setthathirat.

The grounds are open to visitors from 8 to 11.30 am and 2 to 4.30 pm, Tuesday to Sunday. Admission is 500 kip. Pha That Luang is about 4km north-east of the city centre at the end of Thanon That Luang. Any bus going north of Thanon Lan Xang will pass within a short walk from the compound.

If you happen to be in Vientiane in mid-November, don't miss the That Luang Festival, the city's biggest annual event.

Haw Pha Kaew

About 100m from Wat Si Saket along Thanon Setthathirat is a former royal temple of the Lao monarchy. It has been converted into a museum and is no longer a place of worship.

According to the Lao, the temple was originally built in 1565 to house the so-called Emerald Buddha. Pha Kaew means Jewel Buddha Image, though the image is actually made of jade. The Siamese removed the Emerald Buddha (originally from a northern Thai kingdom) to Bangkok's royal temple in 1779. During the Siamese-Lao War of 1828, Haw Pha Kaew was razed.

The temple was rebuilt between 1936 and 1942 in a rather Bangkok-style rococo. Today, the veranda shelters some of the best examples of Buddhist sculpture in Laos. Royal requisites, Khmer stelae, wooden carvings and palm-leaf manuscripts are on display inside.

Hours and admission for Haw Pha Kaew are the same as for Pha That Luang.

Wat Si Saket

This temple is near the Presidential Palace and is at the corner of Thanon Lan Xang and Thanon Setthathirat. Built in 1818, by King Anouvong (Chao Anou), it is the oldest extant temple in Vientiane.

Wat Si Saket has several unique features. The interior walls of the cloister are riddled with small niches that contain silver and ceramic Buddha images – over 2000 of them. Over 300 mostly Lao-style Buddhas of varying age, size and material (wood, stone and bronze) rest on long shelves below the niches. A Khmer-style Naga (Snake-god) Buddha, brought from a Khmer site at nearby Hat Sai Fong, is also on display.

The hours and admission are the same as for Haw Pha Kaew.

Wat Sok Pa Luang

The full name for this forest temple (wat paa) in south Vientiane's Sisattanak district is Wat Mahaphutthawongsa Pa Luang Pa Yai. It's famous for its rustic herbal saunas, after which you can take tea while cooling off. Massage is also available. A donation is requested for sauna and massage services.

Taxi, jumbo and samlor drivers all know how to get to Wat Sok Pa Luang. The temple buildings are set back in the woods, so all that is visible from the road is the tall ornamental gate.

Patuxai (Victory Monument)

This large monument, very reminiscent of the Arc de Triomphe in Paris, is known by a variety of names. Ironically, it was built in 1969 with US-purchased cement that was supposed to have been used for the construction of a new airport. Since it commemorates the Lao who had died in prerevolutionary wars, current Lao maps typically label it Old Monument (Ancien Monument in French, or Anusawali Kao in Lao) in order to draw attention to the newer Unknown Soldiers Memorial, erected since the revolution.

Beneath the arch is a small outdoor cafe with snacks. A stairway leads to the top of the monument, where you can look out over the city (there's a small entry fee to climb the stairs).

Lao Revolutionary Museum

Housed in a well-worn classical mansion on Thanon Samsenthai and originally built in 1925 as the French governor's residence, this museum mostly contains a collection of arte-facts and photos from the Pathet Lao's lengthy struggle for power. Many of the dis-plays consist of historic weaponry; some labels are in English as well as Lao.

Posted hours (which are not scrupulously followed) for the museum are from 8 to 11.30 am and 2 to 4.30 pm weekdays; entry is 200 kip.

Xieng Khuan

Often called Buddha Park (Suan Phut), this collection of slightly bizarre Buddhist and Hindu cement sculpture in a meadow by the side of the Mekong River lies 24km south of the city centre off Thanon Tha Deua. It's open daily from 7.30 am to 6 pm; entry is 800 kip, plus 400 kip for still cameras, 600 kip for video cameras. A few vendors in the park offer fresh young coconuts, soft drinks, beer and Lao food.

Talaat Sao

Talaat Sao (Morning Market) is on the north-east corner of the intersection of Thanon Lan Xang and Thanon Khu Vieng. It actually runs all day, from about 6 am to 6 pm. The sprawling collection of stalls offer fabric, ready-made clothes, hardware, jewellery, electronic goods and just about anything else imaginable.

Other Markets

East of Talaat Sao and beyond the bus termi-nal on Thanon Khua Vieng, **Talaat Khua Din** (Khua Din Market) offers fresh produce and meats, as well as flowers, tobacco and assort-ed goods.

A bigger fresh market is **Talaat Thong Khan Kham**. The market is open all day but is best in the morning. It's the biggest market in Vientiane and has virtually everything. You'll find it north of the city centre in Ban Thong Khan Kham, at the intersection of Thanon Khan Kham and Thanon Dong Miang.

Talaat That Luang is just a little south-east of Pha That Luang on Thanon Talaat That Luang. The speciality here is exotic foods, like snakes (favoured by the Vietnamese and Chinese).

Places to Stay

Many hotels and guesthouses in Vientiane quote US dollar or Thai baht rates; some of the more expensive places require payment in US currency, despite the ban on all currencies other than kip. All offer 5 to 20% discounts for long-term stays.

Places to Stay – Budget

Guesthouses The multistorey *Ministry of Information & Culture (MIC) Guest House* (☎ 21 2362) at 67 Thanon Manthatulat is still the cheapest place in town. Large three-bed fan rooms cost 9000 kip per person a night all with attached toilet/bath, add 3000 kip for air-con. Rates are payable in kip, baht or dollars. The rooms are reasonably clean and it's a good value.

Just up Thanon Manthatulat from the MIC Guest House, on a corner on the same side of the street, the private *Phantavong Guest House* (☎ 21 4738) offers 19 basic rooms for US$6/8 single/double with shared toilet and shower, US$10/12 with private bath and air-con. Cleanliness is not a strength of this place and some of the rooms are rather stuffy.

Santisouk Guest House (☎ 21 5303), above the Restaurant Santisouk on Thanon Nokeo Kumman, has plain but clean rooms with wooden floors, high ceilings and shared bath for US$10 to US$12 depending on the size. The restaurant downstairs is a good breakfast spot.

A centrally located place is the friendly *Vannasinh Guest House* (☎ /fax 22 2020) at 51 Thanon Phnom Penh at the edge of Chi-natown (a block north of Thanon Samsenthai). Small but clean rooms with high ceilings and fans cost US$8 with shared toilet and hot shower, or US$10 with private toilet and shower, while much larger rooms with air-con and hot shower cost US$20 (US$16 if you stay three nights or more). Breakfast is available in a small dining room. The popular Vannasinh tends to fill up by noon.

Also well located is the friendly *Syri Guest House* (☎ 21 2682) in a large house in the old Chao Anou residential quarter. Spacious fan rooms are US$10 with shared hot-water bath, US$15 double with attached hot-water bath and US$20 for air-con rooms with attached hot-water bath, TV, fridge and phone.

Half a block north of the fountain square, at 72/6 Thanon Pangkham, a narrow four storey building houses the new *Pangkham Guest House* (☎ 21 6382). Small rooms with fan and attached toilet and hot-water shower

CENTRAL VIENTIANE

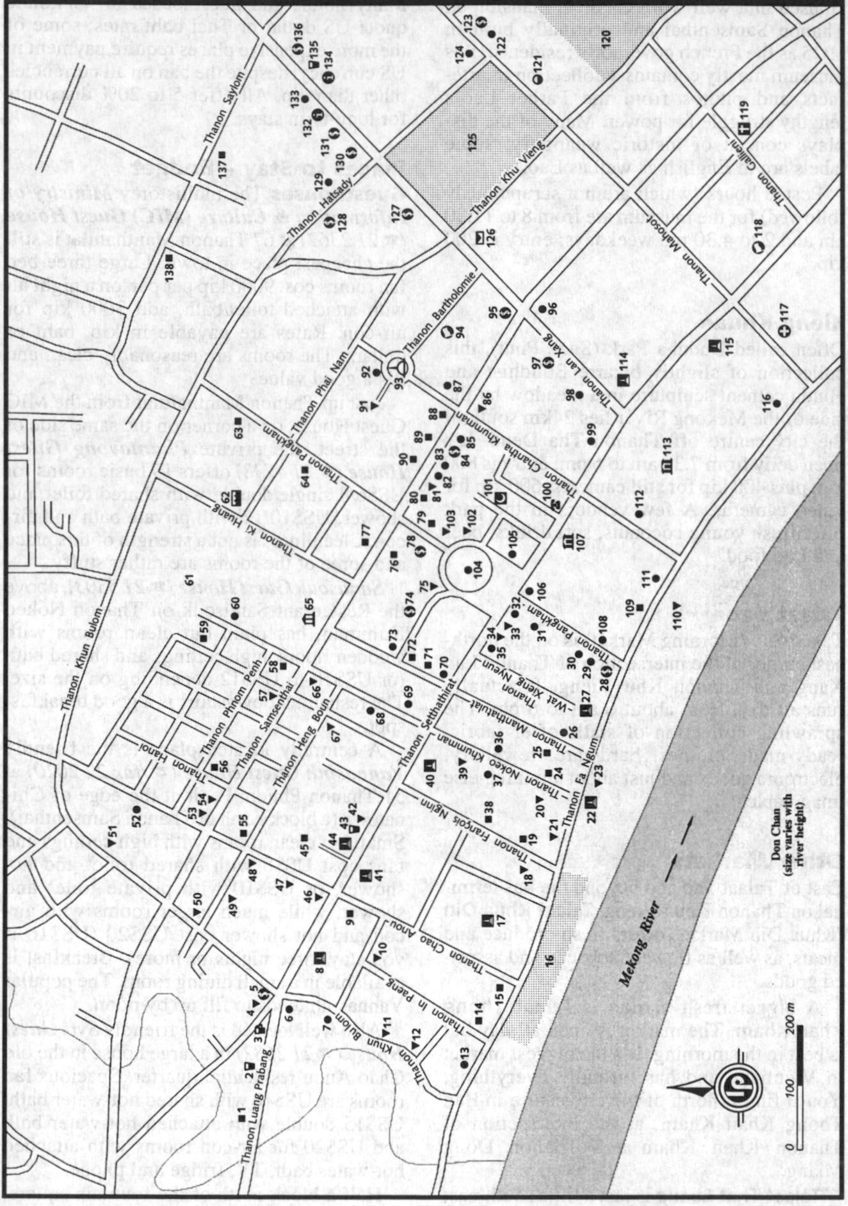

Thanon Saylom

Thanon Hatsady

Thanon Mahosot

Thanon Khu Viente

Thanon Bartholonie

Thanon Lan Xang

Thanon Phai Nam

Thanon Chantha Khumman

Thanon Pangkham

Thanon Ki Huang

Thanon Khun Bulom

Thanon Khun Bulom

Thanon Phnom Penh

Thanon Hanoi

Thanon Samsenthai

Thanon Heng Boun

Thanon Setthathirat

Thanon Manthatulat

Thanon Nokeo Khumman

Thanon Fa Ngum

Thanon Pangkham

Wat Xieng Ngeun

Thanon In Paeng

Thanon Chao Anou

Thanon François Nginn

Thanon Khun Bulom

Thanon Luang Prabang

Thanon Gallieni

Mekong River

Don Chan
(size varies with
river height)

0   100   200 m

CENTRAL VIENTIANE

PLACES TO STAY
1 Vientiane Hotel
9 Saysana Hotel
14 Phornthip Guest House
15 Inter Hotel
19 Tai-Pan Hotel
24 Douang Deuane Hotel
25 Samsenthai Hotel
38 Lao International Guest House
45 Lani I Guest House
55 Anou Hotel
56 Vannasinh Guest House
58 Santisouk Guest House; Restaurant Santisouk
59 Syri Guest House
63 Belmont Settha Palace Hotel (under construction)
64 Day Inn Hotel
71 MIC Guest House
72 Phantavong Guest House
76 Settha Guest House
77 Lao Hotel Plaza; Raintrees; Malaysia Airlines
79 Pangkham Guest House
80 Lao Paris Hotel
88 Hotel Ekalath Metropole; Phimphone Market
89 Asian Pavilion Hotel
90 Hua Guo Guest House
109 Lane Xang Hotel
137 Lani II Guest House
138 Saylomyen Guest House

PLACES TO EAT
4 Phikun
10 Restaurant Le Vendôme
11 Xang Coffee House
12 Nang Kham Bang
16 Night Vendors
18 Le Bistrot Snack Bar
20 Le Safran
21 Nazim Restaurant
23 John Restaurant
33 Healthy & Fresh Bakery & Eatery
34 Lo Stivale Deli Café
39 La Terrase
42 Le Bayou Bar Brasserie
46 Nai Xieng Chai Yene
47 Sweet Home Bakery; Liang Xiang Bakery House
48 Le Chanthy (Nang Janti)
49 Nang Suli/Vieng Sawan Restaurants
50 Maningom Supermarket

51 Aahaan Pheua Sukhaphaap
53 Moey Chin
54 Samsenthai Fried Noodle
57 Thai Food (Phikun) Restaurant
66 Uncle Fred's
67 Restaurant Ha-Wai
75 Scandinavian Bakery; Restaurant Le Provençal
81 PVO
86 Kua Lao
91 Soukvimane Lao Food
102 L'Opera Italian Restaurant
103 The Taj
110 Salongxay Restaurant

TEMPLES
8 Wat In Paeng
17 Wat Chan
27 Wat Xieng Nyeun
40 Wat Mixai
41 Wat Ong Teu
44 Wat Hai Sok
114 Wat Si Saket
115 Haw Pha Kaew

OTHER
2 Win West Pub (Bane Saysana)
3 Shell Station
5 Thai Military Bank
6 Russian Cultural Centre
7 Culeur d'Asie
13 SODETOUR
22 Haw Kang (Chinese Shrine)
26 The Art of Silk
28 BCEL (Lao Foreign Trade Bank)
29 Thai Airways International
30 Raintrees
31 Lane Xang Travel
32 Inter-Lao Tourisme
35 Lao Air Booking
36 Mixay Massage
37 Raintrees
43 Samlo Pub
52 Vietnamese Association
60 Vientiane Tennis Club
61 National Stadium
62 Public Pool
65 Lao Revolutionary Museum
68 Lao Gallery
69 Lao Textiles

70 State Book Shop
73 IMF
74 Bank of Lao PDR
78 Nakhornluang Bank
82 Souvenir & Handicraft Shops
83 Vinotheque La Cave
84 Money Exchange
85 Phimphone Minimart
87 Kanchana Boutique
92 Champa Gallery
93 That Dam (Black Stupa)
94 US Embassy
95 Siam Commercial Bank
96 EDL (Électricté du Laos)
97 Krung Thai Bank
98 Ministry of Education
99 Ministry of Information and Culture
100 Public Call Office
101 Mosque
104 Fountain Circle
105 Diethelm Travel Laos
106 National Library
107 Colonial Villas
108 Lao Aviation
111 Former National Treasury
112 Presidential Cabinet
113 Presidential Palace (Haw Kham)
116 Lao People's Revolutionary Youth Union
117 Mahasot Hospital
118 French Embassy
119 Catholic Church
120 Talaat Khua Din
121 Bus Terminal
122 Pharmacie Sengthong Osoth
123 Siam Commercial Bank
124 Pharmacie Kamsaat
125 Talaat Sao (Morning Market)
126 Post, Telephone & Telegraph (PTT) Office
127 Vientiane Commercial Bank
128 Bangkok Bank
129 Immigration Office
130 Joint Development Bank
131 Bank of Ayudhya
132 Tourist Authority of Thailand
133 Centre de Langue Française
134 NTAL (National Tourism Authority of Laos)
135 Nightclub Vienglatry
136 Thai Farmer's Bank

LAOS

cost US$10, while similar rooms with air-con cost US$15. Slightly larger rooms are available for US$16. Rooms at the back are quieter than those facing Thanon Pangkham.

Saylomyen Guest House (☎ 21 4246), a two storey shophouse-style place on Thanon Saylom, has eight simple, clean rooms for 200B with fan and cold-water shower, 300B with air-con and hot-water shower. There's some street noise in the front so take a room towards the back if you have a choice.

Towards the river, the *Lao International Guest House* (☎ 21 6571) on Thanon François Nginn, north of the Tai-Pan Hotel, offers 11 rooms with varying prices. Bare rooms with fan and shared bath start at US$10, while rooms with attached bath are US$12.

Three blocks west, tucked away on parallel Thanon In Paeng, is the similarly varied but better-designed *Phornthip Guest House* (☎ 21 7239). Spacious, clean, basic rooms with bath and fan cost US$10/12 single/double, while air-con rooms go for US$14/16. The guesthouse enforces a 11.30 pm curfew, when the front door is locked.

Hotels *Hotel Ekalath Metropole* (☎ 21 3420) on the corner of Thanon Samsenthai and Thanon Chantha Khumman has undergone at least three incarnations, starting with the pre-1975 Imperial Hotel. The latest version is basically a mid-range hotel, but a semi-attached annex contains cheap, plain fan rooms for US$5.50 to US$6.60 single and US$7.70 to US$8.80 double with fan and shared cold-water shower, or US$12 single and US$14 double with fan and attached cold shower (but shared toilet).

The *Inter Hotel* (☎ 21 5137) at the corner of Thanon Chao Anou and Thanon Fa Ngum is near the river. Rates here are US$12 to US$16, depending on the size of the room; all rooms come with air-con. Larger, two-room units with hot-water showers are priced at US$20. Formerly the Lao Chaleune Hotel, this hotel is well located and often full, although the rooms are nothing special. One definite drawback is the hotel's bar/disco, which when active causes the whole building to shake.

The *Samsenthai Hotel* (☎ 21 2166) at 15 Thanon Manthatulat near the river has gone through its ups and downs but at last pass was looking OK again. Simple rooms with fan and shared bath go for US$6; with fan and attached toilet/bath it's US$8, while for US$12/15 single/double you can get air-con

and a private toilet/hot-water shower. Downstairs is a restaurant serving Chinese and European food.

Places to Stay – Mid-Range
Guesthouses The centrally located *Lani I Guest House* (☎ 21 6103) is at 281 Thanon Setthathirat, near Wat Hai Sok. Twelve large, comfortable air-con rooms in an old house cost US$25 single and US$30 to US$35 double. Each room comes with phone and attached hot-water shower, and there is a pleasant terrace dining area. A second branch, *Lani II* at 268 Thanon Saylom (☎ 21 3022), is also located well off the street in a large house – if anything it's quieter than Lani I. Seven large, nicely decorated rooms start at US$15/20 single/double with air-con, fan, phone and a basin in the room, with toilet and hot-water shower down the hall. With private toilet, hot-water shower and fridge it's US$20/25.

Next to Honour International School, very near Wat Si Muang and a short stroll from the river, friendly *Villa Manoly* (☎ 21 2282) is a very large villa sitting on quiet, nicely landscaped grounds. The house is furnished with antiques, there's a sitting terrace off the 2nd floor and service is generally excellent. The 12 high-ceiling rooms come with attached hot-water showers and cost US$20/25 single/double.

Hotels The *Asian Pavilion Hotel* (☎ 21 3430) at 379 Thanon Samsenthai is a good mid-priced choice. 'Standard' (read 'old') rooms in the back of the hotel are a reasonable US$18 with fan, air-con, telephone and private hot-water bath. More modern and slightly larger 'superior' rooms with TV, fridge and bathtub are US$25. It's relatively quiet, since there is no disco.

The freshly renovated *Anou Hotel* (☎ 21 3630) at the corner of Thanon Heng Boun and Thanon Chao Anou has smallish rooms for US$30/45 single/double (including breakfast), all with air-con, hot water, satellite TV, operator-assisted phone and minifridge.

The *Douang Deuane Hotel* (☎ 22 2301) on Thanon Nokeo Khumman near the river is a four storey place with simple but very clean, medium-sized rooms with fridge, TV, air-con, soft beds and hot-water showers with tubs for US$22 single/double.

Vientiane's original luxury hotel, the *Lane Xang Hotel* (☎ 21 4102, fax 21 4108) faces the Mekong on Thanon Fa Ngum, around the corner from Lao Aviation, THAI and BCEL. This four storey wonder was until very recently the LPDR's classiest place and the hotel of choice for visiting high-rollers. The 109 clean and spacious rooms have a socialist-era feel – some of the spacious bathrooms still feature funky Russian hot-water heaters (but state-of-the-art Japanese air-con) as well as huge lavatories with bidets. Other amenities include a lift (the second one installed in all of Laos), restaurant, bar, nightclub, business office, swimming pool, putting green, snooker club, two badminton courts, gift shop and a fitness centre out the back with sauna and exercise equipment. At the time we visited, the Lane Xang was a great deal, with rooms costing just US$22/25 single/double, spacious junior suites US$45 and huge apartment-sized executive suites for US$55; all rates include breakfast, service charge, tax and free taxi service to and from the airport. Credit cards are accepted.

Places to Eat

Vientiane is good for eating options, with a wide variety of cafes, street vendors, beer halls and restaurants offering everything from rice noodles to filet mignon. Nearly all fit well into a shoestring budget.

Breakfast A popular street breakfast is *khào jĭi pá-tĕh*, a split French baguette stuffed with Lao-style paté (which is more like English or American luncheon meat than French paté) and various dressings. Vendors who sell breakfast sandwiches also sell plain baguettes (*khào jĭi*) – there are several regular bread vendors on Thanon Heng Boun between Thanon Chao Anou and Thanon Khun Bulom.

Two side-by-side cafes on Thanon Chao Anou, *Liang Xiang Bakery House* and *Sweet Home Bakery*, sell passable croissants and other pastries in the morning, and strong brewed coffee.

Healthy & Fresh Bakery & Eatery, two doors east of Lo Stivale Deli Café on Thanon Setthathirat, features yoghurts, sandwiches, fruit and a large selection of baked goods; it's good, if a little expensive. It's open Monday to Saturday 7 am to 7 pm.

Xang Coffee House, on the east side of Thanon Khun Bulom towards the river, sports innovative decor – a vibrant colour scheme and vaguely south-western American/Mexican theme. The creative menu covers a broad range of light international fare, European and American breakfasts, burgers, sandwiches, salads, ice cream, pastries, espresso coffee, fresh juices and cocktails; prices average 1500 to 3000 kip. Lots of English-language magazines and newspapers – including the *Bangkok Post* – are available to read, and an upstairs room features a TV tuned to CNN or BBC. It's open Wednesday to Monday 9 am to 9 pm.

Lao In the heart of the central area, the best *pîng kai* (grilled chicken) *vendors* are found opposite the Maningom Supermarket near the corner of Thanon Khun Bulom and Thanon Heng Boun from around 5.30 pm to 8 or 9 pm. You can eat at tables behind the vendors, though most people do takeaways.

Towards the northern end of Thanon Chao Anou, on the right-hand side before it crosses Thanon Khun Bulom, a slightly smaller group of *vendors* also offer slightly cheaper pîng kai, along with *tăm* (spicy mortar-pounded salads) made with shredded green papaya or green beans, all for takeaway only.

If you're looking to eat pîng kai with a roof over your head, the clean, popular and inexpensive *Nang Bunmala* (no Roman-script sign) on Thanon Khu Vieng is your best choice. The chickens cooked here are much plumper than the Lao norm and roasted to perfection for 3000 kip per half, 5000 kip for a whole chicken. Also available are *pîng pét* (grilled duck), *pîng pǫa* (grilled fish), *tam màak hung* (spicy papaya salad), sticky rice and draught beer. It's open daily 11 am to 10 pm.

Along Thanon Fa Ngum, facing the river between Wat Xieng Nyeun and Wat Chan, is an intermittent sprinkling of *Lao food shops* specialising in *làap, năem,* fried rice and other simple dishes. *John Restaurant* on Thanon Fa Ngum looks like all the other little shops in the area but features an English-language menu offering Lao dishes and rice plates, American breakfasts, salads and sandwiches.

Thai On Thanon Samsenthai, just past the Lao Revolutionary Museum, is the *Phikun* (the English sign reads 'Thai Food') restaurant, which has all the Thai standards. Curries are good here – something you don't see much of in Lao cuisine. There's a second branch of the Phikun on Thanon Luang Prabang, near the Thai Military Bank just west of Thanon Khun Bulom.

The *Vientiane Department Store* (part of

Talaat Sao) has a small but very popular food centre with an extensive variety of Thai, Lao and western dishes in the 1500 to 2000 kip range.

Noodles, Chinese & Vietnamese Noodles of all kinds are very popular in Vientiane, especially along *Thanon Heng Boun*, the unofficial Chinatown. Basically, you can choose between *fõe* (flat rice noodles) and *mie* (the traditional Chinese wheat noodles).

Samsenthai Fried Noodle on Thanon Samsenthai around the corner from Vannasinh Guest House specialises in large plates of delicious *fõe khùa* (fried rice noodles), with your choice of chicken, pork, or shrimp. Order *phii-sēht* (special) and they'll add more green vegies to the mix. It's open Monday to Saturday 10 am to around 9 pm.

Le Chanthy (Nang Janti) Cuisine Vietnamienne, a small shop on Thanon Chao Anou, one door south of the corner of Thanon Chao Anou and Thanon Heng Boun, makes very good Lao-style *khào pûn* with a choice of three toppings – it's probably the best place in the city centre to try this dish. Janti also offers Vietnamese *nãem neūang* (barbecued pork meatballs) and *yáw* (spring rolls), usually sold in 'sets' *(sut)* with cold khào pũn, fresh lettuce leaves, mint, basil, various dipping sauces, sliced starfruit and sliced green plantain.

Indian *The Taj* on Thanon Pangkham opposite Nakhonluang Bank (just north of the fountain) has an extensive menu of well prepared north Indian dishes. Service is good and the place is very clean, though prices are a bit on the high side for Vientiane. The Taj also has a sizable daily lunch buffet for 3800 kip and set evening dinners for 3700 to 4500 kip.

Cheaper Indian food can be found at *Nazim Restaurant* on Thanon Phonexay near the Aussie embassy, opposite the Phonexay Hotel. A newer branch can be found on Thanon Fa Ngum. The extensive menu includes mostly north Indian dishes along with a few south Indian items, such as *masala dosa* and *idli*.

European Several commendable French, French-Lao and Italian restaurants can be found in Vientiane. Most are costly by local standards but definitely better value than restaurants in Vientiane hotels.

At the cheaper end of the spectrum, and

particularly good value, is *Restaurant Santisouk* (long ago known as Café La Pagode) on Thanon Nokeo Khumman, near the Lao Revolutionary Museum. While decor is bland and slightly tatty, the cuisine is of the simple 'French grill' type and quite tasty. A filling plate of steak or filet mignon (served on a sizzling platter) or filleted fish or roast chicken with roast potatoes and vegies costs less than 5000 kip. Breakfasts are also very good. It's open daily 7 am to 10 pm.

Le Bistrot Snack Bar (☎ 21 5972), opposite the Tai-Pan Hotel on Thanon François Nginn, is owned by an older Lao couple who spent most of their lives in Paris. It's good value, and the fare includes good, relatively inexpensive French dishes.

Le Bayou Bar Brasserie on Thanon Setthathirat, diagonally opposite Wat Ong Teu, is a simple, charming spot with a choice of seating in the air-con dining room or narrow beer garden alongside. Prices are very reasonable and the fare includes draught beer, breakfasts, pasta, pizza, sandwiches, fondue and brochettes. The various salads and fruit shakes are especially good.

Opposite the Restaurant-Bar Namphu on the Fountain Circle is *L'Opera Italian Restaurant*, a branch of a restaurant of the same name in Bangkok. The mostly Italian menu includes pizzas, pasta, antipasto, seafood, salads, plus Italian coffees and wines. Quality is consistent, prices medium high.

The newer *Lo Stivale Deli Café* at 44/2 Thanon Setthathirat takes the prize for best pizza and gnocchi in town. Prices are a bit higher than the norm for Vientiane, even for European food.

Vegetarian *Aahaan Pheua Sukhaphaap* (the English sign reads 'Vegetarian Food') is a stall on the east side of Thanon Khun Bulom just north of the Thanon Samsenthai intersection. Not surprisingly, it's owned and operated by a Thai woman (comparatively, vegetarianism hasn't caught on yet in Laos). The food is 100% vegan, with tofu, gluten and mushrooms sitting in for meat. It's very inexpensive and open daily 7 am to around 2 pm.

Just for Fun, a small shop on Thanon Pangkham next to Raintrees bookshop, has a few vegetarian dishes inspired by Thai, Lao and Indian cuisine, plus Lao coffee and lots of herbal teas. It's open Monday to Saturday from 9 am to 10 pm.

Entertainment

Bars *Samlo Pub*, next door to Restaurant Sourichanh on Thanon Setthathirat (opposite Wat Ong Teu), is a small, well stocked bar that's popular with visitors and expats alike. Draught Beerlao is available on tap.

Beer Gardens Vientiane abounds in casual outdoor places built of bamboo and thatch where patrons while away the hours drinking Lao beer and eating traditional snacks, or *káp kâem.*

Right in the centre of town stands the Croatian-owned *Namphou Garden*, a set of tables and chairs encircling the renovated fountain (lit with coloured lights in the evening) where you can get Lao, European and Indian food, beer and cocktails till around 11 pm. When the weather's hot, this place can be packed with patrons seeking the cooling effects of the large fountain.

A lengthy string of tiny, bamboo-thatch places right on the river can be found near the River View Hotel, the most distinguished of which is *Sala Khounta* about 120m upstream from the hotel. Also known as the Sunset Bar, it's basically a small bamboo platform over the Mekong, decorated with orchids, planters, fishtraps and basketry. Beerlao is the main attraction, but the friendly, enterprising proprietors also offer an array of Lao and Vietnamese snacks.

Farther downriver stands the much more substantial *Bar Brasserie Anousone*, a wooden pavilion on the west side of the road. In the evening, and during cooler weather during the day, the proprietors place tables on the riverbank opposite. Food and service are good, prices reasonable. Nearby *Mekong Riverside* (Sala Khaem Khong in Lao) is popular with the Lao youth who have money to spend on Thai pop music and mood lighting.

Dance Halls Vientiane has at least six 'discos' with live music. Popular places include the huge *Nightclub Vienglatry* on Thanon Lan Xang, a bit north of Talaat Sao (and on the same side of the street), along with clubs attached to the *Anou, Saysana* and *Inter* hotels.

Shopping

The main shopping areas are Talaat Sao (including shops along Thanon Talaat Sao), west along Thanon Samsenthai (near the Hotel Ekalath Metropole) and on Thanon Pangkham.

Lao Textiles Talaat Sao is a very good place to look for traditional and modern fabrics, plus shoulder bags, cushions etc. Lao Antique Textiles in stall A2-4 has a good selection.

Lao Textiles on Thanon Nokeo Khumman (look for an old two storey French-Lao house) sells high-end contemporary fabrics inspired by older Lao artistry. Prices are what you might expect from a weaving house that has exhibited in galleries and museums in major cities around the world.

Getting There & Away

Air Vientiane is the only legal port of entry into Laos for international flights. Lao Aviation (☎ 21 2058) has its main offices at 2 Thanon Pangkham around the corner from the Lane Xang Hotel. Directly across the street from Lao Aviation is the THAI office (☎ 21 6143). Other airlines with offices in town include Malaysia Airlines (☎ 21 8816), 1st floor of Lao Hotel Plaza; Silk Air (☎ 21 7492), 2nd floor of the Hotel Royal Dokmaideng and Vietnam Airlines (☎ 21 7562) on Thanon Dong Palan near Talaat Dong Palan.

Bus The main provincial bus terminal stands next to Talaat Sao on Thanon Khu Vieng. This one handles bus transport to nearby towns in Vientiane Province as well as points south

Senesabay Co (☎ 21 8052) runs a higherclass bus from Vientiane to Savannakhet, advertising on-board beverage/snack service, air-con, assigned seats and an eight hour trip with stops in Paksan and Tha Khaek only. It leaves each morning at 7 am from the Senesabay office opposite the Vientiane Theatre (Odeon Rama) near Talaat Khua Luang market or at 7.15 am from the Talaat Sao terminal. Tickets cost 10,000 kip (same as the government bus), available at the Senesabay office or at the Talaat Sao terminal.

Another terminal recently started up inside the parking lot for Talaat Khua Luang, off Thanon Khua Luang, with buses heading north along Route 13 to Thalat, Vang Vieng and Kasi. Jumbo drivers most often refer to this station as *kíw lōt khua lūang,* or 'Khua Luang bus queue'.

Buses to Luang Prabang leave from just around the corner from the market, on Thanon Khua Luang near its T-junction with Thanon Nong Duang. There are three departures per day at 6.30 and 7.30 am and 11 pm; each costs 13,000 kip. These buses take around 11 hours to reach Luang Prabang; many travellers stop over in Vang Vieng to break up the trip.

Long-Distance River Ferry Few people now take the slow cargo boats to Luang Prabang (which take from four days to a week). These ferries leave from the Kao Liaw pier (Tha Heua Kao Liaw), 7.7km west of the Novotel (3.5km west of the fork in the road where Route 13 heads north) in Ban Kao Liaw. They usually leave between 8 and 9 am and carry a maximum of 20 passengers. You should go to Kao Liaw the day before to make sure a boat is going and to reserve deck space.

Rates are negotiable – many drivers want 35,000 kip. The boats make several stops along the way. Passengers typically sleep on the boat except in Pak Lai, where there are a couple of small guesthouses.

Speedboat Faster boat service is available aboard six-passenger *héua wái* (speedboats), which cost 25,000 kip per person to Pak Lai, 42,000 kip to Tha Deua and 51,000 kip to Luang Prabang. Count on a full day to reach Tha Deua or Luang Prabang, four or five hours for Pak Lai. To charter a speedboat you'd have to pay a fee roughly equal to six passenger fares. Like the slower cargo boats, speedboats leave from the Kao Liaw pier.

Getting Around

Central Vientiane is entirely accessible on foot. For trips into neighbouring districts, however, you'll need vehicular support.

To/From the Airport Wattay international airport is only a 10 minute taxi ride northwest of the city centre. Taxis wait in front of the airport for passengers going into town. The going rate for a jumbo (motorcycle taxi) to the centre of town is 4000 kip, for a car taxi 5000 kip; drivers may ask for more. You'd best pay no more than the kip or baht equivalent of around US$3.

You can also hop a shared jumbo for 1000 kip per person – just follow the Lao who have arrived at the airport.

If you're heading farther – say to eastern Vientiane past Wat Si Muang – you'll have to pay around 1500 kip per person for a jumbo, 6000 kip for a car.

There are no public buses direct from the airport, but if you walk 100m south of the terminal to Thanon Luang Prabang, you can catch a bus into town (turn left) for 300 kip.

Going out to the airport from the town centre, a jumbo costs 2000 kip, a car 2500 to 3500 kip. You can also catch a Phon Hong bus from Talaat Sao for 300 kip.

Bus There is a city bus system but it's for transport to outlying districts to the north, east and west of Chanthabuli. Fares for any distance within Vientiane Prefecture are low – about 300 kip for a 20km ride.

Motorcycle Rental Vientiane Motor, opposite the fountain on Thanon Setthathirat, rents 80cc and 100cc motorcycles for US$10 to US$12 per day.

Taxi A small fleet of car taxis operate in Vientiane, mostly stationed in front of the larger hotels as well as at the airport during flight arrival times. For most short trips within town a pedicab or jumbo is more economical. Within Vientiane, an older car and driver costs US$20 to US$25 for the day; it's US$30 to US$40 a day for trip farther afield.

Motorcycle Taxi Asking fare for jumbos seems to be 1000 kip per foreigner, but the standard local fare for a chartered jumbo should be 600 kip per person for distances of 2km or less; bargaining is mandatory.

Share jumbos which run regular routes around town (eg Thanon Luang Prabang to Thanon Setthathirat, or Thanon Lan Xang to Pha That Luang) cost 400 kip per person; no bargaining is necessary.

Pedicab Recently, bicycle samlors (*sāamlâw*) have almost become extinct. Charges are about 800 kip per kilometre (but don't hire a samlor for any distance greater than 2 or 3km).

Bicycle Rental This is the most convenient and economical way to see Vientiane besides walking. Several guesthouses – including the Syri, Lani I and Lani II – rent bikes on a regular basis for around 2000 kip per day. Kanchana Boutique opposite the Hotel Ekalath Metropole on Thanon That Dam and Queen's Beauty Tailor (on the Fountain Circle) also offer a few bikes for rent.

AROUND VIENTIANE
Lao Pako

Lao Pako (π/fax 31 2234), a rustic bamboo-thatch ecological resort on the banks on the Nam Ngum river about 55km north-east of

Vientiane via Ban Somsamai, is a good spot to enjoy the Lao countryside without leaving Vientiane Province. A wood-and-bamboo longhouse contains a seven bed dorm that costs 14,000 kip per person, plus three rooms for 45,000 kip. Separate bungalows with private bath are 60,000 kip. There is also an open-air *sala* where you can sleep on the floor for 6000 kip a night. All rooms are screened and come with mosquito nets but no electricity. Activities include swimming, boating and hiking, and there are Lao-style buffet meals, weekend barbecues and monthly full-moon parties.

The best way to reach Lao Pako is to drive or take a 1½ hour bus trip to Somsamai (bus No 19 from Talaat Sao, 500 kip, three times daily) on the Nam Ngum river, where a local motorised canoe will take you on to the lodge, a 25 minute journey, for 3000 kip.

Ang Nam Ngum (Nam Ngum Reservoir)

Approximately 90km north of Vientiane, Ang Nam Ngum is a huge artificial lake that was created by damming the Nam Ngum river. A hydroelectric plant here generates most of the power used in the Vientiane valley, as well as the power sold on to Thailand via high-power wires over the Mekong River.

The lake is dotted with picturesque islands and a cruise is well worth arranging (15,000 kip per hour for boats holding up to 20 passengers is the going rate). On the way to the lake you can stop in **Ban Ilai**, in the Muang Naxaithong district, known for a market with basketry, pottery and other daily utensils. Several other villages can be visited along the way.

Places to Stay Ang Nam Ngum can be visited on a day trip from Vientiane. Nam Ngum Tour Company operates a *floating hotel*, with large, clean rooms complete with private hot-water baths and air-con for 15,000 kip per night. The boat is fairly pleasant but rarely leaves the pier except when groups book the entire boat. The dock location is not particularly scenic because of the trashy lumber operations nearby.

A modest *hotel* on Don Dok Khon Kham, an island only 10 minutes by boat from the harbour, has rooms for 12,000 kip; food is available, but running water and electricity only come on in the evening. A shuttle boat to this island costs 2000 kip.

Getting There & Away From Talaat Sao, you can catch the 7 am bus all the way to Kheuan Nam Ngum (Nam Ngum Dam) for 1000 kip. This trip takes three hours and proceeds along Route 13 through Ban Thalat. Taxis in Vientiane charge US$35 to US$40 return to the lake. If you hire one, ask the driver to take the more scenic Route 10 through Ban Keun; the trip is about the same distance as the trip via Ban Thalat. Or make a circle route to see both areas.

Vang Vieng

Surrounded by scenic karst topography, this small town about 70km north of Phon Hong (160km north of Vientiane) via Route 13 nestles in a bend in the Nam Song river. Caverns and tunnels in the limestone are said to be inhabited by spirits.

The most famous of the Vang Vieng caves is **Tham Jang**, a large cavern that was used as a bunker in defence against marauding Chinese Ho (Jiin Haw) in the early 19th century. To find these caves, ask an angler or boatman along the river to show you the way – most will be glad to guide you to two or three caves for a few hundred kip. The section of the river where most of the caves are found is within walking distance (about 2km south-west) of the town centre. You can buy a sketch map to some of the caves from small restaurants near the market for a few hundred kip. Even if you don't plan on any cave exploration, a walk along the river can be rewarding.

Other than the Chinese-built cement factory just outside of town and a little-used airstrip between Route 13 and the town, Vang Vieng is well removed from modernisation.

Places to Stay Off Route 13 in the middle of town, a short roads leads east to *Nana Guest House*, a clean and modern two storey house with five very clean, ample-sized rooms with attached toilet and hot-water shower for 10,000 kip. Just a few metres farther along the same lane stands the larger two storey *Dok Khoun II Guest House*, where all rooms cost 5000 kip. *Siripangna (Siripanya) Guest House*, next to Phonesavang Restaurant, features basic rooms in a one storey building with attached bath for 4000 kip. There are several other similar guesthouses in town.

French-owned *Hotel Nam Song* sits on a slight bluff facing the Nam Song river with a number of very clean and comfortable rooms with fan, fridge, attached toilet and hot-water

LAOS

shower; air-con may be added in the near future. Corner rooms cost US$25, others facing the river are US$20 and rooms around back are US$16. There's a pleasant veranda sitting area in front with river views, plus a spacious garden.

Getting There & Away Route 13 is paved all the way to Vang Vieng. From Vientiane's Talaat Khua Luang terminal or Vang Vieng's market area songthaews leave every 20 minutes in the early part of the day, thinning out a little at night. The fare either way is 5000 kip and the trip takes about three hours.

Buses to/from Luang Prabang cost 11,000 kip per person and take around six hours.

Northern Laos

LUANG PRABANG

The Luang Prabang area was the site of early Thai-Lao meuang that were established in the high river valleys. Luang Prabang remained the capital of the Lan Xang kingdom until 1545.

Even after the Lan Xang period, Luang Prabang was considered the main source of monarchic power. It wasn't until the Pathet Lao took over in 1975 that the monarchy was finally dissolved.

Today, Luang Prabang is a sleepy town of 16,000 inhabitants with a handful of historic temples and old French mansions in a beautiful mountain setting. UNESCO recently added the city to its list of World Heritage sites.

Orientation

The town sits at the confluence of the Mekong and Nam Khan rivers. A large hill called Phu Si (sometimes spelt Phousy) dominates the town skyline. Most of the historic temples are between Phu Si and the Mekong. The whole town can easily be covered, on foot, in a day or two.

Information

Immigration Luang Prabang's immigration is the strictest in the country when it comes to officially checking people in and out of the province. As well as efficient controls at Luang Prabang airport, there are small immigration police posts at the slow-boat and speedboat landings, and one at each bus terminal.

The main immigration office (☎ 21 2435) is on Thanon Wisunalat.

Money Lane Xang Bank, 65 Thanon Phothisalat, will change Thai baht, US, Australian and Canadian dollars, French and Swiss francs, German marks and British pounds – cash or travellers cheques – for kip. The bank normally won't change in the other direction. The rate is a bit lower than in Vientiane.

Post The main post office stands on the corner of Thanon Phothisalat and Thanon Kitsalat, opposite the Phousy Hotel. It's open weekdays from 8.30 am to 5 pm.

Telephone A telephone office around the corner from the post office offers both domestic and international calls via the country's satcom system. It's supposed to be open from 7.30 am to 10 pm, but on our last visit to Luang Prabang the phone office was closed and a sign in Lao read 'Out of Service'. We checked at the post office and were able to make calls there. Domestic and international phone calls can be made at a phone card booth in front of the post office; cards may be purchased inside.

Medical Services The Provincial Hospital on the western side of Thanon Kitsalat and a Chinese-funded clinic opposite are the only public medical facilities in Luang Prabang to speak of. Foreign visitors with serious injuries or illnesses are almost always flown back to Vientiane for emergency transit to hospitals in north-eastern Thailand. If flight services between Luang Prabang and Chiang Mai, Thailand, are initiated (rumours say it will happen by 2000), a direct flight to Chiang Mai would be quicker.

Royal Palace Museum (Haw Kham)

This is a good place to start a tour of Luang Prabang, since the displays convey some sense of local history. The palace was originally constructed beside the Mekong River in 1904 as a residence for King Sisavangvong and his family. When the king died in 1959 his son Savang Vattana inherited the throne, but shortly after the 1975 revolution he and his family were exiled to northern Laos (never to be heard from again) and the palace was converted into a museum.

Various royal religious objects are on display in the large entry hall, as well as rare Buddhist sculpture from India, Cambodia and Laos. One memorable exhibit is a Luang Prabang-style marble standing Buddha.

NORTHERN LAOS

The right front corner room of the palace, which opens to the outside, contains the museum's most prized art, including the Pha Bang, a gold standing Buddha.

The murals on the walls in the king's former reception room depict scenes from traditional Lao life, painted in 1930 by French artist Alix de Fautereau. Each wall is meant to be viewed at a different time of day, according to the changing light.

A highly ornate religious pavilion called the Haw Pha Bang is finally nearing completion in the north-east corner of the museum compound. Eventually the Pha Bang will be moved from the museum proper to this pavilion.

The Royal Palace Museum is open Monday to Friday from 8.30 to 10.30 am, and admission is 1100 kip, except during Pii Mai Lao in mid-April when it's upped to 2100 kip. Shoes and other footwear (socks OK) can't be worn inside the museum, no photography is permitted and you must leave all bags with the attendants. A dress code declares that foreigners must not wear shorts, T-shirts or 'sundresses'.

Wat Xieng Thong

Near the northern tip of the peninsula formed by the Mekong and Nam Khan rivers is Luang Prabang's most magnificent temple, Wat Xieng Thong (Golden City Temple). It was built by King Setthathirat in 1560 and until 1975 remained under royal patronage.

LUANG PRABANG

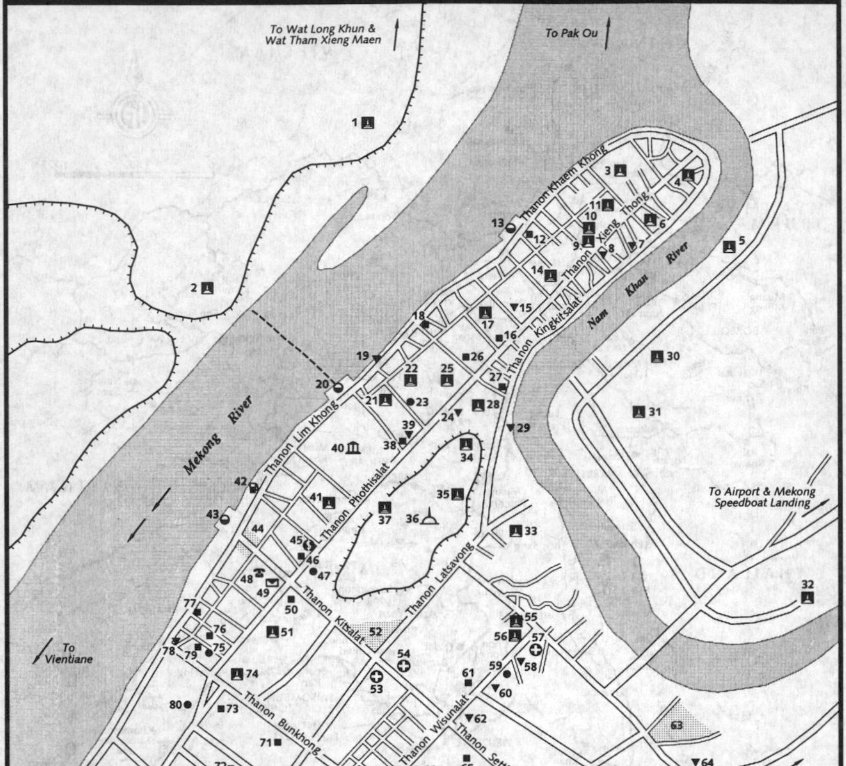

To Wat Long Khun &
Wat Tham Xieng Maen

To Pak Ou

Mekong River

Nam Khan River

Thanon Khem Khong

Thanon Xieng Thong

Thanon Kingkitsalat

Thanon Lim Khong

Thanon Phothisalat

Thanon Phothisalat

Thanon Kitsalat

Thanon Latsavong

Thanon Bunkhong

Thanon Wisunalat

Thanon Setthathirat

Thanon Pha Mehn

Thanon Phu Wao

Thanon Samsenthai

Thanon Pholisan

To Airport & Mekong
Speedboat Landing

To Vientiane

To Ban Phanom,
Wat Paa Phon
Phao & Santi Jedi
Falls

To Northern
Bus Terminal
& Kuang Si
Falls

To Southern
Bus Terminal

0   100   200 m

LUANG PRABANG

PLACES TO STAY
12 Auberge Calao
16 Villa Santi
18 Mekong Guest House
26 Pa Phai Guest House
27 Saynamkhan Guest House
38 Phoun Sab Guest House
46 New Luang Prabang Hotel
50 Phousi Hotel
61 Rama Hotel
65 Viengkeo Hotel
67 Mouang Luang Hotel
69 Somchith Guest House
70 Boun Gning Guest House
71 Souan Savan Guest House
72 Vannida Guest House
73 Hotel Souvannaphoum
76 Viradessa Guest House
77 Vannida 2 Guest House
79 Vanvisa Guest House
84 Sirivongvanh Hotel
88 Suan Phao Guest House
90 Keopathoum Guest
   House
92 Muangsua Hotel
93 Maniphone Guest House
94 Manoluck Hotel
95 Phou Vao Hotel

PLACES TO EAT
7 Bar-Restaurant Duang
   Champa
8 Bo Ben Nyang;
   Baan Khily
15 Lao Food Vegetarian
19 Bane Hous;
   View KhaemKhong

24 Le Saladier
29 Khem Karn Food Garden
39 Luang Prabang Bakery
58 Luang Prabang Restaurant
60 Visoun Restaurant
62 Yoongkhun Restaurant
64 Vieng Mai Restaurant
78 Nang Somchan
   Restaurant
89 Villa Sinxay
91 Malee Lao Food

TEMPLES
1 Wat Chom Phet
2 Wat Xieng Maen
3 Wat Xieng Thong
4 Wat Pakkhan
5 Wat Sa-at
6 Wat Khili
9 Wat Sop
10 Wat Sirimungkhun
11 Wat Si Bun Heuang
14 Wat Saen
17 Wat Nong Sikhunmeuang
21 Wat Chum Khong
22 Wat Xieng Muan
25 Wat Paa Phai
28 Wat Pha Phutthabaat
30 Wat Paa Khaa
31 Wat Phon Song
32 Wat Tao Hai
33 Wat Aphai
34 Wat Thammo
35 Wat Tham Phu Si
37 Wat Paa Huak
41 Wat Mai
   Suwannaphumaham

51 Wat Ho Siang
55 Wat Aham
56 Wat Wisunalat
68 Wat Manolom
74 Wat Pha Mahathat
   (Wat That)
81 Wat Pha Baat Tai
87 Wat That Luang

OTHER
13 Boats to Pak Ou
20 Ferry Pier
23 Ban Xieng Muan
   (future Heritage House)
36 That Chomsi
40 Royal Palace Museum
42 Petrol Station
43 Long-Distance Ferries
   (Tha Heua Meh)
44 Night Market
45 Lane Xang Bank
47 UNESCO Office
48 Telephone Office
49 Post Office
52 Talaat Dala
53 Provincial Hospital
54 Chinese Clinic
57 Lao Red Cross
59 Immigration Office
63 Talaat Vieng Mai
66 Lao Aviation
75 Silversmiths
80 Provincial Office
82 Talaat That Luang
83 Provincial Treasury
85 Petrol Station
86 Finance Department

Like the royal palace, Wat Xieng Thong was placed within easy reach of the Mekong.

The sĩm represents classic Luang Prabang temple architecture, and its rear wall features an impressive 'tree of life' mosaic. Inside, richly decorated wooden columns support a ceiling that's vested with *dhammachakkas* (dharma wheels).

Near the compound's eastern gate stands the royal funeral chapel. Inside is an impressive 12m-high funeral chariot and various funeral urns for each member of the royal family. Gilt panels on the exterior of the chapel depict erotic episodes from the *Ramayana*.

Admission to Wat Xieng Thong is 250 kip.

Wat Wisunalat

This temple, also known as Wat Vixoun, is to the east of the town centre and was original-ly constructed in 1513, making it the oldest continually operating temple in Luang Prabang. It was rebuilt in 1898 following an 1887 fire set by marauding Black Flag Haw.

Inside the high-ceiling sĩm is a collection of wooden Calling for Rain Buddhas and 15th to 16th century Luang Prabang *sima* (ordination stones). In front of the sĩm is That Pathum (Lotus Stupa), which was built in 1514. It's more commonly called That Mak Mo, or Watermelon Stupa, for its hemispherical shape.

Admission costs 400 kip.

Phu Si

The temples on the slopes of Phu Si are all of rather recent construction, but it's likely that other temples were previously located on this important hill site. None of the temples are that memorable, but the top of the hill affords an excellent view of the town.

LAOS

On the lower slopes of the hill are **Wat Paa Huak** and **Wat Pha Phutthabaat**. To continue to the summit of the hill you are required to pay a 650 kip fee, collected at the northern entrance near Wat Paa Huak. At the summit is **That Chomsi**, the starting point for a colourful Lao New Year procession held in mid-April. Behind this stupa is a small cave shrine called **Wat Tham Phu Si**.

Other Temples

Close to the Phousy Hotel and the main post office is **Wat Mai Suwannaphumaham** (New Temple), built in 1796 and at one time a residence of the Sangkharat, or Supreme Patriarch of the Lao Sangha. The front veranda is remarkable for its decorated columns and for the sumptuous gold relief panels on the doors. The Pha Bang, which is usually housed in Luang Prabang's National Museum, is put on public display at this wat during the Lao New Year celebrations.

Across the Mekong River from central Luang Prabang are several temples that aren't remarkable except for the pleasant rural settings. **Wat Tham Xieng Maen** is in a limestone cave almost directly across the river from Wat Xieng Thong. Many Buddha images from temples that have burned down or fallen into decay are kept here. Near Wat Tham Xieng Maen are several other caves that are easily found and explored – bring along a torch (flashlight).

Tastefully restored **Wat Long Khun** is a little to the east of Wat Tham Xieng Maen and features a nicely decorated portico of 1937 vintage, plus older sections from the 18th century. Boats can be chartered from Luang Prabang's northern pier to Wat Long Khun for 3000 kip for a round trip, or you can wait for the infrequent ferry boats which charge just 100 kip per passenger.

At the top of a hill above the previous two wats is peaceful **Wat Chom Phet**, where one can obtain an undisturbed view of the Mekong River.

A few kilometres to the south-east of town is the recently constructed **Santi Jedi**, or Peace Pagoda. This large yellow stupa contains three levels inside plus an outside terrace near the top with a view of the surrounding plains. The interior walls are painted with all manner of Buddhist stories and moral admonitions.

Behind the Talaat That Luang market in town is a modern Vietnamese-Lao Buddhist temple, **Wat Pha Baat Tai**.

Markets

Luang Prabang's main marketplace, **Talaat Dala**, stands at the intersection of Thanon Kitsalat and Thanon Latsavong. It features an impressive array of hardware, cookware, dried or preserved foodstuffs, textiles and local handicrafts.

The main fresh market, **Talaat That Luang**, is at the intersection of Thanon Phothisalat and Thanon Phu Wao near the river and Wat Pha Baat Tai. Also important for fresh produce is **Talaat Vieng Mai** at the northeastern end of Thanon Photisan.

Places to Stay – Budget

Near the Mekong The former silversmithing district near the Mekong River, a neighbourhood known as Ban Wat That, has become a centre for a cluster of modest guesthouses. Facing the river on Thanon Mahin Ounkham (more commonly known as Thanon Lim Khong), *Vannida 2 Guest House* is in a white two storey house. Rooms with high ceilings and shuttered windows cost 6000 kip with shared toilet and shower. Right around the corner in the heart of Ban Wat Thai, another post-independence house contains the friendly *Viradessa Guest House*, where beds in a simple dorm cost 2000 kip or two-bed rooms cost 3500/4000 kip single/double.

Vanvisa Guest House (π/fax 21 2925) features six rooms at the back of a shop selling textiles, antiques and handicrafts. Rates are US$5 with shared bath, US$8 with attached bath. The owner, a very cultured Lao lady, sometimes makes family-style dinners for guests and can even arrange informal cooking workshops.

Historic Temple District In the most concentrated area of colonial architecture and historic monasteries on and off Thanon Phothisalat are a few new places with economic rooms. In an old shophouse between the Royal Palace Museum and the Luang Prabang Bakery, *Phoun Sab Guest House* offers simple but clean two-bed rooms for US$5 with shared hot-water shower, or US$8 with attached hot-water shower. There's a basic cafe downstairs and rental bikes are available.

Opposite Wat Paa Phai, friendly *Pa Phai Guest House* (π 21 2752) occupies a historical two storey French-Lao house with a small garden in front. Bamboo-thatch walls separate the rooms, which cost 8000 kip single, 15,000 kip double with shared bath.

The same family runs the *Mekong Guest House* (same phone), a larger two storey, post-independence house a couple of blocks away towards the Mekong, where a large two bed room with shared bath costs 7000 kip, or 13,000 kip with attached bath.

Places to Stay – Mid-Range

Saynamkhan Guest House (☎ 21 2976) is housed in a restored two storey colonial building near the banks of the Nam Khan, right opposite Wat Si Phutthabaat, on the street that wraps around the peninsula parallel to the river. Clean rooms with air-con, TV and small fridge cost US$20/25 single/double, or US$30 for a large corner room with a bathtub.

The 40 room *Phousi Hotel (☎ 21 2292)* is well located at the intersection of Thanon Kitsalat and Thanon Phothisalat, at the site of the former French Commissariat. Standard one bed rooms are US$28, while standard two-bed rooms cost US$35; larger rooms with slightly better furnishings go for US$40. Tax and service charge are included. All rooms are equipped with air-con, hot-water bath, TV, fridge, minibar and phone.

Places to Stay – Top End

A beautifully restored 1930-vintage colonial house facing the Mekong close to Wat Xieng Thong contains the friendly and welcoming *Auberge Calao (☎ 21 2100)*, also called the Heuan Phak Le Ca-Lao Guest House. A Canadian-Lao joint venture, the stately Sino-Portuguese-style mansion features five capacious rooms, all with air-con, private facilities, and verandas overlooking Thanon Lim Khong and the river. Kudos for one of the best architectural renovations – both interior and exterior – so far seen in Luang Prabang. A terrace restaurant in front serves Lao and western food. Rooms cost a reasonable US$45 in low season, US$55 high season.

Places to Eat

Lao Very good and authentic Lao food is available at *Malee Lao Food*, a casual eatery on Thanon Phu Wao. House specialities include *làap* (mixed with eggplant in the local style) made with water buffalo, deer or fish, *áw pāa-dàek* (fish-sauce curry) and *tām-sòm* (green papaya salad).

Another very good spot for local cuisine is *Nang Somchan Restaurant*, a simple but pleasant outdoor place near the cluster of guesthouses in Ban Wat That near the river.

There's an extensive selection of Lao and Luang Prabang dishes, including the best vegetarian Lao in town so far. It's open daily for lunch and dinner.

A couple of doors down from Villa Santi, *Lao Food Vegetarian* is a small garden cafe in front of an old colonial house. Vegetarian versions of various traditional Lao dishes, including a làap made from tofu are available, as well as Thai curries, salads, noodles, soups, fruit shakes and beer. A few meat and fish dishes also appear on the menu. Service can be very slow.

Yoongkhun Restaurant, across the street from the Rama Hotel, makes a good 'Salad Luang Prabang', a savoury arrangement of local watercress, sliced boiled eggs, tomatoes and onions with a unique dressing.

Along the Mekong River are several small thatched-roof, *open-air restaurants* with passable Lao food.

European *Luang Prabang Bakery* on Thanon Phothisalat (Navang) offers various kinds of homemade pastries, yoghurt, cheese, sandwiches, ice cream and coffee drinks at moderate prices.

Le Saladier in an old colonial shophouse on Thanon Phothisalat, a block north-east of Luang Prabang Bakery and Phoun Sab Guest House (on the opposite side of the street), has a long and varied menu.

Bo Ben Nyang, a cafe contained in the gallery/bookshop Baan Khily on Thanon Xieng Thong, offers a good selection of teas, coffees and snacks with a view of the four temples across the street.

Shopping

Centrally located Talaat Dala market has the best overall selection of textiles and handicrafts, including several silver vendors who sell a variety of old and new pieces at reasonable prices.

Baan Khily, on Thanon Xieng Thong, has unique and carefully selected Lao crafts, including *saa* paper, as well as books, artwork and an upstairs gallery. The German owner is very knowledgeable about the area and is happy to answer questions.

Getting There & Away

Air Lao Aviation flies daily to Luang Prabang airport from Vientiane – sometimes twice a day (US$55). There are four flights per week to/from Phonsavan (US$35) and three flights per week from Huay Xai (US$46), plus one

LAOS

or two flights per week to/from Luang Nam Tha (US$37) and Udomxai (US$28).

Flight frequency to/from Luang Nam Tha and Udomxai depends largely on passenger load and availability of aircraft; the only way to find out for sure is to ask at Lao Aviation a day in advance of scheduled departures.

Bus & Truck In the north, trucks converted into passenger carriers by adding two long benches in the back are called songthaews.

Vientiane From Luang Prabang, buses leave from the new southern terminal on Route 13 a few kilometres outside of town and go all the way to Vientiane for 13,000 kip (10 hours). To Kasi costs 10,000 kip (four hours) and to Vang Vieng costs 11,000 kip (six hours). Buses leave three times a day at 7 and 8.30 am and noon.

Udomxai & Luang Nam Tha Luang Prabang is linked with Udomxai Province by road via Pak Mong (Route 1) and via Muang Xai to Luang Nam Tha Province (Route 2). Songthaews to Pak Mong leave Luang Prabang's northern bus terminal once or twice a day in the morning. The fare is 3000 kip and the trip takes about two hours. From Pak Mong it's another 3000 kip and two hours to Muang Xai. Actual travel durations are quite variable, however.

Nong Khiaw, Xieng Khuang & Hua Phan It's possible to reach Xieng Khuang via Route 7 (which continues east into northern Vietnam), but the road is high and beset with natural and political hazards. For the present the only way to reach Xieng Khuang safely by road from Luang Prabang is to go by bus north to Pak Mong (two hours, 3000 kip), then catch a songthaew to Nong Khiaw and connect to another bus heading south-east along Route 1 till it reaches Route 6 at Nam Noen in southern Hua Phan Province. Here you'll probably have to change to another bus heading south to Phonsavan or north to Sam Neua. There are also daily direct songthaews to Nong Khiaw for 4000 to 4500 kip per person; the trip takes about four hours.

Boat In Luang Prabang the main landing for long-distance Mekong River boats, at the north-west end of Thanon Kitsalat, is called Tha Heua Meh. A chalkboard at the Navigation Office here announces long-distance boat departures, eg to Nong Khiaw and Vi-

entiane – it's all in Lao. A second pier near the Royal Palace Museum is also sometimes used when the river level is too low for the main pier.

Speedboats use a landing at Ban Don, 6km north of Luang Prabang. A jumbo to Ban Don from Talaat Dala can be chartered for 3500 kip. From Ban Don into town foreigners are charged a standard 1000 kip for a shared jumbo; to charter one you must pay 6000 kip.

Pakbeng & Huay Xai As there is no direct road between Huay Xai and Luang Prabang, this is a popular route. By slow river ferry the trip to Huay Xai takes two days with an overnight in Pakbeng. The passenger fare is 28,000 kip from Luang Prabang, only 14,000 kip as far as Pakbeng.

Faster and smaller speedboats reach Pakbeng in three hours, Huay Xai in six or seven. The fares in either direction are 19,000 kip and 38,000 kip respectively. To charter a speedboat the boat pilots usually want the equivalent of six passenger fares but they'll usually go if you pay for four spaces – often they have paid cargo to carry, too.

Vientiane See the Vientiane Getting There & Away section.

Nong Khiaw An alternate way to Luang Prabang from Muang Xai in Udomxai Province is via Nong Khiaw in northern Luang Prabang Province, which is about 127km by road or along the Nam Ou river. The Nong Khiaw landing is sometimes referred to as Muang Ngoi, the village on the opposite bank of the Nam Ou, or as Nambak, a larger village to the west.

Nowadays speedboat departures north to Nong Khiaw are infrequent due to improved road travel. If you insist on going to Nong Khiaw by boat you may have to charter. In Nong Khiaw it will be much easier to find boats farther north to Muang Khua and Hat Sa.

Shared speedboats between Luang Prabang and Nong Khiaw cost 15,000 kip and take around 2½ hours when the water is high enough; during the dry season some stretches of the upper Nam Ou can be treacherous and most pilots won't attempt the trip. From Nong Khiaw it's an hour west to Nambak by passenger truck.

You can also sometimes get on a slow cargo ferry from Luang Prabang to Nong Khiaw (7500 kip per person) and Muang Khua (15,000 kip), but given the fact that a songthaew to Nong Khiaw costs only 4000 to 4500 kip and takes only four hours, you'd have to love river travel for its own sake to prefer to spend two days on a cargo boat.

Getting Around
To/From the Airport Shared jumbos or minitrucks charge a uniform 2000 kip per foreigner (less for Lao) from the airport into town; in the reverse direction you can usually charter an entire jumbo for 2500 to 3000 kip.

Local Transport Most of the town is accessible on foot. Jumbos and motor samlors charge around 800 kip for the first kilometre, plus 500 kip per additional kilometre.

Several guesthouses in town rent bicycles for 2000 to 3000 kip per day.

AROUND LUANG PRABANG
Pak Ou Caves
About 25km by boat from Luang Prabang along the Mekong River, at the mouth of the Nam Ou, are the famous Pak Ou Caves (Pak Ou means Mouth of the Ou). The two caves in the lower part of a limestone cliff are crammed with a variety of Buddha images, most of them classic Luang Prabang standing Buddhas.

On the way to Pak Ou, you can have the boatman stop at small **villages** on the banks of the Mekong, including one that specialises in the production of *lào-láo*, distilled rice liquor.

Getting There & Away You can hire boats from the pier behind the Royal Palace Museum. A long-tail boat seating up to 10 passengers should cost about US$20 to US$25 for the day, including petrol. The trip takes one to 1½ hours one way, depending on the speed of the boat. If you stop at villages along the way, it will naturally take longer.

Kuang Si Falls
This beautiful spot 29km south of Luang Prabang features a wide, multitiered waterfall tumbling over limestone formations into a series of cool, turquoise-green pools. The lower level of the falls has been turned into a public park with shelters and picnic tables, and vendors sell drinks and snacks. A trail ascends through the forest along the left side of the falls to a second tier which is more private (most visitors stay below) and has a pool large enough for swimming and splashing around.

Getting There & Away Guided tours to the falls booked through a local agency cost US$50 to US$60 and include transport and lunch at the falls. Freelance guides in Luang Prabang offer trips by car or motorcycle for US$12 to US$15.

Nong Khiaw (Muang Ngoi)
Anyone travelling by road or river from the capital to Phongsali, Hua Phan or Xieng Khuang provinces stands a good chance of spending some time in Nong Khiaw, a village on the banks of the Nam Ou in northern Luang Prabang Province. Route 1, which extends west to east from Muang Xai to Nam Noen (at the junction with Route 6 in Hua Phan Province), crosses the river here via a steel bridge. Route 14 north from Luang Prabang meets Route 1 about 33km west of town at Pak Mong.

A one day trek into the surrounding forest will take you to **Tham Pha Tok**, a limestone cave where villagers lived during the Vietnam War, and to a nearby waterfall. There are other caves as well, and a few Hmong villages nearby.

The village is little more than a haphazard collection of houses, guesthouses and rustic noodle shops. Sometimes it's referred to as Muang Ngoi, which is actually the group of shacks on the east bank, and sometimes it's called Nambak, which is actually 23km west of Nong Khiaw by road.

Places to Stay & Eat Just across the bridge on Route 1 coming from Xieng Khuang or Hua Phan provinces, the *Philasouk Guest House* is a new two storey wooden house with rooms for 3000 kip per person, though you could probably negotiate to 5000 kip for two. Simple clean rooms have mosquito nets and hard mattresses. Clean bucket baths and toilets are in back of the house. There is an eating area in front downstairs and the food is good.

If you turn left coming from the bridge into town, you'll come to *Si Amphay Guest House*, which is substantially smaller and charges just 1000 kip per person for basic rooms in a slightly cramped house. Candles provide evening lighting. A little farther down on the left, friendly *Somnjot Guest House* features an unusual row of cubicle-like rooms on stilts inside a small building for 1000 kip per person.

A couple of very simple outdoor *noodle shops* opposite Philasouk Guest House offer

LAOS

fish soup, sticky rice and noodles. Philasouk itself has a large menu.

Getting There & Away Songthaews bound for Muang Xai (Udomxai) leave from in front of Philasouk Guest House two or three times each morning and cost 4000 kip per person. You can also take one of the more frequent songthaews south-west to Pak Mong (the junction of Route 1 and Route 13) for 1,500 kip, then change to another songthaew (3000 kip) to Udomxai.

See also the Luang Prabang Getting There & Away entry.

XIENG KHUANG PROVINCE

Virtually every town and village in Xieng Khuang Province was bombed between 1964 and 1973. Flying into the province, one is struck at first by the awesome beauty of high green mountains, rugged karst formations and verdant valleys. But as the plane begins to descend, you notice how much of the province is pockmarked with bomb craters in which little or no vegetation grows.

The province's population of 200,000 is composed of lowland Lao, Thai Dam, Hmong and Phuan. The original capital city, Xieng Khuang, was almost totally bombed out, so the capital was moved to nearby Phonsavan after the 1975 change of government. Not far from Phonsavan is the mysterious Plain of Jars (Thong Hai Hin).

The moderate altitude in central Xieng Khuang, including Phonsavan and the Plain of Jars, means an excellent year-round climate.

Phonsavan

Xieng Khuang's new capital district (population 57,000) grew tremendously in the 1990s – there are several semi-paved main streets lined with tin-roofed wooden shops, a sprinkling of new concrete structures, two markets, a few government buildings, a bank, and several modest hotels and guesthouses.

Take care when walking in the fields around Phonsavan, as undetonated live bombs are not uncommon. The locals use bomb casings as pillars for new structures and as fence posts. Muddy areas are sometimes dotted with pineapple bombs or bomblets, fist-sized explosives that are left over from cluster bombs dropped in the 1970s.

Tourist Offices Sousath Tourism (☎ 31 2031), at the Maly Hotel, is a good source of information.

Money Opposite the Phu Doi Hotel is a branch of Aloun May Bank but it doesn't seem to keep regular hours. Don't count on cashing any travellers cheques here – bring plenty of cash to tide you over. The bank also has an exchange desk at the airport.

Post & Communications There is a post office on the main road near the two central markets. Domestic phone service here has improved greatly since a satellite connection was established.

Places to Stay & Eat The *Hay Hin Hotel*, a simple wooden place on the main street near the market, has basic two-bed rooms with mosquito nets and shared cold-water bath for 5000 kip per night.

Further east along the same street, the well maintained *Dokkhoun Guest House* offers nicer rooms with mosquito nets and better quality mattresses for 5000 kip with shared facilities, or 7000 kip with private shower and toilet.

Continuing east along the same street, the *Muang Phuan Hotel* has similar but more numerous rooms with shared bath for 5000 kip, with attached bath for 6000 kip and four-bed rooms with shared bath for 8000 kip per room.

Back down towards the market are two more fair choices. The two storey *Vanhaloun Hotel* charges 5000 kip for simple rooms with shared bath, 8000 to 10,000 kip for larger rooms with private shower and toilet.

A couple of kilometres south-west of the market-bus terminal area, towards the airport and the Plain of Jars (Site 1), the well run *Hotel Maly (☎ 31 2031)* offers 11 comfortable rooms (with plans to expand to 21) ranging from US$8 to US$20 a night, all with private toilets and hot-water showers. A cosy *restaurant* downstairs has some of the best cooking in town, especially if you order in advance. The owner speaks good English and French, and can easily arrange tours to the Plain of Jars, local villages and places farther afield.

The clean and well run *Sangah (Sa-Nga) Restaurant* near the market and post office offers an extensive menu of Chinese, Thai and Lao foods. Some expats working in Phonsavan have been known to survive on a nightly diet of steak and chips here. Exactly opposite the Sangah, the friendly *Nang Phonekeo* (Phonkaew) serves the best fŏe in town.

Getting There & Away Planes fly to/from Vientiane once or twice daily (US$44) and to/from Luang Prabang thrice weekly (US$35). Delays are common on the latter flight. The Lao Aviation office, a wooden shed off the main street in town, is open daily from 7 to 11 am and 1.30 to 3.30 pm; these hours are not strictly followed.

Potholed Route 1 carries passengers east across Udomxai and northern Luang Prabang till the road terminates at Route 7, where a change of buses at the village of Nam Noen continues southward to Phonsavan. It's best to break this journey by spending the night in Nambak or Nong Khiaw so that you can get an early start and make it from Nambak to Phonsavan in one day – a journey of about 12 hours. You're also more likely to find public transport in the early morning; afternoon buses are few and far between in this part of Laos.

To/from Sam Neua, capital of Hua Phan Province, is a 12 hour, 238km road trip to Phonsavan via Routes 6 and 7. You must change buses at Nam Noen. Logistically, one of the best ways to do this trip is to fly to Sam Neua from Vientiane, then head south by road to Phonsavan. For details see under Sam Neua in the following Hua Phan Province section.

Plain of Jars

A few kilometres south-east of Phonsavan is an area of rolling fields where huge jars of unknown origin are scattered about. The jars weigh an average of 600kg to one tonne each, though the biggest of them weigh as much as six tonnes. They appear to have been fashioned from solid stone, but there is disagreement on this point.

Various theories have been advanced as to the functions of the stone jars: they were used as sarcophagi, as wine fermenters or for rice storage. Many of the smaller jars have been taken away by collectors, but there are still several hundred or so on the plain. In addition to the main site known as **Thong Hai Hin**, or Site 1, there are two other sites which can be visited with the assistance of a guide, available through any guesthouse.

Getting There & Away You can charter a jumbo from Phonsavan to Site 1, 15km from the Phonsavan market, for 10,000 kip round trip. For Sites 2 and 3 your best bet is to arrange a jeep and driver through one of the guesthouses or hotels.

Muang Khun (Old Xieng Khuang)

Xieng Khuang's ancient capital was so ravaged by a century of wars that it was almost completely abandoned by 1975. The old capital is once again inhabited, though the original French colonial architecture has been replaced by a long row of plain wooden buildings, with slanted metal roofs, on either side of the dirt road from Phonsavan. Officially the town has been renamed Muang Khun. Many of the local residents are Phuan, Thai Dam or Thai Neua.

Several **Buddhist temples** built between the 16th and 19th centuries lie in unrestored ruins.

Places to Stay & Eat The town has one funky wooden *hotel* with rooms for 2000 to 3000 kip. Near the market in the centre of town are a couple of noodle shops. *Haan Khai Foe* (an English sign reads 'Restaurant') opposite the market is the best choice for lunch.

Getting There & Away Four buses a day ply the bumpy, torturous 36km route between Phonsavan and Muang Khun for 2500 kip per person.

HUA PHAN PROVINCE

The remote mountainous north-eastern province of Hua Phan is enclosed by Vietnam to the north, east and south-east, Xieng Khuang to the south-west and Luang Prabang to the west. Twenty-two ethnic groups make the province their home, mainly Thai Khao, Thai Daeng, Thai Meuay, Thai Neua, Phu Noi, Hmong, Khamu, Yunnanese and Vietnamese. The Vietnamese influence is very strong.

Textiles in the 'Sam Neua' style – of tribal Thai origins – are a tourist draw. The best textiles are said to come from the areas around Muang Xon and Sop Hao.

Sam Neua

Tucked away in a long narrow valley formed by the Nam Sam river at about 1200m above sea level, Sam Neua is so far one of the country's least visited provincial capitals. Verdant hills, including pointy Phu Luang, overlook the town but other than the natural setting there's not a lot to write home about. District residents are mostly Lao, Vietnamese and Hmong, along with some Thai Dam, Thai Daeng and Thai Lü. For local residents, Sam Neua boasts what is perhaps the largest and fastest-growing **market** in the region. Consumer products from China and Vietnam line up alongside fresh produce and domestic goods.

Places to Stay & Eat Welcome to Laos' rat capital. The *Lao Houng Hotel*, near the south end of a bridge spanning the Nam Sam near the market, is a crumbling Chinese/Vietnamese-style place built around a couple of courtyards by the Vietnamese in 1975. Ordinary rooms with two beds, mosquito nets and shared facilities cost US$8, while the same with private shower and toilet costs US$10. Larger rooms with hot showers cost US$12, while suites with spacious sitting rooms, one large bed, private toilet and hot-water shower are US$15. The hotel also has a major rat problem. An attached beer garden serves cold Beerlao, and the hotel hosts dances on Sunday nights until midnight.

In the market, diagonally across from the Lao Houng Hotel, *Kheam Xam Guest House* is a new three storey cement place and the tallest building in town. On the ground floor is a cafe with TV and VCR, while the 2nd and 3rd floors hold three rooms each. Each room contains two or three twin beds with mosquito nets and shared, clean bathrooms for 6,000 kip. Apparently the rats haven't made a home here – yet.

Around the corner from Lao Houng on a perpendicular street up from the market, new *Phanh Sam Guest House* is a two storey cement building with a balcony on the upper floor. The 20 small rooms are bare save for a few sticks of wooden furniture, and they cost 5000 kip single/double. The staff are friendly and meals can be arranged here.

Good fõe is available at the clean and new *Sam Neua May Restaurant* near the market. For a variety of Lao dishes try the *Mitsampanh Restaurant* about 20m down a side lane opposite the Sam Neua May.

Getting There & Away Lao Aviation has scheduled flights between Vientiane and the renovated airport at Sam Neua thrice weekly (US$70).

Sam Neua can be reached by road from both Xieng Khuang and Udomxai provinces. Route 6 from Xieng Khuang is quite good by Lao standards between Phonsavan and Nam Noen, a small truck stop at the junction of Routes 6 and 1 just north of the Hua Phan Province border. It's usually necessary to change buses (actually large converted Russian or Chinese diesel trucks) in Nam Noen. From Phonsavan to Nam Noen takes four to five hours and costs 5000 kip, while from Nam Noen to Sam Neua takes six hours and costs 6000 kip.

South-east of Sam Neua, Route 6 links with Route 1 from Nong Khiaw (Luang Prabang Province) and Muang Xai (Udomxai Province).

Vieng Xai

Originally called Thong Na Kai (Chicken Field) because of the abundance of wild junglefowl in the area, the postwar name for this former Pathet Lao revolutionary headquarters means Walled City of Victory. The district sits in a striking valley of verdant hills and limestone cliffs riddled with caves, several of which were used to shelter Pathet Lao officers during the Vietnam War.

The district capital itself is a small town that seems to be getting smaller as Sam Neua grows larger. The central market is a poor collection of vendors who can't afford transport to the provincial capital, 29km away.

There are 102 known **caves** in the district, around a dozen with war history. The Vieng Xai caves are supposed to be open to the public, but local authorities may or may not let you tour them. When the caves are open, visitors must first pay a 1500 kip fee at a mustard-coloured building in front of Tham Thaan Souphanouvong.

Tham Thaan Kaysone, the office and residence of the Lao People's Party/Pathet Lao chief – who served as prime minister and president from 1975 till his 1992 death – extends 140m into a cliffside that was scaled by rope before steps were added. **Tham Thaan Souphanouvong** was deemed fit for royalty and housed Prince Souphanouvong, the so-called Red Prince.

Getting There & Away The 29km journey from Sam Neua to Vieng Xai takes around 45 minutes by private vehicle or about an hour by public bus (1500 kip). You can hire a motorcycle to take you from Sam Neua to Vieng Xai and back for US$7, assuming a half day's charter.

LUANG NAM THA PROVINCE

Bordered by Myanmar to the north-west, China to the north, Udomxai to the south and east and Bokeo to the south-west, Luang Nam Tha (Nam Tha for short) is a mountainous province with a high proportion of Lao

Sung and other minorities. The province population includes Hmong, Akha, Mien, Samtao, Thai Daeng, Thai Lü, Thai Neua, Thai Khao, Thai Kalom, Khamu, Lamet, Lao Loum, Shan and Yunnanese. As in Udomxai the Chinese presence is increasing rapidly with the importation of skilled labour from Yunnan for construction and road work.

The CIA's Air America heroin and opium traffic ran through Luang Nam Tha in the 60s. Westerners still seem to carry a romance for Nam Tha, and there is a higher than average number of aid-based and commercial projects in the province.

Luang Nam Tha
Rising from the ashes of war, Luang Nam Tha's capital is expanding rapidly in its burgeoning role as trade entrepôt for commerce between China, Thailand and Laos. There are two town centres, one in the older, southern section of the district near the airfield and boat landing, and a second 7km to the north where the highway comes in from Muang Sing, Boten and Udomxai. The main market is in the latter section.

Places to Stay & Eat Conveniently located three doors down from Lane Xang Bank and across from the main street market, *Many Chan Guest House* is a two storey wooden place with simple but well kept rooms for 2000/4000 kip single/double, or 6000 kip for a big corner room with three beds and its own wash basin.

Farther north up the road is *Sinsavanh Guest House*, in a brightly painted two storey wooden house. Rooms with two beds and mosquito nets cost just 2500 kip, making this the cheapest place in town.

Moving just a little upmarket, *Darasavath Guest House*, opposite the road leading to the provincial hospital, offers OK rooms behind a very nice outdoor restaurant for 4000 to 8000 kip with bathrooms out back.

Significantly more upmarket – for Luang Nam Tha – is the 28 room *Hongthaxay Somboune Hotel* (☎ 086-312078), another 500m north and then 150m west of the main street. Two-bed air-con rooms with private hot-water shower are priced at 10,000 kip, while similar rooms with better mattresses are 12,000 kip.

The *Phone Xai Restaurant*, just a simple wooden place around the corner from the main street market, serves OK Lao and Chinese fare.

Getting There & Away Lao Aviation flies to Nam Tha from Vientiane thrice weekly (US$80). Flights to/from Luang Prabang are supposed to depart twice weekly (US$37), but in reality the schedule varies with passenger demand. There are also occasional flights to/from Huay Xai (US$41).

Nam Tha can be reached by road via all-weather Route 2 from Muang Xai (117km south-east) in four or five hours. Passenger trucks cost 5000 kip per person (60,000 kip charter), and leave in the early morning and early afternoon from either end. The main truck stop in Nam Tha stands in front of the market, not far from the post office and bank.

A side road north off Route 2 about two-thirds of the way to Nam Tha from Muang Xai leads directly to Boten on the Lao-Chinese border. Passenger trucks bound for Boten leave morning and afternoon from Nam Tha (3000 kip, two to three hours on a very poor road).

Muang Sing
Lying on the broad river plains of the Nam La north-west of the provincial capital, Muang Sing is a traditional Thai Lü and Thai Dam cultural nexus, as well as a trade centre for Lao Huay (Lenten), Akha, Hmong, Mien, Lolo and Yunnanese. A major producer of illicit opium, Muang Sing district boasts the fifth highest opium addiction rate in all of Laos.

Among the buildings left standing from the French era is a 75-year-old brick and plaster **garrison** which once housed Moroccan and Senegalese troops. It's now used as a small Lao army outpost.

The main **market** at Muang Sing – called *talàat nyai* in Lao, *kaat long* in Thai Lü – was once the biggest opium market in the golden triangle, a function officially sanctioned by the French. Today it's a venue for fresh produce, meats, food and clothing staples bought and sold by a colourful, polyglot crowd.

A number of Lao Theung and Lao Sung **villages** in the vicinity – particularly those of the Akha – can be visited on foot from Muang Sing.

During the full moon of the 12th lunar month, which usually occurs sometime between late October and mid-November, all of Muang Sing and half the province turn out for the **That Muang Sing Festival** (Bun Thâat Meúang Sīng).

Places to Stay & Eat *Viengxay Guest House*, a large two storey place on the main street, offers rooms for 3000 kip with two beds, 5000 kip for three beds, all with shared facilities. There's a sizable restaurant downstairs, with decent food. The *Vieng Phon Guest House* and *Senkhatiyavong Guest House* on either side of the Viengsay are quite similar.

Farther north along the main street, across a stream towards the north edge of town, is *Noy Vanasay Guest House*. Run by a very friendly Lao family, it offers three basic but clean two-bed rooms for 4000 kip, with bathrooms downstairs. There are a few tables downstairs with food service.

Farther north yet, about 400m from the market, is the larger and well run *Sangdaeone Hotel*. This new concrete/plaster rectangular building contains six upstairs rooms and a balcony along the front for 6000 kip each. There are good views across to the mountains from the balcony.

The *Singxai Hotel* is a concrete establishment behind the market with three-bed rooms for 6000 kip; each room has attached toilet and bathing facilities. This hotel is a little quieter than the others as it's set back from the main street.

Aside from the guesthouses, the only places to eat are a few simple *fōe shops* along the main street and in the market.

Getting There & Away Three or four trucks a day ply between Nam Tha and Muang Sing, a journey of around two hours (3000 kip).

Boten

Other than the lines of parked Japanese cars, thick with dust, waiting to be smuggled into China, there's nothing much to see here.

Now that Boten is a legal border crossing for all nationalities, and with the upgrading of the road to Luang Nam Tha, the village is becoming a town of sorts, complete with basic guesthouses and restaurants. Overnight facilities are available in Mengla on the Chinese side.

The Lao border crossing is open from 8 am to noon and 2 to 4 pm; the Chinese crossing is open from 8 am to 5 pm.

See also the Luang Nam Tha Getting There & Away section.

BOKEO PROVINCE

Laos' smallest and second least populous province, wedged between the Mekong River border with Thailand and Luang Nam Tha Province, was known as Hua Khong (Head of

the Mekong) in earlier times; its current name means 'Gem Mine', a reference to sapphire deposits in Huay Xai district. Bokeo is an important focus of the much-ballyhooed 'Economic Quadrangle', a four-nation trade zone envisioned mainly by corporate entities in Thailand and China.

Despite its diminutive size Bokeo harbours 34 ethnicities, including the Lahu hill tribe and Lao Huay.

Huay Xai

Huay Xai today is a bustling riverside town whose main commercial district centres on the vehicle and passenger ferry landings for boats to Chiang Khong in Thailand. Many new shophouses are under construction along the main street, which curves along the base of a hill overlooking the river.

A set of naga stairs ascends this hillside to Shan-style, 1880 vintage **Wat Jawm Khao Manilat**, a thriving temple that overlooks the town and river.

Huay Xai is a valid border entry/exit point for any visitor regardless of nationality. You don't need special permission to cross into Laos here, just a valid visa.

Places to Stay & Eat Up from the Mekong ferry landing is the well run *Manilat Hotel*, with basic but clean rooms with fan and private bath for single/double 8000 kip/200B. There's a good, inexpensive restaurant downstairs. The *Hotel Houei Sai*, nearby on the same side of the street, is similar in over-all appearance and rates but significantly shabbier.

Head north on this street and you'll come to a new place on your right called *Thaveesinh Hotel*, a clean three storey hotel where rooms with one large bed and fan cost 10,000 kip, two beds with fan 12,000 kip. Air-con rooms cost 16,000 kip with one large bed or 20,000 kip with two beds. All rooms have attached hot-water showers.

Another 400m or so north is the friendly *Arimid Guest House*, a collection of thatched bamboo bungalows opposite a petrol station. All bungalows have attached bathrooms with small electric hot-water heaters. Rates are 8000/10,000 kip single/double. The husband-and-wife owners speak French and English The pier for slow boats to Pakbeng and Luang Prabang is only about 200m away.

Getting There & Away Lao Aviation flies between Huay Xai and Vientiane twice weekly and costs US$88. Flights to/from Luang

Prabang operate three times a week (US$46). There are also weekly flights scheduled to/ from Luang Nam Tha (US$41) and Udomxai (US$37).

The road north-east to Luang Nam Tha used to be extremely rough, but upgrading is now under way. Passenger trucks to Luang Nam Tha, 217km north-east, cost 20,000 kip and take 10 hours under good conditions, though during the rainy season it's often impassable. The upgrade should reduce the time to four to six hours, year-round.

The short ferry ride from Chiang Khong on the Thai side costs 20B.

Long-distance ferries down the Mekong to Pakbeng/Luang Prabang cost 300B/600B. The Mekong slow boat landing is situated north of the town centre next to the vehicle ferry crossing for Thailand.

Speedboats to Pakbeng/Luang Prabang cost 400B/800B (you can pay in kip or dollars but baht are preferred) respectively. The speedboat landing is about 2km south of the town centre. Snacks and drinks can be bought from vendors at the speedboat landing.

Southern Laos

In many ways Southern Laos remains the most traditionally 'Lao' region of the country. The Mekong River valley is mostly inhabited by lowland Lao, while the central highlands are populated by a mixture of Phu Thai, Saek (Sek) and Lao peoples. Only two southern provinces, Savannakhet and Champasak, are regularly travelled by tourists.

SAVANNAKHET PROVINCE

Savannakhet is the country's most populous province (670,000) and is a very active trade junction between Thailand and Vietnam.

Savannakhet

Officially known as Muang Khanthabuli, the provincial capital is a busy district of 124,000 inhabitants just across the Mekong River from Mukdahan, Thailand. Savannakhet has a number of French colonial and Franco-Chinese buildings; most are in the small central business district. A local Vietnamese school, Mahayana Buddhist temple and a Catholic church testify to a continued Vietnamese influence.

Foreign Consulates A Thai consulate (☎ 21 2261) maintains a temporary office at the Nanhai Hotel. There is also a Vietnamese consulate (☎ 21 2182) on Thanon Sisavang-vong. Both consulates can arrange visas for their respective countries.

Money You can change money (cash) at the Lao May Bank on Thanon Khanthabuli just north of Thanon Si Muang, or at the BCEL on Thanon Udomsin.

Places to Stay & Eat The *Santyphab Hotel (☎ 21 2277)* on Thanon Tha Dan, two blocks east of the main ferry pier, offers basic rooms for 4500 kip with fan or 6500 kip air-con, both with shared bath.

On the river in an old French colonial villa is the Vietnamese-owned *Mekong Hotel (☎ 21 2249)*, with large, high-ceiling rooms, ceiling fans, air-con, tile floors and lots of wood panelling. The musty rooms are in fairly poor condition, however, and the place seems deserted, except at night when the downstairs nightclub is filled with Vietnamese men and Vietnamese hostesses. Rates here are 8000 kip.

Consisting of four two-storey houses built around a series of courtyards, the *Savanban-hao Hotel (☎ 21 2202)* has the largest variety of rooms in town. Spacious one-bed fan rooms with outside cold-water bath cost 4500 kip (7000 kip with air-con), one or two-bed rooms with air-con and attached cold-water bath cost 7500 kip; one or two-bed rooms with air-con and hot-water attached bath are 9000 kip (12,000 kip with TV). The mid-range rooms are very good value.

If you have an early bus to catch, or if you want to stay in the cheapest place in town, there's a Vietnamese-owned *motel* along one side of the bus terminal north of town with bare two and three-bed rooms for 1500 kip per person.

In the central area are many small *Chinese-Vietnamese restaurants*, none of them outstanding. A small night market called *Savanhlaty Food Garden*, towards the river from the church in the small town plaza, serves good, inexpensive Lao, Chinese and Thai food.

Getting There & Away Lao Aviation flies from Vientiane to Savannakhet daily except Friday (US$61).

Three or four buses per day leave Vientiane's Talaat Sao bus terminal for the eight to nine hour ride to Savannakhet (eight or nine hours; 10,000 kip). To/from Pakse

SOUTHERN LAOS

SAVANNAKHET

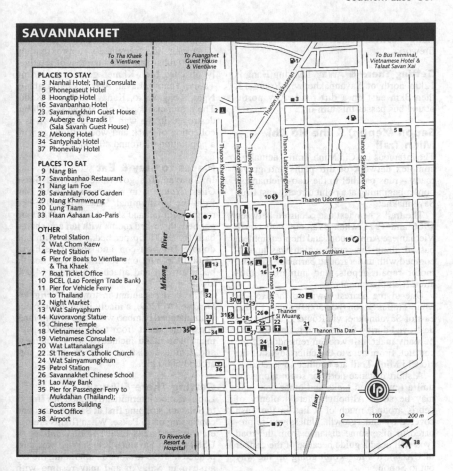

PLACES TO STAY
- 3 Nanhai Hotel; Thai Consulate
- 5 Phonepaseut Hotel
- 8 Hoongtip Hotel
- 16 Savanbanhao Hotel
- 23 Sayamungkhun Guest House
- 27 Auberge du Paradis
  (Sala Savanh Guest House)
- 32 Mekong Hotel
- 34 Santyphab Hotel
- 37 Phonevilay Hotel

PLACES TO EAT
- 9 Nang Bin
- 17 Savanbanhao Restaurant
- 21 Nang Iam Foe
- 28 Savanhlaty Food Garden
- 29 Nang Khamweung
- 30 Lung Taam
- 33 Haan Aahaan Lao-Paris

OTHER
- 1 Petrol Station
- 2 Wat Chom Kaew
- 4 Petrol Station
- 6 Pier for Boats to Vientiane
  & Tha Khaek
- 7 Boat Ticket Office
- 10 BCEL (Lao Foreign Trade Bank)
- 11 Pier for Vehicle Ferry
  to Thailand
- 12 Night Market
- 13 Wat Sainyaphum
- 14 Kuvoravong Statue
- 15 Chinese Temple
- 18 Vietnamese School
- 19 Vietnamese Consulate
- 20 Wat Lattanalangsi
- 22 St Theresa's Catholic Church
- 24 Wat Sainyamungkhun
- 25 Petrol Station
- 26 Savannakhet Chinese School
- 31 Lao May Bank
- 35 Pier for Passenger Ferry to
  Mukdahan (Thailand);
  Customs Building
- 36 Post Office
- 38 Airport

To Tha Khaek & Vientiane

To Fuangnhet Guest House & Vientiane

To Bus Terminal, Vietnamese Hotel & Talaat Savan Xai

To Riverside Resort & Hospital

Mekong River

Huay Long Kong

0   100   200 m

(around six hours; 5000 kip) departure time is usually around 6 am. This trip will be much quicker when Route 13 is finished; for the moment it's a gruelling ride.

Thailand Catch a ferry to get to Mukdahan in Thailand. They cross the Mekong River between Savannakhet and Mukdahan frequently between 8.30 am and 5 pm weekdays, and 8.30 am to 12.30 pm Saturday. The cost is 30B each way.

It's legal for foreigners to enter and exit the country via Savannakhet; no special permission is needed.

Vietnam See the main Getting There & Away section in this chapter.

Getting Around Samlor fares are comparable to those in Vientiane. You can rent bicycles for 3000 kip a day at the Santyphab Hotel.

That Ing Hang

Thought to have been built in the mid-16th century, this well proportioned, 9m thâat is the holiest religious edifice in southern Laos. The monument features three terraced bases topped by a traditional Lao stupa and a gold umbrella weighing 450g. A hollow chamber in the lower section contains an undistinguished collection of Buddha images. By religious custom, women are not permitted to enter the chamber.

On the full moon of the third lunar month

LAOS

(in February or March) is the big **That Ing Hang Festival** featuring processions and fireworks.

Getting There & Away That Ing Hang is 12km north of Savannakhet via Route 13, then 3km east on a dirt road. Any northbound bus passes this turn-off.

Sepon (Xepon) & the Ho Chi Minh Trail

The infamous Ho Chi Minh Trail – actually a complex network of dirt paths and gravel roads – runs parallel to the Lao-Vietnamese border beginning at a point directly east from Savannakhet.

The trail's heaviest use occurred between 1966 and 1971 when over 600,000 North Vietnamese Army troops and their equipment passed along the route, which was honeycombed with underground barracks, fuel and motor repair depots, and numerous antiaircraft emplacements.

One of the nearest towns to the Ho Chi Minh Trail is Sepon (pop 5000), about 170km east of Savannakhet via Route 9. Sepon was destroyed during the war and is now just one of many makeshift wooden reminders of the conflict. From here to the outer edges of the Ho Chi Minh Trail are another 15 to 20km.

A short distance north or south along the trail a few ruined tanks and other war junk may be seen. Although there's plenty of debris around, much of it lies in the bush covered by undergrowth. Unless you're prepared to hike some distance from the road (you will need a guide because of the danger of UXOs), it's not worth going all the way out to Sepon.

Rustic *accommodation* is available in Sepon.

Getting There & Away The bus from Savan to the Vietnamese border stops in Sepon for 4000 kip. Savannakhet Tourism at the Savanbanhao Hotel can arrange car and driver for up to five passengers for about US$100.

SALAVAN PROVINCE

The big attraction in Salavan is the Bolaven Plateau, which actually straddles parts of Salavan, Sekong, Champasak and Attapeu provinces. On the Se Set (Xet) River (a tributary of the Se Don) are several waterfalls and traditional Lao villages. Like the Plain of Jars in Xieng Khuang Province, the Bolaven Plateau has an excellent climate. For details, see the Champasak Province section.

Among the province's approximately 256,000 inhabitants are a number of relatively obscure Mon-Khmer groups, including Ta-oy (Tahoy), Lavai, Alak, Laven, Katang, Ngai, Tong, Pako, Kanay, Katu and Kado. The provincial capital of Salavan was all but destroyed in the war. The rebuilt town is a collection of brick and wood buildings with a population of around 40,000.

Places to Stay & Eat

In Salavan, the government-owned *Saise Guest House* is in a compound about 2km from the bus terminal. Saise offers five-bed rooms with fan and shared bath for 8000 kip per bed, three-bed rooms with fan and shared bath for 9000 kip per bed, rooms with one double bed, air-con and shared bath for 11,000 kip, and one room with two double beds, air-con and attached bath for 14,000 kip.

The best restaurant in town is *Nong Vilaivone* (☎ 3209), a nicely maintained place with thatched bamboo walls and ceiling fans, across the street from the Finance Department. The menu includes Lao, Vietnamese and Chinese dishes, most of which cost around 5000 kip.

Getting There & Away

Lao Aviation intermittently schedules flights to Salavan, stopping first at Savannakhet and continuing on to Pakse. When flights are operating, the fare is US$91 from Vientiane or US$44 from Savannakhet. Service was suspended in 1995 to work on upgrading the US airstrip in Salavan and may resume with flights to/from Pakse only.

You can also get to Salavan by bus or truck from Pakse in Champasak Province.

CHAMPASAK PROVINCE

The Champasak area has a long history that began with Khmer occupation during the Funan (Phanom) and Chenla empires between the 1st and 9th centuries AD. From the 10th to 13th centuries Champasak was part of the Angkor Empire. It broke away from the Lan Xang kingdom in the early 18th century.

Champasak Province has a population of around 500,000 that includes lowland Lao, Khmer, Phu Thai and various Mon-Khmer groups. The province is well known for *matmii*, silks and cottons that are hand-woven of tie-dyed threads.

Pakse

Pakse is French-founded town at the confluence of the Mekong and Se Don rivers. It is now the capital of Champasak Province but has little of interest except the lively **market**.

Pakse is also the gateway for trips to the former royal capital of Champasak and the Angkor ruins of Wat Phu.

Tourist Offices The Tourism Authority of Champasak Province has an office on the banks of the Se Don River near the town centre. The staff can be very helpful.

Vietnamese Consulate Visas for Vietnam can be arranged at the Vietnamese consulate (☎ 21 2058), just off Route 13 in a neighbourhood known as Ban Wat Pha Bat.

Money You can change Thai baht or US dollars (cash) for kip at the BCEL branch near the market (soon to be moving to a new location by the river) and at the Pakse Hotel. It's open weekdays 8.30 am to 3.30 pm, Saturday 8.30 to 10 am. Phak Tai Bank on Route 13 also changes money, albeit at a lower rate than BCEL.

Places to Stay The five storey *Phonsavanh Hotel*, on Route 13 crossing the Se Don from the west, has 18 very basic rooms for 5000/6000 kip single/double, all with shared toilet and cold-water bath. There's a spartan sitting area downstairs and a bulletin board where travellers often post travel info or leave messages.

Near the central market the large *Pakse Hotel* has 38 slightly better rooms starting at 8000 kip for a room with ceiling fan and shared bath at the front of the hotel, 9500 kip for a quieter room of the same sort towards the back, or 12,000 kip with air-con and private cold-water bath. Singles with bath and air-con towards the front cost 11,500 kip. There are also some three-bed rooms with attached bath and fan for 11,500 kip (15,000 kip with air-con).

The clean and friendly *Suksamlan Hotel* on Thanon 14 in the same central area has 24 decent air-con rooms with comfortable beds and private hot-water bath for US$10/12 single/double.

Places to Eat *Restaurant Sedone*, opposite the market area (near the Pakse Hotel), serves

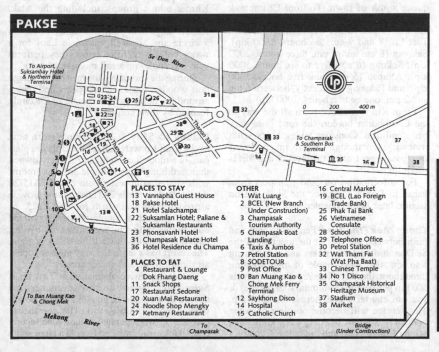

PAKSE

Se Don River

To Airport,
Suksambay Hotel
& Northern Bus
Terminal

To Champasak
& Southern Bus
Terminal

0   200   400 m

To Ban Muang Kao
& Chong Mek

Mekong River

To
Champasak

*Bridge
(Under Construction)*

PLACES TO STAY	OTHER	16 Central Market
13 Vannapha Guest House	1 Wat Luang	19 BCEL (Lao Foreign
18 Pakse Hotel	2 BCEL (New Branch	Trade Bank)
21 Hotel Salachampa	Under Construction)	25 Phak Tai Bank
22 Suksamlan Hotel; Paliane &	3 Champasak	26 Vietnamese
Suksamlan Restaurants	Tourism Authority	Consulate
23 Phonsavanh Hotel	5 Champasak Boat	28 School
31 Champasak Palace Hotel	Landing	29 Telephone Office
36 Hotel Residence du Champa	6 Taxis & Jumbos	30 Petrol Station
	7 Petrol Station	32 Wat Tham Fai
PLACES TO EAT	8 SODETOUR	(Wat Pha Baat)
4 Restaurant & Lounge	9 Post Office	33 Chinese Temple
Dok Fhang Daeng	10 Ban Muang Kao &	34 No 1 Disco
11 Snack Shops	Chong Mek Ferry	35 Champasak Historical
17 Restaurant Sedone	Terminal	Heritage Museum
20 Xuan Mai Restaurant	12 Saykhong Disco	37 Stadium
24 Noodle Shop Mengky	14 Hospital	38 Market
27 Ketmany Restaurant	15 Catholic Church	

LAOS

decent noodle soups, rice dishes, breakfast, Lao coffee and stir-fried dishes. It's open early till late and has a Lao/English menu.

Along the same street opposite the Pakse Hotel, several *Vietnamese-owned restaurants* serve noodles, steamed Chinese-style buns and spring rolls. *Xuan Mai Restaurant*, on the corner opposite the Pakse Hotel, serves good fõe and khào pûn.

Paliane and *Suksamlan* restaurants next door to the Suksamlan Hotel are good and serve mostly Chinese food.

Getting There & Away Lao Aviation flies to Pakse from Vientiane daily (US$95). Pakse can also be reached by road from Salavan.

The intercity bus terminal is split into two separate parts, one 7km north of town and the other 8km south of town. At the northern terminal you'll find buses to Vientiane and Savannakhet. Direct buses between Vientiane and Pakse ply Route 13 once a day for 15,000 kip per person. These leave from either end around 6 am and take a gruelling 13 or 14 hours. Two buses a day go to/from Savannakhet around 5 and 10 am. These cost 5000 kip per person and take about six hours.

For buses south, head to the Km 8 bus queue south of town. To/from Champasak (two hours, 2000 kip) trucks leave at 9 and 11 am and 1 pm. Other destinations include: Taat Lo (7 and 9 am, 2½ hours, 1500 kip); Salavan (8 am and 1 pm, three hours, 2000 kip); Sekong (6 am, five to six hours, 5000 kip); Attapeu (5 or 6 am, five hours, 5000 kip); and Paksong (frequently, between 6 am and 2 pm, one or two hours, 2000 kip).

From Km 8 south of town all the way to the Cambodian border, the road is in very bad condition. Consider taking boats south instead; even though they're much slower than passenger trucks, the level of comfort is much higher.

For information on land transport from Pakse to Don Khong, see the Si Phan Don section later in this chapter.

Chong Mek (Thailand) Ferries run back and forth between the pier at the junction of the Se Don and Mekong rivers and Ban Muang Kao on the west bank of the Mekong throughout the day. The regular ferry costs 500 kip per person (minimum four people) or you can charter a boat across for 2000 kip. This service will become obsolete once the bridge crossing the Mekong a few kilometres south of town is up and operating. Construc-

tion is expected to be completed by March 2001.

From Ban Muang Kao to the Lao-Thai border you can queue up for a share taxi that carries six passengers for 2000 kip each or hire a whole taxi for 9000 kip. The 40km journey to Ban Mai Sing Amphon on the Lao side of the border takes about 45 minutes and operates from 4 am to 6 pm daily.

We've heard rumours that you must now check in with Thai immigration in Phibun Mangsahan, not at the border. If the Thais won't stamp you in at the border, head for Phibun.

See the main Getting There & Away section in this chapter for further detail.

Bolaven Plateau

Centred in north-eastern Champasak Province, the fertile Bolaven Plateau (sometimes spelt Bolovens; Phu Phieng Bolaven in Lao) wasn't farmed intensively until the colonial French planted coffee, rubber and bananas here. Today the Laven, Alak and Katu tribes have revived coffee bean cultivation; other local agricultural products include fruits, cardamom and rattan.

The plateau is a centre for several Mon-Khmer ethnic groups, including the Alak, Laven, Ta-oy, Suay and Katu. The Alak and Katu arrange their palm-and-thatch houses in a circle and are well known in Laos for a water buffalo sacrifice which they perform yearly (usually on a full moon in March).

During the ceremony, the men of the village don wooden masks, hoist spears and dance around the buffalos in the centre of the circle formed by their houses.

Places to Stay & Eat *Tadlo Resort*, next to the Taat Lo waterfall on the Bolaven plateau, is a modest complex of privately owned thatched bungalows. Simple 3rd class rooms with shared cold-water bath cost US$15/20 single/double, while 2nd class rooms provide a private cold-water bath for US$20/25. At the top end are a couple of well appointed bungalows with fan and private hot-water bath that overlook the falls for US$35 a night. The resort has a large and very pleasant open-air dining room and sitting areas.

A less expensive alternative at Taat Lo is *Saise Guest House*, a small government-run operation a couple of hundred metres downstream from Tadlo Resort. The guesthouse consists of two separate sections. One section is set back away from the river in a large white house. This part is rather run-down and unattractive and costs 8000 kip single, 10,000 kip double with shared toilet and shower facilities.

Much better is the so-called 'green house' *(heúan khĭaw)* section farther upstream and directly opposite the Tadlo Resort restaurant. This larger house overlooking the river contains six rooms, all but two of which have attached facilities. VIP rooms with balconies overlooking the falls cost 10,000 kip; other rooms are 8000 kip.

Getting There & Away Passenger trucks between Pakse and Salavan (passing the entrance to Tadlo Resort) cost 1500 kip per person and take about two hours. Tadlo Resort is 100km north-east of Pakse and about 1.5km east of the road to Salavan. The turn-off for Tadlo comes after Lao Ngam, about 30km before Salavan; you should get off the bus at a bridge over the Se Set.

Champasak

This small district of 38,000 on the west bank of the Mekong is a ghost of its former colonial self. An ambitious fountain circle in the middle of the main street looks almost absurd, while either side of the street is lined with French colonial homes in various states of disrepair, along with a couple of noodle shops, a wooden bank building and a single hotel.

A UNESCO office in town, open only part of the year, directs a survey and restoration project at nearby Wat Phu. A collection of religious art dating back nearly 1500 years sits in a warehouse next to the office, awaiting the possible establishment of a museum.

Places to Stay & Eat The *Sala Wat Phou*, a reincarnation of the former Champasak Hotel, is housed in a renovated two storey building next to the provincial offices and near the market. Nine medium-sized rooms with high ceilings, fan and hot water are priced at US$22/25 per single/double, or with air-con US$30. At the back there is also a five bed dorm room that costs US$5 per person. Meals are available in the hotel dining room – it's best if you order in advance.

Mr Sing's House, actually a rice and noodle shop just south of the fountain circle, features a couple of basic rooms for 5000 kip per person. Facilities are shared. During the annual Bun Wat Phu festival (usually in February) every room in Champasak is usually taken, so be sure to arrive a few days in advance to nail down a room.

Between the boat landing and the traffic circle on the east side of the street are three *fŏe shops* usually open from 7 am till around 9 pm.

Getting There & Away Ferries from Ban Muang on the eastern side of the Mekong River to Ban Phaphin on the western side (5km north of Champasak) run regularly throughout daylight hours for 750 kip per person. Buses to Ban Muang from Pakse run regularly throughout the day for 1500 kip per person. From Ban Phaphin a passenger truck to Champasak costs another 500 kip.

Boats between Pakse and Champasak take about 1½ hours down, 2½ hours up, and cost 1000 kip per person. One or two boats typically leave from the Pakse landing between 7 and 8 am, and between noon and 1 pm. Once Route 13 is paved all the way south to the Cambodian border, boat service will probably evaporate entirely.

Wat Phu Champasak

This Angkor-period (10th to 13th centuries) Khmer temple site sits on the lower slopes of Phu Pasak, about 8km south-west of the town of Champasak.

The site is divided into lower and upper parts and joined by a stairway. The lower part consists of two ruined palace buildings at the edge of a pond used for ritual ablutions. The upper section is the temple sanctuary itself, which once enclosed a large Shiva phallus. Some time later the sanctuary was converted into a Buddhist temple but original Hindu sculpture remains in the lintels. The naga stairway leading to the sanctuary is lined with *dok jampa* (plumeria), the Lao national tree. The upper platform affords a good view of the valley below.

The Wat Phu complex is open daily from 8 am to 4.30 pm. Admission (when the booth at the gate is occupied) costs 400 kip plus 800 kip for a still camera permit or 3000 kip for video cameras.

Special Events Near Wat Phu is a large crocodile stone that may have been the site of the purported Chenla sacrifices. Each year, in June, the locals perform a ritual **water buffalo sacrifice** to the ruling earth spirit for Champasak, Chao Tengkham. The blood of the buffalo is offered to a local shaman who serves as a trance medium for the appearance of Chao Tengkham.

Another important local festival is **Bun**

LAOS

Wat Phu, when thousands of pilgrims from throughout Laos come to worship at Wat Phu in its Buddhist incarnation. The festival lasts three days and features Lao boxing matches, cockfights, music and dancing. It's held as part of Magha Puja, which usually falls in February.

Getting There & Away Wat Phu is 46km south from Pakse but only 8km from Champasak. A shared jumbo from Champasak to Bang Thong Khop, the village opposite Wat Phu, should cost 500 kip per person. You can also charter a jumbo from Champasak for 10,000 kip round trip including waiting time, or 4000 kip one way; ask for Wat Phu or Muang Kao (Old City).

Si Phan Don (Four Thousand Islands)

During the rainy season this very scenic 50km section of the Mekong River just north of the Cambodian border reaches a breadth of 14km. During the dry months the river recedes to reveal hundreds of river islands and islets. The largest of the permanent islands are inhabited year-round and offer fascinating glimpses of tranquil river-oriented village life.

The French left behind a defunct short-line **railway** (the only railway ever built in Laos), a couple of river piers and a few **colonial villas** on the islands of Don Khong, Don Det and Don Khon. Other attractions include some impressive **rapids and waterfalls** where the Mekong riverbank suddenly drops in elevation at the Cambodian border, and the rare **Irrawaddy dolphin**.

Places to Stay Near the Muang Khong ferry landing and next door to Don Khong's largest noodle shop, *Done Khong Guest House* contains three simple but clean three-bed rooms with shared facilities for 10,000 kip per room.

Farther north towards Ban Xieng Wang, *Bungalo Souksan* (Suksan Guest House) offers five cottages, each with two small rooms containing fan and private cold-water bath for 10,000 kip. Seven larger bungalows with air-con (6 to 11 pm only) and hot-water showers go for US$35 to US$40 depending on size. A separate building farther back features dorm-style accommodation – basically just a mattress on the floor – for 4000 kip per

bed. The Souksan has a very pleasant restaurant overlooking the river.

Around 200m south of the Muang Khong boat landing, the *Auberge Sala Done Khong* (☎ /fax 21 2077) in Muang Khong offers spacious, nicely decorated rooms in an old teak house for US$20 per night with fan only, US$25 if you use the air-con (available only 5.30 pm to midnight). All rooms come with private toilet and hot-water showers.

Places to Eat Don Khong is nationally famous for its lào-láo, often cited as the smoothest in the country. It's available in the market or at any restaurant.

Near the Muang Khong pier are a couple of adequate *eat-drink shops (hâan kɪn dɛum)*. A large *noodle shop* near the ferry landing also serves khào nĩaw and, with advance notice, khào jâo.

Souksan Guest House has a nice little wooden restaurant overhanging the river. Along the street that leads to the Souksan are several *small cafes* with fõe and Lao snacks.

Getting There & Away There are two passenger trucks per day from Pakse to Hat Xai Khun, directly opposite Muang Khong on the east mainland shore of the Mekong River. The 4000 kip, six hour ride includes the short vehicle ferry ride across to Muang Khong.

There are rumours that the vehicle ferry crossing may move south to Ban Nokhok, opposite Ban Naa on Don Khong, to take advantage of a deeper channel and a slightly shorter crossing. If this transpires, small boats will continue to operate from Hat Xai Khun.

Ferries from Pakse head south around 8 am daily – get to the landing early for space. Be sure to inquire thoroughly before boarding (or the day before) to determine the boat's final destination. Whether or not the boat goes all the way to Don Khong depends upon river height. During and immediately following the rainy season, boats can make it to the landing at Muang Saen on the west side of Don Khong. This trip takes 10 hours and the fare is 5000 kip. From Muang Saen to Muang Khong by jumbo costs 1000 kip per person shared or 6000 kip if you charter.

Getting Around Bicycles can be rented from the Auberge Sala Done Khong for 4000 kip per day; these are quite convenient for seeing the island. Jumbos are also available in Muang Khong and Muang Saen for around 800 kip per kilometre.

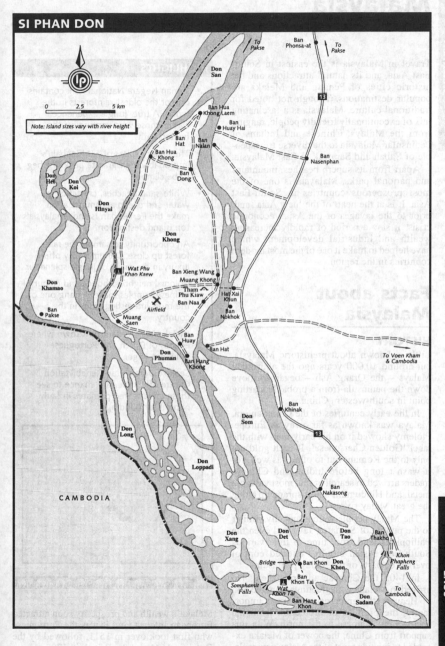

SI PHAN DON

Note: Island sizes vary with river height

0   2.5   5 km

To Pakse

Ban Phonsa-at

To Pakse

Don San

Ban Hua Khong Laem

Ban Huay Hai

Ban Hat

Ban Nalan

Ban Hua Khong

Ban Nasenphan

Ban Dong

Don Hel

Don Koi

Don Hinyai

Don Khong

Don Khamao

Wat Phu Khao Kaew

Ban Xieng Wang

Muang Khong

Tham Phu Kiaw

Ban Naa

Hat Xai Khun

Ban Pakse

Airfield

Ban Nokhok

Muang Saen

Ban Huay

Ban Hat

Don Phuman

Ban Hang Khong

To Voen Kham & Cambodia

Ban Khinak

Don Som

Don Long

Don Loppadi

CAMBODIA

Ban Nakasong

Don Xang

Don Det

Don Tao

Ban Thakho

Bridge

Ban Khon

Don Khon

Khon Phapheng Falls

Somphamit Falls

Wat Khon Tai

Ban Khon Tai

Ban Hang Khon

Don Sadam

To Cambodia

LAOS

Malaysia

Travel in Malaysia is the easiest in South-East Asia, and its natural attractions and the historic cities of Penang and Melaka are popular destinations. Though not noted for traditional culture, Malaysia is a fascinating mix of exceptionally friendly people, ranging from the Malays, Chinese and Indians of Peninsular Malaysia to the diverse tribespeople of Sabah and Sarawak in East Malaysia.

Apart from its superb beaches, mountains and national parks, Malaysia is one of the most prosperous countries in South-East Asia. It is at the heart of the 'new Asia' and, prior to the ravages of the Asian economic crisis, it saw a period of rapidly increasing wealth and industrial development which have helped to make it one of the most modern countries in the region.

Facts about Malaysia

HISTORY

Little is known about prehistoric Malaysia, but around 10,000 years ago the aboriginal Malays – the Orang Asli – began to move down the peninsula from a probable starting point in south-western China.

In the early centuries of the Christian era, Malaya was known as far away as Europe. Ptolemy showed it on his early map with the label 'Golden Chersonese'. It spelt gold not only to the Romans but to others as well, for it wasn't long before Indian and Chinese traders arrived in search of that most valuable metal, and Hindu mini-states sprang up along the great Malay rivers.

The Malay people were ethnically similar to the people of Sumatra, Java and even the Philippines, and from time to time various South-East Asian empires exerted control over all or parts of the Malay peninsula.

In 1405 the Chinese admiral Cheng Ho arrived in Melaka with greetings from the Son of Heaven (the emperor) and, more importantly, the promise of protection from the encroaching Siamese to the north. With this support from China, the power of Melaka extended to include most of the Malay peninsula.

At about the same time, Islam arrived in Melaka and soon spread through Malaya.

HIGHLIGHTS

- Taman Negara National Park contains one of the oldest rainforests in the world. A true 'jungle experience' awaits those who venture off the beaten path.

- The craggy spires of Mt Kinabalu's improbably high granite peak just beg to be climbed.

- White-sand beaches, crystal-clear water and cheap accommodation make the Perhentian Islands Malaysia's top island destination.

- An opportunity to sample the rainforest up close, Danum Valley offers luxury in the midst of jungle splendour.

- Colonial neighbourhoods and colourful Chinese temples make Penang one of the most interesting cities in the country.

- Melaka is a pleasant port town where echoes of Dutch and Portuguese influence linger.

- Sepilok Orang-utan Rehabilitation Centre offers the rare chance to see these endangered primates in fairly natural surroundings.

Melaka's wealth and prosperity soon attracted European interest, and it was the Portuguese who first took over in 1511, followed by the Dutch in 1641 and the British in 1795.

For years, the British were only interested in Malaya for its seaports and to protect their trade routes, but the discovery of tin prompted them to move inland and govern the whole peninsula. Meanwhile, James Brooke, the 'white raja', and the North Borneo Company made British inroads into Sarawak and Sabah respectively. The British, as was their custom, also brought in Chinese and Indians, an action which radically changed the country's racial mix.

Malaya achieved *merdeka* (independence) in 1957, but there followed a period of instability due to an internal Communist uprising and the external 'confrontation' with neighbouring Indonesia. In 1963 the north Borneo states of Sabah and Sarawak, along with Singapore, joined Malaya to create Malaysia.

Relations with Singapore soured almost immediately and, only two years later, Singapore was forced to withdraw from the Malaysian confederation. The demise of Indonesia's megalomaniac leader Soekarno (see the main History section in the Indonesia chapter) ended the disputes with Indonesia and the Communist threat has, as elsewhere, withered away.

In 1969 violent intercommunal riots broke out, particularly in Kuala Lumpur (KL), and hundreds of people were killed. The government moved to dissipate the tensions, which existed mainly between the Malays and the Chinese. Moves to give Malays a larger share of the economic pie have led to some resentment among the other racial groups but, overall, present-day Malaysian society is relatively peaceful and cooperative.

Elections in 1974 resulted in an overwhelming majority for the Barisan, or National Front, of which the United Malays National Organisation (UMNO) is the key party. All elections since have seen power remain with UMNO.

Led by outspoken Prime Minister Dr Mahathir Mohamad, Malaysia's economy was growing at over 8% per year until mid-1997, when a currency crisis in neighbouring Thailand plunged the whole of South-East Asia into a recession. Dr Mahathir was quick to blame western currency speculators for the crisis, a move which did little to improve relations with the west, already angered over his criticisms of 'western decadence' (in contrast to 'Asian Values').

At the time of writing, Dr Mahathir faced strong protests from supporters of Anwar Ibrahim, who had the temerity to question the doctor's responses to the South-East Asian currency crisis. Long considered a shoe-in as Mahathir's successor, Anwar was jailed on questionable charges ranging from sodomy to financial impropriety. While the government has largely succeeded in quieting the opposition, most analysts agree that Mahathir's fate depends on the success or failure of his efforts to resuscitate Malaysia's economy.

GEOGRAPHY

Malaysia consists of two distinct parts. Peninsular Malaysia is the long finger of land extending down from Asia, as if pointing towards Indonesia and Australia, and it accounts for about 40% of the country's area. Although most of the forests have been cleared over the years to make way for plantations of rubber trees and oil palms, there are still stands of virgin forest remaining, largely in the national park of Taman Negara.

The balance of the land area is made up of the states of Sabah and Sarawak, which occupy the northern segment of the island of Borneo. Here too, the forests have been cleared for agriculture and timber exports, and the tracts of virgin rainforest are rapidly diminishing. Mt Kinabalu in Sabah is the highest peak between the Himalayas and Irian Jaya in Indonesia.

CLIMATE

Malaysia has a typically tropical climate – it's hot and humid year-round. The temperature rarely drops below 20°C, even at night, and usually climbs to 30°C or more during the day.

Malaysia gets rain throughout the year, but the west coast of Peninsular Malaysia gets heavier rainfall from September to December. The east coast bears the full brunt of the monsoon rains from November to February, and Sarawak and Sabah are similarly affected. Throughout the region the humidity tends to hover around the 90% mark, but on the peninsula you can escape from the heat and humidity by retreating to the delightfully cool hill stations.

While summer-weight clothing will suffice in most areas of the country, travellers headed up Mt Kinabalu or to the hill stations of the peninsula should bring adequate cold-weather gear.

See the Kuala Lumpur climate chart in the Appendix.

ECOLOGY & ENVIRONMENT

Malaysia attracts more than its fair share of criticism on the environmental front, and it is an issue that the Malaysian government – which remembers the heritage of colonial environmental exploitation – is particularly sensitive about.

Blame for the situation aside, preserving something of Malaysia's environmental heritage before it is all shipped overseas as logs is of utmost importance. Probably more than 60% of Peninsular Malaysia's rainforests have been logged, and similar figures apply to East Malaysia. Government initiatives and the formation of national parks have slowed down logging on the peninsula, but it continues at heavy rates in Sabah and Sarawak despite mounting international and domestic pressure.

In addition to logging, Malaysia has been attacked for undertaking several large dam construction projects, which critics claim are both economically and environmentally unsound. The most controversial of these is the Bakun Dam project in Sarawak. In addition to drowning hundreds of square kilometres of virgin rainforest, construction of the dam will also force thousands of indigenous people from their homes. Fortunately, the current economic slowdown has put this and some of the other megaprojects on an indefinite hold.

More recently, Malaysia's environment has been threatened by a force completely beyond its control: the so-called 'haze' from fires burning in the Indonesian states of Kalimantan and Sumatra. While this problem occurs to some extent every year, the last half of 1997 saw unprecedented levels of air pollution – at times the smoke was so thick that aeroplanes couldn't land at airports in Sabah and Sarawak.

By the end of 1997, most of the smoke had cleared, but experts say that lax enforcement of environmental laws and another dry season could bring a repeat of those smoky months.

FLORA & FAUNA

Malaysia is home to some of the most diverse flora and fauna in the world. Its ancient rainforests, the area's climatic stability, plentiful rainfall and tropical greenhouse heat have endowed Malaysia with a cornucopia of bizarre life forms.

In Peninsular Malaysia alone there are over 8000 species of flowering plants, including 2000 trees, 800 orchids and 200 palms. They include the world's tallest tropical tree species, the *tualang*, and the world's largest flower, the rafflesia, measuring up to one metre across.

Mammals include elephants, rhinos (very rare now), tapirs, tigers, leopards, honey bears, several kinds of deer, *tempadau* (forest cattle), various gibbons and monkeys (including, in Borneo, the orang-utan and the bizarre proboscis monkey), scaly anteaters (pangolins) and porcupines, to name a few.

The bird life features spectacular pheasants, the sacred hornbills, and many groups of colourful birds such as kingfishers, sunbirds, pittas, woodpeckers, trogons and barbets. Snakes include cobras (notably the spitting cobra, which shoots venom into the eyes of its prey), vipers, pythons and colourful tree snakes.

GOVERNMENT & POLITICS

Malaysia is a confederation of 13 states plus the capital district of Kuala Lumpur. Nine of the peninsular states have sultans, and every five years an election is held to determine which one will become the *yang di-pertuan agong*, or 'king' of Malaysia.

The states of Sabah and Sarawak in East Malaysia are slightly different from those of Peninsular Malaysia since they were separate colonies, not parts of Malaya, prior to independence. They still retain a greater degree of local administrative autonomy than the peninsular states.

The political system is a federal one, with each state having its own legislature, but power is concentrated in the national government. General elections are held every five years, but power is firmly in the hands of UMNO.

ECONOMY

Since colonial times, Malaysia has been one of the world's major suppliers of tin, natural rubber and palm oil. Rubber and palm oil plantations cover a large part of the peninsula. In East Malaysia the economy is based on timber, and in Sarawak oil and pepper are major exports. With the decline of these traditional mainstays of the economy, Malaysia has successfully diversified into manufactured goods. The country is a major supplier of electronic components and equipment; along with other goods such as textiles and footwear, manufactured goods now count for over half of all exports.

In the summer of 1997, a currency crisis which started in neighbouring Thailand quickly spread to the rest of South-East Asia and dragged the entire region into a deep recession. While Malaysia's economy seems to be gradually clawing its way back to growth, exchange rates are still down, making this a good time to visit.

POPULATION & PEOPLE

Malaysia's population is currently around 19.5 million. The people of Malaysia come from a number of different ethnic groups – Malays, Chinese, Indians, the indigenous Orang Asli of the peninsula, and the various tribes of Sarawak and Sabah.

It's reasonable to say that the Malays control the government while the Chinese have their fingers on the economic pulse. Approximately 85% of the population lives in Peninsular Malaysia and the remaining 15% in the much more lightly populated states of Sabah and Sarawak.

There are still small, scattered groups of Orang Asli (literally, Original People; in practice, a generic term for minority tribes who don't fall into the government's main racial categories) to be found in Peninsular Malaysia. Although most have given up their nomadic or shifting-agriculture techniques and have been absorbed into modern Malay society, a few groups of Orang Asli still live in the forests.

Dayak is the term used for the non-Muslim people of Borneo. These people migrated to Borneo at times and along routes which are not clearly defined. It is estimated that there are more than 200 Dayak tribes on Borneo, the most important being the Iban and Bidayuh in Sarawak and the Kadazan in Sabah. Other smaller groups include the Kenyah, Kayan and Punan, whose way of life and habitat are rapidly disappearing.

ARTS

It's along the east coast of Peninsular Malaysia, the predominantly Malay part of Malaysia, that you'll find Malay arts and crafts, culture and games at their liveliest and most widely practised. However, the Kelantan government has sought to ban dancing and other un-Islamic folk performances in its push for religious purity.

Dance

There are a variety of dances and dance dramas performed in Malaysia. Though disco dancing is the most popular dance form these days, traditional dance troupes perform for special occasions.

Menora is a dance drama of Thai origin performed by an all-male cast dressed in grotesque masks; *mak yong* is the female version. Performances often take place at Puja Ketek, a Buddhist festival held at temples in Kelantan, near the Thai border.

The upbeat *joget* is the most popular traditional dance in Malaysia today, and is often performed at Malay weddings by professional dancers. In Melaka it is better known as *chakunchak*.

Rebana kercing is a dance performed by young men to the accompaniment of tambourines. The *rodat* is a dance from Terengganu and is accompanied by the *tar* drum.

Music

Traditional Malay music is based largely on the *gendang* (drum), of which there are more than a dozen types. Other percussion instruments include the *gong, cerucap* (made of shells), *raurau* (coconut shells), *kertuk* and *pertuang* (both made from bamboo), and the wooden *celampang*.

Wind instruments include a number of types of flute (such as the *seruling* and *serunai)* and the trumpet-like *nafiri*. Stringed instruments, including the *biola, gambus* and *sundatang,* are also an important component of a traditional ensemble.

The *gamelan*, a traditional Indonesian gong orchestra, is also found in the state of Kelantan, where a typical ensemble will comprise four different gongs, two xylophones and a large drum.

Wayang Kulit

Similar to the shadow-puppet performances of other South-East Asian countries, in particular Java in Indonesia, *wayang kulit* (shadow play) retells tales from the Hindu epic the *Ramayana.*

The Tok Dalang, or 'Father of the Mysteries', sits behind a semi-transparent screen and manipulates the buffalo-hide puppets whose images are thrown onto the screen. Characters include heroes, demons, kings, animals and, ever favourites, clowns.

Performances, which can last for many hours, often take place at weddings or after the harvest.

Wayang kulit used to be an immensely popular form of entertainment, but it was all but killed off with the advent of the all-conquering TV – fifty years ago there were well over 100 wayang kulit masters; these days there are less than half a dozen. The tourist industry has been something of a saviour for the wayang kulit performers, and the art form is unlikely to disappear completely.

Crafts

Batik Originally an Indonesian craft, batik has made itself equally at home in Malaysia. You'll find it in Penang on the west coast, but Kelantan is its true home.

Batik cloth is produced by drawing out a pattern with wax and then dyeing the material. The wax is then melted away by boiling the cloth, and a second wax design is drawn in. After repeated waxing, dyeing and boiling processes, an intricate and beautifully coloured design is produced.

Batik can be found as clothes, cushion covers, tablecloths, placemats or simply as works of art. Malay designs are usually less traditional than in neighbouring Indonesia.

Other Weaving A speciality of Kelantan and Terengganu, *kain songket* is a handwoven fabric with gold and silver threads through the material. *Mengkuang* is a far more prosaic form of weaving using *pandanus* leaves and strips of bamboo to make baskets, bags and mats.

Silver & Brasswork Kelantan is famed for its silversmiths, who work in a variety of ways and specialise in filigree and repoussé work. In the latter, designs are hammered through the silver from the underside. Kampung Sireh at Kota Bharu is a centre for silverwork. Brasswork is an equally traditional skill in Kuala Terengganu.

Arts & Crafts of East Malaysia The indigenous peoples of East Malaysia have a rich legacy of arts and crafts. Perhaps the most famous East Malaysian art is *pua kumbu*, a colourful weaving technique used to produce both everyday and ceremonial items decorated with a wide range of patterns.

Woodcarving is another prized art, and the most skilled carvers of all are held to be the Kenyah and Kayan peoples, who produce enormous, finely detailed burial columns (*kelirieng*) carved from tree trunks. Decaying remnants of kelirieng are still uncovered in the rainforest of Sarawak, and an example can be seen in Kuching Municipal Park. Less formidable, but equally beautiful, the Kenyah and Kayan also produced smaller wooden hunting charms and ornate wooden knife hilts known as *parang ilang*.

Some ethnic groups still produce baskets and other goods in the traditional way, and these can be found in some of the markets of East Malaysia. Others may be offered for sale upon a visit to a longhouse.

SOCIETY & CONDUCT

In common with many Muslim countries in the last decade, Malaysia has been going through a period of increasing concentration on religion and religious activity. It's a world away from the sort of fundamentalism found in other parts of the world, but you still need to be aware of local sensibilities so as not to offend.

It's wise to be appropriately discreet in dress and behaviour, particularly on the stricter Muslim east coast of the peninsula. For women, topless bathing is definitely not acceptable and away from the beaches you should cover up as much as possible. For men, shorts are considered low class away from the beach, and bare torsos are not acceptable in the villages and towns.

RELIGION

The variety of religions found in Malaysia is a direct reflection of the diversity of races living there. Although Islam is the state religion of Malaysia, freedom of religion is guaranteed. The Malays are almost all Muslims. The Chinese are predominantly followers of Taoism and Buddhism, though some are Christians. The majority of the region's Indian population come from the south of India and are Hindu, though a sizeable percentage are Muslim.

Although Christianity has made no great inroads into Peninsular Malaysia, it has had a much greater impact upon East Malaysia, where many of the indigenous people have converted to Christianity, although others still follow their animist traditions.

LANGUAGE

The official language is Bahasa Malaysia, or Bahasa Melayu ('language of the Malays'). You can also get along quite happily with English throughout Malaysia, and it is often the linking language between the various ethnic groups, especially among the middle class.

Other everyday languages include Chinese dialects like Hakka or Hokkien. The majority of the region's Indians speak Tamil, although there are also groups who speak Malayalam, Hindi or other Indian languages.

See the Language section in the Appendix for some useful Malay words and phrases.

Facts for the Visitor

HIGHLIGHTS

Taman Negara National Park is one of the world's oldest rainforests, home to several endangered species and a profusion of exotic plants – excellent jungle trekking and mountain climbing.

Kinabalu National Park features an improbably high granite peak that just begs to be climbed, surrounded by beautiful rainforest with gentle walking trails.

The Perhentian Islands are perhaps the most beautiful islands in all Malaysia, with white-sand beaches and crystal-clear aquamarine water.

Danum Valley offers the ultimate rainforest experience – wake up to the incredible sound of hooting gibbons and a deafening insect chorus.

Penang is a historic British settlement with strong Chinese influences, colourful temples, lots of good food and decent nightlife – perhaps the west coast's most interesting stopover.

Melaka's Dutch and Portuguese heritage is revealed in the port's interesting blend of architecture.

Sepilok Orang-utan Rehabilitation Centre is one of only four such refuges in the world; the antics of these appealing apes are not to be missed.

PLANNING
When to Go

Rain occurs fairly evenly throughout the year, but travel is possible year-round. The exception is the east coast of the peninsula, which receives heavy rain from November to January, when many resorts close down and boat services stop.

Malaysia has many colourful festivals, such as Thaipusam, around January/February, but with such a wide ethnic diversity, celebrations are held throughout the year. During public holidays – especially Chinese New Year, Hari Raya and Christmas – transport is crowded and hotel prices rise in the resorts.

Maps

Mapping in Malaysia is generally poor. Tourist office maps are usually little more than sketch maps, but adequate for getting around. Good maps can be found for the main cities; Periplus and Nelles Verlag each produce a good series.

VISAS & DOCUMENTS
Passport

Passports must be valid for at least six months beyond the date of entry into Malaysia.

Visas

British Commonwealth citizens (except those from India, Bangladesh, Sri Lanka and Pakistan) and citizens of the Republic of Ireland, Switzerland, the Netherlands, San Marino and Liechtenstein do not require a visa to visit Malaysia.

Citizens of Austria, Belgium, Czech Republic, Denmark, Finland, Hungary, Germany, Iceland, Italy, Japan, Luxembourg, Norway, Slovak Republic, South Korea, Sweden and the USA do not require a visa for a visit not exceeding three months.

Citizens of France, Greece, Poland and South Africa do not require a visa for a visit not exceeding one month. Most other nationalities are given a shorter stay period or require a visa. Citizens of Israel cannot enter Malaysia without prior diplomatic arrangement.

Most nationalities are given a 30 day or 60 day permit on arrival. As a general rule, if you arrive by air you will be given 60 days automatically, though coming overland you may be given 30 days unless you specifically ask for a 60 day permit.

Sabah and Sarawak are treated almost like separate countries. Your passport will be checked again on arrival in each state and a new stay permit, usually for 30 days, is issued. Travelling directly from either Sabah or Sarawak back to Peninsular Malaysia, however, there are no formalities and you do not start a new entry period, so your 30 day permit from Sabah or Sarawak remains valid.

Visa Extensions It's possible to get an extension at an immigration office in the country for a total stay of up to three months.

In Sabah and Sarawak your initial 30 day permit can be extended, though extensions can be difficult to get in Sarawak.

Driving Licence

A car can be hired on the production of a valid home licence with a photo. Officially, an International Driving Permit is not required, but it is good to present to overly officious police.

Hostel Cards

A Hostelling International (HI, also YHA) card is of limited use, as only KL, Melaka and Port Dickson have HI hostels, though it can be used to waive the small initial membership fee at some YMCAs and YWCAs.

Student Cards

An International Student Identity Card (ISIC) is also of limited use. Most student discounts, eg on trains, are only available for Malaysian students, but the card can be useful at hostels, and flashing it occasionally brings discounts.

EMBASSIES
Malaysian Embassies

Malaysian embassies abroad include:

Australia
  (☎ 02-6273 1543)
  7 Perth Ave, Yarralumla, ACT 2600
Canada
  (☎ 613-237 5182)
  60 Boteler St, Ottawa, Ontario K1N 8Y7
France
  (☎ 01 45 53 11 83)
  2 bis rue Benouville, 75116 Paris
Germany
  (☎ 228-3768 0306)
  Mittelstrasse 43, 5300 Bonn 2
Japan
  (☎ 03-3476 3840)
  20-16 Nanpeidai-cho, Shibuya-ku,
  Tokyo 150
New Zealand
  (☎ 04-385 2439)
  10 Washington Ave, Brooklyn,
  Wellington
UK
  (☎ 020-7235 8033)
  45 Belgrave Square, London SW1X 8QT
USA
  (☎ 202-328 2700)
  2401 Massachusetts Ave NW, Washington,
  DC 20008

See the other chapters in this book for Malaysian embassies in those countries.

Embassies & Consulates in Malaysia

Countries with embassies in Kuala Lumpur include:

Australia
  Embassy:
  (☎ 242 3122)
  6 Jalan Yap Kwan Seng
Brunei
  Embassy:
  (☎ 261 2800)
  MBF Plaza, 172 Jalan Ampang

Cambodia
  Embassy:
  (☎ 457-3711)
  83-JKR 2809 Lingkungan U Thant
Canada
  Embassy:
  (☎ 261 2000)
  MBF Plaza, 172 Jalan Ampang
France
  Embassy:
  (☎ 249 4122)
  192 Jalan Ampang
Germany
  Embassy:
  (☎ 242 9666)
  3 Jalan U Thant
India
  Embassy:
  (☎ 253 3510)
  Jalan Taman Duta
Indonesia
  Embassy:
  (☎ 984 2011)
  233 Jalan Tun Razak
  Consulate in Penang:
  (☎ 282 4686)
  467 Jalan Burma
  Consulate in Kuching:
  (☎ 24 1734)
  5A Jalan Pisang
  Consulate in Kota Kinabalu:
  (☎ 21 9110)
  Jalan Karamunsing
Ireland
  Embassy:
  (☎ 456-3708)
  4 Jalan Penggawa
Japan
  Embassy:
  (☎ 242 7044)
  11 Pertiaran Stonor
Laos
  Embassy:
  (☎ 248 3895)
  Jalan Bellamy
Myanmar (Burma)
  Embassy:
  (☎ 242 3863)
  5 Jalan Taman U Thant
New Zealand
  Embassy:
  (☎ 238 2533)
  Menara IMC, Jalan Tun Razak
Philippines
  Embassy:
  (☎ 248 4233)
  1 Jalan Changkat Kia Peng
Singapore
  Embassy:
  (☎ 261 6277)
  209 Jalan Tun Razak

Sri Lanka
    Embassy:
    (☎ 456 0917)
    2A Jalan Ampang Hilir
Thailand
    Embassy:
    (☎ 248 8222)
    206 Jalan Ampang
    Consulate in Penang:
    (☎ 226 9484)
    1 Jalan Tunku Abdul Rahman
    Consulate in Kota Bharu:
    (☎ 744 0867)
    4426 Jalan Pengkalan Chepa
UK
    Embassy:
    (☎ 248 2122)
    185 Jalan Ampang
USA
    Embassy:
    (☎ 248 9011)
    376 Jalan Tun Razak
Vietnam
    Embassy:
    (☎ 248 4036)
    Vietnam House, 4 Pesiaran Stonor

CUSTOMS

The following items can be brought into Malaysia free of duty: 1L of alcohol, 225g of tobacco (200 cigarettes), souvenirs and gifts not exceeding RM200. Cameras, portable radios, perfume, cosmetics and watches do not attract duty.

The list of prohibited items is longer – the main thing to avoid is the importation of illicit drugs, which carries the death penalty in Malaysia.

Note that visitors can now carry only RM1000 in ringgit notes in and out of the country. There are no limits on foreign currency, but it must be declared.

MONEY
Currency

The local currency is the Malaysian ringgit (RM), which is divided into 100 sen. Notes in circulation are RM5, RM10, RM20, RM50, RM100, RM500 and RM1000; the coins in use are 1, 5, 10, 20 and 50 sen, and RM1. Old RM1 notes are occasionally seen around, and new RM2 and RM15 notes are coming into circulation.

At the time of writing it was difficult to exchange ringgit outside Malaysia. So best get rid of what you have before you leave the country.

Exchange Rates

In September 1998 Malaysia pegged the ringgit to the US dollar at a fixed rate; other currency rates remain variable.

Exchange rates are as follows:

country	unit		ringitt
Australia	A$1	=	RM2.39
Canada	C$1	=	RM2.46
euro	€1	=	RM4.57
France	10FF	=	RM6.91
Germany	DM1	=	RM2.32
Japan	¥100	=	RM3.18
New Zealand	NZ$1	=	RM2.05
Singapore	S$1	=	RM2.34
UK	UK£1	=	RM6.47
USA	US$1	=	RM3.80

Exchanging Money

American dollars are the most convenient form of currency in Malaysia, but you'll have no problems changing other major currencies.

Banks are efficient and there are also plenty of moneychangers in the main centres. Credit cards are widely accepted, and many ATMs accept Visa and MasterCard if your card has a PIN. Some banks are also connected to networks like Cirrus, Maestro and Plus. Maybank is the most convenient bank for cash advances etc.

Costs

Malaysia is more expensive than other South-East Asian nations, although less so than Singapore. You get pretty much what you pay for – there are lots of hotels where a couple can get a quite decent room for around US$5, or guesthouses in the tourist centres offer dormitory beds for around US$2.50, as well as cheap rooms. Food at hawkers' centres is cheap, and transport is also reasonable and efficient.

Tipping & Bargaining

Tipping is not normal in Malaysia. The more expensive hotels and restaurants already have a 10% service charge added, while at the cheaper places tipping is not expected.

Bargaining is not usually required for everyday goods, unlike in some Asian countries. Always bargain when purchasing souvenirs, antiques and other tourist items, even if prices are displayed. Transport prices are fixed but negotiation is required for trishaws and unmetered taxis around town or for charter.

POST & COMMUNICATIONS

Post

Malaysia has an efficient postal system and a reliable poste restante service at the major post offices. Most post offices are open daily, except Sunday, from 8 am to 5 pm. Aerograms and postcards cost RM0.50 to any destination.

Telephone

There are good telephone communications throughout the country. You can make direct-dial long-distance calls between all major towns in Malaysia. Local calls cost 10 sen for three minutes.

Convenient Telekom card phones are found all over the country and take plastic cards, though two telephone systems – Uniphone and Cityphone – operate using different cards. Credit-card phones are also widely available.

International calls can be direct-dialled from many public phone booths and from most Telekom offices in Malaysia. Reverse-charge international calls can easily be made from any phone by dialling the Home Country Direct numbers that are listed in the telephone book, or you can bill charges to a home phone account. Calls to Singapore are considered long-distance calls, not international calls.

Email & Internet Access

Internet cafes and guesthouses offering Internet facilities have proliferated in recent years. You can also find Internet kiosks in most of the nation's shopping malls, especially in west Malaysia.

Telephone Codes

The country code for Malaysia is 60. The international dialling code is 007. Drop the first zero in the area codes when dialling from outside Malaysia. Following are area codes for some cities.

Peninsular Malaysia

Alor Setar	☎ 04
Cameron Highlands	☎ 05
Cherating	☎ 09
Desaru	☎ 07
Fraser's Hill	☎ 09
Ipoh	☎ 05
Jerantut	☎ 09
Johor Bahru	☎ 07
Kota Bharu	☎ 09
Kuala Besut	☎ 09
Kuala Lipis	☎ 09
Kuala Lumpur	☎ 03
Kuala Perlis	☎ 04
Kuala Terengganu	☎ 09
Kuantan	☎ 09
Langkawi	☎ 04
Marang	☎ 09
Melaka	☎ 06
Merang	☎ 09
Mersing	☎ 07
Penang	☎ 04
Perhentian Islands	☎ 09
Pulau Kapas	☎ 09
Rantau Abang	☎ 09
Singapore	☎ 02
Taman Negara	☎ 09

Taiping	☎ 05
Tioman	☎ 09

Sabah

Beaufort	☎ 087
Kota Kinabalu	☎ 088
Kudat	☎ 088
Labuan	☎ 087
Ranau	☎ 088
Sandakan	☎ 089
Semporna	☎ 089
Sepilok	☎ 089
Tambunan	☎ 087
Tawau	☎ 089
Tenom	☎ 087

Sarawak

Belaga	☎ 084
Bintulu	☎ 086
Kapit	☎ 084
Kuching	☎ 082
Lawas	☎ 085
Limbang	☎ 085
Marudi	☎ 085
Miri	☎ 085
Sibu	☎ 084

BOOKS

There's a wide variety of books available in Malaysia, and a number of good bookshops in which to find them.

Lonely Planet

Lonely Planet's *Malaysia, Singapore & Brunei* has all the information you need for extended travel to these states. Lonely Planet also publishes the *Malay phrasebook*, an introduction to the Malay language.

History & Politics

A Short History of Malaysia, Singapore & Brunei by C Mary Turnbull is straightforward and a good introductory volume on Malaysia's history. *A History of Malaysia* by Barbara Andaya & Leonard Watson is one of the best histories with a post-independence slant.

The prime minister, Dr Mahathir Mohamad, is a prolific writer. *The Malay Dilemma* and his latest offering, *The Voice of Asia*, are interesting polemics of racial stereotyping.

General

Kampong Boy by the cartoonist Lat provides a delightful introduction to Malay life.

Khoo Su Nin's *Streets of Georgetown, Penang* is well worth recommending – it's a fascinating run-down on the town's varied collection of old buildings.

An Analysis of Malay Magic by KM Endicott is a scholarly look at Malay folk religion and the importance of spirits and magic in the world view of Malays.

Chinese Beliefs & Practices in South-East Asia, edited by Cheu Hock Tong, is an excellent introduction to Chinese religion and society.

Vanishing World – The Ibans of Borneo by Leigh Wright has some beautiful colour photographs. Redmond O'Hanlon's *Into the Heart of Borneo* is a wonderfully funny tale of a jaunt through the jungles of northern Borneo. For Bornean wildlife, *A Field Guide to the Mammals of Borneo* by Junaidi Payne, et al is a must.

Malaysia has provided a fertile setting for novelists, and Joseph Conrad's *The Shadow Line* and *Lord Jim* both use the near region as a setting. Somerset Maugham also set many of his classic short stories in Malaya – look for the *Borneo Stories*. Paul Theroux's *The Consul's File* is based in the small town of Ayer Hitam. *The Long Day Wanes* is a reissue in one volume of Anthony Burgess'

classic *Malayan Trilogy* – some of the finest English-language fiction set in South-East Asia.

NEWSPAPERS & MAGAZINES

Malaysia has newspapers in English, Malay, Chinese and Tamil. The *New Straits Times* is the main offering in English, and the *Star* is on line (www.jaring.my/~star). Foreign magazines are widely available.

RADIO & TV

There is a wide variety of radio stations in Malaysia, broadcasting in Bahasa Malaysia, English, and various Chinese and Indian languages and dialects. Around KL the number of English stations is highest, while in East Malaysia, the pickings are pretty scarce.

Malaysia has two government TV channels, RTM 1 and 2, and two commercial stations. Programs range from local productions in the various languages to imports from the USA and UK.

TIME

Malaysia is eight hours ahead of GMT (London). Thus, when it is noon in Kuala Lumpur, it is 8 pm in Los Angeles and 11 pm in New York (the previous day), 4 am in London, and 2 pm in Sydney and Melbourne.

ELECTRICITY

Electricity supplies are reliable throughout Malaysia. Supply is 220-240V, 50 cycles. Power sockets are almost always of the three-square-pin type found in the UK, although some older places have the three-round-pin sockets, also as in the UK.

WEIGHTS & MEASURES

Malaysia uses the international metric system. Some addresses refer to *batu* (literally, stone), the mileposts that are still found on a few roads. So an address might be 'Batu 10, Jalan Ipoh', which means at the 10 mile mark on the Ipoh road, even though the 10 mile marker may have long been replaced by a 16 km post.

Fruit may be sold by the *biji*, eg 'three biji RM1', but the biji is not a unit of weight, but roughly translates as 'piece'. In Malay, it is poor usage to say 'tiga rambutan' (three rambutan) and the proper usage is 'tiga biji rambutan' (three 'pieces' of rambutan), just as in English 'three pieces of paper' is correct, not 'three papers'.

TOILETS

Malaysian toilets are not nearly as horrifying as those in other South-East Asian countries. You will find both western-style and Asian squat-style toilets, the former rapidly replacing the latter. In places with squat-style toilets, toilet paper is not usually provided. Instead, you will find a hose which you are supposed to use as a bidet, or in more budget places, a bucket of water and a tap. If you do not find this to your liking, make a point of bringing packets of tissues wherever you go.

HEALTH

Malaysia enjoys good standards of health and cleanliness. You may be required to show proof of cholera vaccination if you're coming from an infected area, although this is contrary to internationally agreed requirements. The main problem to look out for is malaria in the rural hinterland of Peninsular Malaysia and Sarawak, and throughout Sabah, so take appropriate precautions. Dengue fever also occurs, so it's important to take measures to avoid mosquito bites. The usual rules for healthy living in a tropical environment apply.

For more information on these and other health matters, refer to the Health section in the Appendix.

Tap water is safe to drink in many cities, and bottled water and other soft drinks are widely available.

WOMEN TRAVELLERS

Foreign women travelling in Malaysia have reported some harassment from Malaysian men. The best way to deal with this is to ignore it completely.

It is important to bear in mind that Malaysia is a Muslim country and modesty in dress is important. Though Malaysia is generally a very safe country, don't walk alone at night on empty beaches or poorly lit streets.

Many travellers of both sexes have reported the existence of small peepholes in the walls and doors of cheap hotels. Plug them up with tissue paper, ask for another room or move to another hotel. Remember that in some places the cheap hotels are in fact brothels.

Tampons can be found in supermarkets in the main cities if you hunt around, but pads are more commonly available, so if you use tampons bring your own.

GAY & LESBIAN TRAVELLERS

Gay issues are swept under the carpet in Malaysia. The official attitude seems to be that, as a strongly Muslim country steeped in Asian values, homosexuality in Malaysia doesn't exist and it is a western aberration. Gay groups and venues are thin on the ground, except in the more cosmopolitan and liberal-minded cities such as KL.

DISABLED TRAVELLERS

For the mobility impaired, Malaysia can be hard work. In most cities and towns there are often no footpaths, kerbs are very high, construction sites are everywhere, and pedestrian crossings are few and far between. On the upside, the modern urban rail lines being constructed in KL are at least reasonably accessible.

Both Malaysia Airlines and Keretapi Tanah Melayu (KTM, the national rail service) offer 50% discounts on travel for disabled travellers.

SENIOR TRAVELLERS

Senior travellers get a variety of discounts on admission at most cultural attractions. The usual eligible age for seniors is 65 years. Malaysia Airlines does not offer discounts for foreign seniors, but KTM does offer a 50% discount on all travel for foreign seniors over 65 years of age.

TRAVEL WITH CHILDREN

As elsewhere in South-East Asia, travelling with children in Malaysia can be a lot of fun as long as you come with the right attitude and the usual parental patience – Maureen Wheeler's *Travel with Children* offers practical tips.

There are discounts for children at most attractions, and transport and Chinese hotels charge for the room itself rather than the number of people. However, cots are not widely available in cheap accommodation. Public transport is comfortable and relatively well organised.

For the most part, parents needn't worry too much about health concerns, though it pays to lay down a few ground rules – such as regular hand-washing – to head off potential problems. All the usual health precautions apply (see the Health section in the Appendix for details); children should especially be warned not to play with animals, as rabies occurs in Malaysia.

DANGERS & ANNOYANCES

Malaysia is a relatively wealthy country and theft is not a major problem compared with other countries in the region, though of course the normal precautions should still be taken. Violent crime in the country is virtually unheard of.

See the following Legal Matters section for the grim news on drugs.

Scams

When in KL beware of scammers and flim-flam artists. One of the more common scams involves getting travellers to visit private homes where they are lured into rigged card games. Travellers are often lured into these houses on the pretence of meeting the scam artist's mother (who is invariably worried about a daughter who is soon going abroad to study, surprisingly enough, in the home country of the hapless traveller).

The scam-of-the-day may have changed by the time you read this, but if you use common sense and avoid deals which seem too good to be true, you should be all right.

LEGAL MATTERS

Drugs

As for drugs, the answer is simple – don't. Under Malaysian law all drug offenders are considered equal, and all illegal drugs are the same. Drug trafficking carries a mandatory death penalty, and being a foreigner will not save you from the gallows. A number of foreigners have already been executed in Malaysia, some of them for possession of amazingly small quantities. In almost every village in Malaysia you will see anti-*dadah* (drugs) signs portraying a skull and cross-bones and a noose. Take 'dadah-ism' very seriously. No one can say they haven't been warned!

BUSINESS HOURS

Government offices are usually open Monday to Friday from around 8 am to 12.45 pm, and then again from 2 to 4.15 pm. On Friday the lunch break usually lasts from 12.15 to 2.45 pm. On Saturday morning offices are open from 8 am to 12.45 pm. These hours vary slightly from state to state; on the east coast of the peninsula most government offices are closed on Friday.

Shop hours are also somewhat variable, although from 9.30 am to 7 pm is a good rule of thumb. Major department stores, Chinese emporiums and some shops catering particularly to tourists are open until 9 or 10 pm seven days a week.

PUBLIC HOLIDAYS & SPECIAL EVENTS

Public Holidays

Although some public holidays have a fixed annual date, Hindus, Muslims and Chinese all follow a lunar calendar, which means the dates for many events vary each year.

National Holidays

New Year's Day	1 January
Chinese New Year	January/February
Hari Raya Puasa	January/February
Hari Raya Haji	April
Awal Muharam	April/May
Wesak Day	April/May
Labour Day	1 May
King's Birthday	1st Saturday in June
Birth of the Prophet	July
National Day	31 August
Deepavali	October/November
Christmas Day	25 December

Chinese New Year is the most important celebration for the Chinese community. Dragon dances and pedestrian parades mark the start of the new year. Families hold open house, unmarried relatives (especially children) receive *ang pow*, or money in red packets, businesses traditionally clear their debts and everybody wishes you a *'kong hee fatt choy'* (a happy and prosperous new year).

Hari Raya Puasa marks the end of the month-long fast of Ramadan with three days of joyful celebration. This is the major holiday of the Muslim calendar.

The festival of Deepavali celebrates Rama's victory over the demon King Rawana with the Festival of Lights, where tiny oil lamps are lit outside Hindu homes.

In addition to the national holidays listed, each state has its own public holidays to celebrate the birthdays of the sultans or other state-specific events, such as the Dayak harvest festivals in Sabah and Sarawak.

During school holidays, Hari Raya Puasa and Chinese New Year, accommodation may be difficult to obtain and transport can be fully booked.

Special Events

With so many cultures and religions there is quite an amazing number of occasions to celebrate in Malaysia. The most important and colourful are described here, and Tourism Malaysia puts out a *Calendar of Events* with specific dates and venues of various festivals and parades.

The major Muslim annual events are connected with Ramadan, the 30 days during which Muslims cannot eat or drink from sunrise to sunset.

The Chinese-centred Moon Cake Festival around September celebrates the overthrow of the Mongol warlords in ancient China with the eating of moon cakes and the lighting of colourful paper lanterns.

The Festival of the Nine Emperor Gods involves nine days of Chinese operas, processions and other events honouring the nine emperor gods.

In KL and Penang, in October or November, fire-walking ceremonies are held on the evening of the ninth day. The Dragon Boat Festival is celebrated around June with boat races in Penang.

Thaipusam is one of the most dramatic Hindu festivals, in which devotees honour Lord Subramaniam with acts of amazing masochism. Self-mutilating worshippers make the procession to the Batu Caves outside Kuala Lumpur, usually in January or February.

If you are in Sarawak from 1 to 2 June, don't miss Gawai Dayak, the festival of the Dayaks to mark the end of the rice season. War dances, cockfights and blowpipe events all take place.

ACTIVITIES
Bicycle Touring
Malaysia is one of the best places in South-East Asia for bike touring. Perhaps the most popular route is the one up the east coast of Peninsular Malaysia, with its relatively quiet roads, but some may prefer the hillier regions of the peninsula's interior or East Malaysia.

Birdwatching
Malaysia's tropical jungles and islands are home to a tremendous variety of bird species. On the peninsula, Taman Negara and Kenong Rimba national parks offer excellent birdwatching. In East Malaysia, Kinabalu, Gunung Mulu and Gunung Gading are similarly rich in bird species.

Caving
Malaysia's limestone hills are riddled with caves to lure the spelunker. Some of these are easily accessible and can be visited without

any special equipment or preparation, while others are strictly the terrain of the experienced caver. There are caves both on the peninsula and dotted around East Malaysia, including one of the world's premier caving destinations: Gunung Mulu National Park.

Jungle Trekking
Despite the intense pressures of logging, Malaysia is still home to some of the world's most impressive stands of virgin tropical jungle. Almost all of Malaysia's national parks offer excellent jungle trekking, including Taman Negara on the peninsula and Gunung Mulu in East Malaysia. There are treks to suit all ability levels, from 20-minute jaunts to 10-day expeditions.

Mountain Climbing
Mt Kinabalu is an obvious choice for those interested in mountain climbing. However, this is not the only mountain worth climbing in Malaysia. Gunung Mulu, in Sarawak's Gunung Mulu National Park, is a challenging four day climb. On the peninsula, there are several good climbs in Taman Negara National Park. There are also a few lesser peaks scattered around that make pleasant day outings.

Snorkelling & Diving
With its tropical location and wealth of islands, it's not surprising that Malaysia has some great snorkelling and diving. The main centres include the Perhentian Islands, Pulau Redang, Pulau Tioman and other parts of the Seribuat Archipelago.

COURSES
Several of Malaysia's cultural centres offer classes in traditional Malaysian handicrafts. Kota Bharu and Cherating are perhaps the best places to get a hands-on feel for batik, puppet making and kite making.

ACCOMMODATION
For the budget traveller, the best places to track down are traditional Chinese hotels, which are found in great numbers all over Malaysia. They're the mainstay of backpackers, and in Malaysia you can generally find a good room from RM12 to RM25. Chinese hotels are generally spartan but quite clean.

Couples can sometimes economise by asking for a single, since in Chinese hotel language single means one double bed and double means two beds. Don't think this is being tight – in Chinese hotels you can pack as many into one room as you wish.

The main catch with these hotels is that they can sometimes be terribly noisy. Part of the noise comes from the street, as the hotels are often on main roads, but there's also the traditional dawn chorus of coughing, hacking and spitting, which has to be experienced to be believed. It's worst in the oldest hotels where the walls don't quite reach the ceiling but are meshed in at the top for ventilation.

Malaysia also has a variety of cheap local accommodation, usually at beach centres. These may be huts on the beach or guesthouses (private homes or rented houses divided by partition walls into a number of rooms). A dorm bed will cost RM6 to RM8, and hotel-style rooms can cost anywhere from RM12 to RM40 with air-con.

Camping is also an option in national parks, thinly populated areas and on some islands. A two season tent and lightweight sleeping bag are ideal.

In Malaysia there's a 5% government tax that applies to all hotel rooms. On top of this there's a 10% service charge in the more expensive places. Cheap Malaysian hotels, however, generally quote a price inclusive of the 5% government tax.

FOOD

While travel in some parts of Asia can be as good as a crash diet, Malaysia is quite the opposite. The food is simply terrific, the variety unbeatable and the costs pleasantly low. Whether you're looking for Chinese, Malay, Indian or Indonesian food, or even a hamburger, you'll find happiness!

Chinese

You'll find the full range of Chinese cuisine in Malaysia. If you're kicking round the backwoods of Sabah or Sarawak, however, Chinese food is likely to consist of little more than rice and vegetables.

Indian

Indian food is one of the area's greatest delights. Indeed, it's easier to find good Indian food in Malaysia than in India! You can roughly divide Indian food into southern, Muslim and northern: food from southern India tends to be hotter with the emphasis on vegetarian dishes, while Muslim food tends to be more subtle in its spicing and uses more meat. The rich Mogul dishes of northern India are not so common and are generally only found in more expensive restaurants.

A favourite Indian Muslim dish which is cheap, easy to find and of excellent standard is *biryani*. Served with a chicken or mutton curry, the dish takes its name from the saffron-coloured rice it is served with.

Malay, Indonesian & Nonya

Surprisingly, Malay food is not as easily found in Malaysia as Chinese or Indian food, although many Malay dishes, like satay, are everywhere.

Nonya cooking is a local variation on Chinese and Malay food. It uses Chinese ingredients, but employs local spices like chillies and coconut cream. Nonya cooking is essentially a home skill rather than a restaurant one – there are few places where you can find Nonya food. *Laksa*, a spicy coconut-based soup, is a classic Nonya dish that has been adopted by all Malaysians.

Other Cuisine

Western fast-food addicts will find that Ronald McDonald, the Colonel from Kentucky and Albert & Walter have all made inroads into the regional eating scene.

Tropical Fruit

Once you've tried rambutans, mangosteens, jackfruit and durians, how can you ever go back to boring old apples and oranges? Refer to the Food section in the Regional Facts for the Visitor chapter at the beginning of this book for all the info on these delights.

DRINKS

Life can be thirsty in Malaysia, so you'll be relieved to hear that drinks are excellent, economical and readily available. For a start, water can be drunk straight from the tap in most larger Malaysian cities.

Fruit juices are popular and very good. With the aid of a blender and crushed ice, delicious concoctions like watermelon juice can be whipped up in seconds. Old-fashioned sugar cane crushers, which look like grandma's old washing mangle, can still be seen in operation.

Halfway between a drink and a dessert are *es kacang* and *cendol*. An *es*, or *ais* (ice), kacang is rather like an old-fashioned snocone, but the shaved ice is topped with syrups and condensed milk, and it's all piled on top of a foundation of beans and jellies. It sounds gross and looks lurid but tastes terrific! Cendol consists of coconut milk with brown sugar syrup and greenish noodle-like things topped with shaved ice.

Other oddities? Well, the milky white drink in clear plastic bins sold by street drink sellers is soybean milk, which is also sold in a yoghurty form. Soybean milk is also available in soft drink bottles. Medicinal teas are a big deal with the health-minded Chinese.

Beer drinkers will probably find Anchor beer or Tiger beer to their taste; locally brewed Carlsberg and Guinness are also popular. Alcohol is expensive and sometimes hard to find in the 'dry' east coast states.

Getting There & Away

AIR
The usual gateway to Malaysia is KL, although Penang also has international connections. Singapore is also a handy arrival point as it's just a short trip across the Causeway from Johor Bahru. Singapore also has more international connections and is therefore a better place to shop for tickets.

Penang is a major centre for cheap airline tickets. These days the better agents are usually OK, but beware of places which ask for big advance payments before they issue you the tickets.

Departure Tax
Malaysia levies airport taxes on all its flights. It's RM40 on international flights, RM20 to Singapore and Brunei. If you buy your tickets in Malaysia, the departure tax is included in the price.

Brunei
From Kuching the one way economy fare is RM309 (B$243 from Bandar Seri Begawan), from Kota Kinabalu RM103 (B$81 from BSB) and from Kuala Lumpur RM544 (B$411 from BSB). Because of the difference in exchange rates, it is around 40% cheaper to fly to Brunei from Malaysia than vice versa.

Cambodia
Flights between Kuala Lumpur and Phnom Penh are available with Malaysia Airlines and Royal Air Cambodge (RAC). RAC charges US$190/330 one way/return; with Malaysia Airlines it is US$195/322.

China
From Hong Kong, the cheapest one way flights to Kuala Lumpur cost around US$200 (RM750 from Penang to Hong Kong). Regular fares on Malaysia Airlines from Hong Kong to Kuala Lumpur are US$308/587 one way/return. Dragonair and Malaysia Airlines also have flights to Kota Kinabalu, but they are expensive.

Indonesia
There are several interesting flight options from Indonesia to Malaysia. The short hop from Medan in Sumatra to Penang costs around US$60; from Penang it's RM185. Numerous other flights go to Sumatran destinations from Kuala Lumpur, Penang and other Malaysian cities. One of the more interesting is the Penang-Banda Aceh flight with Pelangi Air. See the Sumatra Getting There & Away section in the Indonesia chapter for more details on Malaysia-Sumatra flights.

There are also weekly flights between Kuching in Sarawak and Pontianak in Kalimantan, the Indonesian part of the island of Borneo, for RM276. Similarly at the eastern end of Borneo there is a twice weekly connection between Tawau in Sabah and Tarakan in Kalimantan.

Malaysia Airlines also has direct flights between Kuala Lumpur and Ujung Pandang in Sulawesi.

For Jakarta, the cheapest connections are from Singapore from as little as US$65, though Malaysia Airlines has competitively priced flights from Johor Bahru.

Myanmar (Burma)
There are flights between Kuala Lumpur and Yangon with Malaysia Airlines (twice weekly) and Myanmar International Airways (also twice weekly).

Philippines
From Sabah you can fly from Kota Kinabalu to Manila with Malaysia Airlines (US$180). You can also fly to Manila or Cebu City from Kuala Lumpur (US$260).

Singapore
It is much cheaper to fly from Malaysia to Singapore than in the reverse direction. See the main Getting There & Away section in the Singapore chapter for details on flights to/from Singapore.

Thailand

Malaysia Airlines and Thai Airways International fly between Penang and Hat Yai, Phuket (RM195) and Bangkok. You can fly from Penang to Bangkok for about RM440, more from KL.

There are also direct flights between Chiang Mai and Kuala Lumpur.

Vietnam

Flights between Kuala Lumpur and Ho Chi Minh City are operated by Malaysia Airlines (four times weekly) and Vietnam Airlines (six times weekly).

Kuala Lumpur-Saigon one way/return is US$150/235. Kuala Lumpur-Hanoi flights cost US$170/340.

LAND
Brunei

To get from Brunei to Miri in Sarawak, take a bus to Seria (B$4), change buses to get to Kuala Belait (B$1), then take a bus to Miri (B$10.20). Immigration and customs formalities are taken care of on both sides of the Brunei/Sarawak border.

Indonesia

A daily express bus (10 hours) runs between Pontianak in Kalimantan and Kuching in Sarawak. The bus crosses at the Tebedu-Entikong border, which is a visa-free entry point into Indonesia.

Singapore

Most travellers enter or exit Singapore by the Causeway connecting Johor Bahru and Singapore Island. Frequent buses do the short run, and a number of long-distance buses operate from the regional centres in Malaysia direct to Singapore city. If the Causeway is jammed with traffic, you can walk across it in 20 minutes or so. The Malaysian rail system also terminates in Singapore.

Thailand

The main border crossings are, west to east: Padang Besar (road or rail), Bukit Kayu Hitam (road) or Keroh-Betong (road) in the west, or at Rantau Panjang-Sungai Kolok in the east.

West Coast Although there are border points at Padang Besar and Keroh, the usual crossing is via Bukit Kayu Hitam on the main north-south highway for Hat Yai. This crossing is made easy by the buses that run from Georgetown in Penang right through to Hat Yai for around RM30. Alternatively, take a bus from Alor Setar to the large border complex at Bukit Kayu Hitam, walk a few hundred metres to the Thai checkpost, then take Thai buses and taxis to Sadao or Hat Yai.

The other alternative is to cross at Padang Besar, where it is an easy walk or taxi ride across. The only reason to go this way by road is if you're heading to/from Langkawi.

The rail route into Thailand is on the Butterworth-Alor Setar-Hat Yai route, which crosses the border at Padang Besar. You can take the *International Express* from Butterworth (across the channel from Georgetown) all the way to Bangkok with connections from Singapore and Kuala Lumpur. From Malaysia, the *International Express* train leaves Padang Besar around 5.20 pm, arrives in Hat Yai at about 6 pm and in Bangkok at around 9.50 am the next day. (Check local schedules for exact times.)

From Hat Yai there are frequent train and bus connections to other parts of Thailand. In addition to the *International Express*, one train a day also goes from Alor Setar to Hat Yai.

East Coast The Thai border is at Rantau Panjang (Sungai Kolok on the Thai side), 1½ hours by share taxi (RM9) from Kota Bharu. From Rantau Panjang, walk across the border, and then it's about 1km to the station, from where trains go to Hat Yai, Surat Thani and Bangkok. The border is only open from 6 am to 6 pm.

Another border crossing at Ban Taba, 32km east of Sungai Kolok, is a shorter and quicker route to Kota Bharu, Malaysia. Eventually, this crossing is supposed to replace Sungai Kolok, but it looks like Sungai Kolok will remain open for a long time.

SEA
Indonesia

Four main services connect Malaysia and Indonesia: Penang-Medan and Melaka-Dumai connecting Peninsular Malaysia with Sumatra; Johor Bahru connecting with Sumatra; and Tawau-Tarakan connecting Sabah with Kalimantan on Borneo.

Penang to Medan The very popular crossing between Penang and Medan is handled by two companies that, between them, have daily services. The journey takes 4½ hours and costs RM110/90 in 1st/2nd class. The boats actually land in Belawan in Sumatra, and the journey to Medan is completed by bus (45 minutes, included in the price).

Melaka to Dumai Daily high-speed ferries operate between Melaka and Dumai (2½ hours, RM80) in Sumatra. From Dumai the ferries run daily at 3 pm (100,000 rp).

Johor Bahru to Sumatra Yet another possibility is to take a boat from the Bebas Cukai ferry terminal in Johor Bahru. Boats go direct to Batu Ampar (RM45) and Tanjung Pinang (RM60), both in Sumatra. See Getting There & Away in the Johor Bahru section for details.

Tarakan/Nunukan to Tawau There are also boats connecting Kalimantan with Sabah on Borneo. For boats from Nunukan to Tawau, go to Pelabuhan Tarakan. There are two speedboats daily (except Sunday) to Tawau, leaving around 1 pm (be at the immigration office by noon). Tickets can be bought at KM Sangalaki Express close to losmen Nunukan (16,000 rp or RM25 from Malaysia). There are many other agencies on the road between the city square and the docks, but they sell tickets for the slower boats. You can also take a speedboat from Tarakan via Nunukan. It leaves at 8.30 am, and you go through immigration in Nunukan. In Nunukan you can catch a speedboat to Tawau (four hours, 30,000 rp). Make sure that you have 1500 rp left for the harbour tax which is collected just before you board the boat.

There are also much slower longboats from Nunukan, leaving daily at around 9 am and arriving in Nunukan 12 hours later.

There is an Indonesian immigration office in Nunukan where you must finalise your paperwork. Note that if you got a two month tourist visa on arrival in Indonesia, you will need an exit permit from the immigration office in Jakarta. If you have a one month tourist visa before coming to Indonesia, Nunukan officials can (but not all will) stamp your passport without an exit permit from Jakarta. Some travellers report an easy exit via this route, but many get turned back because they don't have an exit stamp.

Philippines

Passenger ferries operate between Sandakan and Zamboanga in the Philippines. The trip takes 18 hours and costs from RM60.

The MV *Sampaguita* leaves Sandakan on Saturday at 1 pm, arriving in Zamboanga at 8 am the following day. It leaves the Philippines for Sandakan on Thursday at 1 pm, arriving on Friday at 8 am.

The *Lady Mary Joy* departs from Sandakan on Thursday at 3 pm, arriving Friday at 9 am; the return trip is on Tuesday at 3 pm, arriving in Sandakan on Wednesday at 9 am. The trip costs US$34 and takes 17 hours.

Singapore

The vast majority of people cross on the Causeway, either by train or by road, or at the second land entry via the bridge at Tuas, but a few ferry services exist.

Take bus No 2 from central Singapore out to Changi Village, near Changi airport, and take a bumboat ferry across to Pengerang in Malaysia (S$5).

A car and passenger ferry operates from north Changi (take a taxi from Changi Village) to Tanjung Belungkor, east of Johor Bahru. The 11km journey takes 45 minutes, and costs S$18/28 one way/return. From the Tanjung Belungkor jetty, two bus services operate to Desaru (also east of Johor Bahru), and a Kota Tinggi service is planned. For further information call (☎ 545 3600).

To Pulau Tioman, Auto Batam (☎ 271 4866) at 02-40 World Trade Centre (WTC) in Singapore is the agent for the high-speed catamaran that does the trip in four hours. Departures are at 8.30 am from the Tanah Merah ferry terminal, and the fare is S$85/160 one way/return. There are no services during the monsoon season from 31 October to 1 March.

There are also two daily departures between Johor Bahru and Tanah Merah (RM20).

Thailand

There are some unusual sea routes between Malaysia and Thailand. For example, from Kuala Perlis (the jumping-off point for Pulau Langkawi) you can take a long-tail boat for about RM5 (50B) to Satun (or Satul), just across the border in Thailand. These are legal entry and exit points, complete with immigration and customs posts. On arrival in Satun, it costs about 10B for the 3km ride from the docks to town. You can then take a bus into Hat Yai.

You can also travel by boat between Satun and Langkawi, a large Malaysian island on the Thai-Malaysian marine border. There are about six boats a day between 9 am and 5 pm, and the cost is RM18 or 180B. Though it's cheaper to go straight to Satun from Kuala Perlis, Langkawi is worth a stop if you have the time.

In the main tourist season (around Christmas) yachts also operate irregularly between Langkawi and Phuket in Thailand, taking in Thai islands on the way for around US$70 per person per day for the five day trip.

Getting Around

AIR
Malaysia Airlines is the country's main domestic operator and has an extensive network linking the major regional centres on the peninsula, Sabah and Sarawak and Pulau Langkawi. Pelangi Air is a small regional airline that has useful services to Tioman, Langkawi, Pangkor and Melaka, among other destinations. Reservations for Pelangi flights can be made through Malaysia Airlines. Also note that Malaysia Airlines will change flight reservations etc on the spot in any of its offices free of charge. The Malaysian Airfares chart details some of the main local routes and their one way economy fares.

The main reason to catch flights within Malaysia is to travel between the peninsula and East Malaysia. You can save quite a few

dollars if you are flying to Sarawak or Sabah by flying from Johor Bahru rather than Kuala Lumpur or Singapore. The regular economy fare is RM169 from Johor Bahru to Kuching, against RM262 from KL and S$199 from Singapore. To Kota Kinabalu, the respective fares are RM347, RM437 and S$403. To persuade travellers to take advantage of these lower fares, Malaysia Airlines offers a bus service (S$10) directly from its office at the Novotel Orchid Hotel in Singapore to the Johor Bahru airport.

Malaysia Airlines also has a number of special night flights and advance purchase fares. Seven day advance purchase one way/ 30 day advance purchase return tickets are available for the following flights:

from	to	one way/return (RM)
JB	Kota Kinabalu	295/624
JB	Kuching	144/305
JB	Penang	150/318
KL	Kota Kinabalu	372/689
KL	Kuching	227/425
KL	Miri	359/679
KL	Pulau Labuan	372/656

Domestic Departure Tax
Departure tax is included in the cost of domestic flight tickets.

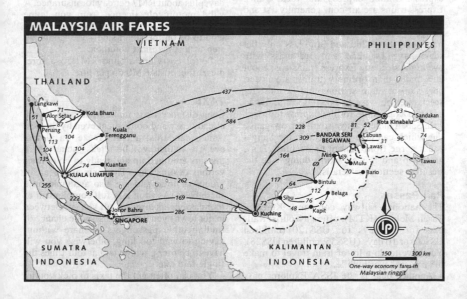

MALAYSIA AIR FARES

One-way economy fares in Malaysian ringgit

BUS

Malaysia has an excellent bus system. There are public buses on local runs and a variety of privately operated buses on the longer trips. In larger towns there may be a number of bus stops, a main station or two, plus some of the private companies may operate directly from their own offices.

Buses are fast, economical and reasonably comfortable, and seats can be reserved. Many routes use air-con buses which usually cost just a few ringgit more than regular buses. They make midday travel a sweat-free activity, but beware – as one traveller put it, 'Malaysian air-conditioned buses are really meat lockers on wheels with just two settings: cold and suspended animation'.

TRAIN

Malaysia has a modern, comfortable and economical railway service, although there are basically only two railway lines. One runs from Singapore to Butterworth and continues on into Thailand. The other branches off from this line at Gemas, south of KL, and runs through Kuala Lipis up to the north-east corner of the country near Kota Bharu (this line is sometimes referred to as the 'Jungle Train').

Classes

Malaysia has three types of rail services – express, limited express and local trains. Express trains are air-con, generally 1st and 2nd class only, and on night trains there's a choice of sleepers or seats. Limited express trains may have 2nd and 3rd class only but some have 1st, 2nd and 3rd class with overnight sleepers. Express trains cost about 20% more than ordinary trains, are faster, only stop at main stations and in most respects are the ones to take. Book as far in advance as possible for the express trains.

In Sabah there's also a small narrow-gauge line which can take you through the Sungai Padas gorge from Tenom to Beaufort. It's a great trip and is well worth doing. See the Beaufort section for details.

Rail Passes

The national railway company, Keretapi Tanah Melayu (KTM), offers a Tourist Railpass for 30 days for US$120 (children US$60) or 10 days (US$55; children US$28). You have to do a lot of train travel to make these passes worthwhile.

Another deal is the ISSA Explorer pass which is available to holders of ISSA student cards (to qualify, you must be under 30 years of age). Seven day passes cost US$36, 14 day passes cost US$48 and 21 day passes cost US$60. These are available from MSL Travel in Kuala Lumpur (☎ 442 4722) and Penang (☎ 227 2655).

CAR & MOTORCYCLE

Road Rules

Basically, driving in Malaysia follows much the same rules as in Britain or Australia – cars are right-hand drive and you drive on the left side of the road. The roads are good and most drivers in Malaysia are relatively sane, safe and slow, though a fair few specialise in overtaking on blind corners and trusting in divine intervention.

Rental

Rent-a-car operations are well established in Malaysia. Major rental operators in Malaysia include Avis, Budget, Hertz, Mayflower, National and Thrifty, although there are numerous local operators. Unlimited distance rates for a Proton Saga, the most popular car in Malaysia, start at around RM150 per day or RM900 per week, including insurance and Collision Damage Waiver. Rates drop substantially for rentals of one month or more.

Motorcycles can be hired in some of the larger tourist areas for RM20 to RM30 per day, plus about RM7 per day for insurance. A valid motorcycle licence from you home country is usually acceptable for rental. Bikes tend to be on the small side – the Honda 70 step-thru is the most common.

Petrol costs are around RM1.15 a litre; diesel fuel costs RM0.65 per litre.

TAXI

Long-distance taxis make Malaysian travel, already easy and convenient even by the best Asian standards, a real breeze. In almost every town there will be a 'teksi' stand where the cars are lined up and ready to go to their various destinations. The taxis are ideal for groups of four, and are also available on a share basis. As soon as a full complement of four passengers turns up, off you go. Between major towns you have a reasonable chance of finding other passengers to share without having to wait too long, otherwise you will have to charter a whole taxi at four times the single fare rate.

You can often get the taxis to pick you up

or drop you off at your hotel. You can also take a taxi to other destinations at charter rates. Shared taxi fares generally work out at about twice the comparable bus fares.

HITCHING

Keep in mind that hitching is never entirely safe in any country in the world, and we don't recommend it. Travellers who decide to hitch should understand that they are taking a small but potentially serious risk. People who do choose to hitch will be safer if they travel in pairs and let someone know where they are planning to go.

Malaysia has long had a reputation for being an excellent place for hitchhiking and it's generally still true. You'll get picked up by expats and by Malaysians and Singaporeans, but it's strictly an activity for foreigners – a hitchhiking Malaysian would probably just get left by the roadside! So if you're going to hitch, the first rule of thumb in Malaysia is to look foreign. Look neat and tidy too, a worldwide rule for successful hitching, but make sure your backpack is in view and you look like someone on their way around the country.

On the west coast of Malaysia, particularly on the busy Johor Bahru-Kuala Lumpur-Butterworth route, hitching is generally quite easy. On the east coast, traffic can often be quite light and there may be long waits between rides. Hitching in East Malaysia also depends on the traffic, although it's quite feasible.

BOAT

There are no services connecting the peninsula with East Malaysia. On a local level there are boats between the peninsula and offshore islands, and along the rivers of Sabah and Sarawak – see the relevant sections for full details.

LOCAL TRANSPORT

Local transport varies widely from place to place. Almost everywhere there are taxis and in most cases these are metered. In major cities there are buses – in Kuala Lumpur the government buses are backed up by private operators.

In many towns there are also bicycle rickshaws – while they are dying out in Kuala Lumpur and have become principally a tourist gimmick in many Malaysian cities, they are still a viable form of transport. Indeed in places like Georgetown, with its convoluted and narrow streets, a bicycle rickshaw is probably the best way of getting around.

Peninsular Malaysia – West Coast

The peninsula is a long finger of land stretching down from the Thai border to Singapore, the tip of which is only 137km north of the equator. It comprises 11 of the 13 states that make up Malaysia. On the western side of the peninsula, you'll find the major cities – oriental Penang, the bustling, modern capital of Kuala Lumpur, historic Melaka – and the restful hill stations.

The following description starts with the capital, Kuala Lumpur, but otherwise follows the route from Johor Bahru, just across the Causeway from Singapore, and moves up the west coast to the Thai border.

KUALA LUMPUR

Malaysia's capital city is a curious blend of the old and the new. It's a modern and fast-moving city, although the traffic never takes on the nightmare proportions of Bangkok. It has gleaming high-rise office blocks beside multilane highways, but the old colonial architecture still manages to stand out proudly.

It's also a blend of cultures – the Malay capital with a vibrant Chinatown, an Indian quarter and a playing field in the middle of the city where the crack of cricket bat on ball can still be heard.

KL, as it's almost always called, started in the 1860s when a band of prospectors in search of tin landed at the meeting point of the Sungai Kelang and Sungai Gombak and named it Kuala Lumpur (Muddy Estuary). The lure of ore quickly turned KL into a brawling, noisy boom town, successively tempered by the rule of sultans, the British and finally, UMNO.

Orientation

The real heart of KL is Merdeka Square, not far from the confluence of the two muddy rivers from which KL takes its name. Just to the south-east of this square is the banking centre of KL and the older Chinatown. Heading east is Jalan Tun Perak, a major trunk road which leads to the Puduraya bus station on the eastern edge of the central district.

To the north-east of Puduraya, around

MALAYSIA

PENINSULAR MALAYSIA

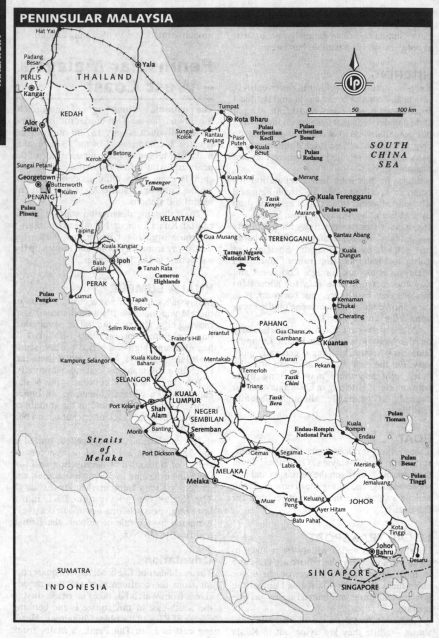

Hat Yai
Padang Besar
PERLIS
Kangar
Yala
THAILAND
KEDAH
Tumpat
Kota Bharu
Alor Setar
Sungai Kolok
Rantau Panjang
Pasir Puteh
Pulau Perhentian Kecil
Pulau Perhentian Besar
Sungai Petani
Keroh
Betong
Kuala Besut
Pulau Redang
SOUTH CHINA SEA
Georgetown
Butterworth
Kulim
Gerik
Temengor Dam
Kuala Krai
Merang
PENANG
Pulau Pinang
Kuala Terengganu
Marang
Pulau Kapas
Taiping
KELANTAN
Tasik Kenyir
TERENGGANU
Rantau Abang
Kuala Kangsar
Gua Musang
Batu Gajah
Ipoh
Tanah Rata
Cameron Highlands
Taman Negara National Park
Kuala Dungun
Kemasik
Pulau Pangkor
PERAK
Lumut
Tapah
Bidor
Kemaman
Chukai
Cherating
Selim River
Fraser's Hill
Jerantut
PAHANG
Gua Charas
Gambang
Kuantan
Kampung Selangor
Kuala Kubu Baharu
Mentakab
Maran
Pekan
SELANGOR
Temerloh
Triang
Tasik Chini
KUALA LUMPUR
Port Kelang
Shah Alam
NEGERI SEMBILAN
Tasik Bera
Pulau Tioman
Morib
Banting
Seremban
Endau-Rompin National Park
Kuala Rompin
Endau
Port Dickson
Gemas
Segamat
Pulau Besar
Straits of Melaka
MELAKA
Labis
Mersing
Pulau Tinggi
Melaka
Jemaluang
Muar
Yong Peng
Keluang
JOHOR
Batu Pahat
Ayer Hitam
Kota Tinggi
SUMATRA
Johor Bahru
Desaru
INDONESIA
SINGAPORE
SINGAPORE

0   50   100 km

Jalan Ampang and Jalan Sultan Ismail, the Golden Triangle is the modern development centre, crammed with luxury hotels, shopping centres and office towers. This is the real heart of the new, booming KL.

Running north from Merdeka Square is Jalan Tuanku Abdul Rahman (also called Jalan TAR) with a number of KL's popular cheaper hotels and more modern buildings. Jalan Raja Laut runs parallel to Jalan TAR and takes the northbound traffic.

The main post office is south of Merdeka Square, and a little further on is the Masjid Negara (National Mosque) and the KL train station. Beyond them, to the west, is KL's green belt, where you can find the Lake Gardens, the National Monument and Malaysia's Parliament House.

On the southern side of the Lake Gardens is the Muzium Negara (National Museum). KL Grand Central (Sentral) station, now under construction immediately south of the museum in the Brickfields area, is to be the city's new public transport hub.

Information

Tourist Offices The biggest and most useful of the many tourist offices is the Malaysia Tourist Information Complex (MATIC, ☎ 264 3929), 109 Jalan Ampang, north-east of the city centre. As well as a tourist information counter (open from 9 am to 6 pm daily), there's an express bus and national parks information counters. MATIC also has audiovisual shows, dance performances, and an expensive restaurant and souvenir shop.

More conveniently located is the small Tourism Malaysia office (☎ 293 6664) in the underground Plaza Putra on Merdeka Square, and the KL Visitors Centre (☎ 238 1832) on Jalan Sultan Hishamuddin near the National Art Gallery.

Tourism Malaysia also has offices at the train station, at the new KLIA airport and at its headquarters in the Putra World Trade Centre on Jalan Tun Ismail in the north-western section of KL.

Immigration The immigration office (☎ 255 5077) is at Block I, Pusat Bandar Damansara, about 1km west of the Lake Gardens. Get there on bus No 18 from Chow Kit or No 21 from the Puduraya bus station.

Money Banks can be found throughout the central area of KL. The biggest concentration is on and around Jalan Silang at the northern edge of Chinatown. In this area, banks include the Hongkong Bank and Maybank, for changing cash and travellers cheques, and for credit-card withdrawals through ATMs.

Post & Communications The huge main post office building is across the Sungai Kelang (Kelang River) from the central district. It is open Monday to Saturday from 8 am to 6 pm, and 10 am to 12.45 pm on Sunday.

For international calls the best place to head for is the Telekom office (☎ 239 6025) on Jalan Raja Chulan, open daily from 8.30 am to 9.30 pm. There's also a Home Country Direct phone at the train station. Some larger shopping complexes have self-service Internet booths.

Travel Agencies MSL Travel (☎ 442 4722), 66 Jalan Putra, is a long-running student travel agency that often has interesting deals on offer.

Merdeka Square & Train Station

At the heart of colonial KL, Merdeka Square is ringed by fine old buildings. The mock-Tudor **Royal Selangor Club** was a social centre for KL's high society in the tin-rush days of the 1890s. Across the road is the impressive **Sultan Abdul Samad building**, designed by the British architect AC Norman and built between 1894 and 1897. Formerly the Secretariat building, it is topped by a 43m clock tower. The old city hall is in a similar Moorish style, and now houses the interesting **Textile Museum** and handicrafts shop. Over the road are the former colonial administration offices, which now house the **Kuala Lumpur Memorial Library** and the **National History Museum**.

To find a building full of eastern promise, head south to KL's magnificent **train station**. Built in 1911, this delightful example of British colonial humour is a Moorish fantasy of spires, minarets, towers, cupolas and arches.

Across from this superb train station is the equally wonderful **Malayan Railway Administration building**. Next door is the **National Art Gallery**, with changing exhibits, usually modern art, from around the world. The art gallery is housed in the once-gracious colonial Majestic Hotel.

Nearby is the modernistic **Masjid Negara** (National Mosque), one of the largest in South-East Asia, but the most delightful of all KL's mosques is the **Masjid Jamek**, or

KUALA LUMPUR

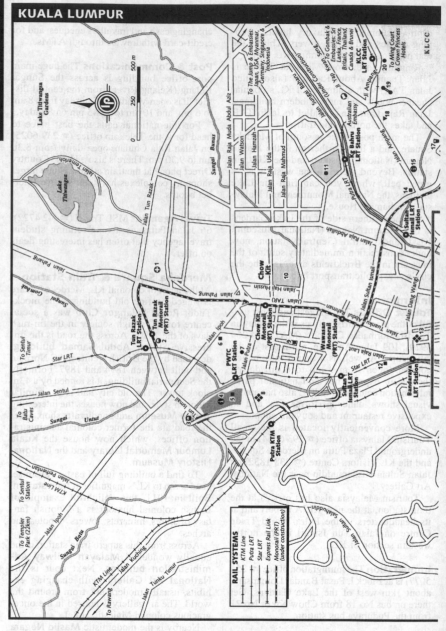

RAIL SYSTEMS

- KTM Line
- Putra LRT
- Star LRT
- Express Rail Link
- Monorail (PRT) (under construction)

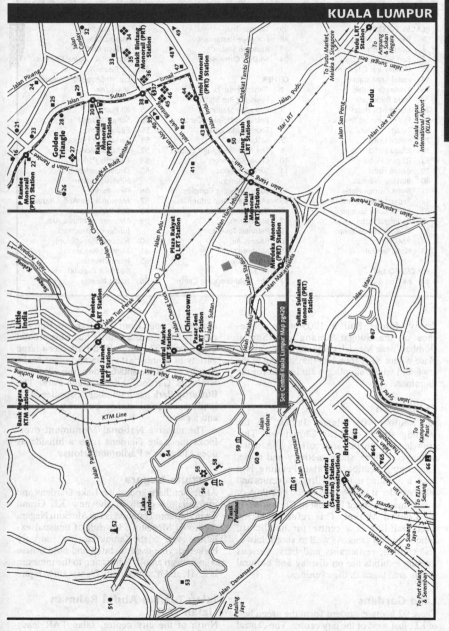

KUALA LUMPUR

KUALA LUMPUR

PLACES TO STAY		39	Tamnak Thai	28	MAS Building
5	Pan Pacific Hotel	48	Fong Lye Restaurant	31	Malibu Cafe
6	Central Hotel	49	Restoran Sakura	32	Budaya Kraf
9	Ben Soo Homestay	64	Sri Devi Curry House	34	Star Hill Shopping Complex
12	Holiday Inn City Centre			35	KL Plaza
14	Hotel Renaissance	**OTHER**		36	Lot 10 Shopping Complex
16	Concorde Hotel;	1	General Hospital	37	Maybank
	Hard Rock Cafe	2	Pekeliling Bus Station	44	Imbi Plaza
22	Shangri-La Hotel	3	Putra Bus Station	45	BB Plaza
24	Holiday Inn on the Park	4	Putra World Trade Centre;	46	Sungei Wang Plaza
25	Equatorial Hotel		Tourism Malaysia	50	Pudu Prison
29	Hilton Hotel	7	MSL Travel	51	Parliament House
30	Istana Hotel	8	The Mall Shopping Complex	52	National Monument
33	Regent Hotel	10	Chow Kit Market	54	Butterfly Park
38	Agora Hotel	11	Sunday Market	55	Orchid Garden;
40	Bintang Warisan		(Pasar Minggu)		Hibiscus Garden
41	Swiss Garden Hotel	13	Sogo Shopping Complex	56	Deer Park
42	Federal Hotel	15	Malaysia Tourist Information	57	Memorial Tun Abdul Razak
43	Melia Kuala Lumpur		Complex (MATIC)	58	Bird Park
47	Parkroyal Hotel	17	Brannigan's	59	Museum of Islamic Arts
53	Carcosa Seri Negara	19	Petronas Towers		(under construction)
62	YMCA	20	Pelangi Air	60	National Planetarium
63	Hotel Sentral	21	Modesto's	61	Muzium Negara
		23	Life Centre	65	International
PLACES TO EAT		26	KL Tower		Buddhist Pagoda
18	Le Coq d'Or	27	The Weld Shopping Centre	66	Istana Negara

Friday Mosque. Built in 1909 at the confluence of the Sungai Kelang and Sungai Gombak near Merdeka Square, this was the place where KL's founders first set foot in the town and where supplies were landed for the tin mines.

Chinatown

Just south of the Masjid Jamek are the teeming streets of KL's Chinatown. This crowded, colourful area offers the usual melange of signs, shops, activity and noise. The central section of Jalan Petaling is a busy, interesting market selling souvenirs and other goods, at its liveliest in the evening.

The main point of interest in Chinatown is the **Central Market**. This refurbished Art Deco building is a centre for handicraft, antique and art sales. As well as shops, hawkers' centres, restaurants and bars, various rotating exhibits are on display and cultural shows are staged in the evenings.

Lake Gardens

These 92 hectare gardens form the green belt of KL, just west of the city centre. The central focus of the gardens is the lake of Tasik Perdana, where boats can be rented on weekends. The gardens contain a host of other attractions, open from 9 am to 6 pm. Entry to most is RM5, and a shuttle bus runs around the gardens. The large **Bird Park** has a large variety of South-East Asian and other birds. Nearby is the **Orchid Garden**, the adjoining **Hibiscus Garden** and the **Deer Park**. The **Butterfly Park** has a number of species in its landscaped enclosure, a butterfly museum and a cafe.

The massive **National Monument** overlooks the Lake Gardens from a hillside as does Malaysia's **Parliament House**.

Muzium Negara

At the southern end of the Lake Gardens and immediately north of the new KL Grand Central (Sentral) station is the Muzium Negara (National Museum). It's full of unusual exhibits, such as the 'amok catcher', an ugly barbed device used to catch and hold a man who has run amok. Admission to the museum is RM1, and it's open daily from 9 am to 6 pm.

Jalan Tuanku Abdul Rahman (Jalan TAR)

North of the city centre, Jalan TAR leads through an old section of the city, passing **Masjid Little India**. Detour along Jalan Masjid India, which is crammed with Indian shops and restaurants. Centred on the mosque, Little India has all the feel of a Middle-Eastern bazaar.

The **Chow Kit Market** is a Malay market, with a gaggle of roadside vendors lining Jalan TAR. On Saturday nights, Jalan TAR is closed to traffic and hosts the liveliest **night market** in the city.

Golden Triangle

The Golden Triangle is the showpiece of Malaysia's economic boom. Crammed with new high-rises, including (for the time being, and depending how you count) the world's tallest buildings, the twin **Petronas Towers**, and the 421m **KL Tower**, it is the place to shop, or dine and drink until the wee hours of the morning. Jalan Sultan Ismail is the main drag, with most of the luxury hotels, shopping malls and nightspots spaced out along its length. The large **Budaya Kraf** handicrafts complex is on Jalan Conlay, just off Jalan Raja Chulan.

At the northern edge of the Golden Triangle, **Jalan Ampang** was built up by the early tin millionaires and is lined with impressive mansions.

Places to Stay – budget

Guesthouses KL has quite a number of guesthouses catering almost exclusively to backpackers. They are quite basic, but provide good value in expensive KL. They all offer similar services: dorm beds as well as rooms, cooking and washing facilities, a fridge and noticeboard.

A new backpackers' favourite is the *Travellers Station* (☎ 273 5588), right at KL's old train station. It's convenient and has good facilities, but with air-con dorms for RM15 and simple air-con doubles for RM45, it's not as cheap as other budget places.

Chinatown is the main budget area. Only a few minutes walk from the Puduraya bus station is the cheap and popular *Travellers' Moon Lodge* (☎ 230 6601) at 36C Jalan Silang. Hot, little plywood-walled singles/doubles cost RM20/25, or the hallway dorm on the top floor is at least cooler and costs RM8. Just a few doors along, the *Travellers Home* (☎ 230 6601), 46C Jalan Silang, is smaller and quieter with larger, nicer rooms for the same price.

Also in Chinatown, at 60 Jalan Sultan, is the popular *Backpackers Travellers Inn* (☎ 238 2473). It has typically small and windowless rooms for RM22/25, up to RM40/50

with air-con. Dorm beds cost RM8, or RM10 with air-con.

The more spacious *Backpackers Travellers Lodge* (☎ 201 0889), 158 Jalan Tun HS Lee, is one of the better guesthouses. Dorm beds cost RM8. Clean rooms start at RM25 with fan, and range up to RM50 with air-con and bathroom.

Smack in the middle of Chinatown at 103 Jalan Petaling, the *CT Guest House* (☎ 232 0417) is scruffy but quite acceptable. Beds in small dorms cost RM10, while rooms are RM17/25.

The *KL City Lodge* (☎ 230 5275), 16 Jalan Pudu, is more a regular, scruffy hotel right opposite the bus station. Air-con dorms cost RM12, while rooms are RM20/30 or RM25/35 with air-con. Nearby, the *Kawana Tourist Inn* (☎ 238 6714), 68 Jalan Pudu Lama, is well kept but lacks atmosphere. A bed in the tiny dorm costs RM12, or good doubles cost from RM35 to RM60.

North of the city centre, just off Jalan Raja Laut, is the very friendly, clean *Ben Soo Homestay* (☎ 291 8096) at 61B Jalan Tiong Nam (opposite the Hotel Wilayah). Airy rooms with fan are RM25/30, with a light breakfast. For a minimal fee, the owner will provide a pick-up from bus or train stations.

Another friendly place is the *TI Lodge* (☎ 293 0261), in the heart of Little India at 20 Lorong Bunus Enam. Good rooms cost RM39 with fan, RM46 with air-con, and RM55 with air-con and bath. Breakfast is included.

Less than 10 minutes walk east of KL train station, the fully air-conditioned *KL International Youth Hostel* (☎ 273 6870) is at 21 Jalan Kampung Attap. Dorm beds cost RM15.

Finally, there are the Ys. Close to KL's new Grand Central station at 95 Jalan Padang Belia is the **YMCA** (☎ 274 1439), with good but simple singles/doubles for RM38/50 and triples/quads for RM65/75.

The **YWCA** (☎ 230 1623) is more central at 12 Jalan Hang Jebat. It has plain but acceptable singles/doubles for women at RM30/50, and for couples from RM50.

Hotels In Chinatown, cheapest of the Chinese cheapies is the well camouflaged *Wan Kow Hotel* (☎ 238 2909) at 16 Jalan Sultan. Very basic rooms with fan and common bath cost RM27. Also very cheap is the *Colonial Hotel* (☎ 238 0336), 39 Jalan Sultan, where rooms go for RM23/30 singles/doubles, or RM37 with air-con. This hotel is more geared

MALAYSIA

CENTRAL KUALA LUMPUR

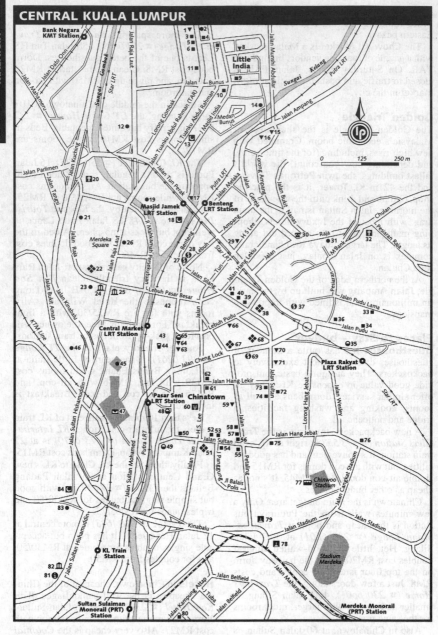

Bank Negara
KMT Station

1 ▼
2 ●
3 ■
4 ■
5 ■
6 ■

▼ 8

Little
India

11 ■

9 ■

Jalan Dato Onn

Jalan Raja Laut

Jalan Munshi Abdullah

Sungai Kelang

Jalan
Bunus

10 ■

Jalan Mahameru

Jalan Parlimen

Sungai Gombak

Star LRT

Lorong Gombak

Jalan Tuanku Abdul Rahman (TAR)

Jalan Tuanku Abdul Rahman

Jalan Tun Perak

Masjid India

Putra LRT

14 ●

Medan
Bunus

▼ 15
▼ 16

Jalan Ampang

0   125   250 m

12 ●

20

Jalan Kuching

Jalan Tangsi

19 ●
Masjid Jamek
LRT Station

17 ▲

18 ●

Benteng
LRT Station

Jalan Melaka

Lorong Ampang

Lorong Bukit Nanas

Jalan Gereja

Putra LRT

21 ●

Merdeka Square

26 ■

Jalan Raja

Jalan Raja Laut

Jalan Mahkamah Persekutuan

Benteng

Lebuh Pasar

Star LRT

28 ●
27 ●

Jalan Tun

Jalan Silang

29 ▼

Ampang

H S Lee

30 ●

Jalan Hang Lekiu

Raja

31 ■

LM Bank

Chulan

Pesiaran Raja

32

Jalan Bukit Aman

Jalan Kinabalu

22 ●

23 ● 24 ● 25 ●

Lebuh Pasar Besar

42

41 ■
40 ■ 39 ■

38 ■

Jalan Pudu Lama

37 ●

33 ■

36 ■

Jalan Pudu

34 ■

KTM Line

Central Market
LRT Station

43

46 ●

45 ◆

65 ▼
64 ▼
63 ▼
44 ▼

Lebuh Pudu

66 ▼

67 ■
68 ■

69 ●

70 ▼
71 ▼

35 ●

Plaza Rakyat
LRT Station

Jalan Cheng Lock

Jalan Sultan Hishamuddin

Jalan Sultan Mohamed

Putra LRT

47 ●

Pasar Seni
LRT Station

48 ●

Chinatown

60 ●
59 ▼

62 ●
61 ■

Jalan Hang Lekir

73 ▼
74 ▼

72 ■

Jalan Sultan

Lorong Hang Jebat

Jalan Wesley

Star LRT

50 ■

49 ●

51 ■

H S Lee

52 ■ 53 ■
54 ■

Jalan Sultan

58 ■
57 ■
56 ■
55 ■

Panggung

Petaling

Jl Balais
Polis

Jalan Hang Jebat

75 ■

76 ■

77 ●
Chinwoo
Stadium

Jalan Cangkat Stadium

84 ●

83 ●

Jalan

Kinabalu

79 ■

78 ■

Jalan Stadium

Jalan Stadium

Stadium
Merdeka

KL Train
Station

82 ●
81 ●

Jalan Sultan Hishamuddin

Jalan Belfield

Jalan Maharajalela

Sultan Sulaiman
Monorail (PRT)
Station

80 ■

Jalan Kampung Attap

Jalan Tuba

Jalan Belfield

Merdeka Monorail
(PRT) Station

CENTRAL KUALA LUMPUR

PLACES TO STAY	PLACES TO EAT		
3 Kowloon Hotel	1 Restoran Insaf	28	Hongkong Bank
4 Noble Hotel	8 Govinda's Vegetarian	30	Telekom
5 Tivoli Hotel	Restaurant	31	KL Stock Exchange
6 Rex Hotel	15 Kapitan's Club	32	St Andrew's Church
7 TI Lodge	16 Bilal	35	Puduraya Bus Station
9 Hotel Champagne	17 McDonald's	37	Mayhank; Numismatic
10 Hotel Chamtan	29 Baba's Curry House		Museum
11 Coliseum Hotel	59 Food Centre	38	Metrojaya Department Store
33 Kawana Tourist Inn	63 Restoran Yusoof	42	Central Market Annexe
34 Hotel Katari	64 McDonald's	43	Central Market
36 KL City Lodge	66 Restoran Wilayah Baru	44	Bull's Head; Riverbank
39 Twin Happiness Inn	70 Meidi-ya	45	Dayabumi Complex
40 Travellers' Home	71 KFC	46	British Council
41 Travellers' Moon Lodge		47	Main Post Office
50 Starlight Hotel	OTHER	48	Jalan Sultan Mohammed
52 Mandarin Hotel	2 Globe Silk Store		Bus Stand
53 Wan Kow Hotel	12 City Hall	49	Kelang Bus Station
54 Hotel City Inn	13 Masjid Little India	51	UDA Ocean Plaza
55 Hotel Lok Ann	14 Little India Night Market	60	Sri Mahamariamman Temple
56 Lee Mun Travellers Inn	18 Masjid Jamek	65	Bus Stand
57 CT Guest House	19 High Court	67	S&M Shopping Complex
58 Excel Inn	20 St Mary's Cathedral	68	Kota Raya Shopping
61 Hotel Malaya	21 Royal Selangor Club		Complex
62 Backpackers Travellers Lodge	22 Plaza Putra; Tourism Malaysia	69	Standard Chartered Bank
72 Hotel Furama	23 KL Memorial Library	77	Swimming Pool
73 Swiss Inn	24 National History Museum	78	Chan See Shu Yuen Temple
74 Backpackers Travellers Inn	25 Textile Museum	79	Khoon Yam Temple
75 Colonial Hotel	(Old City Hall)	81	KL Visitors Centre
76 YWCA	26 Sultan Abdul Samad Building	82	National Art Gallery
80 KL International Youth Hostel	27 Citibank	83	Islamic Centre
		84	Masjid Negara

towards travellers, but the noisy, wire-topped rooms are very run-down.

North of the city on Jalan TAR, the *Coliseum Hotel* (☎ 292 6270) at No 100 is famous for its old planters' restaurant and bar downstairs. The large and quiet rooms are good value at RM25/28 with fan, RM35/40 with air-con. Consequently it is often full. The *Rex Hotel* (☎ 298 3895), nearby at No 132, is a good Chinese cheapie with basic rooms for RM30.

Jalan TAR also has a couple of other basic, cheap hotels. The *Central Hotel* (☎ 442 2981), 510 Jalan TAR (enter from Jalan Ipoh), has simple doubles with fan for RM25; air-con doubles with bath are just RM36.

Places to Stay – Mid-Range

Chinatown has plenty of mid-range hotels. On Jalan Sultan near Jalan Tun HS Lee, the quiet *Hotel City Inn* (☎ 238 9190) has comfortable but small rooms for RM69/81 singles/doubles. Just a few doors along, the *Hotel Lok Ann* (☎ 238 9544), 113A Jalan Petaling, has large rooms for RM70.

More luxurious options in Chinatown include the *Hotel Malaya* (☎ 232 7722) on Jalan Hang Lekir and the *Hotel Furama* (☎ 230 1777) on Jalan Sultan. Both have comfortable rooms from around RM140.

The *Swiss Inn* (☎ 232 3333), 62 Jalan Sultan, is a very popular, newer hotel. Spotless rooms cost RM130 to RM160, and the hotel has a good coffee shop popular for its cheap buffet breakfasts.

On Jalan TAR, the *Kowloon Hotel* (☎ 293 4246) at No 142 is another of the older breed of modern hotels. Rooms from RM80/95 are large and well appointed.

Lively Jalan Bukit Bintang, east of the city centre at the edge of the Golden Triangle, has a good selection of mid-range hotels. The *Bintang Warisan* (☎ 248 8111) at No 68 is a larger hotel and a definite grade above the others. Rooms start at RM130/150, plus 15%.

Down in Brickfields, opposite the new KL Grand Central station at 128 Jalan Tun Sambanthan, is the *Hotel Sentral* (☎ 272 3748), where air-con rooms with modern conveniences cost from RM55/78.

Places to Eat

Hawker Food KL is well endowed with hawker venues dotted all around the city. In Chinatown, street food can be found everywhere, but *Jalan Petaling* and *Jalan Hang Lekir* are good places to start looking. The *Central Market* also has hawkers' food upstairs.

The *Saturday night market* on Jalan Tuanku Abdul Rahman has a large collection of food vendors and a great atmosphere, though it's mostly takeaway. *Chow Kit Market*, just off Jalan Tuanku Abdul Rahman close to the Asia Hotel, is great for Malay food.

Jalan Alor, one street west of Jalan Bukit Bintang in the Golden Triangle, has open-air tables in the evening serving some of the best Chinese hawkers' fare in KL. Most shopping malls have more expensive, air-con food courts – one of the best is in *The Mall* shopping centre on Jalan Putra.

Indian Food Little India is a good hunting ground for Indian food. *Govinda's Vegetarian Restaurant*, upstairs on Jalan Bonus 3, has a cheap vegetarian buffet. *Bangles*, upstairs at 60A Jalan Tuanku Abdul Rahman, is a nearby Indian restaurant with a very good reputation.

In Chinatown's Central Market, *Hameed's* is a thriving, cafeteria-style restaurant with Indian noodles and curries. Facing the market, *Restoran Yusoof* is popular for *roti*, biryani etc.

In Brickfields, a popular south Indian restaurant is the *Sri Devi Curry House* at 144 Jalan Tun Sambanthan opposite the new KL Grand Central station.

Chinese Food Chinese restaurants can be found everywhere, but particularly around Chinatown (surprise) and along Jalan Bukit Bintang.

In the Sungei Wang Plaza on Jalan Sultan Ismail near Jalan Bukit Bintang is the *Super Noodle House*, which is cheap and popular. For superior Cantonese fare try the *Mayblossom* at No 1/F inside the plaza.

Along Jalan Imbi are the more upmarket *Fong Lye Restaurant* at No 94 and the *Restoran Sakura* at No 163.

Malay Food There are Malay *warung* (small eating stalls) and *kedai kopi* (coffee shops) throughout KL, but especially along and just off Jalan Tuanku Abdul Rahman;

look for the *nasi lemak* in the early mornings. The two *Insaf* restaurants on Jalan TAR near the Coliseum Hotel are excellent and cheap.

The stylish *Kapitan's Club*, 35 Jalan Ampang, has a mixed menu that includes Peranakan food along with Chinese and western dishes. Curry *kapitan* is a speciality, as are the savoury Peranakan pastries. Expect to pay RM20 or less per person.

Other Cuisines KL has a surprising variety of western restaurants, and fast-food chains are found everywhere. Not to be missed is the restaurant in the *Coliseum Hotel* on Jalan TAR, which serves excellent steaks at around RM20. The place is quite a colonial experience and has hardly changed over the years.

At 121 Jalan Ampang, *Le Coq d'Or* is another colonial experience in a fine early-20th century mansion. It's not quite as expensive as the elegant surroundings might indicate. The set lunch is excellent value for RM13 plus 15%.

KL also has some good, mid-range Thai restaurants. The *Thai Kitchen* in the Central Market on Jalan Hang Kasturi, and the classier *Tamnak Thai*, 74 Jalan Bukit Bintang, are both recommended and moderately priced.

Entertainment

Bars, Discos & Live Music KL's burgeoning nightlife is mostly found in the Golden Triangle on Jalan Sultan Ismail. The *Hard Rock Cafe* in the Concorde Hotel is still the hottest spot in town, with the usual food-and-rock memorabilia blend. A short stroll behind the Hard Rock Cafe is *Brannigan's*, and nearby on the corner of Jalan Perak and Jalan P Ramlee, is the trendier *Modesto's*.

The *Malibu Cafe* on Jalan Sultan Ismail near the Istana Hotel is open 24 hours and packs in the crowds. Bands play most nights.

Popular discos in the Golden Triangle include *The Jump* in the Wisma Inai on Jalan Tun Razak and *Energy* in the Menara Pan Global on Lorong P Ramlee. Foreign bands often play at *The Venue*, right next door to Energy.

The Central Market is quieter but cheaper. Facing the river on the western side of the market, the *Riverbank* has the occasional jazz band or guitar strummer. A few doors away, the *Bull's Head* is an English-style pub with Eagles on the jukebox and Anchor on tap.

Cultural Shows The *Malaysian Tourist Information Complex* (☎ 264 3929) on Jalan Ampang has traditional dance performances at 3.30 pm on Tuesday, Thursday, Saturday and Sunday. The *Central Market* (☎ 274 6542) has a regular program of events – pick up its monthly calendar from tourist offices.

Shopping

For handicrafts, check out the Central Market complex in Chinatown. Jalan Petaling in the heart of Chinatown is a colourful shopping street and has some craftwork, cheap clothes and copy watches. Bargain hard.

The large Budaya Kraf handicrafts complex, on Jalan Conlay just off Jalan Raja Chulan, displays local craftwork. Jalan Tuanku Abdul Rahman is also worth a browse, especially around the Chow Kit Market.

KL's biggest and most popular shopping malls are in the Golden Triangle on Jalan Sultan Ismail and Jalan Bukit Bintang.

Getting There & Away

Air KL is well served by many international airlines and there are flights to and from Australia, Europe and all regional capitals. All scheduled domestic and international flights operate out of the huge new KL international airport (KLIA), 43km south of the city centre at Sepang.

In the domestic network, KL is the hub of Malaysia Airlines services, and there are flights to most major towns and cities on the peninsula and in East Malaysia. Malaysia Airlines (☎ 261 0555/746 3000 for 24-hour reservations) is in the Malaysia Airlines building, Jalan Sultan Ismail.

Bus Most buses operate from the hot and clamorous Puduraya bus station on Jalan Pudu, just east of Chinatown. There are departures to most places throughout the day, and at night to main towns. Check at the tourist police office or the information counter at the main entrance before you do the rounds of the ticket offices inside. Typical fares from KL are RM23 to Singapore, RM16.50 to Johor Bahru, RM8 to Melaka, RM12.50 to Lumut, RM11 to the Cameron Highlands, RM21 to Penang and RM15 to Kuantan. The bus station has a left-luggage office.

Buses to Kelang and Port Kelang (No 793) and Shah Alam (Nos 337 and 338) leave from the Kelang bus station at the end of Jalan Hang Kasturi in Chinatown.

Buses to Kuala Lipis (four hours, RM8) and Jerantut (for Taman Negara, 3½ hours, RM9) operate from the Pekeliling bus station in the north of the city on Jalan Tun Razak.

Though Puduraya has buses to the east coast, the Putra bus station (☎ 442 9530), opposite the World Trade Centre, handles more express coach services to Kuantan, Kuala Terengganu and Kota Bharu.

Train KL is also the hub of the railway system. From the historic old KL train station there are daily departures (express trains are marked *) for Butterworth (*7.35 am and *2.25, 10.05 and 10.15 pm) and Singapore (*7.40 am and *2.50, 9.05 and 10.30 pm). For the east-coast line to Jerantut (for Taman Negara) and Kota Bharu, you first have to take a southbound train to Gemas and then catch another connection – forget it and take a bus.

Taxi Taxis depart from upstairs in the Puduraya bus station. Per person fares include: Melaka RM17, Johor Bahru RM35, Singapore RM40, Ipoh RM25, Lumut RM35, Cameron Highlands RM35, Penang RM60, Genting Highlands RM10, Fraser's Hill RM20, Jerantut RM18, Kuala Lipis RM15, Kuantan RM35, Kuala Terengganu RM40 and Kota Bharu RM45.

Getting Around

To/From the Airport The new KL international airport (KLIA) situated at Sepang is connected to KL by express train to KL Grand Central (Sentral) station. Taxis from KLIA operate on a fixed-fare system – purchase a coupon at the arrival hall. Going to the airport, count on paying around RM45.

Bus KL's bus system is still chaotic, but is improving as private lines and pink minibuses are merged into two main companies, Intrakota and Cityliner, which run modern air-con buses. Within the city area the maximum fare is 90 sen or RM1; try to have correct change ready when you board, especially during rush hours.

City Train The KTM Komuter service runs via the existing long-distance railway lines, stopping at city and suburban stations, including the old KL train station and the new KL Grand Central (Sentral) station at Brickfields. It is useful for getting to Port Kelang (via Shah Alam and Kelang) or Seremban, 66km south of KL.

Light Rail & Monorail KL's fast, frequent Light Rail Transit (LRT) system has two lines (Star and Putra) which intersect at the Masjid Jamek LRT station. The LRT runs to the KL Grand Central (Sentral) station. A new monorail system, the People-Mover Rapid Transit (PRT) to be completed in late 1999, will further enhance KL's public transport system.

Car All the major car-rental companies have offices at the airport and in the city, eg Avis (☎ 241 7144), Budget (☎ 262 4119), Hertz (☎ 248 6433) and National (☎ 248 0522).

Taxi KL has plenty of taxis, and metered fares are RM2 for the first 1km, then 10 sen for each additional 200m. Because of traffic snarls, drivers may be unwilling to use meters and you'll have to bargain. Count on RM5 for a short ride – RM7 should get you halfway across town. At the train station, buy a taxi coupon from outside platform 4 (the river side of the station).

AROUND KUALA LUMPUR
Batu Caves
The huge Batu Caves are the best known attraction in the vicinity of KL. Just 13km north of the capital and a short distance off the Ipoh road, the caves are in a towering limestone formation and were little known until about 100 years ago. Later, a small Hindu shrine was built in the major cave and it became a pilgrimage centre during the Thaipusam festival. Each year in January or February, tens of thousands of pilgrims flock to the caves to engage in or watch the spectacularly masochistic feats of Thaipusam devotees.

The major cave, a vast open space known as the Temple Cave, is reached by a straight flight of 272 steps. Beyond the stairs is the main temple. There are a number of other caves in the same formation, including a small museum cave, with figures of the various Hindu gods.

To reach the caves take Intrakota bus No 11D from the Central Market annexe or Cityliner bus No 69 from Jalan Pudu in Chinatown. During the Thaipusam Festival, special trains run to the caves from KL station.

National Zoo & Aquarium
East of KL, on the road to Ulu Kelang and about 13km along, is the 62 hectare site of the National Zoo & Aquarium. The zoo is laid out around a central lake and the zoo collection emphasises Malaysian wildlife. It is open daily from 9 am to 5 pm; admission is RM6. Take bus No 20 from Central Market, No 170 from Jalan Ampang or No 17 from Jalan Raja Laut in Chow Kit.

Jungle Park
The Forestry Research Institute of Malaysia (FRIM) has a jungle park at Sungei Buloh, 15km north-west of the city centre, with a museum and arboretum explaining the rainforest habitat and flora. A popular picnic spot, it also has jungle trails, from short strolls to a more strenuous walk up to the waterfall. The park is open from 8 am to 6 pm. Take a Rawang-bound KTM Komuter train to Sungei Buloh station, on the park's northern edge.

Orang Asli Museum
About 19km from KL, on the Genting Highlands road, the Orang Asli Museum is very informative and gives some good insights into the life and culture of Peninsular Malaysia's 70,000 indigenous inhabitants. It's well worth a look.

Templer Park
Beside the Ipoh road, 22km north of KL, Templer Park was established during the colonial period by the British High Commissioner Sir Gerald Templer. The 1200 hectare park is intended to be a tract of jungle, preserved within easy reach of the city. There are a number of marked jungle paths, swimming lagoons and several waterfalls within the park boundaries. To get there, take bus No 66 from the Puduraya bus station.

JOHOR BAHRU
The state of Johor comprises the entire southern tip of the peninsula. Its capital is Johor Bahru (known simply as JB), the southern gateway to Peninsular Malaysia, connected to Singapore by the 1038m-long Causeway.

Johor's entry into the history books goes right back to the early 16th century, when Melaka fell to the Portuguese and the sultans fled, later re-establishing their capital in this area.

Few people stop for long in JB, as both Singapore and Melaka offer better prospects. However, it's worth exploring the **Istana Besar**, the former palace of the Johor royal family and now an impressive museum.

Information

There is an Internet cafe called the Causeway Restaurant on the 4th floor of the JOTIC building.

Places to Stay

About the only budget place is the very basic *Footloose Homestay* (☎ 224 2881), 4H Jalan Ismail, about 20 minutes walk from the Causeway, just off Jalan Gertak Merah. There's one double room for RM28, or a six bed dorm for RM14 per person.

JB's cheaper hotels are mostly clustered in the Jalan Meldrum neighbourhood, just east of the train station. The best in terms of price and comfort is the *Hawaii Hotel* (☎ 224 0633), 21 Jalan Meldrum, where rooms with fan and bath are RM40.

Also good value is the *Top Hotel* (☎ 224 4755) at 12 Jalan Meldrum. All rooms have air-con and attached bath, and cost RM66.

For those willing to spend a little more, the *Causeway Inn* (☎ 224 8811), 6A Jalan Meldrum, is good value for clean, well appointed rooms with air-con, TV and attached bath. Singles/doubles cost RM82/92.

Places to Eat

The *night market*, outside the Hindu temple on Jalan Wong Ah Fook, has a great selection of Chinese, Malay and Indian dishes. The *Restoran Medina*, on the corner of Jalan Meldrum and Jalan Siew Niam, serves excellent *murtabak*, biryani and curries. Inside any of the *large shopping malls* you'll find decent air-con food courts.

Getting There & Away

Air Johor Bahru is well served by Malaysia Airlines (☎ 334 1001) and, as an incentive to fly from JB rather than Singapore, fares to other places in Malaysia are much cheaper than from Singapore.

Pelangi Air (reservations made through Malaysia Airlines) also has direct flights to Padang (RM260) and Palembang (RM280) in Sumatra.

Malaysia Airlines has a coach service (RM4) from the Puteri Pan Pacific Hotel for the 32km trip to the airport.

Bus & Taxi JB has more connections to other towns in Peninsular Malaysia than Singapore. JB's new Larkin bus station is 5km north of town. The bus from Singapore runs there; taxis want an inflated RM6.

Regular buses go from JB to Mersing (RM7), Melaka (RM10), Kuantan (RM15.40), KL (RM16.60) and Butterworth (RM33.60). Melaka buses come through from Singapore, so it pays to book. Long-distance taxis leave from the Larkin bus station.

To Singapore, air-con buses operate roughly every 15 minutes until midnight and cost RM2.10. The regular SBS bus No 170 costs RM1.20. Catch them at the bus station or the Causeway.

Train Daily trains from JB go to KL and Butterworth for west-coast destinations, and there is a 9.38 pm direct east-coast train for Taman Negara and Kota Bharu. Through trains also go to Singapore, although a bus or taxi is easier.

Boat Ferries leave from the Bebas Cukai duty-free shopping complex about 2km east of the Causeway. Sriwani Tours & Travel (☎ 221 1677), in the complex itself, handles tickets to most destinations.

Walking It is possible to walk across the Causeway in both directions. The journey takes about 25 minutes.

MELAKA

Melaka (Malacca), Malaysia's most historically interesting city, has been the site of some dramatic events over the years. The complete series of European incursions into Malaysia – Portuguese, Dutch and English – occurred here. Yet this was an important trading port long before the first Portuguese adventurers set foot in the city.

In 1405 Admiral Cheng Ho, the 'three-jewelled eunuch prince', arrived in Melaka bearing gifts from the Ming emperor, the promise of protection from arch enemies (the Siamese) and, surprisingly, the Muslim religion. Despite internal squabbles and intrigues, Melaka grew to be a powerful trading state and successfully repulsed Siamese attacks.

In 1511 Alfonso d'Albuquerque took the city for the Portuguese and the fortress of A'Famosa was constructed. In 1641 the city passed into Dutch hands after a siege lasting eight months.

In 1795 the French occupied Holland so the British, allies of the Dutch, temporarily took over administration of the Dutch colonies. In 1824 Melaka was ceded to the British in exchange for the Sumatran port of Bencoolen (Bengkulu today).

MELAKA CITY

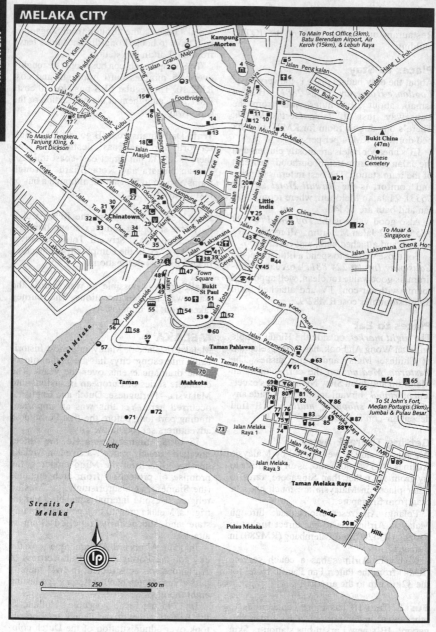

To Main Post Office (3km),
Batu Berendam Airport, Air
Keroh (15km), & Lebuh Raya

Kampung
Morten

Jalan Pengkalan

Jalan Bukit China

Jalan Puteri Hang Li Poh

Bukit China
(47m)

Chinese
Cemetery

Footbridge

Jalan Munshi Abdullah

Little
India

To Muar &
Singapore

Jalan Laksamana Cheng Ho

Chinatown

Town
Square

Bukit
St Paul

Jalan Chan Koon Cheng

Sungai Melaka

Taman Pahlawan

Jalan Parameswara

Jalan Taman Merdeka

Taman

Mahkota

To St John's Fort,
Medan Portugis (3km),
Jumbai & Pulau Besar

Jalan Taman Melaka Raya (Jalan TMR)

Jetty

Jalan Melaka
Raya 1

Jalan Melaka
Raya 4

Jalan Melaka
Raya 3

Taman Melaka Raya

Straits of
Melaka

Bandar

Hilir

Pulau Melaka

0   250   500 m

PLACES TO STAY		PLACES TO EAT		34	Baba-Nyonya Heritage
5	Hotel Grand Continental	24	Sri Lakshmi Vilas		Museum
7	Majestic Hotel	25	Sri Krishna Bavan	37	Tourist Office
8	City Bayview Hotel	30	Old China Cafe	38	Christ Church
9	Hotel Accordian	33	Restoran Peranakan	39	Post Office
10	Renaissance Hotel	35	Jonkers Melaka	40	Karyaneka Handicrafts
11	Ng Fook		Restoran		Emporium; Dulukala
12	Hong Kong Hotel	41	Restaurant Kim	42	Church of St Francis
13	Regal		Swee Huat	46	Telekom
14	May Chiang Hotel	43	Restoran Veni	47	Stadthuys
16	Visma Hotel	45	UE Tea House	48	Tourist Police
17	Malacca Town Holiday	59	Glutton's Corner	49	Hongkong Bank
	Lodge 2	61	Malay Food Stalls	50	St Paul's Church
19	Gold Leaf Hotel	68	Mei Chong	51	Muzium Budaya
20	Valiant Hotel	75	Ole Rasa		(Cultural Museum)
21	Palace Hotel	77	Peppermint Cafe	52	Proclamation of
23	Eastern Heritage	80	Restoran Lim		Independence Hall
	Guest House		(Mee Yoke)	53	Porta de Santiago
26	Chong Hoe Hotel	82	Tandoori House	54	People's Museum
31	Hotel Puri	86	Nyonya Makko	55	Swimming Pool
32	The Baba House	88	Ole Sayang	56	Maritime Museum
36	Heeren House; Cafe			57	Ferries to Dumai
44	Apple Guest House	**OTHER**		58	Royal Malaysian Navy
62	Hotel Equatorial	1	Local Bus Station		Museum
64	Kancil Guest House	2	Taxi Station	60	Sound and Light Show;
66	Hinly Hotel	3	Express Bus Station		Hawkers' Centre
67	Heritage Hotel	4	Villa Sentosa	63	Jin Trading (Bicycle Hire)
69	Robin's Nest	6	Church of St Peter	65	Chinese Temple
72	Century Mahkota Hotel	15	Immigration	70	Mahkota Parade Shopping
74	Melaka Youth Hostel	18	Kampung Hulu Mosque		Complex
76	Grand Star Hotel	22	Sam Po Kong Temple;	71	Mahkota Seaworld
78	Travellers' Lodge		Hang Li Poh Well		(under construction)
81	Sunny's Inn	27	Cheng Hoon Teng	73	Mahkota Medical Centre
83	Hotel Ambassador		Temple	79	Maybank
87	Malacca Town Holiday	28	Kampung Kling Mosque	84	Jam Pub; Orchid Pub
	Lodge 1	29	Sri Pogyatha Vinoyagar	85	Bank of Commerce
90	Harbour Inn		Moorthi Temple	89	Jim's Cottage Pub

Melaka became a sleepy backwater, but it is now stirring from its slumber. New waterfront developments on reclaimed land have seen the historic areas retreat inland, while the construction of an artificial island, Pulau Melaka, just off the new shoreline has turned Melaka into a beach resort.

Despite modernisation, it's still a place of intriguing Chinese streets, antique shops, old temples and cemeteries, and reminders of former European colonial powers.

Information

The helpful tourist office (☎ 283 6538), right in the heart of the city opposite the Christ Church, is open every day from 8.45 am to 5 pm, closed Friday from 12.15 to 2.45 pm. The main post office is located 3km north of the town centre – take bus No 19 from the bus station.

Town Square & Bukit St Paul

The main area of interest in Melaka is the old city centred on Town Square, also known as Dutch Square. Behind is **Bukit St Paul** (St Paul's Hill), site of the original Portuguese fort.

The most imposing relic of the Dutch period in Melaka is the massive red town hall, the **Stadthuys**, built between 1641 and 1660. Believed to be the oldest Dutch building in the east, its typical Dutch architecture features substantial solid doors and louvred windows. It now houses the excellent **Historical, Ethnographic & Literature Museums**, with detailed explanations of Melaka's history, local culture and traditions. The Stadthuys and its museums are open daily from 9 am to 6 pm (closed Friday from 12.15 to 2.45 pm).

Facing the square is the bright red **Christ**

MALAYSIA

Church. The pink bricks were brought out from Zeeland in Holland and faced with local red laterite when the church was constructed in 1753.

From the Stadthuys, steps lead up to St Paul's Hill, topped by the ruins of St Paul's Church. Originally built by the Portuguese in 1571, it was regularly visited by Francis Xavier. Following his death in China, the saint's body was brought here and buried for nine months before being transferred to Goa in India, where it is to this day. The church has been in ruins for over 150 years, but the setting is beautiful, the walls imposing and fine old Dutch tombstones stand around the interior.

From St Paul's Church, steps lead down to the Porta de Santiago. This is the sole surviving relic of the old fort that was originally constructed by Alfonso d'Albuquerque. The Dutch included this gateway in their reconstructed fort of 1670, and it bears the Dutch East India Company's coat of arms.

Nearby, the popular sound-and-light show recreates Melaka's history each evening at 9.30 pm, and costs RM5.

Just along from the Porta de Santiago is a wooden replica of a Melaka sultan's palace which contains the Muzium Budaya (Cultural Museum); entry is RM1.50. The small Proclamation of Independence Hall has historical displays on the events leading up to independence in 1957.

A few steps back along Jalan Kota is the People's Museum (entry RM2), with bizarre exhibits on 'beautification' practices in different cultures. Further around by the river is the Maritime Museum, housed in a huge recreation of a Portuguese ship. Entry (RM2) includes the Royal Malaysian Navy Museum across the street.

Chinatown

A walk through Melaka's old Chinatown, just west of the river, is fascinating. Although Melaka has long lost its importance as a port, ancient-looking schooners still sail up the river and moor at the banks. Riverboat trips, leaving from behind the tourist office, operate several times daily, take 45 minutes and cost RM7.

You may still find some of the treasures of the east in the antique shops scattered along Jalan Hang Jebat, formerly known as Jonkers St (Junk St). At 48-50 Jalan Tun Tan Cheng Lock is a traditional Peranakan (Straits-born Chinese) townhouse which has been made

into the quite small Baba-Nyonya Heritage Museum. The historic Sri Pogyatha Vinoyagar Moorthi Temple, dating from 1781, and the Sumatran-style Kampung Kling Mosque are both in this area. The fascinating Cheng Hoon Teng Temple on Jalan Tokong Emas is the oldest Chinese temple in Malaysia and has an inscription commemorating Cheng Ho's epochal visit to Melaka.

Other Attractions

In the mid-15th century when the Ming emperor's daughter arrived to wed the sultan of Melaka and seal diplomatic relations, she settled with her entourage at Bukit China (China Hill). It has been a Chinese area ever since and is now a Chinese graveyard, with views across Melaka. At the base of the hill is the Sam Po Kong Temple and the Hang Li Poh Well, once an important water supply for Melaka, which was poisoned by various invaders.

The Villa Sentosa, near the Majestic Hotel in Kampung Morten, is a Malay house that functions as a museum of sorts. Family members will show you around, but women are advised against visiting Villa Sentosa alone.

The small Dutch St John's Fort, on a hilltop to the east of town, has fine views but only a few walls and cannon emplacements remain. Further out is the Medan Portugis, where the descendants of the original Portuguese colonists live.

Air Keroh, 15km north of Melaka, is home to a number of manufactured tourist attractions, including a small zoo, butterfly park and Taman Mini Malaysia/Mini ASEAN, a theme park with examples of traditional houses from Malaysia and other ASEAN countries.

Melaka's beaches at Tanjung Kling and Pantai Kundor, to the north-west of town, have plenty of expensive accommodation, but the Straits of Melaka have become increasingly polluted over the years. The small island of Pulau Besar, reached by boat from Umbai, 10km south-east of Melaka, has better beaches.

Places to Stay

Guesthouses Melaka has some excellent, well priced guesthouses. Breakfast is often included in the price. Most are in the new area of Taman Melaka Raya.

On Jalan Melaka Raya 1, just south of the roundabout, Robin's Nest (☎ 282 9142) at

No 205B is very clean and well run with a good atmosphere. Rooms range from RM15 to RM25, and dorm beds are RM8. Further down is the similarly priced *Travellers' Lodge* (☎ 281 4793) at No 214B. This popular place has a large and welcoming common room, and a rooftop garden.

Just east on Jalan Melaka Raya 3, the *Melaka Youth Hostel* (*Asrama Belia*, ☎ 282 7915) is spotless, well run and has spacious dorms for RM10, or RM14 with air-con.

At No 270A-B, *Sunny's Inn* (☎ 283 7990) is a family-run place with dorm beds for RM7. A tiny single costs RM12, but most rooms are RM15, up to RM35/55 for a single/double with air-con.

On Jalan Taman Melaka Raya, the *Malacca Town Holiday Lodge 1* (☎ 284 8830) at No 148B is well kept and has rooms from RM15/20 (no dorms).

The popular *Eastern Heritage Guest House* (☎ 283 3026), 8 Jalan Bukit China, is housed in a superb old Melaka building near the centre of town. It has typical guesthouse rooms from RM15/18 to RM30, or a dorm bed costs RM7.

Nearby, the *Apple Guest House* (☎ mobile 017-671 1203), 24-1 Lorong Banda Kaba, is in a much newer house and offers rooms for RM12.50/18.

Another good guesthouse is the *Kancil Guest House* (☎ 281 4044) at 177 Jalan Parameswara. It's clean, quiet and secure, with dorm beds for RM10 and fan rooms from RM20 to RM35.

North of the river, the *Malacca Town Holiday Lodge 2* (☎ 284 6905), 52 Jalan Kampung Empat, is further out but has good rooms (no dorms) from RM15/20, RM25 to RM35 with bath, or RM50 with air-con.

Hotels Melaka is also well endowed with hotels in all price ranges.

Two cheap hotels near the bus station are the *Ng Fook* at 154 Jalan Bunga Raya and the nearby *Hong Kong Hotel*. Both have very basic rooms from around RM23. The *Valiant Hotel* (☎ 282 2323), 41-A Jalan Bendahara, has simple rooms for RM23, up to RM39 with bath and air-con.

The rambling old *Majestic Hotel* (☎ 282 2367), 188 Jalan Bunga Raya, is a classic place with high ceilings, swishing fans and a bar. Rates range from RM27 for small fan rooms up to RM53 for large air-con rooms.

Mid-range options include the *May Chiang Hotel* (☎ 283 9535) at 52 Jalan Munshi Abdullah. Immaculately clean air-con rooms cost RM40 with bath. Also good value is the quiet and friendly *Gold Leaf Hotel* (☎ 283 6555) at 31 Jalan Kee Ann. Air-con doubles with modern conveniences are RM45.

Places to Eat

Melaka's food reflects its history, with Nyonya cuisine and Portuguese Eurasian food featured among the usual favourites.

Along Jalan Taman Merdeka, on what used to be the waterfront, is a collection of food stalls known as *Glutton's Corner*. The *Bunga Raya* at No 39-40 has steamed crabs.

On Jalan Laksamana, right in the centre of town, the *Restaurant Kim Swee Huat* at No 38 is a cheap restaurant good for Chinese food and western breakfasts.

Good, if slightly expensive, daytime cafes for Nyonya dishes in Chinatown are in the *Heeren House* guesthouse and at the *Jonkers Melaka Restoran*, 17 Jalan Hang Jebat, a craft shop with a few tables.

In the city centre, the *Sri Lakshmi Vilas* and the *Sri Krishna Bavan* next door are good South Indian restaurants. Around the corner at 34 Jalan Temenggong, the *Restoran Veni* is a good Indian place for a *roti canai* breakfast.

The Taman Melaka Raya area has a good range of eateries. A *hawkers' centre* is on Jalan Parameswara opposite the entrance to the sound-and-light show. The *Restoran Lim (Mee Yoke)* is a good late-night coffee shop with Chinese hawkers' fare and tables on the footpath. *Jalan Taman Merdeka* has plenty of other coffee shops and restaurants.

At *Medan Portugis (Portuguese Square)*, you can sample Malay-Portuguese cuisine at tables facing the sea. Excellent seafood is served – a meal will cost around RM30 per person. Pop bands play during the week, and Portuguese/Malay cultural dances are held on Saturday.

Getting There & Away

Air Pelangi Air (☎ 317 4175) has three flights weekly to/from Pekanbaru in Sumatra.

Bus Most bus companies have their offices near the express bus station. There are frequent buses to KL (2½ hours, RM6.80) from 7 am to 7 pm. To Singapore (four hours, RM11.50), buses leave hourly from 8 am to 6 pm; book in advance. Buses to Johor Bahru (3½ hours, RM10) leave roughly every half an hour. To the east coast, two buses per day go to Kuantan (RM14) at 8.30 am and noon, and evening buses go to Kuala Terengganu (RM21) and Kota Bharu (RM24).

Taxi Taxis leave from the taxi station just opposite the local bus station. Sample per person fares are: Port Dickson RM15, KL RM25, Johor Bahru RM30 and Mersing RM35.

Boat Daily high-speed ferries operate between Melaka and Dumai (2½ hours, RM80) in Sumatra. Departure is at 10 am from the river wharf just past the Maritime Museum. It's best to buy your ticket the day before departure. Dumai is a visa-free entry port into Indonesia for most nationalities.

Getting Around
Melaka is easily explored on foot, but one useful town bus service is No 17 from the local bus station to Taman Melaka Raya and on to Medan Portugis.

A bicycle rickshaw is the ideal way of getting around compact and slow-moving Melaka. Any one way trip within the town will cost around RM6. Unmetered taxis cost the same. Many hostels rent out bicycles.

PORT DICKSON
Port Dickson is just a port town, but its popular beach resort starts around the Km 8 peg and stretches south of the town to the lighthouse at **Cape Rachado**, 16km from Port Dickson. Malaysians flock to this mostly upmarket resort on weekends, but it's hard to understand why. The beaches are ordinary, and occasional oil spills from the Straits of Melaka don't help.

Cheap accommodation can be found at the *Port Dickson Youth Hostel* (☎ 647 2188), 6.5km out of Port Dickson. At Km 13, the Chinese *Kong Ming Hotel* (☎ 662 5683) is right by the beach and has doubles for RM25.

Getting There & Away
By bus, Port Dickson is RM4.20 from Melaka and RM5.60 from KL. From Port Dickson town, there are buses which will drop you off anywhere along the beach.

SEREMBAN
Seremban, the capital of Negeri Sembilan, is the centre of the Malaysian Minangkabau area, closely related to the Minangkabau area of Sumatra. Seremban is famed for its attrac-

tive **Lake Gardens**, and the **State Museum**, 3km west of town, has good examples of the Minangkabau style of architecture.

Seremban is linked by bus to all major cities in the peninsula, and is on the main train line. Cheap, central hotels include the scruffy *Chiew Kee*. Slightly better but more expensive are the *Oriental* and the *Hotel Milo*.

From Seremban, a side trip can be made to **Hutan Lipur Ulu Bendol**, a forest park 20km to the east. The primary dipterocarp rainforest has some excellent short walks. Further east, **Sri Menanti**, just off the Seremban to Kuala Pilah road, is the quiet royal capital first settled over 400 years ago by the Minangkabau from Sumatra.

GENTING HIGHLANDS
The Genting Highlands is a thoroughly modern hill station – casinos are the attraction here rather than the jungle walks. Accommodation is relatively expensive.

It's about 50km north of KL, and buses and taxis go there from the Puduraya bus station.

FRASER'S HILL
Fraser's Hill, set at a cool altitude of 1524m, is a quiet and relatively undeveloped hill station. Very few tourists stay here, and it's mostly a middle-class Malaysian resort. It retains more colonial charm than the Cameron Highlands and has some delightful, old-fashioned bungalows run by the Fraser's Hill Development Corporation (FHDC, ☎ 362 2201). Bungalow rooms cost RM89.10 (RM99 on weekends), or the FHDC's *Puncak Inn* has less inspiring, mid-range rooms from RM58.50 (RM65 on weekends).

Getting There & Away
Fraser's Hill is 103km north of KL and 240km from Kuantan on the east coast. The twice-daily bus service from Kuala Kubu Bahru costs RM2.30, and departs at 8.30 am and 12.30 pm. From KL, take a Tanjung Malim bus to Kuala Kubu Bahru (RM3.50) from platform 20 or 21 at the Puduraya bus station.

CAMERON HIGHLANDS
Situated about 60km north from Tapah, off the KL-Ipoh road, this is the best known and most extensive hill station. At an average altitude of 1500m, the weather is pleasantly

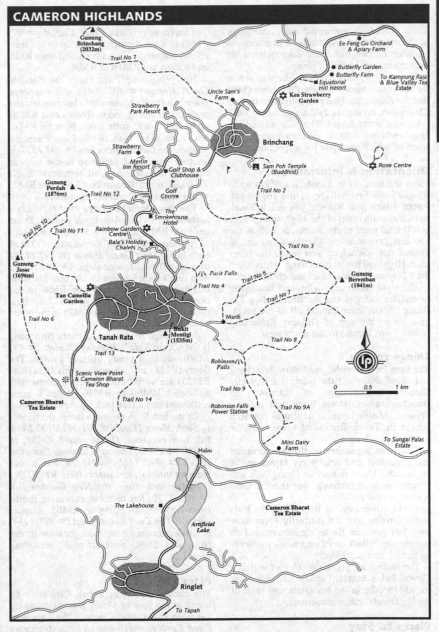

CAMERON HIGHLANDS

Gunung
Brinchang
(2032m)

Trail No 1

Ee Feng Gu Orchard
& Apiary Farm

Butterfly Garden

Butterfly Farm

Equatorial
Hill Resort

To Kampung Raja
& Blue Valley Tea
Estate

Uncle Sam's
Farm

Kea Strawberry
Garden

Strawberry
Park Resort

Brinchang

Strawberry
Farm

Merlin
Inn Resort

Golf Shop &
Clubhouse

Sam Poh Temple
(Buddhist)

Rose Centre

Gunung
Perdah
(1876m)

Trail No 12

Golf Course

Trail No 2

Trail No 10

Trail No 11

The
Smokehouse
Hotel

Rainbow Garden
Centre

Bala's Holiday
Chalets

Trail No 3

Gunung
Jasar
(1696m)

Purit Falls

Trail No 5

Gunung
Bereman
(1841m)

Trail No 4

Trail No 7

Tan Camellia
Garden

Mardi

Trail No 6

Tanah Rata

Bukit
Mentigi
(1535m)

Trail No 8

Trail 13

Robinson/
Falls

Scenic View Point
& Cameron Bharat
Tea Shop

0   0.5   1 km

Cameron Bharat
Tea Estate

Trail No 14

Trail No 9

Robinson Falls
Power Station

Trail No 9A

Habu

Mini Dairy
Farm

To Sungai Palas
Estate

The Lakehouse

Artificial
Lake

Cameron Bharat
Tea Estate

Ringlet

To Tapah

cool, not cold. **Jungle walks** are the thing to do here, and the tourist office and shops in Tanah Rata have somewhat inaccurate maps of the main walks. Most consist of a stroll of an hour or two but some take quite a bit longer and can be tough going.

The only wildlife you are likely to see is the fantastic variety of butterflies. It was here that the American Thai silk entrepreneur, Jim Thompson, mysteriously disappeared in 1967 – he was never found. The hills around the Highlands are dotted with tea plantations, some of which are open for inspection.

Orientation & Information

From the turn-off at Tapah, it's 46km up to Ringlet, the first village of the Highlands. About 14km past Ringlet you reach Tanah Rata, the main town of the Highlands, where you'll find most of the hotels, as well as the bus and taxi stations. Continue on, and at around the 65km peg you reach the other main Highland town, Brinchang, where there are a few more restaurants and cheap hotels.

The road continues up beyond Brinchang to smaller villages and the Blue Valley Tea Estate (90km from Tapah) off to the north-east, or to the top of Gunung Brinchang (80km from Tapah) to the north-west.

Things to See

The **Sam Poh Temple**, just below Brinchang and about 500m off the road, is a typically Chinese kaleidoscope of colours with Buddha statues, stone lions and incense burners. **Mardi** is an agricultural research station in Tanah Rata, and visits must be arranged in advance.

There are a number of **flower nurseries** and vegetable and strawberry **farms** in the Highlands. There is also an Orang Asli settlement near Brinchang, but there's little reason to visit it.

About 10km beyond Brinchang, the **Butterfly Garden** and the **Butterfly Farm** have over 300 varieties fluttering around, and an impressive collection of enormous rhinoceros beetles and scorpions.

The easiest tea plantation to visit is Boh's **Sungai Palas Estate**. Popular half-day tours for RM15 take in the tea estate and most of the Highlands' other attractions.

Places to Stay

Bookings are advisable in the peak holiday periods around April, August and December. Most cheap hotels are in Tanah Rata. Brin-

chang has a number of places, but there's little reason to stay there.

The friendly *Twin Pines Chalet* (☎ 491 2169) is a good place to tune in to the travellers' grapevine. Dorm beds cost from RM6, and rooms are RM16 to RM30.

Just behind the Twin Pines, the *Papillon Guest House* (☎ 491 4069) is a congenial place in a family house with a kitchen, laundry and central sitting room. Rooms cost RM20, up to RM35 with bath. Dorm beds are RM7.

On the same road as the Twin Pines but quieter, the *Cameronian Inn* (☎ 491 1327) is another converted suburban house with an expanse of lawn, a small restaurant and a TV/video room. Rooms cost RM16, or RM25 with bathroom. Dorm beds are RM6.

The new *Daniel's Lodge* (☎ 491 5823) is surrounded by rainforest, yet central. Dorm beds are RM7, and rooms RM16 to RM30.

A short walk from the centre of Tanah Rata is *Father's Guest House* (☎ 491 2484), up a long flight of stone steps. The old Nissen huts don't look like much but provide comfortable accommodation for RM6 in the dorm, and doubles are RM16. Excellent rooms with bathroom cost RM25 in the house nearby on the hill.

Just 1.5km from town towards Brinchang is the scenic *Bala's Holiday Chalets* (☎ 491 1660), set in a pretty hillside garden. The dorm (RM8) and cheaper rooms (RM18 to RM25) are very basic, or better rooms with bath cost RM66 to RM80. It has a good restaurant and a free pick-up service.

Of the hotels on the main street, the friendly *Seah Meng Hotel* (☎ 491 1618), 39 Main Rd, is very clean. Doubles cost RM35, or RM50 with bath. The unpretentious *Cameson Hotel* (☎ 491 1160) at No 29, has a nice wooden interior, and rooms from RM30.

In the mid-range, the *New Garden Inn* (☎ 491 5170) has nice but expensive rooms from RM165, dropping to RM65 in quiet periods. The *Cool Point Hotel* (☎ 491 4914) is a more modern hotel with pleasant rooms from RM125/90 peak/off-peak, including breakfast.

Places to Eat

The cheapest food in Tanah Rata is to be found at the row of Malay food stalls along the main street. Stalls include the *Excellent Food Centre*, which has an extensive menu and steaks on Saturday night. The adjoining *Fresh Milk Corner* sells fresh milk, yoghurt and lassis.

Opposite is Tanah Rata's lively restaurant strip, with tables on the footpath. The *Restaurant Kumar* and the adjacent *Restoran Thanam* both serve good Malay and Indian food. The *Restoran No 14* next to the Malayan Bank also does good Indian food, including the popular *masala dosa*.

Steamboat, a sort of Oriental variation of a Swiss fondue, is the Highlands' real taste treat. You can try it at the *Orient Restaurant* in the main street.

Further along Main Rd is the Chinese *Jasmine Restaurant*, which has good set meals. The *Roselane Coffee House* serves set meals and good breakfasts from RM3.50.

Getting There & Away

Access to the Cameron Highlands is via Tapah, from where buses to Tanah Rata (two hours, RM3.50) run every one to 1½ hours between 8.15 am and 6 pm; most continue to Brinchang.

Most long-distance buses leave from Tapah, and these services can be booked at any of the backpacker places, or at CS Travel & Tours (☎ 491 1200), 47 Main Rd, Tapah. Tanah Rata also has four direct daily buses to KL (five hours, RM10), and two to Penang (six hours, RM14).

From Tanah Rata shared-taxi fares are RM10 to Tapah, RM17.50 to Ipoh and RM37.50 to KL, but you may have to charter.

IPOH

The 'city of millionaires', 219km north of Kuala Lumpur and 173km south of Butterworth, made its fortune from tin mining. It is a thriving Chinese town with some of the best Chinese food in Malaysia and plenty of colonial architecture dating from its heyday. Interesting cave-temples on the outskirts of the town are the **Perak Tong Temple**, the most important temple, about 6km north of town, and the **Sam Poh Temple**, a few kilometres south of town. Both are right on the main road and easy to get to.

Ipoh is also the best take-off point for Lumut and the island of Pangkor.

Places to Stay

Bottom of the barrel is the *Grand Cathay Hotel* (☎ 241 9685), 88 Jalan CM Yussuf, but what it lacks in ambience is more than made up for by the price and the friendly manager. Large, scruffy rooms cost RM23, RM28 with bathroom or RM35 with air-con.

Of a slightly better standard is the *Embassy*

Hotel (☎ 254 9496), 35 Jalan CM Yussuf, where singles/doubles with bath cost RM24/28.50, or RM38.50 with air-con.

The clean but mediocre *New Hollywood Hotel* (☎ 241 5322), 72 Jalan CM Yussuf, has rooms with air-con and bath for RM39/53. The hotel has a good restaurant on the ground floor.

The *Merloon Hotel* (☎ 254 1351), 92-98 Jalan Mustapha Al-Bakri, has clean and very spacious air-con rooms with bathroom and modern conveniences from RM41/62.

Places to Eat

Ipoh has plenty of restaurants, and the rice noodle dish known as *kwayteow* is reputed to be better in Ipoh than anywhere else in Malaysia. The city's best known place for kwayteow is *Kedai Kopi Kong Heng*, on Jalan Bandar Timah between Jalan Pasar and Jalan Dato Maharajah Lela, a bustling restaurant serving a bit of everything.

Ipoh has plenty of food-stall centres. On Jalan Raja Musa Aziz, the large *Medan Selera Dato Tawhil Azar*, better known as the Children's Playground, has stalls arranged around a small square. It's a popular place for Malay food in the evening and is open late.

At night, many of the restaurants in the old town are closed, so a good place to head for is Jalan Yau Tet Shin in the new town. On opposite corners, *Restoran Wong* and *Restoran Onn Kee* specialise in *tauge ayam* (chicken and bean sprouts) and kwayteow.

For Indian food, the *Rahman Restaurant* on Jalan CM Yussuf is very clean and has a wide range of dishes.

Getting There & Away

Air Pelangi Air (☎ 312 4770) flies to KL (RM66) and Medan (RM224). Malaysia Airlines (☎ 241 4155) also has flights to KL.

Bus The long-distance bus station is in the south-west corner of the city centre, a taxi ride from the main hotel area. Destinations (and fares) include Kuala Kangsar (RM2.20), Lumut (RM3.80), Tapah (RM4), Butterworth (RM8), KL (RM9.50), Kota Bharu (RM18) and Hat Yai (RM28) in Thailand. Tickets should be booked in advance if possible.

Most buses to Lumut leave from the Perak Roadway terminus directly across Jalan Tun Abdul Rasak from the bus station.

Train All trains between Singapore and Butterworth stop at Ipoh. North-bound express trains stop at Kuala Kangsar (50 minutes) and Taiping (1½ hours) before continuing to Butterworth (3½ hours).

Taxi Long-distance taxis leave from beside the bus station, and there is another rank directly across the road.

LUMUT

The Malaysian navy has its principal base in this small river port, but Lumut is little more than a departure point for nearby Pulau Pangkor. If you get marooned in Lumut there is a reasonable choice of *Chinese hotels*.

Getting There & Away

Bus & Taxi Lumut is 101km from Ipoh, the usual place for Lumut bus connections. Buses to other destinations include Tapah (for the Cameron Highlands, RM8.50), Butterworth (RM10) and KL (RM13). Per person fares for long-distance taxis are RM11.50 to Ipoh, RM30 to Butterworth, RM35 to KL.

PULAU PANGKOR

The island of Pangkor is close to the coast, off Lumut, and easily accessible via Ipoh. It's a popular resort island known for its fine beaches, many of which can be reached by an interesting round-island loop on bicycle or motorbike. A visit to the island is principally a 'laze on the beach' operation.

Ferries from Lumut stop on the eastern side of the island at Sungai Pinang Kecil and then Pangkor town, where there are banks, restaurants and shops. The main beaches are on the western side of the island. **Pasir Bogak** is the most developed beach, and the next bay to the north, **Teluk Nipah**, is the main budget accommodation beach. **Golden Sands Beach** (Teluk Belanga) at the northern end of the island is the preserve of the Pan-Pacific Pangkor Resort. Between these beaches are a number of virtually deserted beaches, the best being **Coral Bay**.

Emerald Bay on the nearby island of Pulau Pangkor Laut is a beautiful little horseshoe-shaped bay, but the entire island has been taken over by a luxury hotel conglomerate.

Pangkor's one bit of history, a **Dutch fort** dating from 1670, is 3km south of Pangkor village at Teluk Gedong.

Places to Stay & Eat

Teluk Nipah Teluk Nipah has the best beach, and though mid-range hotels are popping up everywhere, it still has a few moderately priced options on expensive Pangkor.

The most popular travellers-only place is *Joe Fisherman Village* (☎ 685 2389). Very basic A-frame huts cost RM25 for two people, or slightly more substantial cottages cost RM35.

Right next door is *Nazri Nipah Camp* (☎ 685 2014), a friendly place at the edge of the rainforest with A-frames for RM20, rooms with bathroom for RM40 and larger chalets for RM30/40 in the high/low season.

The *Coral Beach Camp* (☎ 685 2711) has A-frame huts for RM20, or double rooms for RM45. It lacks atmosphere but the owners arrange reasonably priced boat trips.

The *Takana Juo* (☎ 685 3477) has basic bungalows with bathroom for RM25 right beside its excellent and very popular Indonesian restaurant.

Most places to stay have their own restaurants, or the *Bayview Cafe* is a good spot for a meal overlooking the beach.

Pasir Bogak Accommodation at Pasir Bogak is a varied mixture of upper end and cheaper places.

The cheapest option is the *Pangkor Anchorage* (☎ 685 1363), where small, rustic A-frame huts in a shady grove with mattresses on the floor cost RM10 per person. *Pangkor Village Beach Resort* (☎ 685 2227) has cheap tented accommodation for groups and basic huts for RM40, or RM30 in the low season.

Khoo's Holiday Resort (☎ 685 1164) is a rather ugly concrete conglomeration, but its wooden chalets on the hill behind are good value for RM41 with fan (RM67 with air-con).

The *Pangkor Paradise Village* (☎ 685 1496) on an isolated little beach at the southern end of Pasir Bogak has plain air-con chalets for RM60/70 a single/double.

Pasir Bogak has some good fish restaurants, such as the cheap *Pangkor Restaurant* or the more upmarket *Restoran Number One*, which serves excellent seafood.

Getting There & Away

Air Pangkor airport has reopened after a major upgrade, with flights to/from KL (RM120) and Singapore (RM204).

Boat The Pan Silver Ferry has departures from Lumut to Pangkor town every 20 minutes from 6.30 am to 8 pm. The fare is

RM3 each way. Ferries also service the luxury Pan-Pacific Pangkor Resort and the Pangkor Laut Resort on Pulau Pangkor Laut.

Getting Around
Buses run every hour or so from Pangkor village across the island to the far end of the beach at Pasir Bogak and back again. Pangkor also has plenty of minibus taxis, costing RM5 from Pangkor to Pasir Bogak and RM12 to Teluk Nipah.

Motorcycles can be rented for RM30 per day and bicycles for RM10 per day.

KUALA KANGSAR
The royal town of Perak state has the fine **Ubadiah Mosque**, with its onion dome and the minarets squeezed up against it as if seen in a distorting mirror. Other grand buildings of the sultanate in the eastern part of town include the **Istana Kenangan**, now a museum. Kuala Kangsar is where rubber trees were first grown in Malaysia.

The **Double Lion Hotel**, close to the bus station in the centre of town, has good rooms for RM18/30 singles/doubles.

TAIPING
The 'town of everlasting peace' was once a raucous tin-mining town. Its attractive colonial district is centred on the **Lake Gardens**, which has a **zoo**. The oldest **museum** in the country is nearby. Above the town is **Maxwell Hill**, Malaysia's smallest and oldest hill station. To get there, take a government Land Rover from the station (☎ 807 7243) at the foot of the hill for RM2. You can also walk down in about three hours.

Places to Stay & Eat
The *Swiss Hotel* (☎ 807 4899), at 37 Jalan Panggong Wayang near the central market, has simple rooms with bath for RM20. The *Hong Kong Hotel* (☎ 807 3824) at 79 Jalan Barrack (the entrance is on Jalan Lim Tee Hooi) is a bargain at RM30 for a large room with air-con and bathroom.

Best is the *New Rest House (Rumah Rehat Baru,* ☎ 807 2044), overlooking the beautiful Lake Gardens, about 1km from the town centre. It's clean, secure and very good value at RM31.50 for large doubles, or RM35 with air-con.

Taiping's large *night market* has many open-air eating stalls and satay is one of the city's specialities.

Getting There & Away
The express bus station is at Kamunting near the north-south highway, 7km from town. Take a bus (60 sen) or taxi (RM4) to the town centre. Frequent buses go to Butterworth (RM4), Ipoh (RM4.30) and KL (RM13). The local bus station in the centre of town has non-air-con buses to Kuala Kangsar and Ipoh.

The taxi station near the central market has taxis to Butterworth (RM12), Ipoh (RM12) and Kuala Kangsar (RM5).

PENANG
The oldest British settlement in Malaysia, predating both Singapore and Melaka, is also one of Malaysia's major tourist attractions. This is hardly surprising as the 285 sq km island of Penang has popular beach resorts and an intriguing and historically interesting town, Georgetown, which is also noted for its superb food.

On behalf of Britain's East India Company, Captain Francis Light sailed up and gained possession of the virtually uninhabited island in 1786. Aided by colonial free-trade policies, Georgetown became a prosperous centre as well as a local mecca for dreamers, dissidents, intellectuals and artists.

Sun Yatsen planned the 1911 Canton uprising in Georgetown, probably in one of the local Hainanese coffee shops. Unmistakably Chinese, it's one of the most likeable cities in South-East Asia. With easy-going *kampung* (villages), sandy beaches, warm water, good food and plenty of things to see, who wouldn't like Penang?

Orientation
Penang's major town, Georgetown, is often referred to as Penang, although correctly that is the name of the island (the actual Malay spelling is Pinang and it means 'betel nut'). Georgetown is on the end of a small peninsula at the north-east of the island, the closest point to the mainland, and a 24 hour vehicle and passenger ferry service operates across this 3km-wide channel. South of the ferry crossing is Penang Bridge – the longest in South-East Asia – which links the island with Malaysia's north-south highway.

Georgetown is a fairly compact city, and most places can easily be reached on foot or by bicycle rickshaw. You'll find most of Georgetown's popular cheap hotels along Lebuh Chulia or close to it, while Lebuh Campbell is one of the town's main shopping

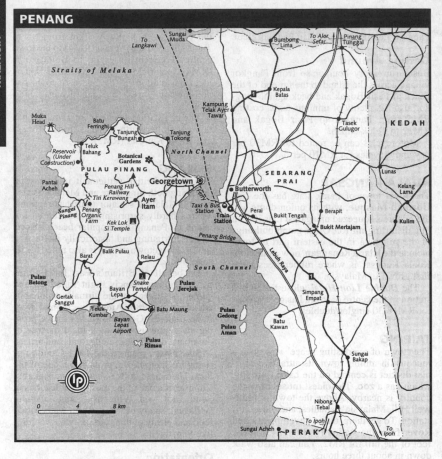

PENANG

streets. Along or near Lebuh Pitt (also called Jalan Masjid Kapitan Keling) are many of Penang's oldest churches, temples and mosques. Jalan Penang is another popular shopping street, and in this area you'll find a number of the more expensive hotels, including the venerable Eastern & Oriental Hotel, at the waterfront end of Jalan Penang.

If you follow Jalan Penang south-west, you'll pass the modern, multistorey blot on the skyline known as the Kompleks Tun Abdul Razak (Komtar).

Information
Tourist Offices The Penang Tourist Association (☎ 261 6663) is on Jalan Tun Syed Sheh Barakbah, close to Fort Cornwallis.

Tourism Malaysia (☎ 262 0066) has an office a few doors along in the same building.

The best of the tourist offices is the Penang Tourist Guides Association (☎ 261 4461) on the 3rd floor of the Komtar building on Jalan Penang. It is open daily from 10 am to 6 pm.

Foreign Consulates Penang has Indonesian and Thai consulates. The Thai consulate (☎ 226 9484), open weekdays from 9 am to noon and 2 to 4 pm, issues two month tourist visas for RM33; many places along Lebuh Chulia will obtain the visa for you for a RM10 fee.

Post & Communications The poste restante facility at the main post office is efficient and popular. The Telekom office next door is open weekdays from 8.45 am to 4.15 pm, and Saturday to 12.30 pm.

Travel Agencies Silver-Econ Travel (☎ 262 9882) at 436 Lebuh Chulia, MSL Travel (☎ 227 2655) in the Ming Court Hotel (on Jalan Macalister near Jalan Rangoon) and Happy Holidays (☎ 262 9222) at 442 Lebuh Chulia are all reliable operators.

Warning! Some trishaw riders offer a variety of drugs, but really only sell heroin, a major problem in Georgetown. Malaysia's penalties for drug use are very severe indeed (death for possession of more than 15g of any contraband).

Fort Cornwallis & Padang

The time-worn walls of Fort Cornwallis are one of Penang's oldest sites. Between 1808 and 1810, convict labour was used to replace the original wooden structure with stone. The fort has a small, interesting **museum** in one of the old gunpowder magazines.

Fort Cornwallis lies next to the Padang – the green, central square laid in colonial times. It is ringed by fine colonial buildings, including the **Penang Museum**, which has interesting exhibits on Penang's history, including gory details of Chinese secret society squabbles, and a small collection of historical paintings and prints.

Kuan Yin Teng Temple

Just round the corner from the museum, on Lebuh Pitt, is the temple of Kuan Yin, the Goddess of Mercy. The temple was built in the 1800s by the first Chinese settlers in Penang. It's neither terribly impressive nor interesting, but it's right in the centre of the old part of Georgetown and is the most popular Chinese temple in the city.

Outside stand two large burners where you can burn a few million in Monopoly money to ensure wealth for the afterlife.

Kapitan Kling Mosque

At the same time as Kuan Yin's temple was being constructed, Penang's first Indian Muslim settlers built this mosque at the junction of Lebuh Pitt and Lebuh Buckingham. In a typically Indian-influenced Islamic style, the yellow mosque has a single minaret. Close by on Lebuh Acheh, the **Acheen St Mosque** has an unusual Egyptian-style minaret.

Khoo Kongsi

The Dragon Mountain Hall is in Cannon Square close to the end of Lebuh Pitt. A *kongsi* is a clan house, a building which is part temple and part meeting hall for Chinese clan organisations (also called kongsi) known variously as ritual brotherhoods, secret societies, triads or heaven-man-earth societies.

The present kongsi, dating from 1906 and extensively renovated in the 1950s, is a rainbow of dragons, statues, paintings, lamps, coloured tiles and carvings. It's a part of colourful Penang which definitely should not be missed.

Sri Mariamman Temple

Lebuh Queen runs parallel to Lebuh Pitt, and about midway between the Kuan Yin Temple and the Kapitan Kling Mosque, you'll find another example of Penang's religious diversity. The Sri Mariamman Temple is a typical South Indian temple, with elaborately sculpted and painted *gopuram*, or pyramidal gateway tower, soaring over the entrance.

Wat Chayamangkalaram

At Lorong Burma, just off the road to Batu Ferringhi, is a major Thai temple – the Temple of the Reclining Buddha. This brightly painted temple houses a 32m-long reclining Buddha, loudly proclaimed in Penang as the third longest in the world – a dubious claim as there's at least one other in Malaysia that's larger, plus six or more in Thailand, Myanmar (Burma) and China.

Penang Hill

Rising 830m above Georgetown, the top of Penang Hill provides a cool retreat from the sticky heat below, as it's generally about 5°C cooler than at sea level. From the summit, you've got a spectacular view over the island and right across to the mainland. There are pleasant **gardens**, a small **aviary**, a cafe and a hotel as well as a **Hindu temple** and a **mosque** on the top. Penang Hill is particularly pleasant at dusk as Georgetown, far below, starts to light up.

Getting There & Away Take the frequent Transit Link bus No 1 or No 101, Lim Seng bus No 91, or minibus No 21 from Pengkalan Weld or Lebuh Chulia to Ayer Itam, then walk five minutes or take Transit Link bus No 8 to the funicular station. The funicular costs RM3/4 one way/return. There are departures every 15 to 30 minutes from 6.30 am

GEORGETOWN

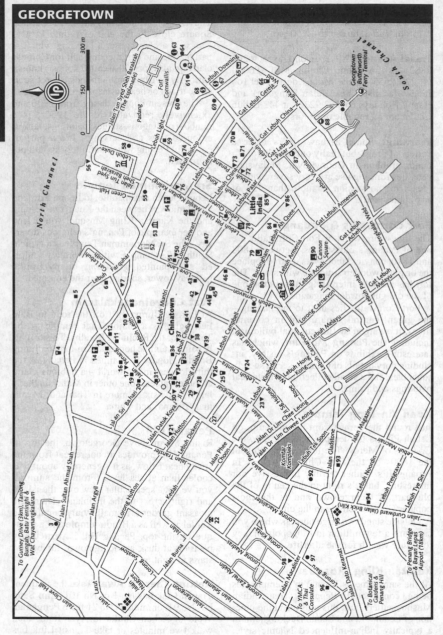

GEORGETOWN

PLACES TO STAY		PLACES TO EAT		44	Hong Kong Bar
1	Sheraton Inn	7	Jaipur Court; 20 Leith Street	45	Hard Life Cafe
5	Eastern & Oriental	13	Polar Cafe	48	Kuan Yin Teng Temple
	Hotel	17	Restoran May Garden	52	Cathedral of the Assumption
6	City Bayview Hotel	21	Tandoori House	53	Penang Museum
8	Waldorf Hotel	23	Kedai Kopi Kimberly	54	St George's Church
9	Cathay Hotel	24	Green Planet	55	Supreme Court
11	Malaysia Hotel	26	Diner's Bakery	57	Penang Library; Art Gallery
12	Hotel Continental	28	Hameediyah Restaurant	58	City Hall
15	Peking Hotel;	29	Taj Restaurant	60	State Assembly Building
	Soho Free House	30	Yasmeen Restaurant	61	Immigration Office
16	Hotel Cititel	34	Tai Wah Coffee Shop & Bar	62	Victoria Memorial Clocktower
18	Merchant Hotel	37	Secret Garden	63	Penang Tourist Association;
19	Towne House Hotel	38	Sin Kuan Hwa Cafe		Tourism Malaysia
20	White House Hotel	39	Hong Kong Restaurant	64	Medan & Langkawi Ferry
31	Oriental Hotel	42	Kafe BB		Offices
32	Hang Chow Hotel	50	Rainforest Cafe	65	Main Post Office; Telekom
33	Eastern Hotel	56	Esplanade Food Centre	66	Flint's Club
36	Blue Diamond Hotel	72	Shusi Banana Leaf Restaurant	67	Hongkong Bank
40	Swiss Hotel	73	Kaliaman Restaurant	68	Standard Chartered Bank
41	Eng Aun Hotel	75	10 King Street Cafe	69	MS Ally
43	Pin Seng Hotel	76	Dragon King	78	Sri Mariamman Temple
46	Honpin Hotel;	85	Meena Cafe	79	Kapitan Kling Mosque
	Coco Island Cafe	86	Restoran Tomyam	80	Post Office
47	Hotel Noble	98	Oriental	81	Market
49	Wan Hai Hotel			82	Syed Alatas Mansion
51	Oasis Hotel	OTHER		83	Thieve's Market
59	Esplanade Pathe Hotel	2	Penang Plaza	87	City Bus Station
70	D'Budget Hostel	3	Singapore Airlines		(Transit Link)
71	GT Guest House	4	Latin Quarter	88	Round Island Buses
74	Hotel Rio	10	Cheong Fatt Tze Mansion	89	Railway Booking Office
77	Broadway Hostel	14	Christian Cemetery	90	Khoo Kongsi
84	Golden Plaza Hostel	22	Telekom	91	Acheen St Mosque
93	Shangri-La	25	Rock World	92	Malaysia Airlines
94	Hotel Grand Continental	27	Chowrasta Bazaar	95	Gama Department Store
96	Sunway Hotel	35	Reggae Club	97	Thai Airways International

to 9.15 pm, until 11.45 pm on weekends (when long queues are common).

The energetic can get to the top by an interesting three hour hike starting from the Moon Gate at the Botanical Gardens – bring along a water bottle. The easier jeep trail to the top starts beyond the Moon Gate and is closed to private vehicles.

Kek Lok Si Temple

On a hilltop at Ayer Itam, close to the funicular station for Penang Hill, stands the largest Buddhist temple in Malaysia. Construction commenced in 1890 and took more than 20 years to complete.

The entrance is reached through arcades of souvenir stalls. Go past a tightly packed turtle pond and murky fish ponds until you reach the Ban Po Thar (Ten Thousand Buddhas Pagoda).

A 'voluntary' contribution is the price to climb to the top of the seven tier, 30m-high tower, which is said to be Burmese at the top, Chinese at the bottom and Thai in between.

Beaches

Penang's beaches are not as spectacular as the tourist brochures would have you believe (there are better beaches elsewhere in Malaysia), but they make a pleasant enough day trip from Georgetown and have accommodation for longer stays. They are mainly along the north coast. **Tanjung Bungah** is the first real beach, but it's not attractive for swimming. **Batu Ferringhi** (Foreigner's Rock) is the resort strip with a string of hotels. It has the best beach and the best facilities. **Teluk Bahang** is a less-developed, overgrown fishing village with a dirty beach.

Places to Stay

Hostels Penang has plenty of cheap travellers' hostels which, though spartan, are relatively clean and offer good travel information.

The *Golden Plaza Hostel* (☎ 263 2388), 32 Lebuh Ah Quee, is very popular and has an air-con lounge. Beds in the large dorm cost RM8, or RM10 in the small dorm. Singles/

doubles start at RM16/25, up to RM45 with air-con, all with common bath.

Another favourite is *D'Budget Hostel* (☎ *263 4794*), 9 Lebuh Gereja, close to the ferry terminal and buses. Dorms cost RM7, small rooms RM16/22 and larger air-con rooms RM38. This hostel is big on security, and the 5th floor rooftop sitting area is a winner.

The *Broadway Hostel* (☎ *262 8550*), 35F Jalan Masjid Kapitan Keling (Lebuh Pitt), is less popular but has good rooms, many with windows, from RM20/25 to RM40 with air-con. Dorms cost RM7.

GT Guest House (☎ *262 5833*), 14 Lebuh China, has large dorms for RM8 and small partitioned rooms for RM15/20.

The *YMCA* (☎ *228 2211*) at 211 Jalan Macalister is at the top of this range. Simple fan rooms cost RM35, or RM45 to RM60 with air-con and bath. To get there, take a No 7 bus.

Hotels Georgetown has a great number of cheap hotels with lots of character, but some sorely need an overhaul. Stroll down Lebuh Chulia, Lebuh Leith or Love Lane and you'll come across them.

Two very popular places are the *Swiss Hotel* (☎ *262 0133*) at 431F Lebuh Chulia and the *Eng Aun* (☎ *261 2333*) directly across the road at No 380. They have cafes and are back from the street, so are insulated from street noise. The well run, if sometimes overrun, Swiss Hotel has tidy rooms with fan and common bath at RM18.70/23.10. The Eng Aun has a variety of decrepit rooms starting at RM16/22 with common facilities, or large rooms with attached showers (toilets shared) from RM18/22.

At 511 Lebuh Chulia is the *Hang Chow Hotel* (☎ *261 0810*), a rickety old wooden hotel with rooms from RM22, but it's well run and has an excellent coffee shop downstairs. The *Eastern Hotel* (☎ *261 4597*) next door has slightly better rooms, but the early-morning call to prayer at the mosque next door is a deterrent.

On the streets just off Lebuh Chulia there are a number of other popular places. At 35 Love Lane, the friendly *Wan Hai Hotel* (☎ *261 6853*) has dorm beds for RM8 and rooms for RM20 with common bath. It's a classic, well run Chinese hotel. Rooms are basic and a little noisy but have some style.

The *Oasis Hotel* (☎ *262 6778*), close by at 23 Love Lane, is a typical older-style Chinese place in a very quiet area. Dorm beds cost

RM8 rooms range from RM20 up to RM35 with private shower (shared toilet).

Also on Love Lane, at No 82 and very close to Lebuh Chulia, is the friendly *Pin Seng Hotel* (☎ *261 9004*), tucked down a little alley. Rooms start at RM18 and vary from the crumbling to the presentable, so it pays to check out a few.

The *White House Hotel* (☎ *263 2385*) at 72 Jalan Penang is a definite notch up in quality, with large spotless rooms for RM25/30, or RM35/40 with air-con. Those which overlook Jalan Penang are noisy – try to get one at the rear.

For a mid-range hotel, the wonderful-looking *Cathay Hotel* (☎ *262 6271*) at 22 Lebuh Leith is a well maintained, grand colonial hotel, and the cavernous lobby nearly equals the exterior. It may look familiar – the Cathay played a fairly starring role in the 1995 film *Beyond Rangoon*. Prices for the huge spotless rooms are RM57 with fan and bath, RM69 with air-con and bath.

There's not much other mid-range accommodation in Penang, though some of those run-down places on Lebuh Chulia might be spruced up as an alternative to the flea bags and big international hotels now available.

During peak travel times it can be difficult to find a room, but there are many more cheap *Chinese hotels* on Lebuh Chulia, Lebuh Campbell and the small connecting streets – a quick wander around will turn up any number of them.

Beach Accommodation Few travellers seem to stay out at the Penang beaches these days, though there are some budget places at Tanjung Bungah, Batu Ferringhi and Teluk Bahang.

The only budget offering at Tanjung Bungah is the *Lost Paradise* (☎ *890 7641*), at the western end of town. Bungalows for RM20/30 are somewhat run-down but have character. The good restaurant in a garden setting overlooks the beach and Georgetown.

Batu Ferringhi has plenty of big hotels and some budget guesthouses clustered together opposite the beach. The *Baba Guest House* (☎ *881 1686*) is a very tidy family home with rooms for RM25, or RM60 with air-con and bath. Next door *Shalini's Guest House* (☎ *881 1859*) is an old, two storey wooden house with a pleasant balcony. Rooms are spartan but cheap for Batu Ferringhi at RM20/30, more with air-con and bath. Next along is *Ali's Guest House* (☎ *881 1316*), with a shady garden. The rooms at the back for RM30 are dank, or the better front rooms with bath cost RM45.

Just on are two similar places, the *ET Budget Guest House* (☎ *881 1553*) and *Ah Beng* (☎ *881 1036*), where simple rooms with polished floorboards cost RM25/30, and air-con rooms with bath are RM50.

At Teluk Bahang, *Miss Loh's* is a comfortable, suburban guesthouse off the main road towards the butterfly farm. Dorm beds are RM8, and doubles RM20 to RM30. *Fisherman Village Guest House* (☎ *885 2936*) is in the Malay fishing kampung and offers simple, tidy rooms for RM18.

Places to Eat

Penang is another of the region's delightful food venues, with many local specialities to tempt you. Penang has two types of laksa. *Laksa assam* is a sour fish soup with tamarind or assam paste, served with white noodles. Originally a Thai dish, *laksa lemak* has been adopted by Penang and has coconut milk substituted for the tamarind.

Seafood, of course, is very popular in Penang and there are many restaurants that specialise in fresh fish, crabs and prawns – particularly along the northern beach fringe.

Despite its Chinese character, Penang also has a strong Indian presence, and there are some popular specialities to savour. Curry kapitan is a Penang chicken curry which supposedly takes its name from a Dutch sea captain asking his Indonesian mess boy what was on that night. The answer was 'curry kapitan', and it's been on the menu ever since.

Murtabak, a thin roti canai pastry stuffed with egg, vegetables and meat, while not actually a Penang speciality, is done with particular flair on the island.

Hawker Food

Georgetown has a big selection of street stalls, with nightly gatherings at places like the seafront *Esplanade Food Centre* behind the Penang Library. This is one of the best hawkers' centres, as much for the delightful sea breezes as the food.

Three kilometres further along the coast on the way to Tanjung Bungah *Gurney Drive* is another popular seafront hawker venue.

Just off Jalan Macalister, *Lorong Baru* is a lively location where food stalls set up in the evenings. Another *market* good for Malay food springs up every night along Lebuh Kimberley on the corner of Lebuh Cintra, not far from the Kompleks Komtar.

Lebuh Chulia is a great place for noodles after 9 pm. Most stalls are found along the street around the Honpin Hotel at No 273.

Indian Food

Penang's Little India is along Lebuh Pasar between Lebuh Penang and Lebuh Pitt and along the side streets between. Several small restaurants and stalls in this area offer cheap north (Muslim) and south (vegetarian) Indian food.

The *Yasmeen Restaurant* at 177 Jalan Penang, near the corner of Lebuh Chulia, is a good place for inexpensive murtabak, biryani or a quick snack of roti canai with dhal dip.

In Chinatown on Lebuh Campbell, the *Taj Restaurant* at No 166 and the *Hameediyah Restaurant* at No 164A are two Indian Muslim coffee shops with prewar decor, and good curries and murtabak at very cheap prices.

A number of unpretentious south Indian restaurants can be found along Lebuh Penang. The *Shusi Banana Leaf Restaurant* serves traditional banana-leaf meals, while the air-conditioned *Kaliaman Restaurant* is a bit more upmarket and offers a broader range of subcontinental dishes.

Chinese Food

There are so many Chinese restaurants in Penang that making any specific recommendations is rather redundant.

At 29 Lebuh Cintra, the *Hong Kong Restaurant* is good, cheap and varied, and has a menu in English. One of Georgetown's 'excellent Hainanese chicken-rice' purveyors is the *Sin Kuan Hwa Cafe*, on the corner of Lebuh Chulia and Lebuh Cintra.

The *Kafe BB* on Lebuh Chulia has Chinese fast food at downmarket prices; you can eat here for around RM6. Also very cheap is *Kedai Kopi Kimberly* on Jalan Kimberly.

Breakfast & Western Food

Lebuh Chulia has some delightfully old-fashioned coffee shops for a leisurely, cheap breakfast at marble-topped tables while you browse the *New Straits Times*. As well as the coffee, tea and toast served at coffee shops everywhere, those on Lebuh Chulia have much more extensive western breakfast menus which include muesli, porridge, toast and marmalade, and other favourites.

The *Yasmeen* (see Indian Food) is the best place in town for roti canai, the perfect Penang breakfast.

Two popular Chinese cafes serving western breakfasts are the coffee shop at the *Hang Chow Hotel* and the *Tai Wah Coffee Shop &*

Bar, which buzzes until late at night. Western breakfasts are also available at the *Eng Aun*, *Swiss* and *Cathay* hotels, and the *Secret Garden* at 414 Lebuh Chulia.

The *Green Planet* at 63 Lebuh Cintra is a popular travellers' restaurant where you can read (and add to) the travel-tips notebooks. It has very stylish decor and good food, but is not the cheapest place in town.

The *Kompleks Komtar* has western fast food, a good hawkers' centre on the 5th floor and a supermarket.

Getting There & Away
Air The Malaysia Airlines office (☎ 262 0011) in the Komtar building is open from 8.30 am to 6 pm, Monday to Saturday, and until 1 pm on Sunday.

See the Getting There & Away section at the start of this chapter for details of flights to other countries in the region.

Bus The main bus terminal is across the channel in Butterworth beside the ferry terminal, but some convenient services leave from Georgetown, mostly from the basement of the Kompleks Komtar. Buy tickets at the Komtar ticket offices or from hotels and travel agents on Lebuh Chulia.

From the Kompleks Komtar there are several daily buses to KL, as well as two buses each to Kota Bharu and Kuala Terengganu – book well in advance. Other east coast services leave from Butterworth. From Georgetown, only two daily buses at 8 am and 3 pm go to the Cameron Highlands (RM15); otherwise, first take a bus to Tapah.

Other services from either Georgetown or Butterworth are: Taiping (RM4), Alor Setar (RM6), Kuala Perlis (RM8), Lumut (RM10), KL (RM17 to RM21), Melaka (RM24) and Singapore (RM33 to RM40).

Hotels or travel agents also sell bus and mini-bus tickets to Hat Yai (RM20), Surat Thani (RM32), Phuket (RM42) and Bangkok (RM75).

Train The train station is, like the bus and taxi stations, right by the ferry terminal at Butterworth. Trains to KL depart at 8 am, and 3.15 and 10 pm. The 8 am train continues to Singapore; it arrives at 8.15 pm and costs RM60/34 in 2nd/3rd class.

The *International Express* to Hat Yai and Bangkok in Thailand departs around 2.30 pm, arriving in Hat Yai at about 6 pm and Bangkok the next morning at about 9.50 am.

You can make reservations at the Butterworth station (☎ 323 7962) or at the railway booking office (☎ 261 0290) at the ferry terminal in Georgetown.

Taxi Long-distance taxis also operate from a depot beside the Butterworth ferry terminal. Typical per person fares include: Alor Setar (RM12.50), Taiping (RM12.50), Kuala Perlis (RM20), Ipoh (RM22), Lumut (RM22), KL (RM42.50) and Kota Bharu (RM47.50).

Boat Kuala Perlis Langkawi Ferry Service (KPLFS, ☎ 262 5630) and Ekspres Bahagia (☎ 263 1943), both near the tourist office on The Esplanade, have ferries to Medan in Sumatra. The journey takes 4½ hours and costs RM110/90 in 1st/2nd class with KPLFS (at 10 am on Tuesday, Thursday and Saturday) and RM90 with Ekspres Bahagia (at 10 am on Wednesday, Friday and Sunday). The boats actually land in Belawan in Sumatra, and the journey to Medan is completed by bus (45 minutes, included in the price).

These companies also run ferries from Georgetown to Kuah on Langkawi (4½ hours) at 8 am daily. The fare is RM45/35 in 1st/2nd class with KPLFS and RM35 with Ekspres Bahagia. The Star Express (☎ 324 4677) runs a faster car ferry from Butterworth to Pantai Tengah on Langkawi at noon and 6 pm (three hours, RM50/75 off-peak/peak).

Getting Around
To/From the Airport Penang's Bayan Lepas airport is 18km south of Georgetown. A coupon system operates for taxis from the airport. The fare to Georgetown is RM19.

Yellow bus No 83 goes to the airport from Pengkalan Weld or Lebuh China from 6 am to 9 pm. Taxis take about 45 minutes from the centre of town, the bus at least an hour.

Bus There are three main bus departure points in Georgetown, and half a dozen bus companies. The Transit Link city buses all depart from the terminal at Lebuh Victoria, which is directly in front of the ferry terminal. Most Transit Link buses also go along Lebuh Chulia, so you can pick them up at the stops along that street.

The other main stand is at Pengkalan Weld, next to the ferry terminal. Transit Link buses all run via Pengkalan Weld, but the other company buses – Yellow Bus, Hin Bus, Sri Negara, Lim Seng and Orient Minibus – all depart from there. Fares around town vary, but are typically under RM1. For the beaches take Hin Bus No 93 from Lebuh Chulia.

For around RM5 you can make the circuit of the island by public transport. Start with a Yellow Bus No 66 and hop off at the snake temple, though this run-down temple is easily missed. This bus will take you all the way to Balik Pulau, from where you have to change to another Yellow Bus, a No 76 for Teluk Bahang. There are only a few per day, roughly every 2¼ hours from 7.30 am to 7.15 pm, so it's wise to leave Georgetown early and check the departure times when you reach Balik Pulau. At Teluk Bahang you're on the northern beach strip, and you simply take a Transit Link bus No 202 or a blue Hin Bus No 93 to Georgetown via Batu Ferringhi.

Taxi Penang's taxis are all metered, but getting the drivers to use the meters is virtually impossible, so it's a matter of negotiating the fare before you set off. Some sample fares from Georgetown are: Penang Hill/Kek Lok Si (RM8), Botanical Gardens (RM10), Snake Temple (RM15), Batu Ferringhi (RM18) and the airport (RM19).

Motorcycle & Bicycle Most of the hotels catering to travellers have bicycles for hire for RM8, as do the shops along Lebuh Chulia. Motorbikes cost from RM25 to RM30.

Trishaw Bicycle rickshaws are ideal on Georgetown's relatively uncrowded streets and cost around RM1.50 per km or, for sightseeing, around RM15 per hour. As with the taxis, agree on the fare before departure.

Ferry There's a 24 hour vehicle ferry service between Georgetown and Butterworth. Ferries run every eight minutes from 7 am to 9 pm, then every 20 minutes until 12 am, then every 40 minutes until 7 am. Fares are only charged from Butterworth to Penang; the other direction is free. The adult fare is 60 sen; cars cost around RM7, depending on the size.

ALOR SETAR

The capital of Kedah state is on the mainland north of Penang on the main road to the Thai border, and it's also the turn-off point for Kuala Perlis, from where ferries run to Pulau Langkawi. People seldom stay long in Alor Setar but it has a few places of interest.

The large, open town square has a number of interesting buildings around its perimeter. The **Balai Besar** (Big Hall) was built in 1898

and is still used by the sultan of Kedah for ceremonial functions. Next door, the **Muzium Di Raja** is a former royal palace with royal family memorabilia. **Zahir Mosque**, the state mosque completed in 1912, is one of the largest and grandest mosques in Malaysia. The **Balai Nobat**, an octagonal building topped by an onion-shaped dome, houses the *nobat* (royal orchestra).

Places to Stay
There are a number of cheap hotels around the bus and taxi stations in the centre of town. The *Sing Tak Sing Hotel* (☎ 732 5482) above the bus station at 74 Jalan Langgar is one of the cheapest in town, with rooms from RM18. The *Hotel Mahawangsa* (☎ 732 1433) at 449 Jalan Raja, opposite the main post office, is a step up and has air-con rooms at RM49.

Getting There & Away
The central bus station on Jalan Langgar has buses to Butterworth (1½ hours, RM4.25) and Kuala Kedah (30 minutes, RM1). The small station north of the centre on Jalan Sultan Badlishah has buses to Bukit Kayu Hitam on the Thai border. The Shahab Perdana express bus station, 4km north of the town centre, has long-distance buses to KL, Melaka, Johor Bahru and Singapore.

The train station is close to the centre of town. The *International Express* to Hat Yai and Bangkok comes through around 4 pm, but you'll need to book well in advance. Alternatively, take the 6 am (approximate time) express train to Hat Yai (three hours, RM8), a scenic alternative to the buses.

KUALA PERLIS
This small port town in the extreme north-west of the peninsula is visited mainly as the departure point for Langkawi. If you get stuck, the *Asia Hotel*, 1.5km from the ferry on the road out of town, has basic rooms for RM25. The *Pens Hotel* (☎ 985 4122) is a good mid-range hotel on the main street in the centre of town.

Getting There & Away
A new bus station is under construction near the ferry terminal. Most services go to Kangar, but there are also direct buses to Butterworth, Alor Setar, KL and Padang Besar (for Thailand). The per person taxi fare to Kangar is RM3.25, or RM11.50 to Padang Besar.

Ferries to Kuah on Pulau Langkawi leave roughly hourly from 8 am to 6 pm, and cost RM12.

LANGKAWI

The 104 islands of the Langkawi group are 30km off the coast from Kuala Perlis, at the northern end of Peninsular Malaysia. They are accessible by ferry from Kuala Perlis, Kuala Kedah, Penang and Butterworth, and by air from Penang and KL.

Langkawi is pleasant enough and has some good beaches, but the mostly upmarket resorts don't have the atmosphere of the islands on the east coast, though they do have beer, and cheap beer at that, thanks to the island's duty-free status. Langkawi has seen a lot of government-promoted tourist development and luxury hotels are popping up everywhere, but it is not yet totally spoiled.

During school holidays, and at the peak time from November to February, Langkawi gets very crowded, but at other times of the year supply far exceeds demand and the prices come down considerably.

By motorbike you can tour the island taking in **waterfalls** (Telaga Tujuh), a rather pathetic **hot spring**, a legendary **tomb** and other points of interest. The best known beaches are **Pantai Tengah**, **Pantai Cenang** and **Pantai Kok**, on the west coast at the opposite side of the island from the main town, Kuah.

Places to Stay & Eat

Kuah Kuah has seen the greatest tourist development in recent years, which is hard to understand given its lack of beaches. If you get stuck, the *Hotel Langkawi* (☎ 966 6248), about 1km from the ferry pier, has small windowless boxes for RM25, and better air-con rooms for RM50. Nearby, the *Asia Hotel* (☎ 966 6216) has air-con rooms with bathroom from RM50.

Pantai Tengah Just south of the headland separating this beach from Pantai Cenang are three budget places all charging RM35 for basic chalets and from RM65 for air-con bungalows – *Green Hill Beach Motel* (☎ 955 1935), the *Sugary Sands* (☎ 955 3473) and the *Tanjung Malie* (☎ 955 1895).

At the mid-range *Sunset Beach Resort* (☎ 955 1751), brick chalets with bathrooms and air-con cost RM55/80/100 for small/medium/large rooms. There is a good restaurant and bar right on the beach.

The *Oasis Beach Pub* also serves more than passable food.

Pantai Cenang Pantai Cenang is easily the liveliest beach strip, with a wide range of accommodation, but the budget places are expensive by Malaysian standards.

2020 Chalets (☎ 955 2806) is a reasonable budget option, with chalets for RM35 and larger chalets for RM70 with air-con. Further north is *Samila* (☎ 955 1964), with cramped and unattractive chalets from RM40 with bath.

The *AB Motel* (☎ 955 1300) is one of the older places facing the beach. Big chalets among palms are reasonable value at RM40, or RM70 with air-con. Next door, the *Sandy Beach Resort* (☎ 955 1308) is popular but can be very crowded. A-frame chalets cost RM50 for a double with fan and bath, or air-con rooms are RM90.

The *Grand Beach Hotel* (☎ 955 1457) has simple beachfront chalets with bath – a good deal at RM35. Larger, more luxurious air-con chalets cost RM100. The *Langkapuri Beach Resort* (☎ 955 1202) offers small, comfortable cottages for RM95 to RM160.

Pantai Cenang has some good restaurants. The *Hot Wok Cafe*, opposite the Semarak Resort, has very good Chinese and western food, and seafood is featured.

Pantai Kok Until recently Pantai Kok was the cheapest and most laid-back beach on the island. The beach is open to the public, but all budget and mid-range accommodation has been removed to make way for a golf course. Only four upmarket resorts remain.

Getting There & Away

Air Malaysia Airlines (☎ 966 6622) has direct daily flights between Langkawi and KL (RM140), Penang (RM56), Johor Bahru (RM199) and Singapore (RM333).

Boat From 8 am to 6 pm ferries operate roughly every hour in either direction between Kuah and the mainland ports of Kuala Perlis (one hour, RM12) and Kuala Kedah (1½ hours, RM15).

Daily ferries also run from Kuah to Georgetown on Penang (4½ hours). The KPLFS ferry (RM45/35 1st/2nd class) leaves at 6.15 pm, and the Ekspres Bahagia ferry (RM35) departs at 5.50 pm. The faster Superstar Express (RM50/75 weekdays/weekends) runs from Langkawi's Teluk Baru jetty to Butterworth, opposite Penang.

There are also up to six daily ferries (between 9 am and 5 pm) from Kuah to Satun (RM18) on the Thai coast. From Satun buses and taxis go to Hat Yai.

Getting Around

Bus The bus station in Kuah is in front of the City Bayview Hotel, but apart from a bus from the jetty to the centre of Kuah (RM1), the only (infrequent) service is to Pantai Cenang (RM1.70).

Taxi Taxis are the main way of getting around, but fares are high. From the Kuah jetty fares are: Kuah town RM5, airport RM15, Pantai Cenang/Pantai Tengah RM12 and Pantai Kok RM20.

Motorcycle & Bicycle The easiest way to get around is to hire a motorbike (usually a Honda 70 step-thru) for RM25 per day or a mountain bike for RM12.

Peninsular Malaysia – East Coast

JOHOR BAHRU TO MERSING

Most travellers head directly to Mersing from Johor Bahru. There are a couple of en-route stops, but they are mainly weekend retreats for Singaporeans.

Around 15km north-west of **Kota Tinggi**, which is 42km from JB, are the waterfalls at **Lumbong**. Accommodation at the falls has become expensive, but there are cheaper options in Kota Tinggi.

Johor Lama was the seat of the sultanate following Melaka's fall to the Portuguese. Today the old fort of Kota Batu, overlooking the river, has been restored. It is best visited by share-taxi from JB or Kota Tinggi.

Beach resorts are mainly the preserve of wealthy Singaporeans in this part of the world. A turn-off 13km north of Kota Tinggi leads down 24km of rather rough road to the sheltered waters of **Jason's Bay**. There are more developed resorts at **Desaru**, 88km east of JB and also reached via Kota Tinggi. If you're really keen, try the *Desaru Golden Beach Hotel* (✆ 822 1205), which has a campground with sites for an inflated RM10 per person. Buses (RM3.50) and taxis (RM20) run from Kota Tinggi to Desaru.

MERSING

Mersing is a small fishing village on the east coast of Peninsular Malaysia. It's the main departure point for boats to Pulau Tioman and other islands of the Seribuat archipelago lying just off the coast in the South China Sea.

Places to Stay

Omar's Backpackers Hostel (✆ 799 5096) on Jalan Abu Bakar is the traveller's place, with clean dorm beds for RM7 and good-value doubles for RM15. Ask about the hostel's one-day island tour and cultural tours.

The *Sheikh Tourist Agency* (✆ 799 3767) has decent dorm beds for RM6, and an in-house travel agency which can provide details about island accommodation and transport. Both places are roughly opposite the post office, a few hundred metres before the boat dock.

Near the second roundabout on Jalan Abu Bakar, the *Comfort Guesthouse* (✆ 799 6911) is another good choice, with clean, semi-partitioned dorm beds for RM10. Those starved for Internet access can log on here for RM7.50 per half hour.

The best value hotel in Mersing is the popular *Hotel Embassy* (✆ 799 3545) on Jalan Ismail near the roundabout, where clean, comfortable rooms with attached bath, hot water and fan cost RM25, or RM35 with air-con.

Places to Eat

There are several places around town for a roti canai and coffee breakfast, the best of which is the *Restoran Al-Arif*, which also serves excellent Indian food for lunch and dinner.

For inexpensive Chinese fare, including breakfast, try the *Ee Lo* restaurant near the second roundabout.

For good seafood, try the air-con *Mersing Seafood Restaurant*, which costs a little more than some but turns out consistently tasty fare.

For Malaysian fare, try the *Plaza R&R*, which has a small food court with hawker stalls selling the usual favourites.

Lastly, for good western-style meals at any hour try the *Rio Del Mar* restaurant on Jalan Abu Bakar. The menu includes tacos, salads, burgers, pizzas and beer.

Getting There & Away

Mersing is 133km north of JB and 189km south of Kuantan. Most long-distance buses start and terminate at the R&R Plaza near the jetty. Destinations include Singapore (RM11), JB (RM11), Melaka (RM11.20), KL (RM16.60), Ipoh (RM26) and Penang (RM35). The ticket booths are at the back of the plaza.

Most north-bound long-distance buses stop at the Restoran Malaysia on the roundabout.

Destinations include Kuantan (RM10.35), Kuala Terengganu (RM16.10) and Kota Bharu (RM25).

The local bus and long-distance taxi station is on Jalan Sulaiman near the river. Taxi destinations include: Kota Tinggi (RM10), JB (RM15), Pekan (RM15), Kuantan (RM20) and Melaka (RM30).

PULAU TIOMAN

Pulau Tioman is the largest and most spectacular of the east coast islands. It may not be the isolated paradise it once was, but its sheer size (39km long and 12km wide) affords a diversity of attractions like **snorkelling**, **diving**, **jungle trekking** or just lazing around on the beach.

Note that the island can get crowded during holiday periods. Also be warned that the island's beaches are home to a large population of sandflies, and some travellers suffer very badly from their bites. The only way to avoid them is to stay off the beach.

Beaches

Air Batang Usually referred to as ABC, Air Batang is a popular beach just over the headland to the north of Kampung Tekek. Along with Salang, it's the main travellers' centre, with a lazy string of chalet operations connected by a concrete path that runs the length of the beach. The northern end of the beach is rocky and poor for swimming; the southern end, near Nazri's, has the best white-sand beach.

Salang In terms of swimming and easy access to a variety of restaurants and activities, Salang is probably Tioman's best place to be based. It is also popular with divers. Two of Tioman's better dive centres are here as well.

Juara The only place to stay on the east coast of the island, Juara is less developed and quieter than most of the other beaches on the west coast. The beach is excellent. This is a place for serious relaxation, since there is little to do except swim and laze away the day under the coconut trees.

Places to Stay & Eat

Most foreign travellers gravitate to Air Batang, Salang or Juara (the southern beaches are more popular with package-tourists from Singapore). Salang is the most crowded of the three, but it is the place to be if you want a variety of restaurants and some drinks in the

evening. Air Batang is less cluttered and more relaxing, while Juara is the place to get away from it all. The main village of Kampung Tekek is too run-down to recommend.

The cheap A-frame accommodation is gradually disappearing and being replaced with chalets. Prices range from RM10 to RM50, though the offerings at the bottom of the scale can be pretty grotty.

As for food, many travellers find Tioman a disappointment. Aside from a few mediocre independent restaurants, most places to eat are attached to chalet operations, with the same limited menu. The best bet is to look for a place offering a barbecue of fresh seafood. There are also small general stores for self-catering in ABC, Tekek and Salang.

Air Batang Stepping off the jetty and heading north, the first place along ABC you come to is *South Pacific* (☎ 419 1176), a basic place offering chalets with fan for RM18, and air-con for RM65. Next along is *Johan's House* (☎ mobile 011-664 257), slightly more attractive, with chalets with fan for RM18, and air-con for RM75.

After Johan's is the *Tioman Guest House* (☎ 419 1196), where clean chalets cost RM25/35 for singles/doubles with fan, and RM70 with air-con.

After the Tioman Guest House, *Rinda House* (☎ 419 1957) has simple, clean chalets with fan for RM15. Given the price, this is one of the better value places in ABC. After Rinda is *Nazri's Beach Cabanas* (☎ mobile 011-333 486). More commonly known as Nazri's II, its bungalows are large and fairly clean, ranging in price from RM30 to RM100.

Just past Nazri's Beach Cabanas is the popular *ABC Bungalows* (☎ 419 1154), with a variety of chalets spread over pleasant, well tended grounds. The simplest huts with fan and no bath cost RM10, while standard huts with fan and bath cost RM25.

Finally, at the far northern end of the beach are the lovely *Bamboo Hill Chalets* (☎ 419 1339, email bamboosu@tm.net.my). With only six chalets ranging in cost from RM50 to RM100, the place is almost always full – calling ahead is a good idea. The owners will refill water bottles with filtered water for RM1 per 1.5l bottle (nonguests are welcome to bring empties). Bamboo Hill also produces an informative leaflet about the island and sells phone cards.

Working south from the ABC jetty, you soon come to *Mawar Resort* (☎ 419 1153),

PULAU TIOMAN (TIOMAN ISLAND)

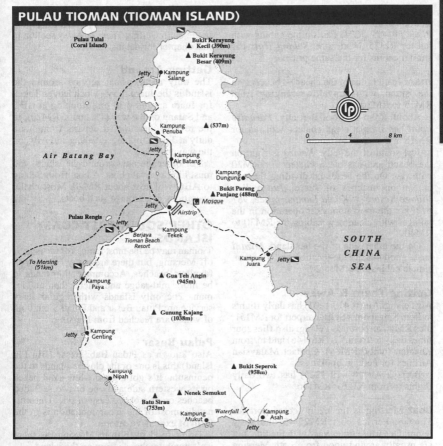

one of the better places on the beach, with clean fan cabins for RM25/30. Next along is *Mohktar's Place* (☎ *419 1148*), a simple place with fan cabins for RM20.

The last place before the headland, *Nazri's Place* (☎ *mobile 011-349 534*) is popular with travellers and lays claim to the best stretch of beach on ABC. Accommodation ranges from RM12 to RM70.

Penuba Bay Over the headland from ABC, the *Penuba Inn Resort* (☎ *mobile 011-952 963*) has 30 chalets with fan and bath for RM30 to RM56, with air-con for RM60 to RM150. The chalets are built on a hill overlooking the bay and are very attractive.

Salang The main places of interest to trav-

ellers are south of the jetty. *Khalid's Place* (☎ *mobile 011-953 421*) is a popular option. Standard chalets cost RM35, or there are larger chalets for RM60/100 with air-con.

Across the small creek is another cluster of chalet outfits. Most of these are cheap but grim. An exception is *Zaid's* (☎ *419 5019*), which has chalets with fan for RM50 for two people and RM65 for three.

The *Indah Salang* (☎ *413 1406*) is the second place north of the jetty, and it sprawls along the beach for some distance. Clean, basic bungalows with fan are RM30, and nicer cabins with air-con are RM80.

The *Salang Beach Resort* (☎ *799 3607*) is another resort-style operation, with a Chinese restaurant and pricey chalets – RM40 with fan, or RM110 and upwards with air-con.

Near the north end of the beach are two small, cheap bungalow operations. *Ella's Place* (☎ *419 5004*) has simple cabins with fan for RM25. Next door, *Salang Huts* has similar cabins for the same price.

Juara Juara is one of the cheapest beaches on the island, with bungalows ranging from RM15 to RM30.

About 150m north of the jetty, *Paradise Point* has simple, clean chalets with fan for RM15 and a small restaurant.

Just south of the jetty, *Kejora* is right on the beach and has clean chalets for RM20 with fan. On the headland dividing the two half-moon beaches of Juara, *Juara Bay Village Resort* (☎ *Kuala Lumpur office, 981 6122*) is the most upmarket operation in the village, with clean new cabins for RM30 to RM40.

On the other side of the headland, *Mizani* has a good beach-side location and pleasant, simple cabins for RM15/20.

Getting There & Away

Air Pelangi Air (☎ *419 1301*) has daily flights to/from Singapore's Seletar airport for RM151, plus RM40 airport tax. Pelangi also flies four times daily to/from KL (RM146) and to/from Kuantan (daily, RM84). Contact Malaysian Airlines for Pelangi bookings.

Berjaya Air (☎ *419 1303*) has two daily flights to/from KL for RM146.

Boat Mersing is the main access port for Tioman. Ferries cost RM25/45 one way/ return. Departure times vary with the tide, but are usually around noon from both Mersing and Tioman (ask at the place you're staying for the next day's sailing times). From Mersing, ferries leave from the main jetty and stop at Genting, Paya, the Resort, Tekek, ABC and Salang, in that order, picking up from those jetties in the reverse order on the return trip. Sailing time averages about two hours.

There are also several speedboat companies that do the trip between Mersing and Tioman in 1½ hours for RM30 one way. These operate from the same jetties as the big ferries and depart several times a day, making them a good option if you've missed the day's ferry sailings.

It may also be possible to go from Tanjong Gemok, 38km north of Mersing. However, at the time of writing, there were no regular ferry services.

There are also direct services to and from Singapore. See the sea entry under Singapore in the main Getting There & Away section in this chapter for details.

Getting Around

The only regular boat service around the island is the Juara ferry, which leaves Tekek for Juara around 4.30 pm, stopping at ABC and Salang on the way (1½ hours, RM20). In the reverse direction, it departs from Juara daily at 3 pm, stopping at Salang and ABC on the way to Tekek.

For other journeys around the island, you must hire a private boat. A boat from Salang to ABC will cost about RM20. Most chalet operations can arrange such boats.

OTHER SOUTH-EAST COAST ISLANDS

Tioman may be the most famous of the islands off Mersing, but there are many others with fabulous beaches. Accommodation tends to be more mid-range and pricier than at Tioman. The only islands with regular ferry service are Pulau Besar and Pulau Sibu, both of which are reached from Mersing.

Pulau Besar

Also known as Pulau Babi Besar (Big Pig Island) this is one of the closest islands to the peninsula. It's got a good white-sand beach on its western side and one or two secluded beaches on its isolated eastern side. Unfortunately, most of the accommodation is in the form of expensive resorts.

Bring food over from Mersing, as there isn't much to choose from on the island.

Places to Stay Budget travellers can try the four *A-frames* in front of the D'Coconut Resort a little north of the jetty which rent for RM30 per night (call D'Coconut below for details).

Further north along the beach, *Pulau Besar Chalet* (☎ *mobile 010-775 8136*) is a simple place with clean bungalows for RM40.

Getting There & Away Regular ferries to Besar (RM18 one way) leave from the main Mersing jetty daily at around 9 am and 12.30 pm. Return ferries leave Besar daily at around 10.30 am and 2 pm. The ride takes a little under an hour.

Pulau Sibu

Easily accessible and quiet, Sibu is a good option for those who want to escape the crowds on larger islands like Tioman. The island has some good white-sand beaches and decent coral.

Places to Stay Most travellers gravitate to *O&H Kampung Huts* (☎ 07-799 5096/mobile 011-354 322) in the middle of the island on the eastern side. It's a friendly place with A-frames without bathrooms for RM27 to RM35, and chalets with bathrooms for RM55 to RM65.

Getting There & Away Boats to Sibu leave from Tanjung Leman, about 30km south of Mersing. Taxis from Mersing to the jetty cost about RM40 for the whole car.

Most resorts operate their own boats to the island, but for RM20 they will take nonguests over to the island. It's best to show up at the jetty around noon to be sure of catching a boat over. The trip takes about 30 minutes.

KUANTAN

About midway up the east coast from Singapore to Kota Bharu, Kuantan is the capital of the state of Pahang and the start of the east-coast beach strip which extends all the way to Kota Bharu.

Kuantan is a pleasant enough city/town but its importance to travellers is mainly as a stopover en route to other places.

Information

The tourist office (☎ 513 3026) is by the local taxi station, opposite the Kompleks Terantum shopping mall. The post office, Telekom office and most of the banks are on Jalan Mahkota near the huge and soaring Sultan Ahmed I Mosque.

Places to Stay

On Jalan Mahkota near the local taxi station, the *Min Heng Hotel* is the cheapest in town at RM16 for rooms with common bath. It should only be considered as a last resort. Not much better is the *Tong Nam Ah Hotel* (☎ 514 4204) on Jalan Besar near the taxi station where rooms start at RM15.

The *Hotel Baru Raya* is better with rooms for RM29 with fan and attached bath, or singles/doubles with air-con for RM39/49. The rooms are clean but the bathrooms are on the dirty side.

For a room with attached bath, the *New Capital Hotel* (☎ 513 5222), 55 Jalan Bukit Ubi, is a good choice. It has clean rooms for RM22 with fan and bath, or RM32 with air-con and bath.

Near the central market are a few good hotels. The *Hotel Makmur* (☎ 514 1363) has rooms with shared bath for RM28, and with attached bath for RM35; all rooms have air-con. Most rooms have no windows, but the place is fairly new and close to the bus station.

Places to Eat

Kuantan has a good selection of places to eat. The small *Muslim food stalls* dotted along the riverbank, across from the Hotel Baru Raya, are a great place to sit and watch the boats pass by. The food stalls set up near the *central market* are also very good.

There are indoor food courts in all of Kuantan's shopping centres, most of which have at least one fast-food place like *KFC*. The best indoor food court is the one in the giant *Megamall shopping centre*, near the long-distance bus station.

There are some good Indian restaurants on Jalan Bukit Ubi, past Jalan Gambut, including the *Restoran Biryani* and the *Restoran Parvathy*. Another good Indian choice is *Restoran Tawakkal* on Jalan Haji Abdul Aziz, near the mosque, which has good daily specials and tasty murtabak.

The best Chinese in town can be had at *New Yee Mee*. Dinners cost from RM10 to RM20 and noodle breakfasts RM5 with tea.

For something resembling a western-style breakfast in the morning and a variety of western and Malaysian dishes throughout the day, try the air-con *Swan Bakery* on Jalan Bukit Ubi. It also serves a variety of fresh juices.

Getting There & Away

Air Malaysia Airlines (☎ 515 7055) has direct flights to Singapore (twice weekly, RM244) and KL (daily, RM74), among others.

Pelangi Air (☎ 538 1177) has flights to Pulau Tioman (daily, RM84).

Bus All the bus companies have their offices on the 2nd floor of the enormous new express bus station on Jalan Stadium. There is an information office on the second floor of the building near the food court.

Destinations include Kuala Terengganu (RM9), Mersing (RM11), KL (RM12), Johor Bahru (RM16), Singapore (RM16.50), and Kota Bharu (RM16). For Taman Negara, direct buses to Jerantut (RM8.50) leave between 9 am and 3 pm.

For Cherating, take the No 27 Kemaman bus from the local bus station for RM2.50.

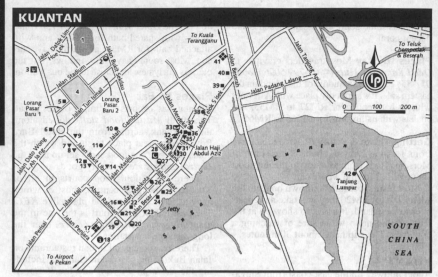

KUANTAN

PLACES TO STAY		7	Food Stalls	18	Tourist Office
5	Hotel Makmur	8	Restaurant Panvathy	19	Taxi Station
6	Hotel Pacific	9	Restoran Biryani	20	Local Bus Station;
12	New Capital Hotel;	13	Food Stalls		Food Stalls
	Restoran Parvathy	14	Swan Bakery	26	Moneychanger;
16	Min Heng Hotel	15	Food Stalls		Hamid Bros Books
21	Hotel Baru Raya	23	Outdoor Food Stalls	27	Local Bus Stop for
22	Tong Nam Ah Hotel	31	Restoran Tawakkal		Northbound Buses
24	Samudra River View Hotel	35	New Yee Mee	28	Mosque Sultan Ahmed I
25	Hotel Classic			29	Maybank
34	Suraya Hotel	**OTHER**		30	Standard Chartered Bank
36	Hotel Embassy	1	Stadium	32	Telekom
37	Titi Hotel	2	Long-Distance Bus	33	Post Office
39	Hotel New Meriah		Station	38	Mr Dobi Laundry Service
40	M.S. Garden Hotel	3	Hindu Temple	41	Megamall Shopping
		10	Immigration		Centre
PLACES TO EAT		11	Malaysia Airlines	42	Kampung Tanjung
4	Central Market	17	Kompleks Teruntum		Lumpur

Taxi The long-distance taxi station is in the same building as the long-distance bus station. Regular destinations include Pekan (RM5), Cherating (RM7), Mersing (RM20), Jerantut (RM20), Kuala Terengganu (RM24), KL (RM30) and Johor Bahru (R45).

AROUND KUANTAN

The coast north of Kuantan has some decent if rather shallow beaches.

Beserah

The small fishing village of Beserah, just 10km from Kuantan, is very pleasant. Unfortunately, there is no accommodation available here.

Buses to Kemaman (No 27), Balok (No 30) and Sungai Karang (No 28) all pass through Beserah. They leave from the main bus station in Kuantan, and the fare is 60 sen. Taxis from Kuantan cost RM6.

Gua Charas

Gua Charas (Charas Caves) is a limestone outcrop with caves that contain some Thai statuary. Take the Sungai Lembing bus (No 48) from the main bus station in Kuantan and get off at the small village of Panching. From there it's a hot 4km walk each way – hitching is possible. A taxi from Kuantan to the caves should cost RM25.

TASIK CHINI

Tasik Chini is a series of 12 lakes, situated about 60km west of Kuantan, and around its shores live the Jakun people, an Orang Asli tribe. It's a very beautiful area and you can walk for miles in jungle territory and stay at the nearby Orang Asli village of **Kampung Gumum**.

Places to Stay & Eat

The *Lake Cini Resort* (☎ 456 7897), on the southern shore of the lake, has good cabins with attached bathroom from RM77 for doubles. Some cabins are also set aside for dormitory accommodation – a bed in a 10-bed cabin costs RM18.50, plus a 10% service charge.

A much cheaper option is *Rajan Jones Guest House* in the Orang Asli settlement of Kampung Gumum, a two minute boat ride from the resort or a 30 minute walk. Accommodation is extremely basic – there's no electricity or running water in the village – but it's a rare opportunity to stay near the jungle. The cost is RM15 per person, including dinner and breakfast.

Getting There & Away

The tourist information stand in Kuantan can arrange day trips to Tasik Chini for RM50 per person, but the cheapest tours are from Cherating at RM35 per person. Doing it yourself is difficult. From Kuantan, catch a bus to Maran and get off at the Tasik Chini turn-off, from where it's 12km to Kampung Belimbing. You will have to hitch or walk, and traffic on this road is light. From Belimbing you can hire a boat to Tasik Chini. The cost is RM60 per boat for the beautiful two hour trip.

The alternative is to take a bus to Felda Chini, south of the lake, from Kuantan or Pekan. Take a Mara No 121 bus marked 'Cini' (two hours, RM5.70) and then hire a motorcycle (RM5) or a taxi to take you the 11km to the lake.

CHERATING

Cherating is one of the most popular travellers' centres on the east coast. Complete with budget shacks by the sea, a handful of bars, some good restaurants and a reasonable beach with windsurfer breezes, Cherating is as close as the east coast gets to southern Thailand.

Cherating is also a good base from which to explore the surrounding area. You can arrange mini-treks and river trips, and most of the places to stay can arrange tours to Tasik Chini and Gua Charas, among others. The two travel agents on the main road also organise tours and bus tickets.

Information

There's no bank in Cherating, but you can change US cash at La Pippins restaurant on the beach. A few other places, including the two travel agents on the main road, will change travellers cheques and cash, but the rate is poor.

Places to Stay

Accommodation ranges from basic A-frame huts, each with a double mattress and light but no fan, to more comfortable 'chalets' with bathrooms. Most of the A-frame huts cost around RM10 and sleep two people; chalets range from RM15 to RM50.

Maznah's Guest House is a good choice for those on a tight budget. Very basic A-frames rent for RM12, and the price includes breakfast and a home-cooked Malaysian dinner!

One of the best places for an extended stay is the *Matahari Chalets* (☎ 581 9126). Large rooms with balcony, fridge (yes, fridge), mosquito net and fan are a bargain at RM20. It's a very relaxed place, and you can do batik courses here.

One of the most interesting places in Cherating is the *Green Leaves Inn* (☎ mobile 010-337 8242). Right on the banks of the river, and set in among low trees, the place invites lengthy stays. Its few chalets are very small and the facilities quite basic, but the cool atmosphere and friendly owner make up for any shortcomings.

On the same side of the road is the *Payung Cafe* (☎ mobile 012-303 3911), also on the riverbank. There are a few chalets around a large lawn; those on the river cost RM20, and those nearer the road cost RM15. Its restaurant is quite good.

Nearby is the attractive *Tanjung Inn*

(☎ 581 9081). It's sited on a pleasant lawn area, and chalets with bath and fan cost RM45; there are also family chalets for RM65.

Towards the eastern end of the main road is the *Ranting Holiday Resort (☎ 581 9068)*. It's one of the better mid-budget choices, with clean cottages with fan and attached bath for RM40 (with air-con for RM60).

This is by no means an exhaustive list of Cherating accommodation – if these places are all full, just take a stroll down any of the streets in town and you'll find loads of other options.

Places to Eat
Most guesthouses have their own restaurants, but there are also a few other restaurants in Cherating, all within easy walking distance of each other.

Mimi's does delicious banana roti canai for breakfast, and gets good reviews for lunch and dinner as well. The *Payung Cafe* is a good spot for dinner, offering two daily specials, one Malay and one western style, for RM10 each.

For Chinese and Malay food, there are the *Lianee Cafe*, the *Restoran Riverside*, the *Blue Lagoon Restoran* and the *Susah Dilupakan* restaurants on the beach road, all of which offer similar dishes and prices.

The *Pop In Steakhouse & Pub* does good steaks for around RM25, and has a few other dishes on the menu as well. Down by the beach, *La Pippins* does good western-style breakfasts and dinners, as well as satay. Located next to La Blues bar, this is a great spot for a late-night snack, as it stays open until 3 am.

Entertainment
There are a few bars scattered around the town, the most popular of which are *The Pop Inn Steakhouse & Pub* and *La Blues Bar*. The Pop Inn often has live music and is a good place to start your evening, as it also serves food. La Blues Bar, pleasantly located right on the beach, is a good place to rage until the wee hours of the morning.

Getting There & Away
To get to Cherating, catch one of the hourly buses (one hour, RM2.50) marked 'Kemaman' from the main bus station in Kuantan. When coming from the north, any bus going to Kuantan will be able to drop you on the main road.

RANTAU ABANG
This is the principal **turtle beach** and the prime area for spotting the great leatherback turtles during the egg-laying season.

The **Turtle Information Centre**, close to the main budget accommodation area, has a few decent displays. The centre is open every day during the turtle-watching season (May to August), but otherwise closed on Friday and public holidays. Note that the nearest bank is at Kuala Dungun, 22km south.

August is the peak egg-laying season, when you have a decent chance of seeing turtles, but you may also be lucky in June and July. Full moon and high-tide nights are said to be best. The turtles are the east coast's primary tourist attraction – unfortunately, this has resulted in a decline in turtle numbers. The government is making a concerted effort to protect the turtles and their egg-laying habitat. The beach is now divided into three sections during the season – prohibited, semi-public (where you have to buy tickets) and free access – in an attempt to control the crowds.

Places to Stay & Eat
Right on the beach, just south of the Turtle Information Centre, are two travellers' places. *Awang's (☎ 844 3500)* is the more popular of the two. Singles/doubles with fan and bath go for RM10/20; there are also air-con family rooms (two double beds and one single) available for RM60 to RM80.

The *Ismail Beach Resort (☎ 844 1054)* next door has similar rooms for RM20 with bath and fan, and RM80 with two double beds and air-con. It's worth having a quick look at both places before making a decision on which to stay at. Both Awang's and Ismail offer discount rates off season.

Both of the above-mentioned guesthouses have attached *restaurants*. You'll also find a *stand* near the Turtle Information Centre selling snacks and drinks.

Getting There & Away
Rantau Abang is only about 22km north of Kuala Dungun, which in turn is 80km south of Kuala Terengganu and 138km north of Kuantan. The nearest airport is at Kerteh, where there are flights to Kuantan, Kuala Terengganu and KL.

Dungun-Kuala Terengganu buses run in both directions every hour from 7 am to 6 pm, and there's a bus stop near the Turtle Information Centre. Rantau Abang to Kuala

Terengganu costs RM4; to Dungun costs RM1.50. Heading south you can try to hail a long-distance bus, or take the bus to Kuala Dungun, from where hourly buses go to Kuantan, as well as to Mersing, Singapore and KL.

MARANG

Marang is a picturesque fishing village on the mouth of the Sungai Marang, though it is being rapidly modernised. The river is dotted with brightly painted boats, the water is clear and thick with fish, and there are good beaches in the south of town. It is also the departure point for Pulau Kapas. Marang is a conservative village, however, especially across the river from the main town, and reserve in dress and behaviour is recommended.

Places to Stay & Eat

Most of the travellers' places are on the lagoon to the north of the jetty.

The most popular spot with travellers is the pleasant *Green Mango Inn* (☎ 618 2040), located on a hill near the jetty. Singles/doubles with fan and common bath go for RM10/15. Chalets with fan and common bath go for RM20.

North of the jetty, *Kamal's Guest House* (☎ 618 2181) has rooms with fan and common bath for RM12, and for M16 with attached bath. Check a few rooms before deciding, as they are a mixed bag.

Nearby, the *Island View Resort* (☎ 618 2006) charges RM20 for rooms with fan and bathroom, and RM40 upwards for air-con rooms. The rooms are a little run-down.

On the hill behind Kamal's is the *Marang Guesthouse* (☎ 618 1976). It's a notch up from the other guesthouses, and has its own restaurant. Rooms with fan are RM20; nicer air-con rooms cost from RM50.

Getting There & Away

Marang is 30 minutes south of Kuala Terengganu, and regular buses run to and from Kuala Dungun and Kuala Terengganu. There is a ticket office near the town's main intersection. Express buses go twice daily to Kuantan/Cherating (RM8), KL (RM21.70) and Johor Bahru (RM22). The local bus fare is RM1 to Kuala Terengganu.

PULAU KAPAS

About 6km offshore from Marang is the beautiful little island of Kapas. There are jungle walks and good snorkelling, but the island is best avoided during holidays and long weekends, when it is overrun with day trippers.

Places to Stay & Eat

The *Kapas Garden Resort* (☎ mobile 011-984 1686) has chalets for RM50 with bath, or rooms for RM75 with bath and fan, including breakfast. The *Mak Cik Gemuk Beach Resort* (☎ 618 1221) has a wide range of accommodation from RM18 to RM50, but is not as nice.

The *Zaki Beach Chalet* (☎ 612 0258) is a cheap place, with longhouse rooms for RM20, or RM35 for chalets with bath, fan and mosquito nets. At the other end of the island, *Lighthouse* (☎ mobile 010-215 3558) is a budget spot popular with backpackers. All the rooms are in one elevated longhouse. Dorm beds go for RM10, and private rooms for RM20.

Getting There & Away

Boats to Kapas leave from the larger of the town's two jetties. Slow boats cost RM7.50 one way, but are gradually being replaced by speedboats which cost RM25 return. Most speedboat operators will only sell return tickets, and you must arrange a pick-up time with them when you purchase your ticket. There are usually departures at 8 and 9 am.

KUALA TERENGGANU

Standing on a promontory formed by the South China Sea on one side and the wide Sungai Terengganu on the other, Kuala Terengganu is the capital of Terengganu state, and the seat of the state's sultan. Oil revenue has transformed Kuala Terengganu from a sprawling, oversized fishing village of stilt houses into a medium-sized modern city. There is little to see or do around town and nothing to do by night. Most travellers use it as a staging post to visit nearby attractions such as **Tasik (Lake) Kenyir**, Merang and Marang.

Things to See

Kuala Terengganu's compact **Chinatown** can be found on Jalan Bandar. It comprises the usual array of hole-in-the-wall type Chinese shops, hairdressing salons and restaurants, as well as a sleepy Chinese temple and some narrow alleys leading to jetties on the waterfront.

MALAYSIA

KUALA TERENGGANU

PLACES TO STAY
1 Awi's Yellow House
2 Seri Malaysia Hotel
4 Terengganu Hotel
11 Seaview Hotel
14 Hotel Grand Continental
15 Ping Anchorage
16 Hotel Ten Tin Midtown
22 Seri Hoover
26 Kenangan Hotel
28 Hotel KT Mutiara
37 Park Royal Hotel
42 Motel Desa

PLACES TO EAT
3 Seri Binjai Restaurant
5 Restoran Cheng Cheng
23 Good Luck Restoran
24 Restoran Kari Asha
25 Sahara Tandori
27 A&W
36 Food Stalls
40 Batu Buruk Food Centre
41 Food Stalls

OTHER
6 Chinese Temple
7 Central Market
8 Istana Maziah
9 State Tourist Office
10 Post Office
12 Express Bus Station
13 Kompleks Taman Selera Tanjung
17 Convenience Store
18 Zainal Abidin Mosque
19 Main Bus Station
20 Long-Distance Taxi Stand
21 Telekom
29 Convenience Store
30 Maybank
31 Public Toilet
32 Immigration Office
33 Tourism Malaysia
34 Malaysia Airlines
35 Mosque
38 Hospital Terengganu
39 Cultural Centre

To Airport (5km), Merang (38km) & Kota Bharu (159km)

To Museum (3km)

To Tasik Kenyir (55km) & Sekayu Waterfall (56km)

South China Sea

Sungai Terengganu

Pantai Batu Buruk

Sports Ground Jalan Pantai Batu Buruk

To Suterasemai Centre (5km) & Marang (15km)

Pulau Wan Embong
Pulau Duyung Kecil
Pulau Duyung Besar
Chinatown

The central **market** is a lively, colourful spot, and the floor above the fish section has a good collection of batik and songket. Across the road from the market is a flight of stairs leading up to **Bukit Puteri**, a 200m hill with the remains of a fort and good views of the city.

The **Istana Maziah** – the sultan's palace – and the nearby **Zainal Abidin Mosque** make for good photographs. The jetty just south of Chinatown is the place for a 40 sen ferry ride to **Pulau Duyung Besar**, the largest island in the estuary.

Places to Stay

Ping Anchorage (☎ 622 0851), upstairs at 77A Jalan Dato Isaac, is the number-one travellers' place. It has a rooftop restaurant and bar, and organises tours to Pulau Kapas, Pulau Redang, Sekayu Falls, Lake Kenyir etc. Dorm beds are RM6; rooms are RM12 to RM15, RM20 with attached bath.

Awi's Yellow House is a unique guesthouse built on stilts over the river. It's in the boat-building village on Pulau Duyung Besar, a 15 minute ferry ride across the river. A bed with mosquito net costs RM5 per night in the open dorm, or the small thatched rooms are RM16. Tea and coffee are free and most people cook their own food, but there is a small restaurant next door. It's a beautiful, relaxed place and highly recommended. Take the ferry from the jetty near the Seri Malaysia Hotel.

The *Terengganu Hotel* (☎ 622 2900), at the western end of Jalan Sultan Ismail, is one of the cheaper options, with rooms at RM33 with fan, or RM38.50 with air-con and attached bath.

Another good mid-range hotel is the *Seaview Hotel* (☎ 622 1911) at 18A Jalan Masjid Abidin, close to the istana (palace). Clean rooms with fan and bath cost RM30, and those with air-con and bath cost RM45.

Places to Eat

The *Batu Buruk Food Centre* down by the beach and the food court on the 2nd floor of the *Kompleks Taman Selera Tanjung* are good places to seek out inexpensive Malay and Chinese food. The 2nd floor of the *central market* also has a good selection of inexpensive food stalls.

The *Restoran Cheng Cheng* at 224 Jalan

Bandar has the standard Chinese favourites for reasonable prices. For better Chinese fare, try the *Good Luck Restoran* on Jalan Kota Lama, which has an extensive menu and outside tables where you can sit and watch life roll by.

There are two decent Indian places on Jalan Air Jernih, *Sahara Tandori* and *Restoran Kari Asha*, both of which serve filling Indian meals for around RM5.

Getting There & Away

Air Malaysia Airlines (☎ 622 1415), 13 Jalan Sultan Omar, services Kuala Terengganu. There are direct flights daily to/from KL (RM104) and to/from Johor Bahru (RM149). A taxi to the airport costs RM15.

Bus Kuala Terengganu has a new bus station on Jalan Masjid Abidin that serves as a terminus for all local and many long-distance buses.

There are regular buses to Marang (RM1), Merang (RM2.30), Rantau Abang (RM3, terminates at Dungun), Kuala Besut (RM6), Kota Bharu (RM7.40), Kuantan (RM9), Mersing (RM18), KL (RM21.70), Johor Bahru (RM22.10), Singapore (RM23.10), Melaka (RM24) and Butterworth (RM24).

Note that some express buses depart from the express bus station in the north of town near the Kompleks Taman Selera Tanjung.

Taxi The main taxi stand is near the bus station. It costs RM4 (per person) to Marang, RM6 to Merang, RM8 to Rantau Abang, RM12 to Jerteh (for Kuala Besut), RM14 to Kota Bharu, RM15 to Kuantan and RM40/50 to KL.

Getting Around

Kuala Terengganu was once the trishaw capital of Malaysia, and while their numbers have dropped, they are still the main form of inner-city transport and cost roughly RM3 per kilometre. If you can't find a trishaw, taxis around town cost about RM5 for a short journey.

AROUND KUALA TERENGGANU
Tasik Kenyir

Tasik Kenyir (Lake Kenyir) has been developed as an 'eco-tourism' site by the state authorities, although the lake itself was formed by the construction of the Kenyir Dam in 1985. Watersports and waterfalls are the chief attractions here. You can also visit caves which border the lake, located within the boundaries of Taman Negara National Park.

Tasik Kenyir is best visited on a package tour from Kuala Terengganu (see the details on Ping Anchorage in the earlier KT Places to Stay section).

MERANG

The sleepy little fishing village of Merang (not to be confused with Marang) is 40km north of Kuala Terengganu. There's nothing to do here, but the beach is decent. Merang is also the place to get boats to Pulau Redang and other nearby islands.

Places to Stay & Eat

The best place to stay is the *Kembara Resort* (☎ 653 1770), about 500m south of the village (follow the signs from the main road). Dorm beds go for RM7, and pleasant chalets with fan and attached bath go for RM25. There are larger family chalets for RM35. A common kitchen is available for those who bring their own food.

In the centre of the village, the *Merang Inn* (☎ 653 1435) is a decent choice, with semi-detached chalets for RM35 with fan and bath, and RM60 with air-con. It also has one of the village's only restaurants.

Getting There & Away

There are daily buses from the main bus station in Kuala Terengganu to Merang (RM2.30). Taxis from Kuala Terengganu costs RM6 per person. Coming from the north is more difficult, and it is easiest to go south as far as Kuala Terengganu and then backtrack. Otherwise, taxis from Kota Bharu cost RM12 per person.

PULAU REDANG

One of the largest and least accessible of the east coast islands, Redang is also one of the most beautiful. Unfortunately, the island has been targeted by big developers, and there are few options for the independent traveller.

A small village is located on a bay at the southern end of the island, and the huge Berjaya Island Resort and golf course are hidden away on the north shore. Of most interest to travellers are the beautiful bays on the east side of the island including **Teluk Dalam**, **Teluk Kalong** and **Pasir Panjang**.

Note that the island basically shuts down

from 1 November to 1 March; the best season to visit is from mid-April to mid-September.

Places to Stay & Eat

Accommodation on Pulau Redang is best organised as a package in Kuala Terengganu. *Ping Anchorage* (see the earlier Kuala Terengganu Places to Stay entry) has the cheapest deal – RM240 for two nights, three days with camping equipment and meals provided. Other than this, you're looking at shelling out big bucks for upmarket resorts.

Getting There & Away

Most visitors to Redang purchase packages which include boat transfer to the island. If you choose to go independently, ferries to Redang leave Merang daily at 10 am, 2 and 6 pm, and cost RM40 (return ferries leave Redang daily at 8 am, noon and 4 pm). Tickets can be purchased at the Merang Inn.

If you go over on the ferry, you'll be dropped in the village where there is no accommodation for travellers. In order to get to the beaches of the island's east coast, you will have to hire a taxi boat for RM20.

KUALA BESUT

Kuala Besut, on the coast south of Kota Bharu, is a staging post for the Perhentian Islands. On the east side of the main square, *Perhentian Ferry & Tours* (☎ 691 9679) is a reliable travel agency that can arrange transport to, and accommodation on, the Perhentians.

Places to Stay

The cheapest option around is *Yaodin Guesthouse* (☎ 697 0887), which has basic singles/doubles with fan and shared bath for RM10/20. It's above Yaodin Holidays & Tours travel agency, a minute's walk from the town square. Close by, *Coco Hut Chalet* (☎ 697 2085) has very basic rooms for RM20 with fan and shared bath.

If you want a little more comfort, the *Nan Hotel* (☎ mobile 010-985 3414) is just down the road from the Perhentian Islands ferry pier. It has clean rooms with attached bathroom and ceiling fan for RM40, and air-con doubles for RM60.

Getting There & Away

From the north or south, take a bus to Jerteh on the main highway (Route 3), from where buses go hourly to Kuala Besut (RM1) from

8 am to 4.30 pm. A share taxi from Jerteh to Kuala Besut costs RM2. A share taxi from Kota Bharu all the way to Kuala Besut costs only RM5 per person. Most guesthouses in Kota Bharu can arrange share taxis. Likewise, a share taxi from Kuala Terengganu costs only RM10 per person.

PERHENTIAN ISLANDS

The islands of Pulau Perhentian Besar and Pulau Perhentian Kecil lie just 21km off the coast. They are arguably the most beautiful islands in Malaysia with great snorkelling and diving. Don't come here looking for Thailand-style partying though, as the Perhentian Islands are virtually alcohol-free.

While both islands have their strong points, most travellers tend to gravitate to Kecil, where there is an abundance of cheap accommodation.

The Perhentians basically shut down during the monsoon (usually from mid-November to early March).

Places to Stay & Eat

Pulau Perhentian Besar Apart from the expensive resort at the northern end of the beach, accommodation is mostly in basic beach huts, with rates from around RM20 to RM50.

At the northern end of the beach, the *Coral View Island Resort* (☎ 691 0943) is a fairly upmarket place where A-frames with fan and bath cost RM80, and RM140 with air-con. Next door, *Paradise Resort* (☎ mobile 010-981 0930) has clean chalets with fan and bath for RM60/80 for singles/doubles.

Next along, *Mama's Place* (☎ mobile 010-981 3359) is a good mid-range option, with standard rooms with fan and bath for RM30, and nicer chalets with fan and bath for RM55. Its restaurant does a nice Malay-style fish dinner with all the trimmings for RM12 if you request early in the day.

Over the headland, the first place you come to is *Cozy*, a group of chalets built on the rocks overlooking the water. Slightly tatty chalets with fan and bath are RM35. Down on the beach, *Co-Co Huts* is a bargain choice, with simple but clean A-frames for RM15 with common bath.

Behind Co-Co, the *Seahorse Caf* manages some decent western and Malay-style food for around RM5 per order. Next along, *ABC Chalets* has so-so A-frames for RM50, but you may not find anyone around to show them to you. The next spot on the beach, *IBI*

Huts, has huts with fan and bath for RM35/ 50, and a good location.

Clambering over the next headland brings you to another nice stretch of beach where you'll find the popular *Abdul's* (☎ *mobile 010-983 7303)*. There's a wide selection here, from longhouse rooms (RM15) with shared bath to chalets with fan and attached bath (RM40).

Camping is possible down the beach beyond Abdul's and the neighbouring government resthouse, although this area can get busy during holiday periods.

An easily missed track leads from behind the second jetty over the hill to Teluk Dalam, a secluded bay on the south side of the island with a long stretch of shallow beach. The first spot you come to is *Pelangi Chalets*, a rather ramshackle operation with A-frames for RM25 and bungalows for RM40.

Next door, *Flora Bay Chalets* (☎ *697 7266)* has a wide variety of slightly run-down accommodation ranging in price from RM30 to RM100.

Next along, *Fauna Beach Chalets* (☎ *691 8919)* is a better choice, offering clean chalets with fan and bath for RM45, and family rooms for RM70.

Last on the beach, *Samudra Beach Chalets* (☎ *mobile 010-983 4929)* is a pleasantly isolated operation, where bungalows with fan and bath for RM50, and A-frames with fan and bath for RM30.

Pulau Perhentian Kecil Accommodation over on Kecil is more basic and prices are generally lower – most places hover at around RM20 for a chalet with two beds, a mosquito net and a well or common shower for washing.

Long Beach is the most popular place on Kecil and it has a great beach. On the rocks at the southern end of the beach, *Rock Garden* has some of the cheapest bungalows at RM10 for rugged, bare-bones huts.

Down the hill, *Chempaka Chalets* – run by the ever-helpful Musky – is a string of simple A-frames for RM18. Next door, *D'Lahar Chalets* has decent chalets with shower for RM60 to RM80.

Set back from the beach, *Mohsin Chalets* (☎ *mobile 010-333 8897)* are a cut above the rest of the offerings at Long Beach. Built on the hillside overlooking the bay, clean and relatively new chalets with fan and bath start at RM60.

In the middle of the beach, set back a bit,

Matahari Chalets is a popular choice. Simple chalets with fan and common bath are RM30, and A-frames with fan and attached bath are RM55. Nearby, *Panorama Chalets* (☎ *mobile 010-912 2518)* has basic chalets for RM12, and chalets with fan and attached bath for RM25. Next along, *Simfony* (☎ *mobile 010-910 8683)* has basic A-frames with common bath for RM15.

At the very northern end of the beach, *Moonlight Chalets* (☎ *mobile 010-985 8222)* is another very popular spot with a wide range of accommodation choices. Rooms in the longhouse start at RM10, and simple chalets with common bath go for RM20. Nicer chalets with attached bath are RM35; family rooms are RM40.

A trail over the narrow waist of the island leads from Long Beach to the quieter Coral Bay (sometimes known as Aur Bay) on the west side of the island. The beach is decent and gets good sunsets. The southernmost spot is *Butterfly Beach Chalet* (☎ *mobile 010-985 8603)*, which has chalets built over the rocks at the end of the beach for RM30/45 for singles/doubles. Next door, *Sunset View Resort* (☎ *697 7703)* has a good location but slightly tatty rooms and chalets from RM45 to RM80.

Centrally located, *Coral Bay Chalets* (☎ *mobile 010-984 7636)* has some of the nicest chalets and A-frames on the beach for RM50. Its restaurant, the *Iguana Bistro*, turns out some of the best food on this side of the island.

Set back a little from the water, *Aur Beach Chalets* (☎ *mobile 010-895 6486)* is the budget choice, with simple chalets for RM20 and dorm beds for RM15. Nearby, *DJ Chalet* (☎ *mobile 010-985 6155)* is also set back from the beach. It has rooms going for RM20 with common bath and RM35 with attached bath.

Built on the rocks at the northern end of the bay, *Rajawali Island Resort* (☎ *mobile 010-985 9807)* has chalets with common bath for RM15. The chalets are a mixed bag, and it's a good idea to have a look at a few before deciding.

If you really want to get away from it all, *D Lagoon Chalets* (☎ *mobile 010-976 0631)* is on Teluk Kerma, a small bay on the northwestern side of the island. Longhouse rooms and chalets range from RM10 to RM40. There's a small restaurant, and tracks lead to a couple of very remote beaches in the northwest corner of the island.

MALAYSIA

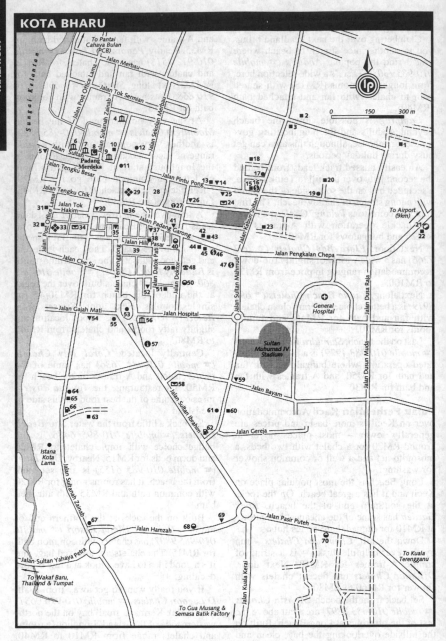

KOTA BHARU

To Pantai
Cahaya Bulan
(PCB)

Sungai Kelantan

Jalan Merbau

Jalan Post Office Lama

Jalan Tok Sermian

Jalan Sultanah Zainab

Jalan Sekolah Merbau

2

3

1

0   150   300 m

4

Jalan Sultan

6 7
8
9 10
Padang
Merdeka

12

18

Jalan Tengku Besar

11

17

20

Jalan Tengku Chik

Jalan Pintu Pong

13 14

Jalan Tok
Hakim

29

28

27

25
26

15 16

19

To Airport
(9km)

31

30

36

Jalan Padang Garong

24

Jalan Kebun Sultan

23

21
22

32

33 34

35

41
37
38

42
43

5

Jalan Hilir Pasar

40

44
45 46

Jalan Post Office Lama

Jalan Che Su

39

Jalan Temenggong

Jalan Datok Pati

49 48
47

Jalan Pengkalan Chepa

50

Jalan Doktor

51

52

Jalan Gajah Mati

53

56

Jalan Hospital

General
Hospital

Jalan Dusa Raja

55

57

Sultan
Muhumad IV
Stadium

Jalan Dusun Muda

58

59

Jalan Bayam

64
65
66

61 60

63

Jalan Sultan Ibrahim

62

Jalan Gereja

Istana
Kota
Lama

Jalan Sultanah Zainab

67

69

68

Jalan Hamzah

Jalan Pasir Puteh

70

To Kuala
Terengganu

To Wakaf Baru,
Thailand & Tumpat

Jalan Sultan Yahaya Petra

Jalan Kuala Krai

To Gua Musang &
Semasa Batik Factory

KOTA BHARU

PLACES TO STAY
1 Johnty's Guesthouse
2 KB Garden Hostel
3 Star Hostel
10 Safar Inn
13 City Guest House
15 Juita Inn
18 Ideal Travellers' Guest House
20 Zeck Traveller's Inn
22 Rainbow Inn
23 Friendly Guest House
31 Hotel New North Malaysia;
    Restoran Donald Duck
32 Diamond Puteri Hotel
36 Temenggong Hotel
38 Thye Ann Hotel
42 KB Backpackers Lodge
43 Kencana Inn
44 KB Inn
45 Yee Guest House
49 Kencana Inn City Centre
51 Hotel Ansar
60 Hotel Perdana; Aris
63 Rebana House
65 Menora Guest House

PLACES TO EAT
5 Food Stalls
14 KFC

25 Muhibah Vegetarian
    Restaurant
26 McDonald's
30 McDonald's
35 Sun Too Restaurant
37 Restoran Razak
41 Night Market Food
    Stalls
52 Family Restaurant
54 Meena Curry House
59 Food Stalls
69 Outdoor Market;
    Food Stalls

OTHER
4 Istana Batu (Royal
    Museum)
6 Bank Kerapu (WWII
    Memorial Museum)
7 Muzium Islam
8 State Mosque
9 Istana Jahar (Royal
    Customs Museum)
11 Istana Balai Besar
12 Kampung Kraftagan
    (Handicraft Village)
16 Mayban Finance
17 ITA Pro Multimedia Café
19 Bird-Singing Place

21 Thai Consulate
24 Post Office
27 Public Toilet
28 Central Market
29 Bazaar Buluh Kubu
33 Hankyu Jaya Department
    Store; KFC
34 Post Office
39 Old Central Market
40 Central Bus & Taxi Station
46 Hongkong Bank
47 Maybank
48 Telekom
50 Taxi Station
53 Clock Tower
55 Malaysia Airlines
56 State Museum
57 Tourist Information
    Centre
58 Post Office
61 Gelanggang Seni
    (Cultural Centre)
62 Petrol Station
64 Silver Shops
66 Caltex Petrol Station
67 Silversmith
68 External (Jalan Hamzah)
    Bus Station
70 Langgar Bus Station

Getting There & Away

Both speedboats and regular slow boats do the run between Kuala Besut and the Perhentians. Speedboats depart from Kuala Besut at 9.30 and 10.30 am, and 2.30 pm daily (30 minutes, RM30/60 one way/return), while slow boats depart approximately every hour from 9.30 am to 4.30 pm daily (about 1½ hours, RM25/40). The boats will drop you off at any of the beaches. In the other direction, speedboats depart from the islands daily at around noon and 4 pm, and slow boats hourly from 8 am to 2 pm.

KOTA BHARU

In the north-east corner of the peninsula, Kota Bharu is the termination of the east-coast road, and a gateway to Thailand. It is the capital of the state of Kelantan, an Islamic stronghold and a centre for Malay culture. It is undoubtedly the most interesting city on the east coast, and many travellers end up staying longer than they planned.

Information

The Kota Bharu tourist information centre

(☎ 748 5534) is on Jalan Sultan Ibrahim, just south of the clock tower. It is open Sunday to Thursday. Other offices in Kelantan are closed Thursday afternoon and Friday, but open on weekends.

The Thai consulate (☎ 744 0867) is on Jalan Pengkalan Chepa, and is open from 9 am to 4 pm Sunday to Thursday, but is usually closed for lunch between 12.30 and 2.30 pm.

Email & Internet Access There are several Internet cafes scattered around town, including the ITA Pro Multimedia Cafe on Jalan Kebun Sultan. You can also log on at KB Backpacker's Lodge (see Places to Stay in this section).

Things to See

Padang Merdeka (Independence Square) is a strip of grass that has only a few historical associations to claim your attention. The real attraction is the cluster of museums close by. They are all open from 10 am to 6 pm, closed Friday, and charge RM3 entry.

The **Bank Kerapu** (WWII Memorial Museum) is dominated by photographic memorabilia. The **Muzium Islam** (Islamic

Museum) celebrates the percolation of Islam into the everyday life of the state. The **Istana Jahar** (Royal Customs Museum), a beautiful old wooden structure, dates back to 1887 and is well worth ducking into. The displays on courtly life are tastefully presented. Also worth a look are the **Istana Batu** (Royal Museum) and the **Kampung Kraftangan** (Handicraft Village).

The **central market** is one of the most colourful and active in Malaysia. It is in a modern octagonal building, with traders selling fresh produce on the ground floor and stalls on the floors above selling spices, basketware and other goods.

Performances held at the **Cultural Centre** (Gelanggang Seni) are very popular. Top-spinning, traditional dance dramas, wayang kulit and other traditional activities are featured regularly. Check with the tourist information centre for more details.

The **State Museum**, next to the tourist information centre, brings together an eclectic array of artefacts, crafts, paintings and photographic displays, all connected in some way or another with Kelantan state.

Places to Stay

Locals count upwards of 60 guesthouse outfits in Kota Bharu. Prices vary only marginally, hovering around RM6 for a dorm bed, RM10/12 for a single/double and RM15 to RM20 for a room with attached bathroom. Many have bicycles for rent and cooking facilities.

For anyone spending more than a couple of days in Kota Bharu, the best places to be based are the 'homestays' on the outskirts of town. The guesthouses in the centre of town are generally noisy and slightly claustrophobic.

Zeck Traveller's Inn (☎ 743 1613) is a popular spot with a friendly, informative owner. It's your standard-issue guesthouse and the rooms are clean, if a little cramped. Five minutes walk away, *Johnty's Guesthouse* is a laid-back place with the air of a 1960s crash pad which might appeal to some.

One of the best places in the centre of town, the *KB Backpackers Lodge* (☎ 743 2125) is a friendly and popular choice. It has both dorm and private rooms, a pleasant common area and cooking facilities. The owners can also help with local and ongoing travel arrangements, and have Internet and fax facilities.

At 3338-D Jalan Sultanah Zainab is the *Menora Guest House* (☎ 748 1669). There's a variety of accommodation, from dorm beds

for RM5 up to large double rooms for RM22. It also has air-con rooms for RM38. This place is cleaner than many other guesthouses in town.

Not far south of the Menora is *Rebana House* – look for the faded sign pointing up an alley next to the Caltex petrol station. It's a lovely house, decorated in Malay style, with lots of artwork around. There's a variety of rooms available, from the RM6 dorm and pokey RM8 singles to some beautiful old rooms and chalets in the garden for RM10 to RM15.

Another option, if you are desperate, is one of the old *Chinese hotels* around the bus station – they are usually noisy and seedy but relatively inexpensive, with rooms at around RM15.

Places to Eat

The best and cheapest Malay food in Kota Bharu is found at the *night market*, opposite the central bus station. The food stalls are set up in the evenings, and there's a wide variety of delicious, cheap Malay food. Just bear in mind the whole thing closes down for evening prayers between 7 and 7.45 pm, and Muslims and non-Muslims alike must vacate the premises. Most of the stalls at the night market deal in variations on the *nasi goreng* theme, but Thai-style *tom yam* soups and Indian *murtabak* are also popular. Local specialities include: *ayam percik* (marinated chicken enclosed between bamboo skewers) and *nasi kerabu* (rice with coconut, fish and spices).

It's easy to write off the rest of Kota Bharu after the night market, but there's a surprising amount of good food around town. More *food stalls* can be found next to the river opposite the Padang Merdeka, by the Jalan Hamzah bus station and at the stadium.

The *Restoran Razak*, on the corner of Jalan Datok Pati and Jalan Padang Garong, is cheap and has good Indian Muslim food. For an excellent lunchtime Malay curry on a banana leaf, try the *Meena Curry House* on Jalan Gajah Mati.

The *Restoran Donald Duck* cooks up a very good Cantonese-style duck and rice.

Vegetarians can try the *Muhibah Vegetarian Restaurant* on Jalan Pintu Pong, which serves meatless Malay, western and Chinese dishes.

Getting There & Away

Air The Malaysia Airlines office (☎ 744 7000) is located opposite the clock tower on

Jalan Gajah Mati. Direct flights go to Penang (RM87), Alor Setar (RM71) and KL (RM104).

Bus The state-run SKMK is the largest bus company, and runs all the city and regional buses, as well as most of the long-distance buses. It operates from the central bus station (city and regional buses) and the Langgar bus station (long-distance buses). All the other long-distance bus companies operate from the Jalan Hamzah external bus station.

SKMK has regular buses to Kuala Terengganu (RM7.40) and Kuantan (RM16) – these buses depart from the central bus station. Buses to Johor Bahru (RM29), Singapore (RM30) and KL (RM25) leave at 8 pm (also 9 pm to KL). The buses to Butterworth (RM20) and Penang leave at 10 am and 10 pm. There is a bus to Jerantut (RM18) at 8.30 am. Other destinations are Alor Setar, Gerik, Kuala Dungun, Kuala Lipis, Melaka, Mersing and Temerloh.

All regional buses leave from the central bus station. Destinations include: Wakaf Baru (Nos 19, 27, 27a, 43), Rantau Panjang (Nos 29, 29a, 36), Tumpat (No 19), Bachok (Nos 2, 23, 29), Pasir Puteh (Nos 3, 3a), Jerteh (No 3a), Kuala Krai (Nos 5, 57) and Gua Musang (No 57).

Train The nearest station to Kota Bharu is at Wakaf Baru, a RM1 trip on bus No 19 or 27. See the following Kota Bharu to Kuala Lumpur section for more details on this railway.

Taxi The taxi station is on the southern side of the central bus station. Main destinations (and costs) are: Kuala Terengganu (RM12), Kuantan (RM25), Kuala Lipis (RM35), Butterworth (RM40) and KL (RM35/45).

Getting Around
The airport is 9km from town – take bus No 9 from the old central market. A taxi costs around RM12.

To Pantai Cahaya Bulan (PCB) take bus No 10. It leaves from the Bazaar Buluh Kubu, or you can catch it at the bus stand in front of the Kencana Inn.

AROUND KOTA BHARU
Beaches
The beaches around Kota Bharu are nothing special, but are OK for a sunny afternoon. **Pantai Cahaya Bulan** (PCB) used to be known

as Pantai Cinta Berahi, the 'Beach of Passionate Love', until local leaders decided the name was too raunchy.

Other beaches are **Pantai Irama** (Beach of Melody) at Bachok and **Pantai Dasar Sabak**, 13km from Kota Bharu, where the Japanese landed in December 1941, 1½ hours before they bombed Pearl Harbor.

Other Attractions
Also in the Kota Bharu vicinity are **waterfalls** (Pasir Puteh area) and a number of Thai temples, including **Wat Phothivihan** (at Kampung Jambu), with its 40m reclining Buddha.

Kota Bharu to Kuala Lumpur

THE JUNGLE RAILWAY
The jungle railway starts at Tumpat and goes through Kuala Krai, Kuala Lipis and Jerantut (for Taman Negara National Park), and eventually meets the Singapore-KL line at Gemas. There are express and local trains running on this line. The nearest station to Kota Bharu is at Wakaf Baru, a RM1 trip on bus No 19 or 27. The times listed here are from Wakaf Bahru.

There is a daily express train all the way through to KL at 6.40 pm, stopping en route at Kuala Lipis, Jerantut and Gemas before arriving in KL the following morning at 6.30 am. There is also a daily express through to Singapore at 8.20 pm, making the same stops en route before arriving the following morning at 8.10 am. Note that both of these trains leave in the evening, which means that you'll miss out on most of the jungle scenery.

A local train leaves daily at 6.21 am and stops at almost every station before arriving at Gemas at 7.55 pm.

KTM has a ticket office (counter No 5) at the Hamzah bus station in Kota Bharu.

KUALA LIPIS
Kuala Lipis is a pretty, well maintained town with fine rows of shops down the main street, and some impressive colonial architecture dating from the time when Kuala Lipis was the state capital.

There's not much to do in Kuala Lipis, but you can arrange good four-day/three-night jungle treks to nearby **Kenong Rimba Park** for about RM35 per day, all inclusive (ask at the two tourist information offices near the station). All visitors to the park must be accompanied by a guide.

Places to Stay

Most of the hotels in town are on Jalan Besar (the main street) and Jalan Jelai (the riverfront street), both of which are a short walk from the bus and train stations.

On Jalan Besar, the **Hotel Tong Kok** (☎ 312 1027), has rooms for RM15 with fan and common bath. Down by the river, the **Hotel Jelai** (☎ 312 1562), at 44 Jalan Jelai, is a very clean hotel with a variety of rooms ranging in price from RM18 with fan to RM40 with air-con. This is probably the best buy in town.

Getting There & Away

There is an express train to Singapore (eight hours, RM21) at 12.45 am and a local train at 7.22 am. The 2.29 pm local to Gemas also allows you to connect to Singapore. There is also an 11 pm express to KL (eight hours, RM18). Any Singapore, KL or Gemas-bound train will stop at Jerantut, for those heading to Taman Negara National Park.

Express trains to Tumpat (five hours) leave at 2.45 and 4.25 am and stop at Wakaf Bharu, the closest station to Kota Bharu (RM16). A slow but interesting local ('jungle') train departs at 12.55 pm and takes 11 hours to Wakaf Bahru (RM16).

Six buses per day run between Kuala Lipis and KL's Pekeliling bus station from 8 am to 6 pm (RM8). Buses also go to Kuantan (RM14) and Kota Bharu (RM14), among others.

Taxis leave from the bus station to Jerantut (RM10), KL (RM25) and Kuantan (RM40).

JERANTUT

Jerantut is the gateway to Taman Negara National Park. Most visitors to the park spend at least one night here, but the town itself has no real attractions.

Places to Stay

Most of the accommodation in Jerantut is on Jalan Besar, south of the train station.

The friendliest and most atmospheric guesthouse is the small **Chong Heng Hotel Travellers Inn** (☎ 266 3693) on Jalan Besar. There are singles/doubles for RM10 with fan, washbasin and a common bath, and similar triples for RM15.

The small, friendly **Green Park Guest House** (☎ 266 3884) on Jalan Besar has four-bed dorms for RM8 and singles/doubles for RM12/20.

The best hotel in town is the clean, friendly **Hotel Jelai** (☎ 266 7412) with air-con rooms with attached bath for RM30 and similar triples for RM40.

Opposite the bus station, the **Hotel Chett Fatt** (☎ 266 5805) is a reasonable place if you can't be bothered walking further. It costs RM15 for a fan room, RM20 to RM28 with air-con.

Getting There & Away

Bus The bus and taxi station is in the centre of town. Buses to KL leave from the ticket offices on the other side of the taxi station from the main bus station.

At present two companies operate to KL's Pekeliling bus station (RM9) going via Temerloh. If you miss the bus to KL, buses go every hour to Temerloh (RM3), from where there are connections to KL and other destinations. Two companies have buses to Kuantan (RM8.50), with departures until 2.30 pm.

Buses to Kuala Tembeling (45 minutes, RM3), for Taman Negara, leave at 7.15 and 10 am, and 1.30 and 3.45 pm. These don't always arrive in time to meet the boat going to the park. The best bet is to take a taxi between Jerantut and Kuala Tembeling. A taxi costs RM16, but the chances of finding other passengers to share this fare are pretty good.

The Sri Emas Hotel and the Green Park Guest House arrange minibuses to Kuala Tembeling for RM4 per person. They can also arrange transport by road all the way to Kuala Tahan for RM23 per person. The minibuses depart at 8.10 am to both destinations from either hotel.

Train Jerantut is on the Tumpat-Gemas railway line. The daily express train to Singapore (seven hours) leaves at 1.30 am and arrives in Singapore at 8.10 am. A local train leaves at 3.50 pm to Gemas, where you can catch another train to Singapore or Kuala Lumpur.

To Wakaf Bahru (the nearest station to Kota Bharu on the Tumpat line) express trains take six hours, and leave at 1.50 and 3.30 am; otherwise a local train leaves at 11.15 am and takes about 11 hours. All northbound trains go via Kuala Lipis.

TAMAN NEGARA

Peninsular Malaysia's great national park covers 4343 sq km and sprawls across the states of Pahang, Kelantan and Terengganu. The part of the park most visited, however, is all in Pahang. Taman Negara is billed, perhaps wrongly, as a wildlife park. Certainly this vast wilderness area is home to endangered species such as elephants, tigers, panthers and rhinos, but numbers are low and sightings are rare, especially around the heavily trafficked park headquarters. The chances of seeing game are greatest if you do an extended trek away from the more frequented parts of the park, but the main reason to visit is to experience the pristine primary rainforest.

The best time to visit the park is in the dry season between February and September, but it doesn't always rain in the rainy season, when the number of visitors drops dramatically.

Orientation & Information

The park headquarters is at the Taman Negara Resort at Kuala Tahan (☎ 266 3500, fax 266 1500). There's a Wildlife Department office, restaurant, cafeteria, hostel, some chalets and a shop selling provisions at inflated prices. You can rent camping, hiking and fishing gear. At the Wildlife Department office you can arrange a guide for trekking or a stay in a hide. At the resort you can also change money (lousy rate) and make phone calls (expensive).

The kampung of **Kuala Tahan**, right across the Sungai Tembeling from the park headquarters, also has a couple of basic shops, cafes and two small lodges.

Entrance to the park costs RM1, and a camera permit is RM5. You get these at the office at the Kuala Tembeling jetty.

What to Bring

Although everyday clothes are quite suitable around Kuala Tahan, you need to be well equipped if heading further afield. River travel in the early morning hours can be surprisingly cold. If overnighting in a hide, you'll need a powerful torch (flashlight).

Mosquitoes can be annoying but you can buy repellent at the park shop. Leeches are generally not a major problem, although they can be a real nuisance after heavy rain.

Hides & Salt Licks

There are several accessible hides and salt licks in the park. A number of them are close to Kuala Tahan and Kuala Trenggan, but your chances of seeing wildlife will increase if you head for the hides furthest from park headquarters. All hides are built overlooking salt licks and grassy clearings.

For overnight stays, take food and your own sleeping bag or sheets from Kuala Tahan (lent free of charge) – you won't need blankets. Each hide costs RM5 per person per night. Even if you're not lucky enough to see any wildlife, the fantastic sounds of the jungle are well worth the time and effort taken to reach the hides. The 'symphony' is at its best at dusk and dawn.

Bumbun Tahan is an artificial salt lick less than five minutes walk from the reception building – no chance of seeing any animals here! Better hides within one to 1½ hours walk from the park HQ are **Bumbun Blau** (you can visit Gua Telinga along the way), **Bumbun Tabing** and **Bumbun Cegar Anjing**. **Bumbun Yong**, on the Sungai Yong, is about 1½ hours past Blau. **Bumbun Kumbang** is about seven hours from Kuala Tahan, or take the riverboat service up the Sungai Tembeling to Kuala Trenggan and then walk. All these hides have sleeping facilities for six to eight people and nearby fresh water.

Mountains & Walks

Trails around the park headquarters are well marked and heavily trafficked. However, relatively few of the 40,000 visitors the park receives each year venture far beyond the headquarters, and the longer walks are far less trammelled.

Short walks around park headquarters include those to the **Canopy Walkway** (RM5, open 9 am to 3 pm Saturday to Thursday, to noon Friday), and on to **Bukit Teresik**. You can continue to **Bukit Indah** or do a loop back via **Lubok Simpon**, a swimming area on the Sungai Tahan.

There's a well marked, five hour trail along the bank of the Sungai Tembeling for 9km to **Kuala Trenggan**. You can continue to **Kuala Keniam** for a two day trek.

Gua Telinga is a cave south-west of the park HQ, and it takes about 1½ hours to walk there, after first crossing the Sungai Tahan. It's a strenuous half-hour walk – and crawl – through the cave. Once back at the main path, it's a further 15 minutes walk to the Bumbun Blau hide, where you can spend the night or walk directly back to Kuala Tahan.

The trek for the really adventurous is the ascent of **Gunung Tahan** (at 2187m, the highest mountain in Peninsular Malaysia), which is 55km from the park HQ. It takes nine days up and down, but can be done in seven with a faster descent. A guide is compulsory and costs RM638 for eight people.

A shorter three day walk is **Rentis Tenor** (Tenor Trail). It's popular but the trail is not always clear and a guide is recommended.

Places to Stay & Eat

Kuala Tahan All accommodation at park HQ is operated by the privately run Taman Negara Resort (☎ 266 3500). Bookings can also be made through its Kuala Lumpur sales office (☎ 245 5585) on the 2nd floor on the Istana Hotel, 73 Jalan Raja Chulan. A 15% tax and service charge is added to all the rates quoted here.

Camping at the *park headquarters* with your own tent costs RM2 per person per night, or you can hire tents. Other campsites with minimal facilities are scattered throughout Taman Negara. There is also a decent *hostel*, which costs RM35 per person, including breakfast.

The *Taman Negara Resort* has overpriced rooms for RM125, and luxurious two-person chalets starting at RM175/260 standard/deluxe.

The resort has one expensive restaurant, and a much cheaper self-service cafeteria.

The village of Kuala Tahan directly across the river from park HQ is slightly less convenient but much cheaper for accommodation and food. Crossing the river is easy: sampans go on demand throughout the day and evening, and are free if you eat at the restaurants or stay in the village.

First on the right as you climb the steps away from the river is the *Tembeling River Hostel & Chalets*. Here, a bed in the hostel costs RM12, two-person chalets cost RM35 with a fan and common bath, and three-person chalets cost RM60 with fan and attached bath.

First on the left as you climb the steps is the *Liana Hostel*, which has a barracks-like but clean hostel with beds for RM10.

About 50m on the right from the top of the steps, the *Ekoton Chalets* are a good mid-range choice, with clean air-con chalets for RM80. It also has a decent dorm, with beds for RM10 with a fan and fridge.

Beyond Agoh Chalets, the *Teresek View Village* (☎ 266 3065) has large dorms for RM10 and small A-frame huts for RM30; newish, good-value chalets with fan and bath are RM50.

Nusa Camp *Nusa Camp* is 15 minutes up the Sungai Tembeling from Kuala Tahan. It's much more of a 'jungle camp' than anything at park HQ. Dorm beds cost RM10 (with no insect nets and a grotty bathroom); slightly run-down A-frames are RM45. Much better value are the clean, spacious double cottages with fan and bath for MR60/80 (semi-detached/detached).

Bookings can be made in KL at the Nusa Camp desk at the Malaysia Tourism tourist centre on Jalan Ampang (☎ 264 3929 ext 112), or at the Jerantut office (☎ 266 2369) at the bus station. The camp runs its own boat from Kuala Tembeling, and a riverbus service between Nusa Camp and Kuala Tahan (see the Getting Around entry later in this section).

Kuala Trenggan & Kuala Keniam About 35 minutes upstream from Kuala Tahan at Kuala Trenggan is the quite luxurious *Trenggan Lodge*. Further upriver is the simpler and more remote *Keniam Lodge*. Both are run by the resort and cost RM80 per double room.

Getting There & Away

The main entry point into the park is by riverboat from Kuala Tembeling, 18km from Jerantut. Boats go at 9 am and 2 pm (2.30 pm on Friday). Boats are operated by the resort and Nusa Camp, whose boats also stop at the park HQ before continuing to Nusa Camp. It's a 2½ to three hour boat trip from Tembeling to the park HQ at Kuala Tahan. The trip costs RM19 one way. Leaving the park, boats also depart at 9 am and 2 pm.

Kuala Tembeling is most easily reached by bus or taxi from Jerantut. From the resort's office at the Istana Hotel in Kuala Lumpur, Reliance Travel has a daily shuttle bus all the way to Kuala Tembeling, leaving at 8 am and costing RM35 (reserve through the resort). Most of the guesthouses in KL can arrange pick-up and drop-off at Kuala Tembeling for the same price.

Getting Around

Nusa Camp has a riverboat service from Kuala Tahan to Nusa Camp (RM3 for Nusa Camp guest, RM5 for nonguests) at 10 am, and 12.30 and 6 pm. In the opposite direction there are departures from Nusa Camp at 8.15 and 11.15 am, and 2.15 and 3.45 pm. To Kuala Trenggan, boats from Kuala Tahan go via Nusa Camp. They leave at 10 am and 3 pm, and cost RM10 from Kuala Tahan, RM5 from Nusa Camp. The return boats leave Kuala Trenggan at 11 am and 3.30 pm.

The resort has a riverboat service which departs at 8.30 am, and 1.30 and 2.15 pm for Kuala Trenggan and Kuala Keniam (30 minutes and RM10 to Trenggan, one hour and RM20 to Keniam). In the reverse direction, boats depart from Kuala Keniam for Kuala Tahan at 10.15 am, and 3.15 and 4.45 pm, stopping at Kuala Trenggan on the way. While they keep pretty much to schedule during peak periods, in the wet season they drop services or stop all together.

For charter boats, the Wildlife office is helpful in trying to arrange groups for those who want to share costs.

Sarawak

Approximately the same size as Peninsular Malaysia, Sarawak is probably the least visited of all Malaysia's states. This is a shame. Sarawak has some excellent national parks, Kuching is one of the most pleasant cities in all of Asia, and upriver is a fascinating diversity of Dayak tribes and (if one travels far enough) untouched jungle. The politics of logging have injured the state's international reputation to be sure, but there remains much that is worthwhile.

The modern history of Sarawak whiffs of Victorian melodrama. In 1838 James Brooke, a British adventurer with an inheritance and an armed sloop arrived to find the Brunei sultanate fending off rebellion from warlike inland tribes. Brooke put down the rebellion and in reward was granted power over part of Sarawak.

Appointing himself Raja Brooke, he pacified the 'natives', suppressed head-hunting, eliminated the much feared Borneo pirates and founded a dynasty that lasted until after WWII. The Brooke family of 'white rajas' continued to bring ever-growing tracts of Borneo into their control throughout their rule.

Today, Sarawak is an economically important part of Malaysia, accounting for major oil and timber exports. It is also an important producer of pepper, rubber and palm oil. The state was hit hard by the Communist insurgency during the 60s, but things are peaceful today.

Visas & Permits

See Visas & Documents in the Facts for the Visitor section at the start of this chapter for more information on visa requirements for entering this region.

If you plan to visit any of the longhouses above Kapit on the Batang Rejang or Batang Balleh you will need a permit, which can be obtained in Kapit without fuss or fee. It can be trickier getting a permit for travel in the interior of the north-east. This is the scene of most logging and where the Dayaks have been most active against the government. Permits are required from the District Office in Miri or Marudi for travel to Bario and the upper reaches of the Batang Baram. You may be interviewed to determine your real reason for travelling to the interior, but most travellers don't have any problems, as long as they have absolutely nothing to do with journalism. Tell them you are a carpenter if you think your profession may be a problem.

Permits are also required to visit national parks but are generally a formality and issued as a matter of course when you check in at the park HQ. National parks close to main settlements can get crowded on weekends and during school holidays, and it's wise to book ahead during these times. The penalty for visiting national parks without a permit is a fine of RM1000 *and* six months in prison (at least it's not death), so always check in at the park HQ before going any further. Permits are required for the Semenggok Wildlife Rehabilitation Centre, but these are issued instantly (along with permits for Bako National Park) at the National Parks & Wildlife booking office in Kuching.

Getting There & Away

Air Malaysia Airlines has flights to Sabah and Peninsular Malaysia. The cheapest way to reach Sarawak is to take a flight from Johor Bahru – see the main Getting Around section at the beginning of this chapter for details. You can fly to Brunei from Sarawak, or skip Brunei by flying from Miri to Kota Kinabalu in Sabah for RM228.

See the following Kuching Getting There & Away section for information on flights to Indonesia.

Land There is no highway linking Sarawak to Sabah. It is possible to travel by road from Brunei to Limbang and Lawas, then right through to Sabah, but it is expensive and there is no public transport. The usual – and cheapest – route is to take a bus from Miri to Brunei. From Brunei there are ferry connections with Sabah.

MALAYSIA

EAST MALAYSIA

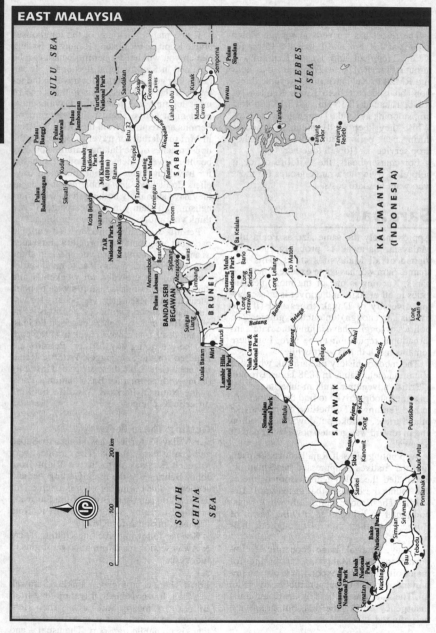

Sea The only regular boat connections from Sarawak are the ferries between Brunei and the isolated outposts of Lawas and Limbang in north-eastern Sarawak.

KUCHING

Kuching is without a doubt the most pleasant and interesting city in Borneo. It is hilly, leafy, has a very pleasant riverside area, and it's very easy to spend a few days exploring the place.

The city contains many beautifully landscaped parks and gardens, historic buildings, an interesting waterfront, colourful markets, one of Asia's best museums, various Chinese temples and the striking state mosque.

Information

Tourist Offices Kuching has two excellent tourist information offices which distribute leaflets on accommodation, sights, national parks and transport.

The Sarawak Tourist Association (STA) office (☎ 24 0620) is in an octagonal building on the waterfront. The Visitors' Information Centre Kuching (☎ 41 0944) is just down from the new wing of the Sarawak Museum. In the same building is the National Parks & Wildlife booking office (☎ 24 8088), which can arrange permits and accommodation for Bako, Gunung Gading and Kubah National Parks, and for Matang and Semenggok Wildlife Rehabilitation Centres.

Look out for the *Official Kuching Guide*, an excellent freebie.

Foreign Consulates The Indonesian consulate (☎ 24 1734) is at 5A Jalan Pisang – take CLL bus Nos 8, 8A, 8B, 14, 14A or 14B from near the Masjid Negeri (State Mosque).

Money The best place to change money is the Hongkong Bank on Jalan Tun Haji Openg. The Standard Chartered Bank and the Bank of Commerce can also change cash and travellers cheques.

Post & Communications The main post office is right in the centre on Jalan Tun Haji Openg. It is open from 8 am to 4 pm from Monday to Friday, from 8 am to 6.30 pm on Saturday and from 9 am to 4 pm on Sunday. International calls can be made at card phones around town.

Travel Agencies Ask the tourist office to recommend travel agents. Interworld Travel (☎ 25 2344) at 85 Jalan Rambutan has longhouse day trips, as well as longer Batang Skrang (Skrang River) trips. CPH Travel (☎ 24 3708), 70 Jalan Padungan, has Skrang and Lemanak river safaris. Borneo Interland Travel (☎ 41 3595), 1st floor 63 Main Bazaar, is a general agency that offers a wide variety of tours.

Bookshops The Mohamed Yahia & Sons bookshop in the basement of the Sarawak Plaza has the best range of books on Borneo and Malaysia. For general reading, Belle's Bookshop on the 2nd floor of the Sarawak Plaza has a very good range, including paperbacks, on every topic.

Fort Margherita

Built by Charles Brooke in 1879 and named after his wife, the Ranee Margaret, Fort Margherita guarded the approach to Kuching against pirates. Sitting on a knoll opposite the waterfront, this little white fort is now a police museum (Muzium Polis). To get there take a *tambang* (ferry boat) from the landing stage behind the Square Tower to the bus stop below the fort, then walk. The fare is 30 sen each way.

Sarawak Museum

This is one of the best museums in Asia and should not be missed. It consists of two sections, old and new, connected by a footbridge over Jalan Tun Haji Openg. The old wing was opened in 1891; the new wing is modern and air-conditioned. Next door is the **Muzium Islam Sarawak** (Islamic Museum), which is also well worth a visit.

Chinese History Museum

The Chinese History Museum is part of the Waterfront development. It has interesting exhibits on the Chinese diaspora, the influence the Chinese have had on Sarawak, trading associations formed and so on.

Cat Museum

Billed as the only one of its kind in the world, Kuching's Cat Museum will delight cat lovers. Several small galleries feature, among other things, the benefits cats have bestowed on their owners. Take Petra Jaya bus No 2B or 2C, or MTC bus No 2; the fare is 60 sen.

Temples, Mosques & Churches

Historically, the most important Chinese temple is **Tua Pek Kong**, just down the road

MALAYSIA

KUCHING

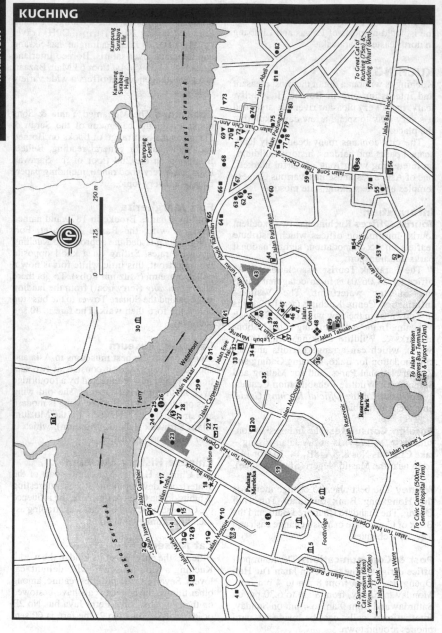

Sungai Sarawak

Kampung Surabaya Hilir
Kampung Surabaya Hulu
Kampung Gersik

To Great Cat of Kuching (75m) &
Pending Wharf (6km)

To Jalan Penrissen
Express Bus Terminal
(5km) & Airport (12km)

To Civic Centre (500m) &
General Hospital (1km)

To Sunday Market,
Cat Museum
& Wisma Satok (500m)

Reservoir Park

Padang Merdeka

Footbridge

250 m

0   125   250 m

PLACES TO STAY
4	Arif Hotel
19	Merdeka Palace Hotel
34	Anglican Diocesan Rest House
36	Fata Hotel
39	River View Inn
40	Kuching Hotel
43	Kuching Hilton Hotel
45	Goodwood Inn
46	Mandarin Lodging House
47	Orchid Inn
49	Borneo Hotel
50	B&B Inn
54	Telang Usan Hotel
57	Liwah Hotel
64	Riverside Majestic; Riverside Shopping Complex
66	Holiday Inn
75	Kapit Hotel
76	Ban Hua Hin Hotel
80	Chung Hin Hotel
81	Hotel Longhouse

PLACES TO EAT
10	Saujana Food Centre
14	Open Air Market
17	Jubilee; Madinah; Malaya
22	National Islamic Cafe
28	Green Vegetarian Cafe
33	Life Cafe
37	Tiger Garden
38	Green Hill Corner

48	Ting & Ting Supermarket
51	San Francisco Grill
52	Hornbill's Corner Cafe
53	See Good Food Centre
60	Top Spot Food Court
65	Beijing Riverbank Restaurant
67	McDonald's
69	Kuching Food Centre
71	Suan Chicken Rice
72	Pizza Hut
73	Benson's Seafood Centre

OTHER
1	Istana
2	STC Buses
3	Masjid Negeri (State Mosque)
5	Muzium Islam Sarawak
6	Sarawak Museum (Old Building)
7	Sarawak Museum (New Building)
8	Visitors' Information Centre Kuching; National Parks & Wildlife Office
9	Sikh Temple
11	CLL Buses
12	Bank of Commerce
13	Petra Jaya Buses
15	Electra House
16	Taxi Stand
18	Central Police Station
20	Anglican Cathedral

21	Main Post Office
23	Court House & Brooke Memorial
24	Square Tower
25	Sarawak Steamship Building
26	Sarawak Tourist Association Office
27	Hongkong Bank
29	Star Bookshop
30	Fort Margherita
31	Borneo Interland Travel; Borneo Adventure
32	Hong San Temple
35	Bishop's House
41	Chinese History Museum
42	Tua Pek Kong Temple
44	De Tavern; The Royalist
55	Easy-Wash
56	Hindu Temple
58	Tourism Malaysia; Royal Brunei Airlines
59	Malaysia Airlines
61	Dragonair
62	Standard Chartered Bank
63	Singapore Airlines
68	Sarawak Plaza
70	Cat City
74	Mr Dobi (Laundromat)
77	Tan & Sons Souvenir & Handicraft Shop
78	Ekspes Bahagia Office
79	CPH Travel
82	British Council

from the Hilton. The nearby **Hong San Temple** is also worth a look if you happen to be in the area. The **Masjid Negeri** (State Mosque) is visually impressive, but otherwise pretty uninteresting.

Places to Stay

Kuching's only backpackers' hostel is the *B&B Inn* (☎ 23 7366), at 30 Jalan Tabuan, next door to the Borneo Hotel. It's close to all attractions, clean and friendly, has left luggage facilities and can help with travel information. Costs – including breakfast – are RM15 in a six bed dorm, RM23 for a single or RM29 for doubles/twins.

The *Anglican Diocesan Rest House* (☎ 41 4027), at the back of the Anglican cathedral, is normally reserved for those on church business, but if it's not full you can probably stay. Rooms with fan and shared bathroom cost RM18 to RM25, while larger, fan-cooled flats with attached bathroom cost RM30 to RM35.

The *Kuching Hotel* (☎ 41 3985) on Jalan Temple has simple rooms fitted with fan and sink costing from RM21/RM22 singles/doubles to RM26/RM27 for twins/triples. The *Ban Hua Hin Hotel* (☎ 24 2351), at 36 Jalan Padungan, has fan-cooled singles/doubles with shared bathroom for RM22. It's clean enough but noisy and dilapidated. The *Arif Hotel* is not far from the State Mosque. It's tatty but reasonable, and fan rooms cost RM25, or RM30 with bath.

On Jalan Green Hill there's a whole group of mid-range 'lodging houses', many of which cater to long-term residents. There's little to choose between them – they are all quite acceptable and cost roughly the same. The *Green Mountain Lodging House* (☎ 23 2828) at No 1 has rooms from RM42, and the *Mandarin Lodging House* (☎ 41 8269) at No 6 has rooms from RM40 to RM45. The *Orchid Inn* (☎ 41 1417) at No 2 has rooms from RM28, and the *Goodwood Inn* (☎ 24 4862) at No 16 has rooms between RM40 and RM45.

Places to Eat

Kuching has the best food in Sarawak, arguably in all of Borneo. The so-called *Open Air Market* (it's covered) on Jalan Market next to the taxi stand is one of the largest and most popular food centres. One section serves mostly Muslim food and the other has mostly Chinese food. The *Top Spot Food Court*, off Jalan Padungan behind the Malaysia Airlines building, is a popular food-stall centre on top of a car park.

The *Green Hill Corner* has a good selection of Malaysian Chinese standards. The *Tiger Garden* nearby has outdoor seating, and is a good place to knock back a couple of beers and enjoy a leisurely meal. They're both in the Jalan Green Hill area.

The *Green Vegetarian Cafe*, 16 Main Bazaar, has a variety of vegetable dishes as well as Indian curries and roti. You can stuff your face at lunch time on the vegetarian platter for RM4.50. *Life Cafe*, 108 Jalan Ewe Hai (the eastern end of Jalan Carpenter), serves delicious Chinese dumplings and rice dishes for RM3 to RM4. It also has an excellent range of Chinese teas and the best coffee in Kuching.

For fast food, check out the area around the Holiday Inn, particularly Sarawak Plaza, where there are branches of *KFC*, *McDonald's*, *Pizza Hut* and local permutations like *SugarBun* and *Hertz Chicken*.

Jalan India has three long-running Indian restaurants: the *Jubilee*, *Madinah* and *Malaya*. They're all very close to each other on the same side of the street and serve inexpensive Malay curries of the kind widely available in Peninsular Malaysia.

Entertainment

Sarawak has a big drinking culture. Pubs are the best places to meet locals and find out more about Sarawak. Opposite the Hilton car park, *De Tavern* is a friendly Kayan-run place frequented by an interesting mix of Malays, Chinese, Indians, Ibans, Kayans and western expats. Next door, *The Royalist* is an English-style pub fitted out with a nautical theme.

Getting There & Away

Air Malaysia Airlines (☎ 24 4144) is on Jalan Song Thian Cheok and has flights to KL (RM262), Johor Bahru (RM169), Sibu (RM72), Bintulu (RM117), Miri (RM164) and Kota Kinabalu (RM228).

Malaysia Airlines also operates two flights per week to Pontianak (RM276) in Indonesia.

Bus Long distance buses leave from the Regional Express Bus Terminal station on Jalan Penrissen, 5km south-east of the city centre. Buses for Sri Aman, Sarikei, Sibu, Bintulu and Miri leave from here, and several bus companies have daily services to all these places; some also have a regular service to Pontianak in Kalimantan.

Very few travellers bother with buses through to Bintulu and Miri because it is faster to travel by boat via Sibu. Sarikei is the main interchange for points further north, but buses to Bintulu and Miri can also be caught from Sibu. Daily buses from Kuching going through to all centres stop at Sarikei.

Companies servicing Kuching and nearby towns are Chin Lian Long (CLL), Matang Transport Company, Petra Jaya Transport (☎ 42 9418), Regas Transport and Sarawak Transport Company (STC, ☎ 24 2967). These services depart from the bus stands near the markets at the west end of the Kuching waterfront.

Pontianak The cheapest buses to Pontianak cost RM34.50, and the trip takes between eight and 10 hours. Kirata Express departs at 7.30 am; Sapphire Pacific leaves at 11 am; and Biaramas Express has buses at 7, 8 and 10.30 am and 12.30 pm. The border crossing at the Tebedu/Entikong border is a visa-free entry point into Indonesia for most nationalities, but check with the Indonesian Consulate first.

Boat Two companies operate daily express boats between Kuching and Sibu, from where you can continue to Niah National Park or head up the Batang Rejang. They are far quicker than the buses (the trip takes around four hours) and cost nearly the same.

Coastal Union Express
   (☎ 33 5516) 177 Jalan Chan Chin Ann; departs at 8.30 am daily; RM33.
Ekspres Bahagia
   (☎ 42 1948) 50 Jalan Padungan; direct service to Sibu at 12.45 pm daily; RM33. An additional service via Sarikei leaves on Monday, Wednesday and Friday at 8.30 am.

Borneo Interland Travel (☎ 41 3595), 63 Main Bazaar, sells tickets for both services. The Coastal Union Express boat is perhaps better because you can sit outside on the ocean leg of the trip. All boats should be booked at least a day in advance to be on the safe side.

All boats leave from Pending, about 6km east of the city centre. Catch CLL bus Nos 17 or 19 from outside the market on Main Bazaar and tell the driver which boat you are catching; the fare is 60 sen.

Getting Around
To/From the Airport STC (green and cream) bus No 12A runs approximately every 50 minutes from 6.30 am to 7.10 pm; the fare is RM1.

A taxi between Kuching airport and the city centre costs RM16.50; there's a booth at the airport where you can buy a fixed price coupon.

Bus There are five local bus services around town, but the only ones you should need are for the Cat Museum, airport, Indonesian consulate and the Sibu ferry wharf in Pending – see the relevant sections for details.

Taxi There is usually no problem flagging down a taxi on the street, and charges start at RM5, though the taxis are unmetered.

AROUND KUCHING
Semenggok Wildlife Rehabilitation Centre
This is Sarawak's equivalent to the orangutan sanctuary at Sepilok in Sabah. It's a low-key place, 32km south of Kuching, that tries to rehabilitate orang-utans, monkeys, honey bears and other unfortunate creatures which have been orphaned or caged illegally. You're not guaranteed to see wild orangutans and it was scheduled to close sometime late in 1998, so check with the National Parks & Wildlife office or tourist offices in Kuching before jumping on a bus.

A permit is required to visit the centre and can be arranged, free of charge, at the National Parks office (☎ 24 8088) in Kuching.

Getting There & Away To get there, take STC bus No 6 from Kuching (40 minutes, RM1.50). Tell the driver you wish to get off at the Forest Department Nursery, then follow a plankwalk through the forest to get to the Centre; the walk takes about 30 minutes.

Bako National Park
Bako protects an unspoilt promontory between the mouths of the Batang Sarawak and Batang Bako. It's a beautiful spot where rocky headlands are indented with clean beaches;

Bako is most famous for its wildlife, and highlights include pitcher plants and the rare proboscis monkey. It's well worth a visit, but being only 37km north of Kuching it is popular with day trippers – bookings are essential on weekends and during school holidays. A permit is needed to visit the park, and this, along with accommodation bookings, can be obtained in advance at the National Parks & Wildlife office (☎ 24 8088) in Kuching.

Places to Stay & Eat There are resthouses, hostels and a camping site at the park. *Resthouses* include fridges, gas burners, all utensils and bed linen. It costs RM80 per resthouse, or RM40 per double room. Four-person *hostel rooms* with shared kitchen and bathrooms and cost RM10 per person. Linen, cooking utensils and a few cups and plates are provided. *Camping* costs RM4 per site; there's a shower block, and lockers can be hired for RM3 per day. The park *cafeteria* sells a good variety of meals and snacks.

Getting There & Away The park is 37km from Kuching and is reached by Petra Jaya bus No 6 (45 minutes, RM2.10), then a 30 minute boat ride from Kampung Bako (RM30 for up to 10 people, or RM3 per person if there are more than 10).

Kubah National Park
Just 20km north-west of Kuching, Kubah National Park is an easy day trip from Kuching. There are waterfalls, walking trails through rainforest and lookouts. Kubah's forest features a wide variety of palms and orchids, but there is less chance of encountering animals than in Bako National Park.

Places to Stay The park's *hostel* rooms sleep two, four or six people and have pillows, linen and ceiling fan; a bed costs RM10 or rooms are RM20, RM40 or RM60, respectively. It's self-catering only, but there's a kitchen with all facilities, including a fridge.

Getting There & Away Take Kuching Matang (yellow and orange) bus No 11 to Kubah (about 30 minutes, RM1.65). The bus will drop you at Sungai Cina, from where it's a 300m uphill walk to the park entrance.

Gunung Gading National Park
The chief attraction here is the **rafflesia**, the world's largest flower, and this is one of the

best places on Borneo to see it. Well marked trails provide access to areas where it is most likely to be found. The flower has no specific flowering season, so ring the park HQ (☎ 73 5714) or the National Parks & Wildlife office (☎ 24 8088) in Kuching before heading out. Rafflesias bloom for only a few days so if one is out, get to Gunung Gading as soon as you can.

Hostel accommodation is available at RM10 per person and there's a couple of cheap *hotels* in nearby Lundu.

Getting There & Away To get there from Kuching, take an STC bus No 2B to Lundu (two hours, RM7.80). From Lundu take a Pandan bus (ask to be dropped off at the park) or you could walk to Gunung Gading in about half an hour.

UP THE BATANG REJANG

The mighty Batang Rejang (Rejang River) is the main 'highway' of central and southern Sarawak, and most of the trade with the interior is carried out along it. It is also the main trading conduit for logs from the forests in the upper reaches of the river (and its tributaries the Balleh, Belaga and Balui rivers). The number of log-laden barges on the river is astounding and depressing.

The best time for a trip up the Rejang is in late May and early June, as this is the time of **Gawai**, the Dayak harvest festival, when there is plenty of movement on the rivers and the longhouses welcome visitors. There are also plenty of celebrations, which usually involve the consumption of copious quantities of *arak* (fiery palm wine) and *tuak* (rice wine).

On the river there is *hotel accommodation* only in Song, Kanowit, Kapit and Belaga.

Visiting a Longhouse

The main reason to travel upriver is to visit a longhouse. There is no guarantee, however, that you will succeed. The Orang Ulu are generally hospitable, but without an introduction they are not going to invite you into their homes – turning up unannounced is not just bad manners, it can, in certain circumstances, be a minor catastrophe, particularly if there has been a recent death or certain rituals are under way.

To arrange a visit, the most important commodity you need is time. Most travellers head for Kapit, a small administrative town upriver. Make yourself known around the

town – sit in the cafes and get talking to people. If you are not the sociable type, it's unlikely that anyone is going to invite to you their home – unless you bring a couple of bottles of Hennessy XO.

If you are invited to a longhouse, don't forget to stock up on gifts to pay for your visit. Alcohol, cigarettes and sweets are most appreciated.

Permits

Before heading upriver from Kapit, you need to get a permit from the Pejabit Am Office on the 1st floor of the State Government Complex. This only takes a few minutes, but permits are not available on Saturday afternoon or Sunday. The permit is merely a formality, and chances are you'll never be asked for it.

What to Bring

Apart from gifts, other indispensable items include a torch, mosquito repellent, a medical kit with plenty of aspirin and paracetamol (acetaminophen in the USA), and some Lomotil, Imodium or other anti-diarrhoeal.

SIBU

Sibu is the main port city on the Batang Rejang and will probably be your first stop. There's not a great deal to do in Sibu, so most travellers only stay overnight and head off up the Rejang the next day. It's worth climbing the tower of the **Chinese temple**, as there are great views of the river from the top of the tower.

Places to Stay

If you can find the caretaker and it's not full, the best place to stay is the Methodist guesthouse, *Hoover House* (☎ 33 2973), next to the church on Jalan Pulau. It's excellent value at RM12 per person for clean, well kept rooms.

The local bus station area has budget accommodation, but a lot of these places are very seedy. The *Mehung Hotel* (☎ 32 4852), at 17 Maju Rd, has small rooms from RM15, and decent rooms with fan and tiny bathroom from RM20.

On the street behind, the *Holiday Hotel* (☎ 31 7440), at 16 Jalan Tan Sri, is a clean boarding house where simple fan-cooled singles/doubles cost RM15/RM20, and aircon rooms with shower and toilet go for RM30.

The *To-Day Hotel* (☎ 33 6499), upstairs at

40 Jalan Kampung Nyabor, is a friendly, well run place where clean air-con rooms with bathroom cost RM25/RM30.

Going up in price and comfort, the *Sarawak Hotel 1992* (☎ *33 3455*), at 34 Jalan Cross on the corner of Jalan Wong Nai Siong, has bright, clean rooms starting at RM35. Opposite is the *New World Hotel* (☎ *31 0311*), at 1 Jalan Wong Nai Siong, which has rooms from RM33/RM35; the Sarawak is slightly better value.

The *Hotel Capitol 88* (☎ *33 6444*), at 19 Jalan Wong Nai Siong, has good rooms for RM35/RM40.

Places to Eat

The best cheap food in Sibu can be found at various *hawker centres* and *food stalls*. There's a small two storey *food centre* at the end of Jalan Market, at the rear of the Palace Cinema, where stalls sell Malay curries, roti and laksa. There are food stalls on the 2nd floor of the *new market*; others are set up in the late afternoon near the market selling delicious snacks such as *pau* (steamed dumplings), barbecued chicken wings and all manner of sweets.

There are loads of Chinese *kedai kopi* in town; if you're taking an early boat up the Rejang, those along the waterfront open for breakfast well before dawn.

For western fast food, *SugarBun* and *McDonald's* are on Jalan Kampung Nyab, and there's a *KFC* outlet on Jalan Wong Nai Siong.

Getting There & Away

Air There are flights to Kapit (RM48), Bintulu (RM64), Kuching (RM72), Belaga (RM76), Miri (RM112) and Kota Kinabalu (RM180).

Bus The main bus lines all have ticket stalls at Sibu's long distance bus station at Sungai Antu. There are services to Bintulu virtually every hour between 6 am and 8 pm; the trip takes around four hours and costs RM16.50.

Boat All express boats to Sarikei and Kuching (change at Sarikei) leave from the Sarikei Wharf in front of the Chinese temple. There are two daily departures to Kuching; the trip takes around four hours and costs RM35.

Getting to Kapit is the first leg of the journey up the Batang Rejang. The *ekspres* launches (RM15) which do this trip cover the 130km or so from Sibu to Kapit in a shade over two hours!

KAPIT

This small town on the eastern bank of the Batang Rejang dates from the days of the white rajas, and still sports an old wooden **fort** built by Charles Brooke.

Information

For travel permits beyond Kapit, go to the Pejabit Am office on the 1st floor of the state government complex. It takes around 15 minutes, but bear in mind that the office is only open business hours.

Places to Stay & Eat

It's worth checking at the *Methodist Guesthouse* to see if there are any vacancies. It is normally reserved for those on church business, but if it's not full you may be allowed to stay. Most travellers head for the *Kapit Rejang Hotel* (☎ *79 6709*), which has good, cheap singles/doubles with fan on the top floor for RM15/RM18, or air-con rooms with bathroom for RM20/RM24 on the lower floors. The management is helpful and welcomes travellers.

If there's no other choice, the *Kapit Longhouse Hotel* (☎ *79 6415*) has air-con rooms with bathroom for RM30.

Food stalls set up in the evening at the *night market*. Kapit has a number of good Chinese coffee shops, particularly around the square and along the riverfront. The *Hua Sin Cafe* is reasonably priced, and the popular *Kah Ping Cafe* on the main square has good pork dishes.

Getting There & Away

Air Malaysia Airlines flies Sibu-Kapit-Belaga and back on Sunday only. From Kapit, the fare is RM47 to Belaga and RM48 to Sibu.

Boat Ekspres launch departures to Sibu (2½ hours, RM15) are from 8 am until around 3 pm. During the wet season, ekspres launches leave for Belaga (six hours, RM25) daily from the main jetty. The first ekspres from Sibu doesn't always reach Kapit in time to connect with the Belaga service.

When the river is low, ekspres boats can't get through the Pelagus Rapids, about an hour upstream of Kapit. Small cargo boats do the run, but they are uncomfortable, take around eight hours and charge RM50.

There are also boats heading up the Batang Balleh on a daily basis as far as Interwau – ask at the fuel barges in Kapit.

BELAGA

Belaga is just a small village and government administration centre on the upper reaches of the Rejang, where the river divides into the Belaga and Balui rivers. There are many Kayan and Kenyah longhouses upriver.

Permits

Permits are required for travel beyond Belaga, though it may be restricted to travel as far as the Bakun Rapids, one hour upstream.

Places to Stay

The *Belaga Hotel* (☎ 46 1244) is the most popular place, with fan doubles for RM18, or RM25 to RM40 with air-con. Next door, the *Bee Lian Hotel* (☎ 46 1416) has rooms for RM25. There's also the *Sing Soon Huat Lodging House* (☎ 46 1257), a basic hotel with cheap fan rooms for RM15.

Getting There & Away

From Belaga, ekspres boats go upriver as far as Long Pangai.

BINTULU

Bintulu is a modern, air-conditioned boom town which is best passed through as quickly as possible. There's nothing of interest for the traveller and unless you're travelling late in the day, there's no need to stop here.

Places to Stay

Bintulu has plenty of hotels. Most are air-con mid range places but there are a couple of cheap options.

The *Capital Hotel* (☎ 33 1167) on Jalan Keppel has a few scruffy fan-cooled rooms with shared toilet and *mandi* (bathing facility) for RM15, and air-con rooms with private toilet and mandi costing from RM30 to RM35.

The *Dragon Inn* (☎ 31 5150), 1 New Commercial Centre, is brighter and has basic fan rooms with shower/toilet for RM20, and air-con rooms with bathroom and TV for RM30.

The *AA Inn* (☎ 33 5733), 107 Taman Sri Dagang, has air-con rooms costing RM32.

Places to Eat

The top floor of the *new market* is the place to go for hawker food. It has dozens of food stalls, and you can sit and look out over the river. The stalls at the *night market*, near the local bus station, are good for takeaway satay, grilled chicken and fish.

By the waterfront, the *Seaview Restoran* is a kedai kopi that also does toasted sandwiches and coffee at breakfast. There are literally dozens of Chinese *kedai kopi* on Jalan Masjid, all offering very similar fare.

Getting There & Away

Air Malaysia Airlines has regular flights to Sibu (four daily, RM64), Kuching (10 daily, RM117), Miri (three daily, RM69) and Kota Kinabalu (two daily, RM127). The airport is smack in the middle of town.

Bus The long distance bus terminal is about 5km from town, although buses to Batu Niah can be caught outside the Li Hua Plaza on the Bintulu waterfront. There are frequent buses to Batu Niah (two hours, RM10) and Miri (four hours, RM18). There are also plenty of daily buses to Sibu (RM16.50).

Boat If you're trying to get to Belaga, ekspres launches go up the Batang Kemena as far as Tubau. Boats leave approximately every hour between 9 am and noon; the journey takes about 3½ hours and costs RM18.

NIAH NATIONAL PARK & NIAH CAVES

A visit to the Niah Caves will probably be one of your most memorable experiences in East Malaysia. The **Great Cave**, one of the largest in the world, is in the centre of the Niah National Park, which is dominated by the 394m-high limestone massif of **Gunung Subis**. Archaeologists have found evidence that humans have been living in and around the caves here for 40,000 years.

Swiftlets construct their nests in crevices in the roof of the Great Cave, and it's these nests which are used in the preparation of that famous Chinese dish, bird's-nest soup. Scattered throughout the Great Cave are many flimsy poles, up which the collectors have to scramble to get to the nests.

The millions of winged inhabitants of the caves provide an unforgettable spectacle as evening comes along. Swiftlets are day fliers and bats are nocturnal animals, so if you arrange to be at the mouth of the cave around 6 pm you can watch the 'shift change' as the swiftlets return home and the bats go out for the night.

Orientation

The park HQ is 4km from the village of Batu Niah and the caves themselves are a further

3km along a boardwalk – an interesting one hour walk. The boardwalk continues inside the caves and it's impossible to get lost, though a torch is essential.

Places to Stay

The *Visitors' Hostel* at the park HQ is a great place to stay. Comfortable four-bed dorms cost RM10 per bed. Also available are four-bed rooms in chalets for RM60.

There are three hotels in Batu Niah; the *Niah Caves Hotel* (☎ 73 7726) is the cheapest and a good option. Simple but clean air-con rooms with shared bathroom cost RM22/RM26 for singles/doubles.

Getting There & Away

Whether you come from Bintulu or Miri you will end up at Batu Niah, the nearest town to the park. Transport to the park HQ is by taxi or by boat. Boats cost RM2 per person if there are five or more of you, or RM10 per boat. Taxis also cost RM10.

From Batu Niah to Bintulu there are seven buses daily (check at the park office for times). The two hour trip to Miri costs RM8.50 and buses depart seven times daily.

LAMBIR HILLS NATIONAL PARK

Lambir Hills is a chain of sandstone hills which, at its closest, is only 20km from Miri. While it doesn't have the spectacular scenery of Niah and Mulu, it's a good day trip from Miri for jungle walks and swimming.

The park HQ is 32km from Miri. Here you'll find the park office (☎ 085-36 637) and information centre, a canteen and chalets.

From Miri, take the Batu Niah bus for RM2.40, or any non-express bus going to Bintulu. From Niah National Park, the buses from Batu Niah to Miri pass Lambir Hills and cost RM6.

MIRI

Miri is another oil boomtown and an 'R&R' retreat for oil workers. It is by no means an unpleasant place but there is little to hold the average traveller. If you've been slogging through the rainforest and are yearning for the bright lights, Miri has plenty of good restaurants and probably the liveliest nightlife in all of Borneo.

Information

The Visitors' Information Centre Miri (☎ 43 4181) is on Jalan Melayu at the southern end

of the town centre. Here you can organise permits and accommodation for Gunung Mulu, Niah Caves and Lambir Hills National Parks.

The post office is about 15 minutes walk from the town centre along Jalan Sylvia, which continues on from Jalan Brooke. The Resident's Office, for permits to Bario and the Kelabit Highlands, is on Jalan Kingsway.

Places to Stay

Miri has little in the way of budget accommodation. The cheaper hotels are in the bus station/market area, and tend to be noisy and seedy. If you can afford it, the mid-range hotels offer much better value for money.

The cheapest option is the dorm in the Chinese *Tai Tong Lodging House* (☎ 41 1072), at 26 Jalan China, although there's little privacy and no security. Dorm beds in the lobby cost RM9, but it's noisy and smoky. Other basic but clean singles/doubles go for RM28/RM32 with fan and shared bathroom, or RM45 for a double with bathroom and air-con. The walls are thin and the dorm is not secure – this place is probably not suitable for solo female travellers.

Slightly better, if dilapidated, choices include the *Mulu Inn*, where fan rooms are RM25, and air-con rooms with bathroom cost RM37/RM42; and the *South East Asia Lodging House* (☎ 41 5488), on the square behind the Cathay Cinema, where all rooms have a common bathroom (RM28 with fan or RM40 with air-con).

The *Fairland Inn* (☎ 41 8981) on the same square is quieter than the preceding and probably the best choice. Small, clean rooms with windows, air-con, attached bathroom and TV cost RM35.

Places to Eat

For hawker food there's a small *food centre* near the Chinese temple where you can choose between Malay food and the usual Chinese dishes. On Jalan Brooke, the *Taman Seroja* is a very pleasant open-air food-stall centre where you can get good satay, more expensive seafood and other dishes.

For good curries and excellent roti, *Bilal Restaurant* is one of the better Indian restaurants you'll find in Sarawak. It is on Jalan Persiaran Kabor, a pedestrian mall, and in the evenings the restaurant sets up tables on the pavement.

Entertainment

Miri has a very lively nightlife scene. The

only problem is that things really don't get going until around 11 pm. There are no cover charges, but like elsewhere in Sabah and Sarawak, beers usually cost around RM9. A good place to start the night is *The Pub*, a friendly watering hole. *The Ranch* is just down the road and offers live music from around 10.30 pm.

Getting There & Away
Air Malaysia Airlines has Twin Otter services to Marudi (three daily, RM29), Limbang (seven daily, RM45), Pulau Labuan (twice daily, RM57), Long Seridan (weekly, RM57), Lawas (four daily, RM59), Long Lellang (twice weekly, RM66), Bario (daily, RM70) and Mulu (three daily, RM74). Bigger aircraft fly to Bintulu (four daily, RM69), Kota Kinabalu (six daily, RM104), Sibu (eight daily, RM112) and Kuching (15 daily, RM164).

Bus There are frequent buses to Bintulu (4½ hours, RM16.50). Buses to Batu Niah (two hours, RM9) depart approximately hourly and pass Lambir Hills (RM2.40) on the highway. Buses to Sibu leave seven times daily (eight hours, RM34).

See the Land entry in the main Getting There & Away section in this chapter for details on travel between Miri and Brunei.

Getting Around
For the long distance bus station, bus No A1 leaves regularly and costs 50 sen. Bus No 7 plies between Miri and the airport from 6.15 am to 8 pm; it costs RM1. Taxis to and from the airport cost RM12.

Miri itself is easy to get around. It is a small place and everything around town can be reached on foot.

MARUDI
Marudi is devoid of attractions, but you might find yourself coming through here on your way to or from the interior. Unless you fly from Miri to Bario, you need to get a permit from the District Office here to head further upstream or to Mulu.

Places to Stay
The *New Alisan Hotel* (☎ 75 5971), at 81 Jalan Kapitan Lim Ching Kiat, has grubby fan rooms for RM20 and bigger air-con rooms for RM30.

The *Hotel Zola* (☎ 75 5311) on Jalan Cinema is a notch better and has air-con rooms from RM31 to RM58.

The *Mayland* (☎ 75 5106), at the western end of the main street, has shabby but acceptable air-con singles/doubles starting at RM26/RM37.

Getting There & Away
Air Malaysia Airlines operates daily Twin Otter flights to Miri (RM29), Mulu (RM40), Long Seridan (RM42), Long Lellang (RM46), Bario (RM55) and Sibu (RM100).

Boat The ekspres boats from Kuala Baram to Marudi operate roughly every hour and cost RM18. Heading up the Batang Baram, there are ekspres boats to Kuala Apoh or Long Terawan (depending on the water level). They leave when they have enough passengers (3½ hours, RM20).

GUNUNG MULU NATIONAL PARK
Gunung Mulu is Sarawak's largest national park and one of the most popular travel destinations in Sarawak. It features rugged mountains, deep gorges with clear rivers, and a unique mosaic of habitats supporting fascinating wildlife; underneath is a 51km-long network of underground passages that includes the world's largest cave chamber, the recently discovered **Sarawak Chamber**. The two major mountains, **Gunung Mulu** and **Gunung Api** (with its spectacular limestone Pinnacles), can be visited on four and three day treks, respectively.

The park is noted for its many caves. The **Deer Cave** and the adjoining **Lang Cave** are an easy 3km walk from the park HQ along a boardwalk. The more spectacular **Clearwater Cave** and **Wind Cave** can also be reached by boat.

Information
Permits for Gunung Mulu should be obtained from the Visitors' Information Centre Miri (☎ 43 4181), where you can also book accommodation. It is possible to get to Mulu without a booking, but you run the risk of park HQ being full and being forced to use more expensive accommodation.

To visit the so-called 'Show Caves' (Lang's, Deer, Wind and Clearwater Caves) you are supposed to hire a guide. This is an expensive nuisance unless you go with a group, or form a group once you are at the park. Guides should be waiting for visitors at the entrances to the caves. For the Show Caves guides cost

RM20 per group – separate guides are needed for Clearwater and Wind Caves, and for Deer and Lang's Caves.

A guide for trekking depends on where and how far, but things will be much cheaper if you're part of a group. Boat hire costs from RM85 for a visit to Clearwater Cave (although you can walk there for nothing – it's about an hour each way) to RM350 for the Pinnacles trek.

Places to Stay & Eat
There's a 15 bed *hostel* where a bed costs RM10, and an *annexe* where five-bed rooms with attached bathroom and fans are RM15 per bed. There are two classes of *chalet* where rooms have ceiling fans and an attached bathroom; rooms in the Class 3 chalets have four beds and cost RM60, and rooms in a Class 2 chalet have three beds and cost RM90 per night.

There's a *cafeteria* at park HQ where you can buy good meals, soft drinks and beer, although you may have to go to the *cafe* over the river for good bottled water.

If you're *self-catering*, there are gas stoves and fridges at the chalets and hostel, although you'll have to ask at the park office for cutlery, crockery, pots and pans. You must bring all your food requirements from Miri.

Outside the park, the place to head for is the *Melinau Canteen* (☎ *mobile 011-29 1641, 65 7884 in Miri*). It is just a few hundred metres downriver from the jetty at the park HQ, around the bend on the other side of the river. This Berawan-owned place costs RM6 per person in bunk rooms. Tour groups occasionally fill the place up, but usually you will have no problem getting a room to yourself. Meals are available, and a provisions shop sells tinned goods, snacks, beer etc.

Further downriver at *Long Pala* are more guesthouses owned by the tour companies, such as Tropical Adventure, Seridan Mulu and Alo Doda. It is possible to stay here for around RM15 upwards per night if they are not full, though they are a long way from the park HQ.

Getting There & Away
Air The quickest – and probably the cheapest – way to get to Mulu is to fly. Malaysia Airlines has flights from Marudi (two weekly, RM40), Limbang (two daily, RM40) and Miri (three daily, RM74). The airstrip is a few minutes upstream from the park HQ (RM5 by boat).

KELABIT HIGHLANDS
If you are planning a long trek into the interior to places such as Bario, Lio Matoh and Long Lellang, the first step is to get a permit from the Resident in Miri. You can also get these permits from the District Officer in Marudi. Bario is the best place to arrange treks, and if you do a long trek to Ba Kelalan or Long Semado, you can then fly out to Lawas. Long Lellang is connected by flights to Miri.

Bario
Bario sits on a beautiful high valley floor in the Kelabit Highlands, close to the Indonesian border and makes an ideal base for treks in the highlands. Bario has shops where you can stock up on supplies and gifts to take to the longhouses, as does Ba Kelalan.

There are treks around Bario to places such as Pa Lungan, Ba Kelalan, Long Semado and Lio Matoh. You need to be well prepared and hire local guides.

Places to Stay & Eat *Tarawe's* is the place to head for. It's run by a local and his English wife. The cost is RM15 per person, and meals are available on request. They welcome travellers and provide good trekking information.

Getting There & Away Malaysia Airlines flies Twin Otters from Bario to Miri daily (RM70), usually via Marudi (RM55). Flights are very much dependent on the weather and it's not uncommon for flights to be cancelled, so make sure your schedule is not too tight. These flights are also fully booked well in advance during school holidays.

LIMBANG
This town is the divisional HQ of the Limbang District, sandwiched between Brunei and Sabah. There is nothing of interest in the town itself, but you may well find yourself coming through on the way to or from Brunei or Gunung Mulu.

The *Muhibbah Hotel* (☎ *21 2488*) is one of the cheapest places around, with some economy rooms costing from RM38.

Getting There & Away
Malaysia Airlines has flights to Lawas (RM25), Gunung Mulu (RM40), Miri (RM45) and Kota Kinabalu (RM60). The airport is 4km from the town centre, and a taxi costs RM4 per person.

An express boat goes to Lawas (RM20)

every morning at 8 am. There are also frequent boats to Bandar Seri Begawan, the capital of Brunei (30 minutes, RM18).

LAWAS

Like Limbang, Lawas is essentially a transit town and you may find yourself here while en route to or from Brunei, on your way up to Bario in the Kelabit Highlands and Ba Kelalan, or in order to take the short flight to Miri (skipping clean over Brunei).

There is no decent budget accommodation in Lawas. The *Soon Seng (☎ 85 871)* on Jalan Punang has fan doubles for RM35 and air-con rooms starting at RM45; it is probably the best of a limited choice.

Getting There & Away

There are flights to Limbang (RM25), Pulau Labuan (RM31), Long Semado (RM40), Ba Kelalan (RM47), Kota Kinabalu (RM47) and Miri (RM59).

There are two buses daily to Kota Kinabalu (RM22) via Sipitang and Beaufort, leaving at 7.30 am and 1.30 pm. Otherwise, catch a bus to Merapok (RM5) on the Sabah border, from where you can catch a bus to Sipitang. At the border you have to go through immigration formalities for both states.

For Brunei, the only boat goes at 7.30 am and costs RM20. One boat a day goes to Pulau Labuan at 7.30 am for RM20 – book at the Bee Hiong Restaurant (☎ 85 137) underneath the Hotel Million. The boat to Limbang goes at 9 am and costs RM20.

Sabah

The chief attractions of Sabah are Mt Kinabalu, the Turtle Islands and the opportunity to see wildlife in the national and state parks. Budget travellers will generally find Sabah more expensive than Peninsular Malaysia and Sarawak, but it is possible to keep costs to a minimum if you stick to the beaten trail – most of the major attractions have inexpensive accommodation and cheap eats.

Before independence Sabah was known as North Borneo and controlled by the British North Borneo Company. Before that, it was part of Brunei's empire and renowned for its pirates. Kota Kinabalu was at one time known as Api Api (Fire Fire) because of the pirates' tiresome habit of repeatedly putting it to the torch.

Today, Sabah is an integral part of Malaysia.

Its economy is based chiefly on oil, timber and agriculture. The road network is generally good, apart from a few horror stretches here and there, and the delightful little railway that meanders from Beaufort to Tenom in the south-west of the state is an interesting jungle trip.

Visas & Permits

For details of the visa requirements of this region, see the Facts for the Visitor section at the start of this chapter.

Getting There & Away

Air Malaysia Airlines has direct flights from Kota Kinabalu to KL and Johor Bahru – see the Getting Around section at the start of this chapter for details. Malaysia Airlines also flies direct to Miri (RM104), Bintulu (RM127) and Kuching (RM228) in Sarawak, and to Pulau Labuan (RM52).

Land The only way to leave Sabah by land is via the crossing to Lawas in Sarawak.

Sea Fast passenger ferries ply between Sabah's capital, Kota Kinabalu, and the Federal Territory of Labuan, with connections to Brunei. Other ferries leave for Labuan from Sipitang and Menumbok.

It is possible to travel between Sandakan on the east coast and Zamboanga in the Philippines, and between Tawau and Kalimantan (Indonesia) by sea. See the main Getting There & Away section earlier in this chapter for details.

KOTA KINABALU

Known as Jesselton until 1963, Kota Kinabalu was razed during WWII to prevent the Japanese using it as a base. Today it's a modern city of wide avenues and tall buildings, with little in the way of historical charm. All the same, KK, as everyone calls it, is not an unpleasant city; there's just not much to do. It is necessary to stop in KK to book accommodation for the trip to Mt Kinabalu, Sabah's number-one tourist attraction.

Orientation

Although the city sprawls for many kilometres along the coast from the international airport at Tanjung Aru to Likas, the centre itself is actually quite small and most places are within easy walking distance of each other.

Information

Tourist Offices Kota Kinabalu has two excellent tourist offices. Tourism Malaysia (☎ 21 1732) is on the ground floor of the Wing Onn Life building on Jalan Segunting at the northern end of the city centre. The Sabah Tourism Promotion Corporation (STPC, ☎ 21 8620), 51 Jalan Gaya, is housed in a historic building.

Foreign Consulates The Indonesian consulate (☎ 21 9110) is on Jalan Karamunsing, off Jalan Kemajuan south of the city centre.

Immigration The immigration office (☎ 28 0772) is on the 4th floor of the tall government building, near Jalan Tunku Abdul Rahman and around the corner from the Diamond Inn.

Money There are plenty of banks that can change cash and travellers cheques in the city centre. You'll find moneychangers on the ground floor of Centre Point and Wisma Merdeka.

Post & Communications The post office is right in the centre of town and has an efficient poste restante counter. International calls can be made from card phones around town.

There are two cybercafes in central KK and Net Card booths at the airport.

National Parks Bookings Accommodation in Mt Kinabalu (including Poring Hot Springs) and Tunku Abdul Rahman National Parks is handled by Kinabalu Gold Resorts (☎ 24 3629), 3rd Floor, Block C, Kompleks Karamunsing. It's about five minutes walk south along Jalan Tunku Abdul Rahman past the Hotel Shangri-La, then off to the left.

Things to See

As an example of contemporary Islamic architecture at its best, the **State Mosque** is well worth a visit. It's on the outskirts of town and you'll see it when you're on your way to or from the airport.

The **Sabah Museum** is on the outskirts of town, next to the State Legislative Assembly Hall on Jalan Tunku Abdul Rahman. For a view of the city, head up **Signal Hill** at the eastern edge of the city centre above the former main post office.

The **central market** is in two sections – the waterfront area for fish and an area in front of the harbour for fruit and vegetables. Next to the main central market on the waterfront is a market known locally as the **Filipino Market** – the stalls are owned by Filipinos, who sell a wide variety of handicrafts.

Places to Stay

The super-clean and friendly *Backpacker Lodge* (☎ 26 1495) at Australia Place has beds in segregated dorms for RM18, including breakfast. Another bright and spotless place is the *Trekkers Lodge* (☎ 21 3888), at 46 Jalan Pantai (enter from the lane at the back). Air-con dorm beds are RM20, and there's a double room for RM45; prices include breakfast.

City Park Inn (☎ 26 0607), at 2 Jalan Pasar Baru, is a combined backpackers' dorm and mid-range hotel. It's very clean and centrally located. Dorm beds are RM20, including linen and pillows; air-con singles/doubles are RM52/RM60.

There are two cheap options in the Kompleks Sinsuran, near the Filipino market. The *Traveller's Rest Hostel* (☎ 22 4720), on the 3rd floor in Block L, is a long-standing budget travellers' hangout that has seen better days. At RM13 including breakfast, the dorm beds are good value. Rooms with fan cost RM20/RM25; air-con rooms are RM36/RM40. The hostel also provides inexpensive tours to destinations around Sabah.

Next door, the *Borneo Wildlife Youth Hostel* (☎ 21 3668) has basic but clean dorm rooms at RM15 per bed for YHA members, and RM20 for others. Other than toilet and shower, the only facilities are a TV, kettle and fridge.

Farida's Bed & Breakfast (☎ 42 8733), at 413 Jalan Saga in Likas, is a delightful place set in quiet suburbia 6km north of town. Although it's a long way from the centre, staff know just what backpackers want, and can arrange transport and tours to sights around KK. Dorm beds are RM16, and double fan or air-con rooms cost RM25 (RM18 for a bed only). To get there, take any minibus that goes along Jalan Tuaran and get off at the Likas Baptist Church. Walk 100m down Jalan Likas and then turn right into Jalan Saga – Farida's is 200m on the left.

The *Seaside Travellers Inn* (☎ 75 0555), at H 30 Gaya Park, Jalan Penampang, is 20km from town past the airport towards Papar. It is not the place to stay if you want to explore KK, but may be ideal if you want a day or two on the beach and you are leaving from the airport. Accommodation ranges from a dorm bed for RM20 to rooms at RM33/RM55, all with a continental breakfast.

MALAYSIA

KOTA KINABALU

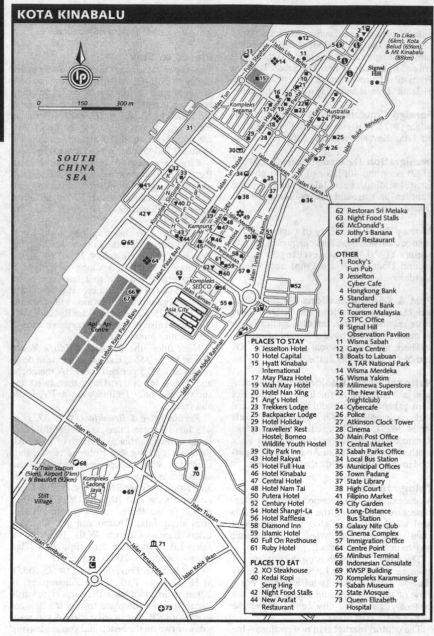

SOUTH CHINA SEA

0   150   300 m

To Likas
(6km), Kota
Belud (69km),
& Mt Kinabalu
(88km)

Signal
Hill

Australia
Place

Komplek
Segama

Kampung
Air

Kampung
Air

Asia City

To Train Station
(5km), Airport (7km)
& Beaufort (92km)

Komplek
Sadong
Jaya

Stilt
Village

62 Restoran Sri Melaka
63 Night Food Stalls
66 McDonald's
67 Jothy's Banana
    Leaf Restaurant

OTHER
1   Rocky's
    Fun Pub
3   Jesselton
    Cyber Cafe
4   Hongkong Bank
5   Standard
    Chartered Bank
6   Tourism Malaysia
7   STPC Office
8   Signal Hill
    Observation Pavilion
11 Wisma Sabah
12 Gaya Centre
13 Boats to Labuan
    & TAR National Park
14 Wisma Merdeka
16 Wisma Yakim
18 Milimewa Superstore
22 The New Krash
    (nightclub)
24 Cybercafe
26 Police
27 Atkinson Clock Tower
28 Cinema
30 Main Post Office
31 Central Market
32 Sabah Parks Office
34 Local Bus Station
35 Municipal Offices
36 Town Padang
37 State Library
38 High Court
41 Filipino Market
49 City Garden
51 Long-Distance
    Bus Station
53 Galaxy Nite Club
55 Cinema Complex
57 Immigration Office
64 Centre Point
65 Minibus Terminal
68 Indonesian Consulate
69 KWSP Building
70 Kompleks Karamunsing
71 Sabah Museum
72 State Mosque
73 Queen Elizabeth
    Hospital

PLACES TO STAY
9   Jesselton Hotel
10 Hotel Capital
15 Hyatt Kinabalu
    International
17 May Plaza Hotel
19 Wah May Hotel
20 Hotel Nan Xing
21 Ang's Hotel
23 Trekkers Lodge
25 Backpacker Lodge
29 Hotel Holiday
33 Travellers' Rest
    Hostel; Borneo
    Wildlife Youth Hostel
39 City Park Inn
43 Hotel Rakyat
45 Hotel Full Hua
46 Hotel Kinabalu
47 Central Hotel
48 Hotel Nam Tai
50 Putera Hotel
52 Century Hotel
54 Hotel Shangri-La
56 Hotel Rafflesia
58 Diamond Inn
59 Islamic Hotel
60 Full On Resthouse
61 Ruby Hotel

PLACES TO EAT
2   XO Steakhouse
40 Kedai Kopi
    Seng Hing
42 Night Food Stalls
44 New Arafat
    Restaurant

Travellers Hostels The travellers' hostels provide better value for money than KK's budget hotels, many of which tend to be noisy and slightly seedy. The *Islamic Hotel*, above the restaurant of the same name at 8 Jalan Perpaduan, has fan rooms and common bath for RM27.

The *Putera Hotel* (π 51 2814) on Jalan Merdeka, near the corner of Jalan Tunku Abdul Rahman, is a fairly clean Chinese hotel with large rooms for RM20/RM25 with fan, or RM35 to RM45 for a double with air-con.

For just a little more, the *Hotel Rakyat* (π 22 2715), in Block I of the Kompleks Sinsuran, is very good value. Rooms in this clean, friendly, Muslim-run hotel cost RM37 with fan and bathroom, and from RM40 to RM55 with air-con and bathroom.

If these are full, the *Central Hotel* (π 51 3522), at 5 Jalan Tugu, has air-con rooms with attached bath for RM40/RM48. Nearby on Jalan Merdeka, you'll find the *Hotel Nam Tai* (π 51 4803). It's fairly clean, and has double rooms for RM35 to RM45.

Places to Eat

KK offers some very good dining. The best *night market* in town is at the Kompleks SEDCO. The speciality is seafood, but other dishes are also available. Hawkers set up stalls around the *Filipino market* at night and in the vacant lot near Asia City on Jalan Pasar Baru. The top floor of the *central market* also has good food stalls.

KK's shopping malls are good foraging grounds for cheap fare. The basement of *Centre Point* has a collection of moderately priced eating places serving Malay and Chinese food. On the 2nd floor of the *Yaohan department store* are some slightly more expensive food stalls in squeaky-clean aircon surroundings; and *Wisma Merdeka* has a small but good food centre on the 2nd floor overlooking the sea.

For Indian Muslim food, try the *New Arafat Restaurant* in Block I of the Kompleks Sinsuran. This 24 hour place is run by very friendly Indians who serve excellent curries, roti and murtabak.

Entertainment

If you feel like checking out what's hip in KK, try *Rocky Fun Pub* or *The New Krash* – a good dance club. These places tend to be deserted before 10.30 pm. There's no cover charge, but drinks are not cheap at around RM9.

Getting There & Away

Air There are regular flights to Pulau Labuan (RM52), Sandakan (RM83), Tawau (RM96), Brunei (RM99), Lahad Miri (RM104), Datu (RM106), Bintulu (RM127) and Kuching (RM228).

Malaysia Airlines (π 21 3555) and Philippine Airlines (π 23 9600) are in the Kompleks Karamunsing, about five minutes walk south of the Hotel Shangri-La along Jalan Tunku Abdul Rahman. On the other side of Jalan Tunku Abdul Rahman is the KWSP building, which also contains a number of airline offices, including Dragon Air (also Cathay Pacific, π 25 4733), Royal Brunei Airlines (π 24 2193), Singapore Airlines (π 25 5444) and Thai Airways International (π 23 2896).

Bus There is no main bus station in KK. Most of the long-distance buses leave from the open area south-east of the council offices along Jalan Tunku Abdul Rahman. These buses cost only a few ringgit more than minibuses and are far more comfortable.

Kampung Likas
  Buses leave every 30 minutes between 6 am and 8 pm; 70 sen.
Lahad Datu
  All buses to Tawau pass through Lahad Datu; the fare is RM40.
Lawas (Sarawak)
  Departures are at 7.30 am and 1 pm; buses pass through Papar, Beaufort and Sipitang; RM25; 4 hours.
Mt Kinabalu
  Buses leave for the national park at 7.30 am every day; the fare is RM15 and the trip takes about three hours. You could also take any bus going to Ranau or Sandakan and asked to be dropped off at the entrance road, from where the park HQ is 100m.
Ranau (for Poring Hot Springs)
  Departures are at 8.30 am and 12.30 pm; RM10; 3½ hours.
Sandakan
  There are several departures daily between 7 and 9 am; 6 hours. Fares hover between RM20 and RM25, and it's advisable to book ahead.
Tawau
  Buses leave at 7.30 am daily; the nine hour trip costs RM50. Buses to Tawau can drop passengers at Lahad Datu.
Tuaran
  Buses leave approximately every 15 minutes between 6 am and 9 pm; RM2.

The large open plot of land behind Centre Point is a very busy minibus park. Most buses from here are local but also go to centres around KK, such as Penampang, Papar and Tuaran. All minibuses leave when full, and there are frequent early-morning departures. There are fewer departures later in the day, and don't count on departures for long-haul destinations in the afternoon. The general rule is travel early, and the further you travel the earlier you should leave. Minibus destinations and fares include: Tuaran (RM2), Beaufort (RM5), Kota Belud (RM10), Ranau (RM10 – all buses pass Kinabalu National Park), Keningau (RM10), Kudat (RM12) and Tenom (RM20).

Train The train station is 5km south of the city centre at Tanjung Aru, close to the airport. There are daily trains to Beaufort and Tenom at 8 and 11 am. The train takes four hours to Tenom and seven hours to Beaufort. Minibuses are quicker.

Taxi Besides the minibuses, there are share taxis available to most places. They also go when full, and their fares are at least 25% higher than the minibuses. Their big advantage is that they are much quicker and more comfortable.

Boat Fast passenger boats leave daily for Pulau Labuan from the jetties behind the Hyatt Hotel; there are connecting services to Muara in Brunei. There's usually no need to book in advance. The trip to Labuan generally takes about three hours, and the fare is RM33/RM28 for 1st/economy class by fast ferry or RM28 on the *Sanergy Rafflesia* catamaran. The *Sanergy Rafflesia* leaves at 7.30 am, *Labuan Express Dua* and *Express Ming Hai* leave at 8 am, *Express Kinabalu* leaves at 10 am and *Duta Muhibbah No 3* leaves at 1.30 pm.

Getting Around
To/From the Airport Take a local bus from outside the council offices for 70 sen and ask to be dropped at the airport. This bus stops opposite the access road, from where it's a 10 minute walk to the terminal. Heading into town, there's a bus stop to the right as you leave the airport.

The 15 minute taxi ride to the airport normally costs RM12.50, but you may be charged more late at night. Leaving the terminal, there's a taxi desk on the ground floor where you can buy a fixed-price coupon for RM12.50 into town.

Taxi Local taxis are plentiful. They are not metered, so it's a matter of negotiating the fare before you set off.

AROUND KOTA KINABALU
Tunku Abdul Rahman National Park
TAR National Park has a total area of nearly 4929 hectares and is made up of the offshore islands of Gaya, Mamutik, Manukan, Sapi and Sulug. Only a short boat ride from the centre of the city, these islands offer some of the best beaches in Borneo, crystal-clear waters and a wealth of tropical corals and marine life.

Places to Stay & Eat Accommodation on the islands is booked through Kinabalu Gold Resorts in KK – see the Kota Kinabalu Information entry for details. There are expensive chalets (from RM140) at Manukan and Mamutik, but it is also possible to camp at Gaya, Sulug, Mamutik and Sapi for RM5 per person if you bring your own tent.

Getting There & Away Boats run seven times daily from the national parks jetty behind Wisma Merdeka. The fare is RM10/RM5 for adults/children, and the trip to Manukan takes about 40 minutes. Depending on demand, most boats also call at Pulau Sapi.

RAFFLESIA FOREST RESERVE
The highway from Kota Kinabalu to Tambunan and the central valley region crosses the forested Crocker Range. Near the top of the range on the highway is the Rafflesia Forest Reserve, devoted to the world's largest flower. The rafflesia is a parasitic plant that is hidden within its host, the stems of jungle vines, until it bursts into bloom and grows up to 1m in diameter.

The Rafflesia Information Centre (☎ 77 4691), on the highway 59km from Kota Kinabalu, has interesting displays and information devoted to the rafflesia. From the centre, trails lead into the forest where the rafflesias can be found (if any are flowering – it's a nonseasonal bloom).

Places to Stay
There is no accommodation available at the reserve, but *Gunung Emas Highlands Resort* (☎ mobile 011-81 1562), at Km 52 on the KK-Tambunan road, is perched on the side of the mountain only 7km from the information centre. The views are superb and the climate

refreshingly mild, if not downright cold. This resort has a variety of accommodation, but apart from the dormitories, it's very expensive. A dormitory bed costs RM21, or RM31.50 with breakfast; on the other side of the highway and a steep climb up the mountain are the hilltop cabins built around tree trunks for RM63. The restaurant is overrun with day-trippers on weekends.

Getting There & Away
Take a Tambunan or Keningau minibus from KK to the reserve or the resort for RM8. From Tambunan the cost is RM4.

TAMBUNAN
Across the Crocker Range, Tambunan is a small agricultural service town about 81km from KK. Tambunan can be used as a base to climb Gunung Trus Madi, Sabah's second highest peak – it's a much more demanding climb than Mt Kinabalu.

Places to Stay
The *Tambunan Village Resort Centre* (☎ 77 4076) on Jalan TVRC is a mid-range resort with some basic rooms in three-bedroom chalets for RM50. A camping ground is also available for those with their own equipment – a camp site costs RM6.

Getting There & Away
There are regular minibuses plying the roads between Tambunan and Ranau (RM6), Keningau (RM7), Tenom (RM8) and KK (RM10).

BEAUFORT
Beaufort is a quiet provincial town on the Sungai Padas. Its two-storey wooden shophouses have a certain dilapidated charm, and the people go out of their way to make you feel welcome, but the only reason to come here is to catch the **train** to Tenom, or to pass through on the way to eastern Sarawak, Brunei or Pulau Labuan.

Heading south to Lawas in Sarawak, you pass through Sipitang, which has cheap accommodation and early morning boats to Labuan.

Places to Stay
The two hotels in town are of the same standard, and have air-con rooms with TV and attached bathrooms. Both charge RM30/RM36 singles/doubles. The *Hotel Beaufort* (☎ 21 1911) is near the mosque, and the

Mandarin Inn (☎ 21 2800) is over the bridge across the river.

Getting There & Away
Bus Express buses leave daily for KK at 10.30 am and 4 pm (1½ hours, RM14). There are frequent minibus departures for KK (two hours, RM5), and less frequent departures for Sipitang (1½ hours, RM6). To Menumbok (for Pulau Labuan), there are plenty of minibuses until early afternoon (one hour, RM6).

Train It's a spectacular trip between Beaufort and Tenom, where the train follows the Sungai Padas through steamy jungle. At times the dense jungle forms a bridge over the narrow track. The railcar is quicker and more comfortable, and costs RM8.35, while the diesel train costs RM2.75. Book as soon as you arrive in Beaufort or at the Tanjung Aru train station in KK (☎ 25 4611). Departures are listed in the table at the station.

PULAU LABUAN
Off the coast from Menumbok, Labuan is the main jumping-off point for Brunei. The island is a federal territory, governed directly from KL, and its main claim to fame these days is as a duty-free centre. There's very little of interest here for the traveller, and it is best avoided.

Places to Stay
Budget accommodation in Bandar Labuan is very limited. The *Pantai View Hotel* (☎ 41 1339), Jalan Bungah Tanjung, has fan rooms with shared bathroom that are comparatively cheap at RM30; there are also air-con rooms for RM45. If you can afford it, you're better off elsewhere.

Around the corner on Jalan OKK Awang Besar, *Hotel Sri Villa* (☎ 41 6369) has large fan rooms for RM35; air-con rooms start at RM40. The nearby *Melati Inn* (☎ 41 6307) has small air-con rooms for RM45; rooms with an attached bathroom cost RM45/RM48 for singles/doubles.

Getting There & Away
Air There are flights to Kota Kinabalu (RM52), Miri (RM66), Kuching (RM199) and KL (RM372). A taxi to the airport should not cost more than RM8 from Bandar Labuan.

Boat The cheapest option is the slow car ferry to Menumbok which leaves at 8 am, and

1 and 4 pm, costs RM5 for passengers and takes around 1½ hours. At least four launches – more at busy times – connect Pulau Labuan and Kota Kinabalu (KK). Tickets can be bought just before departure, or you can book in advance; the fare is RM28, or RM33 in 1st class. The *Duta Muhibbah No 3* leaves Labuan at 8.30 am, and the *Labuan Express Dua* (RM28) departs at 1 pm. These boats can be booked through Sinmatu (☎ 41 2261) on Jalan Merdeka. *Express Kinabalu* leaves Labuan at 3.30 pm and can be booked at the Duta Muhibbah Agency. *Sanergy Rafflesia* departs at 3.30 pm.

TENOM

Tenom is the home of the friendly Murut people, most of whom are farmers. It's a pleasant rural town and is the end of the railway line from Tanjung Aru (just out of KK).

Despite the peaceful setting there's absolutely nothing to do, although the **train trip** to Beaufort is highly recommended.

Places to Stay & Eat

The *Hotel Syn Nam Tai* on the main street is a basic Chinese hotel with fan-cooled singles/doubles for RM18/RM24 with shared bathroom. A little bargaining may be required.

The Indian-run *Sabah Hotel* (☎ 73 5534) is entered through the Bismillah Restaurant. Simple but clean fan rooms cost RM20; air-con rooms are RM37. The *Hotel Kim San* (☎ 73 5485), set back from the main road, has run-down air-con rooms for RM28 a double.

Food stalls set up in the evening in the car park down the main road from the padang. There are plenty of Chinese *kedai kopi* in town selling basic Chinese food. The *Yun Lee Restaurant* on the main street is popular with the locals, but it closes in the early evening; the *Restoran Fon Chi*, not far from the Hotel Kim San, stays open a bit later.

Getting There & Away

Most minibuses go to Keningau (RM5), but some also go to KK (RM25). You may as well take the train to Beaufort if you're here.

KOTA BELUD

Kota Belud is the venue of Sabah's largest and most colourful **market**; it takes place every Sunday – get there as early as possible. It's an easy day trip from KK.

Minibuses go to KK (two hours, RM5) and Kudat (two hours, RM5).

KUDAT

Kudat is right at the far north-eastern tip of Sabah and gets very few foreign visitors. It has a noticeable Filipino influence. The area around Kudat has fine **beaches** and **Rungus longhouses**, though it is difficult to get around without your own transport.

Places to Stay

In the old part of town, the *Hotel Oriental* has worn but OK fan-cooled rooms for RM20, and air-con for RM35. All the other hotels are mid-range air-con places. The *Hotel Sunrise* (☎ 61 1517) is of a reasonable standard; fan/air-con rooms with shared bathroom cost RM20/RM28; single/double air-con rooms with bathroom and TV are RM40/ RM48.

Getting There & Away

Several minibuses a day make the three to four hour trip from Kota Kinabalu for RM15.

MT KINABALU

Sabah's main attraction is the highest mountain between the mighty Himalayas and Mt Puncak Jaya in Irian Jaya. Mt Kinabalu towers 4101m above what's left of the lush tropical forests of North Borneo, and is the centrepiece of the vast 750 sq km Kinabalu National Park. Despite its height, it is one of the easiest mountains in the world to climb, and thousands of people of all age groups and fitness levels climb it every year. All you need is a little stamina, and gear to protect you from the elements – it can get very cold and wet up there.

Information

The climb to the top is best attempted with an overnight stop on the way, so bring plenty of warm clothes – you can hire sleeping bags. A climbing permit and Climber's Personal Accident Insurance are compulsory to climb to the summit. The permit costs RM50 for foreigners and RM25 for Malaysians; insurance costs RM3.50 per person per journey. All this is payable at the park HQ before you climb. A guide is compulsory if you climb beyond Laban Rata, ie to the summit, and the guide's fee is RM25 per day for one to three people, RM28 for four to six people and RM30 for seven to eight (the maximum). Attach yourself to a group to cut down on costs.

On the first day, you get to within around 700m of the summit; set off before dawn the next day to be on the summit before mid-morning, when the clouds roll in. The trip back down to park HQ takes the rest of the day.

It's worth spending a day or so exploring the well marked trails around the park HQ. Guided walks leave daily from the administration building and last for one to two hours.

A slide and video show is presented at the administration building from Friday to Monday at 7.30 pm. It provides an excellent introduction to the mountain.

Places to Stay & Eat
Park Headquarters Advance bookings at Kinabalu Gold Resorts in KK are essential. The cheapest places to stay are the 46 bed *Old Fellowship Hostel* and the 52 bed *New Fellowship Hostel*, which cost RM10 per person, or RM5 for anyone under 18 years of age. Both hostels are clean and comfortable, have cooking facilities and a dining area with an open fireplace. The Old Hostel tends to be less cramped.

The rest of the accommodation at park HQ is good but expensive, and gets even more pricey on weekends and holidays. Twin-bed *cabins* are RM50 (RM80 on weekends) and *annexes* for up to four people are RM100 (RM160). Two-bedroom *chalets* sleeping up to six people cost RM150 (RM200) per night.

The cheaper and more popular of the two restaurants is *Kinabalu Balsam*, down the steps below the park office; it offers Malay, Chinese and western food at reasonable prices. There's also a small shop which sells a limited range of tinned foods, chocolate, beer, spirits, cigarettes, T-shirts, bread, eggs and margarine. The other *restaurant* is in the main administration building, just past the hostels. Both restaurants are open from 6 am until 10 pm (11 pm on weekends).

On the Mountain On your way up to the summit you will have to stay overnight at one of the mountain huts at 3300m or the 54 bed *Laban Rata Rest House*, which costs RM25 per person in four-bed rooms. It has heating, hot water and a restaurant.

There are three huts at 3300m: the 12 bed *Waras* and *Panar Laban* huts, and the 44 bed *Guntin Lagadan Hut*. These cost RM10 per person, or RM5 for those under 18. They are more spartan and unheated, but a sleeping bag is provided and the huts are within walking distance of the *restaurant* at Laban Rata, which is not only open for regular meals but also opens from 2 to 3 am, so you can grab some breakfast before attempting

the summit. The huts have cooking facilities which you can use if you bring your own food.

As far as sleep is concerned, it doesn't make much difference where you stay; you may sleep fitfully – the air is quite thin up there. It's *very* cold in the early mornings (around 0°C!), so take warm clothing with you.

Getting There & Away
All express and minibuses between KK and Ranau or Sandakan pass the park turn-off, from where it is 100m to the park. Air-con express buses leave from the long-distance bus station in KK at 7.30 am every day; the fare is RM15 and the trip takes about three hours. There are several minibuses daily from KK to Ranau which depart up to about 1 pm.

If you're heading back towards KK, minibuses pass the park HQ until mid-afternoon, but the best time to catch one is between 8 am and noon.

RANAU
Ranau is just a small provincial town halfway between Kota Kinabalu and Sandakan. Few travellers stay overnight since the big attraction is Poring Hot Springs, about 19km north of the town.

The *Hotel Ranau* (☎ 87 5661) is the first place you see when entering the town and is opposite the Shell petrol station. Singles/doubles with fan cost RM30/RM45 and range up to RM70 with air-con, TV and bath.

Getting There & Away
Minibuses and taxis depart daily for KK up to about 4 pm, sometimes later, cost RM15 and take about three hours. It is best to catch them in the morning, as the afternoon services are less reliable. There are large air-con buses to Sandakan (3½ hours, RM25) from around 7.30 am until noon. Minibuses go throughout the day but can take a while to fill up, especially in the afternoon.

PORING HOT SPRINGS
The Poring Hot Springs are also part of the Kinabalu National Park, but are 43km away from the park HQ and 19km north of Ranau.

There are tubs for soaking in, walking trails for some exercise and a jungle canopy walk for a monkey's-eye view of the forest.

Places to Stay & Eat
It is essential to make advance bookings at Kinabalu Gold Resorts in KK.

The *Poring Hostel* has two units – one with 24 beds and one with 40 beds. Costs are RM10 per person (RM5 if you are under 18 years of age), and blankets and pillows are provided free of charge. There is a clean, spacious kitchen with gas cookers. A camping ground is also available for RM5 per tent, though you will have to bring your own. Pillows and blankets can be hired for 50 sen each. There are also more expensive cabins from RM60.

There's a good *restaurant* near the park swimming pool and three inexpensive *eating places* opposite the park gate.

Getting There & Away

From Ranau, share taxis to Poring cost RM5 on weekends. On weekdays you may need to hitch or charter a taxi (RM20).

SEPILOK ORANG-UTAN REHABILITATION CENTRE

Sepilok is one of only four orang-utan sanctuaries in the world and one of Sabah's major tourist attractions. The apes are brought here to be rehabilitated to forest life and about 20 still return regularly to be fed. It's unlikely you'll see anywhere near this number at feeding time – three or four is a more likely number.

Information

The apes are fed daily at a platform in the forest about 10 minutes walk from the centre, usually at 10 am and 3 pm. The reserve has a Nature Education Centre and videos are shown daily. Visiting hours are from 9.10 to 11 am and 2.10 to 3.30 pm. To see everything you should arrive at 9 am or 2 pm. Admission is RM10 (RM1 for Malaysians).

Places to Stay & Eat

After KK, Sepilok has the best selection of backpackers' accommodation in Sabah, and there's no need to stay in Sandakan unless they are full. *Sepilok B & B* (☎ 53 2288) is a professionally run place set in peaceful gardens 100m off Jalan Sepilok, about 500m short of the Centre entrance. Dorms beds cost RM15 and fan doubles are RM40.

Sepilok Jungle Resort I (☎ 53 3031) is in the opposite direction off Jalan Sepilok and offers a range of accommodation, including dorms at RM20 a bed and fan doubles/twins for RM50/RM60.

Labuk B & B (☎ 53 3190), Mile 15, Jalan Labuk, is a couple of kilometres back along the KK road. This delightful family-run concern has fan bunk or double rooms costing RM20 per person. Dinner is RM10.

Uncle Tan (☎ 53 1917), Mile 16, Jalan Labuk, is a long-established operator based about 3.5km from the Sepilok turn-off towards KK. A bed in simple dorms costs RM20, including breakfast. It's basic accommodation and it's a little inconvenient for Sepilok.

There is a *cafeteria* at the Rehabilitation Centre, open from 7 am to 4 pm, that serves breakfast, sandwiches, noodle and rice dishes, and drinks.

Getting There & Away

All express buses from KK can drop you at the turn-off to the Centre (Jalan Sepilok), or at Labuk B&B or Uncle Tan's. Just ask the driver and remind him as you get closer. The fare from KK is RM20 to RM25.

Sepilok is 25km from central Sandakan. Take the blue Labuk bus marked 'Sepilok Batu 14' from the local bus stand next to the central market on the Sandakan waterfront (45 minutes, RM1.40).

SANDAKAN

The former capital city of Sabah, Sandakan is today a major commercial centre where the products of the interior are brought to be loaded onto boats for export.

There's nothing much to see or do and the real attractions lie outside the city. If you are only visiting Sepilok there is no need to go to Sandakan; you'll have to pass through if you want to visit **Turtle Islands National Park**, and it's a useful transit point for the **Batang Kinabatangan**.

Information

Bookings and transport for Turtle Islands National Park (Pulau Penyu National Park) are handled by Crystal Quest (☎ 21 2711), 12th Floor, Wisma Khoo Siak Chiew.

Places to Stay

If you are only visiting Sandakan to see the Orang-utan Rehabilitation Centre at Sepilok, it's probably better to stay out there since it's situated about 25km from the town centre (see the Sepilok section for details of budget accommodation).

In Sandakan, most budget travellers head for the *Travellers' Rest Hostel* (☎ 21 6454), 2nd Floor, Block E, Bandar Leila, about 1km west of the town centre. It's a friendly place with fan-cooled dorm beds at RM20 and a couple of simple doubles for RM25. The

Travellers' Rest also runs a jungle lodge on the Batang Kinabatangan (see that section for more information), and can organise tours to other attractions around the city.

The **Hotel Paris** (☎ 21 8488), Lorong Dua, has clean singles/doubles from RM25/RM35 with fan and bathroom, or RM48 for an aircon double with bathroom.

Places to Eat

For no-frills food, try one of the stalls upstairs in the **central market**. A couple of ringgit will get you a decent meal, but choose carefully, as hygiene might not be first-class. There's more market food at the **night market** which sets up outside the post office each evening.

Sandakan has many cheap **Chinese restaurants** and **coffee houses** serving standard rice or noodle dishes, particularly near the waterfront. For good Malay food, try the **Habeeb Restoran** on Jalan Pryer near the market. There are a couple of similar places close by, including the **Citarasa** and **Restoran Gane**.

Getting There & Away

Air There are flights to KK (RM83), Kudat (RM54) and Tawau (RM74).

Bus The long-distance bus station is opposite the community centre, out towards the post office. Most express buses to KK leave at 6.30 or 7 am (last one at 12 pm); the trip takes about six hours and costs RM20 to RM25.

Buses depart daily for Lahad Datu between 6.30 am and 5 pm (three hours, RM15), and for Tawau between 6.30 and 8 am (5½ hours, RM20).

There's also a bus to Semporna at 8 am costing RM20 and taking about 5½ hours. If you miss this you can take one to Lahad Datu, from where there are more frequent minibuses to Semporna.

Getting Around

If you're arriving or leaving by air, the airport is about 11km from the city. A taxi costs RM15. The Batu 7 airport bus runs by the airport, stopping on the main road about 500m from the terminal. The fare to/from the city centre is 70 sen.

TURTLE ISLANDS NATIONAL PARK

Taman Pulau Penyu (Turtle Islands National Park) comprises three small islands which lie 40km north of Sandakan. Pulau Selingan,

Pulau Bakungan Kecil and Pulau Gulisan are visited by marine turtles which come ashore to lay their eggs, mainly between the months of August and October.

Places to Stay & Eat

It is not possible to visit Turtle Islands on a day trip, and any excursion must be arranged through Crystal Quest (see the Sandakan Information entry.)

The only accommodation is in **chalets** on Pulau Selingan, and meals and transfers are included in the tour packages. Currently these cost RM150 per person per night, including dinner and breakfast, or RM170 including three meals a day. These prices are on a twin share basis, so if you're travelling alone, try to team up with someone or you're in for even more expense. Extra meals are available for a set RM20 per person.

Getting There & Away

Transport to the islands is included as part of a tour, and Crystal Quest will try to put individuals in with a group.

BATANG KINABATANGAN

The Batang Kinabatangan (Kinabatangan River) is Sabah's longest river, measuring 560km from its headwaters in the south-west side of the state to where it empties into the Sulu Sea east of Sandakan. Logging and clearing for plantations have devastated the upper reaches of the river, but by a strange irony the riverine forest near the coast is so hemmed in by oil palm plantations that an astonishing variety of wildlife is both common and easy to see. This is one of the best places in Borneo – indeed, in all of south-east Asia – to observe wildlife, and the Kinabatangan will be a highlight of any nature lover's trip to Sabah.

Independent travel to the Kinabatangan is virtually impossible, but if wildlife is your passion, make room in your budget to visit this incredible place.

Places to Stay & Eat

Backpackers and budget travellers are catered for in jungle camps, and there's a cluster of more expensive lodges near the riverside village of Sukau.

Travellers' Rest Jungle Camp is run by the backpackers' hostel of the same name in Sandakan; bookings and transport can be arranged through the hostel. This place gets good reports, and wild orang-utans are occasionally seen around the sleeping huts.

Accommodation and meals cost RM15 per day.

Uncle Tan's Jungle Camp is a longstanding budget option. It's ultra-basic accommodation, but among diehards it's a legend – the food is very good, and many return for a second visit. Tan also charges RM15 per person per day for accommodation and meals.

Getting There & Away
Camp operators arrange transport to and from the river; both Travellers' Rest and Uncle Tan charge RM130 per person for the return trip, so obviously it's better if you stay a few days.

SEMPORNA
Most foreigners who pass through Semporna are en route to or from **Pulau Sipadan**, which is renowned for its superb diving. Accommodation on the island is provided by expensive resorts.

Places to Stay & Eat
The main hotel in Semporna is the ridiculously expensive *Dragon Inn Hotel* (☎ 78 1088), built in traditional floating-village style over the water. The bamboo and thatch air-con rooms cost an outrageous RM165; family rooms are cheaper at RM110 but are usually full.

The only alternative is the friendly but rundown *Hotel Semporna* (☎ 78 1378), on the main street in town, where poor-value air-con rooms start at RM40.

Getting There & Away
Minibuses leave from the town centre for Lahad Datu (2½ hours, RM8) and Tawau (1½ hours, RM4). There are also share-taxis to Tawau for RM10.

TAWAU
A mini-boomtown on the very south-east corner of Sabah close to the Indonesian border, Tawau is a provincial capital and commercial centre. There is nothing of interest in town and it is generally only visited by travellers en route to or from Tarakan in Kalimantan.

Information
There's no tourist office, although the reception desk at the Belmont Marco Polo Hotel may be able to help with inquiries.

The Indonesian consulate (☎ 77 2052) is on Jalan Apas, 3km from the centre on the main road coming into town.

Places to Stay
The so-called budget hotels in Tawau are poor value for money. There's a couple of basic lodging houses that aren't brothels, but they are not recommended for women travellers.

The cheapest is the *Penginapan Kinabalu Lodging House*, Jalan Chester, where basic singles/doubles can be bargained down to RM15/RM20. Much better is the *Hotel Soon Yee* (☎ 77 2447), 1362 Jalan Stephen Tan, where a simple fan cooled room costs RM18, and air-con rooms with bathroom start at RM28. It's a clean, well run place.

The *Tawau Hotel* (☎ 77 1100), 73 Jalan Chester, has basic, musty and tatty fan-cooled rooms for RM27.50, or air-con rooms with attached bathroom for RM38.50.

The *Loong Hotel* (☎ 76 5308), on Jalan Abaca, is probably the best bet in this price range. Clean air-con rooms start at RM38/RM48 for singles/twin share, and a room with a double bed is RM53.

Places to Eat
Hawkers' stalls seem to spring up wherever there's a vacant lot and you won't have to walk far for a cheap feed. Indonesian and Malaysian favourites can found at the *old* and *new markets*, along the waterfront near the public library, and next to the mosque on Jalan Klinik.

For good Malay food, try the *Restoran Sinar Murni* near the waterfront; there's a good Chinese *kedai kopi* downstairs at the Loong Hotel. The centrally located *Restoran Yasin* does good murtabak and curries.

There are also a couple of branches of *SugarBun* and *KFC* around town.

Getting There & Away
Air Malaysia Airlines has flights between Tawau and Kota Kinabalu (RM96) and Sandakan (RM74).

See the main Getting There & Away section at the beginning of this chapter for details of flights to Indonesia.

Bus Air-con express buses to Sandakan (5½ hours, RM20) and KK (nine hours, RM50) leave daily from 5.30 until 8.30 am. There are also frequent minibuses to Semporna (1½ hours, RM5).

Boat See the main Getting There & Away section at the beginning of this chapter for details of boats to Indonesia.

Myanmar

Charming, chaotic, controversial and serene, Myanmar (formerly Burma) remains to the visitor an intriguing culture.

Already one of the world's least western-influenced countries, Myanmar was virtually sealed off from the outside world in 1962, when a dictatorial regime took control of the government and economy. The country has come under increasing international scrutiny following a popular uprising in 1988 and the military's refusal to relinquish power following national elections in 1990. Simultaneous efforts to attract tourism have done nothing to lessen widespread international criticism of its harsh policies.

Charming, chaotic, controversial and serene, Myanmar remains as insular as it is intriguing.

Should You Visit Myanmar?

Myanmar remains under tight military rule. Dissent of any sort is suppressed, and political prisoners have plenty of company in jail or labour camps.

SLORC (State Law & Order Restoration Council), the abominable military junta that has run Myanmar since 1962, recently changed its name to the less catchy SPDC (State Peace & Development Council). But most observers of the political scene are reluctant to give up the nasty-sounding SLORC moniker, and its use is still common.

As a ruling group, it is continuing a tradition that has existed in Myanmar for centuries. Most Burmese monarchs, up to and including the last, King Thibaw, came to power by killing off all persons with claims to the throne. In many regards, Myanmar is still a hundred years behind the rest of South-East Asia. Corvée – involuntary civilian service to the state – was practised in Thailand, Laos, Vietnam and Cambodia until early this century. It is still practised in Myanmar. It is not uncommon in small towns and on isolated roads to see gangs of teenaged girls and boys doing road work in 10-hour shifts for which they make about K100.

Some refugee and human rights groups urge non-Burmese not to visit Myanmar, believing that tourism contributes to government repression in Myanmar. Others believe that international visitation helps educate the world as to what's really going on in the

country, filling in the gaps left by sharply focused refugee and activist reports. Until the country began opening up to investment and tourism in 1989, almost no one in the international community – certainly not in the international media – seemed to care about what had been going on in Myanmar for the last 35 years. The National Coalition Government of the Union of Burma, formed by refugee MPs who were elected in 1990 but prevented from taking office, has advised: 'Tourists should not engage in activities that will only benefit SLORC's coffers and not the people of Burma. However, responsible individuals and organisations who wish to verify the facts and to publicise the plight of the Burmese people are encouraged to utilise SLORC's more relaxed tourist policies.'

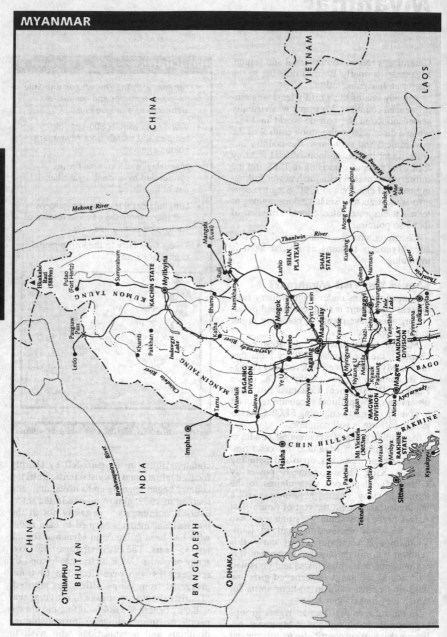

MYANMAR

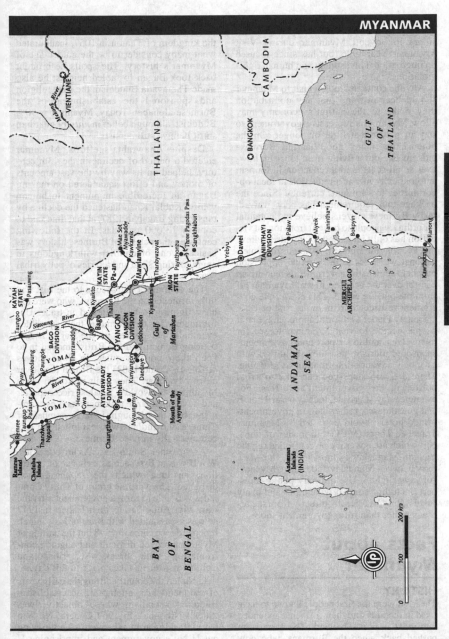

MYANMAR

National League for Democracy (NLD) spokesperson Aung San Suu Kyi urged outsiders to boycott Myanmar during Visit Myanmar Year 1996, but has since focused on international investment and human rights violations.

Anyone contemplating a visit to Myanmar should bear in mind that any contribution they make to the nation's economy may allow Myanmar's repressive government to stay in power that little bit longer. On the other hand, many good-hearted Burmese citizens eke out a living from tourism, however small-scale, and a reduction in tourism automatically means a reduction in local opportunities to earn hard currency. Since the package-tour requirement has been waived, many Burmese citizens believe the potential for ordinary people to benefit from tourist visitation has only increased. Many also believe that keeping the Burmese isolated from international witnesses to the internal oppression may help cement the government's fear-driven control over the people and seal Myanmar off from the outside world. This is why the government restricts tourism in the first place.

Lonely Planet's editorial approach is that if people decide to visit Myanmar to see for themselves, and to support non-government-sponsored tourism, that they should go with as much advance information as possible. There are also steps you can take to avoid bolstering the government's coffers. For example: stay at private, locally owned hotels and guesthouses, rather than in government-owned hotels; avoid tours led by Myanmar Travel & Tours (MTT) and modes of transport which are government-controlled (eg the Yangon-Mandalay express trains, the MTT ferry between Mandalay and Bagan, Myanma Airways flights). Use ordinary public transport (including some private trains and many flights); buy handicrafts directly from the artisans rather than from government shops.

Facts about Myanmar

HISTORY

The Mon were the first people known to have lived in the area and their influence extended into what is now Thailand. The Mon were pushed back when the Burmans, who now comprise two-thirds of the total population, began arriving from the Tibetan Plateau to the north around the 9th century.

King Anawrahta took the throne of Bagan (Pagan) in 1044 and, with his conquest of the kingdom of Thaton in 1057, inaugurated what many consider to be the golden age of Myanmar's history. The spoils he brought back took Bagan to fabled heights; he also made Theravada Buddhism the state religion and sponsored the establishment of the Burmese alphabet. Today, Myanmar is 90% Buddhist, although belief in *nats*, or guardian spirit beings, still persists.

Despite Anawrahta's efforts, Myanmar entered a period of decline in the 13th century, helped on its way by the vast amounts of money and effort squandered on making Bagan an incredible monument to human vanity. Kublai Khan hastened the decline by ransacking Bagan in 1287, at that time said to contain 13,000 pagodas. In the following centuries, the pattern of Burmese history was basically one of conflict with kingdoms in neighbouring Siam and a series of petty tribal wars.

The coming of Europeans to the east had little influence on the Burmese, who were too busy fighting to be interested in trade. Unfortunately for the Burmese, their squabbles eventually encroached on the Raj in neighbouring Bengal and the British moved in to keep their borders quiet. In three moves (1824, 1852 and 1883) the British took over all of Myanmar. They built railroads, made Myanmar the world's greatest rice exporter and developed large teak markets. Less commendably, they brought in large numbers of Chinese and Indians who exploited the less commercially minded Burmese.

As in other South-East Asian countries, WWII was at first seen as a chance of liberation, an idea which the Japanese soon dispelled. The wartime group of Thirty Comrades was able to form a government after the war, with Aung San as their leader. In 1947 he was assassinated with most of his cabinet. Independence came in 1948 but the uniting of Myanmar proved difficult and ongoing confrontation with breakaway tribes and Communist rebels takes place to this day.

U Nu led the country during the early years of independence, attempting to establish a Buddhist socialism whose objective was 'Social Nibbana'. In 1962 General Ne Win led a left-wing army takeover. After throwing out U Nu's government and imprisoning U Nu for four years, Ne Win set the country on the 'Burmese Way to Socialism'. The path was all downhill. He nationalised everything in sight, including retail shops, and quickly crippled the country economically. The Burmese saw their naturally well-endowed economy stumble as exports of everything plummeted.

Myanmar's crumbling economy reached a virtual standstill when, in 1987 and 1988, after a long period of suffering, the Burmese people had had enough of their incompetent, arrogant government. They packed the streets in huge demonstrations, insisting that Ne Win had to go. He finally did go in July 1988 but in the following month massive confrontations between pro-democracy demonstrators and the military contributed to an estimated 3000 deaths over a six week period.

Ne Win's National Unity Party (formerly the Burmese Socialist Programme Party) was far from ready to give up control and the public protests continued as two wholly unacceptable Ne Win stooges followed him. The third Ne Win successor came to power after a military coup in September 1988 which, it is generally believed, was organised by Ne Win.

The new State Law & Order Restoration Council (SLORC) established martial law under the leadership of General Saw Maung, commander-in-chief of the armed forces, and promised to hold democratic National Assembly elections in May 1989. The opposition quickly formed a coalition party and called it the National League for Democracy (NLD) and in the following months it campaigned tirelessly.

The long-suppressed Burmese population rallied around the charismatic NLD spokesperson, Aung San Suu Kyi, the daughter of national hero Aung San. Nervous, SLORC tried to appease the masses with new roads and paint jobs in Yangon (Rangoon), and then attempted to interfere in the electoral process by shifting villages from one part of the country to another. Just prior to the election the government placed Aung San Suu Kyi under house arrest.

In spite of all preventive measures, the National Unity Party lost the May National Assembly elections to the NLD, which captured over 85% of the vote. Even though an ex-military man, U Aung Shwe, would have become prime minister, the military refused to allow the opposition to assume their parliamentary seats and arrested most of the party leadership. Most were later released.

Aung San Suu Kyi was awarded the Nobel Peace Prize in 1991 and finally released from house arrest in July 1995, although she hasn't been allowed to travel in Myanmar outside Yangon. She has continually refused offers of freedom in exchange for exile from the country. At first there was cautious optimism regarding her chances of developing a dialogue with the military but very little progress has actually occurred. And despite an on-going debate in the pro-democracy movement over future strategy, her stature throughout Myanmar is as great as ever.

The government's rhetoric and deeds are as abrasive as ever. Harassment of Shan refugees near the Thai border continues, primarily through the work of the Democratic Karen Buddhist Army (DKBA). Yangon disavows control of the DKBA which has conducted frequent raids on the Huay Kalok refugee camp near Mae Sot (Thailand), just across the Moei River. Observers have reported the burning of villages and the forced repatriation of 'adult males' back to Myanmar, as well as apparent complicity by Thai army units which have left their posts prior to the raids. The only good news on the horizon is that the United Nations High Commission for Refugees (UNHCR) has become involved and has agreed to administer the camps and to move them deeper into Thai territory.

GEOGRAPHY

Myanmar covers an area of 671,000 sq km. It is sandwiched between Thailand and Bangladesh, with India and China bordering to the north. The centre of the country is marked by wide rivers and expansive plains, and mountains rise to the east along the Thai border and to the north, where you find the easternmost end of the Himalaya.

Most of the country's agriculture is situated along the floodplains of the 2000km Ayeyarwady River (formerly spelt Irrawaddy), which flows south from its source 27km north of Myitkyina to a vast delta region along the Gulf of Martaban (the upper Andaman Sea) south-west of Yangon. Other major rivers are the Chindwinn, the Kaladan, the Sittoung and the Thanlwin, which has its headwaters in China and for some distance forms the border between Myanmar and Thailand before eventually reaching the sea at Mawlamyine. The Mekong River forms the border between Myanmar and Laos.

The Himalaya rise in the north of Myanmar, and Hkakabo Razi, right on the border between Myanmar and Tibet, is 5889m. West of Bagan towards Rakhine, Mt Victoria rises to 3053m. A wide expanse of comparatively dry plain stretches north of Yangon, but hill ranges running north-south separate the central plain from Myanmar's neighbours.

The country is rich in timber, gems, oil, natural gas and mineral deposits, all of which are major sources of hard currency for the Tatmadaw, the armed forces.

Name Changes

One of the cursory changes instituted by the government since the 1988 uprising has been a long list of geographic name changes in an effort to further purge the country of its colonial past. The official name of the country has been changed from the Socialist Republic of the Union of Burma to the Union of Myanmar.

According to the government, 'Myanmar' avoids national identification with the Burman ethnic group; 'Burma' is an English corruption of 'Bamar', the Burmese term for that ethnic group. 'Myanmar' has in fact been the official Burmese name for the country since at least the time of Marco Polo's 13th century writings.

In most of the name changes, the new Romanised versions bring the names phonetically closer to the everyday Burmese pronunciation. The 'r' at the end of 'Myanmar' is merely a British English device used to lengthen the preceding 'a' vowel; it is not pronounced. State enterprises that use 'Myanmar' in their titles typically spell the word without an 'r', eg Myanma Airways, Myanma Five Star Line, Myanma Timber Enterprise and so on.

old name	new name
Burma	Myanmar
Rangoon	Yangon
Mandalay	no change
Maymyo	Pyin U Lwin
Moulmein	Mawlamyine
Myohaung	Mrauk U
Pagan	Bagan
Pegu	Bago
Prome	Pyay
Sandoway	Thandwe
Yaunghwe	Nyaungshwe
Irrawaddy River	Ayeyarwady River
Salween River	Thanlwin River

CLIMATE

The rainy season lasts from mid-May until mid-October. For the next few months, the weather is quite reasonable. In fact, it is actually cool in Mandalay at night and near freezing in Kalaw, near Inle Lake. From mid-February, it gets increasingly hot until the rains arrive once more. The Burmese New Year in April, at the peak of the hot season, means much fun and throwing water at all concerned. November to February are the best months to visit.

See the Yangon climate chart in the Appendix.

ECOLOGY & ENVIRONMENT

From the snow-capped Himalaya in the north to the coral-fringed Mergui Archipelago in the south, Myanmar's 2000km length crosses three distinct ecological regions: the Indian subregion along the Bangladesh and India borders; the Indochinese subregion in the north bordering Laos and China; and the Sundaic subregion bordering peninsular Thailand. Together these regions produce what is quite likely the richest biodiversity in South-East Asia.

Very little natural history research has been carried out in Myanmar due to the country's self-imposed isolation from the academic world since independence. Myanmar claims to have three national parks and 17 wildlife sanctuaries (including two marine and three wetland environments), which together protect about 1% of the nation's total land surface. Compared with international averages, this is a very low coverage (Thailand, by comparison, has 12% coverage); the government plans to raise protection to 5% by the end of the century.

At the moment, deforestation by the timber industry poses the greatest threat to wildlife habitats. The state-owned Myanma Timber Enterprise (MTE) accounts for most of the logging undertaken throughout the country. The latest government plan calls for the complete elimination of all log exports, figuring that the greatest potential revenue comes from processed wood products rather than raw timber. If this plan is carried out, cutting should slow even further. Unfortunately illegal logging in areas of the country controlled by insurgent armies – particularly in the Shan and Kayin states – is not controlled. These areas – rather than the MTE – are the greatest source of timber smuggled to neighbouring countries.

Wildlife laws are seldom enforced due to corruption and a general lack of manpower. While many animals are hunted for food, tigers and rhinos are killed for the lucrative overseas Chinese pharmaceutical market. Among the Chinese, the ingestion of tiger penis and bone are thought to have curative effects. Taipei, where at least two-thirds of the pharmacies deal in tiger parts (in spite of the fact that such trade is contrary to Taiwanese law) is the world centre for Burmese tiger consumption.

Marine resources are threatened by a lack of long-range conservation goals. For the moment, Myanmar's lack of industrialisation means the release of pollutants into the seas is relatively low. But overfishing, especially in the delta regions, is a growing problem.

Financed primarily by oil giants Unocal and Total, a major gas pipeline from the Andaman Sea to Thailand is currently under construction at Ban-I-Thong and poses a significant environmental hazard, especially on the Thai side where the short-sighted planners pointed the pipeline directly at Sai Yok National Park. Thai environmentalists have gone to court, creating the current stand-off.

FLORA & FAUNA

As in the rest of tropical Asia, most indigenous vegetation in Myanmar is associated with two basic types of tropical forest: monsoon forest (with a distinctive dry season of three months or more) and rainforest (where rain falls more than nine months per year). There is much overlap of the two – some forest zones support a mix of monsoon forest and rainforest vegetation.

In the mountainous Himalayan region above the Tropic of Cancer, Myanmar's flora is characterised by subtropical broadleaf evergreen forest up to 2000m; temperate semideciduous broadleaf rainforest from 2000m to 3000m; and evergreen coniferous and subalpine snow forest passing into alpine scrub above 3000m.

The country's most famous flora includes an incredible array of fruit trees, over 25,000 flowering species, a variety of tropical hardwoods and bamboo. Myanmar may possibly contain more species of bamboo than any other country outside China. Cane and rattan are also plentiful.

According to the UN's World Development Report, Myanmar currently boasts natural forest cover of 43% and is ranked 33 among the top 100 countries. It also holds 75% of the world's teak reserves; teak is one of Myanmar's most important exports, for which the biggest consumers are (in descending order) Hong Kong, Singapore, Thailand and India.

When Marco Polo visited Myanmar in the 13th century, he described 'vast jungles teeming with elephants, unicorns and other wild beasts'. Though Myanmar's natural biodiversity has no doubt altered considerably since that time, it's difficult to say just how much because of the lack of scientific data available. Myanmar is rich in bird life, with an estimated 1000 resident and migrating species. Coastal and inland waterways of the delta and the southern peninsula are especially important habitats for South-East Asian waterfowl.

Distinctive mammals of renown – found in dwindling numbers within the more heavily forested areas of Myanmar – include the leopard, jungle cat, fishing cat, civet, Indian mongoose, crab-eating mongoose, Himalayan bear, Asiatic black bear, Malayan sun bear, gaur (Indian bison), banteng, serow (an Asiatic mountain goat), wild boar, sambar deer, barking deer, mouse deer, tapir, pangolin, gibbon, macaque, dolphin and dugong (sea cow). An estimated 2000 tigers are thought to inhabit the primary forests, about four times as many as in neighbouring Thailand. Around 10,000 Asiatic elephants are widely distributed in Myanmar.

Both the lesser one-horned (Javan) rhinoceros and the Asiatic two-horned (Sumatran) rhinoceros are believed to survive in very small numbers near the Thai border in the Kayin State. The rare red panda (or cat bear) was last sighted in northern Myanmar in the early 1960s but is still thought to live in the Kachin State forests above 2000m.

GOVERNMENT & POLITICS

The State Peace & Development Council (SPDC) has officially replaced SLORC as the governing arm of the military. Like SLORC, the council is made up of four top generals and 15 military commanders. They have added a 14 member cabinet and separate 14 member advisory board. The big four are SPDC chairman Gen Than Shwe, vice chairman Gen Maung Aye, secretary one Khin Nyunt (head of MI) and secretary two Gen Tin Oo. The SLORC name persists in daily conversation.

The Tatmadaw and their political junta, the SPDC, currently rule Myanmar with an iron fist. The only political party with any actual power is Ne Win's National Unity Party.

Burmese citizens have relative economic freedom in all but state-owned trade spheres (naturally these are the big ones, like timber

MYANMAR

and oil), but their political freedom is strictly curtailed.

Peaceful political assembly is banned and citizens are forbidden to discuss politics with foreigners – though many relish doing so as long as they know potential informers aren't listening. All government workers in Myanmar, regardless of level and status of their occupation, must sign a pledge not to discuss the government among themselves or they risk losing their jobs.

The opposition movement that began in 1988 appears to be quelled now, with the military firmly in control. Amnesty International and UN human rights reports state that the junta has effectively silenced the democracy movement through the systematic use of terror and torture.

The streets in Yangon and the country roadways are festooned with huge red signboards (in English and Burmese) bearing slogans: 'Oppose those relying on external elements, acting as stooges, holding negative views', 'Anyone who tries to break up the union is our enemy'.

The once well-attended weekly gatherings outside Aung San Suu Kyi's Yangon home, where she spoke to the crowds on the importance of persevering towards democracy, have been stopped, replaced by barricades at the end of University Ave near her home. Her former house-arrest might now be termed 'city arrest'; a well documented attempt by Suu Kyi to testify at a political trial in Mandalay ended when the train to Mandalay was unable to move that day.

A round of student demonstrations in late 1996 were considerably smaller than those in 1988 and 1990 – both in number and in geographical scope. They were limited to Yangon and Mandalay and mostly consisted of street sit-ins rather than marches. In all cases demonstrators quickly moved when security forces turned up. Not coincidentally, universities in Myanmar have been closed since 1996.

ECONOMY

In 1997 Myanmar was admitted to the Association of Southeast Asian Nations (ASEAN), an economic alliance of nine countries in the region. What effect this will have on the economy and the majority of people is unclear.

In the 1980s, Myanmar was one of the 10 poorest countries in the world. Beginning with the left-wing military takeover in 1962,

consumer goods just fell apart, went out of stock or simply became unusable. The official economy went nowhere – though a secondary, black-market economy flourished – until the state finally relinquished control of all industry in 1989. Now everything is available – at a price.

The new open-door economic policy, launched in 1989 to attract foreign investment, has had some success, despite the fact that few investors have been willing to risk their cash while the political situation remains so volatile. In 1996 and 1997, Pepsi, Carlsberg and Heineken all pulled out of joint ventures with government. Much of the profit the nation takes in is absorbed by the Tatmadaw, which directs all foreign trade in timber, gems, fisheries and oil (the main moneymakers), though there is a small but growing middle class in urban areas. Tourism is the only potentially large-scale industry to which ordinary Burmese have access, and the only locally based economic activity besides smuggling that offers them an opportunity to earn hard currency. Meanwhile Tatmadaw officers live in colonial-style villas in Yangon's best suburbs.

As of 1997 the economy was growing at a rate of 5.8% per year, down from the previous year's 6.5%, the highest since before Ne Win took power in the early 1960s. Myanmar now ranks sixth in world rice exports. According to UN statistics, processing and manufacturing have tripled over the last eight years and provide more of the country's GDP than agriculture. Nominal per capita income is around US$300, but when adjusted for purchasing power parity amounts to US$600 to US$900, still the lowest in Asia. Inflation runs at an estimated 31% per annum when adjusted for dollar usage. In 1998, a school teacher could expect to be paid about K1000 a month. For the majority of Myanmar's citizens who don't have access to hard currency, life is still very tough.

Tourism

The government has gradually extended tourist visas over a 10 year period from seven days, to 15 days, to the current 28 days allowed.

Tourism, an obvious source of hard currency, was brought to a halt following the 1988 uprising but it is steadily building up again with the new visa regulations and expanding tourist infrastructure.

During the highly touted 'Visit Myanmar Year 1996', the national tourist industry predicted half a million visitors. This figure was wildly unrealistic given the deficiency of the accommodation and transport infrastructure, Myanmar's lack of promotion outside the country and the country's poor human rights image. Most observers put the figure at closer to 150,000. Since then, it has declined to less than 100,000 though statistics are scarce. Yearly receipts earned via tourism so far amount to less than US$1 million, much of which is spent by business travellers.

POPULATION & PEOPLE

No reasonably accurate census has been taken since the colonial era but the generally recognised population estimate as of 1996 is 46 million, with an annual growth rate of 2.1%. The population is made up of several racial groupings indigenous to Myanmar, including the Bamar (Burman, around 65%), Shan (10%), Kayin (Karen, 7%), Mon (less than 3%), Kachin (less than 3%), Chin (less than 3%), Kayah (less than 2%) and Rakhine (Arakanese, less than 2%). There are still quite a few Indians and Chinese in Myanmar, but not many other foreigners or immigrants.

The largest cities, in declining order, are Yangon, Mandalay, Pathein, Mawlamyine, Taunggyi and Sittwe.

ARTS

Burmese fine art, at the court level, has not had an easy time since the collapse of the last kingdom – architecture and art were both royal activities which, without royal support, have floundered and faded. On the other hand, at the street level, Burmese culture is vibrant and thriving.

Pwe

Popular drama, one of the keys to understanding modern Burmese culture, is accessible and enjoyable for visitors. The *pwe* (show) is the everyday Burmese theatre: a religious festival, wedding, funeral, celebration, fair, sporting event – almost anything can be a good reason for a pwe. Once under way, a pwe traditionally goes on all night, which is no strain – if the audience gets bored at some point during the performance, they simply fall asleep and wake up when something more to their taste is on.

Myanmar's truly indigenous dance forms are those that pay homage to the *nats,* or members of the spirit world. In special *nat pwes,* one or more nats are invited to possess the body and mind of a medium; sometimes members of the audience are possessed instead, an event that is greatly feared by most Burmese. Nat dancing styles are very fluid and adaptable, and are handed down from older pwe dancers to their offspring or apprentices.

Marionette Theatre

Yok-thei pwe, or Burmese marionette theatre, presents colourful puppets up to a metre high in a spectacle that many aesthetes consider the most expressive of all the Burmese arts. Developed during the reign of King Bagyidaw in the Konbaung period, it was so influential that it became the forerunner to classical dance as later performed by actors rather than marionettes. The genre's 'golden age' began with the Mandalay kingdoms of the late 18th century and ran through the advent of cinema in the 1930s. Marionette theatre declined following WWII and is now mostly confined to tourist venues in Mandalay and Bagan. Rather less frequently it appears at pwes sponsored by wealthy patrons.

Burmese Music

Traditional Burmese music is primarily two-dimensional in the sense that rhythm and melody provide much of the musical structure, while repetition is a key element in developing this structure. There is also a significant amount of improvisation in live performance, an element traditional Burmese music shares with jazz.

The original inspiration for much of Myanmar's current musical tradition came from Siam after the second conquest of Siam in 1767 when Siamese court musicians, dancers and entertainers from Ayuthaya were brought to Myanmar by the hundreds in order to effect 'cultural augmentation'.

The *saing waing* ensemble accompanies classical dance-dramas which enact scenes from the *jatakas* (stories of the Buddha) or from the Indian epic *Ramayana*. Musical instruments are predominantly percussive, but even the circle of tuned drums, or *pat waing*, may carry the melody. In addition to the pat waing, the traditional Burmese ensemble of seven to 10 musicians will usually play: the *kyaynaung,* a circle of tuned brass gongs; the *saung kauk,* a boat-shaped harp with 13 strings; the *pattala,* a sort of xylophone; the *hne,* an oboe-type instrument related to the Indian shanai; the *palwe,* a bamboo flute; the *michaung*, or crocodile lute; the *patma*, a bass drum; and the *yagwin* (small cymbals) and *wa-let-khoke* (bamboo clappers), which are purely rhythmic in nature and are often played by Burmese vocalists. It is also not uncommon to see a violin or two in a saing, and even the dobro (an American acoustic slide guitar played on the lap) is occasionally used.

Older still is an enchanting vocal folk music tradition still heard in rural areas where the Burmese may sing without instrumental accompaniment while working. With a bit of luck, you might hear such songs in an up-country guesthouse.

Via radio, TV and cassette tapes, Myanmar's urban ears are fed by a huge pop music industry based in Yangon. Younger Burmese listen to heavily western-influenced sounds – the pervasive power of rock music has even penetrated the SLORC prohibition on western music (except for lyrics, which must always be sung in Burmese). Burmese heavy metal groups with names like Iron Cross, Wild Ones and Emperor have become very successful in recent years, with fans among the 'motorcycle and Marlboro' crowd.

Art & Architecture

Early Burmese art was always a part of religious architecture – paintings were something you did on the walls of temples, sculpture something to be placed inside them. Since the decline of temple-building, the old painting skills have considerably deteriorated. Modern Burmese paintings in western style reflect only a pale shadow of the former skill and the one painter of any renown, U Ba Kyi, paints murals and canvases commissioned for hotels and government offices.

Burmese woodcarving was mainly reserved for royal palaces, which were always made of timber and were showpieces for the skilful woodcarver. When royal palaces ceased to be built, the woodcarving skills rapidly declined although the new construction boom has brought about a small but growing woodcarving renaissance – again mostly seen in hotels.

Remarkably little research has been carried out on the topic of Burmese religious sculpture other than that from the Bagan and Mandalay eras. A rich Buddhist sculptural tradition in wood, bronze, stone and marble existed among the Shan, Mon and Rakhine peoples, but these have received short shrift from both Burman and foreign scholars. Even Burman sculpture is hard to come by in the country.

It is in architecture that one sees the strongest evidence of Burmese artistic skill and accomplishment. Myanmar is a country of stupas, or Buddhist reliquaries, often called 'pagodas' in English. The Burmese seem unable to see a hilltop without wanting to put a religious monument on top of it. Wherever you are – boating down the river, driving through the hills, even flying above the plains – there always seems to be a stupa in view. It is in Bagan that you see the most dramatic results of this national enthusiasm for religious monuments; for over two centuries a massive construction program here resulted in thousands of shrines, stupas, monasteries and other sacred buildings.

Payas *Paya* (pa-YAH), the most common Burmese equivalent to the often misleading English term 'pagoda', literally means 'holy one' and can refer to people, deities and places associated with religion. For the most part it's a generic term for what students of Hindu-Buddhist architecture call a 'stupa'. There are basically two kinds of payas: the solid, bell-shaped *zedi* and the hollow square or rectangular *pahto*. A zedi, or stupa, is usually thought to contain 'relics' – either objects taken from the Buddha himself (especially pieces of bone, teeth or hair) or certain holy materials such as Buddha images and other religious objects blessed by a famous *sayadaw* (Burmese Buddhist master). The relics are usually placed inside a *tabena*, or relic chamber, embedded deep in the centre of the zedi. Both zedis and pahtos are often associated with Buddhist monasteries, or *kyaung*.

Payas function basically as a focus for meditation or contemplation. In the case of solid payas (zedis), if there is a need for some sheltered gathering place or a place to house images or other paraphernalia, then this will usually be an ancillary to the paya. There may be small shrines, pavilions, covered walkways or other such places all around a major paya. These are often more heavily ornamented than the zedis themselves.

SOCIETY & CONDUCT

The social ideal for most Burmese citizens – no matter what their ethnic background may be – is a standard of behaviour commonly termed *bamahsan chin*, or 'Burmese-ness'. The hallmarks of bamahsan chin include showing respect for elders; acquaintance with Buddhist scriptures (and the ability to recite at least a few classic verses); the ability to speak idiomatic Burmese; showing discretion in behaviour towards the opposite sex; dressing modestly; and most importantly exhibiting modes of expression and comportment that value the quiet, subtle and indirect rather than the loud, obvious and direct.

Dos & Don'ts
Myanmar is a land of temples, and your visit can begin to feel like a procession from one of them to another. One should dress neatly (no shorts or sleeveless shirts) when visiting religious sites. The Burmese are insistent that you barefoot it in the temple precincts, and that includes the steps from the very bottom of Mandalay Hill, the shop-lined arcades to Shwedagon Paya and even the ruins of Bagan. Carry your shoes and socks with you.

As elsewhere in Asia it is unseemly to show too much emotion – losing your temper over problems and delays gets you nowhere; it just amazes people. Stay calm and collected at all times. The Burmese frown on such displays of anger just as much as they frown on too open a display of affection. Patience and quiet will carry the day more often than not.

As in other Buddhist countries the head is the highest part of the body – spiritually as well as literally. You should never deliberately touch somebody else on the head or pat a child on the head. Equally, the feet are the lowest part of the body – don't point your feet at anyone.

Buddha images are sacred objects, so don't pose in front of them for pictures and definitely do not climb onto them.

Monks are not supposed to touch or be touched by women. If a woman wants to hand something to a monk, the object should be placed within reach of the monk, not handed directly to him.

If ever you find yourself having to bathe in a public place you should wear a *longyi* (cotton wraparounds for men and women); nude bathing is not the norm.

RELIGION
Around 87% of Myanmar's citizens are Theravada Buddhists, but there is also a strong belief in nats, the animist spirits of the land, and many of the hill tribes are Christian. Smaller Hindu and Muslim communities are common throughout the country.

Buddhism
For the average Burmese Buddhist everything revolves around the 'merit' (*kutho*, from the Pali *kusala*, or 'wholesome') one is able to accumulate through rituals and good deeds. One of the more typical rituals performed by individuals visiting a stupa is to pour water over the Buddha image at their astrological post (determined by the day of the week they were born) – one glassful for every year of their current age plus one extra to ensure a long life. Asked what they want in their next life, most Burmese will put forth such seemingly mundane and materialistic values as beauty and wealth – or rebirth somewhere beyond the reach of SLORC.

Socially, every Burmese male is expected to take up temporary monastic residence twice in his life: once as a *samanera*, or novice monk, between the ages of five and 15 and again as a fully ordained monk, or *pongyi*, sometime after age 20. Almost all men or boys under 20 years of age participate in the *shinpyu*, or novitiation ceremony – quite a common event since a family earns great merit when one of its sons takes robe and bowl.

Though there is little social expectation to do so, a number of women live monastic lives as *dasasila*, or 'Ten-Precept' nuns. Burmese nuns shave their heads, wear pink robes and take vows in an ordination procedure similar to that undergone by monks.

Nat Worship
The widespread adoption of Buddhism in Myanmar has suppressed but never replaced the pre-Buddhist practice of nat worship. Nat figures and Buddhist images are often found side by side. Originally animistic – associated with hills, trees, rivers, lakes and other natural features – the Burmese nat has evolved into a spirit that may hold dominion over a place (natural or artificial), person or field of experience.

In spite of King Anawrahta's 12th century attempt to ban it, the nat cult remains strong. The Burmese merely divide their devotions and offerings according to the sphere of influence: Buddha for future lives, and the nats – both Hindu and Burman – for problems in this life. A misdeed, for example, might be redressed by offerings made to the nat Thagyamin (related to the Hindu deity Indra), who once a year records the names of those who perform good deeds in a book made of gold leaves, those who do evil in a book made of dog skin.

A village may have a nat shrine off in a wooded corner somewhere for the propitiation of the village guardian spirit. Such tree and village shrines are simple dollhouse-like structures of wood or bamboo; their proper placement is divined by a local *saya*, a 'teacher' or shaman trained in spirit lore.

Knowledge of the complex nat world is fading fast among the younger Burmese generation, many of whom pay respect only to the coconut-head house guardian. Red and white are widely known to be nat colours; drivers young and old tie red and white strips of cloth onto the side-view mirrors and hood ornaments of their vehicles for protection from the nats.

LANGUAGE

There is a wide variety of languages spoken in Myanmar – fortunately, English is one of them. The Burmese alphabet is most unusual and looks like a collection of interlocked circles. If you would like to tackle Burmese (the main language), look for Lonely Planet's handy *Burmese phrasebook*. The best Burmese-English dictionary is *1993 Myanmar Language Commission One*.

See the Language section in the Appendix for some useful Burmese words and phrases.

Facts for the Visitor

HIGHLIGHTS

Now that visitors may stay nearly a full month, and new areas have been opened up, Myanmar's plentiful attractions are even more accessible.

Historic Temple Architecture
Bagan, Bago, Salay, Mrauk U, Amarapura, Ava, Thayekhittaya, Yangon
Handicrafts
Mandalay (kalaga tapestries, antiques), Inle Lake (shoulder bags, Shan textiles), Bagan (lacquerware)
Hiking
Kalaw, Pindaya, Inle Lake, Kyaingtong
Beaches
Thandwe, Chaungtha, Letkhokkon, Myeik
Traditional Culture
Yangon, Mandalay, Kyaiktiyo, Mawlamyine, Hsipaw, Pa-an

PLANNING
Maps

Good, up-to-date maps of Myanmar are virtually nonexistent. For a country map, Nelles' *Myanmar* is sufficient for most purposes.

Myanmar Travel & Tours (MTT) publishes very useful and fairly detailed city maps of Yangon, Mandalay and Bagan. All are available from the main MTT office in Yangon on Sule Pagoda Rd, or from individual MTT offices in the respective cities. A good new map of Yangon was published in 1996 by Design Printing Services (☎ 28 1861) and is available in some bookshops and the souvenir shop at the Traders Hotel.

TOURIST OFFICES

Myanmar Travel & Tours, once known as Tourist Burma, is part of the Ministry of Hotels & Tourism (MHT), the official government tourism organ in Myanmar. Its main office (☎ 27 5328, 27 8386; fax 28 2535) is at 77/91 Sule Pagoda Rd in Yangon, beside Sule Paya. MTT has little in the way of brochures or leaflets. The information it has to hand out is sparse and uninteresting, although timetables and costs for places where they do business will usually be right on hand.

There are MTT offices in Mandalay, Bagan, Nyaungshwe (Inle Lake) and Taunggyi, but they sometimes give the impression that their purpose is to hinder travellers rather than to be useful.

With the privatisation of the tourist industry in the country, it's no longer difficult to avoid using MTT while travelling round Myanmar.

VISAS & DOCUMENTS
Visas

The tourist visa situation in Myanmar has been in a state of flux since the upheavals in mid-1988, when the country was briefly closed to all visitors, then reopened under more strict regulations, then opened up wider than it had been at any time since 1962. By early 1994, 28-day tourist visas were being issued with regularity at Burmese embassies abroad; it is no longer necessary to book a package tour in advance.

Once you've arrived in Yangon, you're free to plan your own itinerary and go almost wherever you like (see Travel Permits later in this section).

The cost of the visa itself is around US$10. Tourist visas are readily available through most Myanmar embassies or consulates abroad. At the embassy in Bangkok you can usually receive a visa the same day you apply for it.

Visa Extensions Although some Myanmar embassies abroad will say tourist visa extensions aren't permitted, once in Myanmar you can usually extend your visa up to 30 days (two week extensions are the norm) beyond the original 28 day validity – at the discretion of the Department of Immigration & Manpower. The usual procedure requires five photos plus payment of a US$36 fee, but this can vary from office to office. If you're refused at one office, try again at another location – in low-tech Myanmar there are no computer checks or other easily communicated records of visa extension applications. Some offices are slower than others; allow two or three days for the extension to go through. The type of permit issued for such extensions is called a 'Stay Permit'.

Travel Permits

The xenophobic government does try to keep tabs on you while you are in Myanmar, though less so than before 1994. In general it doesn't want you wandering off into 'touchy' regions and that's part of the reason for the 28 day visa. Also, with the emphasis on earning hard currency through the FEC-for-dollars system (see the Money section below), the government obviously wants to keep you within reach of the government banking and tourism system. The farther off the beaten track you get, the less likely you'll have to pay for anything in dollars or FECs, which is the only way the government wants your money.

Travel anywhere in the standard tourist quadrangle – Yangon, Mandalay, Bagan, Inle Lake and Taunggyi and to any points between or near these destinations – is freely allowed for anyone holding a valid passport and tourist visa. This also includes places a little off the main linking routes such as Kyaiktiyo, Mawlamyine, Pyay, Shwebo, Magwe, Monywa, Lashio, Taungoo and Pyinmana – basically anywhere in central Myanmar between the Shan Yoma to the east and the Ayeyarwady River to the west – plus most places in the Ayeyarwady Delta region (Pathein, Twante, Thanlyin, Letkhokkon).

Even for these places, your passport is likely to be checked from time to time. In fact every airport arrival, anywhere in Myanmar, requires a passport and visa check and the filling in of some papers with your name and passport number. Hotel staff also check passports and visas.

Travel to just about anywhere else in Myanmar requires a permit – actually a typed letter stamped with various government seals – issued by the MHT and approved by the Ministry of Defence (which even has its own 'military-tour operator', Myawaddy Travel & Tours). Such permits are available directly from MTT in Yangon or through many private travel agencies. Travel agencies usually require that you contract the services of a guide or driver before they'll arrange for a permit.

MTT will show you a list of officially approved destinations, including areas requiring 'prior permission from the authorities concerned'. In actual practice, the authorities concerned may never have seen the list. It's a good idea to inquire more than once about reported permit areas. In another office in another city, the story may be different. In information-starved Myanmar, it really becomes a guessing game as to which places you're allowed to visit and which you aren't.

At some point in your Myanmar travels, you come to realise that the country is still run like a loose-knit collection of warlord states. Even when you're just moving from one Burman-majority division to another, your papers are checked. On top of this, every time you enter a small town or village by car, someone appears to exact tribute from the driver in the form of a 'road tax' (the same thing happens to Burmese road travellers).

Because what is 'officially' open seems to change from week to week, sometimes it's better just to set off for your intended destination rather than ask MTT or wait around for permits. Your fellow travellers will be the most up-to-date source of info on what's possible and what's not.

At the time of writing, areas that elicit an immediate 'no way' response include the Kayah State and the Chin State. At the same time, we were told that travel to the Kayah capital of Loikaw may open up. The same goes for possible package tours to the Chin hills. Travel is currently prohibited to Loilem, between Taunggyi and Kyaingtong. Military checkpoints placed at close intervals along every government-controlled road leading to sensitive areas will usually net anyone trying to enter from Myanmar proper; some areas are in fact more accessible from Thailand – albeit illegally.

The following areas have been officially declared 'open' to package tourists: Putao; Muse at the Chinese border to Lashio; Mogok.

See other individual destinations for details on various permit or tour requirements.

EMBASSIES
Myanmar Embassies
Myanmar embassies abroad include:

Australia
(☎ 02-6273 3811)
22 Arkana St, Yarralumla, ACT 2600
Bangladesh
(☎ 02-60 1915)
89B Rd No 4, Banani, Dhaka
Canada
(☎ 613-232 6434)
85 Range Rd, Apt 902-903, The Sandringham,
Ottawa, Ont K1N 8J6
China
(☎ 010-532 1584)
6 Dong Zhi Men Wai St, Chaoyang District,
Beijing
UK
(☎ 020-7629 6966)
19A Charles St, London W1X 8ER
USA
(☎ 202-332 9044)
2300 'S' St NW, Washington, DC 20008

See the other chapters in this book for Myanmar embassies in those countries.

Embassies in Myanmar
Myanmar is usually a good place to get visas for other countries. You can often pay for them with free-market kyat (see the Money section later in this chapter), so they can be very cheap and, as relatively few tourists come to Myanmar, embassy officials can usually issue them quickly.

Countries with diplomatic representation in Yangon include:

Australia
(☎ 28 0711) 88 Strand Rd
Bangladesh
(☎ 55 1174) 56 Kaba Aye Pagoda Rd
Canada
See UK Embassy
China
(☎ 22 1280) 1 Pyidaungsu Yeiktha Rd
Indonesia
(☎ 28 1714) 100 Pyidaungsu Yeiktha Rd
Japan
(☎ 55 2288) 100 Natmauk St
Laos
(☎ 22 2482) A-1 Diplomatic Quarters, Taw
Win Rd
Malaysia
(☎ 22 0248) 82 Pyidaungsu Yeiktha Rd
Thailand
(☎ 22 1713) 45 Pyay Rd
UK
(☎ 28 1700) 80 Strand Rd
Vietnam
(☎ 54 8905) 40 Thanlwin Rd

Other foreign embassies in Yangon include Israel, Egypt, India, Nepal, Pakistan, South Korea and Sri Lanka.

CUSTOMS
The following items cannot legally be taken out of the country: prehistoric implements and artefacts; fossils; old coins; bronze or brass weights (including opium weights); bronze or clay pipes; *kammawas* or *para-baiks* (palm-leaf manuscripts); inscribed stones; inscribed gold or silver; historical documents; religious images; sculptures or carvings in bronze, stone, stucco or wood; frescoes or fragments thereof; pottery; national regalia and paraphernalia.

MONEY
Currency
The kyat (pronounced 'chat') is no longer divided into smaller pyas. These once-confusing coins are now for sale as souvenirs since the rapid depreciation of the kyat over the last few years.

The government has a nasty habit of demonetising large denomination notes from time to time. The theory is that anybody who has some large denomination notes sitting around must have obtained them by less than legal means. So the government simply declares that (say) all even-numbered denominations are no longer legal tender.

At present the following kyat banknotes are in use: K1, K5, K10, K15, K20, K45, K50, K90, K100, K200 and K500. Make sure that any K50 or K100 bills you're offered are labelled 'Central Bank of Myanmar' rather than 'Union of Burma Bank', although even these can be OK. To discourage the black market, K50 and K100 notes were demonetised in the 1960s, and K25, K35 and K75 notes underwent a similar fate in 1987; unscrupulous money dealers occasionally try to foist these older bills on unsuspecting visitors. Just remember, any note reading 'Myanmar' rather than 'Burma' should be OK.

Foreign Exchange Certificates (FECs)
As soon as you exit the immigration check at Yangon international airport you're supposed to stop at a counter and exchange US$300 for 300 FECs – Myanmar's second legal currency. Printed in China, these Monopoly-like notes issued by the Central Bank of Myanmar 'for the convenience of tourists visiting Myanmar' come in denominations equivalent to US$1, US$5, US$10 and US$20.

Payment for FECs is accepted *only* in US dollars or UK pounds sterling, in the form of cash or travellers cheques. Credit cards are not accepted in payment for FECs. One US dollar always equals one FEC; the pound equivalent fluctuates according to pound-dollar variance. Reconversion of kyat to dollars or pound sterling is possible only for conversions in excess of US$300 and only when accompanied by the FEC voucher. However, some pavement moneychangers will reconvert your excess kyat for a better-than-nothing rate.

FECs can be spent anywhere in Myanmar. No special licence or permit is necessary for a citizen of Myanmar to accept FECs; this is not the case for dollars. Officially approved hotel rooms, airlines, Myanma Railways (some stations) and larger souvenir shops require payment either in dollars or FECs. So the required US$300 purchase of FECs is not something necessarily to avoid since they can be used to pay your hotel costs.

FECs can also be legally exchanged for kyat – at the free-market rate – at shops or from moneychangers that accept FECs (at a slightly lower rate – usually about 5%). On the other hand, FECs aren't absolutely necessary for Myanmar travel, and if you can get away without having to purchase them you might as well. The staff at the FEC exchange booth at Yangon airport doesn't seem to be too concerned about dragging each and every newly arrived visitor over to the booth and many travellers are able to simply walk past without buying FECs. Upon request, couples are usually permitted to exchange US$300 for both persons rather than US$300 each. Some travellers on a short visit have reported being able to purchase a smaller amount of FECs.

This entire complicated system revolves around the desire of virtually every Burmese – and of course the government – to get their hands on hard currency, commonly referred to as 'FE' (foreign exchange, pronounced like one word, 'effee').

Dollars The 'effee' most desired is the US dollar, Myanmar's third currency – and the most basic to the country's overall economy. Cash dollars can legally be used only at establishments possessing a licence to accept dollars. In reality all merchants are happy to take them. They can also be exchanged for kyat on the black market or at licensed moneychangers.

Exchange Rates

With the FEC system in place, it's quite rare – and plain stupid – for any foreign visitor to exchange money at the ridiculously low official exchange rate. In fact, you might have trouble convincing someone you were serious. Since it's legal for Burmese to possess FECs without any special permit, the visitor doesn't need to consider the official exchange rate and can instead concentrate on getting the best free or 'black' market rate. Moreover, because licensed moneychangers are as common as banks, it's unclear just what the term 'official rate' even means in Myanmar.

In any case, the old whisky-and-cigarette scheme – buying a bottle of Johnny Walker scotch and a carton of 555s at Bangkok airport's duty-free shop to sell for free-market kyat – is no longer necessary. In fact you'll lose money if you do it! These items are usually less expensive in Yangon than in Bangkok.

In short, the official rates are essentially meaningless. At the time of writing, the 'official' rate was 6.2 kyat per US dollar, while the free market rate was running around 385 per US dollar. This is basically a risk-free activity, especially if you use licensed moneychangers.

Following are the free market rates:

country	unit		kyat
Australia	A$1	=	244K
Canada	C$1	=	249K
euro	€1	=	468K
France	10FF	=	708K
Germany	DM1	=	238K
Japan	¥100	=	333K
New Zealand	NZ$1	=	206K
UK	UK£1	=	654K
USA	US$1	=	385K

Credit Cards, ATM Cards & Travellers Cheques

There are no ATM machines in Myanmar, and credit cards (Visa and American Express, but not MasterCard) are accepted only at large expensive hotels, or by MTT for travel costs. Some travel agents can take a credit card, but it's usually a hassle and the fee can range up to 14%!

Travellers cheques are only slightly less of a bother. Again, large hotels and MTT take them, and any foreign exchange bank will convert travellers cheques to US dollars for a modest 2% fee, usually earning such a bank the nick-name '2% bank'.

Costs

Travel in Myanmar today is cheaper than it has been at any time since the 1988-89 disturbances. Costs depend largely on where you decide to go and which hotels you choose to stay in. Generally speaking the farther off the beaten track you go, the cheaper travel becomes.

Goods and services may be priced either in kyat or in US dollars/FECs. Hotel rooms, some train tickets, air tickets, car rental and guide services are generally priced in dollars/FECs – for some of these services dollars/FECs may be the only currencies accepted.

Food, taxis, buses and just about everything else in Myanmar are priced in kyat. In keeping with this two-currency system, prices in this chapter are quoted in either US dollars or kyat; anytime dollars are quoted, FECs are equally acceptable.

Daily Expenses It's possible to get basic rooms in well touristed areas of Myanmar for as low as US$3 per person per night. For shoestring travellers this is high compared with Thailand and Indonesia, but about the same as in Laos and Vietnam. In very out-of-the-way places where you can pay entirely in kyat, room rates drop as low as K200 to K300 per person.

Except for those transport services monopolised by MTT (notably tickets for the Yangon-Mandalay express train), public ground transport is inexpensive and so slow that you're unlikely to be able to spend more than US$5 a day maximum on long-distance movement.

Although it's difficult to pin down a one-figure travel budget due to all the variables in the equation – particularly whether or not your desired itinerary requires travel permits – you can expect to spend a rock-bottom minimum of about US$10 a day. This assumes always taking the cheapest room available, using public ground transport and eating in local restaurants and teashops rather than hotel restaurants or places geared to foreign tourists.

Inflation It's important to remember that Myanmar has an annual inflation rate of 25 to 30%, so any prices quoted in this book will probably need to be adjusted accordingly.

Tipping & Bribes

Minor bribes – called 'presents' in Burmese English (as in 'Do you have a present for me?') – are part of everyday life in Myanmar. Much as tips are expected for a taxi ride or a restaurant meal in the west, extra compensation is expected for the efficient completion of many standard bureaucratic services. A visa extension or customs inspection will move a little more quickly if a 'present' – a little cash, a packet of cigarettes, a tube of lipstick, a ballpoint pen – is proffered along with whatever the regular fee is. T-shirts and up-to-date western calendars – basically anything that can be sold for cash – will work minor miracles.

No matter how this system might bruise your sensibilities, you probably won't get through a Myanmar trip without paying at least a couple of minor bribes – even if you're not aware you've paid.

POST & COMMUNICATIONS

Making overseas telephone calls is reasonably straightforward, though incoming post and telephone services are notoriously unreliable.

Post

International postage rates are a bargain K15 per letter to the USA and Europe, K5 to Asia. For registered mail anywhere in the world add K15.

Parcels can be mailed safely since the recent arrival of DHL Worldwide Express, with offices in both Yangon (☎ 66 0515) and Mandalay (☎ 39 274). Rates are high for anything heavier than a letter, however.

Telephone

Domestic Calling other places in Myanmar is relatively simple and very inexpensive from the Central Telephone & Telegraph (CTT) office at the corner of Pansodan and Mahabandoola Sts in Yangon. Only larger cities with area codes can be dialled direct. Smaller towns still use manual switchboards, so you must ask the national operator to connect you to a specific town operator, then request the local number.

International There are two ways to make an international call. The fast and expensive way is to use an IDD phone available in some hotels in Yangon, Mandalay and Bagan. Rates are by the minute, usually about US$12 to anywhere outside of Asia.

The cheaper way is from the CTT office in Yangon or Mandalay, or in Yangon from several shops in the centre of town; there is one on the south-east corner by Sule Paya.

Telephone Codes

The country code for Myanmar is 95. The international dialling code is 00. Following are area codes for some cities. You must dial the zero when calling from within Myanmar.

Bagan	☎ 062
Bago	☎ 052
Kyaiktiyo	☎ 035
Lashio	☎ 082
Mandalay	☎ 02
Mawlamyine	☎ 032
Pathein	☎ 042
Pyay	☎ 053
Pyin U Lwin	☎ 085
Taunggyi	☎ 081
Yangon	☎ 01

These trunk calls must be booked and you may have to wait from 10 to 30 minutes to place a call. Three-minute calls to Thailand cost K180, to Japan K300, to Europe K480 and to the USA K500.

The CTT phone offices are open Monday to Friday 8 am to 4 pm, weekends and holidays 9 am to 2 pm.

BOOKS

Lonely Planet

For more information about travelling in Myanmar look for Lonely Planet's *Myanmar*.

Guidebooks

Several books offer histories and descriptions of the temple architecture at Bagan. The older *Pictorial Guide to Pagan* contains illustrated descriptions of many of the important Bagan buildings plus a map inside the back cover. It's a useful book that you'll find fairly easily in Myanmar. *Pagodas of Pagan* is also readily available, but not so detailed or interesting.

Top of the line is *Pagan: Art and Architecture of Old Burma* by Paul Strachan. One of the few books available with any information at all about archaeological sites other than Bagan or Mandalay is *A Guide to Mrauk U* by Tun Shwe Khine.

Travel

George Orwell's *Burmese Days* is the book to read in order to get a feel for the country

under the British Raj. *Golden Earth* by Norman Lewis is a reprint of a classic account of a visit to Burma soon after WWII.

History & Politics

The most comprehensive sociopolitical account of pre-1988 Myanmar is *Burma: A Socialist Nation of Southeast Asia* by David Steinberg. *Burma – Insurgency & the Politics of Ethnicity* by Martin Smith contains a well researched history and analysis of insurgent politics in Myanmar from the 1940s through to 1988.

Outrage: Burma's Struggle for Democracy by journalist Bertil Lintner chronicles the violent suppression of Myanmar's prodemocracy movement from 1987 to 1990, with particular focus on the events of 1988. It is a somewhat polemic look at the student uprisings, but basically it's very informative.

Another revealing book which gives some startling details about politics within Burma is *Hidden Agendas* by Australian investigative journalist John Pilger.

General

Anyone interested in quickly obtaining a broad understanding of Burmese customs and etiquette should pick up a copy of *Culture Shock! Burma* by Saw Myat Yin. This book simply and accurately explains male and female roles, business protocol, common Burmese ceremonies and festivals, the naming system, how to extend and accept invitations, and even how Burmese perceive westerners.

Freedom from Fear & Other Writings by Aung San Suu Kyi is a collection of essays by and about the Nobel Peace Prize winner.

NEWSPAPERS & MAGAZINES

The only English-language newspaper readily available in Myanmar is the *New Light of Myanmar*, a thin, state-owned daily that's chock-full of Orwellian propaganda of the 'War Is Peace' or 'Freedom Is Slavery' nature, mixed in with a fair amount of noncontroversial wire news and sports scores.

Recent issues of international magazines like *Time*, *Newsweek* or the *Economist* are quite often available at The Strand Hotel in Yangon. Whenever a feature about Myanmar appears in one of these magazines, however, that issue mysteriously fails to appear. Older issues are sold on the street by pavement vendors.

A relatively new tourist-oriented publication called *Today*, available at the MTT office and at many hotels, contains short, safe articles on Myanmar's culture and the tourism industry, along with useful lists of embassies, current festivals, airlines and long-distance express bus services.

RADIO & TV

All legal radio and television broadcasts are state-controlled. Radio Myanmar broadcasts news in Burmese, English and eight other national languages three times a day. Only music with Burmese-language lyrics goes out on the airwaves.

TV Myanmar operates nightly from 6 to 10 pm. Regular features include military songs and marching performances, locally produced news and weather reports and a sports presentation.

Many hotels have satellite TV, if only in the lobby. CNN is available on these sets.

Educated Burmese generally listen to short-wave BBC and VOA broadcasts for news from the world outside. Every Friday at 12.20 and 4.30 pm, the American Center at 14 Taw Win St, behind the Ministry of Foreign Affairs in Yangon, packs them in for the satellite broadcast of the ABC World News Weekly Highlights. CBS News and the Jim Lehrer Newshour are shown Monday through Friday at 10.30 and 11 am respectively.

PHOTOGRAPHY & VIDEO

Myanmar is a very photogenic place so bring lots of film. Colour print film – mostly Kodak, Fuji and Konica brands – is readily and inexpensively available in shops in Yangon and Mandalay. Slide film is harder to find but some shops stock it. In Yangon, Anawrahta St just east of Sule Pagoda Rd is lined with camera and film shops.

Outside Yangon and Mandalay, film is scarce. Most film you might see on sale in the hinterlands will have come from visitors who sold it while in the country – with no guarantee on age or quality. Photographic processing services are available and very cheap, and the quality is said to be improving. You may prefer to wait until you've returned home – or have your film processed in Bangkok, where decent colour labs are plentiful.

A benefit of Myanmar's low tourist flow is that the Burmese are not overexposed to camera-clicking visitors and are not usually unhappy about being photographed. Even monks like to be photographed although, of course, it's rude to ask them to pose for you and it's always polite to ask anybody's permission before taking photographs.

It is forbidden by law to photograph any military facility or any structure considered strategic – this includes bridges and train stations – and any uniformed person.

WEIGHTS & MEASURES
Weight

The most common units of weight used in Myanmar are viss *(peiktha)*, pounds *(paun)* and ticals *(kyat tha)*. One viss equals 3.6 pounds (1.6kg) or 100 ticals. One tical equals 16g.

Volume

At the retail level, rice and small fruits or nuts are sold in units of volume rather than weight; the most common measure is the standard condensed milk can, or *bu*. Eight *bu* equals one small rice basket, or *pyi*, and 16 *pyi* make a jute sack, or *tin*.

Petrol and most other liquids are sold by the imperial gallon (4.55l). One exception is milk, which is sold by the viss.

Length & Distance

Cloth and other items of moderate length are measured by the yard (91.5cm), called *gaik* in Burmese. A half yard is a *taung* (45.7cm), which is divided into two *htwa* (22.8cm). Half a htwa is a *mait* (11.4cm), roughly equivalent to an Anglo-American foot.

Road distances are measured in miles (one mile equals 1.61km). Shorter distances in town or in the countryside may be quoted in furlongs. There are eight furlongs in one mile; thus one furlong equals about 200m.

LAUNDRY

Inexpensive laundry services are available through virtually all hotels and guesthouses. In Yangon and Mandalay you'll also find independent laundry shops in the town centres – generally even less expensive than at your lodgings. Techniques employed favour the 'rub and scrub' method, so wash anything delicate yourself.

HEALTH

Malaria risk exists in rural areas and is not usually a problem in the areas most frequented by foreign travellers. You should take appropriate precautions if necessary. Dengue fever also occurs, and there is a very small risk of Japanese encephalitis. Food and water-borne diseases, including dysentery, cholera and hepatitis, occur, so it pays to be careful with food and drink. For more information on these and other health matters, refer to the Health section in the Appendix.

All water should be boiled or otherwise treated before consumption. Bottled water is available at most tourist destinations.

DANGERS & ANNOYANCES

Theft from tourists seems quite rare in Myanmar, but don't tempt fate by leaving valuables lying around.

PUBLIC HOLIDAYS & SPECIAL EVENTS

Traditionally Myanmar follows a 12 month lunar calendar, so the old holidays and festivals will vary in date, by the Gregorian calendar, from year to year. Myanmar also has a number of more recently originated holidays whose dates are fixed by the Gregorian calendar. Festivals are drawn-out, enjoyable affairs in Myanmar. They generally take place or culminate on full-moon days, but the build-up can continue for days.

Independence Day
    4 January – A major public holiday marked by a seven day fair at Kandawgyi Lake in Yangon. There are fairs all over the country at this time.
Union Day
    12 February – Celebrates Bogyoke Aung San's short-lived achievement of unifying Myanmar's disparate racial groups. For two weeks preceding Union Day, the national flag is paraded from town to town, and wherever the flag rests there must be a festival.
Shwedagon Festival
    February/March – The largest pagoda festival in Myanmar.
Peasants' Day
    2 March
Armed Forces Day
    27 March – Celebrated with parades and fireworks. Since 1989 the Tatmadaw has made it a tradition to pardon a number of prisoners on Armed Forces Day.
Buddha's Birthday
    April/May – Commonly called the 'water festival,' also celebrates the day of the Buddha's enlightenment and the day he entered nirvana. Thus it is known as the 'thrice blessed day'. One of the best places to observe this ceremony is at Yangon's Shwedagon Paya, where a procession of girls carry earthen jars to water the three banyan trees on the western side of the compound.

Workers' Day
    1 May – Although the government renounced socialism in 1989, the country still celebrates May Day.
Buddhist 'Lent'
    June/July – Laypeople present monasteries with stacks of new robes for resident monks, since during the three month Lent period monks are restricted to their monasteries. Ordinary people are also expected to be rather more religious during this time – marriages do not take place and it is inauspicious to move house.
Martyr's Day
    19 July – Commemorates the assassination of Bogyoke Aung San and his comrades on that day in 1947. Wreaths are laid at his mausoleum north of Shwedagon Paya in Yangon.
Festival
    July/August – Lots are drawn to see who will have to provide monks with their alms. If you're in Mandalay, try to get to Taungbyone, about 30km north, where there is a noisy, seven-day festival to keep the nats happy.
Boat Races
    September/October – This is the height of the wet season, so boat races are held in rivers, lakes and even ponds all over Myanmar. The best place to be is Inle Lake, where the Buddha images at the Phaung Daw U Kyaung are ceremonially toured around the lake in the huge royal barge, the Karaweik.
Festival of Lights
    September/October – Celebrates Buddha's return from a period of preaching. For the three days of the festival all Myanmar is lit by oil lamps, fire balloons, candles and even mundane electric lamps. Every house has a paper lantern hanging outside and it's a happy, joyful time all over Myanmar.
Tazaungdaing
    October/November – Another 'festival of lights'. It's particularly celebrated in the Shan State. In Taunggyi there are fire balloon competitions. In some areas there are also speed-weaving competitions during the night – young Burmese women show their prowess at weaving by attempting to produce robes for Buddha images between dusk and dawn. The results, finished or not, are donated to the monks. The biggest weaving competitions occur at Shwedagon Paya in Yangon.
Kathein
    October/November – A one-month period at the end of Buddhist Lent during which new monastic robes and requisites are offered to the monastic community. Many people simply donate cash; kyat notes are folded and stapled into floral patterns on wooden 'trees' called padetha and offered to the monasteries.
National Day
    Late November/early December
Spirit Festivals
    November/December

Christmas
25 December – Despite Myanmar's predominantly Buddhist background, Christmas Day is a public holiday in deference to the many Christian Karen.

Karen New Year
December/January – Considered a national holiday. Karen communities throughout Myanmar celebrate by wearing their traditional dress of woven tunics over red *longyis* (the sarong-style cloth covering the lower body) and by hosting folk dancing and singing performances. The largest celebrations are held in the Karen suburb of Insein, just north of Yangon, and in Pa-an, the capital of the Kayin State.

Ananda Festival
December/January – Held at the Ananda Pahto in Bagan.

COURSES
Meditation Study

In Yangon there are several centres for the study and practice of *satipatthana vipassana*, or insight-awareness meditation, based on instructions in the Maha Satipatthana Sutta (Sutra) of the Theravada Buddhist canon. The most famous centre in Yangon is the Mahasi Meditation Centre (Mahasi Thathana Yeiktha in Burmese), founded in 1947 by the late Mahasi Sayadaw, perhaps Myanmar's greatest meditation teacher. The Mahasi Sayadaw technique strives for intensive, moment-to-moment awareness of every physical movement, every mental and physical sensation, and ultimately, every thought.

To obtain the necessary 'special-entry visa' for a long-term stay, applicants must receive a letter of invitation from the centre where they would like to study, which may in turn require a letter of introduction from an affiliated meditation centre abroad. This invitation is then presented to a Burmese consulate or embassy, which will issue a visa for an initial stay of six to 12 weeks, as recommended by the centre. This may be extended in Yangon at the discretion of the centre and Burmese immigration. The special-entry visa takes eight to 10 weeks to be issued and cannot be applied for while in Myanmar on a tourist visa.

Food and lodging are provided at no charge at the centres but meditators must follow eight precepts, which include abstaining from food after noon and foregoing music, dancing, jewellery, perfume and high or luxurious beds. Daily schedules are rigorous and may involve nearly continuous practice from 3 am till 11 pm. Westerners

who have undergone the training say it is not recommended for people with no previous meditation experience.

For further information, write to:

Chanmyay Yeiktha Meditation Centre
(☎ 66 1479) 655-A Kaba Aye Pagoda Rd,
Yangon
International Meditation Centre
(☎ 53 1549) 31-A Inya Myaing Rd, Yangon
Mahasi Meditation Centre
16 Thathana Yeiktha Rd, Yangon
Panditarama
(☎ 53 1448) 80/A Shwetaunggyaw Rd,
Yangon

For further information on the teachings of Mahasi Sayadaw, U Ba Khin and Mogok Sayadaw, read *Living Buddhist Masters* by Jack Kornfield.

ACCOMMODATION

Until recently, Myanmar was the hottest hotel market in the world as dozens of large and small developers tried to meet the pent-up demand created by years of mismanagement by the Ministry of Hotels & Tourism (MHT). There are now very few government-owned places left in Myanmar. However, the hotels have been going up faster than the tourists are coming; consequently rates have fallen quite a bit.

Technically, any hotel or guesthouse that accepts foreign guests must have a special lodging licence – this is usually displayed somewhere on the wall behind the reception desk. The newer private hotels tend to represent better value than government-owned hotels or hotels that were previously government-owned. Many of the latter are now owned or managed by former MHT hotel managers who have long been accustomed to charging high rates for indifferent service and mediocre room quality. Of the countless new places, among the best are the small, family-run places with fewer than 10 rooms.

Rates and overall variety have improved tremendously over the last few years, though many of Myanmar's hotels are still a bit overpriced by most South-East Asian standards. Almost all hotels follow a two-tiered pricing system – charging one rate for locals in kyat and another for foreigners in US dollars/FECs. A typical middle-of-the-road, Burmese-owned hotel might charge K900 for Burmese and US$30 for foreigners – over three times the local price figured at the real exchange rate. A dingy guesthouse in the hinterlands might take K100 from locals and US$5 from foreigners – more than a tenfold increase!

Fortunately for travellers on a tight budget there are a smattering of places in the US$5 to US$10 per person range. Typically this gets a bare cubicle with two beds and a cold-water bathroom down the hall. Rooms with a private cold-water bath cost a few dollars more. A toast-and-egg breakfast is usually included.

You can usually find a few kyat-priced hotels in out-of-the-way areas, and even in fairly accessible but relatively untouristed Shwebo, Magwe, Myingyan and Pakkoku. Guesthouses in some towns cost no more than K200 a night, sometimes as low as K100. The rooms in such places are very basic – perhaps two hard beds in a room surrounded by wood partitions that stop 30cm short of the ceiling. Once the local government begins enforcing the foreign guest licence law this kind of place may become more difficult to find.

FOOD

Despite an international reputation to the contrary, you can eat very well and very inexpensively in Myanmar. Until recently it could often be difficult to find Burmese food in local restaurants, but the economic development in urban areas has brought substantial improvements in the availability and quality of Burmese cuisine. Chinese and Indian food are also quite popular in the larger towns and cities. Street and market stalls tend to provide the regional dishes, but with these you must be a little wary of cleanliness.

Mainstream Burmese cuisine represents an intriguing blend of Burman, Mon, Indian and Chinese influences. Rice *(htamin)* is the core of any Burmese meal, to be eaten with a choice of curry dishes *(hin)*, most commonly fish, chicken, prawns or mutton. Very little beef or pork is eaten by the Burmese – beef because it's considered offensive to most Hindus and Buddhists, pork because the nats disapprove.

Burmese curries are the mildest in Asia in terms of chilli power – in fact most cooks don't use chillies at all in their recipes, just a simple *masala* of turmeric, ginger, garlic, salt and onions, plus plenty of peanut oil and shrimp paste. Heat can be added in the form of *balachaung*, a table condiment made from chillies, tamarind and dried shrimp pounded together, or from the very pungent, very hot

ngapi kyaw – shrimp paste fried in peanut oil with chilli, garlic and onions.

Almost everything in Burmese cooking is flavoured with *ngapi*, which is a salty paste concocted from dried and fermented shrimp or fish, and can be very much an acquired taste. A thin sauce of pressed fish or shrimp called *nganpya-yay* may also be used to salt Burmese dishes.

Noodle dishes are most often eaten for breakfast or as light meals between the main meals of the day. By far the most popular is *mohinga* (pronounced 'moun-hinga'), rice noodles served with a thick, yellow fish soup. Another popular noodle dish, especially at festivals, is *oh-no khauk-swe*, rice noodles with pieces of chicken in a spicy sauce made with coconut milk.

Shan khauk-swe, or Shan-style noodle soup – thin wheat noodles in a light broth with chunks of chilli-marinated chicken – is a favourite all over Myanmar but is most common in Mandalay and the Shan State. A variation popular in Mandalay is made with rice noodles and called *myi shay*. Another Shan dish worth seeking out is *htamin chin*, literally 'sour rice', a turmeric-coloured rice salad.

See the Language section in the Appendix for food vocabulary.

DRINKS
Nonalcoholic Drinks

Only drink water when you know it has been purified – bottled water is available in most restaurants and many stalls. One should be suspicious of ice although we've had lots of ice drinks in Myanmar without suffering any ill effects. Myanma Mineral Water is sold in bottles and is quite safe.

Burmese tea, brewed in the Indian style with lots of milk and sugar, is cheap. Many restaurants, the Chinese ones in particular, will provide as much weak Chinese tea as you can handle – for free. It's a good, safe thirst quencher and some people prefer it to regular Burmese tea. Teashops are a good place to drink safely boiled tea and munch on inexpensive snacks like *nam-bya, palata* or Chinese pastries.

Soft drinks are more costly but reasonable by Asian standards. Made-in-Myanmar soft drinks are mostly terrible, but a few come in pleasant flavours.

Sugar-cane juice is a very popular street-side drink – cheap, thirst quenching and relatively healthy.

MYANMAR

Alcoholic Drinks

Beer Since foreign trade was freed up in the early 1990s, the beer brands most commonly seen in Myanmar are international: Tiger, Bintang, ABC Stout, Singha, San Miguel, Beck, Heineken and other beers brewed in Thailand, Singapore and Indonesia. At one time these brands were available only on the black market; they are now sold freely in shops and restaurants throughout the country and typically cost K90 to K120 per can or bottle.

Myanmar has its own brand, Mandalay beer, which is very similar to Indian or Sri Lankan beer – light, but not bad on those hot and dusty occasions when only a beer will do. Mandalay Beer only comes in large bottles, and costs about K275 on average.

Toddy Throughout central Myanmar and the delta, *hta yei*, or toddy juice, is the farmer's choice of alcoholic beverage. Hta yei is tapped from the top of a toddy palm, the same tree – and the same sap – that produces jaggery or palm sugar. The juice is sweet and nonalco-holic in the morning but by mid-afternoon naturally ferments to a weak beer-like strength. By the next day it will have turned. The milky, viscous liquid has a nutty aroma and a slightly sour flavour that fades quickly.

The toddy is sold in the same roughly engraved terracotta pots the juice is collected in for about K80 per pot (or K15 in a bottle to go), and drunk from coconut half-shells set on small bamboo pedestals. Favourite toddy accompaniments include prawn crackers and fried peas. Some toddy bars also sell *hta ayet*, or toddy liquor (also called jaggery liquor), a much stronger, distilled form of toddy sap, for around K30 per bottle.

SHOPPING

Now that free-market kyat may be used openly for purchases, shopping in Myanmar is easier than ever before. Bartering is also quite acceptable and many merchants would love to trade their wares for designer watches, pocket calculators, jeans, T-shirts with English writing on them, and so on.

There is nice lacquerware available, particularly at Bagan. The black and gold items probably aren't as good quality as in Chiang Mai in Thailand, but coloured items are much more vibrant. Look for flexibility in bowls or dishes and clarity of design. Opium weights are cheaper than in Thailand. Beautiful shoulder bags are made by the Shan tribes. *Kalagas*,

tapestries embroidered with silver thread, sequins and colourful glass beads, are a good buy.

Be very careful if you decide to buy gems. Many foolish travellers buy fake gemstones. It's another of those fields to dabble in only if you really know what is and what isn't. Precious stones are supposed to be a government monopoly and they are very unhappy about visitors buying stones anywhere except at licensed retail shops. If *any* stones are found when your baggage is checked on departure, they may be confiscated unless you can present a receipt showing they were purchased from a government-licensed dealer. See also the earlier Customs section for information on items which cannot be taken out of the country.

Getting There & Away

AIR

There are several major air route options. First, and most commonly, is to travel out and back from Bangkok in Thailand. The second possibility is to slot Myanmar in between Thailand and Bangladesh, India or Nepal – many people travelling from South-East Asia to the subcontinent manage a few weeks in Myanmar in between. The third alternative is to travel out and back from Calcutta. Kuala Lumpur, Singapore, Osaka and Kunming round out the possibilities.

Bangkok is a good place to look for tickets to Myanmar.

Airlines

Myanma Airways International (MAI) is the country's international carrier. MAI is much more reliable than its domestic counterpart, Myanma Airways.

Reconfirmation

If you are counting on flying out of Yangon on your scheduled date of departure, then you must reconfirm your outbound flight either at the appropriate airport ticket counter or at the relevant airline office in town. This applies regardless of whether your flight is officially confirmed ('OK' status) on the ticket or not. You may notice a sign in the airport waiting lounge which reminds you of this requirement. If you do not reconfirm, the airlines (this goes for any of the airlines flying in and out of Yangon) cannot guarantee your outbound seat. Especially during the height of the tourist season (November-February), most flights out of Yangon seem to be intentionally overbooked. If you have an international flight to catch in Bangkok with an airline that has no Yangon office, you might try the Thai Airways office, which can sometimes help reconfirm.

Departure Tax
A US$10 departure tax, payable in dollars or FECs, is collected at the airport before flight check-in.

Bangladesh
Biman Bangladesh Airlines flies Bangkok-Yangon Dhaka (via Chittagong) once a week. It is usually the cheapest operator although not always that reliable. If you plan on overnighting in Dhaka, be sure to get a hotel voucher from Biman before leaving Yangon; in fact it might be best to get it in Bangkok (or wherever you buy the ticket) first, just to be safe.

MAI flies to Dhaka once a week.

China
Air China flies between Kunming (Yunnan) and Yangon once a week. If you are travelling around China and then continuing to South-East Asia this can be an economical choice, since from western China you would not have to backtrack all the way east to Hong Kong, then fly all the way west to Bangkok.

MAI flies to Hong Kong three times weekly.

India
MAI flies Bangkok-Yangon-Calcutta for around US$150.

Japan
All Nippon Airline (ANA) flies to Yangon from Osaka twice weekly, but the return flight is via Bangkok.

Malaysia
There are flights between Kuala Lumpur and Yangon with Malaysia Airlines (twice weekly). MAI also flies to Kuala Lumpur twice a week.

Nepal
MAI also flies Bangkok-Yangon-Kathmandu for around US$200.

Singapore
Silk Air, a subsidiary of Singapore Airlines, flies to Yangon four times weekly from Singapore (around US$250 return).

MAI flies to Singapore four times a week.

Thailand
Typical costs for Bangkok-Yangon-Bangkok tickets are around US$230 on Thai Airways International, US$220 on MAI and as low as US$144 on Biman Bangladesh.

Thai Airways International currently flies Bangkok-Yangon-Bangkok daily. Although slightly more expensive than the equivalent MAI flight, Thai's departure times are much more sane and the service more reliable.

MAI flies from Bangkok to Yangon and vice versa daily.

Air Mandalay, Myanmar's new, privately owned domestic carrier, has recently started flying between Chiang Mai and Yangon on Wednesday and Sunday.

LAND
The government has announced the opening of the Thai-Burmese border between Mae Sai (Thailand) and Tachilek. However, overland travel is limited to Kyaingtong. You must fly out of Tachilek to get to Mandalay or elsewhere in Myanmar.

It's also possible to enter Myanmar at Kawthoung by boat from Ranong in Thailand. However, you must fly out of Kawthoung, as there is no road travel from Kawthoung to Myeik.

There are two other possible border crossings to/from Thailand, but they are for brief excursions only. Payathonzu, opposite Three Pagodas Pass, is open on and off but was closed at the time of writing. There is now a bridge between Myawaddy and Mae Sot on the Thai side, but this crossing also is open only on and off. Check before attempting either of these crossings.

Getting Around

Travel in Myanmar is not easy – it's uncertain and often uncomfortable by whatever means of travel you choose. Airline schedules often change without notice, and buses may be delayed due to flooded roads or even during popular festivals.

AIR
Myanmar has 66 airstrips around the country, 23 of which are served by scheduled domestic flights. Most are short, one-strip fields that

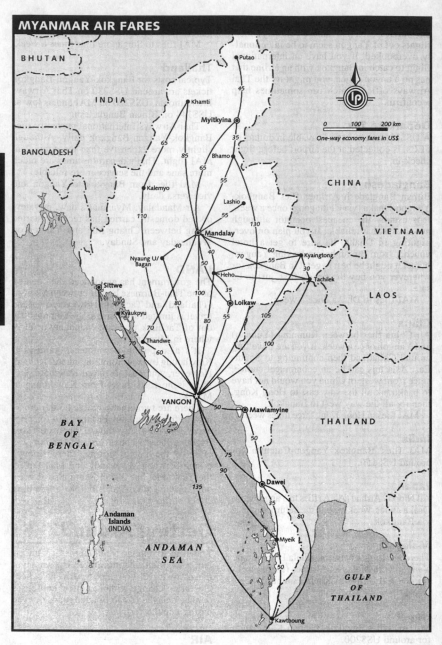

MYANMAR AIR FARES

BHUTAN

INDIA

BANGLADESH

Putao

Khamti

45

Myitkyina

35

Bhamo

65

85

65

55

Lashio

55

110

55

130

Kalemyo

Mandalay

CHINA

VIETNAM

40

40

70

60

Kyaingtong

Nyaung U/
Bagan

50

55

30

Sittwe

Heho

35

Tachilek

LAOS

Kyaukpyu

100

80

Loikaw

80

55

105

70

70

60

100

Thandwe

85

YANGON

50

Mawlamyine

THAILAND

BAY
OF
BENGAL

50

75

90

Dawei

135

35

Andaman
Islands
(INDIA)

80

ANDAMAN
SEA

Myeik

50

GULF
OF
THAILAND

Kawthoung

0   100   200 km

One-way economy fares in US$

can land only one plane at a time. None have instrument landing capability, a situation which can be especially tricky during the May to November monsoon season even though all 23 are considered 'all-weather aerodromes'.

Construction has slowed or stopped on a planned international airport outside Yangon near Bago, on a site used by B-29 bombers during WWII. Airports at Mandalay and Heho are soon to add sorely needed runways and expanded passenger facilities.

Domestic Air Services

Myanma Airways Myanma Airways' small fleet of aircraft are in a decidedly tatty condition and the whole operation seems to be a little on the haphazard side, which does not do wonders for one's nerves when flying with Myanma Airways.

Schedules for Myanma Airways don't mean all that much – if the passengers turn up early the flight may go early. If insufficient passengers show up the flight may not go at all. It's wisest in Myanmar to travel as lightly as possible and carry your own baggage out to the aircraft rather than trust that it will find its own way there.

Foreigners must purchase all tickets using FECs or US dollars cash. Burmese citizens pay lower fares in kyat.

Air Mandalay & Yangon Airways There are two private carriers in Myanmar.

Air Mandalay or Yangon Airways saves visitors a whole list of headaches. In the first place they fly to places for which permits aren't necessary, so that's one layer of bureaucracy eliminated in their ticket lines. Secondly, both Air Mandalay and Yangon Airways are usually punctual in arrivals and departures. Finally, both Air Mandalay and Yangon Airways planes are new and substantially more comfortable.

Air Mandalay appears to have been created so that foreigners won't compete with Burmese citizens for perpetually tight seating space on Myanma Airways aircraft. In other words the government would just as soon see you fly with upscale Air Mandalay (or Yangon Airways) rather than with government-subsidised Myanma Airways.

Both Air Mandalay and Yangon Airways flights cost a bit more than Myanma Airways flights to the same destinations. Fares are slightly higher during the busier November to February period. Tickets are cheaper from travel agents than from the airlines.

BUS & TRUCK

In general, buses in Myanmar operated by the state-owned Road Transport Enterprise tend to be crowded and unreliable. Foreigners are permitted to buy bus tickets of any class, using kyat, to any destination within or near the main Yangon-Mandalay- Bagan-Taunggyi triangle. Buses are generally easily boarded in most other places, too, except for 'brown' areas towards the Thai border.

Within the last couple of years a fleet of new private, air-con express buses have caught on for services from Yangon to Meiktila, Pyay, Mandalay, and Taunggyi – with more sure to come with the ongoing privatisation of the transport industry. These new express buses beat Myanma Railway's express trains in both speed and ticket price; they also stop for meals or snacks along the way. Another major difference between bus and train is that all bus tickets may be purchased using kyat; if there's a dollar/FEC fare posted it's usually equivalent to the kyat fare figured at the free-market rate. Fares are the same for locals as for foreigners. These buses fill up fast, so book a day or two in advance.

There are also many modern Japanese pick-up trucks installed with bench seats (rather like a Thai *songthaew*), carrying 20 or more passengers plus cargo. Sometimes you can pay a bit more for a seat by the driver, worth considering on longer trips.

TRAIN

Apart from the daily Yangon to Mandalay special express, the ordinary-class trains are better forgotten – they are dirty, slow, unreliable and very dark at night due to a national shortage of light bulbs! Travel in upper class (equivalent to 1st class) and 1st class (equivalent to 2nd class) is generally better.

Except for the main tourist routes, you may find it impossible to buy railway tickets through MTT and the station is not supposed to sell tickets to foreigners, who should get them from MTT! The answer is to ask somebody at the station to buy them for you, although we've bought tickets at several points not watched over by MTT and had no trouble.

BOAT

River

A huge fleet of riverboats, heir to the old Irrawaddy Flotilla Company, still ply Myanmar's major rivers. The main drawback is speed; where both modes of transport are available, a boat typically takes three to four times as long as road travel along the same route.

There are 8000km of navigable river in Myanmar, with the most important river being the Ayeyarwady. Even in the dry season boats can travel from the delta all the way north to Bhamo, and in the wet they can reach Myitkyina. Other important rivers include the Twante Canal, which links the Ayeyarwady to Yangon, and the Chindwinn, which joins the Ayeyarwady a little above Bagan.

Only a few riverboat routes are regularly used by visitors. Best known is the Mandalay-Bagan service. A new express ferry runs five times a week. The regular ferry departs Mandalay in the early morning twice weekly and arrives at Nyaung U, just north of Bagan. If you take the slower local boats, this trip can be extended to Pyay or all the way to Yangon; it's two days travel downriver from Bagan to Pyay, where you change boats and have another couple of days travel before reaching Yangon.

Coast

Although the obstacles standing in your way are daunting, it's possible to travel along Myanmar's coastline via Myanma Five Star Line (MFSL), the country's state-owned ocean transport enterprise. MFSL maintains just 21 craft, which sail north and south from Yangon about twice a month. Only eight vessels offer passenger service. Shipping dates vary from month to month and are announced via a public chalkboard at the main MFSL office in Yangon.

Southbound ships sail regularly to Kawthoung, a two night voyage from Yangon, with occasional scheduled calls at Dawei and Myeik. Northbound ships call at Thandwe (a full day from Yangon) and Kyaukpyu (one night) before docking in Sittwe (five more hours) for cargo from India and Bangladesh.

Since to book passage on any MFSL ship you must show an MHT travel permit that specifies travel by ship, and since you must wait around for up to two weeks for a ship going your way, this is by far the most difficult public transport to arrange.

LOCAL TRANSPORT

Larger towns in Myanmar offer a variety of city buses (kaa), bicycle rickshaws or trishaws (sai-kaa), horse carts (myint hlei), vintage taxis (taxi), more modern little three-wheelers somewhat akin to autorickshaws

(thoun bein, or 'three wheels'), tiny four-wheeled Mazdas (lei bein, or 'four wheels') and modern Japanese pick-up trucks (also kaa) used like Indonesian bemos or Thai songthaews.

Small towns rely heavily on horse carts and trishaws as the main mode of local transport. In the five largest cities (Yangon, Mandalay, Pathein, Mawlamyine and Taunggyi), public buses ply regular routes along the main avenues for a fixed per-person rate, usually no more than K2. Standard rates for taxis, trishaws and horse carts are sometimes 'boosted' for foreigners. A little bargaining may be in order; ask around locally to find out what the going fares are. The supply of drivers and vehicles usually exceeds the demand, so it's usually not hard to move the fare down towards normal levels.

You can rent bicycles in Mandalay, Bagan, Pyin U Lwin and Nyaungshwe.

Yangon (Rangoon)

The capital of Myanmar for just over 100 years, Yangon (formerly called Rangoon) is 30km upriver from the sea and has an air of seedy decay along with a great pagoda – Swedagon Paya – that is one of the real wonders of South-East Asia. A city of wide streets and spacious architecture, it looks run down, worn out and thoroughly neglected, although with the roadwork and new coats of paint ordered by SLORC, your initial impression will probably be favourable. The streets are lively at night with hordes of stalls selling delicious-looking food, stacks of clothing and piles of huge cigars and cheroots.

History

As Myanmar's capital city, Yangon is comparatively young – it only became capital in 1885 when the British completed the conquest of Upper Myanmar and Mandalay's brief period as the centre of the last Burmese kingdom ended. Previous to the British conquest, Yangon was very much a small town in comparison with places like Bago, Pyay or Thaton. In 1755 King Alaungpaya conquered Lower Myanmar and built a new city on the site of Yangon, which at that time was known as Dagon. Yangon means End of Strife: the king rather vainly hoped that with the conquest of Lower Myanmar his struggles would be over. When the British arrived, they rebuilt the capital to its present plan and corrupted the city's name to 'Rangoon'.

Orientation

The city is bounded to the south and west by the Yangon River (also known as the Hlaing River) and to the east by Pazundaung Canal, which flows into the Yangon River. The whole city is divided into townships, and street addresses are often suffixed with these (eg 52nd St, Botataung Township). Addresses in this northern area often quote the number of miles from Sule Paya – the landmark paya (pagoda) in the city's centre. For example, 'Pyay Rd, Mile 8' means the place is eight miles north of Sule Paya on Pyay Rd.

Central Yangon's grid-style layout is relatively simple to find your way around and pleasant enough to explore on foot. Many of the major roadways were renamed after independence, but some of the old names persist and this can be confusing. Anawrahta St, for example, is still often called Fraser Rd, even though most of the street signs have changed.

Maps The *Yangon Tourist Map*, put out by MTT, is cheap and useful enough for most people. If you anticipate spending a lot of time in the capital, it's worth seeking out the more detailed and more up-to-date *Yangon Guide Map* (Ministry of Forestry, Survey Department).

Information

Tourist Offices Myanmar Travel & Tours (☎ 27 5328), 77/91 Sule Pagoda Rd, at the corner of Mahabandoola St, is next to Thai Airways.

Money With the Foreign Exchange Certificate system in place, no one bothers to change money at the so-called official rate. Yangon and Mandalay are the best places in the country for changing money at the free-market rate. Ask around first to establish what the current rate is. If you've bought FECs at the airport, the best place to change them is at a hotel or shop licensed to accept FECs.

Post The GPO is a short stroll east of The Strand Hotel on Strand Rd. It's open Monday to Friday from 9.30 am to 4.30 pm. The GPO is considered the safest place to post letters.

Telephone The Central Telephone & Telegraph (CTT) office is on the corner of Pansodan and Mahabandoola Sts. The office is open Monday to Friday from 8 am to 4 pm, weekends and holidays from 9 am to 2 pm. IDD calls can also be made from many hotel lobbies; trunk calls are quite cheap, and can be made from many shops in the central area.

Bookshops Yangon has quite a few bookshops, most along Bogyoke Aung San St opposite the Bogyoke Aung San Market, where you can find some really interesting books. Also check the Pagan Bookshop at 100 37th St, not far from The Strand Hotel. You never know what will turn up in this little shop that specialises in worthwhile English-language material – much of it is vintage stuff.

Shwedagon Paya

Dominating the entire city from its hilltop site, this is the most sacred Buddhist temple in Myanmar. Nearly 100m high, it is clearly visible from the air as you fly in or out of Yangon. You may see it as a tiny golden dot while flying over Myanmar to Kathmandu – magic! Visit in the early morning or early evening when the gold spire gleams in the sun and the temperature is cooler. Or see its shimmering reflection from across Kandawgyi Lake at night. In 1587 a European visitor wrote of its 'wonderful bignesse' and that it was 'all gilded from foote to the toppe'. The Shwedagon has an equally impressive appearance at night when it glows gold in the spotlights.

A few facts and figures: the current stupa dates from the 18th century, though the site is undoubtedly much older; there are over 8000 gold plates covering the monument; the top of the spire is encrusted with more than 5000 diamonds and 2000 other precious or semiprecious stones; and the compound around the pagoda has 82 other buildings – it is this sheer mass of buildings that gives the place its awesome appeal.

In the compound's north-western corner is a huge bell which the butter-fingered British managed to drop into the Yangon River while carrying it off. Unable to recover it, they gave the bell back to the Burmese, who refloated it by tying a vast number of bamboo lengths to it.

The official admission fee for Shwedagon is US$5, which includes an elevator ride to the raised platform of the stupa. There are separate elevators for Burmese and foreigners. Of course, you may walk up one of the long graceful entrances. If you come before 7 am, you may be able to get in for free.

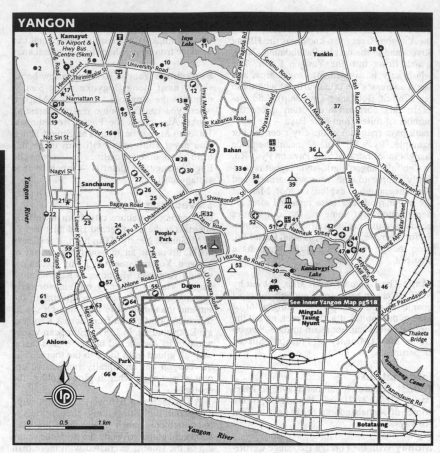

YANGON

Sule Paya

Also over 2000 years old and right in the centre of town, 46m Sule Paya makes a fine spectacle at night and the inside of the complex is lit up by pulsating neon. It's also a popular meeting place for Burmese.

National Museum

The national museum collection is unspectacular and cavernous; most explanations are in Burmese. Nevertheless, you can find several interesting exhibits, including the 8m-high Sihasana Lion Throne, returned to Burma in 1908 by Lord Mountbatten. The main floor contains jewellery, old photos, royal relics, Hintha opium weights and inscribed tablets. The upper floors exhibit art and archaeology. The museum is on Pyay Rd,

about 1km north of Bogyoke Aung San St, and is open from 10 am to 3 pm; closed Mondays. Admission is US$5.

Other Sights

There's a mirror maze in the stupa of Botataung Paya. Yangon has a fine open-air market and the extensive Bogyoke Aung San Market is always worth a wander. It's a very pleasant stroll around Kandawgyi Lake, where you can visit the huge Karaweik non-floating restaurant. The Karaweik, a local attraction in its own right, is a reinforced concrete reproduction of a royal barge. Yangon has a British-built zoo with a collection of Burmese animals, and on Sunday there is a snake charmer and an elephant performance.

Maha Wizaya (Vijaya) Paya, almost op-

YANGON

PLACES TO STAY		18	Hsimmalaik Bus Centre	44	Kandawgyi Clinic
4	Aurora Inn		(for Bago, Pathein & Kyaikto)	45	Worker's Hospital
13	Windermere Inn	19	Orthopaedic Hospital	46	Mingala Zei (Market)
28	Winner Inn	20	San Pya Fish Market	47	UNDP & FAO
		21	Police Station	48	Kandawgyi Palace Hotel
PLACES TO EAT		22	Htee Dan Jetty (Passenger		(landmark)
14	Green Elephant Restaurant		Ferry to Dalah)	49	Yangon Zoological Gardens
31	ATK: Aung Thu Kha	23	Kohtatgyi Paya	50	National Aquarium
		24	Malaysian Embassy	51	Japanese Embassy
OTHER		25	Yuzana Supermarket	52	Jivitdana Hospital for Monks
1	Institute of Marine	26	Singaporean Embassy		& Nuns
	Technology	27	Czech & Slovak Embassy	53	Maha Wizaya Paya
2	Myanma Dockyards	29	Traditions Gallery	54	Shwedagon Paya
	Enterprise	30	Vietnamese Embassy	55	Thai Embassy
3	Hledan Train Station	32	Martyrs' Mausoleum	56	Pyithu Hluttaw (National
5	Hledan Zei (Market)	33	Home for the Aged Poor		Assembly)
6	Judson Baptist Church	34	Air Mandalay	57	Ahlone Road Train Station
7	University of Yangon (Main	35	Mahasi Meditation Centre	58	Pakistani Embassy
	Campus)	36	Chaukhtatgyi Paya	59	West Yangon Hospital
8	University Post Office	37	Kyaikkasan Grounds	60	Thirimingala Zei (Market)
9	Institute of Foreign Language		(Sports Field)	61	Myanma Fisheries
10	UNICEF	38	Bauktaw Train Station		Enterprise
11	Tatmadaw Boat Club	39	Ngahtatgyi Paya	62	Myanma Timber Enterprise
12	South Korean Embassy	40	Bogyoke Aung San Museum	63	Police Station
15	Institute of Medicine 1	41	Mogok Meditation Centre	64	Chinese Embassy
16	Myanma TV & Radio	42	Nepalese Embassy	65	Children's Hospital
	Department	43	Eye, Ear, Nose & Throat	66	Myanma Electric Power
17	Police Station		Hospital		Enterprise

MYANMAR

posite the southern gate to Shwedagon Paya, features a well proportioned zedi built in 1980 to commemorate the unification of Theravada Buddhism in Myanmar. The king of Nepal contributed sacred relics for the zedi's relic chamber, and Burmese strongman Ne Win had it topped with an 11 level *hti* (the umbrella or decorated top of a pagoda) – two more levels than the hti at Shwedagon.

The **Kaba Aye Paya** (World Peace Pagoda) is about 11km north of the city and was built in the mid-1950s for the 2500th anniversary of Buddhism. The huge reclining Buddha at **Chaukhtatgyi Paya** is also close by.

An interesting excursion from Yangon is a bus trip to **Kyauktan** with its small island pagoda. Another is to take a longer river/canal trip to the famed pottery village of **Twante**, two or three hours away.

Places to Stay

Since the privatisation of the hotel industry in 1993, there has been an explosion of hotel and guesthouse development in Yangon. With so many new rooms in the city, many places have lowered their rates, and bargaining is often worth a try. Prices quoted at the following places almost always include tax and service, and some travellers have been able to bargain down US$1 by declining the rudimentary eggs-and-toast breakfast. Payment is accepted in US dollars cash or FECs only.

There are several very cheap places to stay in Yangon, including the conveniently located *Zar Chi Win Guest House* (☎ 27 5407) on the western side of 37th St, just south of Merchant St and near the book vendors and Pagan Bookshop. The usual windowless cubicles cost US$5/10 a single/double with shared bath and toilet or US$20 with private bath. Rates include breakfast, and a left-luggage service is available.

A few blocks west, *Pyin Oo Lwin II Guest House* (☎ 24 3284) on Mahabandoola Garden St, just south of Anawrahta St, is better than it looks from the outside. Single/double rooms with hot water cost US$10/18.

Nearby, on busy Mahabandoola St, between 37th and 38th Sts, the friendly *Myanmar Holiday Inn* (☎ 24 0016) charges US$6/12 a single/double without breakfast for an economy room (separate bath and toilet) or US$12/22 with breakfast and attached bath.

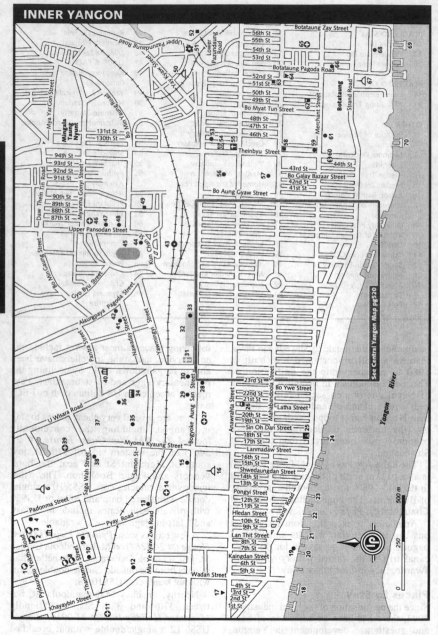

INNER YANGON

INNER YANGON

PLACES TO STAY
49 Sunflower Inn 1
52 Motherland Inn 2
58 YMCA
63 Three Seasons Hotel

PLACES TO EAT
17 Maw Shwe Li Restaurant
64 Home Sweet Home

OTHER
1   Egyptian Embassy
2   Indonesian Embassy
3   French Embassy
4   National Archives
5   National Museum
6   Ein Daw Yar Paya
7   Lao Embassy
8   Sri Lankan Embassy
9   Ministry of Foreign Affairs
10 American Center & USIS
11 Central Women's Hospital
12 Mary Chapman Deaf &
    Dumb School
13 Than Zei (Market)
14 New General Hospital
15 Institute of Medicine
    No. 1

16 Thayettaw Kyaung
18 Wadan St Jetty
19 Inland Water Transport
    Office
20 Kaingdan St Jetty
21 Lan Thit St Jetty
22 Hledan St Jetty
23 Pongyi St Jetty
24 Sin Oh Dan St Jetty
25 Kheng Hock Keong
    (Chinese Temple)
26 Pick-ups to Bago
27 Yangon General Hospital
28 Institute of Dental
    Medicine
29 School
30 School
31 St Mary's Cathedral
32 Bogyoke Aung San Market
33 FMI Centre
34 National Swimming Pool
35 National Theatre
36 Tatmadaw Military Hall
37 Myoma Ground
38 School
39 No 2 Military Hospital
40 War Museum
41 Yuzana Pickle Tea

42 School
43 Yangon Train Station
44 City Ticket Offices for
    Long-Distance Buses
45 Aung San Stadium
46 Infectious Diseases Hospital
47 School
48 School
50 Shwe Pon Pwint Paya
51 Pazundaung Garden
53 Ivy Gallery
54 Sikh Temple
55 Salvation Army Church
56 School
57 Ministers' Offices
59 Myanma Five Star Line
    Office
60 Foreign Exchange Counter
61 Myanma Railways Office
62 50th Street Bar & Grill
65 General Hospital
66 University of Yangon
    (Botataung Campus)
67 Botataung Paya
68 Sawmill
69 Botataung Jetty
70 Myanma Five Star Line Cargo
    Jetty

Half a block north of Sule Paya is the *Mayshan Guest House* (☎ 28 3599) at 115/117 Sule Pagoda Rd. It is clean, well managed and centrally located with single/double rooms at US$16/28. They also have four single economy rooms at US$10.

Near the train station at the north-west corner of U Pho Kya Rd and Bo Min Yaung Rd is one of the best of the budget places. The *Sunflower Inn 1* (☎ 27 6503) offers very clean if small rooms with communal bath for US$10/16 a single/double including breakfast. Or for US$16/24 you can have a room with private hot-water bath, air con, fridge and TV.

A newer and slightly more expensive *Sunflower Inn 2* (☎ 24 0014) at 259/263 Anawrahta St, on the corner of Shwebontha St, in the downtown Indian quarter, offers similar rooms at US$15/20 for a single/double with common bath, and US$20/30 for a single/double with bath and air con.

The spartan and reliable *Yangon YMCA* (☎ 29 4128) at 263 Mahabandoola St in Botataung Township, has clean economy rooms (common bath) with a fan for US$8/15 a single/double, and US$10/16 with air con. Air con rooms with private bath cost US$20/30 a single/double.

Seven blocks east of the YMCA is one of the best values in the downtown area, the *Three Seasons Hotel* (☎ 29 3304) at 83/85 52nd St in Pazundaung Township, a few doors north of Mahabandoola St. Clean, well lit rooms cost US$18/22 a single/double. Farther east near Pazundaung Canal is the reliable *Motherland Inn 2* at 433 Lower Pazundaung Rd. Clean rooms with fan and shower cost US$8/10 a single/double.

North of the centre between Inya Lake and Shwedagon Paya in a quieter part of Yangon, *Winner Inn* (☎ 53 1205) at 42 Thanlwin Rd is excellent value with rooms for one or two at US$24. The dining room overlooks a lovely garden. At the nearby *Windermere Inn* (☎ 53 3846) at 15 Thanlwin Rd rooms cost US$20/30 a single/double.

In the same vicinity, near the University of Yangon and Hledan Zei (Market), *Aurora Inn* (☎ 52 5961) at 37 Thirimingalar St, has decent rooms with common bath for US$10/16 a single/double; larger rooms with private bath cost US$20/30.

Places to Eat

There are numerous Indian restaurants along Anawrahta St west of Sule Pagoda Rd. The

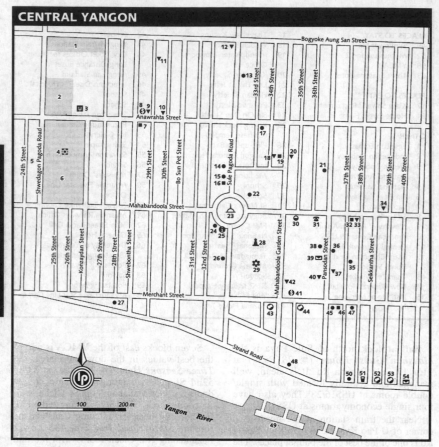

CENTRAL YANGON

New Delhi Restaurant between 29th St and Shwebontha St and nearby *Shwe Htoo Restaurant* both serve good north and south Indian dishes, including biryani (spiced rice with chicken).

On Mahabandoola St, at the corner of Seikkhantha St, is the dependable and cheap *Bharat Restaurant*, which is similar to the New Delhi. A bit more expensive is the excellent *Royal Taj Restaurant* at 232 29th St, just south of Bogyoke Aung San St, serving mostly north Indian food, including good vegie curries.

You can get yoghurt or lassi (a delicious yoghurt drink) at *Nilar Win's Cold Drink Shop* at 377 Mahabandoola St, next to the Myanmar Holiday Inn, midway between the YMCA and Sule Paya.

Try the genuine Burmese food at *ATK: Aung Thu Kha*, 17 1st St, just north of Shwegondine St in Bahan Township. Like most Burmese eateries, it's buffet style so you can look before ordering. Figure on spending no more than K300 per person for a full spread, not including beverages. If you want to splurge on Burmese cuisine in a fancier garden setting, try the upscale *Green Elephant Restaurant* at 12 Inya Rd.

For traditional Shan-style food, try the excellent *999 Shan Noodle Restaurant*, or 'Triple 9,' on 34th St between Anawrahta St and City Hall. Shan sour rice salad and sour noodle soup with tamarind are among the specialities. Most dishes are less than K100.

Another excellent Shan eatery is *Maw Shwe Li Restaurant* at 316 Anawrahta St in

CENTRAL YANGON

PLACES TO STAY	OTHER		29	Mahabandoola Garden
7 Sunflower Inn 2	1	New Bogyoke Market	30	Pick-ups to Thanlyin
16 Mayshan Guest House	2	Open-Air Market	31	CTT Office
19 Pyin Oo Lwin II Guest	3	Sri Kali Temple	35	Pagan Bookshop
House	4	Moseah Yeshua Synagogue	36	Biman Bangladesh Airlines
32 Myanmar Holiday Inn	5	Theingyizei Plaza; Nightclubs	38	Supreme Court
46 Zar Chi Win Guest House	6	Theingyi Zei (Market)	39	Township Post Office
	8	Myanma Oriental Bank	41	Myanma Foreign Trade Bank
PLACES TO EAT	13	Inwa Book Store	43	US Embassy
9 New Delhi Restaurant	14	Yangon Duty-Free Store	44	Indian Embassy
10 Shwe Htoo Restaurant	15	Myanma Airways International	45	Silk Air
11 Royal Taj Restaurant	17	Camera/Film Shops	47	Sarpay Beikman Book Centre
12 Traders Hotel	21	Ava Tailoring	48	Customs
18 999 Shan Noodle Restaurant	22	City Hall	49	Myanma Five Star Line
20 Theingi Shwe Yee Tea House	23	Sule Paya		Passenger Jetty
33 Nilar Win's Cold Drink Shop	24	Thai Airways International	50	Myanma Airways
34 Bharat Restaurant	25	MTT Office	51	The Strand Bar
37 Donburiya	26	Air France	52	Australian Embassy
40 Nan Yu Restaurant	27	Ministry of Commerce	53	UK Embassy
42 Tokyo Fried Chicken	28	Independence Monument	54	Main Post Office

Lanmadaw Township, west of the city centre. This small and friendly out-of-the-way place is usually crowded with Burmese, and the curries are excellent and cheap; Shan specialities include *pei pot kyaw* (sour bean condiment) and *hmo chawk kyaw* (fried mushrooms).

You can sample the whole range of Chinese cuisine in Yangon – from the familiar Cantonese through to the less well known Shanghai, Sichuan, Beijing or Hokkien dishes. *Nan Yu Restaurant* at 81 Pansodan St is clean, air-conditioned and serves acceptable Cantonese fare at reasonable prices.

Modest western-style fast-food ('short eats') restaurants with sandwiches, burgers, pizza, chicken, spaghetti and the like are multiplying quickly in the city. Typical of the genre are *Home Sweet Home*, on the corner of Mahabandoola and 52nd Sts, and *Tokyo Fried Chicken* at 156 Mahabandoola Garden St, just north of Merchant St.

There's even a new 24 hour restaurant in town, *Donburiya* at 112 Pansodan St across from the High Court, serving good Japanese rice and noodle dishes.

For an expensive splurge on a Sunday morning, you'll get your fill at the *Traders Hotel*, at the corner of Sule Pagoda Rd and Bogyoke Aung San St. The lavish Sunday brunch includes very well prepared Burmese curries, Chinese steam pot, roast duck, souffles, desserts, you name it. While you're there, be sure to check out the player piano in the lobby.

Entertainment

Yangon entertainment, never the highlight of any foreigner's Myanmar visit, was dealt a near death-blow by the 11 pm curfew imposed from 1988 to late 1992. The main form of local recreation still seems to be hanging out in the teashops or 'cold drink' shops.

One of the best teashops in Yangon, *Theingi Shwe Yee Tea House* at 265 Seik-kanthar St, offers an assortment of Burmese snacks and sweets, including *bain mok* (opium cakes). They are semi-sweet and made with rice flour, brown sugar, coconut and in the past were sprinkled with opium seeds – hence the enduring name.

To enjoy a cup of tea after 9 pm, you must pull up a small stool at one of the impromptu collections of small tables that suddenly appear after dark on the streets of Yangon. One of the most popular is in front of the fire station just north-west of Sule Paya.

Cinema Half a dozen or so cinemas along Bogyoke Aung San St, east of Sule Paya, show films for K15 or less per seat. The normal fare is pretty awful; a succession of syrupy Burmese dramas, kungfu smash-ups and European or American action thrillers.

The American Center, behind the Ministry of Foreign Affairs at 14 Taw Win St, shows free American movies every Monday at noon.

Bars & Cafes *The Strand Bar*, far more sophisticated than its funky predecessor, is open from 11 am to 11 pm. Any foreign liquors you may be craving are bound to be among the huge selection of bottles behind the polished wooden bar. Modern watercolours of Burmese scenes decorate the walls and occasionally there's someone around to play the baby grand.

The Nawarat Hotel's popular *Zawgyi Lounge* is a small but pleasant bar decorated with a series of original paintings by well known Yangon muralist U Ba Kyi. The series depicts various episodes in the life of a typical *zawgyi*, or accomplished Burmese alchemist. A pop band performs Monday through Saturday nights. There is no cover charge.

Worth a look for the swank interior is *50th Street Bar & Grill* at 9/13 50th St near the corner of Merchant St. On Saturday nights, a local house band performs upstairs. No cover charge, but prices are in US dollars.

Shopping

The sprawling, 70-year-old Bogyoke Aung San Market (sometimes called by its British name, Scott Market), appropriately located on Bogyoke Aung San St, has the largest selection of Burmese handicrafts you'll find under one roof (actually several roofs).

Another major market, especially for locals who find Bogyoke Aung San Market a little too pricey, is Theingyi Zei, the biggest market in Yangon. This rambling affair extends four blocks east to west from Konzaydan St to 24th St, and north to south from Anawrahta St to Mahabandoola St. The majority of the merchandise for sale here represents ordinary housewares and textiles, however the market is renowned for its large section purveying traditional Burmese herbs and medicines.

The FMI Centre just east of Bogyoke Aung San Market is a recent and upscale addition to the downtown shopping scene with music stores, jewellery and clothing shops.

Arts & Crafts Traditions Gallery at 24 Inya Myaing Rd has quality reproductions of traditional Burmese handicrafts. Ivy Gallery, 159 45th St between Bogyoke Aung San and Anawrahta Sts, features a fine collection of modern Burmese art.

Yone Yang Antique Shop, 1B Kabaaye Pagoda Rd at Inya Rd, is a fine shop to browse in, even if much of its stock is not for export.

Getting There & Away

Bus Most public and private buses to destinations outside of Yangon leave from the Hwy Bus Centre at the intersection of Pyay and Station Rds, just south-west of Yangon's airport in Mingaladon. Each bus line has an office at the station; for the most part these offices are lined up according to general route, eg one section for Nyaung U/Bagan, another for the Mandalay area, another for Taunggyi/Inle Lake and one for Mawlamyine/Dawei. You can buy tickets at the station (a day or two in advance is recommended) or at several downtown locations, mostly opposite the Central Train Station.

Air-con express buses run to Pyay, Meiktila, Mandalay, Taunggyi and Mawlamyine. Typical fares are K2000 (or US$10/FEC) for Mandalay, Meiktila or Taunggyi; K800 to Pyay or Mawlamyine. These lines also may stop in Bago and Taungoo, where small offices are maintained at roadside restaurants.

The major players on the popular Yangon to Mandalay route are Leo Express, Kyaw Express and Transnational Express, all of whom maintain offices at the Hwy Bus Centre as well as in central Yangon across from the train station at Aung San Stadium. Meals, snacks and water are usually provided. Most companies transfer passengers from several downtown locations to the Hwy Bus Centre in vans or pick-ups for no extra charge.

Train The 716km trip from Yangon to Mandalay is the only train trip most visitors consider – there are daily and nightly reserved cars on express trains on this route, where you can be sure of getting a seat. The express trains are far superior to the general run of Burmese trains. Upper class has reclining seats and is quite comfortable. Sleepers are available but hard to reserve.

In addition to the many trains operated by state-owned Myanma Railways, one private company runs out of Yangon train station along the Yangon-Mandalay line. Dagon Mann (☎ 24 9024) reserves just four berths and six upper-class seats for foreigners on its private express train (No 17 Up on the public schedule), which departs Yangon at 3.15 pm three times a week, arriving in Mandalay at 5.40 am the next day.

Boat Along the Yangon River waterfront, which wraps around southern Yangon, four main passenger jetties service long-distance ferries headed up the delta towards Pathein or north along the Ayeyarwady to Pyay, Bagan and Mandalay: Pongyi, Lan Thit, Kaingdan and Hledan. Named for the respective streets that extend north from each jetty, all four are clustered in an area just south of Lanmadaw Township and south-west of Chinatown. When you purchase a ticket for a particular ferry from the Inland Water Transport Company (IWT) office at the back of Lan Thit St jetty, be sure to ask which jetty your boat will be leaving from.

Myanma Five Star Line ships leave from the MFSL jetty – also known as Chanmayei-seikan jetty – next to Pansodan St jetty.

Getting Around
To/From the Airport
Hotel desks just outside the arrival area can arrange buses into Yangon for US$2 per person, or taxis for US$6 per vehicle (up to four passengers). Some hotels will provide free transport if you book a room at their airport hotel desk. You can also book your own taxi from the motley collection of old, battered vehicles parked outside the airport for around US$3 to the destination of your choice.

Getting to the airport from Yangon you can pay in free-market kyat, though the fare works out to be about the same (about K500 to K600).

If you happen to be flying out of Yangon on Union Day, 12 February, you need to get out to the airport before noon because the road to the airport is closed to non-parade traffic after that time.

Bus
Over 40 numbered city bus routes connect the townships of Yangon. Many buses date back to the 1940s and carry heavy teak carriages. Often they're impossibly crowded; a Burmese bus is not full until every available handhold for those hanging off the sides and back has been taken. Other routes use newer Japanese and Korean buses that aren't too bad; some routes also use pick-up trucks with benches in the back. If you manage to find a space, you can get anywhere in central Yangon for K5 or less. Longer routes cost up to K10.

Train
An interesting way of seeing the city, suburbs and surrounding countryside is to take the 'circle line' train from Yangon station. It's crowded with commuters on weekdays but on Saturday morning you can make a 2½ hour loop, allowing you to see the outskirts of the city and surrounding villages.

Taxi
Licensed taxis carry red licence plates, though there is often little else to distinguish a taxi from any other vehicle in Yangon. The most expensive are the car-taxis – usually older, mid-sized Japanese cars. Fares are highly negotiable – most trips around the central area shouldn't cost more than K150 to K200. You can hire a nonregistered cab for the whole day for no more than K4000 or US$20 (always check the vehicle before you settle on a price).

Cheaper, but increasingly difficult to find, are the tiny three-wheeled and four-wheeled Mazda taxis, close relatives of the Indian autorickshaws or Thai *tuk-tuks*. A short trip of six to eight blocks or so should cost no more than K75, longer distances downtown K100 to K150.

Trishaw
The Burmese-style pedicab, or *sai-kaa*, costs roughly K25 per person every kilometre or so. Trishaws are not permitted on the main streets between midnight and 10 am. They're most useful for side streets and areas of town where traffic is light, especially in the evening. Despite rumours about their imminent ban, the trishaws continue to survive.

Around Yangon

THANLYIN (SYRIAM) & KYAUKTAN
If you've got a morning or afternoon to spare in Yangon, you can make an excursion across the river to Thanlyin and on to the paya (pagoda) at Kyauktan. Thanlyin was the base during the late 1500s and early 1600s for the notorious Portuguese adventurer Philip De Brito.

If you continue 12km farther until the road terminates at a wide river, you can visit the **Yele Paya**, or Mid-River Pagoda, at Kyauktan. It's appropriately named since the complex is perched on a tiny island in the middle of the river.

Getting There & Away
With the opening of a Chinese-built bridge over the Bago River a few years ago, the journey from Yangon to Thanlyin no longer requires a ferry trip. Large pick-ups to Thanlyin (K5) leave frequently throughout the day from a location on Sule Pagoda Rd opposite city hall, a little to the east of Sule Paya.

MYANMAR

AROUND YANGON

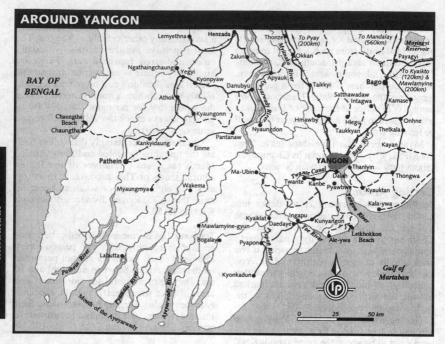

TWANTE

It's an interesting day trip from Yangon to Twante, a small town noted for its pottery and cotton-weaving, and for an old Mon paya complex. One can travel there by public jeep from Dalah (on the opposite bank of the Yangon River) or by ferry along the Yangon River and Twante Canal. The latter mode of transport is slower but provides a glimpse of life on and along the famous canal, which was dug during the colonial era as a short cut across the Ayeyarwady Delta.

BAGO

Bago is 80km north-east of Yangon on the Mandalay railway line. Founded by the Mon, the city was a major seaport until the river changed course. This event, coupled with Bago's destruction by a rival Burmese king in 1757, was the city's downfall.

Shwemawdaw Paya

The Great Golden God Pagoda was rebuilt after an earthquake in 1930 and is 14m higher than Shwedagon Paya in Yangon. Murals tell the sad story of the quake. Note the large

chunk of the hti (the umbrella or decorated top of a pagoda), which was toppled by a quake in 1917, embedded in the north-eastern corner of the pagoda. Admission to the paya for foreigners is US$2.

Shwethalyaung

This huge reclining Buddha image is 9m longer than the one in Bangkok and very life-like. A terrific signboard gives the dimensions of the figure's big toe and other vital statistics. Foreigner admission is US$2, though you can glimpse the image without actually entering.

Other Sights

Bago has other attractions. Beyond the Shwe-mawdaw is **Hintha Gon Paya**, a hilltop shrine guarded by mythical swans. On the Yangon side of town, **Kyaik Pun Paya** has four back-to-back sitting Buddhas. Just before the Shwethalyaung is the **Maha Kalyani Sima** (Hall of Ordination) and a curious quartet of standing Buddha figures.

Carry on beyond the Shwethalyaung and you soon come to **Mahazedi Paya**, where you can climb to the top for a fine view of the surrounding country. **Shwegugale Paya**, with 64 seated Buddha images, is a little beyond the Mahazedi.

Places to Stay

The best budget places are on the busy main road. As usual, rooms towards the back are quieter. The six storey, modern-looking *Emperor Hotel* (☎ 21 349) on the main avenue through town between the railway and the river has a friendly, English-speaking manager. Small but clean rooms cost US$6/10 a single/double with fan and attached toilet and bath, US$8/14 with air-con and hot water.

Slightly fancier is the *Shwe See Seim Motel* (☎ 22 118), 354 Ba Yint Noung St near the bus terminal. Bungalow units cost US$25/30 a single/double.

Farther south-west near the railway crossing, the *San Francisco Guest House* (☎ 22 265) has mostly shabby rooms with shared toilet and bath for US$4 to US$6 per person, or US$8/12 a single/double with attached bath. Rooms in the new wing (west) are cleaner and brighter looking.

Places to Eat

The friendly but shabby *555 Hotel & Restaurant*, a few doors west of the Emperor Hotel, is a very popular eatery. The menu is a combination of Burmese, Chinese, Indian and European; the food is cheap and good.

The *Panda Restaurant*, just west of the river, offers a good standard Chinese menu. Around the corner is the excellent and quieter *Shwe Le Restaurant* at 194 Strand St; the menu features Shan, Indian and Malaysian curries, all under K200.

In the centre of town near the market are a number of food stalls, including good Indian biryani stalls. The *Hadaya Cafe*, opposite the Emperor Hotel, is a teashop with a good selection of pastries, ice cream and good-quality tea.

Getting There & Away

The buses from Yangon (two hours, K150) operate approximately hourly from 5 or 6 am and depart from the Hwy Bus Centre near the airport. GEC Bus Co and Taung Hta Ban Co both make the Bago trip. Pick-ups to Bago depart from Hsimmalaik Bus Centre. The fare is K100 (or K150 for a front seat). Avoid Sundays as Bago is a popular excursion from Yangon and the buses get crowded. It can also be difficult to get back to Yangon.

If you can't get the bus back to Yangon, try catching the train coming from Mawlamyine back to Yangon, which is supposed to arrive in Bago at 7.30 pm but is often one or two hours late. The fare is US$3 for ordinary class; US$6 for first class. Pick-ups to Kyaikto (six hours, K500) depart from in front of Hadaya Cafe.

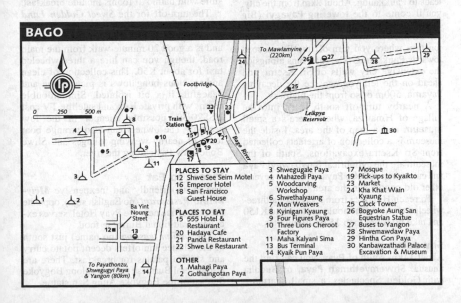

BAGO

To Mawlamyine (220km)

Footbridge

0   250   500 m

Train Station

Leikpya Reservoir

Bago River

Ba Yint Noung Street

To Payathonzu, Shwegugyi Paya & Yangon (80km)

PLACES TO STAY
12 Shwe See Seim Motel
16 Emperor Hotel
18 San Francisco Guest House

PLACES TO EAT
15 555 Hotel & Restaurant
20 Hadaya Cafe
21 Panda Restaurant
22 Shwe Le Restaurant

OTHER
1 Mahagi Paya
2 Gothaingotan Paya

3 Shwegugale Paya
4 Mahazedi Paya
5 Woodcarving Workshop
6 Shwethalyaung
7 Mon Weavers
8 Kyinigan Kyaung
9 Four Figures Paya
10 Three Lions Cheroot Factory
11 Maha Kalyani Sima
13 Bus Terminal
14 Kyaik Pun Paya

17 Mosque
19 Pick-ups to Kyaikto
23 Market
24 Kha Khat Wain Kyaung
25 Clock Tower
26 Bogyoke Aung San Equestrian Statue
27 Buses to Yangon
28 Shwemawdaw Paya
29 Hintha Gon Paya
30 Kanbawzathadi Palace Excavation & Museum

MYANMAR

Getting Around

Trishaw is the main form of local transport in Bago. A trip in the central area should cost no more that K20 to K25. If you're going farther afield – say from Shwethalyaung at one end of town to Shwemawdaw Paya at the other – you might as well hire one for the day, which should cost no more than K200 to K300.

PYAY (PROME)

Six hours north of Yangon by road or an overnight riverboat trip south of Bagan, the town of Pyay lies on a sharp bend in the Ayeyarwady. Nearby are the ruins of the ancient Pyu capital of Thayekhittaya (Sri Ksetra). Very few visitors make their way to this remote site, although it has been the centre of the most intensive archaeological work in Myanmar almost all this century.

In the centre of the small town of Pyay itself, **Shwesandaw Paya** is the main point of interest. A lift (K2) takes visitors from street level to the elevated main stupa platform, which, like the Shwedagon in Yangon, is perched on top of a hill. All in all, it's also one of the country's more impressive zedis, especially on its hillside setting.

Thayekhittaya & Hmawza

The ancient site of Thayekhittaya – known to Pali-Sanskrit scholars as Sri Ksetra – lies 8km north-east of Pyay along a good road that leads to Paukkaung. About 2km from the city, you'll come to the towering **Payagyi** (Big Paya), an early, almost cylindrical stupa. A few kilometres further along brings you to the junction where you turn off the Bagan road towards Paukkaung. The road runs alongside the extensive city walls of Sri Ksetra, and ahead on the left you can see the decaying **Payama**, 500m or so from the highway.

A nearby turn-off south leads into the village of Hmawza, where there's a small **museum** and a map of the area. Inside the museum is a collection of artefacts collected from Sri Ksetra excavations. South of the museum are the cylindrical **Bawbawgyi Paya** and cube-shaped **Bebe Paya**. There are several other old pagodas in the area.

To reach Hmawza from Pyay take a three-wheeled taxi, which should cost around K150 and take no more than 15 or 20 minutes.

Shwedaung

About 14km south of Pyay, you can find the unusual **Shwemyethman Paya,** or Buddha with Golden Spectacles, a small charming paya with a friendly attendant whose main duty seems to be clapping his hands whenever a few birds alight on the huge pair of classic gold wire-rims. To find it, look for the small green and white English sign by the main road pointing to 'Shwemyethman Buddha Image – 1 furlong.'

The most convenient way to reach Shwedaung is by three-wheeled taxi, which should cost around K150 and take no more than 15 or 20 minutes.

Places to Stay

Near the Bogyoke Aung San statue in the middle of town, not far from the train station, is *Aung Gabar Guest House* (☎ 22 743) at 1436 Bogyoke St. Although the rooms here are a bit small and dark, they're clean and the management is helpful. Bath and toilet are down the hall. Rates run from US$3 (or kyat equivalent) per person, with breakfast.

The *Yoma Royal Hotel* (☎ 21 824) at 43 Pyay-Yangon Rd has small but decent economy rooms at US$4/7 a single/double, and larger rooms with bath at US$24/36 a single/double, including breakfast.

The recently privatised *Pyay Hotel* (☎ 21 890) at the corner of Strand and Kan Sts is very comfortable and friendly and off the main road just a bit, not far from the river. Economy rooms (common bath) cost US$6/9 a single/double, and go up to US$24/30 for a suite with bath. All rooms include breakfast.

The turn-off for the *Sweet Golden Land Motel & Restaurant* (☎ 053-22 526) at 12 Nawaday Rd is just south of the town gate and is a good 20 minute walk from the main road, though you can hire a three-wheeled taxi for about K50. This collection of clean and spacious bungalows is picturesque and peaceful, if a bit isolated. Single/double rooms with private bath and satellite TV cost US$20/30, possibly cheaper in the low season. The owners can also arrange boat tours of nearby weaving villages and Shwe Bone Daw Paya along the river.

Places to Eat

The clean, friendly and inexpensive *Meiywetwar Restaurant* (no English sign), opposite the post office near the Pyay Hotel, serves excellent traditional Burmese food.

The *Indian teashop* (no name) just south of the Chittee Inn offers decent potato curry and stuffed palatas for breakfast. There are also several Burmese teashops along Bogyoke St, east of the Bogyoke Aung San statue.

Getting There & Away

Bus There are many choices from the Hwy Bus Centre at the northern end of Yangon, such as Rainbow Express's air-con, 45 seat bus with door-to-door delivery for US$4 (or the kyat equivalent).

The Nawade Bridge across the Ayeyarwady allows for easy road access to Ngapali Beach and Thandwe on the Rakhine coast 215km to the west over a good, but hilly, road. The eight hour bus trip from Pyay to Thandwe costs K600. A car can be hired, but you may have to pay the round-trip price, about US$50 or kyat equivalent.

Boat By riverboat from Bagan it's a two day trip to Pyay with an overnight stop at Magwe. The boat leaves Nyaung U jetty twice a week and arrives the following evening in Pyay. Deck class costs a steep US$9 for ordinary class; US$18 for a reserved seat on the upper deck. Bring your own food and water, as the food served at the deck canteen is of questionable quality.

LETKHOKKON BEACH

Letkhokkon, about three hours by road from Dalah, is the closest beach to the capital. Located in Kunyangon Township near the mouth of the Bago River, it's a delta beach facing the Gulf of Martaban with fine powder-beige sand and a very wide tidal bore that tends towards mud flats at its lowest ebb. Copious coconut palms along the beach help make up for the less than crystalline waters; not really for swimming.

Getting There & Away

Vehicle ferries cross the Yangon River to Dalah from Sin Oh Dan St jetty between 18th and 19th Sts in Yangon; the fare is K5. The road between Dalah and Letkhokkon is in very poor condition in spots, and it's a three hour trip without stops. At the row of restaurants and teashops on the Dalah side you'll see a cluster of pick-up trucks and jeeps; ask around to see if anyone's going to Letkhokkon. A minitaxi should cost about K200 to K300.

PATHEIN

Situated on the eastern bank of the Pathein River (also known as the Ngawan River) in the Ayeyarwady Delta about 190km west of Yangon, Pathein is the most important delta port outside the capital despite its distance from the sea.

The scenic waterfront area, markets, umbrella workshops and colourful payas make the city worth a stay of at least a night or two. It also serves as a jumping-off point for excursions to the small beach resort of Chaungtha and farther north to Thandwe in the Rakhine State.

Shwemokhtaw Paya, in the centre of Pathein near the riverfront, is a huge golden, bell-shaped stupa. The hti consists of a top tier made from 6.3kg of solid gold, a middle tier of pure silver and a bottom tier of bronze; all three tiers are gilded and reportedly embedded with a total of 829 diamond fragments, 843 rubies and 1588 semiprecious stones.

Settayaw Paya is perhaps the most charming of the several lesser known payas in Pathein. It is dedicated to a mythical Buddha footprint left by the Enlightened One during his legendary perambulations through mainland South-East Asia. The paya compound wraps over a couple of green hillocks dotted with a number of well constructed *tazaungs* (shrine buildings).

Around 25 **parasol workshops** are scattered throughout the northern part of the city, off Mahabandoola Rd. The parasols come in a variety of colours; some are brightly painted with flowers, birds and other nature motifs. One type which can be used in the rain is the saffron-coloured monks' umbrella, which is waterproofed by applying various coats of tree resin over a two day period.

Places to Stay & Eat

Delta Guest House (☎ *22 131*) at 44 Mingyi Rd is a good downtown choice. Small and simple though well kept rooms cost US$4 per person with common bath downstairs, US$12 for special singles/doubles upstairs with air con and private bath.

The nearby *Tan Tan Ta Guest House* on Merchant St offers economy fan rooms from US$7/10 for a single/double to US$12/16 with air-con and private bath.

Among the more well known and longest-running Chinese places is the *Zee Bae Inn* on Merchant St.

Shwezinyaw Restaurant at 24/25 Shwezedi St near Merchant St is a Burmese/Indian Muslim hybrid with good curries and biryani. It's open from 8 am to 9 pm daily. The biryani at nearby *Mopale Restaurant* is even better, though it closes down around 6 or 7 pm.

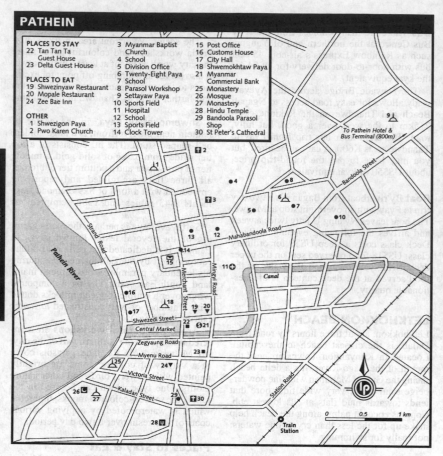

PATHEIN

PLACES TO STAY
22 Tan Tan Ta
   Guest House
23 Delta Guest House

PLACES TO EAT
19 Shwezinyaw Restaurant
20 Mopale Restaurant
24 Zee Bae Inn

OTHER
1 Shwezigon Paya
2 Pwo Karen Church

3 Myanmar Baptist
   Church
4 School
5 Division Office
6 Twenty-Eight Paya
7 School
8 Parasol Workshop
9 Settayaw Paya
10 Sports Field
11 Hospital
12 School
13 Sports Field
14 Clock Tower

15 Post Office
16 Customs House
17 City Hall
18 Shwemokhtaw Paya
21 Myanmar
   Commercial Bank
25 Monastery
26 Mosque
27 Monastery
28 Hindu Temple
29 Bandoola Parasol
   Shop
30 St Peter's Cathedral

To Pathein Hotel &
Bus Terminal (800m)

Pathein River

Strand Road
Bandoola Street
Mahabandoola Road
Merchant Street
Mingyi Road
Canal
Shwezedi Street
Central Market
Zegyaung Road
Myenu Road
Victoria Street
Kaladan Street
Station Road
Train Station

0   0.5   1 km

Getting There & Away

Bus Buses are available from both Hsim-malaik Bus Centre and the Hwy Bus Centre for K400. Tickets should be purchased at least a day in advance.

Boat New Chinese triple-deckers ('Bala' series) have recently started making the Yangon-to-Pathein trip, and foreigners have to pay in dollars; ordinary class costs US$7 per passenger and puts you on the middle deck. Express boats leave Yangon's Lan Thit St jetty at 3 and 5 pm, arriving the next morning in Pathein at 7 and 9 am respectively. Foreigners must buy tickets from the deputy division manager's office next to Bldg 63 at Lan Thit St jetty.

CHAUNGTHA BEACH

West of Pathein on the Bay of Bengal coast, Chaungtha Beach has recently opened to foreign tourists. As western coast beaches go, this one fits somewhere between Letkhokkon farther south and Ngapali to the north in terms of quality.

Places to Stay & Eat

All accommodation traditionally closes down from 15 May to 15 September.

Several new bungalows, including *Delta 3* and *Co-op Chaungtha*, go for US$4 to $8 per person in economy and four-bed dorm rooms with mosquito nets, high ceilings and attached shower and bath.

A few chalet/bungalow-type hotels (*Ambo;*

See Seim; Dini) have opened recently to compete with the long-standing but somewhat shabby *Chaungtha Beach Hotel*. Room rates average US$16/24 a single/double with private bath, breakfast included.

The main street into the village from the beach is lined with rustic seafood restaurants. The better ones include *Pearl, Golden Sea* and *May Khalar*, all of which serve fresh lobster, clams, scallops and fish.

Getting There & Away
Several buses make the four hour trip over the rough 36km road to Chaungtha (K150) from Pathein, starting at 7 am from the Pathein bus terminal.

Mandalay Region

MANDALAY
Mandalay was the last capital of Myanmar to fall before the British took over, and for this reason it still has great importance as a cultural centre. It is Myanmar's second largest city with a population of around 500,000 and was founded, comparatively recently, in 1857. Dry and dusty in the hot season, Mandalay is a sprawling town of busy streets, stunning pagodas and a lively cultural scene. The 'ancient cities' around Mandalay are equally worthwhile.

Information
Tourist Offices The MTT office (☎ 27 193) is in the Mandalay Swan Hotel at the corner of 68th and 27th Sts. It's open from 8.30 am to 6.30 pm daily.

The Ministry of Information's *Map of Mandalay* is useful for getting to the main tourist sites, and has a fairly extensive restaurant and hotel key.

The Central Telephone & Telegraph (CTT) office is at the corner of 80th and 25th Sts. The GPO is at the corner of 22nd and 81st Sts. A DHL Worldwide Express office is next door.

Admission Fees Seeing historical Mandalay can add up quickly – US$3 per person for Mandalay Hill, US$5 for Kuthodaw Paya and Sandamuni Paya together, US$5 for both Shwenandaw Kyaung and Atumashi Kyaung, US$5 for Mandalay Palace and US$4 for Mahamuni Paya. If you continue on to the ancient cities, add US$3 to see Mingun, US$4 to visit Sagaing Hill and US$6 to visit Ava.

On the other hand, the five minute ferry ride to Ava is only K10.

Admission fees can be paid at each site. The MTT office will also collect fees for the various tourist attractions around the city, but most people pay as they go.

The Ministry of Hotels & Tourism (MHT) receives a steady trickle of complaints about these relatively high entrance fees. They typically respond by either raising the fees or creating new ones.

Mandalay Fort & Palace
King Mindon Min ordered the construction of his imposing walled palace compound in 1857. A channel from the Mandalay irrigation canal fills the moat. On 20 March 1945, in fierce fighting between advancing British and Indian troops and the Japanese forces which had held Mandalay since 1942, the royal palace within the fort caught fire and was completely burnt out.

Because recent renovations were notorious for their use of draft labour, many locals as well as visitors refuse to enter the new 'palace'. Apparently, an old term for the west gate, Gate of Ill Omen, still applies for the same reasons.

Mandalay Hill
An easy half-hour barefoot climb up the sheltered steps brings you to a wide view over the palace, Mandalay and the pagoda-studded countryside.

A US$3 fee is collected at the bottom of the hill, though you could take a minitaxi the back way to the top of the hill and enter freely, then walk down. Two immense carved lions guard the south-west entrance to the hill and the south-east entrance is watched over by the Bobokyi Nat.

Kuthodaw Paya
This pagoda's 729 small temples each shelter a marble slab inscribed with Buddhist scriptures. The central pagoda makes it 730. Built by King Mindon Min around 1860, it is the world's biggest book. Don't confuse it with **Sandamuni Paya**, which is right in front of it and which also has a large collection of inscribed slabs. The ruins of the **Atumashi Kyaung** (Incomparable Monastery) are also close to the foot of Mandalay Hill.

Shwenandaw Kyaung
Once a part of King Mindon Min's palace, this wooden building was moved to its present site and converted into a monastery after his

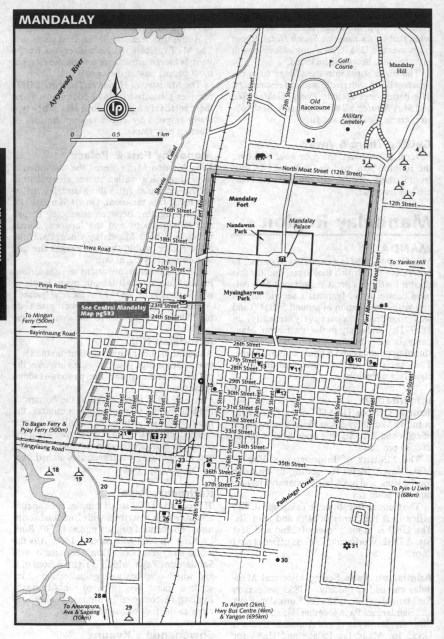

MANDALAY

MANDALAY

PLACES TO STAY		3	Kyauktawgyi Paya	19	Thakawun Kyaung
12	Tam Byu (Silver Cloud)	4	Kuthodaw Paya	20	Jade Market
	Hotel	5	Sandamuni Paya	21	Kachin Traditional
25	Great Guest House	6	Shwenandaw Kyaung		Clothing
		7	Atumashi Kyaung	22	Judson Baptist Church
PLACES TO EAT		8	School of Fine Arts,	23	Bamboo Fan Factory
11	Sakantha Restaurant		Music & Drama	24	Gold-Leaf Workshop
13	Tu Tu Restaurant	9	Mandalay Marionettes	26	Moustache Brothers
14	Marie-Min Vegetarian	10	MTT Office		Comedy Troupe
	Restaurant	15	Kachin Traditional Clothing	27	Kin Wun Kyaung
			(2nd location)	28	Buddha Image Makers
OTHER		16	Main Post Office	29	Mahamuni Paya
1	Yadanapon Zoo	17	Buses to Monywa	30	Mandalay University
2	Novotel Hotel (Landmark)	18	Shwe In Bin Paya	31	Royal Garden

death. This is the finest remaining example of traditional wooden Burmese architecture in Mandalay since all the other palace buildings were destroyed during WWII.

Shwe In Bin Kyaung

This large and elegant wooden monastery was commissioned in 1895 by a pair of wealthy Chinese jade merchants. The wood-carved ornamentation along the balustrades and roof cornices is of exquisite quality, and the sandy compound can be a peaceful change from Mandalay Hill. No admission fee.

Mahamuni Paya

Mahamuni Paya, or Arakan Pagoda, stands to the south of town. It's noted for its huge, highly venerated, Rakhine-style Buddha image, which is thickly covered in gold leaf. Around the main pagoda are rooms containing a huge five tonne gong and Khmer-style bronze figures. Outside the pagoda are streets full of Buddha image makers. Admission is US$4.

Other Sights

The **Zegyo Market** in the centre of town really comes alive at night. The 19th century **Eindawya Paya** and the 12th century **Shwe-kyimyint Paya** are also close to the centre. The latter is older than Mandalay itself. Several of the town's pagodas have amusing clockwork coin-in-the-slot displays. Mandalay's **museum** is tatty and entry costs US$2.

Places to Stay

Room rates at the bottom end now average US$4 to US$8 per person – high by Burmese standards but the lowest they've been in years.

The tidy *Sabai Phyu Guest House* (☎ 25 377), a multistorey, modern building at 58 81st St, offers economy fan rooms with common bath for US$4 to US$8 a single, US$8 to US$12 a double. Another popular place in the same general vicinity is the well managed *Royal Guest House* (☎ 22 905) at 41 25th St. Clean, if small, rooms here cost US$4/8 for singles/doubles with common toilet and cold-shower facilities, or US$10/12 with attached toilet and hot-water shower. There are two triple rooms with bath, air-con and small fridge for US$15.

The *Garden Hotel* (☎ 25 184) at 174 83rd St is a typical Burmese-style hotel with decent economy rooms with common bath for US$8/12 a single/double, and rooms with private bath for US$10 to US$20. All rooms come with air-con, TV, fridge and breakfast.

Around the corner is the popular *Nylon Hotel* (☎ 33 460) with clean economy single rooms with fan and common bath for US$4. Larger rooms with air-con, fan, TV and bath range from US$8 to US$10 a single and US$15 to US$20 a double.

Taim Byu (Silver Cloud) Hotel, on the corner of 73rd and 29th Sts, is good value with economy rooms for US$10 per person, and larger superior rooms for US$20/30 a single/double. *Great Guest House* on the northern side of 39th St, between 80th St and the railway, sees few foreigners. This location is convenient to where the Moustache Brothers and other pwe troupes often perform. Rooms cost US$5 per person.

AD-1 Hotel, just east of Eindawya Paya near the corner of 87th and 28th Sts, is one of the best bargains in Mandalay. Clean and basic rooms with fan and hot-water shower cost $4/6 a single/double, with breakfast.

CENTRAL MANDALAY

Another dollar will get you a better room with air-con.

The friendly and quiet *Classic Hotel* (☎ 25 635) at 59 23rd St, between 83rd and 84th Sts, has air-con rooms and attached bath for US$10/16 a single/double, breakfast included.

Places to Eat

The long-running *Tu Tu Restaurant*, on the southern side of 27th St between 74th and 75th Sts, serves traditional Burmese food from pots lined up on a table, in typical fashion.

The best Shan restaurants are found in the vicinity of 23rd St west of the moat. The popular *Lashio Lay Restaurant*, next to the Classic Hotel on 23rd St, offers spicy Shan dishes which changes on a daily basis and

usually includes four or five vegetarian dishes. For good Burmese sweets, walk across the street to the *Mingalar Confectionery*.

There's a selection of Chinese eating places on 83rd St, between 26th and 25th Sts, not far from Zegyo Market. Here you'll find the popular *Mann Restaurant* – one of the city's better Chinese eateries. The nearby *Min Min*, on 83rd St between 26th and 27th Sts, has Chinese Muslim food (indicated by the number '786' throughout Myanmar) – it's reasonably cheap, and the food is quite OK.

The strictly vegetarian *Marie-Min Vegetarian Restaurant*, on 27th St between 74th and 75th Sts, serves delicious chapatis, pappadums, curries, pumpkin soup and eggplant dip, plus such non-Indian delights as straw-

CENTRAL MANDALAY

PLACES TO STAY
2 Classic Hotel
6 Garden Hotel
14 Royal Guest House
18 Sabai Phyu Guest House
38 AD-1 Hotel

PLACES TO EAT
1 Lashio Lay Restaurant
10 Min Min Restaurant
11 Mann Restaurant
22 Punjab Food House
23 Everest Restaurant
26 Chan Myae South Indian
    Restaurant

OTHER
3 Mosque

4 Shwekyimyint Paya
5 Bank
7 CTT Office
8 Zegyo Market
9 Clock Tower
12 Main Bus/Pick-up Centre
    (Pyin U Lwin, Hsipaw, Lashio)
13 Bank
15 Sacred Heart
    Cathedral
16 Mandalay Museum
17 Myanma Airways
    Office
19 Central Mosque
20 Air Mandalay Office
21 Sikh Temple
24 Hindu Temple
25 Train Station

27 Penta Moneychanger
28 Buses to Hsipaw
29 Fire Lookout Tower
30 Yangon Airways Office;
    Mayflower Moneychanger
31 Police
32 Hindu Temple
33 Night Market
34 Mosque
35 Pick-ups to Amarapura,
    Ava & Sagaing
36 Bank
37 Eindawya Paya
39 Setkyathiha Paya
40 Small Pagoda
41 Buses to Taunggyi
42 Buses to Bagan
43 Buses to Yangon

MYANMAR

berry lassis (yoghurt shakes), muesli, guaca-mole, hash-brown potatoes, pancakes and various western-style breakfasts (served all day). The menu, written in 12 languages, is priced quite reasonably. This traveller-friendly oasis also offers a 'breakfast box' for early riverboat or train trips. It's open from 8 am to 9 pm daily.

More traditional Indian places can be found near the Hindu and Sikh temples and the Central Mosque near the corner of 81st and 26th Sts. *Punjab Food House* on 80th St near 27th is a friendly, small Sikh-run curry shop with chapatis, rice and vegetarian curries. Across the street from Punjab Food House, next to the Nepalese temple, is the slightly larger *Everest Restaurant*, with a tasty 'morn-ing nasta' of chapati with vegetables, dosai and aloo puri on occasion. The roomy *Chan Myae South Indian Restaurant* is on 81st St near the corner of 28th St.

Sakantha, on 72nd between 27th and 28th Sts, is a very pleasant upscale Burmese res-taurant in a patio setting.

Entertainment

Mandalay Marionettes, on 66th St between 26th and 27th Sts opposite the Sedona Hotel, is a small theatre where marionette shows, music and dancing are performed nightly at 8.30 pm. The show lasts around an hour and features selections from the zat pwe and yama pwe traditions. The admission fee seems to fluctuate between K300 and K500 per person depending on the number of tourists in town.

Pwe Mandalay is the cultural heart of Myanmar, and there is an active entertain-ment scene. Most notable are the dozens of pwe troupes which perform at important Burmese social functions, including paya fes-tivals, novitiations, weddings and ear-boring ceremonies. Among the most famous of the pwe troupes is the *Moustache Brothers Comedy Troupe*. The Moustache Brothers gained unwanted notoriety on 4 January 1996 when the oldest brother, U Pa Pa Lay, was arrested following an Independence Day per-formance at the invitation of Aung San Suu Kyi, at a gathering of 2000 members of the opposition National League for Democracy outside her Yangon home. His crime was to tell a joke on the government: 'In the past, thieves were called thieves. Now they are known as cooperative workers'. He is cur-rently serving a seven-year prison term at Myitkyina Prison, north of Mandalay.

Performances at the small theatre on 39th St are narrated in English by brother Lu Maw, a master of improvisation. The family of dancers, musicians and story-tellers are as talented as they are dedicated to the fine line between art and politics. In true pwe fashion, performances always include improvised ma-terial about news of the day – from selling of Shan girls to the increasing price of cooking oil.

The family performs nightly at 8 pm in a small theatre-room facing the street. The price for a group of up to seven people is K3000. If you go alone, a donation may be acceptable. The family will also do a daytime performance by appointment. The brothers also make 'old-looking' marionettes which are reasonably priced.

Shopping

Markets Zegyo Market – a redundant term since zegyo *(zei gyo)* means 'central market' – encompasses two large buildings on 84th St; one between 26th and 27th Sts, the other between 27th and 28th Sts. You can find just about anything made in Myanmar here, from everyday consumer goods to jewellery and fine fabrics.

Mandalay is a major crafts centre and you can get some really good bargains if you know what you're looking for. There are many little shops in the eastern part of the city near the Mya Mandalar and Mandalay Swan hotels selling a mixture of gems, carvings, silk, kalaga tapestries and other crafts. If you enter without a tout (most of the younger trishaw or horse cart drivers are into this), you'll get better deals than with a tout, as they are usually paid high commissions.

You can visit a bamboo fan factory on 80th St between 36th and 37th Sts. Here the artisans make fans of paper and bamboo for weddings and banquets.

Arts & Crafts Try the east entrance of Mahamuni Paya for religious crafts. Thein Hteik Shin Myanmar Handicrafts is a reliable shop with fair prices. A good shop for longyis, ready-made silk and cotton clothing (also in big sizes) and shoulder bags is Manaw Myay Kachin (MMK) Traditional Store with two locations: on 84th St between 33rd and 34th Sts; and on 30th St between 77th and 78th Sts.

Sein Myint Artist at 42 Sanga University Rd in Nan Shei Quarter makes excellent kalaga tapestries. You're also free to wander around the indoor-outdoor workshop, which is adorned with antique looms and a fine collection of Burmese artwork. Check out Myanmar Handicrafts Workshop at 97/99 Mandalay-Sagaing Bypass Rd opposite the Myohaung Warehouse for weavings and traditionally-styled wood crafts.

Getting There & Away

Air Myanma Airways, Air Mandalay and Yangon Air fly daily to Mandalay from Yangon (US$100).

Bus Private air-con buses from Yangon's Hwy Bus Centre cost less than US$10 (K1800 to K2000), payable in kyat. Both Leo Express

(☎ 31 885) and Kyaw Express (☎ 27 611) depart for Yangon at 5 pm from the corner of 83rd and 33rd Sts. The fare is K2000. For most other destinations outside Mandalay, the usual mode of transport is Japanese pick-up truck.

Minibuses make the trip from Mandalay to Bagan (K650) in about seven hours (roads permitting) and leave three times daily from the Hwy Bus Centre, which is 4km south of the centre of town. Buy tickets in advance from Nyaung U Mann Bus Co, inside the second building under the circular stairway. Several companies run pick-ups to Bagan, including Bagan Express at the corner of 82nd and 32nd Sts.

Buses bound for Taunggyi leave from the Hwy Bus Centre. Golden minibuses (25 seats) depart at 5.30 am (K1000). Slightly larger and more expensive (K1500) Tiger Head (Kya Khaung; ☎ 28 814) and Lion King (Chinthay Min; ☎ 21 280) express buses depart for Taunggyi at 5 am. All three companies also do downtown pick-ups.

Train Although there are a number of trains each day between Yangon and Mandalay, you should consider only the day or night expresses since the other trains represent everything that can be wrong with Burmese rail travel – slow, crowded and subject to long delays en route. Additionally, it's possible to reserve a seat on the express services, and on these special 'impress the tourists services' you really do get a seat – not a half or a third of a seat. Upper class even has reclining seats and is quite comfortable. Sleepers are available but hard to reserve.

Myanma Railways operates daily trains from Mandalay to Myitkyina, Monywa (Ye U), Hsipaw and Lashio.

Boat The Inland Water Transport office (☎ 86 035) is on 68th St near the Mandalay Swan Hotel. For information on ferries to Bagan or Bhamo, see the Getting There & Away sections under those cities.

Getting Around

Bus Mandalay's city buses are virtually always crowded, particularly during the 7 to 9 am and 4 to 5 pm 'rush hours'. The fare from Zegyo Market to Mahamuni Paya is K15.

Taxi Around Zegyo Market you'll find hordes of three and four-wheelers. They operate within the city for around K75 to K100 per trip. It's possible to hire cars, jeeps or pick-ups by the day for tours around Mandalay. Count on around K2000 to K2500 for a trip to Amarapura and Sagaing that includes an English-speaking guide; the trucks can take up to eight people so it needn't be expensive.

Trishaw The familiar back-to-back trishaws are the usual round-the-town transport. Count on K50 for a short ride in a trishaw, K80 for a longer one – say, from the Mya Mandalar Hotel to Zegyo Market. Figure on K500 to K800 a day per trishaw for all-day sightseeing in the central part of the city. You must bargain for your fare, whether by the trip, by the hour or by the day. In the evening, expect to pay a bit more.

Unless you know the driver, it is best not to shop in a trishaw, as drivers often have 50% deals with shop owners. Shops that refuse to go along with this may still be hassled by the driver later on, or the driver might tell you that a particular shop is now closed.

Bicycle There are several places downtown to rent bicycles, including near the Royal Guest House on 25th St and opposite the Mann Restaurant on 83rd St. The average cost ranges from K50 to K60 per hour or K300 to K400 per day, depending on the bike's condition.

AROUND MANDALAY

Close to Mandalay are four 'ancient cities', which make very interesting day trips. You can also visit Pyin U Lwin, farther to the north-east, which probably requires an overnight stop, and Mogok, which requires a permit.

Amarapura

Situated 11km south of Mandalay, the 'City of Immortality' was the capital of Upper Burma for a brief period before the establishment of Mandalay. Among the most interesting sights is the rickety 1.2km-long **U Bein's Bridge** leading to **Kyauktawgyi Paya** and small Taungthaman village with tea and toddy shops. There's also a good teashop (no name) at the bottom of a cement stairway about two-thirds of the way across the bridge.

Just out of town on the road to Sagaing, **Kyaw Aung San Hta Kyaung** is one of Myan-

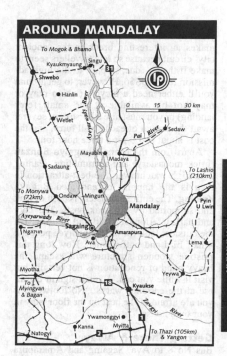

AROUND MANDALAY

mar's largest and most active wooden monasteries, dating from the mid-19th century. Admission is free.

Sagaing

If you continue a little farther beyond Amarapura, you'll reach the Ava Bridge, the only bridge across the Ayeyarwady River. Built by the British, it was put out of action during WWII and not repaired until 1954. Crossing the bridge will bring you to Sagaing with its temple-studded hill.

Most pilgrims make their way to **Soon U Ponnya Shin Paya** overlooking the Ayeyarwady River. Sagaing is the meditation centre of Myanmar; many foreigners come to **Kyazwa Kyaung** to practice Buddhist meditation.

Sagaing's best known pagoda is not on Sagaing Hill – you have to continue 10km beyond the town to reach **Kaunghmudaw Paya**, which is said to have been modelled on a well endowed queen's perfect breast; admission for foreigners is US$3.

Ava (Inwa)

The ancient city of Ava, for a long time a capital of Upper Burma after the fall of

Bagan, is on the Mandalay side of the Aye-yarwady River close to the Ava Bridge. Ava makes an interesting break in the 'ancient city' circuit because so few travellers seem to make it there – due, in part, to the high admission fee of US$6. However, to get around you'll either need a bicycle (which may or may not be available at the small ferry landing) or you must hire a horse cart; several await the arrival of each small ferry, and the cost is about K400 for a three hour tour.

Apart from the **Maha Aungmye Bonzan** (brick monastery) and a crumbling, leaning 27m-high watchtower, the best attraction in Ava is the happily unrenovated **Bagaya Kyaung**. The entire monastery is built of teak and supported by 267 teak posts. The cool and dark interior feels old and inviting. On the outside, look for the Keinarayee peacock – half bird and half woman. How long this pristine wooden structure will escape the heavy hand of renovation is not certain, but visit it while you can. A small sign in Burmese at the entrance warns: 'No footwear; if you are afraid of the heat on the floor, stay in your own house.'

Getting There & Away
Bus No 8 to Ava, Sagaing and Amarapura leaves from the Clock Tower near Zegyo Market. Pick-ups leave from the corner of 84th and 29th Sts.

Mingun
The fourth of the old cities is Mingun, on the opposite bank from Mandalay, a pleasant 11km trip upriver, and the easiest of the ancient cities to visit. Get a riverboat from the bottom of 26th St (B Rd). The cost is around K200 and takes about an hour. It's a pleasant trip, and makes a very good introduction to Burmese river travel, particularly if you do not take the boat to Bagan.

Principal sights at Mingun are the huge ruined base of **Mingun Paya** and the equally grandiose **Mingun Bell**. The bell is said to be the largest uncracked bell in the world – there is a bigger one in Russia but it is badly cracked. The **Mingun Sanitarium** (or Buddhist Infirmary) is well worth a visit for the friendly information on Mingun.

Admission for foreigners to Mingun is US$3.

Monywa
Thanboddhay Paya here is one of the largest in Myanmar and is said to contain 582,357 Buddha images. The town of Monywa, a trade centre for the Chindwinn Valley, is 135km north-west of Mandalay. Starting at 6 am, buses leave for Monywa regularly from the corner of 83rd St and 27th Rd (near the Clock Tower) in Mandalay, cost around K200 and take about three hours. You can also take a Ye U train from Mandalay for only K50, but this trip takes five or six hours.

Of the five guesthouses currently in town, the best value is probably *Shwe Taung Tan Hotel & Restaurant* (☎ 21 478) near the Moonlight Cinema. Single or double rooms with air-con and bath cost US$5, including breakfast.

Pyin U Lwin (Maymyo)
This old British hill station, formerly called Maymyo after the British Colonel May, lies just 60km north-east of Mandalay and about 800m higher.

The chief pleasure of Pyin U Lwin is wandering among the many old Tudor-style mansions and paying a visit to the former British bachelor's quarters of Candacraig, now a government hotel. You can read a delightful description of Candacraig in Paul Theroux's *Great Railway Bazaar*.

There is also an impressive **botanical gardens**, designed by the British colonialists and built with Turkish POW labour. Another legacy of colonial times are the numerous dairies in town started by the families of British-Indian army Gurkhas from India and Nepal.

Places to Stay & Eat The *Golden Dream Hotel* (☎ 22 142) on the main Lashio-Mandalay road and close to the tower and HMV pick-up stop is a rambling place where rooms with shower and toilet down the hall cost US$4 per person, with larger rooms with bath at US$8/15 a single/double, including Indian or western breakfast.

The *Grace Hotel* (☎ 21 230) at 114 Nann Myaing Rd is a one storey inn, with rooms US$8 to US$10 per person. Bicycles can be rented for the short ride to town.

The *Da Shanghai Hotel* (☎ 22 397) at 55 How Go Rd off the main road is a large Chinese place with lots of economy rooms for US$5/8 a single/double, and standard rooms with bath for US$10/15.

The new *Dahlia Motel* (☎ 22 255) at 105 Eindaw Rd is a bit far from the town centre, but easily the best value. Tidy economy rooms cost US$5 per person, and the larger standard rooms with bath, TV and fan go for US$10/20 a single/double, breakfast and free transport to town included.

The ex-colonial, teak *Candacraig* – now officially known as the *Thiri Myaing Hotel* (☎ *22 047)* – has small singles with common bath for US$10, plus larger, high-ceiling rooms with attached bathroom from US$18/24 to US$30/36 a single/double. Rates include breakfast.

Apart from Candacraig there are a number of assorted eating places in the town centre near the market and clock tower, including several inexpensive Chinese and Indian places. *Aung Padamya Restaurant*, farther east near the Shan market at 28 Thu Min Galar Zaythit Rd serves excellent and reasonably priced Indian food from about 11 am to 6 pm daily. A block west of the Hindu Temple is *Yoe Yar Restaurant*, serving very good Burmese/Thai/Chinese dishes.

Getting There & Away From Mandalay, you can take a pick-up truck to Pyin U Lwin for K300 or K400 (front seat) per person. These depart from one central location: in the alley lot on 82nd St between 26th and 27th Sts.

From Pyin U Lwin, there are five places to get pick-ups to Mandalay, including frequent departures from the clock tower/Golden Dream Hotel area and the municipal market. The trip takes about three hours up, and about two down. At the time of writing, it was not uncommon for foreigners to be told they were not allowed to go by pick-up to Pyin U Lwin one day, whereas the next day it was fine.

There is also a daily train but it's more for railway enthusiasts, as it takes about four hours to negotiate the many switchbacks. However, if you go by train, buy your ticket the day before at the train station. A private taxi to Mandalay costs about K3000 or US$15.

Getting Around Most of the town's colourful horse coaches are stationed near the mosque on the main street downtown. Fares are steep by Myanmar standards: figure on K60 to K80 to travel from the mosque to the Shan market, K200 for the round trip to Candacraig or the Botanical Garden, K800 for all-day sightseeing. You can hire bicycles to explore the town at the Grace Hotel, the Golden Dream Hotel and Pacific World Curio on the Mandalay-Lashio road. The going rate is K50 per hour or K300 per day.

Mogok

Mogok is roughly 200km north of Mandalay. Famed for the surrounding natural beauty and for the brilliant rubies and sapphires pulled from its red earth, the township of Mogok was until recently completely off limits to foreigners. A travel permit is now required. Contact MTT or Myawaddy Travel & Tours, the government 'military-tour operator.' The going rate for a restricted tour is US$220 per person for a two-night/three-day trip, which includes hotel, meals and air-con van to and from Mandalay.

In Yangon, contact Myawaddy Travel & Tours (☎ 27 8900) at 189 Sule Pagoda Rd. In Mandalay, Myawaddy (☎ 27 618) is on 35th St between 81st and 82nd Sts.

Bagan Region

BAGAN (PAGAN)

One of the true wonders of Asia, Bagan (formerly spelt Pagan) is a bewildering, deserted city of fabulous pagodas and temples on the banks of the Ayeyarwady, to the south-west of Mandalay. Bagan's period of grandeur started in 1057 when King Anawrahta conquered Thaton and brought back artists, artisans, monks and 30 elephant-loads of Buddhist scriptures.

Over the next two centuries, an enormous number of magnificent buildings were erected, but after Kublai Khan sacked the city in 1287 it was never rebuilt. A major earthquake in 1975 caused enormous damage but everything of importance has now been restored or reconstructed. Unhappily, the plunderers who visit places like Bagan to scavenge for western art collectors have also done damage, but it is definitely the place in Myanmar not to be missed.

Orientation

Bagan Archaeological Zone (and the village of Old Bagan) contains just four hotels and the offices of Myanma Airways and Air Mandalay, as well as MTT. The latter is usually open from 9 am to 6 pm daily; its main function seems to be to administer the admission fee system for the Bagan Archaeological Zone and post timetables on the wall.

Nyaung U is the area's largest settlement, from where most public transport departs, including buses and the Mandalay ferry. Bagan airport is also near Nyaung U, and the Yangon Airways office is there.

AROUND BAGAN

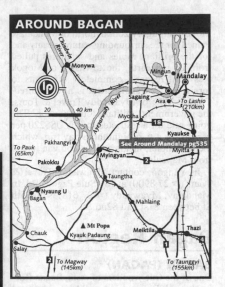

Maps You can purchase two useful maps at the MTT office in the Bagan Archaeological Zone, MTT's own *Bagan Tourist Map* and the independently produced *Tourguide Map of Bagan Nyaung U.*

Information
The entry fee into the Archaeological Zone is US$10 per day for the first two days, US$2 per day thereafter (although seldom collected). The fee is collected at the airport, the ferry jetty or at local hotels and guesthouses.

Things to See
Tharaba (Sarabha) Gateway The ruins of the main gate on the eastern wall are all that remains of the old 9th century city wall. Traces of old stucco can still be seen on the gateway. The gate is guarded by highly revered brother and sister nats, the male (Lord Handsome) on the right, the female (Lady Golden Face) on the left.

Ananda Pahto One of the finest, largest, best preserved and most revered of the Bagan temples was built in 1091 and houses four standing Buddhas and two sacred Buddha footprints. Facing outward from the centre of the cube, four 9.5m standing Buddhas represent the four Buddhas who have attained nirvana. On the full moon of Pyatho (mid-

December to mid-January), a huge pagoda festival attracts thousands to Ananda.

Thatbyinnyu Pahto The highest temple in Bagan, this huge structure consists of two cubes; the lower one merges into the upper with three diminishing terraces from which a *sikhara* (Indian-style finial) rises.

Gawdawpalin Pahto Also close to the village of Bagan, Gawdawpalin looks like a slightly smaller Thatbyinnyu. Built between 1174 and 1211, this temple was probably the most extensively damaged in the 1975 quake but has been completely restored.

Mingalazedi The Mingalazedi, or Blessing Stupa, was built in 1277 and was the very last of the late Bagan period monuments to be built before the kingdom's decline, the final flowering of Bagan's architectural skills. It's noted for its fine proportions and for the many beautiful, glazed jataka tiles around the three square terraces. Mingalazedi is a particularly good spot for panoramic afternoon views of all the monuments to the east.

Shwesandaw Paya A cylindrical stupa on top of five ultra-steep terraces with good views from the top. In the shed beside the stupa is a 20m reclining Buddha. This monument and Mingalazedi now offer the highest accessible points within the Archaeological Zone.

Shwezigon Paya Standing between the village of Wetkyi-in and Nyaung U, this traditionally shaped gold pagoda was started by King Anawrahta. The stupa's graceful bell shape became a prototype for virtually all later stupas all over Myanmar. Figures of the 37 pre-Buddhist nats which were first endorsed by the Burman monarchy can be seen in one of the *zayats,* or open-air resthouses, surrounding the zedi. Check out the revolving wishing wheel, where worshippers squeeze money through a cage and pick from a wish list ranging from love to lotteries to school exams.

Manuha Paya This temple was built by King Manuha, the 'captive king', in the village of Myinkaba. The four Buddhas are impossibly squeezed in their enclosures – said to be an allegorical representation of the king's own discomfort with captivity. Note the north-facing Buddha: north and east positions represent death (with hands flat and

BAGAN REGION

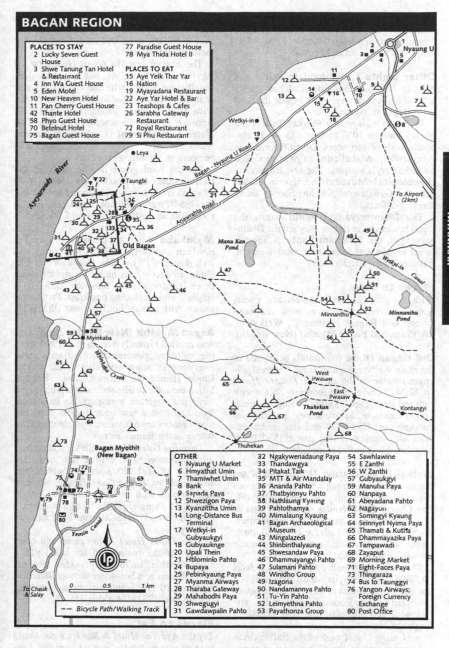

PLACES TO STAY
2 Lucky Seven Guest House
3 Shwe Tanung Tan Hotel & Restaurant
4 Inn Wa Guest House
5 Eden Motel
10 New Heaven Hotel
11 Pan Cherry Guest House
42 Thante Hotel
58 Phyo Guest House
70 Betelnut Hotel
75 Bagan Guest House

77 Paradise Guest House
78 Mya Thida Hotel II

PLACES TO EAT
15 Aye Yeik Thar Yar
16 Nation
19 Myayadana Restaurant
22 Aye Yar Hotel & Bar
23 Teashops & Cafes
26 Sarabha Gateway Restaurant
72 Royal Restaurant
79 Si Phu Restaurant

OTHER
1 Nyaung U Market
6 Hmyathat Umin
7 Thamiwhet Umin
8 Bank
9 Sapada Paya
12 Shwezigon Paya
13 Kyanzittha Umin
14 Long-Distance Bus Terminal
17 Wetkyi-in Gubyaukgyi
18 Gubyaukge
20 Upali Thein
21 Htilominlo Pahto
24 Bupaya
25 Pebinkyaung Paya
27 Myanma Airways
28 Tharaba Gateway
29 Mahabodhi Paya
30 Shwegugyi
31 Gawdawpalin Pahto
32 Ngakywenadaung Paya
33 Thandawgya
34 Pitakat Taik
35 MTT & Air Mandalay
36 Ananda Pahto
37 Thatbyinnyu Pahto
38 Nathlaung Kyaung
39 Pahtothamya
40 Mimalaung Kyaung
41 Bagan Archaeological Museum
43 Mingalazedi
44 Shinbinthalyaung
45 Shwesandaw Paya
46 Dhammayangyi Pahto
47 Sulamani Pahto
48 Winidho Group
49 Izagona
50 Nandamannya Pahto
51 Tu-Yin Pahto
52 Leimyethna Pahto
53 Payathonza Group
54 Sawhlawine
55 E Zanthi
56 W Zanthi
57 Gubyaukgyi
59 Manuha Paya
60 Nanpaya
61 Abeyadana Pahto
62 Nagayon
63 Somingyi Kyaung
64 Seinnyet Nyima Paya
65 Thamati & Kutila
66 Dhammayazika Paya
67 Tampawadi
68 Zayaput
69 Morning Market
71 Eight-Faces Paya
73 Thingaraza
74 Bus to Taunggyi
76 Yangon Airways; Foreign Currency Exchange
80 Post Office

Bicycle Path/Walking Track

feet parallel); south and west represent the relaxed or sleeping position (hands at head, feet crossed). Excellent lacquerware workshops can be visited in Myinkaba.

Other Sights The **Htilominlo Pahto** was built in 1211 and has fine Buddhas on the ground and upper levels. It's beside the road from Bagan to Nyaung U.

In Bagan village, the **Pitakat Taik** is the library built in 1058 to house those 30 elephant-loads of scriptures. Down towards the Ayeyarwady, **Mahabodhi Paya** is modelled on Indian-style temples. The new **Bagan Archaeological Museum** (admission US$4) near the Gawdawpalin Pahto houses many Bagan artefacts.

The **Dhammayangyi Pahto** boasts the finest brickwork in Bagan. Beyond the Dhammayangyi, the **Sulamani Pahto** is another larger temple with interesting, though recent, frescoes on its interior walls.

Places to Stay

With the privatisation of hotels and guesthouses, accommodation is now scattered among Old Bagan, Nyaung U, Wetkyi-in, Myinkaba and Bagan Myothit (New Bagan).

Old Bagan Of the four hotels permitted in the main Archaeological Zone, the best all-around value is the private *Thante Hotel* (☎ *70 144)* where small economy rooms with bath and air-con are US$10/15 a single/double. Larger rooms in the two storey 'guesthouse' building cost US$16/20 and fancier bungalows with small verandas cost US$30/35. A patio breakfast buffet is included.

Wetkyi-in & Nyaung U This end of the Bagan area is becoming a budget accommodation centre. In Wetkyi-in, the comfortable *Pan Cherry Guest House*, just north-east of Shwezigon Paya, has fan-cooled singles/doubles with shared bath for US$6/10, three rooms with air-con and attached cold-water shower for US$10/15.

The small and friendly *New Heaven Hotel* (☎ *70 061)* at Thiripyitsaya Rd (Block 5) is a few blocks south-east of Shwezigon in a quiet courtyard setting. Rooms come with fan, air-con, bath and breakfast and cost US$4/8 a single/double.

In Nyaung U just west of the traffic circle and central market, there's a cluster of guesthouses, including the *Lucky Seven Guest House,* which has rooms with ceiling fans

for US$4/7 a single/double. Rates include a substantial breakfast (or skip breakfast and save a dollar); toilet and cold-water shower facilities are shared.

The nearby *Inn Wa Guest House* (☎ *70 125)* is slightly higher, but a good value. Small clean rooms with fan and hot shower cost US$6/10 a single/double. Larger rooms with air-con and a fridge cost US$10/20. Across the street, the new *Shwe Tanung Tan Hotel & Restaurant* is another good deal with clean, air-con rooms with bath for US$4 per person, including breakfast.

On the road going due south from the traffic circle and market, *Eden Motel* (☎ *70 078)* has small rooms with fan and hot shower for US$4/7 a single/double, and larger air-con rooms off an upstairs terrace for US$12/15.

Myinkaba Next to Gubyaukgyi at the northern end of the village is the quiet and well managed *Phyo Guest House* (☎ *70 086).* Eight air-con rooms along a corridor share three bathrooms; the rates are US$7/10 a single/double including breakfast. Two larger rooms with private hot bath cost US$10/15.

Bagan Myothit (New Bagan) This village was created virtually overnight in 1990 when the military government arbitrarily gave everyone in town a week to clear out of Bagan (hence the names Old/New Bagan). Since then, the resilient residents who stayed have put together a respectable existence. You can find a few budget spots here, but many places are a bit more upscale than elsewhere in the Bagan area.

Paradise Guest House offers spartan rooms with common bath, ceiling fans and hard beds for US$6/12/15 a single/double/triple, with breakfast. *Bagan Guest House* has clean, large rooms with air-con, fridge and bath at US$10/15 a single/double, though prices may be as high as US$15/20 from November to January.

Mya Thida Hotel II has clean and quiet rooms off the main road for US$10/16 a single/double, including breakfast. Rooms have air-con and hot-water shower. *Betelnut Hotel* (☎ 70 110) features clean and airy bungalows for US$18/24 a single/double.

Places to Eat

Try the *Aye Yar Hotel & Bar* for a good cold beer as you watch the sun set over the Ayeyarwady River from the veranda.

Just outside Tharaba Gateway, the friendly

Sarabha Gateway Restaurant serves well seasoned and reasonably priced Burmese, Chinese and Thai food in a simple, quiet, indoor-outdoor setting; however, service can be slow.

Three popular places outside the Archaeological Zone towards Wetkyi-in and Nyaung U are the *Nation* (opposite Shwezigon Paya), *Aye Yeik Thar Yar* (also near Shwezigon) and the friendly *Myayadana Restaurant*. The menus at all three are similar, mostly Chinese with some Burmese. There is also a cluster of cheap cafes and teashops next to the boat landing below the Aye Yar Hotel.

There are a couple of teashops in Myinkaba, and a good cafe at the *Phyo Guest House*. Near Bagan Myothit, *Si Phu Restaurant* stands above the river off the western side of the road. Prices on the Burmese/Chinese menu are moderate to high; a full course is about K600 to K800, and cheaper for small groups. Check out the large lacquer mural.

The nearby *Royal Restaurant* is clean and dependable, and the largely Chinese menu is reasonably priced.

Getting There & Away

Air Myanma Airways, Air Mandalay and Yangon Airways fly to Nyaung U-Bagan airport from Yangon, Mandalay and Heho. A taxi from the airport to Nyaung U costs around K300; to Old Bagan it's K700; to New Bagan K900.

Bus Buses from Bagan to Mandalay (K650) and Taunggyi (K1000) depart from Nyaung U near Shwezigon Paya starting at 6 am. The fare to Mandalay is K650.

Train There is a 10 pm daily departure from Mandalay to Bagan, which should arrive at 6 am. Upper class fare is US$9, US$4 for ordinary class. Tickets must be purchased at the station the day before.

Boat The MTT Mandalay-Bagan ferry departs Mandalay at 5.30 am every Wednesday and Sunday at a cost of US$11 deck class or US$33 for a stuffy cabin.

A better alternative is the new Mandalay-Bagan express ferry which departs every Monday, Tuesday, Thursday, Friday and Saturday. The trip takes about nine hours and costs US$16. Food is available on board, but it's pricey.

A slower, much cheaper ferry does the same route every day, taking roughly 26 to 29 hours and costing just K80 for deck class. The slower boat stops overnight at Pakkoku.

Getting Around

The Nyaung U-Bagan airport is about 5km south-east of Nyaung U, which is 5km north-east of Old Bagan. Car taxis and small vans are available for K300 to K900, depending on the destination; from the jetty it's K200 to K400.

There is a bus service (pick-up trucks) between Nyaung U and Bagan for K5.

You can hire horse carts from place to place or by the hour; count on an hourly rate of around K200, K800 for a half-day, K1500 for the whole day, depending on the number of passengers.

Bicycles – available for hire at most hotels and guesthouses – are a great way to get around. The usual cost is K75 per hour, or K300 to K500 per day.

AROUND BAGAN
Mt Popa

Near Kyauk Padaung, the monastery-topped hill of 1520m Mt Popa can be visited as a day trip from Bagan. Pick-ups cost K150 each way; a taxi is about US$20 for the round trip. If you get a group together to charter a taxi-truck to the Thazi junction or Inle Lake, a detour can be made to visit it. It takes 30 minutes or so to make the stiff climb to the top of the hill. This is the centre for worship of the nats in Myanmar.

Salay

During the late 12th and 13th centuries, Salay developed as the expanding spiral of Bagan's influence moved southward along the Ayeyarwady River. Today's Salay is much more of a religious centre than Bagan, with many more working monasteries than found in Bagan today. A trip to Salay is warranted for anyone who develops a passion for Bagan-style architecture.

Among the named sites worth a look is **Payathonzu**, a 19th century shrine which shelters a large lacquer Buddha known as **Nan Paya**. The fingertips alone measure about two metres high.

On the other side of the main road from Kyauk Padaung is **Yoe Soe (Youpson) Kyaung**, the oldest surviving wooden monastery hall in the Bagan area south of Pakkoku.

Getting There & Away By public transport you can catch an early morning pick-up

MYANMAR

from Nyaung U to Kyauk Padaung (K60, 48km) and change to a Salay-bound pick-up (K80, 58km). Salay can easily be visited as a day trip from Bagan if you hire your own vehicle and driver (about US$25). You could also take a 5 am Pyay-bound ferry from Nyaung U, getting off in Salay around midday. The fare is around K30.

MEIKTILA

Only a short distance west of Thazi, Meiktila is the town where the Bagan-Taunggyi and Yangon-Mandalay roads intersect. The town sits on the banks of huge Lake Meiktila, bridged by the road from Nyaung U. From one end of this bridge, a wooden pier extends out over the lake to small **Antaka Yele Paya**, a cool spot to rest on warm evenings.

Places to Stay & Eat

Honey Hotel, a converted mansion on Pan Chan St next to the lake, offers large rooms with high ceilings, air-con, private hot showers and good mattresses for US$15/25, or similar rooms with shared bath for US$8/15. A few single rooms with fan cost US$3. Breakfast is available for US$1.

Most famous of the local restaurants is *Shwe Ohn Pin* on the main street; a couple of the major express buses between Mandalay and Yangon stop here. One of the house specialities is a delicious 'curd curry', big hunks of Indian-style cheese (hlan no kei) mixed with cauliflower and okra in a thick and spicy sauce.

THAZI

Thazi is really nothing more than a place people find themselves in when travelling to or from Bagan or Inle Lake. It's also a rail junction.

You can stay at the clean, well managed *Moon-Light Rest House*, upstairs from the Red Star Restaurant, run by the same friendly family. Single rooms with fan are US$3; larger air-con rooms cost US$8/15 a single/double.

Getting There & Away

The Thazi bus stop is a couple of hundred metres from the railway station. Pick-ups to Kalaw cost K200 for a seat in the back, K300 up the front; there's usually only one departure a day at around 7 am. A passenger pick-up between Meiktila and Thazi costs around K20 to K30.

Shan State

Nearly a quarter of Myanmar's geographic area is occupied by the Shan State. Before 1989 the area was broken into several administrative divisions collectively known as the 'Shan States'. It's the most mountainous state in the country, divided down the middle by the huge north-south Thanlwin River. About half the people living in the Shan State are ethnic Shan; the state's major ethnic groups include the Palaung, Kachin, Kaw (Akha), Lahu (Musoe), Kokang, Wa, Padaung and Taungthu.

KALAW & PINDAYA

There are several excursions you can make en route to Inle Lake, the main destination of most visitors to the Shan State. The Thazi to Taunggyi road passes through Kalaw, once a popular British hill station.

At Aungban, you can turn off the main road and travel north to Pindaya, where the **Pindaya Caves** are packed with countless Buddha images, gathered there over the centuries. Admission is US$3.

From either Kalaw or Pindaya, it's possible to make day treks to nearby tribal villages (Palaung, Pao, Danu, Taungyo); inquire at guesthouses or hotels for guides, who charge around US$5 a day.

Places to Stay & Eat

In Kalaw there are several places to stay on or close to the main road. The *Golden Kalaw Hotel* offers clean if spartan rooms with common bath for US$3 per person. Larger rooms with bath cost US$5. *Eastern Paradise Motel* has large rooms with private bath for US$10/14 a single/double.

The *Winner Hotel* is good value with basement single rooms with common bath for US$5 per person, and much larger rooms with bath going for US$15/18 a single/double. This is a good place to ask about local treks.

For excellent curries, fresh juice and dry chapatis, try *Everest Nepali Restaurant*, a block from the main road on Aung Chan Tha St. *Thirigayhar Restaurant* is a very popular Shan-Chinese spot on the main road.

May Pa Laung Restaurant, three blocks west of the market, offers a good menu of Shan and Burmese dishes. Near the cinema, try *Lakmi* teashop and *Royal* teashop for good tea and sweets. For a splurge the famous *Kalaw Hotel* offers high tea and mostly European set meals.

In Pindaya, there are four places to stay, including the *Pindaya Hotel*, a clean and comfortable place about halfway between the town and the caves. Standard singles/doubles with fan and attached shower and toilet cost US$8/12.

Getting There & Away

From Kalaw it costs K250 to Pindaya by public transport (pick-up). A taxi can be hired for about US$15 for the round trip from Kalaw. A bus from Kalaw to Bagan costs K1300, or K900 to Meiktila.

INLE LAKE

The 22km-long lake itself is extraordinarily beautiful and famous for its Intha leg rowers, who propel their boats by standing at the stern on one leg and wrapping the other leg around the oar. This strange technique has arisen because of all the floating vegetation – it's often necessary to stand up to plot a path around all the obstacles.

Half-day boat tours include visits to the **floating gardens** of Keta, **Phaung Daw U Kyaung**, **Nga Pha Kyaung** (nicknamed 'jumping cat' monastery) and the **Ywama floating market** (or 'five-day market'), which happens every fifth day; other days it's just souvenir oriented.

One of the best times of the year to be here is during September and October. The ceremonial Phaung Daw U Festival, which lasts for almost three weeks, is closely followed by the Thadingyut Festival, when the Inthas and Shan dress in new clothes and celebrate with fervour the end of Waso, or Buddhist Lent.

Small and friendly Nyaungshwe has a village atmosphere. You can walk around easily or rent a bike if you want to explore. The **Yadana Man Aung Kyaung** and **Shwe Yaunghwe Kyaung** are a couple of temples worth a quick visit.

Orientation

There are four place names to remember in the lake area. First, there's Heho, where the airport is located. Continue east from there and you reach Shwenyaung junction, where the railway terminates and where you either turn south to get to Nyaungshwe and the lake, or continue farther east to reach Taunggyi, the main town in the area.

Information

To enter the Inle Lake Zone, tourists are required to pay a US$3 entry fee at the MTT

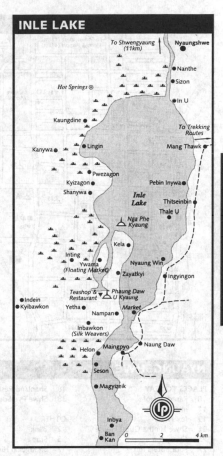

office in town, or more commonly at one of the hotels or guesthouses. You can arrange a boat tour at your guesthouse, or from a couple of places near the canal leading to the lake.

Places to Stay

Nyaungshwe New places continue to open in Nyaungshwe. Near the main canal, the friendly *Shwe Hintha Guest House* offers economy rooms with common toilet and hot-water shower for US$3/6 a single/double. All rates include breakfast.

The *Joy Hotel* has 12 basic but clean rooms in a two storey house for US$3/6 with shared toilet and hot-water shower, or US$5/10 with hot-water shower and toilet attached. Breakfast comes with the rooms. The *Gypsy Inn*, facing the canal near the MTT office,

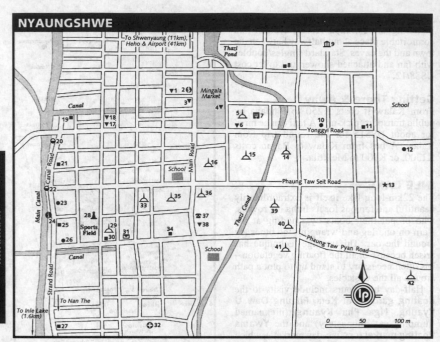

NYAUNGSHWE

PLACES TO STAY
8 Paradise Hotel
11 Inle Inn
19 Joy Hotel
21 Shwe Hintha Guest House
25 Gypsy Inn
27 Four Sisters Inn
30 Little Inn
34 Mingalar Hotel

PLACES TO EAT
1 Hu Pin Restaurant
3 Shwe Inlay Bakery
4 Teashop
6 Teashop
17 Chow Su Ma Restaurant

18 Shanland Restaurant
38 Shwe Pye Soe Restaurant

OTHER
2 Bank
5 Stupa
7 Sri Jagdish Hindu
   Temple
9 Shan Museum
10 Puppet Theatre
12 Township Office
13 Police
14 Hlain Kyu Kyaung
15 Yangon Kyaung
16 Monastery
20 Boat Landing

22 Boat Landing
23 Moe Ma Kha Boat Hire
24 MTT Office
26 Handicrafts
28 Independence Monument
29 Shwe Zali Paya
31 Post Office
32 Hospital
33 Stupas
35 Yadana Man Aung Kyaung
36 Stupas
37 CTT Office
39 Shwe Gu Kyaung
40 Kan Gyi Kyaung
41 Monastery
42 Nigyon Taungyon Kyaung

has small clean rooms with bath and breakfast for US$4/6 a single/double.

Four Sisters Inn used to be a well known dining spot, and it still is. The sisters have expanded it into a quiet guesthouse between the canal and a large rice field, about 1km south of the main village. Rooms with fan, hot shower and good beds cost US$7/12 a single/

double. Like most places in town, they arrange boat tours and rent bicycles.

East of Mingala Market is the long, two storey **Evergreen Hotel**. Basic economy rooms here with common toilet and hot-water shower cost US$5/10 a single/double, and larger rooms with hot shower cost US$10/20.

The well run and quiet **Inle Inn** is one of

the oldest privately owned inns in the country. Rooms in the main building and in a new wing off to the side come with attached toilet and hot-water shower for US$15/22 a single/double, breakfast included.

The *Paradise Hotel* is fancier than most places in Nyaungshwe, and pricier at US$30/36 a single/double for most rooms. Hot shower, fridge, TV and air-con are included, as well as breakfast. The staff here are quite helpful with travel arrangements.

Little Inn opposite Shwe Zali Paya has bright clean rooms with fan and hot shower for US$8/12 a single/double, breakfast is included.

The cheapest place in Nyaungshwe is the friendly but shabby *Mingalar Hotel* with small rooms at US$2 a person, including breakfast.

Places to Eat

Best for Chinese food is the clean *Hu Pin Restaurant*. Nearby *Shwe Inlay Bakery* is good for Chinese pastries, tea and good cafe au lait. The impecunious can find cheaper food in the market, including plenty of *Shan khauk swe* (noodle soup). *Four Sisters Inn*, run by an Intha family, serves excellent food in a cosy family setting.

Near the main canal are several Chinese/Burmese places, including *Chow Su Ma Restaurant* and *Shanland Restaurant*. *Shwe Pye Soe Restaurant*, near the hospital, is a very popular Burmese eatery.

Getting There & Away

Air Myanma Airways, Yangon Airways and Air Mandalay fly to Heho, which is 30km from Shwenyaung, from where it is an additional 11km south to Nyaungshwe or 20km east to Taunggyi. Car taxis from Heho to Nyaungshwe cost K2500 or about US$15. If you wait for a collective pick-up, you can get a ride as far as the Shwenyaung junction for K60; from Shwenyaung another pick-up goes to Nyaungshwe for K50.

Bus & Pick-up The fare for the better Meiktila/Thazi-Taunggyi pick-ups varies from K150 to K350 depending on the type of vehicle and number of passengers. If you're heading for Inle Lake, get off at the Shwenyaung junction and catch one of the frequent pick-ups (6 am to 6 pm only) to Nyaungshwe, 11km south, for K60.

Several buses leave from Yangon's Hwy Bus Centre bound for Taunggyi, and cost K600 to K800. Get down at Shwenyaung junction for the short ride south to Inle and Nyaungshwe.

The staging area for most public transport in and out of Nyaungshwe is the street that runs south of the Hu Pin Hotel, one block west of Mingala Market. Minibuses to Mandalay cost around K1000; pick-ups about K600.

Tiger Head Express operates a bus from New Bagan to Taunggyi for K700 which leaves at 4 am; as usual, get off at Shwenyaung and continue on to Nyaungshwe by public pick-up for K60.

Getting Around

Bicycles generally rent for about K200 a day, or K150 a half-day. Longtail boats can be hired for around K1500 for a half-day tour of the lake and the most popular spots; extra stops can be made for K200 each.

TAUNGGYI

Situated at 1430m, the pine-clad former hill station of Taunggyi provides a cool break from the heat of the plains. There are some pleasant walks if you are in the mood, but basically it's a just a growing trade centre for the south-western area of the Shan State.

Taunggyi is the official end of the line for eastern-bound foreigners in Myanmar; travel eastward was prohibited at the time of writing, and there are armed checkpoints. However, it's possible to fly from Yangon or Heho to Kyaingtong (Kengtung) near the Chinese and Lao borders.

For those interested in the Shan State's cultures, the modest **Shan State Museum** (admission US$2) and **Shan State Library** (free) near the Taunggyi Hotel are worth a visit.

Places to Stay

An old stand-by in Taunggyi, the *May Khu Guest House*, is a rambling, dark and shabby wooden structure on the main road with foreigner rates of US$2 to US$3 per person in stark two-bed rooms with common bath. The newer, cleaner *Khemarat Guest House* at 4B Bogyoke Aung San St has economy rooms with shared bath for US$8/10 a single/double plus rooms with attached bath for US$15/20.

The privatised and somewhat efficient *Taunggyi Hotel* sprawls over landscaped grounds near the southern end of town. Spacious rooms with attached hot-water bath cost from US$30 to US$40. The old MHT-style bar and restaurant attract a mix of well heeled businesspeople and military types.

Places to Eat

A row of small food stalls in the market serve decent Chinese and Shan dishes. On the main street near the Khemarat Guest House, the *Coca Cola Restaurant* has a decent all-Chinese menu. The nearby *Lyan Yu Restaurant*, with several kinds of noodles in a window display, is another popular Chinese spot.

Getting There & Away

Air There are daily flights from Yangon and Mandalay to Heho, 32km west of Taunggyi. A taxi costs K2000, or US$10.

Bus & Pick-up Trucks to Taunggyi from Inle Lake charge K80 and leave frequently from the Nyaungshwe market area between 7 am and 5 pm for the 45 minute trip. A taxi along the same route costs around US$10 or K2000. There's one pick-up per day from Taunggyi to Pindaya at 2 pm, which arrives at 5.30 pm and costs K100. There are frequent pick-ups to Pindaya from the Shwenyaung junction, starting at 6 am.

From New Bagan and Mandalay, pick-ups cost K400 to K500 per person and take seven or eight hours to reach Taunggyi. A minibus from Bagan costs K1300. A bus departs from Taunggyi for Yangon at 1.30 pm. It's a long 18 hour trip and costs K1500.

KYAINGTONG (KENGTUNG)

Tucked away in the south-eastern corner of the Shan State and surrounded by Wa, Shan, Akha and Lahu villages, Kyaingtong is the sleepy but historic centre for the state's Khün culture. Built around a small lake, and dotted with aging Buddhist temples and crumbling British colonial architecture, Kyaingtong is possibly the most scenic town in the Shan State.

There are two ways to reach Kyaingtong: by air from Yangon, Heho and Tachilek (although the airport was temporarily closed at the time of writing); or by road from Tachilek via the bridge over the Sai River at the Thai border. Four-day/three-night excursions can be arranged through any Mae Sai (Thailand) guesthouse or travel agency or you can do it on your own by pay-ing US$18 for a four-day/three-night permit at the border, plus a mandatory exchange of US$100 for Myanmar's FECs. These FECs can be spent on hotel rooms or exchanged for kyat at the going rate.

The road between Taunggyi and Kyaingtong allows glimpses of Shan, Akha, Wa and Lahu villages but is currently closed to foreigners.

Places to Stay

The *Noi Yee Hotel* in Kyaingtong costs US$10 per person per night in dorm rooms. MTT tries to steer tourists towards the more expensive, government-run *Kyainge Tong Hotel*, where rooms cost US$30 to US$40.

Harry's Guest House & Trekking (☎ 101-21 418) at 132 Mai Yang Rd, Kanaburoy Village, is operated by an English-speaking Kyaingtong native who spent many years as a trekking guide in Chiang Mai. His simple rooms go for US$5 per person, payable in US, Thai or Burmese currency.

Getting There & Away

The cheapest form of transport to Kyaingtong is the 60B songthaew that leaves each morning from Tachilek. Count on at least six to 10 gruelling hours to cover the 163km stretch between the border and Kyaingtong.

The road is slowly being improved and will eventually be paved all the way to the Chinese border, 100km beyond Kyaingtong.

HSIPAW

Newly opened Hsipaw between Mandalay and Lashio is becoming a popular destination, possibly because it is so peaceful and there is little to do but enjoy the friendly atmosphere. A sign in some guesthouse lobbies warns tourists not to visit gypsum mines or SSA (Shan State Army) occupied areas, and not to raft down the river with inner tubes.

This small Burmese town offers simple accommodation and several good Shan-style restaurants. Bicycles are available for lending or rent at most guesthouses. Rates are K25 per hour, or K200 for the day.

Things to See

The **Shan Palace** on the northern outskirts of town is worth a visit for the story it holds about vanquished royalty (the topic of *Twilight over Burma: My Life as a Shan Princess*, a recently published memoir by American Inge Sargent who became the popular Mahadevi of Hsipaw in the 1950s, until the military takeover in 1962).

There are walking tours and boat trips to nearby villages, and a cheroot/cigar factory in town near the market. Visit the friendly and well informed book-seller Ko Zaw Tun (known as Mr Book to many travellers) on the main road for reliable advice on moving around Hsipaw. **Mahamyatmuni Paya** at the southern end of the main road is an active religious site.

Places to Stay

There are several basic accommodation places in Hsipaw, most with separate bath and toilet facilities. Cost is similar at all the guesthouses – about K250 per person.

Aung Tha Pye Rest House at 43 Aung Tha Pye Rd has clean rooms with mosquito nets and is the quietest of any guesthouse in town.

Mr Charles/Myat Yatana Rest House just off the main road at the north end of town has small clean cubicles with mosquito net for K250 a person, and larger doubles above the lobby for the same price. On most days at about 8 am, Mr Charles leads a three hour 'morning excursion' to a village or nearby waterfall.

East of the clock tower on Bogyoke St, *Nam Khae Mao* has double and triple rooms plus a large lobby with TV. On the same street and west of the clock tower, *Yamin Shwe Zin* has clean spartan rooms with screens, but no nets.

Places to Eat

Most of the good Shan and Chinese restaurants are found along the main road (Numptu Rd) near the cinema and across the street from the Yoma bus stop. *Hwai Ta* and *Law Chun* both serve very good rice and noodle dishes. A few doors south is *Yin Kyan* (sign in Burmese), an excellent small Shan restaurant. On the north-east corner of the main road and Lanmadaw Rd is a tasty *Shan noodle shop*, open for breakfast and lunch (Burmese sign).

Near the market and just around the corner from the *U Kyin Yi Cafe* and Duhtawadi bus stop is another good *Shan restaurant* (Burmese sign). There are several tea and snack shops in town, including *Flower Master Teashop* on Aung Tha Pye Rd.

Getting There & Away

Bus, Van & Pick-up Both Yoma Express and Duhtawadi Express run between Mandalay and Hsipaw. Cost is K400, and buses depart Hsipaw at about 5.30 am daily. Buses to Lashio (K200) depart from opposite the market and half a block down from Duhtawadi Express stop. Pick-ups and vans to Pyin U Lwin and Lashio are usually parked by the market on Lanmadaw Rd.

Train The Mandalay-Lashio train departs Mandalay at 4.45 am and – with any luck – arrives in Hsipaw at 3 pm. Ordinary class costs US$4; 1st class (a step down from upper) is US$9. Buy train tickets at least a day ahead at the Mandalay train station between 6 am and 4 pm. The same train leaves Hsipaw at about 3.30 pm, arriving in Lashio at 7.30 pm.

LASHIO

This township of 103,000 mostly Shan-Chinese and Chinese inhabitants is at the southern end of the infamous 'Burma Road'. Until recently Lashio was off limits to foreigners because of its proximity to China and to ethnic insurgent territory. It's also a major smuggling route for teak, opium and Shan girls bound for Kunming.

It's possible to reach Lashio from the Chinese border via Mu-se (and nearby Namkhan and Kyu Koke) on the old Burma Road if you have a visa and a border pass. Officially, a package tour is required to proceed south to Lashio by car, but this requirement may loosen if the region remains under Yangon's control. Travel north from Lashio, however, remains subject to military checkpoints at the north-eastern edge of town, and you may need special permission from the regional army command.

Orientation

Lashio is divided into two main districts, Lashio Lay (Little Lashio) and Lashio Gyi (Big Lashio), connected by Theinni Rd. Lashio Lay is the newer and bigger of the two districts.

Things to See

Mansu Paya Mansu Paya stands between Lashio Lay and Lashio Gyi on a hill to the western side of Theinni Rd and is said to be over 250 years old. More impressive is the **Sasana 2500-Year (Pyi Lon Chantha) Paya**, reportedly built by the last Shan *sawbwa* (chieftain) in the area, Sao Hon Phan. More interesting than any of the Buddhist shrines in town is the large and busy **Quan Yin San Temple** in Lashio Lay.

Places to Stay & Eat

Just about any hotel or guesthouse in Lashio seems prepared to accept foreign guests. Rates quoted bounce back and forth between kyat and dollars. *Nadi Ayeyar Guest House* (☎ 21 725) on Theinni Rd in Lashio Gyi, 1km from the town centre, has clean but small rooms with carpet and good mattresses for US$5 per person. Both the *New Asia Hotel* with single rooms for K500 and *Thida Aye Hotel* with rooms for US$5 per person are clean and central.

The three storey *Lashio Motel* (☎ *081-21 702*), at the intersection of the Mandalay-Lashio road and Station Rd, charges a hybrid US$/kyat rate totalling around US$12 for good rooms with air-con, TV, fridge, toilet and hot-water shower. The price includes breakfast.

The famous *Lashio Restaurant*, on Theinni Rd just east of the New Asia Hotel, is one of the most reliable for both Chinese and Shan cuisine. Another good restaurant serving both Chinese and Shan meals is *Lite Lite Restaurant*, near the New Asia Hotel on Chinese Temple St. For Yunnanese cuisine, the *Winlight Chinese Muslim Restaurant*, downtown near the Aung Dagon Hotel, is inexpensive and good.

Getting There & Away

Air Yangon Airways flies to Lashio from Mandalay twice a week, and there are two Myanma Airways flights weekly from Yangon. The airport is north of Lashio Gyi. A pick-up from the airport costs around K500.

Bus, Van & Pick-up From Mandalay there are buses to Lashio for K500 to K600, some of which operate from the main bus centre (in Mandalay), others from the Shan neighbourhood around 23rd St. In either direction the 220km ride takes a slow nine to 11 hours on a rough, dusty road. To break the trip up, it's a good idea to schedule at least a day's stopover in Pyin U Lwin or Hsipaw along the way.

Train Although it's expensive and sometimes takes longer, travel to Lashio by train is definitely more comfortable than by pick-up. The No 131 Up leaves Mandalay at 4.45 am and arrives in Lashio around 6 pm - when it's not delayed by track conditions (9 pm arrivals aren't unusual). Along the way you'll crawl across the famous Gokteik Bridge and wind around four monumental switchbacks. The Mandalay to Lashio fare is US$5 for ordinary class, US$12 in the only 1st class coach on the train. From Pyin U Lwin the fare drops to US$10. (Officially, ordinary class isn't available to foreigners, but if 1st class is full, it's worth asking; in a pinch, you can just board the train and wait for the ticket collector to come by.)

Kachin State

Myanmar's northernmost state borders India and China to the north and east, the Sagaing Division to the west and the Shan State to the south.

Hkakabo Razi Peak near the India border measures 5881m, considered south-east Asia's highest. Burmese refer to this area as the 'ice mountains.'

The Jingpaw, who are known to the Burmese as Kachin, are the majority. Following the 1993 signing of a truce with the Yangon government, the Kachin Independence Army (KIA) has ceased active insurgency. As a result, the Burmese government has relaxed travel restrictions somewhat. And since the government's super-hyped 'Visit Myanmar 1996' campaign, things have opened up a bit more. It is possible to visit both Bhamo and Myitkyina without a permit. But travel to Putao in the far north requires permission from MHT or Myawaddy Travel & Tours, the government's 'military tour operator.' The lucrative jade trade may also have something to do with travel restrictions in the state.

BHAMO

Bhamo's daily market draws Lisu, Kachin and Shan participants from the surrounding countryside. The overgrown city walls of **Sampanago**, an old Shan kingdom, can be seen around 5km east of town. **Theindawdye Paya** downtown features an older stupa.

Places to Stay & Eat

The *Shwe Naga (Golden Dragon Hotel)* accepts foreigners for K300 per person. *Friendship Hotel* charges K500 per person. Either place can provide a guide to nearby Kachin villages such as Aungtha. The Chinese *Sein-Sein Restaurant* is the best of an average lot.

Getting There & Away

Air Myanma Airways flies to Bhamo from Mandalay (US$55) on Wednesday and Sunday.

Boat A double-decker express ferry plies the Ayeyarwady River between Mandalay and Bhamo three times a week. Upper deck class costs $9 for foreigners, and takes two days. The downriver trip back is the same price and takes only a day. Purchase tickets from Inland Water Transport (☎ 86 035) in Mandalay. The scenery along the upper reaches of the Ayeyarwady is very fine.

MYITKYINA

Set in a flat valley that becomes extremely hot in the hot season and very rainy during the monsoon, the town itself is not especially interesting. Myitkyina is the capital of the Kachin State. The majority of the population is Christian and there is a sizable Punjabi community.

Rice produced in this valley, known as *khat cho*, is considered the best in Myanmar. Highly valued for its delicate texture and fine fragrance, khat cho is scarce and expensive outside the Kachin State.

There are plenty of Kachin villages in the area, though you may need a guide to visit them. **Myit-son**, the confluence of the Maikha and Malikha rivers, 45km north of town, forms the beginning of the great Ayeyarwady River.

Places to Stay & Eat

At the friendly *YMCA*, decent rooms with common bath cost US$5 per person. The central *Patsun Hotel* has large, comfortable rooms with air-con and hot water for US$10/15 a single/double.

Most of the restaurants in town serve Chinese food. One of the better ones is the family-run *Khine Shwe Wa*. Nearby *Shwe Ein Zay* is reasonably good. The expensive *Sumpra Hotel* has a dining room with set European and Chinese meals.

Getting There & Away

Air Yangon Airways flies to Myitkyina from Mandalay (US$65) on Tuesday and Saturday. Myanma Airways flies to Myitkyina three times a week. The fare is US$55 (US$65 by F-28).

Myanma Airways also has one 25 minute flight on Wednesday to/from Bhamo for US$30/35. On Friday there is also a flight between Myitkyina and Putao which costs US$40/45.

Train The government's No 55 Up train from Mandalay leaves daily at 3 pm and is supposed to take 22 hours to reach Myitkyina (US$27). In everyday practice it often takes longer – up to 50 hours due to the poor condition of the track, especially in rainy July and August.

Two private companies (Malikha and San Thawdar) run better trains to Myitkyina from the railway station on Tuesday, Wednesday, Friday and Sunday. The fare is US$30 for a seat, US$60 for a sleeper, and includes breakfast and lunch. Both the No 57 Up and the No 59 Up train depart Mandalay at 7.30 pm, arriving 23 hours later barring delays.

Road There are no regular public transport services along the road between Mogok and Myitkyina as road conditions are especially bad between Mogok and Bhamo.

PUTAO

A permit is required to visit Putao and surroundings. The highlands north of Putao are considered among the most pristine Himalayan environments in Asia and could become a major trekking, hiking and ecotourism destination if made more accessible to foreigners. During the late British colonial era, a military post called Fort Hertz was based in Putao. Most of the population of around 10,000 are Kachin and Lisu, followed by Burman, Shan and various other smaller tribal groups.

Individual travellers can obtain permits to Putao, but it's unclear so far whether you'll be allowed to venture farther north where the real mountains begin. Plans are afoot to bring tourism here, and the runway at Putao is being extended to accommodate jets. Inquire at MTT or a private travel agent in Mandalay about current restrictions.

If you go, it's possible to stay at the expensive *Government Guest House* or the cheap *Tokyo Guest House*.

Getting There & Away

Foreigners are not allowed to travel to Putao by road. Even then, the narrow, unsurfaced 356km road is passable only in dry weather. Myanma Airways flies to Putao twice a week from Mandalay via Myitkyina.

South-Eastern Myanmar

Most of south-eastern Myanmar lies between the Andaman Sea and Thailand. The Thanlwin River empties into the Gulf of Martaban at Mawlamyine, where most of the country's original Mon inhabitants now reside.

KYAIKTIYO

One of the most interesting formerly 'off-limits' trips is to the incredible balancing boulder stupa at Kyaiktiyo. The small stupa, just 7.3m high, sits atop the Gold Rock, a massive, gold-leafed boulder delicately balanced on the very edge of a cliff at the top of Mt Kyaikto. Like Shwedagon Paya in Yangon or Mahamuni Paya in Mandalay, Kyaiktiyo is one of the most sacred Buddhist sites in Myanmar. Any time of year, but especially between October and March, you're sure to be in the company of devout Buddhists making their pilgrimage to this holy site.

Kinpun, about 9km in from the highway and the small town of Kyaikto, lies at the base of the mountain. This is the starting point for either beginning the four hour hike up or catching one of the frequent trucks-with-benches up the winding road. No vehicles are permitted near the top, so you still have about a 45 minute walk up to the stupa area.

There is a US$6 entrance fee to the stupa area, payable at the tourist office (open daily from 6 am to 6 pm) opposite the pilgrim truck-loading area. There is a table-and-chair checkpoint near the top, where you can also pay.

Places to Stay & Eat

Although Kyaiktiyo can be visited as a day trip from Bago, the advantage of staying at the top is that you can catch sunset and sunrise – the most magical times for viewing the boulder shrine.

The cheapest places to stay are in Kinpun, the base village. Many of the new guesthouses have a temporary feel to them, but three are worth looking for. All of them have separate shower and toilet facilities. The best value is the well managed *Pann Myo Thu Guesthouse*. The rooms are clean and light and they cost US$5/6 a single/double. Friendly *Htet Yar Zar Guesthouse* is the cheapest of the lot, with rooms for one or two people at K600. *Sea Sar Guesthouse* is behind the Sea Sar Restaurant & Bar. Rooms are very basic, with wooden slats and mosquito nets. The cost is US$4/5 a single/double.

Because Kinpun is the starting point for this popular Burmese site, there are a number of good Chinese and Burmese restaurants up and down the main street.

Along the ridge at the top of Mt Kyaikto, the well situated and government-owned *Kyaikto Hotel* features a couple of long wooden buildings overlooking the valley below. Standard rooms with attached bath cost US$36/44 a single/double. 'Economy' rooms with two beds and two buckets of water cost US$15/24. All rates include the

standard toast-and-egg breakfast. Compared with other accommodation in the area, rooms here are rather shabby; Its appeal is its proximity to the stupa.

Prices at the new *Golden Rock Hotel* (☎ 70 174) are similar to the Kyaiktiyo Hotel, but it's much better value – with the exception that it's just up the path from the last truck stop – a 40 minute walk from the top. Attractive standard rooms with TV, fridge and phone cost US$36/48 a single/double. Smaller economy rooms, also with attached bath, cost US$24/30.

The new *Mountain View Motel* is the best value of the upscale places. It's closer to Kyaiktiyo town than Kinpun, although you can usually get a free lift to either location. Very comfortable bungalow-type rooms with fan and cold-water shower are US$15/20 a single/double. Larger 'superior' rooms with a desk and hot-water shower cost US$30/40. Breakfast is included with all rooms, and there is an indoor-outdoor restaurant.

In the town of Kyaikto at the foot of the mountain, there are several guesthouses, none of them very appealing. Of the lot, *Nilar Guesthouse* on the main road at the corner of Hospital St is the most conveniently located. Rooms cost K400 per person. Bucket bath and toilets facilities are separate. Nearby *La Min Tha Guesthouse* on Station Rd is similar.

Getting There & Away

Bus & Pick-up Buses straight from Yangon to Kyaikto cost K350 from the Hwy Bus Centre; it's much wiser to start from Bago, where a large bus costs K250. Pick-ups from Bago to Kyaikto cost around K150 and take around five hours. From Kyaikto town to Kinpun, pick-ups charge K30.

Train A direct train from Bago to Kyaikto leaves daily at 4.30 am, arriving two and a half to three hours later, substantially quicker than the equivalent bus trip. The foreigner fare is US$7 per seat.

MAWLAMYINE (MOULMEIN)

The atmosphere of post-colonial decay is more palpable here than in fast-developing Yangon or Mandalay; it's also an attractive, leafy, tropical town with a ridge of stupa-capped hills on one side and the sea on the other.

The **Mon Cultural Museum** is dedicated to the Mon history of the region. In the city's east, a hilly north-south ridge is topped with five separate monasteries and shrines. At the northern end is **Mahamuni Paya**, the largest temple complex in Mawlamyine. It's built in the typical Mon style with covered brick walkways linking various square shrine buildings. Farther south along the ridge stands **Kyaikthanlan Paya**, the city's tallest and most visible stupa. It was probably here that Rudyard Kipling's poetic 'Burma girl' was 'a-setting' in the opening lines of *Mandalay*: 'By the old Moulmein Pagoda, lookin' lazy at the sea'.

Below Kyaikthanlan is the 100 year old **Seindon Mibaya Kyaung**, a monastery where King Mindon Min's queen, Seindon, sought refuge after Myanmar's last monarch, King Thibaw Min, took power. On the next rise south stands the isolated silver and gold-plated **Aung Theikdi Zedi**. A viewpoint on the western side of the ridge a bit farther south looks out over the city and is a favoured spot for catching sunsets and evening sea breezes.

Mawlamyine's central market, **Zeigyi**, is a rambling area on the western side of Lower Main Rd just north of the main pedestrian jetty for Mottama.

Gaungse Kyun, commonly known in English as Shampoo Island, is a picturesque little isle off Mawlamyine's north-western end. You can hire a boat out to the island for K150.

Places to Stay

The cheapest place is the funky but quite adequate *Breeze Rest House* at 6 Strand Rd. Rooms with two beds, fan and shared facilities cost US$5 per person. The English-speaking owner has recently added air-con to a few rooms with private bath for US$7 per person.

The renovated *Thanlwin Hotel* (☎ 21 976) on Lower Main Rd is friendly and spacious, with wide stairways and open verandas. Economy rooms with separate shower and toilet cost US$10/15 a single/double. Air-con rooms with bath attached cost US$15/20.

In the north-western corner of the city, not far from the Mottama vehicle ferry landing, the recently privatised *Mawlamyine Hotel* (☎ 22 560) offers well spaced bungalows for a steep US$36/48 a single/double including breakfast.

Getting There & Away

Air Myanma Airways flies direct from Yangon to Mawlamyine on Wednesday, and via Dawei on Saturday. From Yangon to Mawlamyine the fare for the 35 minute flight is US$35 (US$50 by F-28). From Dawei, an hour away by plane, the fare is US$50/55. A taxi to town is K500.

Bus & Pick-up Several overnight buses costing K800 to K1000 leave Yangon for Mawlamyine at 8 pm and arrive at Mottama at about 6 am. From there, you take a ferry (K5) or much faster 25 passenger outboard motorboat (K30) across the river to Mawlamyine. Bus tickets can be purchased from the offices opposite the central Yangon train station downtown, and most companies provide free shuttles to the Hwy Bus Centre. The fare ranges from K800 to K1000.

Pick-ups leave from west Yangon's Hsimmalaik Bus Centre in the morning for around K500.

Permits have been required recently to proceed south by road into Taninthayi Division. However, since travel has been opening up in the nearby Mon State and elsewhere, it may be possible to go overland despite the official restrictions. Mawlamyine's main terminal for southbound buses or pick-ups is near the southern end of town off the road to Ye, where public vehicles go to Thanbyuzayat, Kyaikkami (previously Amherst), Dawei or Payathonzu on the Thai border.

Train Two express trains run from Yangon to Mottama daily. When the trains are running on time the trip takes 7½ hours – beating even the fastest bus lines by several hours. The foreigner fare for an upper class seat is US$17.

Boat Double-decker passenger ferries depart for Mawlamyine from the Mottama landing on the Thanlwin River every half hour; the fare is K5 and the trip takes 20 to 30 minutes depending on tides. If you don't feel like waiting for a ferry, you can take a much faster 25 seat outboard across the river for K30.

Getting Around

Motorised *thoun bein* (three-wheelers) are the main form of public transport. The going rate is K50 for a short hop within the centre of town, and as much as K100 or K150 for a ride up the ridge to Kyaikthanlan.

AROUND MAWLAMYINE

The area south of Mudon was recently considered a 'brown area', and most locals may still warn against travelling along the roads here after 3 pm due to the possibility of bandit activity. The local authorities, when pressed, seem to frown upon foreigners travelling even as far south as **Kyaikkami** and **Setse**, and the tidal-flat beaches at these towns aren't worth even a moderate risk.

Mottama (Martaban)

The narrow, patched and potholed road from Bago terminates at Mottama, where the wide Thanlwin River empties into the Gulf of Martaban. The railway from Yangon also terminates here, although an extension picks up on the other side in Mawlamyine and continues 145km to Ye, where a new line leads farther south to Dawei.

Getting There & Away See the Mawlamyine Getting There & Away section for details on transport to Mottama.

Kyaikmaraw

This small but charming town 24km southeast of Mawlamyine is accessible via a good sealed road. Mon-style **Kyaikmaraw Paya** is well worth a visit. A pick-up is K100 each way; a taxi is K1000 round trip.

PA-AN

Pa-an, capital of the Kayin (Karen) State, was recently removed from the restricted list of travel destinations. It's possible to reach it by road from Yangon or by river ferry from Mawlamyine – a very scenic trip. In 1997 a new bridge south-west of town opened over the Thanlwin River, thus linking Pa-an with Thaton.

Even though Pa-an is a small but busy commerce centre, it still has something of a village atmosphere. Away from the jetty, which is crowded with trucks and motorcycles, you can see farmers coming to town in horse carts or trishaws stacked with baskets or mats to sell in the market.

The townspeople are a mixture of Mon, Burman and Muslim. Burmese is the primary language, but Karen is spoken by many. The mosque seems to be the town hub, and there are numerous teashops around, along with pick-ups to Thaton and Kyaikto.

Pa-an is famous among Burmese for the Buddhist village at **Thamanyat Kuang** and the highly respected monk U Winaya, whose solid support of democracy leader Aung San Suu Kyi is well known throughout Myanmar. Thamanyat monastery is about 40km southeast of Pa-an, and there is a daily flow of small buses (K70) to this busy religious site.

Places to Stay & Eat

There are only two places worth staying at in Pa-an. Near the jetty is the *Royal Guesthouse*, managed by the ever-helpful Mr Robin. The rooms are adequate, with separate shower and toilet, and cost US$3 per person.

Slightly better value is the *Parami Hotel* a few blocks away. Rooms with fan, mosquito net and common bath cost US$4 per person. There are a few rooms with attached bath and toilet which cost US$7.

Khit-Thit Restaurant (New Age) and *Dream Restaurant* are near the guesthouses, although the food is quite ordinary.

Getting There & Away

Bus & Pick-up Shwe Chin (The Golden Lion) buses leave from Yangon's Hsimmalaik Bus Centre, departing at 8 pm and arriving at about 7 am. The fare is K600. Pick-ups from Pa-an to Kyaiktiyo depart from in front of the green mosque and cost around K400 or K500 for a front seat. Pick-ups from Thaton cost about K200. Buses depart from near the Parami Hotel at about 6 pm for Kyaiktiyo and Bago.

Boat Double-decker ferries from the Pa-an jetty in Mawlamyine leave daily at 7 am and noon for the four hour trip up the Thanlwin River to Pa-an on the river's eastern bank. The fare for foreigners is US$2 for upper deck class and US$12 for a stuffy cabin. There is a good Chinese restaurant across from the loading dock in Mawlamyine.

DAWEI (TAVOY)

Dawei is a sleepy, tropical seaside town only recently connected to the rest of Myanmar by road and rail. Among local religious monuments, **Shinmokhti Paya** is the most sacred. Reportedly constructed in 1438, this is one of the four shrines in the country that house a Sinhalese Buddha image supposedly made with a composite of cement and pieces of the original Bodhi tree.

Beaches & Islands

Foreigners have recently been permitted to visit coastal areas around Dawei, though details are still sketchy. The best local beach area reportedly lies on the coast around 18km west of Dawei in Maungmakan Township. Here a sand beach stretches 8km and has some government bungalows usually reserved for VIPs.

Opposite Maungmakan is a collection of

three pretty island groups which were named the Middle Moscos Islands by the British – they are now known as Maungmakan, Henze and Launglon (or collectively as the Maungmakan Islands).

Places to Stay

Thitsar Guest House on Arzarni St lodges government officials and foreigners for US$10 per person.

Getting There & Away

Air Myanma Airways fields four flights a week from Yangon to Dawei and twice weekly flights from Mawlamyine and Kawthoung.

Bus Buses from Mawlamyine may require an overnight at Ye since drivers have been reluctant to drive at night to Dawei. The fare from Yangon on Golden Arrow Express is K2000; from Mawlamyine, about K1000.

MYEIK (MERGUI)

The Taninthayi coast, in the extreme south of Myanmar where Myanmar and Thailand share the narrow peninsula, is bounded by the beautiful islands of the Myeik (Mergui) Archipelago. Myeik – known to the colonials as Mergui and locally as Beik or Myeit – sits on a peninsula that juts out into the Andaman Sea.

The city's most venerated Buddhist temple, **Theindawgyi Paya**, contains a European-pose Buddha and a reclining Buddha.

Boats to nearby islands can be chartered for US$60 per day from Myeik's harbour.

Places to Stay

Myeik Shwe Palei Guest House on Pyitawthar St accepts foreigners and charges US$15/20 a single/double. *Mergui Guest House* may also accept foreigners. The current rate is K200 per person.

Getting There & Away

Air Myanma Airways flies daily from Yangon for US$85. Yangon Airways flies twice weekly for US$70. There are also flights from Mawlamyine, Dawei and Kawthoung.

Bus There are daily buses and pick-ups from Dawei, 249km north, but it's highly unlikely any foreigner will be permitted to travel by bus to Myeik.

KAWTHOUNG

This small fishing port at the southernmost tip of Taninthayi Division – and the southernmost point of mainland Myanmar – is separated from Thailand only by a broad estuary in the Pakchan River. To the British it was known as Victoria Point and to the Thais it's known as Ko Sawng, which means Second Island in Thai. The main business here is trade with Thailand, followed by fishing. Among the Burmese, Kawthoung is perhaps best known for producing some of the country's best kickboxers.

Most foreigners enter from Ranong, Thailand.

Places to Stay

There are now two hotels in Kawthoung which accept foreigners. The *Kawthoung Motel* is about a 10 minute walk from the waterfront. For simple double rooms with private cold-water bath, Thais pay 350B, foreigners US$20/30 a single/double. The *Honey Bear Hotel* is on the waterfront past the immigration office and charges US$35/45.

Getting There & Away

Air Myanma Airways flies to Kawthoung from Yangon, Myeik and Dawei. Yangon Airways expects to make flights here, but recently stopped its routes to Mawlamyine, so it may be a while.

Boat Myanma Five Star Line occasionally sails weekly between Yangon, Dawei, Myeik and Kawthoung but travel is very slow.

From Thailand Most foreigners enter from Ranong, Thailand, where longtail boats depart for Kawthoung regularly for 35B per person. Immediately as you exit the Kawthoung jetty there's a small immigration office on the right, where you must pay US$5 for a day permit. Nearby Thahtay Kyun island is home to a popular though expensive resort, the Andaman Club. There's a frequent ferry service from Ranong several times a day.

Western Myanmar

The Rakhine Yoma (Arakan Range) separates the Rakhine and Chin states from the central Ayeyarwady River plains. Isolated from the Burman heartland, in many ways the inhabitants of both states have more in common with the peoples of eastern India and Bangladesh.

Travel to the Chin State is prohibited for individuals, but the government's Myawaddy Travel & Tours says that package tours may soon be allowed. If true, independent travellers may follow, but when is anybody's guess.

The Rakhine

Rakhine ethnicity is a controversial topic – are the Rakhine actually Burmans with Indian blood, Indians with Burman characteristics or a separate race (as is claimed by the Rohingya insurgents)? Although the first inhabitants of the region were a dark-skinned Negrito tribe known as the Bilu, later migrants from the eastern Indian subcontinent developed the first Hindu-Buddhist kingdoms in Myanmar before the first Christian millennium. These kingdoms flourished before the invasion of the Tibeto-Burmans from the north and east in the 9th and 18th centuries.

The current inhabitants of the state may thus be mixed descendants of all three groups, Bilu, Bengali and Burman.

The Burmese government denies the existence of a Rohingya minority, a group of around three million people who distinguish themselves from the Rakhine majority by their Islamic faith. Many Rakhine Muslims – or Rohingyas as they prefer to be called – have fled to neighbouring Bangladesh and India to escape Burman persecution.

The Chin

The Chin State, to the immediate north, is hilly and sparsely populated. The people and culture exhibit an admixture of native, Bengali and Indian influences similar to that found among the Rakhine, with a much lower Burman presence. As in the Rakhine State, there have been clear government efforts in recent years to promote Burmese culture at the expense of Chin culture, and many Chin have fled west to Bangladesh and India.

Of Tibeto-Burman ancestry, the Chin call themselves Zo-mi or Lai-mi (both terms mean Mountain People) and share a culture, food and language with the Zo of the adjacent state of Mizoram in India. Outsiders name the different subgroups around the state according to the district in which they live: Tidam Chins, Falam Chins, Hakha Chins etc.

SITTWE

Known to the Bengalis as Akyab and to the Rakhine as Saitway, this port city of the Rakhine State sits at the mouth of the Kaladan River, where it empties into the Bay of Bengal. Offshore delta islands form a wide protected channel that has served as an important harbour for many centuries. Sittwe has at least a 2000 year history of habitation, though in its modern form the city started as a trading port around 200 years ago and further developed after the British occupation of 1826.

Highly revered **Payagyi** sits in the centre of town and features a large plain shed supported by pillars decorated with glass mosaic. A large sitting image beneath the shelter was cast in 1900 in the Rakhine style. The **Buddhistic Museum**, on the grounds of Mahakuthala Kyaungtawgyi, is the best place in Myanmar to view Rakhine-style Buddha images. Admission is free. The new **Rakhine Cultural Museum** is worth a look. Admission for foreigners is US$2.

The Point is a land projection at the confluence of the Kaladan River and Bay of Bengal. A large terrace constructed over the flat, shale-and-sandstone point is a good spot to catch the breeze and to cool off on hot afternoons. South-west of The Point is a beach area with grey-brown sand.

Places to Stay

The *Prince Guest House* at 27 Main Rd in the centre of town features basic but clean rooms with ceiling fans and bathroom down the hall at a cost of K500. *Mya Guest House* is housed in a massive colonial building with a colonnaded carriageway. The interior is disappointing, however, with unkempt rooms created from wooden partitions and mosquito nets for K500 per person. Toilet facilities are down the hall.

Places to Eat

Seafood and spicy Rakhine curries are what Sittwe kitchens do best. The top place in town is the all-wood, brightly painted *Innpaukwa Restaurant*, directly opposite the main post office on the waterfront. Service can be slow and perhaps only two of three dishes served will actually correlate with your order, but it still has good food. *Mopale Restaurant,* diagonally opposite the new cultural museum, serves both Rakhine and Burmese food, and it's open from 9 am to 10 pm.

Aung Tea Shop near the market opens early and by 7 am is full of locals savouring the shop's delicious chapati, *nam-bya, palata*

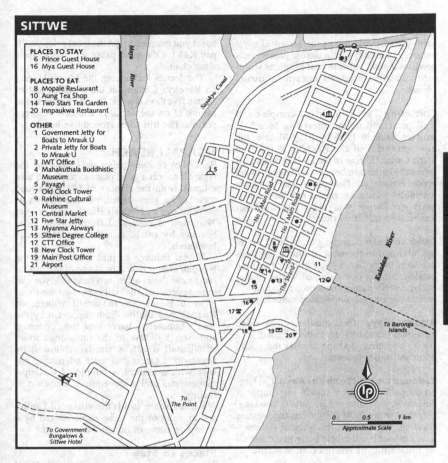

SITTWE

PLACES TO STAY
6 Prince Guest House
16 Mya Guest House

PLACES TO EAT
8 Mopale Restaurant
10 Aung Tea Shop
14 Two Stars Tea Garden
20 Innpaukwa Restaurant

OTHER
1 Government Jetty for
   Boats to Mrauk U
2 Private Jetty for Boats
   to Mrauk U
3 IWT Office
4 Mahakuthala Buddhistic
   Museum
5 Payagyi
7 Old Clock Tower
9 Rakhine Cultural
   Museum
11 Central Market
12 Five Star Jetty
13 Myanma Airways
15 Sittwe Degree College
17 CTT Office
18 New Clock Tower
19 Main Post Office
21 Airport

Mayu River

Sayokya Canal

Kaladan River

No 2 Main Road

No 1 Main Road

The Strand

To Baronga Islands

To The Point

To Government Bungalows & Sittwe Hotel

0   0.5   1 km
Approximate Scale

MYANMAR

and potato curry. Still popular *Two Stars Tea Garden*, opposite Sittwe Degree College, was a student favourite before the college was closed by the government.

Getting There & Away
Air Air Mandalay makes the Yangon to Sittwe flight (US$80) on Wednesday and Sunday. Myanma Airways fields direct flights from Yangon on Tuesday and Friday (US$60/70 by F-27/F-28). Sittwe's tiny airport is only 10 minutes from town. A taxi costs K350.

MRAUK U
Once a centre for one of Myanmar's most powerful kingdoms, Mrauk U straddles the

banks of Aungdat Chaung, a tributary of the Kaladan River, 72km from the coast. The Rakhine king Minzawmun founded Mrauk U ('Myauk U' in the Burmese pronunciation) in 1433, though in the common practice of the times, dynastic legends endowed the kingdom with a make-believe 3000 year history. A network of canals allowed access by large boats, even ocean-going vessels.

Today the original city lies in ruins and a small, poor town with simple buildings of brick, wood and thatch has grown up adjacent to the old city site.

One of the best times – or worst depending on your tastes – to visit Mrauk U is during the huge Paya Pwe (Pagoda Festival) held in mid-May.

Things to See

Walls and gateways of sandstone blocks and earth are all that's left of the Mrauk U royal palace. A museum within the old palace walls contains a good collection of religious sculpture and other artefacts unearthed around Mrauk U.

Shittaung This is the most complex and well preserved of the surviving Mrauk U temples, built in 1535 by King Minbin, the most powerful of the Rakhine kings. The name means 'Shrine of the 80,000 Images', a reference to the number of holy images found inside. A maze-like floor plan – which vaguely resembles a square-cornered pinwheel – suggests the shrine was originally used for Tantric-like initiation rituals.

Dukkanthein Standing on a bluff 100m opposite and to the west of Shittaung, Dukkanthein looks like a huge bunker from the outside. Simple dome-shaped stupas similar to those at Shittaung stand atop receding terraces over a large, slope-sided sanctuary.

Andaw Paya This smaller, eight sided monument features 16 zedis aligned in a square-cornered U-shape around the south, north and west platforms.

Yadanapon (Ratanabon) Paya The largest stupa in the area stands just north of Andaw Paya. Damaged by WWII bombing, only the bottom 'bell' portion and base remain standing. Even minus the original sikhara – now a pile of brick rubble lying to the sides – the brick structure reaches 60m in height.

Places to Stay & Eat

The very basic *Myanantheingi Guest House* costs K100 for locals, K300 for foreigners. The new *Mrauk U Hotel* is a joint (government with private financing) venture near the ruins area, and room rates are US$30/40 for a single/double.

An *unnamed restaurant* opposite Khite San Tailor on the main street serves fried rice, noodles, fried vegetables and noodle soup. The *Dhanyawady Tea & Cold Drink Shop* (no English sign) opposite the market isn't bad.

Getting There & Away

Both government and private ferries make the river trip between Sittwe and Mrauk U. On the government boat foreigners are supposed to pay US$4 to Inland Water Transport for a round-trip ticket in 'sling-chair class' but if you manage to get the local price you'll pay K11 for the basic passage plus K15 for a sling chair.

The ferries leave from the Mrauk U jetty on Sayokya Chaung at the northern end of Sittwe five days a week. Private ferries sail to Mrauk U on the off days and cost K50 per person. The trip takes around five hours.

NGAPALI BEACH

Backed by swaying palms and casuarinas, the Ngapali area is a good place to relax and take a break from the rigours of Myanmar road travel. The very broad, pristine stretch of sand known as Ngapali Beach reaches over 3km, and is separated from several more beaches by small, easily negotiated rocky headlands.

If you manage to rent a bicycle (at the Ngapali Beach Hotel, or at one of the restaurants near the hotel or in Thandwe), you can tour several of the villages. Just north of Ngapali Beach are the small villages of **Ngapali** and **Lintha**, both supported by the area's bounteous harvest of fish, coconuts and rice. **Kyiktaw** to the immediate south of Ngapali Beach is similar, followed by **Myabyin**, a larger and more interesting village with a market, a couple of teashops, monasteries and a government rice-storage facility.

Farther south still is the village of **Lontha** and an inlet of the same name backed by a sweeping curve of mangrove and sand.

Places to Stay

The mainstay is the *Ngapali Beach Hotel* (☎ *Thandwe 28)*, where two-room wooden bungalows with louvred walls and shaded verandas cost US$20/30 for a single/double.

Good budget places near the beach are *Lin Thar Oo Guest House* and *Christian Baptist Guest House*, both costing US$5 per person.

Places to Eat

The *Ngapali Beach Hotel* has an open-air beachside restaurant with decent and reasonably priced food (kyat acceptable). Almost opposite the New Ngapali Beach Hotel section is *Kyi Nue Yake (Reik) Restaurant*, a small, friendly family-run place with fresh seafood plus Burmese and Chinese dishes – and an English menu. *Zaw Restaurant*, opposite the hotel, is very similar. Prices at both are low to moderate.

Getting There & Away

See the Thandwe section below for details on air and road travel to Thandwe, the transport hub for the region.

Getting Around

A jeep taxi from Thandwe or Thandwe airport to Ngapali Beach costs K1000 and takes 30 minutes. Thandwe, Kyiktaw, Myabyin, Lintha and Lontha are all linked by narrow sealed roads and can be visited by bicycle. Though there are no regular bike rental places, you should be able to find one at the hotel or one of the restaurants across the road.

THANDWE (SANDOWAY)

Thandwe (also spelt Thantwe), around 9.5km north-east of Ngapali Beach, is the seat of a township by the same name. The town boasts a network of sealed and unsealed streets lined with two-storey buildings around 50 to 100 years old, constructed of masonry on the ground floors and wood on the upper floors.

A former British jail in the centre of town is now used as a market where vendors sell medicinal herbs, clothes, textiles, hardware and free-market consumer goods. Among the many small shops surrounding the market are a number of gold shops, which suggests that the area is marked by some wealth.

Three stupas perched on hillsides at the edge of town are of mild interest.

Places to Stay & Eat

The *San Yeik Nyein Guest House*, a set of bare but adequate wooden rooms with shared facilities set over a video house a block south of the market, charges K60 per person. This guesthouse was not accepting foreigners when we came along but it may be worth a try.

Next to the market, almost opposite a large mosque, is a very good teashop called *Point*, which offers whitewashed chairs instead of the usual tiny stools. Sticky rice and palatas are usually available here. There are several other tea and cold drink shops in this area, and in the market itself there are a few questionable-looking noodle vendors.

Getting There & Away

Air Air Mandalay flies from Yangon to Thandwe (US$65) three times a week. Myan-

ma Airways also flies to Thandwe from Yangon on two different days. The fare from Yangon is US$50/55 by F-27/F-28. There are also infrequent flights from Sittwe.

Bus & Taxi A government bus between Thandwe and Yangon costs only K600, with an overnight in Pyay when heading north or Sinde (opposite Pyay) when heading south, but anyone who would endure this 24 hour trip without planning a more appealing stopover must be either crazy or in a big hurry.

If you decide to break the trip up into sections, there are two different routes to choose from. The longer and more trying, but more scenic, route from the south starts in Pathein, the northern route from Hinthada on the Ayeyarwady River – or better yet use the shorter route from Pyay. Direct buses from Pyay to Thandwe cost K400 – there are only one or two per day, starting early in the morning. It takes around six hours from Pyay to Taungup on the coast, then another three hours from Taungup to Thandwe.

SOUTHERN CHIN STATE

Travel to any destination in the Chin State has been prohibited of late. Even so, one traveller reported making it there recently, only to be told a few days later by a uniform that he had '10 minutes to leave the state.' If you're able to stay longer, there's a lot to see.

Although it's possible to enter the north by road from Kalewa in the Sagaing Division, the true heart of traditional Chin culture is found in the south. **Paletwa**, just over the state line from the Rakhine State, can be reached via boat along the Kaladan River from Sittwe or Kyauktaw. A new road under construction between Mahamuni and Paletwa will also allow vehicle travel direct from Mrauk U when completed.

In the Chin Hills some women still tattoo their faces, though it's a custom that's fading fast. At higher elevations they wear thick, striped cotton blankets draped over the body and ornaments of copper and bronze. Among the Khamui, a sub-tribe that inhabits the lower elevations of southern Chin State, unmarried women wear short skirts and little else. Chin men tend to wear simple western-style dress such as shirts and trousers.

Philippines

A little off the fashionable South-East Asia route, the Philippines are the forgotten islands of the region. But you won't forget this place if you *do* make the effort to visit. The food's good, accommodation is easy to find and there's an incredible 7000 islands to hop between. Flights are cheap, and boats, buses and those glorious home-grown jeepneys go just about everywhere.

It's hard not to have a good time in a land where travel options are as varied as the country itself, the people are friendly, English is spoken well and widely, and there's a colourful festival happening somewhere just about every day of they year. In fact, many pleasantly surprised travellers reckon the Philippines is their favourite country in the whole region.

Facts about the Philippines

HISTORY

The Philippines is unique among the countries of South-East Asia, both for the variety of its colonisers and for its energetic attempts to cast off the colonial yoke. Little is known about pre-colonial Filipino society, as the Spaniards – who ruled the country for over 300 years – tried to eradicate every trace of what they felt was 'pagan' in the culture.

Ferdinand Magellan, a Portuguese who had switched sides to arch-rival Spain, set off from Europe in 1519 with instructions to sail around the world, claim anything worth claiming and bring back some spices.

Finally reaching the Philippines in 1521, our dubious hero claimed the lot for Spain from his first stop – Cebu Island. He even managed to make a few Christian conversions to boot. Unfortunately, he then decided to display Spanish military might to his newly converted flock by dealing with an unruly tribe on the nearby island of Mactan. This backfired when Chief Lapu-Lapu, the first of many modern Filipino independence heroes, swiftly killed Magellan. The surviving invaders scuttled back to Spain after collecting a cargo of spices on the way, arriving home in the sole remaining ship in 1522.

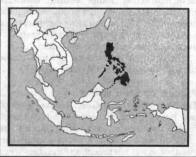

The Philippines, named after the somewhat minor King Philip II of Spain, was more or less left alone until 1565, when Miguel de Legaspi stormed the no-longer-friendly island of Cebu and made the first permanent Spanish settlement. In 1571 they moved headquarters to Manila and from there gradually took control of the entire region – or more correctly converted the region, since Spanish colonial rule was very much tied up with taking the cross to the heathen natives.

The Spanish were not alone in the area. In fact, when the Spanish originally claimed the country as the Eastern Islands, the Portuguese were sailing from the other direction to dub

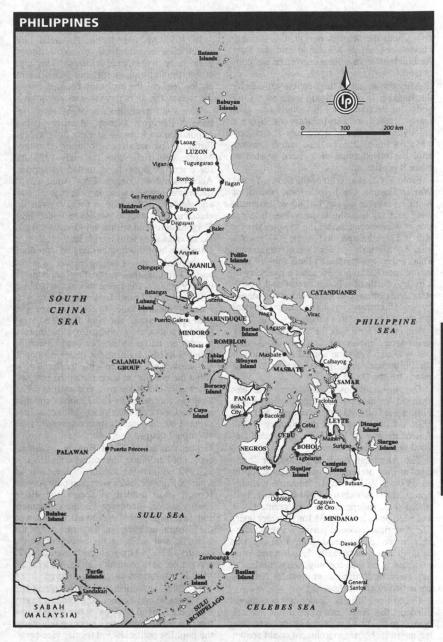

PHILIPPINES

0   100   200 km

Batanes Islands

Babuyan Islands

Laoag
LUZON
Vigan   Tuguegarao
Bontoc   Ilagan
Banaue
San Fernando
Hundred   Baguio
Islands
Dagupan   Baler

Angeles   Polillo Islands
Olongapo
MANILA

Batangas   LUZON
Lubang   Lucena   CATANDUANES
Island
Puerto Galera   MARINDUQUE   Naga   Virac
MINDORO   Burias   Legaspi
Roxas   ROMBLON   Island
Tablas   Sibuyan   Masbate
Island   Island   Calbayog
MASBATE   SAMAR
Boracay
Island   Tacloban
PANAY
Cuyo   Iloilo   LEYTE
Island   City   Bacolod   Dinagat
Cebu   Island
CEBU   Maasin   Siargao
Island
PALAWAN   Puerto Princesa   BOHOL
Surigao
NEGROS   Tagbilaran
Dumaguete   Siquijor   Camiguin
Island   Island
Butuan

SOUTH
CHINA
SEA

PHILIPPINE
SEA

CALAMIAN
GROUP

Dipolog
Cagayan
de Oro
MINDANAO

Balabac   SULU SEA
Island
Davao

Turtle
Islands   Zamboanga
Jolo   Basilan
Sandakan   Island   Island   General
SABAH   Santos
(MALAYSIA)   SULU   CELEBES SEA
ARCHIPELAGO

PHILIPPINES

the place the Western Islands. The Japanese and Chinese also made forays into area and, throughout the Spanish period, the strongly Muslim regions of Mindanao and the Sulu Archipelago were neither converted nor conquered.

After the defeat of the Spanish armada by the English in 1588, Spain entered a long period of decline. The Philippines was generally treated as a subsidiary of Spain's colony in 'New Spain' – Mexico. The colony was a continual drain on the Spanish treasury until the introduction of tobacco started to make it profitable.

From 1762, as a result of the Seven Years' War in Europe, the British took control of Manila for over a year, but never extended their rule far into the countryside. Internal events were more threatening to Spanish rule and it is estimated that over 100 revolts against Spanish power were organised. Finally the Spanish sealed their fate by executing Jose Rizal in 1896, after a mockery of a trial. A brilliant scholar, doctor and writer, Rizal had preferred to work for independence by peaceful means, but his execution sparked the worst revolt to that time.

Nevertheless, it was the USA who finally pushed the Spanish out. The Spanish-American War of 1898 soon spread from Cuba to the Philippines and Spanish power was no match for the USA.

One colonial power, however, was exchanged for another and once the inevitable Filipino revolt had been stamped out, the USA set out to convert the country to the American way of life. They succeeded beyond their wildest dreams.

The American colonial period, or 'tutelage' as they preferred to call it, was abruptly ended by WWII, when the Japanese military occupied the islands until 1944. At the close of the war, independence was granted – it had been promised in 1935 for 10 years later. The American colonial period was considerably more enlightened than that of the Spanish, but it left equally deep impressions, particularly on the economy, since ruthlessly opportunistic American companies had become firmly entrenched.

In addition, Filipino democracy was modelled on the American pattern and events were to prove that a system wide open to vote buying in its home environment could spawn spectacular abuses in Asia. So in the 1950s and 1960s the Philippines bounced from one party to another (usually similar) party until

the future dictator Ferdinand Marcos was elected in 1965.

In 1972 Marcos declared martial law, which soon became total control. Although previously widespread violence was curtailed, the Philippines suffered from stifling corruption and the economy became one of the weakest in an otherwise booming region.

The 1983 assassination of Marcos' opponent Benigno 'Ninoy' Aquino pushed opposition to Marcos to new heights and further shook the already tottering economy. Marcos called elections for early 1986 and for once the opposition united to support Aquino's widow, Corazon 'Cory' Aquino. With the world's media watching closely, Marcos and Aquino both claimed to have won the election. But 'people power' rallied behind Cory Aquino, and within days Ferdinand and his shoe fetishist wife Imelda had slunk off to Hawaii, where the former dictator later died.

Aquino's job on taking power was not easy. The coalition supporting her was an uneasy one and she failed to win the backing of the army and other former pro-Marcos elements. She also failed to come to grips with land reform issues; the New People's Army (NPA), who were pushing for a communist revolution; and the Moro National Liberation Front (MNLF), fighting for independence in the south. This, coupled with her inability to solve the corruption endemic in the country, eventually led to her own downfall in 1992. She was succeeded by Fidel Ramos, the man who had leapt off the sinking Marcos ship to support Aquino and help her survive seven attempted coups.

The Protestant Fidel Ramos, a distant cousin of Ferdinand Marcos, won the election in 1992 without the support of the Catholic Church. Equipped with sweeping new powers, Ramos soon moved to secure the ailing energy sector, encourage foreign investment and, in a surprise move, even lifted the ban on the Communist Party in an attempt to end the guerrilla war draining the resources of the country. This policy was vindicated in 1996 when a peace agreement was signed with the MNLF, after much tough negotiating.

In 1998, with critics baying for blood and all the same old economic problems pretty much unchanged, Ramos' sober presidential term ended and a massive election win swept the populist politician and former vice-president Joseph Estrada into power. An ageing B-grade movie idol, Estrada immediately promised to redirect government funding to help the poor and fight for the rights of the long-neglected average Filipino. Sound like an over-the-top movie script? Welcome to the Philippines ...

Estrada's first real test as president has been to keep the struggling national carrier, Philippines Airlines (PAL), up and running. Lengthy negotiations between the PAL workers' union, management and creditors look to have saved the vital transport link, for now.

GEOGRAPHY

The official statistics state that the Philippines comprises more than 7000 islands and islets – depending on the tide. Together, they make up a land area of about 307,000 sq km, 94% of which is on the 11 largest islands.

The Philippines can be conveniently divided into four areas:

Luzon – the largest island (site of the capital, Manila), and the nearby islands of Mindoro, Batanes, Catanduanes and Marinduque.

The Visayas – the scattered group of islands south of Luzon. The Visayan islands include Cebu, Bohol, Leyte, Biliran, Samar, Romblon, Panay, Guimaras, Negros and Siquijor.

Mindanao – the Muslim trouble centre in the south and the second-largest island in the country, along with the string of islands in the Sulu Archipelago, like stepping stones to Borneo.

Palawan Island – nearly 400km long but averaging a width of only 40km.

CLIMATE

The Philippines is typically tropical – hot and humid all year round. Instead of four seasons, it simply has a January-June dry period and a July-December wet period. From May to November there may also be typhoons. January, February and March are probably the best months for a visit, as it starts to get hotter after March, peaking in May. In some places it seems to rain all year round and, in others, it hardly rains at all.

The biggest thing to hit the Filipino climate recently has been an unusually strong 'El Niño' (literally 'The Boy') event, a weather phenomenon bringing long and merciless dry spells to the western Pacific region. El Niño's effects will be felt for many years to come, particularly on the islands of Palawan and Mindanao, where rice yields have shrivelled by almost half. As often occurs, El Niño's evil sister, La Niña, took over in the latter

half of 1998, unleashing brutally heavy rainstorms and flash floods.

See the Manila climate chart in the Appendix.

ECOLOGY & ENVIRONMENT

The Philippines is not alone in its tendency to talk rather than act when it comes to respecting nature. Nor is it the only nation allowing big business to plunder land and sea with little regard for the future.

Particularly short-sighted activities, made all the more lethal by foreign funding, include cyanide and dynamite fishing, as well as compressor diving and unchecked net and trawler fishing. Cyanide is used to stun fish such as the prized lapu-lapu, which are then collected and shipped off live – mostly to Japan. Apart from killing countless other sea creatures, the poison slowly destroys coral reefs. Dynamite does the same thing, only faster and louder. On the island of Palawan attempts have been made to stop this wanton destruction but vested interests, ranging from corrupt government officials and policemen to the fishermen themselves, remain an obstacle.

Still, environmental awareness is increasing and government agencies such as the Department of Environment and Natural Resources (DENR) are trying to reverse the trend of putting the economy before the environment. For example, schemes have been introduced to re-employ those who lose their jobs when wood-cutting employers move on to greener pastures. In Manila, the newspaper *Today*, together with other sponsors, has published full page ads with photos of dead fish, appealing to people to stop polluting 'before toxic wastes lead our rivers and lakes to extinction'. The Department of Interior and Local Government, with the full support of the president, publishes a yearly list of the 'cleanest and greenest towns, cities and provinces'. And it's beginning to matter to people whether their area is at the top of the list, or at the bottom among the 'dirty dozen'.

FLORA & FAUNA
Flora

The country's flora includes well over 10,000 species of trees, bushes and ferns, most of which are endemic to the Philippines. In spite of uncontrolled tree felling in the 1980s, the islands of the Philippines are still covered with around 10% tropical rainforest. As well as stands of magnificent giants of the forest and rare tree ferns, over 900 species of orchid contribute to the astounding variety of jungle flora.

Important cash crops include coconut palm, rice, corn and sugar cane, as well as many different kinds of tropical fruits. One crop unique to the Philippines is that of the *pili* nut, which is used in chocolate, ice cream and even soap production. It's harvested from May to October, mostly around Sorsogon in South Luzon. The pretty yellow flowering *narra* is the national tree of the Philippines, but the unofficial national tree must surely be the *nipa* palm – which lends its name and timber to the traditional nipa hut found in villages and many tourist resorts all over the country.

Fauna
Countless species of animal are at home in the Philippines, many of them endemic. A number of small mammals, like the rare mouse deer and the tarsier, a pocket-size saucer-eyed primate, are endangered, as is the *tamaraw* (a species of dwarf buffalo) of Mindoro, the Palawan bearcat and the flying lemur. The best known representative of the bird family is the *haribon*, or Philippine eagle, only about 100 of which are left in their natural habitat on Mindanao. Even further south, the Sulu hornbill of Sulu, Jolo and Tawi-Tawi is another amazing and elusive mountain-dwelling bird.

Of the reptile family, South-East Asia traveller's will be most familiar with the little gravity-defying, mosquito-chomping gecko and its raspy 'tap tap tap' mating call. More elusive scaled beasts include the sailfin dragon and the flying lizard – discovered by national hero Jose Rizal while he was exiled in Dapitan on Mindanao – and a wide variety of venomous and nonvenomous snakes, including pythons.

There's an unbelievable array of fish, seashells and corals, as well as the sea cow, or dugong (known locally as the *duyong*), once found in great numbers in Philippine waters but now rare. You're more likely to spot dolphins and, if your timing's just right, whale sharks (*butanding*) near Sorsogon in South Luzon. The local tourism industry there is desperately hoping these plankton-feeding gentle giants will continue their present habit of surfacing from around November to May each year (see the Donsol entry in the South Luzon section).

Endangered Species Apart from those already mentioned under Fauna, the following animals are on the endangered list: the scaly anteater, Palawan peacock pheasant, Luzon bleeding-heart pig-eon, flying fox, hawksbill and green sea turtles, and Philippine and estuarine crocodiles. Filipino seahorses (*kabayo-kabayo*), despite a 70% population plunge, aren't on the list because there's too much money to be made exporting them live, or selling them dead and dried as souvenirs or aphrodisiacs. Environmental groups recently warned that the seahorse may be wiped out within 10 years.

For heaps more info on Filipino creatures clinging to existence, contact the Haribon Foundation (☎/fax 712 2601, email emc010 @wtouch.com.ph) 3rd floor, AM Bldg, 28 Quezon Ave, Quezon City, Manila. It also has a Web site (www.haribon.org.ph).

National Parks
A visit to one or more of the national parks is a must for any traveller. Nature is still intact, to a large extent, in Mt Apo National Park on Mindanao, Mt Kanlaon National Park on Negros and St Paul National Park on Palawan. On the other hand, illegal wood cutters in Bicol National Park have left behind a totally denuded environment.

GOVERNMENT & POLITICS
In a process that's part religious festival, part circus, the president of the Philippines is elected directly by the voters for a six year term. During the 1998 elections, newspapers reported that banks nationwide had run out of P100 and P500 bills because party officials needed them to buy votes. The average vote was selling for around P300 to P500. During the last elections, it was P20 and P50 bills that became scarce at banks – it seems the price of votes has skyrocketed. Accusations of vote rigging during elections are commonplace, and usually greeted with a buck-passing shrug by authorities. This recently prompted one provincial leader to ask of his country: 'Where else can you see registered names of voters belonging to newborn babies, every child in the family, maybe even the dogs and chickens?'

But nobody's accusing the newly installed President Joseph Estrada of cheating. A landslide election victory in 1998 catapulted Estrada onto the presidential throne with such force that even his supporters were surprised.

The country's shell-shocked intellectual elite were left to bitterly claim that Estrada is a dopey latter-day Ferdinand Marcos bent on plunging the nation back into the darkest days of cronyism and shady deals. But the *masa*, or masses, are convinced Estrada's trademark 'Robin Hood' screen persona will play just fine in the theatre of politics.

The Philippines has a constitutional form of government. The legislative power is vested in Congress, which is composed of the Senate and House of Representatives. The Republic of the Philippines is divided into 12 administrative regions (plus Metro Manila as the National Capital Region) consisting of 76 provinces. Every province comprises a provincial capital and several municipalities, which in turn consist of village communities, or *barangays*. This setup may change in Mindanao as the Muslim province gathers support from both Muslim and non-Muslim politicians to amend the constitution and create a 'two-nation state'.

ECONOMY

In 1998 the nation recorded a 1.7% Gross Domestic Product (GDP) growth rate, which was trumpeted as great news by the then Ramos government because, well, it could have been worse. The fact is, the GDP growth rate was cancelled out by a 2.3% annual population growth rate and more than 40% of families are living below the poverty line. Only a politician could twist that into something worth cheering about. Likewise, only political hype and economic sorcery could have spawned the impossibly low one year inflation rate of 7.3% in 1998. Even self-confessed economic dunce President Estrada could work out that such a figure doesn't add up in a year when average rental prices rose by around 30%, water rates by as much as 100%, transport costs by 40%, food prices by 30% and labour costs by 15%.

Despite all the talk of economic reform under the former Ramos administration and the billions of dollars repaid to creditors, the nation's foreign debt is bigger than it's ever been – far bigger than it was even during the Marcos dictatorship. Add the combined climatic forces of El Niño and La Niña to what is principally an agrarian economy, and Estrada looks to be the proud owner of a bankrupt government. Like several other countries in the region, the Philippines is potentially self-sufficient in rice and other important foods but, mainly because of poor yields and the evils of absentee landlords in a peasant society, it generally ends up having to import rice, fish and meat.

Copra, sugar and *abaca* (a fibre from a relative of the banana plant), tobacco, bananas and pineapples are the principal agricultural exports. Gold and silver mining are other important economic activities. There is some industry and it had been growing in recent years, but widespread corruption, inefficiency, ruthless foreign interests and that almighty Asian financial crisis has meant that the economy of the Philippines has, at best, merely stayed alive.

POPULATION & PEOPLE

The population of the Philippines is estimated to be about 75 million and still growing too fast for comfort. The people are mainly of the Malay race although there's a sizable Chinese minority and a fair number of *mestizos* – Filipino-Spanish or Filipino-American. Pre-Malayan communities include the Irayan Mangyan tribes in the mountainous interior of Mindoro, the Tagbanua of Palawan and the former head-hunters of North Luzon including the Ifugao, the Luplupa, the Ambato and the Kalinga.

ARTS
Dance

Filipinos are talented dancers, whether it be disco, folk, modern or classical ballet. Traditional dance is derived from Malay, Spanish and Muslim origins. Among the most beautiful Malay dances are *tinikling* (bamboo or heron dance) and *pandanggo sa ilaw* (dance of lights); the best known Filipino-Muslim dance is *singkil* (court dance). You will also often see performances of the Philippine variations of the Spanish dances *habanera*, *jota* and *paypay* (the fan dance).

Music

While 'civilised' Filipinos have fallen for western pop music and imitated it perfectly, more and more musicians are rediscovering their cultural heritage and bringing old melodies back to life, using traditional instruments like bamboo flutes, gongs and wooden drums, and are singing in Tagalog. The most popular social critic in the Philippines is without a doubt Freddie Aguilar, whose song 'Bayan Ko' (My Country) became the anthem of the Marcos opponents during the uprising of 1986.

PHILIPPINES

Besides Imelda Marcos and her wailing karaoke performances, the Philippines' most famous musical export must be Joey Santiago, guitarist for the hugely influential and sadly missed Boston rock band, the Pixies.

If you're already in South-East Asia, check out the Asian MTV channel to get an idea of just how big, hip and healthy the Filipino rock scene is.

Pirated music tapes by local and foreign artists are sold at many street markets for about P65; premium quality tapes in department stores and music shops go for about P130. CDs start at around P250.

Painting

The best known local painters of the 19th century are Felix Hidalgo and Juan Luna. Luna's *Spolarium* won a gold medal at the 1884 Madrid Exposition. In the mid-20th century Fernando Amorsolo, Vicente Dizon and Vicente Manansala were all internationally renowned, and today there's a lively, if disorganised, contemporary art scene based mainly in Manila. In 1998 the capital was the venue for Asia's prestigious ASEAN Art Awards.

Cartoons & Comics

It's a well kept secret, but many international animation giants such as Disney, Marvel and Hanna Barbara produce substantial portions of their animation in Manila. Filipino cartoonists are renowned for their low rates, speed and ability to copy. Filipinos also excel at original comic artwork, and many have earned cult followings in the superhero genre at home and in the USA.

Cinema

The Philippines is easily South-East Asia's most prolific and diverse filmmaker, but the industry has certainly had its ups and downs. Launched by foreigners around the turn of the century, it peaked during the 1950s and troughed in the 1970s under the Marcos regime. Swashbuckling good guy-bad guy movies remain a firm favourite and it's no coincidence that the nation's latest president made his name exclusively playing a gun-toting good guy.

In contrast, Kidlat Tahimik's surreal anti-colonial opus, *The Perfumed Nightmare*, is about a Filipino boy taken to Paris by an American – see it, and you'll never look at being abroad the same way again.

If you're staying at a hotel in the Philip-pines that has cable TV, look for the Pinoy Blockbuster channel for hours of Filipino schlock classics.

SOCIETY & CONDUCT
Traditional Culture

The Philippines has developed a unique mixed culture from the historical blending of foreign influences with indigenous elements. Today, the Muslims and some of the isolated tribes are the only people whose culture remains unadulterated by Spanish and American influences.

The results of this foreign influence can be seen every day in the Philippines. For example, every afternoon even the smallest village square is converted into a basketball court. Ever since American colonial times Filipinos have been crazy about this sport. They also love to gamble, and cockfighting gives them a great chance to indulge in this. The average Filipinos are not great savers anyway. They live more to enjoy today and survive it if they can; tomorrow will take care of itself. This philosophy is reflected in the Tagalog term *bahala na* (roughly translated as 'confidence despite a lack of responsibility or organisation') – a shameful national trait according to some.

The ability of the Filipinos to improvise and even outdo their former colonial masters is nowhere more apparent than in the jeepney. The army jeeps left behind by the Americans after WWII were converted into colourful, shining chrome communal taxis through painstaking work. Nowadays, these vehicles are produced locally.

Perhaps as a reaction to the residual influence of occupying foreign powers, people have begun to rediscover their cultural heritage. As a result, the national language is finding more and more favour and is widely used today in cinema and literature, while *kundimans* – romantic and sentimental love songs – are also popular again.

Dos & Don'ts

As in other Asian countries, always allow locals a way of extracting themselves from an awkward situation. Above all, they want to avoid 'losing face'. Also, if people stare at you, don't get annoyed; they find you interesting – even exotic – and they want to get a good look at you.

Treatment of Animals

A pet is an unaffordable luxury for most

Filipinos. Household cats and dogs are usually expected to work for their keep, and stray dogs are regularly rounded up and shot to keep rabies outbreaks down. Pigs, chickens, fish and, in some regions, dogs, all end up in the pot without ceremony. Only the hard-working water buffalo is treated in a friendly way, along with the rooster, or fighting cock, who is pampered like a royal prince – at least until his fighting career comes to its inevitable bloody end. In Mindanao, it's often stallions rather than roosters which are taunted into attacking one another as spectators cheer them on.

RELIGION

While visitors could be forgiven for thinking basketball is the dominant religion, Catholicism is still number one. The Philippines is unique for being the only Christian country in Asia – over 90% of the population claims to be Christian and over 80% are Roman Catholic. The Spanish did a thorough job! The largest religious minority group are the Muslims, who live chiefly on Mindanao and in the Sulu Archipelago.

Religion and travel go hand in hand in the Philippines. Jeepneys and tricycles are usually dripping with Catholic good-luck charms, several ferry companies screen a video prayer for safe sailing, bus passengers often cross themselves as the journey begins and traffic is regularly brought to a standstill by long, slow funeral processions.

LANGUAGE

As in Indonesia, there's one nominally national language and a large number of local languages and dialects. It takes 10 languages to cover 90% of the population! Although not as widespread as in the American days, English remains the language of secondary school education, commerce and politics – although President Estrada, long the butt of jokes for his poor English skills, recently broke with tradition by delivering his inaugural speech in his native Tagalog.

Tagalog, the local language of Manila and parts of Luzon, is now being pushed – with some alterations – as the national language, called Pilipino. It sounds remarkably like Indonesian – listen to them roll their rrrs. By the way, for a bit of foul-mouthed fun, try wrapping your tongue around the excellent Filipino Dirty Words Web site (pubweb. acns.nwu.edu/~flip/dirty.html).

See the Language section in the Appendix for some useful Pilipino words and phrases. For more detailed information on the language get Lonely Planet's *Pilipino phrasebook*.

Facts for the Visitor

THE BEST & WORST

Some of the most magnificent scenery in the Philippines can be found in the **Central Cordillera** mountain range in North Luzon. The journey from **Baguio to Banaue** via Sagada, although not the easiest, is unforgettable. And then you have the absolute highlight: the **rice terraces** of Banaue and Batad.

The impressive countryside around **Mt Pinatubo** was created by the forces of nature, as was – in a very different sense – the nearby city of Angeles, the prostitution capital of the country.

The active, cone-shaped **Mayon volcano** at Legaspi, in South Luzon, is considered to be one of the most beautiful volcanoes in the world.

Despite signs it is moving in the direction of upmarket tourism, the little island of **Boracay** still has that certain something.

On Palawan, **St Paul Subterranean National Park** and **Underground River** as well as **El Nido** and **Bacuit Archipelago** are attractive places worth visiting.

The Philippines without fiestas? Unimaginable. The colourful **Ati-Atihan Festival** in Kalibo, on the island of Panay, is the most spectacular in the country. But quieter, less 'wild' local town **fiestas** have an attraction of their own.

Now for the bad news. Even if you leave aside the extreme of **Angeles**, most Philippine towns don't have much in the way of flair or charm, but of all the tourist attractions in the country, **Pagsanjan**, south-east of Manila, gets the worst marks. This is not because of the waterfall and the raft ride up to it, but because of the high tips the often aggressive boat operators demand.

SUGGESTED ITINERARIES

Anyone who wants to travel intensively around the Philippines needs plenty of time. Days and weeks pass quickly, particularly if you want to go island hopping. You should plan a two or three week stay fairly well if you want to experience some of the country's more unusual aspects. If you only have a little time, say a week, and don't particularly want to get to know Philippine airport architecture intimately, you would do well to restrict yourself to a round trip of North Luzon (eg Manila-Banaue-Sagada-Baguio-Bauan-Manila).

The following is a list of a few of the possibilities, but there are endless opportunities to discover the island world for yourself:

• From Manila to Mindoro via Batangas City (Puerto Galera-Calapan-Roxas), on to Tablas/Romblon, then to Panay via Boracay. From Kalibo back to Manila or from Iloilo City to Manila. You should allow about two weeks for this trip.
• From Panay (Iloilo City) or Cebu (Cebu City) to Palawan (Puerto Princesa), then to northern Palawan, returning to Manila from El Nido or from Busuanga.
• From Cebu to Mindanao (Zamboanga, Davao), then from northern Mindanao (Surigao) on to Leyte and Samar, returning to Manila via South Luzon.

Island Hopping in the Visayas

With so many islands in the Visayas, such relatively short distances between them and so many ferries and boats, the possibilities for island hopping are immense.

All things considered, the following route makes an interesting and adventurous loop that takes in most of the Visayan Islands with minimal backtracking. Starting from Manila, you could travel to South Luzon. From Matnog at the southern tip of Luzon there are ferries every day to Allen at the northern end of Samar.

The new road down the west coast of Samar means it's now a quick and relatively easy trip through Calbayog and Catbalogan, then across the bridge to Tacloban on the island of Leyte. From Tacloban or Ormoc, or from Bato and Maasin, there are regular ships to Cebu City. From Cebu there are daily ferries to the neighbouring island of Bohol, famed for its Chocolate Hills. Ferries also cross daily between Cebu and Negros, either in the south of the island to Dumaguete or, closer to Cebu City, from Toledo to San Carlos. You can then continue by bus to Bacolod, from where ferries cross to Iloilo City on Panay.

From Iloilo City, in the south of Panay, you can travel to Caticlan at the north-west tip and make the short crossing by outrigger to the popular island of Boracay. After a spell of lazing on the beach you can find another outrigger to cross to Tablas Island in the Romblon group, usually to Looc in the south. Take a jeepney to San Agustin and a boat from

there to Romblon on Romblon Island. Finally, there are boats twice weekly to Manila.

PLANNING
When to Go

Generally, the best time to travel is from the middle of December to the middle of May – that's off season for typhoons. However, you would be well advised not to travel during the Christmas and Easter holiday periods: find yourself a pleasant base, because the entire country is on the move at these times and you'll hardly find a seat on any transport.

January and May are the months with the most colourful festivals. In the provinces along the Pacific coast, where vast amounts of rain can fall between November and January, the dry season usually begins in the second half of February at the latest. The rice terraces in North Luzon show themselves at their best in March and April. Those are the pleasant, warm summer months, when island hopping is the most fun. It really heats up in May, when you'll be glad of the slightest breeze.

Maps

The Nelles Verlag *Philippines* map is an excellent map of the islands at a scale of 1:1,500,000.

What to Bring

A big towel or a sarong can help you feel more comfortable on the bare boards or plastic sheets covering the beds on many overnight ferries.

A tough plastic rubbish bag will keep your gear dry when outrigger boat trips get splashy. It can also keep out the dust on long, dry bus trips.

A good torch (flashlight) is essential in country areas where electricity can't be taken for granted.

Ear plugs can be a godsend for muffling everything from crowing roosters to ship engines or your neighbour's TV.

Tampons are fairly widely available (average price: P150 for a box of eight), but it's a good idea to stock up.

What Not to Bring

Umbrellas and raincoats can be bought cheaply along the way when the need arises. Don't weigh yourself down unnecessarily.

Mosquito nets are also a bulky inconvenience – and places that have mosquitoes *do* tend to have mosquito nets.

TOURIST OFFICES

The Department of Tourism (DOT) office in Manila isn't all it's cracked up to be. Staff are friendly, but computer print-outs for specific areas are out of date and the piles of brochures available can be found at the various regional DOT offices around the country, usually along with more practical and current information. The towering Philippine Convention & Visitors Corporation (☎ 525 9318), 4th floor, suite 10-17, Legaspi Towers, Roxas Blvd has a tiny but jam-packed library and helpful staff.

Local Tourist Offices

Bacolod City
   (☎ 29021) Bacolod Seawall
Baguio
   (☎ 442 7014) DOT Complex
   Governor Pack Rd
Boracay
   (☎/fax 288 3689) Balabag
Butuan City
   (☎ 225 5712) City Hall Compound
Cagayan de Oro
   (☎ 72 6394) Pelaez Sports Complex,
   Velez St
Cebu City
   (☎ 254 2811) 3rd floor, GMC Plaza Bldg,
   Legaspi St
Cotabato
   (☎ 21 1110) Elizabeth Tan Bldg,
   De Mazenod Ave
Davao City
   (☎ 221 6798) Door No 7, Magsaysay Park
   Complex
Iloilo City
   (☎ 75411) Provincial Capitol Ground,
   Bonifacio Drive
Laoag
   (☎ 712 0467) Ilocano Heroes Hall
Legaspi City
   (☎ 24 3215) 3rd floor, M Dy Bldg,
   Rizal St
Manila
   (☎ 523 8411) Room No 208, DOT Bldg,
   TM Kalaw St, Ermita
San Fernando (La Union)
   (☎ 41 2411) Mabanag Bldg, Capitol Hills
San Fernando (Pampanga)
   (☎ 961 2665) Paksuhan Village
Tacloban
   (☎ 321 2048) Children's Park,
   Senator Enage St
Tuguegarao
   (☎ 844 1621) 2nd floor, Tuguegarao
   Supermarket
Zamboanga
   (☎ 991 0218) Lantaka Hotel,
   Valderrosa St

Tourist Offices Abroad

Australia
   (☎ 02-9267 2695)
   Highmount House, Level 6, 122 Castlereagh
   St, Sydney, NSW 2000
China
   (☎ 0852-2866 6471)
   c/o Philippine Consulate, 6F United Centre,
   95 Queensway, Hong Kong Central
France
   (☎ 01 42 65 02 34)
   c/o Philippine Embassy, 3 Faubourg Saint
   Honoré, 75009 Paris
Germany
   (☎ 069-20893)
   Kaiserstrasse 15, 60311 Frankfurt-
   am-Main
Japan
   (☎ 03-3464 3630)
   c/o Philippine Embassy, 11-24 Nampeidai
   Machi, Shibuya-ku, Tokyo;
   (☎ 06-535 5071)
   Philippine Tourism Center, 2nd floor Dainan
   Bldg, 2-19-23 Shinmachi, Nishi-ku,
   Osaka 550
Singapore
   (☎ 235 2184)
   c/o Philippine Embassy, 20 Nassim Rd,
   Singapore
UK
   (☎ 020-7499 5443)
   c/o Philippine Embassy, 17 Albemarle St,
   London WlX 7HA
USA
   (☎ 213-487 4527)
   Suite 285, 3660 Wilshire Blvd, Los Angeles,
   CA 90010;
   (☎ 818-956 4050)
   Suite 507, 447 Sutter St, San Francisco,
   CA 94108;
   (☎ 212-575 7915)
   Philippine Center, 556 Fifth Ave, New York,
   NY 10036

VISAS & DOCUMENTS
Visas

Visa regulations vary with your intended length of stay. The easiest procedure is to simply arrive without a visa, in which case you will be permitted to stay for up to 21 days. However, your passport has to be valid at least six months beyond the 21 day period you intend to stay. If you obtain a visa overseas it will usually allow a 59 day stay. This is free of charge in Australia and New Zealand, and usually about US$35 elsewhere. If you already have a visa on arrival make sure the immigration officers know this or your passport will still be stamped for just 21 days.

PHILIPPINES

Visa Extensions To extend the 21 day stay period to 59 days, apply with your passport and the relevant documents to the immigration office in Manila, Cebu City or Angeles. The Manila office is at the Department of Immigration & Deportation, Magallanes Drive, Intramuros, Manila. The extension costs P500 for the visa waiver plus P10 for a legal research fee. The four hour express service costs an additional P250. You must be neatly dressed if you apply in person – rubber thongs (flip-flops) will invite an instant refusal. A number of travel agencies and hotels will handle the extension application for anything from about P200 to P700.

After 59 days it gets really complicated, although it's possible to go on extending for about a year. Such extensions cost P200 per month, plus alien head tax (P200), alien certificate of registration (P400), emigration clearance certificate (P500) and a series of legal research fees.

Staying beyond six months involves a certificate of temporary residence (P700) and after one year there's a travel tax on departure (P1620).

Other Documents

Apart from Philippine Airlines (PAL), some bus and shipping companies offer student discounts, so a student ID card could come in handy.

EMBASSIES & CONSULATES
Philippine Embassies & Consulates

For Philippine diplomatic offices in countries covered in this book, see the relevant country chapter.

Australia
  (☎ 02-6273 2535)
  1 Moonah Place, Yarralumla, ACT 2600
Canada
  (☎ 416-922 7181)
  Suite 365, 151 Bloor St West, Toronto
France
  (☎ 01 42 65 02 34)
  3 Faubourg Saint Honoré, 75009 Paris
Germany
  (☎ 0228-267990)
  Argelanderstrasse 1, 53115 Bonn
Japan
  (☎ 03-3496 6555)
  11-24 Nampeidai Machi, Shibuya-ku, Tokyo
New Zealand
  (☎ 04-472 9921)
  50 Hobson St, Thorndon, Wellington

South Africa
  (☎ 012-342 6920)
  Southern Life Plaza Bldg, Schoeman St, Pretoria
UK
  (☎ 020-7499 5443) 17 Albemarle St, London WIX 7HA
USA
  (☎ 202-467 9300) 1600 Massachusetts Ave NW, Washington, DC 20036

Embassies & Consulates in the Philippines

The following diplomatic offices are all in Manila:

Australia
  (☎ 817 7911) Doña Salustiana Ty Tower, 104 Paseo de Roxas, Makati
Canada
  (☎ 810 8861) Allied Bank Bldg, 6754 Ayala Ave, Makati
France
  (☎ 810 1981) Pacific Star Bldg, Gil Puyat Ave, Makati
Indonesia
  (☎ 892 5961) 185 Salcedo St, Makati
Japan
  (☎ 895 9050) 375 Gil Puyat Ave, Makati
Malaysia
  (☎ 817 4581) 107 Tordesillas St, Makati
New Zealand
  (☎ 818 0916) Gammon Center Bldg, Alfaro St, Makati
Singapore
  (☎ 816 1767) ODC International Bldg, 219 Salcedo St, Makati
Thailand
  (☎ 815 4219) Marie Cristine Bldg, 107 Rada St, Makati
UK
  (☎ 816 7116) LV Locsin Bldg, 6752 Ayala Ave, Makati
USA
  (☎ 521 7116) 1201 Roxas Blvd, Ermita
Vietnam
  (☎ 50 0364) 554 Vito Cruz, Malate

CUSTOMS

Personal effects, a reasonable amount of clothing, toiletries, jewellery and perfume are allowed in duty free. Visitors may also bring in 200 cigarettes or two tins of tobacco and 2L of alcohol free of duty.

It's strictly prohibited to bring illegal drugs, firearms and pornographic media into the country.

Visitors carrying more than US$3000 are requested to declare the amount at the Central

Bank counter at the customs area. Foreign currency taken out upon departure must not exceed the amount brought in. Departing passengers may not take out more than P1000 in local currency.

It's forbidden to export coral and mussels, certain types of orchid, or parts of animals such as turtle shells and python skins.

MONEY
Currency
The unit of currency is the peso (P, also spelt piso), divided into 100 centavos (c). Banknotes come in denominations of 5, 10, 20, 50, 100, 500 and 1000 pesos. Coins are most common in 10 and 25 centavos, and 1 and 5 pesos.

Exchange Rates
Exchange rates are as follows:

country	unit		peso
Australia	A$1	=	P27.21
Canada	C$1	=	P27.96
euro	€1	=	P52.01
France	10FF	=	P78.70
Germany	DM1	=	P26.39
Japan	¥100	=	P36.21
New Zealand	NZ$1	=	P23.33
UK	UK£1	=	P73.62
USA	US$1	=	P43.26

Exchanging Money
There are no particular hassles with exchanging or carrying pesos, although you'll need an exchange receipt if you want to convert any back on departure. Of course, US dollars are preferred and accepted with glee everywhere. Around the tourist haunt of Ermita, along Mabini St in particular, moneychangers seem to outnumber tourists by about 10 to one. These places are much faster than the banks and give a better rate for cash. The rate varies with the size of the bill – US$50 and US$100 bills are best.

Cash
'Sorry, no change' becomes a very familiar line. Stock up on notes smaller than P100 at every opportunity.

Travellers Cheques
The Philippines seems to have something against travellers cheques. Even in Manila, banks and moneychangers can be reluctant to cash them. And don't be surprised if those banks that do change cheques only do so between 9 and 10 am, or only at limited branches – or only on Friday during a lunar eclipse when Mars is in Virgo and your name is Reginald. Of the banks, the best bet is usually the PCI Bank, or the Hongkong & Shanghai Bank on Ayala Ave, Makati. Don't forget to take along your passport and purchase receipts. Cash tends to get a better rate than cheques.

ATMs
There are ATMs in cities and towns throughout the country, but it's a good idea to use them only during banking hours (9 am to 3 pm, Monday to Friday).

With most major credit cards you can withdraw as much as P20,000 (debited from your account back home) per day from any Equitable or PCI Bank ATM. Some ATMs, however, limit withdrawals to as little as P3000 for no apparent reason.

Credit Cards
Major credit cards, such as American Express, Diner's Club, MasterCard and Visa, are accepted by many hotels, restaurants and businesses. Most of the big-name cards let you withdraw cash in pesos at any branch of the Equitable Bank or PCI Bank (almost every big city has branches). Unlimited cash advances on credit cards are also available at Swagman Travel offices in Manila, Angeles, Bauang, Olongapo, Puerto Galera, Sabang (Mindoro), Boracay, Coron, and Apuao Grande Island. But unlike the banks, Swagman charges a killer 8% commission. You'll need your passport and, of course, your magic piece of plastic.

Costs
Despite the price-plunging Asian financial crisis, dining and accommodation in the Philippines are still a bit pricey compared with many neighbouring countries. You'll get the best value for money in the mountains of North Luzon (Banaue, Batad, Sagada), while in the more crowded tourist areas, such as the islands of Boracay and Cebu, you'll have to dig deeper into your pockets. Still, some things seem amazingly cheap – local transport and beer are two good examples. Air fares within the Philippines are also good value.

Tipping & Bargaining
Restaurant staff generally expect a tip (it's part of their wage), even if the menu states

PHILIPPINES

that a service charge is included. The money then goes into a kitty and is shared later with the cook and the cashier. If the service was particularly good, a tip of around 5 to 10% of the bill will show your appreciation.

Taxi drivers will often try to wangle a tip by claiming not to be able to give change. If the charge on the meter appears to be accurate, the passenger should voluntarily round up the amount: for example, if the fare is P44, then P50 would be appropriate.

When shopping in public markets or even shops, Filipinos try to get a 10% discount. They almost always succeed. Foreign customers will automatically be quoted a price that is around 20% more than normal or, in places which deal mainly with tourists, up to 50% more.

POST & COMMUNICATIONS
Post
The postal system is generally quite efficient. Poste restante is available at the main post office in all major towns. Depending on the distance from Manila, it can take up to three weeks to be delivered.

Opening hours in Philippine post offices vary widely, but the following hours can usually be relied upon: Monday to Friday from 8 am to noon, and from 1 to 5 pm.

Air mail letters (per 20g) within the Philippines cost P6 (ordinary/three weeks), P11 within Asia, P13 to Australasia and the Middle East, P15 to Europe and North America, and P18 to Africa and South America. Aerograms and postcards cost P8, regardless of their destination.

Telephone
You don't find telephones everywhere in the Philippines; in an emergency try the nearest police station, which in many areas will have the only telephone. Phone numbers are always changing, so obtain a local directory before calling, or try directory assistance on 114.

Local calls are full of problems. It can take a ridiculously long time to be connected and the lines over long distances are bad. International calls are simple in comparison.

International calls can be made from many hotels or from one of the many offices of the Philippine Long Distance Telephone Company (PLDT), Philippine Telegraph & Telephone Corporation (PT&T), or other such companies. The average deal is you pay about P375 for the first five minutes, and P60 for every minute after that. For collect (reverse charges)

Telephone Codes

The country code for the Philippines is ☎ 63. The international dialling code is ☎ 00. Following are area codes for some cities. You must dial the first zero when calling from within the Philippines.

Angeles	☎ 0455
Bacolod	☎ 034
Baguio	☎ 074
Banaue	☎ 073
Batangas	☎ 043
Bauang	☎ 072
Borocay	☎ 036
Butuan	☎ 08521, ☎ 08522
Cagayan de Oro	☎ 08822
Cebu City	☎ 032
Cotabato	☎ 064
Davao City	☎ 082
Dipolog	☎ 065
Dumaguete	☎ 035
General Santos	☎ 083
Iloilo City	☎ 033
Kalibo	☎ 036
Laoag	☎ 077
La Union	☎ 072
Legaspi City	☎ 05221
Lucena	☎ 042
Mambajao	☎ 088
Manila	☎ 02
Naga	☎ 054
Olongapo	☎ 047
Ormoc	☎ 05351
Puerto Princesa	☎ 048
San Fernando (La Union)	☎ 072
San Fernando (Pampanga)	☎ 045
San Jose	☎ 046
Sorsogon	☎ 056
Surigao	☎ 08681
Tacloban	☎ 053
Tagaytay	☎ 096
Tagbilaran	☎ 038, ☎ 03823
Tuguegarao	☎ 078
Vigan	☎ 077
Virac	☎ 052
Zamboanga	☎ 062

calls, a flat fee of about P11 is charged. You can also make reverse charges yourself by dialling ☎ 105 followed by your country code.

Call ☎ 108 for international call assistance.

Fax & Telegraph

Sending a fax overseas from a hotel can be quite expensive (for example, P350 for one page to Europe). On the other hand, telecommunications companies such as Eastern Telecom and PLDT charge about P95 for the first minute (one page) and P85 for each minute after that.

You may be surprised to hear the antique sound of Morse code telegraphing coming from little offices in towns around the Philippines. This cheap, reliable and fast medium is used mainly for sending 'socialgrams'.

Email & Internet Access

Internet cafes are setting up at a rapid rate in even the smallest of towns. Some are franchises, some are one-offs. One of the biggest names is MosCom (mozcom4.mozcom.com/help/sitemap.html), which has outlets in 32 cities and towns, from Angeles to Zamboanga. In Manila, most of the big shopping malls have one or more cybercafes. Costs vary from place to place – expect anything from P25 to P75 per half hour.

INTERNET RESOURCES

For a fantastically thorough pile of local news and views, go to the Philippine News Link (www.philnews.com), which includes links to all the main daily newspapers. To help you survive the country's crazy capital, the Manilaguide (www.manilaguide.com) and Metro Guide (www.metromanila.com.ph) Web sites list the latest concerts, movies and other often needed escapist pursuits. Great overall Philippine sites include the highly informative Go Philippines! site (www.gopi.com) and the vast Tanikalang Ginto web directory (www.filipinolinks.com).

BOOKS
Lonely Planet

For in-depth coverage of travel in the Philippines, look for Lonely Planet's *Philippines* and the pocket-size language guide, *Pilipino phrasebook*.

General

Manila has a good selection of bookshops. Notable titles in the last few years have included *A Journey Through the Enchanted Isles* by Amadis Ma Guerrero; *Who's Who in Philippine History* by Carlos Quirino; *In Our Image – America's Empire in the Philippines* by Stanley Karnow; the excellently researched *Power from the Forest – The Politics of Logging* by Marites Dañguilan Vitug; and the chillingly entertaining insight into the Manila police force, *Ghosts of Manila* by James Hamilton-Paterson.

NEWSPAPERS & MAGAZINES

After 20 years of press censorship under Marcos, the change of government brought a flood of new national and local newspapers and magazines indulging in a marvellous journalistic free-for-all; many are in English.

There are about 20 English-language publications, the best daily broadsheets being the *Manila Bulletin*, the *Philippine Daily Inquirer* and *Today*. Well stocked newspaper stands can be found in towns and cities all over the country.

RADIO & TV

Radio and TV operate on a commercial basis, and there are 22 TV channels. Seven of these broadcast from Manila, sometimes in English and sometimes in Tagalog.

Many hotels offer cable TV with international channels as part of their service.

PHOTOGRAPHY & VIDEO
Film

Take sufficient slide film with you as there is not a lot of choice in the Philippines. This is especially true of the provinces, where the use-by date has often expired. Kodak Ektachrome 100 ASA costs about P170, 200 ASA costs P215 and 400 ASA costs about P250.

There's no problem with normal colour film, which is often preferred by Filipinos. Development is fast and good value. High gloss prints (9cm by 13cm) can be processed in an hour at a cost of P2.50 per print; cheaper processing takes longer.

Technical Tips

The usual rules for tropical photography apply in the Philippines. Remember to allow for the intensity of the tropical light, keep your film as cool and dry as possible and have it developed as soon as possible after exposure.

Photographing People

Remember that cameras can be one of the most intrusive and unpleasant reminders of the impact of tourism – it's polite to ask people before you photograph them. A smile always helps.

PHILIPPINES

Airport Security

Although airport X-ray equipment is said to be safe for film, it's certainly not *good* for film. If you're passing through numerous airports, have your film inspected separately.

TIME

The Philippines is eight hours ahead of GMT. Official time in Davao, the capital of Mindanao is – believe it or not – about 10 minutes ahead of the rest of the country. While Davao residents aren't too sure how or why it happened, nobody's in a hurry to synchronise watches.

ELECTRICITY

The electric current is generally 220V, 60Hz, although the actual voltage is often less. In some areas the standard current is the USA-style 110V. An adaptor may be needed for Philippine plugs, which are usually like the US flat two-pin type.

Blackouts are common even in the tourist centres, and the chug-a-chug of emergency generators becomes a familiar sound.

WEIGHTS & MEASURES

In general, the metric system is in use, although both metric and imperial are normal. Measurements of length are more often given in feet and yards than in centimetres and metres, while weight is normally expressed in grams and kilograms and temperature in Celsius.

LAUNDRY

Only a few of the laundries open to the public in the Philippines are equipped with modern machinery. Self-service laundrettes with coin-operated machines are completely unknown.

If you don't want to wash your clothes yourself, hand them in to your hotel or guesthouse and you'll get them back within one or two days. It costs about P15 to have a shirt or blouse washed and ironed, or about P20 to P50 per kilogram.

TOILETS

A toilet is referred to as a 'comfort room', or 'CR'. In Tagalog, men are *lalake* and women are *babae*. There are no public toilets and it's not unusual to see men relieving themselves in the street. If you're not keen to join them, head for the nearest fast-food restaurant.

HEALTH

There have been recent large outbreaks of dengue fever, so you should take appropriate precautions to avoid mosquito bites. Malaria exists in rural areas, and is not usually a risk to travellers. Food and water-borne diseases, including dysentery, hepatitis and liver flukes, are a risk. You should be particularly careful of shellfish, as it is periodically affected by algae ('red tide'), causing diarrhoea and vomiting, visual disturbances and even breathing problems. Schistosomiasis (bilharzia) occurs in the southern Philippines – avoid bathing or even paddling in freshwater lakes or rivers.

For more information on these and other health matters, refer to the Health section in the Appendix.

State-owned hospitals and provincial private practices are often poorly equipped. In case of an emergency, you should try to reach the nearest town and check into a private hospital. Dental treatment is adequate, at least in the towns and cities (look for the quaint 'Lady Dentist' signs).

WOMEN TRAVELLERS

Many Filipinos like to think of themselves as being irresistible macho types, but can also turn out to be surprisingly considerate gentlemen. They are especially keen to show their best side to foreign women. They will address you respectfully as 'Ma'am', shower you with friendly compliments and engage you in polite conversation.

Filipinas too rarely miss the chance to ask questions out of curiosity: for example, about your home country, family, marital status etc. It's worth packing a few stock answers to these questions for cheerful distribution.

GAY & LESBIAN TRAVELLERS

While gay Filipinos boast of their *gayday*, or 'innate ability to spot another gay man no matter how well he hides it', homosexuality is generally out in the open in the Philippines. Even if jokes are told about them (never meant in an insulting or prejudiced way), gay men (*bakla*) and lesbians (*binalaki*) are almost universally accepted.

There are well established gay cruising places or 'beats' in Manila, but you should still beware of police and hustlers.

For brilliant, up-to-date info about being gay, bi or lesbian in the Philippines, check out the Filipino Queer Directory Web site (www.tribo.org/bakla/bakla.html).

DISABLED TRAVELLERS

Judging by facilities in buildings, the Philippines is really not suited for disabled people. Only a few hotels and guesthouses are equipped with a suitable ramp for wheelchairs, and only rarely has an architect thought of providing roomy toilets with big doors.

On the other hand, those deficits are largely made up for by the sheer humanity of the people. When they see a disabled person, Filipinos are not stunned into inaction because they're so concerned, nor do they turn away helplessly. They behave perfectly naturally, without ingratiating themselves in an embarrassing way. And if needed, there's always someone there with a helping hand.

SENIOR TRAVELLERS

The older generation is treated with respect and deference in the Philippines and this applies equally to visitors. On the practical side, if you're over 60 years of age, PAL will give you a 20% rebate on all inland flights.

TRAVEL WITH CHILDREN

A Philippine child is never alone, so a foreign child will definitely never spend a moment without someone to play with. Filipinos are simply crazy about children. If you travel with a child, people will often strike up a conversation with you and you'll have to talk a lot.

DANGERS & ANNOYANCES

The Philippines has rip-offs like anywhere else and new tricks pop up every year. Beware of people who claim to have met you before. 'I was the immigration officer at the airport when you came through' is one often used line. There are also phoney police officers, and a favourite scam is to ask to check your money for counterfeit notes, only to hand it back with notes missing or replaced with fakes. Look out for pickpockets in crowded areas of Manila or on tightly packed jeepneys or buses. Favourite places are around Ermita. Sleight-of-hand scams by street moneychangers are another speciality, as are invitations to join in rigged card games.

As for annoyances, you'll probably find you don't share the average Filipino's enthusiasm for roosters – especially at 3 am after a long, hot day when that hideous squawk has torn you from your sleep for the 10th time in a long, hot night. And don't expect to escape the little beasts on boats or buses – fighting cocks travel often, and usually in more style than their doting owners. Pack a pair of ear plugs.

Your ears may also notice that the Filipinos have a unique greeting for male (and sometimes female) westerners: 'Hey Joe!' or 'Hey Kano!' Both are hangovers from American colonial days and both are used ad nauseam. Of course, if your name's Joe and you're American then you'll feel pretty special. If not, you may start to feel like a clown sent especially from the USA to give the locals a laugh. Pack a big supply of patience.

LEGAL MATTERS

If you're arrested, contact your nearest embassy or consulate immediately. However, they may not be able to do much more than provide you with a list of local lawyers and keep an eye on how you're being treated. Remember you are subject to Philippine law when in the Philippines.

BUSINESS HOURS

Businesses first open their doors between 8 and 10 am. Most offices, banks and public authorities work a five day week, with some offices also open on Saturday morning. Banks open at 9 am and close at 3 or 3.30 pm. Embassies and consulates are open to the public mainly from 9 am to 1 pm.

Offices and public authorities close at 5 pm. Large businesses like department stores and supermarkets continue until 7 pm, and smaller shops often stay open until 10 pm.

PUBLIC HOLIDAYS & SPECIAL EVENTS

Offices and banks are closed on public holidays, although shops and department stores stay open. Good Friday is the only time in the year when the entire country closes down. Even public transport stops running, and PAL remains grounded on that day. The public holidays are:

New Year's Day	1 January
Maundy Thursday, Good Friday and Easter Sunday	March/April
Bataan Day	9 April
Labour Day	1 May
Independence Day	12 June
All Saints' Day	1 November
Bonifacio Day (National Heroes Day)	30 November
Christmas Day	25 December
Rizal Day	30 December

PHILIPPINES

ACTIVITIES

The most popular activities are diving and windsurfing, but mountain biking and surfing are also growing in popularity.

Diving

Mindoro (Puerto Galera), Palawan (Puerto Princesa), Bohol (Alona Beach) and Cebu (Moalboal) are the points of departure for the most popular diving places in the archipelago. Boracay is ideal for beginners (there are lots of diving schools), and for wreck divers Subic Bay (Luzon) and Busuanga Island (in the Calamian group) are the places to go.

Windsurfing

The island of Boracay is the Philippine mecca for windsurfers. The best conditions for both beginner and advanced levels can be found on the east coast.

Mountain Biking

The island of Guimaras, between Negros and Panay, looks as if it was made for mountain biking: sparsely populated, with a lack of traffic and other hindrances, its rolling hills and fields are crisscrossed with trails and streams. Enterprising people at Moalboal, on Cebu, are attracting more and more bikers by organising exciting tours. Bike hire companies are on the increase, as is the standard of bikes on offer.

Surfing

In the early days, practically the only place for surfers to go was the island of Catanduanes. Nowadays, the number one place on their list is Siargao Island, north-east of Mindanao. There is also Surf Beach at San Juan on the west coast of Luzon, which is a bit more accessible.

WORK

Nonresident aliens may not be employed at all, nor theoretically even look for work, without a valid work permit, while foreign residents need the necessary work registration; both can be obtained from the Department of Labor & Employment (DOLE, ☎ 527 3585), Palacio del Gobernador, General Luna St, Intramuros, Manila.

If you're interested in doing voluntary work, contact: the Voluntary Services Organisation (VSO, ☎ 722 6033), Unit 1, Fersal Executive Homes, No 53, 14th St, New Manila, Quezon City.

ACCOMMODATION

Depending on where you are, if your budget for a night's accommodation only stretches to P100, there are only a few hotels available. Prices for quite basic accommodation start at around P200.

The exceptions are the guesthouses in the mountains of North Luzon, although some will be pretty rudimentary. For P35 to around P75, these places offer basic sleeping quarters, with hot shower extra.

The best selection of well equipped, medium priced hotels can be found in the red-light city of Angeles, near Mt Pinatubo. On the popular little island of Boracay during the high season from December to May, only a handful of resorts offer cottages for less than P500; however, during the off season all sorts of attractive discounts are available. Reasonably priced accommodation from P150 up to P500 can be found on Palawan, the 'last frontier' of the Philippines.

Maintenance in many hotels is a little lackadaisical so it's well worth checking if the electricity and water are working before you sign in. Beware of fires in cheap hotels – Filipino hotels don't close down, they burn down. Check fire escapes and make sure windows will open. Finally, it's often worth asking for a discount or bargaining a little on prices, as they'll often come down.

FOOD

The Filipinos have taken to US fast foods wholeheartedly, so there are plenty of hamburgers and hot dogs. Chinese food is also widely available. Filipino food, usually called 'native' food, is a bit like Indonesian *nasi padang* in that it's all laid out on view – and to western palates it would often taste a lot better if it were hot. It's worth a splurge to try good, authentic Filipino food as it can be really delicious. But whatever the cuisine, vegetarianism is a pretty foreign concept in the Philippines. One solution is to buy your own fresh fruit and vegetables at the many excellent street markets.

Favourite Filipino dishes include:

adobo – a national dish: salty stewed chicken, pork or squid
arroz caldo – thick rice soup with chicken, garlic, ginger and onions
balut – a boiled chicken egg containing a partially formed embryo
bangus – milkfish, lightly grilled, stuffed and baked
crispy pata – crispy fried pig skin

inihaw – grilled fish or meat
lechon – spit-roast baby pig with liver sauce
lumpia – spring rolls filled with meat or vegetables
mami – noodle soup, like mee soup in Malaysia or Indonesia
menudo – stew with vegetables, liver or pork
pancit – thick or thin noodle dish
pinangat – Bicol region vegetable dish laced with hot peppers – 'the Bicol express'

See the Language section in the Appendix for more food and drink vocabulary.

DRINKS
Nonalcoholic Drinks
buko juice Buko juice is young coconut juice with floaty flesh. It's usually sold in a pre-sealed cup and is said to stave off dehydration.
calamansi The popular little lemons known as calamansi are turned into a refreshing cordial or served with black tea. They are thought to have amazing curative effects.
guyabano juice This is a sweet but surprisingly refreshing juice, made from the soursop.
halo-halo This is a colourful dessert of crushed ice, ice cream and fruit. It means 'all mixed together' and is similar to an *es kacang* in Malaysia.
water Tap water should be avoided in most places. Local mineral and distilled bottled water is fine, and sold in shops everywhere.

Alcoholic Drinks
San Miguel This must be one of the cheapest beers in the world (P12 to P28). It's also very good, but make sure it's cold.
Tanduay Rhum This is a perfectly drinkable travelling companion (P20 to P28 per 375ml bottle) – and a handy antiseptic!
tuba This coconut wine can be very strong.

ENTERTAINMENT
The Filipinos are very keen on their nightlife. There are bars and clubs in every city, and cinemas are a popular, inexpensive pleasure. Also popular are karaoke bars, where Filipinos can sing their hearts out.

But there's no doubt that cockfights *(sabong)* are what the Filipinos get most excited about. All over the country, every Sunday and public holiday, irritable and expensive fighting birds are let loose on one another. The cockpits are full to bursting, the audience is high with excitement and as much as P100,000 may be wagered on a big fight.

SPECTATOR SPORTS
Basketball is *the* sport of the Philippines, and the basketball shirt is just about the national dress. You can catch a game on just about every street corner and in many towns basketball courts dominate the town square. Games in the professional league of the Philippine Basketball Association take place three times a week (see Spectator Sports in the Manila section), but it's US basketball that brings this nation to a virtual standstill. In mid-1998, government officials in Cebu City were forced to deploy security men in all the bars and eateries around the city hall to stop staff sneaking out to watch Game 1 of the NBA finals on TV.

SHOPPING
There are a wide variety of handicrafts available in the Philippines and you will find examples of most crafts on sale in Manila. Clothing, cane and basket work, woodcarving and all manner of regional specialities can be found. In Manila, Davao and other commercial centres, many shops sell those wonderful lights, mirrors and ornaments you see hanging off jeepneys.

If you're feeling a bit travel frazzled, one of the best things you can buy is a haircut (around P30), massage (P90) and/or shave (P30) from one of the many barber shops (as opposed to the hairdressers) around the country – men and women are both welcome.

Getting There & Away

AIR
Airports & Airlines
Manila's airport is the Ninoy Aquino international airport (NAIA). If Manila is your first stop on a first visit to Asia, hold your breath, because it's pure chaos out there. For some reason the Filipinos are unable to make the airport work – in contrast to the relatively smooth operations at Hong Kong, Bangkok or Singapore.

Although Cebu City, Davao and Laoag have international airports, Manila is unfortunately still the main gateway to the country. Cebu City's Mactan Island international airport is a much more pleasant first stop, and its popularity is growing thanks to services by the likes of Cathay Pacific, Malaysia Airlines and Singapore's regional feeder airline, Silk Air.

At the time of writing, Philippine Airlines (PAL) – the national carrier and Asia's oldest airline – was experiencing some very heavy turbulence. Big debts and a crippling strike in mid-1998 saw a number of domestic and international routes cancelled (including all services to Australia) before the airline itself closed for two weeks in late September 1998.

PAL routes and prices in this chapter (and elsewhere in the book) were current to PAL's temporary closure, but though PAL has risen from the ashes of bankruptcy, the situation may remain rather up-in-the-air for some time. How many routes and flights operate (and who runs them with what aircraft), and what tickets cost, are questions best answered on the ground.

If you're looking for a bargain flight out of Manila, forget it. Travel agents here don't seem to be in the business of offering competitive prices.

Departure Tax

International departure tax is P500.

China

Hong Kong is the regional gateway to the Philippines. Fares from Hong Kong to Manila or Cebu City cost around US$140.

Indonesia

Garuda flies four times a week between Manila and Jakarta (US$220), and there are also direct flights between Bali and Manila.

Bouraq Airlines flies between Davao, in the south of Mindanao, and Manado in the north of Sulawesi (US$180 from Davao; US$150 from Manado).

Malaysia

From Sabah you can fly from Kota Kinabalu to Manila with Malaysia Airlines (US$180). You can also fly to Manila or Cebu City from Kuala Lumpur (US$260).

Singapore

Singapore to Manila or Cebu City with Silk Air costs around US$270, or there are twice weekly flights between Singapore and Davao.

Thailand

You can also look for cheap fares from Bangkok – Bangkok to Manila can cost you around US$210.

Vietnam

Manila-Saigon one way/return is priced at US$165/290.

SEA

Although there are plenty of ship routes *within* the Philippines, international services are more scarce.

Indonesia

One of the most popular routes is the monthly run between Davao and Bitung, the port for Manado in northern Sulawesi (US$10 to US$65; 164,000 rp in *ekonomi* class from Bitung; 36 hours), with Pelni's *Tilongkabila*.

Malaysia

Passenger ferries operate between Sandakan and Zamboanga. The trip takes 18 hours and costs from RM60.

The MV *Sampaguita* leaves Sandakan on Saturday at 1 pm, arriving in Zamboanga at 8 am the following day. It leaves the Philippines for Sandakan on Thursday at 1 pm, arriving on Friday at 8 am.

The *Lady Mary Joy* departs Sandakan on Thursday at 3 pm, arriving Friday at 9 am; the return trip is on Tuesday at 3 pm, arriving in Sandakan on Wednesday at 9 am. The trip costs US$34 and takes 17 hours.

Getting Around

AIR
Domestic Air Services

At the time of writing, Philippine Airlines (PAL), despite financial and industrial troubles, still had the biggest range of domestic flights and its fares are reasonable (eg Manila to Cebu City for around P1500).

Regardless of who is flying PAL's routes when you read this, the main problem with its routes is that there are often flights from Manila to town A, B or C, but rarely flights *between* towns A, B and C.

Student card holders under 26 years of age are eligible for a 20% discount on round-trip domestic flights and there's a Golden Age Discount of 20% for passengers over 60 years. Also, you'll save around P200 if you can book four days before departure; and even more if you can book eight days beforehand.

For bookings, ring PAL in Manila (☎ 816 6691), or visit the main PAL offices. There's one at the airport, another in Roxas Blvd, Malate, and another in Legaspi St, Makati.

With PAL's future unclear, it's a good thing there are several other domestic airlines offering a wide range of fares, flights and standards. These include (all in Manila):

PHILIPPINES AIR FARES

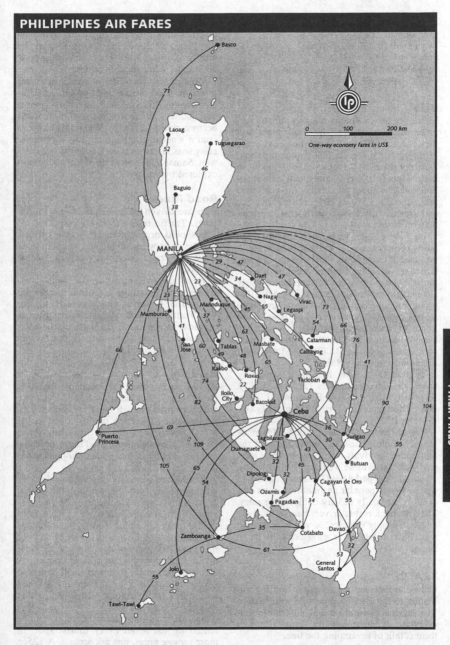

One-way economy fares in US$

0   100   200 km

Basco

71

Laoag

52

Tuguegarao

46

Baguio

38

MANILA

29   47

23   34   Daet   47

Naga   Virac

Mamburao   Marinduque   45   55   Legaspi   73

41   37   63   54   66

San   Tablas   Masbate   Catarman   76

Jose   60   49   48   Calbayog   41

Kalibo   65

74   Roxas   Tacloban

22

Iloilo   90   104

City   Bacolod   55

82

Cebu   36   Surigao

Puerto   69   30

Princesa   109   Tagbilaran   43   Butuan

Dumaguete   32   45   Cagayan de Oro

105   65   Dipolog   32

54   Ozamis   34   38   55

Pagadian   Davao

Zamboanga   35   Cotabato   53   32

61   General

Jolo   Santos

55

Tawi-Tawi

Air Ads (☎ 833 3264)
Air Philippines (☎ 843 7770)
Asian Spirit (☎ 551 1723)
Cebu Pacific (☎ 636 4938)
GrandAir (☎ 524 1784)
Pacific Airways (☎ 832 2731)

BUS

There are an enormous number of bus services running all over the Philippines and they are generally very economical. As a rule of thumb, on a regular bus you cover about 2km per peso and average about 50km an hour. Thus a 100km journey will cost about P50 and take about two hours. Air-con buses are generally 15% to 20% more expensive and trips on gravel roads are normally pricier than on sealed roads.

Departures are very frequent although buses sometimes leave early if they're full – take care if there's only one bus a day! People like to travel early, when it's cool, so there'll probably be more buses. Air-con buses nearly always leave early in the morning. Note that on Luzon, all roads lead to Manila and so do all bus routes. If you're heading from South Luzon to North Luzon you'll have to take one bus into Manila and another out. The main companies include BLTB, JAM, Victory Liner and Philippine Rabbit.

Typical fares from Manila for ordinary buses include: Alaminos (237km, P115), Baguio (250km, P120), Batangas (110km, P60), Olongapo (126km, P80) and Legaspi (544km, P260).

You should also look out for L-300 minibuses, which are used in many parts of the Philippines as rivals to regular buses. Operated privately, these vehicles usually hang around the car parks near bus depots and take passengers to popular destinations in air-con comfort, normally at very competitive rates. The drawback is that drivers hate to head off with half empty vehicles, so you may have to wait indefinitely – or pay extra to leave straight away.

TRAIN

Only one rail service remains: south from Manila to the Bicol region of South Luzon. The service is so slow and unreliable that everyone recommends the bus, although there is talk of revamping the line.

CAR & MOTORCYCLE

Traffic is getting steadily worse in the major cities, despite new road systems and all sorts of innovative schemes. In Manila, one plan involves vehicles being forced to park on only one side of the street in a desperate attempt to reduce double parking.

On the less travelled islands, roads are often unsealed even around provincial capitals, making tricycle and motorbike jaunts very juddery. In the wet, many of these roads become rivers of sludge. When this happens (and it's not restricted to the July-December rainy season), islands such as Mindoro, Palawan, Samar and even parts of Luzon are best explored by sea or air.

Road Rules

Cars are driven on the right in the Philippines. Traffic rules are rarely respected, so you should drive defensively at all times. Whatever happens, avoid the temptation to copy the crazy overtaking style of local drivers.

As a pedestrian, be aware that zebra (pedestrian) crossings are often merely for decoration. Never assume cars will stop for you. Traffic lights also tend to be regarded as optional information. Be particularly wary after dark, when some drivers don't even slow down for a red light.

Rental

Apart from international companies like Avis (☎ 526 2847) and Hertz (☎ 832 0520), there are more than enough local car rental companies, many of which can be found in the Manila tourist area, Ermita. Swagman Travel (☎ 524 5816) also has a good range of deals, and cars can be picked up and dropped off at the various offices.

Rentals are generally offered on a daily or weekly basis, with or without the added expense of a driver. The average newish drive-yourself four-seater sedan will cost around P1000 per day (plus fuel). Most places demand that you be not less than 21 and not more than 65 years of age. An international driver's licence shouldn't be necessary. A clause in the rental agreement small print also says cars can only be driven on surfaced roads: this really cramps your style in this part of the world.

Motorcycles and motor scooters can be rented in just about every tourist spot. In more remote areas, just ask around. A 125cc Honda or Suzuki will cost you P500 to P700 per day. A helmet should be worn, but finding one can be difficult.

BICYCLE

Touring the Philippines by bike is still a bit unusual. A German couple who rode from Davao in the south of Mindanao via the islands to Manila in four weeks caused quite a stir.

HITCHING

As transport costs are so low, it's hardly worth anyone's while to hitchhike, as jeepneys are cheap, plentiful and always willing to pick you up. No Filipino would ever dream of sticking their thumb out for a lift, even if they didn't have the money for a ticket. In any case, drivers usually expect a few pesos if they give lifts 'because of the high price of petrol'. Needless to say, hitching in the guerilla territory of Mindanao is positively suicidal.

WALKING

This is definitely a good way to meet people and discover the joys of nature. There's always a way to finish the rest of your journey, as the entire archipelago is crisscrossed with paths and trails. With the right planning, a hiker can avoid practically all contact with cobbles, asphalt and exhaust gases.

BOAT

Getting around by boat is much easier than in Indonesia – it's not so much 'Will there be a boat this week?' as 'Will there be a boat today?' – and the answer is often 'Yes, this morning'. Boats are cheap, usually comfortable and pretty fast. They range from the high class multidecked WG&A/SuperFerry ships and luxury passenger catamarans, to the smallest of outriggers (known locally as *bangcas*, or pumpboats). Whatever the vessel, be prepared for long unscheduled stops and try to keep a flexible schedule.

Ferry prices vary widely, but as a guide, the average fare between Manila and Cebu City is around P700 (22 hours), and between Manila and Puerto Princesa it's about P550 (20 hours). Inquire about student discounts: some shipping lines give 20 or 30%.

Travellers should note that there are a number of infamous routes, most of which involve bangcas attempting open sea crossings in rough weather (eg Palawan to Panay, and Panay to Mindoro) or ageing tubs being dangerously overcrowded (eg the MV *Romblon* to/from Romblon Island).

On most ferries, food and drinks are available, but the on-board menu is often limited to instant noodles and soft drinks. Camp beds or bunks are standard on most of the long-haul ferries – but make sure you choose a bed well away from the deafening engine.

The following shipping companies cover most of the Philippines:

Delta Fast Ferries
  (☎ 232 6237) Cebu City
Milagrosa Lines
  (☎ 433 4806) Puerto Princesa
Negros Navigation/SeaAngel
  (☎ 434 5926) Cebu City
Sulpicio Lines
  (☎ 241 9701) Manila
WG&A/SuperFerry
  (☎ 894 3211) Manila

LOCAL TRANSPORT
Bus

Philippine buses come in all shapes and sizes, from rusty boxes on wheels to luxury air-con coaches. Bus depots are dotted throughout town and country, and most buses, unless crammed to the ceiling, will stop if you wave them down. Destinations are usually marked on the front of the bus.

On islands such as Palawan, long-haul road trips are made by jeepney-bus hybrids (overgrown jeepneys with the seats facing forward). On these and other long-distance vehicles, sit on the right and you'll swallow less dust from the oncoming traffic.

Jeepney

The recipe for this Filipino specialty is: take one ex-US Army jeep, put two benches in the back with enough space for about 12 people, paint it every colour of the rainbow, add badges, horns, lights, aerials, air fresheners, mirrors, a tape deck with a selection of Filipino rock music, a chrome horse (or a whole herd of them) and anything else you can think of. Then stuff 20 passengers on those benches for 12, add four more in front, and drive like a maniac. But they're cheap, and you'll find them in cities and doing shorter runs between centres.

The average price for a short trip is P3, and jeepney drivers are generally as honest as Manila taxi drivers are crooked. You pay at the end of the line, or anywhere along the way if you have a rough idea of the price. The driver usually has change. When you want to get off, you can rap on the ceiling, hiss or use the correct term: *'pára'*, Tagalog for 'stop'.

PHILIPPINES

For longer journeys in the country, it's wise to find out what the fare should be before you set off. Try not to be the first person to get into an empty jeepney, because if the driver suddenly takes off you may find you've chartered a 'special ride'. Take care also if several men suddenly get into a jeepney and all try to sit near you. Chances are you're being set up to be pickpocketed – get off and find another vehicle.

Jeepneys are infamously overcrowded in rural areas and you may actually feel safer on the roof, or hanging off the back – but most drivers will insist that all hangers-on hop off (or inside) before reaching a town (or police station).

Taxi

So many horror stories, so little space – suffice to say that Manila taxi drivers are about as crooked as they come. But at least when they rip you off they do it with a smile. Insist that drivers turn on the meter, watch that it works properly, keep your pack beside you or on your lap, and get out straight away if you suspect you're being taken for a ride in more ways than one. But don't write off every Filipino cab driver – in many smaller Philippine cities, taxi drivers can be disconcertingly honest.

Tricycle

Found in various forms in most cities and towns, the tricycle is the Filipino rickshaw: a little roofed sidecar bolted to a bicycle or motorcycle. Often garishly decorated à la the jeepney, the tricycle has a carrying capacity of two or three people, but six and seven is not unknown.

There are basically three types of tricycle rates: the rate for locals, the rate for tourists, and the outrageous rate for tourists. In many touristy areas, tricycle riders of the motorbike variety will quote P150 as a matter of course – especially if night is coming on and/or the trip involves unsealed roads. Locals would pay a fraction of this price, so feel free to haggle.

For the record, the official tricycle rates are: P3 for every 2km, 50c for every kilometre after that, or P50 per hour.

Calesa

Calesas are two-wheeled horse carriages found in Manila's Chinatown, Vigan (North Luzon) and Cebu City (where they're known as *tartanillas*).

Bangca

The jeepney of the sea, the bangca (also known as a pumpboat) is a narrow outrigger with or without a roof. Bangcas ply regular routes between islands and are also available for hire per day for diving, sightseeing or just getting around. On many islands, the bangca is a far better option than going overland. Standard bangcas are licensed to carry six people. Trips should be priced per boat, rather than per person, and the average day trip costs about P600.

Manila

The capital of the Philippines and by far the largest city, Manila has a population of over 12 million. It's not a city of great interest in itself; it's really just an arrival and departure point for the rest of the Philippines. Although bitter fighting at the end of WWII did a pretty thorough job of flattening the city, there are still some places of interest in Intramuros, the oldest part of the capital. But once you've seen the Spanish ruins here, you've pretty much seen all Manila has to offer in an historical sense.

The other attraction is entertainment – there are countless reasonably priced restaurants, pubs and clubs.

Orientation

Although it sprawls a great distance along Manila Bay, the main places of interest and/or importance to the visitor are fairly central and concentrated just south of the Pasig River. Immediately south of the river is Intramuros, the old walled Spanish town, where many of Manila's historic buildings are situated. South of that is the long rectangle of Rizal Park (the Luneta), the lungs of the central area.

Farther south again, the districts of Ermita and Malate provide the so-called tourist belt with numerous hotels, restaurants and travel agencies. Here you'll find not only the big international hotels but many of the medium and low-priced places. This is the visitor's central area; the businessperson's centre is Makati – several kilometres away.

By the way, locals won't know what you're talking about if you pronounce Roxas Blvd as it looks – it's actually pronounced 'ro-hoss'.

Maps The giant Philippine Auto Club Metro-Manila map, with a scale of 1:20,000, is sold at all National Book Store outlets (P145).

Information

Tourist Offices DOT's grand office (☎ 523 8411) is in Ermita at the Taft Ave end of Rizal Park (see Tourist Offices in the earlier Facts for the Visitor section). There's also a smaller DOT office at Manila's Ninoy Aquino international airport (NAIA).

Money Most moneychanging facilities are open daily until 10 pm. Mind you, after 9 pm, and on the weekend and public holidays, the exchange rate is not the best. The larger department stores also offer moneychanging services outside regular banking hours. American Express (☎ 815 9311) is in the Ace Bldg, Makati. It's open Monday to Friday from 9 am to 5.30 pm. All branches of the Equitable Bank give cash advances on major credit cards (see also Money in the earlier Facts for the Visitor section).

Post & Communications The main post office, for poste restante, is near the river in Intramuros. There's a small office at the harbour end of Rizal Park, near the Manila Hotel, which is generally not so busy.

There are several communication companies in Manila. Eastern Telecom, PLDT and PT&T all have several branches where telephone and fax services are available.

Email & Internet Access Most of Manila's big shopping malls have at least one Internet cafe. A common name is Universe Cybercafe, which has a branch at the Glorietta shopping centre (☎ 840 1088) in Makati, among others.

Also, the painfully groovy Coffee California Internet group has several Internet outlets, including one on the 2nd floor of the brand new Pan Pacific Hotel, on the corner of Adriatico and General Miguel Malvar Sts, Malate. It's called the Indiana Cafe. The average rate is around P60 per half hour, and snacks and coffee are available in most cases.

Travel Agencies Manila's travel agents are much of a muchness, but for organised tours, as well as domestic and international air tickets, check out Interisland Travel & Tours (☎ 522 1405), 1322-H Roxas Blvd, Ermita, and Blue Horizons Travel & Tours (☎ 813 5011), Shangri-La Hotel Manila, Ayala Ave, Makati.

Bookshops The National Book Store, at 665 Rizal Ave in Santa Cruz, is the largest bookstore in the Philippines; it has a number of other branches in Metro Manila, eg at Harrison Plaza. The Solidaridad Book Shop at 531 Padre Faura St, Ermita, is particularly good for political books.

Libraries The National Library (☎ 525 1314) is on TM Kalaw St, Ermita.

Cultural Centres Alliance Française (☎ 813 2681) is in the Keystone Bldg, Gil Puyat Ave, Makati.

The British Council (☎ 721 1981) is on 73rd St, Quezon City.

The Goethe Institut Manila (☎ 722 4671) is at 687 Aurora Blvd, Quezon City.

Laundry The Laundryette Britania in Santa Monica St, Ermita, between Mabini and MH del Pilar Sts, is fast and reliable. Same-day service is possible and the average price for shirts is P15. It's open daily from 7.30 am to 10 pm.

Medical Services Reliable hospitals in Manila include:

Makati Medical Center
(☎ 815 9911) 2 Amorsolo St, Makati
Manila Doctors Hospital
(☎ 523 3010) 667 United Nations Ave, Ermita

Emergency In case of emergency, the Tourist Assistance Unit (☎ 524 1728) is available around the clock.

Other useful phone numbers: Emergency police ☎ 59 9011, Information ☎ 114.

Dangers & Annoyances Beware of overfriendly Filipinos in Manila. Unwary tourists are often pick-pocketed around Rizal Park. Beware of the Manila slum areas such as Tondo too. It's here that 'a mad scramble to pick your pockets ensues', as one visitor commented! See also Dangers & Annoyances in the earlier Facts for the Visitor section.

Intramuros

The Spanish rebuilt this former Chinese settlement as a wooden fort, replacing the timber with stone in 1590 and gradually extending it until it became the walled city of Intramuros. The walls were 3km long, 13m thick and 6m high. There were seven main gates to the city, and inside there were 15 churches, six monasteries and lots of Spanish – who kept the Filipinos at arm's length.

The walls are just about all that was left

METRO MANILA

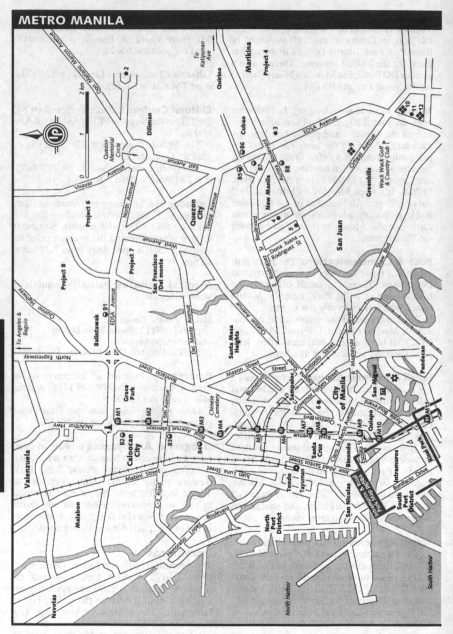

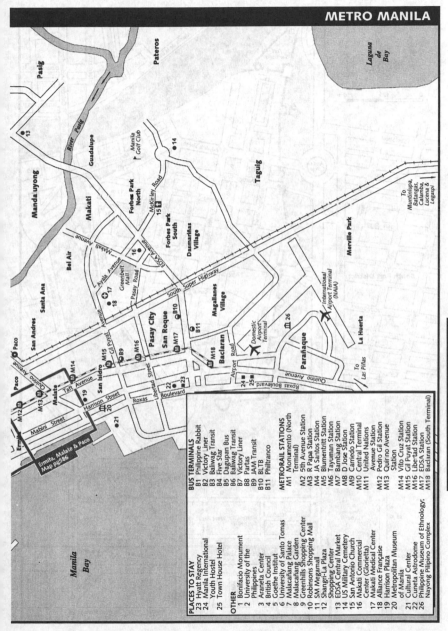

METRO MANILA

PLACES TO STAY
23 Hyatt Regency
24 Manila International
   Youth Hostel
25 Town House Hotel

OTHER
1 Bonifacio Monument
2 University of the
   Philippines
3 Araneta Center
4 British Council
5 Goethe Institut
6 University of Santo Tomas
7 Malacañang Palace
8 Malacañang Garden
9 Greenhills Shopping Center
10 Robinsons Shopping Mall
11 SM Megamall
12 Shangri-La Plaza
   Shopping Center
13 EDSA Central Market
14 US Military Cemetery
15 San Antonio Church
16 Makati Commercial
   Center (Glorietta)
17 Makati Medical Center
18 Alliance Française
19 Harrison Plaza
20 Metropolitan Museum
   of Manila
21 Cultural Center
22 Cuneta Astrodome
26 Philippine Museum of Ethnology;
   Nayong Pilipino Complex

BUS TERMINALS
B1 Philippine Rabbit
B2 Victory_iner
B3 Baliwag Transit
B4 Five Star
B5 Dagupan Bus
B6 Baliwag Transit
B7 Victory Liner
B8 Partas
B9 JAM Transit
B10 BLTB
B11 Philtranco

METRORAIL STATIONS
M1 Monumento (North
   Terminal)
M2 5th Avenue Station
M3 R Papa Station
M4 JA Santos Station
M5 Blumentritt Station
M6 Tayuman Station
M7 Bambang Station
M8 D Jose Station
M9 Carriedo Station
M10 Central Terminal
M11 United Nations
   Avenue Station
M12 Pedro Gil Station
M13 Quirino Avenue
   Station
M14 Vito Cruz Station
M15 Gil Puyat Station
M16 Libertad Station
M17 EDSA Station
M18 Baclaran (South Terminal)

PHILIPPINES

INTRAMUROS & RIZAL PARK

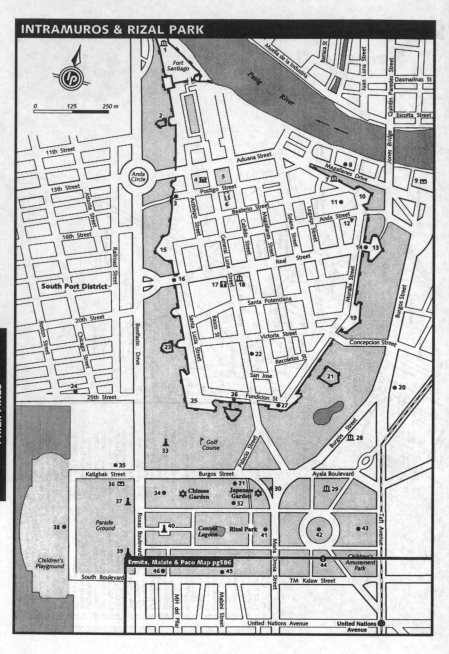

0   125   250 m

Pasig River

Muelle de la Industria

Barraca St

Juan Luna Street

Quintin Paredes St

Dasmariñas St

Jones Bridge

Escolta Street

1 Fort Santiago

2

11th Street

Anda Circle

13th Street

Atlanta Street

16th Street

Railroad Street

Aduana Street

Postigo Street

Archbigo Street

4 5

3

6

Beaterio Street

Cabildo Street

General Luna Street

Magallanes Street

Solana Street

Legaspi Street

Anda Street

Real Street

Muralla Street

Magallanes Drive

8

7

9

11

10

12

14 13

15

South Port District

Bonifacio Drive

Chicago Street

Boston Street

20th Street

16

17 18

Santa Potenciana

Basco St

Santa Lucia Street

19

Concepcion Street

Burgos Street

23

Victoria Street

22

Recoletos St

San Jose

21

20

24

25th Street

25

26 Fundicion St

27

33

Golf Course

Palacio Street

28

Burgos Street

35

Katigbak Street

Burgos Street

Ayala Boulevard

29

36

34

Chinese Garden

31

Japanese Garden

32

30

37

Parade Ground

Roxas Boulevard

38

40

Central Lagdon

Rizal Park

41

42

43

Taft Avenue

39

Children's Playground

South Boulevard

Emita, Malate & Paco Map pg586

46

45

Maria Orosa Street

44

Children's Amusement Park

MH del Pilar

Mabini Street

TM Kalaw Street

United Nations Avenue

United Nations Avenue

PHILIPPINES

INTRAMUROS & RIZAL PARK

1	Rizal Shrine Museum	17	San Agustin Church	32	Concerts in the Park &
2	Revellin de San	18	Casa Manila Museum;		Open-Air Stage
	Francisco		San Luis Complex	33	Legaspi & Urdaneta
3	Puerta del Postigo	19	Bastion de Dilao		Monument
4	Palacio del Gobernador	20	Manila City Hall	34	Rizal's Execution Site
5	Plaza Roma	21	Revellin de Recoletos	35	Manila Hotel
6	Manila Cathedral	22	Philippine Art, Craft &	36	Rizal Park Post Office
7	Puerta Isabel II		Culture Center	37	Carabao Statue
8	Immigration Office	23	Fortin San Pedro	38	Quirino Grandstand
9	Main Post Office	24	Bureau of Quarantine	39	Tamaraw Statue
10	Bastion de San	25	Bastion de San Diego	40	Rizal Memorial
	Gabriel	26	Puerta Real	41	Floral Clock
11	Letran College	27	Bastion de San Andres	42	Agrifina Circle & Skating Rink
12	McDonald's	28	National Museum	43	Philippines Model Map
13	Revellin del Parian	29	National Museum of the	44	Department of Tourism
14	Puerta del Parian		Filipino People		(DOT) Office
15	Bastion de Santa Lucia	30	Artificial Waterfall	45	National Library
16	Puerta de Santa Lucia	31	Planetarium	46	Rizal's Fountain

after WWII finished off what US General Douglas MacArthur had started. During the 1930s he had his HQ there and 'modernised' the place by knocking down lots of old buildings and widening those nasty narrow streets. A few years ago, renovations finally started on the remaining buildings. Worth seeing are the beautifully restored **Casa Manila** in the San Luis complex and **Philippine Art, Craft & Culture Center,** both on General Luna St.

The church and monastery of **San Agustin** is one of the few buildings left from the earliest construction. It was here in 1898 that the last Spanish governor of Manila surrendered to the Filipinos.

The **Manila Cathedral** is also in Intramuros and has a history that reads like that of many other Spanish-built churches in the Philippines: built 1581, damaged (typhoon) 1582, destroyed (fire) 1583, rebuilt 1592, partially destroyed (earthquake) 1600, rebuilt 1614, destroyed (earthquake) 1645, rebuilt 1654-71, destroyed (earthquake) 1863, rebuilt 1870-79, destroyed (WWII) 1945, rebuilt 1954-58; on that average an earthquake should knock it down again in 2006.

The ruins of the old **Fort Santiago** stand just north of the cathedral. They are now used as a pleasant park – you can climb up top for the view over the Pasig River. The fort's darkest days took place during WWII, when it was used as a prison by the Japanese. Today, the most interesting part of the fort is the **Rizal Shrine Museum,** which contains many items used or made by the Filipino martyr. The room in which he was imprisoned before his execution can be seen here.

The fort is open daily from 8 am to 10 pm, and admission is P15, children P5.

Rizal Park

Intramuros is separated from Ermita, the tourist centre, by Rizal Park (also known as the Luneta). It's a meeting and entertainment place for all of Manila – particularly on Sunday when there are all kinds of activities.

At the bay end of the park is the **Rizal Memorial.** Close by is **Rizal's execution site,** where a firing squad pointing their weapons at Rizal forms the dramatic theme of a group of statues.

The **planetarium** is flanked by a **Japanese** and a **Chinese garden** – favourite meeting spots for young couples, although it's a little difficult to hide behind a bonsai tree for a passionate clinch. Further up there are **fountains,** a **floral clock,** a **roller-skating circuit** and the tourist office.

At the Taft Ave end there's a gigantic pond with a three-dimensional **map of the Philippines.** Once you know a little about the geography of the country, it's fascinating to wander around it and contemplate just how many islands there are. Also at this end of the park is a popular **children's amusement park,** with some impressive dinosaur and monster figures.

Museums

Manila has lots of museums, including the **National Museum** on Burgos St, adjacent to Rizal Park. Admission is free, and it's open Tuesday to Saturday, 9 am to noon and 1 to

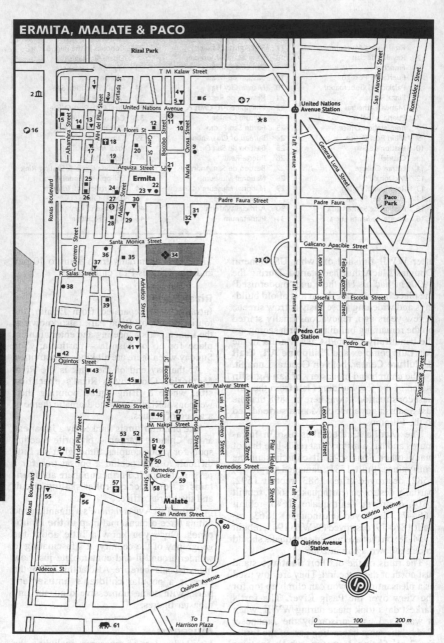

ERMITA, MALATE & PACO

ERMITA, MALATE & PACO

PLACES TO STAY		PLACES TO EAT		OTHER	
6	Holiday Inn; Avis	1	Hong Kong Tea House	2	Museo Pambata
12	Hotel Soriente; International	3	Maxim's Tea House		(Children's Museum)
	Supermarket	4	KFC	7	Manila Doctors Hospital
14	Swagman Hotel	5	McDonald's	8	Western Police Station
15	Bayview Park Hotel	10	Max's	9	Court of Appeals
19	Yasmin Apartelle;	13	7-Eleven	11	Equitable Bank
	Tadel Apartelle	17	Myrna's	16	US Embassy
20	City Garden Hotel	21	Sea Food Market	18	Ermita Church
24	Royal Palm Hotel	23	Kashmir; Kamayan	22	Solidaridad Book Shop
25	Sandico Apartel	29	München Grill Pub	27	Philippine National Bank
26	Iseya Hotel;	30	7-Eleven		(PNB)
	Rooftop Restaurant	31	Mrs Wong Tea House	33	Philippines General Hospital
28	Mabini Pension	32	Food Stalls	34	Robinsons Shopping Mall
35	Centrepoint Hotel	37	7-Eleven	36	Laundryette Britania
39	Ermita Tourist Inn	40	Cafe Mondial	38	Philippine Airlines (PAL)
42	Manila Diamond	41	Zamboanga Restaurant	44	Endangered Species
	Hotel	48	Sala Thai		Cafe Bar
43	Pension Natividad	49	Racks	47	Verve Room
45	Pan Pacific Hotel	50	Cafe Adriatico	51	Ten Years After
46	Joward's Pension	54	Shakey's Malate	56	WG&A; Super Ferry
52	Malate Pensionne;	55	Aristocrat	57	Malate Church
	Post 1771	58	Cafe Adriatico 1900	60	San Andreas Market
53	Juen's Place	59	Penguin Cafe Gallery	61	Manila Zoo

5 pm. The **Ayala Museum** on Makati Ave, Makati, is open Tuesday to Sunday from 9.30 am to 7.30 pm; entry is P40. It has a series of dioramas and a wide range of regularly changing exhibitions focusing on Philippine history.

In Intramuros, there's the **San Agustin Museum** in the Augustine monastery at the San Agustin Church. The **Casa Manila** is a fine restored colonial-era home right across the road. The museum is open Tuesday to Sunday from 9 am to noon and 1 to 6 pm, and entry costs P30.

The **Cultural Center Museum** is in the bayside Cultural Center in Malate (see the Metro Manila map), which is open Tuesday to Sunday from 9 am to 6 pm. Also at the Cultural Center complex is the **Coconut Palace**, a guesthouse erected for a visit by the pope in 1981. It's open daily except Monday from 9 am to 4 pm, and admission costs P100, including a guided tour which takes just under an hour. The **Metropolitan Museum of Manila** in the Central Bank Complex on Roxas Blvd, Malate, has various changing displays. It's open Tuesday to Sunday from 9 am to 6 pm. Admission is free.

Other museums include the **Museum of Arts & Sciences** at the University of Santo Tomas in Sampaloc, and the **Philippine Museum of Ethnology** – which has displays depicting Filipino minority groups – at the Nayong Pilipino Complex in Pasay City.

The **Museo ng Malacañang** is on Jose P Laurel St. When you visit the Malacañang Palace in San Miguel, across the Pasig River from central Manila, it seems as if the family of former president Marcos has just left. This impressive place was built by a Spanish aristocrat and was used as a presidential home until Cory Aquino opened the main building as a museum. It's open for guided groups on Monday and Tuesday from 9 am to noon and from 1 to 3 pm, and Thursday and Friday to noon; admission is P200. Sometimes the palace is closed for official functions so call (☎ 521 2307) to check before you go. Jeepneys run from Quiapo Market at Quezon Bridge to the palace.

A great place for the kids is the **Museo Pambata** (Children's Museum), on Roxas Blvd, Ermita. Look for the helicopter in the car park. It's open Tuesday to Saturday from 9 am to 5 pm, and Sunday from 1 to 5 pm (lunch break noon to 1 pm). Admission is P50, children P30.

Chinatown & Chinese Cemetery

North of the river, Chinatown is interesting to wander through. The luxurious Chinese Cemetery, about 2km north of Chinatown near the JA Santos Metrorail station, is a

PHILIPPINES

bizarre attraction. It's in the north of Santa Cruz, just where Rizal Ave becomes Rizal Ave Extension. A tricycle from the station to the South Gate will be about P10.

Places to Stay

Hostels About 3km north of the airport in the direction of Malate and Ermita, you'll find the *Manila International Youth Hostel* (☎ 832 0680). It's located on Tomas Claudio St, Parañaque, near Roxas Blvd, and has dorm beds only for P150 with fan or P200 with air-con. Hostelling International (HI) members get a P30 discount.

Guesthouses A few of the cheaper guesthouses and pension houses offer dormitory accommodation. There are numerous small places around Ermita and Malate, ranging from rock bottom upwards in standards and price.

The *Town House Hotel* (☎ 833 1939) on Bayview Drive, Parañaque, has everything from dorm beds (P120) to big doubles with private bath, air-con and TV (P900). Although some rooms are a little too close to thunderous Roxas Blvd for light sleepers, it's a short cab drive to the airport, does good, cheap meals and is great for meeting like-minded travellers.

There are several inexpensive places to stay in the Remedios Circle area of Adriatico St in Malate. The big one here is the *Malate Pensionne* (☎ 523 8304) at 1771 Adriatico St. Although still popular, this place lost a lot of its simple, friendly charm when its room rates rose sharply and a pretentious glasshouse cafe was installed. A dorm bed costs P220/242 with fan/air-con. Rooms cost P440/P550 without/with fan, P770 with fan and bath, P825 with air-con and bath and, lastly, P1485 with air-con, TV, kitchen and bath. Lockers can be rented and luggage left without charge for up to one week – thereafter it costs P5 per day per piece.

Down the ramshackle lane running off Adriatico St beside the Malate Pensionne, the unassuming little *Juen's Place* is a friendly, family-run guesthouse with singles/doubles at P180/240. It's a mattresses-on-the-floor kind of place, but it's cheap and decent.

Joward's Pension House (☎ 521 4845) at 1726 Adriatico St, Malate, is a great little place for the price: rooms are P180/280, all with fan and common bath. The entrance is next to Joward's Hot Pot Restaurant.

The *Pension Natividad* (☎ 521 0524) at 1690 MH del Pilar St, Malate, has replaced the Malate Pensionne as *the* place to stay for budget travellers in the know. Here you can enjoy a rare, relaxing escape from the usual Manila chaos and, unlike other places, you can sit outside in comfort. It has dorm beds with fan for P200, singles with fan and bath for P650 and doubles with air-con and bath for P900. There's also a coffee shop and staff will look after left luggage.

In the Ermita area, the long-established *Mabini Pension* (☎ 524 5404) at 1337 Mabini St has singles with fan from P350, doubles with fan and bath from P550 to P650 and air-con doubles with bath for P850. The rooms are not all necessarily attractive, but the staff will help take care of visa extensions and look after left luggage.

There are two self-styled apartelles, or, more appropriately, little pension houses, on Arquiza St between Mabini and MH del Pilar Sts in Ermita. The more pleasant of the two is the *Yasmin Apartelle* (☎ 524 5134), which is quiet with a little courtyard and friendly rooms. Singles/doubles with fan and common bath are P250/500. Doubles with air-con and cable TV start at P750. At the *Tadel Apartelle* (☎ 521 9766) next door, singles with fan go for P450, or P700 with air-con. Twins with air-con are P800.

Hotels Manila has a number of mid-range hotels; some are only slightly more expensive than the pension houses and guesthouses, but most cost at least twice as much.

The *Sandico Apartel* (☎ 523 8130) on MH del Pilar St, Ermita, has passable, though ageing, rooms with air-con, bath and TV; singles/doubles cost P600/P650.

At 1549 Mabini St, the *Ermita Tourist Inn* (☎ 521 8770) is pleasant and fairly clean; air-con rooms with bath for P610 to P650 are worth the money.

Directly above the International Supermarket, the *Hotel Soriente* (☎ 523 9480) is at 595 A Flores St, on the corner of JC Bocobo St, Ermita, and has OK rooms with bath and cable TV for P1195.

The *Iseya Hotel* (☎ 523 8166) at 1241 MH del Pilar St, Ermita, has a 24 hour rooftop restaurant and quite comfortable singles/doubles with TV, fridge, phone, air-con and bath for P1050/1150. Be choosy though – the rooms facing MH del Pilar St are quite noisy.

One block farther on, at 1227 Mabini St, the clean, friendly and accommodating *Royal Palm Hotel* (☎ 522 1515) has well maintained rooms complete with air-con, bath, fridge and TV for P1716/2145.

Also on Mabini St, Ermita, the *City Garden Hotel* (☎ 536 1451) is owned by the same company as the Royal Palm. It has clean rooms for US$48/56, plus a complimentary breakfast.

Other places in the middle bracket include the central and convenient *Centrepoint Hotel* (☎ 521 2751) at 1430 Mabini St, Ermita. It has a big, swanky lobby with a small Internet cafe. Swish air-con rooms with bath, fridge and cable TV start at P1450 – and you get a free drink when you check in.

The *Swagman Hotel* (☎ 523 8541) at 411 A Flores St, Ermita is the frenetic headquarters of the Australian-run Swagman chain of travel agents and hotels. Slightly gloomy rooms with cable TV, fridge, air-con and bath start at P2260.

Places to Eat

Manila is full of places to eat – with all types of food and all types of prices. Apart from Filipino food and a variety of other Asian cuisines, there are also western fast-food operators and a choice of fixed-price buffets at the best hotels.

The recommendations that follow are essentially in Ermita and Malate because most visitors will be staying there. There are plenty of other restaurants in Makati, Binondo, Santa Cruz and other parts of Manila.

Breakfast You can get a good coffee for about P35 at the *Coffee Beanery*, which has branches at the Greenbelt Mall, Makati, and on the 3rd floor of Robinsons shopping mall, Ermita.

If you want to combine coffee with a bit of Internet surfing, see the Manila, Internet Resources entry.

For fresh fruit concoctions for around P65, try the little *Cafe Mondial* on Adriatico St near the corner of Pedro Gil St, Malate. It's open from 7 am daily.

If you like your breakfast huge and meaty, there's a carnivore's breakfast (average dish P90) at *Racks*, specialising in ribs. This new chain includes stores inside Robinsons shopping mall, Ermita, and at Remedios Circle, Malate. It's open from 7 am daily.

The little *München Grill Pub* on Mabini St near the corner of Padre Faura St, Ermita, does hearty 'international breakfasts' for around P100. It opens daily around 10 am.

If you really want to fill up for the day, try the all-you-can-eat breakfast buffets at Manila's big hotels. The Holiday Inn, United Nations Ave, Ermita, charges P394. The Hyatt Regency, Roxas Blvd, Pasay City, charges P595. They start serving around 6 or 7 am.

Filipino In Ermita, a good hunting ground for tasty and cheap Filipino food is provided by several *food stalls* on JC Bocobo St, between Padre Faura St and Robinsons shopping mall. The average cost of a meal for one, with rice and one vegetable or meat serving, is around P60. On MH del Pilar St, Ermita, *Myrna's* is a popular little place appealing essentially to local people. The speciality here is grilled chicken and *bangus* (milkfish). A meal typically costs about P80. It's open daily 7 am to 11.30 pm, closed on Sunday.

Definitely more expensive – but worth it – is the *Kamayan* on Padre Faura St in Ermita. The name means 'bare hands' because that's what you eat with – knives and forks aren't used. The food is authentic, delicious and well prepared. Across the back of the restaurant is a line of tapped water jars for you to wash your hands before and after eating. A meal costs about P300.

Despite its name, the *Aristocrat*, on the corner of Roxas Blvd and San Andres St, Malate, is good value. This big Filipino restaurant is the most popular of the six Aristocrats in Manila and is open 24 hours. Try lapu-lapu fish (expensive) or the fish soup here – a meal costs about P200.

The *Sea Food Market* at JC Bocobo St, Ermita, positively bounces. You select your fish or other seafood from a display area on one side and it's cooked up by a squad of short-order cooks lined up along an open window on the street side. They're all frantically stirring woks, scooping pots and juggling frying pans while flames leap high. It's wonderful entertainment for passers-by. But beware: fish, shrimps, crabs etc are sold by weight. The prices given are per 100g.

Chinese Manila has a great number of Chinese restaurants. For simple and economical Chinese food try *Mrs Wong Tea House* next to the food stalls near Robinsons shopping mall, Ermita. A meal will cost from P75 to P200.

Other good, inexpensive Chinese restaurants include the *Hong Kong Tea House* and *Maxim's Tea House*, both on MH del Pilar St, Ermita. The Hong Kong Tea House is open 24 hours daily. There are far more *Chinese restaurants* across the river in China-town and Binondo.

Indian Next to the Kamayan Restaurant on Padre Faura St there's good north Indian food at *Kashmir*. It's about P400 for a meal.

Thai The *Sala Thai* at 866 JM Napkil St, Malate, specialises in spicy *tom yum* soup. Dinner is about P300 per head.

Western There are plenty of western restau-rants. For example, the very pleasant *Cafe Adriatico* at 1790 Adriatico St, Malate, is a good place for a drink or a meal: there are tables outside and others, upstairs, overlook the Remedios Circle street scene. The food ranges from burgers to pasta. It's not cheap, but it's a relaxed, stylish place to dine. Di-rectly opposite is *Cafe Adriatico 1900*, which is a pretty good clone.

Near the Natividad Pension on MH del Pilar St, Malate, the *Endangered Species Cafe Bar* offers huge servings of (no, not en-dangered species) grills, seafood, pasta and pizza for around P250. Despite the environ-mental theme, there's not much here for vegetarians. Desserts are excellent.

There's 24 hour food and beer at the *Rooftop Restaurant*, on top of the Iseya Hotel at the corner of Padre Faura and MH del Pilar Sts, Ermita. Mexican food can be found at *Tia Maria's* on Remedios St, on the corner of Madre Ignacia St, Malate. *Max's* on Maria Orosa St, Ermita, is one of 16 branch-es around the city and offers a variety of chicken dishes for about P150.

Vegetarian Vegetarian restaurants are ex-tremely thin on the ground in Manila. The *Bhodi*, inside the Tutuban Mall in Tondo, is a dedicated vegetarian restaurant which serves a wide selection of dishes. The average meal is P90. The *Kashmir* (see under Indian) does fine dhal dishes for P140.

Fast Food & Cheap Eats Manila has bucketloads of the usual high-profile, low-stimulus fast-food chains. *Jollibee* is a local burger chain with numerous branches, but the fastest growing local fast-food chain is *Kenny Rogers Roasters*, which just opened its 18th flesh-friendly store in Luzon. If you have trouble finding any of these places dotted all around the city, just head for a shopping mall. Even in the old Spanish walled city of Intra-muros there's now a McDonald's!

Self-Catering Apart from numerous 24-hour 7-Elevens, one of the best and handiest food markets is the *San Andres Market*, a few blocks east of Remedios Circle in Malate. It's open daily, piled high with every kind of fruit and vegie, and surrounded by bustling shops.

Entertainment

Cinemas Movies, both local and foreign, are advertised in the daily press. The best cinemas can be found in shopping centres such as Robinson's in Ermita, and they're usually beautifully air-conditioned! Admis-sion is P40 to P60.

Nightclubs & Bars The grooviest places in town at the moment are the *Verve Room*, on trendy JM Nakpil St, Malate, and the chic *Giraffe*, ground floor, Ayala Land Bldg, 6750 Ayala Ave, Makati.

Post 1771 on Adriatico St, Malate, is a rowdy place that's open late. In Quezon City, hip nocturnal types hang out at *Katips*, 209 Katipunan Rd.

Bistros & Music Lounges Places for drinking and snacking have become very popular. *Cafe Adriatico* at 1790 Adriatico St, Malate (on the Remedios Circle), started the craze and is still a favourite. Next door, *Ten Years After* has an aeroplane 'crashed' into the roof and shows music videos.

The *Penguin Cafe Gallery*, on Remedios St, Malate, is a popular bohemian haunt open Tuesday to Friday till 1.30 am.

Folk Dances The *Zamboanga Restaurant* on Adriatico St, Malate, has nightly Filipino and Polynesian dancing.

Concerts In idyllic Paco Park, San Marcel-ino St, Paco Park Presents puts on free chamber music at 6 pm on Friday. A free Concert at the Park takes place every Sunday at 5 pm in Rizal Park.

Spectator Sports

Basketball Games of the Philippine Bas-ketball Association (PBA) are mostly played at the Cuneta Astrodome on Roxas Blvd, Pasay City, on Tuesday, Friday and Sunday from around 4 to 7.30 pm. Admission costs anything from P50 to P250. For more infor-mation, call the PBA (☎ 833 4103), or visit the PBA Web site (www1.pba.com.ph/).

Shopping

Manila is certainly not the best place for handicrafts, although in Intramuros there's the Philippine Art, Craft & Culture Center, at 744 General Luna St, which houses Silahis Art & Artifacts, Chang Rong Antiques and the Galeria de las Islas. There's hours of browsing potential here. On Mabini St, Ermita, towards Rizal Park, there are a number of interesting antique shops.

Bargaining is not done as much in the Philippines as in other South-East Asian countries, but you should still haggle a little.

The SM department store, at the Makati Commercial Center, and the Landmark, on Makati Ave, are good for souvenirs if you can't get around the country. Prices are fixed and competitive. Other shopping centres include Robinsons in Ermita, Harrison Plaza in Malate, Glorietta (Makati Commercial Center), Araneta Center in Cubao, SM City in Quezon City and Greenhills in San Juan.

Getting There & Away

Air Most airlines have offices in and around the domestic and international terminals of Manila's airport in Baclaran, but the bigger players such as PAL also have offices in Ermita and Makati. See the Philippines Getting Around section.

Bus Unfortunately, there's no single central long-distance bus station in Manila. Several terminals, including those on EDSA Ave in south Manila, can be reached by Metrorail.

Coming into Manila from other centres, buses will generally display their terminal in Manila. The sign may simply announce that the bus is heading for 'Avenida', 'Cubao' or 'Pasay' and it's assumed you know that these are destinations within Manila. See also Bus in the Philippines Getting Around section.

The following are Manila's main bus companies and depots:

Baliwag Transit (☎ 364 0778), at 199 Rizal Ave Extension, Caloocan City (and EDSA Ave, Quezon City), has buses going north to Aparri, Bulacan Province, Baliwag, San Jose and Tuguegarao.
BLTB (☎ 833 5501) is on EDSA Ave, Pasay City (near Victory and Five Star lines). Buses operate to Nasugbu, Calamba, Batangas, Santa Cruz (for Pagsanjan), Lucena, Naga and Legaspi.
Dagupan (☎ 929 6123) is on New York St, Quezon City. Buses go to Baguio, Dagupan and Lingayen.
Five Star (☎ 361 2781) is at 27 Rizal Ave Extension, Caloocan City. Buses go to Alaminos and Dagupan.

JAM Transit (☎ 932 2914) is on Taft Ave, Pasay City. Buses go to Batangas and Laguna.
Partas (☎ 724 9820) in Aurora Blvd, Quezon City, has buses going north to Laoag, San Fernando (La Union) and Vigan.
Philippine Rabbit (☎ 361 4821) is at 1240 EDSA Ave, Quezon City. Buses operate to various destinations in north-west and central Luzon, including Angeles, Baguio, Balanga, Laoag, Mariveles, San Fernando (Pampanga and La Union), Tarlac and Vigan.
Philtranco (☎ 833 5061) is on EDSA Ave, Pasay City. Get a jeepney towards Baclaran from Taft Ave or MH del Pilar St, or Metrorail to EDSA station. Buses from here run to Daet, Naga, Tabaco, Legaspi, Sorsogon, Samar, Leyte and Mindanao.
Victory Liner (☎ 361 1506) is at 713 Rizal Ave Extension, Caloocan City and 683 EDSA Ave, Quezon City. Buses go to Alaminos, Dagupan, Iba, Olongapo and Mariveles.

Train The Philippine long-distance rail system has contracted to just one route south from Manila to the Bicol region. Although cheap, it's much slower and less reliable than the bus services and it's not recommended. Manila residents claim trains regularly get pelted with stones as they head through the slum areas.

Boat Shipping companies generally advertise departures in the Manila English-language dailies. There are plenty of departures from Manila. Many travel agents in Manila's tourist areas sell tickets for the main passenger lines such as WG&A and Negros Navigation. See the Philippines Getting Around section for details.

Nearly all inter-island departures are made from North Harbor in Manila. If you have trouble finding it, ask a guard opposite Pier 8. A taxi from Ermita to North Harbor should cost about P60. Travelling in the other direction – to Ermita from the harbour – is likely to be more expensive: nobody's meter seems to work properly and the fare is likely to be P100 or more. The jeepney route between the harbour and Ermita is circuitous and slow.

Getting Around

To/From the Airport Domestic and international flights go from the same airport but the terminals are some distance apart. A constant throng of opportunistic taxis awaits you at both terminals (rough prices are P250 to Pasay, P350 to Ermita, P350 to Makati and P380 to Quezon City). Before hailing a cab, ensure you have plenty of spare change. If you want to get into town from the international terminal for around half the price, take the stairs up to the departure level, where you can wait for a taxi dropping off passengers. Mind you, lots of drivers know this trick and wait for victims at the departure level with bargain 'deals'.

An economic alternative is to take a taxi to the Baclaran (South Terminal) Metrorail station for about P40 (provided one will take you this short distance). Baclaran is only 2km from the airport. From there, ride the train to Pedro Gil or UN Ave Metrorail stations near Ermita and Malate tourist areas for P10.

Going to the airport you can take any taxi – and you'll probably have better luck at getting a properly working meter.

Bus There's a comprehensive bus system around Manila, but it's a little difficult to find your way around until you've got some idea of the city's geography and can recognise the destination names.

Buses, like jeepneys, generally display their destinations on a board in front. This might be a large complex like NAIA (the airport), a street name like Ayala (Ayala Ave, Makati) or a whole suburb like Quiapo. Fares are around P3 on regular buses.

Train Metrorail (or Metro Rail Transit, MRT) trains let you sail along above the nightmare traffic on a gloriously elevated line which runs along Taft Ave beside Ermita. Trains get very crowded during rush hour, but they still move faster than the road traffic. The line extends north as far as Monumento (North Terminal) in Caloocan City, and south to Baclaran (South Terminal), quite close to the airport. The fare is a flat P10 and trains run daily from 5 am until 9 pm.

In a tale of pure Manila madness, it was recently revealed that a pylon supporting the Metrorail has blocked the massive viaduct under EDSA Ave. The result: regular flooding of a multilaned arterial by a rail system built to ease traffic congestion.

Car & Motorcycle You might have already guessed that driving and parking in Manila are not much fun. In most areas, on-street parking is limited to three hours and cars overstaying their welcome are towed away (retrieving your impounded car costs P500). On a number of streets, the same applies to cars left after 5 pm. It can also be

illegal to park on such streets between 7 and 10 am. These rules have been made deliberately strict in an effort to encourage drivers off the streets and into parking lots, where the standard rate recently rose to P25 for the first three hours, and P10 every hour after that.

Taxi Sedan taxis have a flag-down rate of P20, which includes the first 500m; thereafter it's P2 for every 250m. With fuel prices steadily rising, however, expect a price hike by the time you read this. Nearly all taxis in Manila nowadays are equipped with air-con.

See also the Taxi entry in the main Getting Around section in this chapter.

Jeepney Jeepneys are very reasonably priced, with fares from P2. As with the buses, it can be a little difficult to find the right one, but they're so cheap it's no great loss to get on the wrong jeepney. Most pass by the city hall, north of Rizal Park. Heading north, they usually split there and either head north-west to Tondo, straight north to Monumento and Caloocan City or north-east to Quezon City, Cubao and beyond.

Heading south, the routes from north of the river converge at City Hall, then split to either go down Taft Ave or MH del Pilar St.

Around Manila

Luzon is the largest island in the Philippines and has a lot to offer apart from Manila. The places in this section can all be visited as day trips from the capital, although a number are worth overnight stops, or can be combined with visits to places further afield. To the north and west of Manila respectively, the attractions are Mt Pinatubo and the WWII battle site of Corregidor at the entrance to Manila Bay. South of Manila there are beach resorts, the Pagsanjan rapids and the Lake Taal volcano. These can be visited en route to South Luzon or to the island of Mindoro.

CORREGIDOR
This small island at the mouth of Manila Bay was the site of the US-Filipino last stand against the invading Japanese. The island certainly wasn't impregnable, as planned, but it held out for a long time. Now it's a national shrine and you can have a look around the underground bunkers and inspect the rusty relics of the fortress armaments.

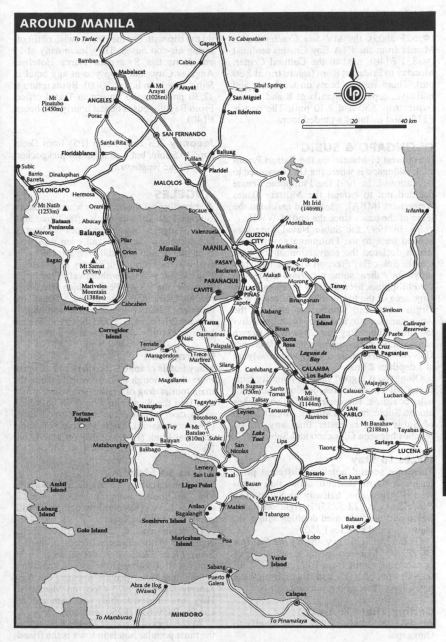

AROUND MANILA

To Tarlac

To Cabanatuan

Bamban

Gapan

Cabiao

Mabalacat

Arayat

Sibul Springs

Dau

Mt
Arayat
(1026m)

San Miguel

Mt
Pinatubo
(1450m)

ANGELES

San Ildefonso

Porac

SAN FERNANDO

Santa Rita

Baliuag

Floridablanca

Pulilan

Plaridel

Subic

Dinalupihan

MALOLOS

Ipo

Barrio
Barreta

OLONGAPO

Hermosa

Bocaue

Mt Irid
(1469m)

Infanta

Mt Natib
(1253m)

Orani

Valenzuela

Montalban

Bataan
Peninsula

Abucay

QUEZON
CITY

Morong

Balanga

Pilar

MANILA

Marikina

Manila
Bay

PASAY

Antipolo

Orion

Baclaran

Taytay

Tanay

Bagac

Limay

PARAÑAQUE

Makati

Mt Samat
(553m)

LAS
PIÑAS

Morong

Binangonan

CAVITE

Siniloan

Mariveles
Mountain
(1388m)

Zapote

Alabang

Talim
Island

Cabcaben

Tanza

Binan

Caliraya
Reservoir

Mariveles

Dasmariñas

Carmona

Santa
Rosa

Laguna de
Bay

Paete

Corregidor
Island

Naic

Palapala

Lumban

Santa Cruz

Temate

Trece
Martirez

Silang

Canlubang

CALAMBA

Pagsanjan

Maragondon

Los Baños

Magallanes

Mt Sugnay
(750m)

Santo
Tomas

Mt Makiling
(1144m)

Calauan

Majayjay

Lucban

Fortune
Island

Nasugbu

Tagaytay

Talisay

Tanauan

SAN
PABLO

Lian

Bosoboso

Leynes

Alaminos

Mt Banahaw
(2188m)

Tuy

Mt
Batulao
(810m)

Subic

Lake
Taal

Tayabas

Matabungkay

Balayan

Balibago

San
Nicolas

Lipa

Tiaong

Sariaya

LUCENA

Ambil
Island

Calatagan

Lemery
San Luis

Taal

Bauan

Rosario

San Juan

Ligpo Point

Lubang
Island

Golo Island

Anilao

Mabini

Bagalangit

Tabangao

Bataan

Laiya

Sombrero Island

BATANGAS

Maricaban
Island

Pisa

Lobo

Verde
Island

Sabang

Abra de Ilog
(Wawa)

Puerto
Galera

Calapan

To Mamburao

MINDORO

To Pinamalaya

0   20   40 km

PHILIPPINES

Getting There & Away
Under the aegis of the Corregidor Foundation
(☎ 523 5605), the MV *Sun Cruiser* leaves
Manila from the PTA Bay Cruises terminal
(☎ 831 8140), next to the Cultural Center,
Monday to Friday at 8 am (return trip at 2.30
pm). There are two boats on weekends and
holidays, departing Manila at 8 and 10 am
(return trip 2.30 and 4.30 pm). The cost is
P1150 and includes a guided tour.

OLONGAPO & SUBIC
North-west of Manila, on the Bataan Peninsula, Olongapo is where the US Navy used to
be stationed. In 1991 the Philippine Senate
decided not to extend the Military Bases
Agreement (MBA), which had regulated the
lease of the bases since the end of WWII.

So, in 1992 the Subic Naval Base was
handed back to the Philippine government,
which declared the conversion of the base
into the Subic Bay Freeport a top national priority. Only then, some historians argue, did
the Philippines become truly independent. A
large area of the former base is covered with
virgin rainforest, which was used by the
Americans for survival training. A great diving area, Subic Bay has 20 wrecks strewn
across its floor, among them the battle cruiser
USS *New York*, sunk in 1941 and now lying
at a depth of 27m.

Olongapo is a good starting point for trips
to the Mt Pinatubo area or along the Zam-
bales coastline. There are some so-so beaches
around Subic, but San Miguel, slightly north
of Subic Bay, is better than any of the
beaches between Olongapo and Subic.

Places to Stay
There are several hotels of different price
ranges in Barrio Barretto, about 5km north-
west of Olongapo, halfway to Subic. The
Pynes Inn (☎ 222 5755) is right on Baloy
Beach and has balconied doubles with good
views, fan and bath for P350.

On the National Hwy, the *By the Sea Inn*
(☎ 222 4560) offers a whole selection of
comfortable rooms from P550 to P2000, all
with air-con, bath, TV and fridge. Both these
hotels have their own restaurants.

Getting There & Away
Air PAL has daily flights from Manila to
Olongapo.

Bus It's a two to three hour bus ride from the
Victory Liner station in Manila (P80). Between

Angeles City and Subic, Victory Liner buses
run hourly (two hours, P65), but most tourists
do the trip with Fly the Bus, a swish outfit offering air-con buses. They leave daily at 10
am from the Swagman Narra Hotel in
Angeles City, and drop you at any hotel in
Subic Bay (two hours, P300). Buses return at
12.30 pm from the Swagman Travel office.
From Baguio, buses depart hourly (six hours,
P140).

Jeepney It's only 12km (P5) from Olongapo to Subic, but watch out for pickpockets
on the blue jeepneys.

ANGELES
A sprawling brothel of a city where breakfast
is served all day and hotels offer 'three hour
rates', Angeles is nothing if not resilient. It
has somehow survived and even prospered
from two potentially fatal events in 1991. The
first was the eruption of nearby Mt Pinatubo.
The second was the withdrawal of the city's
clientele, the US Air Force, which abandoned
nearby Clark Air Base in the wake of the
eruption. Pinatubo's eerie ashen landscape is
now a tourist attraction, and the city's clientele
has successfully shifted to civilian tourists.

Information
Many hotels change US dollars and there are
more than enough moneychangers along the
main tourist drag of Fields Ave, where you'll
also find the Swagman Travel office, which
gives cash advances on major credit cards
(8% commission). There's also a Philippine
National Bank (PNB) nearby on MacArthur
Hwy.

Places to Stay
Since most visitors are paying for more than
just the room, accommodation rates in
Angeles have remained low compared with
many other tourist spots.

Down the end of Raymond St, off Fields
Ave, one of the cheapest places in town is
Some Place Else, where decent rooms with
fan cost P130. Around the corner, straddling
a long tree-lined private avenue, the *New
Liberty Hotel* (☎ 602 4588) on MacArthur
Hwy, has singles/doubles with bath and air-
con for P450/650 (P250 with fan).

At the opposite end of Fields Ave, one of
the most popular hotels in town is the friendly *Sunset Garden Inn* (☎ 378 1109). It has
tip-top clean rooms with fan and bath for
P460 (P560 with air-con). There's also a

swimming pool. Nearby, the ritzy *America Hotel* (☎ 785 1022) has a swimming pool too, and doubles/twins with bath and air-con at P780/890 – or suites with Jacuzzi for P2850.

A little removed from the general Angeles hustle and bustle, the *Woodland Park Hotel* (☎ 785 3311), off MacArthur Hwy, is set on huge leafy grounds and offers the biggest swimming pool in town. Cool, spacious doubles with air-con and bath are P695 to P1000. Officially in the neighbouring town of Dau, this place is actually only a 10 minute walk from Fields Ave.

Places to Eat

There is an enormous range of international restaurants in Angeles. *Margaritaville* on Fields Ave probably has the widest choice on its menu. In addition to American and Filipino food, it offers excellent Thai dishes from P60. There are also excellent *fresh-food stalls* on Fields Ave.

Getting There & Away

There are several Philippine Rabbit buses daily from Manila (two hours, P50), but make sure the bus is marked 'Expressway/ Dau'. Alternatively, there are many bus services operating to North Luzon via Dau, from where you can catch a jeepney (P3) or tricycle (P40) for the short trip back to Angeles.

In addition, for P300 there are several daily air-con buses from Manila. Departures from the Swagman Hotel on A Flores St, Ermita, are at 11.30 am and 3.30 and 8 pm.

There are hourly Victory Liner services from Olongapo which take two hours. Victory Liner also has hourly buses from Baguio. They're marked 'Olongapo' and take four hours. Many of the services between Manila and North Luzon go via Dau, a short tricycle ride from Angeles.

AROUND ANGELES
Mt Pinatubo

The violent eruption of Mt Pinatubo – its worst ever – on 15 June 1991 was like a bad dream for many. Clouds of steam and ejecta shot up to 40km into the stratosphere, darkening the sky, and incredible amounts of ash and sand settled in a wide area around the volcano. West of Angeles, the grey mass of coagulated material reached heights of up to 20m, and today this impressive terrain is crisscrossed with bizarre ravines which you can wander through for hours. Other areas are better explored with a vehicle.

Several hotels and travel agents in Angeles offer tours to Pinatubo and can arrange guides. Four to five-hour hikes with guide cost about P500 per person.

San Fernando

Not to be confused with San Fernando (La Union), north-west of Baguio, this town is famous for its Easter celebrations, during which about a dozen religious fanatics have themselves nailed to crosses.

LAS PIÑAS

On the way to Lake Taal many people stop at Las Piñas to see the **Sarao Jeepney Factory** and a small church, famous for its **pipe organ**. The organ, which has over 800 bamboo pipes, was built between 1816 and 1824; after restoration in Germany in the early 70s, it still sounds good. On non-holiday weekdays it can only be seen from 2 to 4 pm.

Getting There & Away

Zapote or Cavite buses from Taft Ave in Manila will get you to Las Piñas in half an hour. You can continue to Tagaytay on a Nasugbu bus coming through from Manila.

TAGAYTAY (TAAL VOLCANO)

The volcanic lake of Taal makes a pleasant excursion from Manila. There's a lake in the cone of the Taal volcano from which emerges a smaller volcano, inside of which is another lake. The view from Tagaytay Ridge is incredible.

You can climb the volcano, and there are plenty of boats to the island which can be chartered from **Talisay** for around P600 per round trip. As protection against sharp, high grass and pointed lava stones you should wear long trousers and suitable shoes.

Talisay is easily reached from Batangas or Pagsanjan. It's also possible, but less convenient, to take a jeepney from Tagaytay to the lake and a boat across from there.

Places to Stay

Villa Adelaide (☎ 413 1267) at Foggy Heights has rooms for P1200 (up to 20% more on weekends) and a swimming pool and restaurant. When coming from Manila, instead of turning right to Tagaytay, you must turn left. The Villa is near the road going down to the lake towards Talisay.

Getting There & Away

Take a BLTB bus from Manila heading for Nasugbu – the trip takes about one hour. It's about 17km down from Tagaytay to Talisay at the lake side, and several jeepneys a day make the dusty journey (P15). Manila to Talisay direct takes about two hours. First, take a BLTB bus marked 'Lemery' or 'Batangas' as far as Tanauan, then a jeepney from the public market to Talisay.

NASUGBU & MATABUNGKAY

Matabungkay is the most popular beach near Manila and it gets busy on weekends. Nasugbu (pronounced nass-U-boo) has better beaches, including **White Sands**, about 4km north of the town. You can get there by tricycle or outrigger.

Places to Stay & Eat

In the hotter months from February to June, resorts here host 'exclusives', which means companies book out all the rooms for the weekend or longer.

In Nasugbu, *Freddie Reyes Beach Resort* (☎ 931 1403) has air-con doubles with bath for P1500. It's a gay-friendly place right on the beach where you might find Freddie himself, a former hairdresser to Imelda Marcos. Next door is the *Maryland Beach Resort* (☎ 96 2771), with cottages for P950 and air-con rooms for P2000, all set around a swimming pool.

The *Swiss House Hotel* (mobile ☎ 0912 322 4631) in Matabungkay has pleasantly furnished double rooms with fan and bath for P650, or there's the *Coral Beach Club* (mobile ☎ 0912 318 4868) at P1600 for attractive rooms with air-con and bath.

Most resorts have their own *restaurants*.

Getting There & Away

BLTB buses for Nasugbu take about two hours from Manila and leave almost hourly. For Matabungkay, get off the bus at Lian and travel the last few kilometres by jeepney. Crow buses run from Nasugbu and Matabungkay regularly to Batangas (around two hours, P50).

BATANGAS

Batangas can make a good base for visiting Lake Taal, the nearby old town of Taal and sites along the coast, but the main reason for coming here is to take the ferry across to Mindoro or Palawan.

Places to Stay & Eat

Most of the inexpensive hotels in town are in poor condition. The relatively centrally located *Avenue Pension House I* (☎ 725 3720) at 30 JP Rizal Ave is acceptable – decent doubles with fan and bath cost P300, with air-con and bath P350.

On the outskirts of town, the upmarket *Alpa Hotel* (☎ 2213) has rooms with air-con and bath and cost from P850 to P2000. Oh well, at least it has a swimming pool.

Getting There & Away

Several BLTB and JAM buses leave Manila daily for Batangas (three hours, P73.50). BLTB air-con buses are only a few pesos more, but not all of them go to the pier. Boats from Batangas to Puerto Galera operate all day. Boats to Busuanga, north Palawan, leave twice a week.

LOS BAÑOS & CALAMBA

The **Los Baños Botanic Gardens** has a big swimming pool and the town is noted for its **hot springs** (most resorts are outside of town, along the highway as far as Calamba). Los Baños is also the location of the **International Rice Research Institute**, where the rice varieties that prompted the Asian 'green revolution' were developed.

Just before Los Baños is Calamba, where national hero Jose Rizal was born. **Rizal House** is now a memorial and museum.

Getting There & Away

Buses from Manila for Los Baños or Santa Cruz will get you to both towns. Calamba is the junction town if you're travelling to Batangas, Talisay or Lake Taal.

SAN PABLO & ALAMINOS

San Pablo is a good area for hiking. There's an easy hour's stroll around **Sampaloc Lake**, which is in an extinct volcanic cone. Alternatively, make the longer half-day trip to the twin lakes of **Pandin** and **Yambo**, north-east of San Pablo.

Near here, at Alaminos, **Hidden Valley** is a private park with lush vegetation, natural springs, a swimming pool and a hefty admission charge of about P1200, which includes a drink on arrival, a buffet lunch and use of facilities such as the pool.

Mt Makiling (1144m) is best reached from Alaminos or Los Baños, while from San Pablo you can climb 2188m-high **Mt Banahaw**.

Getting There & Away

Buses going from Manila to Lucena, Daet, Naga and Legaspi in South Luzon, or San Pablo-direct buses, all run via Alaminos en route to San Pablo (about two hours).

From Pagsanjan, take a jeepney to Santa Cruz and another from there to San Pablo. It's about 5km from Alaminos to Hidden Valley and drivers often demand P150 for this short trip.

PAGSANJAN

About 70km south-east of Manila in the Laguna Province, this is where you can shoot the **rapids** by canoe. The standard charge for a canoe is P500 for one or two people, including the entry fee. You are paddled upriver to the falls (a good place for a swim), and then go rushing down the rapids – getting kind of wet on the way.

You'll probably get hassled for extra money since plenty of rich tourists come here and throw pesos around. It's reported that if you're unwilling to give in to demands for increased payment, you will not enjoy the rest of the trip. Some boatman aggressively demand P500 or even P1000 as a tip. You have been warned!

The final scenes of *Apocalypse Now* were shot along the river but, despite all the tourist hype, this is no nail-biting white-water maelstrom – more a gentle river cruise most of the time. The water level is highest, and the rapids are at their best, in August and September. The best time to go is early in the morning before the tourist hordes arrive, so spend the night in Pagsanjan. The various hotels will all arrange boats for you. On weekends it's terribly crowded.

Places to Stay

Ignore the accommodation 'guides' at Pagsanjan, as their commission will cost you extra and there is plenty of accommodation, particularly along Garcia St, which runs along the river and doubles back from beside the post office.

The *Willy Flores Guesthouse* at 821 Garcia St has pleasant rooms for P250; with fan and bath it's P350. It's a simple, clean place with a homey atmosphere and staff will help you organise boat trips. The *Pagsanjan Garden Resort* has rooms starting at P142.

Places to Eat

There are plenty of good eating places in Pagsanjan, such as the *Me-Lin Restaurant* in Mabini St near the plaza. You'll find good food, nice staff and genuine home-made pizza.

Getting There & Away

Several BLTB and JAM buses leave Manila daily for Santa Cruz (two hours, P70), from where jeepneys run the last few kilometres to Pagsanjan.

LUCENA

The capital of Quezon Province, Lucena is a departure point for boats to Marinduque and Romblon. They leave either from Dalahican or from the river harbour of Cotta Port, just outside the town.

The **Quezon National Park**, between Lucena and Atimonan, is one of the largest wildlife reserves in Luzon. This is a great place for hiking; take along water and food.

Places to Stay & Eat

The *Lucena Fresh Air Hotel & Resort* (☎ 71 2424) is in the Isabang district, at the edge of town as you enter from Manila. This place has pretty good rooms set in generous grounds: singles/doubles with fan cost P155/185, with fan and bath P240 and with air-con and bath P440/785. There's also a nice swimming pool, and a restaurant with good meals for about P80.

Getting There & Away

Philtranco, Inland Trailways, Superlines and BLTB buses operate to Lucena from Manila, taking about two hours.

North Luzon

After a spell on the beaches at Hundred Islands, most travellers continue north to the famed rice terraces in the Mountain Province. The Ifugao villages around Banaue and their superb rice terraces have been dubbed the 'eighth wonder of the world'. North Luzon also has the popular summer capital of Baguio and the interesting old town of Vigan, with its many reminders of the Spanish period.

HUNDRED ISLANDS, LUCAP & ALAMINOS

Alaminos is the gateway to Lucap, and Lucap is the gateway to the Hundred Islands – that intriguing speckle of dots in the Lingayen Gulf. Officially a national park, the islands are quite a sight from the popular little resort

PHILIPPINES

town of Lucap. Green and rounded, they appear on the horizon like a line of giant turtles swimming out to sea.

Because of dynamite fishing the snorkelling and diving here isn't as good as it should be, but Lucap is a peaceful place to stay, and a good base from which to explore the caves and reefs of the Hundred Islands. As for Alaminos, it only gets a mention because it's where the bus will drop you off.

Information
There is a tourist office on the Lucap Pier which has a map of the islands and arranges boats. Also, most hotels and stores in Lucap can arrange boat trips to the Hundred Islands.

Places to Stay
Prices vary considerably with the season, jumping up at Easter week and April and May weekends.

A simple *nipa hut* on Children's Island, one of the prettiest of the Hundred Islands, costs P560 (with two beds, a kerosene lamp, toilet and a drum of water). Bring your own food. For more information, contact the resident manager (☎ 551 2505).

In Lucap, 1km from the pier, on the road from Alaminos, is the quiet *Kilometer One Lodge Youth Hostel* (☎ 551 2510). A twin room in this homely place is P150 for one person, P250 for two. Rooms come with fan and bath (shared between two rooms). There's also a little restaurant.

Nearer the pier, set back from the main road is the ageing but friendly *Gloria's Cottages* (☎ 551 2637). Double rooms (with bath) jutting out over the water go for P300. Across the road you'll find the *Ocean View Lodge* (☎ 551 2501), where roomy upstairs twins with fan and bath are very good value at P300 (P750 for a triple with air-con). There's also a restaurant.

Turning right at the Caltex station before the pier, a man-made peninsula supports a string of hotels. These include: the *Last Resort* (☎ 551 2440), which has good twins with fan and bath for P450, or P550 with air-con and cable TV; *Maxine by the Sea* (☎ 551 2537) with darkish air-con twins with bath P600; and the stately *Vista del Mar* (☎ 551 4455), featuring balconied air-con doubles and twins with the lot for P1000.

Places to Eat
The *Vista del Mar* has a breezy rooftop restaurant with good views, but the food

doesn't justify the high prices. You'd be better off at the restaurants attached to the *Last Resort* or *Maxine by the Sea*, which serves a Filipino or American breakfast for P80.

Getting There & Away
From Manila, Dagupan, Five Star, Philippine Rabbit and Partas buses run hourly from Manila to Alaminos (six hours, P180). You can also catch these buses at Dau, near Angeles (four hours, P85). From Olongapo, Victory Liner has several buses daily (seven hours, P180). From the north, Dagupan and Byron buses do the Baguio-Alaminos run throughout the day (four hours, P60).

Getting Around
Tricycle It's a quick P25 ride between Alaminos and Lucap.

Boat An outrigger from Lucap to the Hundred Islands costs P300 for up to six people, plus a P5 entry fee per person. For about P100 extra you can be dropped off and picked up later. Four or five hours is enough for most people, especially where there is no shade. Quezon is the most popular island and you can get drinks at the kiosk there.

LINGAYEN, DAGUPAN & SAN FABIAN
At the southern end of Lingayen Gulf, Dagupan is mainly a transport hub. There are also some beaches in the vicinity, none of them particularly memorable. Between Lingayen and Dagupan you could try **Lingayen Beach** (15km from Dagupan) and **Blue Beach** (3km away at Bonuan), while **White Beach** is 15km north-east at San Fabian. White Beach is really brownish grey.

AGOO & ARINGAY
Between San Fabian and Bauang is Agoo, where a **basilica**, rebuilt after an 1892 earthquake, is worth going to see. It is probably the most beautiful church in La Union Province. In Aringay you can visit the small **Don Lorenzo Museum**, opposite the old church.

SAN FERNANDO (LA UNION)
The 'city of the seven hills' is the capital of La Union Province, and the **Museo de La Union** next to the Provincial Capitol building gives a cultural overview of the region. The Chinese **Ma-Cho Temple** on the northern edge of town is also well worth a visit.

Information

The tourist office (☎ 41 2411) is in the Matanag Justice Hall, General Luna St, Town Plaza.

Places to Stay

The centrally located four storey *Plaza Hotel* (☎ 41 2996) on the main drag of Quezon Ave (which becomes the main highway) has a wide variety of passable rooms. Singles/doubles with fan and common bath cost P280/350, and with air-con and bath P650/750.

At the north end of town, a better multi-storey option is the *Sea & Sky Hotel and Restaurant* (☎ 41 5279), where big rooms with views and balcony go for P700. Book ahead if you can here, especially if you want a sea view. This place also has a nice pool.

Places to Eat

The *Cafe Esperanza*, next to the town square on Gomez St, is the perfect place for a sweet-tooth's breakfast.

For lunch and dinner, the *New Society Restaurant* has good Chinese food (about P60 per dish). It's in P Burgos St, opposite the market.

Getting There & Away

There are numerous daily buses from Manila (seven hours, P180).

AROUND SAN FERNANDO

A long brown-sand **beach** stretches between San Fernando in the north and Bauang in the south. There are better beaches in the Philippines, but this particular stretch of sand is only a couple of hours bus travel from Baguio and its wide range of beachside resorts attracts an equally wide range of tourists.

Places to Stay & Eat

The best way to see what's on offer here is simply to wander along the beach. The main places to stay are about 3km from Bauang and about 4km from San Fernando. Most of these places have restaurants attached. From the road, look for the Mark Terese Apartments and from here take the narrow paved road opposite through to the beach. You'll emerge alongside the lively bamboo eatery, *Michaela Snack Bar*.

The big three resorts just to the north of the Michaela Snack Bar are the *Coconut Grove Resort* (☎ 41 4276), the *Cabaña Beach Resort* (☎ 41 2824), and the *Bali Hai Beach Resort* (☎ 41 2504). All have good standard rooms for P900 to P1100. All three also have swimming pools, with the Cabaña even throwing in a bowling green.

At the southern end of the beach things are bit more downmarket. Here you'll find the *Hide Away Beach Resort* (mobile ☎ 0912 311 2421), where tatty but decent rooms upstairs cost P550 (with bath and air-con). About 500m away, the *Leo Mar Beach Resort* has excellent, breezy upstairs rooms with fan and bath for P400 to P500 – great value if you don't mind the derelict eye-sores next door.

Getting There & Away

Bus There are many buses from Manila to Bauang (seven hours, P140) and some continue north to Vigan and Laoag. It takes over an hour from Baguio on Philippine Rabbit or Eso-Nice Transport (P40) and slightly less by jeepney (P25). It's a nice trip down the winding road to the coast – sit on the left side for the best views.

Jeepney Jeepneys take about 30 minutes to get from Bauang to San Fernando (P8).

San Juan

About 10km north of San Fernando, the small town of San Juan is on an elongated bay. The **beach** here is wider and cleaner than the one in Bauang and it has become known as a surfing beach; from November until February you may come across some surfers, but otherwise there's not much going on. Several resorts here rent out surfboards for around P100 per hour.

Places to Stay About 2km south of San Juan, in Urbiztondo, the *La Union Surf Resort* (☎ 242 4544) has tiny single rooms with fan and common bath for P300, and pretty cottages with bath and fan for P600. It also has a nice garden and restaurant right on the beach.

A good stand-by about 200m farther on is the *Hacienda Beach Resort* (☎ 242 1109) – but watch out for the guard geese! This place has basic cottages with fan and bath for P350. Rooms are P250, and a self-contained flat in the main building is P500.

Another 200m south is the homely *Monaliza Beach Resort* (☎ 41 4892) – this time, watch out for the guard dog! Good basic rooms (with fan and bath) right on the edge

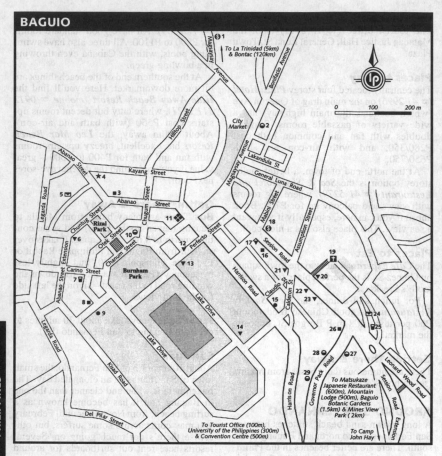

BAGUIO

To La Trinidad (5km) & Bontac (120km)

City Market

Magsaysay Avenue
Bonifacio Avenue

Hilltop Street

Lakandula St

General Luna Road

Kayang Street

Abanao Street

Abanao Street

Legarda Road

Chugum Street

Chugum Street

Otek Street

Chanum Street

Rizal Park

Burnham Park

Lake Drive

Lake Drive

Kisad Road

Legarda Road

Abanao Street Extension

Carino Street

Carino Street

Del Pilar Street

Perfecto Street

Mabini Street

Assumption Street

Session Road

Harrison Road

Claude St

Calderon St

Harrison Road

Governor Pack Road

Leonard Wood Road

Session Road Extension

To Matsukaze
Japanese Restaurant
(600m), Mountain
Lodge (900m), Baguio
Botanic Gardens
(1.5km) & Mines View
Park (2km)

To Tourist Office (100m),
University of the Philippines (300m)
& Convention Centre (500m)

To Camp
John Hay

0   100   200 m

of the sand are P350. Bigger rooms with fridge (but still no air-con) are P500. Cheap meals are also available here.

On the northern side of San Juan, in Montemar Village, the friendly ***Sunset German Beach Resort & Restaurant*** (☎ 41 4719) has rugged little stone rooms with fan and bath for P450, or P650 with air-con. This is a well tended place with lots of plants.

Getting There & Away The San Fernando jeepneys to Urbiztondo are P3, and to Montemar Village P4 (get off at the turn-off in Ili Norte – it's approximately 200m from there to the beach). To/from Vigan, Philippine Rabbit buses run daily (two to three hours, P101).

BAGUIO

Ah, Baguio – the City of Pines, the City of Lovers, the City of Countless Affectionate Nicknames. At an altitude of about 1500m, Baguio (BAHG-ee-oh) is much cooler than Manila and for this reason once served as a summer capital. Still popular as an escape from the lowland heat, this laid-back town has plenty of **parks** and an interesting **market**. It's also good for buying handicrafts (although you have to bargain aggressively).

Baguio is also famed for its faith healers, to whom many people flock each year. To most travellers, however, the town serves mainly as a gateway to the mountain provinces of the Central Cordillera and the amazing rice terraces.

BAGUIO

PLACES TO STAY				
3	Swagman Attic Inn	22	Sizzling Plate Restaurant	11 Sunshine Department Store
8	Benguet Pine Tourist Inn	23	Shakey's Pizza	15 Avis Rent-a-Car; PAL
16	Hotel 45			18 Philippine National Bank
26	Baden Powell Inn		**OTHER**	(PNB)
		1	Equitable Bank	19 Immaculate Heart of Mary
	PLACES TO EAT	2	Dangwa Tranco Bus	Cathedral
6	Café by the Ruins		Terminal; Lizardo Trans	24 Post Office
12	Food Stalls		Bus Terminal	25 Perk Cafe
13	New Ganza Restaurant	4	Police Station	27 Victory Liner Bus Terminal
14	Solibao Restaurant	5	Post Office; Town Hall	28 Byron Bus Terminal;
17	McDonald's	7	Spirits Disco; E3 Bar	Dagupan Bus Terminal;
20	Mister Donut & Swiss Baker	9	Baguio City Orchidarium	Partas Bus Terminal
21	Jollibee; Benguet	10	Eso-Nice Transport Bus	29 Philippine Rabbit Bus
	Supermarket		Terminal	Terminal

Orientation

It can be tricky getting your bearings in this steep, sprawling metropolis. Roads tend to snake all over the place and the bottle-necked pedestrian overpasses in the town centre don't help. Two handy landmarks are: the Immaculate Heart of Mary Cathedral, perched high above the main drag of Session Rd; and Burnham Park, the vast rectangular park, lake, sports arena and market area in one, around which many central streets curve.

Information

The tourist office (☎ 442 7014) is at the DOT complex on Governor Pack Rd.

Things to See

The **City Market** has local produce and crafts, including basketwork, textiles, wood carvings and jewellery. There's a small **Mountain Provinces Museum** in **Camp John Hay**, a well kept recreation area in the south-eastern suburbs of town. When you're there don't miss the **Cemetery of Negativism**, with its amusing gravestones; it's right next to **Liberty Park**. To the east, the **Baguio Botanic Gardens** are about 1.5km out of the town centre. There are scenic views of the surrounding countryside from **Mines View Park** a little further on (P3 by jeepney).

In **La Trinidad**, the provincial capital north of Baguio, visit the governor's offices and see the **Kabayan mummies**. These remarkably well preserved mummified bodies were brought from burial caves in the north.

Places to Stay

Air-con rooms are unheard of in this refreshingly cool climate – instead, it's worth hunting down a room with an electric blanket if you tend to feel the cold. It's also a good idea to book ahead – Baguio fills up faster than any other Philippine tourist spot.

Squeezed between the numerous shops on Session Rd, *Hotel 45* (☎ 442 6634) – formerly the Baguio Goodwill Lodge – has windowless boxes with common bath for P250 to P300.

A far more attractive budget option is the *Benguet Pine Tourist Inn* (☎ 442 7325), a four storey place on the corner of Otek and Chanum Sts, right opposite the Baguio City Orchidarium and Burnham Park. Dorm beds are P220, attic-style doubles with common bath (and common balcony) are P525 and doubles with private bath are P690. All prices include breakfast.

Just off the top end of Session Rd, on Governor Pack Rd, near no less than three bus terminals, is the surprisingly quiet *Baden Powell Inn* (☎ 442 5836). It's made up of two separate buildings, but the main one housing the restaurant and reception area has the best-value rooms: six-bed dorms are P300 per head; bright little doubles with bath are P850 (P950 with TV and breakfast). Rates for the dorm beds jump by P250 on the weekend. Major credit cards are accepted.

About 1km east of town on Leonard Wood Rd (grab a La Trinidad-Mines View jeepney) is the *Mountain Lodge* (☎ 442 4544). This big old place has a restaurant, a hunting-lodge lounge area, and an array of variously ageing rooms with common bath at P650, or with private bath at P700 to P800. A room for four with bath is P1000.

More salubrious rooms are available at the *Swagman Attic Inn* (☎ 442 5139) on Abanao

PHILIPPINES

St in town, where big well furnished doubles are P1142 (with bath and cable TV). But be warned: rooms facing the street here can be very noisy. This place has its own restaurant, and major credit cards are accepted.

Places to Eat
The *Dangwa Tranco Bus Terminal* off Magsaysay Ave has astoundingly good, cheap food – including excellent cakes. The *Swiss Baker* on Session Rd is good for breakfast, and there are heaps of excellent *fresh-fruit stalls* tucked inside the City Market, on Magsaysay Ave.

At the *New Ganza Restaurant* and the *Solibao Restaurant* in the very central Burnham Park, you can eat outside. Nearby, on Perfecto St, there are rows of excellent Filipino *food stalls* which stay open late.

There are various restaurants along Session Rd, including the *Sizzling Plate*, a good place for a meat lovers. But if you'd like to try traditional Cordillera cooking and drinks, the *Cafe by the Ruins*, opposite the town hall, is the place to go. The name's a bit misleading – the cafe *is* the ruins. It's an amazing amalgam of bamboo and bullet-riddled remains of the former governor's residence. The place was virtually destroyed in 1944 when US forces turned on their own favourite summer retreat, which had been over-run by the Japanese. The cafe has mouth-watering seasonal specials (for around P110) and a tranquil ambience.

There's also a very good Japanese Restaurant, *Matsukaze*, up towards the Mountain Lodge at the intersection of General Luna, Leonard Wood and Brent Rds. If money's not a problem, then try the P180 mixed sashimi.

Entertainment
There are a number of good live music places in town, the most vibrant being *Spirits disco* and the *E3 Bar*, both housed in the impressive two storey building on the corner of Otek and Carino Sts. Also pretty damn groovy is the *Perk Cafe*, at the top end of Session Rd, a short climb up from the Baden Powell Inn.

Shopping
Look for Ifugao wood carvings and for interesting hand-woven fabrics. The cottons are produced in such limited quantities that they rarely even reach Manila. The baskets and wooden salad bowls are remarkably cheap, but a little bulky to carry home.

Getting There & Away
Air PAL has 50-minute flights from Manila to Baguio daily. There's a PAL office (☎ 442 2734) on Harrison St, opposite Burnham Park. Jeepneys to the airport leave from Mabini Rd, between Session and Harrison Rds.

Bus Philippine Rabbit, Victory Liner, Dangwa Tranco and Dagupan Bus all operate daily from Manila to Baguio (six hours, P140); Victory Liner has the most extensive schedule and comfortable buses. You can also catch these buses from Dau, near Angeles.

There are hourly Victory Liner buses from Olongapo to Baguio (six hours), a few Dagupan Bus and Byron buses from Dagupan (two hours) and several Philippine Rabbit and Eso-Nice Transport buses from San Fernando (two to three hours, P27).

Dangwa Tranco has two daily bus services to Banaue (eight hours, P150) which depart early in the morning. Departures to Bontoc are also in the morning (eight hours). Lizardo and Dangwa Tranco operate between Baguio and Sagada, with several morning buses daily (six to seven hours, P136).

RICE TERRACES
The main provinces of the Cordillera mountain ranges, Mountain Province and Ifugao, start 100km north-east of Baguio and are famed for interesting tribes and spectacular rice terraces. If you've spent much time in South-East Asia, going to a place just to see more rice terraces may seem a little weird, but these are definitely special.

Some 2000 to 3000 years ago the Ifugao people carved terraces out of the mountainsides around Banaue, which are as perfect today as they were then. They run like stepping stones to the sky – up to 1500m high – and if stretched end to end would extend over 20,000km.

In more remote areas, the Ifugao still practice traditional ways – this no longer includes head-hunting.

The terraces are best seen from Bontoc, Banaue and Batad.

Getting There & Away
You can approach the Central Cordillera from two directions. The more spectacular route, the Halsema Rd, climbs up from Baguio to Bontoc, the capital of Mountain Province. Halsema Rd reaches a height of 2255m and is the highest road in the Philippines. Try to get a seat on the right-hand side to get the best

views. Expect rough, winding mountain roads in buses which are robust but lack the most comfortable suspension. The trip takes about seven hours and from Bontoc you can make side trips to places like Sagada, or continue to Banaue, the main town for rice terraces.

The faster alternative route is direct from Manila via Nueva Viscaya Province – on occasionally good roads the bus trip takes 10 hours. The Baguio-Bontoc-Banaue road is often cut off during the wet season, but it's far more interesting, so you should try to make the trip in at least one direction by this route. July to September is the wettest period.

BONTOC

Bontoc is the first major town you come to from Baguio and the main town of the area. It's possible to walk from here to the villages of the Igorot people – they build their rice terraces with stone dikes, unlike the earth terraces of Banaue. Take food and water for yourself and dried fish or other gifts for the villagers.

The village of **Malegcong** is a two or three hour walk into the mountains. You have to follow a narrow creek for about 200m before you reach the footpath leading to the village. There's a chance that one or two jeepneys a day will make the trip between Bontoc and the **rice terraces**. Because of the high fare (P40) most locals decide to walk instead.

The excellent **Bontoc Museum** is run by the local Catholic mission and includes headhunting relics, Chinese vases and photos of the mountain tribes; admission is P20.

Places to Stay & Eat

Let's put it this way: accommodation in Bontoc was obviously at its best a long time ago. The *Pines Kitchenette & Inn*, behind the market, is the only acceptable place; quite nice, big doubles with common bath cost P100 per head, or P450 for a room with bath.

Though lacking in good accommodation, Bontoc has loads for little *cafes*, *restaurants* and *bakeshops*.

Shopping

Bontoc is a good place to buy locally woven materials, woodcarvings and other handicrafts of Mountain Province.

Getting There & Away

There are five Dangwa Tranco buses daily between Baguio and Bontoc, generally de-

parting in the early morning (eight hours, P130).

Between Bontoc and Banaue, one bus leaves daily from both towns, sometime between 7.30 am and 1 pm (two to three hours, P60). Jeepneys also do this run all morning (two to three hours, P40) – but it can be a hair-raising, dust-raising trip. These jeepneys also operate between Bontoc and Sagada (one hour, P20).

As elsewhere in the Central Cordillera, transport is somewhat unreliable. If you can't find regular transport you can charter a jeepney.

SAGADA

Only 18km from Bontoc, the tranquil little village of Sagada is famed for its **burial caves** and **hanging coffins**. Guides can be arranged at the info centre in the town hall, just below the bus depot. One guide (with a lamp) will cost around P300, for one to four people.

About 500m from the town, heading towards Bontoc, the **Eduardo Masferré Studio** has photographs of life in Mountain Province from the 1930s to the 50s.

Information

Although perfectly comfortable, Sagada is quite isolated. There are no telephones, only telegraph, and no banks.

For an entertaining map of the area (P7), drop into the Shamrock Cafe, near the town hall.

Places to Stay

All hotels except the brand new Prime Hotel have a policy of charging around P75 per person. And in most places, you must order a bucket of hot water the evening before if you don't want a cold shower in the morning – and when they say cold water in Sagada they really mean cold! You should note also that many hotels here have early check-out times (9.30 or 10 am).

The *Sagada Guesthouse*, perched prominently above the bus depot, is a simple place with a common balcony aimed out across the valley. On the lower road, the *Masferrés Inn* is very popular – 'quaint, charming, cosy and rustic' was how one traveller described it. It's hidden behind the Country Cafe & Restaurant. Other places include the *St Joseph Resthouse*, at the end of a steep footpath that leaves the main road opposite the hospital.

It's also friendly, with tidy rooms as basic as they come, although new rooms with private bath are on the way.

The *Mapiyaaw Pensione* is idyllically located in a natural rock garden about 1km from town on the road to Bontoc. It's a three storey building, but it manages to be cosy with a fireplace and big balcony on each floor. There's no restaurant as such, but food can usually be rustled up.

Then there's the big, ugly exception to the P75-per-head rule: the *Prime Hotel*, just down the road from the Country Cafe & Restaurant. Charmless, overpriced and already showing signs of wear and tear, it offers one thing that the other hotels do not – a hot shower (but only in the P1000 rooms!). The P800 room with common bath has showers as cold as anywhere else in town. And as for the restaurant here, both the food and the service can only improve.

Places to Eat

Most of the *hotels* here serve decent, hearty breakfasts and main meals (although it's a good idea to order well in advance). But the best food in town is served at the cosy little *Log Cabin*, up past the Sagada Guesthouse. You should *definitely* reserve a table here, as numbers are limited.

Getting There & Away

Bus To Baguio, Dangwa Tranco and Lizardo buses leave each morning until about 9 am (six to seven hours, P136).

Jeepney Jeepneys to Bontoc take an hour (P20), leaving between 8.30 am and 4.30 pm daily. From Sagada to Baguio, jeepneys leave between 6 and 10.30 am.

BANAUE

From Bontoc, the road turns south and runs through incredibly spectacular countryside to Banaue, the heart of the **terrace scenery**. It's a narrow, rough road and travel is slow – but what a view. Take the right side of the bus to best appreciate it. There are many **hiking trails** around Banaue.

Information

The tourist information office has a good map of Banaue's surroundings for P6.

There is no bank in Banaue, but some hotels change money, and there's a money-changer in the main market area.

Places to Stay & Eat

All the following places have restaurants – nothing fancy, but the *People's Lodge Restaurant* is usually the busiest.

The *Jericho Guest House* above the main market area is the cheapest in town at P50 per head – but you miss out on some great views. For P25 more, you can virtually float above the glorious Banaue valley at the three-tiered *People's Lodge* (☎ 386 4014), just down from the main market area. It's a deservedly popular place, charging P75 to P100 per head, or P400 for a big room with bath and hot shower. Even the views from the toilet here are spectacular!

Next door, the attractive timber-lined *Green View Lodge* (☎ 386 4021) has some excellent rooms with common bath at P100 per head, or P400 for a room with a hot shower.

A few doors down is the *Stairway Lodge* (☎ 386 4053), good value at P75 to P150 per head, P100 for a dorm bed, and P250 for rooms with private bath. Next door, the *Halfway Lodge* (☎ 386 4082) has rooms with common bath for P100 and rooms with bath for P350.

Heading up, out of town, and to the left, you'll find the *Banaue Hotel & Youth Hostel* (☎ 386 4087). The hotel's expensive, but the hostel has big, segregated dorm rooms for P175 per head – and some very impressive views. The vast grounds here include a swimming pool and a lot of carefully labelled shrubbery.

Getting There & Away

You can reach Banaue from either direction but, while the Bayombong route is faster, the Bontoc route is much more interesting. From Baguio, there are two daily Dangwa Tranco buses via Bayombong (eight hours, P150). They leave early in the morning, but at busy times they will leave when they're full.

From Manila, the daily Dangwa Tranco bus leaves at 7 am (10 hours, P240). If you miss this direct bus, take a Baliwag Transit bus to Solano, just before the Banaue turn-off. From there, jeepneys run to Lagawe and then to Banaue, and take another two or three hours.

BATAD

The wonderfully remote village of Batad is surrounded by breathtakingly beautiful **rice terraces**. It's a two hour, sometimes steep, walk to Batad after a 12km jeepney or tricycle ride from Banaue.

A 45 minute walk beyond the village itself, over a steep saddle, is the gorgeous 21m-high **Tapplya Waterfall** and swimming hole. Ask for directions at the friendly Foreigner's Inn, in the middle of Batad. Keen walkers could include the waterfall in a day trip from Banaue, but it would be a pity to rush Batad.

Places to Stay & Eat

Batad accommodation is spartan, particularly in the shower and toilet department, but considering the tiny prices and the huge views, these are some of the best hotel rooms in the world!

For the widest, highest views, stop at the ridge above Batad itself, where a mini-village of hotels looks out over the valley. Hotels here include: *Rita's Mount View Inn*, a breezy place with rooms for P35 per head; the excellent *Hillside Inn* (P35 to P50 per head); and the popular *Simon's Inn*, in the prime spot at the tip of the ridge, with views of both sides of the valley and rooms at P35 per head. Simon's also has a great menu including pizza and pita bread rolls.

For a stronger taste of village life, and impressive close-up views of the terraces, clamber down to Batad itself (if the concrete steps here were any steeper you'd need a safety harness). There are several small hotels with rooms for the going rate of P35 per head, with the most prominent place being the *Foreigner's Inn*, which has a nice balcony restaurant.

Getting There & Away

You can get a jeepney (P20) or tricycle (P100 to P150) 12km of the way to Batad from Banaue – and some drivers even brave the trail up to the saddle above Batad (for a price, of course). But you must still walk the rest of the way.

If taking a tricycle to Batad for a day trip, it's a good idea to get the driver to wait for you (average return trip P300), or you may get stranded – don't pay the full fare until you return. Buses which ply the route between Banaue and Mayoyao pass the turn-off for Batad. It takes approximately two hours along the signposted path between Dalican and Bangaan. Beware of self-appointed, but expensive 'guides'.

VIGAN

About 130km north of San Fernando (La Union), this interesting old town was second only to Manila during the Spanish era and today is the best-preserved Spanish town in the country. Its **Cathedral of St Paul** dates from 1641 and is one of the oldest and largest churches in the country. If you're interested in old Spanish architecture and ancient churches, this region of Ilocos is a prime hunting ground.

It's fascinating just wandering around the town very early in the morning, taking in the narrow streets around Mena Crisologo St, listening to the clip-clop of horse-drawn calesas.

Places to Stay

The *Vigan Hotel* (☎ 722 3001) on Burgos St is the cheapest of the old-style Spanish villas cum hotels. Good basic singles/doubles with fan and common bath go for P375/475. Rooms with air-con, cable TV and fridge are P575/895. There's also the 'antique room' for P775, with the antique touch supplied by the four-poster bed.

Around the corner, on Mena Crisologo St, the much grander *RF Aniceto Mansion* (☎ 722 2383) has an eclectic range of rooms from P300 (with fan and bath) to P650.

On the other side of town, on Liberation Blvd, is the well preserved *El-Juliana Hotel* (☎ 722 2994), with good rooms with air-con and bath from P475 to P575. The upstairs suites are P750. There's also a swimming pool but you have to pay extra to use it (P35 by day, P50 by night).

Over the road, on Quirino Blvd, behold the magnificent *Villa Angela*. More like a museum than a hotel, this stunning time capsule has rooms with fan and common bath for P500, or with air-con and bath for P1000. It's worth it just for the furniture.

Places to Eat

The *Cool Spot Restaurant*, at the back of the Vigan Hotel, is a lovely, airy place known for its good Ilocano cooking. For the opposite in ambience, there are hearty P60 meals served at the ugly concrete video arcade/pool hall eatery known as the *88.8 Restaurant*. It's on the corner of Del Pilar and General Luna Sts.

While you're in Vigan you should try *empanadas* – these are tasty vegetable or meat-filled pastries of Spanish origin. You can get them from around 4 pm until quite late at the *Plaza Burgos* (the market square between Florentino and Burgos Sts) for P5 each.

Getting There & Away

From Manila, the trip takes about eight hours (around P200) with Partas Lines, Philippine

Rabbit, or Times Transit. Some buses continuing north to Laoag bypass the town, in which case you will have to take a tricycle from the highway for about P10. Buses also connect from San Fernando, Aparri and Laoag. You can reach Vigan from Baguio via San Fernando, or by the coast from Hundred Islands and Dagupan, again via San Fernando (three hours, P110).

It's about two hours beyond Vigan to Laoag and you can continue right around the north of Luzon to Claveria, Aparri, Tuguegarao and back down to Manila.

LAOAG
In 1818, when Ilocos Province was divided in two, Laoag (lao-AHHG), on the Laoag River, became the capital of Ilocos Norte, one of Luzon's most beautiful provinces.

Things to See
There are many old Spanish churches in the Ilocos Norte Province and Laoag has **St William's Cathedral**, built between 1650 and 1700. Near Laoag, in **Bacarra**, the town's church has a massive, earthquake-damaged bell tower.

South-east of the town is **Sarrat**, birthplace of the former president, Ferdinand Marcos. In the centre of town is the restored **Sarrat Church & Convent**, built in 1779 by Augustinian monks.

About 15km south of Laoag, the town of Batac is home to the **Marcos Mansion**, a creepy villa stuffed with yellowing scraps of the infamous ex-president's life and wardrobe (including his tennis outfit). Until recently, Ferdinand's refrigerated body was on display here. The mansion is in the centre of Batac, opposite the huge **Batac Church** (built in 1587). To get there from Laoag, hop on a Batac jeepney at the corner of Jose Rizal St and Don Severo Hernando Ave (P7), or catch a roaming Batac bus (P10).

A few kilometres south-west of Batac is the fortress-like **Paoay Church**, built in a style referred to as 'earthquake baroque'. The coastline between Laoag and Paoay, with its extensive sand dunes, is most impressive. Buses headed in all directions from Batac mill at the front gate of Batac Church.

Places to Stay
The *Texicano Hotel* (☎ 722 0290) is on Rizal St and, despite an ugly exterior, it has plenty of character. Huge rooms in the newer annex, with air-con, cable TV, fridge and bath, are

P750. Bright doubles in the older building range from P135 (with fan and common bath) to P350 with air-con.

Casa Llanes (☎ 722 1125), on Primo Lazaro Ave, looks almost derelict from the outside. Inside, it's a rambling collection of big, darkly ageing rooms (P220 with fan and common bath; P350 with air-con).

The brand new, four storey gelati-pink *Hotel Tiffany* (☎ 770 3550), on General Fidel Segundo Ave, has small, sterile singles/ twins (with air-con and cable TV) for P400/ 600 – no double beds, except in the P1000 family room.

Places to Eat
Breakfast possibilities include the very cheap *Town Bakery*, one block from the Texicano Hotel, or *Kookee*, a bakery near the Hotel Tiffany.

The friendly, unpretentious little *La Preciosa Restaurant*, on Rizal St diagonally opposite the Texicano Hotel, is fantastic. It serves delicious Ilocos Province dishes (for around P60) from a menu bound to please both carnivores and vegetarians – a rarity in this fast-food filled town.

Getting There & Away
Air PAL has two weekly flights between Manila and Laoag (P1570). Jeepneys run all day between the airport and Laoag proper (P4).

Bus Companies such as Philippine Rabbit (on General Antonio Luna St) and Fariñas Trans (on the corner of FR Castro Ave and Fariñas St) have air-con buses running to/from Manila from 6 am to 11.30 pm (11 hours, P370).

For Vigan (two hours, P45), catch the bus from the corner of Jose Rizal and Bagumbayan Sts. Less frequent buses travel around the north coast to Claveria (three hours), Aparri (five hours) and Tuguegarao (seven hours).

TUGUEGARAO
In an area known for its many caves, the **Callao Caves** can be found 15km north-east of Tuguegarao (tug-EG-ar-ow), about 9km north of Peñablanca. However, many of the caves in this area are for divers only. There are some good walks in the **Sierra Madre**.

Places to Stay
The *Pensione Abraham* (☎ 844 1793) on Bonifacio St has acceptable rooms at a rea-

sonable price: singles/doubles with fan cost P80/110, with fan and bath P150/280 and with air-con and bath P250/350.

The *Pensione Roma* (☎ *844 1057*) on the corner of Luna and Bonifacio Sts has rooms with fan and bath for P300 and with air-con and bath for P550/600.

Getting There & Away
PAL flies daily between Manila and Tuguegarao.

Baliwag Transit buses from Manila take 11 hours and depart hourly (P240).

South Luzon

With its impressive contours and countless bays and inlets, the south of Luzon meanders its way from Manila in the direction of Samar, the most easterly island of the Visayas. The major attraction of Bicol, as South Luzon is also called, is the majestic Mayon volcano at Legaspi, claimed to be the most perfectly symmetrical volcano cone in the world. Between Sorsogon and Matnog lies the so-called 'Switzerland of the Orient': beautiful Mt Bulusan with its extensive foothills.

SAN MIGUEL BAY
San Miguel Bay, with its beaches and islands, is an interesting detour on the route south. **Daet** is a good overnight stop en route to the bay.

Mercedes, a small coastal village about 10km north-east of Daet, has a lively fish market from 6 to 8 am, and from here you can reach **Apuao Grande Island**, with its white sand beach, in San Miguel Bay.

Places to Stay
In Daet the centrally located *Karilagan Hotel* (☎ *721 2314*) has quite good singles/doubles with fan and bath for P150/200, and with air-con and bath for P400/550.

On the white sand beach on Apuao Grande Island, the *TS Resort* has dorm accommodation for P100 and a good number of attractive cottages with fan and bath from P350 to P700. They also offer facilities like a swimming pool, golf course and tennis courts.

Places to Eat
Near the Karigalan Hotel, a pleasant place with good food is the *Sandok at Palayok*. It's on the second floor, so you have to manage a few stairs. A few streets away, the *Golden*

House Restaurant is recommended for its Chinese dishes.

Getting There & Away
Air PAL has flights to Daet from Manila twice a week.

Bus Buses from Manila take about seven hours to Daet and some continue to centres further south. It's three to four hours further south to Legaspi via Naga.

Jeepney Jeepneys go to Mercedes, the jumping-off point for the San Miguel Bay islands.

NAGA
In late September this friendly and noticeably clean town holds the **Peñafrancia Festival**, which includes a huge and colourful procession. Hotel prices at this time can be two or three times as much as normal.

Places to Stay
The friendly and fairly good *Sampaguita Tourist Inn* (☎ *21 4810*) on Panganiban Drive has singles with fan and bath for P185 (good value), singles with air-con and bath for P285 and doubles with air-con and bath for P400 to P550.

The *Moraville Hotel* (☎ *811 1807*), on Dinaga St, has singles/doubles with fan and bath for P175/275; with air-con, bath and TV it's P400/500. The rooms are quiet and comfortably furnished.

Places to Eat
The *Ming Chun Foodhouse* on Peñafrancia Ave serves good Filipino and Chinese dishes. The *New China Restaurant* on General Luna St offers daily specials for about P60, and *Carl's Diner* at Plaza Rizal is a clean, inexpensive and popular 50s-style fast-food restaurant.

Shopping
Pili nuts are a popular favourite in the Bicol region. There is a shop in the market at Naga which sells all varieties of pili nuts. See the Philippines Flora & Fauna section for details.

Getting There & Away
PAL has a daily flight from Manila. Buses take about nine hours from Manila, and there are also buses from Daet (one to two hours) and Legaspi (two hours).

LEGASPI

The main city of the Bicol region hugs the waterfront in the shadow of the **Mayon** volcano.

Information

Legaspi is divided into two parts: the central area around the port, and the Albay district further inland. The two areas are linked by Rizal St.

The tourist office (☎ 24 3215) is on Rizal St.

Things to See

South-east of the city, **Kapuntukan Hill** provides a fascinating panoramic view of Legaspi harbour with the impressive Mayon volcano in the background.

In the **St Rafael Church**, on Aguinaldo St across from the Rex Hotel, the altar is a 10 tonne volcanic rock from Mayon.

Places to Stay

There are plenty of cheap hotels around Legaspi, but none will win any prizes for high standards.

There is quite a choice along Peñaranda St, parallel to the waterfront. *Catalina's Lodging House* is a friendly place with basic singles/doubles with fan for P80/120, with fan and bath for P140/200, and with air-con and bath for P300/400.

On the same street, the *Hotel Xandra* (☎ 22688) has reasonable, clean rooms with fan for P120/150, with fan and bath priced at P180/200 or with air-con and bath for P220/300.

Places to Eat

Legaspi offers a wide choice of places to eat – like the *New Legaspi Restaurant* on Lapu-Lapu St, where the special meal for about P60 can be recommended. The food here is basically Chinese with some Filipino dishes.

The *Mamalola Bakery & Snack House* on Peñaranda St will surprise you not only with its plucky karaoke singers but also with its excellent cooking. The *Legaspi Ice Cream House* in Magellanes St makes wonderful ice cream.

Getting There & Away

Air PAL has daily fights from Manila.

Bus Buses from Manila to Legaspi all pass through Naga. BLTB, Inland Trailways and Philtranco buses depart from their terminals on EDSA Ave in Pasay City, and the trip takes 11 to 12 hours. The fare to Legaspi is about P280, depending on the bus.

AROUND LEGASPI

Santo Domingo

This long, black-sand beach is 15km north-east of Legaspi and sometimes has quite high surf. Jeepneys run from Legaspi to Santo Domingo and tricycles run from there to the resorts along the beach.

Daraga & Cagsawa

The eruption of Mayon in 1814 totally destroyed the villages of Camalig, Cagsawa and Budiao on its southern side. The **Cagsawa Church** was rebuilt in a baroque style at nearby Daraga. It's just a 15 minute jeepney ride from Legaspi. The **Cagsawa ruins** are a short distance west of Daraga.

Camalig

The interesting **Hoyop-Hoyopan Caves** are about 10km from Camalig – hire a tricycle there and back or take a jeepney. The **church** in Camalig has artefacts that were excavated from the caves in 1972. Camalig is about 14km from Legaspi and is reached by jeepney or bus.

MAYON

Derived from the word 'beautiful' in the local dialect, Mayon is claimed to be the world's most perfect volcano cone. You can best appreciate it from the ruins of Cagsawa church. In 1814 Mayon erupted violently and killed 1200 people, including those who took shelter in the church. To get to Cagsawa, take a jeepney bound for Camalig and alight at the Cagsawa sign, from where it's a few minutes walk.

Mayon is said to erupt every 10 years and recently it's been doing even better than that. A spectacular eruption in 1968 was followed by another in 1978 and then another in late 1984. The last serious eruption was in February 1993, when 70 people died and a further 50,000 were evacuated.

If you want to appreciate Mayon from closer up, you can climb it in a couple of days – the tourist office in Legaspi will fix you up. The usual cost for two people is around P1800, including a guide, a porter and a tent. Take warm clothing and a sleeping bag; provisions are extra – take enough for two days.

Count on P400 per person for food and for a second porter if you don't want to carry your own food and gear.

You take a jeepney to Buyuhan (extra cost) and then climb two hours to Camp 1 (Camp Amporo), at about 800m. If you start late, you spend the night in the simple hut there. Another four hours takes you to Camp 2 (Camp Pepito), at about 1800m. Here you have to use a tent, as there is no hut. From here it's a four hour climb to the summit, with the last 250m a scramble over loose stones and steep rocks; it's advisable to be roped. Going down takes three hours from the crater to Camp 2, two hours to Camp 1 and two hours to the road.

You can also try hiring a guide and porter in Buyuhan for about P500 a day. To try the ascent without a guide is reckless and irresponsible, because many of the harmless-looking canyons turn out to be dead ends with sheer drops.

TABACO

Tabaco is just a departure point for the Catanduanes ferry.

Getting There & Away

Buses go direct to Tabaco from Manila, or it's just 45 minutes from Legaspi and another half-hour on to Tiwi.

SORSOGON

Sorsogon, the capital of the southernmost province of Luzon, was until recently just a transit region to the Visayas. Now it's known as the gateway to **Donsol**, the town made famous by the appearance of tourist-friendly, plankton-feeding **whale sharks**. Although lacking the basic infrastructure for a tourism boom, Donsol (about 50km from Sorsogon) is set to become a focus for divers and general tourists – as long as the whale sharks keep coming to the party.

Places to Stay

The *Dalisay Hotel* at 182 VL Peralta St, Sorsogon, is simple and fairly clean; singles/doubles are P75/130 with fan and P100/150 with fan and bath.

Getting There & Away

Buses to Sorsogon, from Legaspi, leave every half hour and take 1½ hours. It's 3½ hours from Legaspi to Bulan.

BULUSAN & IROSIN

Mt Bulusan is a 1560m-high volcano at the centre of the triangle between Juban, Bulusan and Irosin. It is a fascinating area: hundreds of different kinds of trees, giant ferns, rare orchids and other flora cover its slopes, and there's a small crater lake, also called Bulusan, a pleasant 6km walk from Bulusan village.

Irosin is another good base for a stay in the so-called Switzerland of the Orient.

Places to Stay

The *Bartilet's Lodging House* behind the town hall in Bulusan has clean singles/doubles at P100/200 with fan. At the pleasant *Villa Luisa Celeste Resort* in Dancalan, Bulusan, the rooms are clean and spacious, with fan and bath for P250/350, and with air-con and bath for P450. The Villa Luisa has a swimming pool.

At the very peaceful *Mateo Hot & Cold Springs Resort* in Irosin, the rooms are basic but passable, and cost P125/250. This pleasant establishment is in a forest about 4km north-east of Irosin (3km in the direction of Sorsogon, then 1km north-east). There is a signpost at the point where the path leaves the road. The resort has two pools (one lukewarm and one hot).

Getting There & Away

Buses from Legaspi go to Irosin or to Bulan via Irosin in about two hours.

MATNOG

Right at the southern tip of Luzon, this is the departure point for boats to Allen, on Samar.

Places to Stay

Mely's Snack House costs P30 per person. It's a basic place and the only one left in Matnog. If they miss the last ferry, most Filipinos prefer to sleep in the big waiting room at the pier.

Getting There & Away

Buses run from Legaspi to Irosin, from where you continue by jeepney. You can do the trip with all connections in three hours. There are also direct Philtranco and BLTB buses, but they come straight through from Manila so it can be difficult to get a seat. It's probably easier to take local services to Sorsogon or Irosin and change there. Coming from Allen there are usually jeepneys waiting to meet the ferry.

PHILIPPINES

Islands Around Luzon

Although Luzon is the main island of the Philippines and offers a lot of attractions, it is only the start – there are still nearly 7000 islands left to explore.

Islands around Luzon include the Batanes, which are scattered off the far northern coast; Catanduanes, off the south-eastern coast near Legaspi; the smaller islands of Masbate and Marinduque; and lastly, the large island of Mindoro, which has become a very popular escape because of its beautiful beaches and relaxing accommodation possibilities.

BATANES

The Batanes Islands are surprisingly unspoilt and different; they display a raw beauty, varying greatly with the tides. Many houses here are built of solid rock and have roofs thickly thatched with grass. There is next to no traffic on the roads, which makes the islands ideal for hiking.

Places to Stay

In Basco, *Mama Lily's Inn* offers unpretentious but pleasant and friendly accommodation; clean rooms with fan cost P400 per person, including three meals.

Getting There & Away

PAL flies to Basco from Manila three times a week.

CATANDUANES

There are some excellent beaches and pleasant waterfalls on this island, but few tourists come here. The main town and accommodation centre is **Virac**.

About 30km north-east of Virac, **Puraran** has a wonderful long, white beach.

Places to Stay & Eat

Sandy's Blossoms Pension House (☎ 811 1762) at Piersite, Virac, has basic singles/doubles with fan for P120/220; there is a little garden restaurant where snacks are served. The more expensive *Catanduanes Hotel* on San Jose St has rooms with fan and bath for P290/400. It's unpretentious but quite cosy, and has a good restaurant on the roof. Both places are within walking distance of the pier.

On the beach at Puraran, the *Puting Baybay Resort* charges P350 per person for a simple room, including three meals.

Getting There & Away

PAL flies daily to Virac from Manila.

The ferry to Virac, on Catanduanes, departs Tabaco daily (four hours, P60).

MARINDUQUE

The small island of Marinduque is sandwiched between Mindoro and Luzon. It's noted for its **Easter Moriones festivals**, in particular at Boac. On Good Friday, the *antipos* (flagellants) engage in a little religious masochism as they flog themselves with bamboo sticks.

From Buenavista, on the south coast, you can climb **Mt Malindig**, a 1157m-high dormant volcano. The weekend **Buenavista Market** is worth seeing.

The **Tres Reyes Islands** are 30 minutes by outrigger from Buenavista – **Gaspar Island** has a small village and a nice coral beach. **White Beach**, near Torrijos, is probably the best beach on Marinduque. The towns of **Gasan** and **Mogpog** are also heavily involved in the Easter passion play.

Getting There & Away

Air PAL has flights three times a week to Marinduque from Manila.

Boat There are usually one or two boats daily from Lucena in Luzon to Balanacan (three hours, P70). Jeepneys meet the boats and go to Boac. Crossings are also made between Lucena and Buyabod, the harbour for Santa Cruz.

There's a daily service from Gasan, between Boac and Buenavista, to Pinamalayan on Mindoro. The crossing takes about three hours.

Boac

One of the most colourful religious ceremonies in the Philippines takes place at Boac from Good Friday until Easter Sunday. Dressed as Roman centurions wearing large carved masks, the participants capture Longinus, the centurion who was converted after he had stabbed Christ in the side with his spear. The festival ends with a *pugutan* (mock beheading) of the hapless Longinus.

Places to Stay On Nepomuceno St, the primitive *Boac Hotel* is probably the best of the handful of places offering basic accommodation in the town. Singles/doubles with fan cost P100/200, and with fan and bath P180/350.

Directly on the sea front at Balaring, 5km south of Boac, the *Marinduque Marine* dive resort has immaculate rooms with fan and bath for P400. About 1km further south, on the pebbly beach at Caganhao between Boac and Cawit, is the *Cassandra Beach Resort*, where fairly tired little cottages with fan and bath cost P175; use of the kitchen is possible.

MINDORO

The relatively undeveloped island of Mindoro is the nearest 'last frontier' to Manila – the Philippines has quite a few last frontiers. The population is concentrated along the coastal strip and inland is mainly dense jungle and mountains.

Because you can get to Mindoro easily from Manila, many travellers make the trip to try the beautiful beaches of Puerto Galera and Sabang on the north-east tip of the island.

Another, albeit less popular, destination is the small island of **North Pandan** just off the west coast.

Getting There & Away

Air PAL, Air Philippines, Asian Spirit and Pacific Airways have flights from Manila to Mamburao, San Jose and Sablayan.

Bus & Boat The usual route to Mindoro is from Batangas, on Luzon, to Calapan or Puerto Galera. Buses run directly to Batangas from the BLTB terminal in Manila (three hours, P74), but beware of pickpockets – they work overtime on this route.

Ferries and outriggers operate all day (until about 6 pm) between Batangas and Puerto Galera (or Sabang). The crossing takes one to two hours, depending on the craft, and prices range from P65 for the Viva ferry and outriggers to P150 for the swish Si-Kat ferry (which sails from Batangas at 11.30 daily).

On Mindoro, you can continue from Pinamalayan to Marinduque, and from Roxas on to Boracay (Panay) or Romblon. The Mindoro to Boracay route is becoming quite popular and combines the two beach destinations of Puerto Galera and Boracay. Be careful, as some of the boats on this route are leaky tubs and are often dangerously overloaded.

There's a big outrigger from Roxas to Boracay on Monday and Thursday (six hours, P250). From December to May it can leave as often as every other day.

Puerto Galera

In recent years, the excellent sailing and snorkelling spot of Puerto Galera has been out-gunned by nearby Sabang. Now something of a haven for western retirees, beautiful little Puerto Galera is a very quiet spot compared with its hipper, younger neighbour.

Information The Rural Bank in Puerto Galera changes cash, as does the Swagman Travel office.

Places to Stay & Eat Inexpensive rooms in Puerto Galera generally cost around P200. If you're trying to save money, the modest *Melxa's Greenhill Nipa Hut* has rooms with fan for P200 – make the most of the place by staying in the beachside annexe. Right at the wharf, the *Coco Point* has rooms with fan and bath for P400.

The row of *restaurants* beside the Puerto Galera pier are much of a muchness, with the emphasis on meaty western stodge. The *Typhoon Restaurant*, however, does a tasty chilli fish with rice for P130.

Getting There & Away Jeepneys leave for Sabang when full from just above the wharf (P10), and tricycles can also be hired for the ride (P60 to P150).

Ferries leave several times a day for Batangas, and bangcas can be hired for the trip around to Sabang (P180) or any other beach you fancy. There's a list of bangca hire rates on a board at the pier.

Sabang

Sabang's beachfront is packed with tropical resort-style hotels/restaurants and dive shops. Rowdier than anywhere else on the island, Sabang still has plenty of quiet patches of paradise to explore. The place tends to be geared towards divers, with most hotels offering dive trips of varying standards and prices.

If you don't dive, it's still worth hiring a snorkel and mask for the day (P100) to check out the fantastic coral at nearby places such as Long Beach.

Places to Stay At the eastern end of Sabang Beach is the *Villa Sabang Beach Resort* (mobile ☎ 0912 313 4486). A very popular place, it has powder-blue rooms with air-con and marble floors for P990. Cottages with kitchenette (fan only) cost P650.

The nearby *Seashore Lodge* (mobile

☎ *0912 304 9340)*, a leafy compound, has balconied huts going for P800 with air-con, fridge, cable TV and bath (it's P500 minus the air-con). *At Cans Inn*, a few doors along, is big and plain and good value, with balconied rooms right on the water. Rooms cost P350 with fan, P800 with air-con.

On the western side of Sabang Beach, hidden up behind the maze of dive shops, the *Terraces Garden Resort Bar & Restaurant* has cute thatched huts (fan only) on the hillside for P600.

Places to Eat & Drink To start the day in style, the *Sunshine Coast Bar & Restaurant* offers the 'Feeling Shitty Breakfast' (coffee, two cigarettes and one Coke – all for P50). This place is right on the beach where the boats pull in and has a great little shady eating area facing the water.

Also among the throng of restaurants worth trying is the tasty *Relax Thai Restaurant*, hidden down a small alley, and the *Tropicana*, on the main drag heading up the hill. The Tropicana has a big menu including seafood, Italian dishes and even imported wines.

A short walk along the Sabang Beach towards the neighbouring Small La Laguna Beach is *The Point*, a bar perched above the walking path. It's open till midnight, does bar snacks and has a big, eclectic CD collec-

tion. And if you really want to drink like a fish, there's always the floating bar, moored about 300m from Sabang's central shore.

Getting There & Away Bangcas come and go all day from Sabang's central shore. Most are running back and forth between Batangas, while others can be hired for trips to Puerto Galera (P180) or elsewhere. Jeepneys and tricycles to Puerto Galera head off from the steep main road inland.

Around Puerto Galera & Sabang

Puerto Galera or Sabang may be where the boat from Batangas drops you, but they're certainly not the only accommodation options in the vicinity.

Places to Stay & Eat More secluded beaches with places to stay include **Small La Laguna** and **Big La Laguna**, **White Beach** and **Aninuan Beach**. All are within 10km of Puerto Galera or Sabang. Most of the prices quoted here are for double occupancy. The places that follow are just a small selection of the numerous possibilities. Most places have their own restaurant/bar.

Small La Laguna Beach You can walk along the beach from Sabang to Small La Laguna Beach, where the *El Galleon Beach Resort* (☎/fax 865252) has spacious poolside hut-

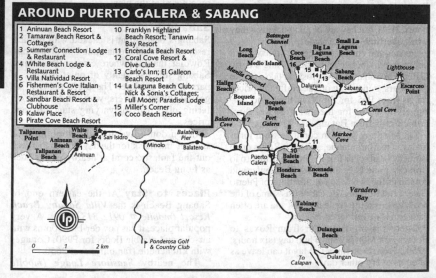

AROUND PUERTO GALERA & SABANG

1 Aninuan Beach Resort
2 Tamaraw Beach Resort & Cottages
3 Summer Connection Lodge & Restaurant
4 White Beach Lodge & Restaurant
5 Villa Natividad Resort
6 Fishermen's Cove Italian Restaurant & Resort
7 Sandbar Beach Resort & Clubhouse
8 Kalaw Place
9 Pirate Cove Beach Resort
10 Franklyn Highland Beach Resort; Tanawin Bay Resort
11 Encenada Beach Resort
12 Coral Cove Resort & Dive Club
13 Carlo's Inn; El Galleon Beach Resort
14 La Laguna Beach Club; Nick & Sonia's Cottages; Full Moon; Paradise Lodge
15 Miller's Corner
16 Coco Beach Resort

style rooms with fan for P912 (P1444 with air-con).

At the other end of the beach, *Carlo's Inn (mobile ☎ 0912 301 0717)* is a fun place with wacky decor. Rooms here are stacked all the way up the steep hill, ensuring great views and firm calf muscles. Rooms start at P450, climbing to P850 for deluxe with air-con.

Big La Laguna Beach Right next to Small La Laguna, Big La Laguna has plenty of accommodation options, including *Nick & Sonia's Cottages* and *Full Moon*, which both have pleasant, quite comfortable cottages from P350. The *Paradise Lodge (☎/fax 375 6348)* has rooms for P550, and the *La Laguna Beach Club (mobile ☎ 0912 306 5622)* has a swimming pool and comfortable rooms with fan and bath for around P700 (P1100 for air-con).

White Beach A little bit like Sabang but with a lot more sand, White Beach to the west has a lively cluster of hotels and restaurants. While it's an easy enough 15 minute jeepney ride from Puerto Galera, White Beach is at its most attractive when approached by boat. Many places to stay in White Beach have mosquito nets 'just in case', and the beach's dazzling expanse of sand can make it extremely hot by day.

Places to stay include the *Summer Connection Lodge & Restaurant* at the western end of White Beach, which has cottages for P500 (fan only). An old favourite, the *White Beach Lodge & Restaurant* has basic P400 to P500 cottages (fan only), and the newer *Villa Natividad (mobile ☎ 0912 391 1825)* has beachy, basic fan rooms for P500 (P1200 with air-con).

Aninuan Beach White Beach's western neighbour is Aninuan Beach, home to the German-run *Aninuan Beach Resort*, with quite spacious cottages with fan for P800; and the *Tamaraw Beach Resort & Cottages*, run by Captain Jesus and his wife. Cottages here go for P500. They may be a little flimsy, but what a location!

Other Areas About 1km from Puerto Galera, on the road to Sabang, is a choice bunch of places to stay for those seeking privacy and panoramic views. The *Franklyn Highland Beach Resort (mobile ☎ 0912 314 8133)* is a friendly new place on the high ridge above the main road. Roomy nipa huts here go for

P500 to P700. The restaurant and pool here have great views of Varadero Bay to the south.

Next door, on a vast plot of prime land, is the luxurious *Tanawin Bay Resort (☎/fax 526 0117)*, featuring such crazed architectural delights as the 'Snail House' and the 'Circle House'. Great views, weird cottages (P1200 to P1600).

Just to the north, on a point overlooking Port Galera, is *Kalaw Place (☎ 0912 301 4778)*. As unique for its low-key approach to tourism as it is for its stunning position and accommodation, it has several cottages and one vast timber villa. Rates range from around P650 to about P2400.

Nearby, the top value *Pirate Cove Beach Resort (mobile ☎ 0912 270 9428)* has comfortable cottages for P500. Carl, the Swedish part-owner, can pick you up from any beach in the area if you ring ahead.

The *Encenada Beach Resort (mobile ☎ 0912 312 9761)*, on the beach of the same name, is in a lovely spot. But the rooms and cottages hardly deserve their US$60 to US$80 price tags.

On Boquete Island, clinging to Mindoro by a narrow land bridge, is the *Sandbar Beach Resort & Clubhouse (mobile ☎ 0912 385 1904)*. Big, well spaced out cottages complete with kitchen, bath and chunky furniture cost a hefty P1500. Nearby, back on the main road, the *Fishermen's Cove Italian Restaurant & Resort (mobile ☎ 0912 306 8494)* comes with a secluded beach and pretty nipa hut cottages for P750.

East of Sabang, the *Coral Cove Resort & Dive Club (mobile ☎ 0973 771571)* has cute, well kept rooms with fan for P800. This sleepy, secluded place has a restaurant with great views and a pool table. Dive trips are a speciality, and there's a private jeep or boat available to pick you up from Sabang.

Over on the west side of Sabang is the exclusive *Coco Beach Resort (mobile ☎ 0917 890 1426)*, with about 90 meticulously finished nipa huts hidden among the palms of a big, beautiful beach. Huts start at US$38 per person, but that includes round-trip transport (Manila-Coco Beach-Manila), buffet breakfast and a guaranteed air of superiority.

Roxas & Mansalay

Roxas doesn't exactly make you feel like staying for long, but from there you can get boats to Boracay. From Mansalay, farther south from Roxas, you can walk to the villages of the Mangyan tribes.

Places to Stay Roxas has the *Santo Niño Hotel*, which has basic singles/doubles with fan for P80/160; with fan and bath for P150/200.

The *Catalina Beach Resort* at Bagumbayan has simple rooms with fan for P60/120 and with fan and bath for P100/200. It's 1.5km from Roxas.

Getting There & Away From Calapan buses take three hours to Bongabong and four hours to Roxas. See Getting There & Away in the earlier Mindoro section for boat information.

San Jose

From the fairly uninviting town of San Jose it may be possible to visit the Mangyan tribes, or you can rent a boat to **Ambulong** or **Ilin Island** for swimming and snorkelling. **Apo Reef**, a popular diving spot well offshore, can be reached from San Jose or Sablayan.

Places to Stay The *Sikatuna Town Hotel* (☎ 697) on Sikatuna St is cheap and OK, with rooms (with fan) starting at P260. The place comes with a very good, very cheap restaurant which does big breakfasts.

Getting There & Away It usually takes several stages to round the southern end of Mindoro between Roxas and San Jose, and the road is often bad. Boats leave from Caminavit Pier, south of town.

Cebu

The most visited of the Visayan islands, Cebu is the major travel hub of the southern Philippines, and flights and shipping services radiate in all directions. This is also where Magellan introduced Christianity to the Philippines with the erection of a cross – and where he was killed in a skirmish on Mactan Island in 1521.

Getting There & Away

Air A huge flock of airlines currently connects Cebu City with Luzon, Mindanao, Palawan and the rest of the Visayas. Cebu's own Cebu Pacific flies to Manila daily, and to Davao.

There are also flights between Cebu City and Hong Kong, Singapore and Kuala Lumpur.

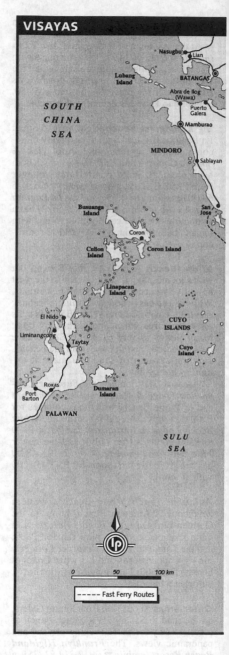

VISAYAS

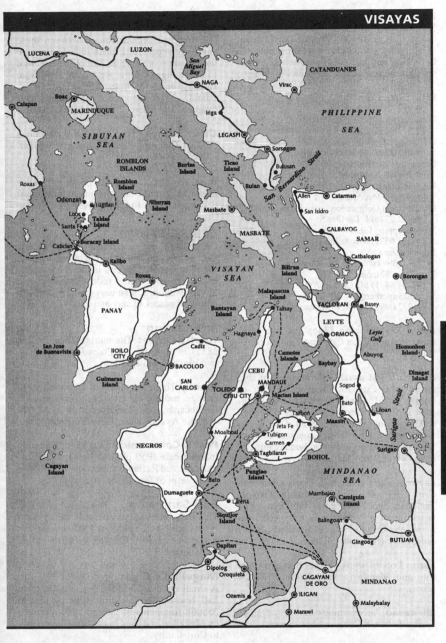

Boat WG&A/SuperFerry sails between Manila and Cebu City five times a week (about 11 hours, P700). There's a vast amount of shipping companies operating between Cebu City and just about everywhere else in the Philippines. These companies include:

Bullet Express
(☎ 91272) Pier 1
Cebu Ferries
(☎ 232 0490) Pier 4, Reclamation Area
Cokaliong Shipping Lines
(☎ 253 2262) 46 Jakosalem St
George & Peter Lines
(☎ 75914) Jakosalem St
K&T Shipping Lines
(☎ 90633) MacArthur Blvd
Lite Shipping Corporation
(☎ 253 7776) L Lavilles St
Socor Shipping Lines
(☎ 253 6531) MacArthur Blvd
Sulpicio Lines
(☎ 73839) 1st St, Reclamation Area
Trans-Asia Shipping Lines
(☎ 254 6491) MJ Cuenco Ave
WG&A/SuperFerry
(☎ 232 0490) Pier 4, Reclamation Area

Bohol VG Shipping Lines has five ships daily between Cebu City and Talibon (three hours, P75).

Camiguin The usual route is by air or ship from Cebu City to Cagayan de Oro or Butuan, in Mindanao, then a bus to Balingoan. From there ferries run across to Benoni, on Camiguin, three times daily. Or you can take another ship from Cagayan de Oro. Sometimes there's a ship on Sunday directly from Cebu City to Mambajao.

Leyte A variety of ships operate between Cebu City and Baybay, Maasin, Ormoc, Tacloban and other ports on Leyte. The fastest are the connections by speed boat from Cebu City to Maasin (two hours, P200) and Ormoc (two hours, P200).

Luzon Lots of ships operate between Cebu City and Manila (around P700; 10 to 14 hours).

Mindanao An enormous number of ships operate between Cebu and Mindanao.

Negros There are four departures daily between Toledo on Cebu and San Carlos on Negros; the trip takes 30 minutes. There are connecting buses between San Carlos and Bacolod.

Other less regular routes between these narrowly separated islands include Bato, in the far south of Cebu, to Tampi; from Tangil to Guihulngan on the west coast; and from Hagnaya in the north to Cadiz, via Bantayan Island. Ships also operate between Dumaguete and Cebu City (five hours, P180).

Other Islands There are also connections between Cebu and Panay, Samar and Siquijor.

Getting Around
Buses run from Cebu City's Southern bus terminal to Toledo and the other west-coast departure points for nearby Negros.

CEBU CITY
Cebu City is the capital and main town, and Colon St is claimed to be the oldest street in the Philippines. The city is currently undergoing considerable redevelopment and modernisation. It's an easy-going place with plenty of places to stay and eat.

Information
Tourist Offices The tourist office (☎ 254 2811) is opposite the Plaza Independencia, two blocks from Pier 1.

Money There are plenty of banks happy to change money or give cash advances on credit cards. American Express (☎ 232 2970) is at the Ayala Center, Cebu Business Park.

Post & Communications There's a handy Internet cafe (P50 per half hour) at the centrally located Ruftan Internet Cafe & Pensione on Legaspi St (see Places to Stay).

Fort San Pedro
This is the oldest Spanish fort in the country. It was built by Legaspi in 1565 to keep out marauding pirates. Entry is P10. It's closed on Monday.

Magellan's Cross
A small circular building, opposite the town hall, houses a hollow cross which is said to contain fragments of the cross brought here by Magellan and used in the first conversions to Christianity.

Basilica Minore del Santo Niño
Not far from the Magellan shrine, the Santo

Niño statuette is the main attraction in this basilica, built in 1740. This image of Jesus as a child was said to have been given to Queen Juana of Cebu by Magellan on the queen's baptism in 1521. It's the oldest religious relic in the country.

Casa Gorordo Museum
In the central Parian district, the impressive Casa Gorordo Museum is a beautifully restored, period-furnished home dating from the early 20th century. Admission costs P15; it is closed on Sunday.

Taoist Temple
Overlooking the town, in the ritzy Beverly Hills residential area, is a magnificent Taoist temple. To get to the temple take a Lahug jeepney and ask to stop at Beverly Hills – you've then got a 1.5km walk uphill. Alternatively, take a taxi for about P40.

Places to Stay
The amiable *Ruftan Internet Cafe & Pensione* (☎ 79138) on Legaspi St has unassuming but clean doubles with fan from P165 to P440.

A good bet is the *Cebu Elicon House* (☎ 253 0367) on Junquera St. It has decent singles/doubles with fan and common bath for P130/200, and with air-con and bath for P380/430.

Also in an acceptable price range, the *McSherry Pension House* (☎ 52749) is a good place despite a dingy reception area. Rooms with fan and bath are P250/300, and P350/450 with air-con. It's a pleasant central place in a lane off Pelaez St, next to the Hotel de Mercedes.

The *Mayflower Pension House* (☎ 253 7233) on Villalon Drive, near Escario St's massive white Capitol building, has smallish rooms with fan and common bath for P210/275, or with air-con and bath for P435/540.

If you're looking for a pleasant, old-style place to stay, check out the popular older-style *Kukuk's Nest Pension House* (☎ 412 2026) at 157 Gorordo Ave. Its cosily furnished rooms with fan and common bath cost P224/392, and it's P616 for air-con, bath and cable TV. There's a nice garden restaurant, but the intersection traffic spoils it a bit.

Finally, the *Verbena Pension House* (☎ 253 3430) is a quiet place on A Don Gil Garcia St, behind Osmeña Blvd. Big, simple rooms here go for P360/410. A room for four is P530. All rooms have air-con and bath.

If you're looking for cheaper accommodation, it's worth asking if the better quality places in Cebu City have rooms without air-con. These places always try to steer you towards air-con first.

Places to Eat
There are lots of places to eat in Cebu City, many of them along *Colon St* – you can, of course, eat much more cheaply off this beaten track. Notable for its excellent, inexpensive food, the *Visayan Restaurant* on V Gullas St has big portions (for P60 to P70) and friendly service. Vegetarians should note: the bean curd soup has meat in it, the fried rice has meat in it ...

The *Snow Sheen Restaurant*, on Osmeña Blvd, has good, low-priced Chinese and Filipino food for about P80. There's a smaller *Snow Sheen* around the corner on Colon St. *Pete's Kitchen* on Pelaez St also has reasonably priced Chinese and Filipino food. Nearby is *Pete's Mini Food Center*, a big, partly open-air restaurant.

For a good breakfast, try the *Ruftan Internet Cafe & Pensione* on Legaspi St. For affordable western food (P80) and cold beer, *Our Place* on Pelaez St is the place to go.

Maxilom Ave has lots of places to eat, including a *Shakey's Pizza*; the *Lighthouse* for Filipino food (P150); and the *Swiss Chalet Restaurant*, with excellent, although not exactly cheap, European food, including imported wine and cheese.

Getting There & Away
There are several buses daily from the Southern bus terminal on Bacalso Ave for the 1½ hour trip from Cebu City to Toledo on the other coast. You also find buses at the Southern bus terminal for Bato (another departure point for Negros) and Moalboal.

If you want to travel to northern Cebu (eg Hagnaya for Bantayan Island or Maya for Malapascua Island), Cebu City's new Northern bus terminal on Soriano St is where you will normally get on the bus.

Getting Around
To/From the Airport The easiest option is a taxi (although the 'fixed rate' into town can range from about P100 to as much as P200) – try to find a few fellow travellers to share the fare.

There used to be a shuttle bus running between Mactan international airport and the city centre but the contract ended, and that was that.

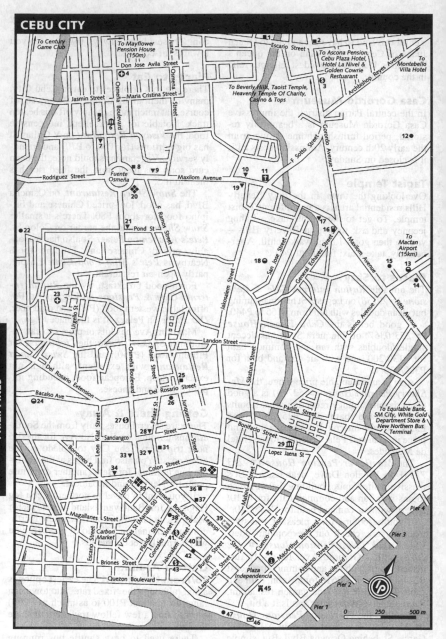

CEBU CITY

CEBU CITY

PLACES TO STAY		17	Lighthouse	20	Robinson's Department
1	Cebu Grand Hotel;	19	Shakey's Pizza		Store
	The Apartelle; Bouraq	21	McDonald's	22	Anzar Coliseum
	Airlines; Grand Air; KLM;	28	Our Place	23	Sacred Heart Hospital
	PAL; Hertz Rent-a-Car	32	Pete's Kitchen;	24	Southern Bus Terminal
2	Kukuk's Nest Pension House;		Pete's Mini Food Center	26	San Carlos University
	Tonros Apartelle;	33	Snow Sheen	27	Central Bank
	Duty-Free Shop		Restaurant	29	Casa Gorordo Museum
5	Verbena Pension House	34	Snow Sheen	30	Gaisano Main Department
8	Park Place Hotel		Restaurant		Store
25	Cebu Elicon House			35	Gaisano Metro Department
31	Hotel de Mercedes;	**OTHER**			Store
	McSherry Pension House	3	PCI Bank; US Consulate	38	PAL
36	Hotel Victoria de Cebu;	4	Cebu Doctors Hospital	39	Cebu Cathedral
	Visayan Restaurant	6	Rizal Memorial Library &	40	Basilica Minore del
37	Ruftan Internet Cafe &		Museum		Santo Niño
	Pensione	11	Iglesia Ni Kristo	41	Equitable Bank
		12	Ayala Center; American	42	Magellan's Cross
PLACES TO EAT			Express; Qantas Airways	43	Philippine National Bank
7	Fruit Stalls	13	Old Northern Bus Terminal		(PNR); City Hall
9	McDonald's	14	Chinese Cemetery	44	Tourist Office
10	Swiss Chalet Restaurant;	15	Caretta Cemetery	45	Fort San Pedro
	Ball's Disco; Robinson's	16	Steve's Music Bar	46	Main Post Office
	Foodorama	18	ABC-Liner Bus Terminal	47	Immigration Office

Taxi Officially, the rate is P20 for the first 500m, and P1 for every 200m thereafter. Between the pier area in the south and the uptown northern area of town, P35 is about right. It you're lucky, your driver will even use the meter.

Jeepney Jeepneys around Cebu City cost about P2.

AROUND CEBU
Mactan Island

The island where Magellan met Lapu-Lapu (and lost) is now the site of Cebu's airport and is joined to Cebu by a bridge. **Guitars**, one of the big industries in Cebu, are manufactured here, and there are **monuments** to both Lapu-Lapu and Magellan.

Places to Stay Around the island there are a number of fine but expensive (US$100) *beach resorts*.

In Lapu-Lapu, near Mactan Bridge, there are a couple of less expensive hotels. The small *Mactan Bridgeside Hotel* (☎ 340 1704) has rooms with cable TV, fan and bath for P385, and with air-con and bath for P700. It also has motorcycles for rent.

Getting There & Away Several jeepneys ply between Cebu City and Lapu-Lapu daily (P4). A taxi should cost about P100.

Bantayan Island

Beautiful Bantayan Island, off the north-west coast of Cebu, has some good beaches on its south coast. The island can also be used as a stepping stone to Negros. The wonderful little town of **Santa Fe**, on the island's south-east coast, is connected by ferry to Cebu Island. With perfect beaches and excellent, relaxed resorts, it attracts a small but steady stream of tourists.

About 10km from Santa Fe, **Bantayan town** is the island's largest (and ugliest) town. It has a lively port with ferries to/from Negros, but it lacks the pristine beaches of Santa Fe – not to mention the Obtong Cave, a small freshwater swimming hole about 10 minutes walk from town (P20 entrance fee).

Places to Stay & Eat A short walk or tricycle ride north from the pier is the stark white *Santa Fe Beach Club* (*Cebu City office* ☎ *255 0676*), where swish air-con twins cost P1000, and cottages with fan and bath are P500. There's a good beach here but just about the only shade is provided by the Caltex oil tanks behind the main building.

On the other side of Santa Fe, the *Kota Beach Resort* (☎ *254 5661*) is set among palm trees and offers rooms with fan for P610, cottages with fan and bath for P840, and with air-con and bath it's P1200. The air-con cottages are too plain for the price, but

PHILIPPINES

the *Ding Dong Bar & Restaurant* here makes up for it – great ocean view and excellent Filipino seafood cuisine for around P90. Right next door, the better value accommodation of the *Budyong Beach Resort* comprises cottages with fan for P350 to P500 and air-con rooms for P900, all laid-out amid shady palms.

One of Bantayan's best kept secrets must surely be *Moby Dick's Beach Resort* (☎ 352 5269), on the road from Bantayan town to Madridejos in the north (turn left at San Pedro Chapel). It's a fun seaside retreat with large cabins for P400 (P500 for full board), a pool, restaurant and free transport from Santa Fe.

Two eateries well worth trying in Santa Fe are *Yaga's Kitchenette*, for local cuisine, and *Moby Dick's* (known locally as Little Dick's), for imported Australian beef, great decor and lots of dick jokes.

Getting There & Away Look for the comfy yellow air-con buses of the Phil-Cebu Bus Lines at Cebu City's new Northern bus terminal. They leave for the northern port town of Hagnaya (via Bogo) at 5 and 6 am, and at 1.30 and 2.30 pm (three hours, P73). From here, pay your P1 pier fee (and get a cute little souvenir ticket) and then hop on a Santa Fe boat (one hour, P55) – there are three a day each way, from 5.30 am to 8.30 pm.

Bantayan town has boats to Cadiz on Negros (3½ hours, P120).

Malapascua Island

Beautiful little Malapascua Island is about 8km north-east of Cebu and 25km west of Leyte. The blindingly white **Bounty Beach** located on the south coast is a gorgeous bathing beach.

Places to Stay In Logon village, *BB's Lodging House* offers basic singles/doubles for P100/200. The *Cocobana Beach Resort* will set you back a bit more: roomy, generously appointed cottages with bath cost P850, although in the off season (May to November) they cost P700.

Places to Eat The best places to eat on the island are *La Isla Bonita Restaurant*, *Ging Ging's Flower Garden* and *Sally's Eatery*.

Getting There & Away Buses leave from Cebu City's Northern bus terminal for Maya early in the morning (3½ hours, P65). Outrigger boats leave Maya for Malapascua at

around 11 am (40 minutes, P15 to P30). There is a boat connection between Maya and San Isidro on Leyte.

Moalboal

There's good, reasonably priced scuba diving at **Pescador Island**, near Moalboal (hard to pronounce – try 'mo-all-bo-all'), and a number of beach resorts near the town along **Panagsama Beach**. From Moalboal, tours with mountain bikes are getting more and more popular.

Places to Stay There's a wide range of accommodation, from simple huts right through to comfortable, air-conditioned rooms.

At the lower end of the price scale, with basic cottages for P150 to P250, try *Emma's Store & Restaurant*, *Pacita's Nipa Hut*, *Virgie's* and the very good value *Eve's Kiosk* (fan rooms P200 to P250, air-con P560 to P700).

Worthwhile mid-range places (around P350 to P450) include the *Roxy Music Pub*, the new cottages of the *Quo Vadis Beach Resort & Visaya Divers*, the nearby *Sunshine Pension-House* (complete with swimming pool) and the more basic beachside *Kukuk's Nest* and *Cora's Palm Court*. The *Sumisid Lodge* (mobile ☎ 0918 770 7986) next door offers excellent rooms in the upper price bracket of P550 (for doubles with fan) to P950 (with air-con) – with a hearty breakfast included in both prices.

Places to Eat & Drink Most places to stay have good restaurants, although there are plenty of other eateries worth a look.

The *Last Filling Station* is famous for its breakfasts, while *BB's Seaview Restaurant* does fine, cheapish Filipino seafood.

There are plenty of pizza and pasta joints, including the new *Francesca's Corner* near Eve's Kiosk, and the fancy *Hannah's Place* nearby.

Lively drinking holes include *The Abyss*, the *Chief Mau Station* and the *Roxy Music Pub* (the Roxy has jam sessions every Saturday night).

Getting There & Away Numerous buses make the daily 90km trip from Cebu City (2½ hours, P40) to Moalboal. A friendly bus driver may even take you right down to the beach, so it's worth asking. Otherwise, take a tricycle from Moalboal for about P25.

ABC or Albines buses run all day to Bato

from Cebu City via Moalboal. In Moalboal, just wait by the main road and be prepared for standing room only. From Moalboal to Bato, it takes about 1½ hours (P27). The Roxy Music Pub can also arrange six-seater minibuses to take you to Bato (P900) and several other spots around Cebu.

Bohol

It's a short ferry trip from Cebu City to the island of Bohol, an easy-going, quiet sort of place with some fine beaches, relatively untouched forests and interesting old churches. The famous Chocolate Hills here are strangely rounded and look rather like chocolate drops when the vegetation turns brown in the dry season. They are about 60km north-east of Tagbilaran, the main town.

There's some superb diving around Bohol. **Balicasag Island**, just 10km south-west of Panglao Island, is surrounded by a coral reef. **Pamilacan** is a beautiful little island, 20km south-east, that gets very few visitors. **Cabilao Island**, 30km north-west of Tagbilaran, has excellent diving and snorkelling.

Getting There & Away

Air Most people get to Bohol via Cebu. There are PAL flights daily from Manila to Tagbilaran.

Boat From Cebu City there are four fast, air-con daily ferries to Tagbilaran (1½ hours, P200), a number of daily ferries to Tubigon (three hours, P75) and a couple to Talibon (three hours, P75).

From Ubay, on the east coast, daily boats run to Leyte (three hours, P65); a weekly ship to Manila (26 hours); and a number of services to ports in Mindanao.

TAGBILARAN

There's not much in Tagbilaran (tag-bil-AR-an), the capital and main port, but you can make worthwhile day trips from the city.

Places to Stay

The *Nisa Travelers Inn* (☎ 411 3731) on Carlos P Garcia Ave is this town's backpacker haven. Despite the closed-down-looking entrance (make a U-turn left up the stairs), it's a friendly place with a lovely timber common balcony area. The windowless singles with common bath (P140) are best avoided, but the doubles with fan for P160 are fine for

the price. Rooms with air-con and bath are P500.

Directly opposite, the *Charisma Lodge* (☎ 411 3094) isn't exactly charismatic, but it does have passable, clean singles with common bath for P150, doubles with fan and bath for P225 and doubles/twins with air-con for P375/395.

Two blocks north, just off Carlos P Garcia Ave on MH del Pilar St, the *Gie Gardens Hotel* (☎ 411 3182) is plushly carpeted and has reasonable singles/doubles with air-con and bath for P490/590.

Way up the north end of town, the *Hotel La Roca* (☎ 411 3179) on Graham Ave has comfy rooms ranging from P600 to P850. There's a swimming pool as well.

Places to Eat

The restaurant at the *Gie Garden Hotel* has good, cheap food. The *Garden Cafe* is a pleasant place next to the church on JS Torralba St which specialises in fruit shakes.

AROUND TAGBILARAN

The old **Punta Cruz pirate watchtower** is 15km north, near Maribojoc. **Loon**, a few kilometres north-west of Maribojoc, has a beautiful old church dating from 1753. **Antequera**, 10km north-east of Maribojoc, has a Sunday market where basketwork is sold.

At **Bool**, 3km east of Tagbilaran, there's a monument commemorating the blood compact between Legaspi and Rajah Sikatuna. **Baclayon**, 4km east of Bool, is the oldest town in Bohol and has one of the oldest churches in the Philippines, dating from 1595. Boats go from there to nearby Pamilacan Island.

Loay has an old church. Outrigger boats go up the Loboc River. The large **San Pedro Church** in Loboc dates from 1602, and there is a remarkable naive painting on its ceiling.

CHOCOLATE HILLS

Legend has it that the Chocolate Hills (there are more than 1000 of them, up to 50m high) are either the teardrops of a heartbroken giant or the debris from a battle between two giants. The scientific explanations for these curious, similarly shaped hills are more mundane: some think they are the result of volcanic eruptions when the area was submerged; others believe they were formed by the weathering of marine limestone over impermeable claystone.

Hiking in the area is best in the dry season, from December to May, when the vegetation has turned brown and the hills are at their most 'chocolate'-like.

Places to Stay & Eat

The sole occupant of the utterly spectacular lookout area is the utterly disappointing *Chocolate Hills Complex*, a grotty place with tired old rooms with bath (P250) and a dorm (P75 per head) that even the lethargic staff seem embarrassed about. Of course the Hills deserve better, but for the price – and the view – it's a crusty old bargain. New rooms are being built and were scheduled to be ready by mid-1999. The complex includes a restaurant, two snakes and a poor little caged tarsier.

Getting There & Away

Buses for Carmen (4km north of the Chocolate Hills) leave from the Tagbilaran bus depot near the Central Public Market hourly, on the hour (two hours, P20). St Jude Line buses make this bumpy trip, and they're often full to overflowing. A few air-con L-300 minibuses also hang around these buses, with drivers offering to get you to the Chocolate Hills for P50 – the only problem is they'll wait there at the depot all day (and so will you) if no other passengers turn up.

From the Chocolate Hills drop-off point, there are usually a few motorbike riders keen to whisk you up the steep hill for P5. The same bikers will take you to/from Carmen for P10. From Carmen, buses to/from Talibon, Tubigon and Tagbilaran can be found (Talibon to Carmen, two hours, P20).

TALIBON

The relatively large town of Talibon on Bohol's north coast has shipping services to Cebu and is the jumping-off point for nearby Jao (pronounced *how*) Island.

Places to Stay & Eat

On the main street, just before the pier, the *Sea View Lodge* has simple little singles/doubles with fan and bath for P75/150, P400 for an air-con room.

Directly opposite is an excellent *fresh food market* and, next to the FCRB bank, the friendly little *Costancia's Restaurant* does good main meals and great halo-halo (P30).

Getting There & Away

From Tagbilaran to Talibon, it's a four hour

bus ride (P40), with the Chocolate Hills almost exactly half way (two hours, P20). VG Shipping Lines has five ships daily between Talibon and Cebu City (three hours, P75).

Panglao Island

Two bridges connect Bohol to Panglao Island, where there are now several beach resorts. Located on the south-west coast, **Alona Beach** is the most popular, especially for diving and whale watching. Unfortunately, bathing is spoilt a bit by the sea urchins that lurk in the sea grass – care is required. **Doljo Beach** is also good, although the water is very shallow.

Hinagdanan Cave at Bingag on the northeast of the island is worth a look.

Places to Stay & Eat

There are about a dozen resorts to choose from at Alona Beach. The best offering for a single/double with fan, at P150/200, is the *Alonaville Beach Resort* (☎ 411 3254). It has good, rustic rooms with common bath for P250 and attractive little rooms and cottages (mostly twins) with fan for P500.

At the quieter end of the beach, a really nice place to spend the night is the *Alona Tropical (mobile ☎ 0918 770 4709)*, which also has a deservedly popular restaurant. Cottages with fan and bath cost a rather high P800.

If you like to be surrounded by lots of greenery, try the *Alona Kew White Beach (mobile ☎ 0912 516 2904)*. It has fairly extensive grounds and offers cottages with fan and bath from P750 to P950 (depending on size), with air-con and bath for P1700 to P2000. There is a fine, big restaurant on the grounds; staff can also arrange excursions.

Getting There & Away

Bus JG Express buses go several times a day from Tagbilaran to the island (45 minutes). Just ask for the bus to Alona. Buses leave from the new bus/jeepney terminal on E Butalid St (at the end of C Marapao St).

Tricycle The simplest way to reach Alona in a hurry is to hire a tricycle from anywhere in Tagbilaran (30 minutes, P100 to P150).

Car From Alona, there are often jeeps or minibuses hanging around after dropping off passengers in Alona. You can usually commandeer one of these for around P200 for a quick trip back to Tagbilaran.

Getting Around

Most places in Alona Beach rent out motorbikes for around P600 per day.

Leyte

Another of the Visayan Islands, Leyte is notable for being the island where MacArthur fulfilled his promise to return to the Philippines – towards the end of WWII Allied forces landed here and started to push out the Japanese.

Like the neighbouring island of Samar, few westerners get to Leyte, so you can expect to be stared at a lot. Although there are some outstanding national parks and an impressive mountain region, there is little tourist development.

Getting There & Away

Air PAL flies to Tacloban daily from Cebu City and Manila.

Bus The San Juanico Bridge connects Leyte with neighbouring Samar. There are daily buses from Tacloban, via Catbalogan and Calbayog on Samar, right through Luzon to Manila – a 28 hour trip in total.

Boat Ships operate between Cebu City and a variety of ports around Leyte. Outriggers operate daily between Carmen on Cebu and Isabel on Leyte (four hours) and between Maya in northern Cebu and San Isidro (two hours).

Daily outriggers connect Ubay on Bohol with Bato and Maasin (four hours, P120). Buses to Mindanao run from Tacloban to Liloan in the south of the island; from there a ferry takes you across to Lipata, 10km north-west of Surigao, and buses continue to Cagayan de Oro or Davao. The ferry crossing takes three hours. There are also ships from Maasin to Surigao.

Getting Around

Buses go hourly between Tacloban and Ormoc (2½ hours, P60). Ormoc to Baybay and Tacloban-Baybay-Maasin also have regular bus services.

TACLOBAN

The small port of Tacloban is the main city of Leyte and home town of the great shoe collector, Mrs Marcos. About 7km out of town, **Red Beach** (it isn't red – that was just its

WWII code name) is the spot where General MacArthur fulfilled his famous 'I shall return' pledge in October 1944. There's a memorial showing MacArthur wading ashore here. Take a jeepney there, but return by getting another jeepney in the same direction; it loops back via Palo.

Information

The tourist office (☎ 321 2048) is on Senator Enage St, at Children's Park.

Places to Stay

Tacloban offers a wide variety of places to stay. *Cecilia's Lodge* (☎ 321 2815) at 178 Paterno St is basic but reasonably good value: singles/doubles from around P100/200 – more expensive with bath or air-con.

Manabó Lodge (☎ 321 3727) on Zamora St has fairly good rooms from P150/240.

Leyte Normal University House (☎ 321 3175) on Paterno St has good value rooms from around P310 to P465.

Places to Eat

You can start the day at the *Good Morning Square* or nearby *Alpha Bakery* in Rizal Ave.

Feel like some Italian food for a change? Then check out *Giuseppe's* on Avenida Veteranos. But if it's seafood you're after, try the inexpensive but excellent *Agus Restaurant*. You can find it on the southern outskirts of town, about 2km from the centre, on San Pedro Bay.

ORMOC

Ormoc is just the jumping-off point for boats to Cebu. The 40km **Leyte Mountain Trail** starts near Ormoc. It crosses over the island from Lake Danao, at about 700m altitude, to Lake Mahagnao. From there you can go down to Burauen, where there's a bus connection to Tacloban (last bus leaves about 3 pm).

Places to Stay

The *Don Felipe Hotel* (☎ 64661) on Bonifacio St has singles/doubles with fan and bath for P190/290; the more expensive rooms with air-con (P900) are among the best in Ormoc. On the same street, the *Pongos Lodging House* has no-frills rooms starting at P100.

Places to Eat

The *Bahia Coffee Shop* in the Don Felipe Hotel is a good restaurant, or try *Chito's Chow Bar & Restaurant* down by the water.

Samar

The large Visayan island of Samar acts as a stepping stone from Luzon to Leyte. There's a regular ferry service from Matnog, at the southern end of Luzon, to Allen and San Isidro at the northern end of Samar. From there, the Pan-Philippine Hwy runs along the picturesque coast and a bridge connects Samar with Leyte.

This road has made transport through Samar much easier. Elsewhere, the island is fairly undeveloped, so finding transport can be hard going. Samar also experiences guerrilla activity – check the situation before venturing there.

The northern part of Samar and the west coast are usually OK. **Sohoton National Park**, near Basey in southern Samar, is the island's outstanding attraction.

Getting There & Away
Bus Buses between Catbalogan and Tacloban, on Leyte, take two hours.

Boat There are a number of ferries daily between Matnog and Allen, and between Matnog and San Isidro. The crossing takes 1½ to two hours.

CALBAYOG

Calbayog is just another 'through' town, although the road there from Allen runs along the coast almost the entire way. The views are especially fine around **Viriato**, between Allen and Calbayog. The **Blanca Aurora Falls** are about 50km south-east of Calbayog. They're reached by boat to Buenavista (one hour) from near the village of Gandara.

Places to Stay & Eat
At the *San Joaquin Inn* (☎ *91125*), at the market on the corner of Nijaga and Orquin Sts, basic singles/doubles with fan cost P90/150 and with fan and bath P260/350. Its restaurant serves good food, despite its appearance; and it's cheap too.

The best hotel in Calbayog is the *Central Inn* on Navarro St, where very clean rooms with air-con and bath cost P550. It also has a rooftop restaurant.

Getting There & Away
There are a couple of daily Philippine Eagle buses and several jeepneys between Catarman and Calbayog, via Allen. Several buses

a day go from Catbalogan to Calbayog (two hours). There are some slower jeepneys.

CATBALOGAN

There are beaches around Catbalogan, but it's really just a stepping stone to Tacloban on Leyte. Buses cross to the east coast from here.

Places to Stay
There is not much choice in Catbalogan. Try the *Domsowir Hotel* on Real St. Singles/doubles with fan and bath are P125/250.

Getting There & Away
At least four buses run daily from Catbalogan, via Borongan (three hours, P480), to Guiuan on the south-east coast of Samar (five hours, P73).

Romblon Islands

This scattering of small islands in the Visayan group is in the middle of the area bordered by South Luzon, Masbate, Panay and Mindoro. It's noted for its marble: quality marble is exported and an extensive range of carved marble souvenirs is produced. There are some good beaches and the tranquil town of Romblon has a notable cathedral. The three main islands of the group are Romblon and the larger islands of Sibuyan and Tablas.

Getting There & Away
Boat Regular boats operate between Lucena on Luzon and Magdiwang on Sibuyan, and between Lucena and Romblon town on Romblon. There are also services twice a week between Manila and Romblon town. Other boats, some of them large outriggers, operate between Romblon ports and Masbate, Mindoro and Panay.

Mindoro to Tablas and Tablas to Boracay, used by some intrepid travellers as a route between the two popular beach centres of Puerto Galera and Boracay, can be a bit risky. There have been some unhappy incidents at Boracay (no deaths, but people have lost all their gear), and the Roxas (Mindoro) to Tablas (Romblon) boats are particularly bad.

ROMBLON

The small port of Romblon on Romblon Island is the capital of (what else?) Romblon province. **San Andres** and **Santiago Hill forts** were built by the Spanish in 1640, while

San Joseph's Cathedral dates from 1726 and houses a collection of antiques. There are good views from the **Sabang** and **Apunan** lighthouses.

Lugbung Island shelters the bay and has a beautiful white beach, as does nearby **Ko-brador Island**.

Places to Stay & Eat

Your best bet here is probably the *Marble Hotel*, where singles/doubles with fan and bath cost P120/150.

You can stay at the *Palm Beach Resort* at Lonos, about 4km south of Romblon town; it's P100/200 for rooms and P150 per person for balconied cottages. There's good food cooked here by your hosts, the friendly Atoy and Inday.

In Romblon town, the *Kawilihan Food House* is by the harbour, but the *Tica Inn* is probably the best restaurant in town.

Getting There & Away

Boats go about four times weekly between Romblon town and Sibuyan in two hours. Daily outriggers to San Agustin, on Tablas, take 45 minutes.

TABLAS

Tablas is the largest island in the Romblon group. The main towns are San Agustin, Odiongan, Looc and Santa Fe.

Places to Stay

The *Kamella Lodge* in San Agustin has singles/doubles with fan for P100/200, rooms with fan and bath for P400 and with air-con and bath for P450/650.

In Odiongan, the *Shellborne Hotel* costs P125/250 with fan and common bath, and P380/550 with air-con and bath.

In Looc, the drably generic *Tablas Pension* across from the market costs P110/220.

Tugdan has the *Airport Pension House*, where modest but clean rooms with fan cost P125/150 (P160/300 with bath).

Getting There & Away

Air Flights to Tugdan from Manila are almost always heavily booked. Jeepneys meet the plane and go to San Agustin (one hour), Santa Fe (one hour) and Looc (45 minutes).

Boat San Agustin is the port for boats to Romblon town. Odiongan's small harbour is just outside the town and, from here, boats go to Batangas on Luzon and Roxas on Mindoro.

Looc is the port for boats to Boracay, and there's a connecting jeepney service from the airport in Tugdan.

There's also a daily boat from Santa Fe to Carabao (the island between Tablas and Boracay), Boracay and Caticlan on Panay. The two hour trip to Boracay costs P90.

SIBUYAN

Sibuyan is more mountainous and less developed than the other islands. There are several **waterfalls** and the 2050m-high **Mt Guiting-Guiting**.

Panay

The large, triangular island of Panay in the Visayan group has a number of decaying forts and watchtowers – relics from the days of the Moro pirates. There are also some interesting Spanish churches, especially on the south coast, which stretches from Iloilo City around the southern promontory at Anini-y to San Jose de Buenavista.

The Ati-Atihan Festival in January, in Kalibo, is one of the most popular in the Philippines.

Last, but far from least, the delightful little island of Boracay, off the north-west tip of Panay proper, can get so packed it's a wonder its famous white sand is still above sea level.

Getting There & Away

Air There are a variety of flight services to Panay from Manila, Cebu City and other major centres. Air Philippines flies from Manila to Iloilo City; PAL flies from Manila to Iloilo City, Kalibo and Roxas, and from Cebu City to Iloilo City and Kalibo, and Air Ads, Asian Spirit and Pacific Airways fly from Manila to Caticlan. Travellers bound for Boracay head for Kalibo or Caticlan, but the Kalibo flights are often heavily booked.

Boat You can reach Panay by boat from Cebu, Leyte, Luzon, Mindanao, Mindoro, Negros, Palawan and Romblon. The shortest crossing is the two hour trip from Bacolod on Negros to Iloilo City. There are several boats daily.

It's possible (with some difficulty) to travel from Mindoro to Boracay (San Jose to Caticlan P150; six hours), but this can be a dangerous trip as the outrigger boats are often no match for severe conditions in the Tablas Strait.

ILOILO CITY

Iloilo (ill-o-ill-o) City is the capital of Iloilo Province and the main city on Panay. It is a large town which was very important during the Spanish era. There's the interesting and large **Museo Iloilo** in the city, plus the coral **Molo Church**.

Iloilo has wide, leafy streets and its curving riverside lay-out make it a great place to explore, either on foot or with the help of a jeepney.

Iloilo City is noted for its *jusi* (raw silk) and *piña* (pineapple-fibre) weaving. The very colourful **Dinagyang Festival** is held here in January.

Information

The tourist office (☎ 337 5411) is on Bonifacio Drive.

Places to Stay

For true budget accommodation, you can't go past the *Centercon Hotel* (☎ 73431). Actually, you can very easily go past it – it's hidden down a narrow lane off JM Basa St (look for the lane entrance next to the Rose Pharmacy). Single/doubles with fan and bath are P150/250, or P406/519 with air-con. Cable TV is P50 extra.

A couple of blocks north, past the Museo Iloilo on Bonifacio Drive, there's the *Castle Hotel* (☎ 81021) and, 200m on, the *River Queen Hotel* (☎ 337 6667). Both have seen better days, and both have entrances far more impressive than their rooms, but they offer livable rooms with air-con (P433/522 at the Castle and P485/585 at the River Queen).

Around the corner, the popular *Family Pension House* (☎ 335 0070), on General Luna St, has clean, acceptable rooms with fan and bath for P225/300, or air-con doubles with bath and cable TV from P400.

The best value place to stay is the ritzy new *Four-Season Hotel* (☎ 336 1070) on Delgado St. Run by four friends fresh out of college, this place looks far pricier than it is, with sparkling rooms (with air-con, cable TV, phone and great hot showers) for P550/680. The swanky lobby also features a good restaurant.

Places to Eat

You can eat Filipino food with your fingers at *Nena's Manokan* restaurant on General Luna St. However, the most popular, and probably the best, local restaurant is *Tatoy's Manokan & Seafood*; it's at Villa Beach on the western edge of town, about 8km from the city centre.

For breakfast, or general munchies, try the big *Tibiao Bakery* on General Luna St, opposite the Iloilo Supermarket.

Shopping

Apart from fabrics such as *barong* shirts made from *piña*, Iloilo City is well known for its local shellcraft and is a good town in which to look for *santos*, antique statues of the saints.

Getting There & Away

Air There are flights between Iloilo and Manila, Cebu City, Puerto Princesa and General Santos City, among other places.

Bus Ceres Liner buses run between Iloilo City and Estancia, Roxas, Kalibo and Caticlan. The depot is near the corner of Ledesma and Rizal Sts. If you're bound for Boracay, it's best to catch the 10.45 am bus to Caticlan (six hours, P94) so you have enough time to grab a boat across to Boracay.

Getting Around

To/From the Airport The airport is about 7km out and a taxi there costs about P100. Taxi drivers (and their meters) are fairly reliable in this town.

AROUND ILOILO CITY

Guimaras

Guimaras, an island province between Panay and Negros, makes a pleasant day trip from nearby Iloilo City.

Alubihod Beach, with its white sand, is good for swimming; it's about 45 minutes walk from Nueva Valencia.

The walk to **Daliran Cave** from Buenavista is pleasant, although the cave itself is not that memorable.

There's a beautiful view over Iloilo Strait from **Bondulan Point**, near Jordan, which has a giant cross standing on it.

Places to Stay The *Colmenaras Hotel & Beach Resort* has rooms with fan and bath for P120, or cottages for single/double P100/200; there's no bathing beach here, although there is a pool.

Getting There & Away Small ferries cross from Iloilo City to the island almost hourly (30 minutes, P8).

KALIBO

The only real interest here is the annual **Ati-Atihan Festival** in January – the Mardi Gras of the Philippines. Similar festivals are held elsewhere in the country but this one is the most popular.

Places to Stay

During the huge Ati-Atihan Festival in January, you'll be lucky to find a decent room for anything less than triple the normal price.

Gervy's Gourmet & Lodge (☎ 262 4190), on quiet R Pastrada St, has simple, clean rooms with bath and fan for P125.

On Martelino St, parallel to Pastrana St, the *Glowmoon Hotel & Restaurant* (☎ 868 5167) is a similar sort of place, although with a wider range of rooms. Singles/doubles with fan and common bath are P250/350, or P500/800 with air-con.

On the town's main thoroughfare of Roxas Ave, up three floors at No 159, the spruce *Garcia Legaspi Mansion* (☎ 262 5588) is the best budget deal in town. Doubles with fan and common bath are P300, or P350 to P650 with private bath. Big air-con rooms start at P700. There's also a good little coffee shop here.

Places to Eat

The *Peking House Restaurant* on Martyrs St has outstanding Chinese food; the set menu for P65 is recommended. The *Glowmoon Hotel* also has a restaurant with excellent, if not so cheap, food.

The little *Willhelm Tell Deli-Shop & Restaurant* on Roxas Ave specialises in European sausages and US and Australian steaks, with dishes starting at around P160.

Getting There & Away

Air PAL flights between Manila and Kalibo are very heavily booked, so make reservations well ahead of time and reconfirm as early as possible. PAL also flies between Cebu City and Kalibo. Other airlines worth checking are Air Philippines and Asian Spirit.

Bus Ceres Liner buses operate from Iloilo City to Kalibo daily (six hours, P74). From Kalibo, the buses leave from the service station on the southern edge of town.

The trip from Kalibo to Caticlan, where boats cross to Boracay, takes about two hours by jeepney from Roxas Ave (P30). If you arrive by plane from Manila in the early afternoon, you might be able to get to Boracay before sunset. After the flight from Manila arrives, comfortable air-con buses leave the airport for Caticlan. The trip takes about 1½ hours (P175, including the boat transfer, which costs P16.50).

Jeepney Jeepneys run back and forth all day between Kalibo and Caticlan (two hours, P30).

CATICLAN

Outrigger boats cross from Caticlan to Boracay and there's also a small airport for the increasingly popular flights from Manila. Sunday – market day – merits a trip from Boracay.

Getting There & Away

There are direct buses from Iloilo City to Caticlan but it takes about seven hours – five to Kalibo and two more to Caticlan.

Jeepneys from Kalibo leave several times daily (two hours, P30).

Boracay

This superb little island, off the north-western tip of Panay, has beautiful clear water and splendid beaches. It's about 9km long, only 1km wide in the middle, and you can walk across it in just 15 minutes.

Beach and water activities, general lazing and watching the sunset are daily attractions at this popular spot. Although electricity has arrived on Boracay it's still a good idea to bring along a torch (flashlight).

White Beach is the centre of Boracay's tourist area, and three 'Boat Stations' are stretched out across its sands. These are hard to spot, being simply designated patches of beach where the regular bangcas drop off and pick up passengers. The beach is dominated by a sandy pedestrian highway – the White Beach Path – where motorised vehicles are banned and it's almost compulsory to go barefoot.

Information

Tourist Offices DOT runs a friendly and efficient office about halfway along White Beach in front of Boat Station 2. Further south, the big Boracay Tourist Center, near

PHILIPPINES

WHITE BEACH BORACAY

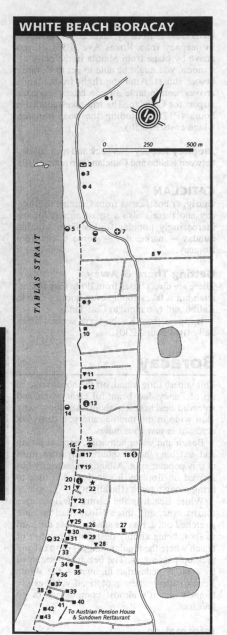

WHITE BEACH BORACAY

PLACES TO STAY
10	Red Coconut Beach Resort; Seabird Resort Bar & Restaurant
17	Nigi Nigi Nu Noos; Victory Restaurant; Victory Divers
26	Michelle's Bungalows
27	Trafalgar Garden & Lodge
30	La Isla Bonita; Mona Lisa White Sand; Beach Life Bar & Restaurant; Pizza da Baffo; Beach Life Diving Center
31	Queen's Beach Resort
35	Noe's Place
37	South Sea Beach Resort; Dive Right Dive Shop
39	Melinda's Garden
40	Moutain View Inn; The Orchids Resort
41	Moreno's Place
42	Villa Camilla; English Bakery; Swagman Travel
43	Tin-Tin's Cottages

PLACES TO EAT
8	English Bakery & Tea Room
11	Mango-Ray Restaurant & Laser Disc Cine Club; True Food; Lapu-Lapu Diving Center
19	Alice in Wonderland Bar & Restaurant
21	Diamond Garden Restaurant
23	Dalisay Bar & Restaurant
24	English Bakery; Boracay Scuba Diving School
25	Casa Pilar
28	Honey Bee Restaurant; Lolit's
33	Sulu Tha Thai Restaurant; Swiss Inn Restaurant; Aqualife Diving; Sulu Bar
36	Cocoloco Bar & Restaurant

OTHER
1	Boracay Horse Riding Stables
2	Post Office
3	Swagman Travel
4	Far East Scuba Diving Institute
5	Boat Station 1
6	710 Boracay Shuttle Office
7	Boracay Medical Clinic
9	Aquarius Diving
12	Sea World Dive Center
13	DOT Tourist Office
14	Boat Station 2
15	PT&T Office
16	Charlh's Bar
18	Allied Bank
20	Boracay Tourist Center
22	Police Station
29	Fausto's Shiatsu
32	Boat Station 3
34	Star Fire General Store
38	PAL

the Alice in Wonderland Restaurant, has more general info and a noticeboard that's always worth perusing. Both places sell maps of the island.

Money The Allied Bank along the main road will change travellers cheques and cash. Many resorts change cash and travellers cheques, and the Boracay Tourist Center and Swagman Travel offices will give cash advances on major credit cards (with an 8% commission).

Post & Communications Several resorts have phone and fax facilities, but the rates are a lot higher than at the Boracay Tourist Center or the PT&T office near Charlh's Bar. The nearby resort of Nigi Nigi Nu Noos is, so far, the only place with Internet access.

Things to See & Do
Besides doing absolutely nothing, you can easily arrange **snorkelling** and **diving** trips on Boracay. The island is surrounded by spectacular reefs, and White Beach is packed with diving resorts and dive shops. Snorkelling gear costs about P200 to hire; diving trips cost around P750.

Half-day **boat excursions** (with food laid on) are about P450 (ask at just about any resort).

Boracay Horse Riding Stables (☎ 288 3311) do great one hour **horse rides** for P390.

Or if you're only up to a **massage**, try Fausto's Shiatsu (☎ 288 3305), near Boat Station 3 (P300 for one hour).

Places to Stay
Boracay accommodation rates are ruled by the high season (1 December to 31 May) and the low season (1 June to 30 November). Time your trip right and you'll get a P800 cottage for P400 (or, time it wrong, and you'll get a P400 cottage for P800).

There are so many cottages along White Beach that the best thing to do is just to start at one end and keep going until you find something you like. With this many options, you can afford to be fussy. And don't just stick to the beachfront – keep your eyes open for signs to places hidden down the narrow paths leading away from the water.

Starting at the southern end of White Beach (near Boat Station 3), there's the peaceful *Austrian Pension House & Sundown Restaurant* (☎ 288 3406), where rooms with fan and bath cost P250 to P350.

Then there's the glaring-white *Tin-Tin's Cottages* (☎ 288 3051), a popular place with singles/doubles for P300/500 (with fan and bath).

Close by is the stylish *Villa Camilla* (☎ 288 3354), which has great Spanish-style rooms with fan and bath for P600, or P1200 with air-con.

Next up, take the path leading away from the beach and you'll find *Moreno's Place*, where cottages with bath are P300. Next door is the hidden gem known as *Melinda's Garden* (☎ 288 3021). Run by the tireless Horst and Melinda, it has roomy, jungley cottages ranging form P400 to P750. Discounts are often possible, the staff are helpful and there's an excellent restaurant offering imported European wines.

Back on White Beach Path, you can't miss the lavishly landscaped *Mona Lisa White Sand* (☎ 288 3012), where very nice cottages are pretty pricey at P1200.

For better value, head down the next path leading off the beach (next to the Beach Life Bar) and look for *Michelle's Bungalows*, a tranquil courtyard of cottages priced at P400.

Nearby is the crowded little *Trafalgar Garden & Lodge* (☎ 288 3101), 'an oasis in the middle of the epicentre', according to one satisfied customer. The Trafalgar's friendly owners, Julia and Joel, offer a wide range of comfy rooms and cottages, from P150 to around P400. Their breakfasts also come highly recommended.

Back on the beachfront, about 500m on, is *Nigi Nigi Nu Noos* (☎ 288 3101), which lives up to its fantastic name with towering nipa huts (P1200 with fan and bath; 1800 with air-con) all hidden in a veritable jungle of palms and ferns.

Towards Boat Station 1, the fancy *Red Coconut Beach Resort* (Manila office ☎ 522 1405) has nice enough rooms for US$30 and, set back from the beach, outrageously luxurious rooms for US$60.

Just behind the Red Coconut's front building, the great value *Seabird Resort Bar & Restaurant* (☎ 288 3047) is a new place with an excellent range of rooms, starting at P390 for doubles with fan and spotless common bath. Doubles/twins with hot shower are P750.

Places to Eat & Drink
There are so many restaurants here that some places tempt customers in with surprisingly inexpensive, yet sumptuous, buffets (ranging

from P135 to P160). Others have concentrated on one particular kind of food to attract business. Nearly every eatery here does great fruit shakes, and the **English Bakery** (with three outlets) is a big breakfast favourite.

Needless to say, White Beach is also one very long shelf when it comes to alcohol. Most places have a happy hour starting at 5 pm and finishing at 7, 8 or even 9 pm.

Starting at the southern end of White Beach, your eating and drinking orgy should include the **Cocoloco Bar & Restaurant**, which does a fine pizza for around P100. **Melinda's Garden** nearby specialises in European cuisine. Down the busy lane starting near the Queen's Beach Resort, savour cheap local flavours at the popular **Honey Bee Restaurant** and, opposite, **Lolit's**.

Back on the beach, past Mona Lisa White Sand, the big open-air **Casa Pilar** has nightly grills. Two doors along, the **Dalisay Bar & Restaurant** is renowned for its P150 all-you-can-eat buffet.

On the south side of the Boracay Tourist Center, the 24 hour **Diamond Garden Restaurant** does low price Filipino dishes, as does the 24 hour **Alice in Wonderland Bar & Restaurant** on the north side of the tourist centre.

The nearby **Victory Restaurant** (set back a little from the rest) is a pleasant place serving small helpings of Thai food, among other styles. **Nigi Nigi Nu Noos**, next door, has a big menu, reasonable prices, and great jazz and blues music (sometimes live). Close by, the little shack of **Charlh's Bar** also has good music, usually quite loud, usually quite late.

Further afield, up near the Lapu-Lapu Diving Center, you'll find the relaxed setting of the **Mango-Ray Restaurant & Laser Disc Cine Club**. The Mango-Ray does good pasta and pizza for around P140.

The Cine Club has a pool table and board games. Next door, the cosy, cushiony **True Food Restaurant** is a fine but quite pricey Indian restaurant.

Getting Around

This compact island is perfect to explore on foot. Tricycles cost about P20 for short trips, mountain bikes can be hired for around P300 per day, and motorbikes for about P800.

Getting There & Away

Getting to Boracay from Manila is either quick, relatively expensive and heavily booked or else it's time-consuming. Caticlan, just across the narrow strait on Panay, is the departure point whether you arrive by bus, jeepney or air.

Air The quickest (and most expensive) way to Boracay from Manila is to fly to Caticlan with Air Ads, Air Philippines, Asian Spirit or Pacific Airways. PAL flies to Kalibo, from where it's two hours by road to Caticlan.

PAL also flies to Tugdan on Tablas Island, in the province of Romblon, but the sea crossing from there to Boracay via Santa Fe is not always easy. You can also fly from Manila to Iloilo City, but it's a long bus ride from there to Caticlan.

Boat Outriggers shuttle back and forth between Caticlan and Boracay (P16.50). The crossing takes only 20 minutes, but operators are inclined to grossly overload the boats and more than one traveller has lost gear after a capsize. During the south-western monsoons from June to November, the sea on the west side of Boracay can get too rough for outriggers. They then tie up on the east coast, at or near Bulabog, or at Manoc-Manoc.

There's a big outrigger between Boracay and Looc, on Tablas, twice a week, which takes about two hours in good conditions. There's also a daily one to Santa Fe on Tablas (1½ hours). There are jeepneys from Santa Fe and Looc to Tugdan, the airport on Tablas. The boat departs from Tablas when passengers arrive from the airport.

There are also several ports in north Panay, including Dumaguit and New Washington, both near Kalibo.

Negros

Sandwiched between Cebu and Panay, and well connected by ferry services in both directions, Negros is the sugar island of the Philippines. **Kanlaon volcano** may, it is hoped, become a similar tourist attraction to the famous Mayon volcano in South Luzon, but at the moment the volcano has a 4km danger zone around it due to recent ominous rumblings. The east and south-east coasts of Negros can offer Spanish-style charm – perhaps a reason why foreigners often spend a few days in and around the pleasant little town of Dumaguete.

Getting There & Away

Air PAL flies to Bacolod and Dumaguete from Cebu City and from Manila.

Boat There are four ferry departures daily between Toledo on Cebu and San Carlos on Negros. The crossing takes just 30 minutes. Other regular services across the comparatively narrow waters between the two islands are from Tampi to Bato in the far south, Tangil to Guihulngan in the centre and Hagnaya via Bantayan Island to Cadiz in the north. Ships also operate between Cebu City and Dumaguete.

The next island north is Panay; the popular route from Negros to Panay is the Bacolod-Iloilo City boat service, but you can also go via Guimaras Island. The Bacolod to Iloilo City ferry operates two or three times daily (two hours, P50). Allow an hour to get by jeepney from Bacolod to the Banago wharf. Other Negros-Panay connections include the daily boats from Victorias to Culasi and Malayuan, both near Ajuy, on the east coast of Panay.

There are also frequent shipping connections between Negros and other islands, including Siquijor, Luzon (a 20 hour trip) and Mindanao.

Getting Around
Along the north and east coasts it's 313km between Bacolod and Dumaguete, which are at opposite ends of the island. The trip takes 7½ hours (P150), and it's wise to take an express bus, as it avoids the many small village stops. Bacolod to San Carlos takes four hours. The route along the west coast – from Bacolod to Kabankalan and then cutting across the island to Dumaguete via Mabinay – is shorter and faster (5½ hours).

BACOLOD
Bacolod is a typical Filipino city of no great interest. You can visit the huge **Victorias Milling Company**, one of the world's largest sugar refineries, 35km north of the city. Bacolod is also one of the major **ceramics** centres of the Philippines.

Information
The tourist office (☎ 29021) in the city plaza has first-hand information about climbing – or avoiding – Mt Kanlaon.

Places to Stay
The *Pension Bacolod* (☎ 23883) on peaceful 11th St offers good value for money: immaculate singles/doubles with fan cost P95/145, or P155/200 with fan and bath; with air-con and bath it's P260/335. No wonder it's often fully booked.

The small, well managed *Ester Pension* (☎ 23526) on Araneta St has tiny rooms with fan and bath for P150/200, and with air-con and bath from P300. It's OK for the money.

The centrally located *Bacolod Pension Plaza* (☎ 27076) on Cuadra St has more than 60 friendly, quiet rooms with air-con and bath from P575 to P790.

The *Bascon Hotel* (☎ 23141) on Gonzaga St is neat and clean, and has comfortable air-con rooms at P550/650.

Places to Eat
Reming's & Sons Restaurant in the city plaza serves good Filipino fast food, as does the air-con *Gaisano Food Plaza* on Luzuriaga St.

The *Ang Sinugba Restaurant* on San Sebastian St is clean, well kept and does first-class native food, while *Mira's Cafe* on Locsin St serves native coffee.

You can get barbecues and beer at the many all-night restaurants at the *Manokan Country*, in the Reclamation Area.

Getting There & Away
There are a number of Ceres Liner buses daily between Bacolod and Dumaguete via San Carlos, and two Royal Express buses via Mabinay.

Jeepneys run to Ma-ao, Silay and Victorias.

Getting Around
To/From the Airport A cab from the airport to the centre shouldn't cost more than P30, or you can stop a passing jeepney, as they all go to the city plaza.

Bus After the arrival of a ferry from Iloilo City, air-con shuttle buses will take you to the city plaza for P20.

Jeepney Banago Wharf is about 7km north – about P7 by jeepney or P40 by cab. The Northern bus terminal is a P2 trip on a jeepney labelled 'Shopping'.

AROUND BACOLOD
Sugar Plantations
Old steam locomotives, used on the sugar cane fields until recently, can possibly be seen at the MSC (Ma-ao Sugar Central) – check at the tourist office in Bacolod. Ma-ao is an hour by jeepney from Bacolod. The **Hawaiian-Philippine Sugar Company** in Silay has a 180km rail network and some fine steam engines. Silay is only half an hour from Bacolod.

Informative and efficient guided tours of the **Vicmico** (Victorias Milling Company) plant are operated from Tuesday to Friday. Arrangements can be made at the company's Public Relations building. Again, there are some fine old steam locomotives, but the town of Victorias also has the quirky **St Joseph the Worker Chapel**, with its famous mural of the Angry Christ. Victorias is an hour by bus (P13) or jeepney (P8) from Bacolod, and it's a further 15 minutes by jeepney (P3) to the 'VMC'.

DUMAGUETE

Dumaguete (doo-ma-GET-ay) is a pleasant, leafy little town, centred on the large Silliman University campus, where there's the very interesting **Anthropology Museum & Center for the Study of Philippine Living Culture**. The museum is at the eastern end of the university's big, grassy area (enter from Hibbard Ave, the extension of Perdices St). It's open weekdays from 8 am to 12 noon, and 2 to 5 pm. Admission is P5. **Silliman Beach**, just north of Dumaguete, is fine for swimming.

Information

Money There are several banks in town, including the PNB on Silliman Ave.

Post & Communications The post office is on the corner of Legaspi and Santa Catalina Sts.

Email & Internet Access Two doors along from Opeña's Pension House & Restaurant (see Places to Stay) is the Surf Station Internet Cafe. It's open late and charges only P40 per hour.

Laundry The Brightwash Laundry is handily placed below the Home Quest Flats (see Places to Stay).

Places to Stay

The cheapest places in town are around Silliman University (near the ferry pier). On noisy Silliman Ave, *Jo's Lodging & Restaurant* has rock-bottom P100 fan rooms. It's above a raucous fried chicken joint – but there's a very generous check-out time of 6 pm! Also on Silliman Ave, over Perdices St (the town's main drag), *Home Quest Flats* (☎ 225 3327) has windowless singles with fan and common bath for P176, and doubles for P283. Air-con singles/doubles (with common bath) are P292/395.

On the other side of Silliman University, at 27 Katada St, *Opeña's Pension House & Restaurant* (☎ 225 0595) has rooms with fan for P385/440, and with air-con for P495/577.50. All rooms have private bath and cable TV – and, except for the screaming blue carpet, they're nice and quiet.

At the southern end of Perdices St, on Santa Rosa St, rooms at the *OK Pensionne House* (☎ 225 5925) are indeed OK, as long as you can live without windows. Single rooms with fan are P275, and singles/doubles with air-con range from P385/440 to P550/770. The air-con rooms are set around an Arabian-style courtyard worthy of a Humphrey Bogart movie.

By the water, on Rizal Blvd, the swish *Bethel Guest House* (☎ 225 2009) is a multi-storey place with spotless 'studios' (singles) and doubles with modern conveniences for P630.50 and P660.

Along the coast south of Dumaguete there are a few nice resorts, including the *El Dorado Beach Resort* in Dauin, *Hans & Nenita's Malatapay Cottages* in Maluay, the *Salawaki Beach Resort* in Zamboanguita and the *Kookoo's Nest Beach Resort* on Tambubo Bay.

Places to Eat

There's excellent food at the Chinese *Chin Loong Restaurant* on Rizal Blvd; particularly recommended is the special dinner for P100, which includes bird's-nest soup.

One block down, the *Music Box* and *Chico's Pizza Snack & Bar* are popular, cheap eating and drinking hang-outs.

Getting There & Away

Air PAL and Cebu Pacific fly regularly between Cebu City and Dumaguete. PAL has an office at Dumaguete airport (☎ 225 1352), just north of town. Pacific Airways should be able to get you over to Siquijor Island.

A tricycle into town from Dumaguete airport costs about P10-20.

Bus The fastest bus connection from Bacolod to Dumaguete is with Royal Express via Mabinay (5 hours). From both Bacolod and Dumaguete, buses leave daily at 6 and 10 am, and 1.30 pm. There are also Ceres Liner buses operating around the southern end of the island via Hinoba-an (12 hours).

Boat Delta Fast Ferry and SeaAngel both have hydrofoil 'fastcrafts' daily between Dumaguete and Dipolog on Mindanao (one to two hours, P185 to P210), as well as from Dumaguete to Larena (Siquijor Island). In Dumaguete, the hydrofoil offices are at the central wharf, on Rizal Blvd.

At Dumaguete's port in Tampi (20 minutes from town by jeepney, P10), boats sail to/ from Bato on Cebu Island every 90 minutes or so daily, from 5.30 am to 5 pm (45 minutes, P27).

Several shipping firms operate between Dumaguete (Tampi wharf) and Cebu City (five hours, P180). The WG&A SuperFerry also stops at Dumaguete on its weekly run between Manila and Dipolog (on Mindanao).

Getting Around
There are tricycles everywhere, and motor-bikes can be hired next to the Chin Loong Restaurant on Rizal Blvd. From Chico's Pizza Snack & Bar nearby, a free shuttle bus goes to the El Dorado Beach Resort at 11.30 am daily (20 minutes).

AROUND NEGROS
Siquijor
The island of Siquijor (sick-YAW) lies about 20km east of southern Negros and is one of the smallest provinces in the Philippines. A surfaced road encircles this hilly island, connecting its tidy villages and small towns. **Larena** is its main port, Siquijor town is the capital. The most popular beaches are at **Sandugan**, 6km north of Larena, and along the west coast at **Paliton**, 2km north of San Juan.

Among Filipinos, Siquijor is known for its witches, magicians and faith healers. Indeed, many strange events take place on this island, especially in the mountain village of **San Antonio**.

Places to Stay In Larena, the *Luisa & Son's Lodge* near the noisy wharf has basic singles/doubles with fan for P200/250. It also offers good local cuisine. The *Larena Pension House*, just a few minutes walk uphill from the wharf, has unpretentious rooms with fan for P100/150.

On Sandugan Beach, you can stay for P300 to P500 in pleasantly decorated cottages with fan and bath at *Casa de la Playa*, *Kiwi Dive Resort* and *Paradise Beach*.

Getting There & Away There are daily hydrofoil 'fastcrafts' between Dumaguete on Negros and Larena, three boats weekly between Cebu City and Larena (seven hours),

three boats a week between Plaridel on Mindanao and Larena (five hours) and one boat weekly between Tagbilaran on Bohol and Larena (four hours).

Getting Around Jeepneys and tricycles are the main means of transport. A tricycle from Siquijor town to Larena costs P5 to P10 per person.

Mindanao

South of the Visayas is Mindanao, the second largest of the Philippine islands and also the country's biggest trouble spot. Its predominantly Muslim population has long chafed at Christian rule: Islam had already gained a toehold by the time the Spanish arrived, and throughout the Spanish era the situation varied from uneasy truce to outright rebellion.

More recently, the Mindanaoans have campaigned hard for separation from the rest of the country. Armed at one time by Libya's Colonel Moammar Gaddafi, the Mindanao guerrilla force (the Moro National Liberation Front, or MNLF) staged a long-running battle with government forces. Although the government and the MNLF concluded a peace agreement in 1996, it was no surprise to anybody that the peace was not kept for long.

A splinter group of the MNLF, known as the Moro Islamic Liberation Front (MILF), has been responsible for some of the most ferocious terrorist attacks in recent years.

Both the Philippine and foreign media dutifully report on 'Muslim' violence in Mindanao, but the background for the fighting is rarely touched on. Government moves to weaken and displace the Muslim majority, crush all resistance without question and offer what many see as token autonomy, only serves to fuel the fire. With the island's rich resources long exploited by outsiders, it's hardly surprising that Muslim terrorist groups have evolved. These are desperate, endangered people and travellers should stay out of their way. Kidnappings are common in many areas. Before straying too far from Mindanao's main cities, check thoroughly with tourist offices, bus companies and locals to make sure your destination – and the roads to and from you destination – are safe.

Getting There & Away
Air You can fly to Mindanao from Cebu City or Manila with airlines including PAL, Air Philippines and GrandAir, for around P1000.

GrandAir also flies between Cagayan de Oro and Manila daily (one hour, P1589). Most major cities in Mindanao are covered, including Zamboanga, Davao, Cagayan de Oro and Surigao. The number of flights to General Santos City has recently been increased also.

International flights are available between Davao and Manado (Sulawesi) and Singapore.

Boat WG&A/SuperFerry sails weekly beween Dipolog and Manila via Dumaguete on Negros (34 hours, P636). Sulpicio Lines has a weekly boat doing the same run, as well as a weekly service from Dipolog to/from Cebu City. Delta Fast Ferry and SeaAngel both operate swish hydrofoil 'fastcrafts' daily between Dumaguete and Dipolog (one to two hours, P185 to P210).

There are also regular weekly ships to neighbouring Bohol, and Balingoan on Mindanao is the departure point for visits to friendly little Camiguin Island.

Indonesia's Pelni line has a monthly service between Davao and Bitung (north Sulawesi). See the Philippines Getting There & Away section earlier in this chapter for details.

Getting Around

Air PAL flies between most major cities in Mindanao, with the slack being taken up by Air Philippines and GrandAir. Another option is the new Mindanao Express airline, which flies at least twice a week between Cagayan de Oro, Camiguin, Cotabato, Davao and General Santos City – but it's not cheap (eg Cagayan de Oro to Davao is P1501).

Bus The dangers may often be exaggerated, but you should still be careful when travelling by bus in Mindanao – guerrilla shoot-ups *do* occur. Tourist offices in most cities will advise you on which routes are safe and which ones to forget. At the time of writing, for example, buses between Cagayan de Oro and Zamboanga were said to be regular targets of terrorist attacks.

Boat There are shipping services around the coast, with most major companies represented in the port cities.

SURIGAO & SIARGAO ISLAND

There are a number of beautiful small islands east of Surigao (SURRY-gao), which is on the north-eastern tip of Mindanao. They can best be reached from **General Luna** on the island of Siargao, where foreigners usually head for. It's the number one destination for **surfing** in the Philippines. The best time to drop in is from April to June.

Places to Stay

Surigao The *Garcia Hotel* on San Nicolas St has a variety of singles/doubles starting at P85/160. On Borromeo St, the *Tavern Hotel* (☎ 87300) starts at around P80/180 for the simplest fan-cooled rooms, and goes up to around P600 for an air-con double with bath.

Siargao Island There are a number of places to stay on Siargao Island. In General Luna, the *BRC Beach Resort* has wooden cottages, set in grassy grounds, with bath for P75 per head or P300 for full board. The *Latitude 9 Beach Resort* is in a beautiful location, in the village of Union on the south coast of Siargao. The owner's wife takes care of the cooking; P60 per meal.

Getting There & Away

Air PAL flies three times a week to Surigao from Manila (two hours) and Cebu City (one hour).

Bus Several buses travel daily from Surigao to Butuan (two hours, P54), Cagayan de Oro (six hours, P135) and Davao (eight hours, P165).

From Surigao, you can travel by bus, taking the ferry across to Leyte, and on through Leyte, Samar and right through Luzon to Manila.

Boat A ferry operates daily from Surigao to Siargao Island (four hours, P40). The ferry between Cebu City and Surigao no longer operates.

Getting Around

A tricycle between the airport and town is about P10.

Most boats use the wharf south of town, but the ferries to and from Leyte operate from the Lipata wharf, about 10km north-west. A regular tricycle trip should be about P5 per person.

BUTUAN

Butuan (BOO-twan) is a junction town two hours south of Surigao by bus. Ever since the discovery of ancient human bones and artefacts here in 1984, it's thought that this might also be the oldest settlement in the Philippines.

Places to Stay

The *Hensonly Plaza Inn* (☎ 225 1340) on San Francisco St has basic, clean, window-less rooms from P90, more expensive rooms with fan and bath for P200. The *Embassy Hotel* on Montilla Blvd has fancier singles/doubles with fan, bath and cable TV for P350/450 (air-con P450/550).

Getting There & Away

Air PAL has four flights a week between Butuan and Manila (two hours), and three flights weekly between Butuan and Cebu City (50 minutes).

Bus Butuan is about two hours by bus from Surigao with onward connections to Davao (seven hours, P110) and Cagayan de Oro (three to four hours, P80).

CAGAYAN DE ORO

On the north coast, Cagayan de Oro is a friendly, clean, prospering university town. It's also the centre of the Philippine pineapple industry. On Corrales Ave, the **Xavier University Folk Museum** (Museo de Oro) is worth a visit, but otherwise there's not much to see. The giant **pineapple fields** are about 34km outside of town, at Camp Phillips.

Information

There's a tourist office on T Neri St in the centre of town.

Places to Stay

The *Parkview Lodge* (☎ 72 3223), on T Neri St near the corner of General Capistrano St, is a big, well organised place with singles, doubles and twins with fan, bath and cable TV for P360 (P600 with air-con). This place is fantastic value between March and June, when there's a 40% discount on all room rates.

Nature's Pensionne (☎ 72 3718), on T Chavez St, has slightly time-worn singles, doubles and twins with air-con, bath and cable TV starting at P470.

Places to Eat

The *Blueberry Coffee Shop*, one block from Nature's Pensionne, is the place for a decadent breakfast of cake and caffeine. Healthier breakfasters might prefer the fresh fruit shops on nearby T Niro St.

You can get big, cheap meals at the *Bagong Lipunan Restaurant* on A Velez St.

About 100m south you'll find the *Persimmon Fastfoods & Bakeshoppe*, an inexpensive self-service restaurant with good, standard Filipino dishes. *Paolo's Ristorante*, on Velez St, one block from the Blueberry Coffee Shop, is a romantic candlelit place that that's not as pricey as it appears. Home-made pasta dishes cost around P90.

Getting There & Away

Air PAL has an office on T Niro St a few doors from the Parkview Lodge. Mindanao Express also has a little office on T Niro St, down the other end past the tourist office. Other airlines can be found at the city's Lumbia airport.

Bus Ceres Liner buses go to/from Davao daily (nine hours, P180). The long haul trip between Cagayan de Oro and Zamboanga is done by Fortune Liner and Almirante buses (15 hours, P244) – but ask around about the safety of this route in particular.

To/from Dipolog (via Dapitan), there's Lilian Liner buses leaving every hour or so all morning, with air-con buses heading off around 5.30 am (six hours, P168.50 including vehicle ferry fare).

Getting Around

To/From the Airport Lumbia airport is about 10km west of town (20 minutes, average taxi ride P70).

Jeepney The main bus terminal is on the edge of town beside the Agora Market, and jeepneys run between there and the town centre. Look for a Divisoria jeepney from the station or a Gusa/Cugman jeepney from the town. By taxi it's P40. The wharf is 5km out.

DIPOLOG

The busy, compact town of Dipolog (dee-PO-log) is the capital of Zamboanga del Norte, and it appears to have paid the price for the grand title. Unlike nearby Dapitan, industry has robbed the town of most of its beauty, but it has some fine accommodation deals. It's also a lively place to wander about, and there are some interesting **markets** around the central streets of General Luna Ave and Quezon Ave.

Information

There's a tourism office at the City Hall on Rizal Ave. If you're planning to catch a bus out of Dipolog, check here to see what your chances of being kidnapped by Muslim guerillas might be.

Places to Stay

On Jones St, one block from the Lilian Liner bus depot, you'll find the cheapest rooms in town at the *Casbaj Lodging House*. Clean, no-frills rooms with common bath are P75 per head. Right opposite, on the corner of General Luna and Jones Sts, the *Golden Royal Pension* (☎ *212 4543*) has good value doubles with bath and air-con for P425.

The vast *Hotel Arocha* (☎ *212 2656*) on Quezon Ave near the corner of General Luna Ave has good singles/doubles with fan and bath for P200/250, or P571 with air-con.

The pick of the bunch is the narrow, four storey *Ranillo Pension House* on Bonifacio St, near the corner of Burgos St. Ground floor singles/twins with fan and common bath (P100/120) are OK, but the place to be is in the upper-storey rooms (with fan, bath, balcony and good views) for P200/250. With air-con, they cost P300/350.

Also unique is the *Casa Jose Pension House* (☎ *212 4240*) in the tranquil Riverside area, near the bridge. It's a big, family-run place in a great position right beside the river. Singles/doubles with a view (plus air-con and bath) are P500/600. Smaller rooms with fan and common bath start at P150/200.

Places to Eat

Bakeshops can be found all over town, and there are a few fast-food joints, but by far the best nosh spot is the friendly *Alison's Food Plaza*. On General Luna Ave, behind the Caltex service station, it has open-air dining areas and does a wide range of freshly cooked Filipino dishes for about P50. Strict vegetarians should probably bring a packed lunch – even Alison's vegetable chop suey has meat in it.

Smartie's Pizza, on Jones St, might also be worth a try.

Getting There & Away

Air PAL flies twice weekly between Dipolog and Zamboanga (one hour), Dipolog and Cebu (45 minutes), and Dipolog and Manila (two hours).

Bus Buses to/from Zamboanga take about 13 hours via Pagadian, where you may have to change buses. This route is not always safe – check with the tourism office. Lilian Liner buses run all day to/from Cagayan de Oro (see Getting There & Away under Cagayan de Oro).

Boat See the Mindanao Getting There & Away section for details.

DAPITAN

Dapitan (da-PEE-tan) is the prettier little sister of Dipolog. It's here that many boats from Dumaguete on Negros pull in, and it's here that revolutionary hero Jose Rizal lived in exile for five years. Rizal's rather eccentric legacy here is the grassy knoll relief **map of Mindanao**. It's in front of **St James Church**, with its twin bell towers and groovy swirly pattern ceiling, in the town square (central plaza). When not mowing the lawn, Rizal was busy discovering and naming this area's native animals, such as the flying lizard.

Just beyond Dapitan, take a walk (and a supply of water) along the trails of **Rizal National Park**, which offers stunning 360-degree views of Dapitan Bay and Dakak Bay. **Dakak** has some very good diving beaches and several classy resorts. Boats between Dapitan and Dakak run daily.

Places to Stay

About 10 minutes walk from Dapitan's beautiful town square is the aptly named Sunset Blvd, a westward road on the town's peaceful, brown sand beach. Here you can stay at the simple *Casa Patricia Pension House* (twins with fan and common bath P250, with private bath P350), or the slightly fancier *Aplaya Lodge & Aplaya Vida Restaurant* (P450 for twins with air-con and bath).

Getting There & Away

Buses, jeepneys and tricycles run all day between Dipolog and Dapitan. For boat info, see the Mindanao Getting There & Away section.

ZAMBOANGA

One of the most visited cities in Mindanao is Zamboanga, which acts as the gateway to the Sulu Archipelago. In early 1996 there was a series of bombings right in town; though it's been relatively peaceful since then, check the latest situation first if you intend to visit.

Information

The tourist office (☎ 991 0218) is in the Lantaka Hotel, by the water on Velderrosa St.

Fort Pilar & Rio Hondo

Fort Pilar is an old Spanish fort on the waterfront south of the city. Some restoration is going on and there's now a **Marine Life Museum**. From the fort battlements, you get a good view to Rio Hondo, the Muslim village on stilts a little further down the coast.

Parks

The **Pasonanca Park** is a large park in the hills, a little beyond the airport – the main attraction here is a famous tree house. Nearby is **Climaco Freedom Park**, named after a murdered mayor of Zamboanga.

Islands

Ten minutes across the bay by outrigger is the island of **Santa Cruz**, which has good swimming and a beautiful beach. It costs around P200 to rent a boat for the round trip.

The island of **Basilan**, about a two hour boat ride away, is the centre for the colourful Yakan tribe – but it's also a volatile stronghold of the rebel Muslim faction Abu Sayyaf.

Places to Stay

At 160-A Mayor Jaldon St, *L'Mirage Pension House* (☎ *991 3962*) has well kept, good value rooms with fan for P140, and with aircon and bath for P350.

The centrally located *Paradise Pension House* (☎ *991 1054*) on the corner of Barcelona and Tomas Claudio Sts has reasonable rooms with air-con, bath and cable TV for P500.

An-An's Pension House (☎ *881 4974*), on Governor Camins Ave out near the airport, has decent air-con rooms starting at P450.

Places to Eat

There are lots of places to eat around the centre of Zamboanga. Right next to the George & Peter Lines office on Valderrosa St is the inexpensive *Flavorite Restaurant*.

The *Food Paradise* on Tomas Claudio St is a popular meeting spot, with a fast-food outlet on the ground floor and a Chinese restaurant upstairs. There are also good *food stalls* on Justice RT Lim Blvd near the water.

The pleasant waterfront *Talisay Bar* at the Lantaka Hotel on Valderrosa St is a good place for a beer; a reasonably priced buffet dinner is served and it's also a good spot for breakfast.

Getting There & Away

Air PAL flights, among others, connect Zamboanga with other towns in Mindanao and further afield in the Philippines, including Cebu City (one hour).

Bus Several buses travel daily to Pagadian (eight hours) and Cagayan de Oro (15 hours, P244), but both routes pass through guerilla territory.

Boat There are numerous shipping services between Zamboanga and the Sulu Islands and other destinations including General Santos City (12 hours).

Getting Around

To/From the Airport Although the airport is only 2km from the city you'll probably have to pay as much as P50 for a tricycle. A taxi will set you back at least P70.

Bus The bus terminal is in Guiwan, about 4km north of town. A tricycle shouldn't cost more than P30. Within town a ride costs about P5, depending on the distance.

DAVAO

This fast growing, cosmopolitan metropolis on the south coast of Mindanao is the third largest city in the Philippines. It's also the capital of durian country. The **durian**, a fruit much loved and much hated, is so smelly it's banned by many hotels and airlines. It's at its most pungent in September, and can be bought at fruit stalls all around the city for much of the year.

Orientation

Just to keep you on your toes, Davao has changed the names of many of its streets – former names may or may not be included on current street signs.

Information

The tourist office (☎ 221 0070) is at Magsaysay Park near the Santa Ana Wharf. Check here for official word on the safety of Mindanao regions you fancy visiting.

The Equitable Bank and the main post office are on CM Recto Ave, near the University Mall (which contains an Internet cafe).

Dangers & Annoyances Definitely in the strange-but-true category is the fact that Davao clocks are generally 10 minutes ahead of standard Philippines time. Keep this in mind if you're the type of traveller who leaves things to the last minute – in Davao at least, you might miss the bus.

DAVAO

PLACES TO STAY AND EAT
3 McDonald's
4 Sychar Garden Hotel
5 Food Street Restaurants
10 BS Inn
14 Alta Pension House & Cafe
15 Osakaya Restaurant
17 Trader's Inn
21 Kusina Dabaw; New Sunya Restaurant

22 Merco Restaurant
24 Le Mirage Family Lodge
28 Men Seng Hotel & Restaurant
29 Sunny Point Lodge & Cafe
30 El Gusto Family Lodge

OTHER
1 University of Southern Philippines
2 Agdao Market

6 WG&A
7 Sulpicio Lines
8 Tourist Office
9 Equitable Bank
11 NCCC Department Store
12 Jeepney Ornament Stores
13 Gaisano Mall
16 PAL
18 Main Post Office
19 University Mall

20 Equitable Bank
23 House of Lord Anthony
25 St Peter's Cathedral
26 Philippine National Bank
27 City Hall

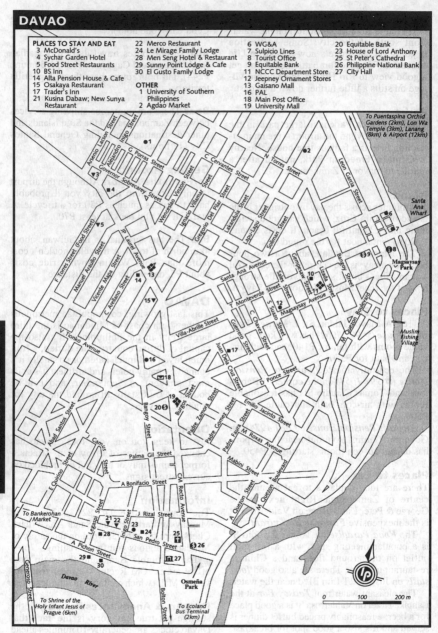

To Puentaspina Orchid Gardens (2km), Lon Wa Temple (3km), Lanang (8km) & Airport (12km)

Santa Ana Wharf

Magsaysay Park

Muslim Fishing Village

To Bankerohan Market

Davao River

To Shrine of the Holy Infant Jesus of Prague (6km)

Osmeña Park

To Ecoland Bus Terminal (2km)

0   100   200 m

PHILIPPINES

Things to See

It's worth taking the time to see the **Lon Wa Temple** with its 'Buddha with 1000 hands'. Davao also has the **Puentaspina Orchid Gardens**, the **Shrine of the Holy Infant Jesus of Prague** and some pleasant **parks**.

Places to Stay

The city's cut-price accommodation is mostly found around the colourful shopping area at the southern end of CM Recto Ave, which runs down through the middle of the city. Here, at 51 A Pichon St, you'll find the little entrance to the *El Gusto Family Lodge*, where surprisingly bright and tidy rooms with fan and common bath cost P120 (for one or two people).

A few doors along, the *Sunny Point Lodge* (☎ 221 0155) has similarly good, basic singles/doubles for P168/240. Guests here get free coffee 24 hours a day at the great little Sunny Point Cafe downstairs.

One block over, on San Pedro St, the *Men Seng Hotel & Restaurant* (not to be confused with the much dearer Men Seng Hotel on A Pichon St) is a giant place with a certain dilapidated charm – right down to the moss on the bathroom tiles. Large rooms with fan and mossy bath are P180 (for one or two people). Rooms with air-con are P220/280.

Down a lane, just off San Pedro St, *Le Mirage Family Lodge* has good value rooms with fan and common bath for P140 (for one or two people), and big, simple timber-floored rooms with fan and bath for P250/300. For air-con, you'll pay P400/500.

Towards the northern end of CM Recto Ave, on Juan Dela Cruz St (just off Magsaysay Ave), the ugly but serviceable *Trader's Inn* (☎ 22 14071) has roomy accommodation with fan and bath for P230 (for one or two people). With air-con, it's P300/400.

Heading up a little in price and comfort, the *Alta Pension House* (☎ 222 2058) on JP Laurel Ave (the northern extension of CM Recto Ave) is right on the doorstep of the huge Gaisano Mall. It has tidy, if a little cramped, rooms with fan, bath and cable TV for P400/450. For air-con, you'll pay P600/700.

Further north on JP Laurel Ave, near the drive-through McDonald's, the *Sychar Garden Hotel* (☎ 224 0603) has air-con rooms only, starting at P600.

Another good value upper-bracket place is the five storey *BS Inn* (☎ 221 3980). It's a few blocks from the pier, on the corner of Gempesaw and T Monteverde Sts, near the

NCCC department store. Cavernous singles/doubles/twins with air-con, bath and cable TV cost P660/825/850.

Places to Eat

If you can't quite stomach one of Davao's prize durians for breakfast, try the cafe at the *Alta Pension House* (see Places to Stay), the numerous coffee shops at the *Gaisano Mall* right opposite or the countless *eateries* on and around San Pedro and A Pichon Sts further south.

The *Sunny Point Cafe* on A Pichon St, below the Sunny Point Lodge (see Places to Stay), does great budget meals from P24 – it even serves oh-so-rare vegetarian dishes.

Nearby, San Pedro St has the *Kusina Dabaw* for Chinese and Filipino dishes and the ever popular *New Sunya Restaurant* and *Merco Restaurant*.

Excellent, and astonishingly cheap, Japanese lunch and dinner is available at the *Osakaya Restaurant* at the busy intersection of CM Recto Ave, JP Laurel Ave and Santa Ana Ave. About 500m further on, F Torres St – or *Food St* – offers an assortment of eateries specialising in Japanese, Mongolian and Filipino cuisine.

Shopping

If you're after souvenirs that are a little out of the ordinary, have a rummage around in the magnificent House of Lord Anthony, at 172 San Pedro St. An eccentric sort of army surplus store, this place is crammed with uniforms, badges, medals, hats and musical instruments. There are branch stores on nearby Inigo St and at the University Mall on CM Recto Ave.

Also, check out Magsaysay Ave, where rows of low-price jeepney decorations (lights, horns, hood ornaments) make for the perfect Philippine souvenirs.

Getting There & Away

Air PAL, Cebu Pacific and GrandAir fly daily to Manila (one to two hours, P1800 to P2900) and Zamboanga (one hour). Mindanao Express flies daily from Cagayan de Oro (35 minutes).

Beyond the Philippines, Davao is linked by air to Kuala Lumpur, Singapore, Jakarta and Manado.

Bus Buses take about seven hours from Butuan (P110), nine from Cagayan de Oro (P218), four from General Santos City (P56)

PHILIPPINES

and more than eight from Surigao (P142). Davao's bus terminal is in Ecoland, about 2km south of the town centre.

Boat There's one weekly ship between General Santos and Davao (nine hours, P98), and between Surigao and Davao (17 hours, P170).

For those interested in a route to Indonesia, Pelni's *Tilongkabila* operates monthly to Bitung, the port for Manado in north Sulawesi (36 hours).

Getting Around

To/From the Airport
Bangoy airport is about 12km north-east of the town centre – say, P70 by taxi. To town, take the jeepney 'San Pedro'; from town to the airport junction, take the 'Sasa' jeepney.

AROUND DAVAO

Beaches
There are a variety of black beaches around the city, like **Talomo** (8km south), but probably the best beach is the white **Paradise Island Beach** on Samal Island. **Samal Island** is only a short bangca ride away (outriggers leave near Sasa Bridge – just before Lanang towards the airport).

Mt Apo
At 2954m, Mt Apo is the highest mountain in the Philippines. It overlooks Davao and can be climbed in four to five days. On your way to the top you'll pass waterfalls, hot springs and pools of boiling mud, and you might even spot the rare Philippine eagle. No special equipment is needed for the climb. March to May are the driest (hence best) climbing months. The tourist office can offer advice and arrange guides.

Camiguin

Located off the many bays on the north coast of Mindanao, Camiguin (cam-EE-gan) is an idyllic, small get-away-from-it-all sort of place. The tiny island actually has seven volcanoes; Hibok-Hibok, the best known, last erupted in 1951. The beaches are nothing special but the people are great.

Getting There & Away
There may be occasional ships from other islands, but the usual route is from Balingoan in Mindanao to Benoni on Camiguin. A ferry crosses seven times daily (1½ hours, P25).

If you leave Cebu City in the evening you can reach Cagayan de Oro on Mindanao in about 10 hours, make the 1½ hour bus trip to Balingoan and then ferry across to Camiguin, arriving by the early afternoon.

A boat leaves from Cagayan de Oro on Tuesday, Thursday and Saturday at 8 am for Guinsiliban on the southern tip of Camiguin (three hours, P60 to P95).

Getting Around
The 65km circuit of the island takes about three hours actual travelling time. While it's possible to travel around the island on jeepneys and tricycles, there are not many vehicles between Yumbing and Catarman. You're more independent of public transport with a hired motorcycle. Many resorts rent out mountain bikes for P250 and motorcycles for P500 a day.

MAMBAJAO
Mambajao is the capital and main town of Camiguin.

Information
You'll find the Camiguin tourist office in the Provincial Capitol building. The Philippine National Bank (PNB) will change your travellers cheques.

Places to Stay
Tia's Pension House (☎ 87 1045), near the town hall, has singles/doubles with fan for P75/150. There is also *Tia's Beach Cottages*, just a few minutes from the centre, where cottages with bath start at P300; straight across is the beautiful *Shoreline Cottages* (☎ 87 1091), where rooms with fan are P85 per person.

Between Kuguita and Bugong are several *beach bungalows*.

AROUND THE ISLAND
Starting from Mambajao, and travelling anticlockwise, at **Kuguita** there's a beach and some coral where you can snorkel. The *Turtles Nest Beach Cottages* (☎ 87 1000) has cottages for P350 (with fan and bath), and singles/doubles with fan for P170/300.

Another 4km takes you to **Agoho**, where the *Caves Resort* (☎ 87 9077) is an ageing dive resort near the beach with rooms from P200 to P350. Some other possibilities are the *Camiguin Seaside Lodge* and the *Morning Glory Cottages*, both with dorm beds, rooms and cottages.

Beyond Yumbing, **Bonbon** has some interesting church ruins and a huge cross in the sea marking the **Sunken Cemetery**. Near Catarman, a track leads to the **Tuwasan Falls**. Down at the southern end of the island, there's a 300-year-old **Moro watchtower** at Guinsiliban.

Benoni is near the artificial Tanguine Lagoon, where the peaceful *J & A Fishpen* (☎ 87 4008) has basic but attractive cottages, with big verandas over the water. With fan and bath cottages cost P300 (with air-con, P500/600).

Hibok-Hibok Volcano

The 1320m-high Hibok-Hibok volcano can be climbed in the dry season; from Ardent Hot Spring it takes at least four hours. A guide (P350) is useful, as the weather on the mountain is changeable and you can easily get lost. The volcano erupted disastrously in 1951 and it's now monitored from the Comvol station.

Katibawasan Waterfall

The waterfall, with good swimming, is 3km from Pandan, which in turn is only 2km from Mambajao. Near here the **Ardent Hot Spring**, a favourite for weekend outings, has a beautifully designed swimming pool.

White Island

About 3km off Agoho, this small island is just a sand bar. There is no shade, but there is good swimming and snorkelling. Count on about P250 to rent a boat for the round trip, but arrange a definite time to be picked up.

Palawan

Off to the west of the Visayas, Palawan is the long thin island stretching down to the Malaysian state of Sabah. Things to do and see here are strongly connected with nature: islands, scuba diving and caves with underground rivers, and wildlife. On no other island in the Philippines are people as attuned to nature and aware of the environment as on Palawan. The protection of wildlife and commitment to the environment is a serious way of life for many Palaweños.

Getting There & Away

Air As well as flying from Cebu City via Iloilo (2½ hours), PAL flies daily between Manila and Puerto Princesa (one hour, P2269),

as does Air Philippines (one hour, P1614). Air Ads flies twice a week to Busuanga (1½ hours, P2000).

Boat WG&A/SuperFerry ships sail to Puerto Princesa twice a week (20 hours, P459). Negros Navigation ships do the Puerto Princesa-Cebu trip via Bacolod and Iloilo (48 hours, P450). Milagrosa sails between Puerto Princesa and Iloilo via the Cuyo Islands (28 hours, P330).

Several ships also sail twice weekly from Batangas to Coron (around P300; 18 hours).

Getting Around

Puerto Princesa, the capital, is roughly half way down the island. Buses and jeepneys run up and down: south, as far as Brooke's Point (four hours, P94), or north to Roxas (four hours, P65), Port Barton (P100; five hours), Taytay (eight hours, P160) and El Nido (about 12 hours, P250).

PUERTO PRINCESA

The remarkably clean capital of Palawan has a population of about 130,000 and is a good base for excursions to elsewhere on the island.

Information

Tourist Offices There's a city tourist office (☎ 433 2983) at the airport, and a provincial tourist office in the Provincial Capitol building on Rizal Ave at the corner of Fernandez St.

Money There are several big banks and moneychangers along the main drag of Rizal Ave, and the Go Palawan travel agent next door to the Trattoria Inn (see Places to Stay) gives cash advances on major credit cards (with a hefty 10% commission).

Post & Communications A number of telephone offices can be found along Rizal Ave, and the main post office is just off Rizal Ave on Burgos St. There are three Internet cafes in town, one of them being the Hexagon Cafe (P45 per half hour) near the post office on Roxas St.

Places to Stay

The *Duchess Pension House* (☎ 433 2873), at 107 Valencia St, has tiny cell-like singles for P120, and more livable doubles with fan and bath for P300.

Diagonally opposite the Duchess is the *Backpackers Cafe, Bookshop & Inn*. A friendly, relaxed hang-out, it has basic singles/doubles for P150/220 and a dorm (or four-bed room) for P100 per head. This place also does great food for about P100, hires out bikes (P100 per day) and provides plenty of ideas on what to do in and around Puerto Princesa.

The *Trattoria Inn (☎ 433 2719)* at 353 Rizal Ave, towards the airport, is a very popular place (especially with Germans) where doubles with common bath start at P350. Doubles with bath, fan and cable TV cost P750.

Over the road, down little Trinidad Rd, is the classy *Casa Linda Tourist Inn (☎ 433 2606)* with its big, manicured garden courtyard. Rooms with fan and bath here are P350/425, and with air-con they're P650/750.

Next door, back on Rizal Ave, is the ugly facade of the *Badjao Inn (☎ 433 2380)*. It looks much better from the inside, where big, good value rooms with fan and spotless bath are P400 (with air-con, P650 to P750).

The *Puerto Pension (☎ 433 2969)*, well placed on Malvar St between the pier and the main bus/jeepney depot, has rooms with fan and 'semi-private' bath for P200/300 (with private bath, P350/450) and air-con rooms for P645. This place was built from indigenous materials and has the best views in town from its little rooftop restaurant/bar.

Places to Eat

For breakfast or a light lunch, the *Cafe Kamarikutan & Galeri*, just past the airport on Rizal Ave, serves an incredible range of coffees – all in a huge, airy bamboo mansion and an enormous oasis of a garden. Great fresh-fruit pancakes (along with an ever-changing lunch and dinner menu) are available at the *Backpackers Cafe, Bookshop & Inn* (see Places to Stay).

Among the diverse eateries of central Rizal Ave is the fancy *Cafe Puerto* (closed Wednesday), whose slightly over-attentive staff will serve you a good European lunch and dinner.

Opposite is the traditional *Filipino Kamayan Folkhouse & Restaurant*, set on a large, leafy plot complete with a tree-house dining area.

A few blocks along, out the back of the Trattoria Inn, is the lively *Swiss Bistro* – a great place if you're craving hearty western meat dishes or pizza. If not, try the brilliant *Kalui Restaurant* nearby, serving sophisticated Filipino set meals including a succulent seaweed appetiser (no, really). The giant P275 set meal should be enough for two people.

There are three *Pho Vietnamese Restaurants* in town, the most authentic being about 2km past the airport on Rizal Ave Extension.

Getting Around

Tricycle feeding frenzies are the norm in Puerto Princesa, especially around the market, the wharf, the bus depot and the strolling tourist. Unless you're happy to pay extra for being a 'Kano', insist on the official tricycle fare rate of P3 for every 2km.

AROUND PUERTO PRINCESA

There are various places within day-trip distance of Puerto Princesa. For example, **Irawan** has the Irawan Crocodile Farming Institute, and **Iwahig** has Iwahig Prison and Penal Farm (far more interesting than it sounds).

The diving is good at **Honda Bay**, off Tagburos (Santa Lourdes Pier), only 10km from Puerto Princesa. There are many small islands in the bay. White **Nagtabon Beach** lies on a beautiful, calm bay on the west coast and is another good swimming spot.

Sabang

Sabang is famed for the **Underground River** in **St Paul Subterranean National Park** – a highlight of Palawan. From the beach in Sabang you can either take a boat to the mouth of the river for P400 or walk there over the **monkey trail** through the beautiful jungle of the national park – it takes about two hours. Of the river itself, you'll only get to see about 2km of its 8km total because most of the river is currently off-limits except for research purposes.

Places to Stay & Eat It's a pretty nasty old road out to Sabang (about 2½ hours even by tourist minibus) but it's well worth it. Day trippers take note: the trip back to Puerto Princesa, and the sheer beauty of the Sabang area, may have you wishing you'd brought your luggage from Puerto Princesa after all.

The best place has got to be the simply idyllic *Mary's Beach Resort*. At the opposite end of Sabang Beach to the pier, it's hidden just around the point, has a giant shady tree with hammocks right on the sand and has its very own beach (and island!). It costs P200 for no-frills cottages, or P300 for cottages with bath. It also has a basic little restaurant.

Within the national park itself, you can stay at the *ranger station cottages* for P100, or in one of the ranger's tents for P50. Beyond the Underground River, there's the reclusive *Panaguman Beach Resort*, with big rooms with common bath for P290, or deluxe cottages for P480. The resort's boat leaves from the Sabang pier daily at 1 pm. For more information, contact the Trattoria Inn in Puerto Princesa (see Puerto Princesa Places to Stay).

Good food can be found at *Cafe Sabang*, on the main road into Sabang, about 500m from the beach.

Getting There & Away There are jeepneys from Puerto Princesa to Sabang.

SOUTH PALAWAN

Unlike the north of Palawan, the south of the island doesn't have too much to offer the traveller. **Quezon**, halfway from Puerto Princesa to the southern end of the island, is the jumping-off point for the **Tabon Caves**. There's a small **National Museum** in Quezon and the caves have yielded some interesting stone-age finds. It takes half an hour by boat to the caves.

Places to Stay

In Quezon you can stay in basic little rooms for P70 per person at the *New Bayside Lodging House*.

The nicely laid out *Tabon Village Resort* at Tabon Beach, about 4km north-east of Quezon, has singles/doubles at P100/120 and cottages with bath for P250/350.

Getting There & Away

More than a dozen buses travel between Puerto Princesa and Quezon (three hours, P55) daily.

NORTH PALAWAN
Port Barton

On the west coast, the sleepy and refreshingly quiet town of Port Barton is something of a travellers hang-out. There are a number of fine islands in the bay, some beautiful beaches and good snorkelling.

Places to Stay & Eat Port Barton has several beachside cottage places to stay. The swishest of these is the central *Swissippini Lodge & Resort*, with big A-frame balconied huts in a giant garden setting for P600 (by the

water) and P400 (set back a little). Swissippini accepts major credit cards, changes money and travellers cheques and organises boat trips. A few doors along is *Elsa's Beach Cottages*, with good little huts for P300 (P400 for a triple), and the *El Busero Inn*, with cottages a tad simpler for P300 and tawdry rooms for P150. All cottages have private bath.

Over the creek at the north end of town is the new *El Dorado Sunset Cottages*. The front ones go for P300, the back ones for P275. All have private bath. Note: El Dorado's owner will only accept guests planning to stay for two nights or more.

All places mentioned here have restaurants and bars attached, but the fish curry (P65) at the *Filipiniana Restaurant*, opposite Elsa's Beach Cottages, would put the fanciest of resorts to shame.

Taytay

A half-day journey north-east of Port Barton is Taytay, the former capital of Palawan. Here you can visit the ruins of a **fort** built in 1667 by the Spaniards.

Places to Stay In Taytay, you can stay cheaply at *Publico's International Guest House*, where basic rooms surround the plants of the inner courtyard and cost P60/150 for singles/doubles with fan and P200 with fan and bath. The price is right for what you get.

Pem's Pension & Restaurant on the bay at the fort is a little more expensive. Basic cottages with fan and bath are P250 to 300, P500 to 600 for larger ones; or it's a flat P150 for singles.

El Nido

Right up in the north-west of Palawan, a beautiful bay jealously guards El Nido. This picturesque little village is surrounded by rugged, steep limestone cliffs and a stunning beach. It's not easy to get to, but it's well worth the effort. A boat trip to the offshore islands of the **Bacuit Archipelago** is an absolute must.

Information Power in El Nido cuts out at midnight officially (and at any other time unofficially).

There are now several moneychangers (dealing mainly in US dollars), including the friendly El Nido Boutique & Art Shop near the wharf. This place also organises boat trips to the nearby islands.

Places to Stay & Eat Stumbling off the boat and across the pile of rocks making up El Nido's new wharf, look for the *Bayview Inn*, with largish rooms for P200 to P400. It also sports a big, broad balcony on the second floor facing the beautiful bay and a couple of badly behaved showers. Next, set back from the beach at the foot of the spooky cliffs is the popular *Cliffside Cottages*, with separate huts with bath for P350 to P450.

Back on the beach strip is the *Marina Garden Beach Resort*, with rooms starting at P150 and cottages for P450. A few doors along is the two storey timber villa known as *Ric Son's Lodge & Restaurant*. It has cheap but airless rooms for P150 to P300 upstairs, and a good restaurant with the best views in town downstairs.

Clumped together you have *Gloria's Beach Cottages* (shady, balconied cottages with bath for P400, and a bigger four person cottage with bath for P630), *Dara Fernandez Cottages* (P400 to P500 per cottage with bath) and *Tandikan Cottage* (P500 with bath).

At the far end of town from the wharf is the *Lally & Abet Cottages*, with roomy, balconied bungalows with bath (P700 to P800), and rooms with shared bath right by the water (P350).

Busuanga Island

Coron Town Offering up a paradise for wreck divers as well as snorkellers, Coron town on Busuanga Island is also great base for sun-worshipping explorers (the town itself has no beach). The best value thing to do is hire a bangca (around P700, limit eight people) and snorkelling gear (about P100 per day) through the hotels or dive shops, and inspect the nearby islands all day long. Don't miss the magical **Lake Cayangan** on Coron Island, opposite Coron town itself. Crystal clear, this semi-freshwater lake has sheer rock walls and is only accessible on foot (a short walk over a steep rocky rise). This island is also home to the **Tagbanua people**, famed for their elusiveness as much as for their pottery skills.

Another activity often included in a bangca day trip is a soak in the **hot spring** just out of Coron town.

Places to Stay & Eat A short tricycle ride (about P5) from the Coron town wharf will bring you to the market area, the centre of Coron town, half of which is perched on bamboo stilts. Places to stay here include: the *Bayside Lodge & Restaurant* (starting with dorm rooms for P150 per head, up to big rooms with a view and bath for P600), the *Bayview Lodge* with a similar deal and the *Sea Breeze Lodge* (singles for P100 to P150, doubles P200). A 20 minute walk onwards, up the sloping main road past the Swagman tourist office (or grab a tricycle for about P10), is the *Kokosnuss Garden Resort & Restaurant*, by far the best place if you don't mind the relative isolation. Cottages and nipa-style rooms in this large garden compound range from P400 (with possibly the fanciest common bath in South-East Asia) to P800 (for big rooms complete with bathroom murals).

All places to stay have their own *restaurants*, and while the food won't exactly entrance your taste buds, the tastiest dishes are served at the Bayview Lodge (which does a great pizza).

Getting There & Away Air Ads, Pacific Airways and Asian Spirit all serve the little YKR airport on the north side of Busuanga Island (about a one hour bumpy jeepney ride from Coron town). There are flights three times a week to/from Manila (P2000), Boracay (P1260) and Puerto Princesa (P2000). There's an Air Ads office in Coron town next door to the Bayside Lodge & Restaurant.

MBRS Lines has a big passenger/car ferry doing the Manila-Coron-Liminangcong-Coron-Manila trip each week. Leaving Monday at noon from Pier 8 in Manila, it hits Coron town around 8 am Tuesday and costs P250 for a standard ticket to Liminangcong (eight hours). The same boat returns at 1.30 pm Wednesday for the run back to Manila.

Viva Lines has solid little wooden ferries sailing between Batangas and Coron town. They leave Coron on Monday and Friday at noon and cost P330 (17 hours – up to 22 hours if the ship's heavily laden). From Batangas, they leave around 6 pm Sunday and Thursday.

Getting Around If you're game, you can hire 125cc Suzuki motorbikes from the Blue Heaven Hang-Out Bar on the road to the Kokosnuss Garden Resort & Restaurant. The usual charge is P500 per day, without petrol.

Singapore

Singapore is a small island at the tip of the Malay Peninsula. It thrives on trade and, through a combination of hard work and efficient, if at times repressive, government, has become one of the most affluent countries in Asia. It's a hub for travellers, but also offers a wide variety of places to visit, shopping opportunities and some of the best food in Asia.

Singapore, with its preoccupation with cleanliness and orderliness, can be a pleasant break from the more hectic travelling you find elsewhere in the region, but it's also less traditional and more antiseptic.

Facts about Singapore

HISTORY

Singapore's improbable name, which means Lion City, came from a Sumatran prince who thought he saw a lion when he landed on the island – it was much more likely a tiger. Singapore would have drifted on as a quiet fishing village if Sir Stamford Raffles had not decided, in 1819, that it was just the port he needed. Under the British it became a great trading city and a military and naval base, but that didn't save it from the Japanese in 1942.

In 1959 Singapore became internally self-governing, in 1963 it joined Malaysia and, in 1965, this federation was in tatters and Singapore became independent. The reason behind this was a basic conflict of interest between 'Malaysia for the Malays' and Singapore's predominantly Chinese population. Under Prime Minister Lee Kuan Yew, Singapore made the best of its independence. Trade, tourism and industrialisation soon made up for the loss of British military bases.

Mr Lee's somewhat iron-fisted government also turned Singapore into a green, tidy garden city where no one dares to litter the streets, or even carelessly drop cigarette ash. The economy is dynamic, the water from the taps is drinkable, smoking in public places is forbidden, cars are heavily taxed and all drivers are discouraged from venturing into the city centre during rush hour.

Singapore's progressive attitudes have another side: criticism of the government is not

a recommended activity, the press is tightly controlled and the minuscule elected opposition has always had a hard time. It has even been loudly mooted as to whether the country actually needs any opposition to the People's Action Party (PAP). Lee Kuan Yew finally stepped down from the leadership in 1990 and handed over the reigns to Goh Chok Tong, though Lee is still Special Minister and exerts a major influence.

Goh Chok Tong instituted a series of liberalising reforms. Goh's social reforms saw a relaxation of censorship laws, a flourishing in the arts and a greater awareness of the quality-of-life issues that concern most

SINGAPORE

645

SINGAPORE

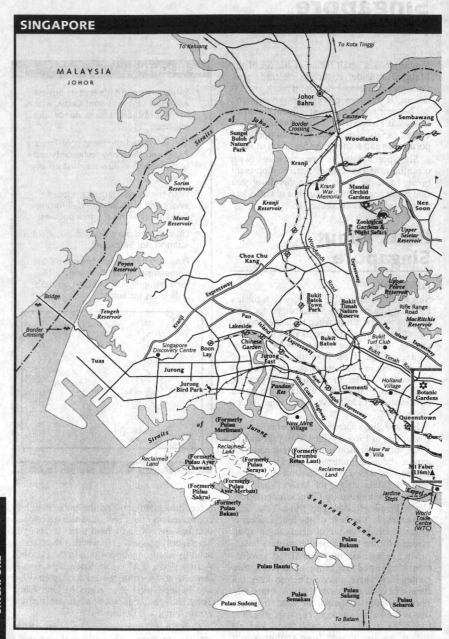

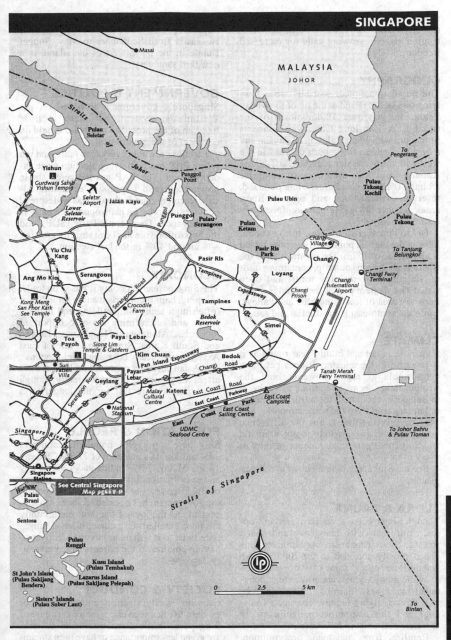

modern industrialised nations. However, few real steps have been made towards democratisation, despite growing calls for increased freedom.

GEOGRAPHY

The population squeezes itself into a low-lying 646 sq km island at the tip of the Malay Peninsula, just over 100km north of the equator. A 1km-long Causeway connects Singapore with Johor Bahru in Malaysia, and a bridge connects the suburb of Tuas in the west with the Malaysian mainland at Tanjung Kupang. Built-up urban areas comprise around 50% of the land area, while parkland, reservoirs, plantations and open military areas occupy 40%. Remaining forest accounts for only 4%.

Bukit Timah (Hill of Tin), in the central hills, is the highest point on Singapore Island at an altitude of 162m. The central area of the island is an igneous outcrop, containing most of Singapore's remaining forest and open areas. The western part of the island is a sedimentary area of low-lying hills and valleys, while the south-east is mostly flat and sandy.

CLIMATE

Singapore is hot and humid year-round as it is so close to the equator. It does get more comfortable at night, however, and the weather never seems to be quite as sticky as in Bangkok, 1500km to the north. November to January tend to be the wettest months, and May to July the driest, but the difference between these two periods is not dramatic and Singapore gets an abundance of rainfall every month.

See the Singapore climate chart in the Appendix.

FLORA & FAUNA

Though Singapore was once covered in tropical rainforest, with mangrove and beach forest in the coastal areas, very little remains and is mostly confined to the Bukit Timah Nature Reserve and some offshore islands.

While many animals are now extinct, long-tailed macaques, squirrels, flying squirrels, tree shrews, flying lemurs, civet cats (musang) and the distinctive pangolin (scaly anteater) still exist in forest areas.

Reptiles, frogs and toads are common. Snakes are still found in urban areas, including the reticulated python, poisonous pit viper and black spitting cobra.

Singapore has over 300 bird species and migrant species are observed in the migratory season from September to May. Sungei Buloh, in the north-west of the island, is a new bird sanctuary.

GOVERNMENT & POLITICS

Singapore's government is based on the Westminster system, but there is little freedom of the press and a tight lid is held on criticism of the government.

Elections are held every five years, and the ruling PAP has won every election since independence. The PAP has delivered stable government and impressive economic advancement, and undoubtedly has widespread popular support. The main opposition party is the Singapore Democratic Party (SDP), and the opposition vote has been steadily growing – to around 40% in the last election.

ECONOMY

The Singaporean economy is based on trade, shipping, banking, tourism and light industry (often high-tech). Shipbuilding and maintenance and oil refining are also important industries. Along with Hong Kong, Taiwan and South Korea, Singapore is one of East Asia's economically booming 'mini-dragons'. The Asian currency crisis of late 1997 did not affect Singapore's economy directly, though some jitters were felt for the longer-term outlook.

POPULATION & PEOPLE

Singapore's polyglot population numbers 3.04 million. It's made up of 77.3% Chinese, 14.1% Malay, 7.3% Indian and 1.3% of any and every nationality you can imagine. Curiously, after years of promoting birth control, the government has decided it's been too successful and the joys of the three child family are now extolled. Of course, it has a Singapore twist to it – there are extra incentives to having children if the parents have university degrees.

SOCIETY & CONDUCT

Growing westernisation and the pace of modern life has seen changes in the culture of Singapore. While some traditional customs are given less importance or have been streamlined, the strength of traditional religious values and the practice of time-honoured ways remain.

For the Chinese, the moment of birth is strictly recorded; it is essential for astrological consultations that are important in later life. Funerals are traditional, colourful and expensive affairs. Paper houses, cars, TV sets and even paper servants are offered and burnt so that the deceased can enjoy all these material benefits in the next life. The importance of the grave and its upkeep remains, and most Chinese will pay their respects to the elders on All Souls Day. The major Chinese celebration is Chinese New Year.

Islam provides the focus for Malays, but *adat* (customary law) guides the important ceremonies and events in life, such as birth, circumcision and marriage. Many aspects of adat exhibit Hindu and even pre-Hindu influences. The most important festival for Malays is Hari Raya Puasa, the end of the fasting month.

Most Singaporean Indians come from southern India, so the customs and festivals that are more important in the south, especially Madras, are the most popular in Singapore. Deepavali, the Festival of Lights, is the major Indian festival in Singapore and many homes are decorated with oil lamps to signify the victory of light over darkness. The spectacular Thaipusam is the most exciting festival.

RELIGION

The variety of religions found in Singapore is a direct reflection of the diversity of races living there. The Chinese are predominantly followers of Buddhism and Shenism (deity worship), though a significant number are Christian. Malays are overwhelmingly Muslim, and most Indians are Hindus from southern India, though a significant number are Muslim.

See the Appendix for more information on the various religions.

LANGUAGE

English is widely spoken, as is Malay, Tamil and a number of Chinese dialects. After a spell in Singapore, you may come to the conclusion that Chinese is not a language to be whispered or even spoken. It is a language to be howled, yowled, shrieked and screamed. In any Chinese restaurant, you will witness just how. The 'official' Chinese dialect is Mandarin – you may see public signs urging Chinese citizens to 'Speak Mandarin, Not Dialect!'.

Facts for the Visitor

HIGHLIGHTS

The best way to get a feel for Singapore is to wander around its inner city. Though the ethnic areas are quickly becoming dining and drinking venues rather than repositories of traditional culture, **Chinatown**, **Little India** and **Arab St** are still fascinating areas to explore.

The historic **Singapore River** is a lively stretch of restoration and redevelopment, especially in the evening when the restaurants and bars of Boat Quay and Clarke Quay are packed.

The **Singapore Zoological Gardens** are among Singapore's most popular attractions, and nothing like the animal jails you normally find in South-East Asia. Highly recommended is the **Night Safari** next to the zoo, which allows you to view animals along jungle paths at night. The **Jurong Bird Park** has a huge variety of birdlife in similarly well-tended enclosures.

Green and clean Singapore also has plenty of gardens, the pick of which is the **Botanic Gardens**. For a walk in the jungle, **Bukit Timah Nature Reserve** is about as far away from the city as you can get.

The theme park island of **Sentosa** is Singapore's answer to Disneyland, though the comparison is a loose one. The fun park activities are mostly for families, but it has enough to keep adults amused.

Last but not least, every visitor ends up at **Orchard Rd**, a dazzling strip of modern delights. Singapore has plenty of other attractions to keep you amused from a day in transit to a week's exploration.

PLANNING
When to Go

Anytime. Climate is not a major consideration, as Singapore gets a fairly steady annual rainfall. Your visit may coincide with various festivals – Singapore has something happening every month. Thaipusam, which usually falls in January or February, is one of the most spectacular festivals, or if shopping and eating are your major concerns, July is a good month as the Singapore Food Festival and Great Singapore Sale are held.

Maps

Various good give-away maps are available at tourist offices, the airport, some hotels and shopping centres. Nelles and Periplus are the best of the commercial maps. The best reference of all is the *Singapore Street Directory*, a bargain at S$9 plus GST. It's available at most bookshops, though stocks are depleted fairly quickly.

TOURIST OFFICES

The Singapore Tourism Board (STB) has a Tourist Information Centre at its head office (☎ 1800 738 3778) at 1 Orchard Spring Rd, off Cuscaden Rd in the Orchard Rd area. Another is conveniently located at 02-34 Raffles Hotel Arcade (☎ 1800 334 1335) on North Bridge Rd in the colonial district. Both can answer most queries and have a good selection of hand-outs. Pick up a copy of the excellent *Singapore Official Guide*, which is updated monthly.

VISAS & DOCUMENTS

Most western nationalities do not require visas. You are granted an initial two weeks on entry and a one month permit is usually not a problem if you ask for it. You can easily extend a 14 day permit for another two weeks, but extensions beyond a month become increasingly hard. The government obviously feels that a month is long enough for anybody to do their shopping. Inquire at the Immigration Department (☎ 1800 391 6400), 10 Kallang Rd, opposite the Lavender MRT station (see the Central Singapore map).

An international student card is not of much use as student discounts are almost invariably for Singaporeans only, and Singapore has no Hostelling International (HI; formerly YHA) hostels in which to use a Hostelling International card.

EMBASSIES
Singaporean Embassies Abroad

Some Singaporean embassies and high commissions overseas include:

Australia
   (☎ 02-6273 3944)
   17 Forster Crescent, Yarralumla,
   ACT 2600
France
   (☎ 01 45 00 33 61)
   12 Square de l'avenue Foch, 75116 Paris
Germany
   (☎ 228-951 0314)
   Südstrasse 133, 53175 Bonn 2
Japan
   (☎ 3-3586 9111)
   5-12-3 Roppongi, 5-Chome, Minato-ku,
   Tokyo 106

New Zealand
   (☎ 04-479 2076)
   17 Kabul St, Khandallah, Wellington
UK
   (☎ 020-7235 8315)
   9 Wilton Crescent, London, SW1X 8SA
USA
   (☎ 202-537 3100)
   3501 International Place NW, Washington,
   DC 20008

For Singaporean embassies in other countries in South-East Asia, refer to the relevant chapters in this book.

Embassies in Singapore

Singapore is generally a good place to get visas. Embassies in Singapore include:

Australia
   (☎ 836 4100) 25 Napier Rd, 258507
Brunei
   (☎ 733 9055) 325 Tanglin Rd, 247955
Canada
   (☎ 325 3200) 14-00 IBM Towers, 80 Anson
   Rd, 079907
France
   (☎ 466 4866) 5 Gallop Rd, 258960
Germany
   (☎ 737 1355) 14-00 Far East Shopping Centre,
   545 Orchard Rd, 238882
India
   (☎ 737 6777) 31 Grange Rd, 239002
Indonesia
   (☎ 737 7422) 7 Chatsworth Rd, 249761
Japan
   (☎ 235 8855) 16 Nassim Rd, 258390
Malaysia
   (☎ 235 0111) 301 Jervois Rd, 238856
Myanmar (Burma)
   (☎ 735 0209) 15 St Martin's Drive, 257996
New Zealand
   (☎ 235 9966) 15-06/10 Tower A Ngee Ann
   City, 391A Orchard Rd, 238873
Philippines
   (☎ 737 3977) 20 Nassim Rd, 258395
Thailand
   (☎ 737 2644) 370 Orchard Rd, 238870
UK
   (☎ 473 9333) 100 Tanglin Rd, 247919
USA
   (☎ 476 9100) 27 Napier Rd, 258508
Vietnam
   (☎ 462 5938) 10 Leeden Park, 267887

CUSTOMS

Visitors to Singapore are allowed to bring in 1L of wine, beer or spirits duty-free, and most other goods are already duty-free. Singapore does not allow duty-free concessions for cigarettes and tobacco. The importation of chewing gum was banned after anti-social elements started gumming up the doors of the Mass Railway Transit (MRT) subway system. Duty-free concessions are not available if you come from Malaysia or if you leave Singapore for less than 48 hours.

The importation or exportation of illegal drugs carries the death penalty for more than 15g of heroin, 30g of morphine, 500g of cannabis or 200g of cannabis resin, or 1.2kg of opium. Trafficking in lesser amounts ranges from a minimum of two years jail and two strokes of the rotan to 30 years and 15 strokes of the rotan.

MONEY
Currency
Singapore uses 1c, 5c, 10c, 20c, 50c and S$1 coins, while notes are in denominations of S$2, S$5, S$10, S$50, S$100, S$500 and S$1000; Singapore also has a S$10,000 note – not that you'll see too many.

Exchange Rates
Exchange rates at the time of writing are as follows:

country	unit		S dollar
Australia	A$1	=	S$1.02
Canada	C$1	=	S$1.05
euro	€1	=	S$1.95
France	10FF	=	S$2.95
Germany	DM1	=	S$0.99
Japan	¥100	=	S$1.36
New Zealand	NZ$1	=	S$0.87
Thailand	100B	=	S$4.25
UK	UK£1	=	S$2.76
USA	US$1	=	S$1.62

Exchanging Money
There are no pitfalls in changing money in Singapore but if you're watching every cent it is worth shopping around the banks – exchange rates tend to vary and many banks also make a small service charge on a per-cheque or per-transaction basis. Bring with you any major hard currency in cash. US dollars are probably your best bet.

Singapore is one of the major banking centres of Asia so it is a good place to transfer money. Moneychangers can supply currency from almost anywhere, and they delightedly calculate complicated double exchanges – the conversion of Thai baht into Indonesian rupiah, for example. They are found everywhere – almost every shopping centre has one – and generally, they're better than banks for changing cash.

All major credit cards are accepted and cash advances on Visa and MasterCard can be readily obtained over the counter at banks, or through the many ATMs that display credit symbols. Some banks are connected to international networks that allow you to withdraw funds from overseas savings accounts if you have a card with a PIN number (check with your home bank).

Costs
Singapore is much more expensive than other South-East Asian countries. The only cheap accommodation is in guesthouse dormitories, which cost around S$9, or a double room in a cheap hotel or guesthouse costs from S$22 to S$45.

Singapore has plenty of cheap dining possibilities, public transport is good value and many attractions are free. It is possible to stay in Singapore for as little as S$25 per day, but be prepared to spend a lot more if you want to indulge in some of the luxuries you may have craved in less developed countries.

Tipping & Bargaining
Tipping is not usual in Singapore. Most expensive hotels and restaurants have a 10% service charge, in which case tipping is discouraged.

Many shops have fixed prices and it is unnecessary to bargain for everyday goods or transport, as in many Asian countries. A fair number of small shops in the tourist areas, especially electronic shops, don't display prices. In this case bargaining is almost always required. For handicrafts and other tourist-oriented items, a price tag doesn't mean you can't bargain, and you often should.

Taxes & Refunds
A 3% GST is applied to all goods and services in Singapore. Visitors purchasing goods worth S$300 or more through a shop participating in the GST Tourist Refund Scheme can apply for a refund of GST, but it's a hassle.

In addition to the 3% GST, a 10% service charge and 1% 'cess' (government entertainment tax) is added to the more expensive hotel and restaurant bills, as well as at most nightspots and bars. Most of the cheaper establishments don't add taxes but absorb them into the quoted price.

SINGAPORE

POST & COMMUNICATIONS
Post
The main post office on Fullerton Rd, near Raffles Place, is currently closed for renovations and letters addressed to poste restante c/- GPO are being held at the Robinson Rd post office near the Tanjong Pagar MRT station.

The Comcentre, 31 Exeter Rd, very near the Somerset MRT station on Exeter Rd, is the place to go to make phone calls, send faxes or apply for a phone connection. It is open from 8 am to 6 pm Monday to Friday and until 2 pm on Saturday. Singapore is an efficient place from which to send parcels, and rates are good compared with many other South-East Asian countries.

Telephone
There are several Telecom centres, such as the one in the Comcentre, where it is easy to make international calls. The phone centres also have Direct Home phones (press a country button for direct connection with your home country operator or automated service and then reverse the charges to your home account) and credit-card phones.

International calls can also be dialled from public payphones with a stored-value phone card. They cost from S$2 to S$50 and are available at Telecom centres and retail outlets.

For directory information call ☎ 100; the police emergency telephone number is ☎ 999; and the talking clock is 1711.

Telephone Codes

The country code for Singapore is ☎ 65. The international dialling code is ☎ 001. There are no area codes in Singapore.

BOOKS
Lonely Planet
The Lonely Planet *Singapore city guide* is a detailed guidebook to the city-state and includes detailed, colour maps, suggestions for excursions and details of more upmarket accommodation, restaurants and entertainment. If you're planning to explore Malaysia as well as Singapore, Lonely Planet's *Malaysia, Singapore & Brunei* provides comprehensive information about both countries.

History & Politics
Singapore has experienced something of a literary boom, especially after Goh Chok Tong's relaxation of censorship laws, and bookshops are packed with Singaporean titles.

Lee Kuan Yew – The Man and His Ideas by Han Fook Kwang has been a surprising best seller since its release in November 1997 and stocks in bookshops have even been depleted on a few occasions. It naturally presents the still-influential politician in a favourable light, but nonetheless makes for a good read.

A History of Singapore by CM Turnball is the best choice for a detailed overview of Singapore's history. Books on politics range from the pro-government *Governing Singapore* by Raj Vasil to *Dare to Change – An Alternative Vision for Singapore* by Chee Soon Juan, the leader of the opposition Singapore Democratic Party.

Bookshops
Singapore probably has the best bookshops in South-East Asia. The main MPH shop (☎ 336 3633) at 71-77 Stamford Rd in the colonial district (see the City Centre map) is excellent, but there are numerous other good bookshops around the city, including other MPH branches, Borders, Times and Kinokuniya bookshops. Centrepoint shopping complex on Orchard Rd has branches of Times and MPH.

NEWSPAPERS & MAGAZINES
Singapore has three Chinese daily newspapers with a combined daily circulation of over 450,000 and three English newspapers with a slightly higher circulation. There is also a Malay daily and a Tamil daily. The English daily newspapers are the establishment *Straits Times*, the *Business Times* and the tabloid *New Paper*. *Time*, *Newsweek* and many other foreign magazines are readily available.

HEALTH
Health worries are not generally a problem in Singapore, though heat exhaustion and dehydration can occur as in any tropical country. Dengue fever occurs, so it's worth taking measures to avoid mosquito bites. Malaria is not a risk in Singapore – the cases you hear reported in the media are imported cases, usually in Singaporeans returned from holidaying in neighbouring islands.

Singapore possesses the best medical facilities in the region and many people come here from neighbouring countries for medical attention.

See the Health section in the Appendix for more information.

DANGERS & ANNOYANCES

Singapore is a very safe country with low crime rates. The usual precautions apply and pickpockets are not unknown, but in general, crime is not a problem.

The importation of drugs carries the death penalty and, quite simply, drugs in Singapore should be avoided at all costs, not that you are likely to come across them.

BUSINESS HOURS

Government offices are usually open from Monday to Friday and Saturday mornings. Hours vary, starting around 7.30 to 9.30 am and closing between 4 and 6 pm. On Saturday, closing time is between 11.30 am and 1 pm. Banks are open from 9.30 am to 3 pm weekdays and until 11.30 am on Saturday.

Shop hours are variable. Small shops are generally open Monday to Saturday from 10 am to 6 pm, while department stores and large shopping centres are open from 10 or 10.30 am to 9 or 9.30 pm, seven days a week. Most small shops in Chinatown and Arab St close on Sunday, though Sunday is the big day in Little India.

PUBLIC HOLIDAYS & SPECIAL EVENTS

The following days are public holidays. For those not based on the western calendar, the months they are likely to fall in are given:

New Year's Day	1 January
Chinese New Year	January or February
Thaipusam	January or February
Hari Raya Puasa	January
Good Friday	March or April
Hari Raya Haji	April
Vesak Day	April or May
Labour Day	1 May
National Day	9 August
Deepavali	November
Christmas Day	25 December

Singapore's polyglot population celebrates an amazing number of festivals and events. Chinese New Year is the major festival, and even Chinese who profess no religion will clear out the old and bring in the new. The house is given a spring clean, and all business affairs and debts brought up to date before the new year. It falls in late January or early February and goes on for a week. It's more a stay-at-home holiday than one offering lots of attractions, and hotels will be packed out, taxis scarce, restaurants often closed and prices temporarily higher.

Other special events include the biennial Singapore Festival of Arts, held around May. It alternates with the Festival of Asian Performing Arts, held every odd year. Around July, the month-long Singapore Food Festival celebrates the national passion with special offerings at everything from hawker centres to gourmet restaurants. During the Great Singapore Sale, also held around July, merchants are encouraged by the government to drop prices in an effort to boost Singapore's image as a shopping destination.

ACCOMMODATION

Singapore's hotels run the full range from dormitories in travellers' guesthouses to five star high-rises and old world luxury at Raffles.

See Places to Stay later in this chapter for a rundown on budget and mid-range accommodation, but if you want to splash out and stay in luxury, Singapore has scores of international standard hotels, and Orchard Rd has the biggest concentration. When competition hots up, the big hotels offer large discounts – if you arrive by air, check out the latest rates at the airport.

FOOD

Singapore is far and away the food capital of Asia. When it comes to superb Chinese food, Hong Kong may actually be a step ahead but it's Singapore's sheer variety and low prices that make it so good. Equally important, Singapore's food is so accessible – you don't have to search out obscure places, you don't face communication problems and you don't need a lot of money. Cheap, hygienic hawker centres are everywhere or, if you have the cash, Singapore has a mind-boggling array of restaurants serving cuisine from all over the world.

Singapore has all the favourites found in Malaysia (see the Food section in that chapter for details), such as *roti chanai* (Indian) and *satay* (Malay), though the availability and variety of Chinese food is greater. If Singapore has a national dish, then it is Hokkien fried *mie*, otherwise known as Singapore noodles. Thick, yellow egg noodles are fried with prawns, pork, bean sprouts and vegetables in a rich stock and served with chilli and lime.

Getting There & Away

AIR

Singapore is a major travel hub and there are direct flights to all the capital cities in South-East Asia and to regional centres, such as Phuket and Hat Yai in Thailand, Cebu in the Philippines, and many destinations in Malaysia and Indonesia.

Sample Fares

Some sample one-way air fares from Singapore to popular destinations are:

destination	price
Auckland	S$550
Bangkok	S$200
Jakarta	S$120
Kuala Lumpur	S$129
London	S$620
Los Angeles	S$650
Sydney	S$500

Singapore is a very good place to look for cheap airline tickets. Some typical rock-bottom discount fares being quoted in Singapore at the time of writing included South-East Asian destinations like Bangkok from S$200 one way, Denpasar from S$220 and Jakarta S$120. To the subcontinent, you can fly to Delhi or Kathmandu for S$450, to Madras for S$400.

Fares to Australia include Sydney or Melbourne for S$500 one way or S$650 excursion return, Perth from $420 one way or S$500 return. London, or other European destinations, costs from S$550 one way with the Eastern European airlines and from S$620 one way with the better airlines. One-way fares to the US west coast are around S$650 direct or with a stop in Manila.

Travel Agents

Reputable travel agents include:

Airpower Travel
(☎ 294 5664, fax 293 1215)
2A Pahang St and 131A Bencoolen St
Harharah Travel
(☎ 337 2633, fax 337 4973)
171-C Bencoolen St
STA Travel
(☎ 737 7188, fax 737 2591)
Orchard Parade Hotel, 1 Tanglin Rd 02-17

Departure Tax

The airport departure tax (Passenger Service Charge; PSC) from Changi is S$15 and is included automatically in your air ticket price.

Cambodia

Silk Air and Royal Air Cambodge (RAC) have flights from Singapore to Phnom Penh. RAC tickets cost about US$250/360 one way/return, while Silk Air flights are about US$260/440. Kampuchea Airlines are a cheaper option at US$145/168.

Indonesia

The most popular flight is from Singapore to Jakarta. Many airlines do this route for around US$65 one way. Bali to Singapore costs around US$150.

Silk Air, the regional offshoot of Singapore Airlines, and Garuda have a number of direct flights to regional Indonesian cities, including Manado and Ujung Pandang (Sulawesi); Solo and Surabaya (Java); Pontianak (Kalimantan); and Palembang, Pekanbaru, Padang and Medan (Sumatra).

Laos

Silk Air flies between Singapore and Vientiane twice weekly for US$355. See also the Air entry in the main Getting There & Away section of the Laos chapter.

Malaysia

Singapore International Airlines (SIA) has flights to the main cities, though Malaysia Airlines is the main carrier. Flights (and one-way fares) from/to Singapore include: Kota Kinabalu (S$403/RM515), Kuala Lumpur (S$110/RM140), Kuantan (S$158/RM204), Kuching (S$199/RM255), Langkawi (S$211/RM270) and Penang (S$176/RM225).

Pelangi Air and Silk Air have flights from/to other destinations, including Pulau Tioman (S$125/RM197), Melaka and Ipoh. Almost all flights go from Changi airport, but a few regional flights, such as those to Tioman, leave from Seletar airport.

There is no discounting on flights between Malaysia and Singapore, but note that it's much cheaper to fly from Malaysia to Singapore than Singapore to Malaysia – at the time of writing the Malaysian ringgit was worth around 50% less than the mighty Singapore dollar.

It's much cheaper to fly to Malaysian destinations from Johor Bahru, just across the Causeway from Singapore, than directly from

Singapore. Malaysia Airlines operates a connecting bus service for S$12 from the Novotel Orchid, 214 Dunearn Rd, to the Johor Bahru airport. In Singapore, tickets for internal flights originating in Malaysia are only sold by Malaysia Airlines (☎ 336 6777), 02-09 Singapore Shopping Centre, 190 Clemenceau Ave.

Myanmar (Burma)

Silk Air flies to Yangon four times weekly from Singapore (around US$250 return).

Philippines

Singapore to Manila or Cebu City with Philippines Airlines costs around S$485, or there are twice-weekly flights between Singapore and Davao.

Vietnam

Silk Air and Vietnam Airlines both have at least daily flights between Singapore and Ho Chi Minh City.

Singapore-Saigon one way/return is priced at US$180/350. One way Singapore-Hanoi costs US$225.

LAND
Malaysia

Bus For Johor Bahru, buses leave from the Queen St bus station on the corner of Queen and Arab Sts; the Bugis MRT station is within walking distance. Air-con express buses (S$2.40) depart every 15 minutes between 6.30 am and midnight, or take public SBS bus No 170 (S$1.10). Buses stop at the Singapore checkpoint, but don't worry if yours leaves while you clear immigration – keep your ticket and just hop on the next one that comes along. Three buses per day also go to Kuala Lumpur (KL) from this terminal.

Long-distance buses to Melaka, KL and the east coast of Malaysia leave from the bus station on the corner of Lavender St and Kallang Bahru, near the top end of Jalan Besar (the continuation of Bencoolen St). Pan Malaysia Express (☎ 294 7034) has buses to KL (S$25), Kuantan (S$16.50), Kota Bharu (S$35.10) and Mersing (S$13.10). Hasry (☎ 294 9306) has buses to KL (S$17) and Melaka (S$11). Melacca-Singapore Express (☎ 293 5915) has eight buses daily to Melaka (S$11; 4½ hours). It is preferable to buy your tickets the day before departure. Many travel agents also sell bus tickets. Buses to KL take between five and six hours.

To Thailand and northern Malaysian destinations on the way, such as Ipoh, Butterworth, Penang and Alor Setar, most buses leave from the Golden Mile Complex, 5001 Beach Rd, at the north-east end near Jalan Sultan. The Lavender MRT station is 0.5km away. Buses to Penang cost around S$33, and most leave in the afternoon and evening. Bus agents line the outside of the building, tickets are also available from Morning Star Travel (☎ 292 9009) at the Lavender MRT station.

Train Singapore is the southern termination point for the Malaysian railway system (Keretapi Tanah Malayu, or KTM). The Singapore train station (☎ 222 5165) is on Keppel Rd, south-west of Chinatown.

Three trains go every day to KL. Fares range from S$19 in 3rd class to S$68 in 1st class on the express trains, and from S$14.80 to S$60 on the ordinary trains. The express train *Ekspres Rakyat* leaves at 8.15 am (arriving 2.11 pm), the *Ekspres Sinaran* leaves at 2.25 pm (arriving 8.15 pm) and the *Senandung Malam* leaves at 10.30 pm (arriving 6.20 am). The 8.15 am *Ekspres Rakyat* continues on to Butterworth, arriving at 9.25 pm. There is also the *Ekspres Timuran* to Tumpat (in the very north-east of Malaysia) at 9.15 pm, which reaches Jerantut at 3.29 am for Taman Negara National Park.

For further details check out the KTM Web site (www.ktmb.com.my) or you can email directly (passenger@ktmb.com.my).

Taxi For Johor Bahru, long-distance taxis leave from the Queen St bus station. They cost S$7 per person, but as foreigners take longer to clear the border you will most likely have to charter a whole taxi for S$28. The bus is quicker if there are delays at the Causeway.

SEA
Indonesia

Curiously, there are no direct shipping services between any of the major towns of Indonesia and its near neighbour, Singapore. You can, however, travel by sea between the two countries via the Riau Archipelago, the Indonesian islands to the south of Singapore, and then on to Sumatra or Java.

Numerous high-speed ferry services go from the World Trade Centre (WTC), opposite Sentosa Island, to Batam and from the Tanah Merah Ferry Terminal to Bintan (the two major islands closest to Singapore). Ferries go every day to Sekupang (S$17; half an hour) on Batam, at least every half hour from 7.30 am to 8.15 pm. From Sekupang, high-speed ferries go to Pekanbaru and other destinations in Sumatra. This is a popular route to Sumatra.

Ferries go to Tanjung Pinang (S$39; 1½ hours), on Bintan, from the Tanah Merah Ferry Terminal at 9.20 and 11.10 am, and 1.20 and 3.25 pm. From Bintan, Pelni boats and the MV *Samudera Jaya* go to Jakarta.

You don't require a visa to enter Indonesia via Batam or Bintan. For full details of onward travel from Batam and Bintan, see under Sumatra in the Indonesia chapter.

Malaysia

The overwhelming majority of travellers coming to or from Malaysia will either be coming through Changi airport or either crossing the main Causeway by road or rail, or the second land entry via the bridge at Tuas, but a few ferry services exist.

Take bus No 2 from central Singapore out to Changi Village, near Changi airport, and take a bumboat ferry across to Pengerang in Malaysia (S$5).

A car and passenger ferry operates from north Changi (take a taxi from Changi Village) to Tanjung Belungkor, east of Johor Bahru. The 11km journey takes 45 minutes, and costs S$18/28 one way/return. From the Tanjung Belungkor jetty, two bus services operate to Desaru, and a Kota Tinggi service is planned. For further information call (☎ 545 3600).

To Pulau Tioman, Auto Batam (☎ 271 4866), 02-40 World Trade Centre, is the agent for the high-speed catamaran that does the trip in four hours. Departures are at 8.30 am from the Tanah Merah Ferry Terminal, and the fare is S$85/160 one-way/return. There are no services during the monsoon season from October 31 to March 1.

Getting Around

TO/FROM THE AIRPORT

Singapore's ultra-modern Changi airport, 20km east of the city, is one of those efficient miracles that Singapore specialises in. It has banking, money changing, post and telephone facilities, hotel reservation counters, left-luggage facilities, nearly 100 shops, hotel rooms, a fitness centre and a business centre. There are free films, audiovisual shows, bars with entertainment, hairdressers, medical fa-

cilities and a mini Science Discovery Museum, and if you're in transit for a long time you can even take a free two hour tour of the city.

Changi is divided into Terminal 1 and Terminal 2 – each in themselves international airports to match the world's best, connected in less than two minutes by the Changi Skytrain. A third terminal is currently under construction.

If you are one of the many air travellers fed up with overpriced and terrible food at airports, then Changi airport with its myriad of excellent restaurants serving food at normal prices will be a welcome change. Even better, Changi has hawker centres in the basement of Terminal 1 and just outside Terminal 2.

Leaving the airport, catch public buses from the basement bus stop. Public buses No 16 and 16 E (express) stop on Stamford Rd for the Bencoolen St-Beach Rd cheap accommodation enclave and continue on to Orchard Rd. The fare is a flat S$1.50 and you have to tender correct money, so get some coins when you change money on arrival. Going to the airport, catch these buses on Orchard or Bras Basah Rds. The buses operate every eight to 12 minutes from 6 am to midnight, and take about half an hour.

Alternatively, the convenient Airbus service runs roughly every 20 minutes from 6 am to midnight. Three routes service all the big hotels in the colonial district (it also drops off on Bencoolen St) and Orchard Rd. The cost is S$5.

Taxis from (but not to) the airport are subject to a S$3 supplementary charge on top of the metered fare, which is around S$12 to S$15 to most city centre destinations.

Singapore has another 'international' airport – forgotten Seletar, which primarily handles the Pelangi flights to Pulau Tioman in Malaysia, but also the private jets of high-flying businesspeople. It is in the north of the island, and the easiest way to get there is to take a taxi (S$11), or bus No 103 from the city centre (S$1.30). The nearest MRT station is Yio Chu Kang from where you can take bus No 59 to the airport (S$1.30). Note, however, that buses only take you to the gates of the Seletar base. From the gates you take an internal base bus to the Seletar terminal itself.

BUS

Singapore has a comprehensive bus network with frequent buses. You rarely have to wait more than a few minutes for a bus and they go almost everywhere. If you intend to do a lot of travelling by public transport in Singapore, a copy of the *Transitlink Guide*, S$1.50 from bookshops or MRT stations, listing all bus and MRT services, is a good investment.

Bus fares start from 60c (70c for air-con buses) for the first 3.2km and go up in 10c increments for every 2.4km to a maximum of S$1.20 (S$1.50 air-con). Drop the exact fare into the change box when boarding – change is not given.

Singapore Explorer bus passes cost S$5 for one day or S$12 for three days of unlimited travel, but you have to do a lot of bus travelling to get your money's worth.

MASS RAPID TRANSIT (MRT)

Singapore's ultra-modern MRT system is the easiest, fastest and most comfortable way of getting around the city. The Somerset, Orchard and Newton MRT stations are all close to Orchard Rd. The Dhoby Ghaut station is closest to Bencoolen St. The Bugis and City Hall stations are close to Beach Rd.

Tickets vary from 60c to S$1.60, and are bought at ticket vending machines at MRT stations. You can also buy Transitlink stored-value 'Farecard' tickets for a minimum of S$10 (plus S$2 refundable deposit); the exit machine electronically deducts fares from the encoded card and returns the card to you until its full value has been utilised. The cards can also be used on buses that have validator machines.

Trains run from around 6 am to midnight and operate every three to eight minutes.

TAXI

Singapore has plenty of taxis, all air-con, metered, neat and clean, with drivers who know their way around and have been taught to be polite, believe it or not!

Taxis cost S$2.40 for the first 1.5km then 10c for each additional 240m. From midnight to 6 am, there is a 50% surcharge over the metered fare. Comfort CabLink (☎ 552 1111) is one of the biggest companies.

Cars entering Singapore's Central Business District (CBD) between 7.30 am and 6.30 pm Monday to Friday, and 10.15 am and 2 pm on Saturday, are subject to a surcharge which is displayed on a small electronic unit on the taxi's windscreen. A S$1 surcharge also applies for trips from the CBD in afternoon peak times.

OTHER TRANSPORT

You still see a few bicycle rickshaws in Chinatown, near Bugis St and on Orchard Rd. Always agree on the fare beforehand.

You can easily rent cars in Singapore, although it is rather pointless when you consider the excellent public transport available. Expensive surcharges apply if you take a rental car into Malaysia, where rental rates are cheaper anyway.

Check the following Things to See & Do section for details on the ferries out to various islands.

Cycling in Singapore may not have too much appeal but if you want a bicycle to ride further afield, Singapore could be a good place to buy it. Check the yellow pages of the phone directory. Bicycles can be hired at a number of places on the East Coast Parkway, but they are intended mostly for weekend jaunts along the foreshore.

ORGANISED TOURS

A wide variety of tours are available in Singapore. Operators are listed in the tourist office's *Singapore Official Guide*. Most half-day tours cost between S$20 and S$40, while full-day tours can range up to S$70. Some of the most popular tours are river boat and harbour tours (see Things to See & Do section following).

Things to See & Do

Singapore offers an accessible selection of varied Asian flavours in a small package. There's a modern CBD, the nearby renovated Chinatown and relics of a British colonial past, as well as colourful Little India and Arab St.

River & Central Business District

The Singapore River is no longer the city-state's commercial artery but it's still in the heart of Singapore, flanked by the CBD, Chinatown and the colonial district.

Raffles Place is the trading centre of a city that thrives on trade. The banks, offices and shipping companies are clustered around here. At the southern end of the CBD, on Raffles Quay, **Lau Pa Sat Festival Centre** is essentially a food market, with souvenir shops and a host of food stalls housed in the restored Telok Ayer Centre, a fine old cast-iron Victorian marketplace. From **Clifford Pier**, you can get a good view over the teeming

CENTRAL SINGAPORE

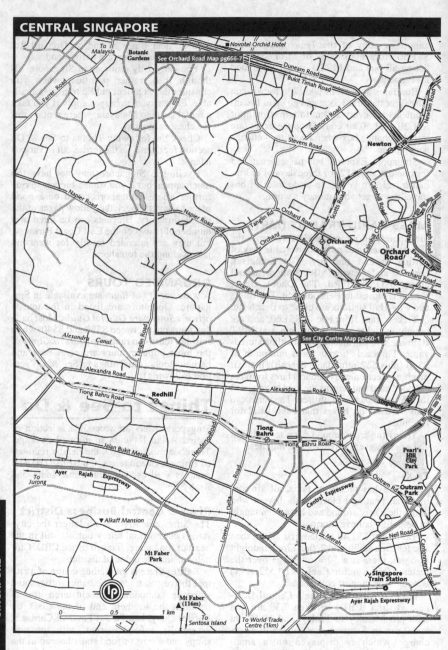

To Malaysia

Botanic Gardens

Novotel Orchid Hotel

See Orchard Road Map pg666-7

Farrer Road

Dunearn Road

Bukit Timah Road

Balmoral Road

Stevens Road

Newton

Napier Road

Scotts Road

Cairnhill Road

Cavanagh Road

Central Expressway

Napier Road

Tanglin Rd

Orchard Road

Orchard

Orchard Boulevard

Cairnhill Rd

Orchard Road

Grange Road

Orchard Road

Somerset

Alexandra Canal

Tanglin Road

Choa Chu Kang Road

See City Centre Map pg660-1

Singapore River

Alexandra Road

Redhill

Alexandra Road

Kim Seng Road

Tiong Bahru Road

Tiong Bahru

Tiong Bahru Road

Pearl's Hill City Park

Jalan Bukit Merah

Henderson Road

Delta Road

Outram Rd

Outram Park

Ayer Rajah Expressway

To Jurong

Lower Delta Road

Jalan

Central Expressway

Bukit Merah

Neil Road

Cantonment Rd

Alkaff Mansion

Mt Faber Park

Singapore Train Station

Mt Faber (116m)

To Sentosa Island

To World Trade Centre (1km)

Ayer Rajah Expressway

0   0.5   1 km

CENTRAL SINGAPORE

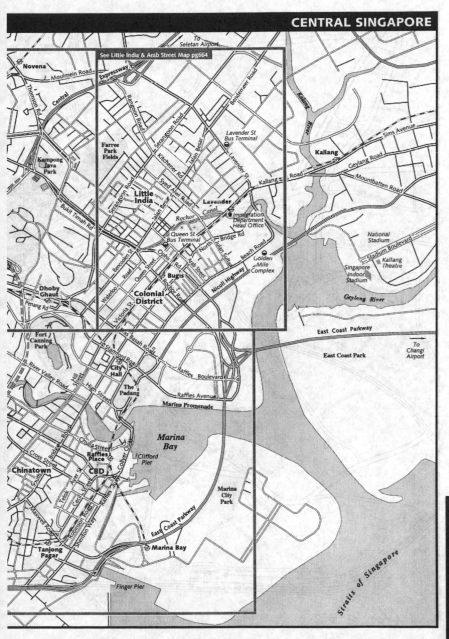

See Little India & Arab Street Map pg664

To Seletan Airport

Novena

Moulmein Road

Thomson Rd

Central

Expressway

Rangoon Road

Serangoon Road

Bendemeer Road

Kampong Java Park

Farrer Park Fields

Jalan Besar

Kitchener Rd

Lavender St Bus Terminal

Lavender St

Kallang River

Kallang

Sims Avenue

Geylang Road

Mountbatten Road

Bukit Timah Rd

Serangoon Road

Syed Alwi Road

Little India

Jalan Besar

Lavender

Canal

Rochor

Kallang Road

Immigration Department Head Office

Queen St Bus Terminal

Bridge Rd

North Bridge Rd

Beach Road

National Stadium

Stadium Boulevard

Kallang Theatre

Dhoby Ghaut

Bencoolen St

Queen Street

Ophir Rd

Arab Street

Victoria St

Bugis

Nicoll Highway

Golden Mile Complex

Singapore Indoor Stadium

Penang Rd

Waterloo Street

Rochor Road

Colonial District

Geylang River

Fort Canning Park

Jalan Besar Road

East Coast Parkway

East Coast Park

To Changi Airport

River Valley Road

Stamford Road

Hill St

High Street

City Hall

Raffles Boulevard

The Padang

Raffles Avenue

Marina Promenade

Chinatown

Cross Street

South Bridge Road

Chulia Street

Raffles Place

CBD

Clifford Pier

Marina Bay

Collier Quay

Telok Ayer St

Cecil Street

Robinson Road

Raffles Quay

Shenton Way

Marina City Park

Maxwell Road

Tanjong Pagar

East Coast Parkway

Marina Bay

Finger Pier

Straits of Singapore

SINGAPORE

CITY CENTRE

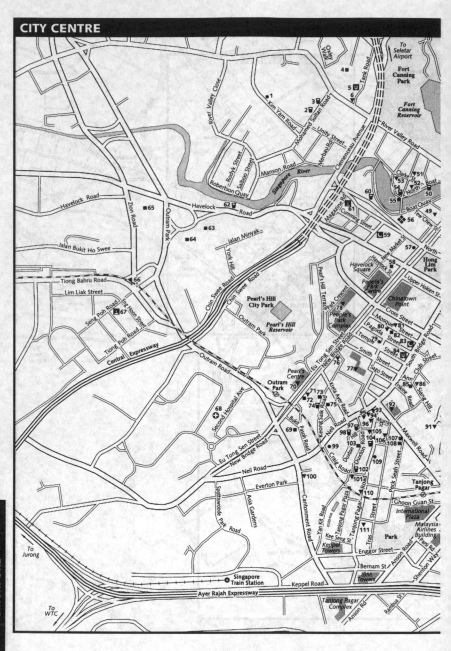

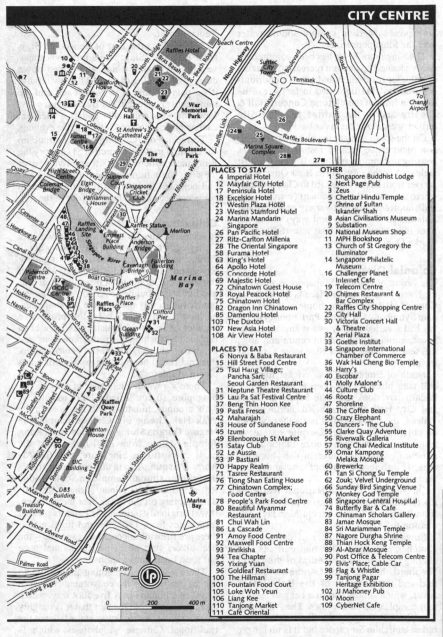

CITY CENTRE

PLACES TO STAY
4 Imperial Hotel
12 Mayfair City Hotel
17 Peninsula Hotel
18 Excelsior Hotel
21 Westin Plaza Hotel
23 Westin Stamford Hotel
24 Marina Mandarin Singapore
26 Pan Pacific Hotel
27 Ritz-Carlton Millenia
28 The Oriental Singapore
58 Furama Hotel
63 King's Hotel
64 Apollo Hotel
65 Concorde Hotel
69 Majestic Hotel
72 Chinatown Guest House
73 Royal Peacock Hotel
75 Chinatown Hotel
82 Dragon Inn Chinatown
85 Damenlou Hotel
103 The Duxton
107 New Asia Hotel
108 Air View Hotel

PLACES TO EAT
6 Nonya & Baba Restaurant
15 Hill Street Food Centre
25 Tsui Hang Village; Pancha Sari; Seoul Garden Restaurant
31 Neptune Theatre Restaurant
35 Lau Pa Sat Festival Centre
37 Beng Thin Hoon Kee
39 Pasta Fresca
42 Maharajah
43 House of Sundanese Food
45 Izumi
49 Ellenborough St Market
51 Satay Club
52 Le Aussie
53 JP Bastiani
70 Happy Realm
71 Tasree Restaurant
76 Tiong Shan Eating House
77 Chinatown Complex; Food Centre
78 People's Park Food Centre
80 Beautiful Myanmar Restaurant
81 Chui Wah Lin
86 La Cascade
91 Amoy Food Centre
92 Maxwell Food Centre
93 Jinrikisha
94 Tea Chapter
95 Yixing Yuan
96 Goldleaf Restaurant
100 The Hillman
105 Fountain Food Court
105 Loke Woh Yuen
109 Liang Kee
110 Tanjong Market
111 Café Oriental

OTHER
1 Singapore Buddhist Lodge
2 Next Page Pub
3 Zeus
5 Chettiar Hindu Temple
7 Shrine of Sultan Iskander Shah
8 Asian Civilisations Museum
9 Substation
10 National Museum Shop
11 MPH Bookshop
13 Church of St Gregory the Illuminator
14 Singapore Philatelic Museum
16 Challenger Planet Internet Cafe
19 Telecom Centre
20 Chijmes Restaurant & Bar Complex
22 Raffles City Shopping Centre
29 City Hall
30 Victoria Concert Hall & Theatre
32 Aerial Plaza
33 Goethe Institut
34 Singapore International Chamber of Commerce
38 Wak Hai Cheng Bio Temple
3R Harry's
40 Escobar
41 Molly Malone's
44 Culture Club
46 Rootz
47 Shoreline
48 The Coffee Bean
52 Crazy Elephant
54 Dancers - The Club
55 Clarke Quay Adventure
56 Riverwalk Galleria
57 Tong Chai Medical Institute
59 Omar Kampong Melaka Mosque
60 Brewerkz
61 Tan Si Chong Su Temple
62 Zouk; Velvet Underground
66 Sunday Bird Singing Venue
67 Monkey God Temple
68 Singapore General Hospital
74 Butterfly Bar & Cafe
79 Chinaman Scholars Gallery
83 Jamae Mosque
84 Sri Mariamman Temple
87 Nagore Durgha Shrine
88 Thian Hock Keng Temple
89 Al-Abrar Mosque
90 Post Office & Telecom Centre
97 Elvis' Place; Cable Car
98 Flag & Whistle
99 Tanjong Pagar Heritage Exhibition
102 JJ Mahoney Pub
104 Moon
109 CyberNet Cafe

SINGAPORE

harbour, or take a harbour boat tour. From there, walk along to **Merlion Park**, where Singapore's Merlion symbol spouts water over the Singapore River.

The Singapore River has been comprehensively cleaned up and is a recreational stretch of colonial restoration and photo opportunities. **Raffles' Statue** – two in fact – can be found in front of the **Victoria Concert Hall & Theatre** and at the **Raffles Landing Site** further west along the river bank.

On the south bank of the river, **Boat Quay** is a picturesque area of restored old shops housing restaurants and bars. It's the liveliest nightspot in the city. North Boat Quay leads upriver from River Valley Rd to **Clarke Quay**, where the restored old *godowns* (warehouses) and shopfronts house a variety of shops and restaurants. One of the best ways to see the river is to take a river boat tour (S$9) from Clarke Quay.

Colonial District

The centre of colonial Singapore is north of the river. Near Empress Place is the **Victoria Concert Hall & Theatre**, home of the Singapore Symphony Orchestra. **Parliament House** has had a varied history as a mansion, courthouse, colonial government centre and now, the seat of independent Singapore's parliament.

North of Empress Place, cricket matches still take place on the open expanse of the **Padang**, overlooked by the **Supreme Court** and **City Hall**. On Beach Rd, north of the Padang, the **Raffles Hotel** is another symbol of colonial Singapore. Despite extensive restoration, it continues to ooze tradition. The museum on the 3rd floor in the shopping area, featuring old photographs and postcards, is free.

On Stamford Rd, the **National Museum** has rotating exhibitions and is open every day from 9 am to 5.30 pm, except Monday. Admission is S$3.

Singapore has a number of colonial-era churches and other Christian edifices, including the Catholic **Cathedral of the Good Shepherd**, the Anglican **St Andrew's Cathedral** and the **Convent of the Holy Infant Jesus**, which is now part of a bar and restaurant complex called Chijmes. The Armenian **Church of St Gregory the Illuminator** is the oldest church in Singapore but it is no longer used for services. The former St Joseph's Institution is one of the finest colonial buildings and now houses the **Singapore Art Museum**.

These buildings are all near Bras Basah Rd and the travellers' accommodation centre of Bencoolen St.

Also in this area, east of Bencoolen St, is **New Bugis St**, Singapore's infamous transvestite playground which was ripped down during the building of the MRT. Now rebuilt, it's a pale shadow of its former self and the transvestites have left, but Bugis St has a few food and souvenir stalls and is a pleasant enough place for alfresco dining in the evening.

To reach **Fort Canning Hill**, continue up Coleman St past the Church of St Gregory the Illuminator where there's a good view over the city, some minor remains of the old fort and poignant gravestones from the Christian cemetery set into walls at the foot of the hill.

Chinatown

It seems strange to have a Chinatown in a Chinese town, but the area bounded by South Bridge and Robinson Rds, the Singapore River and Maxwell Rd is just that. Much of this area, one of the most picturesque in Singapore, was ploughed over for development but more recently many of the old shophouses have been restored. In the process, a number of traditional businesses have been replaced by fashionable restaurants, bars and expensive shops. Despite the gentrification, this traditional heart of Singapore still holds plenty of interest.

There's a whole dictionary of religions in Singapore, so you'll find a lot of temples. A walk around Chinatown will take you to the **Wak Hai Cheng Bio** Chinese temple, the **Nagore Durgha Shrine**, the **Thian Hock Keng Temple**, dating from 1840 and one of the most colourful in Singapore, and the **Al-Abrar Mosque**. Also in this intriguing area is the **Sri Mariamman Temple** on South Bridge Rd, a technicolour Hindu shrine with brilliant statuary on the tower over the entrance. It was originally built in 1827 and its present form dates from 1862. Several times a year there are firewalking ceremonies inside – the firewalkers start at a slow ceremonial pace but soon break into a sprint.

There's always something interesting to see as you wander the convoluted 'five foot ways' of Chinatown. A five foot way, which takes its name from the fact that it is roughly five feet wide, is a walkway at the front of the traditional Chinese shophouses which is enclosed, veranda-like, at the front of the building. The difficulty with them is that every shop's walkway is individual – one may well be higher or lower, or closer to or further from the street, than the next.

The **Tanjong Pagar** conservation area, the first major restoration project in Chinatown (wedged between Neil and Tan-jong Pagar Rds) is the showpiece of restored Chinatown.

Little India

Although Singapore is predominantly Chinese, there's a colourful Indian district around Serangoon Rd, just north of the colonial district. The smell of spices and curries wafting through the area is as much a part of the district's flavour as the colours and noises.

Attractions in Little India include the **Zhujiao Centre** market, the restored **Little India Arcade** and the backstreets off Serangoon Rd, with their exotic little shops and temples, including the **Sri Veeramakaliamman** and **Sri Srinivasa Perumal** temples. The **Temple of 1000 Lights** on Race Course Rd at the northern edge of Little India has a fine 15m-high seated Buddha, illuminated, for a small fee, by the promised 1000 lights. There is also a mother-of-pearl replica of the Buddha's footprint.

The seedy alleyways behind Desker Rd house Singapore's most infamous brothels, and the coffee shops with outdoor tables here do a roaring trade. It is the successor to old Bugis St, without the tourists and carnival atmosphere. Later in the evenings the transvestites strut their stuff here.

Arab St

South-east of Little India is Arab St, the Muslim centre. Here, especially along North Bridge Rd, you'll find old shops with Malaysian and Indonesian goods, and the **Sultan Mosque** on North Bridge Rd, the biggest mosque in Singapore. It was originally built in 1825 but was totally replaced a century later. The **Istana Kampong Glam** was the centre for Malay royalty, resident here before the arrival of Stamford Raffles.

It's always interesting to wander around the picturesque streets, with evocative names like Baghdad St, Kandahar St and Haji Lane. Bussorah St has recently been renovated and it comes to life during Ramadan, when food stalls set up after dark for the faithful who fast during the day.

Orchard Rd Area

This area is a corridor of big hotels and busy shopping centres. Beyond Orchard Rd are the fine old colonial homes where the wealthy elite of Singapore still live. Holland Village is an expat enclave out on the western continuation of Orchard Rd.

Peranakan Place, at Orchard and Emerald Hill Rds, is one old-fashioned exception to the glass and chrome gloss of Orchard Rd. In recent times, there has been a resurgence of interest in Peranakan culture in Singapore. Peranakan is the term for Straits-born Chinese, also called *nonyas* (women) and *babas* (men). Traditionally, the Straits-born Chinese have spoken their own patois and practiced their own customs, a hybrid of Chinese and Malay. This is probably the nearest Singapore comes to having a cultural identity. Peranakan Place is a lane of restored shophouses, one of which is a small, interesting museum (entry S$4).

The **Istana** (President's Palace) is open to the public on selected public holidays, such as New Year's Day. The recently rebuilt **Chettiar Hindu Temple** is on Tank Rd near the intersection of Clemenceau Ave and River Valley Rd. It's a short walk from Orchard Rd and most active during the spectacular Thaipusam festival.

Jurong

Jurong town, west of the city centre, is a huge industrial complex but it also has a few tourist attractions.

On the way out to Jurong is **Haw Par Villa** (formerly the Tiger Balm Gardens), originally built with the fortune amassed from the Haw Par brothers' miracle medicament. Fun park additions have changed much of the gory and crazy charm of the old gardens, though some of the grotesque statuary telling tales from Chinese mythology survives. Entry is S$5. Take the MRT to Clementi and then bus No 10.

Out at Jurong, there are the adjoining **Chinese Gardens** and **Japanese Gardens**, right by the Chinese Garden MRT station. They are open from 9 am to 6 pm, and entry is S$4.50.

The **Jurong Bird Park** is interesting, even if you're not a feathered-friend freak. The impressive enclosures and beautifully landscaped gardens house over 8000 birds. The bird park is open Monday to Friday from 9 am to 6 pm and on weekends from 8 am to 6 pm. Admission is S$10.30. Get there on bus No 194 or 251 from the Boon Lay MRT station. Right opposite the bird park is **Jurong Reptile Park**, open from 9 am to 6 pm daily, and costing S$7.

SINGAPORE

LITTLE INDIA & ARAB STREET

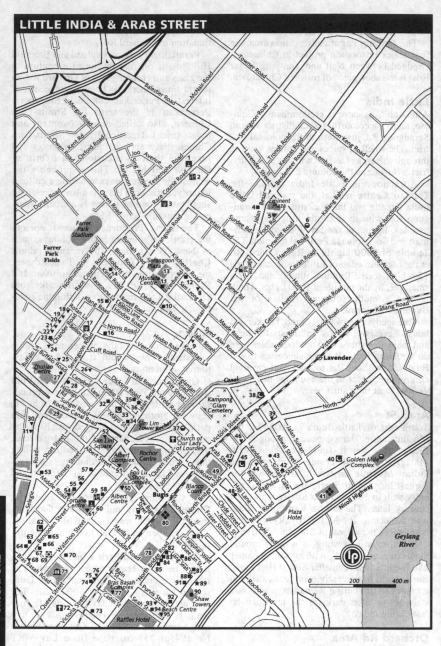

SINGAPORE

LITTLE INDIA & ARAB STREET

PLACES TO STAY		
4	Kam Leng	
7	International Hotel	
10	Grandmet Hotel	
11	Mustafa Hotel	
12	Tai Hoe Hotel	
13	New Park Hotel	
14	Ali's Nest	
15	Broadway Hotel	
16	Little India Guest House	
23	Kerbau Hotel	
29	Albert Court Hotel	
32	Perak Lodge	
34	Mayo Inn	
35	Dickson Court Hotel	
36	Boon Wah Hotel	
49	Golden Landmark Hotel	
53	Sun Sun Hotel	
55	Peony Mansion Travellers' Lodge; Green Curtains	
57	Goh's Homestay; Hawaii Hostel	
58	South-East Asia Hotel	
63	Bencoolen House	
64	Strand Hotel	
65	Lee Boarding House; Peony Mansions	
66	San Wah Hotel	
67	Bayview Inn	
70	Waterloo Hostel	
73	Carlton Hotel	
74	Allson Hotel	
78	Hotel InterContinental	
81	New 7th Storey Hotel	
82	Ah Chew Hotel	
83	Waffles Homestay	
84	Sunderbone Homestay	
85	Willy's	
86	New Backpackers Lodge	

87	Cozy Corner Lodge	
88	Beach Hotel	
91	Lee Traveller's Club	
92	Shang Onn	
94	Metropole Hotel	

PLACES TO EAT		
5	Lavender Food Centre	
8	Fut Sai Kai	
9	Berseh Food Centre	
18	Muthu's Curry Restaurant	
19	Nur Jehan Restaurant	
20	Delhi Restaurant	
21	Banana Leaf Apolo Restaurant	
22	D' Deli Pubb & Restaurant	
24	Andhra Curry	
25	Komala Vilas	
76	Madras New Woodlands Restaurant	
30	Ananda Bhavan	
31	Sri Krishnan Vilas	
39	Islamic Restaurant	
44	Rumah Makan Minang	
46	Jubilee Classic Restaurant	
47	Victory; Zam Zam Restaurant	
50	Albert Centre	
51	Fatty's Eating House	
52	Tenco Food Centre	
54	OM Moosa Restaurant	
61	ABC Eating House; Eastern Vegetarian Food; Golden Dragon Inn	
68	Regency Palace	
75	Victoria St Food Court	
76	Koh Fong Restaurant	

77	Esquire Kitchen	
93	Yet Con	
95	Tropical Makan Palace	

OTHER		
1	Leong San See Temple	
2	Temple of 1000 Lights	
3	Sri Srinivasa Perumal Temple	
6	Lavender St Bus Station	
17	Sri Veeramakaliamman Temple	
27	Jewellery Shops	
28	Little India Arcade; Food Court	
33	Abdul Gaffoor Mosque	
37	Queen St Bus Station	
38	Malabar Muslim Jama-Ath Mosque	
40	Hajjah Fatimah Mosque	
41	Concourse Shopping Centre	
42	Airpower Travel	
43	Istana Kampung Glam	
45	Sultan Mosque	
48	Kazura Perfumes	
56	Airpower Travel	
59	Kuan Yin Temple	
60	Sri Krishnan Temple	
62	Bencoolen Mosque	
69	Maghain Aboth Synagogue	
71	Singapore Art Museum	
72	Cathedral of the Good Shepherd	
79	Boom Boom Room	
80	Bugis Junction Shopping Centre; Sketches; Sumo's	
89	Central Police Station	
90	Cinemas	

The **Singapore Science Centre**, on Science Centre Rd, has handles to crank, buttons to push and levers to pull – all in the interest of making science come alive. It is open Tuesday to Sunday from 10 am to 6 pm, and admission is S$3. Take the MRT to the Jurong East station and then walk 500m west or take bus No 66 or 335 from the station.

Tang Dynasty City, about 2km south of the Chinese and Japanese gardens at 2 Yuan Ching Rd, is a huge theme park re-creation of old Chang'an, China's Tang Dynasty capital from the 6th to 8th centuries AD. It is open every day from 10 am to 6.30 pm; admission is S$15.45. Take the MRT to Lakeside then bus No 154 or 240.

East Coast & Changi

The East Coast district, out towards the airport, has a popular beach with recreational and dining facilities along the foreshore. **East Coast Park** has swimming, windsurfing and bicycle rentals.

If you want to find the Malay influence within Singapore, head inland from East Coast Park to the **Katong** district. Along East Coast Rd you'll find old terraces, excellent Nonya restaurants and antique shops.

Nearby **Geylang**, a Malay residential area, is easily accessed by the Paya Lebar MRT station. On Geylang Rd is the **Malay Cultural Centre**, a Malay theme park with a museum and entertainment for kids, or you can wander

SINGAPORE

ORCHARD ROAD

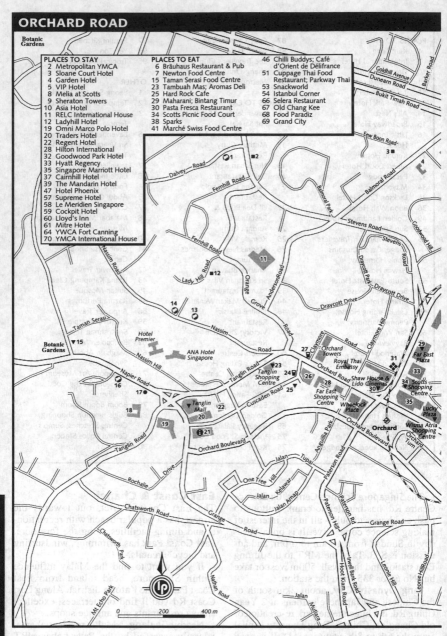

PLACES TO STAY
2 Metropolitan YMCA
3 Sloane Court Hotel
4 Garden Hotel
5 VIP Hotel
8 Melia at Scotts
9 Sheraton Towers
10 Asia Hotel
11 RELC International House
12 Ladyhill Hotel
19 Omni Marco Polo Hotel
20 Traders Hotel
22 Regent Hotel
28 Hilton International
32 Goodwood Park Hotel
33 Hyatt Regency
35 Singapore Marriott Hotel
37 Cairnhill Hotel
39 The Mandarin Hotel
47 Hotel Phoenix
57 Supreme Hotel
58 Le Meridien Singapore
59 Cockpit Hotel
60 Lloyd's Inn
61 Mitre Hotel
64 YWCA Fort Canning
70 YMCA International House

PLACES TO EAT
6 Bräuhaus Restaurant & Pub
7 Newton Food Centre
15 Taman Serasi Food Centre
23 Tambuah Mas; Aromas Deli
25 Hard Rock Cafe
29 Maharani; Bintang Timur
30 Pasta Fresca Restaurant
34 Scotts Picnic Food Court
38 Sparks
41 Marché Swiss Food Centre

46 Chilli Buddys; Café
   d'Orient de Délifrance
51 Cuppage Thai Food
   Restaurant; Parkway Thai
53 Snackworld
54 Istanbul Corner
66 Selera Restaurant
67 Old Chang Kee
68 Food Paradiz
69 Grand City

ORCHARD ROAD

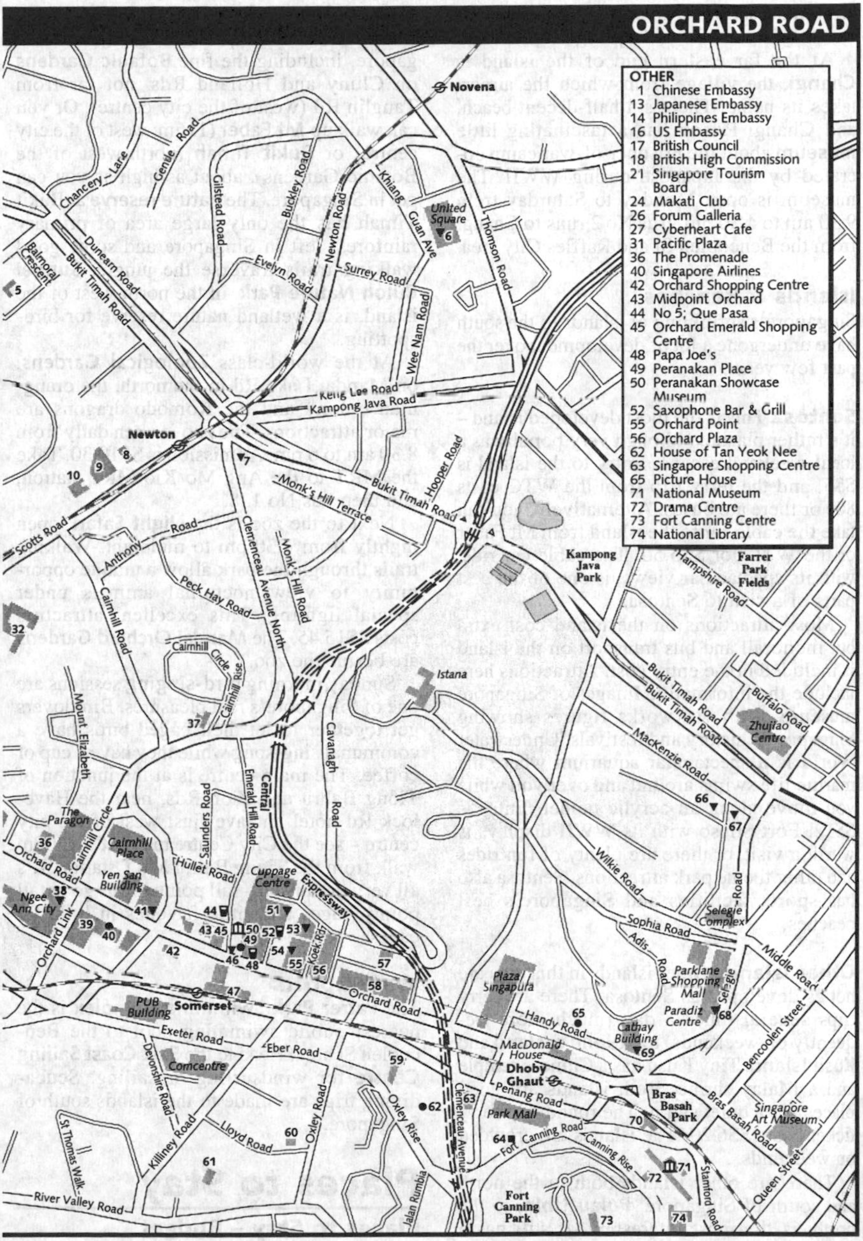

OTHER
1 Chinese Embassy
13 Japanese Embassy
14 Philippines Embassy
16 US Embassy
17 British Council
18 British High Commission
21 Singapore Tourism Board
24 Makati Club
26 Forum Galleria
27 Cyberheart Cafe
31 Pacific Plaza
36 The Promenade
40 Singapore Airlines
42 Orchard Shopping Centre
43 Midpoint Orchard
44 No 5; Que Pasa
45 Orchard Emerald Shopping Centre
48 Papa Joe's
49 Peranakan Place
50 Peranakan Showcase Museum
52 Saxophone Bar & Grill
55 Orchard Point
56 Orchard Plaza
62 House of Tan Yeok Nee
63 Singapore Shopping Centre
65 Picture House
71 National Museum
72 Drama Centre
73 Fort Canning Centre
74 National Library

around the shops for free. Next door is the interesting, old-fashioned **Geylang Serai market**.

At the far eastern end of the island is **Changi**, the village from which the airport takes its name. There's a half-decent beach, and Changi Prison has a fascinating little **museum** about the prisoner-of-war camp operated by the Japanese during WWII. The museum is open Monday to Saturday from 9.30 am to 4.30 pm. Bus No 2 runs to Changi from the Bencoolen St and Raffles City area.

Islands & Beaches

Singapore's sprinkling of islands to the south have undergone a lot of development over the past few years.

Sentosa This is the most developed island – it's rather plastic, although very popular as a local weekend escape. Entry to the island is S$5, and the ferry trip from the WTC costs 80c or there are buses. Alternatively, you can take the cable car to the island from Mt Faber or the WTC for S$5.50. The cable-car ride, with its spectacular views, is one of the best parts of a visit to Sentosa.

Most attractions on the island cost extra but monorail and bus transport on the island is included in the entry cost. Attractions here include the informative Images of Singapore museum, with waxworks figures showing Singapore's history and festivals. Underwater World is a spectacular aquarium where the marine life swims around and over you while you move along an acrylic tunnel. Entry is S$12. Fort Siloso with its WWII displays is worth a visit, or there are plenty of fun rides and other theme park attractions. Sentosa also has sports facilities and Singapore's best beaches.

Other Islands Other islands in this area are not as developed as Sentosa. There are ferry trips several times a day (much more frequently on weekends) to **St John's Island** and **Kusu Island**. Tiny Kusu has a Chinese temple and a Malay shrine. Both islands are good places for a quiet swim. The round-trip ferry ticket costs S$6.20. The islands are crowded on weekends.

There are other islands both to the north and south of Singapore. **Pulau Ubin**, to the north, is the most interesting. It still has a rural feel and can be explored by bicycle – a good day trip. Bumboat ferries to Pulau Ubin leave from Changi Village and cost S$1.50 per person.

Other Attractions

There are numerous parks and gardens in Singapore, including the fine **Botanic Gardens** on Cluny and Holland Rds, not far from Tanglin Rd (west of the city centre). Or you can walk up **Mt Faber** (116m; west of the city centre) or **Bukit Timah** (north-west of the Botanic Gardens), about as high as you can get in Singapore. The **nature reserve** at Bukit Timah has the only large area of primary rainforest left in Singapore and some good walking trails traverse the jungle. **Sungei Buloh Nature Park**, in the north-west of the island, is a wetland nature reserve for bird-spotting.

At the world-class **Zoological Gardens**, on Mandai Lake Rd in the north, the orang-utan colony and the Komodo dragons are major attractions. The zoo is open daily from 8.30 am to 6 pm. Admission is S$10.30. Take the MRT to the Ang Mo Kio MRT station, and then bus No 138.

Next to the zoo is the **Night Safari**, open nightly from 7.30 pm to midnight. Walking trails through the park allow a unique opportunity to view nocturnal animals under special lighting. This excellent attraction costs S$15.45. The **Mandai Orchard Gardens** are beside the zoo.

Sunday morning **bird-singing** sessions are one of Singapore's real pleasures. Bird lovers get together to let their caged birds have a communal sing-song while they have a cup of coffee. The main centre is at the junction of Tiong Bahru and Zion Rds, near the Havelock Rd hotel enclave (just west of the city centre – see the City Centre map). It's a 500m walk from the Tiong Bahru MRT station. It's all very organised – tall pointy birds go in tall pointy cages and little fat ones in little fat cages.

Watersports

The **Farrer Park Swimming Complex** is the nearest public swimming pool to the Bencoolen St area. Head to the **East Coast Sailing Centre** for windsurfing or sailing. Scuba-diving trips are made to the islands south of Singapore.

Places to Stay

Places to Stay – Budget

Budget accommodation is found in the guesthouses and cheap Chinese hotels. Guesthouses offer the only really cheap accommodation in Singapore, with dormitory beds and cheap rooms (often small spartan cubicles with a fan). Free tea and coffee are standard offerings, and a basic breakfast is usually thrown in. They are the best places to meet other travellers.

Most of the cheap hotels have seen better days, but they do have more character than the guesthouses. Rooms range from around S$25 to S$60. This will get you a fairly spartan room with a bare floor, a few pieces of furniture, a sink and a fan. Couples can ask for a single room – a single usually means just one double bed, whereas a double has two.

The main area for budget accommodation is in the colonial district. Bencoolen St and Beach Rd have the most options. Other cheap possibilities are found further north in Little India and nearby Jalan Besar, and in Chinatown (south of the river).

Bencoolen St Area Singapore's original and biggest backpackers' centre is at 46-52 Bencoolen St. There's no sign at all; go around the back and take the lift.

At the top, at least in elevation, *Lee Boarding House* (☎ *338 3149*) has its reception at room No 52 on the 7th floor. It's a large place with dorms for S$9 or less crowded air-con dorms for S$10. Rooms range from standard singles/doubles with fan for S$22/28, and air-con rooms range from S$30/45 right up to some good hotel-style rooms with air-con and bathroom for S$45 to S$60.

Peony Mansions (☎ *338 5638*), one of the original guesthouses, is on the 4th floor. Dormitory beds cost S$8 or S$9 with air-con, singles with a fan cost S$18 and doubles are S$22. The dorms aren't great but many of the rooms are quite good.

On the other side of Bencoolen St, between the Strand and Bencoolen hotels, is *Bencoolen House* (☎ *338 1206*) at No 27. The reception area is on the 7th floor. Dorm beds cost S$7, a few singles cost S$20 but most rooms cost from S$25 to S$45 with air-con. It's a bit run-down but OK.

In the thick of things, the *Peony Mansion Travellers' Lodge* (☎ *334 8697*) 131A Bencoolen St is a popular place with an excellent 24 hour Indian restaurant downstairs. It has a variety of reasonable rooms from S$25 for a fan room with two bunk beds, to S$50 for rooms with air-con and shower.

Green Curtains (☎ *334 8697*), next door within the same building, is an offshoot of Peony Mansions with well maintained rooms.

The S$25 fan rooms are fairly small and dark but better rooms range up to S$45.

Another centre for guesthouses is at 171 Bencoolen St. *Goh's Homestay* (☎ *339 6561*), up a long flight of stairs to the 3rd floor at 169-D, has an eating/meeting area where you can get breakfast, snacks and drinks. The rooms are clean but small, without windows and fairly pricey at S$36/46 for singles/doubles; dorm beds cost S$14. There is Internet access at S$6 per hour.

The *Hawaii Hostel* (☎ *338 4187*), 2nd floor, 171-B Bencoolen St, is an impersonal place with ten-bed dorms for S$10, pokey singles for S$25 and better air-con doubles for S$35. Basic breakfast is included.

Redevelopment in the area has seen the demise of most of the old hotels. The *San Wah* (☎ *336 2428*), 36 Bencoolen St, is a little better than the cheapest Chinese hotels. Singles/doubles cost S$45/50, S$5 more with air-con. At 260-262 Middle Rd, the good, spotlessly clean *Sun Sun Hotel* (☎ *338 4911*) has single/double rooms for S$40/45, or air-con doubles cost S$50.

Beach Rd Area *Lee Traveller's Club* (☎ *339 5490*), 6th floor, Fu Yeun building, 75 Beach Rd, is a large, popular place and not as cramped as some others. The air-con dorm costs S$8, singles start at S$15, and air-con doubles cost S$35 and S$40.

Willy's (☎ *332 1585*), 494 North Bridge Rd, is reasonable but a bit cramped. Open dorms cost S$8, while air-con dorms are S$12. Air-con doubles cost S$26.

Waffles Home Stay (☎ *334 1608*), 3rd floor, 490 North Bridge Rd, is a friendly place with dorms for S$8 and S$12, and a few basic double rooms for $26.

Liang Siah St, which runs onto Beach Rd, has a couple of good guesthouses. The popular *New Backpackers Lodge* (☎ *338 7460*) at No 18A has dorm beds for S$8 and most rooms go for S$25. *Cozy Corner Lodge* (☎ *296 8005*) at No 2A tries harder and offers a slightly better standard of rooms. Dorms cost S$9 and double rooms with fan go for S$25. Breakfast is included.

The traditional Chinese hotels are rundown but good for the price. The *Shang Onn* (☎ *338 4153*), 37 Beach Rd, is a little more expensive at S$30/34 for singles/doubles. The rooms are very clean and have character but not much else.

On the corner of Liang Seah St and North Bridge Rd, the *Ah Chew Hotel* (☎ *336 3563*) is very basic but friendly. The S$30 rooms are decrepit, but at least the eyeball-sized holes have been taped over.

Chinatown The friendly *Chinatown Guest House* (☎ 220 0671), 5th floor, 325D New Bridge Rd, has dorm beds for S$10 and reasonable rooms for S$30 up to S$45 with air-con. It's about the cheapest option in Chinatown and handy to the Outram Park MRT station.

On Peck Seah St are a couple of carpeted, air-con hotels. The *New Asia Hotel* (☎ 221 1861), on the corner of Maxwell Rd and Peck Seah St. Most rooms are small but reasonable value for S$40/58 for singles/doubles or S$5 extra with TV. A couple of doors down at 10 Peck Seah St, the *Air View Hotel* (☎ 225 7788) is a bit better than the New Asia, and costs S$60 for doubles or S$75 with two double beds. All rooms have a shower cubicle and TV.

Little India & Jalan Besar There are a couple of good guesthouses that are hanging on in Little India. The more popular is the friendly *Ali's Nest* (☎ 291 2938), 23 Roberts Lane. Dorms cost S$9, a few small singles go for S$20 or better doubles cost S$30. Breakfast is included.

The other is the *Little India Guest House* (☎ 294 2866), 3 Veerasamy Rd, which is more a small hotel than a guesthouse. Small, well-appointed rooms with a fan and a shared bathroom cost S$38/50.

Jalan Besar has a couple of cheap hotels, convenient for the Malaysia bus station but not much else. The old Palace Hotel at 407A-B Jalan Besar – a hotel with history, where Tony and Maureen Wheeler wrote the 1st edition of this book in a back room – had been gutted for renovations at the time of research. Whether it will re-emerge as the New Palace Hotel remains to be seen.

Otherwise, further south down Jalan Besar at No 383, is the *Kam Leng* (☎ 298 2289), a run-down old hotel with rooms for S$28, S$35 with air-con. At No 290A, the architecturally interesting *International Hotel* (☎ 293 9238) has singles without a bath for S$35 or large doubles for S$40 or S$50 with bath, and most have balconies.

Other Areas In the colonial district, the *Mayfair City Hotel* (☎ 337 4542) is at 40-44 Armenian St near Orchard Rd, behind the National Museum. Good singles/doubles with air-con, shower and TV cost S$60/70.

The *Mitre Hotel* (☎ 737 3811), 145 Killiney Rd, is the cheapest hotel anywhere near Orchard Rd (500m to the north). It would have to be the most dilapidated flea pit in Singapore, but it does have a good deal of character. It is in an old villa set back off the street in large grounds with a dingy bar which is popular with oil-rig workers. Rough singles cost S$24, or passable doubles with air-con and attached bath cost S$36.

The Ys Singapore has three YMCAs, which provide mostly mid-range accommodation. Though expensive, they are still very popular, so advance bookings in writing with one night deposit are usually essential. Non-YMCA members pay a small charge for temporary membership.

The *YMCA International House* (☎ 336 6000), 1 Orchard Rd, is in a handy position with good facilities, including a fitness centre, swimming pool, restaurant and a McDonald's. Average mid-range singles/doubles with air-con, TV and bathroom cost S$101/118, plus 13% tax and service charge. A bed in a four-bed dorm costs S$28.

The *YWCA Fort Canning* (☎ 338 4222), 6 Fort Canning Rd, offers good accommodation, though it's still pricey for a 'Y'. Dorms beds are from S$35 to S$45, whereas a standard single room is a whopping S$110.

The *Metropolitan YMCA* (☎ 737 7755), 60 Stevens Rd, also has well-appointed rooms, a pool and a cafe. It is a good 15 minute walk north of Orchard and Tanglin Rds. Singles/doubles with bathroom, TV and air-con range from S$64 to S$98.

Places to Stay – Mid-Range

While Singapore has dozens of high-rise, luxury hotels with all mod-cons, mid-range hotels are in short supply. Most rooms in these hotels have air-con, TV, telephone and bathroom attached. In the major hotels, a 14% government tax and service charge is added to your bill, but many mid-range hotels, like those in the budget range, include this in the price.

The *New 7th Storey Hotel* (☎ 337 0251), 229 Rochor Rd, at the northern end of the colonial district, is an upmarket cheapie with rooms for S$65 or S$80 with attached bathroom. The *South-East Asia Hotel* (☎ 338 2394), 190 Waterloo St, is quiet and good for the money. Doubles cost S$70 or S$86.50 with two double beds.

Smaller modern hotels include the *Strand*

Hotel (☎ 338 1866), 25 Bencoolen St, with rooms for S$95. The new **Beach Hotel** (☎ 336 712) has better quality rooms for $95 to S$120.

The **Broadway Hotel** (☎ 292 4661), 195 Serangoon Rd, in Little India, is an older hotel with singles/doubles for S$80/90 and S$90/100, plus 4% tax.

The new **Tai Hoe Hotel** (☎ 293 9122), 163 Kitchener Rd, is the pick of the new hotels that have sprung up in Little India. Excellent singles/doubles cost a reasonable S$68/78.

Slap-bang in the heart of Little India is the newish and very attractive **Grandmet Hotel** (☎ 297 8797), 65A-75A Desker Rd, with air-conditioned singles/doubles starting at S$58/68. There is a convenient restaurant of the same name underneath the hotel.

Also in Little India, at 12 Perak Rd, is the delightfully tasteful **Perak Lodge** (☎ 296 9072), a small, private guesthouse which has air-con singles/doubles with polished floors for S$80/90. Breakfast is included.

You can find a few reasonably priced hotels around Orchard Rd. On Kramat Rd, one block north of Orchard Rd, the **Supreme Hotel** (☎ 737 8333) is central and a good deal for the position. Doubles cost S$85. **Lloyd's Inn** (☎ 737 7309), 2 Lloyd Rd, is a small, attractive hotel less than a 10 minute walk from Orchard Rd in a quiet street among the old villas of Singapore. Lee Kuan Yew is a neighbour. Well-appointed doubles cost S$85 a double or S$95 with fridge.

In the quiet residential area to the north of Orchard and Tanglin Rds, the **VIP Hotel** (☎ 235 4277), 5 Balmoral Crescent, has a swimming pool and rooms for S$99. The **RELC International House** (☎ 737 9044), 30 Orange Grove Rd, is a quality hotel edging into the top-end category. Large doubles with balcony and fridge are S$110.

Places to Eat

Hawker Food

Traditionally, hawkers had mobile food stalls (pushcarts), set up their tables and stools around them and sold their food right on the streets. Real, mobile, on-the-street hawkers have long-since been replaced by hawker centres, where a large number of stationary hawkers can be found under the one roof. These centres are the baseline for Singapore food, where the prices are lowest and the eating is possibly the most interesting.

Scattered among the hawkers are tables and stools, and you can sit and eat in any area you choose – none of them belong to a specific stall. A group of you can sit at one table and all eat and purchase drinks from a variety of different stalls.

One of the wonders of food-centre eating is how the various operators keep track of their plates and utensils – and how they manage to chase you up with the bill. The real joy of these food centres is the sheer variety; while you're having Chinese food, your companion can be eating a *biryani* and across the table somebody else can be trying the satay. As a rough guide, most single dish meals cost from S$2 to S$3; the price is higher for more elaborate dishes.

Chinatown The Chinatown area has a number of excellent food centres. The **People's Park Complex** has a good, large food centre, and the **Maxwell Rd Food Centre** is an old-fashioned centre on the corner of South Bridge and Maxwell Rds (near the Tanjong Pagar MRT station).

Some of the best Chinese food stalls in town are on the 2nd floor at the **Chinatown Complex**, on the corner of Sago and Trengganu Sts, where there is also a market. Try the **Fu Ji Crayfish**, stall No 02-221, where a superb crayfish or prawn claypot with vegetables and rice costs around S$5.

The **Fountain Food Court** at 51 Craig Rd is more upmarket, with Art Nouveau decor and air-con comfort. It has satay and other Malay food, *popiah* and *kueh*, and good *congee*.

City Centre Near the waterfront is the trendy **Lau Pa Sat Festival Centre**, on Raffles Quay near the Raffles Place MRT station. Hawkers serve Nonya, Korean and western food, as well as more usual fare. Quasi-mobile hawkers set up in the evenings on nearby Boon Tat St.

Colonial District The **Albert Centre**, on Albert Rd between Waterloo and Queen Sts, is an extremely good and popular centre which has all types of food at low prices. On the corner of Bencoolen Sts and Rochor Canal Rd, in the basement of the Sim Lim Square complex, is the **Tenco Food Centre**, a very clean establishment.

Victoria St Food Court, near the Allson Hotel, has an air-con section at the back and a bar with draught beer. The **Tropical Makan**

Palace in the basement of the Beach Centre, 15 Beach Rd, is close to the Raffles Hotel. It has food stalls in the air-con section or you can eat outside.

The famous *Satay Club* has finally fallen to redevelopment, but many of the hawkers have moved from the waterfront to Clarke Quay by the river where the satay is still superb. Specify how many sticks (40c each) you want or they'll assume your appetite is much larger than it is. Watch out here for possible bill padding.

Orchard Rd Area Hawker food is mostly found in slightly more expensive air-conditioned food courts in the shopping centres.

The *Scotts Picnic Food Court* in the Scotts Shopping Centre on Scotts Rd, just off Orchard Rd by the Hyatt Regency, is glossier and more restaurant-like than the general run of food centres, and the stalls around the dining area are international. Similar food centres are the *Orchard Emerald Food Court*, in the basement of the Orchard Emerald shopping centre, near Emerald Hill Rd, and the *Food Life Food Court*, on the 4th floor of the Wisma Atria.

The *Asian Food Mall* in the basement of Lucky Plaza has a good range of local hawker favourites and is as cheap as you'll find anywhere.

Chinese Food

Singapore has plenty of restaurants serving everything from a south Indian rice plate to an all-American hamburger, but naturally, Chinese restaurants predominate.

Chinatown The *Hillman*, 159 Cantonment Rd, near the Outram Park MRT station at the edge of Chinatown, is a straightforward Cantonese restaurant where you can have a good meal for under S$15 per person.

For dim sum, a good bet is the *Tiong Shan Eating House*, an old-fashioned coffee shop on the corner of New Bridge and Keong Saik Rds. A plate of dim sum is around S$1.50, and as good as you'll find anywhere.

Teochew food is a widely available cuisine, and the *coffee shops* on Chinatown's Mosque St are good places to try it. Menus are hard to come by, but a request for suggestions and prices will be readily answered, and the prices are low. *Chui Wah Lin* at 49 Mosque St is a good Teochew eatery.

Chinatown has some moderately priced vegetarian restaurants, including the *Happy*

Realm, on the 3rd floor of Pearl's Centre on Eu Tong Sen St, which is one of the best around. Mains cost around S$5 to S$6, and it serves good claypot dishes.

Colonial District The famous *Fatty's Eating House* at 01-33 Albert Complex on Albert St, near the corner of Bencoolen St, has an extensive menu and consistently good food. Most dishes cost around S$5 to S$8, and go up to S$20 or more for crab.

The *Esquire Kitchen*, 02-01 Bras Basah Complex, is another moderately priced place with air-con, Chinese decor and good food. Good value set lunches and dinners cost S$18 for two people.

Chicken-rice is a common and popular dish all over town. Originally from Hainan in China, chicken-rice is a dish of elegant simplicity, and in Singapore they do it better than anywhere. The *Yet Con*, 25 Purvis St, is claimed by some to be the best of all Singapore's chicken-rice places.

On Bencoolen St, the Fortune Centre (a few blocks north-west of the Raffles Hotel) is a good place for cheap vegetarian food. On the ground floor you'll find the *ABC Eating House* and *Yi Song* food stalls, which have cheap vegetarian food in air-con surroundings. Upstairs on the 4th floor is the *Eastern Vegetarian Food* coffee shop.

Coast Singapore has another local variation on Chinese food. Seafood in Singapore is simply superb, whether it's prawns or abalone, fish-head curry or chilli crabs. Seafood isn't cheap, and a whole fish, crab or prawns start at around S$20 per dish. Many of the seafood places don't have set prices but base dishes on 'market price' and the size of the fish. Make sure you check the price first.

The *UDMC Seafood Centre*, at the beach on East Coast Parkway (several kilometres east of the city centre), has a number of seafood restaurants and is very popular in the evenings. The food and the setting are good, but some places tend to hustle a bit, so definitely check the prices first.

Indian Food

To sample eat-with-your-fingers south Indian vegetarian food, the place to go is the Little India district off Serangoon Rd (just north of the colonial district). The famous and very popular *Komala Vilas*, 12-15 Buffalo Rd, has an open downstairs area where you can have *masala dosa* (S$1.50) and other snacks. The upstairs section is air-conditioned and you can have its all-you-can-eat rice meal for S$5. Remember that it is customary to wash your hands before you start and use your right hand to eat with – ask for eating utensils only if you really have to!

Another contender in the local competition for the best southern Indian food is the **Madras New Woodlands Cafe** at 14 Upper Dickson Rd off Serangoon Rd. A branch of the well known Woodlands chain in India, prices are about the same as at Komala Vilas.

Race Course Rd, a block north-west from Serangoon Rd, is the best area in Singapore for nonvegetarian curry. Try the **Banana Leaf Apolo** at 56 Race Course Rd for superb nonvegetarian Indian food, including Singapore's classic fish-head curry, or the very popular **Muthu's Curry Restaurant** at No 78.

Delhi Restaurant at 60 Race Course Rd is an excellent north Indian restaurant, with tandoori food and curries from S$5 to S$12. Expect to pay around S$20 per person with bread and side dishes.

For Indian Muslim food (chicken biryani for S$3.50, as well as *murtabak* and fish-head curry), there are fine establishments on North Bridge Rd, near the corner of Arab St, opposite the Sultan Mosque. The **Victory** and **Zam Zum** are two of the most well known.

The **OM Moosa Restaurant** at 129 Bencoolen St, near Middle Rd, is a small, basic Indian restaurant with very good food, including fish-head curry. Meals are around S$4 and it is open 24 hours. At the other end of the scale, **Maharani** is on the 5th floor of the Far East Plaza, 14 Scotts Rd (near the Hyatt Hotel). The northern Indian food and the service are good in this casual restaurant. You can eat well for S$20 per person.

Malay, Indonesian & Nonya Food

The Orchard Rd area has a number of good restaurants. **Bintang Timur**, 02-13 Far East Plaza, 14 Scotts Rd, has excellent Malay food and you can try a good range of dishes and eat your fill for under S$20.

Tambuah Mas, 04-10/13 Tanglin Shopping Centre, 19 Tanglin Rd, is a moderately priced Indonesian restaurant with a good selection of seafood dishes and Indonesian favourites, such as *rendang* and *gado gado*.

If you like the fiery food of northern Sumatra, a good *nasi padang* specialist is the cheap **Rumah Makan Minang** in a renovated shophouse on the corner of Muscat and Kandahar Sts, behind the Sultan Mosque.

The **Nonya & Baba Restaurant** is one of the best restaurants to try Nonya food at reasonable prices. Most mains cost around S$6 for small claypots and up to S$15 for large serves. A variety of snacks and sweets are also available. It is at 262-64 River Valley Rd, near the corner of Tank Rd and directly behind the Imperial Hotel.

East Coast Rd in Katong is also a great place to try Nonya food. The **Peranakan Inn**, 210 East Coast Rd, is one of the cheapest places in Singapore to eat Nonya food in an air-con setting. Most dishes cost S$4 to S$6, or more expensive seafood dishes cost S$12 to S$20. During the day, try the **Nonya kueh** (cakes) and curry puffs at the wonderfully old-fashioned **Katong Bakery & Confectionary**, 75 East Coast Rd. The best bus for East Coast Rd is No 14, which goes along Orchard and Bras Basah Rds in the colonial district.

Other Asian Cuisine

The **Golden Mile Complex** at 5001 Beach Rd is a modern shopping centre catering to Singapore's Thai community where you'll find a number of small coffee shops serving Thai food and Singha beer. A good meal costs S$4 to S$5.

On Orchard Rd, **Parkway Thai** in Centrepoint, 176 Orchard Rd, has an extensive menu – small mains range from S$8 to S$15 for seafood.

Singapore has experienced a Japanese restaurant boom, but you don't have to spend a small fortune at a Japanese restaurant. A few food courts also have *teppanyaki* grills with a dining bar. At the Bugis Junction shopping centre on Victoria St in the colonial district, a grill at Sumo's costs around S$6 to S$10, or set meals are S$15. **Teppanyaki Place** in the Tanglin Mall Food Court on Tanglin Rd) is similar.

Western Food

Yes, you can get western food in Singapore too. **McDonald's**, **KFC**, **Burger King**, **Pizza Hut** etc are in profusion.

The **Hard Rock Cafe**, 50 Cuscaden Rd, near the corner of Orchard and Tanglin Rds, is popular for American-style steaks, BBQ grills and ribs. Main meals cost around S$20.

On Bencoolen St, the **Golden Dragon Inn** is a Chinese coffee shop on the 2nd floor of the Fortune Centre that does a reasonable job of western grills. Steak or prawns with chips and eggs served on a sizzler cost only S$6, or cholesterol breakfasts cost S$3.

Singapore has plenty of Italian restaurants. Boat Quay has a good selection. *Pasta Fresca* at 30 Boat Quay is one of the better value places, with a huge range of authentic pastas from S$10 and small pizzas from S$12 to S$15.

Sketches in the Bugis Junction shopping centre does great 'design your own' pasta dishes for around S$10.50.

Breakfast, Snacks & Delis

The big international hotels have their large international breakfast buffets (around S$18 to S$20), of course, but there are still a few old coffee shops which do cheap Chinese and Indian breakfasts – take your pick of *dosa* and curry or *yu-tiao* and hot soy milk.

Many places do a fixed-price breakfast – continental or American. Try the *Silver Spoon Coffee House* at B1-05 Park Mall on Penang Rd near Orchard Rd.

One of the nicest breakfasts is undoubtedly *Breakfast with the Birds* at Jurong Bird Park west of the city centre. The waffles are great and the birds will tell your fortune for free. Although closed at the time of writing it was due to reopen soon after this book's publication. See the Jurong entry in the Things to See & Do section of this chapter.

Old Chang Kee is a chain, with outlets all over town, including one at Lau Pa Sat, that specialises in that old favourite – curry puffs. The *Selera Restaurant*, 15 McKenzie Rd, near Selegie Rd in the colonial district, is a great place for curry puffs. Try its range, washed down with coffee in an old-style *kopi tiam* (coffee shop).

Singapore has plenty of delis that cater for lunching office workers and snacking shoppers in the CBD and Orchard Rd. In the Orchard Rd area, *Aroma's Deli*, 01-05 Tanglin shopping centre on Tanglin Rd, has good coffee and a changing deli menu.

Entertainment

At night, eating out is one of the favourite Singaporean occupations and it takes place at the hundreds of restaurants and countless hawker-centre stalls. Chinese street-operas still take place around the city, especially around September during the Festival of Hungry Ghosts, with fantastic costumes and (to western ears) a horrible noise. Lion dance troupes are increasingly popular and perform at special events, but otherwise traditional entertainment is hard to find. The *Straits Times*

lists cultural performances, and Singapore has a growing local theatre scene and plenty of cinema complexes showing the latest offerings from overseas.

Singapore's nightlife is burgeoning. It's not of the Bangkok sex and sin variety, nor does a wild club scene exist, but the huge number of bars and discos are becoming increasingly sophisticated. *Eight Days*, the weekly TV and entertainment magazine, has the best listings.

Cover charges at discos and clubs are typically S$15 to S$25, but usually include the first drink. A glass of beer will cost around S$8, less during happy hours from around 5 to 8 pm. Many of the bars have bands and no cover charge.

The Orchard Rd area is still the main centre for live music. *Sparks*, level 7, Ngee Ann City on Orchard Rd, is a huge disco with the biggest music system in town, a dazzling laser show and other bars that get some interesting bands. The *Hard Rock Cafe*, 50 Cuscaden Rd, has the usual rock memorabilia and some good bands.

There are some good places that don't usually have a cover charge. *Anywhere* in the Tanglin shopping centre, 19 Tanglin Rd (near the Orchard Parade Hotel), is a long-running rock'n'roll place with a casual atmosphere.

The *Saxophone Bar & Grill*, 3 Cuppage Terrace near the corner of Orchard Rd, is a small place with blues and jazz music.

Emerald Hill Rd has a collection of bars in the renovated terraces just up from Orchard Rd. *No 5*, at 5 Emerald Hill Rd, is very popular with a largely tourist clientele. Next door at No 7, *Que Pasa* is a popular tapas bar.

The happening places in Singapore are on the renovated banks of the Singapore River in the centre of town, especially the incredibly popular Boat Quay. Upmarket *Harry's* at 28 Boat Quay is popular with corporate highfliers and has jazz bands. Around the corner, *Molly Malone's*, 42 Circular Rd, is an Irish pub with Guinness on tap and traditional Irish bands.

Back on Boat Quay, *Culture Club* at No 38 sometimes has decent bands. Right at the end of Boat Quay near the bridge, *The Coffee Bean* at No 82 is a cybercafe with banks of terminals for surfing the net. Further up river, Clarke Quay is less frenetic but also has its fair share of popular bars. The most happening bar is the *Crazy Elephant*.

The Tanjong Pagar area in Chinatown has plenty of quieter bars in the restored terraces. The pick of the bars here is the *JJ Mahoney*

Pub at 58 Duxton Rd. It has a large range of beers, bands, a games-room bar and a karaoke bar. The liveliest night spot in Tanjong Pagar is *Moon*, 62 Tanjong Pagar Rd, a small but happening place with a lively dance floor and a club atmosphere. A cover charge of S$23 (including two drinks) applies on weekends.

Of course you can have a drink at the Raffles, at the *Long Bar* or the *Bar & Billiard Room*. A Singapore Sling, invented at the Raffles, will set you back S$17. A less pretentious and much cheaper place to drink is at New Bugis St. You can have a beer at the food stalls under the stars, and a couple of places have karaoke and bad Filipino bands. The *Boom Boom Room*, 3 New Bugis St, has Singapore's only regular stand-up comic.

If you're wondering what happened to the transvestites, Desker Rd, just off Serangoon Rd in Little India, is the successor to Bugis St. The back alleys are a highly active red-light district, and the *coffee shops* nearby do a roaring trade in noodles and beer. It doesn't have the atmosphere of old Bugis St, but it is lively and the transvestites come out later in the evening.

Shopping

Shopping is a big attraction in Singapore, though with free-market policies applying in many countries around the world it is not the bargain centre it used to be. Duty-free prices for most goods still make shopping in Singapore attractive, but it pays to know prices at home before you seize on anything as a great bargain.

For electronics, Hong Kong may have a slight edge on prices, but Singapore is still the cheapest in South-East Asia and the range is fabulous. Singapore also has a great range of clothes, shoes, sporting goods etc, but prices may be higher than at home (depend-

ing on where 'home' is). Crafts from all over South-East Asia can be found but they are all imported and prices are high.

Fixed-price shops are increasingly becoming the norm but bargaining is still often required, especially in the tourist areas. Many of the small shops, particularly electronic and souvenir shops, don't display prices and you should bargain at these outlets. Even when prices are displayed it doesn't always mean that they are fixed, especially for souvenirs. Fixed-price department stores will give you a rough idea of true prices, but with so many fixed-price discount shops around it hardly seems worth the hassle of bargaining.

Make sure that guarantees are international. It's no good having to bring something back to Singapore for repair. Check that electronic goods are compatible with your home country – voltages vary, and TVs and VCRs made for Japan and the USA operate on a different system to most other countries.

As for where to shop, the answer is almost anywhere. Orchard Rd and its periphery has the biggest proliferation of ultra-modern shopping centres. The People's Park Complex and the People's Park Centre, huge shopping centres in Chinatown, sell almost everything but beware of tourist prices. For modern consumer goods, the fixed-price shops at Changi airport offer surprisingly competitive prices.

For oddities and handicrafts, try Arab St, the Singapore Handicraft Centre in Chinatown Point, Chinatown or Serangoon Rd in Little India. The Serangoon Plaza department stores on Serangoon Rd and the large Mustafa Centre around the corner have electrical and everyday goods as cheap as you'll find anywhere. For luxury goods, it's Orchard Rd again.

The Funan Centre on North Bridge Rd and Sim Lim Square on Bencoolen have inexpensive computer peripherals and software. Film and developing are cheap, as is camera gear, and shops are found everywhere.

Thailand

Thailand has much to interest the traveller: historic culture, lively arts, exotic islands, nightlife, a tradition of friendliness and hospitality to strangers and one of the world's most exciting (and hottest!) cuisines. And if you've got the slightest interest in monastic ruins, restored temples and Buddhism, Thailand is the place to go.

The ease of travel, excellent and economical accommodation and some of the finest beaches in Asia continue to make Thailand the most popular tourist destination in South-East Asia, and with just a little effort one can easily avoid the crowds.

Facts about Thailand

HISTORY

Thailand's history often seems very complex – so many different peoples, kings, kingdoms and cultures have had a hand in it. The Mekong river valley and Khorat Plateau areas of what today encompasses significant parts of Laos, Cambodia and Thailand were inhabited as far back as 10,000 years ago. Currently the most reliable sources for archaeological evidence are the Ban Chiang and Ban Prasat areas of north-east Thailand, where rice was cultivated as early as 4000 BC (China by contrast was growing and consuming millet at the time). The Ban Chiang culture had begun bronze metallurgy before 3000 BC; the Middle East's Bronze Age arrived around 2800 BC, China's a thousand years later.

By the 6th century AD an important network of agricultural, monarch-centred communities was thriving as far south as modern-day Pattani and Yala, and as far north and northeast as Lamphun and Muang Fa Daet (near Khon Kaen). The rise of these kingdoms came to an end with the westward movement of the energetic Khmers, whose influence can be seen throughout north-eastern Thailand and as far west as Kanchanaburi.

Kublai Khan's expansion in China accelerated a south-westward migration of the Thai people and in 1238 Thai king Si Intharathit took over Sukhothai, the first true Siamese capital. Other Thai peoples migrated to Laos and the Shan states of Myanmar.

HIGHLIGHTS

- Mae Hong Son is a crossroads province with diverse ethnic minorities, Asia's longest caves, trekking and rafting.
- Bangkok has highly ornate royal temples, outstanding restaurants and legendary nightlife.
- Kanchanaburi is replete with WWII history; it also has national parks, waterfalls and caves.
- Chiang Mai, the vibrant northern capital, has handicraft markets, massage courses and beautiful teak temples.
- The island resorts of Ko Pha-Ngan and Ko Samui are studded with secluded coves and waterfalls, with lots of opportunities for snorkelling and diving.
- Krabi Province has striking limestone formations, beach resorts, rock-climbing, sea kayaking and diving.

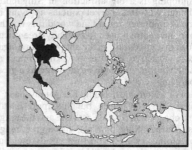

Another Thai kingdom, called Lanna Thai (Million Thai Rice-Fields), formed under King Mengrai in Chiang Rai in the north and later moved to Chiang Mai. In 1350 the Prince of U Thong founded yet another Thai capital – at Ayuthaya – which eventually overshadowed Sukhothai. Ayuthaya was unsurpassed for two centuries: the Khmers were pushed right out of Siam and the Khmer capital of Angkor was abandoned to the jungles, which hid it almost to this century.

In the 16th century the Burmese – archrivals of the Thais – who had become disunited after Kublai Khan's sacking of Bagan, regrouped and wrought havoc in Thailand. Chiang Mai, which Ayuthaya had never absorbed, was captured by the Burmese in 1558, and in 1569 Ayuthaya also fell. However, their success was short lived and the Thais recaptured Chiang Mai in 1595. European influences first appeared in Thailand during the next century, but the execution of Constantine Phaulkon, Greek emissary of the French, ended that little episode.

In the 18th century the Burmese attacked again and in 1767, after a prolonged siege, they took and utterly destroyed Ayuthaya. The Siamese soon regrouped and expelled the Burmese, but Ayuthaya was never reconstructed. In 1782 the new capital at Thonburi was moved across the river to its present site at Bangkok, and the still-ruling Chakri Dynasty was founded under King Rama I. In the 19th century, while all the rest of South-East Asia was being colonised by the French, Dutch and British, Siam managed to remain independent. By deftly playing off one European power against another, King Mongkut (Rama IV) and Chulalongkorn (Rama V) also managed to obtain many of the material benefits of colonialism.

In 1932 a peaceful coup converted the country into a constitutional monarchy, but three years later the king abdicated, without naming a successor, and retired to Britain. The cabinet promoted his nephew, 10-year-old Ananda Mahidol, to the throne as Rama VIII, though Ananda didn't return to Thailand from school in Switzerland until 1945. Phibul (Phibun) Songkhram, a key military leader in the 1932 coup, maintained an effective position of power from 1938 until the end of WWII.

In 1939 the name of Siam was changed to Thailand. During WWII, the Phibul government complied with the Japanese and allowed them into the Gulf of Thailand; as a consequence, Japanese troops occupied Thailand itself. Phibul, the wartime collaborator, came back to power in 1948 and for years Thailand was run by the military. From 1964 to 1973 the Thai nation was ruled by army officers Thanom Kittikachorn and Praphat Charusathien, who had dictatorial power, followed policies of self-enrichment and allowed the USA to develop several bases within Thai borders in support of its campaign in Vietnam.

Reacting to political repression, 10,000 Thai students publicly demanded a real constitution in June 1973. In October of the same year the military brutally suppressed a large demonstration at Thammasat University in Bangkok, but King Bhumibol and General Krit Sivara, who sympathised with the students, refused to support further bloodshed, forcing Thanom and Praphat to leave Thailand. Oxford-educated Kukrit Pramoj took charge of a 14 party coalition government and steered a leftist agenda past a conservative parliament. Among his lasting successes were a national minimum wage, the repeal of anti-Communist laws and the ejection of US forces from Thailand.

It was a short-lived experiment: the government was continually plagued by factionalism, and could never come to grips with Thailand's problems. These were made worse by border unrest following the communist takeovers in Cambodia and Laos, and nobody was surprised when the military stepped in once more in late 1976. An abortive counter-coup in early 1977, elections in 1979 and another abortive counter-coup in 1981 were followed by a long period of remarkable stability.

Thailand's very strong economic growth throughout the 1980s further enhanced the country's prospects. Democratic elections in 1988 brought in the business-oriented Chatichai Choonvahan, who shifted power from the military to the business elite and relentlessly pursued pro-development policies.

In February 1991 the military regained control through a bloodless coup, reasoning that the Chatichai government was corrupt (allegedly most of his cronies – if not Chatichai himself – got into power through vote-buying) and that society and the economy were on the verge of spinning out of control. Bloody demonstrations in May 1992 led to the reinstatement of a civilian government led by Prime Minister Chuan Leekpai.

In 1996 Chuan lost out to Banharn Silapaarcha. Amid a spate of corruption scandals the Banharn government collapsed and was replaced by Chavalit Yongchaiyudh in the November national elections. Following the general economic meltdown that occurred throughout South-East Asia in mid-1997, Chavalit was forced to leave office amid an almost total lack of confidence in his ability to deal with the economy. Chuan retook the helm, appointed a new finance minister, and watched as the Thai currency lost 40% of its value against the US dollar over a period of four months.

THAILAND

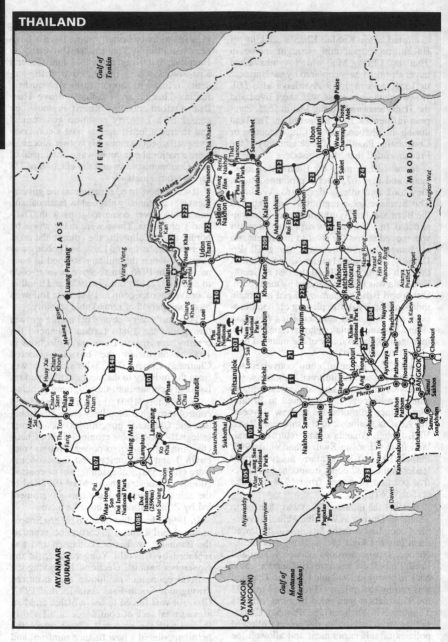

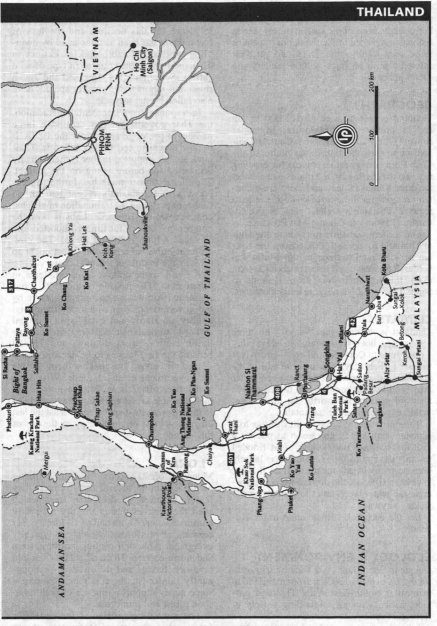

By early 1998 the baht had stabilised but the economy was still having a rough time. Fortunately, none of the violent unrest seen in Indonesia surfaced in Thailand, but it remains to be seen whether the Thais can get their economy back on track without undergoing social upheaval.

GEOGRAPHY

Thailand covers an area of 517,000 sq km and is bordered by Malaysia, Myanmar (Burma), Laos and Cambodia. Central Thailand comprises the flat, damp plains of the Chao Phraya river estuary, ideal for growing rice. To the north-east, the plains rise to meet the drier Khorat Plateau and there are mountain ranges in the northern and southern regions. Thailand's highest peak is Doi Inthanon (2596m), in Chiang Mai Province.

The eastern coastline runs along the Gulf of Thailand for some 1500km from the eastern tip of Trat Province to the Malaysian border. The west coast runs for about 560km along the Andaman Sea, from Ranong to Satun. Dozens of islands hug both coastlines.

CLIMATE

Thailand is tropical year round. The three seasons are: hot – from March to May; rainy – from June to October; and cool – from November to February. Towards the end of the hot season the north-east can get even hotter than Bangkok, although it's a drier heat. In the cool season, the north can almost get 'cold', especially in the mountains.

The rainy season rarely brings things to a complete halt and is no reason to put off a visit to Thailand. Bangkok is often flooded towards the end of the season; this is largely because many canals meant to drain the city have been filled in, the myriad wells are lowering the water table, and the whole place is sinking anyway!

See the Bangkok climate chart in the Appendix.

ECOLOGY & ENVIRONMENT

Unique in South-East Asia because its north-south axis extends 1800km from mainland to peninsular South-East Asia, Thailand provides habitats for an astounding variety of flora and fauna.

Like all countries with a high population density, there is enormous pressure on Thailand's ecosystems: 50 years ago about 70% of the countryside was forest; by 1998 an estimated 20% of the natural forest cover remained. Logging and agriculture are mainly to blame for this decline, and the loss of forest cover has been accompanied by dwindling wildlife. Notable species extinct in Thailand include the kouprey (a type of wild cattle), Schomburgk's deer and the Javan rhino, but innumerable smaller species have also fallen by the wayside.

In response to environmental degradation, the Thai government has created a large number of protected areas since the 1970s. It is now illegal to sell timber felled in Thailand, and all imported timber is theoretically accounted for before going on the market. The illegal timber trade has further diminished with Cambodia's recent ban on all timber exports and the termination of all Thai contracts by the Burmese. Laos is now the number one source for timber imported into Thailand – both legal and illegal. The government hopes to raise total forest cover to 40% by the middle of the next century.

Air and water pollution are problems in urban areas. The passing of the 1992 Environmental Act was an encouraging move by the government; it provides environmental quality standards and establishes national authority to designate conservation and pollution control areas. Pattaya and Phuket became the first locales to be decreed pollution control areas, thus making them eligible for government clean-up funds. With such assistance, officials in Pattaya now claim they'll be able to restore Pattaya Bay – exposed to improper waste disposal for at least the last 20 years – to its original purity by the end of this decade.

FLORA

Monsoon forests account for about a quarter of all remaining natural forest cover; they feature a variety of deciduous trees which shed their leaves during the dry season to conserve water. About half of all forest cover consists of rainforests, which are typically evergreen. Although central, north, eastern and north-eastern Thailand mainly contain monsoon forests and the south is predominantly rainforest, there is much overlap – some zones support a mixture of both monsoon forest and rainforest.

The remaining quarter of the country's forest cover consists of freshwater swamp forests in the delta regions, forested crags amid the karst topography of both north and south, and pine forests at higher altitudes in the north. Thailand's most famous flora includes an incredible array of fruit trees, bamboo (more species than any country outside China and possibly Myanmar), tropical hardwoods and over 27,000 flowering species, including many examples of the national floral symbol – the orchid.

FAUNA

The indigenous fauna of Thailand's northern half is mostly of Indochinese origin while that of the south is generally Sundaic (ie typical of Malaysia, Sumatra, Borneo and Java). There is a large overlap of habitat for plants and animals from both zones, extending from around Prachuap Khiri Khan on the southern peninsula to Uthai Thani in the lower north.

Thailand is particularly rich in bird life: over 1000 resident and migrating species have been recorded – approximately 10% of all world bird species. Indigenous mammals – mostly found in dwindling numbers in national parks and wildlife sanctuaries – include the tiger, leopard, elephant, Asiatic black bear, Malayan sun bear, gaur (Indian bison), banteng (wild cow), serow (an Asiatic goat-antelope), sambar deer, barking deer, mouse deer, tapir, pangolin, gibbon, macaque, dolphin and dugong (sea cow).

Endangered Species

Thailand is a signatory to the UN Convention on International Trade in Endangered Species (CITES). Forty of Thailand's 300 mammal species, including the clouded leopard, Malayan tapir, tiger, Irrawaddy dolphin, jungle cat, dusky langur and pileated gibbon, are on the International Union for Conservation of Nature (IUCN) list of endangered species.

Corruption impedes government attempts to shelter species coveted by the illicit global wildlife trade and to preserve Thailand's sensitive coastal areas. The Forestry Department is currently under pressure to take immediate action in those areas where preservation laws have gone unenforced, including coastal zones where illegal tourist accommodation has flourished. There has also been a crackdown on restaurants serving 'jungle food' *(aahāan pàa)*, which often consists of endangered wildlife, such as barking deer, bear, pangolin, civet and gaur.

As elsewhere in the region, the tiger is one of the most endangered of large mammals. Tiger hunting or trapping is illegal, but poachers continue to kill the cats for the lucrative overseas Chinese pharmaceutical market. Around 200 to 300 wild tigers are thought to be hanging on in the national parks of Khao Yai, Kaeng Krachan, Thap Lan, Mae Wong and Khao Sok.

National Parks

Despite Thailand's rich diversity of flora and fauna, it's only in recent years that most of the 79 national parks (only 50 of which receive an annual budget), 89 'non-hunting areas' and wildlife sanctuaries and 35 forest reserves have been established. Eighteen of the national parks are marine parks that protect coastal, insular and open-sea areas. Together these cover 13% of the country's land and sea area, one of the highest ratios of protected to unprotected areas of any nation in the world (compare this figure with India's 4.2%, Japan's 6.5%, France's 8.8% and the USA's 10.5%).

GOVERNMENT & POLITICS

Since 1932 the government of the Kingdom of Thailand has nominally been a constitutional monarchy, inspired by the bicameral British model but with myriad subtle differences; frequent military coups d'état and occasional vote-buying sprees stretch the definition considerably. In Transparency International's annual Corruption Perception Index, however, Thailand doesn't even make the top 10.

Thailand's 16th constitution was enacted on 11 October 1997 by parliamentary vote. Because it was the first charter in the nation's history not written under military order, it is commonly called the 'people's constitution' *(ratthammanuun prachaachon)*. Among other changes promulgated, the new charter makes voting in elections compulsory; allows public access to information from all state agencies; mandates free public education for 12 years; allows local communities to manage, maintain, and use natural resources in their areas; and establishes commissions devoted to anti-corruption and human rights.

The Thai monarchy, though constitutionally only a figurehead institution, in reality wields considerable decision-making power during times of crisis. Born in 1927, His Majesty Bhumibol Adulyadej (pronounced 'Phumíphon Adunyádèt') is the ninth king of the Chakri Dynasty. Since 1988 Bhumibol has been the longest-reigning king in Thai history; he also claims the longest reign of any current monarch worldwide.

For administrative purposes, Thailand is divided into 76 *jangwàat*, or provinces. Each province is subdivided into *amphoe*, or districts, which are further subdivided into *kìng-amphoe* (subdistricts), *tambon* (communes or village groups), *mùu-bâan* (villages), *sukhã-aphibaan* (sanitation districts) and *thêtsàbaan* (municipalities). Urban areas with more than 50,000 inhabitants and a population density of over 3000 per sq km are designated *nákhon*; those with populations of 10,000 to 50,000, and not less than 3000 per sq km, are *muang* (or *meuang*). The term is also used loosely to mean metropolitan area (as opposed to an area within strict municipal limits).

A provincial capital is an *amphoe muang*. An amphoe muang takes the same name as the province of which it is capital, eg amphoe muang Chiang Mai (often abbreviated as 'muang Chiang Mai') means the city of Chiang Mai, capital of Chiang Mai Province.

ECONOMY

Agriculture remains the mainstay of the Thai export economy. Thailand is the world's number-one rice exporter and rubber producer. Other major export products are tapioca, coconut, maize, sugar, tin, cement, pineapple, tuna, sugar, soybean, jute, processed food products, textiles and electronics. Since 1987 tourism has become a leading earner of foreign exchange, occasionally surpassing even Thailand's largest single export, textiles.

The recession that began in 1997 continues to ravage Thailand's economy at virtually all levels. The economy has been shrinking by 0.4% per year; along with currency devaluation and an inflation rate of 10%, it means that Thailand's average per capita income of US$2450 will continue to decline until the regional economy stabilises.

POPULATION & PEOPLE

Thailand's population is about 61 million. Although basically homogeneous, there are many hill tribes in the northern area and some Malays in the south, as well as numbers of Lao, Mon, Khmer, Phuan and other common South-East Asian ethnic groups. About 10% of the population is Chinese, but they're so well assimilated that almost no one bothers to note the difference.

EDUCATION

The literacy rate in Thailand runs at 94%, one of the highest in mainland South-East Asia. In 1993 the government raised compulsory schooling from six to nine years. Although a high social value is placed on education as a way to achieve material success, at most levels the system itself favours rote learning over independent thinking.

Thailand's public school system is organised around six years at the *pràthõm* (primary) level beginning at age six, followed by three years of *mátháyom* (middle) and three years of *udom* (high) school. In reality less than nine years of formal education is the national norm. These statistics don't take into account the monastic schooling at Buddhist *wat* (Thai Buddhist temple-monasteries), which may provide the only formal education available in remote rural areas.

ARTS
Music
Traditional Music From a western perspective, traditional Thai music is some of the most bizarre on the planet. However, acquiring a taste for it is well worth the effort: classical, central Thai music is spicy, like Thai food, and features an incredible array of textures and subtleties, hair-raising tempos and pastoral melodies.

The classical orchestra is called the *pìi-phâat* and can include as few as five players or more than 20. Among the more common instruments is the *pìi*, a woodwind instrument with a reed mouthpiece; it is heard prominently at Thai boxing matches. The *pìi* is a relative of a similar Indian instrument, while the *phin*, a banjo-like stringed instrument whose name comes from the Indian *vina*, is considered native to Thailand. A bowed instrument, similar to examples played in China and Japan, is aptly called the *saw*. The *ranâat èk* is a bamboo-keyed percussion instrument resembling the western xylophone, while the *khlui* is a wooden flute.

The *pìi-phâat* ensemble was originally developed to accompany classical dance-drama and shadow theatre, but these days it can be heard in straightforward performance in temple fairs and concerts.

In the north and north-east there are several popular reed instruments with multiple bamboo pipes, which function basically like a mouth-organ. Chief among these is the *khaen*, which originated in Laos; when played by an adept musician it sounds like a rhythmic, churning calliope organ. The funky *lûuk thûng*, or 'country' (literally 'children of the fields') style, which originated in the north-east, has become a favourite throughout Thailand.

Modern Music Popular Thai music has borrowed much from the west, particularly its instruments, but retains a distinct flavour. The best example of this is the famous rock group Carabao. Recording and performing for 20 years now, Carabao is by far the most popular musical group Thailand has ever seen and has even scored hits in Malaysia, Singapore, Indonesia and the Philippines. This band and others have crafted an exciting fusion of Thai classical and lûuk thûng forms with heavy metal.

Another major influence on Thai pop was a 1970s group called Caravan. They created a modern Thai folk style known as *phleng phêua chii-wít*, or 'songs for life', which feature political and environmental topics rather than the usual moonstruck love themes. During the dictatorships of the 1970s many of Caravan's songs were officially banned by the government.

Yet another inspiring movement in modern Thai music is the fusion of international jazz with Thai classical and folk motifs.

Traditional Sculpture & Architecture

A visit to the Bangkok National Museum is a good way to acquaint yourself with Thailand's canonical art periods: works from each of the periods are on display. Then, as you travel upcountry and view old monuments and sculpture, you'll know what you're seeing, as well as what to look for.

A part of the Thai government's national economic development plan is the restoration of nine key archaeological sites. As a result, the Fine Arts Department, under the Ministry of Education, has developed nine historical parks: Sukhothai and Si Satchanalai Historical Parks (HPs) in Sukhothai Province; Phra Nakhon Si Ayuthaya HP in Ayuthaya Province; Phanom Rung HP in Buriram Province; Si Thep HP in Phetchabun Province; Phra Nakhon Khiri HP in Phetburi Province; Phimai HP in Nakhon Ratchasima Province; Muang Singh HP in Kanchanaburi Province; and Kamphaeng Phet HP in Kamphaeng Phet Province.

Painting

Apart from prehistoric and historic cave or rock-wall murals found throughout the country, not much formal painting predating the 18th century exists in Thailand. Presumably a great number of temple murals in Ayuthaya were destroyed by the Burmese invasion in 1767. The earliest surviving temple examples are found at Ayuthaya's Wat Ratburana (Ratburana Temple Monastery, 1424), Wat Chong Nonsii in Bangkok (1657-1707) and Phetburi's Wat Yai Suwannaram (late 17th century).

Nineteenth-century religious painting has fared better; Ratanakosin-style temple art is in fact more highly esteemed for painting than for sculpture or architecture. Typical temple murals feature rich colours and lively detail. Some of the finest are found in Wat Phra Kaew's Wihaan Phutthaisawan (Buddhaisawan Chapel) in Bangkok, and at Wat Suwannaram in Thonburi.

Theatre & Dance

Traditional Thai theatre consists of six dramatic forms: *khŏn*, formal masked dance-drama depicting scenes from the *Ramakian* (the Thai version of India's *Ramayana)* and originally performed only for the royal court; *lákhon*, a general term covering several types of dance-dramas (usually for non-royal occasions) as well as western theatre; *lí-khe* (likay), a partly improvised, often bawdy folk play featuring dancing, comedy, melodrama and music; *mánohra*, the southern Thai equivalent of lí-khe, but based on a 2000-year-old Indian story; *năng*, or shadow plays, limited to southern Thailand; and *hùn lŭang* or *lákhon lék*, puppet theatre.

SOCIETY & CONDUCT
Traditional Culture

Thai culture is rooted in the history of Thai migration throughout South-East Asia, and shares features with the Lao of neighbouring Laos, the Shan of north-eastern Myanmar and the numerous tribal Thais found in isolated pockets from Dien Bien Phu, Vietnam, all the way to Assam, India.

Although Thailand is the most 'modernised' of the existing Thai societies, the cultural underpinnings are evident in virtually every facet of everyday life. Those aspects that might be deemed 'westernisation' – eg the wearing of trousers instead of *phâakhamáa*, the presence of automobiles, cinema and 7-elevens – show how Thailand has adopted and adapted tools invented elsewhere.

Dominant hallmarks of Thai culture include the three concepts of *sanuk* (fun), *naa* (face) and *phuu yai – phuu nawy* (big person –

little person). In Thailand anything worth doing, even work, should have an element of sanuk, otherwise it automatically becomes drudgery. Thais believe strongly in the concept of 'saving face' – that is, avoiding confrontation and endeavouring not to embarrass themselves or other people (except when it's sanuk to do so!). Finally, all relationships in traditional Thai society – and virtually all relationships in the modern Thai milieu as well – are governed by connections between phuu yai and phuu nawy. Phuu nawy are supposed to defer to phuu yai following simple lines of social rank defined by age, wealth, status and personal and political power.

For the most part casual visitors needn't worry too much about such social distinctions, although the more that you are able to recognise the differences, and behave accordingly, the more you will be accepted by the Thais.

Dos and Don'ts

Monarchy and religion are the two sacred cows in Thailand. Thais are tolerant of most kinds of behaviour as long as it doesn't insult one of these.

Monarchy The monarchy is held in considerable respect and visitors should be respectful too – avoid disparaging remarks about the king, queen or anyone in the royal family. One of Thailand's leading intellectuals, Sulak Sivarak, was once arrested for describing the king as 'the skipper' – a passing reference to his fondness for sailing.

While it's OK to criticise the Thai government and even Thai culture openly, it's considered a grave insult to Thai nationhood – as well as to the monarchy – not to stand when you hear the royal anthem (composed by the king, incidentally).

Religion Correct behaviour in temples entails several guidelines, the most important of which is to dress neatly (no shorts or tank tops) and to take your shoes off when you enter any building that contains an image of the Buddha. Buddha images are sacred objects, so don't pose in front of them for pictures and definitely do not clamber upon them.

Monks are not supposed to touch or be touched by women. If a woman wants to hand something to a monk, the object should

be placed within reach of the monk and not handed directly to him.

When sitting in a religious edifice, keep your feet pointed away from any Buddha images. The usual way to do this is to sit in the 'mermaid' pose: fold your legs to the side with the feet pointing backwards.

Social Gestures Traditionally, Thais greet each other not with a handshake but with a prayer-like palms-together gesture, known as a *wai*. If someone wais you, you should wai back (unless wai-ed by a child).

The feet are the lowest part of the body (spiritually as well as physically), so don't point your feet at people or point at things with your feet. In the same context, the head is regarded as the highest part of the body, so don't touch a Thai on the head.

Thais are often addressed by their first name with the honorific *Khun* or a title preceding it. Friends often use nicknames or kinship terms like *phii* (elder sibling) or *nong* (younger sibling).

Dress & Attitude Beach attire is not considered appropriate for trips into town and is especially counter-productive if worn to government offices (eg when applying for a visa extension). As in most parts of Asia, anger and emotions are rarely displayed and generally get you nowhere. Remember the paramount rule in any argument or dispute is to keep your cool.

RELIGION

Practised by about 95% of the population, Buddhism is the dominant religion. Orange-robed monks, and sitting, standing or reclining Buddhas made of gold, marble and stone are common sights. The prevalent form of Buddhism practised is the Theravada (Council of the Elders) school. Also known as Hinayana, it is the same as that found in Sri Lanka, Myanmar, Laos and Cambodia. Theravada Buddhism emphasises the potential of the individual to attain Nibbana (Nirvana) without the aid of saints or gurus.

Every Thai male is expected to become a monk for a short period in his life, optimally between the time he finishes school and the time he starts a career or marries. Men or boys under 20 years of age may enter the Sangha (Buddhist brotherhood) as novices, and it is not unusual, since a family earns great merit when a son takes robe and bowl. Traditionally, the length of time spent in a wat is three months, during the Buddhist lent (phansāa), which begins in July and coincides with the rainy season. However, nowadays men may spend as little as a week or 15 days to accrue merit as monks. There are about 32,000 monasteries and 200,000 monks in Thailand.

There's a large Muslim minority in Thailand's four southernmost provinces: Yala, Narathiwat, Pattani and Satun.

See the Religion section in the Appendix for more detail on religions.

LANGUAGE

Although Thai is a rather complicated language with a unique alphabet, it's fun to try at least a few words. The *Thai phrasebook* by Lonely Planet gives a handy basic introduction to the language and contains many helpful words and phrases.

See the Language section in the Appendix for a list of useful Thai words and phrases.

Facts for the Visitor

HIGHLIGHTS

In Thailand the basic threads most visitors follow include beaches/islands, historic temple architecture, trekking, handicrafts, museums, and national parks.

Beaches & Islands

Thailand's coastline boasts some of the finest beaches and islands in Asia. Head to southern Thailand if you have a week or more to spare and will be using ground transportation. Which side of the peninsula you choose – the Gulf of Thailand (for Prachuap Khiri Khan, Ko Samui, Songkhla) or the Andaman Sea (Phuket, Krabi, Trang) – might be determined by the time of year. Both sides are mostly rain-free from March to May, both are somewhat rainy from June to November, while the Gulf side is drier than the Andaman side from November to January.

For shorter beach excursions, check out the beaches and islands along the eastern Gulf coast of central Thailand (Pattaya, Ko Samet, Ko Chang) or upper peninsular Gulf (Cha-am, Hua Hin). Or, if you can afford it, plan to fly to one of the airports in the southern beach resort areas (eg Ko Samui, Phuket).

Historic Temple Architecture

The former Thai capitals of Ayuthaya, Lopburi, Kamphaeng Phet, Sukhothai, Si Satchanalai and Chiang Mai offer a wide range of Buddhist temple architecture, most of it from the 11th to 17th centuries. The Thai government has developed several of these sites into historical parks, complete with on-site museums and impressive temple restorations. For Khmer and Lao temple architecture, head to north-eastern Thailand (known locally as Isaan). Hundreds of Khmer ruins dating from the 8th to 13th centuries, including many Angkor-period monuments, dot the Isaan countryside.

Handicrafts

Thailand's ethnic diversity means a wide range of handicrafts is available for study or purchase throughout the country, especially in Chiang Mai, Nakhon Ratchasima, Khon Kaen, Roi-Et, Udon Thani, Nakhon Phanom, Nong Khai, Nakhon Si Thammarat, Ubon Ratchathani, Songkhla, Yala, Pattani, and Narathiwat.

Museums

Thailand's Department of Fine Arts maintains a good national museum system with regional branches throughout the country, and there are also a few idiosyncratic collections sponsored by other public and private organisations. Among the better ones are the Chao Sam Phraya National Museum and Chan Kasem Palace, Ayuthaya; Dr Thawi's Folk Museum, Phitsanulok; Folklore Museum, Ko Yo (Songkhla Province); Nan National Museum, Nan; National Museum, Bangkok; and Phimai National Museum, Phimai.

National Parks

Thailand boasts more than 80 national parks, a number expected to exceed 100 by the end of the century. See the National Parks entry in the Facts about the Country section for general information about the country's protected areas, and the destination chapters for details on the parks covered in this book. The book *National Parks of Thailand* by Denis Gray, Colin Piprell and Mark Graham is the most comprehensive source of English-language material on the parklands. Top parks include Doi Inthanon NP, Chiang Mai; Kaeng Krachan NP, Phetburi & Prachuap Khiri Khan; Mu Ko Similan National Marine Park, Phang-Nga; Phu Kradung NP, Loei.

SUGGESTED ITINERARIES

The standard tourist visa is valid for two months, though only a relatively small percentage of visitors stays that long. The 30 days granted to visitors from most countries who arrive without a visa usually suffices and can be extended by simply crossing the border into a neighbouring country and re-entering Thailand the same day.

The itineraries suggested below assume you want to see as much of the country as possible within a given interval. Another approach would be to spend more time in fewer places rather than less time in many.

One Week

Temples & Gulf Beaches For a short Thailand sampler, start with a two day taste of Bangkok's heavily gilded temples and urban intensity, then flee toward the former royal capital of Ayuthaya to take in 400-year-old temple and palace ruins, right in the centre of the city. A day in Ayuthaya is enough for most people in a hurry.

Transit back through Bangkok and head south-east to Ko Samet for two or three nights on this all-season island before saying farewell to Thailand. Substitute Jomtien Beach near Pattaya for Samet if your taste runs towards international-class hotels rather than simple beach bungalows.

Floating Market/River Kwai/Lopburi From Bangkok get an early morning start for one of the floating markets south-west of the city – Damnoen Saduak is the most well known but there are several others in the vicinity (see the Nakhon Pathom section for details of another one).

Spend the night in Nakhon Pathom and take in the world's largest Buddhist monument, Phra Pathom Chedi (Phra Pathom Stupa). Continue to Kanchanaburi by bus or train to see the world-famous 'Bridge on the River Kwai' and experience a fairly typical provincial Thai town.

Return to Bangkok via Suphanburi and Lopburi, passing through the country's 'rice bowl' and stopping for a night in Lopburi to catch the Khmer and Thai temple ruins there.

Two Weeks

Northern Thailand After completing one of the above circuits, take an overnight train (or fly) to Chiang Mai. Shop till you flop at the Chiang Mai Night Bazaar, sample the city's excellent Northern Thai cuisine, and decide whether to move north-west to Mae Hong Son or north-east to Nan. Both areas offer mountain trekking, national parks, and large hill tribe populations.

North-Eastern Thailand Start with one of the Central Thailand loops, then take a train from Bangkok to Nakhon Ratchasima and visit the nearby Angkor-period ruins at Phimai. If you want to see more Khmer architectural splendour, make a short journey to Wat Prasat Hin Phanom Rung in Buriram Province.

Finish with a travel sector along the Mekong river – from Chiang Khan to Si Chiangmai if you prefer small towns and villages, from Nakhon Phanom to Ubon Ratchathani if you like cities.

Bangkok to the Malaysian Border After you've had your fill of Bangkok – three or four days does the trick for most people who have two weeks to spend in the country – start your roll down the Malay Peninsula with a two night, one day stopover in Phetburi, a city of venerable late-Ayuthaya-period temples and a hilltop royal palace.

After Phetburi, take your pick among beaches at Cha-am, Hua Hin or in the vicinity of Prachuap Khiri Khan – all places where middle-class Thais like to vacation. And/or visit Khao Sam Roi Yot National Park, good for coastal and hillside hiking.

For some serious beach time, zero in on one or more of the three major islands off the coast of Chumphon and Surat Thani provinces – Ko Tao, Ko Pha-Ngan and Ko Samui – depending on your tastes (see the relevant destination entries later in the chapter for details).

When you're ready for a little culture, sail back to the mainland and see Chaiya (Sriwijaya-era ruins and a world-famous meditation monastery) or Songkhla (Sino-Portuguese architecture and a national museum).

Follow with a night or two in Hat Yai to sample some of Thailand's best Chinese food outside Bangkok and shop for Southern Thai or Malay textiles. For your entry into Malaysia, take the east coast route via Narathiwat for the best natural scenery, the west coast if you're in a rush to reach Penang or Kuala Lumpur.

One Month

Temples, Trekking & Beaches In a month you can sample many of Thailand's major highlights. After a few days in Bangkok (or leave the city for the end), take a slow ride north with two-night stopovers in Lopburi, Phitsanulok and Sukhothai to take in some of Thailand's most historic temple architecture, ancient as well as modern. From the latter, head south-west to Mae Sot, amid a zone of Karen and Burmese influence, and explore the less-than-beaten path stretching from Um Phang to Mae Sariang. Here you will find waterfalls, trekking, rafting and working elephants. Continue north from Mae Sariang along the Mae Hong Son loop to Tha Ton on the Kok river, and either boat down the Kok to Chiang Rai or take a *songthaew* (a small truck with benches, used as a bus/taxi) through the mountains along the Burmese border to the Yunnanese settlement of Mae Salong.

With roughly a week left in your itinerary, choose a beach or island along the upper Gulf of Thailand coast (Pattaya, Ko Samet, Ko Chang or Hua Hin) if you want to get there quick via Bangkok, or pick from either the Andaman coast (Phuket, Khao Lak, Krabi, Trang) or southern Gulf coast (Ko Samui, Ko Pha-Ngan, Ko Tao) if you don't mind a longer trip by air, road or rail. If you like your beaches untrammelled it might be worth the extra effort to visit one of the national marine parks off the Andaman coast; Mu Ko Tarutao, Mu Ko Similan or Mu Ko Surin.

If you have time while in the South, make a side trip to Khao Sok National Park, one of Thailand's most important refuges for tigers and rainforest.

North by North-East If beaches don't matter much to you, go for a major intake of culture and nature by starting with the Lopburi to Mae Salong route described above. From the latter continue eastward to Nan and Phrae, two of the North's less-travelled provinces, then head across to Loei Province for the Mekong river loop from Chiang Khan to Ubon.

If there's time at the end of the latter, head into the interior to visit Prasat Hin Phanom Rung and/or Prasat Hin Phimai. The more adventurous can substitute a whirl along the Cambodian border from Ubon to Aranya Prathet via Surin and Si Saket, provinces that are home to a number of smaller, lesser-known Khmer temple sites. Or if temple-trekking has paled by this point, go hiking in Khao Yai National Park, one of Thailand's largest and oldest protected areas.

PLANNING
When to Go
The best overall time for visiting most of Thailand vis-à-vis climate falls between November and March – during these months it rains least and is not so hot. Temperatures are less extreme in the south, so the south makes a good refuge when the rest of Thailand is miserably hot from April to June. The north is best from mid-November to early December, or in February when it begins warming up again. If you're spending time in Bangkok, be prepared to roast in April and do some wading in October – probably the two worst months, weather-wise, for the capital.

The peak months for tourist visitation are November, December, February, March and August, with secondary peak months in January and July. Consider travelling during the least crowded months of April, May, June, September and October if avoiding crowds is your main objective and you want to take advantage of discounted rooms and other low-season rates.

Maps
Lonely Planet publishes the 1:1,150,000 scale *Thailand travel atlas*, a 44-page country map booklet designed to combine maximum accuracy with maximum portability. Nelles and Bartholomews each publish decent 1:500,000 scale maps of Thailand with general topographic shading. The Bartholomews map is more up-to-date and accurate than the Nelles, though both maps could use updating and corrections.

The Roads Association of Thailand publishes a large format, 48-page, bilingual road atlas called *Thailand Highway Map*. The atlas includes 1:1,000,000 Highway Department maps reduced to a manageable size with dozens of city maps, driving distances and lots of travel and sightseeing information.

In Bangkok, you can buy an invaluable bus map which lists all the Bangkok bus routes. The flip side of the bus map has a pretty good map of Thailand with Thai script as well. Make sure any map you get has names on it in Thai as well as English.

What to Bring
Pack lightweight clothes, but if you're going to the north in the cool season you'll need a pullover. Sunglasses are cheap in Bangkok and most provincial capitals. Slip on shoes or sandals are highly recommended – besides being cooler than lace-ups, they are easily removed before entering a Thai home or temple.

Most toiletries are available anywhere in Thailand. Sun block and mosquito repellent are available, although they can be expensive and often of poor quality.

Pick up a *phâakhamáa* (men's short Thai sarong) or a *phâasîn* (a longer sarong for women), to wear in your room, on the beach or bathing outdoors. The sarong has many uses, including to sleep on or as a: light bedspread (many guesthouses do not supply top sheets or bedspreads); makeshift 'shopping bag'; turban/scarf to keep off the sun and absorb perspiration; towel; small hammock; or a device with which to climb coconut trees.

If you're planning to spend much time in the coastal regions, you might want to bring snorkelling gear, to ensure quality and fit which are a bit risky with rented gear.

Most Thai women don't use tampons and so they can be difficult to find. In general only the o.b. brand is available, usually in middle class pharmacies or mini-marts that carry toiletries. In Bangkok more upscale pharmacies may also carry the Tampax brand. If you're coming for a relatively short time it's probably best to bring your own.

TOURIST OFFICES

The Tourist Authority of Thailand (TAT) has an office at the airport in Bangkok, another in central Bangkok and quite a few in regional centres around the country. TAT has a lot of useful brochures, booklets and maps and will probably have an information sheet on almost any Thai subject. TAT is probably the best tourist office in South-East Asia for the production of useful information sheets rather than (often useless) pretty colour brochures.

Each regional office also puts out accommodation guides that include cheap places to stay.

Local Tourist Offices

Locations of TAT offices in Thailand include:

Ayuthaya
  (☎ 24 6076)
  Thanon Si Sanphet (temporary office),
  Ayuthaya 13000
Bangkok
  (☎ 694 1222)
  Le Concorde Bldg (temporary office),
  202 Thanon Ratchadaphisek,
  Bangkok 10310
  (☎ 281 0422)
  4 Thanon Ratchadamnoen Nok,
  Bangkok 10100
Cha-am
  (☎ 47 1005, fax 47 1502)
  500/51 Phetkasem Hwy,
  Amphoe Cha-am,
  Phetburi 76120

Chiang Mai
  (☎ 24 8604, fax 24 8605)
  105/1 Thanon Chiang Mai-Lamphun,
  Chiang Mai 50000
Chiang Rai
  (☎ 71 7433, fax 71 7434)
  Thanon Singhakai,
  Chiang Rai 57000
Hat Yai
  (☎ 24 3747, fax 24 5986)
  1/1 Soi 2, Thanon Niphat Uthit 3,
  Hat Yai, Songkhla 90110
Kanchanaburi
  (☎/fax 51 1200)
  Thanon Saengchuto,
  Kanchanaburi 71000
Khon Kaen
  (☎ 24 4498, fax 24 4497)
  15/5 Thanon Prachasamoson,
  Khon Kaen 40000
Lopburi
  (☎ 42 2768, fax 42 2769)
  HM the Queen's Celebration Bldg
  (temporary office), Provincial Hall,
  Thanon Narai Maharat,
  Lopburi 15000
Nakhon Phanom
  (☎ 51 3490, fax 51 3492)
  184/1 Thanon Sonthonvichit,
  Nakhon Phanom 48000
Nakhon Ratchasima (Khorat)
  (☎ 21 3666, fax 21 3667)
  2102-2104 Thanon Mittaphap,
  Nakhon Ratchasima 30000
Nakhon Si Thammarat
  (☎ 34 6515, fax 34 6517)
  Sanam Na Meuang,
  Thanon Ratchadamnoen Klang,
  Nakhon Si Thammarat 80000
Narathiwat (Sungai Kolok)
  (☎ 61 2126, fax 61 5230)
  Asia Hwy 18,
  Sungai Kolok, Narathiwat 96120
Pattaya
  (☎ 42 7667, fax 42 9113)
  382/1 Thanon Chai Hat, Pattaya Beach,
  South Pattaya 21000
Phitsanulok
  (☎ 25 2743, fax 25 2742)
  209/7-8 Surasi Trade Centre,
  Thanon Boromtrailokanat,
  Phitsanulok 85000
Phuket
  (☎ 21 2213, fax 21 3582)
  73-75 Thanon Phuket,
  Phuket 83000
Rayong
  (☎ /fax 65 5420)
  153/4 Thanon Sukhumvit,
  Rayong 21000

Surat Thani
(☎ /fax 28 2828)
5 Thanon Talaat Mai,
Ban Don, Surat Thani 84000
Trat (Laem Ngop)
(☎ /fax 59 7255)
100 Muu 1 Thanon,
Trat-Laem Ngop, Laem Ngop,
Trat 23120
Ubon Ratchathani
(☎ 24 3770, fax 24 3771)
264/1 Thanon Kheuan Thani,
Ubon Ratchathani 34000
Udon Thani
(☎ /fax 32 5406)
16/5 Thanon Mukkhamontri,
Udon Thani 41000

Tourist Offices Abroad

TAT offices can be found in the following countries:

Australia
(☎ 02-9247 7549, fax 9251 2465,
email info@thailand.net.au)
Level 2, 75 Pitt St,
Sydney, NSW 2000
France
(☎ 01 53 53 47 00, fax 45 63 78 88,
email tatpar@wanadoo.fr)
90 Avenue des Champs Elysees,
75008 Paris
Germany
(☎ 069-138 1390,
email tatfra@e-online.de)
Bethmannstrasse 58,
60311 Frankfurt/Main
Malaysia
(☎ 03-262 3480, fax 262 3486,
email tatkl@sawatdi.po.my)
Suite 22.01, Level 22, Menara Lion,
165 Jalan Ampang,
50450 Kuala Lumpur
Singapore
(☎ 235 7694, fax 733 5653)
c/o Royal Thai Embassy,
370 Orchard Rd,
Singapore 0923
UK
(☎ 0171-499 7679, fax 629 5519,
email info@tat.uk.demon.co.uk)
49 Albemarle St,
London WIX 3FE
USA
(☎ 212-432 0433, fax 912 0920)
5 World Trade Center, Suite 3443,
New York, NY 10048
(☎ 213-461 9814, fax 462 9834,
email tatla@ix.netcom.com)
611 North Larchmont Blvd,
Los Angeles, CA 90004

Tourist Police

Under the auspices of TAT, the Tourist Police headquarters (☎ 255 2964), 29/1 Soi Lang Suan, Thanon Ploenchit in Bangkok, is in charge of handling complaints tourists may have regarding, crime, gem scams and so on. You can also contact the TP through any TAT office or via the telephone hotline number ☎ 1699 which connects with the Tourist Police from any phone in Thailand.

VISAS & DOCUMENTS

You've got a variety of choices in the visa game for Thailand. First of all, citizens of 56 different countries can enter Thailand without any visa and be granted a 30 day stay. (Those from Sweden, Denmark, New Zealand and South Korea can travel in Thailand for up to 90 days without a visa.) Officially, you must have an outward ticket but in practice this does not seem to be rigidly enforced.

The one month visa is free. Next in length of validity is the tourist visa, which is good for 60 days and costs around US$15, depending on the country of application. Three passport photos must accompany all applications.

Visa Extensions

Sixty-day tourist visas may be extended up to 30 days at the discretion of Thai immigration authorities. The Bangkok office (☎ 287 3101) is on Soi Suan Phlu, Thanon Sathon Tai, but you can apply at any immigration office in the country – every province that borders a neighbouring country has one.

The usual fee for extension of a tourist visa (up to one month) is 500B. Bring along one photo and one copy each of the photo and visa pages of your passport. Normally only one 30 day extension is granted.

The 30 day visa can be extended for seven to 10 days (depending on the immigration office) for 500B. You can also leave the country and return immediately to obtain another 30 day stay. There is no limit on the number of times you can do this, nor is there a minimum interval you must spend outside the country.

Hostel, Student, Youth & Seniors' Cards

Hostelling International (HI) cards are required for stays at member HI hostels in Bangkok, Chiang Mai and Phitsanulok. Student, youth and seniors' cards aren't much use in Thailand.

EMBASSIES & CONSULATES
Thai Embassies

Thai embassies abroad include:

Australia
(☎ 02-6273 1149)
111 Empire Circuit, Yarralumla, ACT 2600
Canada
(☎ 613-722 4444)
180 Island Park Dr, Ottawa,
Ontario K1Y 0A2
France
(☎ 01 47 27 80 79)
8 rue Greuze, 75116 Paris
Germany
(☎ 228-35 5065)
Ubierstrasse 65, 53173 Bonn
New Zealand
(☎ 04-476 8618)
2 Cook St, Karori, Wellington 5
UK
(☎ 0171-589 0173)
29-30 Queen's Gate, London SW7 5JB
USA
(☎ 202-944 3600)
1024 Wisconsin Ave NW,
Washington, DC 20007

See the other chapters in this book for Thai embassies in those countries.

Embassies & Consulates in Thailand

Countries with diplomatic representation in Bangkok include:

Australia
(☎ 287 2680) 37 Thanon Sathon Tai
Cambodia
(☎ 254 6630) 185 Thanon Ratchadamri
Canada
(☎ 636 0540) 15th fl, Abdulrahim Bldg,
990 Thanon Rama IV
China
(☎ 245 7032) 57 Thanon Ratchadaphisek
France
(☎ 266 8250) 35 Soi Rong Phasi Kao (Soi 36),
Thanon Charoen Krung
Germany
(☎ 287 9000) 9 Thanon Sathon
India
(☎ 258 0300) 46 Soi Prasanmit (Soi 23),
Thanon Sukhumvit
Indonesia
(☎ 252 3135) 600-602 Thanon Phetburi
Japan
(☎ 22 6151) 1674 Thanon Phetburi Tat Mai
Laos
(☎ 538 3696) 520/1-3 Soi 39,
Thanon Ramkhamhaeng

Malaysia
(☎ 254 1700) 15th fl, 183 Thanon Ratchadamri
Myanmar (Burma)
(☎ 233 2237) 132 Thanon Sathon Neua
New Zealand
(☎ 254 2530) 93 Thanon Withayu
Philippines
(☎ 259 0139) 760 Thanon Sukhumvit
Singapore
(☎ 286 2111) 129 Thanon Sathon Tai
UK
(☎ 253 0191) 1031 Thanon Withayu
USA
(☎ 205 4000) 120-122 Thanon Withayu
Vietnam
(☎ 251 5835) 83/1 Thanon Withayu

In Chiang Mai the following countries are represented:

Australia (Honorary)
(☎ 22 5975) 165 Thanon Sirimangkhalajan
Canada
(☎ 85 0147) 51 Thanon Chiang Mai-Lamphun
China
(☎ 27 6125) 111 Thanon Chang Law
India
(☎ 24 3066) 344 Thanon Faham (Charoenrat),
Faham
UK
(☎ 20 3405) Airport Business Park,
Thanon Mahidon
USA
(☎ 25 2629) 387 Thanon Wichayanon

CUSTOMS

Like most countries, Thailand prohibits the import of illegal drugs, firearms and ammunition (unless registered in advance with the Police Department) and pornographic material. Visitors are permitted to bring the following into the country without paying duty: a reasonable amount of clothing and toiletries for personal use; professional instruments; one movie/video camera with three rolls of film/ videotape or one still camera with five rolls of film; up to 200 cigarettes, or 250g of other smoking materials; and 1L of wine or spirits.

Electronic goods like personal stereos, calculators and computers can be a problem if customs officials have reason to believe you're bringing them in for resale. As long as you don't carry more than one of each, you should be OK. Occasionally, customs will require you to leave a hefty deposit for big-ticket items (eg a laptop computer or midi-component stereo), which is refunded when you leave the country with the item in question. This is quite uncommon.

MONEY
Currency

The baht (B) is divided into 100 satang, although 25 and 50 satang are the smallest coins you'll see. Coins come in 1B (three sizes), 5B (two sizes) and 10B denominations. Notes are in 10B (brown – but gradually being phased out of circulation), 20B (green), 50B (blue), 100B (red) and 500B (purple) and 1000B (beige) denominations of varying shades and sizes. A 10,000B bill is on the way. Changing 500B or larger notes can be difficult in small towns and villages.

Exchange Rates

Exchange rates are as follows:

country	unit		baht
Australia	A$1	=	24B
Canada	C$1	=	25B
euro	€1	=	46B
France	10FF	=	69B
Germany	DM1	=	23B
Japan	¥100	=	32B
New Zealand	NZ$1	=	21B
Singapore	S$1	=	23B
UK	UK£1	=	65B
USA	US$1	=	38B

Since the Thai government floated the currency in June 1997, the baht has been on a roller coaster ride against the American and European currencies. At one point in early 1998 the exchange rate fell as low as 55B per US dollar. Expect more foreign exchange volatility at least until the middle of 1999.

Exchanging Money

Banks give the best exchange rates. Avoid hotels, which give the worst rates. In the larger towns and tourist destinations, there are also foreign exchange kiosks that are open longer hours, usually from around 8 am to 8 pm.

All banks deduct a 10 to 13B service charge per cheque – thus you can save money by using larger denomination travellers cheques (eg cashing a US$100 cheque will cost you 10B to 13B, while cashing five US$20 cheques will cost 50B to 65B).

ATMS All major Thai banks offer ATM (automatic teller machine) services; many of the machines will accept foreign ATM cards and/or credit and debit cards.

Credit Cards Credit cards are widely accepted at upmarket hotels, restaurants and other business establishments. Visa and MasterCard are the most commonly accepted, followed by American Express and Diners Club. Cash advances are available on Visa and MasterCard at many banks and exchange booths.

Black Market There is no black market for US dollars, but Bangkok is a good centre for buying Asian currencies, particularly those of neighbouring countries where black market moneychanging flourishes (eg Laos and Myanmar) – try the moneychangers on Thanon Charoen Krung (New Rd).

Costs

Thailand is an economical country to visit, probably the best value dollar for dollar in South-East Asia. Transport is reasonably priced, comfortable and reliable; accommodation is inexpensive and finding a place to stay is rarely difficult, although during the high seasons (December-January and July-August) it can be a little tight. The food is also very good and cheap.

Bangkok is more expensive than elsewhere in the country, partly because lots of luxuries are available there which you simply won't be tempted with upcountry. However, with so many cheap guesthouses in the Banglamphu area of the city, accommodation needn't be more expensive than elsewhere. Of course, the Bangkok hassles – noise and pollution being the main ones – may drive you to look for extra comfort, and air-conditioning can be very nice.

One good way to save money is to travel in the off season, which in Thailand means from May/June to September or October. During these periods, tourist destinations are less crowded and prices for accommodation are generally lower. In the remainder of the year, hotels and guesthouses often raise their prices to whatever the market will bear.

Budget-squeezers should be able to get by on 250B per day outside Bangkok if they really watch their expenses. This estimate includes basic guesthouse accommodation, food, nonalcoholic beverages and local transport, but not film, souvenirs, tours, long-distance transport or vehicle hire. Add another 55B to 80B per day for every large beer (30B to 45B for small bottles) you drink.

Tipping & Bargaining

Tipping is not customary except in the big tourist hotels of Bangkok, Pattaya, Phuket

THAILAND

and Chiang Mai. Even here, if a service charge is added to the bill, tipping isn't necessary.

Bargaining is mandatory in almost all situations. Arab and Indian traders brought bargaining to Thailand early in the millennium and the Thais have developed it into an art. Nowhere in South-East Asia is it more necessary to not accept the first price, whether dealing with Bangkok non-metered taxi drivers or village weavers. While bargaining, it helps to stay relaxed and friendly – gritting your teeth and raising your voice is almost always counter-productive.

POST & COMMUNICATIONS
Post
The Thai postal system is relatively efficient and few travellers complain about undelivered mail or lost parcels. Poste restante can be received at any town in the country that has a post office, and most hotels and guesthouses will gladly hold mail for guests as long as the envelopes are so marked.

Telephone
The telephone system is also fairly modern and efficient, with IDD universal. The central post office in any *amphoe muang* will usually contain, or be located next to, the international telephone office. There is generally someone at this office who speaks English. In any case, the forms are always bilingual.

Email & Internet Access
CompuServe and IBM Global are the only 'international' providers so far that include Bangkok nodes. Rates are very high for these services, so if you plan to do a lot of emailing and Internet access it's better to go with a local Internet services provider (ISP). Loxinfo (www.loxinfo.co.th) is currently receiving the best overall reviews; this ISP also offers temporary accounts.

Many guest houses, bars and cafes in Bangkok, Chiang Mai, Krabi, Phuket and Ko Samui offer email and Internet service. The going rate is 3B to 5B per on-line and off-line minute. As these services become more popular, other places around the country where Webheads congregate will surely follow suit.

INTERNET RESOURCES
TAT maintains a Web site (www.tat.or.th). Although limited in scope, it's better than many commercial sites. The well tuned National Electronics and Computer Technology

Telephone Codes

The country code for Thailand is 66. The international dialling code is 001. Following are area codes for some cities. Drop the first zero when dialling from outside Thailand.

Ayuthaya	☎ 035
Bangkok	☎ 02
Buriram	☎ 044
Cha-am	☎ 032
Chiang Mai	☎ 053
Chiang Rai	☎ 053
Hat Yai	☎ 074
Hua Hin	☎ 032
Kamphaeng Phet	☎ 055
Kanchanaburi	☎ 034
Khon Kaen	☎ 043
Ko Samui	☎ 077
Loei	☎ 042
Lopburi	☎ 036
Mae Sai	☎ 053
Mae Salong	☎ 053
Mae Sot	☎ 055
Mae Hong Son	☎ 053
Nakhon Phanom	☎ 042
Nakhon Pathom	☎ 034
Nakhon Ratchasima	☎ 044
Nakhon Si Thammarat	☎ 075
Nan	☎ 054
Nang Rong	☎ 044
Narathiwat	☎ 073
Nong Khai	☎ 042
Pattaya	☎ 038
Phitsanulok	☎ 055
Phuket	☎ 076
Prachuap Khiri Khan	☎ 032
Ranong	☎ 077
Ratchaburi	☎ 032
Rayong	☎ 038
Saraburi	☎ 036
Songkhla	☎ 074
Sukhothai	☎ 055
Surat Thani	☎ 077
Surin	☎ 045
Tak	☎ 055
Trat (Laem Ngop)	☎ 039
Ubon Ratchathani	☎ 045
Udon Thani	☎ 042

Center (NECTEC, www.nectec.or.th) site exhibits great depth and breadth, and contains links on everything from a list of all Thai embassies and consulates abroad and details of visa requirements to weather updates. Another Web site sourced from Thailand is ThaiIndex (www.thaiindex.com). Pages include general information, government office listings, travel listings, a hotel directory and other WWW links.

Lonely Planet's own Web site (www.lonely planet.com) contains Thailand updates from travellers, occasional author updates for this edition, and other salient info; for a direct link to Thailand-related material, go to www. lonelyplanet.com.au/dest/sea/thai.htm.

Mahidol University in Bangkok maintains a very useful site (www.mahidol.ac.th/Thailand/ Thailand-main.html) that's searchable by keyword.

The *Bangkok Post* Web site (www.bangkok post.net) runs around 60 pages of stories as well as photos. Utopia, a gay/lesbian centre in Bangkok, maintains an informative site (www. utopia-asia.com/tipsthai. htm).

BOOKS
Bangkok has some of the best bookshops in South-East Asia. See under Bookshops in the Bangkok section later in this chapter for details.

Lonely Planet
Lonely Planet's *Thailand* and *Thailand's Islands & Beaches* provide much more detail on the country than can be squeezed into this chapter. Lonely Planet also publishes a *Bangkok city guide*, *Thailand travel atlas*, *Thai phrasebook* and *Thai Hill Tribes phrasebook.*

Guidebooks
Discovering Thailand by Clarac & Smithies is good for architectural and archaeological points of interest, although it's a bit dated.

Arts
Several books on Thai arts have appeared over the years. Perhaps the easiest to find (if not necessarily the most accurate) is *Arts of Thailand* (hardback) by Bangkok's dynamic duo, writer Steve Van Beek and photographer Luca Invernizzi Tettoni.

William Warren and Tettoni have authored a worthy book on Thai design called *Thai Style.*

Culture
Denis Segaller's *Thai Ways* and *More Thai Ways* are readable collections of cultural vignettes relating to Thai culture and folklore.

Mai Pen Rai by Carol Hollinger is often suggested as an introduction to Thai culture but is more a cultural snapshot of Thailand in the 1960s. More useful as a cultural primer is Robert & Nanthapa Cooper's *Culture Shock! Thailand*, part of a series that attempts to educate tourists and business travellers in local customs.

Hill Tribes
The Hill Tribes of Northern Thailand by Gordon Young covers 16 tribes, including descriptions, photographs, tables and maps. Young was born of third-generation Christian missionaries among Lahu tribespeople, speaks several tribal dialects and is an honorary Lahu chieftain.

From the Hands of the Hills by Margaret Campbell has beautiful pictures of hill tribe handicrafts. The photo-oriented *Peoples of the Golden Triangle* by Elaine & Paul Lewis (hardback) is also good – but expensive.

History & Politics
The Indianized States of South-East Asia by George Coedes, *The Thai Peoples* by Erik Seidenfaden (hardback, out of print), *Siam in Crisis* by Sulak Sivarak and *Political Conflict in Thailand – Reform, Reaction, Revolution* by David Morrell & Chai-anan Samudavanija are all worth reading.

Two of the best modern histories are David Wyatt's *Thailand – A Short History* and *The Balancing Act – A History of Modern Thailand* by Joseph Wright Jr.

Thailand's role in the international narcotics trade is covered thoroughly in Alfred McCoy's *The Politics of Heroin in Southeast Asia* and Francis Belanger's *Drugs, the US, and Khun Sa.*

The fictional *Red Bamboo,* by ex-prime minister Kukrit Pramoj, vividly portrays and predicts the conflict between the Thai Communist movement and the establishment during the 60s and 70s. His book *Si Phaendin – Four Reigns* (1981), the most widely read novel ever published in Thailand, covers the Ayuthaya era. Both novels are available in English.

FILMS
Probably the most famous movie associated with Thailand is *The Bridge on the River Kwai.* Although based on events in Thailand during WWII, much of the film was shot on location in Sri Lanka (then Ceylon). Another early film of some notoriety was *The Ugly*

American (1962), a vehicle for Marlon Brando based on the novel by William J Lederer.

The Man with the Golden Gun, a pedestrian 1974 James Bond film starring Roger Moore and Christopher Lee, brought the karst islands of Ao Phang-Nga (Phang-Nga Bay) to international attention for the first time.

Virtually every film set during the Vietnam War has been shot either in the Philippines or in Thailand. Relative logistical ease means Thailand tends to be the location of choice.

NEWSPAPERS & MAGAZINES

Two English-language newspapers – the *Bangkok Post* (morning) and the *Nation* (afternoon) – are published daily in Thailand and distributed in most provincial capitals. The *Post* is the better of the two for international news and, in fact, is regarded by many journalists as the best English daily in South-East Asia. The *Nation* has better local and regional news coverage.

Bangkok Metro, a slick lifestyle magazine started in 1995, brings a new sophistication to Bangkok publications dealing with art, culture and music.

Many popular magazines from the UK, USA, Australia and Europe – particularly those about computer technology, cars, fashion, music and business – are available in bookshops that specialise in English-language publications.

RADIO & TV

Thailand has more than 400 radio stations, including 41 FM and 35 AM stations in Bangkok alone. Radio Thailand broadcasts English-language programs at 97MHz FM from 6 am to 11 pm. Most of the programs comprise local, national and international news, sports, business and special news-related features. Another public radio station, 107 FM, is affiliated with Radio Thailand and Channel 9 on Thai public television.

Thailand's five public and private TV networks are all based in Bangkok, and satellite and cable services are swiftly multiplying. Of the many regional satellite operations aimed at Thailand, the most successful so far are STAR, Channel V (a Hong Kong-based music video telecast), Zee TV (Hindi programming) and Thailand's own IBC.

Turner Broadcasting (CNN International), BBC World Service, ESPN, HBO and various telecasts from Indonesia, Malaysia, the Philippines, Brunei and Australia are available.

VIDEO SYSTEMS

The predominant video format in Thailand is PAL, a system compatible with that used in most of Europe (France's SECAM format is a notable exception) as well as in Australia. Some video shops (especially those that carry pirated or unlicensed tapes) sell NTSC as well as PAL and SECAM tapes. A 'multi-system' VCR has the capacity to play both NTSC and PAL, but not SECAM.

PHOTOGRAPHY & VIDEO

Print film is inexpensive and widely available throughout Thailand. Slide film is also inexpensive but it can be difficult to find outside Bangkok, Chiang Mai and Phuket – be sure to stock up before heading upcountry. Film processing is generally quite good in the larger cities and also quite inexpensive. Kodachrome slide film must be sent out of the country for processing, which can take up to two weeks.

Photographing People

Hill tribespeople in some frequently visited areas expect money if you photograph them, while certain Karen and Akha flee a pointed camera. Use discretion when photographing villagers anywhere in Thailand, as a camera can be a very intimidating instrument. You may feel better leaving it behind when visiting certain areas.

Airport Security

The X-ray baggage inspection machines at Thailand's airports are all deemed film safe. Nevertheless, if you're travelling with high-speed film (ISO 400 or above), you may want to have your film hand-inspected rather than X-rayed. Security inspectors are usually happy to comply.

THAI CALENDAR

The official year in Thailand is reckoned from 543 BC, the beginning of the Buddhist Era, so that 2000 AD is 2543 BE.

ELECTRICITY

Electric current in Thailand is 220V, 50Hz. Electrical wall outlets are usually of the round, two-pole type; some outlets also accept flat, two-bladed terminals, and some will take either flat or round terminals. Any electrical supply shop will carry adaptors for any international plug shape and voltage converters.

WEIGHTS & MEASURES

Dimensions and weight are usually expressed in the metric system in Thailand. The exception is land measure, which is often quoted using the traditional Thai system of *waa*, *ngaan* and *râi*. Old-timers in the provinces will occasionally use traditional weights and measures in speech, as will boat builders, carpenters and other craftspeople when talking about their work.

LAUNDRY

Virtually every hotel and guesthouse in Thailand offers a laundry service. Rates are generally geared to room rates; the cheaper the accommodation, the cheaper the washing and ironing. Cheapest of all are public laundries, where you pay by the kilogram.

Many Thai hotels and guesthouses also have laundry areas where you can wash your clothes at no charge; sometimes there's even a hanging area for drying.

TOILETS

In Thailand, as in many other Asian countries, the 'squat toilet' is the norm except in hotels and guesthouses geared towards tourists and international business travellers.

Next to the typical squat toilet is a bucket or cement reservoir filled with water. A plastic bowl usually floats on the water's surface or sits nearby. Toilet-goers scoop water from the reservoir with the plastic bowl and use it to clean their nether regions while still squatting over the toilet. When (usually) there is no mechanical flushing device attached, a few extra scoops must be poured into the toilet basin to flush waste into the septic system. In larger towns, flushing systems are becoming increasingly common, even with squat toilets. More rustic toilets in rural areas may simply consist of a few planks over a hole in the ground.

Even in places where sit-down toilets are installed, the plumbing may not be designed to take toilet paper. In such cases the usual washing bucket will be standing nearby, or there will be a waste basket in which to place used toilet paper.

Public toilets are common in cinema houses, department stores, bus and train stations, larger hotel lobbies and airports. While on the road between towns and villages, it is perfectly acceptable to go behind a tree or bush, or even to use the roadside when nature calls.

BATHING

Some hotels and most guesthouses in the country do not have hot water, though places in the larger cities will usually offer small electric shower heaters in more expensive rooms.

Many rural Thais bathe in rivers or streams. Those living in towns or cities may have washrooms where a large jar or cement trough is filled with water for bathing purposes. A plastic or metal bowl is used to sluice water from the jar or trough over the body. Even in homes where showers are installed, heated water is uncommon. Most Thais bathe at least twice a day, and never use hot water.

If ever you find yourself having to bathe in a public place you should wear a *phâa-khumáa* or *phâasîn* (the cotton wrap-arounds); nude bathing is not the norm.

HEALTH

Of the insect-borne diseases, there have been recent large outbreaks of dengue fever in the region, so you should take appropriate measures to avoid mosquito bites. Malaria is mostly restricted to a few rural areas – notably the islands of the eastern seaboard (Rayong to Trat) and the provinces (but not the capitals) of Kanchanaburi, Chaiyaphum, Phetchabun, Mae Hong Son and Tak. There are small epidemics of Japanese encephalitis in northern Thailand each rainy season, so you should consider getting vaccinated if you're planning to spend long periods of time in these areas – discuss this with your doctor.

Food and water-borne diseases, including dysentery, cholera, hepatitis and liver flukes, occur, so it's worth paying attention to basic food and water hygiene. The main risk of liver flukes (*wiwâat bai tàp* in Thai) is from eating raw or undercooked food. Travellers should in particular avoid eating *plaa ráa* (sometimes called *paa daek* in north-east Thailand), an unpasteurised fermented fish used as an accompaniment for rice in the north-east. Plaa ráa is not commonly served in restaurants but is common in rural areas of the north-east, where it's considered a great delicacy. The Thai government is currently trying to discourage north-easterners from eating plaa ráa or other uncooked fish products. Liver flukes are endemic to villages around Sakon Nakhon Province's Nong Han, the largest natural lake in Thailand. You can become infected (from swallowing small amounts of water) by swimming in this lake.

As of January 1998 Thailand's Ministry of Public Health estimated there were approximately 700,000 HIV-positive cases in Thailand. Of these an estimated 17,000 are thought to be full-blown AIDS cases, but the number will undoubtedly have increased by the time you read this. In spite of rumours to the contrary, the Thai government keeps all AIDS-related records open to public scrutiny and is vigorously educating the general public about AIDS prevention. Infection rates have dropped drastically since 1994 due to successes in these areas. In Thailand, the disease is associated with heterosexual intercourse in over 80% of all cases; intravenous drug use and homosexual contact account for much smaller percentages. If you're going to have sex in Thailand, use condoms (preferably ones made outside Thailand, as Thai condoms have an estimated 11% failure rate).

See the Health section in the Appendix for more information.

WOMEN TRAVELLERS
Attitudes Towards Women
The UNDP Human Development Report for 1995 noted that on the gender-related development index (GDI) Thailand ranks 31st of 130 countries, thus falling into the 'progressive' category. According to the report, Thailand 'has succeeded in building the basic human capabilities of both women and men, without substantial gender imparity'. Thailand's work force is 44% female, ranking it 27th on a worldwide scale, just ahead of China and the United States.

Thai Buddhism commonly holds that women must be reborn as men before they can attain nirvana, though many Thai dharma teachers point out that this presumption isn't supported by the sutras (discourses of the Buddha) or by the commentaries. Men may divorce their wives for committing adultery, but not vice versa, for example. Men who take a foreign spouse continue to have the right to purchase and own land, while Thai women who marry foreign men lose this right.

On the other hand, in rural areas female family members typically inherit land and throughout the country they tend to control family finances.

Safety Precautions
Foreign women have been attacked while travelling alone in remote parts of Thailand. Everyday incidents of sexual harassment are much less common than in India, Indonesia or Malaysia, and this may lull women who have recently travelled in these countries into thinking that travel in Thailand is safer than it is.

If you're a woman travelling alone, try to pair up with other travellers when travelling at night or in remote areas. Urban areas seem relatively safe. Make sure hotel and guesthouse rooms are secure at night – if they're not, demand another room or go somewhere else.

GAY & LESBIAN TRAVELLERS
Thai culture is very tolerant of homosexuality, both male and female. The nation has no laws that discriminate against homosexuals and there is a fairly prominent gay/lesbian scene around the country. There is no 'gay movement' in Thailand, since there's no anti-gay establishment to move against. Whether speaking of dress or mannerism, 'butch' women and 'feminine' men are generally accepted without comment.

Public displays of affection – whether heterosexual or homosexual – are frowned upon.

DISABLED TRAVELLERS
Thailand presents one large, ongoing obstacle course for the mobility-impaired. With its high kerbs, uneven pavements and nonstop traffic, Bangkok can be particularly difficult – many streets must be crossed via pedestrian bridges flanked with steep stairways, while buses and boats don't stop long enough for even the mildly handicapped. Rarely are there any ramps or other access points for wheelchairs.

For wheelchair travellers, any trip to Thailand will require a good deal of advance planning; fortunately a growing network of information sources can put you in touch with those who have wheeled through Thailand before. There is no better source of information than someone who's done it.

Organisations
In Thailand you can contact:

Association of the Physically Handicapped of Thailand
(☎ 951 0569, fax 580 1098 ext 7)
73/7-8 Soi Thepprasan (Soi 8),
Thanon Tivanon, Talaat Kawan,
Nonthaburi 11000
Disabled Peoples International – Thailand
(☎ 583 3021, fax 583 6518)
78/2 Thanon Tivanon, Pak Kret, Nonthaburi
11120

Handicapped International
87/2 Soi 15, Thanon Sukhumvit,
Bangkok 10110.

SENIOR TRAVELLERS
Senior discounts aren't generally available in Thailand, but the Thais more than make up for this in the respect they typically show for the elderly. In traditional Thai culture status comes with age; there isn't as heavy an emphasis on youth as there is in the west. Thais will go out of their way to help older people in and out of taxis or with luggage, and – usually but not always – in waiting on them first in shops and post offices.

TRAVEL WITH CHILDREN
Like many places in South-East Asia, travelling with children in Thailand can be a lot of fun as long as you come well prepared with the right attitudes, physical requirements and the usual parental patience. Lonely Planet's *Travel with Children* contains useful advice on how to cope with kids on the road and what to bring along to make things go more smoothly, with special attention paid to travel in developing countries.

Thais love children and in many instances will shower attention on your offspring, who will find ready playmates among their Thai counterparts and temporary nanny service at practically every stop.

For the most part parents needn't worry too much about health concerns, though it pays to lay down a few ground rules; children should especially be warned not to play with animals encountered along the way since rabies is relatively common in Thailand.

DANGERS & ANNOYANCES
Thailand is one of the safest countries in the region for travelling. Nevertheless it's wise to be a little cautious, particularly if you're travelling alone.

Precautions
Theft in Thailand is still usually a matter of stealth rather than strength – you're more likely to have your pockets picked than to be mugged. Take care of your valuables, don't carry too much cash around with you and watch out for razor artists who ingeniously slit bags open in crowded quarters.

Don't take one of Bangkok's often very unofficial taxis (black and white licence tags) – better a licensed taxi (yellow and black tags) or even the public bus.

Don't trust hotel rooms, particularly in the beach-hut places like Ko Chang and Ko Pha-Ngan. Try not to place your bag on the roof of buses or in under-floor luggage compartments except when taking government buses, which are usually safe.

Also, take care when leaving valuables in hotel safes. Many travellers have reported unpleasant experiences after leaving valuables in Chiang Mai guesthouses: on their return home, they received huge credit card bills for purchases (usually jewellery) charged to their cards in Bangkok. The cards had, supposedly, been secure in the hotel or guesthouse safe while the guests were out trekking!

Women in particular, but men also, should ensure their rooms are securely locked and bolted at night. Inspect cheap rooms with thin walls for strategic peepholes.

Thais are a friendly lot and their friendliness is usually genuine. Nevertheless, on trains and buses, particularly in the south, beware of strangers offering cigarettes, drinks or chocolates. Several travellers have reported waking up with a headache sometime later to find their valuables have disappeared. Travellers have also encountered drugged food or drink from friendly strangers in bars, and from prostitutes in their own hotel rooms.

Keep zippered luggage secured with small locks, especially while travelling on buses and trains. This will not only keep out most sneak thieves, but prevent con artists posing as police from planting contraband drugs in your luggage. That may sound paranoid, but it happens.

Armed robbery does occur in remote areas of Thailand, but the risk is fairly low. Avoid going out alone at night in remote areas and, if trekking in north Thailand, always walk in groups.

Scams
Over the years, LP has received dozens of letters from victims who've been cheated of large sums of money by con men posing as 'friendly Thais'. All of the reports have come from Bangkok and Chiang Mai, and they always describe invitations to buy gems at a special price or participate in a card game.

If you happen to become involved in one of these scams, the police (including the tourist police) are usually of little help: it's not illegal to sell gems at outrageously high prices and everyone's usually gone from the card game by the time you come back with the police.

Remember: gems and card games are this year's scam so, no doubt, some totally new and highly original scheme will pop up next year. The contact men are usually young, friendly, personable, smooth-talking 'students'. They prey on younger travellers – if you're in your 20s you're a prime target. We've even heard of combining the old drugging games with the new selling ones.

Tuk-Tuks
Any *tuk-tuk* (three-wheeled motorcycle taxi) driver in Bangkok or Chiang Mai that offers you a ride for only 10B or 20B is a tout who will undoubtedly drag you to one or more 'factory' showrooms selling gems, clothes or handicrafts – no matter that you've already agreed on another destination in advance! To avoid this extremely frustrating situation, avoid tuk-tuks in Bangkok and use metered taxis instead – they're just as cheap.

Drugs
Penalties for drug offences are stiff: if you're caught using marijuana, you face a fine and/ or up to one year in prison; for heroin use, the penalty can be anywhere from six months' to 10 years' imprisonment, or worse. Remember that it is illegal to buy, sell or possess opium, heroin or marijuana in any quantity (although the possession of opium is legal for consumption, but not for sale, among hill tribes).

Touts
Touting – grabbing newcomers in the street or in train stations, bus terminals or airports to sell them a service – is a long-time tradition in Asia, and while Thailand doesn't have as many as, say, India, it has its share. In the popular tourist spots it seems like everyone – young boys waving flyers, tuk-tuk drivers, *samlor* (three-wheeled pedicab) drivers, schoolgirls – is touting something, usually hotels or guesthouses. For the most part they're completely harmless and sometimes they can be very informative.

But take anything a tout says with two large grains of salt. Don't believe them if they tell you the hotel or guesthouse you're looking for is 'closed', 'full', 'dirty' or 'bad'. Sometimes (rarely) they're right but most times it's just a ruse to get you to a place that pays more commission. Since touts work on commission and get paid just for delivering

you to a guesthouse or hotel (whether you check in or not), they'll say anything to get you to the door. Always have a careful look yourself before checking into a place recommended by a tout.

BUSINESS HOURS
Most businesses are open from Monday to Friday. Many retailers and travel agencies are also open on Saturday. Government offices are open from 8.30 am to 4.30 pm and some close for lunch from noon to 1 pm. Banks are generally open from 8.30 am to 3.30 pm Monday to Friday (except in Bangkok, where they're open 10 am to 4 pm).

PUBLIC HOLIDAYS & SPECIAL EVENTS
There's always a festival happening somewhere in Thailand. Many are keyed to Buddhist or Brahmanic rituals and follow a lunar calendar. Thus they fall on different dates (by the western solar calendar) each year, depending on the phases of the moon.

Such festivals are usually centred on the wats and include: Makkha Bucha (full moon in February – commemorating the gathering, without prior summons, of 500 monks to hear the Buddha speak); Wisakha Bucha (full moon in May – commemorating the birth, enlightenment and death of the Buddha); Asanha Bucha (full moon in July – commemorating the Buddha's first public discourse); and Khao Phansaa (full moon in July – celebrating the beginning of the Buddhist Rains Retreat). For other holidays, the Thai government has assigned official dates that don't vary from year to year, as follows:

New Year's Day	1 January
Chakri Memorial Day	6 April
Songkran Festival	
(Thai New Year)	12-14 April
National Labour Day	1 May
Coronation Day	5 May
Queen's Birthday	12 August
Chulalongkorn Day	23 October
King's Birthday	5 December
Constitution Day	10 December
New Year's Eve	31 December

Government offices and banks close on the above dates; some businesses will also choose to close. As in any other country, the days before and after a national holiday are marked by heavy air and road traffic, and full hotels.

Regional Holidays

Many provinces hold annual festivals or fairs to promote their specialities, eg Chiang Mai's Flower Festival, Kamphaeng Phet's Banana Festival, Yala's Barred Ground Dove Festival and so on. A complete, up-to-date schedule of events around the country is available from TAT offices in each region or from the central Bangkok TAT office.

ACTIVITIES

Thailand isn't all temples and museums. Those interested in outdoor activities can take up diving, snorkelling, windsurfing, canoeing, kayaking, trekking and cycling – either independently or in the company of guides and groups.

Cycling

Details on pedalling your way around Thailand can be found in the Getting Around section later in this chapter.

Diving & Snorkelling

Thailand's two coastlines and countless islands are popular among divers for their mild waters and colourful marine life. The most popular diving centre is still Pattaya, simply because it's less than two hours drive from Bangkok. There are several islands with reefs a short boat ride from Pattaya and this little town is packed with dive shops.

Phuket is the second biggest jumping-off point, with the most dive operations, and offers the largest choice of places, including small offshore islands less than an hour away; Ao Phang-Nga (a one to two hour boat ride), with its unusual rock formations and clear green waters; and the world-famous Similan and Surin islands in the Andaman Sea (about four hours away by fast boat).

In recent years dive operations have multiplied rapidly on the palmy islands of Ko Samui, Ko Pha-Ngan and Ko Tao off Surat Thani, in the Gulf of Thailand. Chumphon Province, another up-and-coming area just north of Surat Thani, has a dozen or so islands with undisturbed reefs.

Newer frontiers include the so-called Burma Banks (north-west of Mu Ko Surin), Khao Lak and islands off the coast of Krabi and Trang provinces. All of these places, with the possible exception of the Burma Banks, are suitable for snorkelling and scuba diving, since many reefs are no deeper than 2m.

Masks, fins and snorkels are readily available for rent at dive centres and through guesthouses in beach areas. However, if you're particular about the quality and condition of the equipment you use, you might be better off bringing your own.

Sea Canoeing & Kayaking

Touring the islands and coastal limestone formations around Phuket and Ao Phang-Nga by inflatable canoe or kayak has become an increasingly popular activity over the last decade. A typical sea canoe tour seeks out half-submerged caves called 'hongs' (*hâwng*, Thai for 'room'), and is timed so you can paddle into the caverns at low tide. The locals have been doing this for centuries; the tour operators latched on only recently. Several outfits and guesthouses in Phuket and Krabi offer equipment and guides.

Trekking

Wilderness walking or trekking is one of northern Thailand's biggest draws. Typical treks run for three or four days (though it is possible to arrange everything from one to 10-day treks) and feature daily walks through forested mountains and overnight stays in hill tribe villages to satisfy urges for both ethno- and eco-tourism.

Other trekking opportunities are available in Thailand's larger national parks, where rangers may be hired as guides and cooks for a few days at a time at reasonable rates.

Windsurfing

The best combinations of rental facilities and wind conditions are found on Pattaya and Jomtien beaches in Chonburi Province, on Ko Samet, on the west coast of Phuket and on Hat Chaweng on Ko Samui. Some rental equipment is also available on Hat Khao Lak (north of Phuket), Ko Pha-Ngan, Ko Tao and Ko Chang.

Windsurfing gear for rent at Thai resorts is generally not the most complete or up-to-date.

COURSES
Cooking

More and more travellers are coming to Thailand just to learn how to cook. Recommended schools include:

Oriental Hotel Thai Cooking School
(☎ 439 7587) Soi Oriental, Thanon Charoen Krung, Bangkok – features five-day courses under the direction of well known chef Chali (Charlie) Amatyakul.

Chiang Mai Cookery School
(☎ 20 6388) 1-3 Thanon Moon Muang – three-day courses include market and herb garden visits.

Nipa Restaurant Cooking School
(☎ 254 0404 ext 48) Landmark Hotel, Bangkok – a five day cooking course.

Language

Several language schools in Bangkok, Chiang Mai and other places where foreigners congregate offer courses in Thai language. Some places will let you trade English lessons for Thai lessons; if not, you can usually teach English on the side to offset tuition costs.

If you have an opportunity to shop around it's best to enrol in programs that offer lots of linguistic interaction, rather than rote learning or the 'natural method', which has been almost universally discredited for the overattention paid to teacher input.

The American University Alumni (AUA) Language Centre (☎ 252 8170) at 179 Thanon Ratchadamri, Bangkok, is one of the most popular places to study Thai; in fact it's the largest private language school in the world! AUA also has branches in Chiang Mai, Lampang, Phitsanulok, Khon Kaen, Udon, Mahasarakham, Ubon, Songkhla and Phuket. Most of these are housed on Thai college or university campuses. Not all AUAs schedule regular Thai classes, but study can usually be arranged on an ad hoc basis. Teaching methodologies in upcountry AUAs tends to be more flexible than at the Bangkok unit.

The YWCA's Siri Pattana Thai Language School (☎ 286 1936), 13 Thanon Sathon Tai, Bangkok, gives Thai language lessons and preparation for the Baw Hok exam necessary for public school teaching certification in Thailand. Siri Pattana also has a second branch at 806 Soi 38, Thanon Sukhumvit, Bangkok.

Massage

Thailand offers ample opportunities to study its unique tradition of massage therapy. Wat Pho in Bangkok is considered the master source for all Thai massage pedagogy, although northern Thailand boasts its own 'softer' version. Chiang Mai has become a major centre for Thai massage instruction; practically every guesthouse in town offers or can arrange for lessons.

The oldest and most popular place to study is the Old Medicine Hospital (☎ 27 5085) on Soi Siwaka Komarat off Thanon Wualai, opposite the Old Chiang Mai Cultural Centre.

The 11 day course costs around 2500B, including all teaching materials.

Other places in Chiang Mai with similar instruction include: Chaiyuth Priyasith's School of Thai Remedial Massage at 52 Soi 3, Thanon Tha Phae and International Training Massage (☎ 21 8632) at 171/7 Thanon Morakot in Santitham.

Meditation

Thailand has long been a popular place for western students of Buddhism, particularly those interested in a system of meditation known as *vipassana* (Thai: *wípàtsanãa*), a Pali word which roughly translated means 'insight'. Foreigners who come to Thailand to study vipassana can choose among dozens of temples and meditation centres (*sãmnák wípàtsanãa*) which specialise in these teachings. Details on some of the more popular meditation-oriented temples and centres are given in the relevant sections.

Short-term students will find that two-month tourist visas are ample for most courses of study. Long-term students may want to consider getting a three or six-month Non-Immigrant Visa. A few westerners become ordained as monks or nuns to take full advantage of the monastic environment; they are generally (but not always) allowed to stay in Thailand as long as they remain in robes.

Some places require lay-persons staying overnight to wear white clothes. For even a brief visit, dress respectfully, eg clean long trousers or skirt, and sleeves that cover the shoulder.

Muay Thai (Thai Boxing)

Many westerners have trained in Thailand, but few last more than a week or two in a Thai camp – and fewer still have gone on to compete on Thailand's pro circuit.

An Australian, Patrick Cusick, occasionally directs *muay thai* (Thai boxing) seminars for *farang* (foreigners of European descent) in Thailand. Contact him at Thai Championship Boxing (☎ 234 5360), Box 1996, Bangkok.

Pramote Gym (☎ 215 8848) at 210-212 Thanon Phetburi, Ratthewi, offers training in Thai boxing as well as other martial arts (judo, karate, tae kwon do, krabi-krabong) to foreigners and locals.

Those interested in training at a traditional muay thai camp might try the Sityodthong-Payakarun Boxing Camp in Naklua (north of Pattaya). Outside Bangkok there's Fairtex

Boxing Camp (mailing address c/o Bunjong Busarakamwongs, Fairtex Garments Factory, 734-742 Trok Kai, Thanon Anuwong, Bangkok).

Lanna Boxing Camp in Chiang Mai (64/1 Soi Chang Kian, Thanon Huay Kaew, Chiang Mai 50300, ☎ /fax 273133) and Patong Boxing Club in Phuket (59/4 Muu 4, Thanon Na Nai, Patong Beach, ☎ 978 9352, fax 29 2189) specialise in training for foreigners.

Be forewarned, though, that muay thai training is gruelling and features full-contact sparring, unlike tae kwon do, kenpo, kungfu and other East Asian martial arts. For more information about Thai boxing, see the Spectator Sports section later in this chapter.

WORK
Thailand's recent economic problems have reduced the variety of work opportunities for foreigners. As in the rest of East and South-East Asia, there remains a high demand for English speakers to provide instruction to Thai citizens. This is not because of a shortage of qualified Thai teachers with a good grasp of English grammar; rather, it represents the desire to have native speaking models in the classroom.

A 1979 royal decree closed 39 occupations to foreigners, including civil engineering, architecture, legal services and clerical or secretarial services.

Voluntary and paid positions with organisations that provide charitable services in education, development or public health are available for those with the right education or experience.

Work Permits
All types of work, including volunteer positions, in Thailand require a Thai work permit. Thai law defines work as 'exerting one's physical energy or employing one's knowledge, whether or not for wages or other benefits.' Permits may be obtained through an employer, who should file for the permit before the foreigner enters Thailand. The permit is not issued until the employee enters Thailand on a valid Non-Immigrant Visa.

ACCOMMODATION
For consistently good value, Thai budget hotels are among the best in the region. Almost anywhere in Thailand, even Bangkok, you can get a double for 200B or less. There can be an amazing variation in prices at the same hotel. You'll find fancy air-con rooms at over 400B and straightforward fan-cooled rooms at a third of that price.

There will be a choice of hotels in even the smallest towns, although 'hotel' will often be the only word written on them in English. Finding a specific place in some smaller towns can be a problem if you don't speak Thai.

A typical 150B to 200B Thai hotel room is plain and spartan, but will include a toilet, a shower and a ceiling fan. Rooms with a common toilet can cost from 80B to 140B. Guesthouses vary from 60B to 120B for a single, 100B to 160B a double, and are likely to be a little more basic and not have bathrooms. At the less touristed beach centres in southern Thailand, you'll find pleasant individual beach cottages for less than 200B.

As in Malaysia, many of the hotels are Chinese-run and couples can often save money by asking for a single – a single means one double bed, a double means two.

Camping
All but four of Thailand's 80 national parks permit camping for fees of only 5B to 10B per person per night. Tents may usually be rented at national park camping grounds, so it's really not necessary to carry any camping equipment. Accommodation in beach areas is so inexpensive there's rarely an incentive to pitch a tent.

Temple Lodgings
If you are a Buddhist or can behave like one, you may be able to stay overnight in some wats for a small donation. Facilities are very basic, though, and early rising is expected. Temple or monastery lodgings are usually for men only, unless the wat has a place for lay-women to stay. Neat, clean dress and a basic knowledge of Thai etiquette are mandatory.

A species of traveller known to Thais as *faràng baanglamphuu* (meaning those wearing shorts and/or sleeveless shirts) is definitely *not* welcome to stay at Buddhist monasteries.

FOOD
Thai food is like Chinese with a sting – it can be fiery. Eating Thai style involves knowing what to get, how to get it and how to get it for a reasonable price. Outside of tourist areas, few places have a menu in English, and fewer have prices on the menus. To make matters worse, your mangled attempts at asking for something in Thai are very unlikely to be

understood. Make the effort though, for there are some delicious foods to be tried. Lonely Planet's *Thai phrasebook* contains an extensive food section with English descriptions, roman transliteration and Thai script.

Khâo phàt (fried rice) is a common dish – a close cousin to Chinese fried rice or Indonesian nasi goreng. It usually comes with sliced cucumber, a fried egg on top if you ask for *phii-sèht* (special) and a small dish of super hot peppers floating in fish sauce. When you don't know what else to order, this will almost always be available. *Kài phàt bai ka-phrao*, a fiery stir-fry of chopped chicken, chillies, garlic and fresh basil, is another Thai favourite. *Phàt thai* is fried rice noodles, bean sprouts, peanuts, eggs, chillies and often prawns – good value at any street stall.

Many Thai restaurants are actually Chinese – serving a few of the main Thai dishes among the Chinese, or some Thai-influenced Chinese ones. In the south, look for delicious seafood and thick, coconut-laced curries, while in the north and north-east there are various local specialities centred on 'sticky rice' *(khâo niaw)*.

DRINKS

Soft drinks are cheaper than almost anywhere in South-East Asia. Tea and coffee are prepared strong, milky and sweet. Thais prefer to drink most fruit juices with a little salt mixed in. Unless a vendor is used to serving farangs, your fruit juice or shake will come slightly salted. If you prefer unsalted fruit juices, specify *mâi sài kleua* (without salt). Sugar cane juice *(náam âwy)* is a Thai favourite and a very refreshing accompaniment to curry-and-rice plates. Many small restaurants or food stalls that don't offer any other juices will have a supply of freshly squeezed náam âwy on hand.

More dairy products are available in Thailand than anywhere else in South-East Asia – including very good yoghurt.

Water

Water purified for drinking purposes is simply called *náam dèum* (drinking water), whether boiled or filtered. *All* water offered to customers in restaurants or to guests in an office or home will be purified.

In restaurants you can ask for *náam plào* (plain water), which is always either boiled or taken from a purified source; it's served by the glass at no charge, or you can order by the bottle. A bottle of carbonated water (soda) costs about the same as a bottle of plain purified water but the bottles are smaller.

ENTERTAINMENT
Bars & Nightclubs

Urban Thais are night people and every town of any size has a selection of nightspots. For the most part they are male-dominated, though the situation is changing rapidly in the larger cities, where young couples are increasingly seen in bars.

The 'go-go' bars seen in lurid photos published by the western media are limited to a few areas in Bangkok, Chiang Mai, Pattaya and Phuket's Patong Beach. These are bars in which girls typically wear swimsuits or other scanty apparel. In some bars they dance to recorded music on a narrow raised stage. To some visitors it's pathetic, to others paradise.

All bars and clubs which don't feature live music or dancing are required to close by 1 am. Many get around the law by bribing local police.

Discos & Dance Clubs

Discos are popular in larger cities; outside Bangkok they're mostly attached to tourist or luxury hotels. The main disco clientele is Thai, though foreigners are welcome. Some provincial discos retain female staff as professional dance partners for male entertainment, but for the most part discos are considered fairly respectable nightspots for couples.

A new trend in Thai dance clubs is the 'kitchen disco' *(disco khrua)*, where small round tables dot the dance floor. This allows patrons to dance at their tables, within easy reach of their drinks and personal belongings – an eminently sensible arrangement.

Thai law permits discotheques to stay open till 2 am.

Cinemas

Movie theatres are found in towns and cities throughout the country. Typical programs include US and European shoot-'em-ups mixed with Thai comedies and romances.

English-language films are shown with their original soundtracks only in a few theatres in Bangkok, Chiang Mai and Hat Yai; elsewhere all foreign films are dubbed in Thai.

Every film in Thailand begins with a rendition of the royal anthem, accompanied by projected pictures of the royal family. Viewers are expected to stand during the anthem.

Coffee Houses

Apart from the western-style cafe, which is becoming increasingly popular in Bangkok, there are two other kinds of cafes or coffee shops in Thailand. One is the traditional Hokkien-style coffee shop (ráan kaa-fae), where thick, black, filtered coffee is served in simple, casual surroundings. These coffee shops are common in the Chinese quarters of southern provincial capitals, though less common elsewhere. Frequented mostly by older Thai and Chinese men, they provide a place to read the newspaper, sip coffee and gossip about neighbours and politics.

The other type, called kaa-feh (cafe), is more akin to a nightclub, where Thai men consort with a variety of Thai female hostesses. This is the Thai counterpart to farang go-go bars, except girls wear dresses instead of swimsuits. A variation on this theme is the 'sing-song' cafe, in which a succession of female singers take turns fronting a live band. Cafes that feature live music are permitted to stay open till 2 am.

SPECTATOR SPORTS
Muay Thai (Thai Boxing)
Almost anything goes in this martial sport, both in the ring and in the stands. If you don't mind the violence in the ring, a Thai boxing match is worth attending purely for the spectacle – the wild musical accompaniment, the ceremonial beginning of each match and the frenzied betting around the stadium.

Bouts are limited to five three-minute rounds separated with two-minute breaks. Contestants wear international-style gloves and trunks (always either in red or blue) and their feet are taped. As in international-style boxing, matches take place on a 7.3 sq m canvas-covered floor with rope retainers supported by four padded posts, rather than the traditional dirt circle.

All surfaces of the body are considered fair targets and any part of the body except the head may be used to strike an opponent. Common blows include high kicks to the neck, elbow thrusts to the face and head, knee hooks to the ribs and low crescent kicks to the calf. A contestant may even grasp an opponent's head between his hands and pull it down to meet an upward knee thrust. Punching is considered the weakest of all blows and kicking merely a way to 'soften up' one's opponent; knee and elbow strikes are decisive in most matches.

Matches are held every day of the year at the major stadiums in Bangkok and the provinces (there are about 60,000 full-time boxers in Thailand), and they are easily found.

Takraw
Tàkrâw, sometimes called Siamese football in old English texts, refers to games in which a woven rattan ball about 12cm in diameter is kicked around. The rattan (or sometimes plastic) ball itself is called a lûuk tàkrâw.

The traditional way to play takraw in Thailand is for players to stand in a circle (the size of the circle depends on the number of players) and simply try to keep the ball airborne by kicking it. Points are scored for style, difficulty and variety of kicking manoeuvres.

A popular variation on tàkrâw – and the one used in intramural or international competitions – is played with a volleyball net, using all the same rules as in volleyball except that only the feet and head are permitted to touch the ball. It's amazing to watch the players perform aerial pirouettes, spiking the ball over the net with their feet. Another variation has players kicking the ball into a hoop 4.5m above the ground – basketball with feet, but without a backboard!

SHOPPING
Many bargains await you in Thailand if you have the space to carry them back. Always haggle to get the best price, except in department stores. And don't go shopping in the company of touts, tour guides or friendly strangers as they will inevitably – no matter what they say – take a commission on anything you buy, thus driving prices up.

Textiles are possibly the best all-round buy in Thailand. Thai silk is considered the best in the world and is very inexpensive. Cottons are also a good deal – common items like the phâakhamáa (reputed to have over a hundred uses in Thailand) and the phâasîn (the slightly larger female equivalent) make great tablecloths and curtains. The north-east is famous for mát-mìi cloth – thick cotton or silk fabric woven from tie-dyed threads, similar to Indonesia's ikat fabrics. Tailor-made and ready-made clothes are relatively inexpensive.

Thai shoulder bags (yâam) are generally quite well made. They come in many varieties, some woven by hill tribes, others by northern Thai cottage industry.

In Chiang Mai there are shops selling handicrafts. It's worth shopping around for the best prices and bargaining. The all-round best buys of northern hill tribe crafts are at the Chiang Mai Night Bazaar – if you know how to bargain. Thailand produces some good lacquerware, much of it made in Myanmar and sold along the northern Burmese border; try Mae Sot, Mae Sariang and Mae Sai for the best buys.

In Bangkok, Chiang Mai and all the tourist centres, there is a flourishing black market street trade in fake designer goods; particularly Benetton pants and sweaters, Lacoste and Ralph Lauren polo shirts, Levi's jeans, and Rolex, Dunhill and Cartier watches. Tin-Tin T-shirts are also big. No-one pretends they're the real thing, at least not the vendors themselves. The European and American manufacturers are applying heavy pressure on the Asian governments involved to get this stuff off the street.

Real antiques cannot be taken out of Thailand without a permit from the Department of Fine Arts. No Buddha image, new or old, may be exported without permission – if in doubt go to the Fine Arts Department, or, in some cases, the Department of Religious Affairs, under the Ministry of Education for inspection and licensing of goods. Too many private collectors smuggling and hoarding Siamese art (Buddhas in particular) around the world have led to strict controls. Some antiques (and many fakes) are sold at the Weekend Market in Chatuchak Park. Objects for sale in the tourist antique shops are fantastically overpriced, as can be expected. In recent years northern Thailand has become a good source of Thai antiques – prices are about half what you'd typically pay in Bangkok.

Thailand is one of the world's largest exporters of gems and ornaments, rivalled only by India and Sri Lanka. Although rough stone sources in Thailand itself have decreased dramatically, stones are now imported from Australia, Sri Lanka and other countries to be cut, polished and traded here. Gold ornaments are sold at a good rate because labour costs are low. The best bargains in gems are jade, rubies and sapphires.

Warning For gems, shop around and *don't be hasty*. Remember: there's no such thing as a 'government sale' or a 'factory price' at a gem or jewellery shop; the Thai government does not own or manage any gem or jewellery shops. Buy from reputable dealers only, unless you're a gemologist. Never make purchases in the company of a newly found Thai 'friend'. The Asian Institute of Gemological Sciences (☎ 513 2112, fax 236 7803), 484 Thanon Ratchadaphisek (off Thanon Lat Phrao in the Huay Khwang District, north-

east Bangkok), offers short-term courses in gemology as well as tours of gem mines for those interested. See the Dangers & Annoyances section earlier in this chapter for detailed warnings on gem fraud.

Getting There & Away

AIR
Airports & Airlines
Thailand has three international airports: Bangkok, Chiang Mai and Phuket. Chiang Rai and Sukhothai are both designated as 'international', but at the time writing they did not actually field any international flights.

Two domestic carriers, Thai Airways International (THAI) and Bangkok Airways, make use of international and domestic airports in 26 cities around the country.

Departure Tax
The departure tax on international flights is 500B. When you're flying out of Thailand, the tax must be paid at separate booths in the airport before entering the departure lounge.

Buying Cheap Tickets
With the baht devaluation of 1997-98 Bangkok is once again the number-one bargain centre of the region, with international air tickets costing at least 15 to 20% less than tickets purchased almost anywhere outside Thailand. Over the years, we have had a lot of letters complaining about various travel agencies in Bangkok – and a few saying what a good deal they got. Remember nothing is free, so if you get quoted a price way below other agencies, be suspicious. In smaller agencies, insist on getting the ticket before handing over your cash. And don't sign anything.

A favourite game of some agents has been getting clients to sign a disclaimer saying that they will not request a refund under any circumstances. Then, when the client picks their ticket up, they find it is only valid for one week or something similar – not very good when you're not planning to leave for a month or two. Alternatively, the ticket may only be valid within certain dates, or other limitations may be placed upon it.

Another catch is you may be told that the ticket is confirmed (OK) only to find on closer inspection that it is only on request (RQ) or merely open. Or even worse, the ticket actually has OK on it when in fact no reservation has been made at all. So read everything carefully and remember – *caveat emptor*, let the buyer beware.

Cambodia

Flights between Phnom Penh and Bangkok are available daily with THAI, Royal Air Cambodge (RAC) and Bangkok Airways, and, somewhat infrequently, Kampuchea Airlines. Flights are cheaper in Bangkok than Phnom Penh.

Kampuchea Airlines is the cheapest, but it has an erratic reliability record, and its schedule is constantly shrinking. Fares are US$80/99 one way/return. RAC charges US$120/220, THAI flights are US$140/280 and Bangkok Airways' Phnom Penh flights are US$142/284; it also flies daily to Siem Reap from US$155/310.

China

You can fly from Hong Kong direct to Bangkok or Chiang Mai.

Laos

Bangkok to Vientiane flights operate daily, alternating between Lao Aviation and THAI. In each case the fare is US$100, though specials as low as US$75 are occasionally available.

Some people save money by flying from Bangkok to Udon Thani in Thailand first, then carrying on by road to Nong Khai and over the new Friendship Bridge to Vientiane. Udon Thani is 55km south of Nong Khai and a Bangkok-Udon air ticket aboard THAI costs US$52. THAI operates an express van direct from Udon airport to Nong Khai for 100B per person, or you can take a local bus for 20B; count on around 35 minutes for the former, a bit over an hour for the latter.

Lao Aviation flies between Vientiane and Chiang Mai every Thursday and Sunday. The one hour flight costs US$70. Flights between Chiang Mai and Luang Prabang have commenced on Thursday for $US70 one way; Lao visas must be obtained in advance.

See also the Air entry in the main Getting There & Away section of the Laos chapter.

Malaysia

For travel between Malaysia and Thailand, there are direct flights from Kuala Lumpur to Bangkok and Chiang Mai; and from Penang to Bangkok (RM440), Hat Yai and Phuket (RM195).

Myanmar (Burma)

Typical costs for Bangkok-Yangon-Bangkok tickets are around US$230 on THAI, US$220 on Myanmar Airways International (MAI), and as low as US$144 on Biman Bangladesh Airways.

THAI and MAI currently fly Bangkok-Yangon-Bangkok daily. Although slightly more expensive than MAI.

Air Mandalay, Myanmar's new, privately owned domestic carrier, has recently started flying between Chiang Mai and Yangon on Wednesday and Sunday.

Philippines

Cheap fares from Bangkok to Manila cost around US$210.

Vietnam

Bangkok, only 80 minutes flying time from Ho Chi Minh City, is the main port of embarkation for air travel to Vietnam. Bangkok-Ho Chi Minh City tickets are US$95 to US$115 one way; round-trip tickets cost about double.

There are also direct Bangkok-Hanoi flights (about US$100 one way) and open jaw tickets from Bangkok-Ho Chi Minh City/Hanoi-Bangkok, or vice-versa, for US$210 return.

LAND
Cambodia

Poipet The land border between Cambodia and Thailand at Poipet was opened to foreigners in February 1998. A steady number of travellers have come and gone this way since, and the roads from the crossing to either Siem Reap or Battambang were safe at the time of writing, but in terrible condition. If things remain stable, this will no doubt become a common way to reach Phnom Penh from Thailand.

To enter Cambodia here you need to obtain a Cambodian visa from Bangkok in advance. Sometimes the border may be closed for a short time if the Thai authorities wish to return Khmer refugees to Cambodia. Check the current situation before heading to the border. There is no departure tax by land, but guards may ask for a dollar.

It is worth noting that the road between Sisophon and Siem Reap can become impassable at times during the wet season. From Poipet, you must take a tuk-tuk or songthaew (4B) to Aranya Prathet, from where there are two trains a day to and from Bangkok and buses every two hours.

Coastal Border The coastal border between Krong Koh Kong (Cambodia) and Trat Province in Thailand is also officially open. Fast boats between Koh Kong and Sihanoukville cost 500B and leave Sihanoukville at 10.30 am and 12.30 pm, although the earlier one may not leave unless full. The boat leaves Koh Kong at 8 am. It takes about 3½ hours.

When entering Cambodia, it is best to take a share taxi (100B per vehicle) or moto (50B) from the border to Koh Kong and pick up the fast boat to Sihanoukville from its point of origin.

When leaving Cambodia, jump off the boat at the commune of Pak Long, just before Koh Kong, and you can take a small speedboat (30 minutes) to the border post of Hat Lek for about 100B. Friendly immigration police usually suggest this as passports are also checked at Pak Long. This is faster and easier than continuing right into Koh Kong.

From the Thai side there are regular 20B songthaews to Khlong Yai from where you can take a 60B per person share taxi to Trat. Bear in mind that buses to Bangkok leave regularly until 6 pm and then break until 11 pm. Move fast unless you don't mind hanging around in Trat.

Laos

Official Thai-Lao border crossings that are open to foreigners include Chong Mek (near Pakse), Mukdahan (opposite Savannakhet), Nakhon Phanom (opposite Tha Khaek), Nong Khai (near Vientiane) and Chiang Khong (opposite Huay Xai). No special permits are necessary to use these crossings; many visitors travelling overland from Vietnam arrive in Thailand via Laos.

Nong Khai The Thai-Lao Friendship Bridge spans the Mekong river between Nong Khai Province on the Thai side and Vientiane Province on the Lao side and is the main land crossing into Laos at the moment. In spite of all the hoopla raised upon its 1994 opening, the bridge has done little to fulfil its design potential. Shuttle buses ferry passengers back and forth across the bridge from designated terminals nearby for 10B per person; there are departures every 20 minutes from 8 am to 5.30 pm. You must arrange your own transport to the bridge bus terminal from Nong Khai.

The bus stops at Thai immigration control on the bridge, where you pay 10B to have your passport stamped with an exit visa. Passengers then reboard the bus and after crossing the bridge stop at Lao immigrations and customs, where you pay a fee of 20B to have your passport stamped (40B between 12 and 2 pm and on weekends).

From the bridge it's 100B by jumbo (Lao tuk-tuk) or 150B by car taxi to Vientiane, about 20km away; the drivers prefer baht. You can also catch bus No 14 into town for 400 kip; around fifteen buses a day (6.30 am to 5 pm) pass the bridge area on their way from Tha Deua (Deua Pier, the old ferry pier) to Vientiane's Morning Market.

Chong Mek There's also a land crossing from Chong Mek in Thailand's Ubon Ratchathani Province to Champasak. Specially endorsed visas are no longer necessary when using this crossing – any visa will do.

To get to Chong Mek from Ubon, take a bus first to Phibun Mangsahan (15B), then switch to a Phibun-Chong Mek songthaew (18B). At Chong Mek you simply walk across the border (Lao immigration and customs are open 8 am to noon and 1 to 4.30 pm) to Ban Mai Sing Amphon, the village on the Lao side of the border. It is about an hour from here to Pakse by bus/taxi and ferry. See under Pakse in the Champasak Province section in the Laos chapter for details on transport to Pakse.

Chiang Khong In 1996 a Thai company announced plans to construct a second bridge over the Mekong between Chiang Khong and Huay Xai but so far nothing has materialised. When (and if) constructed, this bridge is supposed to connect with the 250km road running north-east to the Chinese border via Bokeo and Luang Nam Tha provinces. Meanwhile the ferry is still operating.

Malaysia

West Coast The main border crossings are, west to east: Hat Yai-Padang Besar (road or rail), Sadao-Bukit Kayu Hitam (road), Betong-Keroh (road) or Sungai Kolok-Tantau Panjang (road or rail). The most common mode of transport between Penang and Hat Yai is by taxi – generally big old Thai-registered Chevrolets or Mercedes – or express bus/minivan. In Penang, you'll find them at the various travellers' hotels around Georgetown. In Hat Yai, they'll be at the train station or along Niphat Uthit 2.

You can also easily walk or take a taxi across the border at Sadao (Bukit Kayu Hitam on the Malaysian side) or Padang Besar. Buses run from either side of the border; Padang Besar is also on the rail link between Butterworth and Hat Yai.

All trains heading north from Padang Besar will pass through Hat Yai. There are also connecting services to or from Singapore and Kuala Lumpur aboard the *International Express*. The train operates every day and, it appears, without the border delays which used to be a problem.

From Malaysia, the *International Express* train leaves Padang Besar at 3.27 pm, arrives in Hat Yai at 5.52 pm and in Bangkok at 9.30 am the next day. Fares from Padang Besar to Hat Yai are 15B for 2nd class and 33B for 1st, not including supplementary charges. From Padang Besar to Bangkok is 360B and 767B respectively, exclusive of surcharges.

There is an additional express surcharge on the *International Express* of 70B. For berth charges see the Getting Around section below. Altogether these charges, plus the basic fares, really add up; if you're looking for the cheapest way across the border, take the bus.

Buses from Padang Besar to Hat Yai cost 23B, leave frequently throughout the day and take 1-1/2 hours. From Butterworth or Penang there are two or three air-con bus departures a day (320B; about four hours). From Kuala Lumpur private companies run air-con buses (RM30 to RM40; 12 hours). From Singapore, air-con buses cost RM45 including all meals; 'super VIP' buses with only 24 seats cost 550B.

East Coast From Kota Bharu (Malaysia), you can take a share taxi to Rantau Panjang (45km, RM9). It's then just a 500m (maybe nearer 1km) stroll across the border to the town of Sungai Kolok. From here, trains run to Hat Yai and Bangkok. The border is only open from 6 am to 6 pm. Another border crossing at Ban Taba, 32km east, is a shorter and quicker route to Kota Bharu, Malaysia. See the Sungai Kolok & Ban Taba section for details.

Myanmar

Crossings are occasionally permitted from Thailand at two points as day trips only. Payathonzu, opposite Three Pagodas Pass in Kanchanaburi Province, is open on and off to foreign tourists. As we went to press it was closed.

Myawaddy, opposite Tak Province's Mae Sot, lies at the head of a route to Mawlamyine (Moulmein) via Kawkareik along a rough road that has long been off limits to foreigners due to Mon and Karen insurgent activity in the area. A bridge across the Moei River between Myawaddy and Mae Sot was finally completed and opened in 1997, then quickly closed due to international bickering over reclamation of the river banks. In 1998 it was open for a short time, then closed again. So far when the bridge has been open, travel has only been allowed between Myawaddy and Mae Sot – travel beyond Myawaddy wasn't permitted. Myanmar's Yangon junta claims it has plans to open the road from Myawaddy all the way to Pa-an in the Kayin State.

Contrary to popular belief, you don't have to leave Myanmar via the border crossing at which you arrived, which means there are now two major ways to enter Thailand from Myanmar without flying.

Mae Sai Between Mae Sai and Tachilek is a legal international border crossing between Myanmar and Thailand, but on the Myanmar side road travel in the immediate area is only permitted between Tachilek and Kyaingtong (or as far as Mong La on the Chinese border) in the Shan State. You can also use this border as a quick way to renew your Thai visa if you happen to be in Northern Thailand. You can fly to or from Tachilek via several points in the interior of Myanmar, including Mandalay, Heho and Yangon.

Kawthoung The crossing between Kawthoung (Victoria Point) and Ranong is now open for international entry/exit to or from either country. On the Myanmar side you cannot travel by road to or from Kawthoung, but must fly in or out of Kawthoung via Myeik, Dawei or Yangon.

The only way to reach Ranong from Kawthoung is by boat. Public longtail boats run throughout the day for 50B per person in a shared boat of at least three passengers or 150B to 200B for a chartered one. Few people have used this entry into Thailand so far but it is permitted – Joe Cummings accomplished this crossing in late 1998 without any problem.

SEA
Malaysia

There are also some interesting sea routes between Malaysia and Thailand. For example, from Kuala Perlis (the jumping-off point for

Pulau Langkawi) you can take a long-tail boat for about RM5 (50B) to Satun (or Satul), just across the border in Thailand. These are legal entry and exit points, with immigration and customs posts. On arrival in Satun, it costs about 10B for the 3km ride from the docks to town. You can then bus into Hat Yai.

You can also travel by boat between Satun and Langkawi, a large Malaysian island on the Thai-Malaysian marine border. There are about six boats a day between 9 am and 5 pm, and the cost is RM18 or 180B. Though it's cheaper to go straight to Satun from Kuala Perlis, Langkawi is worth a stop if you have the time.

In the main tourist season (around Christmas) yachts also operate irregularly between Langkawi and Phuket in Thailand, taking in Thai islands on the way for around US$70 per person per day for the five day trip.

ORGANISED TOURS

Many tour operators around the world can arrange guided tours of Thailand. Most of them simply serve as brokers for tour companies based in Thailand; they buy their trips from a wholesaler and resell them under various names in travel markets overseas. Hence, one is much like another and you might as well arrange a tour in Thailand at a lower cost.

Two of Thailand's largest tour wholesalers are World Travel Service (☎ 233 5900, fax 236 7169) at 1053 Thanon Charoen Krung, Bangkok 10500; and Diethelm Travel (☎ 255 9150, fax 256 0248) at Kian Gwan Bldg II, 140/1 Thanon Withayu, Bangkok.

Several Bangkok-based companies specialise in ecologically oriented tours, including:

Friends of Nature Eco-Tours
  (☎ 642 4426, fax 642 4428)
  133/21 Thanon Ratchaprarop,
  Ratthewi
Khiri Travel
  (☎ 629 0491, fax 629 0493)
  Viengtai Hotel, 42 Thanon Rambutri,
  Banglamphu
Nature Travellers
  (☎ 377 7959)
  495 Kankheha Soi 19,
  Thanon Sukhaphiban 1,
  Bang Kapi

The better overseas tour companies build their own Thailand itineraries from scratch and choose their local suppliers based on which ones best serve these itineraries.

Getting Around

AIR
Domestic Air Services

Thai Airways International (THAI) operates both international and domestic routes. They have a useful flight network around Thailand. It's not much used by budget travellers because ground-level transport is generally so good.

The country's second carrier, Bangkok Airways, has three main routes: Bangkok-Sukhothai-Chiang Mai; Bangkok-Samui-Phuket; and U-Thaphao/Pattaya-Samui.

Air Passes

THAI offers special four-coupon passes – available only outside Thailand for purchases in foreign currency – in which you can book any four domestic flights for one fare of US$200 to US$250 as long as you don't repeat the same leg. Unless you plan carefully this isn't much of a savings, since it's hard to avoid repeating the same leg in and out of Bangkok.

For information on the four-coupon deal, known as the 'Discover Thailand fare', inquire at any THAI office outside Thailand.

Domestic Departure Tax

Domestic departure tax costs 30B and is usually collected at the airline check-in counter.

BUS

The Thai bus service is widespread and phenomenally fast – terrifyingly so, much of the time. There are usually air-con buses as well as 'normal' ones, and on major routes there are also private, air-con tour buses. The air-con buses are so cold that blankets are handed out as a matter of routine and the service is so good it's embarrassing. You often get free drinks, pillows, free meals and even 'in-flight movies' on some routes. There are often a number of bus terminals in a town – sometimes separate public and private stations.

Warning

Beware of the low-priced 'VIP' buses and minivans that leave from the Thanon Khao San area. Rarely do these bus lines provide the services promised in advance; Thanon Khao San buses have even left passengers stranded alongside the highway halfway between Bangkok and the supposed destination. The government buses from the official bus terminals are generally safer and more reliable.

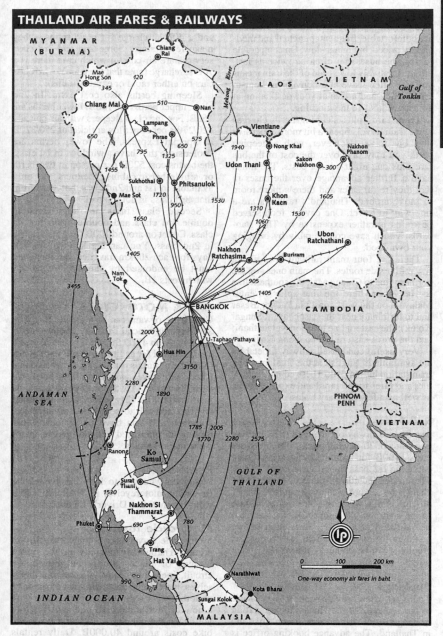

THAILAND AIR FARES & RAILWAYS

MYANMAR
(BURMA)

LAOS

VIETNAM

Gulf of
Tonkin

Mae
Hong Son
345

Chiang
Rai

120

Chiang Mai

510

Nan

Mekong River

Vientiane

Lampang
650

Phrae
795

575

1940

Nong Khai

Nakhon
Phanom

650

1325

Udon Thani

Sakon
Nakhon

300

1455

Sukhothai

Phitsanulok

1720

950

1530

Khon
Kaen

1310

1605

1530

Ubon
Ratchathani

Mae Sot

1650

1060

1405

Nam
Tok

Nakhon
Ratchasima

Buriram

3455

555

905

1405

BANGKOK

CAMBODIA

2000

U-Taphao/Pathaya

Hua Hin

3150

ANDAMAN
SEA

2280

1890

PHNOM
PENH

VIETNAM

1785

2005

1770

2280

2575

Ranong

Ko
Samui

GULF OF
THAILAND

Surat
Thani

1530

Nakhon Si
Thammarat

Phuket

690

780

Trang

Hat Yai

0   100   200 km

One-way economy air fares in baht

Narathiwat

Kota Bharu

990

INDIAN OCEAN

Sungai Kolok

MALAYSIA

TRAIN

The government-operated trains in Thailand are comfortable, frequent, punctual and moderately priced, but rather slow. On comparable routes, the buses can often be twice as fast, but the relatively low speed of the train means you can often leave at a convenient hour in the evening and arrive at your destination at a pleasant hour in the morning.

Train fares plus sleeping-berth charges make train travel appear a bit more expensive than bus travel. However, with a sleeping berth you may save over the cost of the bus fare plus one night's hotel costs. The trains have a further advantage over the buses in that they're far safer and there's more room to move around. Thailand's railways are a fine way to travel. One caveat: food served on trains is rather expensive by Thai standards; you'll save considerably by bringing your own food.

There are four main railway lines plus a few minor side routes. The main ones are: the northern line to Chiang Mai; the southern line to Hat Yai (where the line splits to enter Malaysia on the west coast via Padang Besar and to terminate near the east coast at Sungai Kolok); the eastern line to Ubon Ratchathani; and the north-eastern line to Nong Khai.

Very useful condensed railway timetables are available in English at the Hualamphong train station in Bangkok. These contain schedules and fares for all rapid and express trains, as well as a few ordinary trains.

Rail Passes

The State Railway of Thailand (SRT) offers two kinds of 20-day rail passes. The blue pass costs 1100B for unlimited 2nd class travel, while the red pass for 1st class costs 2000B. These rates include all rapid or express surcharges but do not include sleeping berths or air-con, which will cost you extra according to the standard SRT schedule. Passes must be validated at a local train station before boarding the first train. Seat reservations, if required, can be obtained at any SRT ticket office.

Bookings

Trains are often heavily booked, so it's wise to book ahead. At the Hualamphong station in Bangkok, you can book trains on any route in Thailand. The advance booking office is open from 7 am to 4 pm daily. Seats, berths or cabins may be booked up to 60 days in advance.

Costs

There is a 60B surcharge for express trains and a 40B surcharge for rapid trains – they make fewer stops. Some 2nd and 3rd class services are air-con, in which case there is a 70B surcharge (note that there are no 3rd class cars on either rapid or express trains).

Sleeping berths also cost extra. In 2nd class, upper berths are 100B, lower berths are 150B. For 2nd class sleepers with air-con add 220/270B per upper/lower ticket or 250/320B in Special Express, The lower berths are cooler since they have a window. In 1st class, the berths cost 520B per person in two-berth or single-berth cabins. Sleepers are only available in 1st and 2nd class, but apart from that, 3rd class is not too bad.

Second class fares are approximately double 3rd class and double again for 1st class. Count on around 190B for a 500km trip in 2nd class. You can break a trip for two days for each 200km travelled, but the ticket must be endorsed by the station master, which costs 1B.

CAR & MOTORCYCLE

Cars, jeeps or vans can be rented in Bangkok and large provincial capitals. The best deals are usually on 4WD Suzuki Caribians, which can be rented for as little as 800B per day for long-term rentals or during low seasons. Check with travel agencies or large hotels for rental locations. Always verify that a vehicle is insured for liability before signing a rental contract and ask to see the dated insurance documents. If you have an accident while driving an uninsured vehicle, you're in for some major hassles.

Permits

Foreigners who wish to drive a motor vehicle (including motorcycles) in Thailand need a valid International Driver's Licence.

Motorcycle Touring

Motorcycle travel is a popular way to get around Thailand, especially in the north. Dozens of places along the guesthouse circuit, including many guesthouses themselves, have set up shop with just a couple of motorbikes for rent. It is also possible to buy a new or used motorbike and sell it before you leave the country – a good used 125cc bike costs around 40,000B. Daily rentals range from 100B to 150B a day for a 100cc step-through to 500B a day for a good 250cc dirt bike. If you've never ridden a motorcycle before, stick to the smaller 100cc step-through bikes with automatic clutches.

Motorcycles can be rented in major towns and in many smaller tourist centres, including Krabi, Ko Samui, Ko Pha-Ngan, Mae Sai, Chiang Saen and Nong Khai. Motorcycle rental usually requires that you leave your passport.

While motorcycle touring is one of the best ways to see Thailand, it is undoubtedly one of the easiest ways to cut your travels short – permanently. You could also run up very large repair and/or hospital bills in the blink of an eye. But with proper safety precautions and driving conduct adapted to local standards, you can see parts of Thailand inaccessible by other modes of transport and still make it home in one piece. Some guidelines to keep in mind:

- Always check a machine thoroughly before you take it out. Look at the tyres to see if they still have tread, look for oil leaks, test the brakes. You may be held liable for any problems that weren't duly noted before your departure. Newer bikes cost more than clunkers, but are generally safer and more reliable. Street bikes are more comfortable and ride more smoothly on paved roads than dirt bikes; it's silly to rent an expensive dirt bike if most of your riding is going to be along decent roads. A two-stroke bike suitable for off-roading generally uses twice the fuel of a four-stroke bike with the same engine size, thus lowering your cruising range in areas where roadside pumps are scarce.
- Wear protective clothing and a helmet (most rental places will provide a helmet with the bike if asked) otherwise, a minor slide on gravel can leave you with concussion, cuts, bruises and a lot less skin. Long pants, long-sleeved shirts and shoes are highly recommended as protection against sunburn and as a second skin if you fall. If your helmet doesn't have a visor, then wear goggles, glasses or sunglasses to keep bugs, dust and other debris out of your eyes. It is practically suicidal to ride on Thailand's highways without taking these minimum precautions. Gloves are also a good idea; if nothing else they prevent blisters caused by holding on to the twist-grips for long periods of time.
- Get insurance with the motorcycle if at all possible. The more reputable motorcycle rental places insure all their bikes; some will do it for an extra charge. Without insurance you're responsible for anything that happens to the bike. To be absolutely clear about your liability, ask for a written estimate of the replacement cost for a similar bike – take photos as a guarantee. Some agencies will only accept the replacement cost of a new bike.

BICYCLE

Bicycles can also be hired in many locations; guesthouses often have a few for rent at only 20B to 30B per day. Just about anywhere outside Bangkok, bikes are the ideal form of local transport because they're cheap and non-polluting and keep you moving slowly enough to see everything. Carefully note the condition of the bike before hiring; if it breaks down, you are responsible and parts can be very expensive.

Many visitors bring their own touring bikes to Thailand. Gradients in most of the country are moderate; exceptions include the far north, especially Mae Hong Son and Nan provinces, where you'll need iron thighs. There is plenty of opportunity for dirt-road and off-road pedalling, especially in the north, so a sturdy mountain bike would make a good alternative to a touring rig. Favoured touring routes include the two-lane roads along the Mekong river in the north and the north-east – the terrain is mostly flat and the river scenery is inspiring.

No special permits are needed to bring a bicycle into the country, although bikes may be registered by customs – which means if you leave the country without your bike you'll have to pay a huge customs duty.

Most larger cities have bike shops – there are several in Bangkok and Chiang Mai – but they usually stock only a few Japanese or locally made parts. All the usual bike trip precautions apply – bring a small repair kit with plenty of spare parts, a helmet, reflective clothing and plenty of insurance.

HITCHING

Although hitching is not the relatively easy proposition it is in Malaysia, it is possible to hitch through Thailand. In places, traffic will be relatively light and the wait for a ride can be quite long, but it is certainly done (see the section on hitching in the introductory Getting Around chapter).

BOAT

There are lots of opportunities to travel by river or sea. You can take boats to offshore islands and riverboats operate on Thailand's numerous waterways. The traditional Thai runabout for river trips is the long-tail boat, so called because the engine operates the propeller via a long, open tail shaft. The engines are often car engines mounted on gimbals – the engine is swivelled to steer the boat.

LOCAL TRANSPORT

A wide variety of local transport is available in Thailand. In the big cities you'll find taxis, although they only have meters in Bangkok. Always negotiate your fare before departure.

Samlor (Pedicab)

Samlor, Thai for 'three wheels', are pedal rickshaws, and you'll see them in a few towns in the north-east and in Chiang Mai. Then there are the motorised samlors, which are usually known as tuk-tuks because of the nasty noise their two-stroke engines make. Tuk-tuks can be found in all the larger towns, as well as in Bangkok.

In Bangkok they are notoriously unreliable – either the drivers can't find the destination you want or make time-consuming detours to shops, where they are hoping for commissions. You must bargain and agree on a fare before taking samlors and tuk-tuks, but in many towns there is a more-or-less fixed fare anywhere in town.

Songthaew

Songthaew literally means 'two-rows' and these small pick-ups with a row of seats down each side serve a similar purpose to tuk-tuks or minibuses. In some cities, certain regular routes are run by songthaews or minibuses.

Bus

Finally, there are regular bus services in certain big cities. In Thailand fares are usually fixed for any route up to a certain length – in Bangkok up to 10km.

Bangkok

Thailand's coronary-inducing capital has a surprising number of quiet escapes if you make your way out of the busy streets. But before you leave, you will have to put up with noise, pollution and some of the worst traffic jams in Asia. Add annual floods and sticky weather, and it's hardly surprising that many people develop an instant dislike for the place.

However, beneath the surface Bangkok has plenty to offer, including cheap accommodation, excellent food and great nightlife. There are lots of sights – step out of the street noise and into the calm of a wat, for example. The Chao Phraya river is refreshing compared with the anarchy of the streets, and a canal cruise through Thonburi will show you

how delightful the *khlong* (canals) were and, occasionally, still are.

Bangkok, or Krung Thep as it is known to Thais, became the capital of Thailand after the Burmese sacked Ayuthaya in 1767. At first, the Siamese capital was shifted to Thonburi, across the river from Bangkok, but in 1782 it was moved to its present site.

Orientation

The Chao Phraya river divides Bangkok from Thonburi. Almost the only reason to cross to Thonburi (apart from the Southern bus terminals or the Bangkok Noi train station) is to see Wat Arun (Temple of the Dawn).

The main Bangkok railway line virtually encloses a loop of the river; within that loop is the older part of the city, including most of the interesting temples and the Chinatown area, and the popular travellers' centre of Banglamphu.

East of the railway line is the new area of the city, where most of the modern hotels are located. Thanon Rama IV is one of the most important roads: it runs right in front of the Hualamphong train station and eventually gets you to the Malaysia Hotel area. A little to the north, and approximately parallel to Rama IV, is Thanon Rama I; it passes Siam Square and eventually becomes Thanon Sukhumvit, where many of the popular hotels, restaurants and entertainment spots are located.

Small streets or lanes are called *soi*.

Maps One thing to buy as quickly as possible is a Bangkok bus map. *Bangkok Thailand Tour'n Guide Map* has the most up-to-date bus map of Bangkok on one side and a fair map of Thailand on the other. The bus map is necessary if you plan to use Bangkok's very economical bus system. The map usually costs around 40B and is available at most bookshops in Bangkok that carry English-language materials. *Nancy Chandler's Map of Bangkok* is a colourful map of the unusual attractions. It has all the *Chao Phraya River Express* stops in Thai script and costs 70B.

Information

Tourist Offices There are tourist offices at the airport and in Bangkok – the Thai tourist office is very good for detailed leaflets and information sheets. You'll find the city office of the Tourist Authority of Thailand (TAT, ☎ 282 9773) at 4 Thanon Ratchadamnoen Nok. It's open from 8.30 am to 4.30 pm daily.

Money Thai banks have currency exchange kiosks in many parts of Bangkok, though they are concentrated in the Thanon Sukhumvit, Thanon Khao San, Siam Square and Thanon Silom areas. Hours vary, but most are open from 8 am to 8 pm daily. Regular bank hours in Bangkok are from 10 am to 4 pm.

Try the moneychangers along Thanon Charoen Krung (New Rd), close to the main post office if you want to buy another Asian currency, such as Burmese kyats or Indian rupees.

Post The main post office on Thanon Charoen Krung (New Rd) has an efficient poste restante service, open from 8 am to 8 pm on weekdays and to 1 pm on weekends and holidays. Every single letter is recorded in a large book and you're charged 1B for each one. There is also a packing service if you want to send parcels home.

When the main post office is shut you can send letters from the adjacent central telegraph office, which is open 24 hours. You can also make international telephone calls here at any time of day or night. Hotels and guesthouses usually make service charges on every call, whether they are collect or not.

Branch post offices throughout the city also offer poste restante and parcel services.

Telephone Bangkok's Communications Authority of Thailand (CAT) international phone office, next to the main post office on Thanon Charoen Krung, is open 24 hours.

At the airport, and in some post offices and shopping centres, special telephones with Home Direct service are available. On these you can simply push a button for a direct connection with long-distance operators in 20 countries, including Australia, Canada, Denmark, Germany, Hong Kong, Italy, Japan, New Zealand, the UK and the USA.

Email & Internet Access Places offering Internet access and email services are numerous, especially along Thanon Khao San in Banglamphu.

Travel Agencies Bangkok is packed with travel agents of every manner and description, but if you're looking for cheap airline tickets, it's wise to be cautious. Ask other travellers for advice about agents. The really bad ones change their names frequently, so saying J Travel, for example, is not to be recommended is useless when it's called

something else next week. Wherever possible, try to see the tickets before you hand over the money.

STA Travel has a Bangkok branch at Wall Street Tower (☎ 233 2582), 33/70 Thanon Surawong, Room 1405. It sells discount air tickets and seems reliable – we have yet to receive a negative report about them.

Two agents permitted to issue Thai railway bookings directly, at regular State Railway of Thailand (SRT) fares, are: Songserm Travel Centre (☎ 255 8790), 121/7 Soi Chalermnit, Thanon Phayathai, and 172 Thanon Khao San (☎ 282 8080); and Thai Overland Travel & Tour (☎ 635 0500), 407 Thanon Sukhumvit, between Soi 21 and Soi 23. Other agencies can arrange rail bookings but will slap on a surcharge of 50B to 100B per ticket. The TAT head office has the addresses of all the different sales agencies.

Bookshops The bookshops in Bangkok are among the best in South-East Asia. Asia Books at Soi 15-17, Thanon Sukhumvit, stocks an excellent selection of English-language books. There are also branches in the Landmark Hotel on Thanon Sukhumvit, opposite Soi 5; on the 3rd floor of the World Trade Centre, Thanon Ploenchit; on the 3rd floor of Thaniya Plaza, Thanon Silom; in the Peninsula Plaza on Thanon Ratchadamri; and in the new Siam Discovery Center. Duang Kamol (DK) Books, with branches in Siam Square, the Mahboonkrong Centre, Soi Patpong and Soi 8, Thanon Sukhumvit, also has a wide selection, though much less well organised.

Merman Books, 2nd Floor, Silom Complex, 191 Thanon Silom, takes its used book collection very seriously, with a focus on South-East Asia. You can also find decent book departments in various branches of Central department store and in many of the better hotels.

On Thanon Khao San in Banglamphu, at least three streetside vendors specialise in used paperback novels and guidebooks, including many Lonely Planet titles. Shaman Books at 71 Thanon Khao San carries a good selection of guidebooks, maps and books on spirituality in several languages.

Medical Services There are several good hospitals in Bangkok:

Bangkok Adventist (Mission) Hospital
 (☎ 281 1422)
 430 Thanon Phitsanulok

THAILAND

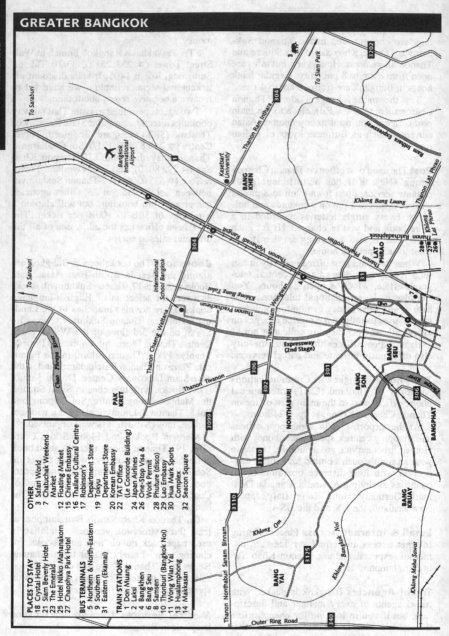

GREATER BANGKOK

To Saraburi

To Saraburi

To Saraburi

To Siam Park

Bangkok International Airport

Kasetsart University

BANG KHEN

Khlong Bang Luang

Thanon Ram Inthara

Ram Inthara Expressway

Thanon Lat Phrao

Khlong Lat Phrao

286
278
266

Thanon Vibhavadi Rangsit

Thanon Phaholyothin

Thanon Ratchadaphisek

LAT PHRAO

International School Bangkok

Thanon Chaeng Wattana

Thanon Pradaduen

Khlong Bang Talu

Thanon Nam Wongwan

Expressway (2nd Stage)

BANG SEU

Bang Pu Khlong

BANG SON

Thanon Tiwanon

PAK KRET

Chao Phraya River

306

302

3099

3110

301

NONTHABURI

BANGPHAT

BANG KRUAT

Khlong Om

Khlong Bangkok Noi

3110

3125

BANG YAI

Khlong Maha Sawat

Thanon Nonthaburi Sanam Binnam

Khlong Bangkok Noi

Outer Ring Road

340

PLACES TO STAY
18 Crystal Hotel
21 Siam Beverly Hotel
23 The Emerald
25 Hotel Nikko Mahanakorn
27 Chaophya Park Hotel

BUS TERMINALS
5 Northern & North-Eastern
9 Southern
31 Eastern (Ekamai)

TRAIN STATIONS
1 Don Muang
4 Laksi
2 Bangkhen
6 Bang Seu
8 Samsen
10 Thonburi (Bangkok Noi)
11 Wong Wian Yai
13 Hualamphong
14 Makkasan

OTHER
3 Safari World
7 Chatuchak Weekend Market
12 Floating Market
15 Chinese Embassy
16 Thailand Cultural Centre
17 Robinson's Department Store
19 Tokyu Department Store
20 Korean Embassy
22 TAT Office (Le Concorde Building)
24 Japan Airlines
26 One-Stop Visa & Work Permit
28 Phuture (disco)
29 Lao Embassy
30 Hua Mark Sports Complex
32 Seacon Square

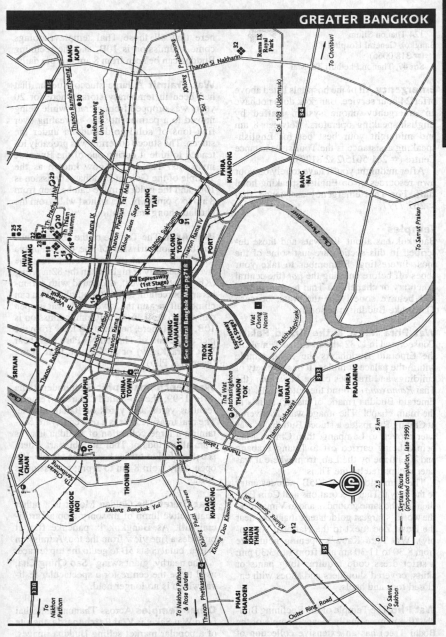

GREATER BANGKOK

Bangkok Christian Hospital
(☎ 233 6981)
124 Thanon Silom
Bangkok General Hospital
(☎ 318 0066)
Soi 47, Thanon Phetburi Tat Mai

Emergency All of the hospitals listed above offer 24 hour service. Bangkok does not have an emergency phone system staffed by English-speaking operators. Between 8 am and midnight your best bet for English-speaking assistance is the Tourist Assistance Centre (☎ 281 5015/282 8129).

After midnight you'll have to rely on your own resources or on English-speaking hotel staff. For Thai emergency assistance, dial ☎ 267 7777.

Temples
Bangkok has about 400 wats and those described in this section are just some of the most interesting. Remember to take your shoes off before entering the *bot* (the central sanctuary or chapel in a Thai temple). Dress and behave soberly in the wats, because Thais take Buddhism seriously.

Wat Phra Kaew & the Grand Palace
Consecrated in 1782, the so-called Temple of the Emerald Buddha is the royal temple within the palace complex. It has a variety of buildings and frescoes of the *Ramakian* (the Thai *Ramayana*) around the outer walls. The Emerald Buddha (made of jasper) stands in the main chapel. The image was discovered at Chiang Rai inside a stucco Buddha. It was later moved to Lampang, then Chiang Mai, before being carried off to Luang Prabang and Vientiane by the Lao, from where it was later recaptured by the Thais.

The admission fee of 125B includes entry to the Royal Thai Decorations and Coin Pavilion (on the same grounds), and to Vimanmek, the world's largest golden teak mansion, near the Dusit Zoo (next to the National Assembly). Wat Phra Kaew's opening hours are from 8.30 to 11.30 am and from 1 to 3.30 pm; a strict dress code requires long pants or skirts, covered shoulders and shoes with enclosed toes and heels.

Wat Pho The Temple of the Reclining Buddha (the name actually means Temple of the Bodhi Tree) has an extensive collection of panels, bas reliefs, *chedi* (stupas) and statuary to view, as well as the celebrated 46m reclining Buddha, which looks like a beached whale with mother-of-pearl feet. This is the oldest and largest wat in Bangkok, and it's from here that all those Thai temple rubbings come. Admission is 10B, and the reclining Buddha can be seen from 8 am to 5 pm daily.

Wat Traimit A large stucco Buddha that had been in temporary storage here for 20 years was dropped from a crane while being moved to a permanent site – revealing over five tons of solid-gold Buddha under the stucco. The stucco covering was probably intended to hide it during one of the Burmese invasions. The wat is now known as the Temple of the Golden Buddha. Admission is 10B, and the golden image can be seen from 8 am to 5 pm daily. It's a short walk from the Hualamphong train station.

Wat Arun The Temple of the Dawn stands on the Thonburi side of the Chao Phraya river. It's seen at its best from across the river, especially at night when the 82m *prang* (Khmer-style tower), decorated with ceramics and porcelain, is lit by spotlights. You can climb halfway up the tower. This wat is open daily from 8.30 am to 5.30 pm; admission is 10B. To get there, hop on a 1B ferry from the pier at the end of Thanon Na Phra Lan (near Wat Phra Kaew) or at Thanon Thai Wang (near Wat Pho).

Wat Benchamabophit Built under Rama V in 1899, the so-called 'Marble Temple' features yards and yards of Italian marble. The real treasure here is a rear courtyard containing a large collection of Buddha images from all periods of Thai Buddhist art. There is a pond full of turtles beside the temple. It's open daily from 8 am to 5 pm; admission is 10B.

Wat Saket The Golden Mount is a rather unattractive lump of masonry atop an artificial hill. As Bangkok is pancake flat, it provides a fine view from the top. Admission is free, but it costs 5B to get to the top terrace.

The nearby 'giant swing', **Sao Ching Cha**, used to be the centre for a spectacular festival which is no longer held.

Other Temples Across Thanon Mahachai from Wat Saket is **Wat Ratchanatda**, the site of a popular market selling Buddha images, amulets and charms. **Wat Bowonniwet** on Thanon Phra Sumen in Banglamphu is the headquarters of the minority Thammayut monastic sect and the monastery where the current Thai king ordained as a monk temporarily. **Wat Intharawihan**, just north of Banglamphu on Thanon Wisut Kasat (near the junction with Thanon Samsen), has an enormous standing Buddha image.

A small Hindu Shaiva temple, **Maha Uma Devi Temple**, sits on the corner of Pan and Thanon Siloms. It contains three main deities: Khanthakumara, Ganesh and Uma Devi (Parvati), although a whole pantheon of Hindu and Buddhist statuary lines one wall.

National Museum

Supposedly the largest museum in South-East Asia, this is a good place for an overview of Thai art and culture before you start exploring the former Thai capitals. All the periods and styles of Thai history and art are shown.

Located on Thanon Na Phrathat near the river in Banglamphu, the museum is open from 9 am to 4 pm, Wednesday to Sunday – admission is 20B. There are free tours conducted in English on Wednesday (Buddhism) and Thursday (Thai art, religion, culture); each begins at 9.30 am from the ticket pavilion.

Jim Thompson's House

Located on Soi Kasem San 2, Thanon Rama I, this is the beautiful house of the American Thai silk entrepreneur Jim Thompson, who disappeared without trace back in 1967 in the Cameron Highlands in Malaysia. His house, built from parts of a number of traditional wooden Thai houses and replete with a superb collection of Thai art and furnishings, is simply delightful. Pleasantly sited on a small khlong, it is open daily from 9 am to 5 pm. Admission is 40B for anyone under 25 years of age and 100B for everyone else.

Floating Markets

The Wat Sai floating market in Thonburi is really a tourist trap – all the boats here are now tourist boats. The trip to the market is picturesque, but with the tourist shops, snake farms and the like, it all looks very artificial. We recommend skipping the Wat Sai market for the less touristy floating market at Khlong Damnoen Saduak, beyond Nakhon Pathom. See under Nakhon Pathom in the Around Bangkok section later in this chapter for details.

Massage

Massage as a healing art is a centuries-old tradition in Thailand, and it is possible to get a really legitimate massage in Bangkok – despite the commercialisation of recent years. One of the best places for a traditional massage is **Wat Pho**, Bangkok's oldest temple. Massage here costs 180B per hour or 100B for half an hour. For those interested in studying massage, the temple also offers two 30-hour courses – one on general Thai massage, the other on massage therapy. Next to Wat Mahathat (opposite Thammasat University at the south-east corner of Thanon Maharat and Thanon Phra Chan) is a strip of Thai herbal medicine shops offering good massage for a mere 80B an hour.

A more commercial area for Thai massage as well as Thai herbal saunas is Thanon Surawong. Here you'll find **Marble House**, **Vejakorn** and **Eve House**. Eve House charges 150B per hour and accepts women only. The rest of these charge 200B to 300B per hour and offer Thai herbal sauna as well as massage.

There are plenty of massage-and-sex places around, including a new strip of very high-end places along Thanon Ratchadaphisek in the north of the city. The sex massage places generally have private massage rooms, while in the traditional places beds are placed side by side, occasionally curtained off, in one big room,. However this doesn't hold 100% since some legit high-class hotel massage operations have private rooms. Often in the sex-type parlours, the bank of masseuses sit on tiered platforms behind one way glass, divided into sections according to skill and/or appearance. A smaller section is reserved for women who are actually good at giving massages, with no hanky-panky on the side.

Before contemplating anything more than a massage at a modern massage parlour, be sure to read the Health section in this book for information on sexually transmitted diseases. There is a definite AIDS presence in Thailand; condom use lowers the risk considerably, but remember that an estimated 11% of commercial Thai condoms are defective.

Other Attractions

An interesting **river tour** can be made by taking a Chao Phraya river taxi from Tha Wat Ratchasingkhon (Wat Ratchasingkhon pier; lots of buses go there) as far north as Nonthaburi. This is a three hour, 15B trip with plenty to see along the way. The Klong Bangkok Noi canal taxi route from Tha Phra Chan, next to Thammasat University, only costs 10B and takes you along a colourful 45 minute route, seemingly far from Bangkok.

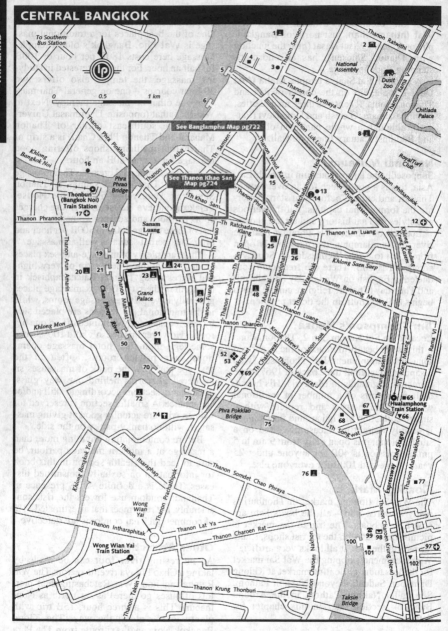

CENTRAL BANGKOK

To Southern
Bus Station

Thonburi
(Bangkok Noi)
Train Station

Thanon Phrannok

Khlong Bangkok Noi

Phra Phrao
Bridge

Phra Pinklao

Thanon Arun Amarin

Thanon Maharat

Chao Phraya River

Khlong Mon

Sanam
Luang

Grand
Palace

See Banglamphu Map pg722

See Thanon Khao San
Map pg724

Th Khao San

Th Ratchadamnoen
Klang

Th Tanao

Th Din So

Thanon Phra Athit

Thanon Samsen

Th Samsen

Thanon Wisut Kasat

Thanon Ratchadamnoen Nok

Thanon Phra Sumen

Thanon Krung Kasem

Thanon Lan Luang

Khlong Saen Saep

Thanon Bamrung Meuang

Thanon Luang

Thanon Charoen

Krung (New)

Th Chakraphet

Th Chakrawat

Thanon Yaowarat

Phra Pokklao
Bridge

Th Song-wat

Thanon Itsaraphap

Thanon Prachathipok

Wong
Wian
Yai

Thanon Intharaphitak

Thanon Lat Ya

Thanon Charoen Rat

Thanon Krung Thonburi

Wong Wian Yai
Train Station

Thanon Taksin

Khlong Bangkok Yai

Thanon Somdet Chao Phraya

Thanon Charoen Nakhon

Taksin
Bridge

Thanon Mahanakhon

Expressway (2nd Stage)

Thanon Charoen Krung (New)

Hualamphong
Train Station

Th Krung Kasem

Th Rong Meuang

Thanon Rama VI

Thanon Si Ayuthaya

Thanon Luk Luang

Thanon Wora Chak

National
Assembly

Dusit
Zoo

Chitlada
Palace

Thanon Ratwithi

Thanon Rama V

Royal Turf
Club

Thanon Phitsanulok

Khlong Phadung Krung Kasem

Phra Phraya

Th Ratchadamnoen

Th Fuang Nakhon

Th Triphet

Th Mahachai

Thanon Bamrung

Th Sua Pa

Thanon Song-wat

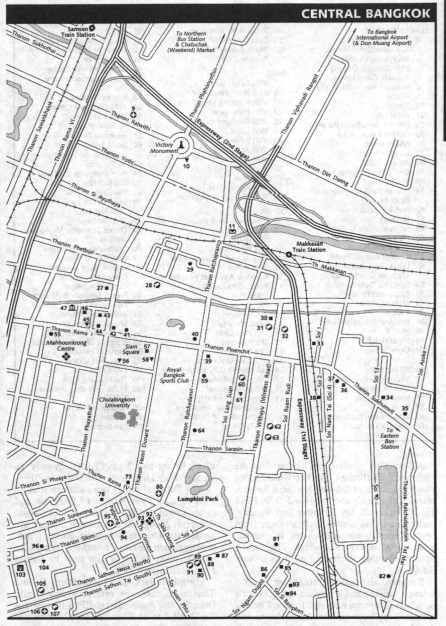

CENTRAL BANGKOK

Samsen Train Station

To Northern Bus Station & Chatuchak (Weekend) Market

To Bangkok International Airport (& Don Muang Airport)

Thanon Sukhothai

Thanon Sawankhalok

Thanon Rama VI

Thanon Ratwithi

9

Thanon Phahonyothin

Expressway (2nd Stage)

Thanon Viphavadi Rangsit

Victory Monument

10

Thanon Yothi

Thanon Din Daeng

Thanon Si Ayuthaya

Thanon Phetburi

11

Thanon Ratchaprarop

Makkasan Train Station

Th Makkasan

29

28

27

47   46

45   43

44

42 41

Thanon Rama I

55

Mahboonkrong Centre

Siam Square

57

56   58

30

31

32

Soi 1

33

40

Thanon Ploenchit

39

Royal Bangkok Sports Club

59

60

61

37

36

Soi 2

Soi 13

Soi Asoke

Soi Sukhumvit

34

35

Chulalongkorn University

Thanon Ratchadamri

Soi Lang Suan

Thanon Withyu (Wireless Road)

Soi Ruam Rudi

Expressway (1st Stage)

Soi Nana Tai (Soi 4)

64

Thanon Sarasin

62

63

To Eastern Bus Station

Thanon Phayathai

Thanon Henri Dunant

38

Thanon Ratchadaphisek Tat Mai

Thanon Si Phraya

Thanon Rama IV

73

80

78

Lumphini Park

Soi 1

Soi 16

95

Thanon Surawong

Pa Pong

93 92

Thanon Silom

94

Th Sala Daeng

Th Convent

96

81

104

103

Thanon Sathon Neua (North)

89 87

91   88

90

86   85

Thanon Sathon Tai (South)

105

Soi Suan Phlu

Soi Ngam Duphli

83

84

82

106 107

Soi Si Bamphen

THAILAND

CENTRAL BANGKOK

PLACES TO STAY
4 Tavee Guest House;
   Sawatdee Guest House;
   Backpacker's Lodge;
   Shanti Lodge; Original
   Paradise Guest House
7 Bangkok International Youth
   Hostel
15 Thai Hotel
27 Asia Hotel
30 Hilton International Bangkok
33 Golden Palace Hotel
34 Miami Hotel
36 Landmark Hotel
38 Atlanta Hotel
39 Grand Hyatt Erawan Hotel
43 A-One Inn
44 Pranee Building; Muangphol
   Building
46 Bed & Breakfast Inn
57 Novotel; Siam Square
65 Sri Hualamphong Hotel
68 New Empire Hotel
77 TT2 Guest House
78 Tawana Ramada Hotel
83 Lee 4 Guest House;
   Madame Guest House
84 Sala Thai Daily Mansion
85 ETC Guest House
86 Malaysia Hotel
87 YWCA
88 Beaufort Sukhothai Hotel
90 YMCA
96 Narai Hotel
101 Oriental Hotel

PLACES TO EAT
10 Saxophone Pub Restaurant
45 Thai Sa Nguan
56 Hard Rock Cafe
58 Coca
61 Whole Earth Restaurant
66 Suki Jea Yuu Seu

69 Royal India Restaurant
93 Delaney's Irish Pub
102 Maria Bakery & Restaurant
104 Madras Café

WATS
1 Wat Ratchathiwat
8 Wat Benchamabophit
20 Wat Rakhang Khositaram
23 Wat Phra Kaew
25 Wat Ratchanatda
26 Wat Saket
48 Wat Suthat
49 Wat Ratchabophit
51 Wat Pho
67 Wat Traimit
71 Wat Arun
72 Wat Kalayanimit
76 Wat Thawng Nophakhun

OTHER
2 Vimanmek Teak Mansion
3 National Library
5 Tha Thewet
6 Tha Wisut Kasat
9 Phra Mongkutklao Hospital
11 Post Office
12 Bangkok Adventist Hospital
13 Ratchadamnoen Boxing
   Stadium
14 TAT Office
16 Royal Barges
17 Siriraj Hospital
18 Tha Phra Chan
19 Tha Maharat
21 Tha Chang
22 Silpakorn University
24 Lak Muang (City Pillar) Shrine
28 Indonesian Embassy
29 Pratunam Market
31 Norwegian Embassy
32 Swiss Embassy; Telephone
   Organisation of Thailand
   (TOT) Office

35 Asia Books
37 Nana Entertainment Plaza
40 World Trade Centre
41 Siam Centre
42 Siam Discovery Centre
47 Jim Thompson's House
50 Tha Tien
52 Pahurat Market
53 ATM Shopping Centre
54 Yaowarat Market
55 National Stadium
59 Peninsula Plaza
60 Israeli Embassy
62 New Zealand Embassy
63 US Embassy
64 AUA Language Centre
70 Tha Ratchin
73 Tha Saphaan Phut
74 Santa Cruz Church
   (Wat Kuti Jiin)
75 Tha Ratchawang
79 Queen Saovabha Memorial
   Institute
80 Chulalongkorn Hospital
81 Lumphini Stadium
82 Queen Sirikit National
   Convention Centre;
   Bangkok Airways
89 French Embassy & Alliance
   Française
91 Malaysian Embassy
92 Silom Complex
94 CP Tower Building
95 Bangkok Christian Hospital
97 Mahesak Hospital
98 Main Post Office
99 CAT Office
100 Tha Meuang Khae
103 Maha Uma Devi (Hindu)
   Temple
105 Myanmar Embassy
106 St Louis Hospital
107 Lao Embassy

All sorts of oddities can be found at the enormous **Chatuchak Market** which takes place just south of the new Northern bus terminal. Take an air-con bus Nos 2, 3, 9, 10 or 13. It's open all day Saturday and Sunday, and you can find almost anything there from opium pipes to unusual posters. It also has lots of other activities to watch. There are a number of other interesting markets around Bangkok.

Bangkok also has a **Chinatown**, with a thieves' market and an Indian district on its periphery. This area is around Thanon Chakrawat, midway between the Grand Palace and the Hualamphong train station.

At the **Queen Saovabha Memorial Institute (Snake Farm)** on Thanon Rama IV, snakes are milked of their venom every day at 10.30 am and 2 pm (10.30 am only on weekends and holidays); admission is 70B.

The **Oriental Hotel** is an attraction in its own right. It's the Raffles of Bangkok and is consistently voted the best hotel in Asia. Somerset Maugham and Joseph Conrad are among the Oriental's historic guests (commemorated in the hotel's Authors' Wing). Be sure to dress nicely or you may be barred from entering the lobby.

Lumphini Park, on Thanon Rama IV and Thanon Ratchadamri, offers a shady respite from the city's noise and traffic. Likewise for the **Dusit Zoo** on Thanon Rama V, which is open from 9 am to 6 pm daily; admission is 20B (children 5B, over 60s 10B).

One of Bangkok's more unusual sights is the **Brahma shrine**, outside the Grand Hyatt

Erawan Hotel, where people come to seek help for some wish they want granted – like their girlfriend to marry them. The person promises that if the grant is made they will pay for something to be done – a favourite promise is to pay for 20 minutes dancing by the Thai dancers who are always ready and waiting for such commissions.

Places to Stay – Budget

There are all sorts of places to stay in Bangkok, with a wide range of prices, mainly concentrated in distinct areas.

Banglamphu is the number one travellers' centre and has an amazing number of budget-priced guesthouses, plus restaurants, snack bars, travel agents and all the other back-up facilities. A big advantage of Banglamphu is that it's central to many of Bangkok's major tourist attractions.

Soi Ngam Duphli is quieter and slightly more expensive; at one time it was the main travellers' centre and it still attracts many visitors. Then there's the Thanon Sukhumvit area, which has some travellers' hotels among the more expensive places. Much more central are the noisy Hualamphong station, Chinatown and Siam Square areas.

Competition in the Banglamphu area is so fierce that you can still get a room in Bangkok for scarcely more than it was 10 years ago. The cheapest rooms start at 80B for a single or 120B for a double in the Banglamphu and Hualamphong areas. The air-con places in Soi Ngam Duphli and along Thanon Sukhumvit now begin at around 400B to 500B. Some hotels give student discounts if you ask.

There's a hotel booking desk at the airport which can book you into many of the cheaper (but not rock bottom) hotels.

Banglamphu Also known as the Thanon Khao San area, Banglamphu is over towards the river, near the Democracy Monument and on the route of Airport Bus No A-2 . Most of the guesthouses are basic, but they can be excellent value: the standard price is around 70B or 80B for a single, and from 100 to 120B for a double. Some very basic guesthouses are even cheaper in the off season, so it doesn't hurt to try bargaining.

It's quite difficult to recommend any of them, since names and management change periodically. Check your room first because, in some cases, a 'room' is just a tiny cubicle, partitioned off with cardboard. Like *losmen*

(guesthouses) at Kuta Beach on Bali, there are so many places around Thanon Khao San that it's just a case of wandering about until you find one that suits. The map shows many, but not all, of them.

Popular places along Thanon Khao San, or on the alleys just off it, include the *Bonny*, *Top*, *Hello*, *Lek*, *Marco Polo 160 Guesthouse*, *Good Luck*, *Chada*, *Nat* and many others, all very similar.

A couple of places do not fit the usual guesthouse mould but rather operate like small hotels. The *Khao San Palace Hotel* (☎ 282 0578), at 139 Thanon Khao San (actually in an alley off Khao San), is Chinese-owned and costs from 250/350B for a room with a fan and bath. Nearby is the popular *New Nith Charoen Hotel* (☎ 281 9872), which has similar rooms and rates but slightly better service.

Off Thanon Chakraphong on Trok Mayom, the soi parallel and just south of Thanon Khao San, you'll find the well run *J & Joe*, *New Joe* and *Ranee*, plus a couple of other less well run places. This soi is significantly quieter than Thanon Khao San.

There's a small soi east off Thanon Tanao (at the end of Khao San) that offers several more cheapies, including the plain and basic *Central* (☎ 282 0667), *PC*, *Sweety* (☎ 281 6756), *CH II* and *Nat II* guesthouses, all at the usual Khao San rates. This network of alleys is fairly quiet, since it's off the main road.

Another relatively quiet area is the network of soi and alleys between Thanon Chakraphong and Thanon Phra Athit, to the west of Thanon Khao San, including Soi Rambutri, Soi Chana and Trok Rong Mai. Good choices include the *New Siam* (☎ 282 4554) on Soi Chana, *Merry V* on Soi Rambutri and *Chai's House* off the southern end of Soi Rambutri near Thanon Chao Fa. On Thanon Phra Athit, near the river, the *Peachy* (☎ 281 6471) and *New Merry V* guesthouses are slightly upmarket for Banglamphu, with rates from 140B to 350B.

The guesthouses along Thanon Chakraphong tend to be a bit noisy, as it's a fairly large thoroughfare.

Around Banglamphu North of Banglamphu, Thanon Chakraphong becomes Thanon Samsen (north of Khlong Banglamphu). About a kilometre further north it crosses Khlong Phadung Krung Kasem then intersects with Thanon Si Ayuthaya. On two

BANGLAMPHU

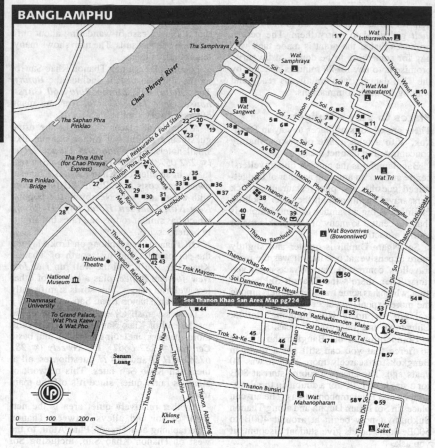

parallel soi off Thanon Si Ayuthaya, west of Samsen, are five guesthouses run by various members of the same extended family: *Tavee Guest House* (☎ 282 5983), *Sawatdee Guest House* (☎ 282 5349), *Backpacker's Lodge* (☎ 282 3231), *Shanti Lodge* (☎ 281 2497) and *Original Paradise Guest House* (☎ 282 4094).

All are clean, well kept, fairly quiet and cost 50B to 60B for a dorm bed, and from 100/150B for singles/doubles. There's a lot of friendly family competition between these places. This area has the distinct advantage of being a short walk from Tha Thewet, a *Chao Phraya River Express* pier; from the pier you walk east along Thanon Krung Kasem to Thanon Samsen, turn left, cross the canal and then take another left onto Thanon Si Ayuthaya.

Close by is the *Bangkok International Youth Hostel* (☎ 282 0950) at 25/2 Thanon Phitsanulok. It has a 70B fan dorm, 80B air-con dorm, and air-con rooms with toilet and shower at 250/300B if you have a youth hostel card. Non-members can purchase a temporary membership for 50B or a full annual membership for 300B. Several readers have written to say that the hostel staff can be quite rude to guests.

Chinatown-Hualamphong Station This is one of the cheapest areas in Bangkok and one of the noisiest. The traffic along Thanon Rama IV has to be heard to be believed. There are a few hotels alongside the station, but these station-area cheapies are no bargain compared with the even cheaper places over

THAILAND

PLACES TO STAY
- 3 Clean & Calm Guest House
- 4 River House
- 5 Villa Guest House
- 6 Truly Yours Guest House
- 7 Rajata Hotel
- 8 Nakorn Pink Hotel
- 9 AP Guest House
- 10 Trang Hotel & Vieng Travel
- 11 Vorapong Guest House
- 12 Mitr Paisarn Hotel
- 13 Vimol Guest House
- 15 New World House Apartments & Guest House
- 17 Gipsy Guest House
- 18 PS Guest House
- 25 New Merry V
- 26 Peachy Guest House
- 29 Apple Guest House
- 30 Rose Garden Guest House
- 31 Mango Guest House
- 32 New Siam Guest House
- 33 Green Guest House
- 34 Merry V Guest House
- 35 My House
- 36 Chusri Guest House
- 37 Sawasdee House
- 41 Chai's House
- 43 Charlie's House
- 44 Royal Hotel
- 45 Palace Hotel
- 46 Smile Guest House
- 47 Hotel Rajdamnoen
- 48 Srinthip Guest House
- 49 Central Guest House
- 51 Nat II Guest House; CH II Guest House
- 52 Sweety Guest House
- 54 Prasuri Guest House
- 57 Thai Waree Hotel

PLACES TO EAT
- 1 Tangtay
- 2 Yok Yor Restaurant
- 14 Aab Aroy
- 19 Joy Luck Club
- 20 Roti-Mataba
- 22 Khrua Nopparat
- 23 108 Yang
- 24 Raan Kin Duem
- 28 Wang Ngar Restaurant
- 53 McDonald's
- 55 Vijit Restaurant
- 58 Arawy Restaurant

OTHER
- 16 Siam Commercial Bank
- 21 Phra Sumen Fort
- 27 UNICEF
- 38 Banglamphu Department Store
- 39 Post Office
- 40 Salvador Dali
- 42 National Gallery; National Film Archives
- 50 Mosque
- 56 Democracy Monument
- 59 City Hall

in Banglamphu, and it's nowhere near as pleasant a place to stay.

Near the Hualamphong train station, the **Sri Hualamphong Hotel** (☎ 214 2610), 445 Thanon Rong Muang, is one of the better ones, with rooms at 120B with fan. There are numerous good, cheap eating places around the station, but take care: some of Bangkok's best pickpockets and razor artists work the station area.

Across Rama IV near Wat Traimit, the **New Empire Hotel** (☎ 234 6990), 572 Thanon Yaowarat, has air-con doubles from 450B up to 800B. It's a bit noisy, but in a good Chinatown location, near the intersection of Thanon Yaowarat and Thanon Charoen Krung (New Rd). There are a number of other Chinatown hotels around, but most don't have signs in English.

The **TT 2 Guest House** (☎ 236 2946) is about a 10 minute walk south from the station, at 516-518 Soi Sawang, Thanon Si Phraya near the junction with Thanon Mahanakhon. It's a short walk from the main post office and river. From the station, turn left and walk a block along Thanon Rama IV, then turn right (south) down Thanon Mahanakhon. There will be signs close to Thanon Si Phraya. It's worth the effort to find this comparatively large, well kept and popular place. Rooms cost 180B; there's a strict midnight curfew.

To find the more hidden **TT 1 Guest House** (☎ 236 3053), 138 Soi Wat Mahaphuttharam, from the station, cross Thanon Rama IV, walk left down Rama IV and then right on Mahanakhon, and follow the signs for TT 1. It's only about a 10 minute walk from the station. Dorm beds are just 40B and rooms go for 150B.

Siam Square On Soi Kasem San 1, off Thanon Rama I opposite the National Stadium, there are several places which are good value, though they tend towards mid-range rather than low-budget accommodation.

Right on the corner of this soi and Thanon Rama I is the **Muangphol Mansion** (☎ 215 3056), which offers decent air-con singles/doubles for 450/550B and has a 24 hour coffee shop downstairs. The **Pranee Building** next door has 300B to 350B fan rooms, air-con rooms starting at 400B, but no restaurant.

More home-like are the family-run **A-One Inn** (☎ 215 3029) and the **Bed & Breakfast Inn** (☎ 215 3004), both of which are at the end of Soi Kasem San 1 and cost 400B to 500B for air-con rooms; rates may drop 100B in the low season. Both have small dining areas on the ground floor. Rates at the Bed & Breakfast Inn include breakfast but rooms are a bit larger at the A-One. Avoid the **Reno** and **Star** hotels on this soi; both are overpriced and rather unfriendly.

THAILAND

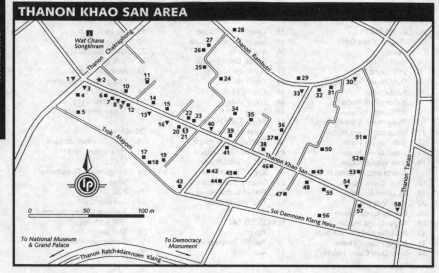

THANON KHAO SAN AREA

PLACES TO STAY			29	Orchid House		56	7-Holder Guest House
4	Ploy Guest House		31	Pannee Guest House I		57	Chada Guest House
5	J & Joe Guest House		32	Pannee Guest House II			
6	Thai Guest House		34	Khao San Palace Hotel		**PLACES TO EAT**	
7	NS Guest House		35	New Nith Charoen Hotel		1	Gaylord Indian Restaurant
10	Sitdhi Guest House		36	Marco Polo Hostel		3	Gulliver's Traveller's Tavern
12	Chart Guest House		37	Pian Guest House		8	Prakorp's House
14	Hello Guest House		38	Nat Guest House		9	Hello Restaurant
15	Mam's Guest House		39	Grand Guest House		13	Bangkok Centre Restaurant
17	Ranee Guest House		41	Dio Guest House		16	Royal India Restaurant
18	New Joe Guest House		42	Bonny Guesthouse; Top		30	Pizza Hut
19	Khao San Privacy			Guesthouse		33	Chabad House
	Guest House		43	Sawasdee Bangkok Inn		40	Orm; Wally House
20	D&D Inn		44	160 Guest House		54	Buddy Beer Garden,
22	Lek Guest House		45	Good Luck Guest House			Restaurant & Swimming
23	Lucky Beer Guest House		46	Siam Oriental			Pool
24	Doll Guest House;		47	Nana Plaza Inn		58	Arawy Det
	Pro Guest House;		48	Siri Guest House			
	Friendly Guest House		49	Classic Place; Central Minimart		**OTHER**	
25	Suneeporn Guest House		50	New Royal Guest House		2	Chana Songkhram Police
26	AT Guest House; Cherry		51	VS Guest House			Station
	Guest House		52	Nisa Guest House		11	Paradise; No-Name;
27	Green House		53	Harn Guest House			Hole in the Wall
28	Viengtai Hotel		55	CH I Guest House		21	Krung Thai Bank

Soi Ngam Duphli Just off Thanon Rama IV, this was for many years the travellers' centre of Bangkok, though the places are no longer the best value. To get there take ordinary bus Nos 4, 13, 14, 22, 27, 46, 47, 74, 109 or 115, or a No 7 air-con bus, and get off just after the roundabout on Thanon Rama IV.

Once, the prime attraction here was the *Malaysia Hotel* (☎ 286 3582), 54 Soi Ngam Duphli – this was one of the hotels quickly thrown together for the R&R trade back in the Vietnam War. It is multistorey and has air-con, a tiny swimming pool and an infamous after-hours coffee shop where Thai bar girls hang out after legal closing time else-where. Standard rooms are 500B, 600B with a TV and small fridge or 700B with a TV, larger fridge and carpet.

Today there are also many smaller guest-houses around Soi Ngam Duphli – in that respect, it's a quieter version of Thanon Khao San. At the northern end of Soi Ngam Duphli, near Thanon Rama IV, the *ETC Guest House* (☎ 286 9424) is an efficiently run, multistorey place with a travel agency downstairs. Rooms are small but clean; rates are 120B with shared bath, 160/200B for singles/doubles with private bath. All rates include a light breakfast.

One of the best deals in this area is *Sala Thai Daily Mansion* (☎ 287 1436), a well run place with very clean rooms for 150B to 200B; it's on an alley that runs north off Soi Si Bamphen. Also on this alley are the simi-larly priced *Lee 4 Guest House* and *Madame*.

The *YWCA* (☎ 286 1936) is close to the Soi Ngam Duphli area at 13 Thanon Sathon Tai. Rooms have air-con and baths, and cost from 567B. This Y takes only women guests and has a restaurant, swimming pool and other facilities. At 27 Thanon Sathon Tai is the more expensive *YMCA* (☎ 286 5134), where rooms start at 1377B – both men and women can stay there.

Apart from the hotels and guesthouses there are also lots of travel agencies, restau-rants, bars and all manner of other 'services' in the area.

Thanon Sukhumvit North of Thanon Rama IV and east of the railway line, Thanon Sukhumvit is a major tourist centre. Take or-dinary bus Nos 2, 25, 40 or 48, or an air-con bus Nos 1, 8, 11 or 13. The hotels are not Bangkok's top-notch places: most are out of the budget traveller's price range, but there are a few worthwhile places scattered about. Staying in this area puts you in the newest part of the city and the furthest from old Bangkok, and while the skytrain is under construction traffic can be tense. All the lanes running off Thanon Sukhumvit are called Soi, and have a number – the bigger the number, the farther east it is; even numbers are to the south and odd to the north.

Starting at the Rama I end (Rama I changes into Thanon Sukhumvit), you'll find the historic *Atlanta Hotel* (☎ 252 1650) at 78 Soi 2. Owned since its construction in the 1950s by Dr Max Henn, a former secretary to the maharaja of Bikaner and sometime In-dochina agent, the Atlanta is a simple but reliable stand-by, with clean, comfortable rooms in several price categories. Simple but well kept rooms cost from 300/400B with fan and private bath, and up to 450/550B with air-con. Facilities include a small coffee shop, garden, swimming pool and a classic 1950s lobby. The heavily annotated coffee shop menu offers a crash course in Thai cuisine that could prove very useful upcountry.

The *Golden Palace Hotel*, 15 Soi 1, Suk-humvit Thanon Si Phraya, has a swimming pool, is well situated and costs 400B to 500B for a double with air-con and bath. The clien-tele here are mostly middle-class tourists 'on a budget', but the Golden Palace has seen better days.

Farther up, at Soi 13, the *Miami Hotel* is one of the cheaper tourist hotels. It's all air-con now and costs 500/550B. There's a pool and coffee shop on the premises.

Places to Stay – Mid-Range

Banglamphu If you're looking for a little more comfort near Thanon Khao San, try the *Viengtai Hotel* (☎ 280 5434) at 42 Thanon Rambutri. Rooms start at 1000B in the old wing, a bit more in the new. All rooms have air-con, TVs, mini-fridges and phones. Of similar quality in this area is the *Thai Hotel* (☎ 282 2833), 78 Thanon Prachatipatai, where singles/doubles cost 1100/1250B.

Besides the Oriental and the Atlanta, the oldest continually operating hotel in the city is the Asian art deco-style *Royal Hotel* (☎ 222 9111), still going strong on the corner of Thanon Ratchadamnoen Klang and Thanon Atsadang near the Democracy Monument. The Royal's 24 hour coffee shop is a favourite local rendezvous; this is one of the few upper mid-range places where there are as many Asian as non-Asian guests. Rooms start at 960B; during low season this can sometimes be negotiated down to around 700B. Most taxi drivers know this hotel as the 'Ratana-kosin' (as the Thai sign on top of the building reads), not as the Royal.

Thanon Sukhumvit A bit nicer are the two *City Lodges* on soi 9 (☎ 253 7680) and soi 19 (☎ 254 4783). Rooms at either location are around 1000B, and include air-con, tele-phone, TV/video and minibar.

Airport If you have to stay near the airport, the least expensive option is *International House (formerly We-Train Guest House,*

THAILAND

☎ *566-1774, fax 566-3481)* at 501/1 Mu 3, Thanon Dechatungkha, Don Muang. Simple but clean fan rooms with private hot-water bath cost 500B or 700B with air-con (extra beds cost 150B). You can also get a bed in a fan-cooled dorm for 150B, air-con 200B.

Right across the road from the airport terminal (take the Airport Hotel pedestrian bridge), the Don Muang town area has lots of little shops, a market, many small restaurants and food stalls, and even a wat.

Places to Eat
Banglamphu & Around There are lots of cheap eating places around Banglamphu, including several on the ground floors of guesthouses in Thanon Khao San. For the most part they serve western food and Thai food prepared for western palates. None of them are particular standouts, though the adjacent *Orm* and *Wally House* produce fair Thai, western and vegetarian meals, while *Prakorp's House* makes good coffee. *Arawy Det*, an old Hokkien-style noodle shop on the corner of Khao San and Thanon Tanao, has somehow managed to stay authentic amid the cosmic swirl.

For more authentic fare, try the many Thai places along Thanon Rambutri, just north of Thanon Khao San. For an all-vegie menu at low prices, seek out the *Vegetarian Restaurant* at 117/1 Soi Wat Bowon, near Srinthip Guest House. Another good Thai vegetarian place in this district is *Arawy* (English sign reads 'Alloy'), which is south-east of Thanon Khao San, across Thanon Ratchadamnoen Klang at 152 Thanon Din So, opposite the City Hall.

The *Yok Yor* on Tha Samphraya has good seafood, a menu in English and main dishes costing from around 50B. The Yok Yor also operates a dinner cruise that offers the same menu with a reasonable 50B surcharge for boat service. Nearby is the similar *Chawn Ngoen*; it has no English sign, but there is an English menu.

Gulliver's Traveller's Tavern, at the corner of Thanon Khao San and Thanon Chakraphong, is a new, all-air-con restaurant-bar with a vaguely Hard Rock Cafe look and a substantial menu of Thai and international dishes.

Thanon Phra Athit, over towards the river, has some inexpensive *Thai restaurants* and *food stalls*.

Hualamphong Lots of good cheap restaurants, mostly Chinese, can be found along Thanon Rong Muang by the station. *Suki Jeh Yuu Seu* (English sign reads 'Health Food'), a Chinese vegetarian restaurant just 70m along Thanon Rama IV from Hualamphong train station, serves excellent, moderately priced vegetarian food in a very clean, air-con atmosphere.

Pahurat The *Royal India* at 392/1 Thanon Chakraphet is one of the better places in the Pahurat District; it's much better than the one on Thanon Khao San.

The ATM Shopping Centre, on Thanon Chakraphet opposite the Royal India, has an *Indian food centre* on the top floor. The alley alongside the centre features cheap *Indian food stalls* as well.

Siam Square The Siam Square sois have plenty of good places in varying price ranges. Try the big noodle restaurant *Coca* on Thanon Henri Dunant, close to Thanon Rama I. At 93/3 Soi Lang Suan, Thanon Ploenchit, the *Whole Earth Restaurant* does good, if somewhat expensive, Thai and Indian vegetarian food. The Whole Earth has a second branch on Soi 26, Thanon Sukhumvit.

Directly opposite Siam Centre on Thanon Rama I, there's a *KFC*, a *Dunkin' Donuts* and a string of other American-style fast-food eateries. *Uncle Ray's* has some of the best ice cream in Bangkok.

The 7th floor of the MBK, or Mahboonkrong Centre (on the south-west corner of Rama I and Thanon Phayathai), there's a good *Singapore-style food centre* with everything from steak and salad to Thai vegetarian fare. It's open from 10 am to 9 pm daily. On the 4th floor of the same building are a number of other *food vendors*, as well as several slightly upmarket *restaurants* serving western or Japanese food. At street level there's a host of *fast food places*.

At the intersection of Soi Kasem San I and Thanon Rama I there's the excellent, inexpensive *Thai Sa-Nguan* (no English sign) restaurant, where curry and rice is 15 to 20B a plate. Good *kuaythiaw* (rice noodles) and *khao man kai* (chicken rice) are also available here.

Silom & Surawong Opposite the Thanon Silom entrance to Soi Patpong, in the CP Tower building, there's a cluster of air-con American and Japanese-style fast food places: *McDonald's*, *Pizza Hut*, *Chester's Grilled Chicken*, *Suzuki Coffee House* and *Toplight*

Coffee House. Several are open late to catch the night-time Patpong traffic.

The *Brown Derby*, on Soi Patpong 1, is good for American-style deli sandwiches. Authentically decorated, *Delaney's Irish Pub* at 1-4 Sivadon Bldg, Thanon Convent in the Silom district serves a reasonably priced set lunch menu Monday to Friday, plus other pub grub daily. It also boasts Guinness on tap, imported wood panelling and live Irish music Tuesday to Saturday.

Halfway along Thanon Silom, across from the Narai Hotel, you can get good *Indian snacks* near the Tamil temple. For south Indian food, try the basic *Madras Cafe* in the Madras Lodge at 31/10-11 Vaithi Lane (Trok 13), off Thanon Silom near the Narai Hotel; it serves *idli* (south Indian rice pudding), *dosa*, a few other south Indian snacks and a selection of north Indian dishes.

There are several other interesting possibilities along Thanon Surawong, which is parallel to Thanon Silom; the reliable and moderately priced *Maria Bakery & Restaurant* at No 311/2-4 serves all manner of Thai and Vietnamese dishes, as well as pizza and pastries.

Thanon Sukhumvit The ancient-looking *Yong Lee Restaurant* at 211 Thanon Sukhumvit, near Soi 15 and Asia Books, does standard Thai and Chinese food – roast duck is a specialty.

On Soi 12, *Cabbages & Condoms*, famous for its name alone, is run by Thailand's hyperactive family planning association. The famous *Djit Pochana* has a branch on Soi 20 and is one of the best-value restaurants in town for traditional Thai dishes. The all-you-can-eat lunch buffet is 90B.

By Soi 17, there's the rather fancy Robinson's Department Store with a branch of *McDonald's* at street level and a basement supermarket and food centre, which features everything from *Dunkin' Donuts* to frozen yoghurt, ice cream, noodles and a variety of Thai food stands.

A few medium-to-expensive restaurants serving Pakistani and Middle Eastern food can be found in the 'Little Arabia' area of Soi 3 (Soi Nana Neua). The best value in the whole area is *Al Hossain*, a roofed outdoor cafe on the corner of a lane (Soi 3/5) off the east side of Soi Nana Neua. A steam table holds a range of vegetarian, chicken, mutton and fish curries, along with *dal* (curried lentils), *aloo gobi* (spicy potatoes and cauli-

flower), *nan* and rice. Dishes cost 20B to 40B each. *Shiraz* on the same soi is a slightly pricier indoor place that provides hookahs for Middle Eastern gentlemen who while away the afternoon smoking out front.

Entertainment

Bars Bangkok has definitely outgrown the days when the only bars around catered to male go-go oglers. The *Front Page*, a one-time journalists' hang-out (before the nearby *Bangkok Post* offices moved to Khlong Toey) on Soi 1, Sala Daeng (off Silom and Rama IV), is a good place for a low-key drink or three.

Brit-style taverns include *Jool's* on Soi 4, Thanon Sukhumvit, near Nana Entertainment Plaza, *Bull's Head* on the ground floor of Angus Steak House, Soi 33/1, Thanon Sukhumvit, and the *Witch's Tavern* at 306/1 Soi 55, Thanon Sukhumvit. The latter features live music on weekends.

Wong's Place at 27/3 Soi Si Bamphen is a low-key hangout for residents and visitors staying in the Soi Ngam Duphli area and sports a good collection of music videos.

Dance Clubs Well-heeled Thais and Thai celebrities frequent the more exclusive, high-tech *Narcissus* at 112 Soi 23, Thanon Sukhumvit. Of course all the major hotels contain discos – one of the most innovative is *CM2* at the Novotel Siam Square.

A string of small *dance clubs* on Soi 2 and Soi 4 (Soi Jaruwan) off Thanon Silom, both parallel to Patpong 1 and 2, attracts a nicely mixed crowd in terms of age, gender, nationality and sexual orientation. Recorded music here includes up-to-date techno, trance, hip-hop and other current dance trends. Check out Soi 4 for *Hyper, Rome Club* and *Sphinx*. The larger places collect cover charges of 100B to 300B depending on the night of the week; the smaller ones are free.

Go-Go Bars Patpong's infamous neon-lit buildings cover roughly four acres, though the typical bar measures 4m by 12m. These days it has more of an open-air market feel as several of the newer bars are literally on the street, and vendors set up shop in the evening hawking everything from roast squid to fake designer watches.

On Patpong's two parallel lanes there are around 38 go-go bars, plus a sprinkling of restaurants and cocktail bars. The downstairs clubs with names like *King's Castle* and *Pussy Galore* feature go-go dancing, while upstairs the sex shows are kept behind closed doors. Don't believe the touts on the street who say the upstairs shows – featuring amazing anatomical feats – are free; after the show, a huge bill usually arrives.

Another holdover from the R&R days is *Soi Cowboy*, a single-lane strip of 25 to 30 bars off Thanon Sukhumvit between sois 21 and 23. *Nana Entertainment Plaza*, off Soi 4 (Soi Nana Tai), Thanon Sukhumvit, is a three storey complex which has surged in popularity among resident and visiting oglers.

Live Music Along Soi Lang Suan and Thanon Sarasin, between Lumphini Park and Thanon Ploenchit, are several bars that feature live western pop, folk, blues, and jazz played by Thai bands. Among the most popular (and better) music bars are *Blue's Bar* and *Old West*.

Opposite the Asia Hotel on Thanon Phayathai is the *Rock Pub*, a hang-out for Thai metalheads. Bangkok has its own *Hard Rock Cafe*, at Siam Square Soi 11, with live music nightly beginning around 10 pm.

The three storey *Saxophone Pub Restaurant* has become an institution for musicians of several genres. It is at 3/8 Victory Monument, Thanon Phayathai, which is actually in a tiny soi south-east of the Victory Monument circle.

The Oriental's famous *Bamboo Bar* hosts live jazz nightly from 5 to 8.30 pm in an elegant but relaxed atmosphere; other hotel jazz bars include *Entrepreneur* at the Asia Hotel (Saturday night only), the Grand Hyatt's *Garden Lounge* (Tuesday through Sunday), the Beaufort Sukhothai Hotel's *Colonnade* (Tuesday through Sunday) and the Hilton's *The Lounge* (Friday night only).

Thai Classical Dance The *National Theatre*, located near the river in Banglamphu, periodically hosts Thai classical dance performances – call ☎ 224 1342 weekdays between 8.30 am and 4.30 pm for the current schedule. Special exhibition performances by the *Chulalongkorn University Dance Club* are offered once a month – ask at TAT for the latest schedule.

To see Thai classical dancing for free, hang out at the *Lak Muang Shrine* near Sanam Luang, or the *Erawan Shrine* next to the Grand Hyatt Erawan.

Several Bangkok restaurants sponsor dinner performances that feature a mix of dance and martial arts, all touristy (the food is usually nothing special), for around 250B to 500B.

Drag Shows Transvestite cabarets are big in Bangkok and several are found in the Patpong area. *Calypso Cabaret*, in the Asia Hotel on Thanon Phayathai, has the largest regularly performing transvestite troupe in town, with nightly shows at 8.30 and 10 pm.

Gay/Lesbian Scene See the comments on the Soi 4 Thanon Silom dance club scene under Dance Clubs for places that attract a gay/straight/bi clientele. Soi 4's *Telephone* is more exclusively gay (male) than other bars on this street. *Khrua Silom*, in Silom Alley off Soi 2, attracts a young Thai gay and lesbian crowd.

There's a cluster of seedier *gay bars* off Soi Anuman Ratchathon, off Thanon Silom opposite the Tawana Ramada Hotel – more or less the gay equivalent of Patpong.

Utopia (☎ 259 9619), at 116/1 Soi 23, Thanon Sukhumvit, is a combination bar, gallery, cafe and information clearing house for the local gay and lesbian community – the only such facility in South-East Asia.

Other lesbian venues include *By Heart Pub* at 117/697 Soi Sainanikhom 1, Bang Kapi, *Be My Guest*, around the corner from Utopia on Soi 31 Thanon Sukhumvit and *Obsession* in the Royal City Avenue Complex.

Muay Thai (Thai Boxing) Thai-style kickboxing can be seen regularly at two stadiums: *Lumphini* on Thanon Rama IV near Soi Ngam Duphli and *Ratchadamnoen* on Thanon Ratchadamnoen Nok. Admission prices start at around 180B and go up to 800B for ringside seats. The out-of-the-ring activity is sometimes even more frenzied and entertaining than that within the ring.

Shopping

Anything you can buy out in the country you can also get in Bangkok – sometimes the prices may even be lower. Thanon Silom and Thanon Charoen Krung (New Rd) are two good shopping areas that cater to tourists. Cheaper Thai-style shopping is available at Siam Square and Mahboonkrong Centre, both at the intersection of Thanon Rama I and Thanon Phayathai.

Better deals yet are available in Bangkok's large open-air markets at Chatuchak Park (Chatuchak Market), Yaowarat (Chinatown), Banglamphu, Pratunam and Pahurat. Things to look for include:

Cotton & Silk Lengths of cotton and the beautifully coloured and textured Thai silk can be made into clothes or household articles. There are some good shops along Thanon Silom but the fabric stalls in the Indian district of Pahurat are cheaper.

Clothes The Thais are very fashion-conscious and you can get stylish clothes ready made or made to measure at attractive prices. Mahboonkrong Centre near Siam Square and the small shops behind the Siam Square cinemas are two of the best places to shop for inexpensive clothes – also Chatuchak Market.

Gems Buyer beware. Unless you know stones, Bangkok is no place to seek out 'the big score'. *Never* accept an invitation from a tout or friendly stranger to visit a gem shop, as the visit will soon turn into a confidence game in which you're the pigeon. See Dangers & Annoyances in the Facts for the Visitor section of this chapter for more on gem scams.

Other Items Silver, bronze and nielloware (silver inlaid with black enamel) items include a variety of jewellery, plates, bowls and ornaments. Antiques are widely available but you'd better know what you're looking for. Temple bells and woodcarvings make nice souvenirs.

Chatuchak Market, opposite the Northern bus terminal is, of course, a great place to look for almost any oddity. Opposite Wat Mahathat or at Wat Ratchanatda, there are amulet markets, where you can buy protection against almost anything.

Getting There & Away
Bangkok is Thailand's travel hub. Unless you cross the border from Malaysia, Cambodia or Laos, this is the place where you're most likely to arrive. It's also the centre from where travel routes fan out across the country.

Air Bangkok is a major centre for international ticket discounting. It's also the centre for THAI's domestic flight schedules.

Some airline offices:

Bangkok Airways
  (☎ 229 3434)
  Queen Sirikit National Convention Centre, Thanon Ratchadaphisek Tat Mai, Khlong Toey
  (☎ 254 2903)
  1111 Thanon Ploenchit
Biman Bangladesh Airlines
  (☎ 235 7643)
  Chongkolnee Bldg, 56 Thanon Surawong

Cathay Pacific Airways
  (☎ 263 0606)
  11th floor, Ploenchit Tower, Thanon Ploenchit
Garuda Indonesia
  (☎ 285 6470/3)
  27th floor, Lumphini Tower,
  1168 Thanon Rama IV
Lao Aviation
  (☎ 236 9821)
  Silom Plaza, 491/17 Thanon Silom
Malaysia Airlines
  (☎ 236 5871; reservations ☎ 236 4705)
  98-102 Thanon Surawong
  (☎ 263 0565)
  20th floor, Ploenchit Tower, Thanon Ploenchit
Myanmar Airways International
  (☎ 267 5078)
  Charn Issara Tower, Thanon Rama IV
Philippine Airlines
  (☎ 234 2483, 233 2350)
  Chongkolnee Bldg, 56 Thanon Surawong
Silk Air
  (☎ 236 0303; reservations ☎ 236 0440)
  12th floor, Silom Centre Bldg, Thanon Silom
Singapore Airlines
  (☎ 236 0303; reservations ☎ 236 0440)
  12th floor, Silom Centre Bldg,
  2 Thanon Silom
Thai Airways International (THAI)
  (☎ 513 0121, reservations ☎ 628 2000/ 280 0060)
  89 Thanon Vibhavadi Rangsit
  (☎ 234 3100)
  485 Thanon Silom
  (☎ 280 0060)
  6 Thanon Lan Luang
  (☎ 215 2020)
  Asia Hotel, 296 Thanon Phayathai
Vietnam Airlines (Hang Khong Vietnam)
  (☎ 251 4242)
  3rd floor, 572 Thanon Ploenchit

Bus The Bangkok bus terminals (all with left-luggage facilities) are:

North & North-East
  Northern & North-Eastern bus terminal (☎ 279 4484), Thanon Phahonyothin. On the road to the airport; for buses to Ayuthaya, Sukhothai, Chiang Mai and Chiang Rai, plus towns in the north-east.
East
  Eastern bus terminal (☎ 391 2504), Soi 40 (Ekamai), Thanon Sukhumvit. For Pattaya and all points east.
South
  Southern bus terminal (☎ 434 5558 ordinary, ☎ 391 9829 air-con), Hwy 338 and Thanon Phra Pinklao. For buses to Nakhon Pathom, Kanchanaburi, Hua Hin, Surat Thani, Phuket, Hat Yai and all other points south.

Train There are two main train stations. The big Hualamphong station on Thanon Rama IV handles services to the north, north-east and most of the services to the south. The Thonburi, or Bangkok Noi, station handles some services to the south. If you're heading south ascertain from which station your train departs.

Getting Around

To/From the Airport Bangkok airport is 25km north of the city centre and there is a variety of ways of getting back and forth.

Airport Bus A relatively new airport express bus service operates from Bangkok international airport to three different Bangkok districts for 70B per person. Buses run every 15 minutes from 5 am to 11 pm.

A-1 goes to the Thanon Silom business district via Pratunam and Thanon Ratchadamri, stopping at big hotels like the Indra, Grand Hyatt Erawan, Regent Bangkok and Dusit Thani.

A-2 goes to Sanam Luang via Thanon Phayathai, Thanon Lan Luang, Thanon Ratchadamnoen Klang and Thanon Tanao; this is the one you want if you're going to the Siam Square or Banglamphu areas.

A-3 goes to the Phrakhanong District via Thanon Sukhumvit.

City Bus Just a few steps outside the airport there's a highway that leads straight into the city. Air-con bus No 29 costs 16B and plies one of the most useful, all-purpose routes into town because it goes to the Siam Square and Hualamphong areas. After entering the city limits via Thanon Phahonyothin (which turns into Thanon Phayathai), the bus passes Thanon Phetburi (where you get off to change buses for Banglamphu), then Thanon Rama I at the Siam Square/Mahboonkrong intersection (for buses out to Thanon Sukhumvit, or to walk to Soi Kasem San 1 for Muangphol Mansion,) and finally turns right on Thanon Rama IV to go to the Hualamphong District. You'll want to go the opposite way on Rama IV for the Soi Ngam Duphli lodging area. Bus No 29 runs only from 5.45 am to 8 pm.

Air-con bus No 4 (16B, from 5.45 am to 8 pm) begins with a route parallel to that of bus No 29 – down Thanon Mittaphap to Thanon Ratchaprarop and Thanon Ratchadamri (Pratunam District), crossing Phetburi, Rama I, Ploenchit and Rama IV, then down Silom, left on Charoen Krung, and across the river to Thonburi.

Alternatively, bus No 13 from the airport goes down Thanon Phahonyothin, it turns left at the Victory Monument to Thanon Ratchaprarop, then travels south to Thanon Ploenchit and east on Thanon Sukhumvit all the way to Bang Na. These air-con buses stop running at 8 pm.

Minibus A THAI minibus goes to most major hotels (and some minor ones, if the driver's in the mood) for 100B per person. Departure times seem to be erratic.

Minibuses depart regularly for the airport from the Thanon Khao San accommodation enclave. They charge 50B.

Train The railway into Bangkok runs near the airport. You can get a train straight to Hualamphong station for 10B in 3rd class, 50B if you happen onto a rapid or express train. Walk over the enclosed pedestrian bridge from the international terminal to the Amari Airport Hotel. The train station is right in front of the hotel. The departure times aren't always that convenient, however, and of course you have to lug your bag(s) a long way. It's timed for commuters to or from work, not for passengers to or from the airport.

Taxi Greedy THAI touts try to steer all arriving passengers towards one of their expensive limousine services, which are just glorified air-con taxi services costing up to twice as much as a regular taxi. Just ignore them and head straight left out of the arrival hall to an exit marked 'Public Taxi'. Outside are two queues, one for metered taxis, and one for flat-fare taxis. Metered taxis from the airport cost 150B to 250B or so, depending on your destination, while the flat-fare taxis cost around 100B more. The catch is that for the metered taxis the passengers must pay highway tolls (up to 50B), plus an airport service charge of 50B, so the fares work out to be about the same either way.

Bus The Bangkok bus service is frequent and frantic, so a bus map is an absolute necessity. Get one from the tourist office or from bookshops and news stands for 35B to 40B. Buses are all numbered and the map is easy to follow. Don't expect it to be 100% correct though, as routes change regularly.

Fares for ordinary buses vary according to the type of bus: from 2.50B (green or blue buses) to 3.50B (red buses) for any journey under 10km; over 10km it jumps as high as 5B – out to the airport for example.

Bus No 17 does a useful circuit of the city attractions terminating near the National Museum and Emerald Buddha.

There are also a number of public air-con buses with numbers that may cause confusion with the regular buses. They start at 6B but jump to 16B on the long trips. Apart from the cool comfort, the air-con buses are less crowded, especially in comparison with the mayhem on the regular buses. Even less crowded are the red Microbuses, which stop taking passengers once every seat is filled and collect a 20B flat fare.

Taxi & Tuk-Tuk Around central Bangkok, metered taxi fares should generally run from 50B to 75B (35B at flagfall, plus 2B for each additional time/distance increment). Although detours may be necessary to avoid traffic snarls, some drivers try to pad fares by driving around in circles. As with bus fares, expect these base fares to rise as the baht lowers in value against the dollar, and fuel prices increase.

You must fix fares in advance for other taxis or the tuk-tuks. The latter are really only useful for shorter trips. When the distances get longer they often become more expensive than regular taxis. You often need real endurance to withstand a long tuk-tuk trip – and half the time the drivers don't know their way around Bangkok anyway.

Motorcycle Taxi Motorcycle taxis have moved from the soi to the main avenues. Fares for a motorcycle taxi are about the same as tuk-tuks except during heavy traffic, when they may cost a bit more. Keep your legs tucked in if you're tall – the drivers are used to carrying passengers with shorter legs than those of the average farang and they pass perilously close to other vehicles while weaving in and out of traffic.

Boat River travel through and around Bangkok is not only much more interesting and peaceful than fighting your way through town in a bus or taxi, it is also much faster. There are a number of regular services along the Chao Phraya river and adjoining khlong. Boats also buzz back and forth across the river from numerous points.

Easiest to use and understand is the *Chao Phraya River Express* – a big, long boat with a number on the roof – that runs up and down

the river, although it only stops at certain landing stages, like the Oriental Hotel. This river-bus service costs 6B to 10B, depending on the distance you travel, and you buy your ticket on the boat.

Bangkok still has quite a few khlong but it's no longer the 'Venice of the east'. Routes still open include Khlong Saen Saep, the canal between the Democracy Monument area and the Ramkhamhaeng University area, along which long-tailed boats run. The boat from Banglamphu to the University costs 10B and takes only 20 minutes; a bus would take nearly an hour under normal traffic conditions.

Around Bangkok

There are a number of interesting places within day-trip distance of Bangkok – some also make interesting stepping stones on your way north, east or south. You can stop at Ayuthaya on your way north, for example, or Nakhon Pathom on your way south.

The **Ancient City** (Muang Boran) is an 80 hectare complex with scaled-down replicas of Thailand's more famous historic sites. It's 33km south of Bangkok. Admission is a reasonable 50B and you can get there by taking bus No 25 or air-con bus Nos 7, 8 or 11 from Thanon Sukhumvit to Pak Nam, and then taking a small local bus. It's open daily from 8 am to 5 pm.

In the same area there is a **Samut Prakan Crocodile Farm & Zoo**, where over 30,000 crocs are kept, as well as elephants, monkeys and snakes. The farm is open from 7 am to 6 pm daily with trained animal shows – including croc wrestling – every hour between 9 and 11 am, and 1 and 4 pm daily. Admission is a steep 300B for adults, 200B for children. items certified under the UN Convention on International Trade in Endangered Species (CITES), such as crocodile hide handbags, belts and shoes are available from the farm's gift shop. You can reach the croc farm on air-con bus Nos 7, 8 or 11, changing to songthaew Nos S1 or S80.

AYUTHAYA

This was the Thai capital until its destruction by the Burmese in 1767. It is 86km north of Bangkok. Built at the junction of three rivers, an artificial channel has converted the town into an island. To find your way around, get a copy of the excellent guidebook and map available from the Chan Kasem Palace Museum here or in Bangkok.

CENTRAL AYUTHAYA

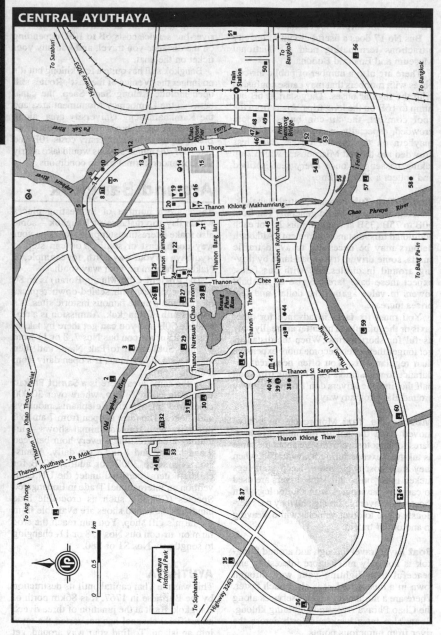

CENTRAL AYUTHAYA

PLACES TO STAY		17	Duangporn Restaurant	31	Wat Phra Si Sanphet
10	U-Thong Hotel	19	Moon Café	32	Royal Palace
12	Cathay Hotel	21	Vegetarian Restaurant	33	Wat Lokaya Sutha
18	Ayothaya Hotel	47	Floating Restaurants	34	Wat Chetharam
20	Ayuthaya Guest House;	53	Phae Krung Kao	35	Wat Kasatthirat
	Old BJ Guest House;			36	Wat Chai Wattanaram
	PU Guest House	OTHER		37	Queen Suriyothai Memorial
22	Thai Thai Bungalow	1	Phu Khao Thong Temple		Pagoda
23	New BJ Guest House		(Golden Mount Chedi)	38	City Hall
24	Thongchai Guest House	2	Wat Phra Mehn	39	TAT Office
43	Suan Luang (Royal Garden)	3	Wat Kuti Thong	40	Tourist Police
	Hotel	4	Elephant Kraal	41	Chao Sam Phraya National
45	Wieng Fa Hotel	6	U Thong Pier (Boat Landing)		Museum
46	Ayuthaya Youth Hostel	8	Chan Kasem Palace	42	Wat Phra Ram
48	Tevaraj Tanrin Hotel	9	Main Post Office	44	Ayuthaya Historical Study
49	Krungsri River Hotel	14	Air-Con Minivans to Bangkok		Centre
50	U-Thong Inn	15	Chao Phrom Market	54	Wat Suwan Dararam
51	Ayuthaya Grand Hotel	16	Bus Station	55	Phet Fortress
52	Phaesri Guest House	25	Chinese Shrine	56	Wat Yai Chai Mongkhon
		26	Wat Suwannawat	57	Wat Phanan Choeng
PLACES TO EAT		27	Wat Ratburana	58	Ayuthaya Historical Study
5	Hua Raw Night Market	28	Wat Phra Mahathat		Centre (Annex)
7	Night Market	29	Wat Thammikarat	59	Mosque
11	Chainam	30	Wihaan Phra Mongkhon	60	Wat Phutthaisawan
13	Rodeo Saloon		Bophit	61	St Joseph's Cathedral

During the 10 days leading to the Songkran Festival in mid-April, there is a sound and light show with fireworks over the ruins of old wats. This is a great time to visit Ayuthaya, but you might want to take refuge in a smaller town during the final water-throwing days of Songkran itself, unless you fancy staying wet for the day. Loi Krathong – when tiny votive boats are floated on rivers and ponds as a tribute to the River Goddess – is another good time to be in Ayuthaya.

On the Island

Places to see are either 'on the island' or 'off the island'. There's a 20B to 30B admission charge to some of the ruins between 8 am and 4.30 pm. The best way to see the ruins is by bicycle, which can be rented at guesthouses. Tuk-tuk tours cost 200B to 300B for a day's sightseeing.

The **Chao Sam Phraya National Museum** is open Wednesday to Sunday from 9 am to 4 pm. Admission is 30B. There's a second national museum at the **Chan Kasem Palace**; the opening hours and admission are the same.

The **Wat Phra Si Sanphet** is the old royal temple and has three restored chedis. The adjacent **Wihaan Phra Mongkon Bophit** houses a huge bronze seated Buddha. **Wat Thammikarat** is particularly appealing because of its

overgrown, deserted feeling and the stone lions guarding a toppling chedi.

Wat Suwannawat was built towards the close of the Ayuthaya period and has been completely and very colourfully restored. **Wat Ratburana** and **Wat Phra Mahathat** are both extensively ruined but majestic.

Off the Island

The **Wat Phra Chao Phanan Choeng** was a favourite of Chinese traders and has a big seated Buddha. **Wat Chai Wattanaram** used to be one of Ayuthaya's most overgrown, evocative-of-a-lost-city type of ruins, with stately lines of disintegrating Buddhas. Today, some hard restoration work (and the wonders of modern cement) has produced a row of lookalike brand-new Buddhas. It's still a lovely wat with nice gardens.

The **Golden Mount** to the north-west of the city has a wide view over the flat country. Also to the north is the **elephant kraal** (enclosure) – the last of its kind in Thailand. **Wat Yai Chai Mongkon** to the south-east has a massive ruined chedi, which contrasts with surrounding contemporary Buddha statues.

For a historical overview of the Ayuthaya period, check out the **Ayuthaya Historical Study Centre** near Suan Luang Hotel on Thanon Rotchana. Japanese-funded, this ambitious facility houses hi-tech displays that cover not only art and archaeology, but also the social and political history of the period.

Wat Phra Mehn, opposite the old royal palace *(wang luang)* grounds via a bridge, is notable because it escaped destruction in 1767. The main *bot* (chapel) was built in 1546 and features fortress-like walls and pillars.

Places to Stay – Budget

Guesthouses The *Ayuthaya Guest House* (☎ 25 1468) is down a soi off Thanon Naresuan, near the bus terminal and the Sri Smai Hotel. Rates are 120/160B for singles/doubles. Next door a branch of the same family runs the *Old BJ Guest House* (☎ 25 1526) at slightly lower rates. Both offer food and bike rentals.

The *New BJ Guest House* (☎ 24 4046), 19/29 Thanon Naresuan, has clean rooms for 60B dorm, 120B, and a nice eating area in front.

Almost directly across the river from the train station, in an old teak house, is the *Ayuthaya Youth Hostel* (☎ 24 1978), also known as Reuan Derm, at 48/2 Thanon U Thong. Plain rooms with ceiling fans and shared bath cost 200B for small rooms, 250B for larger ones.

Hotels The *U-Thong Hotel* (☎ 25 1136), on Thanon U Thong near the boat landing and the Chan Kasem Palace, is noisy but otherwise tolerable; recently upgraded rooms are 260/320B with fan or 370/490B with air-con and hot water. A few shops down, the *Cathay Hotel* (☎ 25 1562) is a less expensive, but grungier, choice at 150/270B with fan, 300B with air-con.

At 13/1 Thanon Naresuan (actually in an alley off Naresuan), the *Thai Thai Bungalow* (☎ 25 1505) has basic but OK rooms with bath from 80/120B up to 300B with air-con.

Places to Stay – Mid-Range

The *Ayothaya Hotel* (☎ 25 2249), formerly Sri Smai Hotel, 12 Thetsaban Soi 2, just off Thanon Naresuan, is a more upmarket place with comfortable air-con rooms with minibar, cable TV and phone for 900B. A swimming pool is available.

Places to Eat

There are lots of places to eat in Ayuthaya, including the *night market* opposite the Chan Kasem Palace. The *Chainam*, opposite Chan Kasem Palace next to the Cathay Hotel, has

tables on the river, a bilingual menu and friendly service; it's also open for breakfast.

The artsy *Moon Cafe*, a tiny spot on the same soi as Ayuthaya Guest House, serves Thai and farang food for 30B to 50B per dish, also beer and espresso.

There are a couple of *floating restaurants* on the river near the Pridi Damrong Bridge, worth considering for a splurge. The *Phae Krung Kao* has a good local reputation – it's on the south side of the bridge on the west bank.

Getting There & Away

Bus There are buses to Ayuthaya from the Northern bus terminal in Bangkok every 10 minutes; the 1½ hour trip costs 22B. The first bus is at 5 am and the last at 7 pm.

Train There are frequent trains from the Hualamphong station; the 3rd class fare is 15B and the travelling time is the same as the buses. The Ayuthaya station is some distance from the town centre, but at the Bangkok end, taking the train saves you trekking out to the Northern bus terminal. After getting off at Ayuthaya, the quickest way to reach the old city is to walk west to the river, where a short ferry ride will take you across to the Chao Phrom pier for 1B.

A tuk-tuk from the Ayuthaya train station into town will cost no more than 20B.

Boat There are no scheduled or chartered boat services between Bangkok and Ayuthaya.

Several companies in Bangkok operate luxury cruises to Bang Pa In with side trips by bus to Ayuthaya for around 1000B to 1200B per person, including a lavish luncheon.

Getting Around

The cheapest way to see the town is by rented bicycle – 40B to 50B per day from the Ayuthaya or New BJ guesthouses. You can also hire a taxi or samlor by the hour (150B) or by the day (400B) to explore the ruins. Or get a group of people together and hire a boat from the Palace pier to do a circular tour of the island and see some of the less accessible ruins. Figure on about 300B for a three hour trip with a maximum of eight passengers.

During the Songkran Festival in April, the local government runs daily boat tours from the U Thong pier for a bargain 50B per person.

Songthaews and shared tuk-tuks ply the main routes for 5B per person.

BANG PA IN

The **Royal Palace** in Bang Pa In has a strange collection of buildings in Chinese, Italian and Gothic style, and a Thai-style pavilion in a small lake. It's not all that interesting, but makes a pleasant riverboat trip from Ayuthaya, which is 20km to the north. Admission is 50B and the palace is open daily from 8.30 am to 3.30 pm. Across the river from the palace is an unusual church-like wat reached by a free trolley-cum-cable-car.

Getting There & Away

There are minibuses (or large songthaew trucks) between Bang Pa In and Ayuthaya every 15 minutes. The short trip costs 10B.

From Bangkok's northern bus terminal, there are ordinary buses to Bang Pa In every half hour from 6 am to 6 pm; the fare is 17B.

LOPBURI

Situated 154km north of Bangkok, this former capital of the Khmer Lavo period (10th century) shows strong Hindu and Khmer influences in its temple and palace ruins.

Orientation & Information

The new town of Lopburi is some distance east of the old fortified town and is centred on two large roundabouts. There is really nothing of interest in the new section, so try to stay at a hotel in the old town if you're interested in the palace and temple ruins.

Tourist Offices There's a TAT office (☎ 42 2768) in the Sala Jangwat (Provincial Hall) in new Lopburi.

Phra Narai Ratchaniwet

This former palace of King Narai is a good place to begin a tour of Lopburi. Built between 1665 and 1677, it was designed by French and Khmer architects – an unusual blend that works quite well. The main gate is off Thanon Sorasak, opposite the Asia Lopburi Hotel. Inside the grounds are the remains of the royal elephant stables, a reservoir, a reception hall, various pavilions and residence halls, and the **Lopburi National Museum**.

The museum is housed in three separate buildings, which contain an excellent collection of Lopburi period sculpture, as well as an assortment of Khmer, Dvaravati, U Thong and Ayuthaya art, traditional farm implements and dioramas of farm life. It's open Wednesday to Sunday from 8.30 am to noon

and from 1 to 4 pm. Admission into the palace grounds is free; museum entry is 20B.

Other Ruins

Most important is the **Prang Sam Yot**, or Sacred Three Spires, which was originally built as a Hindu shrine and is reckoned to be the finest Khmer structure in the region. **Prang Khaek** and **Wat Phra Si Ratana Mahathat** are also notable.

Phaulkon's House, the home of the Greek adviser to Ayuthaya during its heyday, is also in Lopburi. Phaulkon was beheaded by the king's ministers when he began courting French influence in the area.

Places to Stay & Eat

You can do a day trip to Lopburi from Ayuthaya. If you want to stay, the hotels on Thanon Na Kala, close to the train station, are about the cheapest. On Thanon Na Kala, opposite Wat Nakhon Kosa, the *Indra* costs 140B for clean, spacious rooms with fan and bath, or 300B air-con. On the same road, but closer to the train station, the *Julathip* (which doesn't have a sign in English) has rooms with fan and bath for 140B – but ask to see them first.

Still on Thanon Na Kala, the *Supara-phong* is not far from Wat Phra Sri Ratana Mahathat and the train station. It's similar in price and standard to the Julathip. Overlooking King Narai's palace, the *Asia Lopburi* (☎ 41 1892) is on the corner of Thanon Sorasak and Thanon Phra Yam Jamkat. It's clean and comfortable and has two Chinese restaurants downstairs. Rooms are 160/200B with fan and bath, and up to 400B with air-con.

Muang Thong (☎ 41 1036), across from Prang Sam Yot, has noisy but adequate rooms for 130/150B with fan and bath, plus some cheaper rooms without bath for 100B.

There are several *Chinese restaurants* along Thanon Na Kala, parallel to the railway line, but they tend to be a bit pricey. The places on the side streets of Ratchadamnoen and Phra Yam Jamkat are better value.

At 26/47 Soonkangkha Manora, near the Australian Education Placement Centre, there's a *Sala Mangsawirat* (vegetarian pavilion) with inexpensive Thai vegie food; like most Thai vegetarian restaurants, it's only open from around 9 am to 2 pm.

Getting There & Away

Bus Ordinary buses leave about every 10 minutes from Ayuthaya or every 20 minutes

THAILAND

from Bangkok's northern bus terminal – the three hour trip costs 40B; less frequent air-con ones are 72B. From Kanchanaburi, you can get to Lopburi via Suphanburi and Singh-buri on a series of public buses or share taxis.

Train You can reach Lopburi from Bangkok by train for 28/64B in 3rd/2nd class. One way of visiting Lopburi on the way north is to take the train from Ayuthaya (or Bangkok) early in the morning, leave your gear at the station for the day while you look around and then continue north on the night train.

Getting Around

Samlors go anywhere in old Lopburi for 20B. Songthaews run a regular route between the old and new towns for 5B per person.

SARABURI

There's nothing of interest in Saraburi itself, but between here and Lopburi you can turn off to the **Phra Phutthabat**. This small, deli-cate and beautiful shrine houses a revered Buddha footprint. Like all genuine Buddha footprints, it is massive and identified by its 108 auspicious distinguishing marks. In Feb-ruary and March there are pilgrimage festivals at the shrine.

Places to Stay

Try the *Thanin* or *Suk San* at Amphoe Phra Phutthabat – both cost 120B to 200B for fan rooms.

In town, the *Kyo-Un (Kiaw An,* ☎ *22 2022)* on Thanon Phahonyothin has nicer rooms from 450B.

Other hotels include the slightly cheaper *Saraburi (*☎ *21 1646)* opposite the bus stand.

NAKHON PATHOM

Nakhon Pathom is regarded as the oldest city in Thailand – it was conquered by Angkor in the early 11th century and in 1057 was sacked by Anawrahta of Bagan (Burma). At 127m, the gigantic orange-tiled **Phra Pathom Chedi**, in Nakhon Pathom, is the tallest Bud-dhist monument in the world. It was begun in 1853 to cover the original chedi of the same name. There is a museum near the chedi, and outside the town is the pleasant park of **Sanam Chan** – the grounds of the palace of Rama VI. In November, there's a **Phra Pathom Chedi Fair** that packs in everyone from fruit vendors to fortune tellers.

From Nakhon Pathom, you can make an excursion to the **floating market** at Klong Damnoen Saduak. This has become a very popular, less-touristy alternative to the over-commercialised Bangkok floating market. To get there, hop on a bus bound for Samut Songkhram to the south and ask to be let off in Damnoen Saduak or *talaat nam* (floating market). Go early in the morning, around 6 or 7 am, to avoid the tourist hordes from Bangkok.

Places to Stay & Eat

On Thanon Lungphra, near the train station, the *Mitsamphan Hotel (*☎ *24 2422)* has rooms for 180B with fan and bath – more with air-con. The *Mitrthaworn (Mittaowan)*, on the right as you walk towards the chedi from the train station, has rooms at 240/260B with fan and bath, 340B for air-con.

The *Mitphaisan* (its English sign says 'Mitr Paisal') is farther down the alley to the right from the Mittaowan and has rooms from 250 to 300B. All three 'Mit' hotels are owned by the same family. The Mitphaisan seems best this time around.

There's an excellent *fruit market* along the road between the train station and the Phra Pathom Chedi. *Song Saen*, on Thanon Rat-chadamnoen a few blocks directly west of Phra Pathom Chedi, offers a pleasant Thai sala setting with good, medium-priced Thai food.

Getting There & Away

Nakhon Pathom is 56km west of Bangkok. Every weekend there's a special rail trip to Nakhon Pathom and on to Kanchanaburi. Otherwise, you can get there by bus from the Southern bus terminal in Bangkok, or by rail. Buses leave every 10 minutes and cost 16B for the one hour trip. The rail fare is 14B in 3rd class.

RATCHABURI

More often abbreviated Rat-buri, this provin-cial capital is on the way south from Nakhon Pathom, well before you get to the coast and Hua Hin. Ratchaburi is well-known among Thais for its ceramics industry, particularly the large brown-glazed water jars etched with cream-coloured dragon motifs (from which they get their common farang name, 'dragon jars').

The *Kuang Hua Hotel (*☎ *33 7119)*, 202 Thanon Amarin, has reasonable but basic rooms for 150B with fan and bath, or 120B with shared facilities.

KANCHANABURI

Kanchanaburi (pronounced Kan-cha-NA-buri), 130km west of Bangkok, is often referred to as Muang Kan. The infamous bridge over the River Kwai (actually Khwae) was built here during WWII.

The graves of thousands of Allied soldiers can be seen in Kanchanaburi or you can take a train across the bridge and continue farther west, where there are caves, waterfalls and a Neolithic burial site. The bridge that stands today is not the one constructed during the war – that was destroyed by Allied air raids – though the curved portions of the structure are original.

The town was founded by Rama I as protection against Burmese invasion over the Three Pagodas Pass, which is still a major smuggling route into Myanmar. Today it's a favourite spot for Thais and foreigners alike.

Information

There's a TAT office near the bus terminal.

Death Railway Bridge

The bridge made famous by the film *Bridge on the River Kwai* spans the Khwae Yai river, a tributary of the Mae Klong river, a couple of kilometres north of town. The bridge was a small but strategic part of the Death Railway to Burma and was in use for 20 months before the Allies bombed it in 1945.

During the first week of December every year there's a nightly sound and light show at the bridge. It's a pretty impressive scene, with the sounds of bombers and explosions and fantastic bursts of light. The town gets a lot of tourists during this week, so book early.

Get to the bridge from town by catching a songthaew (5B) along Thanon Pak Phraek (parallel to Thanon Saengchuto, close to the river) heading north. You can also take a train from the Kanchanaburi train station to the bridge for 2B.

JEATH War Museum

This interesting little outdoor museum is run by monks. It's set up just like a POW camp on the actual site of a wartime camp. Entry is 30B and it's worth seeing. It's estimated that 16,000 western POWs died in the construction of the Death Railway to Burma but the figures for labourers, many forcibly conscripted from Thailand, Burma, Indonesia and Malaysia, were even worse. As many as 100,000 to 150,000 may have died in this area during WWII.

Other Attractions

There are two Allied **war cemeteries** near Kanchanaburi, one just north of town, off Thanon Saengchuto near the train station, and the other across the river west of town, a few kilometres down the Khwae Noi tributary. The town also has an interesting **Lak Muang**, or city pillar shrine, on Thanon Lak Muang, two blocks north-west of the tourist office.

Wat Tham Mongkon Thong is famous for its 'Floating Nun', who meditates while floating in a pool of water, an attraction that draws daily bus-loads of Thai and Chinese tourists. This cave temple is some distance south-west of town.

Places to Stay

Guesthouses You can stay on the river in a raft house (or over the river in bungalows built on piers) for around 60B to 80B per person. At the junction of the Khwae Yai and Khwae Noi rivers is the well run *Nita Raft House* (☎ 51 4521), where singles/doubles with mosquito net are 100/120B with shared bath.

Two other popular places of this sort are the *River View* and *VN* guesthouses, where small, basic rooms are 70/100B, more with private bath. Both are on the river, not far from the train station. One drawback to these places, especially on weekends and holidays, is the presence of floating disco rafts that cruise up and down blasting pop music nearly all night long.

North of the VN and River View guesthouses is the popular *Jolly Frog Backpacker's* (☎ 51 4579). It costs 60/110B for a room with veranda, mosquito screens and shared bath, or 150B with private bath. Other places come and go but they're all pretty similar. In the floating restaurant area there's the well run *Sam's Place*, where rooms with shared bath start at 100B.

If you want to stay out near the bridge, the *Bamboo House* (☎ 51 2532), 3-5 Soi Vietnam, on the river about a kilometre before the Japanese War Memorial, has quiet double rooms for 100B with shared bath, or up to 450B with air-con. The newer *C&C River Kwai Guest House*, nearby, is also good.

The *VL Guest House*, across the street from the River Kwai Hotel in the middle of town, is good value: clean, spacious rooms with fan and bath are 150B for singles or doubles, and larger rooms holding four to eight people cost 50B per person. The VL has a small dining area downstairs and they rent bicycles and motorbikes.

THAILAND

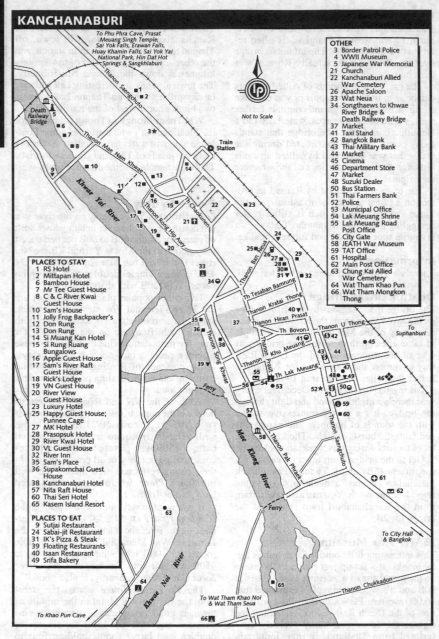

KANCHANABURI

To Phu Phra Cave, Prasat
Meuang Singh Temple,
Sai Yok Falls, Erawan Falls,
Huay Khamin Falls, Sai Yok Yai
National Park, Hin Dat Hot
Springs & Sangkhlaburi

Death
Railway
Bridge

Not to Scale

Train
Station

Khwae Yai River

Mae Klong River

Khwae Noi River

To Khao Pun Cave

To Wat Tham Khao Noi
& Wat Tham Seua

To Suphanburi

To City Hall
& Bangkok

Thanon Chukkadon

PLACES TO STAY
1 RS Hotel
2 Mittapan Hotel
6 Bamboo House
7 Mr Tee Guest House
8 C & C River Kwai
   Guest House
10 Sam's House
11 Jolly Frog Backpacker's
12 Don Rung
13 Don Rung
14 Si Muang Kan Hotel
15 Si Rung Ruang
   Bungalows
16 Apple Guest House
17 Sam's River Raft
   Guest House
18 Rick's Lodge
19 VN Guest House
20 River View
   Guest House
23 Luxury Hotel
25 Happy Guest House;
   Punnee Cage
27 MK Hotel
28 Prasopsuk Hotel
29 River Kwai Hotel
30 VL Guest House
32 River Inn
35 Sam's Place
36 Supakornchai Guest
   House
38 Kanchanaburi Hotel
57 Nita Raft House
60 Thai Seri Hotel
65 Kasem Island Resort

PLACES TO EAT
9 Sutjai Restaurant
24 Sabai-jit Restaurant
31 IK's Pizza & Steak
39 Floating Restaurants
40 Isaan Restaurant
49 Srifa Bakery

OTHER
3 Border Patrol Police
4 WWII Museum
5 Japanese War Memorial
21 Church
22 Kanchanaburi Allied
   War Cemetery
26 Apache Saloon
33 Wat Neua
34 Songthaews to Khwae
   River Bridge &
   Death Railway Bridge
37 Market
41 Taxi Stand
42 Bangkok Bank
43 Thai Military Bank
44 Market
45 Cinema
46 Department Store
47 Market
48 Suzuki Dealer
50 Bus Station
51 Thai Farmers Bank
52 Police
53 Municipal Office
54 Lak Meuang Shrine
55 Lak Meuang Road
   Post Office
56 City Gate
58 JEATH War Museum
59 TAT Office
61 Hospital
62 Main Post Office
63 Chung Kai Allied
   War Cemetery
64 Wat Tham Khao Pun
66 Wat Tham Mongkon
   Thong

Hotels The *Luxury Hotel* (☎ 51 1168) is a couple of blocks north of the River Kwai Hotel and offers clean rooms from 100B.

Places to Eat

There are plenty of places to eat along the northern end of Thanon Saengchuto near the River Kwai Hotel. The quality can usually be judged by the size of the crowds. Good, inexpensive eating can also be found in the markets along Thanon Prasit and between Thanon U Thong and Thanon Lak Muang, east of Thanon Saengchuto.

The *Sabai-jit* restaurant, just north of the River Kwai Hotel, has an English menu and consistently good food.

Down on the river, there are several large *floating restaurants* where it's hard not to enjoy the atmosphere, even if the quality of the food varies. Across from the floating restaurants along the road are several smaller, cheaper *food stalls* which open in the evenings.

Getting There & Away

Bus Regular buses leave Bangkok every 20 minutes daily for Kanchanaburi from the Southern bus terminal in Thonburi. The trip takes about three hours and costs 34B. Air-con buses leave every 15 minutes and cost 62B. The last bus back to Bangkok leaves Kanchanaburi around 10 pm.

Train The regular train costs 28B for 3rd class. There are only two a day and they both leave from the Bangkok Noi station in Thonburi, not from Hualamphong.

Share Taxi & Minivan You can take a share taxi from Thanon Saengchuto to Bangkok for 70B per person. Taxis leave throughout the day whenever five passengers accumulate at the taxi stand. These taxis will make drops at Thanon Khao San or in the Pahurat District. Guesthouses in Kanchanaburi also arrange daily minivans to Bangkok for 90B per person, with drop-offs at Thanon Khao San.

Getting Around

You can hire motorbikes from the Suzuki dealer near the bus terminal. The cost is 150B per day and they are a good way of getting to the rather scattered attractions around Kanchanaburi.

Samlors within the city are 20B a trip. Regular songthaews in town are 5B, but be careful you don't accidentally 'charter' one, because it'll be a lot more.

AROUND KANCHANABURI

Numerous interesting excursions can be made from Kanchanaburi.

Waterfalls

The **Erawan Falls** make an interesting bus trip (1½ to two hours) beyond Kanchanaburi. There's a 25B admission charge to a 2km footpath which goes along the river and past seven waterfalls. There are plenty of good plunge pools, so take along your swimming gear.

To get to the falls take an early morning bus from the station; it costs 21B to the end of the line, from where you have to walk a couple of kilometres to the start of the waterfall trail. Make an early start since the last bus back is at 4 pm. For the lazy – or those with the money – minibuses cruise by the river guesthouses at around 9 am daily and take passengers right into Erawan Park for 60B per person – they return around 3.30 pm.

Other waterfalls are generally too far from Kanchanaburi for a day trip. For overnighters, the **Huay Khamin** falls are one of the most interesting but getting there can be difficult. The 45km road from Erawan is in very bad condition and it takes at least two hours by motorcycle or rugged 4WD (you must bring your own transport). The falls can also be reached by a similarly rugged – and much longer – dirt road from Route 323 north of Thong Pha Phum.

Other Attractions

There are a few places of interest along the road to Sangkhlaburi. From Kanchanaburi, take the Nam Tok Sai Yok road. A few kilometres past the river you can visit the **Phu Phra Cave**. Another pause can be made at the **Prasat Muang Singh Temple**, a western outpost of the Khmer Empire. The **Sai Yok Falls** are 60km out (overnight raft trips head down the Khwae Noi river from here) and another 44km takes you past the **Sai Yok Yai National Park**. Around 107km out, there's the **Hin Dat Hot Springs**, but dress discreetly if you decide to try them out – don't swim in the nude.

SANGKHLABURI & THREE PAGODAS PASS

It's relatively easy to travel up to the pass (Chedi Sam Ong in Thai) and have a peek into Myanmar. Getting there requires an overnight pause in Sangkhlaburi, 223km north from Kanchanaburi. The village on the

Myanmar side of the pass has been the scene of firefights between the Mon and Karen insurgents – both armies want to control the collection of 'taxes' levied on smuggling.

In March 1990, the Burmese government regained control of the area, rebuilt the bamboo village in wood and concrete and renamed it Payathonzu. A row of tourist shops have been built and tourists are allowed over the border for day trips; there is an entrance fee of 150B. There is talk of reopening the road all the way to Mawlamyine. The three pagodas themselves are rather inconspicuous, small, whitewashed monuments.

Places to Stay

At Thong Pha Phum, the last town before Sangkhlaburi, there are several places to stay for around 120B to 150B a night.

In Sangkhlaburi, the **Phornphalin Hotel** is on the first street to the left when you enter town and has rooms from 160B.

About 2km east of the bus terminal, near the lake, the **Burmese Inn**, has lake-view rooms for 70B single, 90B double. The similar **P Guest House**, a bit farther on, has slightly cheaper rooms.

Getting There & Away

Four buses a day go to Sangkhlaburi from Kanchanaburi between 6 am and 1 pm; the ride takes 4½ hours and costs 75B. More expensive, faster air-con minivans are also available.

You can also get to Sangkhlaburi by a rented motorbike from Kanchanaburi. This is not a road for the inexperienced motorcyclist – it has lots of dangerous curves, steep grades and long stretches where there is no assistance. If you go by motorbike, refuel in Thong Pha Phum, 150km north of Kanchanaburi – there isn't another fuel stop before Sangkhlaburi, another 70km away.

From Sangkhlaburi, there are hourly songthaews (35B, 40 minutes) to Three Pagodas Pass all day.

PATTAYA

Thailand's biggest and once most popular beach resort is a long way from being its best. Situated 154km south of Bangkok, a fourth 'S' (for sex) can be added to Sun, Sea & Sand in this gaudy and raucous resort. Pattaya is designed mainly to appeal to European and Russian package tourists, and there are plenty of snack bars along the beach strip proclaiming 'bratwurst mit brot' is more readily available than khao phat.

Pattaya consists of a long beach strip of mainly expensive hotels. The beach is drab and if you venture into the equally uninviting water you run the risk of being mowed down by a lunatic on a ski-boat, an out-of-control jet-ski or simply dropped on from above by a parasailer. Its one real attraction is the rather beautiful offshore islands, where the snorkelling is good. Hat Jomtien (Jomtien Beach) next door is quieter and nicer.

Places to Stay

Although Pattaya is basically a package-tourist, big-hotel deal, there are a handful of cheaper places squeezed in the small soi, back off the main beach road. Cheap in Pattaya would be expensive just about anywhere else in Thailand. This is true even when compared with Ko Samui or Phuket.

Most of the less expensive places are concentrated along and just off Thanon Pattaya 2, near soi 6, 10, 11 and 12. **Lucky House**, between soi 8 and 10, has simple but clean rooms for 150B – you may have to bargain for this price – with fan and bath.

Most other low-end places cost 300B to 400B. One of the best value-for-money places in Pattaya is the modern **Apex Hotel** (☎ 42 9233), 216/2 Thanon Pattaya 2 near Soi 11; it has older rooms with air-con, TV and fridge for 350B.

At nearby Hat Jomtien the **RS Guest House** (☎ 23 1867) rents simple, clean rooms for 300B with fan, or 400B with air-con.

Places to Eat

Most food in Pattaya is expensive – cheap eating here means **Pizza Hut** or **Mister Donut**. Shops along the back street on Thanon Pattaya 2 have decent Thai food. Look for cheap rooms back here, too. **Vientiane Restaurant**, on Thanon Pattaya 2, serves reasonably priced Thai and Lao food. Four places in town now specialise in Russian cuisine.

Entertainment

If there's one thing Pattaya has, it's night life. Two transvestite cabarets on Thanon Pattaya 2 compete for the tourist trade, **Alcazar**, on the east side near soi 4, and **Tiffany's**, on the west side near the roundabout. Both cost around 500B per person.

For a vision of true excess, visit **Pattaya Palladium**, a large, modern entertainment complex at Thanon Hat Pattaya 2. It contains a snooker club, Chinese banquet-style restaurant, karaoke club, cocktail lounge, cinema, disco and massage parlour boasting 200 beds and 180 masseuses.

Getting There & Away
Air Bangkok Airways has a daily flight between nearby U-Taphao and Ko Samui for 1660B each way.

Bus There are departures every half hour from the Eastern bus terminal in Bangkok for the two hour, 40B trip to Pattaya. Air-con buses are 66B. There are also all sorts of air-con tour buses to Pattaya run by a number of tour companies. At 9 am, noon and 7 pm, there are buses direct from Bangkok airport for 200B (150B in the reverse direction).

Getting Around
Songthaews cruise Pattaya Beach and Thanon Pattaya 2 for 5B per person, or go to Jomtien for 10B. Don't ask the fare first or drivers will think you want a charter.

RAYONG
Most of Thailand's *náam plaa* (fish sauce) comes from Rayong. For most travellers it is just a quick bus change on the way to Ko Samet, but there are a few pleasant beaches at this 'real' Thai resort beyond Pattaya. Prices aren't much lower than in Pattaya (for beach places), though they are better value.

Places to Stay & Eat
The *Rayong Hotel* at 65/3 Thanon Sukhumvit and the *Rayong Otani* at No 169 have rooms from 150B.

There are good cheap eats at the *market* near the Thetsabanteung cinemas, and at the string of *restaurants* and *noodle shops* on Thanon Taksin Maharat, just south of Wat Lum Mahachaichumphon.

If you get stuck in Ban Phe, the port town for Ko Samet, you can stay at the *Queen Hotel*, with rooms from 150B, or *TN Place*, with rooms from 200B.

KO SAMET
East beyond Rayong, this small island is off the coast from Ban Phe. It used to be a very quiet and untouristed place but is now packed almost year-round. It cannot compete with the natural attractions of Ko Samui, but the beaches are nice. An advantage of Ko Samet is that the weather is usually good here when Ko

Samui is getting its worst rain; the downside is all the bungalow development and rubbish that's accumulating in places. Water is rationed at some bungalows – a reasonable policy given the scarcity of water on the island.

There are continual rumours that the National Park Service may close down most of the bungalows to preserve the environment, which could make Ko Samet a far more pleasant place to visit. At the moment there is a moratorium on building new accommodation and a 50B park entry fee for non-Thais.

Places to Stay & Eat
Beach accommodation costs from 80B to 300B and is mainly concentrated along the north-east coast.

Naga Bungalows, between Ao Tubtim and Hat Sai Kaew near the concrete mermaid, is recommended, as are *Tok's Little Hut, Ao Phai Hut* and *Tub Tim*. There are plenty of others to choose from, and even a few places on Ao Phrao (Coconut Bay) on the western side of the island, all of which are over 300B a night. Avoid Ao Wong Deuan and Hat Sai Kaew on the central east and north-east coast – they're crowded and overpriced. Another warning: during Thai national holidays all of Ko Samet can get quite crowded.

Most bungalows have restaurants offering mixed menus of Thai and traveller food; prices are typically 30B to 50B per dish. Fresh seafood is almost always available and costs around 60B to 150B per dish. Naga Bungalows has a very good *bakery* with all kinds of breads and cakes. Ao Wong Deuan has a cluster of *restaurants* serving western and Thai food.

Getting There & Away
It's a three hour, 50B (85B air-con) bus ride from the Eastern bus terminal in Bangkok to Rayong, then a 10B bus to Ban Phe (the touts will find you). For 90B you can get a direct air-con bus from Bangkok to Ban Phe, so why bother with Rayong? From Ban Phe, a fishing boat will take you out to Na Dan on the north end of Ko Samet for 30B. Other boats go to Ao Wong Deuan or Ao Thian, on the central east coast, for the same price. A boat to Ao Wai costs 40B.

Many Thanon Khao San agencies in Bangkok organise round-trip transport to Ko Samet for around 150B to 160B one way, including the boat fare. Not only is this more expensive than doing it on your own, but you won't have a choice of which boat to take or where it stops.

KO SAMET

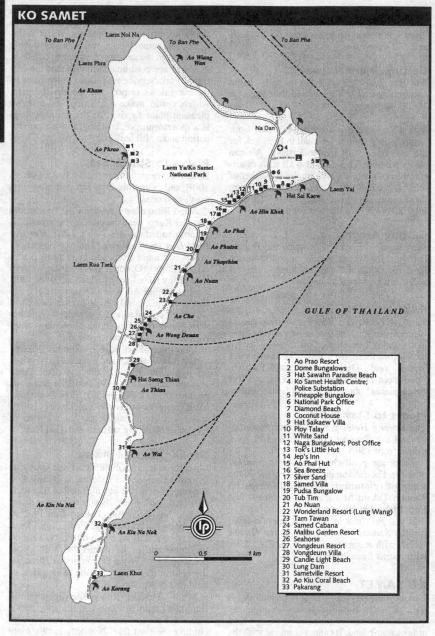

To Ban Phe

Laem Noi Na

To Ban Phe

To Ban Phe

Laem Phra

Ao Wiang Wan

Ao Kham

Na Dan

Ao Phrao

Laem Ya/Ko Samet National Park

Laem Yai

Hat Sai Kaew

Ao Hin Khok

Ao Phai

Ao Phutsa

Ao Thapthim

Laem Rua Taek

Ao Nuan

Ao Cho

GULF OF THAILAND

Ao Wong Deuan

Hat Saeng Thian

Ao Thian

Ao Wai

Ao Kiu Na Nai

Ao Kiu Na Nok

Laem Khut

Ao Karang

0   0.5   1 km

1 Ao Prao Resort
2 Dome Bungalows
3 Hat Sawahn Paradise Beach
4 Ko Samet Health Centre;
   Police Substation
5 Pineapple Bungalow
6 National Park Office
7 Diamond Beach
8 Coconut House
9 Hat Saikaew Villa
10 Ploy Talay
11 White Sand
12 Naga Bungalows; Post Office
13 Tok's Little Hut
14 Jep's Inn
15 Ao Phai Hut
16 Sea Breeze
17 Silver Sand
18 Samed Villa
19 Pudsa Bungalow
20 Tub Tim
21 Ao Nuan
22 Wonderland Resort (Lung Wang)
23 Tarn Tawan
24 Samed Cabana
25 Malibu Garden Resort
26 Seahorse
27 Vongdeun Resort
28 Vongdeurn Villa
29 Candle Light Beach
30 Lung Dam
31 Sametville Resort
32 Ao Kiu Coral Beach
33 Pakarang

Getting Around

Taxi trucks on the island cost from 10B to 50B per person, depending on how far you're going. There are trails all the way to the southern tip of the island, and a few cross-island trails as well.

TRAT PROVINCE

Located about 400km south-east of Bangkok, the province of Trat borders Cambodia. Gem-mining and smuggling are the most important occupations, though tourism is growing at Ko Chang National Marine Park.

As Hwy 318 goes east and then south on the way to Khlong Yai, the province of Trat thins to a sliver between the Gulf of Thailand and Cambodia. Along this sliver are a number of little-known beaches, including **Hat Sai Si Ngoen**, **Hat Sai Kaew**, **Hat Thap Thim** and **Hat Ban Cheun**.

The provincial capital has nothing much to offer – it is a jumping-off point for Ko Chang and other islands. You can get information about Ko Chang National Marine Park in **Laem Ngop**, a small coastal town approximately 20km south-west of Trat. This is also where you get boats to Ko Chang.

Places to Stay

Trat The friendly *NP Guest House* (☎ 51 2564), 1-3 Soi Luang Aet, Thanon Lak Meuang (in a lane which is a south-easterly continuation of Thanon Tat Mai), offers beds in a clean three bed dorm for 50B, or private rooms for 80/100B single/double with shared bath.

The *Trat Inn* (☎ 51 1028) at 66-71 Thanon Sukhumvit and *Thai Roong Roj (Rung Rot, ☎ 51 1141)*, 196 Thanon Sukhumvit, have rooms from around 110B to 200B.

Also good is the *Foremost Guest House* (☎ 51 1923) at 49 Thanon Thana Charoen, towards the canal. Single/doubles here are 70/90B. The same family runs the *Windy Guest House* across the road on the canal.

Laem Ngop There's really no reason to stay here since most boats to Ko Chang leave in the afternoon and it's only 20km from Trat, but the cosy *Chut Kaew Guest House* has rooms from 60/120B.

Places to Eat

The municipal market in the centre of town will satisfy your nutritional needs cheaply, day or night. On the Trat river, north-east of town, is a smaller night market which sells seafood.

Getting There & Away

Regular buses from Bangkok's Eastern terminal to Trat cost 80B and take seven to eight hours. By air-con bus, it's 140B and takes about five hours. Ordinary buses between Chanthaburi and Trat are 25B and take about 1½ hours.

Share taxis to Laem Ngop leave Trat from a stand along Thanon Sukhumvit next to the municipal market; these cost 10B per person shared, or 100B to charter. They depart regularly throughout the day, but after dark you will have to charter.

Getting Around

Samlors, Mazda taxi trucks and motorcycle taxis around town cost 10B per person.

KO CHANG NATIONAL MARINE PARK

Ko Chang is the second largest island in Thailand after Phuket; the park actually covers 47 of the islands off Trat's coastline. The main island has a few small villages supported by coconuts and fishing, but increasing numbers of tourists are attracted to the small bays and beaches, especially along the island's west coast. About 500m inland from the Tha Than Mayom on the east coast, there's a series of scenic waterfalls called **Than Mayom Falls**, or Thara Mayom.

Places to Stay

Ko Chang Starting at the northern end of the island at pretty Hat Sai Khao, there's a string of fairly inexpensive beach bungalows. *Rock Sand*, has rustic wooden huts on a rocky outcrop surrounded by beach on both sides, with a nice two storey restaurant with hammocks to relax in; *KC* is rustic (no electricity, shared bath) and has an herbal sauna; and *Yakha*, has clean bamboo huts with spacious verandas, as well as a swing set for children and a well stocked library. Next are *Tantawan* and *Bamboo* which are very basic but clean bungalow operations; and *Cookie* has 24 hour electricity, fan and attached bath available. All start at 100B for basic huts with shared facilities. There's also a sprinkling of nicer, more expensive huts.

Farther south, on Ao Khlong Phrao, A-frame wooden huts start at 100B at the *Chaichet*. Farther south yet, at Ao Kaibae, *Erawan,* and *Magic* have bungalows with fans for 80B to 100B, but they're none too clean, while the better bungalows with bath cost from 150B to 300B. Magic's best feature is its restaurant built over the bay. *Pikanade Resort* (formerly Chokdee) has nice clean thatch huts. *Coral Resort, Kaibae Hut* and others have cheaper huts at 60B to 150B, plus more expensive ones.

Down along the south coast at Ao Bang Bao is the *Bang Bao Blue Wave* which is a very friendly comfortable place, and has electricity from 6 to 10 pm for 80B to 300B. You may also be able to rent rooms cheaply in nearby Ban Bang Bao.

Menus at all the bungalows on Ko Chang are pretty similar. On Hat Sai Khao, highest marks this time around go to the kitchen at *Tantawan*. Several small *eateries* offer ex-bungalow options along the east side of the main road in Hat Sai Khao. *Ban Nuna Restaurant-Cafe*, an upstairs place where you sit on cushions, is good for Thai lunches and dinners, pizza and western breakfasts, while the *Muk House* next door does huge western breakfasts, homemade bread and a daily changing menu of Thai and farang food.

Swedish-managed *White House Bakery*, across the road from Sabai Beach Bungalow, offers a wide variety of baked goods, fruit shakes and plenty of information on island activities.

The *Salakpet Seafood Restaurant*, in the southern part of Ko Chang, at Ao Salak Phet, serves the very best seafood on the island; prices are moderate.

Other Islands Nearby islands with bungalow accommodation include Ko Kut, Ko Kradat, Ko Kham and Ko Mak.

Getting There & Away

Ko Chang Take a songthaew (10B) from Trat south-west to Laem Ngop on the coast, then a ferry to Ko Chang. Ferries to the beachless east coast are less expensive: Tha Than Mayom 40B, Ao Salak Kok 40B and Ao Salak Phet 60B.

Departures for Ao Sapparot are three or four times daily and the 80B fare includes a truck ride to the west coast beach of your choice. Departures for other bays are once daily, usually in the afternoon. During the rainy season, only boats to Ao Sapparot are available.

From the newer Ko Chang Centrepoint pier, there's also one boat per day, at 7 am for 80B. The boat drops passengers off at Ao Sapparot and the fare includes a songthaew ride to one of the beaches.

Air-con minibuses leave daily from Thanon Khao San in Bangkok and go direct to Laem Ngop for 250B. The fare includes a ferry ride to Ao Sapparot.

Other Islands Two or three fishing boats a week go to Ko Kut from the Tha Chaloemphon pier, on the Trat river towards the eastern side of Trat town. The fare is 90B per person. Coconut boats go to Ko Kut once or twice a month from a pier on the canal.

During the November to May dry season boats to Ko Mak leave daily from the Laem Ngop pier in the afternoon; the fare is 150B per person. Coconut boats go to Ko Mak from the Canal pier once or twice a month – the trip takes five hours and costs 100B per person.

Daily boats to Ko Kham (150B) and Ko Wai (70B) depart around 3 pm.

Getting Around

Songthaews meeting the boats at Ao Sapparot charge 35B per person to any beach along the west coast, although if you paid 80B for the boat, your songthaew fare is already paid for. Between Ao Salak Kok and Ao Salak Phet, a daily jeep service costs 20B per person.

Northern Thailand

The northern area was where early Thai kingdoms (Lanna Thai, Hariphunchai and Sukhothai) first developed, so it's full of interesting temples and ruins. Most visitors tend to cluster around the northern capital of Chiang Mai, while the more adventurous head for the somewhat remote provinces of Chiang Rai, Mae Hong Son, Nan and Phrae. From here, you can make treks through the area inhabited by Thailand's many hill tribes. This too is the region of the infamous Golden Triangle – where Thailand, Laos and Myanmar meet and from where much of the world's opium originates.

Hill Tribe Treks

One of the most popular activities from Chiang Mai, Chiang Rai or Mae Hong Son is to take a trek through the tribal areas in the hills to the north. The best known tribes in this region are the Hmong (Meo), Karen, Lisu, Lahu (Musoe), Mien (Yao) and Akha, but tribal groups are also found across the border in Myanmar and Laos: lines on the political map have little meaning to them.

Unfortunately, these treks have become a bit too popular over the last decade or so and some areas are simply over-trekked. A little care is needed to guarantee a good experience. Finding a good tour guide is probably the key to a good trek: a guide who cannot speak English, let alone the hill tribe languages, is hardly a ticket to an interesting trip. The best guides will be conversant with the tribes and their languages, and have good contacts and easy relations with them. It's also important to check out your fellow trekkers – try to organise a meeting before departure. The best way of finding a good operator is simply to ask other travellers in Chiang Mai. People just back from a trek will be able to give you the low-down on how theirs went.

Treks normally last four days and three nights, although longer treks are also available, and the usual cost is around 1500B to 1800B. Bring a water bottle and medicines, and money – for lunch on the first and last day and for odd purchases.

For an up-to-date list of trek operators, visit the TAT office. Making a recommendation here would be meaningless because guides often change companies, and operators open and close with alarming frequency. Some useful questions to ask include:

- How many people will there be in the group? Six to 10 is a good maximum range.
- Can the organiser guarantee that no other tourists will visit the same village on the same day, especially overnight?
- Can the guide speak the language of each village to be visited (this is not always necessary as many villagers can speak Thai nowadays)?
- Exactly when does the tour begin and end? Some three-day treks turn out to be less than 48 hours in length.
- Do they provide transport before and after the trek or is it just by public bus (often with long waits)?

You can also just head off on your own or hire a guide or porter by yourself, but treks aren't that expensive and it is unwise to go to some areas.

Most people who go on these treks have a thoroughly good time and reckon they're great value. Comments include 'the best experience of my life ... I hope we left the villages as we found them' and 'the area we covered was only recently opened for trekking and the guides were some of the nicest people I have ever met'.

Warning There have been a number of hold-ups and robberies over the years. This area of Thailand is relatively unpoliced, with a 'wild west' feel. Ask around that everything is OK before setting blithely off into the wilds. People who run into trouble often discover afterwards that their guide didn't really know where they were going, or went into areas they should have known were not safe.

Don't bring too much money or other valuables with you. You can leave your gear behind in Chiang Mai with your hotel or the trek operator. Although we've received no reports of pilfering from hotel safes in the last few years, it's always a good idea to get a fully itemised list of any items you leave with a guesthouse while trekking.

Conduct Once on a trek, there are some guidelines for minimising the negative impact on the local people:

- Always ask permission before taking photos of tribal people and/or their dwellings. You can ask through your guide or by using sign language. Because of traditional belief systems, many individuals – and even whole tribes – may object strongly to being photographed.
- Show respect for religious symbols and rituals. Don't touch totems at village entrances or any other object of obvious symbolic value without asking permission. Keep your distance from ceremonies being performed unless you're asked to participate.
- Practise restraint in giving things to tribespeople or bartering with them. Food and medicine are not necessarily appropriate gifts if they result in altering traditional dietary and healing practices. The same goes for clothing. Tribespeople will abandon hand-woven tunics for printed T-shirts if they are given a steady supply. If you want to give something to the people you encounter on a trek, the best thing is to make a donation to the village school or other community fund. Your guide can help arrange this.

Some guides strictly forbid the smoking of opium on treks. This seems to be a good idea, since one of the problems trekking companies have is dealing with opium-addicted guides. Volunteers who work in tribal areas also say opium smoking sets a bad example for young people in the villages.

Hill Tribe Directory
The term hill tribe refers to ethnic minorities living in the mountainous regions of northern and western Thailand. The Thais refer to them

THAILAND

Hill Tribe Directory

Akha (Thai: *I-kaw*)

Population: 50,000
Origin: Tibet
Present locations: Thailand, Laos, Myanmar, Yunnan (China)
Economy: rice, corn, opium
Belief system: animism, with an emphasis on ancestor worship
Distinctive characteristics: head dresses of beads, feathers and dangling silver ornaments. Villages are along mountain ridges or on steep slopes 1000 to 1400m in altitude. The Akha are among the poorest of Thailand's ethnic minorities and tend to resist assimilation into the Thai mainstream. Like the Lahu, they often cultivate opium for their own consumption.

Hmong (Thai: *Meo* or *Maew*)

Population: 111,000
Origin: southern China
Present locations: southern China, Thailand, Laos, Vietnam
Economy: rice, corn, opium
Belief system: animism
Distinctive characteristics: simple black jackets and indigo trousers with striped borders or indigo skirts, and silver jewellery. Most women

wear their hair in a large bun. They usually live on mountain peaks or plateaus. Kinship is patrilineal and polygamy is permitted. They are Thailand's second-largest hill tribe group and are numerous in Chiang Mai Province.

Karen (Thai: *Yang* or *Kariang*)

Population: 353,000
Origin: Myanmar
Present locations: Thailand, Myanmar
Economy: rice, vegetables, livestock
Belief system: animism, Buddhism, Christianity – depending on the group
Distinctive characteristics: thickly woven V-neck tunics of various colours (unmarried women wear white). Kinship is matrilineal and marriage is endogamous. They tend to live in lowland valleys and practice crop rotation rather than swidden (slash and burn) agriculture. There are four distinct Karen groups – the White Karen (Skaw Karen), Pwo Karen, Black Karen (Pa-o) and Kayah. These groups combined are the largest hill tribe in Thailand, numbering a quarter of a million people or about half of all hill tribe people. Many Karen continue to migrate into Thailand from Myanmar, fleeing Burmese government persecution.

as *chao khao*, literally meaning mountain people. Each hill tribe has its own language, customs, mode of dress and spiritual beliefs.

Most are of semi-nomadic origin, having migrated to Thailand from Tibet, Burma, China and Laos during the past 200 years or so, although some groups may have been in Thailand much longer.

The Tribal Research Institute in Chiang Mai recognises 10 different hill tribes but there may be up to 20 in Thailand. The institute's 1993 estimate of their total population was 550,000.

The following descriptions cover the largest tribes, which are also the groups most likely to be encountered on treks. Linguistically, they can be divided into three main groups: the Tibeto-Burman (Lisu, Lahu, Akha); the Karenic (Karen, Kayah); and the Austro-Thai (Hmong, Mien). Comments on ethnic dress refer mostly to the female members of each group as hill tribe men tend to dress like rural Thais. Population figures are 1989 estimates.

The Shan (*Thai Yai*) are not included as they are not a hill tribe group per se; they live in permanent, usually lowland, locations, practice Theravada Buddhism and speak a language very similar to Thai.

Lonely Planet's *Thai Hill Tribes phrasebook* gives a handy, basic introduction to the culture and languages of a number of the tribes.

Getting There & Away

The straightforward way of getting to the north is simply to head directly from Bangkok to Chiang Mai either by bus, train or air. From Bangkok, you can visit the ancient capitals of Ayuthaya, Lopburi and Sukhothai on your way to Chiang Mai. Or, you could take a longer, 'off-the-beaten-track' route by first heading west to Nakhon Pathom and Kanchanaburi, then back-tracking and travelling north-east by bus to Suphanburi and Lopburi.

From Chiang Mai, you can head north to Fang and take the daily riverboat down the Kok river (a tributary of the Mekong) to

Hill Tribe Directory

Lahu (Thai: *Musoe*)

Population: 82,000
Origin: Tibet
Present locations: southern China, Thailand, Myanmar
Economy: rice, corn, opium
Belief system: theistic animism (supreme deity is Geusha); some groups are Christian
Distinctive characteristics: black and red jackets with narrow skirts for women. They live in mountainous areas at about 1000m. Their intricately woven shoulder bags (yaam) are prized by collectors. There are four main groups – Red Lahu, Black Lahu, Yellow Lahu and Lahu Sheleh.

Lisu (Thai: *Lisaw*)

Population: 31,000
Origin: Tibet
Present locations: Thailand, Yunnan (China)
Economy: rice, opium, corn, livestock
Belief system: animism with ancestor worship and spirit possession
Distinctive characteristics: the women wear long multi-coloured tunics over trousers and sometimes black turbans with tassels. Men wear baggy green or blue pants that are pegged in at the ankles. They often wear lots of bright colours. Premarital sex is said to be common, along with freedom in choosing marital partners. Patrilineal clans have pan-tribal jurisdiction, which makes the Lisu unique among hill tribe groups (most tribes have power centred at the village level with either the shaman or a village headman). Their villages are usually in the mountains at about 1000m.

Mien (Thai: *Yao*)

Population: 42,000
Origin: central China
Present locations: Thailand, southern China, Laos, Myanmar, Vietnam
Economy: rice, corn, opium
Belief system: animism with ancestor worship and Taoism
Distinctive characteristics: women wear black jackets and trousers decorated with intricately embroidered patches and red fur-like collars, along with large dark blue or black turbans. They have been heavily influenced by Chinese traditions and use Chinese characters to write the Mien language. They tend to settle near mountain springs at between 1000 and 1200m. Kinship is patrilineal and marriage is polygamous.

Chiang Rai. Or do the Mae Song loop through Mae Sariang and Pai. From there, you can head back through Chiang Mai, get off at Lampang, and either catch a bus via Tak to Sukhothai or take the train to Phitsanulok. From Phitsanulok, you can bus to Lom Sak and then Loei and Udon Thani. There is also a road between Lom Sak and Khon Kaen. Udon Thani and Khon Kaen are both on the rail and bus routes back to Bangkok, but there are a number of other places worth exploring in the north-east before you head back to the capital.

CHIANG MAI

More than 700km north-west of Bangkok, Chiang Mai has over 300 temples – almost as many as Bangkok though the city is far smaller in area – making it visually striking once you get off the main avenues. Doi Suthep rises 1676m above and behind the city, providing a nice setting for this fast-developing northern capital.

Founded in 1296, Chiang Mai was at one time part of the independent Lanna Thai (Million Thai Rice-Fields) kingdom, much given to warring with kingdoms in Burma and Laos, as well as Sukhothai to the south. You can still see the moat that encircled the city at that time, but the remaining fragments of the city wall are mainly reconstructions. Chiang Mai fell to the Burmese in 1556 but was recaptured in 1775.

Despite tourism, which is the city's number-one source of revenue, Chiang Mai is one of the least expensive large cities in Thailand.

Orientation

The old city of Chiang Mai is a neat square bounded by moats. Thanon Moon Muang, along the east moat, is one of the main centres for cheap accommodation and places to eat. Thanon Tha Phae runs east from the middle of this side and crosses the Ping river, where it changes name to Thanon Charoen

CENTRAL CHIANG MAI

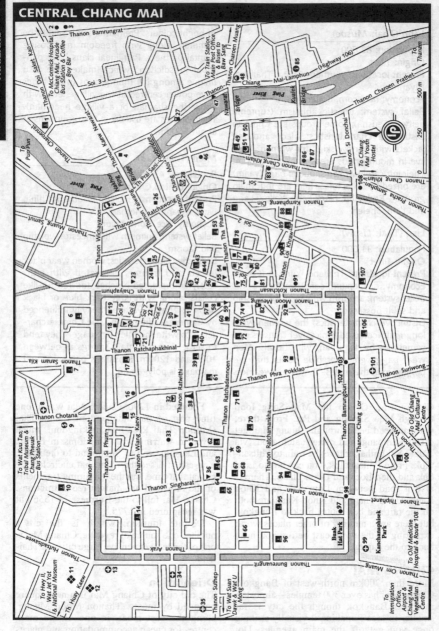

PLACES TO STAY
4 Mee's River View Guest House
18 Ninja SK House; Peter;
   Supreme House; SUP Court
19 Libra Guest House
24 Orchid House
25 Eagle House
26 New Mitrapap Hotel
29 Lek House
31 Eagle House 2
44 VK Guest House
54 Roong Ruang Hotel
56 Daret's House
57 Moon Muang Golden Court
58 Montri Hotel
64 Visaj Guest House
66 Wanasit Guest House
76 Tapae Place Hotel
77 Midtown House;
   Thana Guest House
79 Flamingo; Baan Jongcome
80 Sarah Guest House
92 Muang Thong Hotel
93 Nat Guest House
104 Banana Guest House

PLACES TO EAT
20 Indian Restaurant Vegetarian
   Food
22 Somphet Market
23 Somphet Night Market
30 Crusty Loaf Bakery & Irish Pub
36 Si Phen Restaurant
47 Riverside Bar & Restaurant
50 Khao Soi Fah; Khao Soi Islam
55 American Restaurant & Bar;
   Firenze Pizzeria Steak House
59 JJ Bakery & Restaurant
74 AUM Vegetarian Restaurant
75 Art Café
81 Aroon Rai Restaurant

84 Galare Food Centre
87 Anusan Market
102 Pratu Chiang Mai Night Market

WATS
1 Wat Chetuphon
6 Wat Pa Pao
7 Wat Chiang Yuen
10 Wat Lokmoli
14 Wat Pa Phrao Nai
15 Wat Hua Khwang
17 Wat Chiang Man
21 Wat Lam Chang
39 Wat U Mong Klang Wiang
40 Wat Pan Ping
41 Wat Dawk Euang
43 Wat U Sai Kham
45 Wat Saen Fang
49 Wat Upakhut 'Oopakoot'
52 Wat Bupparam
53 Wat Chetawan
61 Wat Duang Dii
62 Wat Chai Kiat
63 Wat Thung Yu
65 Wat Phra Singh
67 Wat Si Koet 'Srigert'
70 Wat Chedi Luang;
   Wat Phan Tao
71 Wat Phan Tao 'Pundtow'
72 Wat Phan An 'Pun-orn'
78 Wat Mahawan
88 Wat Chang Khong
89 Wat Loi Khraw 'Loikroh'
90 Wat Phan Tawng 'Punthong'
94 Wat Phra Jao Mengrai
95 Wat Meun Ngoen Kong
96 Wat Meh Thang 'Maytung'
100 Wat Sisupan
105 Wat Sai Mun Myanmar
106 Wat Muang Mang
107 Wat Pugchang

OTHER
2 Thai Tribal Crafts
3 British Council
5 US Consulate
8 Chang Puek Hospital
9 BKK Bank
11 Vista 12 Huay Kaew
   Shopping Centre
12 Kad Suan Kaew Shopping
   Centre
13 Chiang Mai Ram Hospital
16 THAI Office
27 The Brasserie
28 Namdhari Sikh Temple
32 Post Office
33 Chiang Mai Central Prison
34 Malaria Centre
35 Maharaj Hospital
37 District Offices
38 Three Kings Monument
42 Money Exchange
46 Warorot Market
48 Buses to Lamphun, Pasang,
   Chiang Rai & Lampang
51 Chiang Mai Mosque
   (Ban Haw Mosque)
60 AUA
68 Post Office
69 Police
73 AUA Thai Language Office
82 Pinte Blues Pub; Sax Music Pub
83 Night Bazaar
85 TAT; Tourist Police
86 Chiangmai Pavilion
91 DK Book House
97 Gim Photo
98 Suan Prung Gate
99 Suan Prung Hospital
101 Ruampaet Hospital
103 Chiang Mai Gate
108 Suriwong Book Centre

Muang. The train station and the main post office are both further down Thanon Charoen Muang, a fair distance from the centre.

Maps Finding your way around Chiang Mai is fairly simple. A copy of Nancy Chandler's *Map Guide to Chiang Mai* is worth its 70B price if you plan extensive exploration of the city.

Information

Tourist Office TAT (☎ 24 8604) is in an office (not shown on some Chiang Mai maps) on Thanon Chiang Mai-Lamphun, a couple of hundred metres south of the Nawarat Bridge. They have piles of useful hand-outs on everything from guesthouse accommodation to trekking.

Foreign Consulates Chiang Mai has several foreign consular posts where you may be able to arrange visas or extend passports. The Indian consulate here is a common stopping-off point for travellers on their way to India; they take about four days to process a visa.

See Embassies & Consulates in the Facts for the Visitor section for details.

Money All major Thai banks have several branches throughout Chiang Mai; most are open from 8.30 am to 3.30 pm. In the well touristed areas – Thanon Tha Phae, Thanon

Moon Muang, Chiang Mai Night Bazaar etc – they also operate foreign exchange booths that are open after bank hours; as late as 8 pm.

Post & Communications The main post office in Chiang Mai is on Thanon Charoen Muang near the train station. It is open Monday to Friday from 8.30 am to 4.30 pm, Saturday and Sunday from 9 am to 1 pm. Overseas calls, telexes; faxes and telegrams can be arranged here from 7 am to 10 pm. Several private offices along Thanon Thaphae can also arrange international calls.

Several places around town offer email and Internet access services. Among the most reliable is Assign Internet 1 (☎ 40 4550), Vista 12 Huay Kaew Shopping Center, Thanon Huay Kaew, to the north-west of the moat, and its second branch Assign Internet 2 (☎ 81 8911), Chiang Mai Pavilion, Thanon Chang Khlan (in the Night Bazaar area).

Bookshops & Libraries The best bookshops in Chiang Mai are the DK Book House on Thanon Kotchasan and the Suriwong Book Centre on Thanon Si Donchai.

The AUA library on Thanon Ratchadamnoen inside the east gate has a selection of English-language newspapers and magazines.

Cultural Centres Several foreign cultural centres in Chiang Mai host film, music, dance, theatre and other socio-cultural events.

Alliance Française
(☎ 27 5277) 138 Thanon Charoen Prathet; French films (subtitled in English) every Tuesday at 4.30 pm, Friday at 8 pm; admission is free to members, 10B students, 30B general public.
British Council
(☎ 24 2103) 198 Thanon Bamrungrat; free British movies every Thursday at 7 pm.
USIS/AUA
(☎ 27 8407, 211377) 24 Thanon Ratchadamnoen; USIS shows US films every second and fourth Saturday at 2 pm and 7 pm; admission is free. AUA also offers English and Thai language courses.

Immigration The immigration office (☎ 27 7510) is off Route 1141 near the airport (bus No 6 will take you there).

Medical Services McCormick Hospital (☎ 24 1107) on Thanon Kaew Nawarat is the budget traveller's best bet. Another good one is the modern Chang Puek Hospital (☎ 22 0022, fax 21 8120) at 1/7 Soi 2, Thanon Chang Pheuak.

Tourist Police The tourist police can be reached in Chiang Mai by dialling ☎ 24 8974 from 6 am to midnight or ☎ 49 1420 after hours. Their office is attached to the TAT office on Thanon Chiang Mai-Lamphun.

Dangers & Annoyances Take care with valuables stored at guesthouses while out trekking. A few years ago, Thailand was swept by a range of credit-card scams: a favourite was to borrow credit cards from trekkers' baggage while they were away. Months later, back in their home country, they would discover enormous bills had been run up. We haven't heard of this happening lately – most guesthouses now place all valuables in a sealed envelope, with your signature across the seal.

Wat Chiang Man

This is the oldest wat within the city walls and was erected by King Mengrai, Chiang Mai's founder, in 1296. Two famous Buddha images – Buddha Sila and the Crystal Buddha – are kept here in the *wihan* (smaller chapel) to the right of the main bot. Like Bangkok's Emerald Buddha, the Crystal Buddha was once shuttled back and forth between Siam and Laos.

Wat Phra Singh

Situated in the centre of town, this well kept wat was founded in 1345. There are a number of interesting buildings here; the supposedly 1500-year-old Phra Singh Buddha image is a subject of some controversy and its exact history is unknown.

Wat Chedi Luang

Originally constructed in 1411, this wat contains the ruins of a huge chedi which collapsed during an earthquake in 1545. A partial restoration has preserved its 'ruined' look while ensuring it doesn't crumble further.

Other Wats

The **Wat Jet Yot** has seven (*jet*) spires (*yot*) and was damaged by the Burmese in 1566. It's near the National Museum and is modelled (imperfectly) after the Mahabodhi Temple in Bodh Gaya, India, where the Buddha attained enlightenment. **Wat Kuu**

Tao has a peculiar chedi that looks like a pile of diminishing spheres.

The **Wat Suan Dawk** was built in 1383. It contains a 500-year-old bronze Buddha image and colourful Jataka murals showing scenes from the Buddha's lives.

Wat U Mong, a forest temple outside the city to the west, also dates from Mengrai's rule and has a fine image of the fasting Buddha, plus an interesting set of brick tunnels constructed into a hillside for meditation.

National Museum
The National Museum has a good display of Buddha images and northern Thai handicrafts. It is open from 9 am to 4 pm Wednesday to Sunday; admission is 20B.

Tribal Museum
At Ratchamangkla Park, off Thanon Chotana north of the city, this renovated museum houses a large collection of artefacts and other displays on the various cultural features and backgrounds of each of the hill tribes in Thailand. It's open Monday to Friday from 9 am to 4 pm.

Other Attractions
Old Chiang Mai Cultural Centre This a touristy 'instant hill tribes' centre. There are Thai and hill tribe dance performances here every night.

You'll often see local hill tribes people in Chiang Mai – check the **night bazaar** which extends along both sides of Thanon Chang Khlan between Thanon Tha Phae and Thanon Si Don Chai. Chiang Mai's **jail**, in the centre of town, has a large, resident population of foreigners – most of whom were incarcerated after drug busts.

Courses
See under Courses in the Facts for the Visitor section of this chapter for details of Thai massage, cooking and muay thai (Thai boxing) courses available in Chiang Mai.

Festivals
The annual dry-season **Songkran** (Water Festival) takes place, with particular fervour, in mid-April in Chiang Mai.

From late December to early January the **Winter Fair** is also a great scene, with all sorts of activities and interesting visitors from the hills.

The biggest festival of all is the **Flower Festival**, held during the first week of Febru-

ary. This festival features parades in which the various *amphoes*, or districts, throughout Chiang Mai Province compete for the best flower-bedecked float and enter their most beautiful young women in the Queen of the Flower Festival contest.

Places to Stay
Guesthouses In Chiang Mai, budget travellers' accommodation is usually in guesthouses. There are plenty of them, ranging from 40B per person for a dorm bed to 300B for a room with private toilet and shower; most places are 80B to 150B. Many of the guesthouses are along the streets on either side of the east moat. Others can be found along the Ping river; on Thanon Charoenrat on the east side, and Thanon Charoen Prathet, on the west. The latter streets are some distance from the city centre, but convenient for the train station and Chiang Rai buses.

TAT lists over 100 guesthouses. During peak periods (from December to March and from July to August), it may be best to go to the TAT office first, pick up a free copy of the guesthouse list and make a few calls to find out where rooms are available.

Banana Guest House (☎ 20 6285), 4/9 Thanon Ratchapakhinai (near Chiang Mai Gate), is a small place with dorm beds for 50B, single rooms with shared facilities for 70B and doubles with private bath for 120B.

Nat Guest House (☎ 21 2878), 7 Soi 6, Thanon Phra Pokklao, is a comfortable, long-established place with 24 rooms for 120/150B. It's a favourite among Israeli visitors.

Visaj Guest House (☎ 21 4016), 104 Thanon Ratchadamnoen, near Wat Phra Singh, offers rooms with private shower and toilet for 100B, or 120B including breakfast; there's a good view of Wat Phra Singh from the rooftop.

Off Thanon Chang Moi is the basic but comfortable *Eagle House* (☎ 23 5387) at 80/100B. The long-standing *VK Guest House*, down an alley off Thanon Chang Moi Kao near Thanon Tha Phae, is quiet and friendly – it costs 80B for small, basic but clean, motel-like rooms; a triple with bath costs 40B per person.

On Thanon Chaiyaphum, in the same area, is the popular *Daret's House*. Rooms cost 70B to 120B depending on facilities and it's usually full, simply because it's so visible.

Farther north, inside the moat along Soi 9, are a number of decent places with rooms for 80/100B with shared bath, or 150/180B with

THAILAND

private bath: *Libra, Ninja SK House, Supreme House, SUP Court* and *Peter*. We've had letters about rude treatment at Ninja SK House, however.

Eagle House 2, located off Thanon Ratwithi inside the old city, is nicer and costs a bit more.

The *Chiang Mai Youth Hostel* (☎ 27 2169) on Thanon Chang Khlan has rooms for 120/150B with fan and bath or 250/300B with air-con.

On Soi 4, off Thanon Tha Phae farther east towards the river, there are several newer, two-storey brick guesthouses with downstairs sitting areas: *Midtown House, Tapae Place Hotel, Thana, Sarah, Flamingo* and *Baan Jongcome* (☎ 27 4823), each with good rooms in the 120B to 200B range.

Two pleasant places along Thanon Charoenrat next to the Ping river are *Mee's River View Guest House* (☎ 24 3534) at No 193/1, where singles/doubles with bath cost 80/100B, and *Pun Pun* (☎ 24 3362) at No 321, where fan rooms are 175B and upgraded air-con rooms 250B. There are lots of others tucked away throughout Chiang Mai.

Hotels There are plenty of hotels, in all price ranges. In Chiang Mai's small Chinatown, at 94-98 Thanon Ratchawong, is the nicer *New Mitrapap* (☎ 23 5436), where recently upgraded rooms cost 310B for a fan cooled single/double, 390B for air-con. There are several good, inexpensive Chinese restaurants to try nearby, as well as the Warorot Market.

The funky *Muang Thong* (☎ 27 8438), at 5 Thanon Ratchamankha, costs 100B for rooms with sagging beds and shared bath, 150B with private bath and similar beds.

Moon Muang Golden Court (☎ 21 2779), off the street at 95/1 Moon Muang, is good value for 150B with fan and hot shower.

The *Roong Ruang Hotel* (☎ 23 2017), at 398 Thanon Tha Phae, near the east side of the moat, has a good location and clean, spacious rooms at 270B with fan and private bath, more with air-con and/or TV.

Places to Eat
Thai South of Thanon Tha Phae, on the moat, the big, open-air *Aroon Rai* specialises in northern Thai food and is a great place to try sticky rice and other northern specialities. Their *kaeng karii kai* (chicken curry) is delicious. Get a group together in order to try the maximum number of dishes. Nearby on Thanon Chaiyaphum, just up from Tha Phae

Gate, the *Thanam Restaurant* is smaller but even better for local food. It's very clean and no alcohol is served.

The highly regarded *Si Phen* (no English sign) at 103 Thanon Intharawarorot, near Wat Phra Singh, specialises in both northern and north-eastern style dishes.

The *Riverside Bar & Restaurant* on Thanon Charoenrat, on the banks of the Ping river, features home-style Thai cooking and country/folk music. On weekend nights it's quite the scene.

Chiang Mai is famed for its fine noodles; *khâo sòi*, a concoction of spicy curried chicken with flat wheat noodles, is the true Chiang Mai speciality. The oldest area for khâo sòi is the Jiin Haw (Yunnanese Muslim) area around the Ban Haw Mosque on Soi 1, Thanon Charoen Prathet, not far from the Night Bazaar. Yunnanese-run *Khao Soi Fuang Fah* and *Khao Soi Islam*, both on this soi, serve khâo sòi for 20B to 25B as well as Muslim curries and Thai-style biryani. Most khâo sòi places are open from around 10 am till 3 or 4 pm, although Khao Soi Islam and Khao Soi Fuang Fah are open 5 am to 5 pm.

Galare Food Centre, opposite the main Night Bazaar building on Thanon Chang Khlan, is a large and very good outdoor food centre; free Thai classical dancing is featured on some evenings.

Western Along either side of the east moat near Tha Phae Gate there are a number of places that pack in the travellers attracted to western food and fruit drinks. The long-running *Daret's House* does some great drinks and westernised Thai food, but service can be slow when it's crowded.

The *American Restaurant & Bar* on Thanon Tha Phae near the Roong Ruang Hotel specialises in pizza, burgers, deli sandwiches, breakfast and Tex-Mex. *Firenze Pizzeria Steak House*, next door, does good pizzas, pastas, steak, fruit juices and espresso drinks at moderate prices. On the corner of Thanon Tha Phae and Thanon Kotchasan, *Art Café* serves very good Italian, Thai and American food and has an extensive wine list. A second branch called *Art Café da Stefano*, nearby at 2/1-2 Thanon Chang Moi Kao, is a more intimate place that focuses on the Italian side of the menu with a better wine selection. Both places have moderate prices and consistently good food and service.

The *JJ Bakery and Restaurant*, beside the Montri Hotel, has a good menu of Thai,

Chinese and western food at very reasonable prices and is air-conditioned.

The slightly more expensive *Crusty Loaf Bakery & Irish Pub* (the main sign merely reads 'Irish Pub') on Thanon Ratwithi offers baked goods, good coffee, yoghurt, muesli, sandwiches, pasta, vegetarian dishes, baked potatoes, ice cream, some Thai food, beer on tap, fruit and vegetable juices and a two-for-one paperback swap. However, service has hit an all-time low recently.

Chinese Chiang Mai has a small Chinatown centred on Thanon Ratchawong, north of Thanon Chang Moi Kao, where you'll find a whole string of Chinese rice and noodle shops. Most offer variations on *Tae Jiu* (*Chao Zhou*) or Yunnanese cooking.

Vegetarian There's a traveller-oriented vegetarian place on Thanon Moon Muang called *AUM Vegetarian Restaurant*. Reports are mixed on this one; we liked it but some people think the food's not so great.

The Asoke Foundation-sponsored *Chiang Mai Vegetarian Centre* operates a dirt-cheap Thai vegetarian restaurant on Thanon Om Muang south of the south-west corner of the city walls; it's open Sunday to Thursday from 6 am to 2 pm only. You can pick up a map that shows the location of 30 vegie restaurants around the city.

Markets *Somphet Market* on Thanon Moon Muang, north of the Thanon Ratwithi intersection, sells cheap take-away Thai food.

On the opposite side of the moat, toward the north end of Thanon Chaiyaphum not far from Eagle House, is the small but thriving *Somphet night market* where you can get everything from noodles and seafood to Yunnanese specialities.

The *Warorot Market*, at the intersection of Chang Moi and Thanon Chang Khlan, is open from 6 am to 5 pm daily. Upstairs, inside the market, vendors serve excellent and very cheap Chinese rice and noodle dishes.

Entertainment

Cinema Movies with English soundtracks are frequently shown at the Vista chain of cinemas; at Kad Suan Kaew shopping centre on Thanon Huay Kaew and Vista 12 Huay Kaew, opposite.

Live Music At 37 Thanon Charoenrat, near the river, *The Brasserie* has become a favourite

late nightspot (from 11.15 pm to 2 am) to listen to a talented Thai guitarist named Took play energetic versions of Pink Floyd, Hendrix, Cream, Dylan, Marley and other gems from the 60s and 70s.

Bars *Pinte Blues Pub* on Thanon Moon Muang near Tha Phae Gate has faithfully provided a low-key place to hang out, talk, drink beer and listen to 100% blues for nearly a decade now. Another good place for recorded music in this area is *Sax Music Pub*.

Nearby are several other bars, most of them staffed with young Thai women (and Thai transvestites) whose purpose is to get male passers-by seated and ordering drinks as directly as possible.

Gay Venues Chiang Mai has several gay men's bars, including the relaxed *Coffee Boy Bar* in a 70-year-old teak house at 248 Thanon Thung Hotel, not far from the Arcade bus terminal; on weekends there's a cabaret show.

Other popular gay meeting places include the low-key *Danny's Bar* at 161 Soi 4, Thanon Chang Phukha, and *Kra Jiap Bar & Restaurant* at 18/1 Soi 3, Thanon Wualai.

Shopping

Long before tourists began visiting the region, Chiang Mai was an important centre for handcrafted pottery, weaving, umbrellas, silverwork and woodcarving, and today it's still the country's number-one source of handicrafts. There are a lot of things to attract your money in Chiang Mai, but a lot of junk is churned out for the undiscerning, so buy carefully. The Chiang Mai Night Bazaar, on Thanon Chang Khlan, is a great place to find almost anything, from handicrafts to cheap jeans, but you'll have to bargain hard.

Warorot Market (also locally called Kaat Luang, or 'Great Market') is the oldest market in Chiang Mai. A former royal cremation grounds, it has been a marketplace site since the reign of Chao Inthawararot (1870-97). Although quite dilapidated, it's an especially good market for Thai fabrics.

Getting There & Away

Air THAI has flights to Chiang Mai several times daily from Bangkok. The flight takes an hour and the normal fare is 1940B – a special night fare is less. There are also flights between Chiang Mai and other towns in the north, including Chiang Rai, Mae Hong

Son and Nan, and to Phuket in the south. Bangkok Airways also operates three flights per week to/from Bangkok via Sukhothai for 1640B.

Internationally, you can reach Chiang Mai by air from Kunming, Kuala Lumpur, Hong Kong and Yangon.

Bus Regular buses from Bangkok take 10 or 11 hours and cost from 170B to 190B (depending on the route); air-con buses cost around 350B and take about nine to 10 hours. Lots of buses leave from the Northern bus terminal between 5.30 am and about 10 pm. A variety of more expensive tour buses also make the trip – a 'VIP' bus with 30 reclining seats is 400B to 500B.

Several travel agencies on Bangkok's Thanon Khao San offer air-con bus tickets from 200B which include a free night's accommodation in Chiang Mai. Some of these trips work out OK, but others are rip-offs in which the Chiang Mai guesthouse charges bathroom and electricity fees in lieu of a room charge. The only real advantage to these trips is that they depart from Thanon Khao San, saving you a trip to the Northern bus terminal. But the entire bus will be loaded with foreigners – not a very cultural experience.

If you intend to hop from town to town on your way north, Chiang Mai buses operate via Phitsanulok, Sukhothai, Uttaradit and Lampang.

For buses to destinations within Chiang Mai Province use the Chang Pheuak station, while for buses outside the province use the Chiang Mai Arcade station. From the town centre, a tuk-tuk or chartered songthaew to the Chiang Mai Arcade station should cost 30 to 40B; to the Chang Pheuak terminal you should be able to get a songthaew at the normal 8B to 10B per person rate.

Train Trains to Chiang Mai from Bangkok are slower than buses, although this is no problem on the overnight service if you have a sleeper. There are four express trains and three rapid trains per day. A 2nd class ticket on the express costs 281B, plus sleeper and express charges. Third class tickets are only available on the rapid trains and cost 151B. Whether travelling by bus or train, you should book in advance if possible.

Getting Around
To/From the Airport An airport taxi service charges 90B from the airport to town. In the reverse direction you can get a red songthaew for only 50B. The airport is only about 3km south-west of the city centre.

Local Transport There is no city bus service in Chiang Mai. Plenty of red songthaews circulate around the city with standard fares of 8B per person, but drivers often try and get you to charter (50B or less). The songthaews don't have set routes; you simply flag them down and tell them where you want to go.

You can rent bicycles (30B a day) or motorbikes (from 150B to 250B) to explore Chiang Mai – check with your guesthouse or one of the rental services along Thanon Moon Muang near Tha Phae Gate.

Hordes of songthaew jockeys meet incoming buses and trains at Chiang Mai. They wave signs for the various guesthouses and if the one you want pops up you can have a free ride.

AROUND CHIANG MAI
Doi Suthep
From the hill-top temple of **Wat Phra That Doi Suthep**, 16km west of Chiang Mai, there are superb views over the city. Choose a clear day to make the hairpin-curved ascent to the temple. A long flight of steps, lined by ceramic-tailed *nagas* (dragons), leads up to the temple from the car park, or you can take a short, steep tram ride.

Phu Ping Palace is 5km beyond the temple – you can wander the gardens on Friday, Saturday and Sunday. Just before the palace car park, a turn to the left leads you to a **Hmong village**, 4km away. It's touristy since it's so close to Chiang Mai, but the opium 'museum' is worth a visit if you're in the vicinity.

Getting There & Away Minibuses to Doi Suthep leave from the west end of Thanon Huay Kaew and cost 30B; the fare back downhill is 20B. For another 5B, you can take a bicycle up with you and zoom back downhill.

Baw Sang & San Kamphaeng
The 'umbrella village' of Baw Sang is 9km east of Chiang Mai. It's a picturesque though touristy spot where the townspeople engage in just about every type of northern Thai handicraft. Beautiful paper umbrellas are hand-painted; huge garden models are around 600B, but postage and packing can add a fair bit more.

About 5km farther down Hwy 1006 is San Kamphaeng, which specialises in cotton and silk weaving.

Getting There & Away Buses to Baw Sang (sometimes spelled Bo Sang or Bor Sang) leave from the north side of Thanon Charoen Muang in Chiang Mai, between the river and the main post office, every 15 minutes. The fare is 8B to Baw Sang and 10B to San Kamphaeng.

Elephants

A daily 'elephants at work' show takes place near the Km 107 marker on the Fang road north of Chiang Mai. Arrive around 9 am or earlier to see bath-time in the river. It's really just a tourist trap, but probably worth the admission price of 40B. Once the spectators have gone, the logs are all put back in place for tomorrow's show.

You can get there on any bus going north to Fang. It's a good idea to have a picture of an elephant to show the bus conductor, or 'elephant' may be interpreted as 'Fang', the town farther north.

Elephants can also be seen at the **Young Elephant Training Centre** at Thung Kwian (Km 37) on the road from Chiang Mai to Lampang. This place is set up for tourists and has seats and even toilets, but nobody seems to know about it. When the trainer feels like it, sometime between 8 am and noon, the show begins and you'll see the elephants put through their paces. The elephants appreciate a few pieces of fruit – 'it feels like feeding a vacuum cleaner with a wet nozzle', reported one visitor. Any bus on the main road south-east will take you to Lampang.

Doi Inthanon

The highest peak in the country, Doi Inthanon (2595m), can be visited as a day trip from Chiang Mai. There are some impressive waterfalls and pleasant picnic spots here. Between Chiang Mai and Doi Inthanon, the small town of Chom Thong has a fine Burmese-style temple, **Wat Phra That Si Chom Thong**, where 26-day vipassana meditation courses are available.

Getting There & Away Buses run regularly from Chiang Mai to Chom Thong for 20B. From there, you take a songthaew the few kilometres to Mae Klang for about 15B and another to Doi Inthanon for 35B.

Lamphun

This town, only 26km south of Chiang Mai, has several interesting wats. **Wat Phra That Haripunchai** has a small museum and a very old chedi, variously dated at 897, 1044 or 1157 AD. There are some other fine buildings in the compound, and the world's largest bronze gong hangs in a reddish pavilion on the grounds. **Wat Chama Thewi**, popularly known as Wat Kukut, has an unusual chedi with 60 Buddha images set in niches. Another Haripunchai-era wat in the town, **Wat Mahawan**, is a source of highly reputable Buddhist amulets.

Places to Stay *Si Lamphun* on the town's main street, Thanon Inthayongyot, has rather grotty rooms for 80B to 140B. *Tareerat Court*, on Thanon Chama Thewi near Wat Kukut, is a clean apartment-style place with rooms for 150B to 300B.

Getting There & Away Buses depart Chiang Mai regularly from the south side of Nawarat Bridge on Thanon Chiang Mai-Lamphun (8B). A bus on to Pasang will cost another 6B.

Lampang

South-east of Chiang Mai, this town is a former home for the Emerald Buddha. The old town's fine wats include **Wat Si Rong Meuang, Wat Si Chum** and **Wat Phra Kaew Don Tao** on the bank of the Wang river north of town.

In the village of Ko Kha, about 18km to the south-west of Lampang, **Wat Phra That Lampang Luang** was originally constructed in the Haripunchai period and restored in the 16th century. It's an amazing temple with walls like a huge medieval castle. Getting there is a little difficult, so start out early in the day.

To get to Ko Kha by public transport, catch a blue songthaew south on Thanon Praisani to the market in Ko Kha (10B), then a Hang Chat-bound songthaew (5B) 3km north to the entrance of Wat Phra That Luang. A chartered motorcycle taxi from the Ko Kha songthaew terminal to the temple costs 20B to 30B.

If you're driving or cycling from Lampang, head south on Asia 2 and take the Ko Kha exit, then follow the road over a bridge and bear right. Note the police station on your left and continue for 2km over another bridge until you see the temple on the left. If you're coming from Chiang Mai via Hwy 11, turn south onto Route 1034 18km north-west of Lampang at Km 13 – this is a 50km short cut to Ko Kha that avoids much of Lampang.

Places to Stay & Eat Friendly *Sri Sangar (Si Sa-Nga)*, 213-215 Thanon Boonyawat, has large rooms with fan and bathroom for 100B up. There are a number of other hotels along Thanon Boonyawat, most with rooms starting at 140B to 160B.

In the vicinity of the Kim and Asia hotels along Thanon Boonyawat there are several good rice and noodle shops. *Mae Hae Restaurant*, on Thanon Upparat, is a diminutive, clean place with cheap northern Thai food.

Getting There & Away There are regular buses between Lampang and Chiang Mai (29B), Chiang Rai, Phitsanulok or Bangkok. The bus terminal in Lampang is some way out of town. It's 10B by songthaew, more if you arrive late at night.

To book an air-con bus from Lampang to Bangkok or Chiang Mai there is no need to go to the bus terminal as the tour bus companies have offices in town; along Thanon Boonyawat near the roundabout.

Pasang

Only a short songthaew ride south of Lamphun, Pasang is a centre for cotton-weaving. The Nantha Khwang shop has fine locally made cotton goods.

PHITSANULOK

This vibrant lower northern city is mainly used as a stepping stone to other places. It's on the rail line between Bangkok and Chiang Mai, and you get off here for Sukhothai. **Wat Phra Si Ratana Mahathat** (known locally as Wat Yai) is an interesting old wat, and contains one of the most revered Buddha images in Thailand, the Phra Jinnarat.

Places to Stay & Eat

The comfortable *Phitsanulok Youth Hostel* (☎ 24 2060), 38 Thanon Sanam Bin (take bus No 3 from the train station), has rooms for 100/140B a single/double; dorm beds are 40B. A Hostelling International membership is mandatory (temporary one-night memberships are 50B; annual membership is 300B). The hostel has a modest restaurant and there are several cheap eateries in the vicinity.

At 11/12 Thanon Ekathotsarot, the *Green House* offers simple comfort and a casual atmosphere for 80B single, or 100B to 120B for a double with shared bath.

If you come out of the train station and go straight ahead, then turn left by the expensive Amarin Nakhon Hotel, on the corner of the first and second intersections on the right you'll find some cheaper hotels. The recently renovated *Unachak* on Thanon Phayalithai has decent rooms for 150B. Farther towards the river on Thanon Phayalithai, the rundown *Chanprasert* has plain fan rooms for 90B to 120B.

Better value than either of these are the 150/200B rooms at the clean and friendly *Siam Hotel* (☎ 25 8844) at 4/8 Thanon Athitayawong, half a block from the river and main post office.

At any of the *flying vegetable restaurants* in town, cooks fling fried morning glory vine through the air from the wok to a plate held by a waiter who has climbed onto the shoulders of two colleagues (or onto a truck in the night market). *Floating restaurants* along the river are also popular.

Getting There & Away

Buses for Sukhothai go from the town centre, but the stations for buses to the east or north are on the other (east) side of the railway tracks, on the outskirts of town. From Chiang Mai or Bangkok, you can reach Phitsanulok by bus or rail. Buses from Bangkok cost 120B, or 185B with air-con. You can also fly here with THAI from Bangkok, Chiang Mai, Mae Sot or Nan.

Getting Around

City buses run between the town centre and the airport or bus terminal for 3B. Samlor rides within the town centre should cost 20B to 30B per person.

SUKHOTHAI

Although Sukhothai was Thailand's first capital, it only lasted a little over 100 years from its foundation in 1257 before being superseded by Ayuthaya in 1379. But if its period of glory was short, its achievements in art, literature, language and law, apart from the more visible evidence of great buildings, were enormous. In general, the ruins visible today at Sukhothai and other cities of the kingdom, like Kamphaeng Phet and Si Satchanalai, are more appealing than Ayuthaya because they are less urbanised and further off the beaten track.

Orientation & Information

Old Sukhothai, known as Meuang Kao, is spread over quite an area. New Sukhothai is 12km from the old town and has a good market, but otherwise it's an uninteresting

SUKHOTHAI HISTORICAL PARK

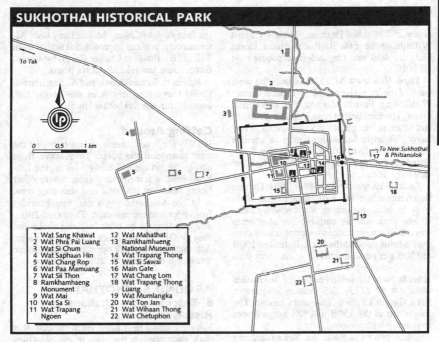

To Tak

0   0.5   1 km

To New Sukhothai
& Phitsanulok

1 Wat Sang Khawat
2 Wat Phra Pai Luang
3 Wat Si Chum
4 Wat Saphaan Hin
5 Wat Chang Rop
6 Wat Paa Mamuang
7 Wat Sii Thon
8 Ramkhamhaeng
   Monument
9 Wat Mai
10 Wat Sa Si
11 Wat Trapang
   Ngoen
12 Wat Mahathat
13 Ramkhamhaeng
   National Museum
14 Wat Trapang Thong
15 Wat Si Sawai
16 Main Gate
17 Wat Chang Lom
18 Wat Trapang Thong
   Luang
19 Wat Mumlangka
20 Wat Ton Jan
21 Wat Wihaan Thong
22 Wat Chetuphon

place. Sukhothai is 55km east of the Bangkok to Chiang Mai road from Tak. A map, available at the old town entrance, is essential for exploring the scattered ruins. The ruins are divided into five zones and there is a 20B admission fee into each zone. Bicycles can be hired to get around.

Ramkhamhaeng National Museum

This museum provides an introduction to Sukhothai history and culture, and is a good place to begin your explorations. They also sell printed guides to the ruins here. It's open daily from 9 am to 4 pm and admission is 20B.

Wat Mahathat

This vast assemblage, the largest in the city, once contained 198 chedis, as well as various chapels and sanctuaries. Some of the original Buddha images remain, including a big one among the broken columns. A large, ornamented pond gives fine reflections.

Wat Si Chum

A massive seated Buddha figure is tightly squeezed into this open, walled building. A narrow tunnel inside the wall leads to views over the Buddha's shoulders and on to the top. Candle-clutching kids used to guide you up and point out the 'Buddha foot' on the way, but the tunnel has been closed to visitors in recent years.

Other Attractions

The **Wat Si Sawai** has three prang and a moat and was originally intended as a Hindu temple. It's just south of Wat Mahathat. **Wat Sa Si** is a classically simple Sukhothai-style wat set on an island. **Wat Trapang Thong**, next to the museum, is reached by the foot-bridge crossing the large, lotus-filled pond which surrounds it. It is still in use.

Somewhat isolated to the north of the city, **Wat Phra Pai Luang** is similar in style to Wat Si Sawai. **Wat Chang Lom** is to the east; the chedi is surrounded by 36 elephants. **Wat Saphan Hin** is a couple of kilometres west of the old city walls on a hillside and features a large Buddha looking back to Sukhothai.

Places to Stay

New Sukhothai is a dull town, although there are some decent hotels and restaurants.

Guesthouses Guesthouses include the *Anasukho Guest House* (☎ *61 1315*), in a large house at 234/6 Soi Panitsan, Thanon Charot Withithong, near the Rajthanee Hotel. Dorm beds are 40B and single/double rooms cost 50/80B.

Yupa House (☎ *61 2578*) is near the west bank of the Yom river at 44/10 Thanon Charot Withithong, Prawet Nakhon, Soi Mekhapatthana. The family that runs Yupa are friendly and often invite guests to share meals. They have 30B dorm beds, plus rooms of various sizes from 60B to 100B. The nearby *Somprasong Guest House* and *Ban Thai* are similarly priced.

Lotus Village (☎ *62 1484*), 170 Thanon Ratchathani, on the east bank of the Yom river, is set in spacious grounds with a garden sitting area, and is suitable for long-term stays. Some rooms are in teak houses on stilts over a lotus pond at the back. Rates are 100B to 150B per person, depending on room size.

Hotels Near the town centre, the *Sukhothai Hotel* (☎ *61 1133*), 5/5 Thanon Singhawat, has a sign in English, Thai and Chinese. The rooms are in the 150B to 180B range (more expensive with air-con).

Other places include the *Sawaddiphong* (☎ *61 1567*), 56/2 Thanon Singhawat, which has rooms from 180B to 250B and isn't bad.

The traveller-oriented *Chinnawat Hotel* at 1-3 Thanon Nikhon Kasem has large single rooms with a double bed, ceiling fan and bathroom for 100B to 160B.

Places to Eat
Both the night market and the municipal market near the town centre are good, cheap places to eat.

The *Chinnawat Hotel* restaurant isn't bad. *Fah Fah (F&F) Fast Food* (no English sign) on Thanon Charot Withithong, west of the Rajthanee Hotel, is a two storey air-con restaurant attached to a department store; it has an extensive menu of Thai, Chinese and western foods.

Getting There & Away
Air Bangkok Airways operates flights from Bangkok (1100B) three times a week.

Bus Air-con buses to Sukhothai from Chiang Mai cost 135B, and from Bangkok are 110/142B without/with air-con. Most services go via Phitsanulok.

From Phitsanulok, buses to Sukhothai depart regularly and cost 20B; the trip takes about an hour. Phitsanulok is also the nearest point on the Bangkok to Chiang Mai railway line. Alternatively, you can approach Sukhothai from Tak (23B). Buses to Chiang Rai go by a more direct route and take about six hours.

Buses to Sawankhalok and Si Satchanalai (20B) leave regularly from the intersection across from the Sukhothai Hotel.

Getting Around
It's 8B for a songthaew or bus between the new town and the ruins. They leave from across the bridge and along a bit on the left-hand side, a fair distance from where other buses depart in the hotel and shopping area.

In old Sukhothai, you can hire bicycles from opposite the museum. They cost 20B a day and tend to be brakeless and shaky but they're OK for the tracks between the ruins. Alternatively, the park operates a tram service through the old city for 20B per person.

AROUND SUKHOTHAI
Si Satchanalai – Chaliang Historical Park
Fifty-six kilometres north of Sukhothai, this park encompasses the ruins of the old cities of Si Satchanalai and Chaliang, which are more isolated and less touristy than those at Sukhothai.

Climb to the top of the hill supporting **Wat Khao Phanom Phloeng** for a view over the town and river.

Wat Chedi Jet Thaew has a group of stupas in classic Sukhothai style. **Wat Chang Lom** has a chedi surrounded by Buddha statues in niches and guarded by the fine remains of elephant buttresses. Walk along the riverside for 2km or go back down the main road and cross the river to **Wat Phra Si Ratana Mahathat**, a very impressive temple with a well-preserved prang and a variety of seated and standing Buddhas. There's a separate 10B admission for this wat.

Sawankhalok Pottery Sukhothai was famous for its beautiful pottery, much of which was exported. The Indonesians were once keen collectors and fine specimens can be seen in the National Museum in Jakarta. Much of the pottery was made in Si Satchanalai. Rejects, buried in the fields, are still being found. Several of the old kilns have been carefully excavated and can be viewed along with original pottery samples at the **Si**

Satchanalai Centre for Study & Preservation of Sangkalok Kilns. The pottery is about 2km north-west of the ruins.

Places to Stay In Sawankhalok, the *Muang In* at 21 Thanon Kasemrat has rooms from 150B. The more centrally located *Sangsin Hotel* at 2 Thanon Thetsaban Damri 3 (the main street) has clean, comfortable rooms with fan for 200B.

There are some newer, more expensive bungalows next to the Si Satchanalai ruins – it's not really worth staying there overnight but it's not a bad place for food and drink.

Getting There & Away Take a bus to Sawankhalok and then change to a Si Satchanalai bus. The ruins are 11km before the new town – tell the bus conductor '*muang kao*' (old city) and look for a big corncob-shaped prang. The river is less than 1km off the road and there is a suspension bridge across it. The last bus back leaves around 4 pm.

KAMPHAENG PHET

This town is only a couple of kilometres off the road from Bangkok to Chiang Mai. There are a number of temple ruins within the old city and the very fine remains of the long city wall. Outside the wall is **Wat Phra Si Ariyabot**, which has the shattered remains of standing, sitting, walking and reclining Buddha images. **Wat Chang Rop**, or 'temple surrounded by elephants', is just that – a temple with an elephant-buttressed wall.

Kamphaeng Phet National Museum, across the road from these temples, displays artefacts from the Kamphaeng Phet area, including terracotta ornamentation from ruined temples and Buddha images in the Sukhothai and Ayuthaya styles. The museum is open Wednesday to Sunday from 8.30 am to 4 pm. Admission is 20B.

Places to Stay & Eat

It can be a little difficult to find places here since few signs are in English. At 114 Thanon Ratchadamnoen, the *Ratchadamnoen Hotel*, in the newer part of the city, has adequate rooms for 130/150B as well as more expensive air-con ones.

Better value, if you can afford the extra baht, is the *Gor Choke Chai (Kaw Chokchai) Hotel* (☎ 71 1247), 7-31 Thanon Ratchadamnoen (Soi 6), where fan-cooled rooms cost around 200B.

A small *night market* sets up every even-

ing in front of the provincial offices, near the old city walls, and there are some *cheap restaurants* near the roundabout.

Getting There & Away

The bus fare from Bangkok is 95B, or 169B with air-con. Most visitors come here from Sukhothai (25B), Phitsanulok (40B) or Tak (24B).

TAK

This is just a junction town from Sukhothai on the way north to Chiang Mai or west to Mae Sot. It's pronounced 'Tahk' not 'Tack'. The southern section of the city harbours a few old teak homes.

Information

TAT (☎ 51 4341) has an office at 193 Thanon Taksin, where you can pick up info and hotel brochures.

Places to Stay & Eat

If you have to stay here, then try the *Tak* (☎ 51 4422) at 18/10 Thanon Mahat Thai Bamrung. It's off the road along a long alley; rooms with fan and shower cost 150 to 250B.

The *Mae Ping* (☎ 51 1807) is very similar but a little more worn; large rooms with fan and bath are an economical 80B to 120B, air-con 250B.

MAE SOT

This outpost sits on Thailand's border facing the Burmese town of Myawaddy and is a big centre for smuggling between the two countries. The area used to be a hotbed of Communist guerrilla activity in the 1960s and 70s, but is now merely a relay point for the highly profitable trade in guns, narcotics, teak and gems. The local population is an interesting mixture of Thais, Chinese, Indians, Burmese and Karen tribespeople.

Songthaews can take you right to the Moei river border from Mae Sot for 8B. If the border is open you may be permitted to cross the footbridge to Myawaddy for the day. The Pan-Asian Hwy (Asia Route 1) continues from here all the way to Istanbul – if only you were allowed to follow it.

Hwy 1085 runs north from Mae Sot to Mae Hong Son Province and makes an interesting trip.

Places to Stay & Eat

At the east end of town towards the river,

the *Mae Sot Guest House* at 736 Thanon Intharakhiri has rooms with shared bath for 100B. They also hand out helpful area maps. The *No 4 Guest House*, a large house well off the road at 736 Thanon Intharakhiri, charges 40B for a dorm bed, 90B for a room with shared bath.

Close to the main market in the south part of town, the new *West Frontier Guest House* (☎ 53 2638), 18/2 Thanon Bua Khun, near Pha-Waw Hospital, has six rooms in a two storey brick and wood house for 70B to 100B per person.

There are also several hotels in town, the cheapest of which is the *Suwannavit Hotel* (☎ 53 1162) on Soi Wat Luang. OK rooms with bath cost 80B in the old wing and 100B in the new building.

There is a good *food centre* next door to the Siam Hotel. The market also has good take away food, and opposite the mosque are several interesting *Burmese food stalls*. There are also several OK *food vendors* at the Mae Moei border market.

Getting There & Away
Air THAI flies to Mae Sot from Bangkok (1865B) four times a week via Phitsanulok (495B) and Chiang Mai (590B).

Bus Air-con minibuses (28B) and share taxis (50B) to Mae Sot leave hourly, from 6 am until 6 pm, from the Tak bus terminal. The trip takes 1½ hours. There is a daily 1st class air-con bus to Mae Sot from Bangkok's Northern bus terminal that leaves at 10.15 pm for 224B; 2nd class air-con buses cost 174B.

MAE HONG SON
North-west of Chiang Mai – 368km away by road and close to the Burmese border – Mae Hong Son is a hub for Burmese visitors, opium traders, local hill tribes and tourists seeking out the 'high north'.

There are several Shan-built wats in the area and a fine view from the hill by the town. It's a peaceful little place that's also a travellers' centre. Treks booked out of this town are generally less expensive than out of Chiang Mai or Chiang Rai.

Information
Tourist brochures and maps can be picked up at the tourist police office (☎ 61 1812) on Thanon Singhanat Bamrung. Open daily from 8.30 am to 9.30 pm, this is also the place to report mishaps such as theft or to lodge complaints.

Places to Stay
All the hotels are on the two main streets, Thanon Khunlum Praphat and Thanon Singhanat Bamrung. *Siam* (☎ 61 1148) and *Methi* (*Mae Tee*, ☎ 61 1121), both on Thanon Khunlum Praphat, are rather dismal at 150B to 170B for a room with fan and bath, 350B to 400B for air-con.

The plethora of inexpensive guesthouses scattered around town are better value. About a kilometre north-west of town is the new location of the long-running *Mae Hong Son Guest House*, along with *Sang Tong Huts*, *Paradise* and *Khon Thai*. Mae Hong Son Guest House is quiet and comfortable, and costs 100B to 120B for a room without bath, from 200B for a bungalow with private bath.

In the Jong Kham Lake area there are several very pleasant guesthouses, including *Jong Kham*, *Holiday House* and *Johnnie House*. All are friendly little places with rates starting at 80B.

Places to Eat
Many guesthouses also offer western-style and northern Thai food. *Paa Dim*, on Thanon Khunlum Praphat, is a warehouse-like restaurant with dishes from every region in Thailand; it's popular with Thai and farang alike because of its reasonable prices and good-sized portions. *Lucky Bakery Kitchen*, west of Thanon Khunlum Praphat on Thanon Singhanat Bamrung, does 'cowboy steak' and baked goods.

Right next to the tourist police office is a *Thai vegetarian restaurant*.

Getting There & Away
Air There are daily flights between Mae Hong Son and Chiang Mai (345B).

Bus By bus, it's nine hours from Chiang Mai to Mae Hong Son via Mae Sariang. There are about five departures a day along two different routes: the northern, through Pai (90B ordinary, 175B air-con, seven to eight hours), and the southern, through Mae Sariang (115B ordinary, 206B air-con, eight to nine hours). The southern route is more comfortable. Although the Pai route is slow and winding, recent road improvements mean the trip can take as little as seven hours (don't count on it to be on time, however). The scenery is quite spectacular in parts and you can break the trip by staying overnight in Pai.

PAI

This little town between Chiang Mai and Mae Hong Son is a mildly interesting, somewhat remote kind of place. It is a good base for exploring the surrounding country and especially for doing self-guided treks. For a view of the town, climb the hill to nearby **Wat Phra That Mae Yen**.

Places to Stay & Eat

Guesthouses line the two main streets in Pai. Across from the bus terminal is the *Duang Guest House*, where clean rooms with shared hot shower cost 50B to 60B a single and 100B to 200B a double.

On the main road through town are *Charlie's House* and *Nunya's*, with rooms from 60B for a single with shared bath, to 200B for a double in a bungalow with private bath.

Spacious rooms are available at the *Wiang Pai Hotel*, a traditional wooden hotel with rooms from 100B to 150B.

There are several bungalow operations along the Pai river east of town, including the *PS Riverside*, *Pai River Lodge* and *Golden Hut*, all with accommodation in the 50B to 80B range.

Most of the eating places in Pai line the main north-south and east-west roads. The *Thai Yai* does a good farang breakfast, plus a few Thai and Shan dishes. For authentic local food, try the *Muslim Restaurant* for noodle and rice dishes, or the *Khun Nu*, which has a variety of Thai dishes. *Bebop Restaurant & Music* has a short menu, but is an interesting place to hang out and hear live music.

Getting There & Away

The Chiang Mai to Pai road is completely paved. It takes just four hours to travel between the towns – the bus fare is 50B.

FANG & THA TON

Fang was founded by King Mengrai in 1268 but there is little of interest today, apart from the earth ramparts of his old city. Tha Ton is, however, a good base for hill tribe visits or for the downriver ride to Chiang Rai. It's situated 152km north of Chiang Mai and there are some points of interest along the way, including the elephant camp mentioned in the Around Chiang Mai section. It's probably better not to stay in Fang itself but at Tha Ton, from where the river boats run to Chiang Rai.

Places to Stay

Fang If you must stay in Fang, the *Fang Hotel* has rooms from 90B. Alternatives are the friendly *Wiang Kaew Hotel*, behind the Fang Hotel, and the *Ueng Khum (Euang Kham) Hotel*, around the corner on Thanon Thaw Phae; both have rooms in the 110B to 180B range.

Tha Ton *Thip's Travellers Guest House* continues to get good reports and costs 50/80B for singles/doubles with shared bath, 80/100B with private shower. On the road nearest the pier, the *Chan Kasem Guest House* has rooms from 60B.

On the opposite side of the river, the long-running *Maekok River Lodge* (☎ 22 2172) has landscaped grounds, a pool and deluxe rooms overlooking the river for 850B to 950B. The staff specialise in 'soft adventure' treks and have lots of ideas for hiking and rafting trips in the area.

Lou-Ta, about 15km to the north-east, is the nearest Lisu village to Tha Ton. *Asa's Guest Home* offers two basic bamboo-walled rooms for 150B per person per night, including two meals. The friendly family who own the house can arrange one and two-day jungle trips in the area. To get there take a yellow songthaew from Tha Ton (10B) or motorcycle taxi (20B) and ask to be let off in Lou-Ta.

Getting There & Away

It takes three hours from Chiang Mai to Fang by bus (45B) from the new bus terminal north of White Elephant (Chang Phuak) Gate. It's 12B and 40 minutes from Fang to Tha Ton.

AROUND FANG & THA TON

Trekking & Rafting

There are pleasant walks along the river near Tha Ton. Treks and raft trips can be arranged through Thip's Travellers Guest House or Mae Kok River Lodge. Thip's arranges economical bamboo house-rafts with pilot and cook for three days for 1200B per person (four person minimum), including all meals, lodging and rafting. The first two days are spent visiting villages and hot springs near the river, and on the third day you dock in Chiang Rai.

You could also pull together a small group of travellers and arrange your own house-raft with a guide and cook for a two or three day journey downriver, stopping off in villages of your choice along the way. A house-raft generally costs around 400B per person per day, including all meals, and takes up to six people – so figure on 1200B for a three day trip with stops at Shan, Lisu and Karen villages along the way.

River Trip to Chiang Rai

The downriver trip from Tha Ton to Chiang Rai is a bit of a tourist trap – the villages along the way sell Coke and there are lots of TV aerials. But it's still fun. The open, longtail boat departs Tha Ton around 12.30 pm. To catch it straight from Chiang Mai, you must leave at 7 or 7.30 am at the latest and make no stops on the way, or take the 6 am bus. The fare on the boat is an expensive 170B and the trip takes about three to five hours. The length of the trip depends on the height of the river. You may even sometimes have to get off and walk.

The trip finishes just in time to catch a bus back to Chiang Mai, so it can really be a day trip from Chiang Mai. It's better to stay in Tha Ton, however, and then travel on through Chiang Rai or Chiang Saen. It's also possible to make the trip (much more slowly) upriver, despite the rapids.

These days, some travellers are getting off the boat in **Mae Salak**, a large Lahu village about a third of the way to Chiang Rai from Tha Ton. From here, it is possible to trek to dozens of tribal villages south in the Wawi area – despite the ease of doing this, it doesn't seem like many foreigners take advantage of the opportunity. The fare to Mae Salak is 60B.

Other Attractions

The **Chiang Dao Caves**, filled with old Buddha images and bizarre cave formations, are 5km off the highway between Fang and Chiang Mai, 72km north of Chiang Mai. The caves are clearly signposted.

CHIANG RAI

Although this town was once the home of the Emerald Buddha, it's of no intrinsic interest – just a stepping stone for other places like Tha Ton, Chiang Saen and Mae Sai. However, it is an alternative starting point for hill tribe treks. Chiang Rai is 105km north of Chiang Mai.

Places to Stay

Chat House (☎ 71 1481), about a kilometre from the Kok river pier (for boats from Tha Ton), at 1 Thanon Trairat, has rooms with shared hot shower for 50B to 80B, dorm beds

for 40B and rooms with private hot shower for 100B to 150B. Nearby, at 445 Thanon Singhakai, is the *Mae Kok Villa*, which has dorm accommodation for 40B and single/double rooms with fan and hot water for 120/150B.

North of here are a couple of places on a large island separated from the city by a Kok river tributary. *Chian House,* 172 Thanon Si Bunruang (just off Thanon Kaw Lawy), has simple but nicely done rooms from 80/100B with hot shower, 100B to 200B for bungalows with hot shower.

Also on the island is *Pintamorn Guest House*, where comfortable singles/doubles are 80/120B with hot water. There are also doubles with air-con in a separate house for 150/250B, and a few cheaper rooms with shared facilities for 50/80B and 70/100B, plus a dorm that costs just 10B per bed.

On a soi off Thanon Singkhlai, the very pleasant *Mae Hong Son Guest House of Chiang Rai* (so named because it was once run by the same family as the original guesthouse in Mae Hong Son) offers rooms for 70/100B with shared hot showers, 100/150B with private ones. This guesthouse has a very nice garden cafe, rents motorcycles and organises treks. English, French, Spanish, Dutch and German are spoken.

Near the clock tower and district government buildings on Thanon Suksathit, the *Chiengrai Hotel* has rooms from 140B. Around the corner from the Chiang Rai Hotel, at 424/1 Thanon Banphraprakan, the *Suknirand Hotel* costs 300B and up for air-con rooms.

The clean and efficient *Krung Thong Hotel* (☎ 71 1033), 412 Thanon Sanam Bin, has large one/two-bed rooms with fan and bath for 200/240B; air-con rooms cost 320B.

Places to Eat

Many restaurants are strung out along Thanon Banphraprakan and Thanon Thanalai. Near the bus terminal there are the usual *food stalls* offering cheap and tasty food.

Near the clock tower on Thanon Banphraprakan are the *Phetburi* and *Ratburi* restaurants, with excellent selections of curries and other Thai dishes.

The *Bierstube*, on Thanon Phahonyothin, south of the Wiang Inn, has been recommended for German food. There are several other western-style pubs along here, and on the street in front of the Wiang Come Hotel.

Noi is a small, family-run Thai vegetarian

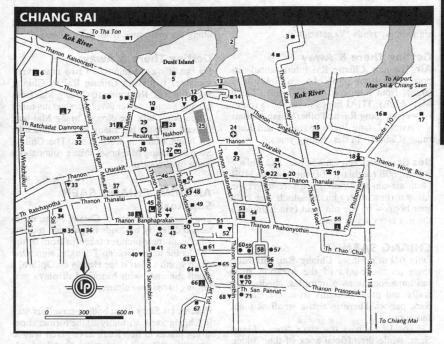

CHIANG RAI

CHIANG RAI

PLACES TO STAY
1 Rimkok Resort
3 Pintamorn Guest House
4 Chian House
5 Dusit Island Resort
9 Chat House
10 Mae Kok Villa
13 Bow Ling Guest House
14 Mae Hong Son Guest
House of Chiang Rai
16 White House
17 Wang Din Place
21 Chiangrai Inn
27 Siriwattana Hotel
30 Ruang Nakhon Hotel
34 Lek House
35 Ben Guest House
36 Ya Guest House
37 Paowattana Hotel
39 Saenphu Hotel
41 Krung Thong Hotel
43 Suknirand Hotel
47 Kijnakorn Guest House
49 Chiengrai (Chiang Rai)
Hotel
51 Siam Hotel
54 Golden Triangle Inn
61 Wang Come Hotel

64 Boonbundan Guest
House
65 Baan Bua
67 Tourist Inn
69 Wiang Inn

PLACES TO EAT
11 Cham Cha
33 Noi
40 Mae Ui Khiaw Restaurant
44 Phetburi Restaurant
52 Nakhon Pathom
Restaurant
58 Night Market
62 Khao Sawy Po Sai
68 Bierstube
70 Muang Thong
Restaurant

OTHER
2 Kok River Pier
6 Wat Phra That Doi Thong
7 Wat Ngam Meuang
8 Government Office;
Town Hall
12 TAT Office
15 Wat Bunreuany
18 King Mengrai Monument

19 Telephone Organisation of
Thailand (TOT) Office
20 Hilltribe Education Centre
22 Xmas Gift Shop/Internet
23 School
24 Provincial Health Centre
25 Police Station
26 Main Post Office
28 Wat Phra Singh
29 Hospital
31 Wat Phra Kaew
32 Communications Authority
of Thailand (CAT) Office
38 Wat Ming Meuang
42 DK Books
45 Mosque
46 Market
48 Bangkok Bank
50 Clock Tower
53 Church
55 Wat Si Koet
56 Bus Station
57 Rama II Theatre
59 Rama I Cinema
60 THAI Office
63 Tossers Bar
66 Wat Jet Yot
71 KM Car Rent

place at a corner of Thanon Utarakit a block west of Thanon Ngam Meuang – an English sign simply reads 'Vegetarian'.

Getting There & Away

Air The new Chiang Rai international airport, about 10km north of town, fields daily flights from Bangkok (1855B) and Chiang Mai (420B). THAI hopes to establish routes between Chiang Rai and other Asian capitals – possibly Luang Prabang (Laos) and Kunming (China) – in the coming years.

Bus Buses between Chiang Mai and Chiang Rai are 60B (regular), 80B (air-con) or 110B (with air-con and video). Be sure to get the *sǎi mài* (new route) buses, which take only four hours – by the old road (via Lampang) the trip takes seven hours.

CHIANG SAEN

Only 61km north of Chiang Rai, this little town on the banks of the Mekong river has numerous ruins of temples, chedis, city walls and other remains from the Chiang Saen period. There is also a small national museum.

Laos lies across the river from Chiang Saen, while the official apex of the Golden Triangle – where the borders of Myanmar, Laos and Thailand all meet – is farther north at Sop Ruak (at the point where the Ruak river meets the Mekong). The area has become very touristy in recent years and even Chiang Saen is beginning to sacrifice its charms to riverside construction.

Boats along the Mekong River

Six-passenger speedboats (*reua raew*) to Sop Ruak (30 minutes) cost 400B per boat one way or 600B round trip, or will go all the way to Chiang Khong (two hours) for 1500/ 2000B.

Places to Stay & Eat

The *Chiang Saen Guest House* is on the Thanon Sop Ruak in Chiang Saen and costs 70/80B for singles/doubles right on the river – a bit more for nicer A-frames. A bit farther along this road, on the same side, is the *Siam Guest House*, which has huts for 70B/100B, or 100/120B with bath.

About 20km from Chiang Rai on the way to Chiang Saen, via Hwy 1129, is the lively Hmong village of Ban Khiu Khan, where the *Hmong Guest House* offers rudimentary huts for 70B a night.

Cheap noodle and rice dishes are available in and near the *market* – on the river road and along the main road from the highway.

Getting There & Away

By bus it's a 40 minute to two hour (very variable) trip from Chiang Rai to Chiang Saen for 20B. Returning to Chiang Mai from Chiang Saen is faster (4½ hours versus nine) if you don't take the direct Chiang Mai bus. Instead, go back to Chiang Rai first and take a Chiang Mai bus from there. The Chiang Saen to Chiang Mai buses take a roundabout route over poor roads.

AROUND CHIANG SAEN

Sop Ruak

Sop Ruak, 9km north of Chiang Saen, is besieged daily by busloads of package tourists who want their pictures taken in front of the 'Welcome to the Golden Triangle' sign. One place worth a visit is the **House of Opium**, a small museum with historical displays pertaining to opium culture.

Places to Stay Most budget travellers stay in Chiang Saen. Virtually all the former shoestring places in Sop Ruak have given way to souvenir stalls and larger tourist hotels. *Jan's Space* is a new Thai-style bar that allows travellers to spend the night on floor mats for just 30B per person.

The second cheapest place to stay is *Debavalya Park Resort* (☎ 053-78 4113), just past the 'Golden Triangle' sign. Simple clean rooms with good beds cost 500B single/double with fan, 600B with air-con; all rooms have hot showers.

Getting There & Away From Chiang Saen to Sop Ruak, a songthaew/share taxi will cost around 10B; these leave every 20 minutes or so throughout the day. It's an easy bike ride from Chiang Saen to Sop Ruak; any of the guesthouses in Chiang Saen can arrange bicycle rentals.

MAE SAI-MAE SALONG AREA

Mae Sai is the northernmost point in Thailand, right across the Sai river from the Burmese trading post of Tachilek. The bridge over the river has recently been opened to foreigners for day trips.

Although Tachilek is not very exciting, Mae Sai makes a good base from which to explore mountain areas like Doi Tung and

GOLDEN TRIANGLE

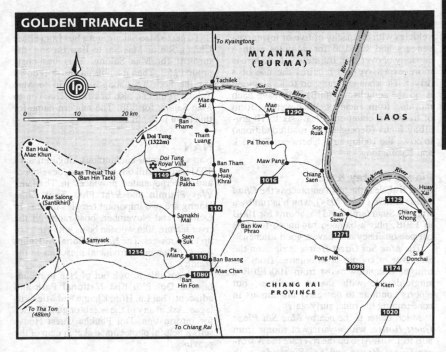

Mae Salong, once infamous for opium cultivation. It is also a good place to shop for gems – if you know what you're doing – lacquerware from Myanmar, and other crafts.

Cross-Border Trips to Tachilek & Kyaingtong

Foreigners may cross the Sai river into Tachilek upon payment of a US$5 fee. Besides shopping for Shan and Burmese handicrafts (which are about the same price as on the Thai side) and eating Shan/Burmese food, there's little to do on the other side. Some visitors use this crossing to obtain a new 30 day visa for Thailand – all you have to do is check out of Thailand, check into Myanmar, turn around and walk back into Thailand and you'll get a fresh Thailand visa.

Three-night/four-day excursions 163km north to the town of Kyaingtong (usually spelt Chiang Tung by the Thais) may be arranged through any guesthouse or travel agency in Mae Sai. You can do it on your own by paying US$18 for a three night permit at the border, plus a mandatory exchange of US$100 for Myanmar's Foreign Exchange Certificates (FECs). These FECs

can be spent on hotel rooms or exchanged on the black market for real kyat (the Burmese currency – see the Myanmar chapter for details on the money system).

Kyaingtong is a sleepy but historic capital of the Shan State's Khün culture – the Khün speak a northern Thai language related to Shan and Thai Lü, and call their town 'Kengtung'. It's a bit more than halfway between the Thai and Chinese borders – eventually the road will be open all the way to China but for now Kyaingtong is the limit. Travel westward to Taunggyi, capital of the Shan State, is also banned.

There's even less to do in Kyaingtong than in Tachilek, but it's a scenic town dotted with Buddhist temples around a small lake. You can catch glimpses of small Shan, Akha, Wa and Lahu villages along the way. The *Noi Yee Hotel* costs US$10 per person per night in multibed rooms. *Harry's Guest House & Trekking* at 132 Thanon Mai Yang, Kanaburoy Village, is operated by an English-speaking Kyaingtong native who spent many years as a trekking guide in Chiang Mai. His simple rooms go for US$5 per person, payable in US, Thai or Burmese currency.

You can rent a jeep on either side: Thai vehicles are charged a flat rate of US$50 for vehicles with a capacity of five or fewer passengers and US$100 for vehicles with a capacity of over five; Burmese vehicle hire is more expensive and requires the use of a driver. The cheapest transport to Kyaingtong is on the songthaews (60B) that leave each morning from Tachilek. Whatever the form of transport, count on at least six to 10 gruelling hours (depending on road conditions) to cover the 163km stretch between Tachilek and Kyaingtong.

Places to Stay & Eat

Mae Sai Near the town entrance is the *Chad Guest House* (☎ 73 2054), which is run by a friendly Shan family and has rooms for 100B to 150B, plus a bamboo rowhouse for 50B per person. They also have a good kitchen.

The *Mae Sai Guest House* is right on the Sai river, a couple of kilometres from the bridge. Bungalows cost from 100/120B a single/double with shared facilities, but reports continue to be nearly unanimous in condemning the rude, surly staff.

Much better is the nearby *Mae Sai Plaza Guest House*, with a variety of rooms from 80B to 150B. Also on the river are the *Northern Guest House* and *Sai Riverside*, with secure, comfortable rooms for 100B to 300B.

Other budget places include the *Sin Wattana* and *Mae Sai* hotels, along the main street, which have rooms from 200B to 400B.

Also along the main street, *Jojo Coffeeshop* makes good Thai curries. There are several other *rice and noodle shops* in the vicinity. Most close early in the evening.

Mae Salong Area In the mostly Yunnanese village of Mae Salong, the old wooden *Shin Sane (Sin Sae) Hotel* has rooms for 50B per person. Information on trekking is available; there is also a nice little eating area and a place for doing laundry. Next to the Shin Sane, *Akha Mae Salong Guest House* (☎ 76 5103) offers cramped, bare rooms for 50/100B with shared bath, 150B with bath – poor value unless the Shin Sane is full.

Getting There & Away

Buses to Mae Sai leave frequently from Chiang Rai for 20B and take 1½ hours. From Chiang Saen it's 18B and from Chiang Mai a bus costs 75B, or 130B with air-con.

To get to Doi Tung, take a 10B bus from Mae Sai to Ban Huay Khrai, then a songthaew up the mountain for 40B going, and 30B returning.

To get to Mae Salong, get a bus from either Chiang Rai or Mae Sai to Ban Basang, the turn-off for Mae Salong. This bus costs around 15B. Then it's 50B up and 40B down for the hour-long songthaew trip to Mae Salong. You can also bus from Tha Ton to Mae Salong for 60B. The modern name for this town is Santikhiri.

NAN

Nan was a semi-autonomous kingdom until 1931 and it is still one of the least 'developed' and underpopulated provinces in Thailand. **Wat Phumin** and **Wat Phra That Chae Haeng** are two important temples in Nan. In October and November, boat races on the river feature 30m wooden boats with crews of up to 50 rowers. The **Nan National Museum** is one of the best provincial museums in the country.

It's possible to trek out of Nan to mountainous **Doi Phu Kha National Park** and adjacent Thai Lü, Htin, Khamu and Mien villages. Ask at any of the hotels or guesthouses for information. Doi Phukha Guest House sells a helpful photocopied sketch map of the province.

Places to Stay

Doi Phukha Guest House (☎ 77 1422), 94/5 Thanon Sumonthewarat (actually on a soi off Sumonthewarat), offers rooms in an old teak house for 70/90B. *Wiangtai House* (☎ 71 0247), 21/1 Soi Wat Hua Wiang Tai (off Thanon Sumonthewarat near the Nara department store), has rooms in a large modern house for 120B (one large bed), 150B (two beds) and 180B (three beds).

Nan Guest House (☎ 77 1849) is in another large house at 57/16 Thanon Mahaphrom (actually at the end of a soi off Thanon Mahaphrom), near the THAI office. Singles/doubles with shared bath cost 60/80B; for rooms with private bath, add 20B per person.

Among Nan's hotels, the least expensive is the *Amorn Si* at 97 Thanon Mahayot, where very basic rooms go for 150B. *Sukkasem* at 29/31 Thanon Anantaworarittidet, has better rooms from 150B to 170B with fan and bath, 300B with air-con.

For more comfort, pick the all air-con *Dhevaraj (Thewarat) Hotel* (☎ 71 0094), 466 Thanon Sumonthewarat, a four-storey place built around a tiled courtyard with a fountain.

Large, clean rooms run from 300B to 900B depending on the amenities.

Places to Eat

One of the most dependable downtown restaurants is the old brick and wood *Siam Phochana* on Thanon Sumonthewarat. It's a very popular spot for rice and noodle dishes, open from 7 am to 9 pm. *Miw Miw*, opposite the Nan Fah Hotel, is a bit cleaner than Siam Phochana and has good *jók* (rice congee), noodles and coffee.

Getting There & Away

Buses run to Nan from Chiang Mai (86B, and 121B to 155B for air-con) and Chiang Rai (77B). The most direct way to Nan is from Den Chai via Phrae. You can also fly from Bangkok, Chiang Mai, Phrae and Phitsanulok.

North-Eastern Thailand

The north-east is the least-visited region of Thailand, although there are a number of places of interest here, and in many ways it's Thailand's most traditional region, culturally speaking. The lack of tourists can be attributed to the region's proximity to Laos and Cambodia, and the history of hold-ups and Communist guerrilla actions in the 1970s and early 1980s. Nowadays it's as safe to travel in as any other part of the country.

Among north-easterners, this region is known as Isaan, from the Sanskrit name for the Mon-Khmer Isana kingdom – a pre-Angkor culture that flourished in what is now north-eastern Thailand and Cambodia. Isaan culture and language is marked by a mixture of Lao and Khmer influences.

Points of major interest in the north-east include the scenic Mekong and the many Khmer temple ruins, especially those from the Angkor period.

Getting There & Away

Railway lines operate from Bangkok to Udon Thani and Nong Khai on the Lao border, in the north-east, and to Ubon Ratchathani, near the Cambodian border, in the east. You can make an interesting loop through the northeast by travelling first to Chiang Mai and other centres in the north and then to Phitsanulok, Khon Kaen, Loei and Udon Thani. Several north-eastern cities are also accessible by air from Bangkok.

NAKHON RATCHASIMA (KHORAT)

Also known as Khorat, Nakhon Ratchasima is mainly thought of as a place from which to visit the Khmer ruins of Phimai and Phanom Rung, although it also has a few attractions in its own right. They include the **Maha-wirawong Museum**, in the grounds of Wat Sutchinda, which has a fine collection of Khmer art objects. It's open from 9 am to noon and from 1 to 4 pm, Wednesday to Sunday.

The **Thao Suranari Memorial** is a popular shrine to Khun Ying Mo, a heroine who led the local inhabitants against Lao invaders during the reign of Rama III.

Information

TAT office in Nakhon Ratchasima can supply you with a map of the city and a list of hotels, restaurants and other useful information. The office is on Thanon Mittaphap at the western edge of town, beyond the train station. A tourist police contingent (☎ 21 3333) is attached to the TAT office.

Places to Stay

The *Doctor's House* (☎ 25 5846), 78 Soi 4, Thanon Seup Siri is quiet and comfortable and has four large rooms ranging from 80B to 160B.

The *Siri Hotel*, 167-8 Thanon Phoklang, is central and friendly; rooms start at 150B. The *Tokyo Hotel* on Thanon Suranari has good, big rooms with bath for 180B or with air-con for 400B.

The *Thai Hotel* (☎ 24 1613), 640 Thanon Mittaphap not far from the main bus terminal, is good mid-range value at 550B to 780B for very comfortable air-con rooms, or 450B to 580B for less expensive fan rooms.

Places to Eat

There are lots of good places to eat around the western gates to the town centre, near the Thao Suranari Memorial. Several inexpensive *Thai-Chinese restaurants* can also be found along Thanon Ratchadamnoen in this vicinity. At night, the *Hua Rot Fai Market* on Thanon Mukkhamontri and the *Thanon Manat night bazaar* offer a great selection and low prices; both are at their best from 6 to 10 pm.

Next to the Siri Hotel, the infamous *VFW Cafeteria*, a hang-out for American ex-GIs who live in the area, has real American breakfasts plus steak, ice cream, pizza and

THAILAND

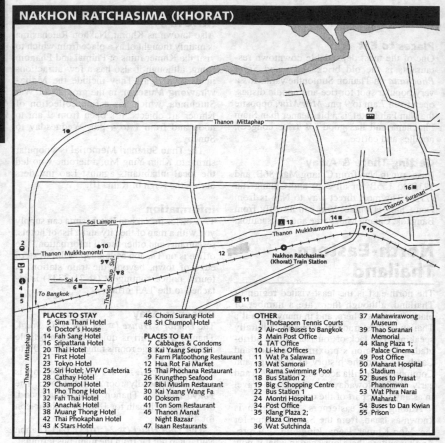

NAKHON RATCHASIMA (KHORAT)

Thanon Mittaphap

Soi Lampru

Thanon Mukkhamontri

Soi 4

To Bangkok

Thanon Mukkhamontri

Thanon Seup Siri

Thanon Mittaphap

Thanon Suranari

Nakhon Ratchasima
(Khorat) Train Station

PLACES TO STAY	46 Chom Surang Hotel	OTHER	37 Mahawirawong
5 Sima Thani Hotel	48 Sri Chumpol Hotel	1 Thotsaporn Tennis Courts	Museum
6 Doctor's House		2 Air-con Buses to Bangkok	39 Thao Suranari
14 Fah Sang Hotel	PLACES TO EAT	3 Main Post Office	Memorial
16 Sripattana Hotel	7 Cabbages & Condoms	4 TAT Office	44 Klang Plaza 1;
20 Thai Hotel	8 Kai Yaang Seup Siri	10 Li-khe Offices	Palace Cinema
21 First Hotel	9 Farm Platoothong Restaurant	11 Wat Pa Salawan	49 Post Office
23 Tokyo Hotel	12 Hua Rot Fai Market	13 Wat Samorai	50 Maharat Hospital
25 Siri Hotel; VFW Cafeteria	15 Thai Phochana Restaurant	17 Rama Swimming Pool	51 Stadium
28 Cathay Hotel	26 Krungthep Seafood	18 Bus Station 2	52 Buses to Prasat
29 Chumpol Hotel	27 Bibi Muslim Restaurant	19 Big C Shopping Centre	Phanomwan
31 Pho Thong Hotel	30 Kai Yaang Wang Fa	22 Bus Station 1	53 Wat Phra Narai
32 Fah Thai Hotel	40 Doksom	24 Montri Hospital	Maharat
33 Anachak Hotel	41 Ton Som Restaurant	34 Post Office	54 Buses to Dan Kwian
38 Muang Thong Hotel	45 Thanon Manat	35 Klang Plaza 2;	55 Prison
42 Thai Phokaphan Hotel	Night Bazaar	Plaza Cinema	
43 K Stars Hotel	47 Isaan Restaurants	36 Wat Sutchinda	

salads. For the best *kài yâang* and *sômtam* (Isaan-style grilled chicken and green papaya salad) in town, try *Kai Yaang Seup Siri*, near Doctor's House on Thanon Seup Siri.

Shopping
Nakhon Ratchasima has many shops specialising in Khorat silk. Several are found along Thanon Ratchadamnoen close to the Thao Suranari Shrine, including Ratri, Thusnee (Thatsani) and Today. Over on Thanon Chomphon are a couple of others – Chompol and Jin Chiang.

Getting There & Away
Bus Buses depart every 20 minutes to half an hour from the Northern bus terminal in

Bangkok – the fare is 70B. Less frequent air-con buses are 115B. The trip takes 3½ to four hours.

Buses to other points in the north-east or in eastern central Thailand leave Nakhon Ratchasima from bus terminal 2, off the highway to Nong Khai in the north. All other buses operate from bus terminal 1 – off Thanon Burin, near the intersection of the Thanon Mittaphap loop and the highway north to Nong Khai.

Train Several trains to Nakhon Ratchasima operate daily from Bangkok's Hualamphong station; fares are 51/117B in 3rd/1st class. The train passes through some excellent scenery.

NAKHON RATCHASIMA (KHORAT)

To Phimai, Khon Kaen & Nong Khai

Thanon Chang Phuak

Thanon Suranari

Thanon Mittaphap

Thanon Burin

Thanon Chakkri

Thanon Ratchadamnoen

Thanon Chumphor

Thanon Suranari

Thanon Phonsaen

Thanon Prajak

Thanon Yommarat

Thanon Phonlan

To Wat Sala Loi

AtsadangThanon

To Wat Thung Sawan

Thanon Manat

Thanon Kudan

Thanon Chumphon

Thanon Thaosura

Thanon Chok Chai

Thryotha

Thanon Phoklang

Thanon Jomsurangyat

Thanon Wacharasritt

Thanon Mahat Thai

Thanon Chainarong

Thanon Sanphasit

Thanon Ratchanikun

Thanon Kamhaeng Songkhram

Chum Thang Train Station

0   250   500 m

To Wat Paa Salawan

To Buriram, Surin, Ubon Ratchathani & Dan Kwian

PHIMAI

The small town of Phimai is nothing much, but staying a night or two is pleasant enough if you're here to visit Prasat Hin Phimai. If you want to visit the ruins as a day trip from Nakhon Ratchasima, an 8 am bus would give you plenty of wandering time at the ruins with time to spare for the return bus trip in the late afternoon. If Nakhon Ratchasima's not your cup of tea, do it the other way around; stay in Phimai and day-trip to Nakhon Ratchasima.

Prasat Hin Phimai National Historical Park is the site of a 12th century Khmer shrine which was constructed in the style of Cambodia's Angkor Wat and was once directly connected by road with Angkor. The main shrine has been restored and is part of the beautiful and impressive Prasat Hin Phimai National Historical Park. Admission to the complex is 40B; hours are from 7.30 am to 6 pm daily.

A **national museum** outside the complex has lots of well-preserved Khmer sculpture.

Places to Stay & Eat The *Old Phimai Guest House*, in an alley off the main street, is comfortable enough for 90B in a four bed dorm or 120/170B for singles/doubles with shared bath.

Around the corner from the bus terminal, the adequate *Phimai Hotel* has rooms ranging from 120B without bath to 400B for an air-con double with bath.

Thai and Chinese food is available at the *Baiteiy (Bai Toey)* restaurant near the hotel and guesthouses. There is also a decent collection of food vendors at a night market just north of the regular day market.

Getting There & Away There are buses every half hour from Nakhon Ratchasima's main bus terminal, behind the Erawan Hospital on Thanon Suranari. The trip takes one to 1½ hours and costs 16B. The bus terminal in Phimai is around the corner from the Phimai Hotel (directly east on Thanon Chomsudasadet) and straight down the street from Prasat Hin Phimai.

PRASAT HIN KHAO PHANOM RUNG HISTORICAL PARK

The restored temple of Prasat Hin Khao Phanom Rung, around 50km south of Buriram, is the most impressive of all Angkor monuments in Thailand. Constructed on top of an extinct volcano between the 10th and 13th centuries, the complex faces east, towards the original Angkor capital. It was originally built as a Hindu monument and features sculpture related to the worship of Vishnu and Shiva. Later, the Thais converted it into a Buddhist temple.

One of the door lintels mysteriously disappeared from the temple between 1961 and 1965. It was later discovered on display at the Art Institute of Chicago. In December 1988, after a long campaign, it was finally returned. Admission to the park is 40B.

Places to Stay & Eat

Buriram There are several inexpensive hotels in Buriram. Right in front of the train station there's the *Chai Jaroen (☎ 60 1559)*, with basic but OK single or double for 120B, or 180B triple. The *Grand Hotel (☎ 61 1089)*, along Thanon Niwat and west of the train station, has fair rooms including fan and bath starting at 160B, or 400B to 800B with aircon.

South-east of the train station on Thanon Sunthonthep, the *Prachasamakhi* is a friendly Chinese hotel with a restaurant downstairs. Adequate rooms here are 100B, or 120B with bath.

At 38/1 Thanon Romburi there's the fairly nice *Thai Hotel (☎ 61 1112)*, where clean rooms start at 200B with fan and bath and go as high as 630B for a deluxe room.

A small *night market*, with good, inexpensive food, is held in the evenings in front of the train station. At the intersection of Thanon Samattakan and Thanon Thani there's a larger *night market*, with mostly Chinese – but also a few Isaan – vendors.

Nang Rong *Honey Inn (☎ 67 1131)*, 8/1 Soi Ri Kun, is run by a local schoolteacher who speaks English. Large, clean rooms cost 100/150B single/double, and meals are also available.

Getting There & Away

Prasat Hin Khao Phanom Rung can be approached from Nakhon Ratchasima, Buriram or Surin. From Nakhon Ratchasima, take a Surin-bound bus and get out at Ban Ta-Ko (20B), which is just a few kilometres past Nang Rong. From the Ta-Ko intersection, occasional songthaews go as far as the foot of Khao Phanom Rung (12km, 15B), or you can catch any one going south to Lahan Sai. Songthaews at the foot of Khao Phanom Rung make the final leg for 5B.

If you take a Lahan Sai songthaew, get off at the Ban Don Nong Nae intersection (there are signs here pointing to Phanom Rung) – this leg is 3B. From Ban Don Nong Nae, you can get another songthaew to the foot of the hill (10B), charter a pick-up (50B one way), or hitch. A motorbike taxi all the way from Ta-Ko to Phanom Rung costs 70B. You may have to bargain hard to get these rates, as the drivers will ask for as much as 200B.

There are also a couple of morning songthaews or buses departing from Buriram Market that go directly to Ban Don Nong Nae; these are met by songthaews that go straight to the ruins.

From Surin, you take a Nakhon Ratchasima-bound bus and get off at the same place on Hwy 24, Ban Ta-Ko, then follow the directions above.

Buses from Nakhon Ratchasima to Buriram leave every half an hour during the day; they take about 2½ hours and cost 40B.

A new airport in Buriram has THAI flights from Bangkok (905B). In the current economic climate, however, this route might not endure.

KHON KAEN

The midpoint between Nakhon Ratchasima and Udon Thani, Khon Kaen is also the gateway to the north-east from Phitsanulok. The branch of the **National Museum** here has an excellent Thai sculpture collection. Otherwise it's just a big, busy town.

Information

Tourist Office TAT (☎ 24 4498) has a branch office in Khon Kaen at 15/5 Thanon Prachasamoson, open daily from 8.30 am to 4 pm. The English-speaking staff distribute good maps of the city and can answer queries on Khon Kaen and surrounding provinces.

Consulates The Lao People's Democratic Republic maintains a consulate (☎ 22 3698) at 123 Thanon Photisan. Foreigners have successfully obtained 15- and 30-day tourist visas here in three days time for around US$25 to US$35, depending on nationality. It's open from 8 to 11.30 am and from 1.30 to 4.30 pm, Monday to Friday.

There is also a Vietnamese consulate (☎ 24 1586) in Khon Kaen at 65/6 Thanon Chatapadung.

Places to Stay & Eat

There are plenty of hotels in Khon Kaen, but not all have their names up in English. Among the least expensive places is the *Suksawat* (☎ 23 9611), off Thanon Klang Meuang, where bare but clean rooms cost 80B with shared facilities, 100B to 160B with fan and bath. The *Saen Samran Hotel* at 55-59 Thanon Klang Muang costs 200B to 250B, but is not as clean as the Suksawat.

Better yet is the *Sawasdee Hotel* (☎ 22 1600), 177-9 Thanon Na Meuang, where fan rooms with hot water cost 200/250B while air-con rooms with TV, minibar and carpet are available at 400B to 500B. There are several other good mid-range places in town – visit TAT for a list.

Khon Kaen has a lively night market, with plenty of *food stalls*, next to the air-con bus terminal. Moderately priced *Khrua Weh* (Tiam An Hue in Vietnamese) is an excellent Vietnamese restaurant in an old house on Thanon Klang Meuang, near Thanon Prachasamoson.

Ob-Un Vegetarian Restaurant (a sign in English reads 'Vegetarian Food'), off the north side of Thanon Si Chan, serves Thai vegetarian dishes for 15B to 25B each and is open daily from 8 am to 9 pm. The *Vegetarian Restaurant* on Thanon Lang Muang is similar.

Getting There & Away

Air THAI flies four times daily between Bangkok and Khon Kaen (1080B).

Bus Ordinary buses arrive at and depart from a terminal on Thanon Prachasamoson, while air-con buses use a depot near the market off Thanon Klang Meuang.

The Phitsanulok to Khon Kaen road runs through spectacular scenery, including a couple of national parks. Ordinary buses to Khon Kaen leave hourly and cost 100B. Air-con buses leave Phitsanulok less frequently for 130B to 160B depending on the company. Air-con buses between Khon Kaen and Chiang Mai (11 to 12 hours) are available for 270B, ordinary for 200B.

Train Khon Kaen is on the Bangkok-Nakhon Ratchasima-Udon Thani rail line, but buses are much faster along this section.

UDON THANI

This was one of the biggest US Air Force bases in Thailand during the Vietnam War era – one of those places from where they flew out to drop thousands of tons of bombs into the jungle in the hope that somebody might be standing under one of the trees. Aside from massage parlours and ice-cream parlours, there are a few shops selling Isaan handicrafts.

Ban Chiang, 50km east, has some interesting archaeological digs – the excavations at **Wat Pho Si Nai** are open to the public, and there's a national museum (admission 10B).

Places to Stay

The *Queen Hotel* at 6-8 Thanon Udon-Dutsadi has rooms with fan and bath from 120B. At 123 Thanon Prajak Silpakorn, the *Sriswast (Si Sawat)* has rooms in an old building for 180B.

Moving up just a bit in quality and price, the friendly *Chai Porn* (☎ 22 1913), at 209-211 Mak Khaeng Rd, costs 200B to 280B for rooms with fan and private bath or 300B with air con.

The *Tang Porn Dhiraksa Hotel* further south along the same street is very similar.

Places to Eat

Udon Thani has plenty of restaurants – many with western food – but you can also find places that specialise in the Isaan food of the north-east region. *Ban Isaan* on Thanon Adunyadet is a good spot to try Isaan-style grilled chicken (kài yâang) with spicy papaya salad and sticky rice.

Try the *Rung Thong* on the west side of the clock tower for good curries (it closes around 5 pm, though).

In the new Charoensi Complex, at the

south-eastern end of Thanon Prajak, there's a good *food centre* and a couple of modern coffee shops and fast food restaurants.

Getting There & Away
There are regular flights to Udon Thani from Bangkok, Chiang Mai and Khon Kaen. Buses from Bangkok depart frequently and cost 140B – the trip takes about nine hours. A bus from Nakhon Ratchasima to Udon Thani is 65B and takes four to five hours. There are regular buses between Udon Thani and Ban Chiang (25B) throughout the day.

Trains from Bangkok cost 219B in 2nd class and take 11 hours overnight. Take a sleeper – it's worthwhile on this long trip.

NONG KHAI
Right on the Mekong river, this is the major crossing point to the Lao capital, Vientiane, via the Thai-Lao Friendship Bridge over the Mekong. It's 624km from Bangkok and only 55km north of Udon Thani.

Information
Visas for Laos Tourist visas valid for 15 days are available on arrival at the Lao immigration post on the Friendship Bridge. See the Laos chapter for further information.

Bookshop Wasambe Bookshop, on the soi leading to Mutmee Guest House, sells new and used English-language novels, guidebooks (especially for Thailand and Laos), maps, and books on spirituality, plus a collection of German, French and Dutch titles. Fax and email services are also available here.

Places to Stay
Guesthouses Long-established *Mutmee Guest House* (☎ 46 0717), on the river off Thanon Kaeworawut, has rooms with shared facilities from 80B to 120B, with private bath from 200B. It has a pleasant garden restaurant overlooking the river.

On Thanon Meechai, the *Sawasdee* offers small but clean rooms in one of the town's historic old shophouses for 80/120B for singles/doubles, and the *Mekong* has rooms overlooking the river for 70B to 150B.

Hotels *Pongvichita (Phongwichit)* at 1244/1-2 Thanon Banthoengjit is fairly clean and efficient and costs 200/350B for a one/two-bed room with fan and bath, 450/500B with air-con.

Places to Eat
Overlooking the Laos ferry pier, *Udom Rot* has good food and a pleasant atmosphere. Another riverside choice is the *Rim Nam Khong,* next to the Mekong Guest House. On Thanon Prajak, the *Thai Thai* has all the usual Thai and Chinese dishes. It's open all night. The French influence in Laos has crept over the border and into the local *pastry shops.*

Getting There & Away
By bus, it's 150B (265B with air-con) from Bangkok and takes nine or ten hours. Udon is only 1¼ hours away, and the fare is 20B.

Nong Khai is the end of the railway line that runs from Bangkok through Nakhon Ratchasima, Khon Kaen and Udon Thani. The basic fare is 238B in 2nd class, not including supplementary charges.

Laos Shuttle buses ferry passengers back and forth across the bridge from a designated terminal near the Thai-Lao Friendship Bridge for 10B per person; there are departures every 20 minutes from 8 am to 5.30 pm. From the Lao side of the bridge you can get a jumbo (Lao tuk-tuk) taxi to Vientiane for 100B or a car for 200B.

AROUND NONG KHAI
About 12km to the south-east of Nong Khai is **Wat Phra That Bang Phuan**. It is one of the most sacred temple sites in the north-east because of a 2000-year-old Indian-style stupa originally found here (it was replaced or built over by a Lao-style chedi in the 16th century). **Wat Hin Maak Peng**, 60km north-west, is a quiet and peaceful place on the banks of the Mekong.

Sala Kaew Ku, also called **Wat Khaek** (Indian temple) by locals, is a strange Hindu-Buddhist sculpture garden established by a Brahmanic yogi-priest-shaman of Lao birth who merges Hindu and Buddhist philosophy, mythology and iconography into a cryptic whole. It's about 5km south-east of town on the road to Beung Kan. Entry costs 10B.

NONG KHAI TO LOEI
Following the Mekong river west from Nong Khai into Loei Province, you'll pass through Si Chiangmai, Sangkhom, Pak Chom and Chiang Khan. Each of these small towns has a couple of guesthouses with accommodation from 100B. Although there are no major at-

tractions along this route, it's a nice area to take a break from the road. Relaxing walks along the Mekong are just the thing for frazzled nerves.

LOEI
From Loei you can climb the 1500m **Phu Kradung** mountain, about 75km to the south. The mountain is in a national park with trails, and cabins are available if you want to stay. The climb takes about four hours if you're reasonably fit.

Places to Stay
Guesthouses The *Friendship Guest House* (☎ 83 2408), south of the post office, features a few rooms in a wooden building by the river for 90B or a large room that will sleep up to five in a modern house for 240B.

Hotels The *Sarai Thong* on Thanon Ruamjit has rooms from 100B to 160B, all with fan and bath; it's off the street, quiet but not particularly clean. The *Srisawat*, nearby on Thanon Ruamjit, is similar but slightly cheaper.

Just off Thanon Chumsai, the recently renovated *Royal Villa Hotel (formerly PR House, ☎ 81 1416)* offers comfortable rooms with air-con and solar-heated shower starting at 380B per night.

Places to Eat
The *market* at the intersection of Thanon Ruamjai and Thanon Charoen Rat has cheap eats, including some local specialities.

Near the Bangkok Bank on Thanon Charoen Rat, the *Chuan Lee* and the *Sawita* are two pastry/coffee shops that also sell a range of Thai and western food.

Getting There & Away
Buses run directly from Bangkok to Loei, or you can get there from Udon Thani for 40B and from Phitsanulok via Lom Sak for 60B. Buses to Phu Kradung leave the Loei bus terminal in the morning. Direct ordinary buses to Chiang Mai cost 140B.

LOM SAK
It's an interesting trip from Phitsanulok to this colourful small town on the way to Loei and Udon Thani. It's also a pleasant trip from here to Khon Kaen. Near the bus stop, the noisy *Sawang Hotel* has rooms for 100B to 120B, and a Chinese coffee shop.

BEUNG KAN
This small dusty town on the Mekong river, 185km north-east of Nong Khai, has a Vietnamese influence. Nearby is **Wat Phu Thawk**, a remote forest wat built on a sandstone outcrop.

NAKHON PHANOM
There's a great view across the Mekong towards Tha Khaek, in Laos, from this otherwise dull city. **Renu Nakhon**, a village south of Nakhon Phanom on the way to That Phanom, is renowned for its daily handicraft market (at its biggest on Saturday).

Information
Tourist Offices TAT (☎ 51 3492) has an office in a beautiful colonial-style building at the corner of Thanon Sala Klang and Thanon Sunthon Wijit. The staff distribute information on Nakhon Phanom, Mukdahan and Sakon Nakhon provinces.

Places to Stay
The *Charoensuk Hotel*, 692/45 Thanon Bamrung Muang, *First Hotel*, 370 Thanon Si Thep, and *Grand Hotel*, on the corner of Si Thep and Ruamjit, offer similarly simple accommodation, in multistorey buildings downtown, for around 140B to 200B per room with fan and private shower, more for air-con.

For 200B to 400B you can get something a bit nicer at either the *Si Thep Hotel*, 708/11 Thanon Si Thep, or the *Windsor Hotel*, 692/19 Thanon Bamrung Meuang.

Places to Eat
Most of the town's better *Thai and Chinese restaurants* are along the river on Thanon Sunthon Wijit. There are several good, inexpensive shops, serving dishes like noodles and curry and rice, along Thanon Bamrung Meuang, north of the Windsor and Charoensuk hotels.

Getting There & Away
There are regular buses from Nong Khai to Nakhon Phanom, via Sakon Nakhon, for 55B. All the way from Udon Thani it's 70B by ordinary bus, 117B air-con.

Nakhon Phanom is a legal border crossing point between Laos and Thailand. A ferry boat across the Mekong to Tha Khaek, Laos costs 30B per person; the fare is 40B in the reverse direction.

THAT PHANOM

This remote north-eastern town, on the banks of the Mekong river, has the famous **Wat Phra That Phanom**, which is similar in style to Pha That Luang in Vientiane, Laos. There's also some interesting French-Chinese architecture around the town, again showing the Lao influence. A Lao market gathers by the river on Monday and Thursday from around 8.30 am to noon.

Places to Stay & Eat

The pleasant *Pom's House* is on a soi near the That Phanom pier. Dorm beds are 60B, singles are 90B and a double is 120B. Pom's also does bicycle rentals and short boat trips on the river.

Chai Von (Wan) Hotel, on Thanon Phanom Phanarak to the north of the arch (turn left as you pass under the arch), is an old wooden hotel with rooms from 80B with shared bath, 100B with bath. There are a couple of Thai restaurants near the Chai Von Hotel.

Getting There & Away

Songthaews from Nakhon Phanom to That Phanom cost 15B and take about 1½ hours. Stay on until you see the chedi on the right. Sakon Nakhon is two to three hours north-west by bus at a cost of 25B. Buses to Ubon Ratchathani cost around 60B ordinary, 100B air-con.

YASOTHON

Although it's a bit out of the way if you're doing the Mekong circuit, the two hour bus trip from Ubon Ratchathani is worth making to witness the annual **Rocket Festival** (8-10 May). This popular north-eastern rain-and-fertility festival is celebrated with particular fervour in Yasothon.

Places to Stay

The *Udomphon Hotel* at 169 Thanon Uthairamrit and *Surawet Wattana* at 128/1 Thanon Changsanit each cost 150B to 200B for rooms with fan and bath. The *Yot Nakhon* at 169 Thanon Uthairamrit costs from 180B for fan rooms, 300B with air-con. These places are all of comparable quality.

Getting There & Away

A bus to Yasothon from Ubon Ratchathani costs 30B.

MUKDAHAN

Around 55km south of That Phanom, 170km north of Ubon Ratchathani and directly opposite the city of Savannakhet in Laos, Mukdahan is known for its beautiful Mekong scenery and as a Thai-Lao trade centre. According to agreements between the Thai and Lao governments, a bridge between Mukdahan and Savannakhet will be built within six years.

A road east from Savannakhet ends at Lao Bao on the Vietnamese border, where it's possible to cross into Vietnam if you hold a valid Vietnamese visa.

Places to Stay

The *Hua Nam Hotel* at 20 Thanon Samut Sakdarak charges 150B for rooms with fan and shared bath, or 300B with air-con and private bath. On the same road is the cheaper *Banthom Kasem Hotel*, but it's a real dive.

The *Hong Kong Hotel*, over at 161/1-2 Thanon Phitak Santirat, is similar in design to the Hua Nam but a bit nicer; rates are 150B to 190B. Better is *Saensuk Bungalow* at 2 Thanon Phitak Santirat, which offers clean, quiet rooms for 120B to 200B fan, more for air-con.

Getting There & Away

There are frequent buses from between here and Nakhon Phanom – 30B ordinary (50B air-con), half that for That Phanom, or 39B (81B air-con) for Ubon.

Savannakhet Ferries cross the Mekong between Savannakhet and Mukdahan frequently between 8.30 am and 5 pm weekdays and until 12.30 pm Saturday; the fare is 30B.

UBON (UBOL) RATCHATHANI

This was the site of another major US Air Force base during the Vietnam War. **Wat Paa Nanachat** at nearby Warin Chamrap has a large contingent of foreign monks in residence. **Wat Thung Si Muang** in the centre of town and **Wat Phra That Nong Bua** on the outskirts are also interesting; the latter has a good copy of the Mahabodhi stupa in Bodh Gaya, India.

Information

Tourist Offices TAT (☎ 24 3770) has a very helpful branch office at 264/1 Thanon Kheuan Thani, opposite the Sri Kamol Hotel.

Places to Stay

Suriyat Hotel at 47/1-4 Thanon Suriyat has bare rooms with fan for 130B to 180B, or 300B with air-con.

A better choice in this range is the *Si Isaan (Far East,* ☎ *25 4204)* at 220/6 Thanon Ratchabut: singles/doubles are 150/180B with fan and private bath, or in a separate building there are air-con rooms for 300B.

The *New Nakornluang Hotel* (☎ *25 4768)*, 84-88 Thanon Yutthaphan, has decent fan rooms with private bath for 150B to 250B, air-con for 250B.

Places to Eat

Several inexpensive rice and noodle shops can be found along Thanon Kheuan Thani, including the *Chiokee*, which is very popular among local office workers and offers Thai, Chinese and western-style breakfasts.

The family-run *Piak Laap Pet* on Thanon Jaeng Sanit (next to a radio relay station) is famous for its namesake *laap pet* (spicy duck salad) and other Isaan food.

Getting There & Away

Air THAI has two daily flights from Bangkok to Ubon (1405B).

Bus There are frequent departures daily from the Northern bus terminal in Bangkok; fares are 164B on the regular buses, 290B air-con. Air-con buses from Nakhon Phanom take six to seven hours and cost 105B.

Train An express train and two rapid trains leave daily from Bangkok. Fares are 95B in 3rd class (rapid and ordinary trains only) and 221B in 2nd class (rapid and express), not including rapid or express surcharges.

SURIN

Surin is best known for the elephant round-up held in late November every year. There are elephant races, fights, tug-of-war and anything else you can think of to do with a couple of hundred elephants. If you've ever had an urge to see a lot of elephants at one time, this is a chance to get it out of your system.

Several minor Khmer ruins can also be visited nearby. A lot of day or overnight trips are available from Bangkok during this time.

Places to Stay

Pirom's House (☎ *51 5140)*, 242 Thanon Krung Si Nai, has dorm beds for 50B per person and singles/doubles for 70/120B. Pirom can suggest day trips around Surin, including excursions to nearby villages and Khmer temple sites.

Run by an expat Texan and his wife, *Country Roads Cafe & Guesthouse* (☎ */fax 51 5721)* is a bit out of the centre at the end of Thanon Sirirat, behind the bus terminal; rooms cost 100B.

Hotel prices soar during round-up time, but normally the *Krung Si* (☎ *51 1037)* on Thanon Krung Si has rooms from 120B to 200B. *Thanachai Hotel*, just off the roundabout on Thanon Thetsaban 1 near the post office, has somewhat dark and dingy rooms for 80/100B.

Getting There & Away

Regular buses from the Northern bus terminal in Bangkok cost 114B. There are many special tour buses at round-up time. You can also get there on the Ubon Ratchathani express and rapid trains for 169B in 2nd class, not including surcharges. Book seats well in advance during November.

Southern Thailand

The south of Thailand offers some of the most spectacular scenery in the country – plus beautiful beaches, good snorkelling, fine seafood and a good selection of things to see. There are roads along the east and west coasts; the east-coast road runs close to the railway line.

Both the geography and the people of the south are very different from the rest of the country. The rice paddies of central Thailand give way to rubber and palm oil plantations, which can be seen right down through Malaysia. Many of the people are related to the Malays in both culture and religion. This 'difference' has long promoted secessionist rumblings and the Thai government still has to grapple with occasional outbreaks of violence in the south.

The two main attractions of the south are the world-famous islands of Phuket and Ko Samui. Both offer a wide range of accommodation (Phuket less so than Ko Samui) and some superb beaches.

Other attractions include the awesome limestone outcrops which erupt from the green jungle and the sea between Phang-Nga and Krabi, and the nearly deserted beaches of Trang, Pattani and Narathiwat. Chaiya has some archaeologically interesting remains and, deep in the south, Hat Yai is a rapidly growing, modern city with a colourful reputation as a weekend getaway from Malaysia.

Getting There & Away

You can travel south from Bangkok by air, bus or rail. The road south runs down the east coast as far as Chumphon, where you have a choice of climbing over the narrow mountain range and going down the west coast (for Ranong, Phuket, Krabi, Trang and Satun) or continuing south on the east coast (for Surat Thani, Ko Samui, Nakhon Si Thammarat, Pattani and Narathiwat).

The railway follows the eastern route and both routes meet again at Hat Yai. From Hat Yai, rail and roads split and you can follow either route to Malaysia: down the west coast to Alor Setar and then Penang, or head to the east and cross the border from Sungai Kolok to Kota Bharu.

PHETBURI (PHETCHABURI)

Phetburi, 160km south of Bangkok, has a number of interesting old temples. A walking tour can take in six or seven of them in two or three hours, including the old Khmer site of **Wat Kamphaeng Laeng** and the Ayuthaya-era **Wat Yai Suwannaram**.

On the outskirts of town, next to the Phetkasem Hwy, is **Khao Wang**, a hill topped by a restored King Mongkut palace. You can walk up the hill to the historical park or take a cable car for 10B one way. Entry to the park is 40B.

The **Phra Nakhon Khiri Fair** takes place in early February and lasts about eight days. Centred on Khao Wang and the city's historic temples, the festivities include a sound and light show at the Phra Nakhon Khiri Palace, temples festooned with lights and performances of Thai classical dance-drama.

Places to Stay & Eat

The *Chom Klao* is on the east side of Chomrut Bridge and has rooms for 100B to 150B. The *Nam Chai*, a block farther east, is similarly priced but not such good value. The *Phetburi* is on the next street north of Chomrut Bridge and behind the Chom Klao; it has overpriced rooms at 150B with fan and bath. The *Ratanaphakdi Hotel* on Thanon Chise-In is better – clean rooms with private bath cost 200.

There are several good *restaurants* in the vicinity of Khao Wang serving a variety of standard Thai and Chinese dishes. The cheap-est food – with plenty of variety – is at the *night market* at the southern end of Thanon Surinluechai, under the digital clock tower.

Getting There & Away

Buses leave regularly from the Southern bus terminal in Thonburi, Bangkok, for 41B or 69B with air-con, and take about three hours. Buses to Phetburi from Hua Hin are 25B.

AROUND PHETBURI

The nearby **Kaeng Krachan National Park** is Thailand's largest. There is public transport from Phetburi as far as Kaeng Krachan village for 25B. From there, you must hitch or charter a truck for the 4km to the park entrance.

HUA HIN

This town, 230km south of Bangkok, is the oldest Thai seaside resort. Hua Hin is still a popular weekend getaway for Thais, but has recently been discovered by a rash of Europeans, who have brought high-rise hotels, western restaurants and bars. Rama VII had a summer residence here and the royal family still uses it.

The Hotel Sofitel Central Hua Hin is fronted by trees and shrubs trimmed to resemble roosters, ducks, women opening umbrellas, giraffes and snakes.

Places to Stay

Accommodation in Hua Hin tends to be a bit on the expensive side as it's so close to Bangkok. Rates are usually higher on weekends and holidays, so go during the week for the best deals.

The cheapest places are along or just off Thanon Naretdamri. Rooms at *Khun Daeng House*, on Thanon Naretdamri, cost 100B to 150B with private bath.

Farther south-east along Thanon Naretdamri are a string of atmospheric wooden places built on piers over the edge of the sea. *Mod (Mot) Guest House* has small but OK rooms for 190B to 290B with fan, 400B to 500B with air-con and hot water. The adjacent *Seabreeze (Sirima)* is similar. A little south-east of here, along a soi that leads toward the beach, *Bird* (☎ 51 1630) is the best of the seaside guesthouses; it's well kept, well designed and charges 300B to 500B.

If you can afford it, the *Hotel Sofitel Central Hua Hin* (☎ 51 2021) is a fine experience. Formerly the Railway Hotel, this delightfully old-fashioned place was built by German railway engineers and leased by a French conglomerate in 1986. It's just off the beach on Thanon Damnoen Kasem. The rooms are big, the ceilings are high and the service is polished. Rooms in the old colonial wing start at 3100B. Movie buffs may recognise the place as the Hotel Le Phnom from the film *The Killing Fields*.

Places to Eat
Hua Hin is noted for its seafood, available near the pier at the end of Thanon Chomsin or at the *night market* (always settle the price before ordering).

Along Thanon Naretdamri there are a number of touristy restaurants with touristy prices, such as the *Beergarden* and *La Villa*.

Getting There & Away
Buses run from the Southern bus terminal in Bangkok. There are frequent departures for the four hour trip and the cost is 51B, or 92B with air-con. Buses from Phetburi are 20B.

Trains en route to Hat Yai in the south also stop at Hua Hin. The trip takes around 4½ hours and costs 44/92B in 3rd/2nd class.

Getting Around
Samlors from the train station to the beach cost 20B; from the bus terminal to Thanon Naretdamri, 25B; and from Chatchai Market to the fishing pier, 30B.

PRACHUAP KHIRI KHAN
This provincial capital is sleepy compared with Hua Hin, but some fine seafood can be found here. South of Ao Prachuap, around a small headland, scenic **Ao Manao** (Lime Bay) is ringed by limestone mountains and islets.

A few kilometres north of town there's another bay, **Ao Noi**, where a small fishing village has a few rooms to let.

Places to Stay & Eat
The centrally located *Yuttichai*, at 35 Thanon Kong Kiat, has fair rooms with fan and bath from 100B to 200B. Around the corner on Thanon Phitak Chat, *Inthira Hotel* has recently renovated rooms for a bit more. The *King Hotel* (☎ 61 1170), farther south on the same street, has rooms from 220B to 270B.

The upmarket but reasonably priced *Hadthong Hotel* (☎ 60 1050), next to the bay in town, has modern air-con rooms with balconies for 600B (mountain view) and 728B

(sea view), plus a 200B surcharge from 20 December to 31 January. A good pool is on the premises.

On Thanon Chai Thale, near the Hadthong Hotel, is a small *night market* that's quite good for seafood. Several good *seafood restaurants* can also be found along the road north of Ao Prachuap on the way to Ao Noi. *Rap Lom* (literally, 'breeze-receiving') is the most popular – look for the Green Spot sign.

Getting There & Away
From Bangkok, buses are 72B, 130B with air-con. Buses from Hua Hin are 30B and leave the bus terminal on Thanon Sasong frequently between early morning and mid-afternoon.

It's also possible to catch a train from Hua Hin to Prachuap for 19B in 3rd class.

RANONG
Ranong lies 600km south of Bangkok and 300km north of Phuket. Only the Chan river separates Thailand from Kawthoung (Victoria Point), in Myanmar, at this point. There's a busy trade supplying Burmese needs – the focus of the sea trade is the Saphaan Plaa pier, which is 8km south-west of town (8B on a No 2 songthaew).

Much of the town centre has a Hokkien Chinese flavour. Just outside of town is the 42°C **Ranong Mineral Hot Springs** at Wat Tapotaram.

Places to Stay & Eat
Along Thanon Ruangrat in Ranong there are a number of cheap places, including the *Rattanasin* (OK rooms; 150B) and the *Suriyanon* (100B). The *Asia* (☎ 81 1113) on the same road offers spacious clean rooms the 200 to 300B range for fan rooms, more with air-con.

The somewhat expensive *Jansom Thara Hotel*, up on the main road, is the place to stay for mineral bathing – all the hotel's water is piped in from the hot springs. Rooms start at 1400B, but sometimes they offer discounted rooms for as low as 780B.

For inexpensive Thai and Burmese breakfasts, try the *morning market* on Thanon Ruangrat, along which there are also several traditional *Hokkien coffee shops* with marble-topped tables.

A couple of kilometres north of town on the highway, between the Caltex and PT petrol stations, the *Mandalay* specialises in Burmese and Thai seafood.

Getting There & Away

Air Bangkok Airways flies twice daily from Bangkok to Ranong airport (1980B), 20km south of town, off Hwy 4.

Bus Buses from Chumphon cost 40B or from Surat Thani 60B (80B air-con). Buses from Takua Pa are 45B, or 80B from Phuket. The bus terminal in Ranong is outside town near the Jansom Thara Hotel. To/from Bangkok, ordinary buses cost 150B, air-con 250B.

AROUND RANONG

Along the coast at the southern end of Ranong Province is **Laem Son National Park**, a wildlife and forest reserve consisting of mangrove swamps, sandy beaches and mostly uninhabited islands.

On nearby **Ko Chang**, several beach places are open November to April, including *Rasta Baby*, *Ko Chang Contex* and *Cashew Resort*, all with simple huts for 100B to 200B a night. Boats to Ko Chang leave from Ranong's Saphaan Plaa twice daily; fares are negotiable depending on how many passengers board.

For **Victoria Point**, boats leave the same pier regularly from around 7 am till 3 pm for 50B per person. Immediately as you exit the Victoria Point jetty there's a small immigration office on the right, where you must pay US$5 for a day permit.

CHAIYA

Just north of Surat Thani, Chaiya is one of the oldest cities in Thailand and has intriguing ruins from the Sumatran-based Sriwijaya Empire. Indeed, some scholars believe this was the real centre of the empire, not Palembang. The name is a Thai abbreviation of 'Siwichaiya'. The restored **Boromathat Chaiya** stupa is very similar in design to the *candis* (shrines) of central Java. A national museum next to the stupa contains artefacts from the Sriwijaya era.

Outside of town, **Wat Suanmok** is a complete contrast, a modern forest monastery established by Thailand's most famous Buddhist monk, the late Ajaan Phutthathat (Buddhadasa).

Places to Stay & Eat

There are guest quarters in *Wat Suanmok* for those participating in monthly 10-day meditation retreats, but most visitors make Chaiya a day trip from nearby Surat Thani. Too many

travellers treat Suanmok and other forest wats as open zoos – visit it only if you are genuinely interested in Buddhism or meditation.

The *Udomlap Hotel*, just off the main road and close to the train station in Chaiya, has rooms with fan for 100B to 140B.

There are several places to eat in the vicinity of the train station. Approximately 10 minutes from town there's a long pier with two restaurants.

Getting There & Away

Chaiya is on the railway line only 20km north of Surat Thani – you can get there by rail, bus or even taxi. Wat Suanmok is about 7km out of Chaiya. Buses run there directly from Surat Thani bus terminal so it isn't necessary to go right into Chaiya. Until late afternoon there are songthaews from Chaiya train station to Wat Suanmok for 8B per passenger, or you can get there from the station by motorbike for 20B.

SURAT THANI

This busy port is of interest for most travellers only as a jumping-off point for the island of Ko Samui, 30km off the coast. See the Getting There & Away entry in the following Ko Samui section for details of boat departures.

Places to Stay & Eat

Many of Surat Thani's hotels are transient specialists and you're likely to sleep better on the night ferry, without all the disturbances of nocturnal customers coming and going. With the rail, bus and boat combination tickets, there's no reason to stay in Surat Thani at all.

Within walking distance of the Ban Don pier are the *Phanfa*, *Ban Don* and *Thai* hotels, each with rooms in the 120B to 300B range. If you want something with a little more comfort, try the *Thai Rung Ruang Hotel* near the bus terminal, where spacious fan rooms cost 310/390B single/double, or with air-con 420/520B.

In nearby Phun Phin, near the train station, the simple *Tai Fah* and *Sri Thani* hotels have rooms for around 100B.

The *market* near the bus terminal has good cheap food or, in Ban Don, try the places on the waterfront. A restaurant marked *Vegetarian Food* on Soi 33, Thanon Talaat Mai, just opposite one of the entrances to Thai Rung Ruang Hotel, has vegetarian kuaythiaw, some very hot curries and other dishes.

Getting There & Away

Air THAI flies to Surat Thani from Bangkok (1785B), Chiang Mai (3115B), Nakhon Si Thammarat (340B), Hat Yai (1200B), Phuket (475B) and Ranong (485B).

Bus & Minivan From the Southern bus terminal in Bangkok, the trip to Surat Thani takes 11 hours and costs 163B, or 294B for an air-con bus. From Surat Thani, buses run to Songkhla, Hat Yai, Phuket and other towns around the south. There are also cramped air-con minivans to tourist centres like Krabi and Phuket; these cost about the same as an air-con bus but are usually a lot less comfortable.

Train By train the fare from Bangkok to Surat Thani is 248B in 2nd class, but Surat Thani station is 14km out of town, at Phun Phin. If you're heading south to Hat Yai you may decide it is easier to take a bus than to risk getting to the station to find there are no seats left.

Getting Around

From the train station to the pier for Ko Samui ferries, buses leave every five minutes and cost 10B. The buses that meet the night express are free, but if you arrive at a time when the buses aren't running, a taxi to Ban Don costs about 80B.

KO SAMUI

This beautiful island, off the east coast, has relatively recently become a fully fledged tourist resort. An airport was finally opened here in 1989 and car ferries have been in operation for several years, so it's hardly 'untouched', but at least you can't drive there over a bridge (as you can to Phuket). There's still accommodation at nearly every budget level.

Coconut plantations are still an important source of income, and visitors go relatively unnoticed outside the beach areas, especially outside the high tourist seasons (December to March and July to August).

Orientation

Ko Samui is the largest island on the east coast and the third largest in Thailand. It's about 25km long and 21km wide and is surrounded by 80 other islands, only six of which are uninhabited. The main town is Na Thon, and most of the population is concentrated there and at a handful of other towns scattered around the coast.

Information

The best time to visit Ko Samui is from February to late June. July to late October is very wet and from then until January it can be very windy. During the on season, from December to March and from July to August, accommodation can get a little tight.

There are several foreign exchange services in Na Thon, Chaweng and Lamai. Mail can be sent to poste restante at the main post office, Na Thon.

Medical Services A modern medical facility, Bandon International Hospital (☎ 24 5236) can be found in Bo Phut.

Things to See

The beaches are beautiful and, naturally, the main attraction, but note the water is not as clear on the north or west coasts as along the east and south. Ko Samui also has scenic waterfalls in the centre of the island – **Hin Lat**, 3km south-east of Na Thon, and **Na Muang**, 10km south-east of Na Thon. Although Hin Lat is closer to Na Thon, Na Muang is the more scenic.

Near Ban Bang Kao, there's an interesting old chedi at **Wat Laem Saw**. The **Wat Phra Yai** (Big Buddha Temple), with its 12m-high Buddha image, is at the north-eastern end of the island, on a small rocky islet joined to the main island by a causeway. The monks are pleased to have visitors, but proper attire (no shorts) should be worn on the temple premises.

Environmental Message

Samui's visitors and inhabitants produce over 50 tonnes of garbage a day, much of it plastic. Not all of this is disposed of properly, and much – including quite a few plastic bottles – ends up in the sea, where it wreaks havoc on marine life. Remember to request recyclable glass water bottles instead of plastic, or try to fill your own water bottle from the large, reusable canisters in the restaurants of guesthouses and hotels.

Places to Stay & Eat

There are over 200 places to stay at the beaches, most ranging in cost from 150B to 500B a night, plus a smattering of luxury places ranging from 1000B to 3000B and over. Hat Chaweng and Hat Lamai are the two most popular spots, and both have beautiful sands and clear, sparkling water. Lamai has a coral reef; Chaweng has the largest beach, with probably the best water, and a

KO SAMUI

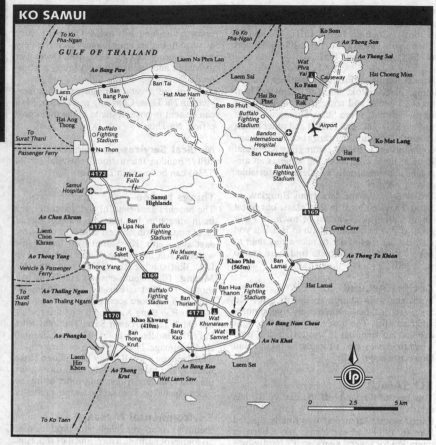

small island opposite. Both are now dotted with discos/beer bars, so are not especially quiet during the high season.

Bo Phut and Big Buddha beaches are on the bay which encloses Ko Faan (the Big Buddha island), and these are rather quieter. Mae Nam and Thong Yang are also very quiet, as are the little coves and tidal flats along the south shore. You can get farther away from it all on the neighbouring island of Ko Pha-Ngan.

Na Thon If you want to stay in the town, there are a number of hotels to choose from. The *Palace Hotel* on the waterfront has clean, spacious rooms starting at 280B with fan, or 400B with air-con. Less expensive is the *Seaview Guest House* on Thanon Wattana,

which has Khao San-style rooms with fan and bath for 150B to 200B. On the southern edge of town, *Jinta Bungalows* has basic rooms for 150B to 250B.

Several restaurants face Na Thon's harbour and offer a combination of western food and Thai seafood; one of the oldest and best is the *Chao Koh*. On the next street back there are two or three *bakeries*, a *pizza joint*, a good *curry shop* and a *Hokkien coffee shop* that has somehow managed to withstand the tourist onslaught.

Chaweng The island's longest beach offers the largest number and variety of places to stay, though they are constantly upgrading themselves to drive room rates higher. The cheaper ones are all much the same and cost from 150B a night for a small bungalow – knock it down a bit for a longer stay or during the off season, when some will go as low as 50B to 80B. Nicer bungalows here go for 300B to 400B.

At the north end of Chaweng, you'll find *Matlang Resort,* which has better than average bungalows for 400B to 650B, as well as, *Venus, Blue Lagoon, Marine, Lagoon Cottages* and *Lazy Wave. JR Chalet,* a new place at the northern end of Chaweng, has a huge restaurant, and clean rooms with modern bathroom facilities for 400B with fan, 600B with air-con.

Towards the centre of the beach, prices rise a bit to the 200B to 350B range in high season, as at *Lucky Mother, Coconut Grove, Charlie's Hut, Charlie's Hut Viking* and *Joy Resort.*

Around the small headland at the south end, the only surviving budget place is *Chaweng Noi,* which costs 150B for a hut. Everything else on Chaweng is upscale and beyond the shoestring budget.

Lamai Samui's second most popular beach is finally succumbing to bigger tourist developments and is feeling the price squeeze, although overall it's still less expensive than Chaweng. Cheaper huts at the north-east end of the beach are at *Beer's House, Island Resort, Rose Garden* and *Suksamer,* all in the 150B to 300B range. *New Hut* also has a few 80B to 100B rooms, but the proprietors have been known to eject guests who don't eat in their restaurant, and we continue to receive complaints of rudeness at this place.

Lamai's central section begins with a string of 150B to 600B places: *Mui, Utopia, Magic* and the *Weekender.* The Weekender has a wide variety of bungalows and activities to choose from, including a bit of nightlife.

Next comes *Thai House Inn, Marina Villa, Sawadee House, Mira Mare, Sea Breeze* and *Varinda Resort* – all with rooms in the 100B to 600B range and with elaborate outdoor dining areas.

At the southern end of central Lamai Beach is a mixture of 80B to 200B places, including the long-standing *Paradise, Bill's Resort, White Sand, Palm, Nice Resort* and *Sun Rise.*

Beyond a headland, between Hat Lamai and Bang Nam Cheut, are some of Ko Samui's cheapest digs, including *Swiss Chalets, Noi, Chinda House* and *Rocky,* all with huts from 100B to 300B.

Big Buddha *Family Village* gets good reviews and costs from 200B to 700B. *Big Buddha Bungalows,* from 200B to 350B, is also OK. *Sun Set* is about the cheapest place here, with simple huts at 80B to 300B.

Como's, Champ Resort, Beach House, Kinnaree and *Number One* are in the 150B to 300B range.

Bo Phut Although there are about 20 places to stay here, this area manages to stay fairly quiet. At the north end, *Bo Phut Guesthouse, Sandy Resort, World Resort, Samui Palm Beach, Calm Beach Resort* and *Peace* have bungalows in the 80B to 300B range.

Towards the village is *Boon Bungalows,* a small operation with 50B to 100B huts. West of Boon is *Ziggy Stardust,* a clean place with huts from 500B to 1500B. Cheaper in this area are *Smile House, Miami* and *Oasis,* all with huts in the 50B to 200B range.

The village has a couple of cheap local-style restaurants and a couple of farang places.

Hat Mae Nam At this beach 14km northeast of Na Thon, the *Friendly* has clean well kept huts for 150B to 300B, all with private bath. We've received one unconfirmed report of vicious dogs' here so beware in case it's true. *New La Paz Villa* is also a good choice for 300B with fan or 600B air-con. *Magic View* and *Silent* are cheap but acceptable.

Moving towards Bo Phut you'll find *Moon Hut Bungalows, Rose Bungalows, Laem Sai Bungalows, Maenam Villa* and *Rainbow Bungalows,* all with old-style Samui huts for 80B to 150B a night.

While the scene at Mae Nam is not quite as picturesque as at Chaweng or Lamai, the swimming and sand are quite OK.

Other Areas Along the southern end of the island you'll find bungalows tucked away into smaller bays and coves. If the development along Chaweng and Lamai is too much for you, this area might be just the ticket – all you need is a motorbike and a Ko Samui map. As at Lamai, the places along the southern end are pretty rocky; they're good for snorkelling but not so good for swimming.

Try Ao Na Khai and Laem Set, just beyond the village of Hua Thanon, for the best southern beaches. Other possibilities include Ao Thong Krut and Ao Bang Kao. Bungalows here start at 60B to 400B with bath.

At Ao Thong Yang and other seaside areas

along Samui's west coast, bungalows are springing up everywhere because the car ferry from Don Sak docks on this side. None of them are anything special, nor are they cheap, and the beaches tend to become mud flats at low tide.

Getting There & Away

You can fly directly to Ko Samui from Bangkok with Bangkok Airways (3150B), or there are three ferry companies running boats from Surat Thani. Altogether, there are four ferry piers on the Surat coast (Ban Don, Tha Thong, Khanom and Don Sak – only three are in use at one time) and two piers on Ko Samui (Na Thon and Thong Yang). This can make things a bit confusing at times, but if you just follow the flow of travellers everything will work out.

The State Railway of Thailand does rail, bus and ferry tickets straight through to Ko Samui from Bangkok or the reverse. You end up paying about 50B more this way than if you book all the segments yourself.

Be cautious when using local agents to make mainland train and bus bookings – they don't always get made, or are not for the class you paid for. Several travellers have written to complain of rip-offs here.

Express Boats from Tha Thong From November to May three express boats go to Samui (Na Thon) daily from Tha Thong, each takes two to 2½ hours to reach the island. The departure times are usually 7.30 am, noon and 2.30 pm, though these change from time to time. From June to October there are only two express boats a day; at 7.30 am and 1.30 pm – the seas are usually too high in the late afternoon for a third sailing in this direction during the rainy season. The express ferry boats have two decks, one with seats below and an upper deck that is really just a big luggage rack - good for sunbathing. Passage is 130B one way, 240B return, but this fare seesaws from season to season; if any rivals to Songserm appear on the scene (as has happened twice in the last four years), Songserm tends to drop its fares immediately to as low as 50B one way to drive the competition quickly out of business.

From Na Thon back to Surat, there are departures at 7.15 am, noon and 2.45 pm from November to May, or at 7.30 am and 2.45 pm from June to October. The morning boat includes a bus ride to the train station in Phun

Phin. The afternoon boats include a bus ride to the train station and to the Talaat Kaset bus terminal in Ban Don.

Night Ferry There is also a slow boat for Samui that leaves the Ban Don pier each night at 11 pm, reaching Na Thon around 5 am. This one costs 80B for the upper deck (including pillows and mattresses), or 50B down below (straw mats only). The locals use this boat extensively and the craft itself is in better shape than some of the express boats. It's particularly recommended if you arrive in Surat Thani too late for the fast boat and don't want to stay in Ban Don. And it does give you more sun time on Samui, after all.

The night ferry back to Samui leaves Na Thon at 9 pm, arriving at 3 am; you can stay on the boat, catching some more sleep, until 8 am. Ignore the touts trying to herd passengers onto buses to Bangkok, as these won't leave till 8 am or later anyway.

Don't leave your bags unattended on the night ferry, as thefts can be a problem. The thefts usually occur after you drop your bags on the ferry well before departure and then go for a walk around the pier area. Most victims don't notice anything's missing until they unpack after arrival on Samui.

Vehicle Ferry From Thanon Talaat Mai in Surat Thani, you can get bus and ferry combination tickets straight through to Na Thon. These cost 80B, or 100B for an air-con bus. Pedestrians, cars and motorbikes can also take the ferry directly from Don Sak. It leaves at 6.50, 8 and 10 am, and 2 and 5 pm, and takes one hour to reach the Thong Yang pier on Ko Samui. The ferry only fares are: pedestrians 50B, motorbikes and driver 80B, and a car and driver 200B. Passengers in private vehicles pay the pedestrian fare.

Don Sak, in Surat Thani Province, is about 60km from Surat Thani. A bus from the Surat bus terminal is 17B and takes 45 minutes to an hour to arrive at the Don Sak ferry. If you're coming north from Nakhon Si Thammarat, this might be the ferry to take, although from Surat the Tha Thong ferry is definitely more convenient.

Tour buses run directly from Bangkok to Ko Samui, via the Don Sak car ferry, for around 400B. From Ko Samui, air-con buses to Bangkok leave from near the pier in Na Thon twice daily, arriving in Bangkok in the early morning (there's a dinner stop in Surat the evening before). Through buses are also available from Ko Samui to Hat Yai and other points south. Check with the travel agencies in Na Thon for the latest routes.

Getting Around
It's about 19km from Na Thon to Bo Phut on the north coast, and 23km to Chaweng in the east. Minibuses and songthaews operate all day. Official fares from Na Thon are 10B to Mae Nam or Bo Phut, 15B to Big Buddha and 20B to Chaweng or Lamai. Farangs are often charged 5B extra because their backpacks take up so much room. From the car-ferry landing in Thong Yang, rates are 20B for Lamai, Mae Nam and Bo Phut/Big Buddha, 25B for Chaweng.

Often you'll be met in Na Thon (even on the ferry at Ban Don) and offered free transport if you stay at the place doing the offering.

You can rent motorbikes on Ko Samui – these are better value at Na Thon than at the beaches. Smaller 100cc bikes cost 150B a day and larger ones are 200B – ask for discounts for multi-day rentals.

KO PHA-NGAN
The island of Ko Pha-Ngan is north of Ko Samui and although nearly as big, it is generally more quiet and tranquil. It also has beautiful beaches, some fine snorkelling and the **Than Sadet Falls**. The lack of an airport and relative lack of paved roads has so far spared it from tourist-hotel and package-tour development.

At **Wat Khao Tham**, on a hilltop on the south-west side of the island, 10-day Buddhist meditation retreats are conducted by an American-Australian couple during the latter half of most months. The cost is 1800B; write in advance to Khao Tham, Ko Pha-Ngan, Surat Thani, for information, or pre-register in person.

Ferries from Surat, Ko Samui and Ko Tao dock at Thong Sala on Pha-Ngan's west coast; there are also smaller boats from Mae Nam and Bo Phut on Ko Samui to Hat Rin on the island's southern end.

Places to Stay
The beaches near Thong Sala are not among the island's best, but since they're close to the main pier, people waiting for an early boat back to Surat Thani or on to Ko Tao sometimes stay here. On Ao Bang Charu, the *Petchr Cottage*, *Sundance*, *Pha-Ngan Villa* and *Moonlight* are all in the 70B to 150B range.

Just north of Thong Sala are the *Phangan* (70B to 300B), *Charn* (80B to 120B), *Siriphun* (100B to 400B) and *Tranquil Resort* (70B to 200B). Farther north, at the southern end of Ao Wok Tum, the basic *Tuk, Kiat, OK* and *Darin* all offer basic huts in the 60B to 80B range with shared facilities, except Darin which also has bungalows with private bath for 120B to 150B.. A little farther down around Laem Hin are *Porn Sawan, Cookies* and *Beach 99*, with the same rates and facilities.

Ban Tai & Ban Khai Between the villages of Ban Tai and Ban Khai there's a series of sandy beaches with well-spaced collections of bungalows, most in the 50B to 100B range. They include *Dewshore, P Park, Liberty Birdville, Jup, Bay Hut, Lee's Garden* and *Golden Beach*.

Laem Hat Rin This long cape has beaches along both sides - Hat Rin Nok (Outer Rin Beach, often referred to as 'Sunrise Beach') along the eastern shore and Hat Rin Nai (Inner Rin Beach) along the western shore. They're getting very crowded these days, especially Hat Rin Nok, the better of the two beaches. The all-night 'full moon' parties here are legendary and have recently begun attracting the attention of the local police.

Most of the places on Hat Rin Nok start at 150B a night; they include *Paradise, Beach Blue, Haadrin Resort, Tommy* and *Palita Lodge*; a couple of slightly cheaper ones, like *Sunrise* and *Sea Garden Bungalows*; and the upscale *Pha-Ngan Bayshore Resort*. Built into the rocky headland at the north end, *Mountain Sea Bungalows* and *Serenity* have huts for 80B to 200B and are quieter at night than the places right on the beach.

All of these places are OK. For 100B, the nicest thatched bungalows (all with attached bath) are those at *Blue Hill*, situated on the hill above the beach.

Along the Hat Rin Nai are the long-running *Palm Beach* and *Sunset Bay Resort*, both of which cost from 80B to 200B. Other places that offer similarly priced accommodation are *Rainbow, Coral, Bird, Star, Bang Son Villa, Sun Beach, Sea Side, Sooksom, Laidback, Sandy* and, down near the tip of the cape, the *Lighthouse* and *Leela Bungalows*.

Ao Chalok Lam & Hat Khuat These two pretty bays on the northern end of Pha-Ngan are still largely undeveloped. Chalok Lam

KO PHA-NGAN

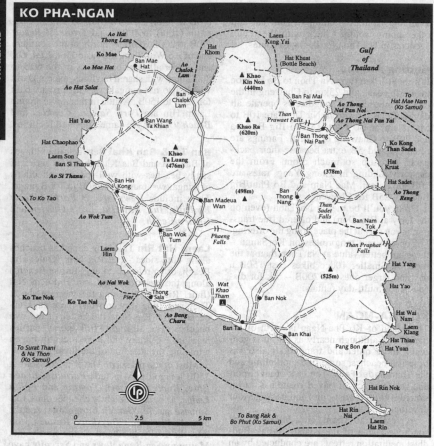

has *Try Tong Resort, Wattana Bungalows* and *Fanta* at 60B to 200B.

Huts at Hat Kuat's *Bottle Beach, Bottle Beach II* and *Sea Love* cost 80 to 200B.

West of Hat Khuat, 2.5km across Laem Kung Yai, is Hat Khom, where the *Coral Bay* charges 50B to 80B.

Ao Mae Hat The beach at Ao Mae Hat isn't fantastic, but there is a bit of coral offshore. *Maehaad Bungalows* has simple huts for 50B plus wood-and-thatch huts with private bath for up to 150B; the *Mae Hat Bay Resort* and *Crystal Island Garden* have small wooden huts in the same price range.

Moving south-westward, nicer wooden huts at the *Island View Cabana* cost from 70B to 250B; there's also a good restaurant.

Ao Si Thanu The *Laem Son* starts at 40B while the *Sea Flower, Seetanu* and *Great Bay* all have huts costing from 100B to 250B, the more expensive ones come with private bath. Several other places come and go in this area with the seasons.

East Coast On the beach at Ao Thong Nai Pan Yai, near Ban Thong Nai Pan on the island's north-east coast, are the *White Sand, AD View* and *Nice Beach* for 60B to 300B.

Up on Thong Nai Pan Noi are the very nicely situated and well maintained *Panviman Resort* (300B and up) and *Thong Ta Pan Resort* (80B to 150B).

Places to Eat

Unlike Ko Samui, Ko Pha-Ngan isn't known

for fabulous cuisine. Virtually all beach accommodation places have their own simple cafes with typical 'farang-ised' versions of Thai food, plus the usual muesli-yoghurt, sandwiches and so on.

In Thong Sala, several cafes near the pier cater to farang tastes and also sell boat tickets. *Cafe de la Poste*, opposite the post office, offers imported cheeses, coffee, sandwiches, pizza, pasta and vegetarian dishes.

Getting There & Away

There are regular ferries from Na Thon, on Ko Samui, to Thong Sala for 60B and occasional boats from Bo Phut to Hat Rin for 50B to 60B. The latter trip requires wading in from the boat to the beach in hip-deep water. The crossing takes about 45 minutes.

The night ferry from Ban Don in Surat stops in Thong Sala – the fare is 100B on the upper deck and 70B on the lower deck for the six hour trip.

Thirty-five-passenger speedboats go between Hat Mae Nam, on Ko Samui, and Thong Sala for 160B per person; this boat only takes about half an hour to reach Thong Sala. From January to September, there is also a slower boat between Hat Mae Nam and Ao Thong Nai Pan, on Pha-Ngan; the fare is 70B.

Subject to weather conditions, there are daily express boats between Thong Sala and Ko Tao, 45km north, at 2.30 pm. The trip takes 2½ hours and costs 150B one way.

Speedboats operate between Thong Sala and Ko Tao a couple of times a day for 350B per person; the crossing only takes about an hour.

KO TAO

Ko Tao, or Turtle Island, is only 21 sq km in area and lies 45km north of Ko Pha-Ngan. Like Ko Pha-Ngan, the island is mostly mountainous with only a few dirt tracks here and there for roads. It has developed very quickly in the past few years and, because of its popularity among divers, it is now considerably more touristed – and more expensive – than Ko Pha-Ngan.

Places to Stay

Accommodation on the island fits more or less between Samui and Pha-Ngan in terms of costs and amenities. Most bungalows now cost 150B to 300B a night, though some are 200B to 600B. During the peak season – December to March – it can be difficult to find accommodation anywhere on the island and people sleep on the beach or in restaurants until a hut becomes available. Some places won't allow you to stay there unless you book a dive trip.

Ao Mae On Ao Mae beach, north of the main pier, *Dam* has nice thatched huts starting at 150B. There's also *Crystal* (150B to 600B), *Queen Resort* (150B to 250B) and *Tommy Resort* (100B to 500B).

On Hat Sai Ri, the *Haad Sai Ree Resort, Ko Tao Cabana* and *SP Cabana* all cost 200B to 250B. *Sai Ri Cottage, New-Way* and *O-Chai* are all in the 80B to 250B price range. *In Touch* is one of the better values at 120B for a bungalow with private shower.

Ao Laem Thian & Ao Tanot On the cape that juts out over the north end of Ao Tanot, *Laem Thian* has huts built among the rocks from 60B.

Ao Tanot, at the southern end of Ko Tao, is one of the best spots for snorkelling and has good bungalow operations. *Tanote Bay Resort* charges 50B to 100B for simple but well-maintained huts, while *Poseidon* has rather shabby huts for 50B to 80B. The friendly *Diamond Beach* offers huts from 50B to 100B. *Bamboo Hut*, a new place, has decked bungalows for 100B.

Ao Chalok Ban Kao & Laem Tato This nicely situated coral beach, about 1.7km south of Ban Mae Hat by road, has become quite crowded. On the hill overlooking the western part of the bay, you'll find *Laem Khlong* (100B to 500B, no beach) and *Viewpoint*, with lots of bungalows for 80B to 350B. Next are *Sunshine* and *Buddha View Dive Resort*, with bungalows in the 150B to 400B range.

Laem Tato can only be reached on foot and at low tide. *Tatoo Lagoon* offers basic huts for 60B, and more elaborate ones for up to 300B.

Getting There & Away

Every third day, depending on the weather, a boat runs between Surat Thani (Tha Thong) and Ko Tao, a seven to eight hour trip for 240B.

Depending on the weather, boats make the three hour trip from Ko Pha-Ngan to Ko Tao daily for 150B. There are also boats daily from Chumphon's Tha Saphan Tha Yang (on the mainland). The trip takes five to seven hours, depending on the boat, and costs 200B. All boats dock at Ban Mae Hat on the island's west side.

A faster speedboat to Ko Tao leaves Chumphon at 8 am, arriving at 10.30 am, for 400B per person. In the reverse direction the speedboat costs 300B.

NAKHON SI THAMMARAT

Nakhon Si Thammarat has the oldest wat in the south, **Wat Phra Mahathat**. Reputed to be over 1000 years old and rebuilt in the mid-13th century, the wat has a 78m-high chedi topped by a solid-gold spire. The town also has an interesting **National Museum** with a good 'Art of Southern Thailand' exhibit.

In the past Nakhon Si Thammarat natives were stereotyped as somewhat rough and prone to criminal activity, but a new civic pride has developed in recent years and the natives are now quite fond of being called *khon khawn* (Nakhon people).

Nakhon Si Thammarat is also noted for its nielloware (a silver and black alloy-enamel jewellery technique) and for the making of leather shadow puppets and dance masks.

Information

A TAT office (☎ 34 6516) is housed in a 70-year-old building in the north-west corner of the Sanam Na Meuang (City Field) off Thanon Ratchadamnoen, near the police station.

Places to Stay – Budget

Most hotels are near the train station and bus terminal. The best budget value is the friendly *Thai Lee Hotel* at 1130 Thanon Ratchadamnoen, where clean rooms with fan and private shower cost 150 to 200B.

On Thanon Yommarat, across from the train station, the *Si Thong* has adequate rooms from 120B with fan and bath. Alternatively, try the similar *Nakhon* at 1477/5 Thanon Yommarat.

Places to Stay – Mid-Range

The *Thai Hotel* (☎ 34 1509), on Thanon Ratchadamnoen, two blocks from the train station, has undergone a relatively recent renovation and now offers air-con rooms with TV, fridge and hot water for 600B to 650B.

Places to Eat

There are lots of funky old *Chinese restau-rants* along Thanon Yommarat and Thanon Jamroenwithi. At night the entire block running south from the Siam Hotel is lined with cheap *food vendors*.

Muslim stands opposite the hotel sell delicious *roti klûay* (banana pancake), *khâo môk* (chicken biryani) and *mâtàbà* (pancakes stuffed with chicken or vegetables) in the evening, and by day there are plenty of *rice and noodle shops*.

Bovorn Bazaar offers several culinary delights, including *Hao Coffee* and the adjacent *Khrua Nakhon*, a large open-air restaurant serving real Nakhon cuisine. Prices are quite reasonable.

Highlights of Nakhon cuisine include *khâo yam* (Southern-style rice salad), *kaeng tai plaa* (spicy fish curry), *khanõm jiin* (curry noodles served with a huge tray of vegies) and seafood.

Getting There & Away

From the Southern bus terminal in Bangkok, it takes 12 hours to Nakhon Si Thammarat; the fare is around 200B, or 350B by air-con bus. Daily buses from Surat Thani cost about 40B (air-con 65B). You can also get buses and share taxis to/from Songkhla, Krabi, Trang, Phuket or Hat Yai; share taxi fares are about twice ordinary bus fares.

PHATTALUNG

The major rice-growing centre of the south, Phattalung is also noted for its shadow puppets. The town has a couple of interesting wats, and **Lam Pang** is a pleasant spot for eating and relaxing beside the 'inland sea' on which Phattalung is situated.

Thale Noi Wildlife Preserve, primarily a waterbird sanctuary, is 32km to the northeast, and the **Tham Malai** cave is just outside town.

Places to Stay

The *Phattalung Hotel*, at 43 Thanon Ramet, is the cheapest place in town, at 150B with fan and bath, although the rooms are dark and dirty. The larger and friendlier *Phattalung Thai Hotel* (☎ 61 1636), on Thanon Disara-Nakarin, off Thanon Ramet near the Bangkok Bank, has spacious rooms for 150/180B single/double with fan and bath, up to 350B with air-con.

The *Ho Fah Hotel*, on the corner of Thanon Poh Saat and Thanon Khuhasawan, has large, clean rooms with fan and bath for 190B to 240B, air-con for 320B to 470B.

Places to Eat

One of the best Thai restaurants in Phattalung is *Khrua Cook* on Thanon Pracha Bamrung. *Boom Restaurant* opposite the train station is more upscale, with dishes in the 50B to 80B range. It's open for breakfast and has an English-language menu.

Getting There & Away

Buses from Phattalung to Nakhon Si Thammarat or Hat Yai take two hours and cost 30B. Air-con buses and minivans to/from Hat Yai are 30B and 35B respectively and take about the same time. There is one minivan a day to/from Songkhla, for 45B.

There are also 3rd class trains to Phattalung from Surat Thani (42B) and Nakhon Si Thammarat (22B).

SONGKHLA

Not much is known about the pre-8th century history of Songkhla, a name derived from the Yawi 'Singora' – a mutilated Sanskrit reference to a lion-shaped mountain (today called Khao Daeng) opposite the harbour. The settlement originally lay at the foot of Khao Daeng, where two cemeteries and the ruins of a fort are among the oldest structural remains. Today it sits on a peninsula between Thale Sap Songkhla (an 'inland sea') and the Gulf of Thailand.

Foreign Consulates

The Malaysian Consulate (☎ 31 1062) is 4 Thanon Sukhum, near Hat Samila. Other foreign missions include a Chinese consulate (☎ 31 1494) on Thanon Sadao, not far from the Royal Crown Hotel and an Indonesian consulate (☎ 31 1544) at the western end of Thanon Sadao, near the junction with Thanon Ramwithi.

Things to See

The main beach, **Hat Samila**, is lined with casuarina trees and seafood restaurants. The city has done much to clean the beach up in recent years and, while not worth going out of your way for, it's a pleasant place for a morning stroll. Offshore are two islands known as 'cat' and 'mouse'.

Songkhla has an active **waterfront**, with a smattering of historic architecture and brightly painted fishing boats; an interesting **National Museum** in an old Sino-Portuguese palace; an **old chedi** at the top of Khao Tang Kuan hill; and **Wat Matchimawat**, which has

frescoes, an old marble Buddha image and a small museum. The National Museum, open from 9 am to 4 pm Wednesday to Sunday (admission 30B), has a collection of Burmese Buddhas and various Sriwijaya artefacts. The building is an old Thai-Chinese palace.

Places to Stay

The popular and clean *Amsterdam* (☎ 31 4890), 15/3 Thanon Rong Muang, has nice rooms with shared bath and toilet for 150 and 180B. It's run by a friendly Dutch woman.

The *Songkhla Hotel* is on Thanon Vichianchom across from the fishing cooperative; rooms cost 150B with common bath or 180B with private bath. Just up the street from the Songkhla Hotel, the *Smile Inn* (☎ 31 1158) is a clean place with medium-size rooms with ceiling fan and private cold-water shower for 200B, or identical rooms with air-con for 300B to 380B.

At the foot of Khao Tan Kuan (the hill overlooking town), the *Narai Hotel*, 14 Thanon Chai Khao, is a long walk from the bus terminal (take a trishaw), though it's a pleasant and friendly place; rooms start at 120B with shared bath.

Places to Eat

As you might expect, Songkhla has a reputation for seafood and there's a string of beach-front *seafood specialists*. None of them are particularly cheap and eating here is mainly a lunchtime activity. Try curried crab claws or fried squid.

At night, the food scene shifts to Thanon Vichianchom in front of the market, where there is a line of *food and fruit stalls*. *Khao Noi Phochana*, on Thanon Vichianchom near the Songkhla Hotel, has a good lunchtime selection of Thai and Chinese rice dishes. Along Thanon Nang Ngam in the Chinese section there are several cheap *Chinese noodle* and *congee shops*.

There are several fast-food spots at the intersection of Thanon Sisuda and Thanon Platha, including *Jam's Quik* and *Fresh Baker*, both with burgers, ice cream and western breakfasts. Of the several expat pubs around town, *The Skillet* on Thanon Saket has the cleanest kitchen and best food, including sandwiches, pizza, chilli, breakfast and steaks.

Getting There & Away

Buses from Surat Thani to Songkhla cost 130B. Air-con buses from Bangkok take 19

THAILAND

SONGKHLA

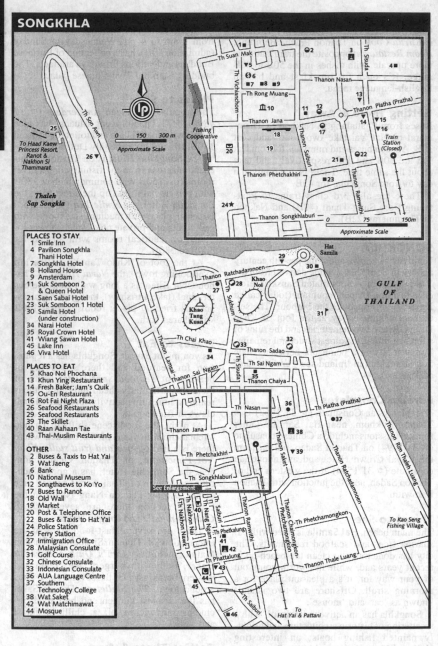

PLACES TO STAY
1 Smile Inn
4 Pavilion Songkhla Thani Hotel
7 Songkhla Hotel
8 Holland House
9 Amsterdam
11 Suk Somboon 2 & Queen Hotel
21 Saen Sabai Hotel
23 Suk Somboon 1 Hotel
30 Samila Hotel (under construction)
34 Narai Hotel
35 Royal Crown Hotel
41 Wiang Sawan Hotel
45 Lake Inn
46 Viva Hotel

PLACES TO EAT
5 Khao Noi Phochana
13 Khun Ying Restaurant
14 Fresh Baker; Jam's Quik
15 Ou-En Restaurant
16 Rot Fai Night Plaza
26 Seafood Restaurants
29 Seafood Restaurants
39 The Skillet
40 Raan Aahaan Tae
43 Thai-Muslim Restaurants

OTHER
2 Buses & Taxis to Hat Yai
3 Wat Jaeng
6 Bank
10 National Museum
12 Songthaews to Ko Yo
17 Buses to Ranot
18 Old Wall
19 Market
20 Post & Telephone Office
22 Buses & Taxis to Hat Yai
24 Police Station
25 Ferry Station
27 Immigration Office
28 Malaysian Consulate
31 Golf Course
32 Chinese Consulate
33 Indonesian Consulate
36 AUA Language Centre
37 Southern Technology College
38 Wat Saket
42 Wat Matchimawat
44 Mosque

hours and cost around 425B. Regular buses are 244B, to get to Hat Yai is a few baht more. By train, you have to go to Hat Yai first. There are buses and share taxis from Hat Yai to Songkhla – 12B by bus and 18B by minivan or share taxi.

Although the usual route north from Songkhla is to backtrack to Hat Yai and then take the road to Phattalung and Trang, you can also take an interesting back-roads route. There's a bus trip to Ranot, 63km north at the end of the Thale Sap lagoon, and more buses connect to Hua Sai (32km) and then Nakhon Si Thammarat (56km).

Getting Around
Motorcycle taxis around Songkhla cost 10B and songthaews are 7B for anywhere on their routes.

AROUND SONGKHLA
On **Ko Yaw**, an island on the inland sea, you can see local cotton weaving and a **Folklore Museum** that emphasises Southern Thai culture. Buses to the island from either Songkhla or Hat Yai cost 10B.

The **Khu Khut Waterbird Sanctuary** is on the eastern shore of Thale Sap Songkhla near Sathing Phra, about 30km north of Songkhla town. This 520 sq km sanctuary is a habitat for over 200 species of waterbirds.

HAT YAI
This is a busy commercial centre where the east and west coast roads and the railway line all meet. Apart from being the south's business capital, Hat Yai is also a popular 'sin centre' for Malaysians who pop across the border on weekends to partake of Thailand's flesh trade.

Orientation & Information
The three main streets, Niphat Uthit 1, 2 and 3, all run parallel to the railway line. The TAT office (☎ 24 3747) is at 1/1 Soi 2, Thanon Niphat Uthit 3.

The immigration office (☎ 24 3019) is on Thanon Rattakan near the railway bridge, in the same complex as a police station.

Things to See
A few kilometres out of town, towards the airport and just off Thanon Phetkasem, **Wat Hat Yai Nai** has a large reclining Buddha image – get a samlor heading in that direction and hop off after the U Thapao Bridge.

On the first Saturday of each month, **bullfights** (bull versus bull) are held at Hat Yai. There's always heavy betting among the Thai spectators.

Places to Stay
Hat Yai has dozens of hotels within walking distance of the train station. During Chinese New Year most room rates at the lower end double. Many places cater for the Malaysian dirty-weekend trade – it's not a traveller's dream town.

Still very popular with travellers is the *Cathay Guest House* (☎ 23 5044), on the corner of Niphat Uthit 2 and Thamnoonvithi. Rooms here start at 160B and there is also a 90B dorm. The management is quite helpful with information on local travel, and travel to Malaysia or farther north in Thailand, and there is a reliable bus ticket agency downstairs.

The *Tong Nam Hotel* at 118-120 Thanon Niphat Uthit 3 is a basic Chinese hotel with good rooms for 150B with fan, up to 300B with air-con and private bath. Another good deal is the *Hok Chin Hin Hotel* (☎ 24 3258), on Thanon Niphat Uthit 1, a couple of blocks from the train station. Very clean rooms with bath and fan cost 150B single, 240B double; there's a good coffee shop downstairs. Hat Yai used to have more hotels like this, but they're closing down one by one.

The clean, friendly and secure *Singapore Hotel* (☎ 23 7478), 62-66 Thanon Suphasan Rangsan, has clean rooms with fan and hot shower for 270/280B single/double, air-con 350B, and air-con rooms with two beds, TV and hot water for 400B.

Very popular with Malaysian visitors as well as travellers is *King's Hotel* (☎ 23 4140) on Thanon Niphat Uthit 1. Rooms with air-con, satellite TV, and hot water cost around 500B.

Places to Eat
Hat Yai has plenty of good places to eat, including lots of shops selling cakes, confectionery, fruit and ice cream. Opposite King's Hotel, the popular *Muslim Ocha* is still going strong, with roti and curry dip in the mornings and rice and curries all day. This is one of the few Muslim cafes in town where women, even non-Muslim, seem welcome; discreet dress is recommended for both sexes.

The extensive night market along Thanon Montri 1, across from the Songkhla bus terminal, specialises in fresh seafood. Inexpensive

HAT YAI

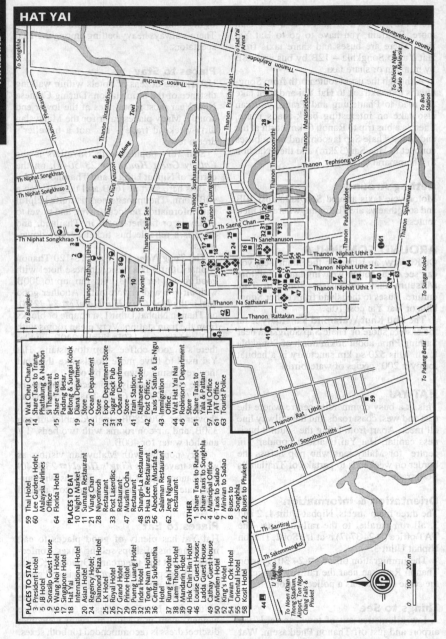

PLACES TO STAY
3 President Hotel
5 JB Hotel
9 Sorasilp Guest House
16 Wang Noi Hotel
17 Singapore Hotel
18 Hat Yai
    International Hotel
20 Asian Hotel
24 Regency Hotel;
    Diamond Plaza Hotel
25 LK Hotel
26 Royal Hotel
27 Grand Hotel
29 Prince Hotel
30 Pueng Luang Hotel
35 Tong Nam Hotel
36 Central Sukhontha
    Hotel
37 Rung Fah Hotel
38 Laem Thong Hotel
39 Mandarin Hotel
40 Hok Chin Hin Hotel
46 Louise Guest House;
    Ladda Guest House
49 Cathay Guest House
50 Montien Hotel
52 King's Hotel
54 Tawan Ork Hotel
58 Kosit Hotel

59 Thai Hotel
60 Lee Gardens Hotel;
    Malaysia Airlines
    Office
64 Florida Hotel

PLACES TO EAT
10 Night Market
11 Sumatra Restaurant
21 Viang Chan
28 Niyomrosh
    Restaurant
33 Post Laserdisc
    Restaurant
47 Muslim Ocha
    Restaurant
48 Shangri-La Restaurant
53 Hua Lee Restaurant
56 Abedeen, Mustafa &
    Salaiman Restaurant
62 Jeng Nguan
    Restaurant

OTHER
1 Share Taxis to Ranot
2 Share Taxis to Songkhla
4 Municipal Office
6 Taxis to Sadao
7 Minivan to Sadao
8 Buses to
   Songkhla
12 Buses to Phuket

13 Wat Cheu Chang
14 Share Taxis to Trang,
    Phattalung & Nakhon
    Si Thammarat
15 Share Taxis to
    Padang Besar,
    Betong & Sungai Kolok
19 Diana Department
    Store
22 Ocean Department
    Store
23 Expo Department Store
31 Sugar Rock Pub
34 Odean Department
    Store
41 Train Station;
    Rajthanee Hotel
42 Post Office;
    Taxis to Satun & La-Ngu
43 Immigration
    Office
44 Wat Hat Yai Nai
45 Robinson's Department
    Store
51 Share Taxis to
    Yala & Pattani
57 THAI Office
61 TAT Office
63 Tourist Police

morning dim sum is available at *Shangrila* on Thanon Thamnoonvithi near the Cathay Guest House. In the evenings the Chinese-food action moves to *Hua Lee* on the corner of Niphat Uthit 3 and Thamnoonvithi; it's open till the wee hours.

Getting There & Away

See the Thailand Getting There & Away section earlier in this chapter for details of travel between Hat Yai and Malaysia.

Air There are at least two flights daily from Bangkok, and Hat Yai is also connected by air with Phuket, Penang, Surat Thani, Chiang Mai and Singapore.

Bus There are many agencies for buses to Bangkok and for taxis to Penang: along Thanon Niphat Uthit 2, towards the THAI and Malaysia Airlines offices, and around the train station. The travel agency below the Cathay Guest House is reliable and also books tour buses.

Buses to/from Bangkok cost 238B ordinary, 440B with air-con, 500B VIP. Buses to Phuket are 126B ordinary, 200B to 250B with air-con; minivans are 200B. Ordinary buses to Satun cost 35B. Buses to Krabi (air-con only) are 150B, while ordinary buses to Surat Thani cost 90B (140B air-con). Buses straight through to Ko Samui, including the ferry, cost 280B to 300B.

It's 23B for a bus, 35B for a share taxi, to Padang Besar on the Malaysian border. If you're crossing on the eastern side, buses to Sungai Kolok (air-con only) cost 96B.

Train Fares from Bangkok, without rapid or express supplements, are 149/345B in 3rd/2nd class. There's no 3rd class on express trains to/from Bangkok. Third class trains to Hat Yai start only as far north as Chumphon (99B) and Surat Thani (55B).

Getting Around

To/From the Airport The THAI van costs 50B per person for transport to the city; count on about 150B for a private taxi or about 70B for a songthaew.

Local Transport Songthaews cost 8B anywhere around town.

AROUND HAT YAI

The **Ton Nga Chang Waterfall**, 24km west of the city, features 1200m, seven-tiered cas-

cades in the shape of a pair of elephant tusks. October to December is the best time to visit. To get to the falls take a Rattaphum-bound songthaew (14B) and ask to get off at the *náam tòk* (waterfall).

SATUN

There's little of interest in this province in the south-west corner of Thailand, but from here you can take boats to Kuala Perlis or Langkawi Island in Malaysia, or visit the Tarutao islands offshore.

Money

If you've just arrived from Malaysia, you can change money at branches of Bangkok Bank and Siam Commercial Bank in the town centre. Both banks also feature ATMs.

Places to Stay

In Satun, the *Rian Thong Hotel* ('Rain Tong' on the English sign), at the end of Thanon Samanta Prasit, has large rooms for 140B. The more modern *Satul Tanee* (Satun Thani) *Hotel* in the town centre is 200B but it's noisy.

The *Udomsuk*, near the municipal offices on Thanon Hatthakam Seuksa, is better value at 130B to 150B.

Places to Eat

There are several cheap Muslim food shops near the gold-domed Bambang Mosque in the centre of town. For Chinese food, wander about the little Chinese district near the Rian Thong Hotel.

Getting There & Away

Share taxis between Hat Yai and Satun cost 50B; air-con buses are 40B and ordinary buses cost 30B. Satul Transport Co, 500m north of the Wang Mai Hotel on the east side of Thanon Satun Thani, sells THAI tickets (for flights out of Trang or Hat Yai), and also operates buses to Trang and Hat Yai.

Frequent boats to Kuala Perlis in Malaysia leave from the Tammalang pier south of town between 9 am and 1 pm for 50B (RM5 in the reverse direction). There are also several boats daily to/from Langkawi Island for 180B or RM18 each way.

Getting Around

An orange songthaew to Tammalang pier costs 15B from Satun.

KO TARUTAO NATIONAL MARINE PARK

Pak Bara, 60km north of Satun, is the usual jumping-off point for the Ko Tarutao archipelago, just north of the Malaysian border. A regular boat services only five of the 51 islands (Tarutao, Adang, Lipe, Rawi and Klang), of which only the first three are generally visited by tourists.

Places to Stay

Officially, the park is only open from November to May. Visitors who show up on the islands during the monsoon season can stay in park accommodation, but they must bring their own food from the mainland unless staying on Ko Lipe, where private accommodation and restaurants are available. Even during other times of year it's advisable to bring extra food for Ko Tarutao and Ko Adang, as the park canteens are a little pricey and not that good.

Park accommodation on Ko Tarutao is in several locations and costs 400B for a large 'deluxe' two room bungalow, or 600B for one of eight cottages which sleep up to eight people. A four bed room in a longhouse costs 280B. All rooms and bungalows must be paid for in full, even if only one person rents it. You may pitch your own tent for 10B per person in designated *camping grounds* at Ao San and Ao Jak.

At Laem Son, on Ko Adang, a bed in a privately owned *longhouse* costs 40B per person, while two-person bungalows are 200B. On Ko Lipe you can stay at *Pattaya Beach Bungalow* for 150B per room with shared facilities, 200B to 270B with attached toilet. *Chao Leh* has huts for 150B with shared bath, or 200B to 300B with attached bath.

Getting There & Away

From Satun to Pak Bara, you first take a bus (18B) or share taxi (30B) to La-ngu and then a songthaew (10B) to Pak Bara. Boats to Tarutao cost 140B per person each way, or you can charter a boat large enough for 10 people for 900B. Boats continue to Lipe and Adang for 200B one way. They run between November and April – the park is closed for the remainder of the year.

PHUKET

Thailand's largest island is barely an island, since it's joined to the mainland by a bridge. Once known as 'Junk Ceylon', Phuket was a major trade entrepôt and tin-mining centre in the 19th century, but these days its well developed resort role has come to the fore. The town of Phuket is pleasant enough, with its Sino-Portuguese architecture, but the beautiful beaches and offshore islands are the main attractions.

Popular beaches are scattered all over the island and virtually all transport radiates from Phuket town. The island is very hilly, and many of the hills drop right into the sea. Beach accommodation is becoming downright high-class these days, with international-class resorts on nearly every beach.

Information

The helpful TAT office is on Thanon Phuket. The THAI office is on Thanon Ranong and the post office is on Thanon Montri.

Phuket Beaches

Patong Ao Patong, 15km west of Phuket town, is the most developed and most crowded of the many beaches. As a result it has a greater variety of accommodation than most of the others, although food is a little more expensive than at Ao Kata Yai or Ao Karon. There's also more going on at night here, including a thriving hostess bar scene. The beach itself is long, white, clean and lapped by picture-postcard clear waters, though plagued by jet-skis.

Karon & Kata Ao Karon is only a little south of Ao Patong and 20km from Phuket town. This is really a triple beach: there's the long golden sweep of Ao Karon, then a small headland separates it from the smaller but equally beautiful Ao Kata Yai; another small headland divides this from Ao Kata Noi, where you'll find good snorkelling. Offshore, there's the small island of **Ko Pu**. All have beautiful beaches with that delightful, squeaky-feeling sand.

Most of the development is centred on the two Kata beaches and the southern end of Karon beach. Development is creeping north, but local hoteliers say they're determined it won't become as saturated as Ao Patong. A new beach promenade with street lights adds a touch of class.

Nai Han South again from Ao Kata Noi is Hat Nai Han, a small, pleasant beach which was one of the last hold-outs for cheap bungalows until the Phuket Yacht Club moved in. Although it's now more of a scene it's still

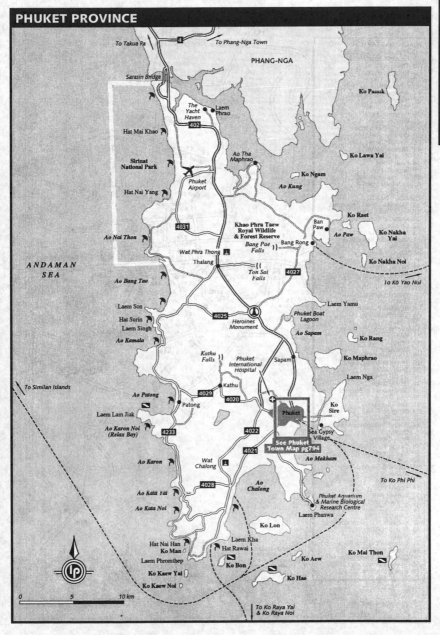

PHUKET PROVINCE

To Takua Pa

To Phang-Nga Town

PHANG-NGA

Sarasin Bridge

Ko Panak

The Yacht Haven

Laem Phrao

402

Hat Mai Khao

Ko Lawa Yai

Ao Tha Maphrao

Sirinat National Park

Ko Ngam

Phuket Airport

Ao Kung

Hat Nai Yang

Ko Raet

4031

Khao Phra Taew Royal Wildlife & Forest Reserve

Ban Paw

Ko Nakha Yai

Ao Nai Thon

Bang Pae Falls

Bang Rong

Ao Paw

Ko Nakha Noi

Wat Phra Thong

Thalang

A N D A M A N S E A

Ao Bang Tao

Ton Sai Falls

4027

To Ko Yao Noi

Laem Yamu

Laem Son

4025

Phuket Boat Lagoon

Hat Surin

Heroines Monument

Ao Sapam

Laem Singh

Ko Rang

Ao Kamala

Kathu Falls

Phuket International Hospital

Sapam

Ko Maphrao

Laem Nga

To Similan Islands

Ao Patong

4029

Kathu

4020

Phuket

Ko Sire

Patong

Laem Lam Jiak

Ao Karon Noi (Relax Bay)

4233

4022

See Phuket Town Map pg794

Sea Gypsy Village

Ao Karon

Wat Chalong

4021

Ao Makham

To Ko Phi Phi

Ao Kata Yai

4028

Ao Chalong

Ao Kata Noi

Phuket Aquarium & Marine Biological Research Centre

Laem Phanwa

Ko Lon

Hat Nai Han

Ko Man

Laem Kha

Hat Rawai

Ko Mai Thon

Laem Phromthep

Ko Bon

Ko Aew

Ko Kaew Yai

Ko Hae

Ko Kaew Noi

0   5   10 km

To Ko Raya Yai & Ko Raya Noi

THAILAND

PHUKET TOWN

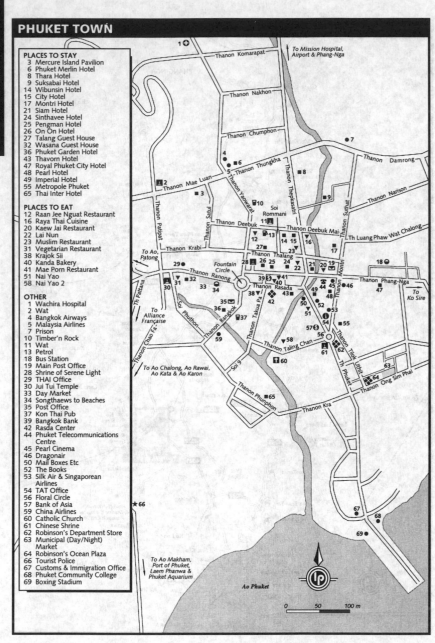

PLACES TO STAY
- 3 Mercure Island Pavilion
- 6 Phuket Merlin Hotel
- 8 Thara Hotel
- 9 Suksabai Hotel
- 14 Wibunsin Hotel
- 15 City Hotel
- 17 Montri Hotel
- 21 Siam Hotel
- 24 Sinthavee Hotel
- 25 Pengman Hotel
- 26 On On Hotel
- 27 Talang Guest House
- 32 Wasana Guest House
- 36 Phuket Garden Hotel
- 43 Thavorn Hotel
- 47 Royal Phuket City Hotel
- 48 Pearl Hotel
- 49 Imperial Hotel
- 55 Metropole Phuket
- 65 Thai Inter Hotel

PLACES TO EAT
- 12 Raan Jee Nguat Restaurant
- 16 Raya Thai Cuisine
- 20 Kaew Jai Restaurant
- 22 Lai Num
- 23 Muslim Restaurant
- 31 Vegetarian Restaurant
- 38 Krajok Sii
- 40 Kanda Bakery
- 41 Mae Porn Restaurant
- 51 Nai Yao
- 58 Nai Yao 2

OTHER
- 1 Wachira Hospital
- 2 Wat
- 4 Bangkok Airways
- 5 Malaysia Airlines
- 7 Prison
- 10 Timber'n Rock
- 11 Wat
- 13 Petrol
- 18 Bus Station
- 19 Main Post Office
- 28 Shrine of Serene Light
- 29 THAI Office
- 30 Jui Tui Temple
- 33 Day Market
- 34 Songthaews to Beaches
- 35 Post Office
- 37 Kon Thai Pub
- 39 Bangkok Bank
- 42 Rasda Center
- 44 Phuket Telecommunications
     Centre
- 45 Pearl Cinema
- 46 Dragonair
- 50 Mail Boxes Etc
- 52 The Books
- 53 Silk Air & Singaporean
     Airlines
- 54 TAT Office
- 56 Floral Circle
- 57 Bank of Asia
- 59 China Airlines
- 60 Catholic Church
- 61 Chinese Shrine
- 62 Robinson's Department Store
- 63 Municipal (Day/Night)
     Market
- 64 Robinson's Ocean Plaza
- 66 Tourist Police
- 67 Customs & Immigration Office
- 68 Phuket Community College
- 69 Boxing Stadium

pleasant and very sparsely developed, thanks to monastic holdings at the beach's centre.

You can walk along a coastal track from Ao Karon to Hat Nai Han in about two hours. In fact, you could probably walk right around the island on coastal tracks. The roads radiate from Phuket town and you have to backtrack into town and out again to get from one beach to another by road – even though they are just a couple of kilometres apart along the coast. **Ao Saen** is a pleasant little place between Kata Noi and Nai Han.

Rawai If you go round the southern end of the island from Hat Nai Han you'll come to Hat Rawai, another tourist development. Again these are mostly more expensive places and the beach is not so special. At low tide, there's a long expanse of mud exposed before you get to the sea. People staying at Rawai often travel out to other beaches to swim. Rawai is a good place to get boats out to the islands scattered south of Phuket. There is good snorkelling at **Ko Hae**.

Other Beaches Between Rawai and Phuket town, there are more places to stay dotted along the nicely beached south-east stretch of coast.

A little north of Ao Patong is **Hat Surin**, a long beach which is less sheltered and where the water is a little rougher than the normal Phuket calm. **Ao Kamala** has a wide calm bay but not such a good beach. It's a kilometre or so south of Hat Surin. Between the two there's an absurdly beautiful little beach, **Laem Singh** – the very image of a tropical paradise.

In the north-west, attractive **Hat Nai Thon** has only one resort, while lengthy **Hat Nai Yang** and **Hat Mai Khao** are protected by Sirinat National Marine Park. Turtles come ashore to lay their eggs from late October to February at Hat Mai Khao.

Other Attractions

If the attraction of beaches starts to pall, Phuket also has a number of waterfalls and other novelties. The **Thai-Danish Marine Biological Research Centre** has an interesting fish collection. It's open from 8 am to noon and from 2 to 4 pm – take a songthaew to Ao Makham.

There is good scuba diving and snorkelling at many points around Phuket, including several small islands to the south and east – **Ko Hae, Ko Raya** (Noi & Yai), **Ko Yao** (Noi & Yai), **Ko Bon, Ko Mai Thon, Ao Patong,**

Hin Daeng and **Shark Point** (a habitat for harmless leopard sharks) off the southern tip of the island. All sites are accessible by boat from various piers at Rawai and Ao Paw (Bang Rong).

Phuket's most important festival is the Vegetarian Festival, which takes place during the first nine days of the ninth lunar month of the Chinese calendar - usually late September or October. The festival activities are centred around five Chinese temples, with the Jui Tui temple on Thanon Ranong the most important, followed by Bang Niaw and Sui Boon Tong temples. The TAT office in Phuket prints a helpful schedule of events for the Vegetarian Festival each year.

Places to Stay & Eat – Phuket Town

Most people head straight out to the beaches, but should you want to stay in town – on arrival or departure night for example – there are some very pleasant places. At 19 Thanon Phang-Nga, the 1929-vintage *On On* has rooms from 100B to 220B and a lot of character. The *Pengman*, nearby at 69 Thanon Phang-Nga, above a Chinese restaurant, costs just 100B for basic but clean single/double rooms with fan and bath.

The *Thara* on Thanon Thepkasatri has rooms with fan and bath for 130B. About 100m south of the Thara on a soi off the same street, the *Suksabai Hotel* is good value with clean, well-kept rooms at similar rates, plus more expensive air-con rooms.

Talang Guest House, on Thanon Thalang, offers rooms in a semi-restored historic shophouse for 250B single/double with fan, 400B air-con; a 30% discount is available May to October. Some of the air-con rooms will sleep up to four.

The big eating centre in town is the *Mae Porn* restaurant, on the corner of Thanon Phang-Nga and Soi Pradit, near the On On Hotel. They have a vast selection of fresh Thai, Chinese and western food at good prices. Even cheaper is the *Raan Jee Nguat*, around the corner on Thanon Yaowarat and across from the closed Siam cinema – fine Phuket-style noodles with curry are 10B; it opens early and closes around 2 pm. The night market on Thanon Phuket is also good.

Places to Stay & Eat – Phuket Beaches

The two main centres for travellers are Ao Patong and Ao Kata/Ao Karon. Ao Patong is more developed and more expensive; Ao Kata/Ao Karon is a bit more laid-back in spite of its Club Med. It's initially a little confusing, since the name Kata seems to encompass places at both the Kata beaches and the south end of Karon. There are numerous other beaches of course, some of them very quiet and peaceful. Nai Han still has the cheapest beach accommodation.

Ao Patong This was the original beach development and is now full of hotels, restaurants, snack bars, motorbike-hire places, dive shops, girlie bars and all manner of things to do. If you want a little more night-time activity, then Ao Patong may appeal to you more than the other, sleepier places. The accent here is on the more expensive places, there are also some cheapies, but they cost a bit more than elsewhere.

Bottom end for Patong hotels and guesthouses is 300B to 500B during the high season, and all of them are at least a block from the beach. During the low season from May to October, you should request a discount of 30% to 50%.

Among the least expensive places are in the multi-storey Paradise Complex, well away from the beach, where you'll find the multi-storey *Asia, Best, Suksan Mansion* and others in the 300B to 400B range. Be warned, the Paradise Complex is filled with sex-oriented bars, both straight and gay. Closer to the beach, *Capricorn Villa* on Thanon Rat Uthit charges 500B fan and 700B air-con for fairly well kept bungalows.

If you can pay a little more, *Sansabai Bungalows* (☎ 34 2948), 171/21 Soi Sansabai, off Thanon Rat Uthit, is a well managed place where rooms with minibar, TV, fan and hot shower cost 850B, while air-con rooms go for 1150B to 1400B. Low season rates are less (700B fan, 850B deluxe air-con). Breakfast is included in high season.

Ao Kata & Karon Although resort rates of 1000B to 3000B now predominate, there are still a few places in the 200B to 400B range. They're all rather similar – pleasant little wooden or cement bungalows with their own toilet, shower and veranda. Popular places include the *Kata Tropicana* with rooms from 150B, a bit off the beach. *Bell's Bungalow* costs only 100B to 300B. *Cool Breeze* at Kata Noi has a few bungalows from 150B.

Down at Kata Noi, the smaller of the two linked beaches, check out the quiet *Chor Tap*

Kaew Bungalow (500B) and *Kata Noi Club Bungalow* (200B to 500B).

Along Karon, there are a number of places with prices from 300B, including *Karon Seaview Bungalow, My Friend* and *Fantasy Hill.*

The accommodation area is backed up with a whole collection of very similar beach restaurants, featuring the usual traveller's dishes from pizza or pancakes to fruit drinks and banana fritters. Prices for accommodation and food go hand in hand at Phuket – Kata/Karon is cheaper than Patong for both accommodation and food.

Nai Han South of Kata and west of Rawai, this used to be a more remote, get-away-from-it-all beach. Now the Phuket Yacht Club has come to the north end, although the centre has remained undeveloped. If you follow the road through the Yacht Club and beyond to the next cape, you'll come to the simple *Ao Sane Bungalows* (☎ 28 8306), which cost 100B to 300B, depending on the season and condition of the huts.

On the other side of the lagoon from the beach, *Romzai Bungalows* has simple rooms for 150B to 300B; it's a short walk to the beach.

Other Beaches Not all the beaches have accommodation, but if you want to get away from it all you can certainly find more remote places. Camping is allowed on both Nai Yang and Mai Khao beaches. The park accommodation on Nai Yang costs 200B in a dorm-like longhouse, 300B for a four bed bungalow, 600B for a 12 bed one. Two-person tents can be rented for 60B a night.

Getting There & Away

Air You can fly to Phuket from Bangkok, Hat Yai, Narathiwat, Nakhon Si Thammarat and Surat Thani. Bangkok Airways also flies between Ko Samui and Phuket daily.

THAI flies between Phuket and several international destinations, including Penang, Langkawi, Kuala Lumpur, Singapore, Hong Kong, Taipei and Sydney.

Bus From Hat Yai to Phuket, it's eight hours and 126B for an ordinary bus, 200B to 250B with air-con, or 200B by minivan.

Buses from the Southern bus terminal in Bangkok take 13 or 14 hours, and cost 250B or 400B with air-con, around 600B VIP.

Buses from Bangkok usually go overnight, which probably helps reduce the scare quota.

Other buses from Phuket include: Phang-Nga in two hours for 33B (56B air-con); Krabi in four hours for 55B (101B air-con); Surat Thani in six to seven hours for 90B; Nakhon Si Thammarat in eight hours for 100B; and Trang in six hours for 95B.

Boat Phuket has become a popular yachting centre. It's sometimes possible to get yacht rides from here to Penang, Sri Lanka, or farther afield. Try Laem Phrao Yacht Marina (☎/fax 32 7109) at Laem Phrao, on the island's north-east tip; The Yacht Haven (☎ 20 6022) nearby; Phuket Boat Lagoon (☎ 23 9055) at Ao Sapam, about 20km from Phuket town on the east shore; and Ao Chalong, south-west of town on the island's south-eastern edge.

Getting Around
To/From the Airport The airport is about 27km out of town. Minivans go to Phuket town for 80B per person. If you want to go direct to one of the beaches, a taxi will cost 360B to 480B depending on where you're going.

Local Transport When you first arrive in Phuket, beware of the local rip-off artists who will be on hand to tell you the tourist office is 5km away, that the only way to get to the beaches is to take a taxi, or that a songthaew from the bus terminal to the town centre will cost you a small fortune.

Actually, songthaews run all over the island from a central area on Thanon Ranong, near the market. The tourist office (which is also in the town centre) puts out a list of the standard charges to all the beaches and other popular destinations, plus the recommended charter costs for a vehicle. Around town, the standard fare is 10B. Out of town, the standard fares to all the beaches vary from 15B (Kata, Karon, Patong and Rawai) to 25B (Nai Han) to 35B (Nai Thon, Nai Yang).

You can also hire motorbikes (usually 100cc Japanese bikes) from around 200B a day at various places at the beaches or in Phuket town.

KHAO SOK NATIONAL PARK
Situated about midway between Phuket and Surat Thani, this 646 sq km national park has wonderful jungle, foliated limestone cliffs and some crystal-clear rivers. You can stay at the national park lodge for 350B per room, or rent tents for 50B per person. Private tree-house bungalows are also available at *Khao Sok Jungle Huts* (100B to 150B), *Bamboo House* (100B to 250B), *Art's Riverview Jungle Lodge* (200B to 600B) and *Our Jungle House* (400B). All places have guides for jungle trips. *Treetops River Huts* near the park entrance is quite rundown. Meals are available at all the accommodations for 40B to 60B.

To get to the park, take a Takua Pa-Surat Thani bus; the park is 1.5km off Route 401 between Takua Pa and Surat Thani at Km 109. Entry to the park is 10B per person, 20B per vehicle.

PHANG-NGA
Situated 94km from Phuket town on the route to Hat Yai, Phang-Nga makes a good day or overnight trip from Phuket by motorbike. On the way to the town, turn off just 5km past the small town of Takua Thung and visit **Wat Tham Suwankhuha**, a cave shrine full of Buddha images. Tha Dan (with the Phang-Nga customs pier), between here and Phang-Nga, is where you hire boats to visit **Ao Phang-Nga**, a huge bay which has Muslim fishing villages on stilts, strangely shaped limestone outcrops soaring out of the sea and water-filled caves. Tours from the pier vary from 200B to 450B; from Phuket they cost at least 400B to 600B per person. The best tours are run by Sayan Tour and Mr Kean Tours, both with small offices next to the bus terminal in Phang-Nga.

Places to Stay & Eat
The hotel with the most character and facilities is *Thawisuk*, the place with the blue facade in the middle of Phang-Nga; it has clean singles/doubles for 150/200B. Along Thanon Phetkasem, Phang-Nga's main street, you'll also find the *Lak Muang* and *Muang Thong*, two typical places with rooms for 200B to 280B.

You can buy good seafood and *khanŏm jiin* at the *stalls* across from the movie theatre in Phang-Nga's main market.

KRABI
This small town offers similar offshore excursions to Phang-Nga, but there are also good local **beaches** to check out: Noppharat Thara, Ao Nang, Phra Nang and Raileh are the most popular. The longest beach is along

Ao Nang, a lovely spot easily reached from Krabi. Phra Nang Bay is perhaps the most beautiful of all the beaches in this area.

World-class **rock-climbing** has become a major activity along the coast near Tham Phra Nang, south-west of Krabi.

Places to Stay & Eat – Town

Guesthouses Most guesthouses in town offer little cubicles over shophouses for 100B to 150B. *Riverside Guest House* and *Swallow Guest House* are among the better cheapies, followed by the slightly more expensive and better *Grand Tower*.

Guesthouses just south-west of the town centre are quieter. Out on Thanon Jao Fah, the *Chao Fa Valley* costs from 200B to 400B, a tad overpriced for the facilities.

On the same side of Thanon Jao Fah, *KR Mansion & Guest House* offers a dorm with 50B beds; rooms for 150B with fan and shared bath; and single to quad rooms with fan and private bath for 200B to 400B.

Hotels The *New Hotel* on Thanon Phattana has OK rooms for 150/200B with fan and bath. The *Thai* on Thanon Itsara is overpriced, so give it a miss. The *Riverside Hotel* at 287/11 Thanon Utarakit is the best hotel deal in town at 230/350B (fan/air-con) for spacious, clean rooms. The same owners operate the friendly *City Hotel* at 15/2-3 Thanon Sukhon, with sparkling rooms for 300/480B fan/air-con.

At night, *food vendors* set up along the waterfront and there is a good morning market in the centre of town. *Thammachart*, below the Riverside Guest House, serves good vegetarian food oriented towards farang palates.

Places to Stay – Beaches

Ao Nang This has been a centre for budget accommodation, though rates are gradually increasing with demand. Down on the beach heading south you'll come to *Wanna's Place* and *Gift's*, both nice spots where large huts with bath cost 250B to 350B.

Up Route 4203, 100m or so from the beach, the small *BB Bungalow* has relatively modern, if simple, huts for 150B to 350B. *Ya Ya* next door is similar.

Farther up the road, away from the beach, are the quite decent *Green Park* (120B to 180B) and *Jungle Hut* (80B to 200B with private bath). During the low season you may be able to get the cheaper huts for 60B a night.

Rai Leh Beach This beach is accessible by boat only and is very crowded from December to March. *Railay Bay Bungalows* packs in nearly 100 huts right across the peninsula to East Hat Rai Leh; rates range from 200B to 400B, depending on size. Nicer *Railay Village* and *Sand Sea* fall in the 500B to 800B range.

Tham Phra Nang Beach This beach is also accessible by boat only and is entirely occupied by the very upmarket *Dusit Rayavadee Resort*. The beach is definately not Dusit's exclusive domain – a wooden walkway has been left around the limestone bluff so that you can walk to Hat Tham Phra Nang from East Rai Leh. From West Rai Leh a footpath leads through the forest around to the beach.

Ao Nam Mao Also known as East Rai Leh, this beach is accessible by boat (or on foot from Tham Phra Nang or West Rai Leh). In addition to Railay Bay Bungalows, this mangrove-lined beach features the unique treehouse-style *Ya-Ya* for 300B to 600B, *Coco Bungalows* for 100B to 150B and *Diamond Cave Bungalows* for 150B and up. This beach tends towards mud flats at low tide – not at all attractive but it's a short walk to Rai Leh. Tex Rock Climbing and King Climbing offer instruction, equipment and guided climbs.

Places to Eat – Beaches

Aside from the simple cafes attached to beach accommodation places, the only place to find food at Krabi's beaches is along the north end of the beach at Ao Nang, past where Hwy 4203 turns inland. Here you'll find a short string of thatched-roof bars and restaurants.

Getting There & Away

Government air-con buses between Krabi and Bangkok cost 328B to 400B air-con or 500B VIP. Buses from Phuket to Krabi are 46B and leave hourly from the terminal just off Thanon Phang-Nga. There are several buses a day from Phang-Nga to Krabi for 36B (52B air-con). From Surat Thani, it's 72B and the trip takes four hours.

Buses to and from Krabi arrive and depart at Taalat Kao, just outside Krabi proper – a songthaew into town is 8B.

Getting Around

Boats to the various beaches at Rai Leh and Phra Nang leave from the Jao Fa pier on the

Krabi waterfront and cost 30B to 50B per person. Noppharat Thara Beach and Ao Nang can be reached by songthaew for 30B.

AROUND KRABI

The **Than Bokkharani National Park** is a 10B songthaew ride from Ao Luk, between Phang-Nga and Krabi. This park makes an interesting excursion with its forest and small waterfalls.

About 5km north and then 2km east of Krabi, **Wat Tham Seua** (Tiger Cave Temple) is one of southern Thailand's most famous forest wats.

KO PHI PHI

Ko Phi Phi, four hours south-west of Krabi by boat, has white beaches, good diving and a huge cavern where the nests for bird's-nest soup are collected. There are actually two islands: Phi Phi Don is inhabited and has lots of accommodation. Phi Phi Le is uninhabited and is the site for the licensed collecting of the nests of swiftlets (often erroneously called swallows); one of the nest caverns has some curious paintings.

Unfortunately, and despite the island being part of a designated national marine park, runaway growth has almost completely spoiled the atmosphere on southern Phi Phi Don (the northern end – taken up by large resorts – remains in fairly good condition). Phi Phi Le remains protected – not because it's part of the park (it isn't) but because the birds' nest collectors make sure no one interferes with the ecology. Because all the accommodation is on Phi Phi Don, it can only be recommended these days if you're quite keen on snorkelling at nearby reefs. Otherwise, give it a miss.

Places to Stay & Eat

During high season, all accommodation on Phi Phi Don tends to be booked solid. The best value on southern Phi Phi Don is *PP Charlie Beach Resort*, a simple but well managed collection of bungalows on a good section of beach. Prices start at 250B for bungalows toward the back and run to 650B near the beach.

On the other side of the peninsula at Hat Yao, *Phi Phi Paradise Pearl Resort* is the most substantial place on the beach, with a variety of well kept bungalows, all with private facilities. *Phi-Phi Long Beach* also offers a wide variety of beach accommoda-

tion. The prices at both places range from 100B to 800B.

Off by itself on a little cove at the southeast end of Hat Hin Khao, *Maphrao Resort* offers thatched A-frame huts in a natural setting for 100B to 320B.

A little village of sorts has developed in the interior of the island near Ao Ton Sai and Hat Hin Khom. Among the gift shops, scuba shops and cafes, there are several basic, budget-oriented places to stay in the 100B to 400B range, none of them very special. For the most part they just take the overflow when all the beach places are full.

Of the many little restaurants near Ton Sai, *Mama Resto* is the most reliable and offers Italian and Thai food, pizza, salads, desserts and a menu in English, French, Japanese and Thai.

Getting There & Away

Ko Phi Phi is equidistant from Phuket and Krabi, but Krabi is the more economical point of departure. From Krabi's Jao Fah pier, there are usually four boats a day, costing 150B one way. Boats run regularly from November to May, but schedules depend on the weather during the monsoon.

There are also daily boats to Ko Phi Phi from Ao Nang, west of Krabi, from October/November to April/May for 150B per person.

TRANG

The town of Trang, between Krabi and Hat Yai, has a history that goes back to the 1st century AD, when it was an important centre for seagoing trade. Trang probably reached its peak during the 7th to 12th centuries, at the height of the Sriwijaya Empire. Today it's a bustling little place and is known as the cleanest city in Thailand. The Vegetarian Festival is celebrated fervently in September/October.

Places to Stay & Eat

A number of hotels are located along the city's two main thoroughfares, Thanon Phra Ram VI and Thanon Visetkul (Wisetkun), which run from the clock tower. *Ko Teng Hotel* is a friendly, traveller-oriented place on Thanon Phra Ram VI. Rates are 180/300B for fan rooms with private bath. The main doors are closed at 7 pm, after which you must use a back entrance.

The *Wattana Hotel*, Thanon Phra Ram VI, offers rooms for 180B to 260B with fan and bath, more for air-con; it's a bit of a brothel.

On Thanon Visetkul, the *Queen Hotel* features large clean rooms with fan for 230B, or 350B with air-con.

Two *khao tom* (rice soup) places on Thanon Phra Ram VI, *Khao Tom Phui* and *Khao Tom Jai Awn*, serve all manner of Thai and Chinese standards from the evening until 2 am. The *Muslim Restaurant*, opposite the Thamrin Hotel on Thanon Phra Ram VI, serves inexpensive *roti kaeng* (flatbread and curry), curries and rice.

Wunderbar, a Thai-European restaurant and bar on Thanon Sathani near the train station has a couple of tables with umbrellas out on the pavement, and a small air-con dining room inside. The menu includes moderately priced sandwiches, cheeses, salads, many Thai dishes, cocktails and fruit shakes.

Getting There & Away
Ordinary buses to/from Satun or Krabi cost around 45B, air-con around 70B. From Hat Yai an ordinary bus is 50B. A share taxi from the same cities costs around 80B. Air-con buses from Krabi cost 70B and take three to four hours. From Phuket it's 95B ordinary, 132B to 169B air-con.

Air-con buses to/from Bangkok are 344B to 443B or 685B for a 24-seat VIP bus. Travel time is about 12 hours.

Getting Around
Samlors around town cost 10B per trip, tuk-tuks 20B.

AROUND TRANG
The geography of the surrounding province is similar to that of Krabi and Phang-Nga, but it's much less frequented by tourists. Trang's coastline has several sandy beaches and coves, especially in the Sikao and Kantang districts. From the road between Trang and Kantang there's a turn-off west onto an unpaved road that leads down to the coast. At the coast, a road south leads to Hat Yao, Hat Yong Ling and Hat Jao Mai. The road north leads to Hat Chang Lang and Hat Pak Meng. There are also several small islands just off the coast, including Ko Muk, Ko Kradan, Ko Ngai (Hai) and Ko Sukon.

SUNGAI KOLOK & BAN TABA
Sungai Kolok in the south-east is the departure point for the east coast of Malaysia. Another border crossing at Ban Taba, 32km east, is a shorter and quicker route to Kota

Bharu, Malaysia. Eventually, this crossing is supposed to replace Sungai Kolok, but it looks like Sungai Kolok will remain open for a long time.

Information
There are a couple of banks in the town centre; Malaysian ringgit can be changed at the bus terminal or in shops. It's easier to buy baht from a Malaysian bank or moneychanger before you cross into Thailand, although it's also possible to change money on the Thai side of the border. There's a TAT office next to the immigration post on the Thai side. The border is open from 5 am to 5 pm (from 6 am to 6 pm Malaysian time).

Places to Stay
There are few English signs in Sungai Kolok. There are a number of places to stay in the centre of town, although they are a bit grotty. The town centre is just a 15B trishaw ride from the border or a five minute walk straight ahead from the train station.

The most inexpensive places are along Thanon Charoenkhet. Cheapies include the *Savoy Hotel* and, next door, the *Thailiang Hotel*, which has rooms from 145B to 180B.

On the corner of Thanon Thetpathom and Thanon Waman Amnoey is the adequate *Valentine* at 200B with fan and 400B with air-con.

Places to Eat
There's a good *Chinese vegetarian restaurant* between the Asia and Savoy hotels that's open daily from 7 am to 6 pm. A cluster of good, reliable *Malay food vendors* can be found at the market and in front of the train station.

Getting There & Away
When you cross the border from Malaysia, the train station is about 1km straight ahead on the right-hand side – 15B by motorcycle taxi. The bus terminal is a farther 1km beyond the train station, down a turning to the left.

Bus & Share Taxi Air-con buses to Hat Yai cost 123B and leave from the Valentine Hotel four times daily. The trip takes about four hours.

Train From Hat Yai, the 3rd class rail fare is 31B. From Bangkok, fares are 180B in 3rd class and 417B in 2nd class, before the rapid, express or sleeper supplements.

Ferry East of the town centre where Asia 18 crosses the Sungai Kolok (Kolok River), a ferry across the river into Malaysia will cost 10B. The border crossing here is open the same hours as in Sungai Kolok. From the Malaysian side you can get buses direct to Kota Bharu for RM2.50.

Vietnam

After the fall of South Vietnam to Communist forces in 1975, Vietnam was virtually isolated from the world. But in 1989 Vietnam flung open the doors to foreign tourists and investors. This now-popular travel destination offers a rich, unique culture and outstanding scenic beauty.

Facts about Vietnam

HISTORY

About 1000 years of Chinese rule over the Red River Delta (all of Vietnam at the time), marked by tenacious Vietnamese resistance and repeated rebellions, ended in 938 AD when Ngo Quyen vanquished the Chinese armies at the Bach Dang River.

During the next few centuries, Vietnam repulsed repeated invasions by China and expanded in a southward direction along the coast at the expense of the kingdom of Champa, which was wiped out in 1471.

The first contact between Vietnam and the west took place in Roman times. Recent European contact with Vietnam began in the 16th century, when European merchants and missionaries arrived. Despite restrictions and periods of persecution, the Catholic Church eventually had a greater impact on Vietnam than on any country in Asia except the Philippines.

In 1858 a joint military force from France and the Spanish colony of the Philippines stormed Danang after the killing of several missionaries. Early the next year, they seized Saigon. A few years later, Vietnam's Emperor Tu Duc signed a treaty that gave the French part of the Mekong Delta region. In 1883 the French imposed a Treaty of Protectorate on Vietnam.

French rule often proved cruel and arbitrary. Ultimately, the most successful resistance came from the Left. The first Marxist group in Indochina, the Vietnam Revolutionary Youth League, was founded by Ho Chi Minh in 1925.

During WWII, the only group that did anything significant to resist the Japanese occupation was the Communist-dominated Viet Minh. When WWII ended, Ho Chi Minh –

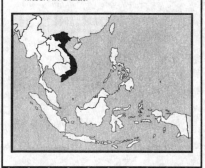

whose Viet Minh forces already controlled large parts of the country – declared Vietnam independent. French efforts to reassert control soon led to violent confrontations and full-scale war. In May 1954 Viet Minh forces overran the French garrison at Dien Bien Phu.

The Geneva Accords of mid-1954 provided for a temporary division of the country into two zones at the Ben Hai River. When the leader of the southern zone, an anti-Communist

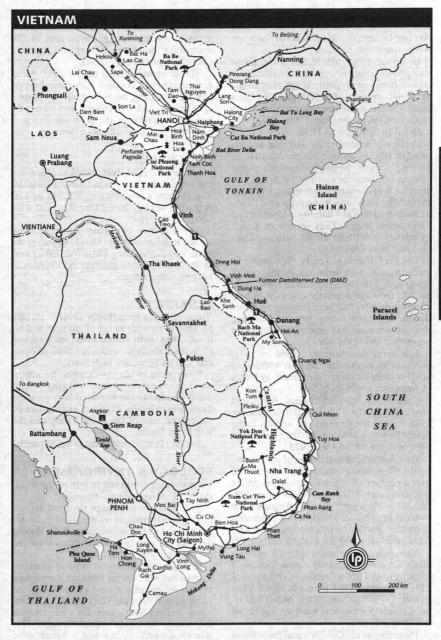

VIETNAM

CHINA

To Kunming

Hekou Bac Ha
Lai Chau Lao Cai
Sapa

Ba Be
National
Park

To Beijing

Nanning CHINA

Phongsali

Dien Bien
Phu

Son La

Tam
Dao

Thai
Nguyen

Pinxiang
Dong Dang

Zhanjiang

Viet Tri

Lang
Son

LAOS

Sam Neua

HANOI

Mai
Chau

Perfume
Pagoda

Hoa
Binh

Haiphong

Nam
Dinh

Halong
City

Bai Tu Long Bay

Halong
Bay

Luang
Prabang

Hoa
Lu

Ninh Binh

Cat Ba National Park

Hainan
Island

VIETNAM

Cuc Phuong
National
Park

Tam Coc

Thanh Hoa

Red River Delta

GULF OF
TONKIN

(CHINA)

VIENTIANE

Cao
Treo

Vinh

1

Tha Khaek

Dong Hoi

Vinh Moc Former Demilitarised Zone (DMZ)

Paracel
Islands

Dong Ha

Savannakhet

Lao
Bao

Khe
Sanh

Hué

1

THAILAND

Bach Ma
National
Park

Danang

Hoi An

My Son

Pakse

Quang Ngai

To Bangkok

Kon
Tum

Pleiku

Central Highlands

SOUTH
CHINA
SEA

CAMBODIA

Angkor

Siem Reap

Qui Nhon

Battambang

Tonlé
Sap

Yok Don
National Park

Tuy Hoa

Mekong River

Buon
Ma
Thuot

Nha Trang

PHNOM
PENH

Moc Bai

Tay Ninh

Dalat

Cam Ranh
Bay

Nam Cat Tien
National
Park

Cu Chi

Phan Rang

Bien Hoa

Ca Na

Sihanoukville

Chau
Doc

Ho Chi Minh
City (Saigon)

Long Hai

Phan
Thiet

Phu Quoc
Island

Ha
Tien

Hon
Chong

Long
Xuyen

Mytho

Vung Tau

Rach
Gia

Cantho

Vinh
Long

GULF OF
THAILAND

Camau

Mekong Delta

0   100   200 km

Catholic named Ngo Dinh Diem, refused to hold elections scheduled for 1956, the Ben Hai line became the de facto border between North and South Vietnam.

In about 1960, the Hanoi government changed its policy of opposition to the Diem regime from one of 'political struggle' to one of 'armed struggle'. The National Liberation Front (NLF), a Communist guerrilla group better known as the Viet Cong (VC), was founded to fight against Diem.

Diem was a brutal ruler and was assassinated in 1963 by his own troops. After Hanoi ordered regular North Vietnamese Army units to infiltrate the south in 1964, the situation for the Saigon regime became desperate. In 1965 the USA (which had supported Diem, then dumped him as a liability) committed its first combat troops. They were soon joined by soldiers from South Korea, Australia, Thailand and New Zealand.

The Tet Offensive of early 1968 marked a crucial turning point in the war. As the country celebrated Tet, the Vietnamese New Year, the VC launched a deadly offensive. Many Americans, who had been hearing for years that the US was winning, stopped believing their government and started demanding a negotiated end to the war.

The Paris Agreements, signed in 1973, provided for a ceasefire, the total withdrawal of US combat forces and the release by Hanoi of American prisoners of war.

North Vietnam launched a massive ground attack across the 17th Parallel in January 1975, routing the demoralised soldiers in the South. Saigon surrendered to the North Vietnamese Army on 30 April 1975.

The takeover and unification of the country by the Communists meant liberation from over a century of colonial repression, but it was soon followed by large-scale internal repression against enemies created by the same external aggression. Hundreds of thousands of southerners fled their homeland, creating a flood of refugees for the next 15 years.

A campaign of repression against Vietnam's ethnic-Chinese community – plus Vietnam's invasion of Pol Pot's Cambodia at the end of 1978 – prompted the Chinese to attack Vietnam in 1979. The war lasted only 17 days, but Chinese-Vietnamese mistrust has lasted well over a decade.

The ending of the Cold War and the collapse of the Soviet Union in 1991 has encouraged Vietnam and former western enemies to seek *rapprochement*.

The USA established diplomatic relations with Vietnam in 1995, a move which opened doors to discrete foreign investment by US companies (others, eg Korean and Japanese interests, were already there).

The lingering effects of the 1997 Asian economic crisis, coupled with natural disasters like flooding, have dramatically curbed investment, and the government currently appears divided over the pace and direction of economic (and political) reforms.

GEOGRAPHY

Vietnam stretches over 1600km along the eastern coast of the Indochinese Peninsula. The country's land area is 329,566 sq km, making it slightly larger than Italy and a bit smaller than Japan.

The country's two main cultivated areas are the Red River Delta (15,000 sq km) in the north and the Mekong Delta (60,000 sq km) in the south. Three-quarters of Vietnam is hilly or mountainous.

CLIMATE

Vietnam has a remarkably diverse climate because of its wide range of latitudes and altitudes. The south is tropical but the north can experience chilly winters – in Hanoi, an overcoat can be necessary in January.

From April or May to October, the southwestern monsoon blows, bringing warm, damp weather to the whole country – except those areas sheltered by mountains, namely the central part of the coastal strip and the Red River Delta.

See the Hanoi climate chart in the Appendix.

ECOLOGY & ENVIRONMENT

Vietnam's environment is not in the worst shape, but there are troubling signs.

Deforestation is perhaps the most serious problem. Government reforestation and environmental awareness programs have slowed the tide, but at current rates, reforestation can not keep up with forest losses.

In addition to rapacious logging practices (curbed in 1992), during what the Vietnamese call the American war (and which Americans know as the Vietnam War), the USA extensively sprayed South Vietnam's jungles with the deadly herbicide Agent Orange. This 'scorched earth' policy had a catastrophic effect on the environment. Agent Orange contains dioxin – the most toxic chemical known – which is highly carcinogenic and mutagenic.

Vietnam's rapid economic and population growth also suggest environmental trouble ahead. The dramatic increase in noisy, smoke-spewing motorbikes over the past few years could be taken as a sign of abominations to come.

FLORA & FAUNA

The forests of Vietnam are estimated to contain 12,000 plant species, only 7000 of which have been identified.

Vietnam's wild fauna is enormously diverse. The country is home to 273 species of mammals, over 800 species of birds, 180 species of reptiles, 80 species of amphibians, hundreds of species of fish and thousands of kinds of invertebrates. Larger animals of special importance in conservation efforts include the elephant, rhinoceros, tiger, leopard, black bear, honey bear, snub-nosed monkey, douc langur (remarkable for its variegated colours), concolour gibbon, rhesus macaque, serow (a kind of mountain goat), flying squirrel, kouprey (a blackish-brown forest ox), banteng (a kind of wild ox), deer, peacock, pheasant, crocodile, python, cobra and turtle.

Endangered Species

Tragically, Vietnam's wildlife is in a precipitous decline as forest habitats are destroyed and waterways become polluted. In addition, uncontrolled illegal hunting has exterminated the local populations of various animals, in some cases eliminating entire species. Officially, the government has recognised 54 species of mammals and 60 species of birds as endangered.

National Parks

Vietnam currently has 10 national parks and an expanding array of nature reserves well worth exploring. Most of these parks remain seldom visited, largely due to travellers getting stuck on the tourist trail, without the time or wanderlust to go.

The most interesting of the ten are Cat Ba, Ba Be and Cuc Phuong national parks in the north; Bach Ma National Park in the centre; and Nam Cat Tien and Yok Don national parks in the south.

Cat Ba National Park is a beautiful island, and during the summer months attracts a steady stream of foreign travellers willing to make the boat journey. Ba Be National Park features spectacular waterfalls and is accessible by rented jeep or motorbike from Hanoi.

Cuc Phuong National Park is less visited, but easily accessible from Hanoi and offers great hiking. Bach Ma National Park near Hué is also seldom visited, but is showing good potential for responsible eco-tourism.

Nam Cat Tien National Park, in the Central Highlands of the south, is a bit difficult to reach and sees few visitors, but is popular with bird watchers. Also in the Central Highlands is Yok Don National Park, which has little scenery but is home to local minority tribes.

GOVERNMENT & POLITICS

The Socialist Republic of Vietnam (SRV) came into existence in July 1976 as a unitary state comprising the Democratic Republic of Vietnam (North Vietnam) and the territory of the defeated Republic of Vietnam (South Vietnam).

Despite the rapid pace of economic reforms in the 1990s, the government shows no sign of moving towards western-style democracy and political control remains firmly in the hands of the Communist Party.

ECONOMY

Vietnam is poor, with an estimated per capita income of US$200 per year. As has long been the case, international economic forces, local bureaucracy and corruption remain the most significant impediments to Vietnam's economic development. However, there are signs that things are improving.

The economy was devastated in the 1960s and 1970s by war, but even the government has admitted that the present economic fiasco is mainly the result of the collectivisation policies and bloated military budgets that followed reunification.

Limited private enterprise was reintroduced in 1986. Since 1991 the loss of trade and aid from the former Eastern bloc has caused Vietnam to greatly accelerate the pace of 'free-market' economic reform. The reforms have breathed new life into an economy that was moribund.

Ironically, the recent flood of money from foreign investors has propped up the state sector, causing it to expand. The bloated bureaucracy is resisting privatisation, and plans to open a stock market keep getting postponed.

POPULATION & PEOPLE

In 1997, Vietnam's population reached 76.5 million, making it the 13th most populous country in the world. There are virtually no government-orchestrated family planning policies and people may have as many children as they wish. Annual population growth is 2.3%.

The population is 84% ethnic-Vietnamese and 2% ethnic-Chinese; the rest is made up of Khmer, Cham (a remnant of the once-mighty Champa kingdom) and members of over 50 ethno-linguistic groups (also known as Montagnards, which means 'Highlanders' in French).

EDUCATION

Although university education is out of reach for most Vietnamese, the country's literacy rate is estimated at 88.6%. Unlike in many other poor countries, women generally receive the same access to education as men.

ARTS
Architecture

The Vietnamese have not been great builders like their neighbours the Khmer, who erected the monuments of Angkor in Cambodia. Most of what the Vietnamese have built has been made of wood and other materials that proved highly vulnerable in the tropical climate.

The grand exception is the stunning towers built by Vietnam's ancient Cham culture. These are most numerous in central Vietnam. The Cham towers at My Son are a major tourist drawcard.

Sculpture

Vietnamese sculpture has traditionally centred on religious themes and functioned as an adjunct to architecture, especially that of pagodas, temples and tombs.

The Cham civilisation produced spectacular carved sandstone figures for its Hindu and Buddhist sanctuaries. The largest single collection of Cham sculpture in the world is at the Cham Museum in Danang.

Water Puppetry

Water puppetry *(roi nuoc)* is a uniquely Vietnamese art form found mostly in the north, though there are shows put on in Saigon.

SOCIETY & CONDUCT
Traditional Culture

The family is the basic unit of Vietnamese society, and anyone who is not married is pitied rather than envied. Most foreigners are asked if they are married – if you're single and under age 30, the best response is 'not

yet'. If you're over 30, perhaps you simply should say 'Yes, and I have one child', even if this is not so. Trying to explain that you are 'happily single' will not make a lot of sense to most Vietnamese.

Dos & Don'ts

Shoes are removed inside most Buddhist temples and often in people's homes, but this is not universal so watch what others do. Don't point the bottoms of your feet towards other people or towards Buddhist statues.

In general, shorts are considered inappropriate wear for all but children or men labouring in the sun. However, the recent influx of foreigners has influenced Vietnamese tastes, and women in fashionable Saigon have started wearing shorts. Nevertheless, such changes have not yet filtered to the hinterlands.

Leaving a pair of chopsticks sticking vertically in a rice bowl looks similar to the incense sticks which are burned for the dead. This powerful death sign is not appreciated anywhere in east Asia.

RELIGION

Four great philosophies and religions have shaped the spiritual life of the Vietnamese people: Confucianism, Taoism, Buddhism and Christianity.

Over the centuries, Confucianism, Taoism and Buddhism have fused with popular Chinese beliefs and ancient Vietnamese animism to form what is known collectively as Tam Giao (Triple Religion), which is sometimes referred to as Vietnamese Buddhism. The religious life of the Vietnamese is also profoundly influenced by ancestor worship, which dates from long before the arrival of Confucianism or Buddhism.

Muslims, mostly ethnic-Khmer and Cham, constitute about 0.5% of the population.

Vietnam has the highest percentage of Catholics (8% to 10% of the population) in Asia outside of the Philippines.

Caodaism is an indigenous Vietnamese sect that was founded with the intention of creating the ideal religion by fusing the secular and religious philosophies of both east and west. It was established in the early 1920s based on messages revealed in seances to Ngo Minh Chieu, the group's founder. The sect's colourful headquarters is in Tay Ninh, 96km north-west of Saigon. There are currently about two million followers of Caodaism in Vietnam.

See the Religions of South-East Asia section in the Appendix for more details.

LANGUAGE

Most of the names of the letters of the Latin-based *quoc ngu* alphabet are the same as the names of the letters in French. Dictionaries are alphabetised as in English, except that each vowel/tone combination is treated as a different letter.

See the Language section in the Appendix for a list of some useful Vietnamese words and phrases.

Facts for the Visitor

HIGHLIGHTS

Some places in the south that have proven particularly popular with travellers include the **Mekong Delta, Dalat, Nha Trang, Hoi An** and **Hué.**

North from Hué, many travellers head for **Hoa Lu, Cat Ba Island, Halong Bay. Sapa** and **Bac Ha** are two of the most colourful hill tribe regions.

PLANNING

When to Go

There are no good or bad seasons for visiting Vietnam. When one region is wet, cold or steaming hot, there is always somewhere else that is sunny and pleasantly warm.

Visitors should take into account that around Tet, the colourful Vietnamese New Year celebration which falls in late January or early February, flights into, out of and around the country are likely to be booked solid and accommodation can be almost impossible to find. The New Year festival is more than just a one day event – it goes on for at least a week. For at least a week before and two weeks after Tet you are likely to encounter some difficulties in booking hotels and flights; this applies also to the whole of eastern Asia.

Maps

Basic road maps of Vietnam are readily available, though fine details are lacking. Lonely Planet's *Vietnam travel atlas* gives an in-depth view of towns, highways and topographic features.

It's easy to find decent maps of the major cities such as Hanoi, Saigon, Hué, Danang and Nha Trang. However, maps of most small to mid-sized cities are virtually nonexistent.

TOURIST OFFICES

Vietnam doesn't have tourist offices as such. Rather, there are state-run travel agencies that masquerade as tourist offices. The names they use, such as Vietnam Tourism and Saigon Tourist, are misleading. They are not in the business of promoting Vietnam as a tourist destination. In fact, they have little information that they're willing to give for free – essentially, they are in business to book pricey tours.

Local Tourist Offices

Every province has a regional tourist office cum travel agency. Although selling tours is their primary function, the staff might be willing to part with some useful travel information if you approach them in a friendly manner. See relevant city entries for the location of local 'tourist offices'.

Tourist Offices Abroad

Some Vietnamese 'tourist offices' abroad include:

France
  Vietnam Tourism
  (☎ 01 42 86 86 37, fax 42 60 43 32)
  4 rue Cherubini, 75002 Paris
  Saigon Tourist
  (☎ 01 40 51 03 02, fax 43 25 05 70)
  24 rue des Bernadins, 75005 Paris
Germany
  Saigon Tourist
  (☎ 030-786 5056, fax 786 5596)
  24 Dudenstrasse 78 W, 1000 Berlin 61
Japan
  Saigon Tourist
  (☎ 03-3258 5931, fax 3253 6819)
  IDI 6th floor, Crystal Bldg, 1-2, Kanda
  Awaji-cho, Chiyoda-ku, Tokyo 101
Singapore
  Vietnam Tourism
  (☎ 532 3130, fax 532 2952)
  101 Upper Cross St, No 02-44 People's Park
  Centre, Singapore 0105
  Saigon Tourist
  (☎ 735 1433, fax 735 1508)
  131 Tanglin Rd, Tudor Court, Singapore 1024

VISAS & DOCUMENTS

Visas

While Vietnamese bureaucracy is legendary, completing the necessary paperwork to obtain a visa is not all that daunting. Bangkok seems to be the fastest and most popular place to get a Vietnamese visa, though Hong Kong is a viable alternative. Keep plenty of visa photos

VIETNAM

handy – you need at least two to apply for a visa (sometimes three or four), and occasionally a couple more photos to get through immigration upon arrival in Vietnam.

Tourist Visas Tourist visas are only valid for a single 30 day stay. To make matters worse, the visa specifies the exact date of arrival and departure. Thus, you must solidify your travel plans well in advance. You cannot arrive even one day earlier than your visa specifies. And if you change your plans and postpone your trip by two weeks, then you'll only have 16 days remaining on your visa instead of 30 days.

Vietnamese visas specify where you are permitted to enter and leave the country – usually Ho Chi Minh City's Tan Son Nhat or Hanoi's Noi Bai airports. Other options worth considering are the Chinese border at Huu Nghi Quan (Friendship Gate) or Lao Cai, or the Cambodian border at Moc Bai and the Lao border at Lao Bao. Make sure this is made clear on your visa application. If you later decide to exit from a place not listed on your visa, amendments can be made at the Foreign Affairs Ministry in Hanoi or Saigon, or even at the local immigration police (Hué is popular for this).

Prices for single-entry tourist visas are around US$45 to US$60. In Bangkok they can be issued in about four days, in Hong Kong five days, but in other places (Taiwan, for example) it can take as long as 10 working days. An 'express visa' takes half the time and is arranged by fax to Hanoi – the drawback is a greater chance of things going awry (paperwork not done properly on the Vietnamese end and the visa being declared 'invalid' on arrival). Many travel agencies offer package deals with visa and air ticket included. In Bangkok, the place to look for competitive prices is Khao San Rd. In Hong Kong, a travel agency specialising in visas and air tickets to Vietnam is Phoenix Services (☎ 0852-2722 7378, fax 2369 8884) in Room B, 6th floor, Milton Mansion, 96 Nathan Rd, Tsimshatsui, Kowloon.

Business Visas There are several advantages in having a business visa: such visas are usually valid for three months; they can be issued for multiple-entry journeys; you are permitted to work in Vietnam; and the visas can be extended with relative ease. Business visas are arranged at travel agencies, who can also normally arrange the requisite 'sponsor'.

Trying to obtain the visa yourself through a Vietnamese embassy is definately more troublesome.

Visa Extensions If you've got the dollars, they've got the rubber stamp. In Saigon and Hanoi, visa extensions cost around US$30, but you should probably go to a travel agency to get this taken care of – fronting up at the immigration police yourself usually doesn't work. Many hotels have a sign on the front desk indicating that they have a visa extension service. The procedure takes one or two days and one photo is needed. You can apply for your extension even several weeks before it's necessary. This process is only readily accomplished in major cities – Hanoi, Saigon, Danang or Hué.

Official policy is that you are permitted one visa extension only for a maximum of 30 days. Be alert for sudden unannounced changes to these regulations.

Travel Permits

Since 1993 internal travel permits supposedly have been abolished. However, local authorities often make up their own rules. Currently, travel permits are required for the following places: Lat Village and Lang Bian Mountain in Dalat; minority villages around Buon Ma Thuot and Pleiku in the Central Highlands; and villages around the Demilitarised Zone (DMZ).

However, policies change frequently, and you may have to inquire locally to see if a permit is required. Furthermore, there have been reports of con artists insisting that police permits are required when in fact this is not the case. Many unsuspecting foreigners have paid for bogus 'permits' that were little more than a photocopied piece of paper with someone's signature scribbled on it.

EMBASSIES & CONSULATES
Vietnamese Embassies & Consulates

Diplomatic representation abroad includes:

Australia
  Embassy:
  (☎ 02-6286 6059)
  6 Timbarra Crescent, O'Malley, ACT 2603
Canada
  Embassy:
  (☎ 613-236 0772, fax 236 2704)
  226 Maclaren St, Ottawa, Ontario
  K2P 0L9

China
  Embassy:
  (☎ 010-532 1125)
  32 Guanghua Lu, Jianguomenwai, Beijing
  Consulate:
  (☎ 020-776 9555 ext 101/604)
  Jin Yanf Hotel, 92 Huanshi Western Rd,
  Guangzhou
  Consulate:
  (☎ 22-591 4510, fax 591 4524)
  15th floor, Great Smart Tower Bldg, 230
  Wanchai Rd, Hong Kong
France
  Embassy:
  (☎ 01 44 14 64 00, fax 01 45 24 39 48)
  62-66 rue Boileau, 75016 Paris
Germany
  Embassy:
  (☎ 228-357021, fax 351866)
  Konstantinstrasse 37, 5300 Bonn 2
UK
  Embassy:
  (☎ 020-7937 1912)
  12-14 Victoria Rd, London W8 5RD
USA
  (☎ 800 874 5100 toll free)
  Vietnamese Liaison Office, Washington, DC
  Visa processing:
  (☎ 202-638 3800)
  Travel Documents Inc, 734 15th St NW,
  Suite 400, Washington, DC 20005

See the other chapters in this book for Vietnamese embassies in those countries.

Embassies & Consulates in Vietnam

Useful embassies/consulates in Hanoi/Ho
Chi Minh City include:

Australia
  (☎ 831 7755, fax 831 7711)
  Van Phuc Diplomatic Quarter, Hanoi
  Consulate:
  (☎ 829 6035, fax 829 6031)
  The Landmark, 5B Duong Ton Duc Thang,
  District 1, Ho Chi Minh City
Cambodia
  (☎ 825 3788, fax 826 5225)
  71 Pho Tran Hung Dao, Hanoi
  Consulate:
  (☎ 829 2751, fax 829 2744)
  41 Duong Phung Khac Khoan, District 1,
  Ho Chi Minh City
Canada
  (☎ 823 5500, fax 823 5333)
  31 Pho Hung Vuong, Hanoi
  Consulate:
  (☎ 824 2000, fax 829 4528)
  203 Duong Dong Khoi, Suite 102, District 1,
  Ho Chi Minh City

China
  (☎ 845 3736, fax 823 2826)
  46 Pho Hoang Dieu, Hanoi
  Consulate:
  (☎ 829 2457)
  39 Duong Nguyen Thi Minh Khai,
  Ho Chi Minh City
France
  (☎ 825 2719, fax 826 4236)
  57 Pho Tran Hung Dao, Hanoi
  Consulate:
  (☎ 829 7231, fax 829 1675)
  27 Duong Nguyen Thi Minh Khai, District 1,
  Ho Chi Minh City
Germany
  (☎ 845 3836, fax 845 3838)
  29 Pho Tran Phu, Hanoi
  Consulate:
  (☎ 829 1967, fax 823 1919)
  126 Duong Nguyen Dinh Chieu, District 3,
  Ho Chi Minh City
Laos
  (☎ 825 4576, fax 822 8414)
  40 Pho Quang Trung, Hanoi
Malaysia
  (☎ 825 3371)
  Bldg A3, Van Phuc Diplomatic Quarter,
  Hanoi
  Consulate:
  (☎ 829 9023; fax 829 9027)
  53 Duong Nguyen Dinh Chieu, District 3,
  Ho Chi Minh City
Myanmar (Burma)
  (☎ 845 3369, fax 845 2404)
  Block A3, Van Phuc Diplomatic Quarter,
  Hanoi
New Zealand
  (☎ 824 1481, fax 824 1480)
  32 Pho Hang Bai, Hanoi
  Consulate:
  (☎ 822 6907, fax 822 6905)
  5th Floor, Yoco Bldg, 41 Duong Nguyen Thi
  Minh Khai, District 1,
  Ho Chi Minh City
Philippines
  (☎ 825 7948, fax 826 5760)
  27B Pho Tran Hung Dao, Hanoi
Thailand
  (☎ 823 5092, fax 823 5088)
  63-65 Pho Hoang Dieu, Hanoi
  Consulate:
  (☎ 822 2637, fax 829 1002)
  77 Duong Tran Quoc Thao, District 3,
  Ho Chi Minh City
UK
  (☎ 825 2510, fax 826 5762)
  31 Pho Hai Ba Trung, Hanoi
  Consulate:
  (☎ 829 8433, fax 822 1971)
  25 Dai Lo Le Duan, District 1,
  Ho Chi Minh City

VIETNAM

USA
   (☎ 843 1500; fax 843 1510)
   7 Pho Lang Ha, Hanoi

CUSTOMS

Travellers occasionally report trouble with Vietnamese customs. Some travellers have even had their Lonely Planet books seized or sections of it torn out! Ditto for video tapes. Keep such dangerous items buried deep down in your luggage or else in your coat pocket.

You are not permitted to take antiques or other 'cultural treasures' out of the country. If you purchase fake antiques, be sure that you have a receipt and a customs clearance form from the seller. Suspected antiques will be seized, or else you'll have to pay a 'fine'.

MONEY
Currency

The dong (d) is the currency of Vietnam. Banknotes in denominations of 200d, 500d, 1000d, 2000d, 5000d, 10,000d, 20,000d and 50,000d are presently in circulation. There are no coins.

The US dollar virtually acts as a second local currency, and hotels, airlines and travel agencies all normally quote their prices in dollars. This is in part because Vietnamese prices are so unwieldy, since US$100 is over one million dong! For this reason, we also quote prices in US dollars. However, realise that you can, and should, pay dong. Indeed, Vietnamese law requires that all transactions be in dong, though in practice many people will accept dollars.

Exchange Rates

Exchange rates are as follows:

country	unit		dong
Australia	A$1	=	8743d
Canada	C$1	=	8985d
euro	€1	=	16,711d
France	10FF	=	25,288d
Germany	DM1	=	8479d
Japan	¥100	=	11,635d
New Zealand	NZ$1	=	7496d
Thailand	B100	=	36,426d
UK	UK£1	=	23,654d
USA	US$1	=	13,900d

Exchanging Money

Large-denomination bills (US$100) are preferred when changing into dong, but a small supply (say US$20 worth) of US1 and US$5 notes will prove useful on arrival to hire a taxi into the city.

Travellers cheques in US dollars can be exchanged for dong at certain banks – most hotels and airline offices will not accept travellers cheques. Lost or stolen travellers cheques cannot be replaced in Vietnam.

Be very careful with your money – travellers cheques and large-denomination cash belongs in a money belt or pockets sewn inside your trousers.

Visa, MasterCard and JCB credit cards are acceptable in major cities. Getting a cash advance from a credit card is also possible, but you'll be charged between 2% and 4% commission.

Black Market There is really no black market in Vietnam. However, black market 'moneychangers' may approach you on the street and offer a fantastic exchange rate. You can be sure that such exchanges will wind up with you getting cheated or robbed.

Costs

Vietnam is very cheap compared with any western country, but not so cheap compared with some travel bargains in Asia, such as Indonesia. It would be dirt cheap if you could pay the same as the locals, but special 'foreigners only' prices are often charged. In hotels, foreigners are normally charged double the price a Vietnamese would pay for the same room. For airline tickets, foreigners pay triple; for trains, foreigners are charged five times the Vietnamese price.

Nevertheless, hotels, food and buses are cheap by western reckoning, and ascetics can get by on less than US$10 a day. For US$15 to US$20, a backpacker can live fairly well.

Tipping & Bargaining

Tipping is not expected but it's enormously appreciated. For someone making under US$50 per month, 10% of the cost of your meal can equal half a day's wages.

Bargaining is common, even with the police if you are fined! Always be polite and smiling when bargaining – nastiness will cause the other party to lose face, in which case they'll dig in their heels and you'll come out the loser.

POST & COMMUNICATIONS
Postal Rates

International postal service from Vietnam is not unreasonably priced when compared with most other countries.

Sending Mail

Take your letters to the post office yourself and make sure that the clerk cancels them *while you watch* so that someone for whom the stamps are worth a day's salary does not soak them off and throw your letters away.

Receiving Mail

Poste restante works in the larger cities but don't count on it elsewhere. There is a small surcharge for picking up poste restante letters. All post offices are marked with the words 'Buu Dien'.

Telephone

International telecommunications charges are among the highest in the world.

The cheapest and simplest way by far to make an international direct dial (IDD) call is to buy a telephone card, known in Vietnam as a 'UniphoneKad'. They are on sale at the telephone company. UniphoneKads can only

---

Telephone Codes

The country code for Vietnam is 84. The international dialling code is 00. Drop the first zero in the area codes when dialling from outside Vietnam.

Following are area codes for some cities.

Bac Ha	☎ 020
Ca Na	☎ 068
Cat Ba	☎ 031
Cho Ra	☎ 026
Dalat	☎ 063
Danang City	☎ 0511
Dien Bien Phu	☎ 023
Haiphong City	☎ 031
Halong Bay	☎ 033
Hanoi City	☎ 04
Hoa Binh	☎ 018
Hoa Lu	☎ 030
Ho Chi Minh City	☎ 08
Hoi An (Faifo)	☎ 0510
Hué	☎ 054
Lao Cai	☎ 020
Mai Chau	☎ 018
Nha Trang	☎ 058
Ninh Binh	☎ 030
Phan Thiet	☎ 062
Sapa	☎ 020
Vung Tau	☎ 064

---

be used in special telephones which are almost exclusively found in Hanoi and Ho Chi Minh City (and mostly in hotel lobbies). The cards are issued in three denominations; 30,000d, 150,000d and 300,000d. The 30,000d card will only work for domestic calls.

Useful Phone Numbers The following special phone numbers are available, but don't be surprised if the person answering only speaks Vietnamese:

Ambulance	☎ 115
Directory Assistance	☎ 116
General Information	☎ 118
Fire Brigade	☎ 114
International Operator	☎ 110
International Prefix	☎ 00
Police	☎ 113
Time Information	☎ 117

Fax, Telex & Telegraph

Most main post offices and many tourist hotels in Vietnam offer domestic and international fax, telegraph and telex services. Hotels are likely to charge more than the post office.

Email & Internet Access

It is only recently that public-access on-line services are back in Vietnam. In the summer of 1997, the government authorities closed down *all* Internet cafes. They are cautiously beginning to re-emerge, hopefully this time to stay, and range from cybercafes to computer terminals in the lobbies of guest houses.

The cost for Internet access ranges from about US$0.06 to US$0.25 per minute. Printing usually costs between US$0.08 and US$0.16 per page.

INTERNET RESOURCES

Perhaps the best all-around site on contemporary Vietnam is Destination Vietnam (www.destinationvietnam.com). Published for years in print form, DV has recently made the full shift over to an electronic magazine. It is a one-stop Vietnam information zone covering travel, art, history, culture and even adoption. The site has an on-line contemporary Vietnamese art gallery, subsections that delve deeper into specific topics, and enough interesting links to keep you wired for weeks.

Another excellent place to begin is the well established Vietnam Adventures Online (www.vietnamadventures.com). It is full of practical travel information and features monthly adventures and special travel deals.

Vietnam Online (www.govietnam.com) has been on the web since 1995 and gets a huge number of hits. The site is loaded with useful travel lore, and boasts good coverage on employment and business opportunities in Vietnam.

BOOKS

Lonely Planet

Lonely Planet's *Vietnam* guide has the full story on the country. Cyclists, hikers and other back-country explorers may want to score a copy of LP's *Vietnam travel atlas*. Our *Vietnamese phrasebook* is not only educational, but will also give you something to do during those long bus rides. And if you'd like some more details on the ins and outs of Saigon, there is the *Ho Chi Minh City guide*.

History & Politics

One of the finest books about the American war written by a Vietnamese is *The Sorrow of War* by Bao Ninh. *Brother Enemy* by Nayan Chanda is an excellent book about the war's aftermath.

General

Two classic books from the French colonial period are Graham Greene's novel *The Quiet American* and Norman Lewis' account of travels in the region in the early 1950s, *A Dragon Apparent*.

FILMS

There are heaps of videos dealing with America's (or Hollywood's) version of the war experience in Vietnam.

Films set during the French colonial period include nostalgic romances like *The Lover* and *Indochine*.

Happily, Vietnamese filmmakers are now getting the chance to tell their own stories – see Tran Anh Hung's *Scent of the Green Papaya* and *Cyclo*.

NEWSPAPERS & MAGAZINES

The English-language *Vietnam News* is published daily in Saigon but is little more than a pamphlet. If you're desperate for some news of the outside world, it will do in a pinch. It's also good for wrapping fish.

Of more interest is the *Vietnam Economic Times* (published monthly), and the *Vietnam Investment Review* (published weekly). VET's free insert, *The Guide*, is an excellent source of leisure information and can be picked up in hotels, bars and restaurants in larger cities. VIT's free supplement, *Time Out*, is another useful tool for finding what's going on in Saigon and Hanoi.

RADIO & TV

Foreign radio services such as the BBC World Service, Radio Australia and Voice of America can be picked up on short-wave frequencies.

Vietnamese TV broadcasts little of interest to foreigners, but satellite dish antennae are rapidly proliferating and many hotels now offer Hong Kong's Star TV, BBC, CNN and other channels.

PHOTOGRAPHY & VIDEO

New film-safe machines have replaced the ancient dental x-ray machines which were at one time notorious for destroying film upon arrival at the airport.

For videos, on both arrival and departure, you are supposed to get a certificate of clearance from the 'Cultural Department'. Of course, the Cultural Department doesn't have branch offices in the airport or at land border crossings. Some travellers have even been hassled over CD disks and music cassette tapes. Usually, the payment of a small 'fine' causes these problems to evaporate.

ELECTRICITY

About 95% of the electric current in Vietnam is 220V at 50Hz, but you can still find 110V (also at 50Hz). Looking at the shape of the outlet on the wall gives no clue as to what voltage is flowing through the wires, so try to find a light bulb to check.

WEIGHTS & MEASURES

Vietnam subscribes to the international metric system.

LAUNDRY

Virtually every hotel offers a cheap laundry service, but they dry clothes in the sun, so this may take longer in the rainy season.

TOILETS

Better hotels will have the more familiar western-style sit-down toilets, but squat toilets still exist in cheaper hotels and public places like restaurants, bus stations etc.

Hotels usually supply it, but you'd be wise to keep a stash of toilet paper with you at all times while travelling around. Whether you sit or squat, throw the used paper in the waste basket provided.

HEALTH

There have been recent large outbreaks of dengue fever, so you should take appropriate measures to avoid mosquito bites. Malaria risk exists year-round in rural areas. Japanese encephalitis, although a small risk to travellers, is endemic in Vietnam, and you may want to consider a vaccination if you are intending to stay for some time, especially in rural areas – discuss this with your doctor. Schistosomiasis (bilharzia) is present in the Mekong Delta, so you should avoid bathing or paddling here.

Food and water-borne diseases, including dysentery, cholera and hepatitis, occur – it's worth paying particular attention to the basic food and water hygiene rules.

For more information on these and other health matters refer to the Health section in the Appendix.

WOMEN TRAVELLERS

While it always pays to be prudent (avoid dark, lonely alleys at night), western women very rarely have problems in Vietnam. But it can be a different story for an Asian woman.

An Asian woman accompanied by a western male will automatically be labelled a 'Vietnamese whore'. The fact that the couple could be married (or just friends) doesn't seem to occur to anyone, nor does it seem to register that the woman might not be Vietnamese at all. If she's Asian then she's Vietnamese, and if she's with a western male then she must be a prostitute.

Women in this situation can expect considerable verbal abuse, though it will be spoken entirely in Vietnamese, which means she may not realise that insults are being hurled at her if she doesn't speak the language. However, there will be no mistaking the hateful stares and obscene gestures. All this abuse will come from Vietnamese men (including teenagers) rather than Vietnamese women.

For racially mixed couples wanting to visit Vietnam, no easy solution exists. Of course, public intimacy (holding hands etc) is best avoided, but even just walking down the street together invites abuse. In an actual confrontation, the woman should shout something at the antagonist in any language *other* than Vietnamese – this might make the person realise that he is confronting a foreigner rather than a 'Vietnamese whore'.

GAY & LESBIAN TRAVELLERS

On the whole Vietnam is a relatively hassle-free place to travel for homosexuals. There are no official laws on same sex relationships in Vietnam, nor much in the way of official harassment.

Still, the government is notorious for closing down gay venues, and places that get written up in the mass media have a mysterious tendency to soon be 'raided'. As such, most gay gathering points keep a fairly low profile. There is, however, a healthy gay scene in Vietnam, especially in Hanoi and Saigon, evident by unabashed cruising around certain lakes in Hanoi and cafe scene in Saigon.

Common local attitudes suggest a general social prohibition, though the lack of any laws make things fairly safe (even if the authorities do break up a party on occasion). Major headlines were made in 1997 when Vietnam's first gay marriage saw two men wed, and again in 1998 at the country's first lesbian wedding, this one in the Mekong Delta.

Perhaps the best way to tap into what's what is on the Internet. Check out www.utopia-asia.com – the site is chock full of information and contacts, including detailed sections on the legality of homosexuality in Vietnam and local gay terminology.

Hot off the presses is Douglas Thompson's *The Men of Vietnam* (1998), a comprehensive gay travel guide to Vietnam. The book can be ordered at the above mentioned Internet site.

DANGERS & ANNOYANCES

Since 1975 many thousands of Vietnamese have been maimed or killed by rockets, artillery shells, mortars, mines and other ordnance left over from the war. *Never* touch any relics of the war you may come across – such objects can remain lethal for decades. Remember, one bomb can ruin your whole day.

Although the amount pinched by snatch thieves and pickpockets pales in comparison with what is raked in by high-ranking kleptocrats, it's the street crime that most worries travellers. The good news is that violent crime is still relatively rare in Vietnam. The bad news is that just about every other kind of crime is not rare at all. Drive-by bag snatchers are common – thieves on motorbikes have been known to snatch bags through the open windows of cars and buses. Travellers on the trains report that on slow sections, gear can be grabbed straight through the windows. Skilled pickpockets work the crowds.

One strong suggestion, in particular for Saigon, is that you not have anything dangling off your body that you are not ready to part with. This includes bags and any jewellery – even of the costume variety.

LEGAL MATTERS
The police in Vietnam are the best that money can buy. Don't expect much help from them unless you pay. Travellers report being charged US$35 to obtain a simple loss report needed to make an insurance claim for stolen property. If you have a traffic accident, your vehicle is likely to be confiscated by the police and you'll have to pay to get it back (regardless of whose fault the accident was).

Most Vietnamese never call the police – they settle legal disputes on the spot (either with cash or fists). If you lose something really valuable (like your passport or visa), then you'll need to contact the police. Otherwise, it's better not to bother.

BUSINESS HOURS
Offices, museums etc are usually open from 7 or 8 am to 11 or 11.30 am, and from 1 or 2 pm to 4 or 5 pm. Most museums are closed on Monday.

PUBLIC HOLIDAYS & SPECIAL EVENTS
Tet (Tet Nguyen Dan), the Vietnamese lunar New Year, is the most important annual festival. The Tet holiday officially lasts three days, but many Vietnamese take the following week off work and all hotels, trains and buses are chock-a-block. It's a good time to avoid Vietnam. For the rest of this century, Tet falls on the following dates: 16 February 1999, 5 February 2000 and 24 January 2001.

The date on which Saigon surrendered to Hanoi-backed forces in 1975, 30 April, is commemorated nationwide as Liberation Day.

ACTIVITIES
Hiking
No doubt the most popular venue for hiking is the north-west region of the country (the Sapa area, including Vietnam's tallest mountain, Fansipan). Travellers also have good things to say about hikes in Cuc Phuong National Park near Hanoi.

The hiking trails in Bach Ma National Park and Nam Cat Tien National Park are improving, but you'll still need a guide. The hike up Lang Bian Mountain in Dalat gets good reviews, but the local government requires you to hire a guide and obtain a permit. Fortunately, Vietnamese trekking guides can be hired cheaply.

Watersports
Without a doubt, Nha Trang is the place to head for if you're interested in windsurfing, snorkelling, scuba diving and boating.

COURSES
Language
To qualify for student visa status, you need to study at a bona fide university (as opposed to a private language centre or with a tutor). Universities require that you study 10 hours per week. Lessons usually last for two hours per day, for which you pay tuition of around US$5.

You should establish early on whether you want to study in northern or southern Vietnam, because the regional dialects are very different.

In the south, the vast majority of foreign language students enrol at the General University of Ho Chi Minh City (Truong Dai Hoc Tong Hop) at 12 Duong Binh Hoang, District 5.

Other options in the south include Ho Chi Minh City Polytechnic (☎ 865 4087) and Lotus College (☎ 829 0841) at 53 Duong Nguyen Du, District 1.

In the north, Hanoi National University (☎ 858 1468) has the largest market share. The Vietnamese Language Centre is actually inside the Polytechnic University, not at the main campus of Hanoi National University at 90 Pho Nguyen Trai. There is a dormitory for foreign students (Nha A-2 Bach Khoa) at the Polytechnic University, and this is a good place to inquire about tuition.

Hanoi's other place to study is the Hanoi Foreign Language College's Vietnamese Language Centre (☎ 826 2468).

WORK
At least 90% of foreign travellers seeking work in Vietnam wind up teaching English, though there is some demand for French teachers too. Pay can be as low as US$2 per

hour at a university and up to US$5 per hour at a private academy. Some travellers even manage US$10 per hour for private tutoring. However, there are plenty of hurdles to overcome, starting with the visa (you'd best get a business visa) to finding a place to live (the Vietnamese authorities don't allow foreigners to rent inexpensive rooms with a family). Many people report being short-changed on their pay. Working in Vietnam will also attract the attention of the local tax authorities.

ACCOMMODATION
Guesthouses
Many Vietnamese have opened up guesthouses in their own homes. These places are licensed by the government, and are expected to meet certain standards for cleanliness and security. Prices are in the range of US$5 to US$25, depending on facilities. In some places you must share the bath, but often your room will have its own bath.

There are a growing number of budget guesthouses providing dormitory beds for foreigners for only about US$3 to US$4 per person. These are not to be confused with the ultra-cheap dormitories for Vietnamese nationals only – staying in these places is considered dangerous and foreigners are prohibited.

Hotels
The good news is that the tourism boom has been accompanied by a boom in high-standard hotel construction. The bad news is that prices are rising. Foreigners are usually not permitted to stay in the really grotty dumps, but finding hotels priced at around US$10 is still fairly easy. Many hotels throw in a simple free breakfast of coffee and baguettes.

FOOD
One of the delights of visiting Vietnam is the amazing cuisine – there are said to be nearly 500 traditional Vietnamese dishes – which is, in general, superbly prepared and very cheap.

Snacks
The Vietnamese bake the best French bread (baguettes) in South-East Asia. A loaf typically costs US$0.08.

Main Dishes
Pho is the Vietnamese name for the noodle soup that is eaten at all hours of the day. *Com* means rice dishes. You'll see signs with 'Pho' and 'Com' everywhere.

A Vietnamese speciality is spring rolls (*nem* in the north, *cha gio* in the south). These are normally dipped in *nuoc mam* (a foul-smelling fish sauce), though most foreigners prefer soy sauce (*xi dau* in the north, *nuoc tuong* in the south).

Because Buddhist monks of the Mahayana tradition are strict vegetarians, Vietnamese vegetarian cooking (*an chay*) is an integral part of Vietnamese cuisine.

Desserts
Vietnamese sweets tend to be a little too sweet for western palates. However, you may want to try *banh it nhan dau*, a gooey pastry made of pulverised sticky rice, beans and sugar. Most foreigners prefer the ice cream (*kem*) or yoghurt (*yaourt*), which are generally good quality.

Fruit
Aside from the usual delights of South-East Asian fruits, Vietnam chips in with its own unique green dragon fruit (*trai thanh long*) grown only along the coastal region south of Nha Trang.

DRINKS
Nonalcoholic Drinks
Whatever you drink, make sure that it's been boiled or bottled. Ice is generally safe in Saigon and Hanoi, but not guaranteed elsewhere. Foreign soft drinks like Coca-Cola and Pepsi are widely available.

Vietnamese coffee is fine stuff but the tea is disappointing. An excellent local treat is carbonated mineral water with lemon and sugar (*soda chanh*).

Alcoholic Drinks
Memorise the words *bia hoi*, which mean draught beer. There are signs advertising it everywhere, and most cafes have it on the menu. Quality varies but is generally OK and very cheap (US$0.30 per litre!). Places that serve bia hoi usually also have good but cheap food.

There are a number of foreign brands of beer that are brewed in Vietnam under licence. These include BGI, Carlsberg, Heineken and Vinagen.

ENTERTAINMENT
Pubs
Hanoi and Saigon are the only places to have a significant pub scene that can appeal to

western tastes. Some of these places feature very elaborate motifs – everything from Bavarian tavern to Aussie pub or American heavy-metal bar with a large-screen TV.

Discos

These are popping up all over the country, though they are especially numerous in Hanoi and Saigon. The most popular places feature a Filipino band and taped music. Interestingly, when the band starts to play, everyone sits down to watch and listen – they get up to dance when the music tapes are played! It's still good fun, and prices are reasonable except at the fancy five-star hotels.

Karaoke

That bizarre Japanese pastime, karaoke, has taken Vietnam by storm. Most westerners find it about as entertaining as watching concrete dry. However, many Asian travellers wax apoplectic as they sing along with a video featuring a bikini-clad model with a faraway gaze. If you sit in a karaoke bar for over an hour, you too will have a faraway gaze, caused no doubt by being blasted with music at 100 decibels.

Classical Music

It's not Vienna, but both Hanoi and Saigon boast a Conservatory of Music (Nhac Vien). Performances are given about twice weekly, but not throughout the year. Make local inquiries.

Rock Music

This is a sore spot with western travellers. The good news is that there are nightly concerts in Saigon and (to a lesser extent) Hanoi. The bad news (depending on your taste) is that the music is almost entirely western bubble-gum pop hits from the 60s and 70s.

SHOPPING

Handicrafts available for purchase as souvenirs include lacquerware items, mother-of-pearl inlay, ceramics (including enormous elephants), colourful embroidered items (hangings, tablecloths, pillowcases, pyjamas and robes), greeting cards with silk paintings on the front, wood-block prints, oil paintings, watercolours, blinds made of hanging bamboo beads, reed mats, Chinese-style carpets, jewellery and leatherwork.

In places frequented by tourists, it's easy to buy what looks like equipment left over

from the American War. However, almost all of these items are reproductions and your chances of finding anything original is slim. The 'Zippo' lighters seem to be the hottest selling item.

The graceful Vietnamese national dress – these days worn almost exclusively by women – is known as the *ao dai*. It consists of a close-fitting blouse with long panels in the front and back that is worn over loose black or white trousers.

Getting There & Away

AIR

The best deal is the 'open jaws' ticket, which allows you to fly into Saigon and exit from Hanoi (or vice versa). This saves you the time and expense of backtracking.

Departure Tax

The airport international departure tax is US$10, which can also be paid in dong.

Cambodia

Vietnam Airlines does the short hop from Ho Chi Minh City to Phnom Penh for US$70/120 one way/return; RAC charge US$65/130.

Phnom Penh-Saigon one way costs US$117. Phnom Penh-Hanoi one way is US$175. Return fares are exactly double.

China

Hong Kong to Saigon costs US$280/530 one way/return. There are also Hong Kong-Hanoi flights (US$255/490 one way/return). The open jaws ticket costs US$525.

Laos

Direct flights between Hanoi and Vientiane leave four times weekly aboard Vietnam Airlines, twice weekly with Lao Aviation (US$90).

Lao Aviation flies between Ho Chi Minh City and Vientiane every Friday for US$170. Vietnam Airlines also has four Vientiane flights weekly to/from Ho Chi Minh City via Hanoi for the same fare. Either airline can issue tickets for the other.

See also the Air entry in the main Getting There & Away section of the Laos chapter.

Malaysia

Flights between Kuala Lumpur and Ho Chi

Minh City are operated by Malaysia Airlines (four times weekly) and Vietnam Airlines (six times weekly).

Kuala Lumpur-Saigon one way/return is US$150/235; Kuala Lumpur-Hanoi flights cost US$170/340.

Philippines

Manila-Saigon one way/return is priced at US$165/290.

Singapore

Silk Air and Vietnam Airlines both have at least daily flights between Singapore and Saigon.

Singapore-Saigon one way/return costs US$180/350. One-way tickets for Singapore-Hanoi cost US$225.

Thailand

Bangkok, only 80 minutes flying time from Saigon, has emerged as the main port of embarkation for air travel to Vietnam. Bangkok-Saigon tickets are US$95 to US$115 one way; round-trip tickets cost about double.

There are also direct Bangkok-Hanoi flights (about US$100 one way) and open jaw tickets from Bangkok-Saigon/Hanoi-Bangkok, or vice-versa, for US$210 return.

LAND

Border Crossings

To enter or exit Vietnam overland your visa must indicate the correct border crossing. Once you've obtained your visa you can still have it amended at the immigration police or Foreign Affairs Ministry.

The Vietnamese police at the land border crossings are known to be particularly problematic. They may only give you a one week stay, rather than the one month indicated on your visa. Most travellers find that it's easier to exit Vietnam overland than to enter the country that way.

Cambodia

Buses run daily except Sunday between Phnom Penh and Saigon via the Moc Bai border checkpoint. The air-conditioned bus costs US$12; the bus without air-con is US$5.

China

Vietnam's two land border crossings with China can be reached from either side by train. The busiest border crossing is at Duong Dang (20km north of Lang Son in north-east

Vietnam), and the nearest Chinese town to this border crossing is Pinxiang. Nanning, capital of China's Guangxi Province, is about four hours by bus or train from the border. The crossing point is known in Vietnamese as Huu Nghi Quan (Friendship Gate). There is a twice-weekly direct Beijing-Hanoi train which passes through Friendship Gate.

There is also an 851km metre-gauge railway, inaugurated in 1910, linking Hanoi with Kunming in China's Yunnan Province. It crosses the border at Lao Cai in north-west Vietnam. The Chinese town opposite Lao Cai is Hekou.

Laos

There are border crossings at Lao Bao, a small town on the Vietnam side of the Lao-Vietnamese border near Sepon, and at Kaew Neua (also called Nam Phao) on the Lao side, across from Cau Treo.

Another border crossing at Sop Hun in Phongsali Province via Tay Trang (32km west of Dien Bien Phu) is currently open only to Lao and Vietnamese citizens. Stay tuned.

Getting Around

AIR

Domestic Air Services

All air travel within Vietnam is handled by Vietnam Airlines and Pacific Airlines. The booking system is fully computerised, so you can even reconfirm your international flight from some quiet backwater like Hué.

White-knuckle flyers will be happy to know that all of Vietnam Airlines' Soviet-made aircraft have been grounded.

Domestic Departure Tax

The domestic departure tax is 20,000d, payable in dong only.

BUS

Vietnam's extensive bus network reaches virtually every corner of the country. Almost all Vietnamese buses suffer from frequent breakdowns, tiny seats or benches, almost no legroom and chronic overcrowding. Prices are so low that bus travel is almost free, though foreigners are always charged more – if you pay only double for your fare, you've done well. There is no such thing as a reservation until you've bought and paid for a ticket, and once you've paid you can forget about refunds.

VIETNAM AIR FARES

One-way economy fares in US$

TRAIN

The 2600km Vietnamese railway system runs along the coast between Saigon and Hanoi and links the capital with Haiphong and points north. Odd-numbered trains travel southward; even-numbered trains go northward.

Even the fastest trains in Vietnam are very slow, averaging 30km/h and slowing to 5 or 10km/h in some sections. The quickest rail journey between Saigon and Hanoi takes 36 hours at an average speed of 48km/h, but most trains are slower than this.

Children frequently throw rocks at the trains – this can easily cause injury and conductors will insist you keep the metal shields down, which spoils the view.

Classes

There are five classes of train travel in Vietnam: hard seat, soft seat, hard berth, soft berth and super berth. Conditions in hard seat and soft seat can be horrible, often worse than the bus. Hard berth has three tiers of beds (six beds per compartment); the upper berth is cheapest.

Reservations

The supply of train seats is often insufficient to meet demand. Reservations for all trips should be made at least one day in advance. For sleeping berths, you may have to book passage three or more days before the date of travel. Bring your passport and visa when buying train tickets.

You do not necessarily need to go to the train station to get your ticket. Many travel agencies, hotels and cafes are into the business of purchasing train tickets for a small commission.

If you arrive early (7.30 am, for example) at a train station in central Vietnam, you may be told that all tickets to Hanoi or Saigon are sold out. However, this may simply mean that there are no tickets *at the moment*, but more may become available after 8 pm when Saigon and Hanoi phone through the details of unsold tickets. You do not have to pay a bribe to get these last-minute tickets – just hang out, be polite and see if anything turns up.

In any given city, reservations can be made only for travel originating in that city. For this reason – and because train stations are often far from the part of town with the hotels in it – it is a good idea to make reservations for onward travel as soon as you arrive in a city.

The salvation for foreigners are the minibuses. These are pricier, faster and more comfortable – you can even pay for two seats on these if you want more legroom.

Most intercity buses and minibuses depart very early in the morning.

Open Date Ticket

In backpacker haunts throughout Vietnam, you'll see lots of signs advertising the 'Open Date Ticket' or just 'Open Ticket'. Basically, this is a bus service catering to foreign budget travellers, not to local Vietnamese. The buses run between Saigon and Hanoi, and you may enter and exit the bus at any major city along the route. You are not obliged to follow a fixed schedule.

Essentially, there are two tickets available to travellers: Saigon-Hué for as cheap as US$27 and Hué-Hanoi for as low as US$16, though you can also buy shorter individual legs (which cost a bit more, but you achieve maximum flexibility).

Despite the feeling of being herded, the Open Tickets are a temptation and many people go for it. Look for them at cafes in Saigon and Hanoi.

Costs

Officially, foreigners are charged five times the Vietnamese price, and prices also vary according to the speed of the train.

Some sample fares (soft seat/top berth) for the second-fastest express train (40 hours) from Hanoi to Ho Chi Minh City (Saigon) are: Ninh Binh (115km, US$4/6), Hué (688km, US$22/32), Danang (791km, US$25/32), Quang Ngai (928km, US$29/43), Tuy Hoa (1195km, US$38/55), Nha Trang (1315km, US$45/65), Saigon (1726km, US$54/78).

CAR & MOTORCYCLE

Road Rules

Basically there's only one: small yields to big, or else. Traffic cops are there to be paid off. Vehicles drive on the right side of the road (usually). Spectacular accidents are frequent.

No driver's licence is needed to drive a motorbike 50cc or under. To drive a motorcycle that is over 50cc, you'll need an international driver's licence endorsed for motorcycle operation to be legal. In practice, many people drive motorcycles without a licence.

Rental

Vietnamese labour is so cheap that many foreigners rent the vehicle complete with driver. This can apply to motorcycles as well as cars. Figure on giving the driver at least US$5 per day, plus US$5 to US$10 for the bike depending on engine size. Hiring a car costs about US$0.35 to US$0.70 per kilometre, usually with a driver included. Travel agencies and some cafes handle vehicle rentals.

If you want to rent a motorcycle and drive it yourself, you'll normally be asked to leave your passport as security. You will almost never be given the owner's registration certificate (you'll be given a photocopy instead). This means that if the police pull you over (likely), they will have a ready-made excuse to fine you because your papers won't be in order. There is nothing you can do other than to bargain for a cheaper 'fine'.

Warning Beware of a motorcycle rental scam which some travellers have encountered in Saigon. What happens is that you rent a bike and the owner supplies you with an excellent lock and suggests you use it. What he doesn't tell you is that he has a key too, and somebody follows you and 'steals' the bike at the first opportunity. You then have to pay for a new bike or forfeit your passport, visa, deposit or whatever security

you left. And the person who rented you the bike still has it!

Purchase

Except for bona-fide foreign residents, buying a motorcycle for touring Vietnam is illegal. However, some travellers have reported that so far the authorities have turned a blind eye to the practice. Apparently, you buy a bike but register it in the name of a trusted Vietnamese friend. Some shops that sell motorcycles will let you keep the bike registered in the shop's name. This requires that you trust the shop owners, but in most cases this seems to work out OK.

The big issue is what to do with the bike when you are finished with it. If you return to the city where you originally purchased the bike, you can simply sell it back to the shop you bought it from (at a discount, of course). Another possible solution is to sell it to another foreigner travelling in the opposite direction. But remember: buying a motorcycle is illegal and a crackdown may come at any time.

BICYCLE

Long-distance cycling is becoming a popular way to tour some parts of Vietnam. The main hazard is the traffic. To get around this, it's wise to avoid certain areas (the Mekong Delta and National Highway 1). The best cycling seems to be in the Central Highlands, though you'll have to cope with some big hills.

Purchasing a good touring bike in Vietnam is hit or miss. You'd be wise to bring one from abroad.

HITCHING

Though hitch-hiking always has an element of risk and we don't recommend it, those who are intent can take some comfort in the fact that westerners have reported great success at hitching in Vietnam. In fact, the whole system of passenger transport is premised on people standing along the highways and flagging down buses or trucks. To get a bus, truck or other vehicle to stop, stretch out your arm and gesture towards the ground with your whole hand. Drivers will expect to be paid for picking you up – negotiate the fare before getting on board.

BOAT

Commercial hydrofoils connect Saigon with Vung Tau, Cantho and Mytho in the Mekong

Delta, and Haiphong with Cat Ba Island near Halong Bay in the north.

The extensive network of canals in the Mekong Delta makes getting around by boat feasible in the far south. Day cruises in Halong Bay are extremely popular.

LOCAL TRANSPORT
Bus
Inner city bus transport exists in Saigon and Hanoi, and nowhere else. Most foreigners rarely use these local buses.

Taxi
Western-style taxis with meters are readily available in Hanoi, Saigon, Danang and Hué. Elsewhere, ask around travel agencies, cafes and hotels about hiring a car.

Honda Om
The *Honda om* is an ordinary motorbike on which you ride seated behind the driver. There is no set procedure for finding a driver willing to transport you somewhere. You can either try to flag someone down (most drivers can always use a bit of extra cash) or ask around. In places frequented by tourists, the drivers will be looking for you.

Cyclo
Travelling by *cyclo* (pedicab) is the most practical and fun way to get around cities. Always agree on a price before setting off. Bargaining with fingers is not a good idea. Some cyclo drivers have tried to cheat travellers by simply holding up one finger, which travellers interpret as US$1, but upon arrival at your destination the driver interprets as US$10. Since cyclo drivers often don't speak English, have a pen and paper available to write down prices.

Beware: when riding in cyclos keep a very tight grip on your bag or belongings – skilful drive-by thieves are common.

ORGANISED TOURS
Cafes catering to foreigners are usually the cheapest places to organise budget tours. You can also ask at travel agencies – some are cheap, but others charge hefty prices. When shopping for tours, be sure that you aren't comparing apples and oranges – a cafe that offers you a dirt cheap tour may also be offering you dirt cheap accommodation in a dormitory. That may or may not be what you want. Shop around.

Hanoi

Hanoi, capital of the Socialist Republic of Vietnam, is different things to different people. Most foreigners find Hanoi to be slow-paced, pleasant and even charming. It's a city of lakes, shaded boulevards, embassies and holy shrines dedicated to the late, great Ho Chi Minh.

But things are changing fast. New highrises are crowding out the charming French colonial houses, the number of cars and motorbikes increases daily, while postcard vendors and cyclo drivers buzz around tourists like flies. On the other hand, the hotels have improved dramatically, once bare shelves in the state stores are now overflowing with goods and even the staid socialist restaurants have improved their menus. What better place than the national capital to witness all the growth, progress, foibles and follies of Vietnam's economic reforms?

Information
Immigration The immigration police office is at 87 Pho Tran Hung Dao.

Money Vietcombank is at 78 Duong Nguyen Du. ANZ Bank is at 14 Duong Le Thai To (on the western shore of Hoan Kiem Lake) and has a 24 hour ATM.

Post The main post office is at 75 Pho Dinh Tien Hoang.

Email & Internet Access There are a growing number of Internet cafes in Hanoi. Emotion Cybernet Cafe at 52 Pho Ly Thuong Kiet is perhaps the best.

There are also several backpacker cafe/tour agents along Pho Hang Bac (in the Old Quarter) offering Internet service; '10 free minutes online' has become the latest gimmick to attract tour customers (it beats 'one free Chinese beer'!). Try the A-Z Queen Cafe, TF Handspan or the Love Planet Cafe (see the following section for contact details).

Travel Agencies There are plenty of travel agencies in Hanoi, both government and private, which can provide cars, book air tickets and arrange tours. These include:

A-Z Queen Cafe
  (☎ 826 0860, fax 825 0000,
  email queenaz@fpt.vn)
  65 Pho Hang Bac

Love Planet
  (☎ 828 4864, fax 828 0913,
  email loveplanet@hn.vnn.vn)
  18 Pho Hang Bac
TF Handspan
  (☎ 828 1996, fax 825 7171,
  email tthandspn@hn.vnn.vn)
  116 Pho Hang Bac

Bookshops At 55 Pho Trang Tien, a short walk from Hoan Kiem Lake, the Thang Long Bookshop is the biggest and best in town. Just next door at No 53 is another good one, the Trang Tien Bookshop.

The air-conditioned Hanoi Bookstore (Hieu Sach Hanoi), 34 Pho Trang Tien, has a decent selection of imported news magazines and novels in English.

Medical Services The best medical facility in Hanoi is the Vietnam International Hospital (☎ 574 0740). The hospital is staffed by international doctors and offers 24 hour emergency service (☎ 547 1111).

Just next door to the International Hospital is the Bach Mai Hospital (Benh Vien Bach Mai, ☎ 852 2004) on Pho Giai Phong. There is an international department where doctors speak English.

The Viet Duc Hospital (Benh Vien Viet Duc, ☎ 825 3531), 40 Pho Tranh Thi, is open 24 hours and can do emergency surgery. It's in the central area where most travellers stay, and the doctors speak English, French and German.

The Friendship Hospital (Benh Vien Huu Nghi, ☎ 825 2231) at 1 Duong Tran Khanh Du has excellent up-to-date equipment, and the doctors speak English.

Lakes, Temples & Pagodas

Hanoi's **One Pillar Pagoda** (Chua Mot Cot) was built by Emperor Ly Thai Tong, who ruled from 1028 to 1054. Tours of Ho Chi Minh's Mausoleum end up here. The entrance to **Dien Huu Pagoda** is a few metres from the staircase of the One Pillar Pagoda. The One Pillar Pagoda is on Pho Ong Ich Kiem near Ho Chi Minh's Mausoleum.

West Lake (Ho Tay), which covers an area of five sq km, was once ringed with magnificent palaces and pavilions. These were destroyed in the course of various feudal wars. **Tran Quoc Pagoda** is on the south-eastern shore of West Lake. **Truc Bach Lake** is separated from West Lake by Pho Thanh Nien.

The **Ambassadors' Pagoda** (Quan Su) is the official centre of Buddhism in Hanoi, at-tracting quite a crowd (mostly old women) on holidays. During the 17th century, there was a guesthouse here for the ambassadors of Buddhist countries. The Ambassadors' Pagoda is at 73 Pho Quan Su; it is open to the public daily from 7.30 to 11.30 am and 1.30 to 5.30 pm.

The **Temple of Literature** (Van Mieu), founded in 1070, is a rare example of well preserved traditional Vietnamese architecture. **Hoan Kiem Lake** is an enchanting body of water right in the heart of Hanoi. Founded in the 18th century, **Ngoc Son Temple** is on an island in the northern part of Hoan Kiem Lake.

Ho Chi Minh's Mausoleum

In the tradition of Lenin, Stalin and Mao, the final resting place of Ho Chi Minh is a glass sarcophagus set deep inside a monumental edifice that has become a pilgrimage site.

The mausoleum is open to the public on Tuesday, Wednesday, Thursday and Saturday mornings from 8 to 11 am. On Sunday and public holidays it is open from 7.30 to 11.30 am. The mausoleum is closed for two months a year (usually from September to early November) while Ho Chi Minh's embalmed corpse is in Russia for maintenance.

All visitors must register and check their bags and cameras at the reception hall on Pho Chua Mot Cot (there is no charge, so don't pay), where you can view a 20 minute video about Ho Chi Minh's life and accomplishments. You'll be refused admission to the mausoleum if you're wearing shorts, tank tops or other 'indecent' clothing. It's also forbidden to put your hands in your pockets, and hats must be taken off inside the mausoleum building. Although the rules do not explicitly say so, it is suggested that you don't ask the guards 'Is he dead?'

After exiting from the mausoleum, the tour will pass by the **Presidential Palace**, constructed in 1906 as the palace of the governor general of Indochina. **Ho Chi Minh's stilt house**, built of the finest materials in 1958, is next to a carp-filled pond. Nearby is what was once Hanoi's botanical garden and is now a **park**.

Museums

The **History Museum**, once the museum of the École Française d'Extrême Orient, is one block east of the Municipal Theatre at 1 Pho Pham Ngu Lao.

The **Army Museum** is on Pho Dien Bien

CENTRAL HANOI

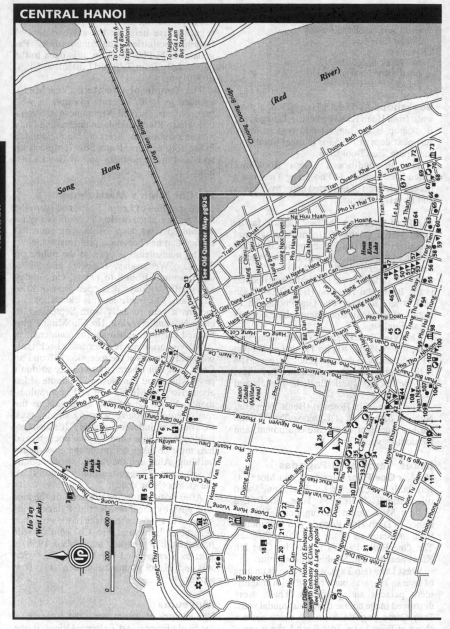

To Gia Lam &
Long Bien
Train Stations

To Haiphong
& Gia Lam
Bus Station

Chuong Duong Bridge

(Red
River)

Song   Hong

Long Bien Bridge

Ho Tay
(West Lake)

Truc
Bach
Lake

Duong Thanh Nien

Pho Yen Ninh

Hanoi Citadel
(Military
Area)

Hoan
Kiem
Lake

See Old Quarter Map pg826

0   200   400 m

CENTRAL HANOI

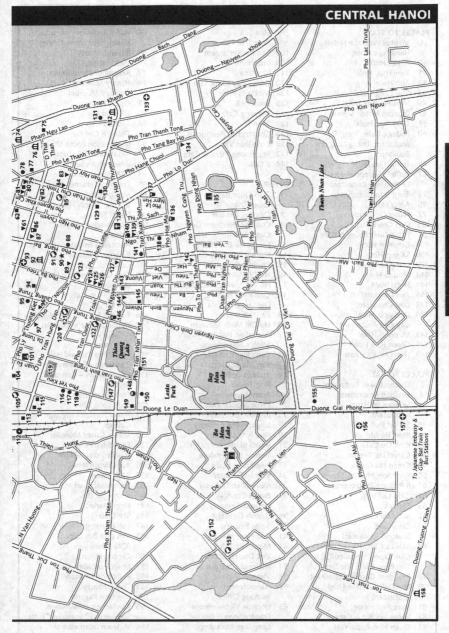

CENTRAL HANOI

PLACES TO STAY
1   Meritus Westlake Hotel
9   Hang Nga Hotel
10   Planet Hotel
11   Tien Thuy Hotel
12   Anh Hotel II
42   Cuu Long Hotel I & II
46   Nam Phuong Hotel
47   Especen Hotel & Tours
56   Thuy Nga Hotel
60   Bodega Café; Trang Tien
     Bookshop; Thang Long
     Bookshop
62   Trang Tien Hotel
67   Sofitel Metropole Hotel;
     Le Beaulieu Restaurant
72   Tong Dan Guesthouse
75   Army Hotel
77   Hanoi Opera Hilton
80   Dan Chu Hotel
94   Lotus Guesthouse & Cafe
104 Guoman Hotel
106 Saigon Hotel
109 Dong Loi Hotel
113 Mango Hotel
114 Hotel 30/4
115 Thu Do Hotel
129 Dan Chu Hotel
130 De Syloia Hotel;
     Cay Cau Restaurant
143 Madison Hotel
145 Green Park Hotel
149 Hotel Nikko Hanoi

PLACES TO EAT
2   Shrimp Cakes Restaurant
4   Seafood Restaurants
6   Seasons of Hanoi
     Restaurant
35   Sunset Pub
40   Kem Tra My
43   Kinh Do Cafe
48   Carvel Ice Cream
49   Green Ho Guom
50   Kem Bon Mua Ice Cream
51   Il Padrino Restaurant
52   Cafe Lac Viet
53   Fanny's
57   Ban Mai Cafe
59   Ciao Cafe
61   Seafood Restaurant
68   Mai La Cafe; Au Lac Cafe;
     Club Opera Restaurant;
     The Press Club; The Deli
70   President Garden Restaurant
79   The Deli; Gustave Eiffel
     Restuarant
81   Miro Restaurant
82   Verandah Bar & Cafe
83   Quan Hué Restaurant
84   Nam Phuong Restaurant
87   Al Fresco's
89   Orient Cafe

96   Hoa Sua
97   Pear Tree Pub
100 San Ho Restaurant
108 Indochine
111 Khazana
120 Com Chay Nang Tam
124 Mother's Pride
125 Soho Deli
126 Meeting Cafe
127 Tiem Pho
134 Countryside Restaurant
139 Com Duc Vien
142 Pepperonis Pizza & Cafe
144 Il Grillo

OTHER
3   Tran Quoc Pagoda
5   Quan Thanh Temple
7   Cua Bac Church
8   Cua Bac (Northern Gate of
     Old Citadel)
13   Long Bien Bus Station
14   Former Botanical Gardens
15   Presidential Palace
16   Ho Chi Minh's Stilt House
17   Ho Chi Minh's Mausoleum
18   One Pillar Pagoda;
     Dien Huu Pagoda
19   Ba Dinh Square
20   Ho Chi Minh Museum
21   Reception Hall for Ho Chi
     Minh's Mausoleum
22   Canadian Embassy
23   Kim Ma Bus Station
24   Russian Embassy
25   Flag Tower
26   Army Museum
27   Lenin Monument
28   Chinese Embassy
29   Singaporean Embassy
30   Fine Arts Museum
31   Hanoi Stadium
32   Temple of Literature
33   Belgian Embassy
34   Korean Embassy
36   Mongolian Embassy
37   British Council
38   German Embassy
39   Danish Embassy;
     Swiss Embassy
41   Cua Nam Market
44   Metal Nightclub
45   Viet Duc Hospital
54   National Library & Archives
55   Vietnam Airlines
58   Hanoi Toserco
     Booking Office
63   Librairie Vietnamienne
     Francophone (French-
     Language bookshop)
64   Main Post Office
65   Hanoi Optic; Theatre de la
     Comedie de Hanoi

66   Hanoi Bookstore (Hieu Sach
     Hanoi); Singapore Airlines
69   Italian Embassy
71   Vietcombank
73   Revolutionary Museum
74   History Museum
76   Geology Museum
78   Opera House
85   UK Embassy
86   Spotted Cow
88   Thang 8 Cinema
90   Immigration Police Office
91   New Zealand Embassy
92   Women's Museum
93   AEA International Clinic
95   Emotion Cybernet Cafe
98   Maison Centrale Museum
     (Former 'Hanoi Hilton')
99   Hanoi Towers
101 Ambassadors' Pagoda
102 Relax Bar
103 Australian Embassy
105 Egyptian Embassy
107 Fanslands Cinema
110 Tran Quy Cap Train Station
     (B Station)
112 Hanoi Train Station
     (Ga Hang Co)
116 Alliance Francaise de Hanoi
117 Hanoi College of Fine Art
     & Gallery
118 Ann Tours
119 Friendship Cultural Hall
121 Cambodian Embassy
122 Lao Embassy – Consular
     Section
123 French Embassy
128 Ham Long Church
131 Hanoi Foreign Language
     College
132 Border Guard Museum
133 Friendship Hospital
135 Hai Ba Trung Temple
136 Apocalypse Now
137 R&R Tavern
138 Hanoi Star Mart
140 Youth Theatre
141 Hom Market
146 VIP Club
147 Lao Embassy
148 Kim Lien Bus Depot
     (City Buses)
150 Central Circus
151 Lenin Park Main Gate
152 Philippine Embassy
153 Thai Embassy
154 Kim Lien Pagoda
155 Polytechnic University &
     Vietnamese Language Centre
156 Vietnam International
     Hospital
157 Bach Mai Hospital
158 Air Force Museum

Phu; it is open daily except Monday from 7.30 to 11.30 am only. The displays include scale models of various epic battles from Vietnam's long military history, including Dien Bien Phu and the capture of Saigon.

The **Ho Chi Minh Museum** is divided into two sections, 'Past' and 'Future'. You start in the past and move to the future by walking in a clockwise direction downwards through the museum from the top of the stairs (right-hand side). The displays are very modern and all have a message (peace, happiness, freedom etc). Some of the symbolism is hard to figure out (did Ho Chi Minh have a cubist period?). The 1958 Ford Edsel bursting through the wall (an American commercial failure to symbolise America's military failure) is a knockout. Upon entering, all bags and cameras must be left at reception.

Many of the exhibits at the **Air Force Museum** are outdoors. This includes a number of Soviet MiG fighters, reconnaissance planes, helicopters and anti-aircraft equipment. Inside the museum hall are other weapons, including mortars, machine guns and some US-made bombs (hopefully defused). There is a partially truncated MiG with a ladder – you are permitted to climb up into the cockpit and have your photo taken. The museum is on Duong Truong Chinh, in the south of the city.

The works in the **Fine Arts Museum** (Bao Tang My Thuat) are fascinating. The museum is at 66 Duong Nguyen Thai Hoc, and is open from 8 am to noon and 1.30 to 4 pm Tuesday to Sunday.

St Joseph Cathedral

Stepping inside the neo-Gothic St Joseph Cathedral (inaugurated in 1886) is like being transported to medieval Europe. The cathedral is noteworthy for its square towers, elaborate altar and stained-glass windows. The first Catholic mission in Hanoi was founded in 1679.

The main gate to St Joseph Cathedral is open daily from 5 to 7 am and from 5 to 7 pm – the hours when masses are held.

Places to Stay – Budget

The *A-Z Queen Cafe* (☎ 826 0860, email queenaz@fpt.vn) at 65 Pho Hang Bac in the Old Quarter has dorm beds going for US$2.50 and very basic fan doubles run US$6 to US$8.

A short walk from the Queen at 116 Pho Hang Bac is the friendly *TF Handspan*

Guesthouse (☎ 828 1996, email tfhandspn @hn.vnn.vn) which has clean air-con doubles (some with bathtub) costing US$10 to US$12.

Lotus Guesthouse (☎ 826 8642) at 42V Pho Ly Thuong Kiet is a quiet, clean and cheap place. There are some dorm beds for US$4, and eight rooms costing US$6 to US$15.

The small but friendly *Mai Phuong Hotel* (☎ 826 5341), 32 Pho Hang Be charges US$6 to US$10 for doubles, or US$12 to US$15 for triples.

The *Bodega Cafe* (☎ 826 7784) at 57 Pho Trang Tien has good cheapish rooms for US$15 to US$20.

Tong Dan Guesthouse (☎ 826 5328), 17 Pho Tong Dan, has doubles from US$9 to US$28. It's east of Hoan Kiem Lake, close to the Red River.

Time Hotel (☎ 825 9498) is a shiny new place at 6 Pho Cau Go in the 'shoe land' part of the Old Quarter. Doubles cost US$15 to US$35. Almost next door at 12 Pho Cau Go is the comparable *Phu Long Hotel* (☎ 826 6074), which charges US$20 to US$40 for clean doubles.

On Pho Hang Be at No 49, *Anh Sinh Hotel* (☎ 826 1331) is a bit dingy, but has dorm beds for US$3 to US$4, and doubles from US$7 to US$12. Across the street at No 50 is the similar *Binh Minh Hotel* (☎ 826 7356), which charges US$4 for a dorm bed and US$8 to US$15 for doubles.

The state-run *Dong Xuan Hotel* (☎ 828 4474) is at 26 Pho Cao Thang. Fan doubles here cost US$6 to US$8, or US$10 with air-con. Triples/quads cost US$15/20.

Van Xuan Hotel (☎ 824 4743) is another government-owned hotel at 15 Pho Luong Ngoc Quyen. Air-con doubles with a shared bath cost US$10. A room with private toilet pushes the tariff to US$15 to US$25.

Next door to Van Xuan at 13 Pho Luong Ngoc Quyen is the popular *Camilla Hotel* (☎ 828 3583), where doubles cost US$15 to US$80.

My Kinh Hotel (☎ 825 5726) at 72-74 Pho Hang Buom has livable rooms for US$12 to US$18.

Especen Hotel (☎ 825 8845), 79E Pho Hang Trong, operates nine mini-hotels around the central area of Hanoi, with rates from US$8 to US$30. There is no point in listing them all here, as its office will give you a map and call ahead to book a room. The hotels all

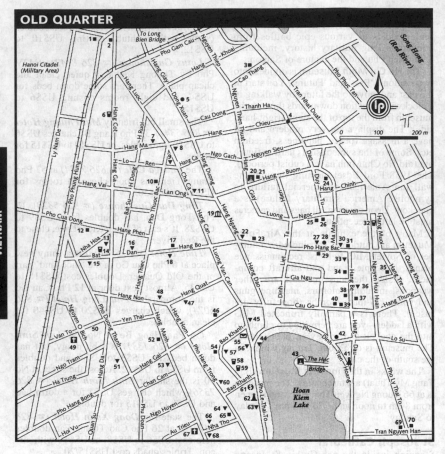

OLD QUARTER

bear imaginative names such as Especen-1, Especen-2 etc.

Tong Dan Guesthouse (☎ 825 2219) at 210 Pho Tran Quang Khai has basic rooms costing US$8 to US$20.

Places to Stay – Mid-Range

Trang An Hotel (☎ 826 8982), 58 Pho Hang Gai, is a good mini-hotel at the north-west corner of Hoan Kiem Lake. Singles/doubles cost US$30/50.

The friendly **Asia Hotel** (☎ 826 9007) at 5 Pho Cua Dong offers nice rooms for $20 to US$40.

The spacious **Mango Hotel** (☎ 824 3704) at 118 Duong Le Duan is near the Hanoi train station. The price range for rooms is US$15 to US$30.

At 32 Pho Thuoc Bac, **Hung Hiep Hotel** (☎ 828 4922) has received some good reports, and has a wide price range from US$15 to US$50.

Win Hotel (☎ 826 7150) is at 34 Pho Hang Hanh, and has spiffy rooms for US$25 to US$50.

Travellers have also had good things to say about **Hang Ngoc Hotel** (☎ 828 5053), 34 Pho Hang Manh, which charges from US$25 to US$94.

Places to Eat

Restaurants One of Hanoi's most popular casual eateries is **Al Fresco's** at 23L Pho Hai Ba Trung, which serves up fantastic pizzas, ribs and salads.

Pepperonis Pizza & Cafe at 71 Pho Mai

OLD QUARTER

PLACES TO STAY		70	Binh Minh Hotel;		63	Five Royal Fish Restaurant
1	Chains First Eden Hotel		China Southern Airlines		64	Thu Huong Chinese
2	Galaxy Hotel					Restaurant
3	Dong Xuan Hotel		PLACES TO EAT		66	Moca Cafe
10	Hung Hiep Hotel	7	Thang Long		68	Mediterraneo Restaurant
12	Asia Hotel	8	Baan Thai Restaurant			
17	Fortuan Hotel	9	Cha Ca La Vong		OTHER	
21	My Kinh Hotel	11	Tuyet Nhung		4	Cua O Quan Chuong
23	TF Handspan Tour	13	Cha Ca 66			(Old East Gate)
	Guesthouse & Office;	15	Pho Gia Truyen		5	Dong Xuan Market
	The Whole Earth	16	Bat Dan Cafe		6	Dai Dong Centropell
24	Anh Dao Hotel	18	Red River Café		14	Bia Hoi Ha Chau Quan
25	Van Xuan Hotel	22	Old Darling Cafe		19	Memorial House
26	Camilla Hotel	27	Sinh Cafe		20	Pagoda
29	A-Z Queen Cafe	30	Love Planet; Kim Cafe		28	The Pan Flute Shop
31	Kim Tin Hotel	33	Tandoor Indian		32	Royal Palace Nightclub
34	Mai Phuong Hotel		Restaurant		41	Martyrs' Monument
35	Royal Hotel	36	Lonely Planet Cafe		42	Municipal Water Puppet
37	Binh Minh Hotel	44	Dinh Lang Restaurant;			Theatre
38	Anh Sinh Hotel		Thuy Ta Café		43	Ngoc Son Temple
39	Time Hotel	45	No Noodles		49	Protestant Church
40	Phu Long Hotel	47	Real Darling Cafe		50	Hang Da Market
46	Trang An Hotel	48	Tin Tin Bar & Cafe		55	Main Post Office
52	Hang Ngoc Hotel	51	Cyclo Bar & Restaurant		58	Polite Pub
54	Nam Phuong Hotel	53	Pho Bo Dac Biet		59	Golden Cock Bar
65	Hoa Long Hotel	56	Mama Rosa		61	ANZ Bank
69	Energy Hotel;	57	Le Café des Arts		62	Le Thai To Statue
	Hanoi Star Mart	60	Sukiyaki		67	St Joseph Cathedral

Hoc De has good cheap pizzas from just US$1.25 to US$4; pasta dishes cost US$1.60.

At 38 Pho Duong Thanh, the *Cyclo Bar & Restaurant* serves up Vietnamese and French food to customers seated in actual cyclos.

There are loads of Italian restaurants in Hanoi to choose from. The *Bat Dan Cafe*, right in the Old Quarter at 10 Pho Bat Dan, dishes up excellent pastas and salads at reasonable prices, and has the best selection of board games in town.

At No 11B Pho Bao Khanh is the casual *Le Café des Arts*, an artsy expat/Vietnamese-run place modelled after a Parisian brasserie.

There is excellent Thai food at *Sukiyaki*, in the rear of a supermarket at 63 Pho Hang Trong.

Recommended for lunch is the open-air *Hoa Sua* – the French pastries from the bakery here are to die for! It's is at 81 Pho Tho Nhuom.

Upstairs at 32 Pho Le Thai To, *Green Ho Guom* is a spacious and funky place serving Vietnamese and western dishes at reasonable prices.

Travellers' Cafes The *Love Planet Cafe* at Pho 18 Hang Bac receives good reports for fine backpacker cuisine, tours and email service.

Another well established backpackers hang-out is *A-Z Queen Cafe* at 65 Pho Hang Bac.

Tin Tin Bar & Cafe, 14 Pho Hang Non, is another backpacker haven. The menu includes good pizza, juices, crepes, fried rice, burgers and so on. It's a friendly place, open from 8 pm until 2 am.

The *Red River Cafe* at 73 Pho Hang Bo is a contender in the cheap eats/tour booking business.

The *Old Darling Cafe*, at 142 Pho Hang Bac, is a well established budget travellers' haven in the Old Quarter.

We can assure you that the *Lonely Planet Cafe* at 33 Pho Hang Be is in no way affiliated with a certain guidebook company. However, as Hanoi cafes go, the food is edible and prices reasonable.

At the *Meeting Cafe*, 59B Pho Ba Trieu, you'll find the usual backpacker cuisine (banana pancakes, milkshakes, cakes, coffee and spring rolls).

Vietnamese A nice spot for Vietnamese food is the *Dinh Lang Restaurant*, which hosts traditional musicians nightly. It's right above the busy *Thuy Ta Café* at 1 Pho Le Thai To, overlooking Hoan Kiem Lake.

One of Hanoi's most famous food specialities is *cha ca*, sumptuous fish hamburgers. *Cha Ca La Vong* is a Hanoi institution at 14 Pho Cha Ca. Other worthy (and cheaper) places to try this local delicacy include *Cha Ca 66* at 66 Pho Hang Ga, and *Thang Long* at 40 Pho Hang Ma.

For a good bowl of casual beef noodle soup, try *Pho Bo Dac Biet* at 2B Pho Ly Quoc Su or *Pho Gia Truyen* at 49 Pho Bat Dan. *Tiem Pho*, at 48-50 Pho Hué, serves up Hué style noodles.

On Pho Cha Ca in the Old Quarter, *Tuyet Nhung* is an excellent place to sample Banh Cuon dumplings. A set meal costs US$1.

There are several restaurants all in a cluster calling themselves *Hué Restaurant*. Consider trying *Quan Hué Restaurant*, 6 Pho Ly Thuong Kiet. On the opposite side of the street is *Huu Ngu Binh* at No 11. The slogan here is 'Our food is more Hué than Hué'.

Vegetarian The best vegetarian restaurant in Hanoi is *Com Chay Nang Tam*, at 79A Pho Tran Hung Dao. Try the superb 'fried snow balls'.

Another excellent vegetarian option is *The Whole Earth* restaurant, inside the TF Handspan tour agency/guesthouse at 116 Pho Hang Bac (in the Old Quarter).

Speciality Streets *Pho Cam Chi* is about half a kilometre north-east of Hanoi train station. It's a very small street – basically an alley – crammed full of lively pavement stalls serving budget-priced, delicious food.

Pho Mai Hac De is in the south-central area, running in a north-south direction. The northern terminus is Pho Tran Nhan Tong, and the line of restaurants continues for several blocks to the south.

Duong Thuy Khue, on the south bank of West Lake, features a strip of 30-odd outdoor seafood restaurants with pleasant lakeside seating.

Pho To Hien Thanh runs in an east-west direction, and also specialises in small seafood restaurants. It's to the south of the city centre, just east of Bay Mau Lake.

Delis & Self-Catering A trendy take-away sandwich joint is *No Noodles* at 51 Pho Luong Van Can.

The Deli whips up tasty sandwiches for about US$1.20 at its two locations in town: 18 Pho Tran Huy Lieu and 25 Pho Trang Tien.

More determined self-caterers can buy fresh vegetables at the *Hom Market* just south of the city centre near the intersection of Pho Hue and Pho Tran Xuan Soan.

Cafes *Au Lac*, a personal favourite, is a delightful garden cafe and bar at 57 Pho Ly Thai To, across from the Sofitel Hotel. It serves perhaps the best coffee in Hanoi.

At 46 Pho Le Thai To, *Cafe Lac Viet* is another contender in Hanoi's prime Java category. Ditto for the *Ciao Cafe*, near the southern end of Hoan Kiem Lake at 2 Pho Hang Bai.

If you're visiting St Joseph's Cathedral, stop in the *Moca Cafe*, at 14-16 Pho Nha Tro, another stylish spot with espresso and the like.

Ice Cream & Desserts The best ice-cream joint in town is *Fanny's* at 48 Pho Le Thai To on the Hoan Kiem Lakefront.

The most popular ice cream with the locals is at *Kem Trang Tien*, 54 Pho Trang Tien. Just look for the mob on the pavement lined up to take away sticks of the tasty treat (US$0.30). There is also an attached indoor place here where you can relax in air-con comfort.

Great ice cream sundaes can be found at *Kem Tra My*, on Pho Nguyen Thai Hoc, towards Ho Chi Minh's Mausoleum.

For some of the best yoghurt, French pastries and coffee in Vietnam, visit the *Kinh Do Cafe* at 252 Pho Hang Bong near the city centre.

Pub Food The *Sunset Pub* is at 31 Pho Cao Ba Quat (several blocks south-east of Ho Chi Minh's Mausoleum). Pizzas and hamburgers are on the menu. There is live jazz on Thursday and Saturday evenings. The pub is run by a Norwegian.

The Brit-run *Verandah Bar & Cafe*, 9 Pho Nguyen Khac Can, is an expat hang-out built in a stylish French villa.

There is a good pool table and light food at *Pear Tree Pub*, 78 Pho Tho Nhuom, just south-east of the Ambassadors' Pagoda.

Entertainment
Pubs & Bars The legendary *Apocalypse Now* is at 5C Pho Hoa Ma. It's best on weekends, and is known for loud and raucous music. Apocalypse opens at 5 pm and closes when the customers trickle away.

The **R&R Tavern** at 17 Pho Le Ngoc Han is run by mellow American Jay, who can regale you with friendly conversation and South-East Asia's best selection of Grateful Dead.

At 6 Pho Thanh Nien, the **C&W Bar** is a funky and popular expat pub, good for a drink or two.

The **Spotted Cow** is one of Hanoi's newer watering holes, featuring pool tables and darts. It's just a few doors down from Al Fresco's restaurant, on Pho Hai Ba Trung.

At 42 Pho Tang Bat Ho, **Cafe Que Huong** offers stylish villa surroundings and three fine pool tables.

The unforgettably named **Golden Cock Bar**, 5 Pho Bao Khanh, is an expat favourite. Next door to the 'GC' is the popular **Polite Pub**. Pho Bao Khanh is right at the northwest corner of Hoan Kiem Lake.

The **Relax Bar** is at 60 Pho Ly Thuong Kiet. From 9.30 am to 8 pm, customers can unwind with a cold beer or cocktail while relishing a US$2 head-and-face massage.

Discos & Karaoke *Metal Night Club*, 57 Pho Cua Nam, is two blocks north-east of Hanoi train station. There is a live band every night and the cover charge is US$4. Opening hours are 11 am to 2 pm and 7.30 pm to 2 am.

The spacious, Japanese-run **Magic Nightclub**, 3 Pho Thai Thinh, is a cool dance place with a US$5 cover charge, but ask around town for free passes.

At 336 Pho Ba Trieu, **Vortex** is on the kinky side and is one of the hottest nightclubs in Hanoi to see and be seen.

The **Queen Bee Nightclub**, 42A Pho Lang Ha, is a long way west of the city centre. The disco is lively.

Cinemas *Fanslands Cinema*, 84 Pho Ly Thuong Kiet, offers the best movies in town. French speakers may also be pleased with what's on offer at *Alliance Française* (☎ 826 6970), 42 Pho Yet Kieu.

The other place in town with foreign films is the **Thang 8 Cinema** on Pho Hang Bai (opposite the Immigration Police Office).

Opposite the Daewoo Hotel near the corner of Pho Ngoc Khanh and Pho Lieu Gai is a 3-D cinema (*phim noi* in Vietnamese) called **Ngoc Khanh**. Admission is a steep US$5.

Circus One Russian tradition that has survived in Vietnam is the **Central Circus** (*Rap Xiec Trung Uong*). Many of the performers

(gymnasts, jugglers, animal trainers etc) were originally trained in Eastern Europe, though new recruits can now learn their skills from their Vietnamese elders.

The circus performs nightly (except Monday) from 8 to 10 pm in a huge tent near the northern entrance to Lenin Park (Cong Vien Le Nin). There is a special show for children on Sunday morning at 9 am. Entry costs US$2.50.

Water Puppets This fantastic art form originated in northern Vietnam, and Hanoi is the best place to see it. Just on the shore of Hoan Kiem Lake is the **Municipal Water Puppet Theatre** (*Roi Nuoc Thang Long*, ☎ 824 9494) at 57B Pho Dinh Tien Hoang. Performances are from 8 to 9 pm every night, except Monday. Admission is US$2.

Shopping

Pho Hang Gai and its continuation, Pho Hang Bong, are a good place to look for embroidered tablecloths and hangings. Hanoi is a good place to have informal clothes custom-tailored. There are also a number of antique shops and art galleries in the city.

A good shop for silk clothing is Khai Silk (☎ 825 4237), 96 Pho Hang Gai. You can also try nearby Duc Loi Silk at 76 Pho Hang Gai.

Greeting cards with traditional Vietnamese designs hand-painted on silk covers are available around town for US$0.10 or so.

There is an outstanding shoe market along Pho Hang Dau at the north-eastern corner of Hoan Kiem Lake.

Souvenir water puppets, costumes and paraphernalia can be purchased from the theatres that do these performances.

For philatelic items, try the philatelic counter at the main post office (in the main postal services hall).

Watercolour paints and brushes are available at a store at 216 Pho Hang Bong. Musical instruments can be purchased from shops at 24 and 36 Pho Hang Gai, and 76 and 85 Pho Hang Bong.

Getting There & Away

Air Vietnam Airlines has nonstop international flights between Hanoi and Bangkok, Dubai, Guangzhou (China), Hong Kong, Seoul, Singapore, Taipei and Vientiane. There are other international flights via Saigon. China Southern Airlines flies Hanoi-Beijing via Nanning.

Pacific Airlines is the only company besides Vietnam Airlines to offer domestic flights.

Contact details for some airline offices are as follows:

Cathay Pacific Airways
    (☎ 826 7298, fax 826 7709)
    49 Hai Ba Trung
China Southern Airlines
    (Binh Minh Hotel, ☎ 826 9233)
    27 Pho Ly Thai To
Lao Aviation
    (☎ 826 6538, fax 822 9951)
    41 Pho Quang Trung
Malaysia Airlines
    (☎ 826 8820, fax 824 2388)
    15 Pho Ngo Quyen
Pacific Airlines
    (☎ 851 5356, fax 851 5350)
    100 Pho Le Duan
Singapore Airlines
    (☎ 826 8888, fax 826 8666)
    17 Pho Ngo Quyen
Thai Airways International
    (☎ 826 6893, fax 826 7934)
    44B Pho Ly Thuong Kiet
Vietnam Airlines
    (☎ 825 0888, fax 824 8989)
    1 Pho Quang Trung

Bus Like Saigon, Hanoi has several main bus stations and each one serves a particular area.

Gia Lam bus station (Ben Xe Gia Lam) is where you catch buses to points north-east of Hanoi. This includes Halong Bay, Haiphong and Lang Son (near the China border). The bus station is 2km north-east of the centre – you have to cross the Red River to get there. Cyclos won't cross the bridge, so you need to get there by motorbike or taxi.

Kim Ma bus station (Ben Xe Kim Ma) is opposite 166 Pho Nguyen Thai Hoc (corner Pho Giang Vo). This is where you get buses to the north-west part of Vietnam. Tickets should be purchased the day before departure.

Son La bus station (Ben Xe Son La) at km 8, Pho Nguyen Trai (next to Hanoi University), also has buses to the north-west.

Giap Bat bus station (Ben Xe Giap Bat) serves points south of Hanoi, including Saigon. The station is 7km south of the Hanoi train station on Duong Giai Phong.

Train The main Hanoi train station (Ga Hang Co, ☎ 825 3949) is at 120 Duong Le Duan, at the western end of Pho Tran Hung Dao; trains from here go to destinations south. The ticket office is open from 7.30 to 11.30 am and 1.30 to 3.30 pm only, and there is a special counter where foreigners can purchase tickets. It's often best to buy tickets at least one day before departure to ensure a seat or sleeper.

Where you purchase the ticket is not necessarily where the train departs. Just behind the main station on Duong Le Duan is Tran Quy Cap station (or 'B station', ☎ 825 2628) on Pho Tran Qui Cap for northbound trains. From the front station entrance to the B station is a two-block walk.

Even more complicated is the fact that some northbound (for Viet Tri, Yen Bai, Lao Cai, Lang Son) and eastbound (for Haiphong) trains depart from both the Gia Lam and Long Bien (☎ 826 8280) train stations (both across the bridge on the east side of the Red River). Some of the local southbound trains leave from the Giap Bat train station (about 7km south of Hanoi train station).

Getting Around
To/From the Airport Hanoi's Noi Bai international airport is about 35km north of the city.

Minibuses from Hanoi to Noi Bai depart from the Vietnam Airlines booking office on Pho Quang Trung. The trip typically takes 50 minutes.

Taxi drivers congregate at the Vietnam Airlines booking office in Hanoi. Needless to say, they are numerous at the airport itself. Drivers will start their opening bid at around US$25, but this can easily be bargained to US$15.

Bus Better tourist maps of Hanoi include bus lines marked in red. Service on most of the bus routes is infrequent.

Motorcycle & Cyclo You'll find cyclos parked every 5 to 10m in central Hanoi, and each driver will enthusiastically try to arm wrestle you into his vehicle. The quoted price is usually three times the real price.

The situation is much the same with motorbikes. You can rent a bike with driver for about US$10 per day.

Bicycle Most budget hotels have bicycles for rent at about US$1 to US$2 per day.

AROUND HANOI
Perfume Pagoda
The Perfume Pagoda (Chua Huong) is a complex of pagodas and Buddhist shrines built into the limestone cliffs of Huong Tich Mountain.

Pilgrims and other visitors spend their time here boating, hiking and exploring the caves.

The Perfume Pagoda is about 60km south-west of Hanoi in Hoa Binh Province, accessible first by road and then by river. There is an obligatory US$7 admission fee which includes a 1½ hour river trip. Cafes in Hanoi book day trips to the Perfume Pagoda for around US$17 (not including the admission fee).

Thay Pagoda

Thay Pagoda (Master's Pagoda) is dedicated to Thich Ca Buddha (Sakyamuni, the historical Buddha). Visitors enjoy water-puppet shows, hiking and exploring caves in the area.

Thay Pagoda is about 40km south-west of Hanoi in Ha Tay Province. Some of Hanoi's cafes catering to budget travellers offer combined day tours of the Thay and Tay Phuong pagodas.

Tay Phuong Pagoda

Tay Phuong Pagoda (Pagoda of the West) consists of three parallel single-level structures built on a hillock said to resemble a buffalo. The 76 figures carved from jackfruit wood, many from the 18th century, are the pagoda's most celebrated feature.

Tay Phuong Pagoda is about 40km south-west of Hanoi in Tay Phuong hamlet, Ha Tay Province. A visit here can easily be combined with a stop at Thay Pagoda.

The North

Stretching from the Hoang Lien Mountains (Tonkinese Alps) eastward across the Red River Delta to the islands of Halong Bay, the northern part of Vietnam (Bac Bo), known to the French as Tonkin, includes some of the country's most spectacular scenery. The mountainous areas are home to many distinct hill-tribe groups.

NINH BINH

Ninh Binh's sudden transformation from sleepy backwater to tourist resort has little to do with Ninh Binh itself, but rather with its proximity to nearby Tam Coc (9km), Hoa Lua (12km) and Cuc Phuong National Park (45km).

Although it is possible to visit these sights as a day trip from Hanoi, most travellers prefer to spend the night in Ninh Binh to appreciate the scenery at a more leisurely pace.

Places to Stay & Eat

Thuy Anh Mini-Hotel (π/fax 87 1602) at 55A Duong Truong Han Sieu has spotless rooms from US$7 to US$25. The food served at the rooftop *restaurant* is superb.

Another backpacker favourite is *Thanh Thuy's Guesthouse* (π 87 1811) at 128 Duong Le Hong Phong. Basic fan rooms cost from US$3 to US$7, and air-con raises the tab to US$10 to US$12.

Queen Mini-Hotel (Khach San Nu Hoang, π 87 1874) is just 30m from Ninh Binh train station, and rooms cost US$6 to US$12.

Star Hotel (Khach San Ngoi Sao, π 87 1522) at 267 Duong Tran Hung Dao is another popular place. Rooms cost US$10 to US$28.

Getting There & Away

Bus Ninh Binh is 93km south-west of Hanoi. Regular public buses leave approximately hourly and make the 2½ hour run for US$1.60. Ninh Binh is also a hub on the north-south 'open tours', and it's possible to travel to/from Hanoi on one of these comfortable air-con buses for US$4.

Train Ninh Binh is a scheduled stop for *Reunification Express* trains travelling between Hanoi and Saigon.

AROUND NINH BINH
Hoa Lu

Vying with nearby Tam Coc for the title of Vietnam's 'Halong Bay without the water', Hoa Lu boasts breathtaking scenery. While Halong Bay has huge rock formations jutting out of the sea, Hoa Lu has them jutting out of the rice paddies.

Hoa Lu was the capital of Vietnam under the Dinh Dynasty (ruled 968-980) and the Early Le Dynasty (ruled 980-1009). The ancient citadel of Hoa Lu, most of which has been destroyed, covered an area of about 3 sq km.

Today there are two sanctuaries at Hoa Lu. **Dinh Tien Hoang**, restored in the 17th century, is dedicated to the Dinh Dynasty. The second temple, **Dai Hanh**, or Dung Van Nga, commemorates the rulers of the Early Le Dynasty.

Hoa Lu is 12km north of Ninh Binh. There is no public transport, so most travellers get there by bicycle, motorbike or car. Some Hanoi cafes may be able to organise a tour to get you here.

Other Sights
Bic Dong Grotto is in the village of Van Lam, a short boat trip from Hoa Lu. Other popular spots include the Tam Coc Caves, 9km south-west of Ninh Binh, Bich Dong, with its cave and built-in temple, and Xuyen Thuy Grotto.

CUC PHUONG NATIONAL PARK
Cuc Phuong National Park is one of Vietnam's most important nature preserves, and home to an amazing variety of animal and plant life. Ho Chi Minh personally took time off from the war in 1963 to dedicate this national park, Vietnam's first. Perhaps the most interesting feature of the park is the Endangered Primate Rescue Center, home to some 50 rare monkeys confiscated from illegal traders or bred in captivity.

The elevation of the highest peak in the park is 648m, and the hills are laced with many grottoes. At the park's lower elevations, the climate is subtropical. During the rainy season (July to September), leeches are everywhere, making trekking impossible.

A guide is not mandatory for short walks, but it would be foolish and risky to attempt a long trek alone through the dense jungle. There are three-day treks to Muong villages.

Admission to the national park costs US$5.

Places to Stay & Eat
Park headquarters charges US$10 for a few basic rooms in a *Muong-style house* (shared toilet and cold showers). Overpriced (but sterile) rooms in the park *guesthouse* also rent for US$35, but at this price you are far better off staying in Ninh Binh. Meals are available for overnight guests, and reservations can be made by contacting: Cuc Phuong National Park, Nho Quan District, Ninh Binh Province (☎ 86 6085), or the office in Hanoi at 1 Pho Doc Tan Ap (☎ 829 2604).

Getting There & Away
Cuc Phuong National Park is 140km from Hanoi (via Ninh Binh); sections of the road are in poor condition. There is no public transport, but with a car or motorbike it is possible to visit the forest as a day trip from Hanoi.

HAIPHONG
Haiphong, Vietnam's third most populous city, is the north's main industrial centre and is one of the country's most important sea-ports. There is precious little to see here, but some travellers use it as a staging post for visiting Halong Bay and Cat Ba Island.

Places to Stay
The cheapest place in town is *Thanh Lich Hotel* (☎ 84 7361) at 47 Pho Lach Tray (about 1km from the city centre). Fan rooms cost US$6 with shared bath, or US$10 with attached bath.

Hoa Binh Hotel (☎ 84 6907) is across from the train station at 104 Duong Luong Khanh Thien. This recently renovated place costs US$10 to US$25.

Thang Nam Hotel (☎ 84 2820) at 55 Pho Dien Bien Phu is another relatively cheap place; rooms cost US$16 to US$25.

Dien Bien Hotel (☎ 74 5264) is at 67 Pho Dien Bien Phu. The hotel's name will probably not enthral French travellers, but the rooms are OK and cost US$15 and US$20.

Directly across the street from the foregoing is the French-era *Hotel du Commerce* (☎ 84 2706) at 62 Pho Dien Bien Phu. The tariff is US$20 to US$60.

Places to Eat
Haiphong is noted for its excellent fresh seafood, which is available from most hotel restaurants.

Com Vietnam at 4 Pho Hoang Van Thu (not far from the post office), is a pleasant little Vietnamese restaurant with reasonable prices.

The *Saigon Cafe* features live music in the evenings. It's at the corner of Pho Dien Bien Phu and Pho Dinh Tien Hoang.

Getting There & Away
Air Both Pacific Airlines and Vietnam Airlines fly Haiphong-Saigon. Vietnam Airlines also offers three flights weekly on the Haiphong-Danang route.

Bus & Train Haiphong is 103km from Hanoi, and the journey by road takes about three hours. The two cities are also linked by rail.

AROUND HAIPHONG
Do Son Beach
Palm-shaded Do Son Beach, 21km south-east of Haiphong, is the most popular seaside resort in the north. This is also the site of Do Son Casino, the first casino to open in Vietnam since 1975.

HALONG BAY

Magnificent Halong Bay, with its 3000 islands rising from the clear, emerald waters of the Gulf of Tonkin, is one of the natural marvels of Vietnam. The vegetation-covered islands are dotted with innumerable beaches and grottoes created by the wind and the waves.

To see the islands and grottoes, a boat trip is mandatory. This can be done from Halong City, though Cat Ba Island is a better alternative for self-propelled travellers.

Orientation & Information

Food, accommodation and all other life-support systems are to be found in the town of Halong City. The seedy town is bisected by a bay – the west side is called Bai Chay. A short ferry ride takes you to the east side, known as Hon Gai. Accommodation can be found on both sides of the bay.

Places to Stay

Bai Chay The hotels are found in several areas. The heaviest concentration is right in the town itself, in the so-called *'hotel alley'*. This is where you'll find countless mini-hotels, plus very competitive prices. Expect to pay something like US$15 for a double with private bath and air-conditioning.

Two nice hillside places are: *Huong Tram Hotel (☎ 84 6365)*, which only costs US$10 for a fan room or US$20 with air-con; and the better-appointed *Hai Long Hotel (☎ 84 6378)* where air-con rooms are priced from US$20 to US$25.

A little farther east and high up in the hills is *Hai An Hotel (☎ 84 5514)*, a fancy place with sea views. Rates here are from US$30 to US$35.

Hon Gai There are not so many places to stay here, but demand is low, so prices have remained cheap. The following places are all on Duong Le Thanh Tong.

The cheapest place in Hon Gai is *Huong Lien Hotel (☎ 82 6608)*, at No 283. Rates are US$7 to US$10.

Phuong Nam Hotel (☎ 82 7242) is a clean place with rooms from US$15 to US$17. Ditto for *Queen Hotel West (☎ 82 5689)* at No 159.

You might also consider *Viet Anh Hotel (☎ 82 6243)*, where rooms are US$10 and US$15; *Thuong Mai Hotel (☎ 82 7258)* at No 269, US$13 and US$15; or *Hai Van Hotel (☎ 82 6279)* at No 78, US$10 to US$12.

Places to Eat

Except for mini-hotels, most hotels have *restaurants*. If you're on a tour, it's likely that meals will be included.

For self-propelled travellers, the area just west of central Bay Chay has a solid row of cheap *restaurants*, all good.

Restaurant Asia is on the 'hotel alley' slope. The Vietnamese food here is very good and prices are reasonable.

Getting There & Away

The 165km trip from Hanoi to Halong City (Bai Chay) takes about five hours by bus (US$6). Budget cafes and travel agencies book a three-day/two-night trip starting at US$25 per person. We recommend these trips over independent travel here – there are too many hassles and it's nearly impossible to do cheaper on your own.

Getting Around

If you're booked into a tour a boat will no doubt already be provided. If you're on your own, it's easy enough to hire a motorised launch to tour the islands and their grottoes. You can probably round up other foreigners to share the boat or even go with a group of Vietnamese tourists. A mid-sized boat can hold six to 12 persons and costs around US$6 per hour. Larger boats can hold 50 to 100 persons and cost US$10 to US$20 per hour.

CAT BA ISLAND

About half of Cat Ba Island was declared a national park in 1986. There are numerous lakes, waterfalls and grottoes in the spectacular limestone hills, the highest of which rises 331m above sea level.

Today, the island's human population of 12,000 is concentrated in the southern part of the island, including the town of Cat Ba.

Beaches

The white sand Cat Co beaches (called simply Cat Co 1 & Cat Co 2) make a great place to lounge around for the day. They are about 1.5km from Cat Ba village and can be reached on foot or by motorbike (US$0.25). There is a US$0.40 entry fee to the beaches.

Cat Ba National Park

You pay US$1 admission to the park, and the services of a guide cost US$5 regardless of group size. A guide is not mandatory but definitely recommended – otherwise, all you are likely to see is a bunch of trees. The guide will take you on a walk through Trung Trang Cave, but bring a torch (flashlight).

It's 17km from Cat Ba town to the park headquarters at Trung Trang. Hotels can book you onto a 12 seat minibus which costs US$30 (round trip) for 12 passengers. You must arrange the time with the driver to come and pick you up at the end of the day. Motorbike drivers want about US$5.

Places to Stay

The long standing *Quang Duc Family Hotel* (☎ 88 8231) was one of Cat Ba's first hotels. Twin rooms cost US$10/12 in winter/summer.

Just next door is *Van Anh Hotel* (☎ 88 8201), one of the most luxurious in town. Air-con rooms with two or three beds cost US$20 year-round.

Also recommended is *Hoang Huong Hotel* (☎ 88 8274), near the ferry pier. Fan twins cost US$8/12. Air-con raises the seasonal prices to US$10/$US15.

Sunflower Hotel (☎ 88 8215) has a billiards bar on the seventh-storey rooftop with the best view of the bay in town. Winter rates are US$12 for fan rooms, US$15 for air-con, and figure on about US$2 less in summer.

Lan Ha Hotel (☎ 88 8299) on a quiet (for now) side street is a very good value. Fan twins cost just US$4/5 winter/summer. The neighbouring *Ngoc Bich Hotel* is similar and costs US$5/10. Ditto for the nearby *Hong Quang Hotel* (☎ 88 8330) and the karaoke-happy *Pacific Hotel* (☎ 88 8331).

Back out on the main drag, we can suggest the friendly *Huong Cang Family Hotel* (☎ 88 8399), which has fan rooms with balconies for US$6/10.

Places to Eat

The friendly *Huu Dung Restaurant* (also known as the 'Coca Cola Restaurant') has some of the best food in town.

Another excellent place to eat is the *Gaulois Restaurant*.

Both of these are also worthwhile choices for booking tours to Cat Ba National Park or Halong Bay.

Getting There & Away

Cat Ba National Park is 133km from Hanoi and 30km east of Haiphong. Both slow boats and hydrofoils sail to Cat Ba from Haiphong every day.

An alternative way to reach Cat Ba is via the island of Cat Hai, which is closer to

Haiphong. A boat departs Haiphong for Cat Hai, makes a brief stop and continues on to the port of Fulong on Cat Ba Island. A bus connects Fulong to Cat Ba Village, a distance of 30km.

Chartered private boats run trips between Cat Ba and Halong Bay. Make inquiries at the pier at either end.

Getting Around

Motorbikes are available for rent in the town for US$1.50 per hour, or US$5 per day. Hotels and restaurants book boat tours around the island.

BAI TU LONG BAY

There's more to Halong Bay than Halong Bay. The sinking limestone plateau, which gave birth to the bay's spectacular islands, continues all the way to the Chinese border. This area is known as Bai Tu Long Bay.

Bai Tu Long Bay is every bit as beautiful as its famous neighbour. Indeed, you could say it's even more beautiful since it has scarcely seen any tourist development. Visitors of any kind are rare, but this will no doubt change – already some of the tourist cafes in Hanoi have made forays into this uncharted region.

You can charter boats at Halong Bay to bring you to Bai Tu Long Bay. A boat capable of holding 20 passengers can be hired for US$10 per hour; the one way sailing time is around five hours. Alternatively, if you get yourself to Cai Rong on Van Don Island, you can travel by public ferry to some of the remote outlying islands, or charter a boat at the usual rates.

At the time of writing there had not yet been any reported incidents of piracy involving foreigners at Bai Tu Long Bay. This is not surprising, since there have been scarcely any visitors to rob. However, security could become a problem if tourists start visiting en masse. A few years ago Halong Bay had a serious problem with piracy until the authorities cracked down with regular police patrol boats. Don't be too surprised if history repeats itself at Bai Tu Long Bay.

Van Don Island

Also known as Cam Pha, this is the largest and most developed island in the archipelago. Cai Rong is the main town on the island.

Places to Stay *Phuc Loc Hotel* (☎ 87 4231) is in the centre of Cai Rong, almost opposite the market. The rooms aren't bad, but check the plumbing – not all of the ancient Soviet toilets are in working condition. A twin room costs US$11 with air-con, or US$7 without.

It's more pleasant to stay near Cai Rong pier on the south-eastern edge of town. About 100m before the pier is *Hung Toan Hotel* (☎ 87 4220). The three rooms on the top floor share a huge balcony which affords superb views of the bay. Twins cost US$10 to US$13.

Getting There & Away Two rickety old ferries run between Cau Ong (Cua Ong Pha; on the mainland) and Tai Xa pier (Tai Xa Pha; on Van Don Island). The passenger ferry (which also carries bikes, motorbikes and chickens) runs once every 30 minutes, while the six-car ferry runs once every two hours (both operate from 5.30 am to 5.30 pm). The journey takes 30 minutes.

There are frequent buses between Hon Gai (in Halong Bay) and Cua Ong bus station, 1km from the pier. There are also a few (rare) buses directly between Hon Gai and Van Don.

If you didn't take a direct bus, you can pay US$0.50 for a ride on a motorbike to take you the 7km between the pier and the town.

The Cai Rong pier is just on the edge of Cai Rong town. This is where you catch boats to the outlying islands.

Quan Lan Island

Quan Lan is the place with the most potential to develop a beach resort. The main attraction here is a beautiful, 1km-long white sand beach shaped like a crescent moon. Quan Lan Island has a **Rowing Boat Festival** (Hoi Cheo Boi) held annually from the 16th to the 18th day of the sixth lunar month. It's the biggest festival in the bay area, and thousands of people turn out to see it.

Ferries between Van Don and Quan Lan islands depart from either side at 7 am and cross during the journey, so a trip to Quan Lan requires an overnight stay.

BA BE NATIONAL PARK

This incredibly beautiful area boasts waterfalls, rivers, deep valleys, lakes and caves set amid towering peaks. The area is inhabited by members of the Dai minority, who live in homes built on stilts.

There are several lakes here, the largest of which is called Ba Be. The lake is about 145m above sea level and surrounded by steep mountains up to 1754m high.

Ba Be (Three Bays) is also the name of the

southern part of a narrow body of water 7km long; the northern section of the lake, separated from Ba Be Lake by a 100m-wide strip of water sandwiched between high walls of chalk rock, is called **Be Kam**. The Nam Nang River is navigable for 23km between a point 4km above Cho Ra and the **Dau Dang Waterfall**, which consists of a series of spectacular cascades between sheer walls of rock.

The 300m-long **Puong Cave** passes completely through a mountain. A navigable river flows through the cave, making for an interesting boat trip.

Foreigners are charged a US$5 entry fee to the park.

Places to Stay

The town of Cho Ra boasts *Ba Be Hotel* (☎ 87 6115), where rooms cost US$15.

Getting There & Away

Ba Be Lake is 240km (eight hours) from Hanoi, 61km from Bach Thong (Bac Can) and 18km from Cho Ra. Most visitors to the national park go from Hanoi by chartered vehicle. Some of the cafes in Hanoi have started organising bus trips.

Reaching this national park by public transport is possible but not easy. Take a bus from Hanoi to Bach Thong (Bac Can), and from there another bus to Cho Ra.

At the Ba Be Hotel in Cho Ra you can book boat rides to the park.

HOA BINH

The city of Hoa Binh (Peace) is 74km southwest of Hanoi. This area is home to many Montagnard people.

Unfortunately, Hoa Binh is the minority village for packaged tours. Hill-tribe clothing is on sale in the market, but in large sizes specially made for tourists. Some of the other genuine Montagnard souvenirs look as if they should have a 'Made in Taiwan' sticker on the bottom. Maybe they do. Give them another year and the Montagnards will be selling banana-muesli pancakes.

None the less, there's no reason why you shouldn't stop in and have a look. However, the traditional Montagnard way of life begins about 50km to the west and continues right up to the border with Laos and beyond.

Places to Stay

Hoa Binh I Hotel (☎ 82 5051) is built in genuine Montagnard stilt-house style, although a few added amenities like hot water and satellite TV are not exactly traditional. Modern intrusions aside, we must admit it's one of the best hotels in north-west Vietnam. The rooms cost US$30 to US$40.

Just opposite is *Hoa Binh II Hotel* (☎ 85 2001).

MAI CHAU

One of the closest places to Hanoi where you can see a real hill-tribe village is Mai Chau. It's a beautiful place, very rural with little in the way of a centre – rather, it's a collection of farms and huts spread out over a large area. The people here are ethnic White Tai (Thai), though only distantly related to tribes in Thailand.

If you are expecting an Indiana Jones adventure, think again. The area is very well touristed and most of the Tai people dress the same as other Vietnamese. Still, many travellers have had great things to say about overnighting in the villages.

Foreigners must pay an admission fee of US$0.50 to enter Mai Chau.

Places to Stay

The only hotel in town is *Mai Chau Guest-house* (☎ 85 1812), where rooms are US$15. However, most travellers prefer to stay a few hundred metres from here in a real *minority house* (US$5 per person) at Lac Village (Ban Lac).

Getting There & Away

Mai Chau is a few kilometres south of National Highway 6 (the direct Hanoi-Dien Bien Phu route), so getting there requires a slight detour.

You'll be hard-pressed to find any direct public transport to Mai Chau from Hanoi. If you're not on a tour or don't have your own chartered vehicle, your best hope would be to take a public bus from Hanoi to Hoa Binh, followed by a motorcycle taxi to Mai Chau. Most cafes in Hanoi run trips to Mai Chau. All transport, food and accommodation is provided for as low as US$25 per person.

LAO CAI

Lao Cai is the major town at the end of the train line and right on the Chinese border. Lao Cai is also a major destination for travellers journeying between Hanoi and Kunming (the capital of China's scenic Yunnan Province).

The border town on the Chinese side is called Hekou, and is separated from Vietnam by a river with a bridge. The bridge and border crossing is open daily from 8 am until 5 pm, and you must pay a small toll to cross.

Orientation

The border is 3km from Lao Cai train station. Making this short journey is best accomplished on a motorbike, which will cost around US$0.50.

Places to Stay

In Hekou, on the Chinese side, budget accommodation is available at the old *Hekou Hotel* or the new, relatively upmarket *Dongfeng Hotel*.

In Lao Cai, closest to the border gate is *Song Hong Guesthouse* (☎ 83 0004). Twin rooms are US$10 to US$15.

Hong Ha Hotel (☎ 83 0007) is a relatively large but lacklustre place. Rooms cost US$10 to US$12.

Hanoi Hotel (☎ 83 2486) is a small but newish place with satellite TV. Air-con rooms cost US$13.

Getting There & Away

There are two trains daily in each direction on the Lao Cai-Hanoi run. One train runs at night and one during the day. Travelling time is 10 to 12 hours. Tickets for foreigners are usually only sold on the day of departure. There is no soft sleeper, just hard seat, soft seat and (on night trains) hard sleeper.

BAC HA

The highlands around Bac Ha are about 900m above sea level, making it somewhat warmer than Sapa (see the following section). There are 10 Montagnard groups living around Bac Ha – Flower Hmong, Dzao, Giay (Nhang), Han (Hoa), Xa Fang, Lachi, Nung, Phula, Tai and Thulao – plus the Kinh (ethnic-Vietnamese).

One of Bac Ha's main industries is the manufacture of alcoholic brews (rice wine, cassava wine and corn liquor). The corn stuff produced by the Flower Hmong is so potent that it can ignite.

Ban Pho Village

If you want to see what a real Montagnard village looks like, this is your chance. The villagers live simply – don't expect bright lights and loud music. Indeed, don't even expect electricity. What they lack in material possessions, they make up for in their extreme

VIETNAM

hospitality. The Hmong villagers are some of the kindest people you'll meet in Vietnam.

Ban Pho is a 7km return trip from Bac Ha. You can take a loop route to get there and back.

Markets

There are several interesting markets around Bac Ha, all within about 20km of each other. You'll see plenty of Flower Hmong – so called because the women embroider flowers on their colourful skirts.

Bac Ha Market This lively and crowded concrete bazaar is the main market in Bac Ha proper. It's chock full with Flower Hmong and as such is *very* colourful.

The market mainly operates on Sunday.

Can Cau Market This interesting open-air market is 20km north of Bac Ha. Can Cau is only 9km south of the Chinese border, and attracts a large number of Chinese traders. The market operates on Saturday.

The road leading to Can Cau is pitiless; without a jeep or strong two-wheeled transport, don't even think about it.

Lung Phin Market This market is between Can Cau market and Bac Ha town, about 12km from the town. It's less busy here than the other markets, and runs on Sunday.

Places to Stay

Sao Mai Hotel (☎ 88 0288) is a popular place. The hotel has three sections – a concrete building where twin rooms cost US$10, and two separate wooden houses where rooms are US$12.

Dang Khoa Hotel (☎ 88 0290) in the centre of town (and the loudspeakers) has rooms for US$5 to US$8. The nearby *Dang Khoa 2 Hotel* (☎ 88 0321) also charges just US$5.

Tran Sin Hotel (☎ 88 0240) is near the market. Rooms are priced at the Bac Ha 'standard rate' of US$10 to US$15.

Also near the market, the friendly and quiet *Anh Duong Guesthouse* (☎ 88 0329) charges US$8 to US$12.

Places to Eat

The *Cong Phu Restaurant* has tasty, low-priced food and an English menu. Ditto for the *Tran Sin Restaurant*, on the ground floor of the Tran Sin Hotel. Both close by about 9 pm.

Getting There & Away

Buses depart from Lao Cai for Bac Ha (63km) daily at 6.30 am and 1 pm. From Bac Ha to Lao Cai buses leave at 5.30 and 11.30 am. The trip takes between three and five hours depending on pick-ups along the way, and costs US$1.20. The road is well maintained and the rural scenery is lovely.

Locals on motorbikes are also willing to make the Lao Cai-Bac Ha run for about US$5, or even Sapa-Bac Ha (110km) for US$12. Sunday minibus tours have also started from Sapa to Bac Ha and cost around US$12, including transport, guide and trekking to a minority village. On the way back to Sapa it is possible to hop off in Lao Cai and catch the night train back to Hanoi.

Bac Ha is 330km (10 hours) from Hanoi. Some cafes in Hanoi offer four-day bus trips to Bac Ha for around US$60, usually with a visit to Sapa included.

SAPA

Sapa is an old hill station in a beautiful valley at 1600m elevation. Don't forget your winter woollies – Sapa is known for its cold, foggy winters (down to 0°C). Thanks to the chilly climate, the area boasts temperate-zone fruit trees (peaches, plums etc) and gardens for raising medicinal herbs. The dry season for Sapa is approximately January to June – afternoon rain showers in the mountains are frequent.

Surrounding Sapa are the Hoang Lien Mountains. These mountains include **Fansipan**, which at 3143m is Vietnam's highest. The trek from Sapa to the summit and back can take four or five days.

The **market** held on Saturday is a major attraction.

Some of the more well known sights around Sapa include **Thac Bac** (Silver Falls) and **Cau May** (Cloud Bridge), which spans the Muong Hoa River.

Places to Stay

The excellent *Auberge Hotel* (☎ 87 1243) is notable for its valley views and superb bonsai garden. Doubles range from US$6 to US$12. The restaurant here is also recommended.

Next to the Auberge is the friendly *Queen Hotel* (☎ 87 1301), which offers rooms with views for US$4 to US$10.

On the other side of the Auberge is the low-cost but viewless *Student Guesthouse* (☎ 87 1308). Dorm beds cost just US$1.20, and twin rooms run from US$3.

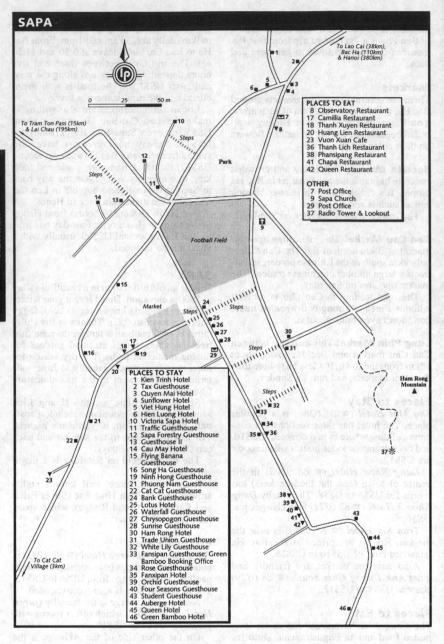

SAPA

To Lao Cai (38km),
Bac Ha (110km)
& Hanoi (380km)

To Tram Ton Pass (15km)
& Lai Chau (195km)

Steps

Park

Steps

Steps

Football Field

Market

Steps   Steps

Steps

Ham Rong
Mountain

To Cat Cat
Village (3km)

PLACES TO EAT
8 Observatory Restaurant
17 Camillia Restaurant
18 Thanh Xuyen Restaurant
20 Huang Lien Restaurant
23 Vuon Xuan Cafe
36 Thanh Lich Restaurant
38 Phansipang Restaurant
41 Chapa Restaurant
42 Queen Restaurant

OTHER
7 Post Office
9 Sapa Church
29 Post Office
37 Radio Tower & Lookout

PLACES TO STAY
1 Kien Trinh Hotel
2 Tax Guesthouse
3 Quyen Mai Hotel
4 Sunflower Hotel
5 Viet Hung Hotel
6 Hien Luong Hotel
10 Victoria Sapa Hotel
11 Traffic Guesthouse
12 Sapa Forestry Guesthouse
13 Guesthouse II
14 Cau May Hotel
15 Flying Banana
    Guesthouse
16 Song Ha Guesthouse
19 Ninh Hong Guesthouse
21 Phuong Nam Guesthouse
22 Cat Cat Guesthouse
24 Bank Guesthouse
25 Lotus Hotel
26 Waterfall Guesthouse
27 Chrysopogon Guesthouse
28 Sunrise Guesthouse
30 Ham Rong Hotel
31 Trade Union Guesthouse
32 White Lily Guesthouse
33 Fansipan Guesthouse; Green
    Bamboo Booking Office
34 Rose Guesthouse
35 Fanxipan Hotel
39 Orchid Guesthouse
40 Four Seasons Guesthouse
43 Student Guesthouse
44 Auberge Hotel
45 Queen Hotel
46 Green Bamboo Hotel

0   25   50 m

Just below the market, the friendly *Ninh Hong Guesthouse* (☎ 87 1334) receives good reports from travellers. The owner, Mrs Hong, is perhaps the only female trekking guide in Sapa.

Song Ha Guesthouse (☎ 87 1273) is set in an attractive villa and also deserves a plug. Rooms are US$4 and US$5 in winter and US$10 to US$15 in summer.

Cat Cat Guesthouse (☎ 87 1387) is very popular and has excellent views from the front terrace. Winter rates are from US$5 to US$8, or US$10 to US$15 in summer.

Near the Cat Cat, *Phuong Nam Guesthouse* (☎ 87 1286) has simple rooms for US$5 to US$10, and a great terrace cafe out the back.

Flying Banana Guesthouse (☎ 87 1580) is of the new concrete variety, but is family-run and very friendly. Rooms here go for US$6 to US$12.

There is a string of cheap, interchangeable guesthouses near the stairs leading down into the market. Rooms average US$3 to US$5 in winter, and US$6 to US$12 in summer. These include: *Rose Guesthouse* (☎ 87 1263), *Fansipan Guesthouse* (☎ 87 1398) and *Sunrise Guesthouse* (☎ 87 1331).

Green Bamboo Hotel (☎ 87 1214) is a mid-range French villa-style place with fine views. Rates are from US$15 to US$25.

Places to Eat

The *Observatory Restaurant* is a Sapa institution and a great place to pick up take-away picnic lunches.

The *Camillia Restaurant* near the market is a worthy expat favourite with a varied menu.

Auberge Hotel is a good breakfast spot, and also has a set vegetarian menu.

The *Chapa Restaurant* is a true travellers' cafe with the usual banana pancakes and spring rolls.

Others to consider nearby include the *Queen Restaurant*, *Four Seasons Restaurant*, and *Thanh Lich Restaurant* – all are good. The *Phansipang Restaurant* is the place to relieve any sudden cravings for antelope.

Entertainment

The first western-style watering hole to open in Sapa is at the *Green Bamboo Hotel* – it stages a free traditional hill tribe music and dance show on Saturday night at 8.30 pm.

For a more 'civilised' drink, there are two stylish bars at the new *Victoria Sapa Hotel*.

Getting There & Away

The gateway to Sapa is Lao Cai, 38km away on the Chinese border. Minibuses make the trip in about two hours. Locals are also willing to drive you up the mountain by motorbike for US$5.

The advertised rate on minibus service for Sapa-Bac Ha (110km) is around US$12 per person; departures from Sapa are at 6 am and departure from Bac Ha is at 1 pm. For Sapa-Hanoi it's US$18 per person, and departure is at 5 am.

Driving a motorbike from Hanoi to Sapa is feasible, but it's a very long trip – start early. The total distance between Hanoi and Sapa is 380km. The last 38km is straight uphill – unless you've been training for the Olympics, it's hell on a bicycle.

Cafes in Hanoi offer four-day bus trips to Sapa for around US$40. This is probably the most hassle-free way to do the journey, but most people prefer to do Sapa on their own.

Once in Sapa, most of the hotels can organise treks.

Getting Around

The best way to move around Sapa is to walk. The town itself is small enough and there are plenty of minority villages in walking distance from the centre.

For excursions further out, you can hire a self-drive motorbike for about US$6 a day, or take one with a driver for about US$10.

DIEN BIEN PHU

History is the main attraction here. Dien Bien Phu seems to hold the same fascination for the French as the DMZ does for Americans.

Dien Bien Phu was the site of that rarest of military events, a battle that can be called truly decisive. On 6 May 1954, Viet Minh forces overran the French garrison at Dien Bien Phu after a 57 day siege, shattering French morale and forcing the French government to abandon its attempts to re-establish colonial control of Indochina.

The **Military Museum** (open daily) tells the story. Admission is US$2.

Places to Stay

The recently renovated *Dien Bien Phu Mini-Hotel* (☎ 82 4319) also runs a large restaurant. Twins with attached bath cost US$20, including breakfast.

Thuong Mai Hotel (☎ 82 5580) has clean doubles for US$16 to US$18. Similar rates exist at *Phuong Hyuen Hotel* (☎ 82 4460).

Airline Guesthouse (Nha Khach Hang Khong, ☎ 82 5052) has a small restaurant and charges US$14; *Bank Guesthouse (Nha Khach Ngan Hang, ☎ 82 5852)* has decent rooms for US$15; and our personal favourite, *Beer Factory Guesthouse (Nha May Bia, ☎ 82 4635)*, charges US$12 to US$15.

Places to Eat
The best eatery in town is the *Lien Tuoi Restaurant*, about 500m from the Army Museum.

You might also try the restaurant in the *Dien Bien Phu Mini-Hotel*, or look for the *Nga Luan Restaurant*, or *food stalls* around the market.

Getting There & Away
During the tourist season (roughly April to September) Vietnam Airlines operates flights between Dien Bien Phu and Hanoi three times a week.

Some travellers rent motorbikes in Hanoi and do a loop trip – Hanoi to Dien Bien Phu, onwards to Sapa, Lao Cai and then back to Hanoi. This takes about 10 days and the roads are sometimes rough or flooded, but it is possible to put the motorbike on the train from Lao Cai to Hanoi. The route passes through a number of towns where the majority are hill tribes (notably the Black Tai and Hmong).

Central Coast

HUÉ
Hué served as Vietnam's political capital from 1802 to 1945 under the 13 emperors of the Nguyen Dynasty. Traditionally, the city has been one of Vietnam's cultural, religious and educational centres. Today, Hué's main attractions are the splendid tombs of the Nguyen emperors, several notable pagodas and the remains of the citadel.

Most of the city's major sights have an admission charge of US$5.

The Citadel
Construction of the moated citadel (Kinh Thanh), whose perimeter is 10km, was begun in 1804 by Emperor Gia Long. The emperor's official functions were carried out in the **Imperial Enclosure** (Dai Noi, or Hoang Thanh), a 'citadel within the citadel' which has a 6m-high wall 2.5km in length.

Within the Imperial Enclosure is the **Forbidden Purple City** (Tu Cam Thanh), which was reserved for the private life of the emperor.

The beautiful hall that houses the **Imperial Museum** was built in 1845 and restored in 1923.

Royal Tombs
The Tombs of the Nguyen Dynasty (1802-1945) are seven to 16km south of Hué.

Nam Giao (Temple of Heaven) was once the most important religious site in Vietnam.

Dong Khanh's Mausoleum, the smallest of the Royal Tombs, was built in 1889. Construction of the **Tomb of Thieu Tri**, who ruled from 1841 to 1847, was completed in 1848.

Perhaps the most majestic of the Royal Tombs is the **Tomb of Minh Mang**, who ruled from 1820 to 1840. The tomb is 12km from Hué on the west bank of the Perfume River (there's a ferry from a point about 1.5km south-west of Khai Dinh's Tomb).

The gaudy and crumbling **Tomb of Emperor Khai Dinh**, who ruled from 1916 to 1925, was begun in 1920 and completed in 1931.

Pagodas, Temples & Churches
The **Thien Mu Pagoda** (also called Linh Mu Pagoda) is one of the most famous structures in all of Vietnam. The pagoda, founded in 1601, is on the banks of the Perfume River, 4km south-west of the citadel.

The **Bao Quoc Pagoda** was founded in 1670. **Notre Dame Cathedral** (Dong Chua Cuu The) at 80 Duong Nguyen Hue is an impressive modern building.

There are quite a few pagodas and Chinese congregational halls in Phu Cat and Phu Hiep subdistricts, which are across the Dong Ba Canal from Dong Ba Market. The entrance to **Dieu De National Pagoda** (Quoc Tu Dieu De), built under Emperor Thieu Tri (ruled 1841-47), is along Dong Ba Canal at 102 Duong Bach Dang. Hué's Indian Muslim community constructed the **mosque**, at 120 Duong Chi Lang, in 1932.

Chieu Ung Pagoda (Chieu Ung Tu), opposite 138 Duong Chi Lang, was founded by the Hainan Chinese congregation in the mid-19th century and was rebuilt in 1908.

The **Cantonese Chinese Congregation Assembly Hall** (Chua Quang Dong) is at 176 Duong Tran Phu.

Tang Quang Pagoda (Tang Quang Tu), just down the road from 80 Duong Nguyen Chi Thanh, is the largest of the three Hinayana (Theravada) pagodas in Hué.

Thuan An Beach
Thuan An Beach (Bai Tam Thuan An), 13km

north-east of Hué, is on a splendid lagoon near the mouth of the Perfume River.

Boat Cruises

All-day boat trips on the Perfume River take in many of the aforementioned sights. Look for boats on the east bank of the river, just north of the Trang Tien Bridge.

Places to Stay

A good place to find cheap rooms near the river is in the narrow alley off Duong Le Loi, between Duong Pham Ngu Lao and Duong Chu Van An. One possibility is the family-run *Thanh Thuy's Guesthouse* (☎ 82 4585) at 46/4 Duong Le Loi, with air-con singles/doubles for US$7/10.

Across the alley is the friendly *Phuong Hoang Hotel* (☎ 82 6736) at 48/3 Duong Le Loi, with nice rooms (some with river views) from US$15 to US$30, including breakfast.

Mimosa Guesthouse (☎ 82 8068), at 46/6 Duong Le Loi, charges $10 to US$15 for air-con rooms. At 46/2 Duong Le Loi, *Guesthouse Hoang Huong* (☎ 82 8509) has US$4 singles, fan twins for US$8 and air-con rooms for US$10.

Near the end of the alley at 48/9 Duong Le Loi, *Guesthouse Tran Van Phuong* (☎ 82 2772) is a tiny place named after its multilingual owner, who charges US$10 for a small twin room.

The popular *Thai Binh Hotel* (☎ 82 8058) is tucked into a quiet alley at 10/9 Duong Nguyen Tri Phuong. Rooms range from US$10 to US$25.

Another nice, family-run place is *Binh Minh Hotel* (☎ 82 5526) at 12 Duong Nguyen Tri Phuong. Rates are US$8 to US$30.

Duy Tan Hotel (☎ 82 5001) at 12 Duong Hung Vuong is another centrally located place. Published rates are US$13 to US$40.

Hung Dao Hotel (☎ 82 3941) is one of the cheapest places in town. It's at 81 Duong Tran Hung Dao, close to the Dong Ba Market.

The enormous *Le Loi Hué Hotel* (☎ 82 2153) at 2 Duong Le Loi is near the train station. Rooms cost US$6 to US$45.

Also near the train station at 3 Duong Dien Bien Phu, *Dien Bien Hotel* (☎ 82 1678) offers fan singles/doubles for US$8/10 and air-con rooms for US$15/20.

Ben Nghe Guesthouse (☎ 88 9106) at 4 Duong Ben Nghe has fair prices. Fan twins cost US$6 with shared bath, or US$10 with attached bath and air-con.

Nearby is *Hoang Long Hotel* (☎ 82 8235), at 20 Duong Nguyen Tri Phuong, with fan rooms from US$6 to US$10 and air-con rooms from US$12 to US$25.

Thang Long Hotel (☎ 82 6462), at 16 Duong Hung Vuong, is new and has twins from US$10 to US$40. A similar standard prevails at *Hung Vuong Hotel* at 2 Duong Hung Vuong. The nearby *Truong Tien Hotel* (☎ 82 3127), at 8 Duong Hung Vuong, has cheaper rooms ranging from US$6 to US$15.

Vong Canh Hotel (☎ 82 4130) at 25 Duong Hung Vuong, is close to the post office. Rooms with a fax cost US$8, or US$10 to US$12 with air-con.

Ngo Quyen Hotel (☎ 82 3278) at 11 Duong Ngo Quyen is a large, old, elegant place with that 'seen better days' appearance. Doubles range from US$15 to US$35.

The popular *Thanh Noi* ('Forbidden') *Hotel* (☎ 82 2478) at 3 Duong Dang Dung boasts an ideal location on the historic west bank of Hué. Rooms cost US$10 to US$25.

Phu Xuan Hotel (☎ 82 3572) at 27 Duong Tran Hung Dao is a newish place with rooms for US$25. It's near the Phu Xuan Bridge and is one of the few hotels on the west bank of the Perfume River.

Also on the west bank is *Hoa Sen Hotel* (☎ 82 5997) at 33 Duong Dinh Cong Trang. This place has a very quiet setting among the trees. Rooms cost US$15 to US$25.

Places to Eat

East Bank There is a solid string of popular *budget cafes* worth checking out along Duong Hung Vuong.

The sign outside the *Xuan Trang Cafeteria* at 14A Duong Hung Vuong reads 'Should be in Lonely Planet'. Having eaten there, we agree. Just next door is the equally popular *News Cafe*.

The *Mandarin Cafe*, in the grounds of the Duy Tan Hotel, is also excellent and tends to stay open late. The sign reads 'Lauded in Lonely Planet ...', so we figure it can't be that bad?

The cafe in the grounds of the Le Loi Hué Hotel, and the *Cafe 3 Le Loi*, just across the street, also dish up fine food and offer the opportunity to swap travellers' tales.

For more upmarket dining, try the pleasant *Paradise Garden Restaurant* on Duong Nguyen Dinh Chieu, on the riverfront near the Hotel Saigon Morin.

West Bank *Lac Thanh Restaurant* at 6A Duong Dien Tien Hoang is a fashionable gathering spot for travellers. To order, see the

HUÉ

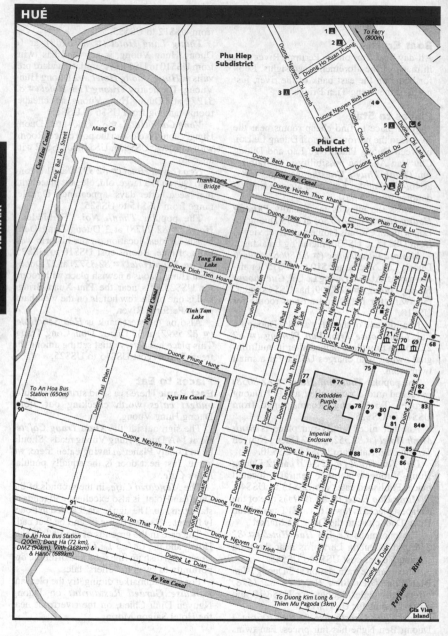

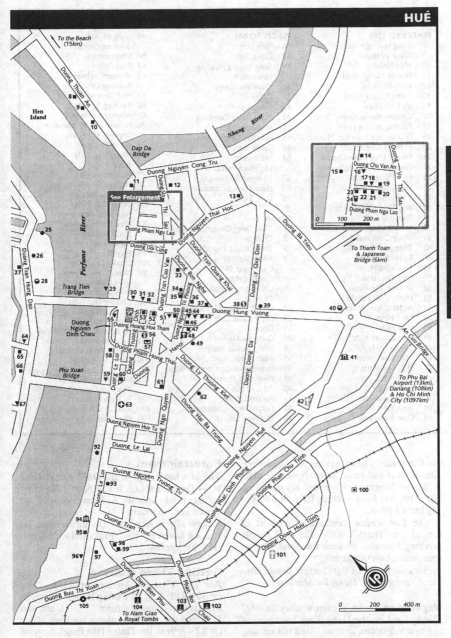

HUÉ

HUÉ

PLACES TO STAY		PLACES TO EAT			
8	Song Huong Hotel	16	Tinh Tam	49	Vietnam Airlines
9	Thon Vy Hotel	18	Dong Tam		Booking Office
10	Vida Hotel	29	Song Huong Floating	56	Vietcombank
11	Huong Giang Hotel		Restaurant	57	Post Office
12	Kinh Do Hotel	30	Travellers' Cafes	62	Vietnam Airlines
13	Thien Duong Hotel	31	Cafes		Booking Office
14	Ky Linh Hotel	44	News Cafe	63	Hué General Hospital
15	Century Riverside Inn	45	Xuan Trang Cafeteria	68	Thuong Tu Gate
17	Phuong Hoang Hotel	51	Mandarin Cafe	69	Military Museum
19	Guesthouse Tran Van Phuong	55	Paradise Garden Restaurant	70	Natural History Museum
20	Mimosa Guesthouse	59	Cercle Sportif	71	Imperial Museum
21	Thanh Thuy's Guesthouse	64	Lac Thanh;	73	Dong Ba Gate
22	Guesthouse Hoang Huong		Lac Thien Restaurant	75	Hien Nhon Gate
23	Hoa Hong 1 Hotel	67	Ba Nhon Restaurant	76	Royal Library
27	Hung Dao Hotel	89	Huong Sen Restaurant	77	Hoa Binh Gate
32	L'Indochine Hotel	96	Cafe 3 Le Loi	78	Halls of the Mandarins
33	Ben Nghe Guesthouse			79	Thai Hoa Palace
34	Thuan Hoa Hotel	**OTHER**		80	Trung Dao Bridge
36	Hoang Long Hotel	1	Chua Ong; Chaozhou Pagoda	81	Ngo Mon Gate
37	Vong Canh Hotel	2	Chua Ba	82	Nine Holy Cannons
43	Thang Long Hotel	3	Tang Quang Pagoda		(Four Seasons)
46	Binh Minh Hotel	4	Assembly Hall of the	83	Ngan Gate
47	Thai Binh Hotel		Cantonese Chinese	84	Flag Tower
50	Duy Tan Hotel		Congregation	85	Quang Duc Gate
52	Truong Tien Hotel	5	Chieu Ung Pagoda	86	Nine Holy Cannons
53	Hung Vuong Hotel	6	Mosque		(Five Elements)
54	Hotel Saigon Morin	7	Dieu De National Pagoda	87	Nine Dynastic Urns
58	Mini Hotel 18	24	DMZ Bar & Cafe	88	Chuong Duc Gate
60	Hue Hotel	25	Dock	90	Nha Do Gate
61	Ngo Quyen Hotel	26	Dong Ba Market	91	Chanh Tay Gate
65	Thanh Loi Hotel	28	Dong Ba Bus Station	92	Perfume River Boat Cruises
66	Phu Xuan Hotel	35	Apocalypse Now	93	National School
72	Hoa Sen Hotel	38	Industrial & Commercial Bank	94	Ho Chi Minh Museum
74	Thanh Noi Hotel	39	Municipal Theatre	100	Tomb of Duc Duc
95	Guesthouse 5 Le Loi	40	An Cuu Bus Station	101	Phu Cam Cathedral
97	Le Loi Hué Hotel; Cafe	41	An Dinh Palace	102	Linh Quang Pagoda;
98	Nam Giao Hotel	42	Notre Dame Cathedral		Phan Boi Chau's Tomb
99	Dien Bien Hotel	48	St Xavier Church	103	Tu Dam Pagoda
				104	Bao Quoc Pagoda
				105	Hué Train Station

book travellers have written in; the owner, Lac, is deaf and mute, so everything is done with sign language. However, his daughter, Lan Anh, has been working hard on improving her English.

The *Lac Thien Restaurant* has sort of cloned Lac Thanh's motif. Six deaf people working here also produce fine food, plus an entertaining atmosphere.

Backpackers on a tight budget should consider eating in the *Dong Ba Market*.

Vegetarian Down a narrow alley at 48/7 Duong Le Loi, the *Dong Tam* has some of the best vegie fare in town – and it's cheap.

An alternative is the excellent *Tinh Tam* vegetarian restaurant, around the block at 4 Duong Chu Van An.

Entertainment

The best bar in Hué is the *DMZ Bar & Cafe* at 44 Duong Le Loi. It is a popular evening eating, pool-shooting and dancing spot for expats and travellers.

Apocalypse Now at 7 Duong Nguyen Tri Phuong has overpriced drinks and an 'aggressive' atmosphere.

Getting There & Away

Air The Vietnam Airlines booking office (☎ 82 3249) is at 12 Duong Hanoi. It is open Monday to Saturday from 7 to 11 am and 1.30 to 5 pm. There is also a booking office (☎ 82 4709) in the Thuan Hoa Hotel. Several flights connect Hué to Saigon and Hanoi.

Bus Tourist minibuses can be booked at most

budget cafes and hotels. Minibuses to Danang and Hoi An leave at 8 am, and cost US$4. Minibuses to Hanoi leave at 5 am and 5 pm, and cost US$22.

Train Hué train station is on the east bank at the south-western end of Duong Le Loi. The ticket office is open from 6.30 am to 5 pm.

Getting Around

Bicycles, motorbikes and cars can be hired from hotels all over town. You can also phone Airport Taxi (☎ 82 5555) or Hué Taxi (☎ 83 3333).

DMZ & VICINITY

From 1954 to 1975, the Ben Hai River served as the demarcation line between South Vietnam and North Vietnam. The Demilitarised Zone (DMZ, dee-em-zee) consisted of an area 5km to either side of the demarcation line.

Most of what you can see nowadays in the DMZ are places where historical things happened. To make sense of it all you really need a guide who can explain just what you're looking at and a good imagination. Day tours are a fixed $25 and can easily be booked in Hué.

Things to See

The remarkable **Tunnels of Vinh Moc** are similar to the ones at Cu Chi, but these are the real thing, not rebuilt for mass tourism.

Truong Son National Cemetery (Nghia Trang Liet Si Truong Son) is a memorial to the tens of thousands of North Vietnamese soldiers killed along the Ho Chi Minh Trail. Row after row of white tombstones stretch across the hillsides.

The gargantuan 175mm cannons at **Camp Carroll** were used to shell targets as far away as Khe Sanh, over 30km away. These days, there is not much to see here except a few overgrown trenches and the remains of their timber roofs.

Set amid beautiful hills, valleys and fields at an elevation of about 600m, the town of **Khe Sanh** (Huong Hoa) is a pleasant district capital once known for its French-run coffee plantations. **Khe Sanh Combat Base**, site of the most famous siege of the American War, sits silently on a barren plateau surrounded by vegetation-covered hills often obscured by mist and fog.

Lao Bao, 18km from Khe Sanh, is right on the Tchepone River (Song Xe Pon), which marks the Vietnam-Laos border. Towering above Lao Bao on the Lao side of the border is Co Roc Mountain, once a North Vietnamese artillery stronghold. About 2km towards Khe Sanh from the border crossing (now open to foreigners) is the lively Lao Bao Market.

DANANG

Vietnam's fourth-largest city, Danang is chiefly of interest to travellers as a transit stop.

Things to See

Danang's most worthwhile sight is the famed **Cham Museum** (Bao Tang Cham). The world's largest collection of Cham artefacts is near the intersection of Duong Nu Vuong and Duong Bach Dang, and is open daily from 8 to 11 am and 1 to 5 pm. Admission costs US$1.60 – make sure you hand over the money to an authorised staff member in the ticket booth and not to some entrepreneurial gardener.

Places to Stay

Danang Hotel (☎ 82 1986) at 3 Duong Dong Da is popular with backpackers. The old wing has spartan, but cheap, rooms costing US$7 to US$12. In the adjacent new wing, plush rooms are priced from US$27 to US$59.

Hai Van Hotel (☎ 82 1300) is at 2 Duong Nguyen Thi Minh Khai. It's an old place, but has large rooms, private bath and hot water. The toll ranges from US$15 to US$20.

Thu Do Hotel (☎ 82 3863), at 107 Duong Hung Vuong, is located just a few blocks from Con Market (Cho Con). It's cheap enough at US$5 to US$10 for fan rooms, US$12 with air-con.

Thanh Thanh Hotel (☎ 82 1230) is a friendly place, but looks dingy. Rooms are priced from US$8 to US$12. The hotel is at 50 Duong Phan Chu Trinh.

The friendly *Vinapha Hotel* (☎ 82 5072) at 80 Duong Tran Phu seems to be popular with long-term expats and business travellers. Rooms go for US$16 to US$18.

Many of the more well-heeled backpackers like *Ami Hotel* (☎ 82 4494). It's at 7 Duong Quang Trung and has rooms for US$16 to US$28.

Places to Eat

Christie's Restaurant (email christies_danang @hotmail.com) at 9 Duong Bach Dang is an absolute haven. The restaurant has nice views of the Han River, a bar, book exchange, western newspapers and satellite TV and email

DANANG

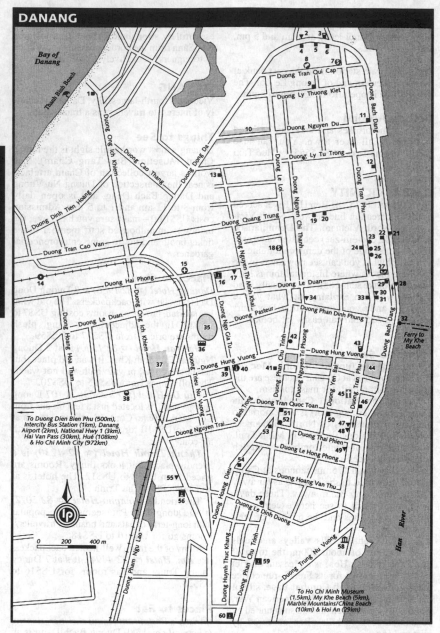

Bay of
Danang

Thanh Binh Beach

Duong Ong Ich Khiem

Duong Cao Thang

Duong Dong Da

Duong Dinh Tien Hoang

Duong Tran Cao Van

Duong Hai Phong

Duong Le Duan

Duong Hoang Hoa Tham

Duong Ong Ich Khiem

Duong Quang Trung

Duong Le Loi

Duong Nguyen Chi Thanh

Duong Nguyen Thi Minh Khai

Duong Ngo Gia Tu

Duong Pasteur

Duong Hung Vuong

Duong Trieu Nu Vuong

D Binh Trong

Duong Nguyen Trai

Duong Pham Ngu Lao

Duong Hoang Dieu

Duong Huynh Thuc Khang

Duong Phan Chu Trinh

Duong Le Dinh Duong

Duong Tran Qui Cap

Duong Ly Thuong Kiet

Duong Nguyen Du

Duong Ly Tu Trong

Duong Le Duan

Duong Phan Dinh Phung

Chu Trinh

Duong Phan Nguyen Tri Phuong

Duong Hung Vuong

Duong Tran Quoc Toan

Duong Yen Bai

Duong Thai Phien

Duong Le Hong Phong

Duong Hoang Van Thu

Duong Bach Dang

Duong Tran Phu

Duong Bach Dang

Ferry to
My Khe
Beach

Han River

Duong Trung Nu Vuong

To Duong Dien Bien Phu (500m),
Intercity Bus Station (1km), Danang
Airport (2km), National Hwy 1 (3km),
Hai Van Pass (30km), Hué (108km)
& Ho Chi Minh City (972km)

To Ho Chi Minh Museum
(1.5km), My Khe Beach (5km),
Marble Mountains/China Beach
(10km) & Hoi An (29km)

0   200   400 m

VIETNAM

DANANG

PLACES TO STAY		PLACES TO EAT			
1	Thanh Binh Guesthouse	2	Cafe Lien	18	Vietcombank
4	Saigon Tourane Hotel	17	My Quang Restaurant	23	Hoa Binh Tourist
	(under re-construction)	21	Hanakim Dinh Restaurant	25	Vietnam & Pacific Airlines
5	Danang Hotel (Old Wing)	28	Christie's Restaurant		Booking Office
6	Danang Hotel (New Wing)	30	Com Chay Nga My	26	East Meets West
9	Thu Bon Hotel	34	Hoang Ngoc Restaurant		Headquarters (NGO)
11	Elegant Hotel	47	Tiem An Binh Dan	27	Post Office
12	Song Han Hotel		Restaurant	32	Ferry Landing
13	Hai Van Hotel	48	Tu Do Restaurant;	35	Danang Stadium
19	Royal Hotel		Kim Do Restaurant	36	Swimming Pool
20	Ami Hotel	49	Tien Hung	37	Con Market
22	Bach Dang Hotel	55	Thanh An Vegetarian	38	Short-Haul Pick-up Truck
24	Binh Duong Mini-Hotel		Restaurant		Station
29	Riverside Hotel			40	Dana Tours
31	Dong Kinh Hotel	OTHER		42	Municipal Theatre
33	Vinapha Hotel	3	Cafe Linh; Free Time;	43	The Cool Spot
39	Thu Do Hotel		Bamboo Cafe	44	Han Market
41	Thanh Thanh Hotel	7	VID Public Bank	45	Danang Cathedral
46	Hai Au Hotel	8	Lao Consulate	52	Bookshop
50	Dai A Hotel	10	Market	56	Phap Lam Pagoda
51	Orient Hotel	14	Danang Train Station	57	Thanh Hong Tour Agency
53	Pacific Hotel	15	Hospital C	58	Cham Museum
54	Minh Tam II Mini-Hotel	16	Caodai Temple	59	Tam Bao Pagoda
				60	Pho Da Pagoda

VIETNAM

service. Christie's also organises tours such as boat trips to Cham Island.

The *Hoang Ngoc Restaurant* is a pleasant place with great service and outstanding food at 106 Duong Nguyen Chi Thanh, near Duong Phan Dinh Phung.

Cafe Lien is at 4 Duong Dong Da. Prices are low and the food is good, plus there is an English menu and friendly staff.

Thanh An Vegetarian Restaurant is a food stall serving vegetable dishes that resemble meat in appearance. The address is 484 Duong Ong Ich Khiem.

There is good vegie fare at *Com Chay Nga My* at 53 Duong Tran Phu, or for dumpling-like *banh cuon*, try *Tien Hung*, about 100m south of Tu Do Restaurant on Duong Tran Phu.

At 1A Duong Ha Phong, near the Cao Dai Temple, is the popular *My Quang Restaurant*, serving casual Vietnamese food.

Entertainment

Not far from the river at 112 Duong Tran Phu (near the corner of Duong Hung Vuong), *The Cool Spot* is a happening bar with moderate prices and a pool table.

There is also a string of cafe/bars in the north, across from the Danang Hotel, which are good places for pub grub and drinks. These include *Cafe Linh*, *Free Time*, and the *Bam-boo Cafe*. *Christie's* (see Places to Eat) keeps a share of lingering boozers into the night.

Getting There & Away

Air There are daily flights to Hanoi and Saigon; four times weekly to Pleiku; three times weekly to Haiphong, Nha Trang and Qui Nhon. Vietnam Airlines (☎ 82 1130) is at 35 Duong Tran Phu.

Bus The Danang intercity bus station (Ben Xe Khach Da Nang) is about 3km from the city centre.

Train Danang train station (Ga Da Nang) is about 1.5km from the city centre on Duong Haiphong.

Pick-up Xe Lams and small passenger trucks to places in the vicinity of Danang leave from the short-haul pick-up truck station opposite 80 Duong Hung Vuong.

HOI AN (FAIFO)

Hoi An (Faifo) was one of South-East Asia's major international ports from the 17th to 19th centuries. Today, parts of Hoi An look exactly as they did a century and a half ago, and there is a whole city block of colonnaded French buildings on Duong Phan Boi Chau.

HOI AN (FAIFO)

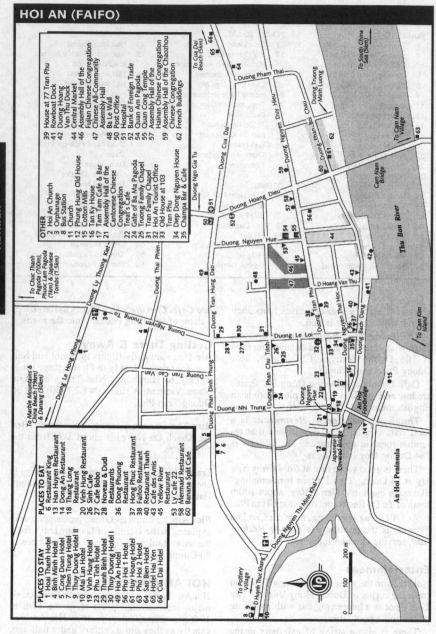

OTHER	
2	Hoi An Church
3	Orphanage
8	Bus Station
11	Church
12	Phung Hung Old House
15	Cotton Mills
16	Tan Ky House
17	Tam Tam Cafe & Bar
19	Assembly Hall of the Cantonese Chinese Congregation
22	Treat's Cafe
24	Gate of Ba Ma Pagoda
25	Truong Family Chapel
31	Tran Family Chapel
32	Hoi An Tourist Office
33	Old House at 103
34	Tran Phu
35	Diep Dong Nguyen House
35	Champa Bar & Cafe
39	House at 77 Tran Phu
41	Rowboat Dock
42	Van Thu Dock
44	Central Market
46	Assembly Hall of the Fujian Chinese Congregation
47	Chinese All-Community Assembly Hall
48	Ba Le Well
50	Hospital
51	Post Office
52	Bank of Foreign Trade
54	Quan Am Pagoda
55	Quan Cong Temple
57	Assembly Hall of the Hainan Chinese Congregation
59	Assembly Hall of the Chaozhou Chinese Congregation
62	French Buildings

PLACES TO STAY	
1	Hoai Thanh Hotel
4	Binh Minh Hotel
5	Cong Doan Hotel
9	Thien Trung Hotel
10	Thuy Duong Hotel II
10	Mai Lan Hotel
14	Vinh Hung Hotel
23	Phu Tinh Hotel
28	Thanh Binh Hotel
30	Thuy Duong Hotel I
49	Hoi An Hotel
56	Pho Hoi 1 Hotel
61	Huy Hoang Hotel
63	Pho Hoi 2 Hotel
64	Sao Bien Hotel
65	Hotel Hai Yen
66	Cua Dai Hotel

PLACES TO EAT	
6	Restaurant King
13	Han Huyen Restaurant
14	Dong An Restaurant
18	Thang Long Restaurant
20	Vinh Hung Restaurant
26	Sinh Cafe
27	Cafe Bobo
29	Noveau & Dudi Restaurants
36	Dong Phuong Restaurant
37	Hong Phuc Restaurant
38	Faifoo Restaurant
40	Restaurant Thanh
43	Cafe des Amis
45	Yellow River Restaurant
53	Ly Cafe 22
58	Mermaid Restaurant
60	Banana Split Cafe

Hoi An was the site of the first Chinese settlement in southern Vietnam.

Japanese Covered Bridge

The first bridge on this site was constructed in 1593 by the Japanese community of Hoi An to link them with the Chinese quarters across the stream.

The French flattened out the roadway to make it more suitable for their motorcars, but the original arched shape was restored during major renovation work in 1986.

Built into the northern side of the bridge is a small temple, **Chua Cau**.

Chinese Assembly Halls

Founded in 1786, the **Assembly Hall of the Cantonese Chinese Congregation** is at 176 Duong Tran Phu.

The **Chinese All-Community Assembly Hall** (Chua Ba), founded in 1773, was used by all five Chinese congregations in Hoi An: Fujian, Cantonese, Hainan, Chaozhou and Hakka. The main entrance is on Duong Tran Phu, but the only way in these days is around the back at 31 Duong Phan Chu Trinh.

The **Assembly Hall of the Fujian Chinese Congregation** is opposite 35 Duong Tran Phu.

The **Assembly Hall of the Hainan Chinese Congregation** was built in 1883. It's on the east side of Duong Tran Phu, near the corner of Duong Hoang Dieu.

The Chaozhou Chinese in Hoi An built the **Assembly Hall of the Chaozhou Chinese Congregation** in 1776. It's across from 157 Duong Nguyen Duy Hieu.

Pagodas & Churches

Serving Hoi An's Caodai community is the small **Caodai Pagoda** (built 1952) between Nos 64 and 70 Duong Huynh Thuc Khang.

The only tombs of Europeans in Hoi An are in the yard of the **Hoi An Church**, which is at the corner of Duong Nguyen Truong To and Duong Le Hong Phong.

Chuc Thanh Pagoda was founded in 1454, making it the oldest pagoda in Hoi An. To get to Chuc Thanh Pagoda, go all the way to the end of Duong Nguyen Truong To and turn left. Follow the sandy path for 500m.

Phuoc Lam Pagoda was founded in the mid-17th century. To get there, continue past Chuc Thanh Pagoda for 350m.

Arts & Crafts Villages

All those neat fake antiques sold in Hoi An's shops are manufactured in nearby villages.

Cross the An Hoi footbridge to reach the **An Hoi Peninsula**, noted for its boat factory and mat weaving factories.

South of the peninsula is **Cam Kim Island**, where you see many people engaged in the woodcarving industry (take a boat from the Duong Hoang Van Thu dock). **Cam Ha**, 3km west of Hoi An, is a village known for it's fine pottery factories. Or cross the Cam Nam bridge to **Cam Nam Village**, a lovely spot also noted for arts and crafts.

Cua Dai Beach

The beach is 5km east of Hoi An out on Duong Cua Dai.

Places to Stay

At 7/2 Duong Tran Phu, *Pho Hoi 1 Hotel* (☎ 86 1633), makes a pleasant choice. Fan doubles cost US$8 or US$25 with air-con. Also recommendable is it's sister hotel, the new *Pho Hoi 2 Hotel* (☎ 86 22628), across the Cam Nam Bridge on the bank of the Thu Bon River. Fan rooms here cost from US$8 to US$15, or US$18 to US$35 with air-con.

Huy Hoang Hotel (☎ 86 1453) at 73 Duong Phan Boi Chau is also by the Cam Nam Bridge. Fan rooms cost US$8 to US$10 and air-con demands US$15 to US$20. There is a lovely riverside garden here to enjoy your coffee.

The atmospheric *Vinh Hung Hotel* (☎ 86 1621), at 143 Duong Tran Phu, is housed in an old Chinese trading house. Standard fan twins cost US$10 with outside bath or US$20 with inside bath.

Also Chinese in style, the nearby *Phu Tinh Hotel* (☎ 86 1297) is at 144 Duong Tran Phu. Fan twins run US$10 or US$15 to US$20 with air-con and bathtubs.

The family-run *Thanh Binh Hotel* (☎ 86 1740) at 1 Duong Le Loi is close to town. Fan twins cost US$8 and US$10, or US$12 to US$25 with air-con.

Sao Bien Hotel (☎ 86 1589), or *Sea Star Hotel* in English, is at 15 Duong Cua Dai. Twins are US$25.

Thien Trung Hotel (☎ 86 1720) at 63 Duong Phan Dinh Phung is built motel-style. Rooms cost US$8 to US$13.

Thuy Duong Hotel 1 (☎ 86 1574) at 11 Duong Le Loi has fan rooms with outside toilet for US$8, or with inside toilet for US$12. Air-con is US$20.

Thuy Duong Hotel II (☎ 86 1394) at 68 Duong Huynh Thuc Khang is right next to the bus station. Twins with bathtubs cost US$10 to US$15.

Mai Lan Hotel (☎ 86 1792) at 87 Duong Huynh Thuc Khang is a good-looking place opposite the bus station. Rooms cost US$8 to US$20.

Binh Minh Hotel (☎ 86 1943) on Duong 12 Thai Phien has twins for US$7 to US$14. Being a little further out from the centre it's not so often full.

Cua Dai Hotel (☎ 86 1722) at 18 Duong Cua Dai is nice in that it's in a rural area, yet still close enough to walk to the centre. Twins cost US$20 to US$35.

Nearby at 22A Duong Cua Dai is the new *Hotel Hai Yen* (☎ 86 2445). Rooms (all with satellite TV & bathtubs) range from US$12 to US$20.

Up at the northern outskirts of town is *Hoai Thanh Hotel* (☎ 86 1242) at 23 Duong Le Hong Phong. Fan rooms cost US$10, or US$20 with air-con.

Cong Doan Hotel (☎ 86 1899) at 50 Duong Phan Dinh Phung is Hoi An's only other state-run hotel. Rooms with fan cost US$10 to US$15 and with air-con US$20.

Places to Eat

The *market* is the cheapest place, even if it does lack aesthetics. The *banh trang* (translucent spring rolls) are particularly nice and cost only US$0.10 each.

One of Hoi An's best eateries is the delightfully atmospheric *Yellow River Restaurant* (Tiem An Hoang Ha) at 38 Duong Tran Phu. It's *all* good.

At 104 Duong Tran Phu is the excellent *Faifoo Restaurant*. Vietnamese food is the house speciality and they serve an excellent full course dinner for US$3.

There have also been good reports on both the *Thang Long Restaurant* at 136 Duong Nguyen Thai Hoc and the tastefully decorated *Vinh Hung Restaurant* at 147B Duong Tran Phu.

Mermaid Restaurant, or *Nhu Y*, is at 2 Duong Tran Phu. It dishes up great food including late breakfasts.

Ly Cafe 22 at 22 Duong Nguyen Hue has become a Hoi An institution.

Cafe des Amis at 52 Duong Bach Dang is along the riverside. This place gets steady rave reviews from satisfied customers.

Also notable on the riverside is the *Hong Phuc Restaurant* at 86 Duong Bach Dang.

Just next door, and also well worth trying, is the *Dong Phuong Restaurant*. Another riverfront spot is the *Restaurant Thanh* at 76 Duong Bach Dang, which does seafood, pizza and vegetarian food.

Other popular spots for backpacker cuisine include *Cafe Bobo*, *Noveau Restaurant* and *Dudi Restaurant*, all on Duong Le Loi.

Restaurant King is next to the Thien Trung Hotel at 63 Duong Phan Dinh Phung. It's a small, unassuming place that specialises in delicious Hué food (try the spring rolls).

The *Banana Split Cafe* can relieve cravings for ice-cream, fresh fruit juices and, of course, banana splits. It's at 53 Duong Hoang Dieu, just at the corner of Duong Nguyen Duy Hieu.

Entertainment

The *Tam Tam Cafe & Bar*, upstairs at 110 Duong Nguyen Thai Hoc, is housed in a unique restored tea warehouse. There is excellent French and Italian food, a wide range of wine, salads, a billiards table, a balcony for summer dining and a collection of over 400 CDs.

Stumbling distance from the Tam Tam, at 75 Duong Nguyen Thai Hoc, is the *Champa Bar & Cafe*. This place offers traditional music shows nightly (except Sundays) staged in the house theatre.

Another popular watering hole in Hoi An that gets good reports is *Treat's Cafe*, on Duong Tran Phu (near the corner of Duong Nhi Trung).

Getting There & Away

All hotels in Hoi An book minibuses to Nha Trang (US$15) and Hué (US$8). Buses to Danang via the Marble Mountains depart from the Hoi An bus station (Ben Quoc Doanh Xe Khach) at 74 Duong Huynh Thuc Khang, 1km west of the town centre.

Getting Around

Motorbike drivers solicit business outside all tourist hotels. The hotels also have bicycles for rent.

AROUND HOI AN
My Son

One of the most stunning sights in the Hoi An area is My Son, Vietnam's most important Cham site. My Son is considered to be the ancient Champa Kingdom's counterpart to the grand cities of South-East Asia's other Indian-influenced civilisations: Angkor (Cambodia), Bagan (Myanmar), Ayuthaya (Thailand) and Borobudur (Java).

The monuments are set in a verdant valley surrounded by hills and overlooked by massive Cat's Tooth Mountain (Hon Quap). Clear brooks (perfect for a dip) run between the structures and past nearby coffee plantations.

My Son became a religious centre in the late 4th century and was occupied until the 13th century – the longest period of development of any monument in South-East Asia (by comparison, Angkor's period of development lasted only three centuries, as did that of Bagan). Most of the temples were dedicated to Cham kings associated with divinities, especially Shiva, who was regarded as the founder and protector of Champa's dynasties.

During the American War, the My Son region was completely devastated and depopulated in extended bitter fighting. Traces of 68 structures have been found, of which 25 survived repeated pillaging in previous centuries by the Chinese, Khmer and Vietnamese. American bombing didn't quite demolish about 20 of these, some of which sustained extensive damage. Today, Vietnamese authorities are attempting to restore the remaining sites.

Elements of Cham civilisation can still be seen in the life of the people of Quang Nam-Danang and Quang Ngai provinces, whose forebears assimilated many Cham innovations into their daily lives.

Entry to the My Son site costs US$4, which includes transportation from the parking area to the site (about 1km). By leaving Hoi An at about 5 am, you will arrive to wake up the gods (and the guards) for the sunrise and can be leaving just as the tour groups reach the area. Remember that it is strictly forbidden to climb on the ancient structures.

My Son is about 60km south-west of Danang and Hoi An. You can get there by rented car or motorbike (Honda Om); Hoi An hotels can also arrange minibus trips (US$6).

Warning During the American War, the hills and valleys around My Son were extensively mined. During mine clearing operations in 1977, six Vietnamese sappers were killed here. Today, grazing cows are sometimes blown up, so as the years pass and the poor beasts clear the mines one by one, the hills around here are becoming less and less unsafe. Nevertheless, it's recommended that you do *not* stray from marked paths.

Marble Mountains & China Beach
Along the road from Hoi An to Danang are the Marble Mountains. These consist of five marble hillocks which were once islands. Local children make enthusiastic and unsolicited tour guides and souvenir pushers – expect to be surrounded. But the kids are generally good-natured, and some of the caves are difficult to find without their help.

China Beach (Bai Non Nuoc) was made famous by an American TV series of that name. There is a fancy tourist hotel here, but the beach is nothing to write home about.

Getting There & Away Buses and minibuses running between Hoi An and Danang can drop you off at the entrance to the Marble Mountains and China Beach. From Danang, it's also possible to reach this area by bicycle.

NHA TRANG
Nha Trang has what is probably the nicest municipal beach in all of Vietnam. The turquoise waters around Nha Trang are almost transparent, making for excellent fishing, snorkelling and scuba diving.

Things to See & Do
The **Po Nagar Cham Towers** were built between the 7th and 12th centuries on a site used by Hindus for worship. The towers are 2km north of Nha Trang on the left bank of the Cai River.

Hon Chong Promontory is a scenic collection of granite rocks jutting out into the South China Sea. The promontory is 3.5km north of central Nha Trang.

Long Son Pagoda is about 500m west of the train station. The **Giant Seated Buddha** is on the hill behind the pagoda.

The **Oceanographic Institute** has an aquarium and specimen room. Nearby **Bao Dai's Villas** (Cau Da Villas) is also worth a visit.

A **boat cruise** to the offshore islands is one of the highlights of Nha Trang. Most hotels in town can book you onto one of the boat tours run by zany Mama Hanh for US$7. There are also boat tours to **Monkey Island** (Doa Khi).

The best place for travellers to rent **watersports** equipment (except scuba gear) is the Nha Trang Sailing Club (☎ 82 6528), 72 Duong Tran Phu. For scuba diving, check out the Blue Diving Club (☎ 82 5390), on the beach side opposite the Hai Yen Hotel.

Places to Stay – Budget
Hotel O-Sin (☎ 82 5064) has earned itself a steady following for good, cheap rooms – US$6

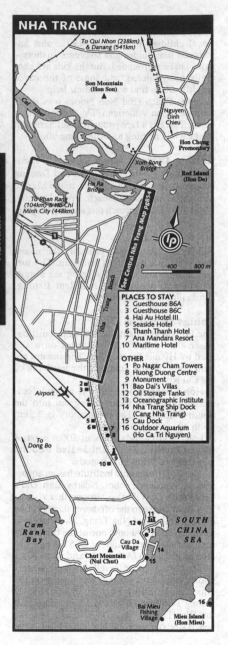

NHA TRANG

To Qui Nhon (238km)
& Danang (541km)

Son Mountain
(Hon Son)

Cai River

Nguyen
Dinh
Chieu

Hon Chong
Promontory

Xom Bong
Bridge

Red Island
(Hon Do)

Ha Ra
Bridge

To Phan Rang
(104km) & Ho Chi
Minh City (448km)

See Central Nha Trang Map Page 854

0   400   800 m

Nha Trang Beach

PLACES TO STAY
2 Guesthouse 86A
3 Guesthouse 86C
4 Hai Au Hotel III
5 Seaside Hotel
6 Thanh Thanh Hotel
7 Ana Mandara Resort
10 Maritime Hotel

OTHER
1 Po Nagar Cham Towers
8 Huong Duong Centre
9 Monument
11 Bao Dai's Villas
12 Oil Storage Tanks
13 Oceanographic Institute
14 Nha Trang Ship Dock
   (Cang Nha Trang)
15 Cau Dock
16 Outdoor Aquarium
   (Ho Ca Tri Nguyen)

Airport

To
Dong Bo

Cam
Ranh
Bay

SOUTH
CHINA
SEA

Cau Da
Village

Chut Mountain
(Nui Chut)

Bai Mieu
Fishing
Village

Mieu Island
(Hon Mieu)

to US$9 – and excellent food. It's at 4 Duong Nguyen Thien Thuat.

Another off-beach spot worthy of a plug is *Tulip Hotel* (☎ 82 1302) at 30 Duong Hoang Van Thu. It offers dorm beds for US$4, and double rooms for US$8 to US$20.

Yen My Hotel (☎ 82 9064) at 22 Duong Hoang Hoa Tham is a friendly spot which charges US$5 to US$8 for fan rooms, or US$8 to US$12 with air-con.

Huu Nghi Hotel (☎ 82 6703), 3 Duong Tran Hung Dao, is another time-honoured backpackers' haunt. Singles/doubles range from US$4/6 to US$15/19.

The friendly *My Hoa Hotel* (☎ 81 0111) is at 7 Duong Hang Ca, nearly across the street from the popular Lac Canh Restaurant. Clean fan rooms here cost US$7 to US$10; air-con raises the tab to US$12 to US$20.

The beachfront *Guesthouse 62* (☎ 82 5095), at 62 Duong Tran Phu, is a popular place with a large courtyard parking area. Rooms cost US$8 to US$12.

Guesthouse 58 (Nha Khach 58, ☎ 82 6303) at 58 Duong Tran Phu has fan rooms for US$7 to US$12, or US$9 to US$17 for air-con.

At 46A Duong Tran Phu is *46A Tran Phu Hotel* (☎ 82 3821). This place has air-con doubles for US$10 and US$12; the seven bed room is a relative bargain at US$20.

Guesthouse 62 (Nha Khach 62, ☎ 82 5095) at 62 Duong Tran Phu has an air of dilapidated elegance. Singles with fan and cold-water bath are US$7, but if you add hot water it's US$8. Air-con raises the tariff to US$15.

Guesthouse 78 (Nha Khach 78, ☎ 82 6342), 78 Duong Tran Phu, is opposite the beach. This motel-style place has singles with shared bath for US$6, doubles with cold/hot-water bath for US$8/10, and doubles with air-con and hot water for US$12. Try to avoid the rooms close to the noisy street.

At 54 Duong Hung Vuong, the new *Phu Quy Mini-Hotel* (☎ 81 0609) has received good reports from travellers. It has fan rooms for US$10, and air-con costs from US$15 to US$18.

Ha Phuong I Hotel (☎ 82 9016), 30 Duong Hoang Hoa Tham, has lots of parking and is a favourite for people arriving with rented vehicles. Doubles are priced at US$12 to US$18. *Ha Phuong II Hotel* (☎ 82 1716) at 26 Duong Nguyen Trung Truc costs the same.

Guesthouse 86A (☎ 82 6526) at 86A Duong Tran Phu belongs to the army and certainly looks much like a barracks. Miserable doubles/triples with fan and cold water only cost US$4/5. Rooms with air-con and hot-water bath cost US$10 and US$12.

Guesthouse 86C (☎ *82 4074*), 86C Duong Tran Phu, is nearby. This place is notable for sea views and the big noisy seafood restaurant on the roof. Rooms with fan and cold-water bath cost from US$5 to US$7, while hot water and air-con raises the rate to US$8 to US$20.

An attractive French-style option is *Duyen Hai Hotel* (☎ *81 1548*), which has rooms for US$10 to US$18. You'll find it near the beach at 72-74 Duong Tran Phu, a short crawl from The Sailing Club.

Places to Stay – Mid-Range
Thanh Thanh Hotel (☎ *82 4657*), 98A Duong Tran Phu, has balconies overlooking the sea. Rooms are US$10 to US$25 in the low season, and US$15 to US$30 in summer.

Even better is *Seaside Hotel* (☎ *82 1178*) just next door at No 96B. It's got satellite TV, and air-con rooms cost from US$20 to US$50.

Vina Hotel (☎ *82 3099*), 66 Duong Tran Phu, is known for its satellite TV, bathtubs and massage services. Rates here are US$16 to US$30.

Post Hotel (*Khach San Buu Dien*, ☎ *82 1250*), 2 Duong Le Loi, is adjacent to the main post office. This place has fancy rooms for US$24 and US$27, plus three budget rooms for US$8.

Places to Eat
Beach Area The *Nha Trang Sailing Club* at 72 Duong Tran Phu has both an excellent Vietnamese restaurant and an authentic Italian ristorante.

There is good vegetarian fare at *Cafe des Amis* at 13 Duong Biet Thu, and the Indian food is worth a try at *Bombay*, next door at No 15.

Right on the beach opposite the Hai Yen Hotel is the *Hai Yen Cafe*, which is adjacent to the *Coconut Cove Resort*. Both are outdoor places with a thatched sun roof to offer protection from the weather.

Central Area *Hanh Cafe*, 5 Duong Tran Hung Dao, next to the Huu Nghi Hotel, is the venerable travellers' cafe cum travel agency for backpackers. Another option is *Sinh Cafe* at 10 Duong Hung Vuong.

One of the best restaurants in town is the *Lac Canh Restaurant*, which is a block east of Dam Market at 11 Duong Hang Ca. Beef,

squid, giant shrimps, lobsters and the like are grilled right at your table.

Hoan Hai Restaurant is near the Lac Canh at 6 Duong Phan Chu Trinh. The menu contains delicious marinated beef, vegetarian dishes and some of the best spring rolls in Vietnam.

For cheap and excellent vegetarian food, try tiny *Au Lac*, near the corner of Duong Hoang Hoa Tham and Nguyen Chanh.

7C Le Loi serves up authentic bratwurst and schnitzel at reasonable prices. The place is named for its address, a short walk from the main post office.

Then there's *Dam Market* itself, which has a collection of stalls in the covered semi-circular food pavilion. Vegetarian food can be found here too.

The *Dua Xanh Restaurant* at 23 Duong Le Loi is a nice spot, with many seafood dishes.

For great ice cream, try one of the neighbouring *'Banana Split' shops* at the roundabout where Duong Quang Trung meets Duong Le Thanh Ton.

Entertainment
Locals head for karaoke lounges, but foreigners congregate at the *Nha Trang Sailing Club* at 72 Duong Tran Phu, right on the beach.

Nearby is the Huong Duong Centre, also known as Paradise Village. Inside you'll find the *Hexagone Disco*, which is open from 8 pm until sunrise.

For something a bit more cultural, there are free nightly ethnic minority song and dance performances at *Vien Dong Hotel*. The show starts at 7.30 pm and makes a good way to start the evening.

Getting There & Away
Air Vietnam Airlines has flights connecting Nha Trang with Saigon two times daily. There are flights to/from Hanoi once daily. Flights to/from Danang fly four times a week.

Vietnam Airlines' main Nha Trang office (☎ 82 3797) is at 12B Duong Hoang Hoa Tham.

Bus Tourist minibuses to Dalat (US$8), Saigon (US$10) and Hoi An (US$15) can be booked from tourist cafes and hotels.

Train The Nha Trang train station is across the street from 26 Duong Thai Nguyen.

VIETNAM

CENTRAL NHA TRANG

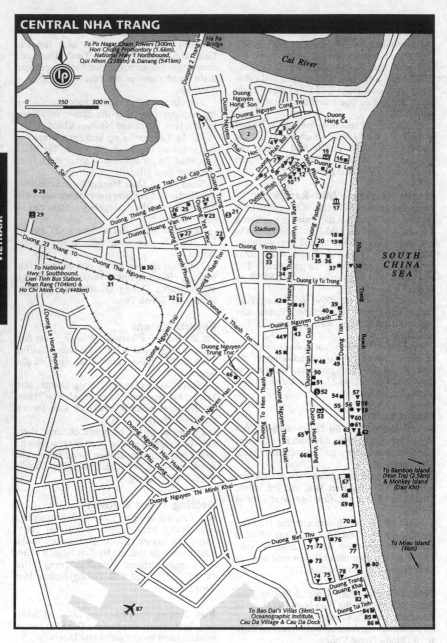

To Po Nagar Cham Towers (300m),
Hon Chong Promontory (1.6km),
National Hwy 1 Northbound,
Qui Nhon (238km) & Danang (541km)

0   150   300 m

Ha Ra
Bridge

Cai River

Duong 2 Thang 4

Duong Nguyen
Hong Son

Duong Nguyen Cong Tru

Duong
Hang Ca

Phuong Sai

Duong Nguyen Thai Hoc

Duong Phan Boi Chau

Duong Dinh Phung

Duong Le Loi

Chu Tinh

Duong Tran Qui Cap

Duong Quang Trung

Duong Phan

Duong Trang Nu Vuong

Duong Pasteur

Duong Thong Nhat

Duong Hoang Van Thu

Duong Yet Kieu

Duong Le Thanh Phuong

Stadium

Duong Yersin

To National
Hwy 1 Southbound,
Lien Tinh Bus Station,
Phan Rang (104km) &
Ho Chi Minh City (448km)

Duong 23 Thang 10

Duong Thai Nguyen

Duong Ly Thanh Ton

SOUTH
CHINA
SEA

Nha Trang Beach

Duong Hoang Hoa Tham

Duong Ly Tu Trong

Duong Le Thanh Ton

Duong Nguyen Trai

Duong Le Hong Phong

Duong Nguyen Trung Truc

Duong Tran Nguyen Han

Duong To Hien Thanh

Duong Nguyen Chanh

Duong Tran Hung Dao

Duong Tran Phu

Duong Nguyen Thien Thuat

Duong Hung Vuong

Duong Nguyen Hieu Huan

Duong Phu Dong

Duong Nguyen Thi Minh Khai

To Bamboo Island
(Hon Tre) (2.5km)
& Monkey Island
(Dao Khi)

To Mieu Island
(4km)

Duong Biet Thu

Duong Trang
Quang Khai

Duong Tui Tinh

To Bao Dai's Villas (3km),
Oceanographic Institute,
Cau Da Village & Cau Da Dock

CENTRAL NHA TRANG

PLACES TO STAY					
3	My Hoa Hotel	66	Phu Quy Mini-Hotel	63	Thuy Duong Cafe;
5	Tulip Hotel	67	46A Tran Phu Hotel		India Gate Restaurant
10	Hoang Ngan Mini-Hotel	68	Guesthouse 58	65	Sinh Cafe
12	Mini-Hotel Van Canh	69	Que Huong Hotel	71	Bombay
14	Thang Loi Hotel;	70	Guesthouse 62	72	Cafe des Amis
	7C Le Loi	76	Khatoco Hotel	74	Truc Mai Vien
16	Post Hotel	77	Vina Hotel	75	Ngoc Linh
18	White Sand III Hotel	79	Duyen Hai Hotel	78	Ngoc Suong
19	White Sand I Hotel	81	Guesthouse 78		
25	Nha Trang Hotel I	83	Ban Me Hotel	OTHER	
26	Nha Trang Hotel II	84	Thanh Binh	1	Short-Haul Bus Station
30	Royal Hotel	85	Quang Vinh	2	Dam Market
35	White Sand II Hotel	86	Thanh Ngoc	15	Main Post Office
36	Thong Nhat Hotel			17	Pasteur Institute;
37	Saigon-Nha Trang	PLACES TO EAT			Yersin Museum
	Hotel	4	Lac Canh Restaurant	21	Vietcombank
39	Duy Tan I lotel	6	Vietnam Restaurant	28	Giant Seated Buddha
40	Hai Au Hotel II;	7	Dua Xanh Restaurant	29	Long Son Pagoda
	Outrigger Hotel	8	Vietnam II Restaurant	31	Nha Trang Train Station
41	Huong Nam Hotel	9	Hoan Hai Restaurant	32	Nha Trang Cathedral
42	Yen My Hotel	11	Kinh Do Restaurant	33	Bien Vien Tinh (Hospital)
43	Hai Au Hotel I	13	Thanh The Resatuarant	34	Vietnam Airlines
45	Ha Phuong I Hotel	20	Restaurant 505	52	Khanh Hoa Tourist
46	Ha Phuong II Hotel	22	'Banana Split' Shops	53	Post Office
47	Hotel O-Sin	23	Restaurant Lys	56	Blue Diving Club
49	Nha Khach Hoc Vien	24	Binh Minh Restaurant	58	Log Bar
	Luc Quan	27	Ngoc Lan Restaurant	61	Vietravel
50	Huu Nghi Hotel	38	Saiga Bar & Restaurant	62	War Memorial Obelisk
51	Vien Dong Hotel	44	Au Lac	73	Vietnam Airlines
54	Hai Yen Hotel	48	Hanh Cafe	80	Nha Trang Sailing Club;
55	Nha Trang Lodge	57	Hai Yen Cafe		Hon Tam Tourist
64	Grand Hotel	59	Coconut Cove Resort	82	Police Station
		60	Four Seasons III Cafe	87	Airport

CA NA

This small town, 312km from Saigon, consists of two hotels and a restaurant along a white-sand beach dressed up by attractive giant boulders. Buses along National Highway 1 can drop you off in Ca Na.

Rooms at the *Ca Na Hotel* (☎ *86 1342*) cost US$12 to US$15, while bungalows close to the beach are US$17.

Prices are similar at the nearby *Haison Hotel* (☎ *86 1318*), which has followed suit by recently building six new cottages.

PHAN THIET

Phan Thiet is best known for its smelly nuoc mam (fish sauce) and fishing industry. The river flowing through the centre of town creates a small **fishing harbour**, which is always chock-a-block with boats and makes for charming photography.

The big attractions are the two nearby beaches. Closest to town is **Phan Thiet Beach**. To get to the beach, turn east at Victory Monument, an arrow-shaped, concrete tower with victorious cement people at the base.

Much more impressive is **Mui Ne Beach**, known for its enormous sand dunes. This could easily rate as Vietnam's best beach. It's 22km east of Phan Thiet proper, near a fishing village at the tip of Mui Ne Peninsula.

Places to Stay & Eat

The charming *Small Garden* (*Vuon Nho,* ☎ *87 4012*), a family-style homestay on Mui Ne Beach run by Swiss Walter and his Vietnamese wife Trang. Costs are US$6 per person, or US$8 including breakfast. It's near kilometre 11.

At kilometre 13 is *Full Moon Resort* (*Trang Tron,* ☎ *84 7008*). This pleasant place has simple but charming bungalows decorated with sea shells and split coconuts. Rates here range from US$25 to US$30.

Hai Duong Resort (☎ *84 7111, email cocobeach@saigonnet.vn)* or 'Coco Beach', is at kilometre 12.5. The resort is absolutely lovely, with swaying palm trees and white sand. Bungalows cost US$60 and villas are US$120.

If you don't want to be surrounded by fellow foreigners, two local places with bungalows and beach front camping are *Mui Ne Beach Resort* and *Coco Beach Resort*.

Staying in town is much less inspiring. You can try *Phan Thiet Hotel (☎ 82 1694)* at 40 Duong Tran Hung Dao, right in the centre of town. Air-con doubles cost US$16 to US$25.

Central Highlands

The Central Highlands cover the southern part of the Truong Son Mountain Range. The most accessible place is Dalat. The region, which is home to many ethno-linguistic minority groups (Montagnards), is renowned for its cool climate, beautiful mountain scenery and innumerable streams, lakes and waterfalls.

DALAT

Dalat (elevation 1475m) is in a temperate region dotted with lakes and waterfalls, and surrounded by evergreen forests. Dalat is often called the 'City of Eternal Spring' – days are pleasant and nights are cool enough for wear-ing a light jacket. The economy is based on tourism and some agriculture, and it's Vietnam's most favoured (and tacky) honeymoon spot.

Information

Travel Agencies Dalat's tourist office cum travel agency is Dalat Tourist (☎ 82 2715). The main office is out on 35 Duong Tran Hung Dao, but for booking tours or vehicle rentals, visit the convenient Dalat Tourist Travel Services Center (☎ 82 2125) at 7 Duong 3 Thang 2 (near the centre).

Things to See & Do

Dalat's **Central Market** is in the Mai building – the street level is the place to find dried fruits and upper levels are a great place to buy clothing. Behind the Mai building is a modern **Vegetable Market**, which offers the finest vegetables in Vietnam (as well as cut flowers and the usual merchandise).

Xuan Huong Lake in the centre of Dalat was created in 1919 by a dam. Paddleboats that look like giant swans can be rented. The **Dalat Golf Course** occupies 50 hectares on the northern side of the lake near the **Flower Gardens** (Vuon Hoa Dalat).

About 500m east of Xuan Huong Lake is a **train station**, and though you aren't likely to arrive in Dalat by train, the station is worth a visit. The **Crémaillère** (cog railway) linked Dalat and Thap Cham (Phan Rang) from 1928 to 1964 – it was closed in 1964 because of repeated Viet Cong attacks. The line has been partially repaired and is operated as a tourist attraction. For US$3 you can ride 5km down the tracks to the suburbs of Dalat and back again.

Hang Nga Guesthouse & Art Gallery, nicknamed the 'Crazy House' by locals, is notable for its Alice-in-Wonderland architecture.

Lam Ty Ni Pagoda, also known as Quan Am Tu, was founded in 1961. More than the pagoda, and its gardens, the attraction here is the lone monk, Mr Thuc, and his mind-boggling collection of self-brushed art works.

About 5km north of Xuan Huong Lake is the **Valley of Love** (Thung Lung Tinh Yeu), so named in 1972 by romantically minded students from Dalat University. This place is heavy on the tourist kitsch – you'll see Vietnamese models dressed up as cowboys for photo opportunities (for a fee). You too can get dressed up as a cowboy and have your picture taken while riding a horse.

Cam Ly Falls is one of those must-see spots for domestic visitors. The grassy areas around the 15m-high cascades are decorated with stuffed jungle animals, which many Vietnamese tourists love to be photographed with. Plenty of 'cowboys' wander around here too.

The **Lake of Sighs** (Ho Than Tho) is a natural lake enlarged by a French-built dam. Horses can be hired near the restaurants. The lake is 6km north-east of the centre of Dalat.

Datanla Falls is south-east of Dalat off Highway 20 about 200m past the turn-off to Quang Trung Reservoir. From the road, it's a pleasant walk downhill.

Prenn Falls is one of the largest and most beautiful falls in the Dalat area. The entrance to Prenn Falls is 13km from Dalat towards Phan Rang; the entrance fee is US$0.50.

The nine hamlets of **Lat Village** are about 12km north-west of Dalat at the base of Lang Bian Mountain. The inhabitants are ethnic minorities. A police permit is required to visit Lat Village.

Lang Bian Mountain (also called Lam Vien) has five volcanic peaks ranging in altitude from 2100 to 2400m. The scenic hike up to the top of Lang Bian Mountain takes three to four hours from Lat Village. A guide and

DALAT AREA

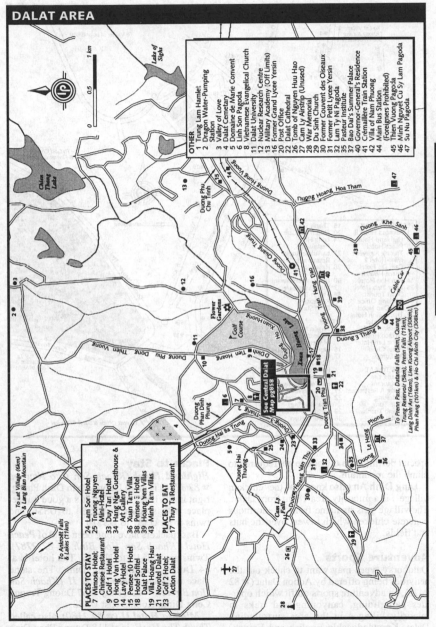

VIETNAM

PLACES TO STAY
7 Mimosa Hotel;
   Chinese Restaurant
9 Golf 1 Hotel
10 Hong Van Hotel
14 Lavy Hotel
15 Pensee 10 Hotel
18 Hotel Sofitel
   Dalat Palace
19 Villa Hoang Hau
21 Novotel Dalat
23 Golf 2 Hotel;
   Action Dalat
24 Lam Son Hotel
25 Truong Nguyen
   Mini-Hotel
33 Duy Tan Hotel
34 Hang Nga Guesthouse &
   Art Gallery
36 Xuan Tam Villa
38 Pensee E Hotel
39 Hoang Yen Villas
43 Minh Tam Villas

PLACES TO EAT
17 Thuy Ta Restaurant

OTHER
1 Trung Lam Hamlet
2 Dragon Water-Pumping
   Station
3 Valley of Love
4 Dalat Cemetary
5 Domaine de Marie Convent
6 Linh Son Pagoda
8 Vietnamese Evangelical Church
11 Dalat University
12 Nuclear Research Centre
13 Military Academy (Off Limits)
16 Former Grand Lycee Yersin
20 Post Office
22 Dalat Cathedral
26 Tomb of Nguyen Huu Hao
27 Cam Ly Airstrip (Unused)
28 War Memorial
29 Du Sinh Church
30 Former Couvent des Oiseaux
31 Former Petit Lycee Yersin
32 Lam Ty Ni Pagoda
35 Pasteur Institute
37 Bao Dai's Summer Palace
40 Governor-General's Residence
41 Crémaillère Train Station
42 Villa of Nam Phuong
44 Main Bus Station
   (Foreigners Prohibited)
45 Thien Vuong Pagoda
46 Minh Nguyet Cu Sy Lam Pagoda
47 Su Nu Pagoda

VIETNAM

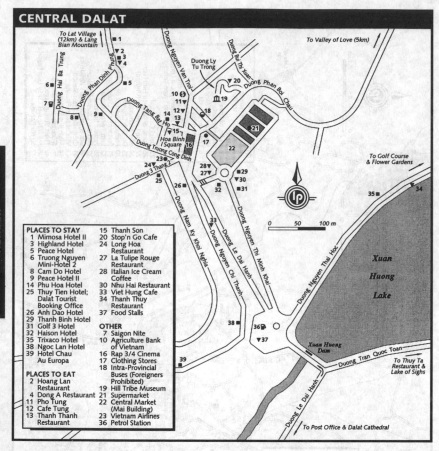

CENTRAL DALAT

PLACES TO STAY
1 Mimosa Hotel II
3 Highland Hotel
5 Peace Hotel
6 Truong Nguyen
  Mini-Hotel 2
8 Cam Do Hotel
9 Peace Hotel II
14 Phu Hoa Hotel
25 Thuy Tien Hotel;
  Dalat Tourist
  Booking Office
26 Anh Dao Hotel
29 Thanh Binh Hotel
31 Golf 3 Hotel
32 Haison Hotel
35 Trixaco Hotel
38 Ngoc Lan Hotel
39 Hotel Chau
  Au Europa

PLACES TO EAT
2 Hoang Lan
  Restaurant
4 Dong A Restaurant
11 Pho Tung
12 Cafe Tung
13 Thanh Thanh
  Restaurant

15 Thanh Son
20 Stop'n Go Cafe
24 Long Hoa
  Restaurant
27 La Tulipe Rouge
  Restaurant
28 Italian Ice Cream
  Coffee
30 Nhu Hai Restaurant
33 Viet Hung Cafe
34 Thanh Thuy
  Restaurant
37 Food Stalls

OTHER
7 Saigon Nite
10 Agriculture Bank
  of Vietnam
16 Rap 3/4 Cinema
17 Clothing Stores
18 Intra-Provincial
  Buses (Foreigners
  Prohibited)
19 Hill Tribe Museum
21 Supermarket
22 Central Market
  (Mai Building)
23 Vietnam Airlines
36 Petrol Station

special permit from the police are required to climb the mountain.

Lang Dinh An (also known as the 'chicken village') is a minority area 18km from Dalat. The village gets its name from an enormous concrete chicken which towers over the huts and fields.

Adventure Sports

Outdoorsy types may want to check out the activities being offered by Action Dalat (☎ 82 9422), an adventure sports outfit which operates paragliding, canyoning and treks to minority villages in the area surrounding Dalat. Knowledgeable English and French-speaking guides lead everything from low-impact hikes to technical rock climbing. It's at 114 Duong 3/2 (next to the Golf 2 Hotel).

Places to Stay

Highland Hotel (*Khach San Cao Nguyen*, ☎ 82 3738) is at 90 Duong Phan Dinh Phung, right in the heart of Dalat. It's a good budget place with singles for US$4 to US$6, and twins from US$7 to US$10.

Backpackers have long been fond of **Peace Hotel** (*Khach San Hoa Binh*, ☎ 82 2787). Twins are US$12 to US$15. The hotel is at 64 Duong Truong Cong Dinh. The same place operates **Peace Hotel II** (*Khach San Hoa Binh II*, ☎ 82 2982) at 67 Duong Truong Cong Dinh. Rooms cost US$8.

Mimosa Hotel II (☎ 82 2180), also called **Thanh The Hotel**, is at 118 Duong Phan Dinh Phung. It offers singles for US$5 to US$8 and doubles US$10 to US$15.

Thanh Binh Hotel (☎ 82 2909) at 40

Duong Nguyen Thi Minh Khai is a good budget hotel right across the street from the central market building. Singles are US$6 to US$8; twins cost US$10 to US$12.

Cam Do Hotel (☎ 82 2732) at 81 Duong Phan Dinh Phung is a standard backpackers' special. It has dormitory beds for US$4, and twins for US$10 to US$30.

Phu Hoa Hotel (☎ 82 2194) at 16 Duong Tang Bat Ho is an old but reasonably pleasant place in the centre. Rates for singles are US$7, and doubles are US$10 to US$12.

Trixaco Hotel (☎ 82 2789) at 7 Duong Nguyen Thai Hoc is a fine place with views of Xuan Huong Lake. Singles are US$8, and twins US$10 to US$30.

Thuy Tien Hotel (☎ 82 1731) is in the heart of the old French section at the corner of Duong 3 Thang 2 and Duong Nam Ky Khoi Nghia. Singles cost US$25 to US$30; twins are US$30 to US$36.

Mimosa Hotel (☎ 82 2656) at 170 Duong Phan Dinh Phung (see the Dalat Area map) is an old Dalat budget institution. Singles cost US$7 to US$8, and doubles US$8 to US$14.

Truong Nguyen Mini-Hotel (☎ 82 1772) at 7A Duong Hai Thuong has singles for US$10, and twins US$15 to US$20. Ditto at *Truong Nguyen Mini-Hotel 2 (☎ 82 9856)* at 5C Duong Hai Ba Trung.

Lam Son Hotel (☎ 82 2362) is in an old French villa at 5 Duong Hai Thuong, 500m west of the centre of town. Singles are US$8 to US$10, and twins US$12 to US$14.

Pensee 3 Hotel (☎ 82 2286), 3 Duong Ba Thang Tu, is plush and costs US$20 for twins.

Highly recommendable is the family-run *Hotel Chau Au Europa (☎ 82 2870)* at 76 Duong Nguyen Chi Thanh. Singles are US$15, and doubles US$25 to $35.

Places to Eat

European fare can be had at *La Tulipe Rouge Restaurant* at 1 Duong Nguyen Thi Minh Khai. *Thanh Thanh Restaurant* at 4 Duong Tang Bat Ho is an upmarket eatery with fine French food.

Across from the Phu Hoa Hotel on Duong Tang Bat Ho, *Thanh Son* has tempting fare, including the house specialty, clay pot stews.

The Chinese restaurant in the *Mimosa Hotel* is excellent and cheap.

The *Long Hoa Restaurant* on Duong 3 Thang 2 is also in vogue with travellers. The *Hoang Lan Restaurant* on Duong Phan Dinh Phung also has excellent food in the budget range.

A good all-round place to eat is the *Dong A Restaurant* at 82 Duong Phan Dinh Phung. This place dishes up Vietnamese, Chinese, western and vegetarian cuisine.

Pho Tung is on the other side of the Rap 3/4 cinema from the central market building; it is not a bad restaurant and has an outstanding bakery.

Cafes *Stop'n Go Cafe*, about half way up the incline to the Hill Tribe Museum, is sort of Dalat's avant-garde hang-out.

The *Cafe Tung* at 6 Khu Hoa Binh Square was a famous hang-out of Saigonese intellectuals during the 1950s.

The specialities at the *Viet Hung Cafe (Kem Viet Hung)* are ice cream and iced coffee. The cafe has entrances across from 22 Duong Nguyen Chi Thanh and on Duong Le Dai Hanh.

Vegetarian If it's fresh Vietnamese vegetables you want, the place to find them is the *Nhu Hai Restaurant* on the traffic circle in front of the central market building.

There are also vegetarian *food stalls* (signposted 'com chay', meaning vegetarian food) in the market area just west of the Xuan Huong Dam. All serve delicious 100% vegetarian food prepared to resemble and taste like traditional Vietnamese meat dishes.

Entertainment

Dalat's only *real* bar is *Saigon Nite*, at 11A Duong Hai Ba Trung.

Getting There & Away

Air There are flights to and from Saigon twice weekly.

Bus Foreigners are not permitted to take the local Vietnamese buses when arriving in or departing from Dalat.

Tourist minibuses to Dalat can be booked from the cafes around Pham Ngu Lao in Saigon. In Dalat, hotels and Dalat Tourist sell tickets to Nha Trang (US$8).

Getting Around

For vehicle rentals, see the Information entry earlier in the Dalat section.

Foreigners are not permitted to rent a private taxi, but travel by motorbike is allowed. Many hotels offer bicycle rentals, and there are places in the tourist scenic spots where you can rent a horse.

Tours are offered through Dalat Tourist and the hotels.

VIETNAM

BUON MA THUOT, PLEIKU & KON TUM

The big three towns of the Western Highlands are Buon Ma Thuot, Pleiku and Kon Tum. Ethnic-Vietnamese make up the majority in these towns, but the surrounding countryside is dominated by Montagnards. There are many small, fascinating villages to explore here, but watch out for the rapacious police (especially in Buon Ma Thuot).

Kon Tum seems to be the area of most interest to travellers. Cyclists are also most enthralled with this area as motorised traffic is quite light, the scenery fine and the climate cool.

Ho Chi Minh City (Saigon)

Vietnam's largest population centre, Ho Chi Minh City covers an area of 2056 sq km, but it's a cartographer's creation – 90% is rural. The 'real city' is District 1, also known as Saigon, a name still used by most people to refer to the whole city. Cholon (District 5) is the Chinese section.

The huge numbers of people and their obvious industriousness give Saigon, capital of South Vietnam for nearly 20 years from 1956 to 1975, a bustling, dynamic and spirited atmosphere.

Orientation

Ho Chi Minh City is divided into 12 urban districts (*quan*, derived from French *quartier*) and six rural districts (*huyen*).

Maps Maps of the city are on sale everywhere. Be aware that a number of maps sold have pre-1975 Saigon printed on one side and post-1975 Ho Chi Minh City on the other. Don't get confused and use the wrong side or you'll have a hard time matching street signs with the map!

Information

Money The airport bank gives the legal exchange rate, but beware of short-changing. The bank is sometimes closed when you'd expect it to be open, so you'd be wise to have sufficient US dollar notes in small denominations to get yourself into the city.

Vietcombank occupies two adjacent buildings at the intersection of Duong Ben Chuong and Duong Nguyen Thi Minh Khai (Duong Pasteur) in central Saigon. The east building is the one that does foreign exchange.

Sacombank at 211 Duong Nguyen Thai Hoc (the corner of Duong Pham Ngu Lao) is right in the heart of budget traveller territory.

In District 1, ANZ Bank at 11 Me Linh Square and Hongkong Bank in the New World Hotel Annex at 75 Duong Pham Hong Thai both have international ATMs.

Post Saigon's French-era main post office (Buu Dien Thanh Pho Ho Chi Minh) is at 2 Cong Xa Paris, next to Notre Dame Cathedral. Postal services are available daily from 7.30 am to 7.30 pm.

Email & Internet Access The best place for Web-junkies to get a fix is the Internet Service Center at Viet Quang Office Systems (☎ 830 0317, fax 830 0741, email vmax.110 @hcm.vnn.vn), 110 Duong Bui Thi Xuan. It's a 10 minute walk from the cafes around Duong Pham Ngu Lao, and is open daily from 8 am to 9 pm.

A more central option is the Tin Cafe (☎ 822 9786, email pqhoi@bdvn.vnmail. vnd.net) at 2A Dai Lo Le Duan. It's a pleasant place to surf the Net over a cappuccino. Tin Cafe is open daily from 7.30 am to 10.30 pm.

Budget Travel Agencies Some local travel agencies catering to the backpacker market are listed here. There are many more, and competition is fierce, so shop around.

All of these places are in the Pham Ngu Lao backpacker's ghetto:

Ben Thanh Tourist/Buffalo Tours
  (☎ 886 0365, fax 836 1953)
  165 Duong Pham Ngu Lao (Zone A)
Fiditourist
  (☎ 835 3018)
  195 Duong Pham Ngu Lao
Kim Cafe
  (☎ 835 9859, fax 829 8540)
  270-272 Duong De Tham (Zone D)
Linh Cafe
  291 Duong Pham Ngu Lao
Sinh Cafe
  (☎ 836 7338, fax 836 9322)
  248 Duong De Tham (Zone D)

One place specialising in domestic and international air ticketing is the Nam Dong Travel Agency (☎ 836 9630, fax 836 9632), at 213 Duong Pham Ngu Lao (Zone G).

Bookshops The best area to look for general map, book and stationery stuff is along the north side of Dai Lo Le Loi, between the Rex Hotel and Duong Nam Ky Khoi Nghia. There are many small privately run shops, and the large government-run Saigon Bookstore is at No 60-62.

Viet My Bookstore, No 41 Duong Dinh Tien Hoang, is at the corner of Duong Dinh Tien Hoang and Dai Lo Le Duan in the Dong Khoi area. This place has a number of imported books and magazines published in English, French and Chinese.

The atmospheric and cosy Tiem Sach Bookstore at 20 Duong Ho Huan Nghiep has a massive library of mostly used English and French titles. The shop is open daily from 8.30 am to 10 pm, and also operates as a cafe and ice cream parlour.

On Duong De Tham in the Pham Ngu Lao area are a handful of shops dealing in used paperbacks and bootleg CDs.

Medical Services The most advanced general medical facility is the Dien Bien Phu Hospital (☎ 829 9480) at 280 Duong Dien Bien Phu, District 3.

The Emergency Centre (☎ 829 2071) at 125 Dai Lo Le Loi, District 1, operates 24 hours. Doctors speak English and French.

The Pasteur Institute (☎ 823 0252) at 167 Duong Pasteur, District 3, has the best facilities in Vietnam for medical tests. However, you need to be referred here by a doctor.

Cho Ray Hospital (Benh Vien Cho Ray, ☎ 855 4137/8, fax 855 7267) with 1000 beds is one of the largest medical facilities in Vietnam. It's at 201B Dai Lo Nguyen Chi Thanh, District 5, and there is a section for foreigners on the 10th floor.

The Medical Consultancy Service (☎ 844 3441, fax 844 3442) at 243 Duong Hoang Van Thu, Tan Binh District, provides a 24 hour service seven days a week, and has doctors who speak English, German, French, Italian and Dutch.

Dangers & Annoyances Saigon has the most determined thieves in all of Vietnam. The pickpockets in the Duong Dong Khoi area are so good that they can snatch your underwear without you even noticing. Beware of the 'under the newspaper trick', practised by cute little children who want to sell you maps, postcards, newspapers and magazines. Snatch thieves on motorbikes may steal the sunglasses right off your face. Ben Thanh Market is another favourite venue for pickpockets.

While it's probably safe to take cyclos during the daytime, it may not be at night – in Saigon, cyclo drivers have been known to take their passengers down some dark, deserted alley and mug them.

Giac Lam Pagoda

This pagoda, in District 10, dates from 1744 and is believed to be the oldest in the city. The architecture and style of ornamentation have not changed since the 19th century. It is open to visitors from 6 am to 9 pm.

Giac Vien Pagoda

The pagoda is right next to Dam Sen Lake in District 11 and is in a more rural setting than Giac Lam is. Giac Vien was founded by Hai Tinh Giac Vien about 200 years ago. The pagoda is open from 7 am to 7 pm.

Emperor of Jade Pagoda

This pagoda, known in Vietnamese as Phuoc Hai Tu and Chua Ngoc Hoang, was built in 1909 by the Canton congregation, and is a gem of a Chinese temple. Filled with colourful statues of phantasmal divinities and grotesque heroes, it's one of the most spectacular pagodas in the city.

The statues, which represent characters from both the Buddhist and Taoist traditions, are made of reinforced papier-mâché. It is at 73 Duong Mai Thi Luu in a part of Saigon known as Da Kao (or Da Cao), north of District 3. To get there, go to 20 Duong Dien Bien Phu and walk half a block north-westward.

Notre Dame Cathedral

The Notre Dame Cathedral, built between 1877 and 1883, is in the heart of Saigon's government quarter in central Saigon. Its neo-Romanesque form and two 40m-high square towers, tipped with iron spires, dominate the skyline. If the front gates are locked, try the door on the side of the building that faces Reunification Palace.

Mariamman Hindu Temple

Mariamman Hindu Temple is a little piece of southern India in central Saigon. There are only 50 to 60 Hindus here, all Tamils, but the temple (referred to in Vietnamese as Chua Ba Mariamman), is also considered sacred by many ethnic Vietnamese and Chinese. The temple, which is at 45 Duong Truong Dinh, was built at the end of the 19th century and dedicated to the Hindu goddess Mariamman. It is open daily from 7 am to 7 pm.

VIETNAM

HO CHI MINH CITY (SAIGON)

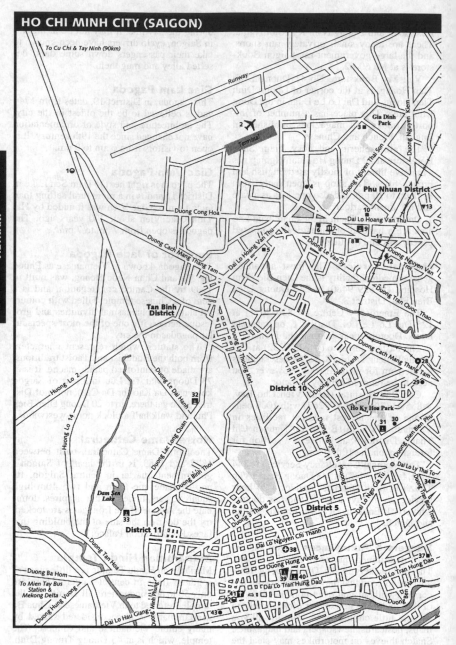

To Cu Chi & Tay Ninh (90km)

Runway

Terminal

Gia Dinh Park

Phu Nhuan District

Duong Nguyen Thai Son

Duong Nguyen Kiem

Duong Cong Hoa

Dai Lo Hoang Van Thu

Duong Le Van Sy

Duong Nguyen Van Troi

Duong Cach Mang Thang Tam

Dai Lo Hoang Van Thu

Duong Tran Quoc Thao

Tan Binh District

Duong Truong Chinh

Duong Le Dai Hanh

Duong Lac Long Quan

Duong Cach Mang Thang Tam

District 10

Duong To Hien Thanh

Ho Ky Hoa Park

Huong Lo 2

Huong Lo 14

Dam Sen Lake

District 11

Duong Binh Thoi

Duong 3 Thang 2

District 5

Dai Lo Ngo Gia Tu

Dai Lo Dien Bien Phu

Dai Lo Ly Thai To

Duong Tran Binh Trong

Duong Tan Hoa

Duong Nguyen Tri Phuong

Dai Lo Nguyen Chi Thanh

Duong Hung Vuong

Dai Lo Tran Hung Dao

Dai Lo Tran Hung Dao

Ben Ham Tu

Duong Ba Hom

To Mien Tay Bus Station & Mekong Delta

Duong Hung Vuong

Dai Lo Hau Giang

Duong Minh Phung

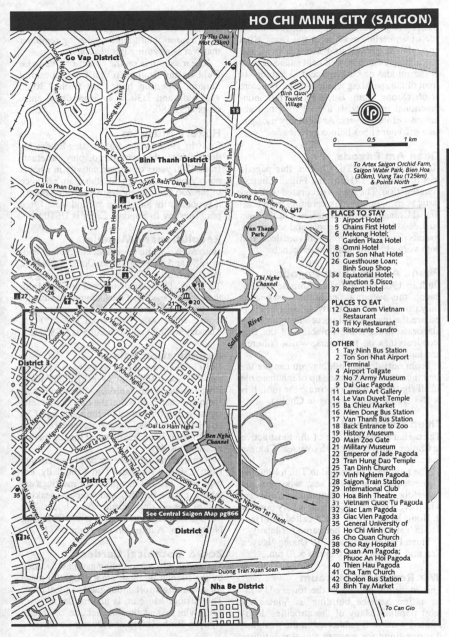

HO CHI MINH CITY (SAIGON)

Go Vap District

Binh Thanh District

District 3

District 1

District 4

Nha Be District

Thi Thu Dau Mot (29km)

Dinh Quai Tourist Village

To Artex Saigon Orchid Farm, Saigon Water Park, Bien Hoa (30km), Vung Tau (125km) & Points North

Van Thanh Park

Thi Nghe Channel

Saigon River

Ben Nghe Channel

See Central Saigon Map pg866

Duong Tran Xuan Soan

To Can Gio

0   0.5   1 km

PLACES TO STAY
3 Airport Hotel
5 Chains First Hotel
6 Mekong Hotel;
  Garden Plaza Hotel
8 Omni Hotel
10 Tan Son Nhat Hotel
26 Guesthouse Loan;
  Binh Soup Shop
34 Equatorial Hotel;
  Junction 5 Disco
37 Regent Hotel

PLACES TO EAT
12 Quan Com Vietnam
  Restaurant
13 Tri Ky Restaurant
24 Ristorante Sandro

OTHER
1 Tay Ninh Bus Station
2 Ton Son Nhat Airport
  Terminal
4 Airport Tollgate
7 No 7 Army Museum
9 Dai Giac Pagoda
11 Lamson Art Gallery
14 Le Van Duyet Temple
15 Ba Chieu Market
16 Mien Dong Bus Station
17 Van Thanh Bus Station
18 Back Entrance to Zoo
19 History Museum
20 Main Zoo Gate
21 Military Museum
22 Emperor of Jade Pagoda
23 Tran Hung Dao Temple
25 Tan Dinh Church
27 Vinh Nghiem Pagoda
28 Saigon Train Station
29 International Club
30 Hoa Binh Theatre
31 Vietnam Quoc Tu Pagoda
32 Giac Lam Pagoda
33 Giac Vien Pagoda
35 General University of
  Ho Chi Minh City
36 Cho Quan Church
38 Cho Ray Hospital
39 Quan Am Pagoda;
  Phuoc An Hoi Pagoda
40 Thien Hau Pagoda
41 Cha Tam Church
42 Cholon Bus Station
43 Binh Tay Market

VIETNAM

Saigon Central Mosque

Built by south Indian Muslims in 1935 on the site of an earlier mosque in the Dong Khoi area, the Saigon Central Mosque is an immaculately clean and well kept island of calm in the middle of bustling central Saigon. In front of the sparkling white and blue structure at 66 Duong Dong Du, with its four non-functional minarets, is a pool for ritual ablutions before prayers. As with any mosque, take off your shoes before entering.

Quan Am Pagoda

At 12 Duong Lao Tu, Cholon, this pagoda was founded in 1816 by the Fujian Chinese congregation. The roof is decorated with fantastic scenes, rendered in ceramic, from traditional Chinese plays and stories. The tableaus include ships, houses, people and several ferocious dragons. The front doors are decorated with very old gold and lacquer panels.

Phuoc An Hoi Quan Pagoda

Built in 1902 by the Fujian Chinese congregation, this pagoda is one of the most beautifully ornamented in the city. Of special interest are the many small porcelain figures, the elaborate brass ritual objects and the fine woodcarvings on the altars, walls, columns and hanging lanterns.

From outside the building you can see the ceramic scenes, each made up of innumerable small figurines, which decorate the roof. It is at 184 Duong Hung Vuong in Cholon.

Thien Hau Pagoda

Thien Hau Pagoda is one of the most active in Cholon and a big hit with overseas Chinese tourists.

The pagoda is dedicated to Thien Hau, the Chinese goddess of the sea, who protects fisherfolk, sailors, merchants and anyone else who travels by sea. Thien Hau is very popular in Hong Kong (where she's called Tin Hau) and in Taiwan (where her name is Matsu).

Thien Hau Pagoda is at 710 Duong Nguyen Trai and is open from 6 am to 5.30 pm.

War Remnants Museum

This museum, housed in the former US Information Service building, is Vietnam's most popular. Many of the atrocities documented were well publicised in the west, but it is one thing for western anti-war activists to protest against Pentagon policies and quite another for the victims of these military/political actions to tell their own story. No matter which side of the political fence you stand on, the museum is well worth a visit – if for no other reason than to get a sobering reminder that war is anything but glorious.

The museum is on the corner of Duong Le Qui Don and Duong Vo Van Tan near central Saigon. Opening hours are from 7.30 to 11:45 am and 1:30 to 4:45 pm daily; entry costs US$0.80.

History Museum

Built in 1929 by the Société des Études Indochinoises, this museum displays artefacts from 3300 years of human activity in what is now Vietnam. Just inside the main entrance to the zoo (on Duong Nguyen Binh Khiem), it is open from 8 to 11.30 am and from 1 to 4 pm, Tuesday to Sunday. Entry is US$0.80.

Revolutionary Museum

Housed in a white neoclassical structure built in 1886 and once known as Gia Long Palace, the Revolutionary Museum is at 27 Duong Ly Tu Trong. There are displays of artefacts from the various periods of the Communist struggle for power in Vietnam. The museum is open from 8 to 11.30 am and from 2 to 4.30 pm, Tuesday to Sunday. Admission is US$0.80.

Reunification Palace

Built in the heart of central Saigon in 1966 to serve as South Vietnam's Presidential Palace, it was towards this building – then known as Independence Hall – that the first Communist tanks in Saigon rushed on the morning of 30 April 1975, the day Saigon surrendered. The building has been left just as it looked on that momentous day.

Reunification Palace is open for visitors from 7.30 to 11 am and 1 to 4 pm daily, except when official receptions or meetings are taking place. English and French-speaking guides are on duty during these hours. The visitors' office and entrance is at 106 Duong Nguyen Du. Admission is a steep US$4.

Zoo & Botanical Garden

The zoo and its surrounding gardens, founded by the French in 1864, are a delightful place for a relaxing stroll under giant tropical trees. The History Museum is just inside the main gate, which is at the intersection of Duong Nguyen Binh Khiem and Duong Le Duan.

Cong Vien Van Hoa Park

Next to the old Cercle Sportif, an elite sporting club during the French period, the bench-lined walks of Cong Vien Van Hoa Park are shaded with avenues of enormous tropical trees.

This place is still an active sports centre but now you don't have to be French to visit. There are tennis courts, a swimming pool and a clubhouse which have a grand colonial feel about them. It's worth a look for the pool alone. There are Roman-style baths with a coffee shop overlooking the colonnaded pool. There is a dressing room but no lockers.

Cong Vien Van Hoa Park is adjacent to Reunification Palace. There are entrances across from 115 Duong Nguyen Du and on Duong Nguyen Thi Minh Khai.

Binh Quoi Tourist Village

Built on a small peninsula in the Saigon River, the Binh Quoi Tourist Village (Lang Du Lich Binh Quoi) is a slick tourist trap. The 'village' is essentially a park featuring boat rides, water-puppet shows, a restaurant, a swimming pool, tennis courts, a camping ground, a guesthouse and amusements for the kiddies. The park puts in a plug for Viet-nam's ethnic minorities by staging traditional- style minority weddings accompanied by music. From 5 to 10 pm, there is a traditional music performance and boat rides along the river.

Binh Quoi Tourist Village is 8km north of central Saigon in the Binh Thanh District. The official address is 1147 Duong Xo Viet Nghe Tinh.

Saigon Water Park

The recently completed Saigon Water Park is a giant oasis in the suburbs of Saigon. It is chock full of pools and water rides: loop-the-loop slides, a kiddie wading pool and even a 'wave pool' which switches on every other 10 minutes to simulate the ocean.

The park is open daily from 11 am to 7 pm, Monday to Saturday, and from 8 am to 8 pm on Sunday and public holidays. The entry fee is US$4.60. People under 1.1m in height pay US$3.85.

Saigon Water Park is on Duong Kha Van Can, in the Thu Duc District (near the Go Dua Bridge). It's too far for cyclos, but you can take a meter taxi for about US$4, or better yet head out on the park's shuttle boat (US$1.50) which leaves from Bach Dang Wharf in central Saigon.

Places to Stay – Budget

District 1 This is far and away the most popular neighbourhood with travellers.

If you don't really know where you want to stay, but you're on a budget, it's best to take a taxi to the Pham Ngu Lao area and proceed on foot. If you don't want to lug your bags around (which also makes you a prime target for cyclo drivers and kids who will persist in taking to you a 'great' hotel) you might consider dropping your gear at one of the travellers' cafes. If you don't want to deal with the commission circus, make reservations in advance – most hotels will be happy to fetch you from the airport.

Pham Ngu Lao Area The three streets Duong Pham Ngu Lao, Duong De Tham and Duong Bui Vien form half a rectangle which is the heart of the budget traveller haven. These streets and the adjoining alleys are dotted with a treasure trove of cheap accommodation and cafes catering to the budget market (at last count there were close to 100 guesthouses and hotels within a 10 minute walk of each other).

Touts from private hotels hang around the airport looking for business. Taxi drivers will often shove hotel name cards into your hands. If the hotels weren't paying sizeable commissions, the touts wouldn't bother.

Near the bottom of the barrel is *Liberty 3 Hotel* (☎ 836 9522) a state-run monstrosity right at 187 Duong Pham Ngu Lao (corner of Duong De Tham). Fan singles/doubles here cost US$5/6.50, and air-con doubles are US$12 to US$16.

An old favourite is the pleasant and friendly *Hotel 211* (☎ 836 7353) at 211 Duong Pham Ngu Lao. Dorm beds go for US$3, while rooms cost US$7/8 with fan or US$10/12 with air-con.

The first place in this neighbourhood to offer dormitory accommodation was *Thanh Thanh 2 Hotel* (☎ 886 1751, email ththanh hotel@hotmail.com) at 205 Duong Pham Ngu Lao (Zone G). Dorm beds start at US$3, and private rooms cost from US$5 to US$10.

Another clean and friendly spot is *Ocean Hotel (Khach San Dai Dong, ☎ 836 8231)* at 217 Duong Pham Ngu Lao (Zone G). Fan rooms go for US$8, and air-con rates are US$12/15. Up the street at 269 Duong Pham Ngu Lao, similar rates and standards prevail at the popular *Hotel 269* (☎ 836 7345).

Many travellers have had good things to say about *Quyen Thanh Hotel* (☎ 836 8570) at 212 Duong De Tham. Air-con rooms begin at US$15, and larger ones equipped with everything cost US$20.

VIETNAM

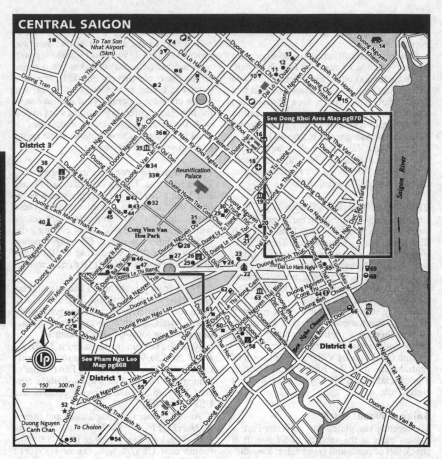

CENTRAL SAIGON

Other good places on this street include *Hotel 265* (☎ 836 1883) at 265 Duong De Tham, with dorm beds for US$3 and air-con rooms from US$10/12. Practically next door is the equally good *Le Le 2* (☎ 836 8585), which has air-con comfort for US$8 to US$15. Ditto for *Peace Hotel* (☎ 836 8824) across the street at 272 Duong De Tham (Zone D).

Lan Anh Hotel (☎ 836 5197) at 252 Duong De Tham (Zone D) is another spiffy place which charges from US$7 to US$18.

The friendly owner at *Anh Dao Guesthouse* (☎ 836 7351), 235 Duong De Tham, has basic fan singles for US$4 and US$5, doubles for US$6 and US$8; add a couple of dollars for air-con.

Warm-hearted Madam Cuc's *Guesthouse 127* (☎ 836 8761) is at 127 Duong Cong Quynh. This place gets raved about by travellers for its welcoming reception. Rooms cost US$7 to US$20.

About 100m south of Duong Pham Ngu Lao is Duong Bui Vien, which is rapidly being transformed into a solid string of *guesthouses* and *mini-hotels* in the US$6 to US$12 range.

We've personally found *Guesthouse 64* (☎ 836 5073), 64 Duong Bui Vien, to be a good one.

Hai Ha Mini-Hotel (☎ 836 5565), at No 78, *Phuong Hoang Mini-Hotel* (☎/fax 836 8631), at No 25, and *Huy Doc Hotel* (☎ 837 0538), 74 Duong Bui Vien all have satellite TV. *Minh Chau Guesthouse* (☎/fax 836 7588, email minhchauhotel@hcm.vnn.vn), 75 Duong Bui Vien, offers email service.

CENTRAL SAIGON

PLACES TO STAY		
1	Saigon Lodge Hotel	
6	Huong Tram Hotel	
7	Que Huong (Liberty) Hotel	
21	Tan Loc Hotel	
27	Hoang Gia Hotel	
29	Tao Dan Hotel	
30	Embassy Hotel	
33	Sol Chancery Hotel	
34	International Hotel	
36	Victory Hotel	
42	Bao Yen Hotel	
43	Chancery Saigon Hotel	
44	Saigon Star Hotel	
46	Rang Dong Hotel	
47	Oriole Hotel	
50	Empress Hotel	
51	Hoang Yen Mini-Hotel	
55	Metropole Hotel	
56	Guesthouse District	
57	Miss Loi's Guesthouse	
60	Hanoi Hotel	
61	Mecure Hotel	

PLACES TO EAT		
3	Tib Cafe	
4	L'Etoile Restaurant	
10	Ciao Cafe	
24	Bavaria Restaurant	
37	ABC Restaurant	
41	Tandoor Indian Restaurant	
48	Annie's Pizza	
62	Tin Nghia	

OTHER		
2	Ho Chi Minh City Association of Fine Arts	
5	Cambodian Consulate	
8	French Consulate	
9	Former US Embassy	
11	Deelite Disco	
12	Tin Cafe	
13	The Home Zone; Vidotour	
14	Zoo & Botanical Garden	
15	No 5 Ly Tu Trong	
16	Main Post Office	
17	Notre Dame Cathedral	
18	AEA Clinic	
19	Revolutionary Museum	
20	Saigon Intershop & Minimart	
22	Tran Nguyen Hai Statue	
23	Ben Thanh Market	
25	Bicycle Shops	
26	Mariamman Hindu Temple	
28	Bus Stop (to Cambodia)	
31	Conservatory of Music	
32	Tao Dan Photocopy	
35	War Remnants Museum	
38	Dien Bien Phu Hospital	
39	Xa Loi Pagoda	
40	Thich Quang Duc Memorial	
45	Vinh Loi Gallery	
49	Viet Quang Office Systems (Internet Service Centre)	
52	Immigration Police Office	
53	Dr Vannoort's Clinic	
54	Saigon Food Centre	
58	Phung Son Tu Pagoda	
59	Dan Sinh Market	
63	Art Museum	
64	Vietcombank	
65	The Old Market	
66	Vung Tau Hydrofoil	
67	Ho Chi Minh Museum	
68	Ferries across Saigon River & to Mekong Delta	
69	Hammock Bar	

VIETNAM

There has been a constant stream of complaints against *Huy Hoang Guesthouse* at 18 Duong Bui Vien – a woman working there seems to have a few too many quarrels with travellers.

Perhaps the greatest concentration of lodgings in Saigon is in the *'mini-hotel alley'* flanked by (and addressed as an extension of) Duong Bui Vien and Duong Pham Ngu Lao. Most are virtually identical: family-run with a price range from US$6 to US$10 for fan rooms, while bigger air-con rooms (some with balconies) generally run between US$12 and US$18.

We can recommend *Mini-Hotel Cam* (☎ 836 7622), 40/31 Duong Bui Vien (Zone C), for cleanliness and safety.

There have been several good reports on the slightly upmarket *Bi Saigon* and *Bee Saigon* (☎ 836 0678) mini-hotels, both at 185/26 Pham Ngu Lao (Zone C).

Other travellers have praised *Hung Mini-Hotel* (☎ 836 7438), 40/14 Duong Bui Vien (Zone B) and *40/18 Guesthouse* (☎/fax 836 7495), 40/18 Duong Bui Vien (send fax for airport pick-up).

Both *Giang Mini-Hotel* (☎ 836 7495), 40/26 Duong Bui Vien (Zone B), and *Hong Hoa Guesthouse* (☎ 836 1915, email honghoa@ bdvn.vnd.net), 182/28 Duong Pham Ngu Lao (Zone C), offer email service, the latter with satellite TV to boot.

Elsewhere in District 1 A quieter alternative about 10 minutes on foot from the Pham Ngu Lao area is a string of fine guesthouses on an alley connecting Duong Co Giang and Duong Co Bac. This area is close to the hoopla, but far enough away not to have to deal with touts in your face every time you step out the door of the hotel.

The first hotel to appear here and probably still the best is *Miss Loi's Guesthouse* (☎ 835 2973) at 178/20 Duong Co Giang. Fan rooms cost US$8 to US$10, and air-con goes for US$12 to US$15. Many of her neighbours are jumping into this business and the area seems destined to develop into another budget travellers' haven. To reach the guesthouses, walk up Duong Co Bac and turn left after you pass the nuoc mam (fish sauce) shops.

District 3 This district seems to attract a large number of French travellers – possibly this is because of the local architecture. Whatever the reason, if you speak French, you'll have a chance to practice it here.

On the north side of Cong Vien Van Hoa

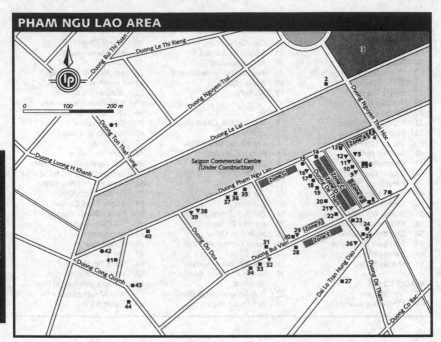

PHAM NGU LAO AREA

VIETNAM

Park at 9 Duong Truong Dinh is *Bao Yen Hotel* (☎ 829 9848). Rooms are a very reasonable US$12 to US$15, and all have air-con.

District 5 (Cholon) *Phuong Hoang Hotel* (☎ 855 1888) is in an eight storey building at 411 Dai Lo Tran Hung Dao. This place is in the middle of central Cholon. Rooms with fan/air-con cost US$13/23.

Song Kim Hotel (☎ 855 9773) is at 84-86 Duong Chau Van Liem. It's a grungy and somewhat disreputable establishment with twins for US$8 with fan, or US$11 with air-conditioning.

Just up Duong Chau Van Liem at 111-117 is *Truong Thanh Hotel* (☎ 855 6044). It's definitely a budget place. Rooms with fan are US$8 to US$10, while air-con costs US$16.

Half a block away, at 125 Duong Chau Van Liem, is *Thu Do Hotel* (☎ 855 9102). It looks very much like a dump, a distinction it shares with the neighbouring Truong Thanh Hotel. Rooms cost a modest US$9.

Places to Stay – Mid-Range
District 1 District 1 boasts a number of slightly upmarket places which cater to both

backpackers who don't mind shelling out a bit more for a nice room and to moneybags who prefer to be where the action is without sacrificing comfort.

Room rates at the attractive *Hanh Hoa Hotel* (☎ 836 0245) at 237 Duong Pham Ngu Lao (Zone G) range from US$20 to US$35, a decent value for the standard (including satellite TV).

Another sleek hotel which managed to inch its way into backpacker central is *Le Le Hotel* (☎ 836 8686) at 171 Duong Pham Ngu Lao (Zone A). This place has a lift and satellite TV. Rooms cost US$15 to US$50.

There have been good reports on the rooms and service at the new *Lan Lan Hotel* (☎ 886 4811), at 42 Duong Bui Thi Xuan (close to the Ben Thanh Market). Rooms here cost US$20 including breakfast.

There are several more options on the streets splintering off from the roundabout with the mounted horseman statue near the New World Hotel. Consider checking out *Oriole Hotel* (☎ 832 3494) at 74 Duong Le Thi Rieng. It's a friendly new mini-hotel with comfortable air-con rooms from US$15 to US$25.

PHAM NGU LAO AREA

PLACES TO STAY
2   Palace Saigon Hotel
3   New World Hotel;
    Hongkong Bank
7   Hong Kong Mini-Hotel
8   Vuong Hoa Guesthouse
10 Hotel Linh Linh
14 Liberty 3 Hotel
17 Le Le 2 Hotel
18 Hotel 265
19 Anh Dao Guesthouse
20 Thanh Ngi Guesthouse
22 Thanh Thanh
    Guesthouse
23 Quyen Thanh Hotel
25 A Hotel
27 Windsor Saigon Hotel
28 Minh Chau Guesthouse
30 96 Guesthouse
31 Hop Thanh Guesthouse
33 Guesthouse 97
34 Tuan Anh Guesthouse
35 Liberty 4 Hotel
36 Hotel 269
37 Vien Dong Hotel;
    Cheers
40 Tan Kim Long Hotel
41 My Man Mini-Hotel
43 Tuan Anh Hotel
44 Guesthouse 127

PLACES TO EAT
5   Margherita
9   Zen
11 Bodhi Tree
12 Nhu Lien
16 Saigon Cafe
21 Cafe 333
26 Cafe Van
    (Sandwich Box)
29 Pho Bo
32 Kim's Guesthouse

38 Kim's Cafe & Bar
39 Linh Cafe

OTHER
1   Ann Tours
4   Sacombank
6   Chua An Lac Temple
13 Bar Rolling Stones
15 Fiditourist
24 Cong Nhan Cinema
42 Thai Binh Market

ZONE A (from right to left)
Nguyen Chat (Bar)
Long Phi Bar
Ben Thanh Tourist/Buffalo Tours
Backpacker Bar
Le Le Hotel
Giant Dragon Hotel

ZONE B (from top to bottom)
Giang Mini-Hotel
40/18 Guesthouse
Hung Mini-Hotel
Titi Mini-Hotel
Linh Mini-Hotel
Hotel Thanh

ZONE C (from top to bottom)
Dung Hotel
Bao Long Mini-Hotel
Mini-Hotel Xinh
Bee Saigon
Viet Thai Restaurant
Bi Saigon
Hong Hoa Guesthouse
Mini-Hotel Cam
Mini-Hotel Huong
Ngu Lan Guesthouse
Mini-Hotel Hau
Quang Guesthouse
Mi Mi Guesthouse

ZONE D (from top to bottom)
Cafe 2
Peace Hotel
Kim Cafe & Booking Office
Hoang Anh Mini-Hotel
Ngoc Dang Mini-Hotel
Lan Anh Hotel
Sinh Cafe & Booking Office
Sasa Cafe
Shanti Indian Restaurant
Ngoc Dung Hotel
Lucky Cafeteria
Cappuccino

ZONE E (from right to left)
Phuong Hoang Mini-Hotel
Hong Quyen Hotel
Vu Chau Hotel
41 Guesthouse
Hotel Hong Loi
Thanh Guesthouse

ZONE F (from right to left)
Minh Phuc Guesthouse
Phuong Lan Guesthouse
Linh Thu Guesthouse
Huy Doc Hotel
Hai Ha Mini-Hotel
Van Trang Hotel
Hai Duong Hotel

ZONE G (from right to left)
Lotus Cafe
Thanh Thanh 2 Hotel
Guns & Roses Bar
Hotel 211
Nam Duong Travel Agency
Ocean Hotel
Roxy Music Bar
Photo Ngu
Hanh Hoa Hotel
Cafe Trang

At *Tao Dan Hotel* (☎ 823 0299), 35A Duong Nguyen Trung Truc (near Reunification Palace), most guests could be described as 'budget business travellers'. Prices are US$20 to US$25 with air-con.

One of the better deals to be had in the Dong Khoi area is *Khach San Dien Luc* (☎ 822 9058) at 5/11 Duong Nguyen Sieu. It has the sterility and look of a new hospital. Rooms cost from US$16 to US$24, and feature satellite TV.

Also in Dong Khoi, *Hotel 69* (☎ 829 1513) is a friendly mini-hotel centrally located at 69 Dai Lo Hai Ba Trung. The rooms are fairly basic, but a decent value for the price; singles/twins start from US$19/25.

Places to Eat

Both Vietnamese and western food are widely available in Saigon, and English menus are becoming more common.

Food Stalls Noodle soup is available all day long at street stalls and hole-in-the-wall shops everywhere. A large bowl of delicious beef noodles costs US$0.50 to US$1. Just look for the signs that say *'Pho'*.

Sandwiches with a French look and a very Vietnamese taste are sold by *street vendors*. Fresh French *baguettes* are stuffed with something resembling pâté (don't ask) and cucumbers and seasoned with soy sauce. A sandwich costs between US$0.50 and US$1, depending on what is in it and whether you get overcharged. Sandwiches filled with imported French soft cheese will cost a little more.

Markets always have a side selection of food items, often in the ground floor or basement. Clusters of *food stalls* can be found in the Thai Binh Market, Ben Thanh Market and Andong Market.

Pham Ngu Lao Area Duong Pham Ngu Lao and Duong De Tham forms the axis of Saigon's budget eatery haven.

A long-running hang-out for budget travellers is *Kim Cafe* at 270-272 Duong De Tham (Zone D). This is a very good place to meet people, arrange trips and get travel information at the tour office next door. An almost identical set up exists at the nearby *Sinh Cafe*.

The *Saigon Cafe* at 195 Duong Pham Ngu Lao (corner Duong De Tham) is also worthy of a plug, and along with *Cafe 333* on Duong De Tham is where the largest numbers of expats congregate. *Cafe 2* at 274 Duong De Tham is also popular and proudly advertises 'no MSG or animal fat' cooking.

The *Lotus Cafe* at 197 Duong Pham Ngu Lao (Zone G) is one of the best in the neighbourhood. The friendly couple who run it prepare excellent Vietnamese and western food at low prices. *Linh Cafe*, at 291 Duong Pham Ngu Lao, is another great little place run by friendly people.

Cafe Van at 169B Duong De Tham, also known as the *Sandwich Box*, whips up excellent sandwiches, baked potatoes, and Saigon's best chilli.

For north-Indian/Pakistani food, try *Cafe Trang* at 237 Duong Pham Ngu Lao (Zone G).

There is decent Italian grub at *Cappuccino*, near Sinh Cafe at 222 Duong De Tham, as well as at *Ngoc Phuong* at 203 Duong Pham Ngu Lao. At 175/1 Pham Ngu Lao, *Margherita* is the cheapest of the lot.

For local point-and-eat fare, try the ground floor of *Kim's Guesthouse* at 91 Duong Bui Vien. There is also good beef noodle soup across the street at *Pho Bo*, next to the 96 Guesthouse, as well as at *Pho Thanh Canh* at 55 Duong Nguyen Cu Trinh, about 300m from Guesthouse 127.

Vegetarian On the first and 15th days of the lunar month, food stalls around the city – especially in the markets – serve vegetarian versions of meaty Vietnamese dishes.

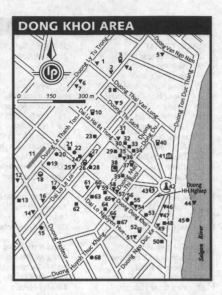

DONG KHOI AREA

Zen is in a narrow alley in Pham Ngu Lao, two streets south of Duong De Tham. The food here is excellent and very cheap. Equally commendable is the nearby *Bodhi Tree*, and if these two places aren't enough, you might try *Nhu Lien* next door.

Tin Nghia is about 200m from Ben Thanh Market at 9 Dai Lo Tran Hung Dao in central Saigon, a short walk from the backpackers' ghetto. It serves an assortment of cheap and delicious traditional Vietnamese foods prepared without meat, chicken, fish or egg.

Vietnamese The following eateries are in the Dong Khoi area.

Along Duong Ngo Duc Ke in District 1 there is a strip of excellent local restaurants serving good, cheap Vietnamese food. At No 19, *Restaurant 19* serves a tasty variation on Hanoi's Cha Ca fish cakes and good Thai dishes. Nearby, the *No 13* is also highly popular with locals and expats alike.

If you're ready to splurge, the popular *Mandarine Cafe* at 11A Duong Ngo Van Nam is perhaps the best Vietnamese restaurant in town.

The *Lemon Grass Restaurant* at 4 Duong Nguyen Thiep, District 1, is another favourite, *the* place for Vietnamese power dining.

Another popular place with traditional decor and fine food is the *Tan Nam Restaurant* at 60-62 Duong Dong Du, in District 1.

DONG KHOI AREA

PLACES TO STAY		PLACES TO EAT		65	Vietnam House
8	Orchid Hotel	1	Sapa Restaurant & Bar	66	Ciao Cafe
13	Norfolk Hotel	2	Indian Heritage;		
17	Rex Hotel		Xuan Huong Hotel	**OTHER**	
21	Asian Hotel	4	Ashoka Indian Restaurant	3	Tex Mex Cantina
23	Park Hyatt Hotel	5	Mandarine Cafe	10	Gecko Bar
	(Under Construction)	6	Bo Tung Xeo Restaurant	11	People's Committee
24	Continental Hotel	7	Blue Gecko Bar &		(Hôtel de Ville)
28	Delta Caravelle Hotel		Restaurant	15	Saigon Centre; Java Cafe
29	Hotel 69	9	Mogambo's Cafe	18	Phnom Penh Bus Garage
31	Khach San Dien Luc	12	Rex Garden Restaurant	19	Vietnam Airlines
32	Nam Phuong Hotel	14	Kem Bach Dang	20	Saigon Tourist
33	Fimex Hotel	16	Kem Bach Dang	22	Tu Do Gallery
34	Chuson Hotel	25	Givral Restaurant	26	Q Bar
35	Bong Sen Annexe	30	Kem Bach Dang	27	Municipal Theatre
39	Saigon Hotel;	36	Indian Canteen	37	Hien & Bob's Place; Wild West
	Cafe Latin	44	Floating Restaurants	38	Saigon Central Mosque
48	Riverside Hotel	46	La Fourchette	40	Apocalypse Now
50	Majestic Hotel; Maxim's	47	Restaurants 19 & 13	41	Ton Duc Thang Museum;
	Dinner Theatre	49	Paris Deli		The Landmark
53	Dong Khoi Hotel	51	Santa Lucia	42	Me Linh Square;
59	Bong Sen Hotel;	54	Paloma Cafe		Tran Hung Dao Statue
	Mondial Hotel	56	Gartenstadt Restaurant	43	ANZ Bank
62	Kim Do Hotel	57	Liberty Restaurant	45	Small Boats for Hire
63	Oscar Saigon Hotel;	58	Liberty Restaurant	52	Montana Hotel
	Starlight Nightclub	60	Brodard Cafe	55	Tiem Sach Bookstore
64	Palace Hotel	61	Lemon Grass Restaurant;	68	Huynh Thuc Khang Street
67	Saigon Prince Hotel		Augustin		Market

International *Annie's Pizza*, at 21 Duong Bui Thi Xuan in central Saigon, does the best peperoni and mozzarella in town.

The best Indian food in District 1 is at *Indian Heritage*, in the Xuan Huong Hotel, 12 Duong Thai Van Lung, in the Dong Khoi area. There is an excellent lunch buffet for US$1. For *really* cheap Indian food, you have to go the atmospheric, cult-like *canteen* behind the mosque at 66 Duong Dong Du (opposite the Saigon Hotel).

Augustin, at 10 Duong Nguyen Thiep, is considered Saigon's best cheap French restaurant. Another choice for reasonable French food is *La Fourchette*. It's also in the Dong Khoi area, at 9 Duong Ngo Duc Ke.

The *Givral Restaurant* at 169 Duong Dong Khoi (across the street from the Continental Hotel) has an excellent selection of cakes, home-made ice cream and yoghurt.

A stone's throw from the Rex Hotel, the *Rex Garden Restaurant* is in an attractive setting and serves good Vietnamese and French dishes.

At 26 Duong Thai Van Lung, the popular Swiss-Vietnamese-run *Sapa Restaurant & Bar* is a fine place to sample bona fide Swiss cooking.

The best authentic Italian food in town is found in District 3 (see the Ho Chi Minh City map) at *Ristorante Sandro*, 142 Duong Vo Thi Sau. Highly atmospheric and somewhat less pricey is *Santa Lucia* at 14 Duong Nguyen Hue, in the Dong Khoi area of District 1.

Mogambo's Cafe at 20 Duong Thi Sach is noted for its stunning Polynesian decor and juicy steaks. This place is a restaurant, pub and hotel.

Cafe Latin at 25 Duong Dong Du is Vietnam's first tapas bar. The attached *Billabong Restaurant* is notable for Aussie tucker and other international flavours.

Ciao Cafe, at 21-23 Duong Nguyen Thi Minh Khai in central Saigon, does excellent pizza, spaghetti, sandwiches, cakes, pastries and ice cream.

The *Paloma Cafe* at 26 Duong Dong Khoi is very popular with young, fashion-conscious Vietnamese.

For a good late night bowl of noodles, try the trendy *ABC Restaurant*, at 172H Duong Nguyen Dinh Chieu in District 3. It's open until about 3 am.

Ice Cream, Coffee & Desserts Some of the best Vietnamese ice cream (*kem*) in Saigon is found in the Dong Khoi area at the three shops called **Kem Bach Dang**. Two of them are on Dai Lo Le Loi on either side of Duong Pasteur (Kem Bach Dang 1 is at 26 Dai Lo Le Loi and the other is at No 28). The third branch is at 67 Dai Lo Hai Ba Trung (at Dai Lo Le Loi, south-east corner).

The stylish **Dong Du Cafe** at 31 Duong Dong Du dishes up great homemade ice cream, coffees, and a bit of Italian food if you're still hungry.

Perhaps the best *real* coffee in town is found at **Java**, in the Saigon Centre at 65 Dai Lo Le Loi (Dong Khoi area).

For fresh-baked pastries and bread, try the **Saigon Bakery** at 281C Dai Lo Hai Ba Trung.

Dinner Cruises Wining and dining while floating around the Saigon River is not the worst way to spend an evening. The *floating restaurants* are all government owned and are docked just opposite the Riverside Hotel in the Dong Khoi area. Most open at 6 pm, depart the pier at 8 pm and return at 10 pm. Prices vary from US$5 to US$10 for dinner à la carte, though you could spend significantly more if you go heavy on the booze.

Tickets for the cruise can be bought at the pier, and you can call for information (☎ 822 5401). Most of the boats feature live music and dancing.

Entertainment

Central Saigon is *the* place to be on Saturday, Sunday and holiday nights. The streets are jam-packed with young Saigonese, in couples and groups, cruising the town on bicycles and motorbikes, out to see and be seen.

Pubs & Bars When it comes to nightlife, the backpacker centre around Duong Pham Ngu Lao has a few hot spots. The **Bar Rolling Stones** at 177 Duong Pham Ngu Lao and the **Backpacker Bar** at No 167 (Zone A) are both known for their late hours, loud music and party atmosphere. A short walk north on Duong Pham Ngu Lao (Zone G) are the **Guns & Roses Bar** and **Roxy Music Bar**.

The real budget-minded should try **Nguyen Chat** at 161 Duong Pham Ngu Lao (Zone A), a Vietnamese place where you can sample local draft beer (bia hoi) for US$0.40 per litre.

Dong Khoi Area For wider nightlife choices, head down to the central area (around Duong Dong Khoi). **Apocalypse Now**, at 2C Duong Thi Sach, has long led the pack. The music is loud, and the patrons are of all walks and apocalyptically rowdy.

For a more civilised atmosphere, try the excellent new **No 5 Ly Tu Trong** (see the Central Saigon map), run by long-term Swiss expat Heinz. Named for its address, the decor of this restored French colonial villa is stylish and sleek.

At 24 Mac Thi Buoi is the legendary, imitation **Hard Rock Cafe**. The music here is more mellow than the name suggests, but it's certainly a popular spot. The real Hard Rock is in the new Delta Caravelle Hotel by the Municipal Theatre in Dong Khoi.

The **Tex-Mex Cantina** at 24 Duong Le Thanh Ton features Mexican food with a Texan twist. It's also notable for its billiards tables.

For wanna-be ranch hands, check out **Wild West** at 33 Dai Lo Hai Ba Trung. The live music here is loud and billiards tables are busy.

The **Gecko Bar** at 74/1A Dai Lo Hai Ba Trung is another expat favourite. There's good food, drinks and satellite TV – and yes, a couple of odd geckos climbing the walls and ceilings.

Built right into one side of the Municipal Theatre is the **Q Bar**, a trendy place with murals on the walls and tables outside by a little garden.

Dancing & Discos **Planet Europe** is the all-new flash place in town. It's in the Saigon Superbowl, close to the airport. Happy hour is from 6.30 to 9 pm.

Cheers is the disco inside the Vien Dong Hotel, at 275A Duong Pham Ngu Lao. This very popular place charges US$7 admission and features live rhythms from the Filipino house band.

Water Puppets The best venue to see water puppets in Saigon is at the **War Remnants Museum** at 28 Duong Vo Van Tan. The schedule changes, so inquire first.

Shopping

In the last few years the free market in tourist junk has been booming – you can pick up a useful item like a lacquered turtle with a clock in its stomach or a ceramic Buddha that whistles the national anthem. But even if you're not into tourist kitsch, Saigon is a good shopping city and there is sure to be something that catches your eye.

Ben Thanh Market (Cho Ben Thanh) in central Saigon is perhaps the best place to start your search. Part of the market is devoted to normal everyday items like vegetables and laundry detergent, but the locals have not overlooked the lucrative tourist trade. Some items have price tags and some don't – polite bargaining should help. Warning: there are *plenty* of pickpockets in this market.

Duong Dong Khoi is the big arts and crafts tourist bazaar, but prices can get outrageous. In this neighbourhood you'd better try to get at least a 50% discount, or try somewhere else.

In the Pham Ngu Lao area are a few small shops plugging ethnic souvenirs, T-shirts and other backpacker paraphernalia.

Getting There & Away

Air Vietnam Airlines also acts as sales agent for Lao Aviation (Hang Khong Lao). Regional airlines include:

Asiana Airlines
 (☎ 822 2663, fax 822 2710)
 141-143 Dai Lo Ham Nghi, District 1
Cathay Pacific (Hang Khong Cathay Pacific)
 (☎ 822 3203, fax 825 8276)
 58 Duong Dong Khoi, District 1
China Southwest Airlines (Hang Khong Nam Trung Hoa)
 (☎ 829 1172, fax 829 6800)
 52B Duong Pham Hong Thai, District 1
Garuda Indonesia (Hang Khong In-do-ne-xia)
 (☎ 829 3644, fax 829 3688)
 132-134 Duong Dong Khoi, District 1
Malaysia Airlines (Hang Khong Ma-lay-sia)
 (☎ 829 2529, fax 824 2884)
 132-134 Duong Dong Khoi, District 1
Pacific Airlines (Hang Khong Pa-ci-fic)
 (☎ 820 0978, fax 820 0980)
 177 Duong Vo Thi Sau, District 3
Philippine Airlines (Hang Khong Phi-lip-pin)
 (☎ 823 0502, fax 823 0548)
 132-134 Duong Dong Khoi, District 1
Royal Air Cambodge
 (☎ 844 0126, fax 842 1578)
 343 Duong Le Van Sy, Tan Binh District
Singapore Airlines (Hang Khong Sin-ga-po)
 (☎ 823 1583, fax 823 1554)
 Saigon Tower Building, Suite 101, 29 Dai Lo Le Duan, District 1
Thai Airways International (Hang Khong Thai Lan)
 (☎ 829 2810, fax 822 3465)
 65 Duong Nguyen Du, District 1
Vietnam Airlines (Hang Khong Vietnam)
 (☎ 829 2118, fax 823 0273)
 116 Dai Lo Nguyen Hue, District 1

Bus Intercity buses depart from and arrive at a variety of stations around Ho Chi Minh City. *Ben xe* means bus station, so if you need to ask for any of these stations just say 'ben xe' first followed by the station name.

Cholon station is the most convenient place to get buses to Mytho and other Mekong Delta towns. The Cholon bus station is just beyond the western end of Dai Lo Tran Hung Dao in District 5, close to the Binh Tay Market.

Less conveniently located than Cholon station, Mien Tay station (☎ 825 5955) nevertheless has even more buses to points south of Ho Chi Minh City. This enormous station is about 10km west of Saigon in An Lac.

Buses to places north of Ho Chi Minh City leave from Mien Dong bus station (☎ 829 4056), which is in Binh Thanh District, about 5km from central Saigon on National Highway 13.

Buses to Tay Ninh, Cu Chi and points north-east of Ho Chi Minh City depart from the Tay Ninh bus station, which is in Tan Binh District.

Vehicles departing from Van Thanh bus station serve destinations within a few hours of Ho Chi Minh City.

Just next to the Saigon Hotel and the mosque on Duong Dong Du is where you catch minibuses to Vung Tau.

Train Saigon train station, or Ga Sai Gon (☎ 824 5585), is in District 3 at 1 Duong Nguyen Thong. The ticket office is open from 7.15 to 11 am and from 1 to 3 pm daily.

Boat Passenger and goods ferries to the Mekong Delta depart from the Nguyen Kiem pier at the end of Dai Lo Ham Nghi, near the Majestic Hotel, in the Dong Khoi area. Hydrofoils to Vung Tau depart from the same wharf.

Getting Around

To/From the Airport Tan Son Nhat international airport is 7km from the centre. The taxis outside the customs hall will try to overcharge, so if they refuse to use the meter, bargain (a fair price into town is about US$5).

Taxi Taxis can be occasionally hailed on the street. If you don't find one straight away, ring up and one will be dispatched in less time than it takes to say 'Ho Chi Minh'. Companies include: Airport Taxi (☎ 844 6666), Cholon Taxi (☎ 822 6666) and Davi Taxi (☎ 829 0290).

VIETNAM

Bicycle Rental bicycles are widely available from many budget hotels and cafes, especially in the Pham Ngu Lao backpacker area.

Cyclo Cyclos are the most interesting way of getting around town, but avoid them at night and always agree on fares beforehand.

Around Saigon

Cu Chi Tunnels

The tunnel network of Cu Chi District, now part of Greater Ho Chi Minh City, became legendary during the 1960s for its role in facilitating Viet Cong control of a large rural area only 30km from Saigon. At its height, the tunnel system stretched from the South Vietnamese capital to the Cambodian border.

In the district of Cu Chi alone, there were over 200km of tunnels. After ground operations against the tunnels claimed numerous US casualties and proved ineffective, the Americans turned their artillery and bombers on the area, turning it into a moonscape.

Parts of this remarkable tunnel network have been reconstructed in the interests of promoting Vietnamese patriotism and mass foreign tourism.

There is a US$4 entry fee to the tunnels.

Getting There & Away Minibuses operated by budget cafes charge around US$4 per person (transport only). Tourist hotels and Saigon Tourist run minibus tours to the area at considerably higher prices.

Tay Ninh

Tay Ninh town, capital of Tay Ninh Province, serves as the headquarters of one of Vietnam's most interesting indigenous religions, Caodaism. The **Caodai Great Temple**, in the Caodai Holy See complex 4km east of Tay Ninh, was built between 1933 and 1955.

The Religion of Caodai Caodaism is the product of an attempt to create the ideal religion through the fusion of secular and religious philosophies from both east and west. The result is a colourful and eclectic potpourri that includes bits and pieces of Buddhism, Confucianism, Taoism, Hinduism, native Vietnamese spiritualism, Christianity and Islam. Victor Hugo is among the westerners especially revered by the Caodai; look for his likeness at the Great Temple.

Caodaism was founded in 1926 after messages were communicated to the group's leaders by spirits. By the mid-1950s, one in eight southern Vietnamese was a Caodai. Today, the sect has about two million followers. All Caodai temples observe four daily ceremonies, which are held at 6 am, noon, 6 pm and midnight.

Getting There & Away Tay Ninh is 96km north-west of Ho Chi Minh City. Many travellers book a one day minibus tour from the cafes in Saigon, which includes both Tay Ninh and the Cu Chi Tunnels.

Vung Tau

Vung Tau is a beach resort 128km south-east of Saigon. Vung Tau's beaches are not Vietnam's best, but are the most accessible from Saigon – therefore the town packs out on weekends.

Although Vung Tau is a relaxing place and worth visiting, the beaches are marred by pollution from raw sewage and nearby offshore oil drilling platforms.

Beaches The main bathing area on the peninsula is **Back Beach** (Bai Sau, also known as Thuy Van Beach), an 8km-long stretch of sand. The northern end of this beach is reasonably pretty, but the southern end is a tacky collection of shops, restaurants and hotels. The water here is the cleanest in Vung Tau, which isn't saying much.

Front Beach (Bai Truoc, also called Thuy Duong Beach) is near the centre of town. It's prettier than Back Beach, but the water is really too dirty for swimming.

Bai Dau (Mulberry Beach), a quiet coconut palm-lined beach, is probably the prettiest stretch of shoreline, though there is little sand. The beach, which is about 3km north of town, stretches around a small bay.

Bai Dua (Roches Noires Beach) is a small beach situated about 2km south of the town centre.

Walks The 6km circuit around Small Mountain (Nui Nho) begins at the southern end of Front Beach and continues on Dai Lo Ha Long along the rocky coastline. The 10km circuit around Large Mountain (Nui Lom) begins at the northern end of Front Beach.

Other Sights The **Hon Ba Temple** is on a tiny island just south of Back Beach. It can be reached on foot at low tide. **Niet Ban Tinh Xa**, one of the largest Buddhist temples in Vietnam, is on the western side of Small

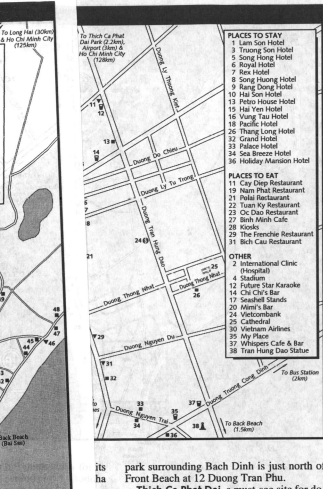

PLACES TO STAY
1 Lam Son Hotel
3 Truong Son Hotel
5 Song Hong Hotel
6 Royal Hotel
7 Rex Hotel
8 Song Huong Hotel
9 Rang Dong Hotel
10 Hai Son Hotel
13 Petro House Hotel
15 Hai Yen Hotel
16 Vung Tau Hotel
18 Pacific Hotel
26 Thang Long Hotel
32 Grand Hotel
33 Palace Hotel
34 Sea Breeze Hotel
36 Holiday Mansion Hotel

PLACES TO EAT
11 Cay Diep Restaurant
19 Nam Phat Restaurant
21 Polai Restaurant
22 Tuan Ky Restaurant
23 Oc Dao Restaurant
27 Binh Minh Cafe
28 Kiosks
29 The Frenchie Restaurant
31 Bich Cau Restaurant

OTHER
2 International Clinic (Hospital)
4 Stadium
12 Future Star Karaoke
14 Chi Chi's Bar
17 Seashell Stands
20 Mimi's Bar
24 Vietcombank
25 Cathedral
30 Vietnam Airlines
35 My Place
37 Whispers Cafe & Bar
38 Tran Hung Dao Statue

VIETNAM

park surrounding Bach Dinh is just north of Front Beach at 12 Duong Tran Phu.

Thich Ca Phat Dai, a must-see site for domestic tourists, is a hillside park of monumental Buddhist statuary built in the early 1960s. Thich Ca Phat Dai is on the eastern side of Large Mountain at 25 Dai Lo Tran Phu.

Places to Stay All the beaches have a range of accommodation options.

Back Beach The cheapest place to stay is *Beach Motel 29* (☎ 85 3481) at 29 Dai Lo Thuy Van, where prices are US$5 to US$10 with fan only, or US$15 to US$20 with air-conditioning.

At the northern end of Back Beach are

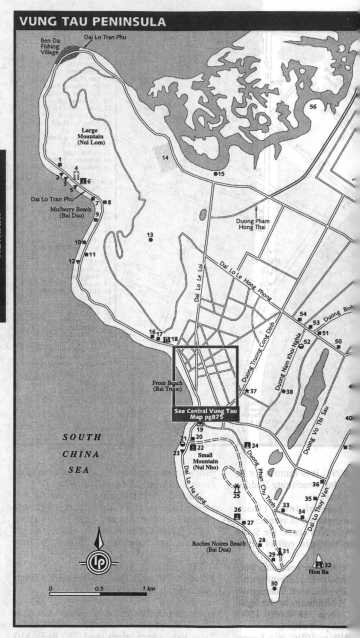

VUNG TAU PENINSULA

Ben Da Fishing Village

Dai Lo Tran Phu

Large Mountain (Nui Lom)

56

14

15

1
4
6
3
5
7 8
9

Dai Lo Tran Phu

Mulberry Beach (Bai Dau)

10
11
12

13

Duong Pham Hong Thai

Dai Lo Le Hong Phong

Dai Lo Le Loi

54
53   Duong Binh
52   51
50

16 17
18

Duong Truong Cong Dinh

Duong Nam Khoi Nghia

Front Beach (Bai Truoc)

37
38

Duong Vo Thi Sau

40

See Central Vung Tau Map pg875

SOUTH
CHINA
SEA

19
20
21
22
23

24

Small Mountain (Nui Nho)

Duong Phan Chu Trinh

25

Dai Lo Ha Long

36

35

26
27

Dai Lo Thuy Van

33
34

Roches Noires Beach (Bai Dua)

28
29 31

30

32
Hon Ba

0   0.5   1 km

VUNG TAU PENINSULA

PLACES TO STAY		43	Hoa Hong Tourist Villas	OTHER	
1	Hai Dang Hotel	44	Cap Saint Jacques	4	Cathedral
7	Nha Nghi My Tho		Hotel	6	Hung Thang Tu Pagoda
8	Nha Nghi 114	45	Thuy Duong Hotel	13	Radar Station
9	Dung Guesthouse	47	Bimexco Beach	14	Thich Ca Phat Dai
10	Nha Nghi 29		Bungalows	15	Market
11	Nha Nghi 68	48	Paradise Marina Club	18	Bach Dinh (White Villa)
16	Tran Phu Hotel	49	Crystal Heart Inn	19	Post Office
17	Guesthouse Ben Tre	50	South-East Asia Hotel	21	Hydrofoil Pier
20	Hai Au Hotel	51	Nu Hoang Hotel	22	Ngoc Bich Pagoda
27	Maritime Safety Hotel	53	Lien Hoa Hotel	24	Linh Son Temple
28	Kim Minh Hotel	54	Phuong Anh Hotel	25	Lighthouse
29	Bai Dua Villas			26	Niet Ban Tinh Xa Temple
33	Phuong Nam Hotel	PLACES TO EAT		30	French Fortifications
34	Dien Luc Hotel	2	Restaurant 73	31	Figure of Jesus
35	Beautiful Hotel	3	Cay Bang Restaurant	32	Hon Ba Temple
36	Saigon Hotel	5	Restaurant 65	37	Immigration Police
39	Beach Motel 29	12	Quan Tre Restaurant	38	Boat-Building Yards
40	Thang Muoi Hotel	23	Vung Tau International	52	Vung Tau Bus Station
41	Phuong Dong Hotel		Club	55	Airport
42	Sammy Hotel	46	Cheap Cafes	56	Docks

VIETNAM

Bimexco Beach Bungalows (☎ *85 9916)*. There are 54 bungalows with rooms from US$10 to US$28.

Close to the beach at 72 Dai Lo Thuy Van is *Saigon Hotel* (☎ *85 2317)*. There are rooms from US$12 to US$38.

Thang Muoi Hotel (☎ *85 2665)* at 4-6 Dai Lo Thuy Van boasts an alluring, garden-like environment. Doubles with fan cost US$12; with air-con it's US$25.

Nearby on Ngoc Tuoc Hill are *Hoa Hong Tourist Villas* (☎ *85 2633)* with rates at US$20 and US$25.

Front Beach Thang Long Hotel (☎ *85 2175)* at 45 Duong Thong Nhat has doubles with fan for US$10 to US$20. Air-con will set you back US$15 to US$20.

You might also check *Truong Son Hotel* (☎ *85 9864)* on Duong Phan Ding Phong, which charges US$14 for air-con doubles.

Song Huong Hotel (☎ *85 2491)* is at 10 Duong Truong Vinh Ky. This was once a dormitory for Russian experts, but has seen some renovation and price increases to match. Twins are US$17 to US$36.

Don't confuse the foregoing with the very similarly named *Song Hong Hotel* (☎ *85 2137)* at 12 Duong Hoang Dieu. Twins with air-conditioning and private bath cost US$24 to US$27.

Hai Yen Hotel (☎ *85 2571)*, at 8 Dai Lo Le Loi, advertises its restaurant, cafe, dance hall,

steam bath and Thai massage. Twins cost US$20 to US$29.

Pacific Hotel (☎ *85 9522)* at 4 Dai Lo Le Loi is a clean and modern place. Room rates depend on whether or not you get a sea view. The price range here is US$16 to US$32.

Mulberry Beach There are dozens of guest-houses *(nha nghi)* in former private villas along Mulberry Beach. This is the cheapest neighbourhood in the Vung Tau area.

Hai Dang Hotel (☎ *85 8536)* at 194 Dai Lo Tran Phu is one of the larger Mulberry Beach hotels. Rooms with fan cost US$10, or US$20 with air-con. The unnamed five room *guesthouse* just next door charges US$5 to US$7.

Nha Nghi My Tho (☎ *83 2035)*, with its rooftop terrace overlooking the beach, is at 47 Dai Lo Tran Phu. A light, airy room with ceiling fan and beach view will cost you US$8 per person.

Nha Nghi 114 (☎ *83 2023)* is at 114 Dai Lo Tran Phu, and charges US$12 for twins. *Dung Guesthouse* (☎ *83 6010)*, at 31 Dai Lo Tran Phu costs US$7 and US$8 for basic twin rooms. *Nha Nghi 29* is right on the seafront. It's a large, good-looking place and is recommended. Rooms with air-con cost US$15. *Nha Nghi 68* is at 68 Dai Lo Tran Phu. Doubles/triples cost US$5/10.

Tran Phu Hotel (☎ *85 2489)* at 42 Dai Lo Tran Phu has a relatively high standard and charges US$12 to US$20.

Next door at No 40, *Guesthouse Ben Tre* (☎ *85 2579*) is cheaper at US$8 to US$10 for fan rooms.

Roches Noires Beach This is a new development area – the small guesthouses have been blown away recently and new tourist pleasure palaces are under construction. At 22 Dai Lo Ha Long are *Bai Dua Villas* (☎ *85 6285*). This 'village of villas' charges US$15 to US$30.

Places to Eat The *kiosks* lining Front Beach do cheap noodle dishes. Opposite these is *The Frenchie Restaurant*, 26 Dai Lo Quang Trung, which does fine French food.

Entertainment Expat bars that get moving in the evening include: *My Place*, 14 Duong Nguyen Trai; *Whispers Cafe & Bar*, 438 Duong Truong Cong Dinh; *Chi Chi's Bar*, 236 Duong Ba Cu; and *Mimi's Bar*, Duong Le Loi.

Getting There & Away The most convenient minibuses to Vung Tau depart roughly every 15 minutes from near the Saigon Hotel, on Duong Dong Du. The 128km trip takes two hours and costs US$4. To return from Vung Tau, catch these minibuses at the petrol station or the Sea Breeze Hotel.

Large public air-con buses depart from Saigon's Van Thanh bus station.

Boat The best way to reach Vung Tau is by hydrofoil (about 1¼ hours, US$10). One hydrofoil can hold 124 passengers.

In Saigon, departures are from the Vina Express office (☎ *822 4621/825 3888*), 6A Duong Nguyen Tat Thanh, District 4, on the Saigon River just south of the Ben Nghe Channel.

In Vung Tau you board the hydrofoil at Cau Da pier opposite the Hai Au Hotel (Front Beach). Vina Express (☎ *85 6530*) has a Vung Tau office by the pier.

Long Hai

To avoid the crowds and commercialised tourism, backpackers are increasingly head-ing to Long Hai, 30km north-east of Vung Tau.

Places to Stay The best place to stay is *Huong Bien Hotel* (☎ *86 8430*). There are five bungalows with two rooms in each. Most rooms have fan and cold-water bath, and cost US$12. With air-con it's US$15.

Palace Hotel (☎ *86 8364*) was originally built to accommodate Emperor Bao Dai, who reigned in Vietnam from 1926 to 1945. Rooms with fan and cold-water bath go for US$14; with air-con and hot water it's US$20.

Military Guesthouse (Nha Nghi Quan Doi, ☎ 86 8316) is also good. The main building has 17 rooms priced from US$10 to US$20. There are also two beach houses (recommended), where rooms cost only US$7.

Rang Dong Hotel (☎ *86 8356*) is memorable chiefly for the karaoke. Rooms cost US$15 to US$20.

The largest hotel currently on offer is *Long Hai Hotel* (☎ *86 8312*). The beach next to the hotel is dirty and the 'massage service' looks rather dodgy. Rooms are priced from US$13 to US$25.

Long Hai Guesthouse (Nha Nghi Long Hai, ☎ 86 8312) is another reasonable option. Twins cost US$10 to US$24.

Long Hai Green Hotel (Khach San Xanh Long Hai, ☎ 86 8337) is far from the best beaches. Rooms with air-con and attached hot-water bath are US$10 to US$12.

Mekong Delta

Flat as a billiards table but lusciously green and beautiful, the Mekong Delta is the southernmost region of Vietnam. It's a rich agricultural region, the breadbasket (or perhaps 'ricebasket') of the nation. The delta is a thick patchwork of rice paddies, swamps and remnant forest interlaced with canals and rivers – an intriguing place to explore.

MYTHO

Mytho is a quiet city of 100,000 easily reached as a day trip from Saigon, and serves as a good introduction to the delta region.

Things to See & Do

Boat Trips Visiting the islands of the Mekong River is the main attraction. However, the Mytho police do not permit foreigners to rent boats cheaply from the locals. Instead you are forced to rent a boat from the government at around US$25 per hour.

Dong Tam Snake Farm About 10km from Mytho is this interesting snake farm where you can wrap yourself in a python (if you dare) or watch the Vietnamese snake handlers milk poison from cobras.

centre of the Mekong Delta); **Chau Doc**, which has a well known mosque across the river in Chau Giang District and a number of pagodas and temples at Sam Mountain; **Rach Gia** on the Gulf of Thailand (where boats depart for Phu Quoc Island); **Phu Quoc Island**, a beautiful island with white-sand beaches; **Ha Tien**, a coastal town almost on the Cambodian border near which there are a number of grottoes and beaches; and **Hon Chong** (32km from Ha Tien), which has the best beach in the otherwise muddy Mekong Delta.

All these places have cheap accommodation and are served by buses, and in some cases, by scheduled ferry services. Cantho and Phu Quoc Island have air service from Ho Chi Minh City.

Appendix

Languages of South-East Asia

CAMBODIA (KHMER)
Basics

Excuse me.	*suom tous*
Good night.	*rear trei suor sdei*
Goodbye.	*lear heouy*
Hello.	*joom reab suor/ suor sdei*
How are you?	*tau neak sok sapbaiy jea te?*
Very well.	*sok touk jea thomada te*
Please.	*suom*
Thank you.	*ar kun*
No.	*te*
Yes. (by men)	*bat*
Yes. (by women)	*jas*

Getting Around

boat	*kopal/tuok*
bus	*lan thom deouk monuos*
train	*rout phleoung*
airport	*veal youn huos*
bus station	*ben lan*
railway station	*sathani rout phleoung*
ticket office	*kanleng luok suombuot*
tourist office	*kariyaleiy samrap puok tesajor*

Where is a/the ...?	*tau ... nouv eir na?*
I want a ticket to ...	*khjoom junh ban suombuot teou ...*
When does it depart?	*tau ke jeng domneur moung ponmann?*
When does it arrive here/there?	*tau ke teou/mouk doul moung ponmaan?*

Accommodation

I want a ...	*khjoom joung ban ...*
single room	*bantuop kre samrap mouy neak*
double room	*bantuop kre samrap pee neak*
bed	*kre mouy*

How much is a room?	*chnoul ... tleiy ...*

Food & Drinks

rice	*bai*
noodles	*mee*
vegetarian	*buong l...*
chicken	*mo-an*
fish	*trray*
beef	*gow*
pork	*chhroul...*
the same	*doi kinn*
water	*tuck*
tea	*thai*
coffee	*caafee*
beer	*bia*
ice	*teckko*

Numbers

1	*mouy*	11
2	*pee*	12
3	*bei*	20
4	*boun*	21
5	*bram*	30
6	*bram-mouy*	40
7	*bram-pee*	100
8	*bram-bei*	500
9	*bram-boun*	1000
10	*duop*	10,000

one million	*muy lia...*

Emergencies

Please call ...	*suom ...*
an ambulance	*lan ...*
a dentist	*pe...*
a doctor	*kra...*
the police	*po...*
It's an emergency.	*nees ...*
I'm allergic to penicillin.	*khjoo... the... tha... pe...*

INDONESIA (BAHASA)

Basics

Good morning.	*Selamat pagi.*
Good day.	*Selamat siang.*
Good afternoon.	*Selamat sore.*
Good evening/night.	*Selamat malam.*
Goodbye. (to one staying)	*Selamat tinggal.*
Goodbye. (to one going)	*Selamat jalan.*
How are you?	*Apa kabar?*
I'm fine.	*Kabar baik.*
Please.	*Tolong.*
Thank you (very much).	*Terima kasih (banyak).*
Yes.	*Yu.*
No.	*Tidak/Bukan.*
Excuse me.	*Maaf/Permisi.*
I don't understand.	*Saya tidak mengerti.*
What is this?	*Apa ini?*
How much (price)?	*Berapa (harga)?*
expensive	*mahal*

Getting Around

What time does the ... leave/arrive?	*Jam berapa ... berangkat/tiba?*
bus	*bis/bus*
ship	*kapal*
train	*kereta api*
I want to go to ...	*Saya mau pergi ke ...*
How far?	*Berapa jauh?*
bus station	*setasiun bis/terminal*
ticket	*karcis/tiket*

Around Town

Where is ...?	*Dimana ...?*
bank	*bank*
post office	*kantor pos*
tourist office	*dinas pariwisata*
here/there	*disini/disana*
left/right	*kiri/kanan*
near/far	*dekat/jauh*
straight ahead	*terus*

Accommodation

guesthouse	*losmen*
bathroom	*kamar mandi*
key	*kunci*
bed	*tempat tidur*

toilet	*WC (way say)/ kamar kecil*
Is there a room available?	*Adakah kamar kosong?*
Can I see the room?	*Boleh saya melihat kamar?*
one night	*satu malam*
two nights	*dua malam*

Food & Drinks

beef	*daging*
chicken	*ayam*
crab	*kepiting*
egg	*telur*
fish	*ikan*
food	*makanan*
fried noodles	*mie goreng*
pork	*babi*
potato	*kentang*
prawns	*udang-udang*
rice with odds & ends	*nasi campur*
fried rice	*nasi goreng*
white rice	*nasi putih*
soup	*soto*
mixed vegetables	*sayur-sayuran*
fried vegetables	*cap cai*
beer	*bir*
coffee	*kopi*
cordial	*stroop*
drinking water	*air minum/air putih*
drinks	*minuman*
milk	*susu*
orange juice	*air jeruk*
tea with sugar	*teh manis, teh gula*
tea without sugar (unthinkable!)	*teh pahit*

Time

When?	*Kapan?*
At what time ...?	*Pada jam berapa ...?*
open	*buka*
close	*tutup*
today	*hari ini*
tonight	*malam ini*
tomorrow	*besok*
yesterday	*kemarin*

Emergencies

Help!	*Tolong!*
Call a doctor!	*Panggil dokter!*
Call the police!	*Panggil polisi!*
I'm ill.	*Saya sakit.*

Numbers

1	*satu*
2	*dua*
3	*tiga*
4	*empat*
5	*lima*
6	*enam*
7	*tujuh*
8	*delapan*
9	*sembilan*
10	*sepuluh*
11	*sebelas*
20	*duapuluh*
21	*duapuluh satu*
30	*tigapuluh*
50	*limapuluh*
100	*seratus*
1000	*seribu*
one million	*sejuta*

LAOS

Basically, Lao is a monosyllabic, tonal language, like various dialects of Thai and Chinese. Many identical phonemes or vowel-consonant combinations are differentiated by tone only. Consequently, the word *sao*, for example, can mean 'girl', 'morning', 'pillar' or 'twenty' depending on the tone. For people from non-tonal language backgrounds, it can be very hard to learn at first. The first rule in learning and using the tone system is to avoid overlaying your native intonation patterns onto the Lao.

Vientiane Lao has six tones (compared with five in Standard Thai, four in Mandarin and nine in Cantonese). Three of the tones are level (low, mid and high), while three follow pitch inclines (rising, high falling and low falling). All six variations in pitch are relative to the speaker's natural vocal range, so that one person's low tone is not necessarily the same pitch as another person's.

Tones

Low tone – produced at the relative bottom of your conversational tonal range – usually flat level (though not everyone pronounces it flat and level), eg *dịi*, 'good'.

Mid tone – flat like the low tone, but spoken at the relative middle of the speaker's vocal range. No tone mark is used, eg *het*, 'do'.

High tone – flat again, but at the relative top of your vocal range, eg *heúa*, 'boat'.

Rising tone – begins a bit below the mid tone and rises to just at or above the high tone, eg *sãam*, 'three'.

High falling tone – begins at or above the high tone and falls to the mid level, eg *sâo*, 'morning'.

Low falling tone – begins at about the mid level and falls to the level of the low tone, eg *kháo*, 'rice'.

Basics

Greetings/Hello.	*sábạai-dịi*
Goodbye.	*sábạai-dịi*
(general farewell)	
Goodbye.	*láa kawn* (lit: leaving
(person leaving)	first)
	pại kawn (lit: going
	first)
Goodbye.	*sọhk dịi* (lit: good
(person staying)	luck)
Thank you	*khàwp jại (lãi lãi)*
(very much).	
Excuse me.	*khãw thọht*
Can you speak	*jâo páak pháasaa*
English?	*ạngkít dâi baw?*
I can't speak Lao.	*khàwy páak pháasaa*
	láo baw dâi
Do you understand?	*jâo khào jại baw?*
I don't understand.	*baw khào jại*

Getting Around

Where is the ...	*... yùu sãi?*
airport	*doen bịn*
bus station	*sathãanii lot pájạm*
	tháang
bus stop	*bawn jàwt lot pájạm*
	tháang
taxi stand	*bawn jàwt lot*
	thaek-sîi

What time will the ... leave?	... já àwk ják móhng?
boat	heúa
bus	lot
minivan	lot tûu
taxi	lot thâek-síi
samlor (pedicab)	sāam-lâw
tuk-tuk (jumbo)	túk-túk

| I want to go to ... | khàwy yàak pại ... |
| How much to ... ? | pại ... thao dại? |

Directions

Which ... is this?	bawn nîi ... nyãng?
street/road/avenue	thanõn
city	méuang
village	muu bâan
province	khwãeng

How far?	kại thao dại?
Turn left.	lîaw sâai
Turn right.	lîaw khwãa
Go straight ahead.	pại seu-seu
far/not far	kại/baw kại
north	thit nẽua
south	thit tâi
east	thit tạawán àwk
west	thit tạawán tók

I'd like to rent a ...	khàwy yàak sao ...
car	lot (ọh-tọh)
bicycle	lot thìip
motorcycle	lot ják

Around Town

Where is the ... ?	... yùu sãi
bank	thanáakháan
hospital	hóhng mãw
pharmacy	hâan khãai yạa
post office	pại-sá-níi/ hóhng sãai
stupa	thâat

| open/closed | pòet/pít |

Accommodation

Do you have a room?	míi hàwng baw?
hotel	hóhng háem
guesthouse	hãw hap kháek

How much ...?	... thao dại?
per night	khéun-la
per week	gathit-la

| single room | hàwng náwn tịang diaw |
| double room | hàwng náwn tịang khuu |

key	kájạe
room	hàwng
soap	sábuu
toilet	sùam

| (I/we) will stay two nights. | si phak sãwng khéun |
| Can (I/we) look at the room? | khaw boeng hàwng dâi baw? |

Food & Drinks

chicken	kai
crab	pụu
fish	pạa
pork	mũu
shrimp/prawns	kûng

fried rice with ...
   khào phát (khào khùa) ...
steamed white rice
   khào nèung
sticky rice
   khào nĩaw
fried egg
   khai dạo
plain omelette
   jẹun khai
fried peanuts
   thua jẹun
fried potatoes
   mán falang jẹun
fried spring rolls
   yáw jẹun
soup with chicken, galingal root & coconut
   tọm khaa kai
fish & lemongrass soup with mushrooms
   tọm yám pạa
plain bread (usually French-style)
   khào jii

| boiled water | nâam tọm |
| cold water | nâam yén |

hot water	*nâam hâwn*
soda water	*nâam sah-dạa*
ice	*nâam kâwn*
weak Chinese tea	*nâam sáa*
hot Lao tea with sugar	*sáa hâwn*
hot Lao tea with milk & sugar	*sáa nóm hâwn*
no sugar (command)	*baw sai nâam-tạan*
hot Lao coffee with milk & sugar	*kạa-féh nâam hâwn*
hot Lao coffee with sugar, no milk	*kạa-féh dạm*
orange juice (or orange soda)	*nâam màak kîang*
plain milk	*nâam nóm*
yoghurt	*nóm sòm*
beer	*bịa*
rice whisky	*lào láo*

Time, Days & Numbers

today	*mêu nîi*
tonight	*khéun nîi*
this morning	*sâo nîi*
this afternoon	*baai nîi*
all day long	*talàwt mêu*
now	*diaw nîi/tạwn nîi*
sometimes	*bạang theua*
yesterday	*mêu wáan nîi*
tomorrow	*mêu eun*

Sunday	*wán ạathit*
Monday	*wán jạn*
Tuesday	*wán ạngkh an*
Wednesday	*wán phut*
Thursday	*wán phahát*
Friday	*wán súk*
Saturday	*wán sáo*

0	*sŭun*
1	*neung*
2	*sãwng*
3	*sãam*
4	*sii*
5	*hàa*
6	*hók*
7	*jét*
8	*pàet*
9	*kâo*

Emergencies

Help!	*suay dae!*
Fire!	*fái mài!*
Call a doctor!	*suai tạam hãa mãw hài dae!*
Call the police!	*suay ôen tam-lùat dae!*
Go away!	*pại dôe!*
Where are the toilets?	*hàwng sùam yuu sãi?*
I'm lost.	*khàwy lõng tháang*
accident	*ú-bát-tí-hèht*
ambulance	*lot hóhng mãw*
allergic (to)	*phâe*
faint	*pẹn lóm*
ill	*puay*

10	*síp*
11	*síp-ét*
12	*síp-sãwng*
13	*síp-sãam*
14	*síp-sii*
...-teen	*síp ...*
20	*sáo*
21	*sáo-ét*
22	*sáo-sãwng*
23	*sáo-sãam*
30	*sãam-síp*
40	*sii-síp*
50	*hàa-síp*
60	*hók-síp*
70	*jét-síp*
80	*pàet-síp*
90	*kâo-síp*
100	*hâwy*
200	*sãwng hâwy*
300	*sãam hâwy*
1000	*phán*
10,000	*meun (síp-phán)*
100,000	*sãen (hâwy phán)*
million	*lâan*
billion	*têu (phan láan)*
first	*thíi neung*
second	*thíi sãwng*

MALAYSIA (BAHASA)
Basics

Good morning.	Selamat pagi.
Good day. (around midday)	Selamat tengah hari.
Good afternoon.	Selamat petang.
Good night.	Selamat malam.
Goodbye. (to one staying)	Selamat tinggal.
Goodbye. (to one going)	Selamat jalan.
Yes.	Ya.
No.	Tidak.
Thank you (very much).	Terima kasih (banyak).
You're welcome.	Sama-sama.
Please.	Tolong/Silakan.
Sorry/Pardon?	Maaf.
Excuse me.	Maafkan saya.
Do you speak English?	Bolehkah anda berbicara bahasa Inggeris?
I understand.	Saya faham.
I don't understand.	Saya tidak faham.
Please write that word down.	Tolong tuliskan perkataan.

Getting Around

How can I get to ...	Bagaimana saya pergi ke ...?
How many km?	Berapa kilometre?
What time does the ... leave?	Pukul berapakah ... berangkat?
bus	bas
train	keretapi
ship	kapal
boat	bot
rickshaw/trishaw	beca

Around Town

Where is a/the ...?	Di mana ada ...?
bank	bank
hospital	hospital
post office	pejabat pos
tourist office	pejabat pelancong
Go straight ahead.	Jalan terus.
Turn left/right.	Belok kiri/kanan.
here/there	di sini/di sana

Accommodation

hotel	hotel
losmen	losmen
room	bilik
bed	tempat tidur
soap	sabun
expensive	mahal
Is there a room available?	Ada bilik kosong?
How much is it per night/person?	Berapa harga satu malam/orang?
Can I see the room?	Boleh saya lihat biliknya?

Food & Drinks

I don't want fish, chicken or meat.
Saya tidak mau ikan, ayam atau daging.

fish	ikan
chicken	ayam
egg	telur
pork	babi
crab	ketam
beef	daging lembu
prawns	udang
fried rice	nasi goreng
boiled rice	nasi putih
rice with odds & ends	nasi campur
fried noodles	mee goreng
soup	sup
fried vegetables	cap cai
potatoes	kentang
vegetables	sayur-sayuran
drinking water	air minum
orange juice	air jeruk/air oren
coffee	kopi
tea	teh
sugar	gula
milk	susu

Time, Days & Numbers

When?	Bila?
How long?	Berapa lama?
tomorrow	besok
yesterday	kelmarin

Emergencies

Help!	*Tolong!*
Call a doctor!	*Panggil doktor!*
I'm lost.	*Saya sesat.*
police	*polis*
hospital	*hospital*

Monday	*hari Isnin*
Tuesday	*hari Selasa*
Wednesday	*hari Rabu*
Thursday	*hari Kamis*
Friday	*hari Jumaat*
Saturday	*hari Sabtu*
Sunday	*hari Minggu*

½	*setengah*
1	*satu*
2	*dua*
3	*tiga*
4	*empat*
5	*lima*
6	*enam*
7	*tujuh*
8	*delapan/lapan*
9	*sembilan*
10	*sepuluh*
11	*sebelas*
12	*dua belas*
13	*tiga belas*
20	*dua puluh*
21	*dua puluh satu*
30	*tiga puluh*
53	*lima puluh tiga*
100	*seratus*
1000	*seribu*

one million *sejuta*

MYANMAR (BURMESE)
Basics

Excuse me.	*kwin pyu baa*
Good morning/ afternoon/evening.	*min ga la baa*
Goodbye.	*pyan dor mai* (lit: I'm going)
Please.	*chay zoo tin baa day*
Thank you.	*chay zoo tin baa dai*

Yes.	*hoke ket*
No.	*ma hoke boo*
How are you?	*mah yeh laa?*
I'm well.	*maa bah day*
Do you understand?	*kin byar har lai tha laa?*
I don't understand.	*chun note nar ma lai boo*
How much?	*bah lout lai?*
Too much.	*myar dai*

Getting Around

Where is the ...?	*... beh mah lai?*
railway station	*boo dah youn*
bus station	*bak skah gait*
When will the bus/ train leave?	*bak skah/miy tah bai kain?*
Is it far?	*waid thlah?*
left	*bay bet*
right	*nya bet*
straight (ahead)	*tay day*

Accommodation

hotel	*hotay*
guesthouse	*tayko gan*
Can foreigners stay here?	*nain ngan gya thah di mah taylo ya thlah?*
How much is it for one night?	*kahn teh yetko bai lauk lai?*

Food & Drinks

bread	*pow mohn*
butter	*taw but*
chicken	*kyet (chet) tar*
egg (boiled)	*chet u byok*
egg (fried)	*chet u chor*
fish	*ngar*
hot	*ah poo*
mutton	*seik tar*
noodles	*kaw swe*
restaurant	*sar tao syne*
rice (cooked)	*ta min*
soup	*hin jo*
sugar	*ta jar*
toast	*pow moh gin*
coffee	*kaw pee*
drinking water	*tao ye*
tea	*la bet ye*

Emergencies

Help!	*kaybah!*
Stop!	*yat!*
I'm lost.	*lahn pyout thwah bee*
doctor	*syah-woon*
hospital	*sayoun*

Numbers

1	*tit*
2	*nit*
3	*thone*
4	*lay*
5	*ngar*
6	*howk*
7	*kun nit*
8	*sit*
9	*co*
10	*ta sei*
11	*sair tit*
12	*sair nit*
20	*na sei*
30	*thone sei*
100	*ta yar*
500	*gar yar*
1000	*(ta)t'aun*
million	*(ta)than*

PHILIPPINES (PILIPINO)
Basics

Good morning.	*Magandáng umága.*
Goodbye.	*Paálam.*
Good evening.	*Magandáng gabí.*
Hello.	*Haló.*
Welcome/Farewell.	*Mabúhay.*
How many?	*Ilán?*
How much?	*Magkáno?*
That one.	*Iyón.*
too expensive	*mahál*
Yes.	*Oó.*
No.	*Hindí.*
good/bad	*mabúti/masamá*

Getting Around

Where is the ...?	*Násaan ang ...?*
bus station	*terminal ng bus*
train station	*terminal ng tren*
road to ...	*daan papuntang ...*

What time does the bus leave/arrive?	*Anong óras áalis/ dárating ang bus?*
Is it far from/ near here?	*Maláyó (malápit) ba díto?*
straight ahead	*dirétso lámang*
to the right	*papakánan*
to the left	*papakaliwá*

Accommodation

camping ground	*kampingan*
guesthouse	*báhay pára sa nga turist*
cheap hotel	*múrang hotél*
price	*halagá*
Do you have any rooms available?	*May bakánte hó ba kayo?*
How much for one night?	*Magkáno hó ba ang báyad pára sa isang gabi?*

Food & Drinks

food	*pagkaín*
restaurant	*restorán*
sugar	*asúkal*
salt	*ásin*
vegetarian	*na walang karne*
beer	*serbésa*
coffee	*kapé*
milk	*gátas*
water	*túbig*

Time & Numbers

What time is it?	*Anong óras na?*
today	*ngayon*
tomorrow	*búkas*
yesterday	*kahápon*

1	*isá*	11	*labíng-isá*
2	*dalawá*	12	*labíndalawá*
3	*tatló*	13	*labíntatló*
4	*apát*	14	*labín-apát*
5	*limá*	15	*labínlimá*
6	*ánim*	20	*dalawampû*
7	*pitó*	30	*tatlampû*
8	*waló*	50	*limampû*
9	*siyám*	100	*sandaán*
10	*sampú*	1000	*sanlibo*

Emergencies

I'm sick.	May sakit ako.
Help!	Saklólo!
Call the police!	Tumawag ka ng pulís!
I'm lost.	Nawáwalá ako.
doctor	doktor
hospital	ospital
chemist	botíká

THAILAND

The main complication with Thai is that it is tonal; the same word could be pronounced with a rising, falling, high, low or level tone and could theoretically have five meanings!

Several different words can be used to mean 'I' but the safest are *phóm* for men and *díichán* for women. You can also omit the pronoun altogether and say, for example, *mâi khâo jai* (do not understand).

Mâi pen rai is a very useful phrase, although it actually has far more meanings than simply 'it doesn't matter': it can also mean 'don't bother', 'forget it', 'leave it alone', 'take no notice', or even 'that's enough'.

The 'ph' in a Thai word is always pronounced like an English 'p', not as an 'f'.

Basics

Hello.	sawàt dii
How are you?	pen yangai?
I'm fine.	sabàay dii
Excuse me.	khāw thôht
Please.	kaa-ru-naa/pròht
Thank you.	khàwp khun
Yes. (female)	khâ
Yes. (male)	khráp
No.	mâi
How much?	thâo rai?
foreigner of European descent	farang
toilet	hâwng sûam

Getting Around

I want to go to ...	yàak pai ...
How far?	klai thâo rai?

Where is the ...?	... yûu thîi nãi?
bus	rót meh
train	rót fai
hotel	rohng raem
post office	praisanii
station	sathaanii
beach	ao
island	ko
house/village	ban

here/there	thîi-nîi/thîi-nûun
near/far	klâi/klai
left/right	sái/khwaa
straight ahead	trong pai

Accommodation

guesthouse	bâan phák
hotel	rohng raem
Do you have a room available?	mii hâwng mãi?
How much is it per night?	kheun-lá thâo rai?

Time

When?	mêu-arai?
What time?	kìi mohng?
today	wan nií
tomorrow	phrûng nií
yesterday	mêua waan

Numbers

1	nèung	9	kâo
2	sãwng	10	sìp
3	sãam	20	yîi sìp
4	sìi	21	yîi sìp èt
5	hâa	30	sãam sìp
6	hòk	100	nèung roi
7	jèt	200	sãwng roi
8	pàet	1000	nèung phan

Emergencies

Help!	chûay dûay!
Go away.	pai láew
police	tam-ruat
doctor	mãw
chemist/pharmacy	ráan khãai yaa

VIETNAM

Perhaps the trickiest aspect of spoken Vietnamese for westerners is learning to differentiate between the six tones, each of which is represented by a different diacritical mark. Thus, every syllable in Vietnamese can be pronounced six different ways. Depending on the tones, the word *ma* can be read to mean 'phantom', 'mother', 'rice seedling', 'tomb' or 'horse'.

đ	with a crossbar; like a hard 'd'
d	without a crossbar; as a 'z' (north) and as a 'y' (south)
gi	as a 'z' (north) and as a 'y' (south)
ng	like the '-nga-' in 'long ago'
nh	as Spanish 'ñ' (as in *mañana*)
ph	as an 'f'
r	as 'z' (north) and 'r' (south)
s	as an 's' (north) and 'sh' (south)
tr	as 'ch' in the north; as 'tr' in the south
th	as a strongly aspirated 't'
x	as an 's'
ch	as a 'k'
ó'	as in 'bird'
ú'	between the 'i' in 'sister' and the 'u' in sugar

Basics

Hello.	*chao*
Good night.	*chuc ngu ngon*
Thank you.	*cam ó'n*
Thank you very much.	*cam ó'n rat nhieu*
Excuse me.	*xin loi*
Yes.	*vang* (north)/ *co, phai* (south)
No.	*khong*
I don't understand.	*toi khong hieu*
How much (price)?	*cai nay bao nhieu tien?*

Getting Around

Where is the ...?	*... ó' đau?*
bus station	*ben xe*
railway station	*ga xe lú'a*
post office	*bú'u đien*
telephone	*đien thoai*
I want to go to ...	*toi muon đi ...*
Is it far?	*co xa khong?*

What time does the ... leave/arrive?	*may gió' ... khoi hanh/ den?*
bus	*xe buyt*
train	*xe lú'a*

Accommodation

hotel	*khach san*
guesthouse	*nha khach*
cheap hotel	*khach san re tien*
air-con	*quat lanh*
toilet	*nha ve sinh*
bathroom	*nha tam*
Do you have any rooms available?	*ong co phong nao trong khong?*
How much is it ...?	*bao nhieu ...?*
per night	*moi dem*
per person	*moi nguoi*

Time & Numbers

What time is it?	*may goi roi?*
today	*hom nay*
tomorrow	*ngay mui*
yesterday	*hom qua*

1	*mot*	11	*mú'ó'i mot*
2	*hai*	19	*mú'ó'i chin*
3	*ba*	20	*hai mú'ó'i*
4	*bon*	21	*hai mú'ó'i mot*
5	*nam*	30	*ba mú'ó'i*
6	*sau*	90	*chin mú'ó'i*
7	*bay*	100	*mot tram*
8	*tam*	200	*hai tram*
9	*chin*	900	*chin tram*
10	*mú'ó'i, chuc*	1000	*mot nghin*

one million *mot trieu*

Emergencies

I'm sick.	*toi bi benh*
Please call a doctor.	*lam ó'n goi bac si*
Help!	*cú'u toi vó'i!*
Thief!	*cú'ó'p/cap!*
police	*cong an*
hospital	*benh vien*
chemist/pharmacy	*nha thuoc tay*
dizziness	*chong mat*
headache	*nhú'c đau*
vomiting	*oi, mú'a*

South-East Asia History Chart

Indonesia	Malaysia & Singapore	Thailand	Myanmar (Burma)	Vietnam	Cambodia & Laos	Philippines
BC						
Java Man 500,000 BC Bronze culture Ban Chiang 2000 BC	Proto Malay Migration from China 2000 BC	Earliest agriculture on Khorat Plateau 8000 BC	Mon arrive 2000 BC Asoka's Buddhist missionaries arrive 3rd C BC	Earliest agriculture in Mekong river valley 8000 BC Rise of Dong Son culture 300 BC		
AD						
			Burmese arrive from Tibet 3rd C	Chinese rule 111 BC-938 AD Hindu Champa kingdom 2nd C	Hindu Funan kingdom 1st-6th C	
500						
Hindu-Buddhist Sriwijaya Empire in Sumatra 7th C Buddhist Sailendras in Java 8th C Borobudur Built 782-84 Hindu Mataram Kingdom Java 9th C	Malay peninsula under loose control of Sriwijaya	Sriwijaya Empire extends to southern Thailand Austro-Thai migrations into lower river valleys 8th C	Bagan founded 849	Mahayana Buddhism Chinese overthrown – 1st Viet dynasty 938	Chenla kingdom 2nd C Sailendras invade Chenla Angkor Founded 889 – Hindu rule	
1000						
Sriwijaya defeats Mataram 1006 Cholas attack Sriwijaya 1025 Majapahit Empire founded in Java 1292 Gajah Mada prime minister 1331-64 Rise of Islam and decline of Majapahits 15th C	Islam comes to Sumatran and Malay peninsula ports Melaka founded 1402 Melaka sultanate converts to Islam	Sukhothai kingdom 1238-1376 Theravada Buddhism and Thai script adopted Ayuthaya founded 1350 Thais attack Khmers and control Malay states 15th C	Bagan dynasty 1044-1287 Theravada Buddhism adopted Mongols sack Bagan 1287 Shan establish capital at Ava 1360s Mon establish capital at Bago 1380s	Ly dynasty 1010-1225 Theravada Buddhism promoted Tran dynasty 1225-1400 Mongol invasion repelled	Angkor Wat built 1112-52 Fa Ngum centres Lan Xang, first Lao kingdom, in Luang Prabang 1353	Islam introduced to Mindanao 15th C

South-East Asia History Chart

Indonesia	Malaysia & Singapore	Thailand	Myanmar (Burma)	Vietnam	Cambodia & Laos	Philippines
1500						
Portuguese in Ternate 1511 Fall of Maja-pahits 1520 Mataram kingdom founded 1582	Portuguese conquer Melaka 1511	Burmese Invasions			Portuguese sign trade treaty with the Mon Lao capital moved to Vientiane 1520	Magellan arrives 1521 Spanish settle Cebu 1565 Legaspi conquers Manila 1571
1600						
	Dutch conquer Melaka 1641	1st European arrivals at Ayu-thaya 1600		French missionaries arrive	Lao Lan Xang kingdom ends 1694	
1700						
	Francis Light arrives in Penang 1786	Burmese sack Ayuthaya 1767	Trading posts established in late 1700s	Tay Son rebellion 1771-1802	Laos overrun by Burma & Siam 1763-69	British occupy Manila 1762-63
1800						
British occupy Java 1811-16 Diponegoro's Java War 1825-30 Ethical Policy 1870-1900	Raffles founds Singapore 1819 British intervention in sultanates Malay Federation 1895	Mongkut (1851-68) and Chula-longkorn (1868-1910) reforms and modernisa-tion	British wars of 1824, 1852 and 1883 see Britain annex Burma	French sieze Saigon (1859), occupy Cochinchina (1862), then Annam and Tonkin (1885)	Cambodia becomes French protectorate 1864	Rizal executed 1896 Independence from Spain, US annexa-tion 1898
1900						
Nationalist movements of Sarekat Islam (1912), PKI (1920) and PNI (1927) Republic of Indonesia 1945 Dutch war 1946-49; Soekarno president Untung coup 1965 Soeharto president 1965-1998 Soeharto ousted after widespread riots 1998	Rubber introduced Chinese and Indians arrive in force Federation of Malaya 1948 Communist Emergency 1948-60 Independence 1957 Singapore goes it alone 1965 Race riots in KL 1969 Dr Mahathir-Mohamad becomes prime minister 1981	Coup sees end of absolute monarchy 1932 Elections restored 1946 but civilian government interrupted by military coups Democracy comes to Thailand 1992 South-East Asian curren-cy crisis hits, several mega-projects put on indefinite hold 1997	Indepen-dence 1948, accompanied by commu-nist and Karen rebellions Ne Win seizes power in left-wing army coup 1962 Democracy movement crushed 1988 Aung San Suu Kyi awarded Nobel Peace Prize 1991	Nationalism suppressed Ho Chi Minh declares north independent 1945 Franco-Viet Minh War 1946-54 Vietnam divided 1955 US bombing of north 1965 Saigon Falls 1975 Diplomatic ties estab-lished with USA 1995	French gain Lao and Me-kong territories 1904 Cambodian and Lao indepen-dence 1954 Cambodian 'killing fields' 1975-78 Vietnam in-vades Cam-bodia 1978 Cambodian elections 1993 Cambodian prime minis-ter Ranariddh overthrown 1997 Pol Pot dies 1998 Hun Sen elected prime minister of Cambodia 1998	Internal self-government 1935 Indepen-dence 1946 Marcos president 1965-86 Marcos ousted, Aquino becomes president 1986 Joseph Estrada wins presidential elections 1998

Religions of South-East Asia

BUDDHISM

Buddhism was founded by Siddhartha Gautama, an Indian prince, in the 6th century BC. After years of ascetic wanderings and contemplation he became the 'enlightened' or 'awakened one', the Buddha. His message is that the cause of life's suffering is the illusory nature of desire, and that by overcoming desire we can free ourselves from suffering. Desire can be conquered by following the Eightfold Path, consisting of right understanding, thought, speech, conduct, livelihood, effort, attentiveness and concentration. The ultimate goal is *nirvana*, the escape from the endless round of births and rebirths and their lives of suffering.

Buddhism is essentially a Hindu reform movement, and its philosophy owes much to the Hindu notions of *maya* (the illusory nature of existence) and *moksha* (enlightenment). The big difference is that Buddhism shunned the Hindu pantheon of gods and the caste system. It was initially not a religion but a practical, moral philosophy free from the priestly Brahman hierarchy.

Buddhism gained wide adherence in India with its adoption by Emperor Ashoka in the 3rd century BC, but later split into two sects: Mahayana (greater path) and Hinayana (lesser path), also known as Theravada (teaching of the elders). Mahayana Buddhism showed greater mysticism and the *bodhisattva*, or saint who attains nirvana, reintroduced the idea of divinity to Buddhism. It spread north to Tibet, China and Japan, and then down to Vietnam. The more scholarly, philosophical Theravada sect found less favour in the royal courts, but continued to thrive in Sri Lanka and lower Burma even after a resurgent Hinduism virtually eliminated Buddhism in India by the end of the first millennium AD.

In South-East Asia, Buddhism, along with Hinduism, was adopted by kingdoms in Indochina, Sumatra and Java in the first millennium. The major change came in the 11th century when the Burmese adopted Theravada Buddhism, and this later spread to Thailand, Laos and Cambodia. Theravada Buddhism remains the dominant faith in these countries today, while Vietnam, with its strongly Chinese influence, follows a form of Mahayana Buddhism.

HINDUISM

Today, the tiny island of Bali is the only place in the region where Hinduism dominates, but Hinduism has strongly influenced the other cultures of South-East Asia.

Hinduism is a complex religion, but at its core is the mystical principle that the physical world is an illusion *(maya)* and until this is realised through enlightenment *(moksha)* the individual is condemned to a cycle of rebirths and reincarnations. Brahma is the ultimate god and universal spirit, but Hinduism has a vast pantheon of gods that are worshipped on a day-to-day level.

The two main gods are Shiva, the Destroyer, and Vishnu, the Preserver. Shivaism represents a more esoteric and ascetic path, and with Shiva's *shakti*, or female energy (represented by his wives Kali and Parvati), destruction and fertility are intertwined. Shivaism found greater acceptance in South-East Asia, perhaps because it was closer to existing fertility worship and the appeasement of malevolent spirits. Vishnuism places greater emphasis on devotion and duty, and Vishnu's incarnations, Krishna and Rama, feature heavily in South-East Asian art and culture through the stories of the *Ramayana* epic.

Hinduism and Buddhism were often intertwined in South-East Asia and many empires accepted the principles and iconography of both religions. Hinduism's rigid caste system had much less relevance in South-East Asia, but the notions of the god-king and the elitist nature of Hindu society were readily accepted by South-East Asian rulers.

ISLAM

In the early 7th century in Mecca, Mohammed received the word of Allah (God) and called on the people to submit to the one true God. His teachings appealed to the poorer levels of society and angered the merchant class. In 622 Mohammed and his followers were forced to flee Medina, and this migration – the *hijrah* – marks the beginning of the Islamic calendar, year 1 AH, or 622 AD. By 630 Mohammed had returned to take Mecca.

Islam is the Arabic word for 'submission', and the duty of every Muslim is to submit to Allah. This profession of faith is the first of the Five Pillars of Islam, the five tenets in the Koran which guide Muslims in their daily lives. The other four are to pray five times a day, give alms to the poor, fast during Ramadan and make the pilgrimage to Mecca.

In its early days Islam suffered a major schism into two streams – the Sunnis and the Shi'ites. The Sunnis comprise the majority of Muslims today, including most Muslims in South-East Asia.

Islam came to South-East Asia with Indian traders and was not of the more orthodox Islamic tradition of Arabia. Islam was adopted peacefully by the coastal trading ports of South-East Asia, and was established in northern Sumatra by the end of the 13th century. The third ruler of Melaka adopted Islam in the mid-14th century, and Melaka's political dominance in the region saw the religion spread throughout Malaysia and Indonesia to Mindanao in the southern Philippines. By the time the Portuguese arrived in the 16th century, Islam was firmly established and conversion to Christianity was difficult. Pre-Islamic traditions exist side by side with Islam in South-East Asia, but with the rise of Islamic fundamentalism, the cries to introduce Islamic law and purify the practices of Islam have increased, especially in Malaysia.

CHRISTIANITY

Christianity first came with the Portuguese in the 15th century. The Portuguese spread Christianity in a few pockets of Indonesia, notably Flores and Timor, but it was the Spanish that were the most successful missionary force. Their former colony, the Philippines, is still the stronghold of Catholicism in Asia today.

The English and the Dutch were mostly pragmatic traders, not proselytisers, and, apart from an obsession with converting headhunters, generally had little desire to spread Christianity. Missionaries were active in Borneo, Irian Jaya and the Batak lands in north Sumatra, and these are strongholds of Christianity, mixed with animism, in Indonesia and Malaysia. Vietnam has long had contacts with Christianity, first through the Portuguese and Spanish, and then under French patronage when the Catholic church flourished.

OTHER RELIGIONS

Animism is in some ways the most pervasive of all religions. The rituals of indigenous religions can still be seen in many levels of belief throughout South-East Asia and pockets of animist worship can be found everywhere. The outer areas of Indonesia, such as Kalimantan, Irian Jaya, Sulawesi and Sumba, and the northern hill tribe areas are the strongholds of nature and spirit worship.

South-East Asia has other religions and different shades of established ones. Of note is *phii* (spirit) worship, which is the major form of non-Buddhist worship in Laos.

Health

Travel health depends on your predeparture preparations, your daily health care while travelling and how you handle any medical problem that does develop. While the potential dangers can seem quite frightening, in reality few travellers experience anything more than an upset stomach.

Predeparture planning

Immunisations Plan ahead for your vaccinations: some of them require more than one injection, while some vaccinations should not be given together. Note that some vaccinations should not be given during

Everyday Health

Normal body temperature is up to 37°C (98.6°F); more than 2°C (4°F) higher indicates a high fever. The normal adult pulse rate is 60 to 100 per minute (children 80 to 100, babies 100 to 140). As a general rule the pulse increases about 20 beats per minute for each 1°C (2°F) rise in fever. Respiration (breathing) rate is also an indicator of illness. Count the number of breaths per minute: between 12 and 20 is normal for adults and older children (up to 30 for younger children, 40 for babies). People with a high fever or serious respiratory illness breathe more quickly than normal. More than 40 shallow breaths a minute may indicate pneumonia.

pregnancy or to people with allergies – discuss with your doctor.

It is recommended that you seek medical advice at least six weeks before travel. Be aware that there is often a greater risk of disease with children and during pregnancy.

Record all vaccinations on an International Certificate of Vaccination, available from your doctor or government health department. Note that, although there is no risk of yellow fever in South-East Asia, you may be required to have proof of vaccination if you are coming from a yellow-fever-infected area (most of sub-Saharan Africa and parts of South America).

Discuss your requirements with your doctor, but vaccinations you should consider for South-East Asia include the following (for more details about the diseases themselves, see the individual entries later in this section):

Diphtheria & Tetanus Vaccinations for these two diseases are usually combined and are recommended for everyone. After an initial course of three injections (usually given in childhood), boosters are necessary every 10 years.

Polio You should keep up to date with this vaccination, which is normally given in childhood. A booster every 10 years maintains immunity.

Hepatitis A Hepatitis A vaccine (eg Avaxim, Havrix 1440 or VAQTA) provides long-term immunity (possibly more than 10 years) after an initial injection and a booster at six to 12 months. Alternatively, an injection of gamma globulin can provide short-term protection against hepatitis A – two to six months, depending on the dose given. It is not a vaccine but is ready-made antibody collected from blood donations. It is reasonably effective and, unlike the vaccine, it is protective immediately, but because it is a blood product, there are current concerns about its long-term safety. Hepatitis A vaccine is also available in a combined form, Twinrix, with hepatitis B vaccine. Three injections over a six-month period are required, the first two providing substantial protection against hepatitis A.

Typhoid Vaccination against typhoid may be required if you are travelling for more than a couple of weeks in South-East Asia. It is now available either as an injection or as capsules to be taken orally.

Cholera The current injectable vaccine against cholera is poorly protective and has many side effects, so it is not generally recommended for travellers. However, in some situations it may be necessary to have a certificate, as travellers are very occasionally asked by immigration officials to present one, even though all countries and the WHO have dropped cholera immunisation as a health requirement for entry.

Meningococcal Meningitis Vaccination is recommended only for travellers in rural north Vietnam who will be staying or travelling long-term. A single injection gives good protection against the major epidemic forms of the disease for three years. Protection may be less effective in children under two years.

Hepatitis B Travellers who should consider vaccination against hepatitis B include those on a long trip, as well as those visiting countries where there are high levels of hepatitis B infection, where blood transfusions may not be adequately screened or where sexual contact or needle sharing is a possibility. Vaccination involves three injections, with a booster at 12 months. More rapid courses are available if necessary.

Rabies Vaccination should be considered by those who will spend a month or longer in most countries in South-East Asia, especially if they are cycling, handling animals, caving or travelling to remote areas, and for children (who may not report a bite). Pretravel rabies vaccination involves having three injections over 21 to 28 days. If someone who has been vaccinated is bitten or scratched by an animal, they will require two booster injections of vaccine; those not vaccinated require more.

Japanese B Encephalitis Consider vaccination against this disease if spending a month or longer in South-East Asia, making repeated trips to a risk area or visiting during an epidemic. It involves three injections over 30 days.

Tuberculosis The risk of TB to travellers is usually very low, unless you will be living with or closely associated with local people. Vaccination against TB is recommended for children and young adults living in South-East Asia for three months or more.

Malaria Medication Antimalarial drugs do not prevent you from being infected but kill the malaria parasites during a stage in their development, significantly reducing the risk of becoming very ill or dying. Expert advice on medication should be sought, as there are many factors to consider, including the area to be visited, the risk of exposure to malaria-carrying mosquitoes, the side effects of medication, your medical history and whether you are a child or an adult or pregnant. Travellers to isolated areas in high risk countries should consider carrying a treatment dose of medication for use if symptoms occur.

Health Insurance Be sure to have adequate health insurance. See Travel Insurance under Visas & Documents in the Regional Facts for the Visitor chapter for details.

Travel Health Guides If you are planning to be away or travelling in remote areas for a long period of time, you might consider taking a more detailed health guide.

CDC's Complete Guide to Healthy Travel, Open Road Publishing, 1997. The US Centers for Disease Control & Prevention recommendations for international travel.

Staying Healthy in Asia, Africa & Latin America, Dirk Schroeder, Moon Publications, 1994. Probably the best all-round guide to carry; it's detailed and well organised.

Travellers' Health, Dr Richard Dawood, Oxford University Press, 1995. Comprehensive, easy to read, authoritative and highly recommended, although it's rather large to lug around.

Where There Is No Doctor, David Werner, Macmillan, 1994. A very detailed guide intended for someone, such as a Peace Corps worker, going to work in an underdeveloped country.

Travel with Children, Maureen Wheeler, Lonely Planet Publications, 1995. Includes advice on travel health for younger children.

There are also a number of excellent travel health sites on the Internet. From the Lonely Planet home page there are links at www.lonelyplanet.com/weblinks/wlprep.htm#heal to the World Health Organization and the US Centers for Disease Control & Prevention.

Other Preparations Make sure you're healthy before you start travelling. If you are going on a long trip make sure your teeth are OK. If you wear glasses take a spare pair and your prescription.

If you require a particular medication take an adequate supply, as it may not be available locally. Take part of the packaging showing the generic name rather than the brand, which will make getting replacements easier. It's a good idea to have a legible prescription or letter from your doctor to show that you legally use the medication to avoid any problems.

Basic Rules

Food There is an old colonial adage which says: 'If you can cook it, boil it or peel it you can eat it ... otherwise forget it'. Vegetables and fruit should be washed with clean (bottled or purified) water or peeled where possible. Beware of ice cream which is sold in the street or anywhere it might have melted and been refrozen; if there's any doubt (eg a power cut in the last day or two), steer well clear. Shellfish such as mussels, oysters and clams should be avoided as well as undercooked meat, particularly in the form of mince. Steaming does not make shellfish safe for eating. Fermented fish (eg *plaa ráa* in Thailand) or other uncooked fish dishes should be avoided because of the risk of liver flukes.

When it comes to places to eat, use your best judgment. Have a good look at the

Nutrition

If your food is poor or limited in availability, if you're travelling hard and fast and therefore missing meals or if you simply lose your appetite, you can soon start to lose weight and place your health at risk. Make sure your diet is well balanced. Cooked eggs, tofu, beans, lentils (dhal in India) and nuts are all safe ways to get protein. Fruit you can peel (bananas, oranges or mandarins for example) is usually safe (melons can harbour bacteria in their flesh and are best avoided) and a good source of vitamins. Try to eat plenty of grains (including rice) and bread. Remember that although food is generally safer if it is cooked well, overcooked food loses much of its nutritional value. If your diet isn't well balanced or if your food intake is insufficient, it's a good idea to take vitamin and iron pills.

In hot climates make sure you drink enough – don't rely on feeling thirsty to indicate when you should drink. Not needing to urinate or small amounts of very dark yellow urine is a danger sign. Always carry a water bottle with you on long trips. Excessive sweating can lead to loss of salt and therefore muscle cramping. Salt tablets are not a good idea as a preventative, but in places where salt is not used much, adding salt to food can help.

place – if it looks dirty, think twice. Street food generally runs a higher risk, but may be better than food in restaurants if it is cooked on the spot before your eyes. In general, places that are packed with travellers or locals will be fine, while empty restaurants are questionable. The food in busy restaurants is cooked and eaten quite quickly with little standing around and is probably not reheated.

Water The number one rule is *be careful of the water* and especially ice. In some places in South-East Asia, the water that comes out of the tap is little better than sewage water. If you don't know for certain that the water is safe, assume the worst. Bottled water is widely available throughout the region. It's expensive at hotels and restaurants, but is reasonably priced in grocery stores or supermarkets. Reputable brands of bottled water or soft drinks are generally fine, although in some places bottles may be refilled with tap water. Only use water from containers with a serrated seal – not tops or corks. Take care with fruit juice, particularly if water may have been added. Milk should be treated with suspicion as it is often unpasteurised, although boiled milk is fine if it is kept hygienically. Tea or coffee should also be OK, since the water should have been boiled. Remember to use clean (bottled or purified) water to brush your teeth with.

Water Purification The simplest way of purifying water is to boil it thoroughly. Vigorous boiling should be satisfactory; however, at high altitude water boils at a lower temperature, so germs are less likely to be killed. Boil it for longer in these environments. You can boil your own water if you carry an electric immersion coil and a large metal cup (most plastic cups will melt).

Consider purchasing a water filter for a long trip. There are two main kinds of filter. Total filters take out all parasites, bacteria and viruses and make water safe to drink. They are often expensive, but they can be more cost effective than buying bottled water. Simple filters (which can even be a nylon mesh bag) take out dirt and larger foreign bodies from the water so that chemical purifiers will work much more effectively; if water is dirty, chemical purifiers may not work at all. It's very important when buying a filter to read the specifications so that you know exactly what it removes from the water and what it doesn't. Simple filtering will not remove all dangerous organisms, so if you cannot boil water it should be treated chemically. Chlorine

Medical Kit Check List

Following is a list of items you should consider including in your medical kit – consult your phamacist for brands available in your country.

☐ **Aspirin** or **paracetamol** (acetaminophen in the US) – commonly used for pain or fever.

☐ **Antihistamine** – for allergies, eg hay fever; to ease the itch from insect bites or stings; and to prevent motion sickness.

☐ **Antibiotics** – consider including these if you're travelling well off the beaten track; see your doctor, as they must be prescribed, and carry the prescription with you.

☐ **Loperamide** or **diphenoxylate** – 'blockers' for diarrhoea; **prochlorperazine** or **metaclopramide** for nausea and vomiting.

☐ **Rehydration mixture** – to prevent dehydration, eg due to severe diarrhoea; particularly important when travelling with children.

☐ **Insect repellent, sunscreen, lip balm** and **eye drops.**

☐ **Calamine lotion, sting relief spray** or **aloe vera** – to ease irritation from sunburn and insect bites or stings.

☐ **Antifungal cream** or **powder** – for fungal skin infections and thrush.

☐ **Antiseptic** (such as povidone-iodine) – for cuts and grazes.

☐ **Bandages, Band-Aids (plasters)** and other wound dressings.

☐ **Water purification tablets** or **iodine.**

☐ **Scissors, tweezers** and a **thermometer** (note that mercury thermometers are prohibited by airlines).

☐ **Syringes** and **needles** – in case you need injections in a country with medical hygiene problems. Ask your doctor for a note explaining why you have them.

☐ **Cold** and **flu tablets, throat lozenges** and **nasal decongestant.**

☐ **Multivitamins** – consider for long trips, when dietary vitamin intake may be inadequate.

tablets (eg Puritabs, Steritabs or other brand names) will kill many pathogens, but not some parasites like giardia and amoebic cysts. Iodine is more effective in purifying water and is available in tablet form (such as Potable Aqua). Follow the directions carefully and remember that too much iodine can be harmful.

Medical Problems & Treatment

Self-diagnosis and treatment can be risky, so you should always seek medical help. Although we do give drug dosages in this section, they are for emergency use only. Correct diagnosis is vital.

Hospitals and private doctors can be found in the main towns throughout the region, but facilities are not always good. The best hospitals are in the capitals, but for serious ailments requiring hospitalisation, have good health insurance that will fly you out.

You can buy virtually any medicine over the counter without a prescription in most countries throughout the region. You shouldn't have trouble finding common western medicines, at least in the main big cities where there are well stocked pharmacies. In rural areas, pharmacies are scarce but grocery stores sell drugs – but check the expiry dates, as they are often long past them. Some of the big tourist hotels also have drugstores.

Note that antibiotics should ideally be administered only under medical supervision. Take only the recommended dose at the prescribed intervals and use the whole course, even if the illness seems to be cured earlier. Stop immediately if there are any serious reactions and don't use the antibiotic at all if you are unsure that you have the correct one. Some people are allergic to commonly prescribed antibiotics such as penicillin; carry this information (eg on a bracelet) when travelling.

Environmental Hazards

Altitude Sickness Lack of oxygen at high altitudes (over 2500m) affects most people to some extent. The effect may be mild or severe and occurs because less oxygen reaches the muscles and the brain at high altitude, requiring the heart and lungs to compensate by working harder. Symptoms of acute mountain sickness (AMS) usually develop during the first 24 hours at altitude but may be delayed up to three weeks. Mild symptoms include headache, lethargy, dizziness, difficulty sleeping and loss of appetite. AMS may become more severe without warning and can be fatal. Severe symptoms include breathlessness, a dry, irritative cough (which may progress to the production of pink, frothy sputum), severe headache, lack of coordination and balance, confusion, irrational behaviour, vomiting, drowsiness and unconsciousness. There is no hard-and-fast rule as to what is too high: AMS has been fatal at 3000m, although 3500 to 4500m is the usual range.

Treat mild symptoms by resting at the same altitude until recovery, usually a day or two. Paracetamol or aspirin can be taken for headaches. If symptoms persist or become worse, however, *immediate descent is necessary*; even 500m can help. Drug treatments should never be used to avoid descent or to enable further ascent.

The drugs acetazolamide and dexamethasone are recommended by some doctors for the prevention of AMS; however, their use is controversial. They can reduce the symptoms, but they may also mask warning signs; severe and fatal AMS has occurred in people taking these drugs. In general we do not recommend them for travellers.

To prevent acute mountain sickness:

- Drink extra fluids. The mountain air is dry and cold, and moisture is lost as you breathe. Evaporation of sweat may occur unnoticed and result in dehydration.
- Eat light, high carbohydrate meals for more energy.
- Avoid alcohol, as it may increase the risk of dehydration.
- Avoid sedatives.

Heat Exhaustion Dehydration and salt deficiency can cause heat exhaustion. Take time to acclimatise to high temperatures,

drink sufficient liquids and do not do anything too physically demanding. Always carry a water bottle with you. Dehydration can be a real problem if you go hiking.

Salt deficiency is characterised by fatigue, lethargy, headaches, giddiness and muscle cramps; salt tablets may help, but adding extra salt to your food is better.

Anhidrotic heat exhaustion is a rare form of heat exhaustion that is caused by an inability to sweat. It tends to affect people who have been in a hot climate for some time rather than newcomers. It can progress to heatstroke. Treatment involves removal to a cooler climate.

Heatstroke This serious, occasionally fatal, condition can occur if the body's heat-regulating mechanism breaks down and the body temperature rises to dangerous levels. Long, continuous periods of exposure to high temperatures and insufficient fluids can leave you vulnerable to heatstroke.

The symptoms are feeling unwell, not sweating very much (or at all) and a high body temperature (39° to 41°C, or 102° to 106°F). Where sweating has ceased, the skin becomes flushed and red. Severe, throbbing headaches and lack of coordination will also occur, and the sufferer may be confused or aggressive. Eventually the victim will become delirious or convulse. Hospitalisation is essential, but in the interim get the victim out of the sun, remove their clothing, cover them with a wet sheet or towel and then fan continually. Give fluids if they are conscious.

Hypothermia Too much cold can be just as dangerous as too much heat. If you are trekking at high altitudes or simply taking a long bus trip over mountains, particularly at night, or sleeping out on the decks of ships at night, be prepared.

Hypothermia occurs when the body loses heat faster than it can produce it and the core temperature of the body falls. It is surprisingly easy to progress from very cold to dangerously cold due to a combination of wind, wet clothing, fatigue and hunger, even if the air temperature is above freezing. It is best to dress in layers; silk, wool and some of the new artificial fibres are all good insulating materials. A hat is important, as a lot of heat is lost through the head. A strong, waterproof outer layer (and a 'space' blanket for emergencies) is essential. Carry basic supplies, including food containing simple sugars to generate heat quickly and fluid to drink.

Symptoms of hypothermia are exhaustion, numb skin (particularly toes and fingers), shivering, slurred speech, irrational or violent behaviour, lethargy, stumbling, dizzy spells, muscle cramps and violent bursts of energy. Irrationality may take the form of sufferers claiming they are warm and trying to take off their clothes.

To treat mild hypothermia, first get the person out of the wind and/or rain, remove their clothing if it's wet and replace it with dry, warm clothing. Give them hot liquids – not alcohol – and some high kilojoule, easily digestible food. Do not rub victims: instead, allow them to slowly warm themselves. This should be enough to treat the early stages of hypothermia. The early recognition and treatment of mild hypothermia is the only way to prevent severe hypothermia, which is a critical condition.

Jet Lag Jet lag is experienced when a person travels by air across more than three time zones (each time zone usually represents a one hour time difference). It occurs because many of the functions of the human body (such as temperature, pulse rate and emptying of the bladder and bowels) are regulated by internal 24-hour cycles. When we travel long distances rapidly, our bodies take time to adjust to the 'new time' of our destination, and we may experience fatigue, disorientation, insomnia, anxiety, impaired concentration and loss of appetite. These effects will usually be gone within three days of arrival, but to minimise the impact of jet lag:

- Rest for a couple of days prior to departure.
- Try to select flight schedules that minimise

sleep deprivation; arriving late in the day means you can go to sleep soon after you arrive. For very long flights, try to organise a stopover.
- Avoid excessive eating (which bloats the stomach) and alcohol (which causes dehydration) during the flight. Instead, drink plenty of noncarbonated, nonalcoholic drinks such as fruit juice or water.
- Avoid smoking.
- Make yourself comfortable by wearing loose-fitting clothes and perhaps bringing an eye mask and ear plugs to help you sleep.
- Try to sleep at the appropriate time for the time zone you are travelling to.

Motion Sickness Eating lightly before and during a trip will reduce the chances of motion sickness. If you are prone to motion sickness try to find a place that minimises movement – near the wing on aircraft, close to midships on boats, near the centre on buses. Fresh air usually helps; reading and cigarette smoke don't.

Commercial motion-sickness preparations, which can cause drowsiness, have to be taken before the trip commences. Ginger (available in capsule form) and peppermint (including mint-flavoured sweets) are natural preventatives.

Prickly Heat Prickly heat is an itchy rash caused by excessive perspiration trapped under the skin. It usually strikes people who have just arrived in a hot climate. Keeping cool, resorting to air-conditioning and bathing often, drying the skin and using a mild talcum or prickly heat powder may help.

Sunburn This can be a problem in South-East Asia. You can get sunburnt surprisingly quickly, even through cloud. Use a sunscreen, a hat and a barrier cream for your nose and lips. You can usually buy sunscreen in better local pharmacies, but it might be safest to bring your own. Calamine lotion or aluminium sulphate spray are good for mild sunburn. Protect your eyes with good quality sunglasses, particularly if you will be near water, sand or snow.

Infectious Diseases

Diarrhoea Simple things like a change of water, food or climate can all cause a mild bout of diarrhoea, but a few rushed toilet trips with no other symptoms is not indicative of a major problem.

Dehydration is the main danger with any diarrhoea, particularly in children or the elderly as dehydration can occur quite quickly. Under all circumstances *fluid replacement* (at least equal to the volume being lost) is the most important thing to remember. Weak black tea with a little sugar, soda water or soft drinks allowed to go flat and diluted by 50% with clean water are all good. With severe diarrhoea a rehydrating solution is preferable to replace minerals and salts lost. Commercially available oral rehydration salts (ORS) are very useful; add them to boiled or bottled water. In an emergency you can make up a solution of six teaspoons of sugar and a half teaspoon of salt to a litre of boiled or bottled water.

You need to drink at least the same volume of fluid that you are losing in bowel movements and vomiting. Urine is the best guide to the adequacy of replacement – if you have small amounts of concentrated urine, you need to drink more. Keep drinking small amounts often. Stick to a bland diet as you recover.

Gut-paralysing drugs such as loperamide or diphenoxylate can be used to bring relief from the symptoms, although they do not actually cure the problem. Only use these drugs if you do not have access to toilets, eg if you *must* travel. For children under 12 years these drugs are not recommended. Do not use these drugs if the person has a high fever or is severely dehydrated.

In certain situations antibiotics may be required: diarrhoea with blood or mucus (dysentery), any diarrhoea with fever, profuse watery diarrhoea, persistent diarrhoea not improving after 48 hours and severe diarrhoea. These suggest a more serious cause of diarrhoea and gut-paralysing drugs should be avoided.

In these situations, a stool test may be necessary to diagnose what bug is causing your diarrhoea, so you should seek medical help urgently. Where this is not possible the recommended drugs for bacterial diarrhoea (the most likely cause of severe diarrhoea in travellers) are norfloxacin, 400mg twice daily for three days, or ciprofloxacin, 500mg twice daily for five days. These are not recommended for children or pregnant women. The drug of choice for children would be co-trimoxazole, a five day course with dosage dependent on weight. Ampicillin or amoxycillin may be given in pregnancy, but medical care is necessary.

Two other causes of persistent diarrhoea in travellers are giardiasis and amoebic dysentery.

Giardiasis is caused by a common parasite, *Giardia lamblia*. Symptoms include stomach cramps, nausea, a bloated stomach, watery, foul-smelling diarrhoea and frequent gas. Giardiasis can appear several weeks after you have been exposed to the parasite. The symptoms may disappear for a few days and then return; this can go on for several weeks.

Amoebic dysentery, caused by the protozoan *Entamoeba histolytica*, is characterised by a gradual onset of low-grade diarrhoea, quite often with blood and mucus. Cramping abdominal pain and vomiting are less likely than in other types of diarrhoea, and fever may not be present. It will persist until treated and can recur and cause other health problems.

You should seek medical advice if you think you have giardiasis or amoebic dysentery, but where this is not possible, tinidazole or metronidazole are the recommended drugs. Treatment is a 2g single dose of tinidazole or 250mg of metronidazole three times daily for five to 10 days.

Fungal Infections Fungal infections occur more commonly in hot weather and are usually found on the scalp, between the toes (athlete's foot) or fingers, in the groin and on the body (ringworm). You get ringworm (which is a fungal infection, not a worm) from infected animals or other people. Moisture encourages these infections.

To prevent fungal infections wear loose, comfortable clothes, avoid artificial fibres, wash frequently and dry yourself carefully. If you do get an infection, wash the infected area at least daily with a disinfectant or medicated soap and water, and rinse and dry well. Apply an antifungal cream or powder such as tolnaftate. Try to expose the infected area to air or sunlight as much as possible and wash all towels and underwear in hot water, change them often and let them dry in the sun.

Hepatitis Hepatitis is a general term for inflammation of the liver. It is a common disease worldwide. There are several viruses that cause hepatitis, and they differ in the way that they are transmitted. The symptoms are similar in all forms of the illness, and include fever, chills, headache, fatigue, feelings of weakness and aches and pains, followed by loss of appetite, nausea, vomiting, abdominal pain, dark urine, light-coloured faeces, jaundiced (yellow) skin and yellowing of the whites of the eyes. People who have had hepatitis should avoid alcohol for some time after the illness, as the liver needs time to recover.

Hepatitis A is transmitted by contaminated food and drinking water. You should seek medical advice, but there is not much you can do apart from resting, drinking lots of fluids, eating lightly and avoiding fatty foods. **Hepatitis E** is transmitted in the same way as hepatitis A; it can be particularly serious in pregnant women.

There are almost 300 million chronic carriers of **hepatitis B** in the world. It is spread through contact with infected blood, blood products or body fluids, for example through sexual contact, unsterilised needles and blood transfusions, or contact with blood via small breaks in the skin. Other risk situations include having a shave, tattoo or body piercing with contaminated equipment. The symptoms of hepatitis B may be more severe than type A and the disease can lead to long term problems such as chronic liver damage, liver cancer or a long term carrier state. **Hepatitis C and D** are spread in the same way as hepatitis B and can also lead to long term complications.

There are vaccines against hepatitis A and B, but there are currently no vaccines against the other types of hepatitis. Following the basic rules about food and water (hepatitis A and E) and avoiding risk situations (hepatitis B, C and D) are important preventative measures.

HIV & AIDS Infection with the human immunodeficiency virus (HIV) may lead to the acquired immune deficiency syndrome (AIDS), which is a fatal disease. It is believed that the incidence of HIV infection is set to increase significantly in the region unless the promotion of safe sex and good hospital practices is improved. The primary risk for most travellers is probably through contact with workers in the sex industry, and the spread of HIV in this region is primarily through heterosexual activity. However, any exposure to blood, blood products or body fluids may put the individual at risk. The disease is often transmitted through dirty needles – vaccinations, acupuncture, tattooing and body piercing can be potentially as dangerous as intravenous drug use. HIV/AIDS can also be spread through infected blood transfusions; many South-East Asian countries cannot afford to screen blood used for transfusions. If you do need an injection, ask to see the syringe unwrapped in front of you, or take a needle and syringe pack with you.

Fear of HIV should never preclude treatment for serious medical conditions.

Intestinal Worms These parasites are most common in rural, tropical areas. The different worms have different ways of infecting people. Some may be ingested in food such as undercooked meat (eg tapeworms) and some enter through your skin (eg hookworms). Infestations may not show up for some time, and although they are generally not serious, if left untreated some can cause severe health problems later. Consider having a stool test when you return home to check for these and determine the appropriate treatment.

Liver flukes Travellers in the Indochinese peninsula, the Philippines and Thailand should be on guard against liver flukes (opisthorchiasis, clonorchiasis). These are tiny worms that are occasionally present in freshwater fish. The main risk comes from eating raw or undercooked fish – in particular, avoid eating *plaa ráa* (called *pla daek* in northern Thailand and *pạa dạek* in Laos), which is fermented fish used as an accompaniment to rice. A much less common way to contract liver flukes is by swimming in lakes and rivers.

Symptoms depend very much on how many of the flukes get into your body. They can range from no symptoms at all to fatigue, a low-grade fever and a swollen or tender liver (or general abdominal pains), along with worms or worm eggs in the faeces.

People suspected of having liver flukes should have a stool sample analysed by a competent doctor or clinic. The usual medication is 25mg per kg of body weight of praziquantel (often sold as Biltricide) taken three times daily after meals for two days.

Meningococcal Meningitis This serious disease can be fatal. The only South-East Asian country where this may be a risk is Vietnam, where epidemics have occurred in the past.

A fever, severe headache, sensitivity to light and neck stiffness which prevents forward bending of the head are the first symptoms. There may also be purple patches on the skin. Death can occur within a few hours, so urgent medical treatment is required. Treatment is large doses of penicillin given intravenously, or chloramphenicol injections.

Schistosomiasis Also known as bilharzia, this disease is transmitted by minute worms which infect certain varieties of freshwater snails found in rivers, streams, lakes and particularly behind dams. The worms multiply and are eventually discharged into the water. The disease is found in some parts of South-East Asia, including the southern Philippines, the Mekong Delta in Vietnam and central Sulawesi.

The worm enters through the skin and attaches itself to your intestines or bladder. The first symptom may be a general feeling of being unwell, or a tingling and sometimes a light rash around the area where it entered. Weeks later a high fever may develop. Once the disease is established abdominal pain and blood in the urine are other signs. The infection often causes no symptoms until the disease is well established (several months to years after exposure) and damage to internal organs irreversible.

Avoiding swimming or bathing in fresh water where bilharzia is present is the main method of preventing the disease. Even deep water can be infected. If you do get wet, dry off quickly and dry your clothes as well.

A blood test is the most reliable way to diagnose the disease, but the test will not show positive until a number of weeks after exposure.

Sexually Transmitted Diseases Gonorrhoea, herpes and syphilis are among these diseases; sores, blisters or rashes around the genitals and discharges or pain when urinating are common symptoms. In some STDs, such as wart virus or chlamydia, symptoms may be less marked or not observed at all, especially in women. Syphilis symptoms eventually disappear completely but the disease continues and can cause severe problems in later years. While abstinence from sexual contact is the only 100% effective prevention, using condoms is also effective. The treatment of gonorrhoea and syphilis is with antibiotics. The different sexually transmitted diseases each require specific antibiotics. There is no cure for herpes or AIDS.

Typhoid Typhoid fever is a dangerous gut infection caused by contaminated water and food. Medical help must be sought.

In its early stages sufferers may feel they have a bad cold or flu on the way, as early symptoms are a headache, body aches and a fever which rises a little each day until it is around 40°C (104°F) or more. The victim's pulse is often slow relative to the degree of fever present – unlike a normal fever where the pulse increases. There may also be vomiting, abdominal pain, diarrhoea or constipation.

In the second week the high fever and slow pulse continue and a few pink spots may appear on the body; trembling, delirium, weakness, weight loss and dehydration may occur. Complications such as pneumonia, perforated bowel or meningitis may occur.

Insect-Borne Diseases

Filariasis, leishmaniasis and typhus are all insect-borne diseases, but they do not pose a great risk to travellers. For more information on them see Less Common Diseases later in the Health section.

Malaria This serious and potentially fatal disease is spread by mosquito bites and is endemic in most countries in the region (exceptions being Brunei and Singapore). If you are travelling in endemic areas it is extremely important to avoid mosquito bites and to take tablets to prevent this disease. Symptoms range from fever, chills and sweating, headache, diarrhoea and abdominal pains to a vague feeling of ill-health. Seek medical help immediately if malaria is suspected. Without treatment malaria can rapidly become more serious and can be fatal.

If medical care is not available, malaria tablets can be used for treatment. You need to use a malaria tablet which is different from the one you were taking when you contracted malaria. The standard treatment dose of mefloquine is two 250mg tablets and a further two six hours later. For Fansidar, it's a single dose of three tablets. If you were previously taking mefloquine and cannot obtain Fansidar, then other alternatives are Malarone (atovaquone-proguanil; four tablets once daily for three days), halofantrine (three doses of two 250mg tablets every six hours) or quinine sulphate (600mg every six hours). There is a greater risk of side effects with these dosages than in

normal use if used with mefloquine, so medical advice is preferable. Be aware also that halofantrine is no longer recommended by the WHO as emergency standby treatment, because of side effects, and should only be used if no other drugs are available.

Travellers are advised to prevent mosquito bites at all times. The main messages are:

* Wear light-coloured clothing.
* Wear long trousers and long-sleeved shirts.
* Use mosquito repellents containing the compound DEET on exposed areas (prolonged overuse of DEET may be harmful, especially to children, but its use is considered preferable to being bitten by disease-transmitting mosquitoes).
* Avoid perfumes or aftershave.
* Use a mosquito net impregnated with mosquito repellent (permethrin) – it may be worth taking your own permethrin; impregnated clothes effectively deter mosquitoes and other insects.

Dengue Fever This viral disease is transmitted by mosquitoes and occurs mainly in tropical and subtropical areas of the world, including South-East Asia. Generally, there is only a small risk to travellers except during epidemics, which are usually seasonal (during and just after the rainy season). With unstable weather patterns thought to be responsible for large outbreaks recently in South-East Asia and elsewhere, travellers to the region may be especially at risk of infection.

The *Aedes aegypti* mosquito, which transmits the dengue virus, is most active during the day, unlike the malaria mosquito, and is found mainly in urban areas, in and around human dwellings.

Signs and symptoms of dengue fever include a sudden onset of high fever, headache, joint and muscle pains (hence its old name, 'breakbone fever') and nausea and vomiting. A rash of small red spots appears three to four days after the onset of fever. Dengue is commonly mistaken for other infectious diseases, including influenza.

You should seek medical attention if you think you may be infected. Infection can be diagnosed by a blood test. There is no specific treatment for dengue, but note that aspirin should be avoided, as it increases the risk of haemorrhaging. Recovery may be prolonged, with tiredness lasting for several weeks. Severe complications are rare in travellers but include dengue haemorrhagic fever (DHF), which can be fatal without prompt medical treatment. DHF is thought to be a result of second infection due to a different strain (there are four major strains) and usually affects residents of the country rather than travellers.

There is no vaccine against dengue fever. The best prevention is to avoid mosquito bites at all times – see the malaria section earlier for more details.

Japanese B Encephalitis This viral infection of the brain is transmitted by mosquitoes. Most cases occur in rural areas, as the virus exists in pigs and wading birds. Symptoms include fever, headache and alteration in consciousness. Hospitalisation is needed for correct diagnosis and treatment. There is a high mortality rate among those who have symptoms; of those who survive many are intellectually disabled.

Cuts, Bites & Stings

See Less Common Diseases for details of rabies, which is passed through animal bites.

Bedbugs & Lice Bedbugs live in various places, but particularly in dirty mattresses and bedding, evidenced by spots of blood on bedclothes or on the wall. Bedbugs leave itchy bites in neat rows. Calamine lotion or a sting relief spray may help.

All lice cause itching and discomfort. They make themselves at home in your hair (head lice), your clothing (body lice) or in your pubic hair (crabs). You catch lice through direct contact with infected people or by sharing combs, clothing and the like. Powder or shampoo treatment will kill the lice and infected clothing should then be washed in very hot, soapy water and left in the sun to dry.

Bites & Stings Bee and wasp stings are usually painful rather than dangerous.

However, in people who are allergic to them severe breathing difficulties may occur and require urgent medical care. Calamine lotion or aluminium sulphate spray will give relief and ice packs will reduce the pain and swelling. There are some spiders with dangerous bites but antivenins are usually available. Scorpion stings are notoriously painful and in some parts of Asia, the Middle East and Central America can actually be fatal. Scorpions often shelter in shoes or clothing.

Certain cone shells found in Australia and the Pacific can sting dangerously or even fatally. There are various fish and other sea creatures which can sting or bite dangerously or which are dangerous to eat – seek local advice.

Cuts & Scratches Wash well and treat any cut with an antiseptic such as povidone-iodine. Where possible avoid bandages and Band-Aids, which can keep wounds wet. Coral cuts are notoriously slow to heal and if they are not adequately cleaned, small pieces of coral can become embedded in the wound.

Jellyfish Avoid contact with these sea creatures, which have stinging tentacles – seek local advice. The box jellyfish found in inshore waters in some parts of Indonesia is potentially fatal, but stings from most jellyfish are simply rather painful. Dousing in vinegar will deactivate any stingers that have not 'fired'. Calamine lotion, antihistamines and analgesics may reduce the reaction and relieve the pain.

Leeches & Ticks Leeches may be present in damp rainforest conditions; they attach themselves to your skin to suck your blood. Trekkers often get them on their legs or in their boots. Salt or a lighted cigarette end will make them fall off. Do not pull them off, as the bite is then more likely to become infected. Clean and apply pressure if the point of attachment is bleeding. An insect repellent may keep them away.

You should always check all over your

body if you have been walking through a potentially tick-infested area as ticks can cause skin infections and other more serious diseases. If a tick is found attached, press down around the tick's head with tweezers, grab the head and gently pull upwards. Avoid pulling the rear of the body as this may squeeze the tick's gut contents through the attached mouth parts into the skin, increasing the risk of infection and disease. Smearing chemicals on the tick will not make it let go and is not recommended.

Snakes South-East Asia has several poisonous snakes, the most notorious being the cobra. There are many other poisonous species. All sea snakes are poisonous and are readily identified by their flat tails. Although not poisonous, giant-sized pythons lurk in the jungle. They do not generally consume humans, but have been known to do so.

To minimise your chances of being bitten always wear boots, socks and long trousers when walking through undergrowth where snakes may be present. Don't put your hands into holes and crevices, and be careful when collecting firewood.

Snake bites do not cause instantaneous death and antivenins are usually available. Immediately wrap the bitten limb tightly, as you would for a sprained ankle, and then attach a splint to immobilise it. Keep the victim still and seek medical help, if possible with the dead snake for identification. Don't attempt to catch the snake if there is a possibility of being bitten again. Tourniquets and sucking out the poison are now comprehensively discredited.

Less Common Diseases
The following diseases pose a small risk to travellers, and so are only mentioned in passing. Seek medical advice if you think you may have any of these diseases.

Cholera This is the worst of the watery diarrhoeas and medical help should be sought. Outbreaks of cholera are generally widely reported, so you can avoid such problem areas. *Fluid replacement is the*

most vital treatment – the risk of dehydration is severe as you may lose up to 20L a day. If there is a delay in getting to hospital, then begin taking tetracycline. The adult dose is 250mg four times daily. It is not recommended for children under nine years nor for pregnant women. Tetracycline may help shorten the illness, but adequate fluids are required to save lives.

Filariasis This is a mosquito-transmitted parasitic infection found in many parts of Africa, Asia, Central and South America and the Pacific. Possible symptoms include fever, pain and swelling of the lymph glands; inflammation of lymph drainage areas; swelling of a limb or the scrotum; skin rashes; and blindness. Treatment is available to eliminate the parasites from the body, but some of the damage already caused may not be reversible. Medical advice should be obtained promptly if the infection is suspected.

Leishmaniasis This is a group of parasitic diseases transmitted by sandflies, which are found in many parts of the Middle East, Africa, Asia, Central and South America and the Mediterranean. Cutaneous leishmaniasis affects the skin tissue causing ulceration and disfigurement, and visceral leishmaniasis affects the internal organs. Seek medical advice, as laboratory testing is required for diagnosis and correct treatment. Avoiding sandfly bites is the best precaution. Bites are usually painless, itchy and yet another reason to cover up and apply repellent.

Rabies This fatal viral infection is found in most parts of South-East Asia. Many animals can be infected (such as dogs, cats, bats and monkeys) and it is their saliva which is infectious. Any bite, scratch or even lick from an animal should be cleaned immediately and thoroughly. Scrub with soap and running water, and then apply alcohol or iodine solution. Medical help should be sought promptly to receive a course of injections to prevent the onset of symptoms and death.

Tetanus This disease is caused by a germ which lives in soil and in the faeces of horses and other animals. It enters the body via breaks in the skin. The first symptom may be discomfort in swallowing, or stiffening of the jaw and neck; this is followed by painful convulsions of the jaw and whole body. The disease can be fatal. It can be prevented by vaccination.

Tuberculosis TB is a bacterial infection usually transmitted from person to person by coughing but which may be transmitted through consumption of unpasteurised milk. Milk that has been boiled is safe to drink, and the souring of milk to make yoghurt or cheese also kills the bacilli. Travellers are usually not at great risk as close household contact with the infected person is usually required before the disease is passed on. You may need to have a TB test before you travel as this can help diagnose the disease later if you become ill.

Typhus This disease is spread by ticks, mites or lice. It begins with fever, chills, headache and muscle pains followed a few days later by a body rash. There is often a large painful sore at the site of the bite and nearby lymph nodes are swollen and painful. Typhus can be treated under medical supervision. Seek local advice on areas where ticks pose a danger and always check your skin carefully for ticks after walking in a danger area such as a tropical forest. An insect repellent can help, and walkers in tick-infested areas should consider having their boots and trousers impregnated with benzyl benzoate and dibutylphthalate.

Women's Health

Gynaecological Problems Antibiotic use, synthetic underwear, sweating and contraceptive pills can lead to fungal vaginal infections, especially when travelling in hot climates. Fungal infections are characterised by a rash, itch and discharge and can be treated with a vinegar or lemon-juice douche, or with yoghurt. Nystatin, miconazole or clotrimazole pessaries or vaginal cream are the usual treatment. Maintaining good personal hygiene and wearing loose-fitting clothes and cotton underwear may help prevent these infections.

Sexually transmitted diseases are a major cause of vaginal problems. Symptoms include a smelly discharge, painful intercourse and sometimes a burning sensation when urinating. Medical attention should be sought and male sexual partners must also be treated. Remember that in addition to these diseases HIV or hepatitis B may also be acquired during exposure. Besides abstinence, the best thing is to practise safe sex using condoms.

Pregnancy It is not advisable to travel to some places while pregnant as some vaccinations normally used to prevent serious diseases are not advisable during pregnancy (eg yellow fever). In addition, some diseases are much more serious for the mother (and may increase the risk of a stillborn child) in pregnancy (eg malaria).

Most miscarriages occur during the first three months of pregnancy. Miscarriage is not uncommon and can occasionally lead to severe bleeding. The last three months should also be spent within reasonable distance of good medical care. A baby born as early as 24 weeks stands a chance of survival, but only in a good modern hospital. Pregnant women should avoid all unnecessary medication; vaccinations and malarial prophylactics should still be taken where needed. Additional care should be taken to prevent illness and particular attention should be paid to diet and nutrition. Alcohol and nicotine, for example, should be avoided.

Climate Charts

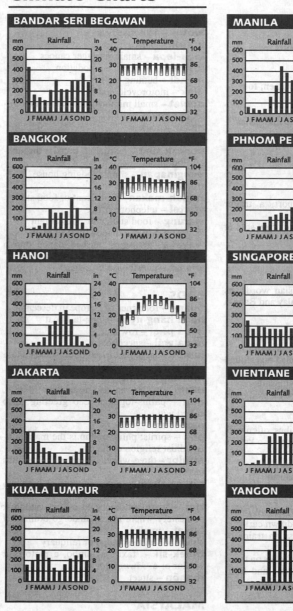

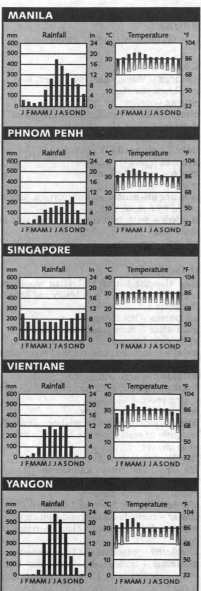

Glossary

BRUNEI
(See the list of Malaysian words)

CAMBODIA
apsaras – shapely dancing women, found on Khmer sculpture
asuras – devils
chunchiets – ethno-linguistic minorities
devaraja – god-king
devas – gods
hols – variegated silk shirts
kramas – checked scarves
moto – motorcycle taxi
prasat – tower
remorque-moto – transport; a trailer pulled by a motorbike
tikalok – fresh fruit smoothie often sold at street stalls
vihara – sanctuary

INDONESIA
(See also the list of Malaysian words, as many are the same in both Malay and Bahasa Indonesia.)
air panas – hot springs
alun alun – main public square of a town
andong – four-wheeled horse-drawn cart
bajaj – motorised three-wheeled taxi, found in Jakarta
balolang – large outrigger with sails
batik – coloured cloth made by waxing and dyeing process
becak – bicycle rickshaw
bemo – pick-up truck or minibus, often with two rows of seats down the side; also known as an *angkot*
bendi – two-person horse-drawn cart
bis air – river ferry in Kalimantan
bisnis – 'business' class on trains
candi – Javanese shrine
cidomo – horse-drawn cart (Lombok)
dokar – two-wheeled horse-drawn cart
ekonomi – 'economy' class on trains or boats
eksekutif – 'executive' (ie 1st) class on trains
gamelan – traditional Javanese and Balinese orchestra with large xylophones and gongs
gang – alley, lane
ikat – cloth in which pattern is produced by dyeing individual threads before weaving
kantor pos – post office

klotok – motorised canoe
kraton – palace
lepa-lepa – small outrigger canoes
losmen – basic accommodation
mandi – bathing facility
ojek – motorcycle taxi
opelet – small minibus; also called a *mikrolet* or a *colt*
pasar – market
Pelni – national shipping line
pencak silat – martial art popular throughout Indonesia
penginapan – simple lodging house
perahu – outrigger
rumah makan – restaurant or food stall
wartel – telephone office
warung – food stall, cheap restaurant
wayang kulit – shadow-puppet play
wayang orang – masked dance drama playing scenes from the *Ramayana*
wisma – guesthouse or lodge

LAOS
falang – foreigner of European descent
héua hãng nyáo – long-tail boat
héua phai – rowboat
héua wái – speedboat
jumbo – large motorised three-wheeled taxi
khwaeng – province
meuang – district
nâam – water; can also mean river
nop – palms-together Lao greeting; also called *wài*
paa – fish
phǐi – spirits; phǐi worship is the main non-Buddhist religion of Laos
samlor – three-wheeled pedicab; sometimes motorised
sǎwng-thǎew – a passenger truck with two rows of benches in the back
sǐm – main sanctuary in a Lao Buddhist monastery where monks undergo ordination
talàat – market
thâat – Buddhist stupa or reliquary
thàek-sii – 'taxi'; a jumbo, a motorised samlor or a *sǎwng-thǎew*
thanõn – street

MALAYSIA
(See also the list of Indonesian words, as many are the same in both Malay and Bahasa Indonesia.)

adat – Malay customary law
air – water
alor – groove, furrow, main channel of river or waterway
bandar – port
batu – stone, rock, milepost
bukit – hill
gunung – mountain
istana – palace
jalan – road
kampung – village
kedai kopi – coffee shop
kota – fort or city
kuala – river mouth, or place where a tributary joins a larger river
labuan – port
masjid – mosque
merdeka – independence
negara – country, national
Orang Asli – Malaysian aboriginal people
padang – open grassy area (usually the city square)
pantai – beach
pasar – market
pulau – island
sungai – river
tuak – rice wine

MYANMAR
hti – pronounced 'tee', the umbrella or decorated top of a pagoda
longyi – Burmese sarong
nats – guardian spirit beings
paya – Burmese equivalent to 'pagoda'
pwe – show or festival
stupa – religious monument, often said to contain relics of Buddha; a type of paya

PHILIPPINES
bangca – local outrigger or pumpboat used for transport and fishing
barangay – local government community
calesas – two-wheeled horse-drawn carriages; known as *tartanillas* in Cebu City
jeepney – wildly ornamented public transport, originally based on WWII US Army Jeeps
mestizos – Filipino-Spanish or Filipino-American people

SINGAPORE
godown – warehouse
MRT – Mass Rapid Transit metro system
Peranakan – Straits-born Chinese (also Nonya)

THAILAND
amphoe – district, next subdivision down from province
ao – bay or gulf
bâan – house or village, often spelt *ban*
bot – central sanctuary or chapel in Thai temple
chedi – stupa; monument erected to house a Buddha relic
farang – foreigner of European descent
hat – beach
jok – rice congee
khao – hill or mountain
khlong – canal
ko – island
kuaythiaw – flat rice flour noodles
muang – city
muay thai – Thai boxing
nakhon – city
nãng – Thai shadow play
prang – Khmer-style tower on temples
samlor – three-wheeled pedicab
soi – lane or small street
songthaew – small pick-up truck with two benches in the back, used as buses/taxis
talaat nam – floating market
tuk-tuk – motorised *samlor*
wai – palms-together Thai greeting
wang – palace
wat – Buddhist temple-monastery

VIETNAM
ao dai – Vietnamese national dress
buu dien – post office
Caodaism – Vietnamese religious sect
cyclo – pedicab
Honda om – motorbike taxi
kem – ice cream
khach san – hotel
nha khach – guesthouse
nuoc mam – fish sauce
pho – noodle soup
Tet – lunar New Year
xe lam – three-wheeled motorised vehicle

Acknowledgments

THANKS

Many thanks to the travellers who used the last edition and wrote to us with helpful hints, useful advice and interesting anecdotes:

Hoy & Doug, Sabine & Carl, Lauren & Cassandra, Arthur & Sandra, Ken & Ina, Nina Aarstrand, Nick Adams, Souhaila Almutawa, Christian Alpers, Gerald van Amerongen, Lisbeth & Jonas Anderson, Stuart Anderson, John Armstrong, Jeroen van As, Emma Astrom, Jaindi Attila, Jeff Backer, E Baird, Steve Ballinger, David Barker, AS Barmoch, David Barnett, Christian Baucharott, Clint Bauld, Penny Bayfield, Karin Baysen, Janet Beale, Josselin Beaulieu, Lee Beckwith, Cheralyn Bell, Jeff Bell, Didier Bellet, S Bennet, Mary Benton, Adam Berg, Jonas Bergenholtz, Robert Berger, Jurgen Berger, T Berndt, Ralph Bernhart, Liz Berry, Jason & Lisa van Beurden, Steve Beutler, Tara Beattie, Anders Bille, Leigh Billett, Emma Birks, A Blackwell, Holger Blanck, M Blyth, Kimden Boer, Susan Bohdan, Andy Bolas, F Bolle, Jean-Marie Boone, Iain Booth, Geoff Botting, Kurt van Bouchout, Antoinette Bouwens, Martin Bowditch, David Boyall, Melanie Boyce, JD Boyes, J Bramson, John Bravel, K Atarina Bremec, David Brighouse, Jennie Brightwell, Annemarie den Broeder, Robert Brookfield, Richard Brooks, Nita T Brown, Danny Brown, Justin Brumelle, Angela Buckingham, Geoff Budge, Rachel Burge, Simone Burgon, Johnathon Burkin, Renske Ter Busch, Lucy Bushell, Kate Butcher, Thomas N Butler, Colin Butler, P Butler

Robert Cadloff, Elkie Calcetas, Neil Caldicott, Michael Caldwell, Heather Cameron, D Ruth Campbell, Aron Campbell, Kenneth Cannaday, Natalie Capelett, Mark Capellaro, Mark Capra, Debbie Carr, Antonio Carro, Ian Carson, W Casker, Natalie Chabierski, Haywood Chapman, Jacques & Liliaue Chapon, Shelley Chen, Wu Yang Xin Cheng, Frank Cheshire, Wong Wai Cheung, Sophia Chiang, Al Chin, Scott Chosed, H Chouanecek, Lee Sek Chu, Chris Clark, Jackie Clement, Ian Cliff, Carl & Diana Clifford, Sandie Codron, Peter Coffin, Brian Cogswell, Donn Colby, MD Comber, M Cook, James Cooke, Cliff Cordy, David Cowans, David & Jill Cowans, Jerry Creedon, Patricia Creighton, David Cross, Elaine Crowe, Christine Cullen, Pat Dagger, Lucinda d'Ambrumenil, Sophy D'Angelo, Victoria Scott D'Angelo, Pat Daniel, Laurie Darian, Will David, Michael Davidson, Kevin Davies, Lucinda Davies, Scott Davis, Irene Day, Lee De St Croix, Alberto Deacon-Morey, Bennett Dean, S Deane, Karine Dedenon, Kara Deringer, Gudrun Devito, Patrick D'haese, Kari Diggins, Doni & Tim Dilworth, Fabiana Dimase, Amanda Dixon, R & M Dixon, Laurel Donaldson, Bjorn Donnis, Mark Donovan, Julia Dotson, P Doucette, Catherine Douxchamps, J Downham, BF Du Sautoy, Russel du Silva, G & J Duffy, M Duffy, A Duflos, Annick Duflos,

Jason Dumphy, Ian & Sonia Duncan, Tania Dunnette, Trang Duong, Hans Durrer, Silvia Durrsperger, Jayne Dyer, T Dykstra, Ian Dyus, Thomas Dyvik, Yoop Ebben, Michael Eckert, Suzanne Ecklund, Donald Edge, RB Edminson, Ian Edmond, Alan Edmunds, Donalyn Edwards, RP Edwards, Sandy Edwards, Martin Egger, Bert Eijnthoven, Ulf Ellervik, Andy & Pravina Ellis, Cathy Ellis, Elissa Epel, H Jonas Eriksson, Gregg Erwin, EV Estey, J Evans, Sara Evans, Sue Evans, Joanna Eveleigh, B Evers, Andrew Ewart, Tim Eyres

Guido Faes, Barry Fagan, Evelyn Falker, Teresa Farnes, James Farrell, Louise Faurett, Evan Fearn, Barrett Feldman, Mark Ferguson, Susie Ferguson, Hanne Finholt, Lyndsay & Jamie Finn, Ulrich Fischer, Syd Fisher, Matthew Flattery, Peter Flegg, Julia Fleming, Michael Fogarty, Andy Forbes, Kent Foster, Jane & Alan Fowler, Steve Fox, Robert Francis, Bruce & Margaret Fraser, MG Frechilla, Edward Freed, Michael Fris-Madsen, Delia Frith, Warren Funnell, Monique Gallway, Ian Ganley, Lance Gatchell, Robert Gatt, William Gaultier, Richard Gee, Anne Giannini, J Gibbons, Roger Gilbert, Cathy Giltrap, Margarita Ginty, Randy Girer, Robert & Louise Giudici, Peter Glanfield, Katherine Glover, John Glover, Erica Goedegebuure, JE Goldsworthy, Arvid Goletz, Andres Gomez, J Goosey, Tim Gourlay, Antonia Gowan, NS Gower, Sascha Grabow, Ewa Grabowska, JA Graham, Rowena Grant, Martin Gray, Julie & Barry Green, Clare Green, Todd Griffin, M Grillenberger, Patrick Groenewegen, Michelle Groleau, Robert Groothuis, Kathryn Guest, Cathy Gulkin, Lawrent Guyor, Art Hacker, Frank Hadam, Bill Haigh, Peter Hajssmann, Jenny & Richard Hall, Russell Hall, Debbie Hall, John Hall, Glen Hall, Keri Hallam, Douglas Hamilton, Michael Hanel, U Hanke, R Hanley, Henry Hanrahan, Peter Hardie, A Hardy, Flemming Harms, Daniel Hart, Tye Hartall, Tom Hartdyne, Rehan Hasan, Claire Hawkins, Lucinda Hayward, Mark Heald, Paul Heester, John Heinzel, Johannes van der Heide, Jenifer Henderson, Douglas Hendrie, Mark Henley, Katri Hentula, Sonia Hernaez, Chris Herzog, Yasuko Higuchi, Jonathon Hill, Richard Hill, Klaus Hille, Philip Himelstein, Tony Hinks, Dave Hirst, Lisa Hirst, Rachel Hobbs, Caroline Hobbs, Rudie Hocke, Graham Hodge, S Hogler, Aste Holen, Joanne Holmes, Lois Holm-Jorgensen, David Horder, Bostjn Horjak, Mark Horowitz, Will Houston, Mike Howlett, Petr Hruska, Charly Hucke, Sue Hucknall, Leow Chun Hui, Sam Huibers, Gordon Hutton, Laura Huxrabue, Lars Hylander

Rodney Jackson, Tim Jacobi, Christian Jacobsen, Sonja Jakoub, Greg & Minke James, Ali James, Helmut Jansch, Helen Jeffs, Fiona & Paul Jeip, Samuel Johnson, Don & Reggie Johnston, N Jones, Wally Jones, Richard Juterbock, Jan Willem Kaal, Dr L Kahansky, Olav Kandel, Ita Kane, Kunalan Kannappan, Pertti Kantanen, Nithya Karpaya-Timm,

Renko Karruppannan, Andrew Kaufman, Mel Kay, Joseph Kellegher, Laura Keller, Rosie Kennedy, Lin Ketchell, Christopher Kickham, Julia Kimber, Erin Kindberg, Lesley King, Rodolfo Kintamar, Dufus Kitten, Debra A Klein, B Klein, Keith Knight, Matthew Konsa, G Kotschenreuther, Julien Kozak, Tim Kretser, Zdenek Kvinta, Wai Shing Kwan, Michael Laird, Ian Lamont, Baylor Lancaster, Christy Lanzl, Sophiede Lara, Andrew Larcom, Paul Lawlor, Eleanor & George Lawson, Mark Leach, Stephen Andrew Lee, Thad Leeper, Tim Leffel, Donna Marcus Leffel, Fiona Lewis, Sheila Lewis, Cas Liber, Steve Lidgey, Inge Light, Cofe Linsbauer, Alison Linsday, Theresa Liu, Yin Lan Lo, Gill Lobel, Paul Lovichi, Louise & Julian Lowry, G Lucania, Lorraine Luciano, Sally Luke, Ben Lupton, E Lynn, Sophia Wai Chee Mah, C Malcolm-Heath, Louis Manne, Stephanie March, Will Markle, Tony Marsden, Ian & Tina Mathiason, Debi Matsuda, Liz Mattock, Melanie Mavromarus, Annette McAllister, Ciara McArdle, N McCallion, Lesley McCann, Barrie McCormick, Francis McEntee, TJ McIntyre, Stuart McLay, J McLoughlin, The Medpower Team, I Mende, Tracey Mercer, Hilda Mertiens, Annette Miller, Danna Millett, Sarah Mitchell, John Mitchell, Vit Mlcoch, Elsa Mock, Alistair Moes, B Monsma, Sheila Montague, Stephen Montgomery, Simon Moore, N Moore, Christopher Morden, H Morris, Dan Morris, Annalie Morris, Julie Morrissey, John Morse, Michael Mortensen, KC Mowbray, Donald Ross Moxley, Karl Muellner, Diana Mundi, Veronica Munk, David Munro, Ian Murphy, Angela Murray

Stephen Neale, Chris Nevmeyer, Gordon Newlands, Kerryn Newton, Kevin Nicholls, Guy Nicholson, Ian Nicholson, N Nicklin, Jeppe Juul Nielsen, Ios Nieuwenhuis, Kala Nobbs, V Noonan, Adrian Nordenborg, Ray Norton, Gail O'Connell, R O'Halloran, Karen Okun, Claes Olesen, Dan Oleskevich, Diane Oliver, Finn Olsen, Frances O'Neill, Shane & Francis O'Neill, Andre Oppe, Mark Orton, Geir Ostrem, Pierre Ostrowski, Tina Ottman, Rick Owen, Mike Pain, Paul & Sherrie Panther, A Parienty, Arnaud Parienty, Nick Park, Kerry Parkin, Vijay K Parmar, James Parsons, Sera Parsons, Ros Passmore, Lynn & Michele Patterson, Lynn Patterson, Johnny Paul, Sarah Pearce, CH Pearce, Naida Pearson, Diana Peh, Paul D Pelczar, Tan Tang Penn, Rena Penna, Oliver Perceval, Mattijs Perdeck, Matthew Peregrine-Jones, Stuart Perkins, David Perlstein, Ann Perrelli, Aidan Perse, Ellie Peters, Anthony Pez, Jochen Pfeuffer, Hoa Pham, Nicolas Philibert, I Philips, Richard Pickard, Yvonne Pickering, Kiekie Piejs, John Piekarski, Jonathon Platt, Lidy van der Ploeg, Bine Pohner, Darren Le Poidevin, Frank Polanco, Julie Polk, Sussan Pongsri, Alison & Simon Porges, Robert Porte, Virginia Porter, M Porup, Joris Postema, Jens Poulsen, Dani Powell, Satya Prakas, Tracey Preiser, Laura Prendergast, Ofer Presente, Russ Preston, Anne Pyke, John Pyke

Clem Read, J Rebecca, J Redfern, Malin Regebro, Lynette & Anthea Reid, Katrin Reiter, Renee Renjal, Anita Rhiner, Louise Riby, Mijk Richfield, Jeff Richter, N Rickaby, Clive Role, L Roberts, Cath Robertson, Jennifer & Alan Robins, Adam Robson,

Sarah Rodgers, Ollie Roger, Ashley Rogers, Steve Rogowski, Joost Rompa, Ron Rook, Johan Ros, Daphne Rose-Jevremor, Marvin & Patricia Rosen, Nina Rosenbladt, Howard Rosenthal, Nicola Ross, Yancey Rousek, Minco Ruiter, Denise Rushton, Petra Russi, A Saez, Jeff Sagalewicz, Alexandra Saidy, Peggy Sailler, N Salloux, Angela Salmon, Damian Sammon, Stefan Samuelsson, Kathy Sawdon, Alain Schellinck, A Schildknecht, Jetta Schmidt-Pederson, Laura Schmuleweitz, Beate Schneider, Marianne Schodt, Mette Schou, Ralph Schwer, Steve Scott, Matthew Scott, Alison Scott, Jess Scruggs, Rayvan Seeters, Anton Segal, Bernd Seidel, Steve Seifert, Peter Sellers, Jack Sellner, Martin & Christina Semler, Alana Serota, Antonio Carru Serranu, Phil & Louise Shambrook, L Sharon, Jenny Shaw, M Shepherd, Joel Shively, Mike Shrimpton, Ann Siebert, Ge Sijm, David Silverman, Anna Silverwood, Julie Simkins, Matthew Simmonds, Fletcher Simpkins, Carl Simpson, Ricki Singer, Thakur Dalip Singh, N Sirak, Marketa Sixtova, Robert Skuy, Peter Slade, Nathalie van der Slikke, Joseph Smallwood, CJ Smith, Janine Smith, Carole Smith, Stuart Smith, L Smith, Michael Smith, Carole Smith, Chad Smolinski, Lorraine Solomon, Arne CA Sorlie, Sandrade Souza, Kathryn Spall, John Spheeris, Amy Spilane, Martin Sprinzl, Christina Squid, Louise Stanley, Judith Starke, DJ Staveley, Keith Stead, Craig Steed, Tatjana Steinecke, C Stenger, Bo Stenson, Linhard Stepf, Sandra St Laurent, Magnus Stomfelt, Bill Stoughton, Robert Strang, Patrick Sullivan, Mark Sunderland, JG Sweetman, Wanda & Barry Syner

Arthur Tan, AA Tan-Keultjes, Steven M Tattersall, Katie Taylor, S Temple, Arthur Teo, Alison Thackray, Howard Thain, E Thebaud, Stephen Theobold, A Thomas, Tracey Thomas, G Thompson, Rasmus Heje Thomsen, Bill Thomson, Kristie Thomson, JM Thomson, David Thorne, Lisette Thresh, Andy Tindle, KE Titchener, Graham Todd, TJ Tolmer-Amos, Ilpo Tornqvist, Rory Towler, R Townsend, N Treacy, K Treharne, Jacques Trouman, Winxie Tse, Phil Tucker, Nicola Turner, Jeffrey Twitchell-Waas, Laurie Ufot, Derek Uhlemann, Filip Verbelen, Koert Vermeulen, Kaj Vetter, Dr Heribert Vollmer, Bjorn von Rimscha, Haroldvan Voornveld, A Voortman, Luc & Josede Vries, Margit Waas, Laszlo Wagner, Roland Wagner, Jens Wahlberg, Nadine Waite, Janet Walker, David Wall, Arthur Walton, Matt Ward, Jan Watson, B & A Watson, Jacob Weismann, Peter Weisshaar, Don Welch, Peter Wellens, Vivian Wesselingh, Honey Weston, Francis Wetzel, L Wharam, Anthony White, Debbie Whitehead, Charlie Wicke, Brett Wigdortz, AR Wilder, Anja Wilke, Chrissie Williams, Louise Williams, NG Williams, Anne Wilshin, GF & J Wilson, Gareth Wilson, Henry Wilson, S Wilson, I Wilson, Charlotte Wilson, Dan Wilton, Stefan Winkler, Mike Witcombe, J Withers, Giles Witittarid, Monica & Christina Wojtaszewski, David Wolff, Emma Wood, Rohan Wood, Helen Woodward, Jackie Wright, Joyce Wu, Anita Wyss, Dina Yael, Ken Yiu, Ricky Yu, YB Yuen, Justin Zaman, RA Zambardino, Yoav Zand, Cathy van der Zee, G & J Zevenboorn

LONELY PLANET

Phrasebooks

Lonely Planet phrasebooks are packed with essential words and phrases to help travellers communicate with the locals. With colour tabs for quick reference, an extensive vocabulary, and use of script, these handy pocket-sized language guides cover day-to-day travel situations.

- handy pocket-sized books
- easy to understand Pronunciation chapter
- clear & comprehensive Grammar chapter
- romanisation alongside script to allow ease of pronunciation
- script throughout so users can point to phrases for every situations
- full of cultural information and tips for the traveller

'...vital for a real DIY spirit and attitude in language learning'

– Backpacker

'the phrasebooks have good cultural backgrounders and offer solid advice for challenging situations in remote locations'

– San Francisco Examiner

Arabic (Egyptian) • Arabic (Moroccan) • Australia *(Australian English, Aboriginal and Torres Strait languages)* • Baltic States *(Estonian, Latvian, Lithuanian)* • Bengali • Brazilian • Burmese • Cantonese • Central Asia • Central Europe *(Czech, French, German, Hungarian, Italian, Slovak)* • Eastern Europe *(Bulgarian, Czech, Hungarian, Polish, Romanian, Slovak)* • Egyptian Arabic • Ethiopian (Amharic) • Fijian • French • German • Greek • Hill Tribes • Hindi/Urdu • Indonesian • Italian • Japanese • Korean • Lao • Malay • Mandarin • Mediterranean Europe *(Albanian, Croatian, Greek, Italian, Macedonian, Maltese, Serbian, Slovene)* • Mongolian • Nepali • Papua New Guinea • Pilipino (Tagalog) • Quechua • Russian • Scandinavian Europe *(Danish, Finnish, Icelandic, Norwegian, Swedish)* • South-East Asia *(Burmese, Indonesian, Khmer, Lao, Malay, Tagalog Pilipino, Thai, Vietnamese)* • Spanish (Castilian) *(also includes Catalan, Galician and Basque)* • Spanish (Latin American) • Sri Lanka • Swahili • Thai • Tibetan • Turkish • Ukrainian • USA *(US English, Vernacular Talk, Native American languages, Hawaiian)* • Vietnamese • Western Europe *(Basque, Catalan, Dutch, French, German, Greek, Irish)*

Lonely Planet Journeys

J OURNEYS is a unique collection of travel writing – published by the company that understands travel better than anyone else. It is a series for anyone who has ever experienced – or dreamed of – the magical moment when they encountered a strange culture or saw a place for the first time. They are tales to read while you're planning a trip, while you're on the road or while you're in an armchair, in front of a fire.

These outstanding titles explore our planet through the eyes of a diverse group of international writers. JOURNEYS books catch the spirit of a place, illuminate a culture, recount a crazy adventure, or introduce a fascinating way of life. They always entertain, and always enrich the experience of travel.

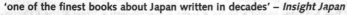

LOST JAPAN
Alex Kerr

Exploring rarely visited temples and shrines, studying calligraphy, talking with Kabuki actors: Alex Kerr draws on more than thirty years of personal experience in presenting this backstage tour of a Japan that outsiders rarely glimpse.

'one of the finest books about Japan written in decades' – *Insight Japan*

ISLANDS IN THE CLOUDS
Travels in the Highlands of New Guinea
Isabella Tree

Isabella Tree travels through the remote and beautiful highlands of Papua New Guinea and Irian Jaya – one of the most extraordinary and dangerous regions on the planet – with a Highlander who introduces her to his intriguing and complex world, changing rapidly as it collides with modern technology.

'a gifted writer and reporter with a lively style . . . she reports on her journeys with compassion and insight' – *Los Angeles Times*

A SEASON IN HEAVEN
True Tales from the Road to Kathmandu
David Tomory

In Iran and Afghanistan, in Rishikesh and Goa, in ashrams, mountain villages and dubious hotels, a generation of young people got hip, got busted, lost their luggage, and sometimes found themselves. From confusion to contentment, from dope to dysentery, A Season in Heaven presents the true stories of travellers who hit the hippie trail in the late 1960s.

Only available in Canada and the USA

SHOPPING FOR BUDDHAS
Jeff Greenwald

In his obsessive search for the perfect Buddha statue in the backstreets of Kathmandu, Jeff Greenwald discovers more than he bargained for. Politics, religion and serious shopping collide in this witty account of an enlightening visit to Nepal.

'Greenwald's quest reveals more about modern Nepal . . . than writings that take themselves much more seriously' – *Chicago Tribune*

LONELY PLANET

Lonely Planet Travel Atlases

L onely Planet has long been famous for the number and quality of its guidebook maps. Now we've gone one step further and produced a handy companion series: Lonely Planet travel atlases – maps of a country produced in book form.

Unlike other maps, which look good but lead travellers astray, our travel atlases have been researched on the road by Lonely Planet's experienced team of writers. All details are carefully checked to ensure the atlas corresponds with the equivalent Lonely Planet guidebook.

- full-colour throughout
- maps researched and checked by Lonely Planet authors
- place names correspond with Lonely Planet guidebooks
- no confusing spelling differences
- legend and travelling information in English, French, German, Japanese and Spanish
- size: 230 x 160 mm

Available now: Chile & Easter Island ● Egypt ● India & Bangladesh ● Israel & the Palestinian Territories ● Jordan, Syria & Lebanon ● Kenya ● Laos ● Portugal ● South Africa, Lesotho & Swaziland ● Thailand ● Turkey ● Vietnam ● Zimbabwe, Botswana & Namibia

Lonely Planet TV Series & Videos

L onely Planet travel guides have been brought to life on television screens around the world. Like our guides, the programmes are based on the joy of independent travel, and look honestly at some of the most exciting, picturesque and frustrating places in the world. Each show is presented by one of three travellers from Australia, England or the USA and combines an innovative mixture of video, Super-8 film, atmospheric soundscapes and original music.

Videos of each episode – containing additional footage not shown on television – are available from good book and video shops, but the availability of individual videos varies with regional screening schedules.

Video destinations include: Alaska ● American Rockies ● Australia – The South-East ● Baja California & the Copper Canyon ● Brazil ● Central Asia ● Chile & Easter Island ● Corsica, Sicily & Sardinia – The Mediterranean Islands ● East Africa (Tanzania & Zanzibar) ● Ecuador & the Galapagos Islands ● Greenland & Iceland ● Indonesia ● Israel & the Sinai Desert ● Jamaica ● Japan ● La Ruta Maya ● Morocco ● New York ● North India ● Pacific Islands (Fiji, Solomon Islands & Vanuatu) ● South India ● South West China ● Turkey ● Vietnam ● West Africa ● Zimbabwe, Botswana & Namibia

The Lonely Planet TV series is produced by: Pilot Productions
The Old Studio
18 Middle Row
London W10 5AT UK

LONELY PLANET

Lonely Planet Online
www.lonelyplanet.com *or* AOL keyword: lp

Whether you've just begun planning your next trip, or you're chasing down specific info on currency regulations or visa requirements, check out Lonely Planet Online for up-to-the minute travel information.

As well as mini guides to more than 250 destinations, you'll find maps, photos, travel news, health and visa updates, travel advisories, and discussion of the ecological and political issues you need to be aware of as you travel. You'll also find timely upgrades to popular guidebooks which you can print out and stick in the back of your book.

There's also an online travellers' forum where you can share your experience of life on the road, meet travel companions and ask other travellers for their recommendations and advice.

And of course we have a complete and up-to-date list of all Lonely Planet travel products including travel guides, diving and snorkelling guides, phrasebooks, atlases, travel literature and videos, and a simple online ordering facility if you can't find the book you want elsewhere.

Lonely Planet Diving & Snorkelling Guides

Known for indispensible guidebooks to destinations all over the world, Lonely Planet's Pisces Books are the most popular series of diving and snorkelling titles available.

There are three series: **Diving & Snorkelling Guides**, **Shipwreck Diving** series, and **Dive Into History**. Full colour throughout, the **Diving & Snorkelling Guides** combine quality photographs with detailed descriptions of the best dive sites for each location, giving divers a glimpse of what they can expect both on land and in water. The **Dive Into History** series is perfect for the adventure diver or armchair traveller. The **Shipwreck Diving** series provides all the details for exploring the most interesting wrecks in the Atlantic and Pacific oceans. The list also includes underwater nature and technical guides.

LONELY PLANET

Guides by Region

L onely Planet is known worldwide for publishing practical, reliable and no-nonsense travel information in our guides and on our web site. The Lonely Planet list covers just about every accessible part of the world. Currently there are nine series: travel guides, shoestring guides, walking guides, city guides, phrasebooks, audio packs, travel atlases, diving and snorkelling guides and travel literature.

AFRICA Africa – the South • Africa on a shoestring • Arabic (Egyptian) phrasebook • Arabic (Moroccan) phrasebook • Cairo • Cape Town • Central Africa • East Africa • Egypt • Egypt travel atlas • Ethiopian (Amharic) phrasebook • The Gambia & Senegal • Kenya • Kenya travel atlas • Malawi, Mozambique & Zambia • Morocco • North Africa • South Africa, Lesotho & Swaziland • South Africa, Lesotho & Swaziland travel atlas • Swahili phrasebook • Trekking in East Africa • Tunisia • West Africa • Zimbabwe, Botswana & Namibia • Zimbabwe, Botswana & Namibia travel atlas
Travel Literature: The Rainbird: A Central African Journey • Songs to an African Sunset: A Zimbabwean Story • Mali Blues: Traveling to an African Beat

AUSTRALIA & THE PACIFIC Australia • Australian phrasebook • Bushwalking in Australia • Bushwalking in Papua New Guinea • Fiji • Fijian phrasebook • Islands of Australia's Great Barrier Reef • Melbourne • Micronesia • New Caledonia • New South Wales & the ACT • New Zealand • Northern Territory • Outback Australia • Papua New Guinea • Papua New Guinea (Pidgin) phrasebook • Queensland • Rarotonga & the Cook Islands • Samoa • Solomon Islands • South Australia • Sydney • Tahiti & French Polynesia • Tasmania • Tonga • Tramping in New Zealand • Vanuatu • Victoria • Western Australia
Travel Literature: Islands in the Clouds • Sean & David's Long Drive

CENTRAL AMERICA & THE CARIBBEAN Bahamas and Turks & Caicos • Bermuda • Central America on a shoestring • Costa Rica • Cuba • Eastern Caribbean • Guatemala, Belize & Yucatán: La Ruta Maya • Jamaica • Mexico • Mexico City • Panama
Travel Literature: Green Dreams: Travels in Central America

EUROPE Amsterdam • Andalucia • Austria • Baltic States phrasebook • Berlin • Britain • Central Europe • Central Europe phrasebook • Czech & Slovak Republics • Denmark • Dublin • Eastern Europe • Eastern Europe phrasebook • Estonia, Latvia & Lithuania • Finland • France • French phrasebook • Germany • German phrasebook • Greece • Greek phrasebook • Hungary • Iceland, Greenland & the Faroe Islands • Ireland • Italian phrasebook • Italy • Lisbon • London • Mediterranean Europe • Mediterranean Europe phrasebook • Paris • Poland • Portugal • Portugal travel atlas • Prague • Romania & Moldova • Russia, Ukraine & Belarus • Russian phrasebook • Scandinavian & Baltic Europe • Scandinavian Europe phrasebook • Slovenia • Spain • Spanish phrasebook • St Petersburg • Switzerland • Trekking in Spain • Ukrainian phrasebook • Vienna • Walking in Britain • Walking in Italy • Walking in Switzerland • Western Europe • Western Europe phrasebook
Travel Literature: The Olive Grove: Travels in Greece

INDIAN SUBCONTINENT Bangladesh • Bengali phrasebook • Bhutan • Delhi • Goa • Hindi/Urdu phrasebook • India • India & Bangladesh travel atlas • Indian Himalaya • Karakoram Highway • Nepal • Nepali phrasebook • Pakistan • Rajasthan • South India • Sri Lanka • Sri Lanka phrasebook • Trekking in the Indian Himalaya • Trekking in the Karakoram & Hindukush • Trekking in the Nepal Himalaya
Travel Literature: In Rajasthan • Shopping for Buddhas

Gigi, Danau (I) 333
Gili Air (I) 274-7, **275**
Gili Islands (I) 26, 274-7
Gili Meno (I) 274-7, **276**
Gili Trawangan (I) 274-7, **277**
Gilimanuk (I) 222
Gita, Danau (I) 333
Gitgit (I) 219
Goh Chok Tong 645-8
Golden Sands Beach (M), see
  Teluk Belanga
Golden Triangle 744, 764, **765**
olkar 121
olo Curu (I) 283
omo (I) 248
eat Cave (M) 474
een Canyon (I) 165
a Charas (M) 451
a Gajah (I) 213
a Jepang (I) 332-3
Kotilola (I) 336
Telinga (M) 463
Wikuda (I) 336
naras (P) 626-7
of Tonkin (V) 833
ng Gading National
rk (M) 471-2
ng Leuser National
k (I) 26, 224, 227, 239
g Mas Tea Plantation (I)

g Mulu National Park
406, 476-7

(V) 879
a, Danau (I) 336
BJ 120, 290
g (V) 832
ay (V) 802, 807, 831,

Pantai (I) 330
25, 820-31, **822-3,**

Internet services 820
nment 828-9
around 830
there & away
0
eat 826-8
stay 825-6
vices 820
829
see & do 821-5
76, 789-91, **790**
06
895-7
& stings 904-5
tal hazards
iseases 900-3

health cont:
  insect-borne diseases 903-4
  less common diseases 905-6
  medical problems &
    treatment 897
  predeparture planning
    893-5
  women's health 906
Hekou (China) 836
Hibok-Hibok volcano (P) 640-1
Hidden Valley (P) 596
hides & salt licks (M) 463
highlights 25-7, see also
  individual countries
Hila (I) 324
Hilimaeta (I) 248
hill tribes 682, 802,
  (T) 745-7
Hin Dat Hot Springs (T) 739
Hin Lat (T) 779
Hinagdanan Cave (P) 622
Hinduism 122, 142, 892
history chart 890-1
hitchhiking 53
Hitigima (I) 336
Hitugi (I) 336
Hkakabo Razi (My) 493, 548
Hmawza (My) 526
Hmong people 340-2, 379,
  744, 746, 754, 836-7, 840
Ho Chi Minh 802, 832
Ho Chi Minh City (Saigon) (V)
  802, 860-78, **862-3, 866,**
  868, 870
  email & Internet services 860
  entertainment 872
  getting around 873-4
  getting there & away 873
  maps 860
  places to eat 869-72
  places to stay 865-9
  postal services 860
  shopping 872-3
  things to see & do 861-5
Ho Chi Minh Trail 337, 339,
  388
Hoa Binh (V) 835-6
Hoa Lu (V) 807, 831
Hoang Lien Mountains (V)
  831, 837
Hoi An (V) 802, 847-50, **848**
Hon Chong (V) 879
Hon Quap (V), see Cat's Tooth
  Mountain
Honda Bay (P) 642
Hsipaw (My) 500, 546-7
Hua Hin (T) 685, 776-7
Hua Phan (L) 342
Hua Phan Province (L) 381-2
Hua Thanon (T) 781
Huay Kalok (My) 493

Huay Khamin falls (T) 739
Huay Xai (L) 384-5
Hué (V) 802, 807, 840-5,
  842-3
Hun Sen 68
Hundred Islands (P) 597-8
Hunimua (I) 324
Huu (I) 279

I
Iboih (I) 237
Ifugao people 563, 602
ikat 284, 286, 288, 293,
  295-7
Ilin Island (P) 614
Iloilo City (P) 626
Imogiri (I) 177
Indonesia 118-336, **119**
  accommodation 132
  books 130
  climate 120
  email & Internet services
    128
  embassies 126
  flora & fauna 121
  food & drinks 132
  geography 120
  getting around 134-40,
    135, 138
  getting there & away 133-4
  health 130-1
  highlights 118, 123-4
  holidays 131-2
  language 123
  maps 124
  money 126-8
  planning 124
  population & people 122
  postal services 128
  religion 122
  safe travel 131
  shopping 132-3
  society & conduct 122
  special events 131-2
  telephone services 128
  tourist offices 124-5
  visas 125
Inerie, Gunung (I) 283
Inle Lake (My) 489, 500,
  543-5, **543**
Internet services & resources 33
Inwa (My), see Ava
Ipoh (M) 433-4
Irama, Pantai (M) 461
Irawan (P) 642
Irian Jaya (I) 124, 326-36, **327**
  getting around 328
  getting there & away 328
Irosin (P) 609
Irrawaddy dolphin 69, 340,
  392

Brunei Darussalam cont:
postal services 58
religion 56
society & conduct 56
special events 59
telephone services 58
tourist offices 56
visas 56-7
Brunei Museum (B) 56, 61
Buddhism 122, 142, 337-9, 341, 492, 499, 684-5, 806-7, 892
Buenavista (P) 610
Bugis people 306
Bukit Barisan Mountains (I) 225-7
Bukit Indah (M) 463
Bukit Lawang (I) 228, 237-9
Bukit Lawang orang-utan sanctuary (I) 123
Bukit Patoi (B) 54, 64-5
Bukit Peninsula (I) 205-6
Bukit Peradayan (B) 64-5
Bukit Teresik (I) 463
Bukit Timah (S) 648, 668
Bukit Timah Nature Reserve (S) 648
Bukittinggi (I) 26, 123, 249-53, **250**
Bulusan (P) 609
Bunaken, Pulau (I) 25, 124, 318-9
Buon Ma Thuot (V) 860
Burauen (P) 623
Burma, see Myanmar
bus travel 52
Busuanga Island (P) 644
Butterfly Garden (M) 432
Butuan (P) 634-5
Buyan, Danau (I) 224

C
Ca Na (V) 855
Cabilao Island (P) 621
Cagayan de Oro (P) 635
Cagsawa (P) 608
Cahaya Bukan, Pantai (M) 461
Cai Rong (V) 834-5
Calamba (P) 596
Calbayog (P) 624
Callao Caves (P) 606
Cam Ha (V) 849
Cam Kim Island (V) 849
Cam Nam Village (V) 849
Cam Pha (V), see Van Don Island
Camalig (P) 608
Cambodia 66-117, **67**
accommodation 78
activities 77
arts 70
books 74

Cambodia cont:
climate 69
email & Internet services 74
embassies 72
entertainment 78-9
flora & fauna 69
food & drinks 78
geography 68
getting around 81-2
getting there & away 79-80
health 75
highlights 66, 70-1
holidays 77
language 70
maps 71
money 72-3
planning 71
population & people 69-70
postal services 73
religion 70
safe travel 76-7
shopping 79
society & conduct 70
special events 77
telephone services 73-4
tourist offices 71
visas 71
work 77-8
Cameron Highlands 430-3, **431**
Camiguin Island (P) 640-1
Camp Carroll (V) 845
Camplong (I) 187, 293
Can Cau Market (V) 837
Candi Bima (I) 166
Candi Ceto (I) 182
Candi Sukuh (I) 182
Candidasa (I) 26, 123, 215-6, **216-7**
Candikuning (I) 223-4
Canggu (I) 222
canoeing (T) 699
Pagsanjan (P) 597
Canopy Walkway (M) 463
Cantho (V) 879
Caodai Great Temple (V) 874
Caodaism 806-7, 874
Cape Fatucama (I) 294
Cape Rachado (M) 430
car travel 52
Carmen (P) 622
Cat Ba Island (V) 807, 833-4
Cat Ba National Park (V) 805, 833-4
Cat Ba town (V) 833-4
Cat Co beaches (V) 833
Catanduanes Island (P) 610
Catbalogan (P) 624
Caticlan (P) 627
Cat's Tooth Mountain (V) 851
Cau May (V) 837

caving (M) 406
Cayangan, Lake (P) 644
Cebu City (P) 616-9, **618**
Cebu Island (P) 614-21
Cemoro Lawang (I) 188
Cempaka (I) 304
Cenang, Pantai (M) 444
Cenderawasih Bay (I) 333-4
Central Cordillera (P) 565
Chaa Ong waterfall (C) 117
Cha-am (T) 685
Chaiya (T) 775, 778
Chakri Dynasty 677, 681
Chaliang (T) 758
Chalok Lam, Ao (T) 783-4
Champa kingdom 802, 851
Champasak kingdom 337, 341-2
Champasak Province (L) 388-92
Champasak town (L) 391
Chan River (T) 777
Chang Lang, Hat (T) 800
Changi (S) 665-8
Chao Phraya River (T) 712
Chau Doc (V) 879
Chaungtha (My) 500
Chaungtha Beach (My) 528-9
Chaweng, Hat (T) 779-82
Cheng Ho 394, 425
Cherating (M) 25
Chiang Dao Caves (T) 762
Chiang Khan (T) 772
Chiang Mai (T) 25, 676, 685, 747-54, **748**
Chiang Rai (T) 761-4, **763**
Chiang Saen (T) 764
Chin people 497, 554, 557
Chin State (My) 553-4, 557
China Beach (V) 851
Chinatown (S) 645, 649, 662-3
Chocolate Hills (P) 558, 621-2
Choeung Ek (C), see Killing Fields
Chom Thong (T) 755
Christianity 122, 398, 565, 614, 806-7, 893
Chuan Leekpai 677-80
Chulalongkorn (Rama V), King 677
Chunchiet people (C) 116
Chunchiet villages (C) 117
Ciater (I) 161
Cibodas (I) 156-7
Cingkes (I) 241
Cipanas (I) 156-7
Cipatujah (I) 165
Cisarua (I) 156-7
Clearwater Cave (M) 476-7
climate charts 907

Co Roc Mountain (V) 845
cockfighting (P) 564
Compang Ruteng (I) 283
Confucianism 806-7
Coral Bay (M) 434
Coron Town (P) 644
Corregidor (P) 592-94
courses 38
Cu Chi Tunnels (V) 874
Cua Dai Beach (V) 849
Cuc Phuong National Park (V) 805, 832
customs 30
cybercafes, see email & Internet services
cycling 52-3; (L) 350, 357; (M) 406; (P) 574, 579; (T) 711; (V) 819
Kon Tum (V) 860
Lombok (I) 267
Moalboal (P) 620

D
Daet (P) 607
Dago (I) 161-2
Dagupan (P) 598
Dakak (P) 636
Dalam Loka (I) 278
Dalat (V) 802, 807, 856-9, **857, 858**
Daliran Cave (P) 626
Danang (V) 845-7, **846**
Danao, Lake (P) 623
Dani people 334
Danum Valley (M) 26, 394, 399
Dapitan (P) 636
Daraga (P) 608
Dasar Sabak, Pantai (M) 461
Data Dawai (I) 301
Datah Bilang (I) 301
Datanla Falls (V) 856
Dau Dang Waterfall (V) 835
Davao (P) 637-40, **638**
Dawei (My) 552-3
Dayak people 298, 300, 397, 465, 472
de Legaspi, Miguel 558
Death Railway (T) 737
Deer Cave (M) 476-7
Democratic Karen Buddhist Army (DKBA) 493
Denpasar (I) 195-8, **196**
Depapre (I) 331
Desaru (M) 445
Dien Bien Phu (V) 802, 839-40
Dieng Plateau (I) 166-7

Dili (I) 294-5
Dili massacre 120
Dipolog (P) 635-6
Diponegoro, Prince 167
disabled travellers 36
diving & snorkelling 38, (C) 77, (M) 406, (P) 574, (T) 699, (V) 814
Alor Island (I) 289
Ambon, Pulau (I) 323
Apo Reef (P) 614
Bali (I) 193
Bandaneira (I) 324
Bandarlampung (I) 261
Biak, Pulau (I) 333
Bintan, Pulau (I) 260
Boracay (P) 629
Bunaken, Pulau (I) 318-9
Depapre (I) 331
Donggala (I) 316
Gili Islands (I) 274
Honda Bay (P) 642
Ko Pha-Ngan (T) 783
Ko Tao (T) 785
Komodo Island (I) 281
Kuguita (P) 640
Kupang (I) 290
Kuta (Bali) (I) 198
Labuanbajo (I) 282
Lombok (I) 264, 267
Lovina (I) 219
Madale, Pantai (I) 315
Maluku (I) 320-1
Menjangan, Pulau (I) 222
Moyo, Pulau (I) 279
Nha Trang (V) 851
Nusa Lembongan (I) 214
Pattaya (T) 740
Perhentian Islands (M) 456
Pescador Island (P) 620
Phuket (T) 795
Port Barton (P) 643
Senggigi (I) 270
Sihanoukville (C) 104-6
Sipadan, Pulau (M) 488
Tanjung Benoa (I) 205
Tioman, Pulau (M) 446
Tujuh Bejas, Pulau (I) 284
Tulamben (I) 218
Weh, Pulau (I) 236
White Island (P) 641
DMZ (V) 845
Do Son Beach (V) 832
Doi Inthanon (T) 680, 755
Doi Inthanon National Park (T) 685
Doi Phu Kha National Park (T) 766
Doi Suthep (T) 747, 754
Doi Tung (T) 764-5
Dokan (I) 241

Doljo Beach (P) 622
Don Det (L) 392
Don Khon (L) 392
Don Khong (L) 392
Donggala (I) 316
Donsol (P) 609
drinks 40
drugs 37, 192-3, 405, 6
Dumaguete (P) 632-3
Dumai (I) 259
durian 637
Dutch East India Com (VOC) 142

E
El Nido (P) 565, 647
El Niño 561
electricity 35
elephants 69, 121
339-40, 495, 7
rides (C) 77, 1
email services 33
embassies 30
Emerald Bay (M
Endangered Pri Center (V)
Ende (I) 284-
Erawan Falls
Estrada, Jose

Gunu
15
Gunu
(M

Faifo (V), s
Fang (T) 7
Fansipan (
Fatumena
fax servic
ferry tra
Flores (I
getti
getti
food 3
forest
Fraser
Frenc
Freti

G
Ga

Ha Tier
Habben
Habibie
Haiphor
Halong
833
Hamadi,
Hanoi (V
826
email &
enterta
getting
getting
829-
places
places
postal se
shopping
things to
Hat Yai (T) 3
health 893-9
basic rule
cuts, bites
environme
897-9
infectious

Bold indicates maps.
Italics indicates boxed text.

Isana kingdom (T) 767
Islam 54, 118, 122, 225, 398, 565, 633, 649, 685, 806-7, 892-3
itineraries 27, see also individual countries
Iwahig (P) 642
Iya, Gunung (I) 284

J

Jakarta (I) 26, 123, 141, 144-53, **145**, **146**, **148**
    entertainment 150-1
    getting around 152-3
    getting there & away 151-2
    places to eat 150
    places to stay 149-50
    postal services 144-5
    telephone services 145
    things to see & do 145-9
    tourist offices 144
Jao Island (P) 622
Jao Mai, Hat (T) 800
Jason's Bay (M) 445
Java (I) 123, 140-89, **140-1**
    getting around 143-4
    getting there & away 143
Jayapura (I) 328-30, **329**
Jempang, Danau (I) 300
Jerantut (M) 462
Jerudong Playground (B) 54, 56, 64
Jimbaran Bay (I) 205
Jiwika (I) 335-6
Johor Bahru (M) 424-5
Johor Lama (M) 445
Jomtien, Hat (T) 740
Jopu (I) 286
Juara (M) 446, 448
Juban (P) 609
Jungle Park (M) 424
jungle railway (M) 461
Jurong (S) 663-5
Jurong Bird Park (S) 645, 649, 663

K

Ka Tieng waterfall (C) 117
Kabonduk (I) 297
Kachin Independence Army (KIA) 548
Kachin State (My) 548-9
Kadidiri, Pulau (I) 317
Kaeng Krachan National Park (T) 685, 776
Kaget, Pulau (I) 303

Kai Islands (I) 321
Kaladan River (My) 555, 557
Kalala (I) 297
Kalaw (My) 500, 542-3
Kalianda (I) 262
Kalibo (P) 565, 625, 627
Kalimantan (I) 124, 298-306, **299**
    getting around 298
    getting there & away 298
Kaliuda (I) 297
Kaliurang (I) 177
Kamala, Ao (T) 795
Kamphaeng Phet (T) 756, 759
Kamping Poy (C) 113
Kampot (C) 70, 107-9, **108**
Kampung Ayer (B) 54, 56, 61
Kampung Gumum (M) 451
Kampung Komodo (I) 280
Kampung Tarung (I) 297
Kanchanaburi (T) 676, 737-9, **738**
Kanlaon volcano (P) 630
Kantang (T) 800
Kapan (I) 294
Kapas, Pulau (M) 453
Kapit (M) 473
Kapuas Kecil, Sungai (I) 304
Karasbik (I) 313
Karen people 746
Karon, Ao (T) 792-5
Kasih, Pantai (I) 237
Kata Yai, Ao (T) 792-5
Katibawasan Waterfall (P) 641
Katong (S) 665
Katupat (I) 317
Kaunghmudaw Paya (My) 535
Kawah Domas (I) 161
Kawah Ratu (I) 161
Kawah Sikidang (I) 166
Kawi, Gunung (I) 123, 189, 213
Kawthoung (My) 553, 777-8
Kefamenanu (I) 294
Kelabit highlands (M) 477
Kelila (I) 336
Kelimutu (I) 118, 123, 263, 281, 285
Kembang, Pulau (I) 303
Kenong Rimba National Park (M) 406, 461-2
Kengtung (My), see Kyaingtong
Kenyir, Tasik (M) 453, 455
Kep (C) 70, 109
Kera, Pulau (I) 293
Kerinci Seblat National Park (I) 27, 227
Kete Kesu (I) 313
Khammuan Limestone NBCA (L) 342
Khao Sok National Park (T) 797

Khe Sanh (V) 845
Khe Sanh Combat Base (V) 845
Khmer people 676
Khmer Rouge 66-8
Khmer ruins (T) 767
Khon Kaen (T) 770-1
Khorat Plateau (T) 680
Khorat Province (T), see Nakhon Ratchasima
Khu Khut Waterbird Sanctuary (T) 789
Khuat, Hat (T) 783-4
Kiematubu, Gunung (I) 326
Killing Fields of Choeung Ek (C) 94
Kimbim (I) 336
Kinabalu National Park (M) 399, 484-6
Kinabatangan, Batang (M) 26, 486-8
Kinchaan waterfall (C) 117
Kinpun (My) 550
Kirirom National Park (C) 69
Ko Adang (T) 792
Ko Chang (T) 25-6, 685, 743-4, 778
Ko Chang National Marine Park (T) 743-4
Ko Faan (T) 780
Ko Kha (T) 755
Ko Kham (T) 744
Ko Klang (T) 792
Ko Kradan (T) 800
Ko Kut (T) 744
Ko Lipe (T) 792
Ko Mak (T) 744
Ko Muk (T) 800
Ko Ngai (Hai) (T) 800
Ko Pha-Ngan (T) 25-6, 676, 783-5, **784**
Ko Phi Phi (T) 25, 799
Ko Rawi (T) 792
Ko Samet (T) 25-6, 685, 741-3, **742**
Ko Samui (T) 25-6, 676, 685, 775, 779-83, **780**
Ko Sukon (T) 800
Ko Tao (T) 25-6, 785-6
Ko Tarutao (T) 792
Ko Tarutao National Marine Park (T) 792
Ko Wai (T) 744
Ko Yaw (T) 789
Kobrador Island (P) 625
Kok, Pantai (M) 444
Komodo dragons 118, 121, 263, 280-1
Komodo island (I) 27, 123, 280-2
Kompong Cham (C) 70, 114-5
Kompong Chhnang (C) 70, 113-4

Kon Tum (V) 860
Korim (I) 333
Kota Ambon (I) 321-3, **322**
Kota Belud (M) 484
Kota Bharu (M) 26, 459-61, **458**
Kota Biak (I) 331-2, **332**
Kota Kinabalu (M) 478-82, **480**
Kota Ternate (I) 325
Kota Tinggi (M) 445
Koto Gadang (I) 254
koupreys 340
Krabi (T) 685, 775, 797-9
Krabi Province (T) 676
Krakatau (I) 261-2
Kratie (C) 115
Kuah (M) 444
Kuala Belait (B) 64
Kuala Belalong Field Studies Centre (B) 64-5
Kuala Besut (M) 456
Kuala Kangsar (M) 435
Kuala Keniam (M) 463-4
Kuala Lipis (M) 461-2
Kuala Lumpur (M) 26, 413-24, **416-7, 420**
    entertainment 422-3
    getting around 423-4
    getting there & away 423
    places to eat 422
    places to stay 419-21
    postal services 415
    shopping 423
    telephone services 415
    things to see & do 415-9
    tourist offices 415
Kuala Perlis (M) 443
Kuala Tahan (M) 463-5
Kuala Terengganu (M) 453-5, **454**
Kuala Trenggan (M) 463-4
Kuang Si Falls (L) 379
Kuantan (M) 449-50, **450**
Kubah National Park (M) 471
Kublai Khan 492, 537, 676-7
Kuching (M) 467-71, **468**
Kudat (M) 484
Kuguita (P) 640
Kupang (I) 290-3, **291, 292**
Kurima (I) 335-6
Kusu Island (S) 668
Kuta (Bali) (I) 25, 123, 198-205, **200**
Kuta Beach (Lombok) (I) 272-3
Kyaikkami (My) 552
Kyaikmaraw (My) 552
Kyaiktiyo (My) 500, 549-50
Kyaikto (My) 550
Kyaingtong (My) 500, 546, 765-6

Kyauk Padaung (My) 541
Kyauktan (My) 523
Kyaw Aung San Hta Kyaung (My) 535
Kyiktaw (My) 556

L

La Laguna Beach (P) 612-3
La Niña 561
Labuan, Pulau (M) 483-4
Labuanbajo (I) 123, 281-3
Labuhan Lalang (I) 222
Labuhan Lombok (I) 273
Ladalero (I) 287
Laem Hat Rin (T) 783
Laem Ngop (T) 743
Laem Set (T) 781
Laem Son National Park (T) 778
Lagundri Bay (I) 26, 247-9
Lahendong Hot Springs (I) 319
Lahu people 747
Lai Tarung (I) 297
Lake Taal (P) 596
Lam Pang (T) 786
Lamai, Hat (T) 779-82
Lamalera (I) 288-9
Lambir Hills National Park (M) 475
Lampang (T) 755-6
Lamphun (T) 755
Lampu'uk (I) 236
Landak, Sungai (I) 304
Lang Bian Mountain (V) 856-8
Lang Cave (M) 476-7
Lang Dinh An (V) 858
Langkawi (M) 444-5
language 880-9, see also individual countries
    Cambodia (Khmer) 880
    Indonesia (Bahasa) 881-2
    Laos 882-4
    Malaysia (Bahasa) 885-6
    Myanmar (Burmese) 886-7
    Philippines (Pilipino) 887
    Thailand 888
    Vietnam 889
Lao Bao (V) 845
Lao Cai (V) 836
Lao Pako (L) 370-1
Lao People's Revolutionary Party (LPRP) 340
Laoag (P) 25, 606
Laoag River (P) 606
Laos 337-93, **338**
    accommodation 351
    activities 350
    arts 341
    books 346-7
    climate 339
    courses 350

Laos cont:
    email & Internet services 346
    embassies 344
    entertainment 352
    flora & fauna 339-40
    food & drinks 351-2
    geography 339
    getting around 355-8, **356**
    getting there & away 353-5
    health 348
    highlights 337, 341-2
    holidays 349-50
    itineraries 342
    language 341
    maps 342
    money 344-5
    planning 342
    population & people 340-1
    postal services 345
    religion 341
    safe travel 348-9
    shopping 352-3
    society & conduct 341
    special events 349-50
    telephone services 345-6
    tourist offices 342
    travel restrictions 343
    visas 342-3
    work 350-1
Laos, Northern 372-85, **373**
Laos, Southern 385-93, **386**
Lapu-Lapu, Chief 558
Larantuka (I) 288-9
Larena (P) 633
Las Piñas (P) 595
Lasa, Pulau (I) 281
Lashio (My) 547-8
Lasiana, Pantai (I) 293
Lat Village (V) 856
Latuhalat (I) 324
Lawang Top (I) 254
Lawas (M) 478
Lee Kuan Yew 645-8
Legaspi (P) 608
Legian (I) 202, **200**
Lembar (I) 272
Lembata Island (I) 288-9
Lembomawo (I) 315
Lemo (I) 314
lesbian travellers 36
Letkhokkon Beach (My) 500, 527
Lewoleba (I) 289
Leyte Island (P) 623
Leyte Mountain Trail (P) 623
Lhok Nga (I) 236
Liang (I) 324
Light, Francis 435
Limbang (M) 477-8
Lingayen Beach (P) 598
Lingga (I) 241

Lintha (My) 556
Lisu people 747
Little India (S) 645, 649, 663, **664**
Loay (P) 621
Loboc (P) 621
Loei (T) 685, 773
Loh Buaya (I) 280
Loh Liang (I) 280
Loh Sabita (I) 281
Lokomata (I) 314
Lom sak (T) 773
Lombok (I) 123, 263-77, **266**
  getting around 265-7
  getting there & away 264-5
Londa (I) 314
Long Apari (I) 301
Long Bagun (I) 300-1
Long Hai (V) 878
Long Iram (I) 301
longhouse visits (M) 472, 484
Lontha (My) 556
Loon (P) 621
Lopburi (T) 25, 735-6
Los Baños (P) 596
Los Palos (I) 295
Lovina (I) 26, 123, 219-21, **220-1**
Luang Nam Tha Province (L) 342, 382-4
Luang Nam Tha town (L) 383
Luang Prabang (L) 26, 337, 341, 372-9, **374**
Lubok Simpon (M) 463
Lucap (P) 597-8
Lucena (P) 597
Lugbung Island (P) 625
Lumbong (M) 445
Lumphat (C) 117
Lumut (M) 434
Lung Phin Market (V) 837
Luzon (P) 561

M
MacArthur, General Douglas 623
Mactan Island (P) 619
Madale, Pantai (I) 315
Madura (I) 118, 186-7
Mae Hat, Ao (T) 784
Mae Hong Son (T) 26, 676, 760
Mae Nam, Hat (T) 780-2
Mae Sai (T) 26, 764-6
Mae Salak (T) 762
Mae Salong (T) 764-6

Mae Sot (T) 759-60
magazines 33
Magellan, Ferdinand 558
Mahagnao, Lake (P) 623
Mahakam, Sungai (I) 300-1
Mahathir Mohamad 395
Mal Khao, Hat (T) 795
Maitara, Pulau (I) 326
Majapahit Empire 118, 142, 186
Makale (I) 310
Malang (I) 141
Malapascua Island (P) 620
Malaysia 394-488
  accommodation 406-7
  activities 406
  arts 397-8
  books 403
  climate 395
  courses 406
  email & Internet services 402
  embassies 400-1
  flora & fauna 396
  food & drinks 407-8
  geography 395
  getting around 411-3, **411**
  getting there & away 408-11
  health 404
  highlights 394, 399
  holidays 405
  language 398-9
  maps 399
  money 401
  planning 399
  population & people 397
  postal services 402
  religion 398
  safe travel 405
  society & conduct 398
  special events 405-6
  telephone services 402
  visas 399-400
Malaysia, Peninsular 413-45, **414**
Malayu kingdom 225
Malegcong (P) 603
Malenge, Pulau (I) 317
Maluk (I) 278
Maluku (I) 25, 124, 319-26, **320**
  getting around 321
  getting there & away 321
Mambajao (P) 640
Manado (I) 124, 306, 317-8
Manao, Ao (T) 777
Mancong (I) 300
Manda (I) 336
Mandai Orchard Gardens (S) 668
Mandalay (My) 489, 500, 529-35, **530**, **532**, **535**

Manila 580-592, **582-3**, **584**, **586**, **593**
  email & Internet services 581
  entertainment 590
  getting around 591-2
  getting there & away 591
  maps 580
  places to eat 589-90
  places to stay 588-9
  postal services 581
  shopping 591
  telephone services 581
  things to see & do 581-8
  tourist offices 581
Maninjau, Danau (I) 254-5
Manokwari (I) 124, 333
Mansalay (P) 613-4
Mansinam, Pulau (I) 333
maps 27
Marang (M) 453
Marang, Sungai (M) 453
Marante (I) 314
Marble Mountains (V) 851
Marcos, Ferdinand 560, 606
Marcos, Imelda 564, 623
Maribaya (I) 161
Maribojoc (P) 621
Marinduque Island (P) 610-1
Marosi, Pantai (I) 298
Martaban (My), see Mottama
Martapura (I) 304
Marudi (M) 476
Maslete (I) 294
Matabungkay (P) 596
Matakakeri (I) 297
Matako, Pantai (I) 315
Mataram (I) 267-9, **268**
Mataram kingdom 118, 142
Matnog (P) 609
Matur (I) 254
Mau Chau (V) 836
Maubisse (I) 295
Maumere (I) 286-7
Maungmakan Islands (My) 553
Maungmakan Township (My) 552
Mawlamyine (My) 550-1
Maymyo (My), see Pyin U Lwin
Mayon volcano (P) 558, 565, 608-9
measures 35
Medan (I) 224, 229-35, **230-1**
Medewi (I) 222
meditation courses 350, 508, 700, 755, 783
Meiktila (My) 542
Meja, Gunung (I) 284
Mekong catfish 69
Mekong Delta (V) 804, 807, 878-9
Mekong River 68, 337, 339, 493, 676, 764, 767, 772-4

Bold indicates maps.
Italics indicates boxed text.

Melak (I) 300-1
Melaka (M) 26, 118, 394, 425-30, **426**
Melolo (I) 296-7
Mengwi (I) 222
Menjangan, Pulau (I) 219, 222
Mentawai Islands (I) 258
Meragang Beach (B) 64
Merah, Pantai (I) 281
Merang (M) 455
Merapi, Gunung (I) 177
Mercedes (P) 607
Mergui (My), see Myeik
Mersing (M) 445-6
Mien people 340-2, 747
Mindanao (P) 561, 633-40
Mindoro Island (P) 558, 611-6
Mingun (My) 536
Miri (M) 475-6
Moalboal (P) 620-1
Moei River (My) 493
Mogok (My) 537
Mogpog (P) 610
Mon people 492, 497-8, 549-51
Mon people 492
Mondolkiri (C) 117
money 30-2
Mongkut (Rama IV), King 677
Moni (I) 285-6
Monkey Forest (I) 274
Montagnard people 806, 835-7, 856, 860
Monywa (My) 536
Moro Islamic Liberation Front (MILF) 633
Moro National Liberation Front (MNLF) 560, 633
Moro watchtower (P) 641
motorcycle travel 52
Mottama (My) 552
Moulmein (My), see Mawlamyine
Moyo, Pulau (I) 279
Mrauk U (My) 500, 555-6
Mt Apo (P) 640
Mt Apo National Park (P) 562
Mt Banahaw (P) 596
Mt Bulusan (P) 609
Mt Faber (S) 668
Mt Guiting-Guiting (P) 625
Mt Ilig-Mt Baco National Wildlife Sanctuary (P) 27
Mt Kanlaon National Park (P) 27, 562
Mt Kinabalu (M) 394, 406, 478, 484-5
Mt Makiling (P) 596
Mt Malindig (P) 610
Mt Pinatubo (P) 565, 592, 595
Mt Popa (My) 541

Mt Victoria (My) 493
Mu Ko Similan National Marine Park (T) 685
Muang Boran (My), see Ancient City
Muang Khun (L) 381
Muang Ngoi (L), see Nong Khiaw
Muang Sing (L) 383-4
Muara Beach (B) 64
Muara Merak (I) 301
Muay Thai (Thai Boxing) 352, 700-1, 703
Mui Ne Beach (V) 855
Mukdahan (T) 774
Mulu, Gunung (M) 406, 476
Munduk (I) 224
Muong Hoa River (V) 837
My Son (V) 850-1
Myabyin (My) 556
Myanmar 489-557, **490-1**
   accommodation 508-9
   arts 497-8
   books 505
   climate 494
   courses 508
   embassies 502
   flora & fauna 495
   food & drinks 509-10
   geography 493-4
   getting around 511-4, **512**
   getting there & away 510-11
   health 506-7
   highlights 489, 500-10
   holidays 507-8
   language 500
   maps 500
   money 502-4
   name changes 494
   permits 501
   planning 500
   population & people 497
   postal services 504
   religion 499-500
   safe travel 507
   shopping 510
   society & conduct 498-9
   special events 507-8
   telephone services 504-5
   tourism 489-92, 496-7
   tourist offices 500
   visas 500-1
Myawaddy (My) 759
Myeik (My) 500, 553
Myitkyina (My) 549
Myit-son (My) 549
Mytho (V) 878-9

N

Na Khai, Ao (T) 781
Na Muang (T) 779

Na Thon (T) 779, 782-3
Nabire (I) 124, 333-4
Naga (P) 607
Nage (I) 283
Nagtabon Beach (P) 642
Nai Han, Hat (T) 792-5
Nai Thon, Hat (T) 795
Nai Yang, Hat (T) 795
Nakai-Nam Theun NBCA (L) 339, 342
Nakhon Pathom (T) 736
Nakhon Phanom (T) 773
Nakhon Ratchasima (Khorat) (T) 767-8, **768-9**
Nakhon Si Thammarat (T) 786
Nam Cat Tien National Park (V) 805
Nam Nang River (V) 835
Namalatu (I) 324
Nan (T) 766-7
Nanggala (I) 314
Narathiwat (T) 775
Nasugbu (P) 596
National League for Democracy (NLD) 492-3
national parks 26-7, (C) 69, (L) 339, (My) 494, (P) 562, (T) 681, (V) 805
   Ba Be National Park (V) 805, 835
   Bach Ma National Park (V) 805
   Bako National Park (M) 471
   Bicol National Park (P) 562
   Bokor National Park (C) 69
   Bromo-Tengger-Semeru National Park (I) 187
   Cat Ba National Park (V) 805, 833-4
   Cuc Phuong National Park (V) 805, 832
   Doi Inthanon National Park (T) 685
   Doi Phu Kha National Park (T) 766
   Gunung Gading National Park (M) 471-2
   Gunung Leuser National Park (I) 26, 224, 227, 239
   Gunung Mulu National Park (M) 406, 476-7
   Kaeng Krachan National Park (T) 685, 776
   Kenong Rimba National Park (M) 406, 461-2
   Kerinci Seblat National Park (I) 27, 227
   Khammuan Limestone NBCA (L) 342
   Khao Sok National park (T) 797

national parks *cont:*
Kinabalu National Park (M) 399, 484-6
Kirirom National Park (C) 69
Ko Chang National Marine Park (T) 743-4
Ko Tarutao National Marine Park (T) 792
Kubah National Park (M) 471
Laem Son National Park (T) 778
Lambir Hills National Park (M) 475
Mt Apo National Park (P) 562
Mt Ilig-Mt Baco National Wildlife Sanctuary (P) 27
Mt Kanlaon National Park (P) 27, 562
Mu Ko Similan National Marine Park (T) 685
Nakai-Nam Theun NBCA (L) 339, 342
Nam Cat Tien National Park (V) 805
Niah National Park (M) 474-5
Pangandaran National Park (I) 162
Phu Kradung National Park (T) 685
Prasat Hin Phimai National Historical Park (T) 769
Quezon National Park (P) 27, 597
Ream National Park (C) 69
Rizal National Park (P) 636
Sai Yok Yai National Park (T) 495, 739
Sirinat National Marine Park (T) 795
Sohoton National Park (P) 624
St Paul Subterranean National Park (P) 562, 565, 642
Taman Nasional Bali Barat (I) 192, 222
Taman Nasional Manusela (I) 320
Taman Negara National Park (M) 26, 394-5, 399, 406, 463-5
Than Bokkharani National Park (T) 799
Tunku Abdul Rahman National Park (M) 482

national parks *cont:*
Turtle Islands National Park (M) 486-7
Virachey National Park (C) 69, 117
Way Kambas National Park (I) 261-2
Yok Don National Park (V) 805
National Zoo & Aquarium (M) 424
nats 499-500
Natsepa (I) 324
Ne Win, General 492-3, 495
Negara (I) 222
Negros Island (P) 630-3
New People's Army (NPA) 560
newspapers 33
Ngadisari (I) 188
Ngapali Beach (My) 528, 556-7
Ngapali village (My) 556
Nggela (I) 286
Ngihiwatu (I) 298
Ngo Dinh Diem 804
Nguyen Dynasty (V) 840
Nha Trang (V) 802, 807, 851-3, **852, 854**
Niah National Park (M) 474-5
Nias, Pulau (I) 25-6, 123-4, 247-9, **248**
Night Safari (S) 649, 668
Niki Niki (I) 293
Ninh Binh (V) 831
Noi, Ao (T) 777
Nong Khai (T) 772
Nong Khiaw (L) 379-80
North Borneo Company 395, 478
North Pandan Island (P) 611
Nusa Camp (M) 464
Nusa Dua (I) 205
Nusa Lembongan (I) 214
Nusa Penida (I) 214
Nusa Tenggara (I) 118, 123, 263, **264-5**
getting around 263
getting there & away 263
Nyuangshwe (My) 543-5, **544**

O

Oecussi (I) 294
Oehala Waterfall (I) 293-4
Oinlasi (I) 293
Olayama (I) 248
Olongapo (P) 594
Omar Ali Saifuddien Mosque (B) 54, 56, 61
Orang Asli Museum (M) 424
Orang Asli people 394, 397, 424, 432, 451

Orang-Utan Rehabilitation Centre (M) 26
orang-utans 121, 471
Orchard Rd (S) 649, 663, **666-7**
Ormoc (P) 623
Osolata Beach (I) 295
overland travel
to/from South-East Asia 45-6
within South-East Asia 48-52

P

Pa-an (My) 489, 500, 552
Pacung (I) 224
Padaido Islands (I) 333
Padang (I) 224, 255-8, **256**
Padangbai (I) 214-5
Pagai Selatan, Pulau (I) 258
Pagai Utara, Pulau (I) 258
Pagan (My), *see* Bagan
Pagsanjan (P) 565, 597
Pai (T) 761
Pak Bara (T) 792
Pak Chom (T) 772
Pak Meng, Hat (T) 800
Pak Ou Caves (L) 379
Pakse (L) 389-90, **389**
Palawa (I) 314
Palawan (P) 558, 561, 641-4
Palembang (M) 225
Paletwa (My) 557
Paliton (P) 633
Palu (I) 315-6
Pamekasan (I) 187
Pamilacan Island (P) 621
Panagsama Beach (P) 620
Panay Island (P) 625-7
Pancasila 121-2
Pandaan (I) 186
pandas 495
Pandin Lake (P) 596
Pangala (I) 314
Pangandaran (I) 123, 141, 162-5, **163**
Pangandaran National Park (I) 162
Pangkor Laut, Pulau (M) 434
Pangkor, Pulau (M) 434-5
Panglao Island (P) 622-3
Pangli (I) 314
Pangururan (I) 243-5
Pantemakassar (I) 294
Paoay Church (P) 606
Paradise Island Beach (P) 640
Parangtritis (I) 177
Parapat (I) 241-3
Pasang (T) 756
Pasir Bogak (M) 434
Pasir Panjang (M) 455

Pasir Sen Babai (I) 333
Pass Valley (I) 336
Pathein (My) 527-8, **528**
Pathet Lao 337
Patong, Ao (T) 792-5
Pattani (T) 775
Pattaya (T) 680, 685, 740-1
Pau (I) 297
Payathonzu (My) 740
Pedewa (I) 221
Pekanbaru (I) 258-9
Penang (M) 26, 394, 399,
    435-43, **436**, **438**
Penanjakan, Gunung (I) 187
Pendolo (I) 314-5
Penuba Bay (M) 447
Penulisan (I) 223
Penyenget, Pulau (I) 260
People's Action Party (PAP)
    645-8
Peradayan Forest Reserve (B)
    56, 64-5
Perak Tong Temple (M) 433
Perfume Pagoda (V) 830-1
Perhentian Besar, Pulau (M)
    456-7
Perhentian Islands (M) 25,
    394, 399, 456-9
Perhentian Kecil, Pualu (M)
    456-7
Pero (I) 298
Pescador Island (P) 620
Petitenget (I) 222
Phan Thiet (V) 855-6
Phan Thiet Beach (V) 855
Phang-Nga (T) 685, 775, 797
Phattalung (T) 786-7
Phetburi (Phetchaburi) (T) 776
Phetburi Khiri Khan (T) 685
Phi Phi Don (T) 799
Phi Phi Le (T) 799
Philip II, King 558
Philippines 558-644, **559**
    accommodation 574
    activities 574
    arts 563-4
    books 571
    climate 561
    email & Internet services 571
    embassies 568
    entertainment 575
    flora & fauna 561-2
    food & drinks 574-5
    geography 561
    getting around 576-80, **577**
    getting there & away 575-6
    health 572
    highlights 558, 565
    holidays 573
    itineraries 565-6
    language 565

Philippines cont:
    maps 566
    money 569-70
    planning 566
    population & people 563
    postal services 570
    religion 565
    safe travel 573
    society & conduct 564-5
    special events 573
    telephone services 570
    tourist offices 567
    visas 567-8
    work 574
Phimai (T) 769-70
Phitsanulok (T) 756
Phnom Bakheng (C) 101
Phnom Chisor (C) 95
Phnom Penh (C) 25, 66, 70,
    82-95, **84-5**, **88**
    email & Internet services 83
    entertainment 91-2
    getting around 94
    getting there & away 92-4
    maps 82-3
    places to eat 90-1
    places to stay 89-90
    postal services 83
    shopping 92
    telephone services 83
    things to see & do 86-8
    tourist offices 83
Phnom Sampeau (C) 112-3
phīī (spirit) worship 341, 893
Phongsali (L) 342
Phonsavan (L) 380-1
photography 34
Phra Phutthabat (T) 736
Phu Kradung (T) 773
Phu Kradung National Park (T)
    685
Phu Phra Cave (T) 739
Phu Quoc Island (V) 879
Phuket (T) 25, 680, 685, 775,
    792-7, **793**
Phuket town 792-7, **794**
Pietriver (I) 336
Pindaya (My) 500, 542-3
pineapple fields (P) 635
Plain of Jars (L) 337, 381
planning 27-8
Pleiku (V) 860
Pol Pot 67-8
Polo, Marco 225, 495
Pontianak (I) 298, 304-6, **305**
Poreng Valley (I) 281
Poring Hot Springs (M) 485-6
Port Barton (P) 643
Port Dickson (M) 430
Poso (I) 315
Poso, Danau (I) 314

postal services 32
Poto Tano (I) 278
Prachuap, Ao (T) 777
Prachuap Khiri Khan (T) 685,
    777
Praigoli (I) 297-8
Prailiu (I) 296
Praiyawang (I) 297
Prambanan (I) 25, 118, 123,
    141-2, 175-6
Prasat Hin Khao Phanom Rung
    Historical Park (T) 770
Prasat Hin Phimai National
    Historical Park (T) 769
Prasat Muang Singh Temple (T)
    739
Prek Toal Bird Sanctuary (C)
    69
Prenn Falls (V) 856
Probolinggo (I) 188-9
Prome (My), see Pyay
Puerto Galera (P) 558, 611,
    612
Puerto Princesa (P) 641-2
Pugima (I) 336
Puncak Pass (I) 156
Punta Cruz pirate watch-
    tower (P) 621
Puong Cave (V) 835
Pupuan (I) 224
Pura Besakih (I) 213-4
Pura Luhur Ulu Watu (I) 205,
    224
Pura Pasar Agung (I) 214
Pura Penataran Sasih (I) 213
Pura Puncak Penulisan (I)
    223
Pura Rambut Siwi (I) 222
Pura Ulun Danu (I) 223
Puraran (P) 610
Puri Lingsar (I) 269
Putao (My) 549
Pyay (My) 526-7
Pyin U Lwin (My) 536-7
Pyramid (I) 336

Q
Quan Lan Island (V) 835
Quezon (P) 643
Quezon National Park (P) 27,
    597

R
Rabbit Island (C) 109
Rach Gia (V) 879
radio 34
Raffles Hotel (S) 26, 662
Raffles, Sir Stamford 645
rafflesia 227, 254, 396, 471-2,
    482

Rafflesia Forest Reserve (M) 482-3
rafting
  Bali (I) 193
  Bukit Lawang (I) 238
  Tha Ton (T) 761
Raja Brooke, *see* Brooke, James
Rakhine people 554
Rakhine State (My) 553-4
Rakhine Yoma (My) 553
Rambut Siwi (I) 123
Ramos, Fidel 560
Ranaka, Gunung (I) 283
Ranamese, Danau (I) 283
Ranariddh, Prince Norodom 67-8
Ranau (M) 485
Ranggase village (I) 286
Rangoon (My), *see* Yangon
Ranong (T) 777-8
Ransiki (I) 333
Rantau Abang (M) 452-3
Rantepao (I) 310, 312-3
Ratanakiri Province (C) 66, 116
Ratchaburi (T) 736
Rawal, Hat (T) 795
Rayong (T) 741
Ream National Park (C) 69
Red Beach (P) 623
Red River Delta (V) 802, 804, 831
Redang, Pulau (M) 455-6
Rejang, Batang (M) 472
religion 892-3, *see also* individual countries and faiths
Rentis Tenor (M) 464
Renu Nakhon (T) 773
rhinoceroses 69, 121, 340, 494-5
  Javan 495, 680
  Sumatran 227, 262, 495
rice terraces (P) 558, 565, 602-4
Rinca island (I) 27, 280-2
Rinjani, Gunung (I) 123, 263, 273-4
Riung (I) 284
Rizal National Park (P) 636
Rizal, Jose 560, 562, 596
Romblon Islands (P) 624-5
Roti (I) 293
Roxas (P) 613-4
Royal Palace (C) 66, 87
Rua, Pantai (I) 298
Ruak River (T) 764

Rubiah, Pulau (I) 237
Rumberpon, Pulau (I) 333
Ruteng (I) 283

S

Sabah (M) 478 88, **466**
Sabang (I) 236-7
Sabang (P) 558, 611-2, 642-3
Sadan (I) 314
Saen, Ao (T) 795
safe travel 36-7
Sagada (P) 603-4
Sagaing (My) 535
Sai Kaew, Hat (T) 743
Sai Si Ngoen, Hat (T) 743
Sai Yok Falls (T) 739
Sai Yok Yai National Park (T) 495, 739
Saigon (V), *see* Ho Chi Minh City
Sakura Hill (I) 254
Sala Kaew Ku (T) 772
Salang (M) 446-8
Salavan Province (L) 388
Salavan town (L) 388
Salay (My) 500, 541-2
Salopa Waterfalls (I) 315
Sam Neua (L) 381-2
Sam Poh Temple (M) 433
Sam Rainsy 68
Samal Island (P) 640
Samar Island (P) 624
Samarinda (I) 300
Samila, Hat (T) 787
Samosir, Pulau (I) 241, 243-6
Sampaloc Lake (P) 596
Samut Prakan Crocodile Farm & Zoo (T) 731
San Antonio (P) 633
San Fabian (P) 598
San Fernando (La Union) (P) 598-9
San Fernando (P) 595
San Jose (P) 614
San Juan (P) 599-600
San Kamphaeng (T) 754-5
San Miguel Bay (P) 607
San Pablo (P) 596-7
San Pedro Church (P) 621
Sandakan (M) 486-7
Sandoway (My), *see* Thandwe
Sandugan (P) 633
Sangeh (I) 222
Sangiran (I) 182
Sangkhlaburi (T) 739-40
Sangkhom (T) 772
Sanjaya, King 142
Santa Cruz Island (P) 637
Santa Fe (P) 619
Santo Domingo (P) 608
Sanur (I) 123, 206-7

Sapa (V) 807, 837-9, **838**
Sape (I) 280
Sarawak (M) 465-78, **466**
  getting there & away 465-7
  visas & permits 465
Sarawak Chamber (M) 476
Sarburi (T) 736
Sarrat (P) 606
Satun (T) 791
Savannakhet Province (L) 385-8
Savannakhet town (L) 342, 385-7, 774, **387**
Sawankhalok (T) 758-9
scams, *see* safe travel
Se Set (Xet) River (L) 388
Sea Garden (I) 237
sea travel 46
Selang (I) 217
Selo (I) 177
Semarapura (I) 214
Semau, Pulau (I) 293
Semenggok Wildlife Rehabilitation Centre (M) 471
Seminyak (I) 202, **203**
Semporna (M) 488
Sen Monorom (C) 117
Sen Ravang (C) 95
Sen Thmol (C) 95
Senggigi (I) 263, 270-2, **271**
Sentani (I) 330-1
Sentani, Danau (I) 331
Sentosa Island (S) 649, 668
Sepilok Centre (M) 26
Sepilok Orang-Utan Rehabilitation Centre (M) 394, 399, 486
Sepon (Xepon) (L) 388
Serasa Beach (B) 64
Seremban (M) 430
Seribu, Pulau (I) 153
Sesean, Gunung (I) 314
Setse (My) 552
Shampoo Island (My), *see* Gaungse Kyun
Shan State (My) 542-8
Shwedagon Paya (My) 489, 515
Shwedaung (My) 526-7
Si Chiangmai (T) 772
Si Phan Don (L) 337, 342, 392-3, **393**
Si Satchanalai – Chaliang Historical Park (T) 758-9
Si Satchanalai (T) 756, 758-9
Si Thanu, Ao (T) 784
Siak, Sungai (I) 258-9
Siargao Island (P) 634
Sibayak, Gunung (I) 239
Siberut, Pulau (I) 258
Sibolga (I) 246-7
Sibu (M) 472-3

Bold indicates maps.
Italics indicates boxed text.

Sibu, Pulau (M) 448-9
Sibuyan Island (P) 625
Siem Reap (C) 95-100, **96**
Sierra Madre (P) 606
Siguntu (I) 314
Sihanouk, King Norodom 66, 87
Sihanoukville (C) 66, 70,
    104-7, **105**
Sikao (T) 800
Sikka (I) 287
Silliman Beach (P) 632
Simanindo (I) 243-4
Sinabung, Gunung (I) 239
Sinatma (I) 336
Singapore 25, 645-75, **646-7**,
    658-9, 660-1
    accommodation 653
    books 652
    climate 648
    embassies 650
    entertainment 674-5
    flora & fauna 648
    food 653
    geography 648
    getting around 656-7
    getting there & away 654-6
    health 652
    highlights 645, 649
    language 649
    maps 649-50
    money 651
    places to eat 671-4
    places to stay 668-71
    planning 649-50
    population & people 648
    postal services 652
    religion 649
    safe travel 653
    shopping 675
    society & conduct 648-9
    telephone services 652
    things to see & do 657-68
    tourist offices 650
    visas 650
Singapore River (S) 649
Singapore Zoological
    Gardens (S) 649
Singaraja (I) 218
Singki (I) 313
Singosari kingdom 142
Sipadan, Pulau (M) 488
Sipora, Pulau (I) 258
Siquijor Island (P) 633
Sirinat National Marine
    Park (T) 795
Sisophon (C) 113
Sitoli, Gunung (I) 248-9
Sittwe (My) 554-5, **555**
SLORC (State Law & Order
    Restoration Council)
    489-93, 495-6

snorkelling, see diving &
    snorkelling
Soa Siu (I) 326
Soe (I) 293
Soeharto, Mohammad 119-20,
    144
Soekarno, Achmad 119-20, 284
Soekarnoputri, Megawati 121
Sohoton National Park (P) 624
Solo (I) 123, 141, 177-82, **178**
Solor Archipelago (I) 288-9
Songkhla (T) 685, 787-9, **788**
Sop Ruak (T) 764
Sorake Beach (I) 247
Sorsogon (P) 609
SPDC (State Peace &
    Development Council)
    489-92, 495-6
Sriwijaya Empire 118, 225,
    778-9
St John's Island (S) 668
St Joseph the Worker
    Chapel (P) 632
St Paul Subterranean National
    Park (P) 562, 565, 642
Stung Treng (C) 115-6
Subic Bay (P) 594
Subis, Gunung (M) 474
sugar plantations (P) 631-2
Sukhothai (T) 756-8, **757**
Sulamadaha (I) 326
Sulawesi (I) 118, 124, 306-19,
    307
    getting there & away 306
Sule Paya (My) 489, 516
Sullukang (I) 313-4
Suluban, Pantai (I) 205
Sumatra (I) 118, 123, 224-63,
    226-7
    getting around 229
    getting there & away 228-9
Sumba (I) 123, 263, 295-8
    getting there & away 295-6
Sumbawa (I) 277-80
    getting there & away 278
Sumbawa Besar (I) 278-9
Sumenep (I) 187
Sungai Kolok (T) 800-1
Sungei Buloh Nature Park (S)
    668
Sunken Cemetery (P) 641
Surabaya (I) 141, 182-6, **184**
Suranadi (I) 270
Surat Thani (T) 778-9
surfing 38, (P) 574
    Bali (I) 193
    Huu (I) 279
    Kuta (Bali) (I) 198
    Kuta Beach (Lombok) (I)
        272-3
    Lagundri Bay (I) 247

surfing cont:
    Lhok Nga (I) 236
    Lombok (I) 264
    San Juan (P) 599
Surigao (P) 634
Surin (T) 775
Surin, Hat (T) 795
Suroba (I) 336
Syriam (My), see Thanlyin

T
Ta Prohm Temple (C) 95
Taal town (P) 596
Taal volcano (P), see Tagaytay
Tabaco (P) 609
Tablas Island (P) 625
Tablolong (I) 293
Tabon Caves (P) 643
Tachilek (My) 764-5, 765-6
Tacloban (P) 623
Tagaytay (P) 595-6
Tagbanua people 644
Tagbilaran (P) 621
Tahan, Gunung (M) 463-4
Tahan, Sungai (M) 463
Taiping (M) 435
takraw 703
Talibon (P) 622
Talisay (P) 595-6
Taliwang (I) 278
Talomo (P) 640
Tam Coc Caves (V) 832
Tam Giao 806
Taman Batang Duri (B) 64
Taman Burung dan Anggrek (I)
    333
Taman Gunung Meja (I) 333
Taman Narmada (I) 269
Taman Nasional Bali Barat (I)
    192, 222
Taman Nasional Manusela (I)
    320
Taman Negara National
    Park (M) 26, 394-5, 399,
    406, 463-5
Taman Rekreasi (I) 223
Taman Safari Indonesia (I) 156
Taman Ujung (I) 216
Tamblingan, Danau (I) 224
Tambunan (M) 483
Tana Toraja (I) 118, 124, 306,
    310-3, **311**
Tanah Lot (I) 123, 222
Tanah Rata (M) 432-3
Tangkuban Perahu (I) 161-2
Tanjong Pagar (S) 645
Tanjung Benoa (I) 205-6
Tanjung Bungah (M) 439
Tanjung Isuy (I) 300
Tanjung Karang (I) 316
Tanjung Pinang (I) 260

Tanjung Ria (I), see Base G, Pantai (I)
Taoism 806-7
Tapplya Waterfall (P) 605
Tarakan (I) 298-300
Tarimbang (I) 297
Tasik Chini (M) 451
Tatmadaw 495-6
Taunggyi (My) 545-6
Tavoy (My), see Dawei
Tawau (M) 488
Tay Ninh (V) 874
Tay Phuong Pagoda (V) 831
Taytay (P) 643
Tek Chhouu Falls (C) 108
Telaga Warna (I) 166
telephone services 33
television 34
Teluk Bahang (M) 439
Teluk Belanga (M) 434
Teluk Dalam (I) 249
Teluk Dalam (M) 455
Teluk Gedong (M) 434
Teluk Nipah (M) 434
Temburong District (B) 56, 64-5
Temburong, Sungai (B) 64
Temkessi (I) 294
Templer Park (M) 424
Tengah, Pantai (M) 444
Tenganan (I) 215
Tenom (M) 484
Tentena (I) 315
Ternate (I) 124, 319
Ternate, Pulau (I) 325
Tet Offensive 804
Tetebatu (I) 274
Tha Khaek (L) 773
Tha Ton (T) 761
Thac Bac (V) 837
Thai boxing, see Muay Thai
Thailand 676-801, **678-9**
  accommodation 701
  activities 699
  arts 682-3
  books 693
  climate 680
  courses 699-701
  email & Internet services 692
  embassies 690
  entertainment 702-3
  flora & fauna 680-1
  food & drinks 701-2
  geography 680
  getting around 708-12, **709**
  getting there & away 704-8
  health 695-6
  highlights 676, 685

Thailand cont:
  holidays 698-9
  itineraries 685-7
  language 685
  maps 687
  money 691-2
  planning 687-8
  population & people 682
  postal services 692
  religion 684-5
  safe travel 697-8
  shopping 703-4
  society & conduct 683-4
  special events 698-9
  telephone services 692
  tourist offices 688-9
  visas 689
  work 701
Thale Noi Wildlife Preserve (T) 786
Thale Sap Songkhla (T) 787
Tham Malai cave (T) 786
Tham Pha Tok (L) 379
Thamanyat Kuang (My) 552
Than Bokkharani National Park (T) 799
Than Mayom Falls (T) 743
Than Sadet Falls (T) 783
Than Shwe, General 495
Thandwe (My) 500, 557
Thanlwin River (My) 493, 552
Thanlyin (My) 523
Thap Thim, Hat (T) 743
That Ing Hang (L) 387-8
That Phanom (T) 774
Thay Pagoda (V) 831
Thayekhittaya (My) 500, 526
Thazi (My) 542
theft, see safe travel
Thibaw, King 489
Thompson, Jim 432, 717
Thong Krut, Ao (T) 781
Thong Nai Pan Noi (T) 784
Thong Nai Pan Yai, Ao (T) 784
Thong Sala (T) 783-5
Thong Yang, Ao (T) 780-2
Three Pagodas Pass (T) 737, 739-40
Thuan An Beach (V) 840-1
Tidore (I) 319
Tidore, Pulau (I) 326
tigers 69, 121, 262, 494-5
Tilanga (I) 314
Timah Nature Reserve (S) 649
time 34-5
Timor (I) 123, 289-95
Tioman, Pulau (M) 25-6, 446-8, **447**
Tirta Empul (I) 213
Tirta Gangga (I) 217

Toba, Danau (I) 26, 118, 123, 241, **242**
Togian Islands (I) 124, 306, 316-7
toilets 35
Toini, Pantai (I) 315
Tolire Besar, Danau (I) 326
Tomohon (I) 319
Tomok (I) 243
Ton Nga Chang Waterfall (T) 791
Tonlé Bati (C) 95
Tonlé Om (C) 95
Tonlé Sap (C) 68
Tonlé Sap River (C) 68
Tonlé Srepok (C) 117
Tonusu (I) 315
Toraja people 118, 310-2
Torrijos (P) 610
Towale (I) 316
Toya Bungkah (I) 223
train travel 52
Trang (T) 685, 775, 799-800
Trat Province (T) 743
trekking 37-8, 604, (L) 350, (M) 406, (My) 500, (T) 699, (V) 814
  Agung, Gunung (I) 214
  Anggi Lakes (I) 333
  Arfak Mountains (I) 333
  Bali (I) 193
  Baliem Valley (I) 335-6
  Banaue (P) 604
  Batur, Gunung (I) 223
  Bittuang (I) 314
  Bukit Lawang (I) 238
  Cameron Highlands (M) 432
  Cherating (M) 451-2
  Chiang Rai (T) 762
  Chocolate Hills (P) 622
  Dalat (V) 858
  Dieng Plateau (I) 166
  Fansipan (V) 837
  Gede, Gunung (I) 156
  Gunung Mulu National Park (M) 476
  hill tribe treks (T) 744-5
  Kelabit Highlands (M) 477
  Kenong Rimba Park (M) 461-2
  Kinabalu National Park (M) 484-5
  Kyaiktiyo (My) 550
  Lambir Hills National Park (M) 475
  Lang Bian Mountain (V) 856-8
  Leyte Mountain Trail (P) 623
  Lombok (I) 264, 267
  Mae Hong Son (T) 760
  Mentawai Islands (I) 258
  Nan (T) 766

Bold indicates maps.
Italics indicates boxed text.

trekking *cont:*
  Pai (T) 761
  Peradayan Forest
    Reserve (B) 64-5
  Putao (My) 549
  Rinjani, Gunung (I) 273-4
  Samosir, Pulau (I) 244
  Sibayak, Gunung (I) 239
  Sierra Madre (P) 606
  St Paul Subterranean
    National Park (P) 642
  Taman Negara National
    Park (M) 463-4
  Tasik Chini (M) 451
  Tha Ton (T) 761-2
  Tioman, Pulau (M) 446
  Ubud (I) 207-10
Tres Reyes Islands (P) 610
Tretes (I) 186
Tribal Research Institute (T) 746
Trikora, Pantai (I) 260
Trowulan (I) 186
Trung Trang (V) 834
Truong Son National
  Cemetery (V) 845
Tu Duc, Emperor 802
Tuban (South Kuta) (I) 198, **199**
Tuguegarao (P) 606-7
Tujuh Belas, Pulau (I) 284
Tuk Tuk (I) 243-5, **244**
Tulamben (I) 218
Tundrumbaho (I) 248
Tunku Abdul Rahman National
  Park (M) 482
Turtle Islands 478
Turtle Islands National
  Park (M) 486-7
turtles 192, 237, 452, 487, 795
Tutuala (I) 295
Tuwasan Falls (P) 641
Twante (My) 524

U

U Winaya 552
Ubin, Pulau (S) 645, 668
Ubon Ratchathani (T) 774-5
Ubud (I) 26, 123, 207-13,
  208-9, 210
Udon Thani (T) 771-2
Udong (C) 94-5
Ujung Pandang (I) 306-10, **309**
Ulu Watu (I) 123
Umabara (I) 297
Underground River (P) 565, 642
United Malays National
  Organisation (UMNO) 395

V

Van Don Island (V) 834-5
Vang Vieng (L) 371-2

Victoria Point (My), *see*
  Kawthoung
Victorias (P) 632
video 34
Vieng Xai (L) 382
Vientiane (L) 337, 341-2,
  358-70, **360-1, 364**
  entertainment 369
  getting around 370
  getting there & away
    369-70
  maps 359
  places to eat 367-8
  places to stay 363-7
  postal services 359
  shopping 369
  telephone 359
  things to see & do 361-3
Viet Cong (VC) 804
Vietnam 802-79, **803**
  accommodation 815
  activities 814
  arts 806
  books 812
  climate 804
  courses 814
  email & Internet services 811
  embassies 808-10
  entertainment 815-6
  flora & fauna 805
  food & drinks 815
  geography 804
  getting around 817-20,
    818
  getting there & away
    816-7
  health 813
  highlights 802, 807
  holidays 814
  language 807
  maps 807
  money 810
  planning 807
  population & people 805-6
  postal services 810-1
  religion 806-7
  safe travel 813-4
  shopping 816
  society & conduct 806
  special events 814
  telephone services 811
  tourist offices 807
  visas 807-8
  work 814-5
Vigan (P) 25, 605-6
Vinh Moc tunnels (V) 845
Virac (P) 610
Virachey National Park (C) 69,
  117
Viriato (P) 624
visas 28-9

Visayas (P) 561, 566, **614-5**
Voen Sai (C) 117
Vung Tau (V) 874-78, **875, 876**

W

Waecicu Beach (I) 282
Waiara (I) 287
Waigali (I) 297-8
Waikabubak (I) 295, 297
Waingapu (I) 295-6
Wairterang (I) 287-8
Wakai, Pulau (I) 317
Wallace Line (I) 121
Wamena (I) 334-5
Wardo (I) 333
Warin Chamrap (T) 774
Wat Banan (C) 113
Wat Ek Phnom (C) 112
Wat Hin Maak Peng (T) 772
Wat Khaek (T), *see* Sala
  Kaew Ku
Wat Khao Tham (T) 783
Wat Laem Saw (T) 779
Wat Paa Nanachat (T) 774
Wat Pho Si Nai (T) 771
Wat Phothivihan (M) 461
Wat Phra That Bang Phuan (T)
  772
Wat Phra That Doi Suthep (T)
  754
Wat Phra That Lampang
  Luang (T) 755
Wat Phra That Si Chom
  Thong (T) 755
Wat Phra Yai (T) 779
Wat Phu Champasak (L) 337,
  342, 391-2
Wat Phu Thawk (T) 773
Wat Suanmok (T) 778
Wat Tapotaram (T) 777
Wat Tham Seua (T) 799
Wat Tham Suwankhula (T) 797
water puppets 806, 829, 872
Way Kambas National Park (I)
  261-2
wayang kulit 141, 397-8
wayang orang 141
Weh, Pulau (I) 224, 236-7
weights 35
Wektu Telu 263
Welirang, Gunung (I) 186
Wesaput (I) 336
West Bali National Park (I), *see*
  Taman Nasional Bali Barat
whale sharks 609
White Beach (Boracay) (P)
  627-30, **628**
White Beach (Luzon) (P) 598
White Beach (Marinduque) (P)
  610

White Beach (Mindoro) (P)
612-3
White Island (P) 641
White Sands Beach (P) 596
wildlife 26-7
Wind Cave (M) 476-7
windsurfing (P) 574, (T) 699
Wodong (I) 287-8
Wogo (I) 283
Wolo Valley (I) 336
Wolonjita (I) 286
Wolowaru (I) 286
women travellers 35-6
Wonosobo (I) 165-6
work 38-9
Wosilimo (I) 336

X

Xieng Khuang Province (L)
337, 380-1

Xuyen Thuy Grotto (V)
832

Y

Yambo Lake (P) 596
Yangon (My) 25, 489, 500,
514-23, **516**, **518**, **520**,
524
entertainment 521-2
getting around 523
getting there & away
522-3
maps 515
places to eat 519-21
places to stay 517-9
postal services 515
shopping 522
telephone services 515
things to see & do 515-7
tourist offices 515

Yangon River (My) 515
Yao, Hat (T) 800
Yasothon (T) 774
Yeak Loam Lake (C) 116
Yeh Pulu (I) 213
Yeh Sanih (I) 218-9
Yele Paya (My) 523
Yogyakarta (I) 26, 118, 123,
141, 167-75, **168**, **171**,
175
Yok Don National Park (V)
805
Yong Ling, Hat (T) 800
Young Elephant Training
Centre (T) 755

Z

Zamboanga (P) 636-7
Zoological Gardens (S) 668

MAP LEGEND

BOUNDARIES

—·—·—·—	International
—·—·—·—	Provincial
— — — —	Disputed

HYDROGRAPHY

	Coastline
	River, Creek
	Lake
	Salt Lake
	Canal
◎ ⇀	Spring, Rapids
⊣⊢	Waterfalls
⅏ ⅏ ⅏	Swamp

MAP SYMBOLS

⊙ CAPITAL	National Capital	⋀	Border Crossing	)(... Pass
◎ CAPITAL	Provincial Capital	⌒	Cave	★ ... Police Station
● CITY	City	🚩	Church	▣ ... Post Office
● Town	Town		Cliff or Escarpment	❖ ... Shopping Centre
○	Point of Interest	◥	Dive Site	☒ ... Sikh Temple
		○	Embassy	血 ... Stately Home
■	Place to Stay	🏯	Hindu Temple	⚶ ... Stupa
Å	Camping Ground	✚	Hospital	✡ ... Synagogue
		◉	Kraal	☎ ... Telephone
▼	Place to Eat	⚑	Monument	▣ ... Temple
ᵺ	Pub or Bar	☪	Mosque	▣ ... Tomb
		▲	Mountain or Hill	❶ ... Tourist Information
✈	Airport	血	Museum	◒ ... Transport
∴	Archaeological Site	🏕	National Park	☖ ... Volcano
♫	Beach	✿	Pagoda	🐗 ... Zoo

ROUTES & TRANSPORT

	Freeway
	Highway
	Major Road
	Minor Road
=======	Unsealed Road
	City Highway
	City Road
	City Street, Lane

	Pedestrian Mall
⊢⊢⊢●⊢	Train Route & Station
⊶Ⓜ⊷	Metro & Station
	Tramway
⊬⊬⊬⊬⊬	Cable Car or Chairlift
— — — —	Walking Track
· · · · · ·	Walking Tour
— — — —	Ferry Route

AREA FEATURES

	Building
✿	Park, Gardens
+ + ×	Cemetery

	Market
	Beach, Desert
	Urban Area

Note: not all symbols displayed above appear in this book

LONELY PLANET OFFICES

Australia
PO Box 617, Hawthorn, Victoria 3122
tel: (03) 9819 1877 fax: (03) 9819 6459
e-mail: talk2us@lonelyplanet.com.au

UK
10a Spring Place, London, NW5 3BH
tel: (0171) 428 4800 fax: (0171) 428 4828
e-mail: go@lonelyplanet.co.uk

USA
150 Linden St, Oakland, CA 94607
tel: (510) 893 8555 TOLL FREE: 800 275-8555
fax: (510) 893 8572
e-mail: info@lonelyplanet.com

France
1 rue du Dahomey, 75011 Paris
tel: 01 55 25 33 00 fax: 01 55 25 33 01
e-mail: bip@lonelyplanet.fr
3615 lonelyplanet *(1,29 F TTC/min)*

**World Wide Web: www.lonelyplanet.com *or* AOL keyword: lp
Lonely Planet Images: lpi@lonelyplanet.com.au**